ENVIRONMENTAL ETHICS: THE BIG QUESTIONS

Philosophy: The Big Questions

Series Editor: James P. Sterba, University of Notre Dame, Indiana

Designed to elicit a philosophical response in the mind of the student, this distinctive series of anthologies provides essential classical and contemporary readings that serve to bring the central questions of philosophy alive for today's students. It presents complete coverage of the Anglo-American tradition of philosophy, including the kinds of questions and challenges that it confronts today.

Aesthetics: The Big Questions
Edited by Carolyn Korsmeyer

Epistemology: The Big Questions
Edited by Linda Martín Alcoff

Ethics: The Big Questions, Second Edition
Edited by James P. Sterba

Metaphysics: The Big Questions, Second Edition
Edited by Peter van Inwagen and Dean W. Zimmerman

Philosophy of Language: The Big Questions
Edited by Andrea Nye

Philosophy of Religion: The Big Questions
Edited by Eleonore Stump and Michael J. Murray

Race, Class, Gender, and Sexuality: The Big Questions
Edited by Naomi Zack, Laurie Shrage, and Crispin Sartwell

Philosophy: The Big Questions
Edited by Ruth J. Sample, Charles W. Mills, and James P. Sterba

Environmental Ethics: The Big Questions
Edited by David R. Keller

Environmental Ethics
The Big Questions

Edited by

David R. Keller

WILEY-BLACKWELL

A John Wiley & Sons, Ltd., Publication

This edition first published 2010
Editorial material and organization © 2010 Blackwell Publishing Ltd

Blackwell Publishing was acquired by John Wiley & Sons in February 2007. Blackwell's publishing program has been merged with Wiley's global Scientific, Technical, and Medical business to form Wiley-Blackwell.

Registered Office
John Wiley & Sons Ltd, The Atrium, Southern Gate, Chichester, West Sussex, PO19 8SQ, United Kingdom

Editorial Offices
350 Main Street, Malden, MA 02148-5020, USA
9600 Garsington Road, Oxford, OX4 2DQ, UK
The Atrium, Southern Gate, Chichester, West Sussex, PO19 8SQ, UK

For details of our global editorial offices, for customer services, and for information about how to apply for permission to reuse the copyright material in this book please see our website at www.wiley.com/wiley-blackwell.

The right of David R. Keller to be identified as the author of the editorial material in this work has been asserted in accordance with the UK Copyright, Designs and Patents Act 1988.

Wiley also publishes its books in a variety of electronic formats. Some content that appears in print may not be available in electronic books.

Designations used by companies to distinguish their products are often claimed as trademarks. All brand names and product names used in this book are trade names, service marks, trademarks or registered trademarks of their respective owners. The publisher is not associated with any product or vendor mentioned in this book. This publication is designed to provide accurate and authoritative information in regard to the subject matter covered. It is sold on the understanding that the publisher is not engaged in rendering professional services. If professional advice or other expert assistance is required, the services of a competent professional should be sought.

Library of Congress Cataloging-in-Publication Data
Environmental ethics : the big questions / edited by David R. Keller.
   p. cm. – (Philosophy: the big questions)
  Includes bibliographical references and index.
  ISBN 978-1-4051-7639-2 (hardcover : alk. paper) – ISBN 978-1-4051-7638-5 (pbk. : alk. paper)   1. Environmental ethics. I. Keller, David R., 1962–
  GE42.E583 2010
  179'.1–dc22

                              2009050308

A catalogue record for this book is available from the British Library.

Set in 9.5/11.5pt Galliard by SPi Publisher Services, Pondicherry, India
Printed in Singapore by Ho Printing Singapore Pte Ltd

04   2011

CONTENTS

Preface   xi
List of Sources   xiii

Introduction: What is Environmental Ethics?   1

PART I   WHY STUDY ENVIRONMENTAL ETHICS?   **25**

George Sessions • Emily Brady • John Granrose • Frederick Ferré • J. Baird Callicott
• Warwick Fox • Eugene C. Hargrove • Ian Smith • Isis Brook • Holmes Rolston III • Clare Palmer
• Kristin Shrader-Frechette • Victoria Davion • Greta Gaard • Peter Singer • James P. Sterba
• Michael E. Zimmerman • Bryan G. Norton •Anthony Weston • David Rothenberg

Contributors to Part I   53

PART II   WHAT IS ANTHROPOCENTRISM?   **57**

   Introduction   59
1 Humans as Moral Ends   63
   Thomas Aquinas
2 The Mastery of Nature   65
   Francis Bacon
3 Nonhumans as Machines   69
   René Descartes
4 Mechanistic Metaphysics   72
   Isaac Newton
5 The Amoral Status of Nature   73
   John Stuart Mill
6 Nature as Economic Resource   77
   John Locke
7 Indirect Duties to Nonhumans   82
   Immanuel Kant

8   In Defense of Anthropocentrism   83
    Wilfred Beckerman and Joanna Pasek

PART III   WHAT IS NONANTHROPOCENTRISM?   **89**

    Introduction   91
9   Walking   93
    Henry David Thoreau
10 The Wild Parks and Forest Reservations of the West and Hetch Hetchy Valley   96
    John Muir
11 Is There a Need for a New, an Environmental, Ethic?   98
    Richard (Routley) Sylvan
12 Attitudes to Nature   103
    John Passmore
13 Should Trees Have Standing? Toward Legal Rights for Natural Objects   110
    Christopher D. Stone
14 The Varieties of Intrinsic Value   120
    John O'Neill
15 Value in Nature and the Nature of Value   130
    Holmes Rolston III
16 The End of Anthropocentrism?   137
    Mary Midgley
17 Is the Crown of Creation a Dunce Cap?   143
    Chip Ward

PART IV   WHAT IS THE SCOPE OF MORAL CONSIDERABILITY?   **147**

    Introduction   149

A   Individualism (Polycentrism)   **154**

Hierarchical Biocentrism   154
18 Persons in Nature: Toward an Applicable and Unified Environmental Ethics   154
    Frederick Ferré

Psychocentrism   161
19 Animals as Subjects-of-a-Life   161
    Tom Regan
20 All Animals are Equal   169
    Peter Singer

Egalitarian Biocentrism   175
21 The Ethics of Respect for Nature   175
    Paul W. Taylor
22 Kantians and Utilitarians and the Moral Status of Nonhuman Life   182
    James P. Sterba

B   Holism (Ecocentrism)   **193**

23 The Land Ethic   193
    Aldo Leopold

24 The Conceptual Foundations of the Land Ethic   201
    J. Baird Callicott

25 Gaia As Seen Through the Atmosphere   211
    James E. Lovelock

C   General Ethics   **213**

26 Developing a General Ethics (with Particular Reference to the Built,
    or Human-Constructed, Environment)   213
    Warwick Fox

**PART V   WHAT ARE THE PROMINENT ALTERNATIVES
           TO GROUNDING ENVIRONMENTAL
           ETHICS IN AXIOLOGY?**   **221**

    Introduction   223

A   Environmental Psychologism   **230**

27 The Shallow and the Deep Ecology Movement   230
    Arne Naess

28 The Heart of Deep Ecology   235
    Andrew McLaughlin

29 The Deep Ecological Movement: Some Philosophical Aspects   240
    Arne Naess

30 Transpersonal Ecology   245
    Warwick Fox

B   Environmental Virtue Ethics   **252**

31 Environmental Virtue Ethics   252
    Ronald Sandler

C   Continental Environmental Ethics   **257**

32 On Environmental Philosophy and Continental Thought   257
    Steven Vogel

D   Political Environmental Ethics   **268**

Social Ecology   268

33 What Is Social Ecology?   268
    Murray Bookchin

34 Socialism and Ecology   275
    James O'Connor

Ecological Feminism   281

35 The Power and the Promise of Ecological Feminism   281
    Karen J. Warren

36 Feminism and the Philosophy of Nature 291
  Carolyn Merchant

37 Nature, Self, and Gender: Feminism, Environmental Philosophy, and
  the Critique of Rationalism 300
  Val Plumwood

E Environmental Pragmatism **311**

38 Beyond Intrinsic Value: Pragmatism in Environmental Ethics 311
  Anthony Weston

39 Methodological Pragmatism, Pluralism, and Environmental Ethics 318
  Andrew Light

F Direct Action **327**

40 Earth First! 327
  Dave Foreman

The Ethics of Ecological Sabotage: An Exchange 333

41 Ecological Sabotage: Pranks or Terrorism? 333
  Eugene Hargrove

42 Earth First! and *The Monkey Wrench Gang* 334
  Edward Abbey

43 More on Earth First! and *The Monkey Wrench Gang* 335
  Dave Foreman

44 Editor's Response 336
  Eugene Hargrove

**PART VI WHAT ARE THE CONNECTIONS BETWEEN
REALISM, RELATIVISM, TECHNOLOGY,
AND ENVIRONMENTAL ETHICS?** **337**

Introduction 339

A Subjectivist Environmental Ethics **342**

45 Meta-Ethics and Environmental Ethics 342
  Robert Elliot

B The Social Construction of Nature **352**

46 How To Construe Nature: Environmental Ethics and the Interpretation of Nature 352
  Roger J. H. King

47 The Trouble With Wilderness 359
  William Cronon

C Ecological Realism **362**

48 Virtually Hunting Reality in the Forests of Simulacra 362
  Paul Shepard

D Environmental Ethics and the Philosophy of Technology   **368**

49   Technology and the Limits of Nature   368
David Rothenberg

PART VII   WHAT ARE THE CONNECTIONS BETWEEN ECOLOGICAL SCIENCE AND ENVIRONMENTAL ETHICS?   **377**

Introduction   379

50   Ecology – A Subversive Subject   380
Paul B. Sears

51   What is Conservation Biology?   384
Michael E. Soulé

52   Environmental Ethics and Ecological Science   392
Mark Sagoff

53   The Metaphysical Implications of Ecology   400
J. Baird Callicott

54   The Ends of the World as We Know Them   409
Jared Diamond

PART VIII   WHAT ARE SOME ETHICAL DIMENSIONS OF ENVIRONMENTAL PUBLIC POLICY?   **413**

Introduction   415

A   The Population/Poverty Debate   **422**

55   An Essay on the Principle of Population   422
Thomas Robert Malthus

56   Impact of Population Growth   426
Paul R. Ehrlich and John P. Holdren

57   The Ecological Necessity of Confronting the Problem of Human Overpopulation   434
Garrett Hardin

58   How Poverty Breeds Overpopulation   443
Barry Commoner

59   More People, Greater Wealth, More Resources, Healthier Environment   447
Julian L. Simon

60   Population: Delusion and Reality   454
Amartya Sen

61   A Special Moment in History   469
Bill McKibben

B   Industrial Agriculture   **476**

62   Nature as the Measure for a Sustainable Agriculture   476
Wes Jackson

63   Putting Food Production in Context: Toward a Postmechanistic Agricultural Ethic   481
     David R. Keller and E. Charles Brummer

C   Socioeconomic Environmental Justice   **491**

64   Environmental Justice for All   491
     Robert D. Bullard

65   Just Garbage   501
     Peter S. Wenz

D   Environmental Ethics and Economic Policy   **509**

66   A Declaration of Sustainability   509
     Paul Hawken

67   The Steady-State Economy   516
     Herman E. Daly

68   Making Capitalism Sustainable   525
     John Elkington

69   The Ignorance Argument: What Must We Know to be Fair to the Future?   534
     Bryan Norton

70   Environmental Justice and Intergenerational Debt   545
     Clark Wolf

E   Globalization   **551**

71   The Environmental Limits to Globalization   551
     David Ehrenfeld

**PART IX   WHAT IS THE FUTURE OF
              ENVIRONMENTAL ETHICS?**   **559**

72   The Future of Environmental Ethics   561
     Holmes Rolston III

Bibliography   575

PREFACE

Teaching is learning. For me, teaching environmental ethics has been as important as solitary study. I did not really begin to understand environmental ethics until I talked with students about the readings included in this volume, and about the world.

This book represents lessons learned over a decade of teaching the environmental ethics course at Utah Valley University.[1] It grew out of the classroom. It is an interdisciplinary text, since during that time I have found it obligatory to mix philosophy with other sources from the social and life sciences, economics, history, legal studies, business, and literature. On account of its origins, I believe this book should work well in the classroom. I also think it should serve well as a historical and thematic introduction to any student eager to learn about ethics and the environment. The readings are challenging, as is the topic.

The idea for this book arose unexpectedly – as good things in life usually do – one pleasant May morning several years ago. I, my wife Anina Merrill, Jim Sterba, and a boatman were floating down the Colorado River through serene Westwater Canyon. Jim had been a visiting scholar at Utah Valley University, and we were immersing ourselves in the solace and beauty of red rock country before he returned to Indiana. The semester had just ended and I had finished teaching environmental ethics. I casually remarked to Jim that I did not find the organizational structure of most textbooks on the market particularly useful in terms of pedagogy.

I ended up, I said, devising my own organizational structure and then bouncing around within a text and between texts, using readings from philosophy and other disciplines. I also commented that I did not think one could understand environmental ethics without contextualizing it within the Western intellectual tradition, and that most textbooks omit or do not adequately treat critical historical background prior to the field's emergence as an identifiable subdiscipline of philosophy in the 1970s. Drifting around a bend into a cool shadow and back again into warm sunlight, Jim invited me to edit an environmental ethics anthology for the *Philosophy: The Big Questions* series, of which he is the editor. I accepted Jim's offer, and spent four years living up to the commitment.

Towards the end of the semester, I find it crucial to use case studies on environmental topics to put the theory to practice. I also think that the case studies which work best are place- and time-dependent, since students relate to issues that are relevant to their lives insofar as they impact their communities. The issue of environmental injustice along the Mississippi River Industrial Corridor might not resonate with Utah kids the way it does with students in southern Louisiana, for example, and the youth of Massachusetts might not be all that engaged with the controversy of nuclear waste storage in Utah. For this reason I decided not to include case studies in this book, and instead to archive case studies from instructors around the world on a Web site – www. environmentalethics.info – continuously updated.

This trove of case studies will complement and explicate the theory outlined in this textbook.

Special thanks to the three peer reviewers – then anonymous – for detailed and constructively critical comments: Michael P. Nelson, Associate Professor of Philosophy, Michigan State University; James P. Sterba, Professor of Philosophy, University of Notre Dame; and Holmes Rolston III, University Distinguished Professor, Colorado State University. Gratitude to Andrew Light and Holmes Rolston for their original contributions to this volume; to Mark Sagoff, Chip Ward, and Clark Wolf for rewriting previously published work for publication herein; and to Bryan Norton for editing his article to conform to space constraints. I must also acknowledge the help and patience of Jeff Dean, executive editor, and Tiffany Mok, philosophy editorial assistant, at Wiley-Blackwell, for bearing with myriad revisions. Also thanks to Ross Green, Senior Library Assistant at Utah Valley University, for serving as a research assistant, and Don LaVange, my friend and colleague, for constructing the case study archive website, and Sarah Dancy, for meticulously copy-editing the text. Most importantly, indebtedness to Richard H. Keller, my father, and as always, for everything, Anina.

Fragments of the editorial material draw from research previously published, from most recent to oldest, as: "A Brief Overview of Basic Ethical Theory," in Peggy Connolly, Becky Cox-White, David R. Keller, and Martin Leever, *Ethics in Action: A Case-Based Approach* (Malden, MA: Wiley-Blackwell, 2009), pp. 11–49; "Deep Ecology," in J. Baird Callicott and Robert Frodeman, eds., *Encyclopedia of Environmental Ethics and Philosophy*, vol. 1 (Farmington Hills, MI: Macmillan Reference USA), pp. 206–11; "Land Ethics," in Ivan I. Mazour, Alexander N. Chumakov, and William C. Gay, eds., *International Global Studies Encyclopedia* (Amherst, NY: Prometheus Books, 2005), pp. 326–8; "Values in Nature: The Contribution of Frederick Ferré to Environmental Philosophy," in George Allan and Merle F. Allshouse, eds., *Nature, Truth, and Value: Exploring the Thinking of Frederick Ferré* (Lanham, MD: Lexington Books, 2005), pp. 177–98; and "Gleaning Lessons from Deep Ecology," *Ethics and the Environment* 2/2 (Fall 1997): 139–48.

Note

1   At Utah Valley University, teaching environmental ethics has been something of an odd odyssey in its own right, which I describe in "Pedagogy in Process: Reflections on Teaching Environmental Ethics in a Community with an Anti-Environmentalist Orientation," *Process Papers* 10 (May 2006): 12–17.

LIST OF SOURCES

The editor and publisher gratefully acknowledge the permission granted to reproduce the copyright material in this book:

In Part I Singer, Peter, "Eating Ethically," *Free Inquiry*, vol. 25, no. 4 (2005): 18–19. © 2005 by Peter Singer. Adapted by permission of the author.

James P. Sterba, "A Demanding Environmental Ethics for the Future," *Ethics & the Environment*, vol. 12, no. 2 (Fall 2007): 146–7. © 2007 by Indiana University Press. Reprinted with permission from the publisher.

1   Thomas Aquinas, "Humans as Moral Ends." From *The Summa Contra Gentiles*, Part II, Book 3, Chapter CXII (London: Burns, Oates & Washbourne Ltd., 1928), pp. 88–92.

2   Francis Bacon, "The Mastery of Nature." From *The Great Instauration*. In James Spedding, Robert Leslie Ellis, and Douglas Denon Heath, eds., *The Works*, vol. VIII. Boston: Taggard and Thompson, 1863, pp. 84–93.

3   René Descartes, "Nonhumans as Machines." From "Discourse on the Method Part V" and "Correspondence," excerpted from John Cottingham, Robert Stoothoff, and Dugald Murdoch, ed. and trans., *The Philosophical Writings of Descartes*, vol. I (Cambridge: Cambridge University Press, 1985). © 1985 by Cambridge University Press. Reproduced with permission of the translators and

Cambridge University Press. And from John Cottingham, Robert Stoothoff, Dugald Murdoch, and Anthony Kenny, ed. and trans., *The Philosophical Writings of Descartes*, vol. III: *The Correspondence* (Cambridge: Cambridge University Press, 1991), pp. 302–4, 365–7. © 1991 by Cambridge University Press. Reproduced with permission of the translators and Cambridge University Press.

4   Isaac Newton, "Mechanistic Metaphysics." From *Opticks* (G. Bell & Sons, Ltd., London, 1931), pp. 401–4.

5   J. S. Mill, "The Amoral Status of Nature." From *Nature* (New York: AMS Press, Inc., 1970), pp. 1, 5–9, 12–13, 15–18, 19–23.

6   John Locke, "Nature as Economic Resource." From *Two Treatises of Civil Government*: Chapter V: "Of Property" (London: J. M. Dent & Sons Ltd., 1970), pp. 129–36, 137–9, 141.

7   Immanuel Kant, "Indirect Duties to Non-humans." From Louis Infield, trans., *Lectures on Ethics* (The Century Co., London, 1930), pp. 239–41. © 1930. Reprinted with permission from Taylor and Francis Books UK.

8   Wilfred Beckerman and Joanna Pasek, "In Defense of Anthropocentrism." From *Justice, Posterity, and the Environment* (Oxford: Oxford University Press, 2001), pp. 129–35. © 2001 by Wilfred Beckerman and Joanna Pasek. Reprinted with permission from Oxford University Press.

9 Henry David Thoreau, "Walking." From *Excursions* (Boston: Houghton, Mifflin & Co., 1883), pp. 260, 275–83, 287–9.

10 John Muir, "The Wild Parks and Forest Reservations of the West and Hetch Hetchy Valley." From *Our National Parks* (Boston: Houghton, Mifflin & Co., 1901), pp. 1–5, and *The Yosemite* (The Century Co., 1912), pp. 255–7, 261–2.

11 Richard (Routley) Sylvan, "Is There a Need for a New, an Environmental, Ethic?" From *Proceedings of the XVth World Congress of Philosophy* (September 17–22, 1973, Varna, Bulgaria), Sofia Press, 1975. © 1973 by Richard Routley.

12 John Passmore, "Attitudes to Nature." From R. S. Peters, ed., *Nature and Conduct* (London: Macmillan Press, 1975), pp. 251–64. © 1975 by Royal Institute of Philosophy. Reprinted with permission from Palgrave Macmillan.

13 Christopher D. Stone, "Should Trees Have Standing? Toward Legal Rights for Natural Objects." From *Southern California Law Review*, vol. 45 (1972), extracts from pp. 450–87. © 1972 by *Southern California Law Review*. Reprinted with permission of the *Southern California Law Review*.

14 John O'Neill, "The Varieties of Intrinsic Value." From *The Monist*, vol. 75, no. 2 (April): 119–38. © 1992, *The Monist: An International Quarterly Journal of General Philosophical Inquiry*. Peru, Illinois, USA. Reprinted by permission.

15 Holmes Rolston III, "Value in Nature and the Nature of Value." From Robin Attfield and Andrew Belsey, eds., *Philosophy and the Natural Environment*, Royal Institute of Philosophy Supplement 36 (Cambridge: Cambridge University Press, 1994), pp. 13–17, 20–30. © 1994 by The Royal Institute of Philosophy and the contributors. Reproduced with permission from Cambridge University Press.

16 Mary Midgley, "The End of Anthropocentrism?" From Robin Attfield and Andrew Belsey, eds., *Philosophy and the Natural Environment*, Royal Institute of Philosophy Supplement 36 (Cambridge: Cambridge University Press, 1994), pp. 103–12. © 1994 by The Royal Institute of Philosophy and the contributors. Reproduced with permission from Cambridge University Press.

17 Chip Ward, "Is the Crown of Creation a Dunce Cap?" An earlier version of this paper appeared in *Catalyst: Healthy Living, Healthy Planet*, vol. 26, no. 1 (January 2008) (Salt Lake City: New Moon Press, Inc.).

18 Frederick Ferré, "Persons in Nature: Toward an Applicable and Unified Environmental Ethics." From *Ethics in the Environment*, vol. 1, no. 1 (1996): 15–25. © 1996 by JAI Press, Inc. Reprinted with permission from Springer Science & Business Media.

19 Tom Regan, "Animals as Subjects-of-a-Life." From "The Case for Animal Rights," in Peter Singer, ed., *In Defense of Animals* (Oxford: Blackwell Publishing, 1985), pp. 13–14. © 1985 by Peter Singer. Reprinted with permission from Blackwell Publishing Ltd. And from "Animal Rights, Human Wrongs," *Environmental Ethics*, vol. 2 (1980): 104–8, 111–13, 114–15, 117–20. © 1980 by Tom Regan. Reprinted with permission from the author.

20 Peter Singer, "All Animals are Equal." From *Philosophical Exchange*, vol. 1, no. 5 (1974): 103–16. © 1974 by Peter Singer. Reprinted by permission of the author.

21 Paul W. Taylor, "The Ethics of Respect for Nature." From *Environmental Ethics*, vol. 3 (1981): 197–200, 205–7, 210–11, 213–18. © 1981 by Paul W. Taylor. Reprinted with permission from the author.

22 James P. Sterba, "Kantians and Utilitarians and the Moral Status of Nonhuman Life." From *The Triumph of Practice Over Theory in Ethics* (Oxford: Oxford University Press, 2005), pp. 58–73. © 2005 by Oxford University Press, Inc. Reprinted with permission from Oxford University Press.

23 Aldo Leopold, "The Land Ethic." From *A Sand County Almanac* (New York: Oxford University Press, 1960), pp. 201–11, 213–19, 220–6. © 1949 by Oxford University Press, Inc. Reprinted with permission from Oxford University Press.

24 J. Baird Callicott, "The Conceptual Foundations of the Land Ethic." From *In Defense of the Land Ethic* (Albany, NY: State University of New York Press, 1989), pp. 75–91. © 1989 State University of New York. Reprinted with permission from SUNY Press.

25 James E. Lovelock, "Gaia As Seen Through the Atmosphere." From *Atmospheric Environment*, vol. 6, no. 8 (1972): 579–80. © 1972 by Elsevier Ltd. Reprinted with permission from Elsevier.

26 Warwick Fox, "Developing a General Ethics." From *A Theory of General Ethics: Human Relationships, Nature, and the Built Environment* (Cambridge, MA: The MIT Press, 2006), 2,500-word extract from pp. 9–15 (with minor modifications). © 2006 by Massachusetts Institute of Technology. By permission of The MIT Press.

27 Arne Naess, "The Shallow and the Deep Ecology Movement." From Peder Anker, "Deep Ecology in Bucharest," The *Trumpeter*, vol. 24, no. 1 (2008): 59–67. © 2008 by Arne Naess. Reprinted by permission of Kit-Fai Naess.

28 Andrew McLaughlin, "The Heart of Deep Ecology." From George Sessions, ed., *Deep Ecology for the Twenty-First Century* (Boston: Shambhala Publications, Inc., 1995), pp. 85–93. © 1995 by Andrew McLaughlin.

29 Arne Naess, "The Deep Ecological Movement: Some Philosophical Aspects." From *Inquiry*, vol. 5 (1986): 10–12, 23–31.

30 Warwick Fox, "Transpersonal Ecology." From *Toward a Transpersonal Ecology: Developing New Foundations for Environmentalism* (Boston: Shambhala Publications, Inc., 1990), pp. 197–206, 213–15, 242–7. © 1990 by Warwick Fox. Reprinted with permission from the author.

31 Ronald Sandler, "Environmental Virtue Ethics." From Ronald Sandler and Philip Cafaro, eds., *Environmental Virtue Ethics* (Lanham, MD: Rowman & Littlefield Publishers, Inc., 2005), pp. 1–7. © 2005 by Rowman & Littlefield Publishers, Inc. Reprinted by permission of Rowman & Littlefield Publishers, Inc.

32 Steven Vogel, "Nature as Origin and Difference: On Environmental Philosophy and Continental Thought." From *Philosophy Today*, vol. 42 (SPEP Supplement, 1998): 169–81. © 1998 by Steven Vogel. Reprinted with permission from the author.

33 Murray Bookchin, "What Is Social Ecology?" From Michael E. Zimmerman, J. Baird Callicott, Karen J. Warren, Irene Klaver, and John Clark, eds., *Environmental Philosophy: From Animal Rights to Radical Ecology*, 4th edn. (Upper Saddle River, NJ: Pearson Education, Inc., 1993), pp. 462–3, 466–78. © 2005, 2001, 1998, 1993 by Pearson Education, Inc. Reprinted by permission of Pearson Education, Inc., Upper Saddle River, NJ.

34 James O'Connor, "Socialism and Ecology." From *Capitalism, Nature, Socialism*, vol. 2, no. 3 (1991): 1–13. © 1991. Reprinted by permission of the publisher, Taylor and Francis Ltd.

35 Karen J. Warren, "The Power and the Promise of Ecological Feminism." From *Environmental Ethics*, vol. 12 (1990): 125–33, 138–44, 145–6. © 1990 by Karen J. Warren. Reprinted with permission from the author.

36 Carolyn Merchant, "Feminism and the Philosophy of Nature." From Irene Diamond and Gloria Orenstein, *Reweaving the World: The Emergence of Ecofeminism* (San Francisco, CA: Sierra Club Books, 1990), pp. 100–5. © 1990 by Irene Diamond and Gloria Feman Orenstein. Reprinted with permission from Sierra Club Books and Carolyn Merchant. And from Carolyn Merchant, *The Death of Nature: Women, Ecology, and the Scientific Revolution* (New York: HarperCollins, 1989), pp. xix–xx, xxi, 1–4, 164, 172, 188–9, 189–93, 290–1. © 1980 by Carolyn Merchant. Reprinted by permission of HarperCollins Publishers.

37 Val Plumwood, "Nature, Self, and Gender: Feminism, Environmental Philosophy and the Critique of Rationalism." From *Hypatia*, vol. 6, no. 1 (1991): 3–18, 22–7. © 1991 by Val Plumwood. Reprinted with permission from Blackwell Publishing Ltd.

38 Anthony Weston, "Beyond Intrinsic Value: Pragmatism in Environmental Ethics." From *Environmental Ethics*, vol. 7 (1985): 321–3, 328–9, 331–9. © 1985 by Anthony Weston. Reprinted with permission from the author.

39 Andrew Light, "Methodological Pragmatism, Pluralism, and Environmental Ethics." Specially written for this volume.

40 Dave Foreman, "Earth First!" From *The Progressive*, vol. 45, no. 10 (1981): 39–42. © 1981. Reprinted by permission from *The Progressive*, 409 E Main St, Madison, WI 53703, USA.

41 Eugene Hargrove, "Ecological Sabotage: Pranks or Terrorism?" From *Environmental Ethics*, vol. 4 (1983): 291–2. © 1983 by Eugene Hargrove. Reprinted with permission from the author.

42 Edward Abbey, "Earth First! and *The Monkey Wrench Gang*." From *Environmental Ethics*, vol. 5 (1983): 94–6.

43 Dave Foreman, "More on Earth First! and *The Monkey Wrench Gang*." From *Environmental Ethics*, vol. 5 (1983): 94–6. © 1983 by Dave Foreman. Reprinted with permission from the author.

44 Eugene Hargrove, "Editor's Response." From *Environmental Ethics*, vol. 5 (1983): 94–6. © 1983 by Eugene Hargrove. Reprinted with permission from the author.

45 Robert Elliot, "Meta-Ethics and Environmental Ethics." From *Metaphilosophy*, vol. 16, nos. 2 & 3 (April/July 1985): 103–17.

46 Roger J. H. King, "How to Construe Nature: Environmental Ethics and the Interpretation of Nature." From *Between the Species*, vol. 6 (Summer 1990): 101–8. © 1990. Reprinted by permission of *Between the Species*.

47 William Cronon, "The Trouble With Wilderness." From *New York Times Magazine* (August 13, 1995), pp. 42–3. Adapted from *Uncommon Ground* (New York: W. W. Norton, 1995), pp. 69–90. © 1995 by William Cronon. Used by permission of W. W. Norton & Company, Inc.

48 Paul Shepard, "Virtually Hunting Reality in the Forests of Simulacra." From Michael E. Soulé and Gary Lease, eds., *Reinventing Nature? Responses to Postmodern Deconstruction* (Washington, DC: Island Press, 1995), pp. 17–29. © 1995 by Island Press. Reproduced by permission of Island Press, Washington, DC.

49 David Rothenberg, "Technology and the Limits of Nature." From David Rothenberg, *Hand's End* (Berkeley: University of California Press, 1993), pp. 1–9, 14–19. © 1993 by The Regents of the University of California. Reprinted by permission of the University of California Press.

50 Paul B. Sears, "Ecology – A Subversive Subject." From *BioScience*, vol. 14, no. 17 (1964): 11–13. © 1964 by American Institute of Biological Sciences (AIBS). Reproduced with permission of the American Institute of Biological Sciences in the format Textbook via Copyright Clearance Center.

51 Michael E. Soulé, "What is Conservation Biology?" From *BioScience*, vol. 35, no. 11 (1985): 727–32, 733–4. © 1985 by American Institute of Biological Sciences (AIBS). Reproduced with permission of the American Institute of Biological

Sciences in the format Textbook via Copyright Clearance Center.

52 Mark Sagoff, "Environmental Ethics and Ecological Science." Specially adapted for this volume by the author. An earlier version appeared as "Environmental Science and Environmental Ethics," in Henk A. M. J. ten Have (ed.), *Environmental Ethics and International Policy* (UNESCO Publishing, France, 2006), pp. 145–63. Reprinted with permission from UNESCO Publishing.

53 J. Baird Callicott, "The Metaphysical Implications of Ecology." From *Environmental Ethics*, vol. 8 (1986): 301–16. © 1986 by J. Baird Callicott. Reprinted with permission from the author.

54 Jared Diamond, "The Ends of the World as We Know Them." From *The New York Times* (Jan. 1, 2005), p. A13. © 2005, *The New York Times*. All rights reserved. Used by permission and protected by the Copyright Laws of the United States. The printing, copying, redistribution, or retransmission of the material without express written permission is prohibited.

55 Thomas Robert Malthus, "An Essay on the Principle of Population." From *An Essay on the Principle of Population as it Affects the Future Improvement of Society with Remarks on the Speculations of Mr. Godwin, M. Condorcet, and Other Writers* (London: J. Johnson, St Paul's Churchyard, 1798), pp. 11–12, 13–17, 18–38.

56 Paul R. Ehrlich and John P. Holdren, "Impact of Population Growth." From *Science*, vol. 171 (1971): 1212–17. © 1971. Reprinted with permission from AAAS.

57 Garrett Hardin, "The Ecological Necessity of Confronting the Problem of Human Overpopulation." From (i) "The Tragedy of the Commons," *Science*, vol. 162 (December 1968): 1243–6. © 1968. Reprinted with permission from AAAS. (ii) "Ethical Implications of Carrying Capacity," in *Managing the Commons* (New York: W. H. Freeman and Co., 1977), pp. 112–16, 123–5. © 1977 by Garrett Hardin. (iii) "The Immorality of Being Softhearted," *The Relevant Scientist*, vol. 1 (November 1971): 17–18. First published in Stanford Alumni Almanac, January 1969. © 1969 by Stanford University. Reprinted with permission from Stanford Magazine.

58 Barry Commoner, "How Poverty Breeds Overpopulation." From *Ramparts*, vol. 13, no. 10

(1975): 21–4, 59. © 1975 by Barry Commoner. Reprinted with permission from the author.

59 Julian L. Simon, "More People, Greater Wealth, More Resources, Healthier Environment." From *Economic Affairs* (April 1994): 22–5, 26–9. © 1994 by *Economic Affairs*. Reprinted with permission from Blackwell Publishing Ltd.

60 Amartya Sen, "Population: Delusion and Reality." From *The New York Review of Books*, vol. 41, no. 15 (September 22, 1994). © 1994.

61 Bill McKibben, "A Special Moment in History." From *The Atlantic Monthly* (1998): 55–60, 72–3, 76–8. ©1998 by Bill McKibben.

62 Wes Jackson, "Nature as the Measure for a Sustainable Agriculture." From F. Herbert Borkmann and Stephen R. Kellert, eds., *Ecology, Economics, Ethics: The Broken Circle* (New Haven and London: Yale University Press, 1991), pp. 43–5, 51–8. © 1991 by Wes Jackson. Reprinted with permission from the author.

63 David R. Keller and E. Charles Brummer, "Putting Food Production in Context: Toward a Postmechanistic Agricultural Ethic." From *BioScience*, vol. 52, no. 3 (2002): 264–71.

64 Robert D. Bullard, "Environmental Justice for All." From *Unequal Protection: Environmental Justice and Communities of Color* (San Francisco, CA: Sierra Club Books, 1994), pp. 3–22. © 1994 by Robert D. Bullard. Reprinted with permission from the author and Sierra Club Books.

65 Peter S. Wenz, "Just Garbage." From Laura Westra and Peter S. Wenz, eds., *Faces of Environmental Racism: Confronting Issues of Global Justice* (Lanham, MD: Rowman & Littlefield Publishers Inc., 1995), pp. 57–71. © 1995 by Rowman & Littlefield Publishers, Inc.

66 Paul Hawken, "A Declaration of Sustainability." From *The Utne Reader* (Sept./Oct. 1993): 54–61.

© 1993 by Paul Hawken. Reprinted by kind permission of the author.

67 Herman E. Daly, "The Steady-State Economy: Toward a Political Economy of Biophysical Equilibrium and Moral Growth." From Herman E. Daly and Kenneth N. Townsend, eds., *Valuing the Earth*, 2nd edn: *Economics, Ecology, Ethics* (Cambridge, MA: MIT Press, 1993), pp. 325–63. © 1992 Massachusetts Institute of Technology, by permission of The MIT Press.

68 John Elkington, "Making Capitalism Sustainable." From John Elkington, *Cannibals with Forks: The Triple Bottom Line of 21st Century Business* (Capstone Publishing Ltd 1999), pp. 24–5, 25–6, 35, 37, 38–9, 70–6, 79–81, 84–6, 87–8, 92–4, 94–6 (notes). © John Elkington, 1997, 1999. Reprinted with permission from Wiley-Blackwell.

69 Bryan Norton, "The Ignorance Argument: What Must We Know to be Fair to the Future?" From Daniel W. Bromley and Jouni Paavola, eds., *Economics, Ethics and Environmental Policy: Contested Choices* (Oxford: Blackwell Publishing, 2002), pp. 35, 36–9, 40–2, 43–52. © 2002 by Blackwell Publishing Ltd. Reprinted with permission from Blackwell Publishing Ltd. Edited by the author.

70 Clark Wolf, "Environmental Justice and Intergenerational Debt." Originally published as "Justice and Intergenerational Debt," in *Intergenerational Justice Review*, 1 (2008): 13–17. Reprinted with minor revisions by permission of Stiftung für die Rechte zukünftiger Generationen.

71 David Ehrenfeld, "The Environmental Limits to Globalization." From *Conservation Biology*, vol. 19, no. 2 (April 2005): 318–20, 321, 322–3, 323–6. © 2002 by Conservation Biology. Reprinted with permission from Blackwell Publishing Ltd.

72 Holmes Rolston III, "The Future of Environmental Ethics." Specially written for this volume.

INTRODUCTION: WHAT IS ENVIRONMENTAL ETHICS?

Environmental ethics is moral philosophy concerning nonhuman nature.

From Socrates to Sartre, ethics has been about humans. This sustained emphasis on human beings for 25 centuries has made moral philosophy in the Western tradition thoroughly *anthropocentric*, or "human-centered." Environmental ethics constitutes critiques of anthropocentrism – some positive, others negative. In the context of the history of the Western intellectual tradition, this critique is both revolutionary and inevitable. Environmental ethics is revolutionary in departing from a bi-millennial tradition in moral philosophy that has identified humans exclusively as the subject-matter of ethics.[1] Environmental ethics is inevitable in that this assumption could not be accepted as an article of faith in perpetuity.

The critique of anthropocentrism asks questions that cut across the main branches of philosophy – metaphysics, axiology, epistemology, aesthetics, and ethics. Is there a firm ontological divide between human culture and wild nature (metaphysics)? Are humans alone intrinsically valuable and, as Protagoras said, the "measure" of all things (axiology)?[2] Or are some nonhuman entities also intrinsically valuable? How do we know (epistemology)? Does natural beauty matter (aesthetics)? Does the preservation of natural beauty and ecological integrity entail ethical responsibility (ethics)? These questions embed environmental ethics firmly in the tradition of Western philosophy. Their answers circumscribe the scope of moral considerability –

that is, the identity of the class of beings worthy of moral consideration – and in some cases dispute the legitimacy of anthropocentrism.

Two points about the status of environmental ethics as a subdiscipline of philosophy are particularly important. First, the breadth and depth of philosophical questions about the human relationship to nonhuman nature suggest that the term "environmental ethics" is not the best description of the field. "Environmental philosophy" is a better name on account of the involvement of all the subdisciplines of philosophy listed above.[3] Yet, while "philosophy" may be a better noun than "ethics," the adjective "environmental" in both terms implies a dualism between human beings and the nonhuman environment – itself a point of contention. To this end, the phrase "ecological ethics" has been proffered.[4] Whatever the case may be, "environmental ethics" is the most common name by inertia of convention.

Second, environmental ethics requires the empirical data of the life sciences and therefore is not "pure philosophy" – that is, a priori non-empirical philosophy. Nor is it appropriate to think of environmental ethics as "applied ethics."[5] As we shall see, environmental philosophers have done far more than "apply" the standard ethical theories of the Western canon – Plato, Aristotle, Mill, Kant, Beauvoir, Rawls – to contemporary environmental problems brought about by technology and industrialization. They have questioned the very authority of that canon.[6]

Ethics is practical reasoning aimed at action; environmental ethics is practical philosophy.[7] Environmental ethics concerns how humans, as moral agents, should best live their lives in their earthly home. It includes the study of human beings, the study of the environment, and the study of relationships between the two. Several questions automatically arise:

- What are human beings?
- What is nature?
- How are humans related to nature?
- How should humans be related to nature?

Here I use the words "nature" and "environment" synonymously, an equivocation common in the literature,[8] but we must be careful to distinguish the different meanings of the words. Let us consider some of the key terms of environmental ethics in greater detail.

Nature, Environment, Ecology, Wilderness, Technology, and Humanness

The vocabulary of environmental ethics involves words loaded with various layers of meaning. Consider the wonderfully polysemous word "nature." The ambiguity of the word is as remarkable as its ubiquity.[9] "Nature" has at least three primary meanings.[10] First, there is a sense (nature$_1$) in which artifacts of human making (paintings, parking structures, polymers) are not considered part of nature. "Nature" in this sense is everything apart from the artificial, which is the approximate sense of the word "wilderness."

Second, "nature" connotes *everything* in the universe apart from the *super*natural (gods, God, souls). Nature in this sense (nature$_2$) includes the products of human artifice (art, architecture, culture, civilization), which are excluded in the definition of nature$_1$.

Third is an Aristotelian connotation: the "nature" of a thing is an innate essence that is disclosed if left to develop unimpeded; acorns grow into oak trees, tadpoles into toads, infants into adults. Living things, then, have "natures" that are manifested through biological processes (nature$_3$). And if entire ecological systems are teleological in this sense, as some ecologists have argued,[11] ecological systems can be considered to have a "nature" in the sense of nature$_3$.

Not only are these different meanings semantically dissimilar, none of them approximates "environment."[12] Consider the last two first. When environmental philosophers talk about "nature," they generally are not talking about distant galaxies and dark matter (which could be consistent with the meaning of nature$_2$); nor are they generally talking about teleological essences (nature$_3$). Instead, they mean that part of "nature" with which human beings interact and influence – the lithosphere, hydrosphere, atmosphere, and biosphere.[13] These four Earth systems comprise the "environment" and include both the inanimate component of living natural systems and an animate nonhuman component.

This description of "environment" parallels the definition of the science of ecology: the study of how the biota and the abiotic features of a locale function together as a living system.[14] The evocation of ecology brings us back to the first connotation: if *Homo sapiens* are biota, then to posit humanity as separate from "nature" (as in the case of nature$_1$) excludes humans from the investigation of the structure and function of ecological systems.[15] The lesson: for the environmental philosopher, the object of investigation is not nature$_1$, either.

For if humans are to be included in the study of environmental ethics, then what about the artifacts of human endeavor? If anthills and beaver dams are to be included in the study of nature$_2$, then should not buildings, pipelines, power lines, roads, dams, locks, and farms also be included? If humans are part of nature$_2$, then "human ecosystems" are "natural."[16] In the main, environmental ethics has been more concerned with *wilderness* and the *wild* than with the human-built environment. Early on in the field's development, Australian philosopher Richard Sylvan (né Routley) pointed out that environmental ethics should include "cities, small parks and household gardens."[17] The human-built environment, that is, must be included in the purview of environmental ethics.[18] Thus there is a fourth sense of "nature" (nature$_4$) that is synonymous with "environment": the four Earth systems, particularly the biosphere, which includes human-constructed systems. We revisit the inclusion of the built environment in environmental ethics in Part IV.

The inclusion of cityscapes shifts the emphasis from wildness as place to wildness as quality. Cast in this light, the urban environment might provide opportunities for surprise and unexpected wonder, just as the untrammeled wilderness does.[19]

A city is a human ecosystem. Cities are human technological strategies for living on Earth. This means that the study of environmental ethics must involve the philosophy of technology.

Aristotle (384–322 BCE) argued that the artifacts of technology (*techne*) are value-neutral and are normatively good or bad only by virtue of how they are used.[20] The invention of a tool is sharply distinguished from the uses to which it is put; technology is a means to an end, not an end itself. From this perspective, technology, in the words of Robert Buchanan, is "essentially amoral, a thing apart from values, an instrument which can be used for good or ill."[21]

Aristotelian philosophy of technology is inadequate for environmental ethics. Technology defines a range of human possibility within the context of nature$_4$. In this sense, through the practice of technology we place under our control a realm that was once beyond it: "the environment." The ambition to expand human power within the context of nature$_2$ is based on a value judgment that to do so is good.

This last point strikes at the core of the first question raised above about the field of environmental ethics: what are human beings? With American philosopher David Rothenberg, we might say that humankind transforms itself through transforming nature.[22] The process begins with the intention of transforming capricious nature into something *manipulable* (from "man," meaning "human"). Such a transformation requires a tool. Once the tool is devised and implemented, the range of possible human activity is expanded, and, in the process, what it means to be "human" is redefined. This redefinition leads to new intentions, and the process begins again. The circular process of intentionality, technological innovation, realization of the goal, and redefinition of humanness is "progress."[24] Intentionality is at the very core of the study of environmental ethics.

On this philosophy of technology, the genesis of the practice of technology begins with the human intention to transform nature. This intention is in the most profound sense value-laden because the use of technology increases the range and scale of human power, and the range and scale of human power affect natural process. If having such an impact makes us responsible for our actions, then the use of technology is inescapably moral.[24]

In short, technology at its very core reflects the values of the human beings who engage in the enterprise of innovation and transformation within the context of nature$_4$. The range of natural process that we have the power to control is the *environment*.

The range of natural process over which we actively refrain from exercising control is *wilderness*.

Let us weave together these key terms. Environmental ethics concerns how humans live and interact with nonhuman nature within the context of ecological systems. Ecology is the study of the interactions of humans with other biota and with the nonbiotic environment. This environment includes not only wilderness but also the human-built environment. The human-built environment is the product of technology. Technology thus provides a nexus to relate the foregoing key terms of the study of environmental ethics – nature, environment, ecology, wilderness, and the essence of *humanness*.

Environmental Metaethics: The Axiology of Nature

Moral philosophers typically divide the enterprise of constructing an ethical theory into two tasks: *metaethics* and *normative ethics*.[25] Normative ethics consists of exhortations to action. Metaethics concerns preparatory considerations *about* those exhortations.

The role of metaethics relative to normative ethics can be framed epistemically or axiologically. In standard moral philosophy it is usually framed epistemically by distinguishing between objectivism and subjectivism. Metaethical objectivism is usually correlated with ethical realism, with normative standards being thought to have a real, objective existence that is independent of human consciousness. Metaethical subjectivism is usually correlated with ethical relativism, with normative standards thought to be relative or subjective; that is, to depend on human consciousness for existence.

The environmental philosopher must also frame metaethics in terms of axiology. Before exhorting people to action, one must first determine exactly what objects or entities the ethical actions should be about. One must determine the class of things that are the proper subject-matter of ethics; that is, the proper objects of moral considerability. Environmental ethics can be conceived as the project of pushing the bounds of moral considerability beyond humans to encompass other entities by the use of theories of value.

Consider environmental metaethics both epistemically and axiologically. Is the kind of value that underpins moral considerability imbedded in nature or projected by humans onto nature? Environmental metaethical objectivism (or metaethical realism) holds that nonhuman natural objects are valuable independently of human consciousness (that is, intrinsically and objectively). Environmental metaethical subjectivism (or metaethical relativism) holds that nonhuman natural objects are valuable only insofar as humans desire them (that is, extrinsically and subjectively). Environmental metaethics can thus be divided into two broad categories: objectivists hold that value inheres in nature; subjectivists hold that value is relative to human consciousness. Subjectivism favors anthropocentrism; objectivism favors nonanthropocentrism.

Axiologically, anthropocentrism holds that human beings, and human beings only, are of intrinsic value (that is, valuable in and of themselves) and that nonhuman nature is valuable only insofar as it is valuable for human purposes (that is, valuable instrumentally – extrinsically – for its ability to serve human ends).[26] American philosopher J. Baird Callicott states the difference succinctly:

> An anthropocentric value theory (or axiology), by common consensus, confers intrinsic value on human beings and regards all other things, including other forms of life, as being only instrumentally valuable, that is, valuable only to the extent that they are means or instruments which may serve human beings. A non-anthropocentric value theory (or axiology), on the other hand, would confer intrinsic value on some non-human beings.[27]

With this definition we have an axiology of two types: entities valued as instruments for the actualization of some other end down a chain of axiological regress (value$_1$), and entities valued as ends-in-themselves at the termination of an axiological chain of regress (value$_2$).

Value$_2$ presupposes some kind of innate attribute or property that gives an entity value independent of its use-value for other ends. Here we have a third sense of value: value qua attribute (value$_3$). If human beings are considered valuable in the second sense (value$_2$), then it must be because we possess some attribute (value$_3$) that gives us the claim to be valued in and of ourselves (value$_2$) independently of our use-value (value$_1$). Anthropocentrists usually view value$_3$ as a quality bestowed by God, a function of being chosen by God as the recipient of love or wrath (as in the Abrahamic religions); by the possession of mental substance (as for Descartes); or by the fact of being sentient (as for Bentham and Mill) or

rational (as for Kant). In fact, the second formulation of Kant's Categorical Imperative – "Act in such a way that you treat humanity, whether in your own person or in the person of another, always at the same time as an end and never simply as a means" – can be understood precisely as treating a human being in terms of value$_1$ when that person should be treated in terms of value$_2$ by virtue of having value$_3$ as a citizen of the Kingdom of Ends.[28]

Value$_3$ is the crucial attribute that makes an entity worthy of moral considerability. The error of limiting "membership in the Moral Club" to humans – which is to say, restricting value$_3$ to humans – is for many environmental philosophers the cardinal sin of anthropocentrism.[29] As we shall see, many environmental philosophers have argued that there are kinds of value$_3$ – sentience or goal-directedness or ecological integrity – that grant citizenship into the moral community to some nonhumans. If this is so, then those entities have value$_2$ and to treat them as if they were only of value$_1$ is morally repugnant – the sin of "human chauvinism," as Sylvan vividly puts it.[30]

Possession of a property or attribute suggests a fourth type of value (value$_4$): value in the sense of having an (objective) existence independent of any (subjective) valuers. This type of value contravenes a long tradition in modern philosophy which holds that there can be no value without valuers (read: humans). Positing value$_4$ is therefore thoroughly nonanthropocentric. The marvel of a buzzing bee at an orchid, the majestic physique of a panther ready to pounce, or the sublime beauty of an Appalachian maple grove blazing in autumnal red might be valuable whether or not a human is around to enjoy it. This is the kind of value that Sylvan (then Routley) evoked in his seminal thought-experiment of 1973: if the last human in existence were to destroy as many other living things as possible before perishing himself, it would be wrong insofar as something valued (value$_4$) would be lost even if there were no sentient beings present to revel in their existence.[31]

Callicott, in the spirit of modern epistemology, argues that objective intrinsic value cannot exist independently of valuing subjects (value$_4$) because "the *source* of all value is human consciousness."[32] This means, objectively, that there is no difference between animate and inanimate objects: "In and of itself an infant child is as value-neutral as a stone or a hydrogen atom."[33]

This line of reasoning could lead to a thoroughly anthropocentric axiology. But not for Callicott, who sees a more complex kind of valuing arising from the phenomenological interaction between valuers and the valued that is not reducible to any of the foregoing four types of value. Though some kind of mentation is the generator of value (the outright rejection of value$_4$), not all value of non-human nature is instrumental (the outright rejection of value$_1$). Callicott is a subjective value theorist who rejects value$_4$ but also argues that not all of the value conferred by humans is instrumental (value$_1$). Some things are valued in and of themselves above and beyond those things' use-value. Think of the way parents value their newborn baby. Part of an infant's value is instrumental in that it brings happiness and joy to them, the proud parents. "But it 'has' – that is, there is conferred or projected upon it, by those who value it for its own sake – *something more* than instrumental value, since it is valued for itself as well as for the joy or other utility it affords them."[34] Similarly, people own pets for a variety of egoistic reasons: protection, companionship, the prestige of owning a Samoyed or Singapura, among others. Yet by also cherishing their pet's unique personality, pet owners value Fido and Fifi's uniqueness. This kind of valuing is non-instrumental, though it does not necessarily ascribe intrinsic value (value$_2$) or intrinsically valuable properties (value$_3$).

To denote this unique type of non-instrumental/non-intrinsic value and to distinguish it from values$_{1-4}$, Callicott suggests we might say that some things are "inherently" valuable. While the *source* of the thing's value is human-generated, the *locus* of value is in the thing's nature.[35] Biotic communities, he says, are wellsprings of the genesis of value, but a value cannot become actual unless it is *valued*. The catalyst of the valuation is anthropogenic and hence external to the valued object. This suggests a type of value (value$_5$) that is independent of human wants, needs, and desires, but is dependent on human cognizance: "In the process," Callicott notes, "the concept of intrinsic value is transformed, or more precisely, truncated."[36] American philosopher Holmes Rolston defines Callicott's axiology as "anthropogenic intrinsic value" in contrast to his own objectivist axiology of "autonomous intrinsic value" (value$_4$) discussed below.[37] American philosopher Bryan Norton defines Callicott's amended axiology as "inherentism."[38]

If the catalyst of valuation is subjective, *why* do humans value some things non-instrumentally? Callicott traces a biosocial moral theory from Adam Smith and David Hume through Charles Darwin to the contemporary sociobiology of E. O. Wilson. According to biosocial moral theory, the propensity to care for others is part of our constitution (nature$_3$) and can be explained in terms of natural selection. Darwin says in *The Descent of Man*:

> [All animals] which defend themselves or attack their enemies in concert, must indeed be in some degree faithful to one another. ... For with those animals which were benefited by living in close association, the individuals which took the greatest pleasure in society would best escape various dangers, whilst those that cared least for their comrades, and lived solitary, would perish in greater numbers.[39]

In social animals, an instinct of sympathy promotes survival. Individuals who are not sociable die without reproducing at a rate comparable to their sociable counterparts. Aristotle recognized "a social instinct ... implanted in all men by nature."[40] How can humans' inclination to live together – their "sympathy" or "beneficence" or "altruism" – be explained evolutionarily? Darwin insists that:

> [I]n however complex a manner this feeling may have originated, as it is one of high importance to all those animals which aid and defend one another, it will have been increased through natural selection; for those communities, which include the greatest number of the most sympathetic members, would flourish best, and rear the greatest number of offspring.[41]

Moral behavior is animal instinct developed through evolution by natural selection. Humans bioempathy, our benevolence with regard to nonhuman nature, is adaptive in the same way. Demonstrating bioempathy amounts to enlightened self-interest (explicit in the forewarnings of George Perkins Marsh). That is, our ability to value nonhuman species beyond our short-term instrumental needs enhances our own species' chance for survival. American philosopher Eugene Hargrove also defends an axiology of anthropogenic intrinsic value in his theory of "weak anthropocentric intrinsic value." On account of the phenomenological dynamism between valuers and the valued, Hargrove deems the anthropocentric/nonanthropocentric dichotomy obsolete, noting that "most values are independent of human judgment, and ... when we do value, we value necessarily from a human perspective but not necessarily in terms of human instrumental interests."[42] Hargrove, with Callicott, posits an anthropogenic inherent value ($value_5$).

In summary:

- instrumental value ($value_1$) is value for some other end;
- intrinsic value ($value_2$) is value for its own sake and not for the sake of any further end;
- moral value ($value_3$) is a property or attribute that gives an entity $value_2$ and consequently makes that entity worthy of moral consideration;
- objective value ($value_4$) is value that inheres in nature and exists independently of being perceived (axiological realism);
- inherent value ($value_5$) is value accorded to non-human nature that is latent (potential) and must be valued in order to become actual; the valuation arises externally (extrinsically) from the entity itself through a valuing subject (anthropogenically), who values it for its own sake (noninstrumentally).

Three observations about this taxonomy are apropos. First, regarding moral value, there is an important difference between *moral considerability* and *moral significance*.[43] Moral properties are qualitative, and some entities possess a property, such as self-awareness, while others do not. Philosophers may agree that a class of entities is worthy of moral considerability but disagree about the entities' moral significance depending on the properties they ascribe to $value_3$. Moral considerability and moral significance are thus connected but not equivalent.

Second, this taxonomy is intended for heuristic purposes, not as a definitive scheme. The categories are general, the boundaries overlapping, the connections fluid. For instance, moral value and objective value are tightly connected but are distinguished here for the purpose of comparing various theories of environmental ethics.

Third, the phenomenology of $value_5$ suggests a truth about the essence of human existence in relation to nonhuman nature. Because humans have a particular evolutionary history and are inextricably and intimately connected with the rest of the biosphere, we *must* believe in an intrinsic value that is independent of our existence, if only for our own well-being. In an essay little noticed by environmental philosophers but well worth reading, American legal scholar Laurence Tribe quotes German political philosopher Max Horkheimer:

> We cannot maintain that the pleasure a man gets from a landscape ... would last long if he were convinced a priori that the forms and colors he sees are just forms and colors, that all structures in which they play a role are purely subjective and have no relation whatsoever to any meaningful order or totality, that they simply and necessarily express nothing ... No walk through the landscape is necessary any longer; and thus the very concept of landscape as experienced by a pedestrian becomes meaningless and arbitrary. Landscape deteriorates altogether into landscaping.[44]

Tribe concludes: "What mind can resist despair at such a prospect? Who can fail to admit that the homocentric logic of self-interest leads finally not to human satisfaction but to the loss of humanity?"[45] Our humanity depends on believing that the more-than-human world has value independently of our awareness; otherwise the cosmos would be an unbearably cold and lonely place. Living in a world bleached of beauty by the logic of anthropocentrism would be intolerable.

The 1970s

The existence of environmental ethics is ironic. Philosophy, the reliable bastion of anthropocentric thinking, is now a cradle for its criticism. During the modern period, Romantic poets, natural historians, and biologists advanced critiques of anthropocentrism. Curiously and conspicuously, philosophers did not.

The 1960s spirit of progressivism (the civil rights, women's, and peace movements) brought a sense of the possibility of a new attitude about the proper human relationship to nonhuman nature. In 1961, building on the work of American author John Muir, environmentalist David Brower published *Wilderness: America's Living Heritage*, drawing attention to the necessity of preserving wilderness as part of the American heritage. In 1962, American biologist Rachel Carson excoriated the hubris of thinking that humans could manipulate and manage the inner workings of ecological systems through the use of chemical tools.[46] Historian Lynn White's celebrated 1967 essay, "The Historical Roots of Our Ecologic Crisis," demonstrated that ecological degradation is a problem of ideology as well as industrialization and argued that issues of environmental crisis are not the sole purview just of natural science but also of the humanities.[47] Biologist Garrett Hardin's equally celebrated 1968 essay, "The Tragedy of the Commons," demonstrated that ecological degradation is a collective cost resulting from the egoistic economic pursuit of profit.

Scholarship about environmental problems commenced in the humanities and social sciences, including law, history, politics, sociology, and economics.[48] These fields all contributed to creating the right atmosphere for the blossoming of the academic field of environmental ethics. It was high time for philosophers to awaken from their 2,500-year dogmatic slumber. The year was 1970.

The first debate was a metaethical one. Can the standard normative paradigm of individualism take into account nonhuman nature (traditionalism), or must existing normative principles be abandoned in favor of new ones (progressivism)? The method of traditionalism is moral extensionism – extending standard normative principles to individuals previously thought to fall outside the scope of those theories.[49] Progressivism renounces extensionism and urges the adoption of new paradigms rooted in holism. This debate continues, but it began in the first half of the 1970s.

The earliest dedicated treatment of the proper scope of moral considerability by a thinker schooled in the Western philosophical tradition was an article published in 1970 by John Cobb. Building on White's earlier insight about the desacrilization of nature by Western European Christianity, and coupling it with Cartesian dualism, Cobb argued that these ideas have led to a depreciation and deprecation of nature that makes the environment vulnerable to "uninhibited investigation and manipulation."[50] Nonhuman organisms exist in a state of brute thinghood.[51] Alternatively, Cobb argued that non-mechanistic process metaphysics provides an axiological basis to deem nonhuman nature worthy of moral consideration against the mainstream view of nature-as-economic-resource. This view can be accurately described as "resourcism."

A conclave of philosophers gathered to address the issue of ethics and the environment at the University of Georgia in 1971. Their goal was to explore the implications of the factual data of ecological science for "social, ethical, political, and legal values."[52] While pathbreaking in historical context, the papers presented at that meeting were generally conservative. William Blackstone asserted, in an Aristotelian manner, that each person has a fundamental right, by virtue of being human, to an unpolluted environment, which "is essential for one to fulfill his human capacities."[53] Employing an "interest principle," Joel Feinberg argued that to have a right means to have an interest in not being harmed.[54] Animals and future generations meet this criterion; plant species, dead persons, human vegetables, and fetuses do not. Animals and future generations, he said, should have proxies (Feinberg may have been thinking about environmental activists) to represent their interests in public policy debates.[55]

American legal scholar Christopher Stone's paper, "Should Trees Have Standing?" was published in a law review in 1972 and then republished as a book two years later. (The latter included Supreme Court Justice William Douglas's famous reference to Stone's argument in his dissenting opinion of *Sierra Club v. Morton*.) Taking a traditionalist stance, Stone argued, along with Blackstone and Feinberg, that existing legal principles, if accurately interpreted and executed, can be expanded to cover nonhuman natural objects.[56]

A radical paper also presented in 1972 marks the rise of unapologetic nonanthropocentrism in environmental ethics. The paper was delivered in September at the Third World Future Research conference in Bucharest, Romania, by the late Norwegian philosopher Arne Naess.[57] Afterward, Naess used his notes from that lecture to pen "The Shallow and the Deep, Long-Range Ecology Movement: A Summary," perhaps the most-cited article in environmental ethics and the preamble to the second full-length book on environmental ethics, Naess's *Økologi, samfunn, og livsstil*.[58]

With perceived global ecological crisis looming, many of the Bucharest participants took a faith-based technological approach and argued that environmental problems can be solved through engineering and management without the need for substantial makeover of social and political structures.[59] Naess disagreed, contrasting anthropocentric environmental ethics (which he called the "shallow ecology movement") with nonanthropocentric environmental ethics (which he called the "deep ecology movement"), a comparison he would continue to develop in the coming years.

Shallow ecology, typical of mainstream environmentalism, is an extension of Western anthropocentrism because the reasons for taking action on environmental issues are invariably framed in terms of human welfare. It finds solutions to pollution and the depletion of natural resources through technological fixes.[60] In contrast, the deep ecology movement questions the fundamental assumptions of Western anthropocentrism – that is, it digs philosophically deeper than the superficial anthropocentrism of shallow ecology. In taking that approach, deep ecology "is not a slight reform of our present society, but a *substantial reorientation of our whole civilization*."[61]

One year later, and not far away, another radical and influential paper was delivered. At the 1973 World Congress of Philosophy in Varna, Bulgaria, Australian philosopher Richard Sylvan (at that time still using his birth surname, Routley) questioned the validity of human subjectivity as the fulcrum for making normative judgments about nonhuman nature. In a famous thought-experiment, Sylvan posed the question mentioned above: what if the Last Man – possibly an allusion to Mary Shelley's novel – in existence systematically destroyed every living thing before perishing himself? Or what if the Last People simplified all wild ecosystems in favor of industrial monoculture to best satisfy their needs before they themselves became extinct? Would the last person or the last people have behaved badly? From an anthropocentric perspective, no, not really.[62] Sylvan later amplified his question in his resolutely nonanthropocentric deep green theory and reached the opposite conclusion.[63] Biodiversity is intrinsically good (value$_4$) independently of human existence. In order to achieve this new ethic, the old normative structures of Western ethical theory would have to be foresworn.

A fellow Australian, Peter Singer, who did not see things as Sylvan did, proffered a traditional extensionist approach that same year by applying the Principle of Utility to sentient animals, just as Bentham had suggested almost 200 years earlier.[64] Singer expanded this argument in "All Animals Are Equal," broaching a subject that will be considered in greater detail below.

Also in 1974, yet another Australian philosopher, John Passmore, published the first book-length manuscript on environmental ethics, *Man's Responsibility for Nature*. Passmore took an unabashedly anthropocentric approach: "I treat human interests as paramount. I do not apologize for that fact."[65] Passmore defended the traditionalist position that human-centered ethics is entirely fit to deal with ecological issues: "The traditional moral teaching of the West, Christian or utilitarian, has always taught men … that they ought not so to act as to injure their neighbors."[66] Most important, Passmore argued, are new moral habits, not new moral principles.[67]

As the ancient Greek period set the stage for the development of the Western philosophical tradition, so the first five years of the 1970s set the stage for the development of environmental ethics. The themes that emerged in the first half of the decade were embellished in the second, culminating in 1979 when Eugene Hargrove established a journal devoted specifically to the topic.

In 1975, a new voice leapt into the conversation, a voice critical of the traditionalism of individualism that would be heard for decades to come. American philosopher Holmes Rolston answered the question "Is There an Ecological Ethic?" in the positive, asserting that ethics should not be merely *about* the environment but should be *informed by* the environment. Formulating such an ethic would require the abandonment of the atomism of traditional humanistic ethics in favor of one "derivative of the holistic character of the ecosystem."[68] Given the human dependence on ecological systems, a shift in emphasis from atomism to holism in ethics is mandatory.

In 1977, American environmental and political studies scholar John Rodman published a seminal critique of the moral extensionism of Singer and Stone. Like Rolston, Rodman perceived a severe deficiency in "moral atomism," which did "not seem well adapted to coping with ecological systems."[69] He called the strategy of extrapolating traditional humanistic ethical systems onto nonhuman individuals "homocentric imperialism" even though the motivation might be couched in nonanthropocentric terms.[70] Rodman adopted a biocentric approach that values the plenitude of living things for what they are – living things.

In that same issue of *Inquiry*, American philosopher George Sessions condemned Western society for erecting an impenetrable ontological divide between human beings and the rest of nature (metaphysical dualism), a tradition that he blamed for a "profound failure of religious, philosophical, and moral leadership."[71] Sessions insisted that all parts of nature are fundamentally interconnected (metaphysical monism). Interestingly, a "continuous minority tradition in the West," particularly

Spinoza, acknowledges this insight.[72] According to Sessions, Spinozistic monism anticipates the insights of the science of ecology, namely, that human beings are an inseparable part of the totality of nature.

Most significant for the history of environmental ethics, Sessions noted the importance of language in disclosing truths about humans' place in nature. Sessions praised the work of American poet Robinson Jeffers as "an expression of the psychology of the emotions,"[73] emotions of the unity of human existence with nature and the ineffable beauty of the living Earth. In noting the importance of language for environmental ethics, Sessions anticipated an entirely different approach to environmental ethics that would not come to fruition for another decade: continental environmental ethics.

Also in 1977, a young philosopher named J. Baird Callicott delivered a paper at a meeting of the Wisconsin Philosophical Association that was published two years later in the inaugural issue of the journal *Environmental Ethics*.[74] In "Elements of an Environmental Ethic," Callicott answered Sylvan's Last People conundrum, creatively applying formal logic to answer the question of the proper objects of moral considerability. These proper objects, Callicott concluded, are ecological wholes inclusive of human and nonhuman biota and the abiotic environment.[75] Further, human beings are moral agents and thus have moral obligations to both biotic and abiotic members of ecological communities, even though those other members are not moral agents themselves and therefore are not saddled with reciprocal moral obligations.[76] On this ethic, for the Last People to systematically destroy all life before perishing would be unconscionable. Callicott sketched a thoroughly holistic and nonanthropocentric environmental ethic that provided a template for his storied career. Aligned with the progressivism of Naess and Rolston, Callicott implied that the worn-out traditional moral paradigm of individualism fails miserably to meet the challenge of the holistic ontology of ecological systems.

In 1978 American philosopher Kenneth Goodpaster defended a traditionalist and individualistic ontology and deontological methodology for environmental ethics. Alsatian polymath Albert Schweitzer had voiced his intuitive spiritual respect for all living things more than a half century earlier,[77] but Goodpaster was the first to give a sophisticated philosophical defense of biocentrism in the mode of analytic philosophy.[78] Goodpaster implicitly agreed with

Feinberg and Singer that individuals are the proper subject-matter of moral consideration, but disagreed that the proper attribute of "moral considerability" (value$_3$) is *sentience*. In his view, the criterion of moral considerability is simply being *alive*. Goodpaster essentially extends Feinberg's "interest principle"[79] to all living things; a living thing need not be conscious to have an interest in flourishing. All living things are worthy of moral considerability insofar as they are alive and vulnerable to injury. This does not mean, however, that all living beings have equal *moral significance*.

In 1979, American philosopher Donald Van De Veer contrasted basic needs and peripheral needs.[80] The basic needs of something as lowly as a cockroach (not to be crushed to death) may trump peripheral needs (repulsiveness for humans).[81] The possible primacy of basic needs over peripheral needs is biocentric. But when basic needs conflict, human interests prevail. This, VanDeVeer admits, amounts to the "speciesism" denounced by Singer.[82] The possible primacy of human basic needs over nonhuman basic needs is hierarchical, and in this VanDeVeer resembles the hierarchical biocentrism of Rolston and Frederick Ferré.

In summary, two schools of thought formed during the first half of the 1970s that framed the discussion for the second half. The traditionalists staked out the position that the standard moral categories of mainstream Western ethics, rooted in ontologies of individualism, are up to the task of grounding an environmental ethic. This school of thought, "extensionism," includes anthropocentrists such as Passmore, who reasoned that nonhuman nature ought to be given moral consideration for the sole reason that doing so benefits humans. It also includes nonanthropocentrists, such as Singer and Stone, who reasoned that individualistic normative paradigms – utilitarianism and the Anglo-American legal tradition, respectively – can and should be extended to nonhuman living beings of various types.

The progressivists took the position that the traditional moral categories of mainstream Western ethics, rooted in ontologies of individualism, are *not* up to the task of grounding an environmental ethic and must be abandoned. What is needed is moral philosophy rooted in ontologies of holism, because ecological systems are characterized by holism.

While the second half of the 1970s seems to have been dominated by the progressivists, the core arguments of the traditionalists remain credible. English philosopher Robin Attfield, for example, has "yet to be persuaded that significantly new moral principles are required," because "the implementation of long-standing principles already requires some radical restructuring of society."[83] American philosopher Kristin Shrader-Frechette insists that "there is a strong rational foundation for using existing utilitarian and egalitarian ethical theories to safeguard the environment."[84] Eugene Hargrove maintains that humans have a duty to affirm good, that natural beauty is a good, and thus that humans have an ethical duty to preserve the environment on aesthetic grounds.[85] Along these lines, American philosopher Gary Varner has argued that the assumption that environmental ethics must be nonanthropocentric is "dogma" and that a sound and workable environmental ethic can indeed be built on an axiological edifice of human-centeredness.[86]

The 10 years between Cobb's essay and the foundation of the journal *Environmental Ethics* constituted an exciting and creative chapter in the history of moral philosophy. In one decade a nascent notion became an official subdiscipline of philosophy – albeit a marginalized one struggling to gain the respect of the "pure" philosophers.[87]

Spheres of Moral Considerability

Anthropocentric philosophers are unanimous in agreeing that moral obligations extend only to other humans. The French philosopher René Descartes (1596–1650 CE), for instance, argued that we have no moral duties to nonhumans because they are machines, and one cannot have moral duties to machines.

The German philosopher Immanuel Kant (1724–1804 CE) agreed with Descartes that humans have no *direct* moral duties to nonhuman animals. For Kant the class of beings worthy of moral consideration is coextensive with the class of moral agents – the Kingdom of Ends.[88] Only rational beings are worthy of moral considerability (ratiocentrism), and only human beings are rational.[89] Humans do, however, have *indirect* moral duties to nonhuman beings. The rationale for these oblique moral duties is anthropocentric.

Kant saw a behavioral link between the treatment of human beings and nonhuman nature. "A propensity to wanton destruction of what is beautiful in inanimate nature … is opposed to a human being's duty to himself; for it weakens or uproots that feeling in him which … greatly promotes morality."[90] Getting into the habit of destroying natural objects desensitizes one to the worth of human life. Since the way we treat our fellow humans is affected by the way we treat natural objects, we have indirect moral duties to nonliving nature. Such indirect duties are even stronger to nonhuman animals:

> With regard to the animate but nonrational part of creation, violent and cruel treatment of animals is far more intimately opposed to a human being's duty to himself, and he has a duty to refrain from this; for it dulls his shared feeling of their suffering and so weakens and gradually uproots a natural predisposition that is very serviceable to morality in one's relations with other men.[91]

Moral duties to nonhumans exist, but they are secondary to the primary imperative to treat rational human beings as ends-in-themselves. "Thus our duties to animals are indirectly duties to humanity."[92]

Environmental ethics can be seen as an outright repudiation of orthodox anthropocentrism. Is anthropocentrism really the proper paradigm for ethics, as philosophers from Socrates to Sartre have assumed? Do human beings really constitute the entire scope of moral considerability? The first philosophers to ask these questions were primarily from the Anglo-American analytic tradition. As we have seen, during the field's gestation during the 1970s these philosophers grounded ethics in axiology; that is, they first asked the metaethical question, "What entities besides humans are intrinsically valuable?"

As axiology requires asking basic ontological questions, metaphysics becomes a necessary condition for the delineation of an environmental ethic. This proclivity for approaching ethics metaphysically is well stated by German-born American philosopher Hans Jonas in a treatise on the philosophy of biology:

> Only an ethic which is grounded in the breadth of being, not merely in the singularity or oddness of man, can have significance in the scheme of things. [An] ethics no longer founded on divine authority must be founded on a principle discoverable in the nature of things, lest it fall victim to subjectivism or other forms of relativity. However far, therefore, the ontological quest may have carried us outside man, into the general theory of being and of life, it did not really move away from ethics, but searched for its possible foundation.[93]

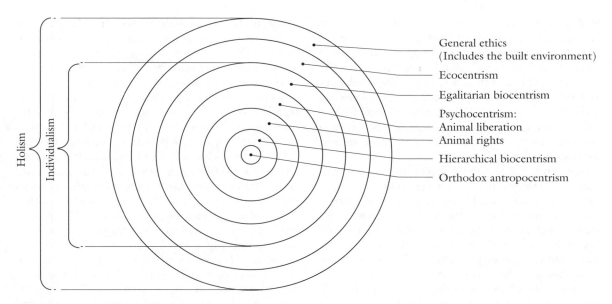

Figure I.1   Spheres of Moral Considerability

Some prominent philosophers, notably Norton, bemoan the fixation on axiology and ontology in environmental ethics. At the end of the day, Norton argues, it makes little difference for ethics and public policy whether the justification is anthropocentric or not; "anthropocentric and nonanthropocentric policies will converge in the indefinite future."[94] Axiological debates about anthropocentrism are thus neither crucial nor productive. (Norton is considered in greater detail in Part V, section E, "Environmental Pragmatism.")

Nonetheless, the question of intrinsic value in nature has undeniably been central to some of the most vigorous and animated debates in environmental ethics.[95] Australian philosopher Robert Elliott, for example, thinks that environmental ethics "is interesting and compelling" because it "attempt[s] to say exactly which kinds of things are morally considerable and why."[96] In my own experience, the most effective way to teach environmental ethics (even if one accepts the validity of Norton's arguments) is to build the course around the basic distinction of anthropocentrism versus non-anthropocentrism and the instrumental value versus the intrinsic value of nature.

The reassessment of whether human beings are the sole loci of intrinsic value can be thought of as the project of pushing the bounds of moral consid-

erability outward to include entities excluded by conventional anthropocentric ethics – the image Leopold imparts in "The Ethical Sequence" (see chapter 23 in this volume). Thus we can picture the development of environmental ethics during its gestational phase as a series of widening concentric spheres of inclusion of membership in the moral community radiating out from a core of orthodox anthropocentrism (see figure I.1).

The first widening of the sphere beyond orthodox anthropocentrism – conceptually, not historically – is the moral philosophy of hierarchical biocentrism.

Hierarchical (anthropometric) biocentrism

A simple and straightforward strategy of extending moral considerability to nonhuman biota is to grant intrinsic value to all living things in the natural order. Such an ethic confers more intrinsic value to beings higher in the hierarchy and less intrinsic value to beings lower in the hierarchy. In the natural order, humans are at the top and therefore have the greatest amount of intrinsic value. Such a biocentric ontology and axiology is anthropocentric, but it acknowledges that all beings in the natural order have at least some intrinsic value. This approach is no better illustrated than by American philosophers Holmes Rolston and Frederick Ferré.

✓ Rolston's environmental ethic is difficult to define. He is confidently Christian, and that view is overtly manifest in his work on the philosophy of science and religion.[97] His environmental ethic resembles a kind of theodicy, seeing the handiwork of God in nature and apprehending a special place in Creation for humans. His hierarchical biocentrism is an attempt to reconcile the ineffable beauty and sublimity of natural process with suffering, misery, and death.

Rolston is not shy about giving humans a special place in Creation, but he is a heterodox anthropocentrist who accords objective, autonomous, intrinsic value to all living things (biocentrism), with human beings providing the benchmark of such intrinsic value (anthropometric). Rolston believes that "humans are of the utmost value in the sense that they are the ecosystem's most sophisticated product. They have the highest per capita intrinsic value of any life form supported by the system. The system is *bio-systemic* and *anthropo-apical*."[98] I place Rolston at the first remove from orthodox anthropocentrism in the outward expansion of the scope of moral considerability for that reason.

Like anthropocentrists Descartes and Kant, Rolston draws a firm ontological divide between the human and the nonhuman. Humans are unique and superior to nonhuman organisms in a number of ways: most obviously, we are self-conscious, use language and reason, have free will, and are moral agents.[99] Human individuals have the potential for radically unique personalities: "the difference between two humans … can be greater and more interesting than the difference between plant species."[100] In Rolston's estimation, nonhumans do not have free will; they cannot choose between alternative actions that shape identity and destiny. Even the actions of higher vertebrates are causally determined. If grizzly bears face extinction, they cannot "consciously change to increase their chance of survival."[101] Nor do nonhumans love. Freedom and love "are emergents at the human level. … Neither is to be looked for in rocks or trees, nor really in animals."[102] Nonhumans are thus "nonmoral forms of life."[103]

Unlike Descartes and Kant, Rolston argues that nonhuman biota are worthy of direct moral consideration. Individual organisms, as teleological centers of life, possess "autonomous intrinsic value"[104] (that is, they are objectively valuable in and of themselves autonomously, or independently, of being valued

subjectively). Here Rolston rejects Callicott's and Hargrove's anthropogenic axiology of nonhuman nature (value$_5$) – the view that the inherent value of nonhuman nature must be recognized by humans in order to become real – in favor of value$_4$.

Ferré's formulation of hierarchical biocentrism is firmly rooted in the tradition of the "organismic" metaphysics of Alfred North Whitehead. In "Persons in Nature" (reprinted herein: see chapter 18) and "Personalistic Organicism," Ferré argues that living things have different intensities of inner experience and different capacities for creativity and freedom of will. He agrees with Rolston that these differences give different organisms varying degrees of intrinsic value. The locus of intrinsic value is to be an experiencing subject: "This need not be self-conscious experience; but intrinsically satisfying experiences of a wide range of sharpness and complexity are not hard to imagine … We need not be talking in metaphors when we speak of contented cows and happy clams."[105] All living things have some intrinsic value insofar as they are the subjects of experience, though the degree of this value differs with the intensity of the subjectivity. Complex organisms with centralized nervous systems have greater intrinsic value than simpler organisms, and hence have more weight in moral calculations. Unlike Rolston, however, Ferré posits a single unified ethical system rather than two discrete ethical systems, one that applies to humans and another that applies to nonhumans.

Hierarchical biocentrism has been criticized for upholding the anthropocentric hierarchies of valuation that some philosophers see as the very task of environmental ethics to dismantle. Sessions protests that any hierarchical axiology merely reinstates a "pecking order in this moral barnyard."[106] "The point is not whether humans in fact do have the greatest degree of sentience on this planet (although dolphins and whales might provide a counter-instance), deep ecologists argue that the degree of sentience is *irrelevant* in terms of how humans relate to the rest of Nature."[107]

Psychocentrism

Why is a face – whether primate, canine, or feline – charming, charismatic, warm, alluring? Because we take that face to be a sign of consciousness (in ancient Greek, *psyche*: soul, mentality, sentience). The possession of sentience, *psyche*, is the attribute (value$_3$)

that provides the axiological foundation for the theories that fall under the heading *psychocentrism*. Emphasizing conation, psychocentrism blurs the line between humanity and animality, and for this reason includes theories generally referred to as "animal welfare ethics."

One way of formulating psychocentrism is to emphasize awareness of oneself as a subject persisting through time in a community of other subjects. Humans are notable for this sort of awareness, but evidence suggests that other primates have it as well. Consider a chimpanzee looking in a mirror. Research suggests that a chimpanzee has the ability to understand that the image staring back is not another chimpanzee but *itself*.[108] It has an awareness of itself as a subject in the world of chimpanzees. American philosopher Tom Regan calls this type of self-awareness "subject-of-a-life":

> Individuals are subjects-of-a-life if they have beliefs and desires; perception, memory, and a sense of the future, including their own future; an emotional life together with feelings of pleasure and pain; preference-and-welfare interests; the ability to initiate action in pursuit of their desires and goals; a psychophysical identity over time; and an individual welfare in the sense that their experiental [*sic*] life fares well or ill for them, logically independently of their utility for others and logically independently of their being the object of anyone's interests.[109]

To be a subject-of-a-life is a moral attribute (value$_3$) that secures intrinsic value (value$_2$). Such beings have a right to be respected by moral agents, and that right entails concordant duties of moral agents. Regan's psychocentric individualistic ethic is thus deontological. On account of the title of his widely read book, Regan's version of animal welfare ethics is appropriately called "animal rights" (see figure I.1 above).

Animal rights has been criticized for employing a necessary condition for moral considerability (value$_3$) that is far too narrow: the subject-of-a-life criterion amounts to mammalian ethics. Some other animal welfare ethicists argue that Regan's scope of moral considerability, albeit wider than anthropocentrism, is too restrictive because it applies only to mammals distinguished by self-awareness – primates. In the tradition of the classical utilitarianism of Jeremy Bentham and John Stuart Mill, Singer argues against Regan that the correct criterion for moral considerability (value$_2$) is the capacity to suffer (value$_3$).

This attribute includes all animals down the scale of nature to, approximately, crustaceans.[110] Singer quotes Bentham approvingly: "The day *may* come when the rest of the animal creation may acquire those rights which never could have been witholden from them but by the hand of tyranny … The question is not, Can they *reason*? nor, Can they *talk*? but, Can they *suffer*?"[111] Singer's psychocentric individualistic ethic is thus utilitarian, and his version of animal welfare ethics is appropriately called "animal liberation" (after his famous book's title) (see figure I.1 above).

Singer's philosophy has been hugely popular with activists, but his colleagues in academe have been less acquiescent. Several criticisms of animal liberation stand out. First is the problem of classical utilitarianism; that is, the exploitation of a class of individuals might be justified if their suffering is outweighed by the pleasure another class of individuals gains from that exploitation.[112] It does not require a huge flight of fancy to imagine the delight of an epicure feasting on veal scaloppine or foie gras offsetting the misery of a calf imprisoned in a puny plastic pen or geese subjected to gavage.

Second, as utilitarians value the pains and pleasures that individuals are capable of (in the sense of value$_3$) rather than the beings themselves (in the sense of value$_2$), animal liberation is susceptible to the "receptacle" problem. Regan uses the analogy of a cup: what is important for the utilitarian is the flavor of the fluid in the cup, not the cup itself:

> What has value are the liquids: the sweeter the better, the bitter the worse. The cup – the container – has no value. … For the utilitarian, you and I are like the cup; we have no value as individuals. … What has value is what goes into us, what we serve as receptacles for; our feelings of satisfaction have positive value, our feelings of frustration have negative value.[113]

Individuals, in other words, have no actual intrinsic value; they only have extrinsic value in serving as receptacles for preferences.

Third, notes Rodman, animal liberation sends a "double message."[114] Some nonhuman animals are granted membership in the moral community by virtue of possessing sentience, an attribute (value$_3$) humans epitomize; semi-sentient nonhuman animals are reduced to inferior status by default.[115] The "rest of nature is left in a state of thinghood, having no intrinsic worth, acquiring instrumental value only as resources for the well-being of an elite of sentient beings. Homocentrist rationalism has widened out into a kind of zoöcentrist sentientism."[116]

Zoöcentrist sentientism might be an improvement over homocentrist rationalism, but the problem of consistency remains: identifying sentience as the attribute that confers moral considerability (value$_3$) is no less arbitrary than identifying rationality (à la Descartes and Kant) as that attribute.[117] As Singer disparages racists and sexists for their indefensible moral fickleness,[118] so Rodman levels the charge of fickleness against Singer.

The criticisms surveyed here do not address problems of animal welfare ethics as an iteration of individualism. That criticism will emerge when we consider animal welfare ethics in relation to holistic environmental ethics.

Egalitarian biocentrism

In the campaign to depose anthropocentrism, animal welfare ethics is a forceful insurrection. Yet for some philosophers, psychocentrism does not go far enough. These philosophers would grant citizenship in the moral community not on the basis of being rational (Kant), being a subject-of-a-life (Regan), or being sentient (Bentham and Singer), but rather for displaying teleological activity. An ethic of this orientation is *biocentric* – centered on life. We have direct moral duties to all living beings based on their intrinsic worth as living beings. For biocentrists, organisms are members of the moral club (see figure I.1 above).

Biocentrism has hierarchical and egalitarian instantiations. The former instantiation, illustrated by Rolston and Ferré, is *anthropometric* insofar as it uses human subjectivity as the apogee of intrinsic valuation. More commonly, biocentrism is given an egalitarian formulation. Egalitarian biocentrists argue that since organisms are either alive or dead, and since simple organisms that are not subjects-of-a-life or even sentient are no less *alive* than complex organisms advantaged by cephalization, all organisms are *equal* in terms of moral considerability. Affirmation of equality is the unconditional rejection of the sort of value hierarchies that are discernible in the works of Rolston, Ferré, Regan, Singer, and others.

The earliest advocates of egalitarian biocentrism were deep ecologists such as Naess and Sessions. The former noted that "*the equal right to live and blossom*

is an intuitively clear and obvious value axiom."[119] Sessions, writing with sociologist Bill Devall, claimed that "all organisms and entities in the ecosphere, as parts of the interrelated whole, are equal in intrinsic worth."[120]

The other prominent formulation of egalitarian biocentrism is the work of American philosopher Paul Taylor. For Taylor, the exhibition of goal-directed activity – in the Aristotelian sense of the actualization of potentiality – is the attribute (value$_3$) that bestows intrinsic value (value$_2$) on an entity. All organisms "have a good of their own around which their behavior is organized. All organisms, whether conscious or not, are teleological centers of life in the sense that each is a unified, coherently ordered system of goal-oriented activities that has a constant tendency to protect and maintain the organism's existence."[121]

Conflict is inevitable on such a model. Parasitic micro-organisms are living things, so the biocentrist must provide a method for arbitrating mutually exclusive interests of parasites and their hosts. For example, the eradication of *Plasmodium falciparum*, the protozoan that causes malaria (as well as *Anopheles quadrimaculatus*, the mosquito that transmits the malarial parasite), would save the lives of innumerable Asians, Africans, Americans, and others. Taylor attenuates conflicting biotic interests with the Principle of Self-Defense, which makes it "permissible for moral agents to protect themselves against dangerous or harmful organisms by destroying them."[122]

As Singer adapts utilitarianism to meet the problem of assuaging nonhuman animal suffering, so Taylor adapts deontology to meet the demand of respect for all living things. Taylor extends Kant's Kingdom of Ends to all living things by swapping rationality with vitality as the attribute that enjoins moral duty:

> In addition to and independently of whatever moral obligations we might have toward our fellow humans, we also have duties that are owed to wild living things in their own right … Our duties toward the Earth's non-human forms of life are grounded on their status as entities possessing inherent worth. They have a kind of value that belongs to them by their very nature, and it is this value that makes it wrong to treat them as if they existed as mere means to human ends. It is for *their* sake that their good should be promoted or protected. Just as humans should be treated with respect, so should they.[123]

Four objections stand out here, two normative (problems related to constructing a workable environmental ethic) and two ontological (problems related to the essence of ecological systems). First, biocentrism in its egalitarian formulation suffers from an internal inconsistency that precludes the construction of any environmental ethic. Richard Watson has shown that, *reductio ad absurdum*, the biocentric egalitarian is compelled to assent to the view that humans' actions, regardless of their effect on other organisms, are natural and perfectly acceptable:

> Human beings do alter things. They cause the extinction of many species, and they change the Earth's ecology. This is what humans do. This is their destiny. If they destroy many other species and themselves in the process, they do no more than has been done by many another species. The human species should be allowed – if any species can be said to have a right – to live out its evolutionary potential, to its own destruction if that is the end result. It is nature's way.[124]

Other species demonstrate no apparent concern for environmental duty, and humans must be exceptional to feel moral obligation at all. In trying to awaken a moral conscience in us, biocentrists cannot avoid making humans exceptional.

Second, egalitarianism is weak when it comes to adjudicating the conflicting interests of biota – the central task of environmental ethics. If the only type of value relevant to moral dilemmas is equivalent, then there is no basis on which to make prescriptions because the kind of value distinctions useful for making ethical judgments about the environment are deliberately disqualified. Warwick Fox contends that:

> [Deep ecology] does itself a disservice by employing a definition of anthropocentrism which is so overly exclusive that it condemns more or less *any* theory of value that attempts to guide "realistic praxis." … Unless deep ecologists take up this challenge and employ a workable definition of anthropocentrism, they may well become known as the advocates of "Procrustean Ethics" as they attempt to fit all organisms to the same dimensions of intrinsic value.[125]

In Norton's judgment, "The 120,000th elk cannot be treated equally with one of the last California condors – not, at least, on a reasonable *environmental* ethic."[126] Environmental ethics is in fact premised on the very ideal of a *nonegalitarian* axiology.

Third, biocentrism does not provide the basis for valuing biodiversity.[127] A tract of African oil palms (*Elaeis guineensis*) could theoretically total the same intrinsic worth as the plenitude of unique Everglades species it replaced. Biocentrism tends to value life generically, but not life in its myriad forms.

Fourth, the individualism of biocentrism is inconsistent with the real ecosystemic structure and function – competition, struggle, death – at the heart of evolutionary process. Irresolvable structural tensions divide biocentric egalitarianism and metaphysical holism within the context of ecological systems. It is simply impossible to affirm both the ability of all individuals to flourish and the integrity and stability of ecosystemic wholes. Although Naess preempts criticism of egalitarian biocentrism with the stipulation "in practice," this does not resolve the inherent incompatibility. The necessity of exterminating feral ungulates to save fragile island ecosystems discussed below is but one example.

Regard for the ecosystem health of wholes requires treating individual organisms differently because individuals of different species have unequal value (or disvalue) for the wholes of which they are a part. Some individuals are destructive to ecological function simply by virtue of their species. Consequently, egalitarian biocentrism and metaphysical holism are mutually exclusive within the context of ecosystemic structure and function. As Callicott says: "Struggle and death lie at the very heart of natural biotic processes, both ecological and evolutionary. An adequate biocentric axiology for environmental ethics could hardly morally condemn the very processes which it is intended to foster and protect."[128]

These last two criticisms point us directly to the holism of ecocentrism.

Ecocentrism

Individualism is polycentric: the loci of moral considerability are multiple discrete organisms. Regan, Singer, and Taylor attempt to construct an environmental ethic, in the spirit of standard moral philosophy, by extending moral considerability to nonhuman individuals. For Regan, those other individuals are subjects-of-a-life. For Singer, they are sentient beings capable of suffering. For Taylor, they are all living things.

Ecocentrism is an attempt to elaborate an entirely new paradigm for a moral philosophy against polycentrism. Voiced first in the 1970s by progressivists Naess, Rolston, Sessions, and Callicott, ecocentrism can be elaborated in a number of ways. One way is a weak holism, such as Rolston's and Ferré's, which grants instrumental value to ecosystemic wholes because they provide the life-support systems for individual living things. Another is a more robust holism that grants intrinsic values to ecological wholes themselves. Naess, Leopold, and Callicott take this approach. Let us look closely at the two eminent approaches to ecocentrism: the deep ecology of Naess and the land ethics of Leopold and Callicott.

Naess asserts that the biosphere consists not of discrete entities but of internally related entities comprising ontologically unbroken wholes:[129]

> An intrinsic relation between two objects A and B implies that it is bound by the definitions or basic constitutions of both A and B. Without this relation, A and B are no longer the same objects. They lose their identity. [In] AB models, totalities with properties ... cannot be deduced from the properties of A and B. The deduction does not give any results because A and B do not exist as separate entities.[130]

This means that an ecological system AB has emergent properties that are not simple summations of the properties of A and the properties of B.

The pedigree of land ethics traces back to American ecologist Aldo Leopold's enormously influential book *A Sand County Almanac*, published in 1949, and its preamble, "The Ecological Conscience," published a year before. Intentionally or not, Leopold fomented a revolution in the history of moral philosophy. Land ethics marks a paradigm shift from individualism to holism.[131] Leopold conjectured that just as moral considerability has expanded during the history of Western civilization to include individuals of previously excluded groups such as blacks and women, its scope should be further expanded to include biotic communities: "The land ethic simply enlarges the boundaries of the community to include soils, waters, plants, and animals, or collectively: the land."[132] (Leopold used "land" as a figure of speech: biotic communities are terrestrial and marine.)

Leopold argued that this schism between economic and ecological paradigms (the "A–B cleavage") is noticeable throughout the scientific disciplines that deal with the land – forestry, wildlife biology, and agriculture. He observed:

> Conservationists are notorious for their dissensions. Superficially these seem to add up to mere confusion, but a more careful scrutiny reveals a single plane of cleavage common to many specialized fields. In each field one group (A) regards the land as soil, and its function as commodity-production; another group (B) regards the land as a biota, and its function as something broader.[133]

Model A is an economic model based on the axiology of resourcism in which the value of the land is its resource, or instrumental, value. English philosopher Francis Bacon and John Locke promoted model A: nature itself has no intrinsic value; human beings, through labor, can transform the latent resource value of land into useful products. Humans should "release" as much value from the land as possible through development.

Model B is an ecological model; the land is a living thing with value above and beyond economic value. Certain members of the biota, in other words, may contribute greatly to ecosystemic integrity and yet have no monetary value. The problem with model A, the economic model, is that it does not recognize ecological value, and decisions made with an eye to profit degrade the integrity of biotic communities. (Or, as Leopold put it a few years earlier, the profit motive precipitates "ecological atrocities."[134]) "The 'key-log' which must be moved to release the evolutionary process for an ethic is simply this: quit thinking about decent land-use as solely an economic problem."[135]

Callicott has given Leopold's insights the systematic philosophical treatment they deserve. Callicott argues that the entire enterprise of mainstream moral philosophy, which has been based on the individual, must be relinquished. Psychocentrism and biocentrism are extensions of traditional moral philosophy in that they simply shift the loci of moral considerability to include select nonhuman animals or all living things. But no living thing exists in an ontological vacuum: living things exist only insofar as they are members of an ecological system. To mourn the death of individuals in the context of food chains is ecologically absurd: predator/prey relationships lie at the very center of evolution by natural selection, and the attempt to secure inviolable "rights" for individual organisms is akin to shutting down ecological process itself.[136]

Land ethics shifts the loci of moral considerability from individual organisms to ecosystemic wholes. Individual organisms should not be thought of as having intrinsic value or rights, because individuals, taken in themselves, do not greatly affect ecosystems. What affects ecosystems is species. An organism has value to the extent that it contributes to the overall integrity and stability of the larger biotic community in which it lives. The upshot, Callicott says, is that the "land ethic manifestly does not accord equal moral worth to each and every member of the biotic community."[137]

Land ethics consists of a nonegalitarian axiology embedded in an ontology of holism. Value is located in the organic whole. Individuals have no value in and of themselves independent of the biotic community:

> An environmental ethic which takes as its *summum bonum* the integrity, stability and beauty of the biotic community is not conferring moral standing on something *else* besides plants, animals, soils, and waters. Rather, the former, the good of the community as a whole, serves as a standard for the assessment of the relative value and relative ordering of its constitutive parts and therefore provides a means of adjudicating the often mutually contradictory demands of the parts considered separately for *equal* consideration.[138]

Land ethics is resolutely nonegalitarian: "Environmental ethics locates ultimate value in the biotic community and assigns differential moral value to the constitutive individuals relatively to that standard."[139] If individuals of a species benefit the biotic community, then those individuals have value. If individuals of a species imperil the biotic community, then those individuals have negative value, or disvalue.

The interests of organisms belonging to species with ecological value – that is, which contribute instrumentally (value$_1$) to the integrity, stability, and beauty of the ecological systems as a whole (value$_2$) – trump the interests of organisms that do not.

Individualism versus holism

The debate over the tenability of individualism (polycentrism) versus holism (ecocentrism) is central to environmental ethics and is no better illustrated than by contrasting animal welfare and land ethics. During the field's formative period during the 1970s, it seemed to be generally assumed that "environmental ethics" included animal welfare ethics. That unstated assumption was abruptly demolished with the publication of Callicott's provocative "Animal Liberation: A Triangular Affair."[140] The divorce of land ethics from animal welfare ethics is

historically significant because many philosophers now consider animal welfare ethics to be outside the purview of environmental ethics proper.

Callicott's article asks, "from the perspective of the land ethic, what the effect upon the natural environment taken as a whole would be if domestic animals were actually liberated."[141] The consequence, he answers, would be ecological catastrophe. Callicott's argument consists of three sub-arguments. First, animal welfare advocates fail to appreciate the differences between wild animals and domestic animals, which "have been bred to docility, tractability, stupidity, and dependency. It is literally meaningless to suggest that they be liberated."[142] Second, the deleterious effects of domestic animals on ecological communities are well documented: "From the perspective of the land ethic a herd of cattle, sheep, or pigs is as much or more a ruinous blight on the landscape as a fleet of four-wheel-drive off-road vehicles."[143] Third, the human vegetarianism that animal welfare ethics encourages would also be ecologically deleterious because it would shift the trophic niche occupied by *Homo sapiens* from omnivore to herbivore.[144] These arguments add up to one conclusion: the dichotomy between anthropocentrism and nonanthropocentrism, taken for granted during the 1970s, is really a triangle whose points are anthropocentric individualism (humanism), nonanthropocentric individualism (animal welfare ethics), and nonanthropocentric holism (land ethics) (see figure V.1 on page 227).

The coupling of moral considerability of individual organisms with ecosystem health led Regan to deliver a most unflattering portrayal of land ethics. Mentioning Leopold, Regan pans land ethics as "environmental fascism."[145] Regan points out, rightly, that if a human being, or any other animal with a high degree of sentience, is identified to have ecological disvalue, then that individual ought to be killed. Consider the problem of feral goats and pigs in Hawaii Volcanoes National Park on the island of Hawaii and Haleakala National Park on Maui. Pigs (*Sus scrofa*) and goats (*Capra hircus*) were introduced to the islands by humans, then escaped domestication and became feral. Tropical island ecosystems are fragile, and these exotic species have caused major ecological damage leading to the extinction of endemic species. Feral pigs, which weigh 200 pounds or more, push over entire trees in order to eat their roots, not only killing the trees but also causing subsequent soil erosion.[146]

To lessen further damage and preserve native species, programs to eradicate feral ungulates were instituted. In Hawaii Volcanoes National Park, around 70,000 goats were killed between 1920 and 1970.[147] Pigs are also regularly hunted and killed.[148] Culling goats in the two national parks includes building fences, hunting with dogs, releasing radio-collared goats to help locate wild flocks, and shooting goats from helicopters.[149] The last technique is needed because goats live on the massive volcanic cliffs beyond the reach of poison bait and hunters with dogs. After being shot, the goats presumably tumble for hundreds or thousands of feet over razor-sharp a´a´ volcanic rock that shreds their flesh. Such a death can only be described as grotesque and ultra-violent. And goats and pigs have a relatively high degree of sentience.

I evoke this dreadful image to make obvious the difference between animal welfare and land ethics. It is given that *Capra hircus* must be killed in order to stave off the extinction of native flora critical for ecosystemic integrity. Land ethics would extirpate the goats using any methods possible because they are of ecological disvalue. According to animal welfare ethics, these highly sentient creatures should not be killed in such a brutal manner regardless of their impact on ecosystemic integrity and stability. For Regan, as for Kant, the inviolable rights of particular beings should not be transgressed for the sake of some greater good, either for ecosystemic integrity or for the greatest good for the greatest number of people. "Individual rights are not to be outweighed by such considerations (which is to say that they are never to be outweighed). Environmental fascism and the rights view are like oil and water: they don't mix."[150]

In liberal democracies, calling someone a fascist is a rather harsh denunciation, although it is undeniably true that some organisms with high levels of sentience are ecologically pernicious. Human beings, in fact, fall into this category, and Regan's criticism of land ethics reflects a tinge of misanthropy in the thinking of ecocentrists. Associate editor of the *Earth First!* journal, Christopher Manes, writing under the pseudonym Miss Ann Thropy, infamously stated that since the biosphere would benefit from a substantial decline in human population, Acquired Immune Deficiency Syndrome (AIDS) might be a welcome palliative.[151]

While it is clear that Callicott initially subscribed to a rather extreme form of holism, he later mitigated

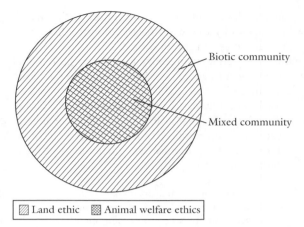

Biotic community

Mixed community

Land ethic   Animal welfare ethics

Figure I.2   Callicott's Theory of Nested Communities.

the holism of land ethics. In his theory of nested communities, Callicott attempts to do exactly what Regan claims is impossible: blend polycentric and ecocentric ethics. Impressed by Mary Midgley's book, *Animals and Why They Matter*, Callicott argues that animal welfare and ecocentric ethicists have overlapping – though not identical – concerns.[152] The mixed community is nested inside the biotic community, like Russian matryoshka dolls. Animal welfare ethics applies to the mixed community, while land ethics applies to the wider biotic community. The land ethic applies to wild animals and does not include the right not to be killed and eaten, while the animal welfare ethic applies to domestic animals as well and does include the right not to be eaten.[153] Therefore, we have two spheres of moral considerability (see figure I.2), and to extend the ethics of the mixed community to the biotic community would be "misplaced morality."[154]

Callicott's ontology of nested communities brings up the contentious issue of moral monism versus moral pluralism. Ethical monists maintain that meta-ethical coherence can be achieved only through the adoption of a single unified normative theory. Ethical pluralists maintain that the variety of entities worthy of moral considerability requires multiple normative theories. The debate between monists and pluralists was among the most interesting exchanges in environmental ethics during the late 1980s and 1990s.

Callicott has forcefully maintained that environmental ethics must rest on one unified normative standard. Ridiculing Stone, he portrays a moral pluralist legislator who capriciously adopts one normative standard (anthropocentric individualism) or another (nonanthropocentric holism) depending on the constituent to be appeased.[155] Since humans, as moral agents, are embedded in various human, mixed, ecological nested communities,[156] "when duties conflict then we must prioritize duties to those who are most proximate to us."[157]

Callicott has been criticized for incoherence here, most pointedly by Varner. Although Callicott seems to prioritize the stability and integrity of ecosystemic wholes over individual human interests, the ontology of nested communities suggests that one might very well support the plight of unemployed loggers, say, over coniferous ecosystems because loggers as humans are more proximate.[158] Callicott's account of the capricious legislator, Varner says, closely resembles Callicott's own system, which chooses duties to other humans in one situation and duties to ecosystems in another.[159] Critics have judged Callicott's environmental ethic to in fact be pluralistic.[160] The debate over monism versus pluralism is interesting, animated, and ongoing, and we will return to the issue when we consider environmental pragmatism.

Conclusion

Aristotle identified two types of rationality: philosophical wisdom (*sophia*) and practical wisdom (*phronesis*).[161] *Sophia* is knowledge of universal truths disclosed by metaphysics and natural science; *phronesis* pertains to the human condition. *Phronesis* instigates action, especially improvement of the quality of life. The phronetic person is able to organize many life-affecting elements into a smoothly functioning existence, a life of well-being, as the legislator organizes the *polis* into a smoothly functioning whole. *Phronesis* is the practical reasoning required of politics as well as ethics.

If humans have been the exclusive focus of ethicists from Socrates to Sartre, this exclusionary emphasis is to some degree justified. Among life forms, human beings certainly stand out. Our capacity to reason, our art, and our skill in technological innovation are unparalleled in the natural order. One cannot listen to the *Eroica*, read the *Odyssey*, or float prone in the sea gazing at fish through a face-mask while breathing through a snorkel and think

otherwise. We are unique and deserve some sort of moral consideration above and beyond that accorded to other life.

But this does not mean, contra the majority tradition in moral philosophy, that nonhumans are worthy of no direct moral consideration whatsoever. The damning fallacy of orthodox anthropocentrism is the association of moral agents with the class of beings deserving of undiluted moral respect. The revolutionary insight of environmental ethics is to call this coextension into question. Environmental ethics can be thought of as the framing of *phronesis* within the context of the natural order.

Environmental ethics discloses a major difference between being a *moral agent* and being *morally considerable*: moral agents are aware of their moral obligations to other beings. Other entities are not moral agents but nonetheless are worthy of moral consideration by agents who are moral. Environmental ethics is premised on the notion that human beings, as moral agents, have obligations to entities other than humans. Depending on the theory, these entities might be sentient animals, living things, or entire ecosystems. Environmental ethicists, as academics, hope to encourage humankind, through the development of theory, to live our lives as best we can, embedded as we are in webworks of ecological relationships. From the environment there is no escape.

The development of environmental ethics was an inevitable consequence of the Western intellectual tradition, although it came surprisingly late. Quality of life is affected by the integrity of the ecological systems with which human beings are inextricably connected. Given the undeniable continuities of all forms of life (the lesson of evolution by natural selection) and the fact that human beings depend on bio-communities for life-support (the lesson of ecological science), the class of entities worthy of moral considerability could not be restricted to *Homo sapiens*, the "wise humans," in perpetuity. In fact, acknowledgment of a wider sphere of moral considerability is compulsory if we are to live up to our self-anointed distinction as "wise." The history of philosophy itself obstructed this insight, but a cadre of philosophers have redeemed their discipline by providing fertile ground in which the field of environmental ethics can flower.

Some evidence suggests that these academics have been marginalized by their "pure philosophy" colleagues and relegated to second-class citizenship in academe.[162] This is predictable given the fact that philosophy itself has been a bastion of anthropocentric thinking. Now, given the quality of the work environmental philosophers have produced in just a few decades – in both creatively extending standard moral paradigms to nonhuman nature and also in developing new paradigms altogether – it is clear that environmental ethics has earned a rightful place in the pantheon of philosophical subdisciplines. Environmental ethics has become integral to the history of moral philosophy in the Western intellectual tradition.[163]

Notes

1 "From the perspective of intellectual history, environmental ethics is revolutionary; it is arguably the most dramatic expansion of morality in the course of human thought." Nash, *The Rights of Nature*, p. 7.

2 Cited by Plato, *Theaetetus* 152a, in *The Collected Dialogues*, ed. Hamilton and Cairns, p. 856.

3 Hargrove, *Foundations of Environmental Ethics*, p. 3.

4 Curry, *Ecological Ethics*, p. 4.

5 Norton, *Toward Unity Among Environmentalists*, p. 266, n. 20.

6 Callicott, "Introduction: Compass Points in Environmental Philosophy," in *Beyond the Land Ethic*, pp. 2–3.

7 See Millgram, "Practical Reasoning: The Current State of Play," in *Varieties of Practical Reasoning*, p. 1.

8 This equivocation is noticeable in Passmore's *Man's Responsibility for Nature*, Brennan's *Thinking About Nature*, and Plumwood's *Feminism and the Mastery of Nature*.

9 Passmore, "Attitudes to Nature," p. 251. (See this volume, p. 105.)

10 This taxonomy follows Ferré, *Philosophy of Technology*, pp. 28–9.

11 See, for example, Clements, *Plant Succession: An Analysis of the Development of Vegetation*. Clements called this teleologically directed biotic community a "superorganism."

12 Using different examples, Jamieson makes the same point in *Ethics and the Environment*, p. 2.

13 One might object that humans do not significantly affect the lithosphere. Scientific evidence suggests, however, that the weight of water in human-constructed reservoirs can trigger sizable earthquakes. See Kerr and Stone, "A Human Trigger for the Great Quake of Sichuan?"

14 Odum, *Fundamentals of Ecology*, p. 8.

15 Keller and Golley, *The Philosophy of Ecology*, p. 320.

16 See Kormondy, "Natural and Human Ecosystems."

17 Sylvan, "A Critique of Deep Ecology," part II, p. 13. Routley changed his surname to Sylvan after his

divorce (his former wife, Val, changed hers to Plumwood). For consistency, I use the surnames he and she died with.

18 See Fox, "Introduction: Ethics and the Built Environment," in Fox, ed., *Ethics and the Built Environment*, pp. 2–3; and Jamieson, *Ethics and the Environment*, p. 1.

19 Rothenberg, "Wildness Untamed: The Evolution of an Ideal," in *Wild Ideas*, p. xvii.

20 *Nicomachean Ethics* 1140a, in McKeon, ed., *The Basic Works of Aristotle*, p. 1025.

21 Buchanan, *Technology and Social Progress*, p. 163.

22 Rothenberg, *Hand's End*, p. 19.

23 Ibid., p. 17.

24 Ferré, *Philosophy of Technology*, p. 11.

25 Nielsen, "Problems of Ethics," in *The Encyclopedia of Philosophy*, vol. 3, pp. 118–19.

26 The following excursus tracks, though not step for step, O'Neill, "The Varieties of Intrinsic Value"; and Jamieson, *Ethics and the Environment*, pp. 68–75.

27 Callicott, "Non-anthropocentric Value Theory and Environmental Ethics," p. 299.

28 Kant, *Grounding for the Metaphysics of Morals*, p. 36.

29 Sylvan (Routley) and Plumwood (Routley), "Against the Inevitability of Human Chauvinism," in Goodpaster and Sayre, eds., *Ethics and Problems of the 21st Century*, p. 38.

30 Sylvan (Routley), "Is There a Need for a New, an Environmental, Ethic?" p. 207. (See this volume, p. 102.)

31 Ibid.

32 Callicott, "On the Intrinsic Value of Nonhuman Species," in *In Defense of the Land Ethic*, p. 133; emphasis in original.

33 Ibid.

34 "Intrinsic Value, Quantum Theory, and Environmental Ethics," in *In Defense of the Land Ethic*, p. 161; originally published in *Environmental Ethics* 7/3 (1985): 357–72.

35 "On the Intrinsic Value of Nonhuman Species," in *In Defense of the Land Ethic*, p. 133.

36 Ibid.

37 Rolston, *Environmental Ethics*, p. 114. Because the source of valuation is external to the valued natural object, Rolston rightly points out that Callicott's axiology of nonhuman nature is more accurately described as "extrinsic." Ibid., p. 115.

38 Norton, *Toward Unity among Environmentalists*, p. 235.

39 Darwin, *The Descent of Man*, pp. 78–9, p. 80.

40 *Politics* 125a30, in McKeon, ed., *The Basic Works of Aristotle*, p. 1130.

41 Darwin, *The Descent of Man*, p. 82.

42 Hargrove, "Weak Anthropocentric Intrinsic Value," p. 202.

43 Elliott, Introduction to *Environmental Ethics*, p. 12.

44 Tribe, "Ways Not to Think about Plastic Trees," pp. 1347–8, quoted from Horkheimer, *Eclipse of Reason*, pp. 37–8.

45 Ibid., p. 1348.

46 Carson, *Silent Spring*, p. 297.

47 "White thus implicitly – and, we daresay, unwittingly – set the agenda for a future environmental philosophy. The first item on the agenda is to criticize the evidently erroneous ideas that we have inherited from our past intellectual tradition about these matters." Frodeman and Callicott's introduction to Callicott and Frodeman, eds., *Encyclopedia of Environmental Ethics and Philosophy*, vol. 1, p. xxiii.

48 Light and Rolston, introduction to *Environmental Ethics: An Anthology*, p. 2.

49 See Mylan Engel Jr., "Ethical Extensionism," in Callicott and Frodeman, eds., *Encyclopedia of Environmental Ethics and Philosophy*, vol. 1, p. 396.

50 Cobb, "The Population Explosion and the Rights of the Subhuman World," p. 41.

51 Ibid., p. 50.

52 Blackstone, introduction to *Philosophy and Environmental Crisis*, p. 1.

53 "Ecology and Ethics," in *Philosophy and Environmental Crisis*, p. 32.

54 "The Rights of Animals and Unborn Generations," in *Philosophy and Environmental Crisis*, p. 51. Much later, Australian philosopher Lawrence Johnson would expand the concept of interest to all living things and even entire ecological systems. See *A Morally Deep World*, especially chs. 3 and 4.

55 Attfield, *Environmental Ethics*, p. 119.

56 Stone, "Should Trees Have Standing?" especially pp. 464–73. (See this volume, pp. 111–14.)

57 See www.deepecology.org/movement.htm (accessed January 18, 2009).

58 Apparently the original paper was lost, although not before it was translated into Romanian. That Romanian version of the original paper was translated into English as "The Shallow and the Deep Ecology Movement" and published in Anker, "Deep Ecology in Bucharest," pp. 59–66. Naess' monograph was later translated into English and reworked by David Rothenberg, in collaboration with Naess, as *Ecology, Community, and Lifestyle*.

59 Anker, "Deep Ecology in Bucharest," p. 57.

60 Naess in ibid., p. 59; Naess, "The Shallow and the Deep, Long-Range Ecology Movement: A Summary," p. 95. (See this volume, p. 230.)

61 Naess, *Ecology, Community, and Lifestyle*, p. 45; emphasis in original.

62 Sylvan, "Is There a Need for a New, an Environmental, Ethic?" pp. 207–8. (See this volume, pp. 100–1.)

63 See Sylvan and Bennett, *The Greening of Ethics*, pp. 142–3.

64 Singer, "Animal Liberation" (review of *Animals, Men and Morals*).

65 Passmore, *Man's Responsibility for Nature*, p. 187. Passmore later tempered his anthropocentrism in "Attitudes to Nature."

66 Ibid., p. 186.

67 Ibid., p. 188.

68 Rolston, "Is There an Ecological Ethic?" p. 98.

69 Rodman, "The Liberation of Nature?" p. 89.

70 Rodman calls this strategy (with which he disagrees), "The Method of Argument from Human Analogy and Anomaly." See ibid., pp. 87, 118.

71 Sessions, "Spinoza and Jeffers on Man in Nature," p. 481.

72 Ibid.

73 Ibid., p. 512.

74 Callicott, "Elements of an Environmental Ethic: Moral Considerability and the Biotic Community," in *In Defense of the Land Ethic*, pp. 63–73; orig. pub. in *Environmental Ethics* 1, no. 1 (1979): 71–81.

75 Ibid., p. 67.

76 Ibid., p. 68.

77 See *Civilization and Ethics*, especially pp. 240–9. Biocentrism is a sort of Western version of Jainism's reverence for the *jiva* ("soul-monad") of each living thing and allied prohibition against injury (*ahimsa*).

78 Goodpaster, "On Being Morally Considerable," pp. 308–25.

79 Goodpaster, "The Rights of Animals and Unborn Generations," in Blackstone, ed., *Philosophy and Environmental Crisis*, p. 51.

80 VanDeVeer, "Interspecific Justice," *Inquiry* 22/1–2 (Summer 1979): 55–79.

81 Ibid., p. 69.

82 Ibid., pp. 72–3.

83 Attfield, *The Ethics of Environmental Concern*, p. 209.

84 Shrader-Frechette, "Environmental Responsibility and Classical Ethical Theories," in *Environmental Ethics*, p. 23.

85 Hargrove, *Foundations of Environmental Ethics*, pp. 191–8.

86 Varner, *In Nature's Interests?* particularly ch. 6 and Conclusion.

87 Callicott, "Introduction: Compass Points in Environmental Philosophy," *Beyond the Land Ethic*, pp. 1–2.

88 Kant, *Grounding for the Metaphysics of Morals*, pp. 39–40.

89 Kant, *The Metaphysics of Morals*, p. 192. Kant's ratiocentrism implies that nonrational human beings are not worthy of moral consideration – a problem that animal welfare theorists have noticed – See, e.g., Regan, "An Examination and Defense of One Argument Concerning Animal Rights."

90 Kant, *The Metaphysics of Morals*, p. 192.

91 Ibid., pp. 192–3.

92 Ibid., p. 213.

93   Jonas, *The Phenomenon of Life*, p. 284.
94   Norton, "Conservation and Preservation," p. 220.
95   Callicott, *Beyond the Land Ethic*, p. 14.
96   Introduction to Elliott, ed., *Environmental Ethics*, p. 12.
97   See Rolston's *Science and Religion: A Critical Survey*, especially pp. 322–45; also his *Genes, Genesis, and God*, ch. 6.
98   Rolston, *Environmental Ethics*, p. 73.
99   Ibid., p. 65.
100 Ibid., p. 68.
101 Rolston, *Science and Religion*, p. 154.
102 Ibid., p. 308.
103 Ibid., p. 139.
104 Rolston, *Environmental Ethics*, p. 114.
105 Ferré, "Persons in Nature," p. 23.
106 "Western Process Metaphysics (Heraclitus, Whitehead, and Spinoza)," appendix D in Devall and Sessions, *Deep Ecology*, pp. 236–42.
107 Sessions, "Spinoza, Perennial Philosophy and Deep Ecology," p. 18.
108 Gallup, "Chimpanzees: Self-Recognition."
109 Regan, *The Case for Animal Rights*, p. 243.
110 Singer, *Animal Liberation*, p. 174.
111 Ibid., p. 7; Bentham, *The Principles of Morals and Legislation*, p. 311n.
112 Regan, "Animal Rights, Human Wrongs," pp. 111–12.
113 Regan, "The Case for Animal Rights," in Singer, ed., *In Defense of Animals*, pp. 19–20.
114 "The Liberation of Nature?" p. 93.
115 Ibid., p. 94.
116 Ibid., p. 91.
117 Ibid.
118 Singer, *Animal Liberation*, p. 3.
119 Naess, "The Shallow and the Deep, Long-Range Ecology Movement: A Summary" p. 96; emphasis in original.
120 Devall and Sessions, *Deep Ecology: Living as if Nature Mattered*, p. 67.
121 Taylor, *Respect for Nature*, p. 122.
122 Ibid., pp. 264–5.
123 Ibid., p. 13.
124 Watson, "A Critique of Anti-anthropocentric Biocentrism," p. 253.
125 Fox, "Deep Ecology: A New Philosophy of Our Time?," pp. 198–9.
126 Norton, *Toward Unity Among Environmentalists*, p. 224; emphasis in original.
127 Palmer, "A Bibliographic Essay on Environmental Ethics," pp. 80–1.
128 Callicott, "Non-anthropocentric Value Theory and Environmental Ethics," p. 301.
129 The holism of deep ecology might be inconsistent with its other central tenet, biospherical egalitarianism. See Keller, "Gleaning Lessons from Deep Ecology," pp. 144–7.
130 Naess, "The Shallow and the Deep Ecology Movement," in Anker, "Deep Ecology in Budapest," p. 60. (See this volume, p. 231.)
131 It is interesting to speculate why such a revolution would come from a non-philosopher. Perhaps disciplines are conservative in inculcating their practitioners with set patterns of thought.
132 Leopold, *A Sand County Almanac*, p. 202. (See this volume, p. 193.)
133 Ibid., p. 221. (See this volume, p. 199.)
134 Leopold, "The Ecological Conscience," p. 112.
135 *A Sand County Almanac*, p. 224. (See this volume, p. 200.)
136 "Review of Tom Regan: *The Case for Animal Rights*," in *In Defense of the Land Ethic*, p. 43.
137 "Animal Liberation: A Triangular Affair," in *In Defense of the Land Ethic*, p. 28.
138 Ibid., p. 25; emphasis in original.
139 Ibid., p. 37.
140 The essay originally appeared in *Environmental Ethics* 2/4 (Winter 1980): 311–38, and is reprinted in his *In Defense of the Land Ethic*, pp. 15–38. Mark Sagoff would also bring attention to the friction of animal welfare and ecocentric ethics in "Animal Liberation and Environmental Ethics: Bad Marriage, Quick Divorce."
141 "Animal Liberation: A Triangular Affair," in *In Defense of the Land Ethic*, p. 25.
142 Ibid., p. 30.
143 Ibid. See also Donahue, *The Western Range Revisited*.
144 "Animal Liberation: A Triangular Affair," in *In Defense of the Land Ethic*, p. 34.
145 Regan, *The Case for Animal Rights*, p. 362.
146 Burdick, "It's Not the Only Alien Invader," p. 55.
147 Loope et al., "Comparative Conservation Biology of Oceanic Archipelagoes: Hawaii and the Galápagos," p. 275.
148 Stone and Keith, "Control of Feral Ungulates and Small Mammals in Hawaii National Parks," pp. 279–80; and Burdick, "It's Not the Only Alien Invader," p. 55.
149 Stone and Keith, "Control of Feral Ungulates and Small Mammals in Hawaii National Parks," pp. 277–9.
150 Regan, *The Case for Animal Rights*, p. 362.
151 Manes, "Population and AIDS."
152 "Animal Liberation and Environmental Ethics: Back Together Again," in *In Defense of the Land Ethic*, p. 49.
153 Ibid., p. 56.
154 Ibid., p. 57.
155 "The Case against Moral Pluralism," p. 115.

156 "Animal Liberation and Environmental Ethics," in
     In Defense of the Land Ethic, p. 58.
157 "The Conceptual Foundations of the Land Ethic,"
     in *In Defense of the Land Ethic*, pp. 93–4.
158 Varner, "No Holism without Pluralism," p. 176.
159 Ibid., p. 177.
160 Domsky, "Evaluating Callicott's Attack on Stone's
     Moral Pluralism," particularly pp. 408–14.
161 *Nicomachean Ethics* 1139a6-11, in McKeon, ed.,
     The Basic Works of Aristotle, p. 1023.
162 In 1989, while a Master's degree student at Boston
     College thinking about doctorate study, I called
     Eugene Hargrove to ask him about the prospects of
     specializing in environmental ethics. To my shock
     and chagrin, Hargrove warned that environmental
     philosophy was disenfranchised by those who
     thought "true" philosophy addresses "pure" topics
     like Truth, Beauty, and Justice (personal communi-
     cation). Yet by 2003 Hargrove had become much
     more optimistic about environmental ethics getting
     the respect it deserves (personal communication).
163 Callicott, "Introduction: Compass Points in Envi-
     ronmental Philosophy," *Beyond the Land Ethic*,
     p. 6.

PART I

WHY STUDY ENVIRONMENTAL ETHICS?

George Sessions

I have been personally and professionally involved in ecological philosophy for 40 years (beginning several years before Earth Day 1970), and my childhood and teenage experiences, it seems, provided the basis for this concern. I was raised in the Central Valley of California in the fairly conservative agricultural community of Fresno. The teen pop culture in the 1950s consisted of "dragging the main" American Graffiti-style. The 1950s were generally a kind of mindless era when America was trying to forget the war, and rampant consumerism was really starting to take off and shape the culture (see the HBO documentary *Earth and the American Dream* and the PBS documentary *Affluenza*). In the Bay Area, the beatnik writers were starting to challenge this, and this led to the countercultural explosion of the 1960s with the hippies, and the ecological revolution of Rachel Carson, David Brower and the Sierra Club, and Paul Ehrlich. My parents were public school teachers and there wasn't much emphasis upon (or extra money for) materialism and consumption. My family was not very ideological – we were moderate Christians and Democrats and there wasn't much talk of politics or religion around the dinner table.

In retrospect, what turned out to be the great saving grace for me from the mindless American teen culture was the immense wall of the Sierra Nevada (John Muir's "Range of Light") rising above the Valley to the east. My parents built a modest cabin at Huntington Lake (at the 7,500-foot level) when I was about 9, and our family would spend all summer up there hiking, fishing, and backpacking in the High Sierra. When I was 12, my dad, brother, and I hiked to the top of Mt. Whitney, and we ran into some mountain climbers with all their gear. This immediately fascinated me, and the mystique of mountaineering (and John Muir and David Brower) became my passion. At age 13, just as Brower was taking the reins as executive director of the Sierra Club in 1952 (see the PBS documentary, *For Earth's Sake: The Life and Times of David Brower*), I hopped onto a bus to attend a Sierra Club practice climb at Indian Rock in Berkeley to learn how to climb from Brower himself. Some of us formed a rock-climbing section of the Sierra Club in Fresno and, all through

high school and college, I was doing roped climbs in Yosemite and Kings Canyon almost every weekend. I got a job with the Park Service while in college, and spent the summers living and climbing in Yosemite Valley.

Religious questions led me to become a philosophy major at Fresno State. After graduation, in September I took a two-week solo backpack down the southern half of the Sierra's John Muir Trail. Halfway through the hike, the backcountry ranger passed me on his way out for the season. For the last week of the trip, I saw no one and was literally alone in the High Sierra. On the backpack, I felt a tremendous sense of freedom. My graduate study at the University of Chicago in analytic and language philosophy and the philosophy of science was very useful but largely ecologically irrelevant. The return to California and a year teaching at Humboldt State University in 1968 was an environmental eye-opener, and the excitement leading to Earth Day I, 1970, was building. *The Sierra Club Bulletins* in the closing years of the Brower era (1967–8) carried articles by Paul Ehrlich on overpopulation and historian Lynn White's indictment of Christian anthropocentrism and the ecological crisis (which greatly influenced me).

When I took a job at Sierra College (east of Sacramento) in 1969, I started doing research on anthropocentrism and the history of Western philosophy. I was also very powerfully moved by the writings of California Pulitzer Prize poet Gary Snyder – particularly his 1969 essay "Four Changes" – which appeared in Garrett DeBell's *Environmental Handbook* that Dave Brower had commissioned to serve as the "Bible" for the nationwide campus teach-ins on Earth Day 1970.[1] "Four Changes" is the first comprehensive statement of a deep ecology position. Snyder started out as a beatnik writer of the 1950s, spent over a decade studying Zen Buddhism in Japan, and wove together a deep ecology position based upon Zen and American Indian philosophies and the "old ways" of life. My narrowly analytic/rational training in philosophy at Chicago had broadened out into an appreciation of Eastern non-dualistic ways of understanding reality, and of overcoming the narrow Western sense of self as isolated ego. My love of the wildness of the mountains and philosophy had finally come together in the realization that Western philosophy, religion, and civilization urgently required an all-inclusive social paradigm shift to deal adequately with the ecological crisis.

In the 1970s I came in contact with the deep ecology writings of the Norwegian philosopher Arne Naess and, by the end of the '70s, I had come to the realization that he had synthesized the approach I had been working on. Naess had started out as a leading expert in the fields of semantics, logical analysis, and philosophy of science. Given his youthful experiences climbing and living in the mountains of Norway, and later as a Himalayan climber, together with his reading of Spinoza and Gandhi, he came to realize that semantics and logical analysis formed too narrow an approach to philosophy. Inspired by Rachel Carson, he distinguished between a shallow and a deep ecology movement in 1972. He set out to develop a philosophy for deep ecology based on the non-dualism of the Western and Eastern approaches of Spinoza and Gandhi.[2]

Perhaps the most radical and insightful approach to an understanding of how humanity has managed to embroil itself in the ecological crisis and destroy the Earth is the Paleolithic understanding of human nature. Many anthropologists, beginning with Claude Lévi-Strauss, claim that the human genome was established by natural selection during our hunting-gathering days in the Pleistocene era. It's as if Darwin's other shoe had dropped. First we learned that humans and other species have a common kinship, and now we realize, like other wild animals, that we have been naturally selected and genetically adapted to wild environments. It's not as if we have to go back to "living in caves" but, to be fully mentally and physically healthy, we have to intimately relate to wild environments. As Thoreau famously said, "In wildness is the preservation of the world."[3] This approach has been worked out by Gary Snyder and Paul Shepard.[4] The ecophilosophers Max Oelschlaeger[5] and Frederic Bender[6] have traced the history of Western civilization (and Western philosophy and religion) in terms of our increasing alienation from wild Nature and our Paleolithic genome. Oelschlaeger has the most insightful descriptions of the positions of Thoreau, Muir, Aldo Leopold, and Snyder in print, and argues that Thoreau, Muir, and Snyder were attempting to re-establish Paleolithic consciousness and a sense of the sacredness of wild Nature. Modern philosophy (and now the French postmodernists) has tended to promote the view

that we are totally cultural beings – Culture and Nature are two separate realms, and rightfully so. By sharply separating humans from Nature and their biological/ecological context, the postmodernists have been referred to as the New Creationists.[7] Fred Bender does an insightful job of showing the serious inadequacy of this view, and how non-dualism plays a crucial role in overcoming the Nature/Culture dichotomy – humans are to a significant extent cultural beings, but there is a necessary interplay between our Pleistocene genetic human nature and culture.[8] As Shepard points out: "[T]he greater the degree to which a person or society conforms to our Paleolithic progenitors and their environmental context the healthier she, he, they, and it will be."[9] This does not bode well for a new younger generation that spends most of its time indoors – playing with computers and living in hyperreality and online in virtual reality and cyberspace – while suffering what psychologists call "Nature-deficit disorder."

But, given that global warming and the ecological crisis are now down upon our heads, we can't sit around and wait for the majority of humans to recapture Paleolithic consciousness. Actually, modern humans are becoming increasingly what Neil Evernden calls "natural aliens"[10] and cyborgs, as their reality is shaped more and more by cyberspace. Al Gore now claims that global warming is the greatest moral and survival challenge that humanity has ever faced, but this can't be limited to global warming.[11] In his best-selling book, Jared Diamond describes 12 major ecological problems (including human overpopulation, biodiversity and wild ecosystem loss, and global warming) each of which could result in the global collapse of civilization.[12] This challenge and awareness must be extended to the full dimensions of the global ecological crisis as described by Diamond and the world scientist's organizations.[13]

A course in environmental ethics should lead to a wider understanding of economics, politics, and the forces that are shaping our world and what we can do about it. In their *One With Nineveh*, Anne and Paul Ehrlich take us through the various aspects of the I = PAT [impact on the biosphere equals the product of human population, affluence, and technology] equation (overpopulation, overconsumption, technology), and the ecological destruction of the Earth, and describe the various economic, political, and lifestyle changes that need to occur.[14] James Speth, a long-time government environmental official (and now dean of the School of Forestry & Environmental Studies at Yale), has also written a very important book that provides a sophisticated analysis of the ecological crisis.[15] He argues, like the Ehrlichs, that modern capitalism and corporations that now "rule the world" (and promote endless growth and overconsumption) have to be turned around, and we must attain a post-growth society that promotes the well-being of humans and Nature. And what's left of wild Nature must be protected as our Paleolithic home and the home of other wild species, and because the wild species and ecosystems of the world literally constitute the life-support systems of the biosphere. As the British scientist James Lovelock (the founder of the Gaia theory) recently pointed out, "there must be no more natural habitat destruction anywhere!"

Notes

1 *The Environmental Handbook: Prepared for the First National Environmental Teach-In* (New York: Ballantine Books, 1970).
2 For two papers that summarize Naess's approach, see "The Deep Ecological Movement," and "Deep Ecology for the Twenty-Second Century," in George Sessions, *Deep Ecology for the 21st Century* (Boston: Shambhala Publications, 1995), pp. 64–84, and pp. 463–7, respectively.
3 Henry David Thoreau, "Walking," in *The Works of Thoreau*, ed. Henry S. Canby (Boston, MA: Houghton Mifflin Company, 1937), pp. 659–60.
4 Paul Shepard, *Coming Home to the Pleistocene*, ed. Florence R. Shepard (Washington, DC: Island Press, 1998); Gary Snyder, *Turtle Island* (New York: New Directions, 1974).
5 Max Oelschlaeger, *The Idea of Wilderness: From Prehistory to the Age of Ecology* (New Haven: Yale University Press, 1991).
6 Frederic Bender, *The Culture of Extinction: Toward a Philosophy of Deep Ecology* (Amherst, New York: Humanity Books, 2003).
7 See George Sessions, "Wildness, Cyborgs, and Our Ecological Future," The *Trumpeter* 22/2 (2006).
8 *The Culture of Extinction*, ch. 4.
9 *Coming Home to the Pleistocene*, p. 34.
10 Neil Evernden, *The Natural Alien: Humankind and Environment* (Toronto: University of Toronto Press, 1985).
11 Al Gore, *Earth in the Balance: Ecology and the Human Spirit* (Boston: Houghton Mifflin, 1992).
12 Jared Diamond, *Collapse: How Societies Choose to Fail or Succeed* (New York: Viking Press, 2005), ch. 16.
13 See Sessions, "Wildness and Cyborgs," pp. 130–3.
14 Anne and Paul Ehrlich, *One with Nineveh: Politics, Consumption, and the Human Future* (Washington, DC: Island Press, 2004).
15 James Speth, *The Bridge at the Edge of the World: Capitalism, the Environment, and Crossing from Crisis to Sustainability* (New Haven: Yale University Press, 2008).

Emily Brady

I love birds. There's the obvious, of course: they can *fly*. This alone inspires a sense of awe in humans who, unfortunately, do not share this phenomenal natural capacity. Not only can (most) birds fly, but they fly vast distances. During their lifetime, swifts may well fly over a million miles. They bathe, "sleep," and can even mate while aloft – a creature more at home on the wing than on land. This is the same bird I hear screaming through the evening sky on summer nights above the rooftops of my village: here and now very much part of my home environment. To this, add the wonders of birdsong, the fascinating behavior of birds, and their great variety, from the modest wren to the great show-stoppers of the avian world – puffins, peacocks, eagles.

The albatross, a beautiful, magnificent bird, is seriously threatened by longline fishing and plastic pollution, among other things. Recently, I was deeply moved by a documentary film about the Laysan albatross, which, as a surface feeder, swallows bits of plastic floating on the surface of the ocean. Adult birds and chicks ingest the plastic, feel full, and die as a result of starvation and dehydration. This is evidenced in thousands of albatross carcasses found on sites in the Northwestern Hawaiian Islands, an area where the world's plastic litter collects.

There, as the birds decay, their remains expose what they swallowed that doesn't degrade: plastic lighters, small plastic toys, etc.[1]

When I first learned about this tragedy, it brought home to me, personally, and yet again, how important it is to change one's practices. "Recycling isn't enough," I thought to myself; "I've also got to curb my use of plastic as much as possible." Despite being a problem occurring far away from my everyday environment (not in my backyard) and affecting a species different from my own, I was moved to work harder at changing old, bad habits. The effect it had on me is at least down to how much I love birds.

What's the point of this brief story of an environmental tragedy and my own very modest environmentalism? It illustrates, first, how experiences of environment connect with personal values, and how, in some cases, there can be positive change, even if on a small scale. It also shows how environmental education conveyed through particular stories rather than just general imperatives (Don't Litter!) have potential for changing attitudes and practices in ways that affect the natural world. Second, beneath the story lies a set of assumptions that throw up a whole range of questions that need answers. Why should I care if another species is harmed, especially a bird living halfway across the world from me? Why should any species be protected – is it for reasons of rarity, biodiversity, or beauty? But what is rarity – after all isn't rarity a relative concept? How does biodiversity confer value on anything? Isn't beauty in the eye of the beholder? What if no one else found that albatross magnificent and beautiful? Would it still be worth protecting?

These are the kinds of questions that concern environmental philosophers, and rightly so. Environmental ethics and environmental aesthetics are areas of philosophy that enable us to dig deeper and develop a greater understanding of the concepts, beliefs, and arguments (or lack thereof!) that produce, shape, and inform decisions, practices, and policies related to the environment around us. The philosophical skills of conceptual analysis, making distinctions, refining or rejecting definitions, evaluating arguments, and so on encourage the careful scrutiny that's required if we want sound ways to back up any claims or arguments relating to the environment.

Let me take beauty, a category of aesthetic value, as a case in point and try to show why reflecting philosophically on beauty matters. It is a commonly held view that beauty is subjective; it's all a matter of opinion, people say. This conclusion is drawn on the basis that there are disagreements among aesthetic judgments. But this sort of mistake is also made in defense of the view that moral judgments are all subjective. In both cases there is a tendency to overestimate disagreement, and thus conclude, too quickly, that value judgments of these kinds must be subjective. Elsewhere, I've argued against strong aesthetic subjectivism, and I've tried to show the importance of a critical understanding of the nature of aesthetic judgments of environment.[2] Why is this understanding so important? An implication of simply assuming that aesthetic judgment is a deeply subjective matter is that aesthetic values are given much less weight in decisions and policy concerning the protection of environments. In this context, objective values carry more weight, inevitably, as they relate to that which, it is believed, can be measured, objectified, quantified, and thus more easily figured into decision-making. But if we assume that only values of the quantifiable kind matter, then we leave out a rich, diverse range of aesthetic experiences which are among the most accessible, immediate ways people discover value in the natural world.

This problem illustrates the need for understanding the complexity of aesthetic value in theory, and how it relates to practice. It points to, I believe, the most important reason for philosophical reflection about aesthetics in relation to the environment. From here, a number of other questions emerge. What if conflicts arise between two kinds of value, aesthetic and ecological? What do we do about a beautiful but invasive plant species that threatens the health of an ecosystem? What about environments, creatures, and other phenomena of the natural world that are not considered beautiful? How does ugliness feature in our aesthetic judgments of nature, and what role do negative judgments have? Can scientific knowledge supplement aesthetic judgments to help us discover value beyond ugliness?[3]

These are the kinds of questions that are thrown up when philosophical aesthetics meets environmental ethics. The problems they raise have their roots in the wonderful, marvelous, awesome, frightening, strange, and tragic experiences we have of the natural environment. In fact, some philosophers have argued that aesthetic valuing of nature might serve as a sound foundation for an environmental ethic.[4] Might this be the case? That's yet another key question – and one that might help us to understand why anyone's love of nature might motivate environmental action. So why study environmental ethics? Because beauty matters!

Notes

1 Rebecca Hosking, *Natural World: Hawaii – Message in the Waves*, BBC Television, May 2, 2007. See also, Greenpeace International, "Plastic Pollution: A growing threat to the health of our oceans": www.oceans.green peace.org/raw/content/en/documents-reports/plastic-pollution.pdf (accessed July 15, 2008).

2 See Emily Brady, *Aesthetics of the Natural Environment* (Edinburgh and Tuscaloosa: Edinburgh University Press/University of Alabama Press, 2003).

3 For discussion of these questions, see, for example, Yuriko Saito, "The Aesthetics of Unscenic Nature," *Journal of Aesthetics and Art Criticism: Special Issue:* *Environmental Aesthetics* 56/2 (1998): 101–11; Allen Carlson, *Aesthetics and the Environment: Nature, Art and Architecture* (New York: Routledge, 2000).

4 Holmes Rolston presents the most recent exploration of this question in "From Beauty to Duty: Aesthetics of Nature and Environmental Ethics," in Arnold Berleant, ed., *Environment and the Arts: Perspectives on Environmental Aesthetics* (Aldershot and Burlington: Ashgate, 2002), pp. 127–42. See also Eugene Hargrove, *Foundations of Environmental Ethics* (Upper Saddle River, NJ: Prentice-Hall, 1989), ch. 6; John Passmore, *Man's Responsibility for Nature* (London: Duckworth, 1980), p. 189; Robert Elliot, *Faking Nature* (New York: Routledge, 1997), ch. 2; A. Carlson and S. Lintott, eds., *Nature, Aesthetics and Environmentalism: From Beauty to Duty* (New York: Columbia University Press, 2008). Mark Sagoff takes the view that loving care for nature can be developed through aesthetic experience in "Has Nature a Good of its Own?" *Hastings Center Report* 21 (1991): 32–40.

John Granrose

The formal study of ethics is not for everyone. Some lack the interest in "theory" which such a study requires. This is not necessarily a bad thing. There is plenty of room in our world for activists, poets, and artists as well as theoreticians. The formal study of environmental ethics will appeal to those with a taste and a talent for philosophy and is certainly worthy of their time and energy. My colleagues contributing to this collection will have made the case for this.

My perspective is a bit different. I want to stress the importance of things outside the philosophy classroom which are nonetheless relevant to environmental ethics.

In 1993 I retired from philosophy teaching at the University of Georgia. Interestingly enough, although my day-to-day activities since then have been more connected to practice than to theory, I can still remember many of the passages about ethics that I discussed with my students.

One such passage is from the British philosopher R. M. Hare. He began his 1963 book *Freedom and Reason* with the following (which I quote from memory): "The reader is invited to think of a difficult moral problem, one which calls for all the resources of thought, imagination and feeling that a person possesses. If the reader cannot think of such a problem, he [or she] had best postpone the reading of this book until having lived a little longer."

I always thought that Hare's opening passage nicely underscored the value and importance of thinking about ethics in a serious way. And, of course, if one reflects for even a moment, it is clear that many issues in environmental ethics qualify as the sort of moral problem that Hare has in mind.

In *Freedom and Reason*, Hare wants to interest the reader in the most theoretical issues in philosophical ethics. I spent 30 years of my professional life wrestling with such issues. Here, however, I want to stress the value of some broader, cultural aspects of our common concern for environmental ethics. For example, I believe that the study of the scientific aspects of environmental problems is just as important as the study of the purely ethical or philosophical theories. We all know that the level of scientific "literacy" in our Western world is at a rather low ebb. Just as during the decades when the tobacco industry managed to cast doubt on the facts of the health consequences of smoking, vested interests still manage to muddle the public's understanding of current issues such as the causes and consequences of global warming. Better understanding of science itself is surely needed here.

In addition to scientific information and sophistication, however, we also need "reminders" that are much less sophisticated than the theories and arguments required for the formal study of environmental ethics. We need metaphors, images, songs, and other cultural reminders of our environmental situation.

In recent years concern for environmental ethics has permeated more and more of our culture. For example, in 1977 the Episcopal Church in the US added a new Eucharistic prayer (prayer "C" on pages 369–72 of the 1977 *Book of Common Prayer*). It includes the following exchange between the priest and the congregation:

> God of all power, Ruler of the Universe, you are worthy of glory and praise.

> *Glory to you for ever and ever.*
> At your command all things came to be: the vast expanse of interstellar space, galaxies, suns, the planets in their courses, and this fragile earth, our island home.
> *By your will they were created and have their being.*

To me, the simple words "this fragile earth, our island home" convey the same powerful perspective as the famous photograph of the Earth as seen from the Moon.

Later, the prayer continues with the statement: "You made us the rulers of creation." But in my parish the priest always alters this to: "You made us the *stewards* of creation." This is another example of how an awareness of environmental ethics has become part of our daily life – quite apart from what is discussed in the philosophy classroom.

There are many roads to an appreciation of the ethical issues about our environment in addition to the study of philosophical theories of ethics. To each his (or her) own.

Frederick Ferré

Sometimes I am tempted to answer this question ("Why study environmental ethics?") as though it were a variant of the question: "Why *should* I be moral in my actions toward the environment?" The most efficient answer to this version is: "If you need to ask why you *should* act according to your moral obligations, you have already branded yourself as hopelessly out of touch." To understand the concept of a moral obligation is to understand, as part of the concept, that moral obligations, when genuine, are obligatory. This is tautologically true.

But of course there are other, more interesting, interpretations of the question. One is: "Why is there a special field called '*environmental*' ethics?" The answer to this is not quite so simple: "All domains of life in which human decisions are needed involve norms of better and worse; and where such decisions have consequences for entities that are capable of being harmed or helped, the relevant norms include ethical issues of right and wrong, moral duties and obligations." What complicates the answer to this question is the prior issue of whether human decisions

affecting the natural environment do or do not have consequences for entities that are capable of being harmed or helped. At one level the answer is obvious: since decisions affecting the natural environment have clear causal consequences for human beings, and since human beings are the sort of entities that have interests – in health, comfort, wealth, general well-being – that can be harmed or helped, an environmental ethics centered around consequences for human welfare is warranted at an obvious minimum.

Many have been content to stop at this level, but an increasing number in our society are concerned about a wider domain of consequences within nature: namely, the consequences for other *non*-human entities they suspect or strongly believe can be helped or harmed as well. Mammals inhabiting both land and sea seem to be able to feel hunger and other sorts of pain, to fear death and thus flee predators; birds too share many of these traits; some fish also seem to fit the pattern. Is this truly the case? Can non-human entities be harmed or helped? If so, then ethical norms come into play along with other aesthetic norms, economic norms, and considerations of human convenience. The sweep of environmental ethics therefore depends on our prior answers to questions about how things really are, what is truly real and what only seems to be. Do even worms and insects have interests? What of grasses and flowers and trees? Do our ethical obligations extend even to them? Environmental ethics is thus complicated (and enriched) by being inextricably entwined with issues in environmental metaphysics.

A third interpretation of our main question might have a different emphasis: "Why *study* environmental ethics?" Are not moral intuitions finally the ground for all felt obligations? If so, then what does study have to do with ethics? Or perhaps religious authority rules in the area of ethics. Who are we to question and probe, when in this area simple obedience is the proper posture? The answer calls for a better understanding of "study." Norms (standards, rules, etc.) do not clarify themselves and do not apply themselves. They have to be understood by limited human beings, for whom conceptual clarity often comes with great difficulty out of a haze of notions and feelings. Even intuitions – perhaps *particularly* intuitions – are often deeply unclear and conflicted. And religious rules are notoriously disputed, even among those who accept the same authorities as normative. "Study," in this sense, means clarifying, distinguishing, and focusing attention on purported obligations. It shows no disrespect; in fact, it manifests the highest respect, to contemplate ideals and standards intensely in order to improve understanding of just what is at stake.

Likewise, norms, even when clarified, do not apply themselves to circumstances. All obligations occur in the context of what is taken to be relevantly the case. We need to judge what we ought to do in the light of correct facts about what is. "Study," in this second

sense, means critically establishing what is really relevant and what is "going on around here." Not having correct facts can lead to terrible actions (and inactions), even while one is intending to maintain the most clarified of righteous intentions. And getting the facts right about what is going on "around here" is always within a wider context that, when seen, may change the meaning of the situation. Inserting a sharp blade into someone's abdomen could be a complex empirical fact, well-attested and verified; but broadening the picture to reveal whether it is being done by a criminal in a dark alley or by a surgeon in an operating room can change the ethical judgment of what is going on. The context is always important. Therefore, "study" in this sense involves the most accurate and most interrelated description of what is broadly so. At its broadest, such study brings one back again to the grand metaphysical understanding of what is going on around here – and everywhere. This, too, is an activity not to disparage but to honor the highest good.

Finally, the question might be asked with existential urgency: "Why should *I* study environmental ethics?" The answer is found deep in the inescapable human condition: Normal human levels of mentality – awareness of causal connections and consequences of our behavior – condemn us to responsibility for our actions, and inactions, whether we like it or not. *Failing* to put some modicum of effort into thinking through and clarifying the norms by which we live in interaction with the natural world, *resisting* critical examination of the facts describing what is going on broadly in nature, and *refusing* to assess the relevance of such facts to our guiding norms – *not* studying, that is, when the means of study are available – is failing morally. Culpable ignorance is no excuse. From this point of view, environmental ethics is not an elective subject. It is a moral requirement for mature human life.

J. Baird Callicott

I started to study environmental ethics in 1971, when I offered the world's first philosophy course with that title at the University of Wisconsin-Stevens Point. That's right, you study hardest and learn the

most when you are teaching a subject – often more than when you are just "taking" it. When I introduce myself to a fresh group of students in that course each semester, I explain that my doctoral specialty in graduate school was ancient Greek philosophy, and that I myself have never taken a course in environmental ethics. I mean, how could I? I taught the first one that ever existed. After I had been at it for about 15 years and had also helped to create a body of academic literature in the field, an irate student complained to my college dean that his professor was teaching a subject that he had never taken as an undergraduate or graduate student! I had to laugh out loud.

So, *why* did I start to study environmental ethics? Maybe my personal experience will strike a chord in you. First off, I was inspired by the first Earth Day the previous year. The Earth Day legislation was sponsored in the US Congress by Gaylord Nelson, one of our senators from Wisconsin. We were right there in the land of the young John Muir and the mature Aldo Leopold, two giants in conservation and precursors of environmental ethics. So the first Earth Day was a huge event at UWSP – a parade of speakers from 9:00 a.m. to 9:00 p.m. to a packed audience in the campus gymnasium. I gave one of them. Afterward, I joined a committee to create a multidisciplinary environmental studies program and rashly offered to teach a philosophy course for it that I called "Environmental Ethics." Philosophy wasn't the only traditional discipline to go green in those heady days; environmental economics and environmental history also emerged at about that same time. UWSP had a College of Natural Resources, so I had good collegial support and a ready clientele of students eager to take anything environmental.

Then too, my formative years were the 1960s. Yes, I know what you're thinking: sex, drugs, and rock and roll. But also think civil rights, the ill-conceived and tragic war in Vietnam, and, not least, the environmental crisis. I was involved in all three of the latter set (I plead the Fifth in regard to the former). My first academic job was at the University of Memphis and, as faculty advisor to the newly formed Black Students Association at that recently desegregated Southern school, I worked alongside Martin Luther King in his last campaign for the sanitation workers' strike. I stayed a jump ahead of the draft with a series of deferments, so I didn't get shipped off to 'Nam. But I certainly protested on behalf of those who did. Yet, as a philosopher, I figured it this way. The philosophical work underlying the civil rights movement had been done in the eighteenth century. So, while I could be a foot soldier for that

cause, I had nothing unique to contribute to it professionally. And the war in Vietnam would end – one way or another, sooner or later. But few, if any, philosophers in the past had considered the ethics of humanity's relationship to nature. Now that was the real challenge – and an opportunity – for me, presented by the environmental crisis.

Twentieth-century philosophy had become ossified and narrowly technical. I wasn't particularly good at it and I certainly was not attracted to it. I wanted to do philosophy in the grand manner of the past, in the manner of Plato and Aristotle, Descartes and Kant. The environmental crisis offered up the opportunity to tackle really big questions. In a 1967 article in *Science*, "The Historical Roots of Our Ecologic Crisis," Lynn White, Jr. implicitly set out an agenda for a future environmental philosophy. He traced the environmental crisis back to the worldview set out in Genesis in which "man" is uniquely created in the image of God, given "dominion" over the Earth and all its other creatures, and commanded to subdue it. In living out this worldview over the next two millennia, humanity had just about succeeded in actually seizing dominion over and subduing the Earth and its creatures. In addition, however, to all the wonderful technological marvels that are the fruits of that worldview, so also is the environmental crisis. Of course, White's analysis is as simplistic as it is lurid and provocative. There are other historical roots of the Western worldview – among them some of my favorites: Plato, Aristotle, Descartes, Locke, and the other Olympians of the philosophical canon. But there were three deep and true insights in White's thesis: (1) what we do, how we act, what choices we make, ultimately comes down to what we think, to our ideas, attitudes, and values; (2) the environmental crisis is negative feedback, the Earth telling us that the actions and choices we have made up to now were based on flawed thinking; and (3) that to change what we do, how we act, and what choices we make, we have to change what we think; we have to change our ideas, attitudes, and values. And until that happens, more science and technology are likely to just make matters worse, because they will be inspired and guided by flawed thinking.

So, who can lift the world out of the environmental crisis? Everybody has to do what they can, but the most important and fundamental job falls to us philosophers. It is our job to dig up, expose to view, and subject to criticism the flawed ideas about the nature of nature, human nature, and the proper relationship between humans and nature that we have inherited from the past. White made a start on that project, but he hardly finished it. And, second, we have to think up new ideas about these same central concerns. So that's one good reason to study environmental ethics. Ultimately, it's the only thing that can save us from ourselves. Call me megalomaniacal, but I still believe that – after nearly 40 years of working at it.

But there's another good reason to study environmental ethics. Being a world saver is a hard job. I mean, you do, in fact, have the weight of the world on your shoulders, don't you? And that's not easy to bear. It would appear to make it difficult to get out of bed in the morning. And you can feel guilty about going to sleep at night, or taking a night off to catch a movie, or going on vacation. If what you are doing is saving the world, and you're serious about it, you better keep at it 24/7, hadn't you? There's a lot at stake. So, it would be nice if there were something about that work which has its own inherent reward. And it does, fortunately. It's a labor of love. You do love the Earth, don't you? But almost as much, and maybe you haven't found this out yet – but you will if you study environmental ethics – the *ideas* about the Earth and our relationship to it are also to love. The work itself has a certain charm and beauty about it. Philosophy – this kind of philosophy, anyway – is enchanting; it's seductive. In this domain of ideas you can go where no one has ever gone before. So, it's a voyage of discovery as well as a labor of love. And for me, that's the best reason of all to study environmental ethics. Try it and see if you feel the same way.

Warwick Fox

What is the world like and how should we act in the light of this? We cannot simply "read off" what we *ought* to do from how we believe the world *is*: to do so is to commit the "is-ought fallacy"; to fail to understand that *descriptive* claims and *normative* claims (i.e., claims about the norms, goals, or standards of being and behaving that we should cultivate, respect, or promote) are logically different kinds of claims. Even so, the kinds of answers we have given to questions regarding how the world *is* have always had a pervasive shaping and constraining influence upon our answers to questions regarding what we *ought* to do, even if they have not directly determined them. For example, if we think that an all-powerful, all-knowing, and all-good being that we refer to as God made the world, then it becomes easy to argue that since God is the source of all goodness (which we can take as an allegedly descriptive premise), and since we ought to strive to partake in the nature of that goodness (which constitutes a rationally appealing normative premise), then we ought to praise, worship, and otherwise follow the guidance of God (which is a normative conclusion).

It turns out, however, that the best *explanatory* answer we have in regard to how the universe *is* is the naturalistic account offered by the sciences, by the kind of patient observation and testing of hypotheses against an independent reality that is undertaken by fields of study such as cosmology, biology, ecology, and psychology. This account shows, among other things, that humans – for all their special features – are an evolutionary outcome of natural processes; that we are relative newcomers to the weird and wonderful parade of life on Earth; that we are related, no matter how distantly, to all other life on Earth; that we are ultimately just as dependent as all other forms of life on Earth on the continuance of suitable life-sustaining conditions in the biosphere (and heating up the atmosphere is not one of them); that we are currently in the throes of the sixth great extinction event in the history of life on Earth; and that, this time, it is human activity (rather than, say, an asteroid impact or sudden, naturally caused climatic change) that is primarily responsible for this reduction in the diversity of life on Earth.

If this is how things *are*, then what should we *do*? Well, for starters, it would seem incumbent upon all of us to think hard about the nature of our relationship with this world of which we are a part, and on which we are ultimately just as dependent as any other species, and to ask ourselves how we ought to act in the light of these reflections. Since the field that specializes in this kind of inquiry is environmental ethics, this suggests that everyone who is capable of doing so should study at least some environmental ethics as part of their general education. The study of environmental ethics is a core component of the ecoliteracy we all need to develop if we are to have a future worth having; a future in which we at least maintain rather than further diminish the present quality, abundance, and diversity of life on Earth. I'm therefore with the renowned Harvard biologist E. O. Wilson when he said back in 1989, "Environmental ethics, still a small and neglected branch of intellectual activity, deserves to become a major branch of the humanities during the next hundred years"[1] – well, I'm with him except for one thing: I'm worried about his timescale!

Note

1 Edward O. Wilson, "Conservation: The Next Hundred Years," in David Western and Mary Pearl, eds., *Conservation for the Twenty-First Century* (New York: Oxford University Press, 1989), p. 7.

Eugene C. Hargrove

There are many reasons for studying environmental ethics. Most important to me is that it helps a person better understand his or her own views about the environment. Our views are shaped by a history of ideas that we are often only dimly aware of, if at all. As a result, we usually express our views either as social facts, which we can't really defend, or as unsupported (subjective) personal opinion. Trapped at this level of understanding, we fall easily into an arbitrary relativism. We say: "There is no right or wrong. It's just a matter of how we feel. I feel one way and you another." This way of thinking assumes that we each independently think up what we feel in isolation, not realizing that most of what we think is derived from historical traditions that we can only vaguely articulate. In the early 1970s, when I was writing my dissertation in philosophy, I was also leading an effort to protect a cave in central Missouri from water pollution. As the political struggle continued, I became curious about why I was saying the things I was saying and why my opponents were saying the things that they were saying.

Later, I researched the views on both sides and discovered that both were based on a history of ideas that were many centuries old. My opponents would say, "I worked that land. What right does anyone have to tell me what to do? No one has that right." It turned out that this view was already held by the Germanic tribes when the Romans first met them around 100 BC. It is part of freehold farmsteading, according to which a free man ("freeman") obtains control of his land by using it. This practice was carried across Europe to England, where it found its place at the level of the shire or county court, the oldest continuous form of government in England. In 1066, William the Conqueror brought this form of land-use practice to an end by imposing feudal law. Six centuries later, when British colonists arrived in North America, they tried to abandon feudal land-use practice in favor of a return to freehold farmsteading. Defended by Thomas Jefferson, drawing on common law and John Locke's theory of property, it eventually became law: the Homestead Act.

My own position was based on an aesthetic tradition, a mixture of natural history, science, and art. At the end of the Middle Ages, educated people were taught that nature was not beautiful. However, this view was transformed over several centuries via landscape gardening, landscape painting, and, later, photography, nature poetry and prose, and natural history science (biology, botany, and geology). The aesthetic experience of nature led naturally to a desire to preserve places of great beauty and scientific interest. My defense of the cave came from this four-century-old tradition. When we don't know the origin of our ideas, they often appear weak (they are just how we feel), and they are, as a result, beyond analysis, criticism, and improvement. Falsely believing that we have made up our ideas, and not realizing that nearly everyone else stands at the end of the same historical traditions, we let economic experts, serving up a naive blend of utilitarianism, pragmatism, and positivism from the late nineteenth century, decide our environmental policies for us.

In his book *1984*, George Orwell writes that he who controls the present controls the past, and he who controls the past controls the future. When we neglect the history of ideas behind our thoughts, we act blindly and are easily controlled by others.

Ian Smith

Back in 1989, when the global climate change issue was beginning to pervade the consciousness of people around the world, I helped raise awareness about the issue. Being part of a local middle school's mentorship program, I was teamed up with another student, David Mitchell, and our mentor Bob Child, a prominent regional politician. With Bob's tremendous help, the three of us crafted legislation that suggested ways to curb global climate change and ozone depletion. We persuaded our local governments to enact the legislation, which directed them to do such things as put bins in town for recycling, give incentives to people using energy-saving devices in their homes, and require that local rental cars' air-conditioning systems be free of ozone-depleting CFCs. Upon hearing about our story, Dr Noel Brown, former director of the North American Office of the United Nations Environmental Programme (UNEP), recognized our efforts by presenting us with a UNEP Leadership award for creative initiatives in the cause of the environment.

At the time, I felt that we were doing the right thing to help curb global climate change and that it was wrong to emit greenhouse gases at excessive levels. However, I lacked the intellectual tools needed to articulate why I believed it was wrong to pollute at such levels and why I believed it was right to change our behavior. This was a problem because, as a dedicated activist, I really should have had these kinds of tools, especially if I was pressed as to why I held such beliefs.

What is fantastic about studying environmental ethics is that it can give you the intellectual tools you need to articulate and critically evaluate your beliefs and those of others. It can help you to think about their implications, to uncover the assumptions on which they depend, and to argue for beliefs you find plausible in a rational manner.

For example, after taking an environmental ethics class, you might find that there are several ways to argue that emitting greenhouse gases at excessive levels is wrong. One route is by appealing to the harm principle. In a relatively simple and widely accepted formulation, the harm principle says that it is wrong to harm others (all else being equal) without their voluntary, informed consent.[1] Now, it turns out that applying the harm principle to such problems as pollution is difficult for many reasons, including that it is very hard to determine each polluter's contribution to the harms that the pollution causes.

However, let us consider a case of how the harm principle could be applied on some level with respect to excessive greenhouse gas emissions. A case can be made that when developed and developing countries release a massively unequal proportion of greenhouse gases into the atmosphere relative to least developed countries, the harm that results to the people in these least developed countries is largely on the shoulders of the developed and developing world. And this means that the developed and developing countries have violated the harm principle, on some level, in relation to the least developed countries. To illustrate, the staggering amounts of CO_2 released by the developed and developing world's fossil-fuel industries help cause desertification, coastal erosion, and more frequent and more powerful hurricanes in the least developed world.

Another route is by appealing to the interests of future generations. Of course, we may not know precisely what future generations will want and need. After all, we do not need nearly as much firewood now as in times past – in times past, firewood was a primary heating source, whereas now it is not. However, there are some things that all future generations will need, as Ernest Partridge has argued.[2]

First, future generations will be humans, with well-known biological needs. Second, if these generations are to flourish, they will need to be sustained by functioning ecosystems. Third, they will require stable social institutions, knowledge, and skills to overcome challenges. Again, excessive CO_2 pollution causes severe problems such as rising sea levels, more serious and frequent hurricanes, desertification, and burning forests. All of these problems can contribute to further troubles relating to what future generations will need. For example, desertification can cause food production to decrease, which will hinder future generations' ability to secure one of their most fundamental needs, food. For another example, rising sea levels can cause problematic emigration from coastal areas, which can destabilize social institutions that were once stable. If we are to take the interests of future generations seriously, then we should curb CO_2 pollution for the above reasons.

Appealing to virtue ethics is yet another route one might take to argue that polluting at excessive levels is wrong. One might argue that a virtuous citizenry is not the kind of citizenry that pollutes at such levels. One might argue that the virtue of humility requires us to have less of an adverse impact on the environment, and so pollute less. Thomas Hill once claimed that "learning humility requires learning to feel that something else matters besides what will affect oneself and one's circle of associates."[3] For example, the developed and developing world's industries could show that people in the least developed world matter by decreasing their levels of CO_2 pollution. And we humans might move beyond ourselves by recognizing that animals and plants matter as well, thus presenting, again, the need for changing our polluting behavior.

In short, you should study environmental ethics because it can help you to articulate and critically evaluate your beliefs and those of others – that is, beliefs about pressing environmental issues. Having a more informed perspective from which to think about environmental problems will help us all in creating a healthier planet.

Notes

1   Donald VanDeVeer and Christine Pierce, eds., *The Environmental Ethics and Policy Book* (Belmont, CA: Thomson/Wadsworth, 2003), p. 589.
2   Ernest Partridge, "Future Generations," in *The Environmental Ethics and Policy Book*.
3   Thomas Hill Jr., "Ideals of Human Excellence and Preserving Natural Environments," in Ronald Sandler and Philip Cafaro, eds., *Environmental Virtue Ethics* (Boulder, CO: Rowman & Littlefield Publishers, Inc., 2005).

Isis Brook

Here are some quick answers to the question "Why study environmental ethics?": because it's new, it's challenging, it's vitally important to our collective future, and it's not possible to develop a comprehensive approach to ethics without it.

Ethics is commonly understood as the study or practice of how we – human beings – should behave toward one another. Unlike some academic subjects, and certainly some other areas of philosophy, ethical questions impress themselves on us from an early age. For example, a favorite toy is taken from a small child by an older sibling and the small child says "It's not fair!" This is said not just as a way of parroting the parents, but with the full emotional force and clarity of vision that an injustice has taken place and that it should not have done. Something is wrong and needs to be put right. We are caught up in ethical questions all our lives and almost everyone thinks about such questions as they regularly encounter dilemmas regarding their own behavior and that of friends, relatives, and those in events relayed to them by the media.

For centuries, the focus of ethics has been on inter-human relationships. What mattered was human beings, not just because they seemed to be the only beings capable of ethical thought, but because they were deemed to be the only beings who mattered; the only beings for whom it made sense to ask questions about how they should be treated. The relatively recent expansion of ethical concern to animals and to the wider environment has been well documented and widely discussed. However, this expansion of ethical concerns has brought with it some seemingly irresolvable dilemmas. How do we weigh up consideration of an ecosystem or the protection of biodiversity against the suffering involved in the eradication of a sentient invasive species? How do we live a culturally rich human life with a small ecological footprint? Environmental ethics is a new area, and exciting in part because of its newness and the opportunity this allows for some original thought. It is also extremely challenging and inherently intriguing. You could see it as concerned with all the problems of inter-human ethics plus a whole lot more besides. Some of this new territory has been mapped and can provide you with a range of concepts and approaches to get you started, but this remains an area with very real challenges for the keen student or researcher.

Beyond the puzzles and opportunities that this new area provides to flex one's intellectual muscles, the study of environmental ethics has a knockout argument going for it: the problems it addresses are among the most important challenges we face – indeed, environmental problems arguably constitute the most important problems we face as a *species*. Although much of the most obvious work in addressing environmental problems occurs at the level of politics and policies, the thinking that informs decisions at this level needs to be underpinned by sound reasoning in ethics, otherwise it can easily be undermined; the reasoned justifications that underpin the "shoulds" and "oughts" of ethics are the lifeblood of rational policy-making.

What kind of thinking is required for environmental ethics? I would like to suggest two provisos. First, it needs to be scientifically literate. Ethicists do not need to be scientists, but it makes sense to be informed – skeptically if you like, but informed nonetheless – by the latest research and thinking. For example, in order to address the problem I referred to above of sentient invasive species, we need to be informed by the latest research on the cognitive abilities of nonhuman animals and the nature of biodiversity and natural processes. Second, but linked to the first point, any workable theory needs to issue in ethical mores that are possible for beings like us; that is, these mores need to be psychologically realistic and take into account our situation as evolved, environed beings.

In addition to these provisos, which I think should apply to any ethical theory regardless of its focus, we can also enrich our general ethical understanding by looking to at least four sources of inspiration for environmental ethics. One is the contemplation of nature; environmental ethics has been shaped and informed by a long tradition of human responsiveness to the wonder of nature and the natural world. Being responsive to nature, listening to something other than human discourse, is a learning experience and one that hones and develops human characteristics that are useful in the domain of human interactions and, some claim, essential for full psychological health. A second, related source is the fact that contemplation of and responsiveness to the world develops our aesthetic sensibilities. This need not be just to nature, but also to the built environment. The movement away from purely inter-human ethics helps us to appreciate nature aesthetically but also allows us to see that what we physically make in the world matters and that the way we respond to our built environments shapes the kind of people we become. A third source is an understanding of ourselves as part of the world, as intimately connected through our evolution and our being-in-the-world. A fourth source of inspiration for environmental ethics is respect for otherness, not just other human beings (or, as historically understood, other human beings like me), but respect for the very difference that separates us from other beings and things in the world.

With these two provisos and four sources of inspiration properly utilized, environmental ethics can lead the way to a workable, comprehensive ethic that can actually guide our actions in the world and help to lead us out of the mistakes of the past.

How people find their way to this area and are inspired enough to work within it is a personal story for each of us, but no doubt there are common themes. My introduction to the strikingly new range of questions this area throws up came in a lecture I attended as a student in 1988 given by Alan Holland on the distinction between deep and shallow ecology. However, a deeper commitment came about through a tangential journey into Goethe's scientific writings and working with his method of observation of nature. The study of natural phenomena using this method created in me a heartfelt engagement with the material world as a place of power, wonder, and fragility, accompanied by a sense of duty to protect and live up to that wonder.

Holmes Rolston III

1.

Study environmental ethics to figure out who you are, where you are, and what you ought to do. "The unexamined life is not worth living" (*Apology*, line 38). The classic search has been to figure out what it means to be human. Socrates, however, was sometimes wrong. I found that out in the Shenandoah Valley of Virginia.

Socrates loved Athens. We live in towns; humans are "political animals" (Greek: *polis*, town; Aristotle, *Politics*, line 1253a). Cultures shape our humanity. That's a main reason you are in college. But Socrates avoided nature, thinking it profitless. "You see, I am fond of learning. Now the country places and trees won't teach me anything, and the people in the city do" (*Phaedrus*, line 230d). I was born in the country, looking at Jump Mountain from my crib; that shaped my childhood worldview.

Out the other window was Bethesda Church, where my father was pastor. The Scots Presbyterians in the Valley loved gospel and landscape. Sundays and schooldays, I was tutored in that culture; otherwise I roamed the hills, fished in Hays Creek, swam in the Maury River.

"Life in an unexamined world is not worth living either." I discovered that when I stumbled, alone, on a whorled pogonia (*Isotria verticillata*) in a secluded glade to exclaim, "Amazing grace!" I needed the gospel words for my awesome landscape. With this more inclusive maxim, I claim to be wiser than Socrates. You will be too. Humans, the only species capable of enjoying culture, are also the only species capable of enjoying the splendid panorama of life.

Become a three-dimensional person. The totally urban (urbane!) life is one-dimensional. One needs experience of the urban, and the rural, and the wild. Otherwise you will be underprivileged. In my Virginia youth I had no electricity, got water from an outdoor cistern, hoed the garden, killed the chicken for Sunday dinner, and knew where the first Trailing Arbutus bloomed in February. My father was educated at the University of Edinburgh in theology, philosophy, mathematics. He taught me gospel, Plato, and Euclid. I was overprivileged.

2.

In environmental ethics you will learn what you most need to know about nature: how to value it. Later in my education, I had found my teachers underprivileged. I had to fight philosophy. Philosophers of science insisted that nonhuman nature was value-free, nothing but a resource for the satisfaction of human desires, abetted by the skills of science. Value was entirely in the eye of the beholder, assigned by the preference of the valuer.

I had to fight theology. In the late 1950s, interest in a theology of nature was disreputable. I was told to seek learning in linear history, not cyclic nature, the distinctive Judeo-Christian redemption history. The Creation stories were problematic myths, a primitive visionary ideal, but the truth was fallen nature, from which by God we are redeemed historically in the biblical covenants.

In the moments when I could escape the philosophers and the theologians, there were the mosses, so luxuriantly developed in the Southern Appalachians, but nobody else seemed much to care about them. There they were, doing nobody any good, yet flourishing on their own, not listening at all to the philosophers and the theologians.

Indeed, there the whole natural world was right "in my face" in the Shenandoah Valley – forests and soil, sunshine and rain, rivers and hills, the cycling seasons, wildflowers and wildlife – all these timeless natural givens that support everything else, all prior to these arrogant humans. That world is not value-free; to the contrary, it is the genesis of value, about as near to ultimacy as we can come.

My college teachers said I was wrong. Almost the first lesson in logic is the naturalistic fallacy; there is no implication from descriptive premises to value or to ethical conclusions. But in the wilderness, hearing a thrush singing to defend its territory, maybe even singing because it enjoyed it, seeing a fox pounce on a squirrel, spooking the deer who fled fearing that I was a hunter, searching for signs of spring after winter, I knew they had to be wrong.

There was life abundant in the midst of its perpetual perishing. These creatures valued life, each in their own way. Something of the meaning of life does lie in its naturalness. "Man is the measure of things," said Protagoras, another ancient philosopher (recalled in Plato, *Theaetetus*, line 152). Yes, humans are the only evaluators who can deliberate about what they ought to do to conserve nature. When humans do this, they must set up the scales; and humans are the "measurers of things," we prefer to say. But do we conclude that all we measure is what people have at stake on their landscapes? Cannot other species display values of which we ought to take some measure?

When you go home and say that you are taking a class in environmental ethics, mom and dad may be doubtful. "Isn't that an ethic for the chipmunks and daisies? Shouldn't you study something more serious? College costs a lot of money!" But, if you study hard, you will have an answer: "I have been searching for a land ethic" (Aldo Leopold). Tell them that an education these days requires becoming environmentally literate, just as much as it does becoming computer literate.

3.

Environmental ethics is vital because the survival of life on Earth depends on it. The main concerns on the world agenda for the new millennium are: war and peace, escalating populations, escalating consumption, degrading environments. They are all interrelated. For the first time in the history of the planet, one species jeopardizes the welfare of the community of life on Earth, as with global warming and extinction of species. Ecology is about living at home (Greek: *oikos*, "house"). Figure out this home planet.

I've been lucky that my own personal agenda has, during my lifetime, become the most inclusive concern of all: figuring out the human place on the planet. Living locally led me to think globally. You should be so lucky.

You don't want to live a denatured life. Humans neither can nor ought to denature their planet. Be a good citizen, and more. Be a resident on your landscape. Study environmental ethics to get put in your place.

Clare Palmer

Global climate change. Species extinction. The felling of rainforests. The peaking of global oil supply. We're bombarded by news stories about environmental problems. But what those stories rarely discuss is why – or even whether – we should care.

Studying environmental ethics is a way of getting behind the news to explore what's at stake in these environmental problems. Indeed, environmental ethics is partly concerned with why something that happens in the world should be seen as a "problem" at all. Let's take species extinction as an example. Sure, we might say, species extinction *sounds* bad. All those forms of life disappearing forever! But, of course, extinction has happened for millions of years: the dinosaurs went extinct long before humans were on the scene. So why should present extinctions worry us? What's *at stake* in species extinction?

Environmental ethicists answer this question in a variety of different ways. Some focus on the *human values* at stake in species extinction. They argue that the divergent genetic material in different species provides vital medical and agricultural resources for humans. Human welfare will be less good without some of these species, and human welfare is an important value. Or it might be argued that we don't know enough about the role any particular species might play in its ecosystem to accept the scale of species loss we're currently seeing. Perhaps the loss of a species will disturb whole systems, causing *cascading* extinctions. Since humans are dependent for survival on the services provided by ecosystems, this might also threaten valuable human welfare. Indeed, an environmental ethicist might argue, we shouldn't only be concerned about humans that are *currently* alive: there are future people to be concerned for too. Perhaps there's a problem about depriving *them* of resources, or impoverishing ecosystems on which they might depend. And – some environmental ethicists argue – there are yet other issues at stake. Perhaps there's something valuable about species in themselves. Maybe they are the kind of thing that have *intrinsic* value, that is, value independent of their usefulness in promoting present and future human welfare.

From this perspective, the loss of a species is the removal of irreplaceable value from the world.

These arguments open up some of the key questions in environmental ethics – ones that lurk behind the environmental headlines, but that are often implicit but neither explained nor justified in the news. These are questions such as: how should we think about future people, and should we take their future interests into account when making decisions now? This is puzzling in itself, because not only do future people not yet exist, but the very policies we choose will determine which particular individuals actually end up existing. And is the environment, or some parts of it at least, valuable independently of its usefulness for us? Suppose there were only one person left on Earth, and that person was about to die. Would there be something morally problematic if that person painlessly extinguished all life on Earth and left a barren planet? After all, no human would have a use for it any more.

These kinds of questions may *seem* esoteric, but actually they underpin both what we take environmental problems to be, and the policies that we make. So, for instance, one of the central policy debates with respect to global climate change has been how much present people should be expected to change their lives now – in particular to restrict their emissions of greenhouse gases – in order to protect people who don't yet exist from the effects of those emissions. It's just these kinds of questions that studying environmental ethics equips you both to understand and to answer. So, if you're interested in environmental policy, then a course in environmental ethics should be top of your list.

But this isn't the only reason environmental ethics is worth studying: it may also require you to examine your *own* beliefs and values. In part, environmental ethics is a challenge to the mind: you'll come to question whether values you've long held, perhaps without much reflection, are consistent with one another and can be supported by sound arguments. But by asking such questions, environmental ethics can also end up challenging everyday practices that such values support – such as eating meat or driving a car. Of course, you might conclude that there's good reason to continue (or to start!) doing both. But the papers you'll read in this book and other books in the field will expose you to a range of often conflicting arguments. Some will infuriate you, others persuade you; some will make you defend your own view, others force you to change your mind. Although it may be going a bit far to buy the line of the ancient philosopher Socrates that "the unexamined life is not worth living," examining one's own life, despite all the discomfort and struggle it might entail, certainly makes life much more interesting. And what more could you want from a college course?

Kristin Shrader-Frechette

"We have no money, but people said you would help us. Many neighborhood children have cancer. We think it's because of pollution from a local facility. Will you help us?"

Nearly every week, I receive phone calls or email messages like this one. Rich people can pay others to protect them. Poor people cannot, so often they call me. Frequently we can help – discovering scientific errors by government assessors who denied that chemical releases from Oak Ridge Laboratories had increased childhood asthma in a Tennessee minority community; or showing violations of citizens' informed consent in environmental-impact assessments (by a multinational corporation siting substandard, unwanted nuclear facilities in a black Louisiana town).[1] Always there are more cases than we can handle. Often pollution victims call us too late. When Hammond, Indiana parents contacted us in 2002, already 16 toddlers (in four blocks of single-family homes near Ferro Chemicals) had rare neurological cancers. Ferro, the top US emitter of ethylene-dichloride, was releasing 40 times the allowed levels of the known carcinogen/neurotoxin. Government was not enforcing safety standards.[2]

Because children (with their undeveloped detoxification systems) are about 10 times more sensitive to toxins than adults are, they are often pollution's first victims, "the canaries in the coal mines." Their sensitivity is one reason that US children's cancer rates are increasing 40 percent faster than adult rates,[3] annually striking 12,500 US children and causing more childhood deaths than do automobile accidents, murder, and child abuse combined.[4] Many scientists say pollution is the main culprit.[5] A long-term *New England Journal of Medicine* study of 90,000 children recently concluded that "the overwhelming contribution" to childhood cancers is "the environment."[6]

In the county where the 16 Hammond, Indiana toddlers lived, government data show that people of color, on average, bear eight times the hazardous chemical releases as whites – while families below the poverty level bear three times the releases as those above the poverty level.[7] The American Public Health Association, US Centers for Disease Control, and most scientists say that such statistics are typical: poor people and minorities face heavier pollution, therefore more disease and death.[8] Pollution, however, harms everyone. Cancer, the leading US cause of premature death for those under 85,[9] kills about 600,000 US citizens annually. Yet the US Office of Technology Assessment says that up to 90 percent of cancers are "environmentally induced and theoretically preventable."[10]

Although the US spends more on per-capita healthcare than any other nation (double to triple what countries like Japan and Australia spend), US children have death rates double or triple those of other Western nations; 54 nations have longer lifespans than the US. The Japanese live on average to 75, Americans to 69.[11] Weaker US pollution standards and less US spending on pollution control are two reasons for poorer US health/longevity, despite higher healthcare expenditures.[12] World Bank data show that the US spends about 0.6 percent of its GDP on pollution control, while Japan and many EU countries spend double that: 1.17 percent. The result? The average Japanese annually inhales 2 pounds of pollutants; the average American, 81 pounds.[13]

Trying to reverse such trends, Notre Dame students and I are annually involved in about 20 community-based, pro bono, environmental justice (EJ) projects. EJ requires more equitable pollution, so people do not breathe dirtier air or drink dirtier water merely because of their age, race, or income level. Our pro bono projects usually are

ethical/logical/scientific analyses of government impact assessments, typically used to set pollution regulations or site/expand polluting facilities. Our work helps stop substandard projects – or ensures they are more ethically and scientifically sound than they would have been.

My parents provided the greatest inspiration for this EJ work. Raised as the only white in Danville, Kentucky's "Colored Town" (as everyone then called it), my mother became a civil rights activist and the first white member of the Kentucky NAACP (National Association for the Advancement of Colored People). When she died at 45, from an environmentally induced cancer (caused by repeated, unnecessary x-rays), she was teaching in the poorest minority high school in Louisville. My favorite memories of her are from the 1960s, when she and Dad led us marching in civil rights demonstrations. They pulled the younger children in our rusted, red, "Radio Flyer" wagon.[14]

An environmental activist, Dad was an avid outdoorsman, president of the local watershed association. Convinced that wilderness experiences could shape people for life, he ran the local orphanage Boy Scout troop for 30 years. With Army surplus tents, sleeping bags, and tarps, he also led family camping trips to different national parks each summer. Riding horseback in the Rockies, listening to park rangers' tales at desert campfires, pitching tents in the driving rains of Hatteras, I learned to love hiking Canyonlands' rim trail, whitewater-rafting the Snake River, or diving the wall off Maui, the way I love home – or the pages of my favorite books.[15]

Doing environmental ethics should remind us that philosophers can be activists. Socrates was killed, and John Locke was hunted and nearly killed, because each criticized government ethical abuses. Bertrand Russell repeatedly was fined and imprisoned for his antiwar and nuclear disarmament activism. If environmental ethicists today are to "make a difference," they too need to engage the real world, to master basic scientific knowledge, and to work with public health and medical experts – so that even anti-environmentalists learn that protecting the environment also saves lives. Migrant laborer activist Cesar Chavez said that, after a day on the picket lines, people would never be the same. My dream is that, after working in EJ, students, faculty, and the world will never be the same.

Why study environmental ethics? Because environmental ethics can save lives.

Notes

1 For a fuller listing of our pro bono environmental justice work, see www.nd.edu/~kshrader/cejch.html, and for descriptions of university course-based, pro bono, environmental justice work, see www.nd.edu/~kshrader/courses/ and click on "Environmental Justice" (both sites accessed October 6, 2009).

2 US Department of Justice, Government and Ferro Corporation Settle Clean Air Act Claims (Washington, DC: DOJ, 2002); www.usdoj.gov/opa/pr/2002/March/02_enrd_157.htm (accessed October 6, 2009), and Kristin Shrader-Frechette, *Taking Action, Saving Lives: Our Duties to Protect Environmental and Public Health* (New York: Oxford University Press, 2007), pp. 3–8.

3 SEER, *Cancer Statistics Review, 1973–97* (Washington, DC: National Cancer Institute, National Institutes of Health, 1998). See also Shrader-Frechette, *Taking Action, Saving Lives*, pp. 213–14; Samuel S. Epstein, "Reversing the Cancer Epidemic," *Tikkun* 17/3 (May 2002): 56–66; Samuel Epstein, *Cancer-Gate* (Amityville, New York: Baywood, 2005); Devra Davis and David Hoel, eds., *Trends in Cancer Mortality in Industrial Countries* (New York: New York Academy of Sciences, 1990).

4 Statistics and citations from Shrader-Frechette, *Taking Action, Saving Lives*, p. 22.

5 E.g., F. Valent, D. A. Little, R. Bertollini, L. E. Nemer, G. Barbonc, and G. Tamburlini, "Burden of Disease Attributable to Selected Environmental Factors and Injury among Children and Adolescents in Europe," *Lancet* 363 (2004): 2032–9; P. J. Landrigan, "Commentary: Environmental Disease – A Preventable Epidemic," *The American Journal of Public Health* 82/7 (1992): 941–3; P. J. Landrigan, "The Prevention of Occupational Cancer," *CA: A Cancer Journal for Clinicians* 46/4 (1996): 254–5; Paul Schulte, "Characterizing the Burden of Occupational Injury and Disease," *Journal of Occupational and Environmental Medicine* 47/6 (2005): 607–22.

6 Paul Lichtenstein, Niels Holm, Pia Verkasalo, Anastasia Iliadou, Jaakko Kaprio, Markku Koskenvuo, Eero Pukkala, Axel Skytthee, and Kari Hemminki, "Environmental and Heritable Factors in the Causation of Cancer," *New England Journal of Medicine* 343/2 (2002): 78–85.

7 Environmental Defense Fund, *Scorecard* (Tabulation of industry toxic release reports to the US Environmental Protection Agency); available at www.scorecard.org/community/ej-summary.tcl?fips_county_code=18089#dist (accessed October 6, 2009).

8 Statistics and citations in Shrader-Frechette, *Taking Action, Saving Lives*, pp. 9–38.

9 American Cancer Society, *Cancer Facts and Figures 2005* (Atlanta: ACS, 2005); available at www.cancer.org/downloads/STT/CAFF2005PWSecured4.pdf. Daniel DeNoon, "Cancer Now Top Killer of Americans Under 85," WebMD (January 19, 2005); available at www.webmd.com/cancer/news/20050119/cancer-now-top-killer-of-american-under-85 (accessed October 6, 2009).

10 J. C. Lashof et al., Health and Life Sciences Division of the US Office of Technology Assessment, *Assessment of Technologies for Determining Cancer Risks from the Environment* (Washington, DC: Office of Technology Assessment, 1981), pp. 3, 6ff.

11 *The Economist, Pocket World 2007* (London: Profile, 2007), pp. 80, 86. US Central Intelligence Agency, *The World Factbook* (Washington, DC: CIA, 2004); www.cia.gov/cia/publications/factbook/rankorder2091rank.htm; accessed January 21, 2005. US Centers for Disease Control, *Infant Mortality Fact Sheet* (Washington, DC: CDC, 2005); www.cdc.gov/omhd/AMH/factsheets/infant.htm (accessed October 6, 2009); see also note 8 above.

12 See note 8 above.

13 Frances Rosenbluth and Michael Thies, "The Political Economy of Japanese Pollution Regulation," paper presented at the American Political Science Association meetings; www.yale.edu/leitner/resources/docs/1999-01/pdf (accessed October 6, 2009). See Jeffrey Broadbent, *Environmental Politics in Japan* (Cambridge: Cambridge University Press, 1998) and Shrader-Frechette, *Taking Action, Saving Lives*, p. 231.

14 Mom's story is in Kristin Shrader-Frechette, *Environmental Justice: Creating Equality, Reclaiming Democracy* (New York: Oxford University Press, 2002), pp. vii–viii.

15 Dad's story is in Shrader-Frechette, *Taking Action, Saving Lives*, pp. ix–x.

Victoria Davion

My study of environmental ethics results from a prior interest in feminist philosophy. Feminist philosophy focuses on various forms of sexism and on how issues of gender, race, and class are used both to justify and to enforce sexism. I find ecological feminism to be extremely useful in providing a framework for understanding these issues. This framework leads directly to questions such as what does it mean to be "human"? What does it mean to be "natural"? What does it mean to have "moral value"?

Ecological feminists such as Val Plumwood[1] and Karen Warren[2] have argued that there are crucial epistemological, ethical, and political links between the exploitation of "nature" and human oppressions such as racism and sexism. They focus on an analysis of dualisms within Western patriarchal culture. A value dualism is a disjunct in which each side is seen as radically different and one side is ranked as morally superior to the other. For example, in sexist societies men and women are seen as radically different from each other and men are seen as morally superior to women.

Ecological feminists have argued that a reason/nature dualism underlies much of traditional Western patriarchal culture, in which whatever is associated with reason is seen as radically different from and morally superior to whatever is associated with nature. This fundamental dualism is said to justify a series of related dualisms such as masculine (reason)/feminine (nature), human (reason)/animal (nature), civilized (reason)/primitive (nature). These pairs are said to justify oppressions based on race, class, and sex within traditional Western patriarchy. Unpacking crucial dualisms, and the reason/nature one in particular, inevitably leads to core philosophical questions such as why is reason seen as opposed to nature? Why is reason seen as superior to nature? What is reason? What is nature? Does reason have special value? If so, why? Hence, one reason to study environmental ethics generally, and ecological feminism in particular, is because they raise key metaphysical issues about being and moral value.

Another reason to study environmental ethics is to discover what things need to change and who has moral responsibility for making needed changes. Some strands of environmental ethics, such as deep ecology, have tended to focus on "human" responsibility for environmental well-being. However, ecological feminists have insisted that we unpack the dynamics of such things as race, class, and gender to discover which groups of humans are responsible for making change, as well as where change is needed.

Ecological feminism encourages us to notice who has power and privilege, who (human and nonhuman) suffers as a result of unfair power and privilege, and how people might go about changing that. For example, on the issue of environmental racism, key ecological feminist questions concern how ethical and economic discourses justify environmental racism, as well as how powerlessness and alienation make fighting back more difficult. Hence, studying environmental ethics leads to core philosophical questions, shows how some problematic assumptions that are entrenched in Western patriarchal culture promote the exploitation of both human and nonhuman beings, and points the way toward policy changes based on the targeting of moral responsibility.

Notes

1 Val Plumwood, *Feminism and the Mastery of Nature* (London: Routledge, 1993).
2 Karen J. Warren, "The Power and Promise of Ecological Feminism," *Environmental Ethics* 12/2 (1990): 125–46.

Greta Gaard

In hindsight, I realize it was the last of our family dinnertime battles, the conclusive conversation that would allow me dietary freedom at the age of 11, and later propelled me to study environmental ethics.

"What if I came up to you, and ripped your arm off, and ate it?" I was practically yelling at my father. "How would you feel about that? And what kind of person would that make me?" Happily, he was silent. "Don't you see? I'm not going to eat Pookie [our

dachshund], I'm not going to eat your arms and legs, and I'm not going to eat anyone else's, either."

This conversation was the formal beginning of my environmental ethic. Of course, I didn't think of it that way at the time.

As a child, I had always had enormous sympathy for animals. Their lack of artifice, their alert wildness even in domesticity, their authenticity spoke to me in a way that I trusted. I saw myself as one of them.

I understood the logic of their desires. I appreciated their kindness and communication with me.

Along with my interspecies affinities, I held conversations with trees. I remember a specific grove of eucalyptus trees, an unmanaged forest that stood on the hillside at the middle of my junior high school. I befriended these trees, spent my recess listening to the murmur of wind in their leaves, the calming presence of their steadfastness easing my early adolescence. Their smell soothed me.

Perhaps because I was an only child, I sought out a wider spectrum of friendships with place, and with the inhabitants of place – avocado trees and ivy, blue jays and skunks, rocks and sage and strawberries. While my peers were busy acquiring toys, I was working the clay soil in our backyard, spreading topsoil and fertilizer, coaxing carrots and beans and tomatoes to grow in a Los Angeles suburb. The red-leaf lettuce thrived; the beans survived; the carrots came out stunted, deformed. The clay soil was impenetrable. I corresponded regularly with relatives in Nebraska, seeking solutions to my gardening problems. At the age of 20 I finally moved to Minnesota, where the land and the culture and community finally aligned with my values, fertile soil for the growth of my own environmental ethic. And then I encountered discrimination.

Feminism wasn't my first choice. It was forced on me through experience with my dissertation committee, a group of five men who, in the mid-1980s, were still able to deny the logic of my innate feminist scholarship as an approach without theory, without foundation. Out of frustration I turned to a feminist scholar, Toni McNaron, whose writing seemed to use the same approach as mine, and asked her to be my advisor. She agreed, with the caveat that I would take the graduate minor in feminist studies. I did, and the world cracked open.

I studied with women who cared deeply about oppression based on gender, race, class, age, sexuality, ability – but saw no connections with oppression based on species, let alone the destruction of forests, rivers, fields. How could they be so oblivious? Feminist studies provided a clear framework for articulating my own environmental ethic: if the point of feminism was that a separate self ("autonomous individualism") was indefensible, that we all grow and flourish in relationship, through connection; if the point was that hierarchy structured beliefs and organizations that quickly became anti-democratic, and led inexorably to the justification of domination – then how could feminists ignore oppression of any kind that relied on a separation of self from other selves? Certain that every-

one would understand this insight if only it were explained clearly to them, I made photocopies of Aviva Cantor's four-page essay linking racism, sexism, and speciesism – "The Club, the Yoke, the Leash" – and placed them in every mailbox of the women's studies department – faculty, students, and staff alike.

No one responded.

It was like dropping a rock down a canyon and hearing nothing, no echo, no affirmation of my words bouncing off stone.

I sought solace in poetry, in the words of Meridel LeSueur, Minnesota labor activist, feminist, mother, journalist. At the 1989 National Women's Studies Association conference I read a paper on "Feminism, animals, the environment" – FATE, I called it – and serendipity coupled me with Marti Kheel, founder of Feminists for Animal Rights, and Ariel Salleh, an Australian environmental feminist. Someone handed me Judith Plant's new volume, *Healing the Wounds: The Promise of Ecofeminism*. At that convention, with Noel Sturgeon and Stephanie Lahar, we founded the Ecofeminist Caucus. An editor from Temple University Press approached me and asked me to write a book on my views. I declined, but promised to collect a bouquet of essays that would articulate the blossoming of this new environmental ethic; four years later, that promise became *Ecofeminism: Women, Animals, Nature* (Temple University Press, 1993).

To envision the volume, solicit contributions, and write my own feminist environmental ethic, I had to read what others had written. My ideas seemed compelling – but were they original? I read volume after volume of the journal *Environmental Ethics*, using these essays as a treasure map to other books and journals, and discovering that others had indeed debated many of these same ideas. But their conclusions weren't mine. Some focused only on animal ethics; others were concerned with wild nature but not with human cultures; those that focused on social justice and the environment still overlooked gender and sexuality, not to mention economics. If I had found an environmental ethic that fully described my own commitment to social and interspecies justice, environmental health, and economic democracy – well, I wouldn't have written the books and articles I've written. I would have focused my creativity on something else. But my viewpoint was absent from the conversation.

Why study environmental ethics? So you can enter the conversation intelligently, informed of what others had already said, and capable of advancing the conversation where others have left off.

Peter Singer

You should study environmental ethics for guidance in everyday life, like eating ethically. Stealing, lying, hurting people – these acts are obviously relevant to our moral character. So too, most people would say, is our involvement in community activities, our generosity to others in need, and – especially – our sex lives. But how about what we eat? Though eating is even more essential than sex, and everyone does it, usually more than once a day, most people don't see it as raising ethical issues. Try to think of a politician whose prospects have been damaged by revelations about what he or she eats.

It wasn't always so. Michel Foucault, the French historian of ideas, has pointed out that in ancient Greece and Rome the ethics of what we eat was considered an important topic, at least as significant as sexual ethics.[1] In traditional Jewish, Islamic, Hindu, and Buddhist ethics, too, discussions of what should and should not be eaten occupy a prominent place. In the Hebrew scriptures, for example, some animals, though edible, are "abominable," and Jewish law prohibits their consumption. (For a witty take on this, see www.God HatesShrimp.com, which aptly mocks fundamentalists who use the Bible as a weapon against gays.)

In the Christian era, however, interest in the ethics of what we eat faded away. Jesus deliberately rejected the Jewish dietary laws, saying, according to Matthew's account, "What goes into a man's mouth does not make him 'unclean,' but what comes out of his mouth, that is what makes him 'unclean.'"[2] As Hub Zwart, who has researched the history of food ethics, comments, "What is so striking in the food ethic proclaimed by Jesus, is the basic atmosphere of carelessness it conveys. All of a sudden, food intake seems to have become completely insignificant, from a moral point of view."[3] Even the later Roman Catholic tradition of avoiding meat on Fridays and during Lent was not intended to suggest that there was anything wrong, in general, with eating meat. True, gluttony is one of the seven cardinal sins. That means that there are ethical concerns about the quantity that one eats, but not about what is eaten.

Perhaps the deliberate decision of Jesus and his followers to rebel against the ethics of the Pharisees by repudiating the Jewish dietary laws has led, as such decisions often do, to an opposite extreme, one that goes too far in its disregard of the moral significance of what we eat. Nobody seriously disputes that eating human flesh – at least if you have killed human beings in order to eat them – is wrong. So at least one kind of food is ethically prohibited. In the West, we also disapprove of eating dogs and cats, but that restriction is a minor one and so widely accepted that it scarcely strikes us as an ethical constraint. With the exception of a few ethical vegetarians, and those who observe religious prohibitions on what they put in their mouths, eating has, until recently, been largely an "ethics-free zone."

Over the past 30 years, however, there have been signs of significant change. Many people show some concern for the treatment of animals in their food choices – avoiding veal because they don't like what they have heard about the treatment of veal calves, or avoiding all factory-farm animal products, or being vegetarian or vegan. Others seek out organically produced food, because they don't want all those pesticides and synthetic fertilizers getting into their bodies or – and here is the broader ethical concern – our land and water. Sales of organic food in America are now growing at about 20 percent per annum, as compared to only a 3 percent rise in food sales in general. That makes organic food the fastest-growing sector of the food market. Then there are trade issues: fair-trade coffee, bought from small growers at a price that assures them a living wage, is increasing its market share. There is a "buy local" movement that points to the fossil-fuel consumption and greenhouse gas emissions required to bring lettuce thousands of miles to your plate. Surveys in several countries have found that more than half of the population claims to have declined to buy something because of conditions under which it was made.

Many Americans are disenchanted with voting because money seems to matter more than votes,

Singer, Peter, "Eating Ethically," *Free Inquiry*, vol. 25, no. 4 (2005): 18–19. © 2005 by Peter Singer. Adapted by permission of the author.

and politicians repeatedly fail to live up to their promises. By bringing ethics into their shopping, they have a political impact that is otherwise denied to them. A consumer who switches from buying conventionally produced fruit to buying organic fruit is giving an incentive to organic producers to maintain or increase their production – and, at the same time, they are diminishing the resources available to the conventional producer. The message does get through to the producers. In a survey of the biggest US farmers, agribusiness executives, academicians, and environmental leaders taken in the summer of 2003, animal welfare was identified as the seventh "megatrend" out of twelve facing American agriculture – entirely because of consumer concern.[4]

When we eat – or, more specifically, when we pay for what we eat, whether at a farmer's market, a supermarket, or a restaurant – we are taking part in a vast global industry. Americans spend more than a trillion dollars on food every year. That's more than double what they spend on motor vehicles and also more than double what the government spends on defense. Food production affects every person on this planet and untold billions of animals as well. It is important, for the sake of the environment, animals, and future generations, that we see our food choices as raising serious ethical issues and learn the implications of what we eat.

Notes

This is a polished version, corrected by the author, of an earlier piece published as "Eating Ethically" in *Free Inquiry* 25/4 (June–July 2005): 18–19. For further details, see Peter Singer and Jim Mason, *The Ethics of What We Eat* (New York: Rodale Press, 2006).

1   Michel Foucault, *Histoire de la sexualité 2: L'Usage des plaisirs* (Paris: Gallimard, 1984) [*The History of Sexuality*, vol. 2: *The Use of Pleasure*, reissue edition (New York: Vintage Books, 1990)]. I owe this reference to Hub Zwart, "A Short History of Food Ethics," *Journal of Agricultural and Environmental Ethics* 12 (2000): 113–26.
2   Matthew 15: 11–17, New International Version.
3   Zwart, "A Short History of Food Ethics," p. 117.
4   Jerry Perkins, "Kinder, Gentler Food," *The Des Moines Register*, March 7, 2004.

James P. Sterba

As we contemplate the present and future effects of global climate change, it is hard not to be disillusioned by what we see. Melting glaciers, rising sea levels, more intense and erratic weather patterns, widescale extinction of endangered species – what can we as environmental philosophers do that might be helpful in this regard? My suggestion is that we respond by drawing on the resources of traditional normative philosophy to ground a demanding environmental ethics that will justify the kind of sacrifices that are needed to cope with our unsettling future.

This is a project that, with a lot of help from others, I have been working on for the past 20 years. I presented it, at least in outline, in my presidential address at the American Philosophical Association Central Division Meeting in 2008, entitled "Completing the Kantian Project: From Rationality to Equality." By equality here I mean substantive intergenerational equality. This will require that we limit our current use of resources to simply meeting our basic needs. So the argument moves from a neutral nonmoral rational foundation to a very demanding set of practical moral requirements. So far sketched, the argument does not yet take into account the requirements that nonhuman living nature places upon us. But surprisingly, so demanding is this morality so far sketched that when additional considerations are introduced to take nonhuman living nature into account not much more is required of us, except for some further constraints on population policy.

Now I know some environmental philosophers are more skeptical about the usefulness of traditional

James P. Sterba, "A Demanding Environmental Ethics for the Future," *Ethics & the Enivronment*, vol. 12, no. 2 (Fall 2007): 146–7. © 2007 by Indiana University Press. Reprinted with permission from the publisher.

moral philosophy than I am. Even I am unhappy with certain debates currently raging among contemporary moral philosophers, such as the realist/antirealist debate. In fact, my argument is designed to make that very debate unnecessary. Still, if we leave most of traditional moral philosophy behind, what do we bring with us, as philosophers, to the new disciplines with which we now propose to collaborate? Do we bring an ability to do values clarification and a good sense of argument? I don't think these skills, and others like them, alone will be enough for the task at hand. We need a very demanding ethics, and if we don't look to philosophy to ground such an ethics, where do we look?

There is also an additional advantage here to grounding a demanding environmental ethics in traditional normative philosophy. Such an approach is more likely to force traditionalists and conservatives, philosophers and otherwise, to take notice of our arguments. If we are out in "left" field just talking to those both inside and outside of philosophy who happen to agree with our practical agenda, it is easier for us to be dismissed by others who are not committed to that same practical agenda. By contrast, if we address our opponents by appealing to very traditional values by which they claim to live their lives, then we do have at least a fighting chance of changing the way they do live their lives. At least, as moral philosophers, we would have then done our best to respond to the environmental crisis, provided, of course, that we are also willing to reach out with our demanding ethics in hand and do that interdisciplinary collaboration that needs to be done to secure fully practical and effective solutions to the problems we face.

Note

This is a slightly revised version of "A Demanding Environmental Ethics for the Future," *Ethics & the Environment* 12/2 (Fall 2007): 146–7.

Michael E. Zimmerman

Studying environmental philosophy is a way in which people with a philosophical bent can discuss aspects of something else that also matters a lot to them as well: the natural world, sometimes called the more-than-human world. Artists can paint pictures of scenic wonders, biologists can explore DNA, and philosophers can pose questions about nature and about humanity's relationship with it. This, at least, helps to explain why I do environmental philosophy.

Aristotle said that philosophy begins in wonder – wonder not only about the stupendous complexity and beauty of things, but even more about the *fact that there are things at all*. Why is there something, rather than nothing at all? Many people are inclined to wonder on occasion about who they are, what their lives mean, how they got here, where they are going, why we must die, and why there is such an achingly beautiful and violent world. For me, environmental philosophy is about pursuing questions like these, which resonate with the wonder that makes life rich and full of questions.

Some people think that environmental philosophy is the same as environmental ethics, that is, the exploration of whether nonhuman beings (plants, animals, even ecosystems) have moral status, and, if they do possess such status, what our moral obligations are toward such beings. This is a worthy pursuit that I myself have followed at times.

For the most part, though, my interest has been in what myth, religious teachings, and modern science have to say about the universe and about the curious self-conscious creatures that have somehow appeared within it. For me, environmental philosophy is akin to what people in the nineteenth century called philosophy of nature. Natural philosophy has been making something of a comeback in the form of cosmology, that is, the study of why and how the cosmos is. The Big Bang theory posits that the universe had a beginning, and if so it has a history about which we can tell narratives and engage in informed speculation. An example of such speculation is that the cosmos is in an important sense "life-friendly," because it is so fine-tuned in terms of its initial conditions and structure. Could human life be understood in part as one way in which the cosmos is becoming conscious of itself? In connection with this question, I highly recommend books by the physicist Paul Davies, including *Cosmic Jackpot: Why Our Universe is Just Right for Life*. Philosophers in particular have an obligation to read widely in the natural and social sciences, as well as in the arts and humanities other than philosophy. By drawing upon findings from these other disciplines, we learn to view complex phenomena from a host of different perspectives.

Speculation about the origin and possible purpose of human consciousness is not "anthropocentric" in the sense of elevating humankind in a way that distracts our attention from preserving wild habitat and limiting pollution. Only because humans are endowed with our special kind of intelligence can we do something called environmental philosophy. Other animals don't philosophize, so far as we know. Animals, plants, ecosystems, the solar system, the Milky Way, and the universe, as far as we can see with our telescopes, manifest themselves within our complex conceptual, linguistic, and perceptual frameworks. What we call "nature" is not simply given, but instead shows up within the limits of such frameworks.

Hence, an important aspect of environmental philosophy involves understanding how cognition and perception work in our encounters with the natural world. Nature is not merely a "social construction," but we must not be naïve when it comes to what is involved in encounters with "nature."

Bryan G. Norton

I answer the question, "Why Study Environmental Ethics?", from the perspective of pragmatism. Our cognitive perceptual apparatus – for very good evolutionary reasons – functions more like a spotlight than a floodlight. To avoid perceptual overload and focus on priorities, our cognitive and conative attention is highly selective and we always encounter our world from a limited perspective. In fact, we notice that, in an increasingly global world, we encounter many perspectives on the world – from both within and outside our own culture – that we often do not understand. All students should take environmental ethics in order to gain deeper understanding of these perspectives. Discussions in environmental ethics allow students to learn about and explore the many ways humans regard nature, how they value it, and how they treat it in their actions.

If one is going to be a responsible citizen in today's global pluriverse, one must sooner or later recognize, interpret, and live according to the norms that are embedded in some perspective; and yet if one is to be responsive to globalism, one must also be able to understand and work with others who have different and sometimes conflicting perspectives. In environmental ethics you will be exposed to multiple "worldviews" or perspectives which embody somewhat different norms of behavior, and in this class you will learn how to compare, analyze, and evaluate normative beliefs and principles that affect human treatment of natural systems and other species.

I prefer to think of environmental ethics as having two traditions. One of these stretches back into prehistory, as cultures have always given meaning and structure to their actions in nature according to narrative stories and myths. At one important juncture in this intellectual history – when the Judeo-Christian Creation story was written down – scriptures accorded humans "dominion" over nature, but with the obligation of stewardship. This set of ideas has become a central narrative within the particular perspective that we call the "Western perspective." This narrative embodied a very specific and powerful ethic that supported thousands of years of human development, as human culture has incorporated much of nature into human activities, and made natural processes a part of their social existence. This narrative, however, has also led to unfathomable destruction of many ecological systems and wildlife habitats, both small and continental in scope. Only sometimes was this destruction an unintended consequence of human need-fulfillment, as the actions perpetrated by humans include not just legitimate uses, but cases of wanton destruction as well. Clearly, within the Western perspective, emphasis has often fallen on the "dominion" and power aspect of the charge from Genesis, but this perspective also offers guidance, however often ignored, by cautioning that use of resources implies stewardship of resources that are not owned, but held in trust. In this sense, in the sense that its stories provide guidance for human actions, every culture has its own "environmental ethic," a narrative or set of stories that give meaning to human action within nature, and guide human decisions as to right and wrong behavior.

Environmental ethics also has a more recent embodiment, in a more professional form, since it has become, within philosophy departments, a study by philosophers of environmental norms and values. This professional form sets as its goal to analyze, evaluate, and correct the theories that would justify environmental action. This field of study initially adopted the task of criticizing the "Western perspective," and the philosophical principles that underlie and give normative shape to this perspective. Much of the early writing on environmental ethics has thus criticized various aspects of the "anthropocentric" perspective. Treating the threat to nature and the human environment as a theoretical problem to be resolved with new theories, many early writers in environmental ethics proposed that we step out of the anthropocentric perspective of Western culture and embrace – either for abstract, philosophical reasons or by appeal to ideas of ancient and foreign cultures – nature as a valued "subject" with value that does not depend on human judgment.

The anthropocentrism/nonanthropocentrism argument has continued, and continues to create great interest, and to challenge students to think through their most cherished, bedrock beliefs about humans, nature, and other species. Another approach to environmental ethical problems, however, has emerged more recently and holds promise to go beyond theoretical analysis to address moral commitments and issues as they are embedded in particular, complex problems. "Environmental pragmatists" believe philosophical analysis is important, but that this analysis is more fruitful when it takes place within specific situations where the unique complexities of the particular controversy about what action to pursue can be taken into account.

Pragmatists thus practice philosophy by addressing conceptual and value issues in the formation of particular policies. While pragmatists recognize the interest of fundamental questions that go to the heart of our Western tradition, and they engage in criticisms of our most cherished principles and ideas, in practice, all environmental problems are ecologically, socially, and culturally complex; and complex problems must be seen from multiple perspectives. In real policy contexts, good responses to actual, complex problems are acceptable to as many perspectives as possible, not judged up or down according to universal, philosophical principles. The goal of environmental ethics should be to use philosophical and ethical theory to tell normative stories appropriate to particular problems, to help communities to develop a narrative that fits their perspectives and environmental challenges, not to support universal principles. A study of environmental ethics that addresses real, situational conflicts, balancing multiple values and principles, is more likely to contribute to saving nature than an ivory-tower search for one-size-fits-all theory.

Anthony Weston

For me, the essential environmental ethical task is to understand the world as vastly bigger than we are. It's a staggering and unsettling realization, but deeply intriguing and inviting at the same time. Physically, the natural world is unimaginably vast; it is more intricately intertwined than we possibly can know, and it is alive and communicating in many, possibly even all, of its parts. And it is not just "out there," somewhere else. We are animals too, we mate and sing and revel in each other's companionship and the sheer joy of life just like a myriad of other creatures, and likewise there are all sorts of supposedly only-human things that other animals do too, like communicate in complex ways. We don't even begin to understand what's going on with whale-song, for example – and perhaps never will: their brains are up to six times larger than ours and far more complex. Yet at the same time there are human languages so shaped by the surrounding bird songs that not only the lilt and rhythm of speech but sometimes whole phrases come straight from the owls and the thrushes – so it is no surprise at all that speakers of those languages can talk with the birds, and vice versa. Many indigenous peoples report that even the stones have a kind of life – not some sort of Disneyesque kind of life where they just turn into rocky-looking people, but something infinitely more mysterious and intriguing: more suited, naturally, to rocks. Everywhere the world watches, communicates, responds. Environmental ethics, at bottom, means finding the will and the grace to join, or, more accurately, to rejoin, this ancient and more-than-human flow.

Philosophy is not the only way. For the sheer sake of waking up to the more-than-human world, you might be better off reading *Walden* or Barry Lopez or taking a sketchbook to the woods or going out into some wild and wonderful places without any books at all. Philosophers can also become particularly adept at resistance and denial. On the other hand, this strange and challenging world of environmental ethical argument may actually give you a unique kind of freedom to begin to relate to the larger world in a new way. You do not have to sort out some stance of your own among the multiple and complex distinctions within the field – in my view they're all totally provisional and incomplete anyhow. But what happens when you find that philosophy's questions and distinctions (any of them, all of them) push the boundaries of ethics-as-usual in some profound way? Maybe you'll end up wondering why we cannot manage to take even our own future seriously enough to sustain the environment that sustains us. That's a real question, not just a rhetorical one. Or how we can justify confining, slaughtering, even torturing other animals who feel it all as acutely, maybe even more acutely, than we would. Or how we could ever imagine that the point of this whole spectacular pageant is to provide a few raw materials for our consumption and disposal. Can you hear the hyenas and the mockingbirds already laughing *that* one out of court? Or how we can even imagine that anything is actually "disposable" in a world where everything that goes around comes around. Just asking these questions – just staying open to them – already invokes unsuspected possibilities for new ethical relations.

We live in perilous as well as parlous times, to be sure – times of environmental emergency. But emergencies are also times of emergence. And *what* is emerging? Well, that's partly up to us.

David Rothenberg

I've always believed that the greatest problem of our era is to figure out how humanity can continue to thrive on Earth without destroying the natural world that makes our life possible. If you read the news, it is hard to have any optimism about this topic: the planet's getting warmer, we're running out of oil, species are disappearing, pollution is spreading, traffic and smog are on the rise. Is there any hope that we'll discover a way out of this madness? Is it better to accept our fate and let some other species take over in our place?

I'd rather dream of a solution than admit defeat, so it seems the first thing we can do as individuals is to think for ourselves, and wonder: is there a different way that each of us can frame our place in the natural world? Can we conceive our way out of this mess, and imagine humanity and nature connected and defined in a whole new relationship? I guess I'm naive enough to say "Yes!" Perhaps that's why I'm a philosopher and not an engineer. Such a course does, though, require a lot of faith, belief in the power of one's own ideas to change the direction of our lives and the future of the world itself.

Environmental ethics is the attempt to define the right and wrong human ways of dealing with the surrounding world. Whenever we gouge out a mountainside or plant a tree, we are taking a moral stand in relationship to the Earth. Sometimes we do this explicitly, but most often it is implicit, where our actions reveal a point of view we've never even bothered to consider. Did we ever *intend* to make the atmosphere warmer through the march of industrialization? Surely not, but that does not mean we are exempt from responsibility for the situation.

The philosopher believes that if we think differently about our place in the scheme of things, then we will act in a whole new way. Ideas *have* made a difference through history: just as there would never have been an American Revolution without the notions of freedom and property championed by Jean-Jacques Rousseau and John Locke, so there would never have been an ecology movement without the outward-looking ethical stance of Aldo Leopold and the conviction that we can live closer to the land right in front of our neighbors as proven by Henry David Thoreau. Rachel Carson's idea of a silent spring with songbirds all felled by DDT moved Americans to champion conservation, preventing any actual tragedy, which never happened because of our public support. Al Gore took the philosophy of environmentalism deep into public scrutiny when he wrote already in the 1980s that we needed "a new idea at the heart of our civilization" to change the human relationship with nature into something sustainable into this new century. Since then, with his efforts to educate America on the facts of climate change, he has proven that a politician can sometimes do more good as a public philosopher than as an elected official – that's because environmental issues touch us way beyond politics. *Everyone* really wants a clean and healthy environment, regardless of whether they expect government or free enterprise to guarantee it.

Religion traditionally tells us what is right and what is wrong, leaving little room for doubt. But philosophy takes human beings far more seriously, urging each and every one of us to figure out for ourselves how to best behave in complex situations. How to strive for greater wealth and prosperity when we know the planet suffers the more each individual human gains? We are better people when we think of the welfare of others, and the greatest sense of other is the vast community of life which we participate in, needing clean air, water, food, and enough energy to continue to flourish long into the future.

Of course, when seen from the perspective of nature, all human civilization, compassion, creation, and destruction are but a blip on the scale of geologic time. To the vast plethora of life on Earth, we cannot matter more than any other species. Yet we are the one species who has evolved a culture that can be altruistic, can care about other forms of life. We are enriched and enhanced by that concern.

How to know what to do? What is right and wrong in connection with the natural world? These are the fundamental concerns of environmental ethics, the one field that will teach you how to stop worrying and learn how to sustain our kind far into the future. Everyone should study it, for we all have to answer these important questions in our own ways. Our relationship to nature is too important to leave to defer to authority instead of good, honest, personal thinking.

Contributors to Part I

Emily Brady is a Senior Lecturer in Human Geography at the University of Edinburgh, Scotland. A philosopher by training, she has research interests in environmental aesthetics, environmental ethics, and Kant's philosophy. She is the author of *Aesthetics of the Natural Environment* (2003); *Environment and Philosophy* (with Vernon Pratt and Jane Howarth, 2000); and co-editor of *Humans in the Land: The Ethics and Aesthetics of the Cultural Landscape* (with Sven Arntzen, 2008).

Isis Brook is a Senior Lecturer, Philosophy Section, International School for Communities, Rights, and Inclusion (ISCRI), University of Central Lancashire. She teaches environmental philosophy for the undergraduate philosophy program and the MA in values and environment program and is managing editor of the journal *Environmental Values*. Her primary research interests centre on the phenomenology of place, environmental aesthetics, Goethean science, and education of the whole person.

J. Baird Callicott is Regents Professor of Philosophy and Chair of the Department of Philosophy and Religion Studies at the University of North Texas. He is the co-editor-in-chief of the *Encyclopedia of Environmental Ethics and Philosophy* and author or editor of a score of books and author of dozens of journal articles, encyclopedia articles, and book chapters in environmental philosophy and ethics. He has served the International Society for Environmental Ethics as president and Yale University as Bioethicist-in-Residence. His research goes forward simultaneously on four main fronts: theoretical environmental ethics, comparative environmental ethics and philosophy, the philosophy of ecology and conservation policy, and biocomplexity in the environment, coupled with natural and human systems (sponsored by the National Science Foundation). He is perhaps best known as the leading contemporary exponent of Aldo Leopold's land ethic and is currently exploring an Aldo Leopold Earth ethic in response to global climate change.

Victoria Davion is head of the Department of Philosophy at the University of Georgia and founding and current editor of the journal *Ethics & the Environment*. Her interests include environmental ethics, ecofeminism, and political philosophy. She publishes in journals including *Environmental Ethics*, *Hypatia*, and *Environmental Values* and is co-editor of *The Idea of Political Liberalism* (with Clark Wolf, 2000).

Frederick Ferré is Professor Emeritus of Philosophy, University of Georgia, now living in Munich, Germany. While at the University of Georgia, he chaired the Department of Philosophy and founded the interdisciplinary Faculty of Environmental Ethics. He was for some years general editor of *Research in Philosophy and Technology*, and is the author of such books as *Shaping the Future* (1976), *Philosophy of Technology* (1988; 1995), and *Hellfire and Lightning Rods* (1993). Now retired, his culminating project was a trilogy of books. The first volume is *Being and Value: Toward a Constructive Postmodern Metaphysics* (1996); the second is *Knowing and Value: Toward a Constructive Postmodern Epistemology* (1998); and the third is *Living and Value: Toward a Constructive Postmodern Ethics, Religion, and Social Ecology* (2001), which brings metaphysics and epistemology down to earth.

Warwick Fox is a Reader in Ethics, at the Philosophy Section, International School for Communities, Rights, and Inclusion (ISCRI), University of Central Lancashire. He has published many papers and articles in environmental philosophy and his books include *A Theory of General Ethics: Human Relationships, Nature, and the Built Environment* (2006); *Ethics and the Built Environment* (2000); and *Toward a Transpersonal Ecology* (1995). His most recent work has focused on the development of a general ethics, which is to say a single integrated approach to ethics that encompasses the realms of inter-human ethics, the ethics of the natural environment, and the ethics of the human-constructed environment. The specific approach that he has developed to general ethics is referred to as the "theory of responsive cohesion."

Greta Gaard's contributions to developing ecofeminist thought include her books *Ecological Politics: Ecofeminists and the Greens* (1998) and *The Nature of Home: Taking Root in a Place* (2007), along with her edited volumes, *Ecofeminism: Women, Animals, Nature* (1993) and *Ecofeminist Literary Criticism* (1998). Her essays appear in *Hypatia*, *Environmental Ethics*, *The Ecologist*, *Frontiers*, *Alternatives*, and other books and journals. She is a professor of English at the University of Wisconsin-River Falls, and a Community Faculty member in Women's Studies at Metropolitan State University in St Paul, Minnesota. You can find links to her work at her website, www.gretagaard.efoliomn2.com/.

John Granrose is a native of Miami, Florida. After graduating from the University of Miami, he was a Fulbright Grantee at the University of Heidelberg, Germany, and then received his PhD from the University of Michigan, where he studied ethics with Charles Stevenson, Richard Brandt, and William Frankena. From 1966 to 1993 he taught in the Department of Philosophy at the University of Georgia. In 1996 he graduated from the C. G. Jung Institute of Zürich, Switzerland, and from 1998 to 2002 served as director of studies there. After several years of living in England, he and his wife reside in Athens, Georgia.

Eugene C. Hargrove is the founding editor of *Environmental Ethics*, the first journal devoted to environmental philosophy. He is the author of *Foundations of Environmental Ethics* (1989), and editor of *Beyond Spaceship Earth: Environmental Ethics and the Solar System* (1986), *Religion and Environmental Crisis* (1986), and *The Animal Rights/ Environmental Ethics Debate: The Environmental Perspective* (1992). He has taught at the University of New Mexico, the University of Georgia, and the University of North Texas. As chair of the Department of Philosophy and Religion Studies at the University of North Texas, he created the first MA and PhD programs devoted to environmental philosophy. His research interests are currently focused on environmental ethics education at the elementary school level, including multicultural value education, and on environmental ethical issues related to the return to the Moon and the exploration of Mars.

Bryan G. Norton is Distinguished Professor of Philosophy, Science, and Technology in the School of Public Policy, Georgia Institute of Technology, and author of *Why Preserve Natural Variety?* (1987); *Toward Unity Among Environmentalists* (1991); *Searching for Sustainability* (2003); and *Sustainability: A Philosophy of Adaptive Ecosystem Management* (2005). Norton has contributed to journals in several fields and has served on the Environmental Economics Advisory Committee of the US EPA Science Advisory Board, and two terms as a member of the governing board of the Society for Conservation Biology. His current research concentrates on sustainability theory and on problems of scale in the formulation of environmental problems. He was a member of the board of directors of Defenders of Wildlife from 1994 to 2005 and is currently on their scientific advisory board. He is also a member of the advisory committee for the MacArthur Foundation Project, Advancing Conservation in a Social Context.

Clare Palmer is an Associate Professor of Philosophy and Environmental Studies at Washington University in St Louis. She is the author of *Environmental Ethics and Process Thinking* (1998) and *Environmental Ethics* (1998), and has recently completed a new book on animal ethics for Columbia University Press. She has edited or co-edited a number of volumes, including *Animal Rights* for the Ashgate International Library of Essays on Rights (2008); a co-edited five-volume collection, *Environmental Philosophy*, with J. Baird Callicott (2005); *Teaching Environmental Ethics* (2006); and a collection co-edited with the Animal Studies Group, *Killing Animals* (2006). She was editor of the journal

Worldviews: Environment, Culture, Religion (Brill Academic Press) for 10 years and is president of the International Society of Environmental Ethics from 2007 to 2010.

Holmes Rolston III is University Distinguished Professor and Professor of Philosophy at Colorado State University. He was Templeton Prize laureate in 2003 and gave the Gifford Lectures, University of Edinburgh, 1997–8. Advocating environmental ethics, he has lectured on seven continents. He is featured in Joy A. Palmer (ed.), *Fifty Key Thinkers on the Environment* (2001). His best-known book is *Environmental Ethics: Duties to and Values in the Natural World* (1988).

David Rothenberg is Professor of Philosophy at the New Jersey Institute of Technology, where he specializes in environmental philosophy, and the aesthetics of the relationship between humanity and nature. He is the author of *Why Birds Sing* (2005), also published in Italy, Spain, Taiwan, China, Korea, and Germany, and turned into a feature-length documentary *Why Birds Sing*, by Endemol UK for BBC 4 in June, 2007. Rothenberg is also the author of *Sudden Music: Improvisation, Art, Nature* (2002); *Blue Cliff Record: Zen Echoes* (2001); *Hand's End: Technology and the Limits of Nature* (1993); and *Always the Mountains* (2003). His most recent book is *Thousand Mile Song: Whale Music in a Sea of Sound* (2008).

George Sessions is Professor Emeritus of Philosophy at Sierra College in Rocklin, California. He is the editor of *Deep Ecology for the 21st Century* (1995).

Kristin Shrader-Frechette is O'Neill Family Endowed Professor in the Department of Biological Sciences and the Department of Philosophy at the University of Notre Dame, where she also directs the Center for Environmental Justice and Children's Health. The Center does pro bono environmental justice work with minority and low-income communities and on behalf of children victimized by pollution. She has written 350 scholarly articles and 15 books, the latest of which is *Taking Action, Saving Lives* (2007). Her scientific research (which has appeared in journals such as *Science* and *BioScience*) has been funded for 25 years by the US National Science Foundation. Her work has been translated into 13 languages. Much of her ethical work focuses on human rights, and much of her philosophy of science work focuses on analyzing methods (especially mathematical and radiobiological methods) of human health and ecological risk assessment. This work appears in philosophy of science journals such as *Philosophy of Science*, *Synthese*, and *Perspectives on Science*. Much of her biological work focuses on endangered species, ecological risk assessment, and radiobiology.

Peter Singer is the Ira W. DeCamp Professor of Bioethics in the University Center for Human Values at Princeton University, and Laureate Professor in the Centre for Applied Philosophy and Practical Ethics at the University of Melbourne. He first became well known internationally after the publication of *Animal Liberation* (1975). His other books include: *Democracy and Disobedience* (1973); *Practical Ethics* (1979); *The Expanding Circle* (1981); *Marx* (1980); *Hegel* (1982); *How Are We to Live?* (1993); *Rethinking Life and Death* (1994); *One World* (2002); *Pushing Time Away* (2003); *The President of Good and Evil* (2004); *The Ethics of What We Eat* (with Jim Mason, 2006); and, most recently, *The Life You Can Save: Acting Now to End World Poverty* (2009). He co-founded The Great Ape Project with Paola Cavalieri, and is currently president of Animal Rights International. In 2005 *Time* named him one of the world's 100 most influential people.

Ian Smith received his PhD from the University of Utah and is now a Visiting Assistant Professor at the Metropolitan State College of Denver. In addition to environmental ethics, he has research interests in environmental aesthetics and ethical theory. He published a piece on a moral principle, the Principle of Double Effect, in the *Journal of Social Philosophy*. He also recently gave a public lecture at the Denver Art Museum on our aesthetic experiences of traditional art, impressionism, and the natural environment.

James P. Sterba is Professor of Philosophy at the University of Notre Dame. He has published 24 books, including *Does Feminism Justice for Here and Now Discriminate Against Men? – A Debate* (2008; co-authored with Warren Farrell); *Triumph of Practice Over Theory in Ethics* (2005); *Terrorism and International Justice* (2003); *Affirmative Action and Racial Preference: A Debate* (2003; co-authored with Carl Cohen); and *Justice for Here and Now* (1998). He is past president of the American Philosophical Association (Central Division), Concerned Philosophers for Peace, the North American Society for Social Philosophy, and the International Association for Philosophy of Law and Social Philosophy (American Section). He has also lectured widely in the US, Europe, Asia, and Africa.

Anthony Weston teaches philosophy and environmental studies at Elon University in North Carolina. His current work centers on the ethical and cultural dimensions of the environmental crisis, very broadly conceived, and on our reconstructive and imaginative resources for more promising responses. He is especially interested in social improvisation and radical social change in general, as we enter a time of dramatic social change in which multiple ecological, social, and conceptual developments are converging and synergizing. His books on environmental philosophy include *Back to Earth: Tomorrow's Environmentalism* (1994) and *An Invitation to Environmental Philosophy* (1999), and he has just finished a collection of essays to appear in 2009 as *The Incomplete Eco-Philosopher: Essays on the Edges of Environmental Ethics.*

Michael E. Zimmerman is Professor of Philosophy, and Director of the Center for Humanities and the Arts at the University of Colorado, Boulder. In addition to publishing a book on environmental philosophy, *Contesting Earth's Future* (1994), and one of the first environmental anthologies, Zimmerman has published dozens of articles and book chapters on a wide variety of topics in environmental philosophy. In 2009, he will publish a book that he co-authored with Sean Esbjörn-Hargens, *Integral Ecology: Uniting Multiple Perspectives on the Natural World.*

PART II

WHAT IS ANTHROPOCENTRISM?

1 Humans as Moral Ends
  Thomas Aquinas

2 The Mastery of Nature
  Francis Bacon

3 Nonhumans as Machines
  René Descartes

4 Mechanistic Metaphysics
  Isaac Newton

5 The Amoral Status of Nature
  John Stuart Mill

6 Nature as Economic Resource
  John Locke

7 Indirect Duties to Nonhumans
  Immanuel Kant

8 In Defense of Anthropocentrism
  Wilfred Beckerman and Joanna Pasek

Introduction

Anthropocentrism is a worldview which places humans, figuratively if not literally (in the case of geocentric astronomy) at the center of the cosmos. Philosophically, anthropocentrism can be parsed into five interconnected themes.

First, anthropocentrists typically see the natural order as arranged in a grand hierarchy (a "Great Chain of Being").[1] In this ranking, humans hold a coveted position, above all other biota and just below supernatural beings such as angels and God, something like this:

God
Other supernatural beings (angels etc.)

Humans
Vertebrate animals
Invertebrate animals
Plants
Simple micro-organisms

Inanimate matter

This idea is no better stated than by the medieval philosopher Thomas Aquinas:

[A] wonderful chain of beings is revealed to our study. The lowest member of the higher genus is always found to border upon the highest member of the lower genus. Thus some of the lowest members of the genus of animals attain to little beyond the life of plants, certain shellfish for instance, which are motionless, have only the sense of touch, and are attached to the ground like plants.[2]

Humans are on a borderline between the supernatural and the natural, just below God and angels: The human soul "is said to be on the horizon and boundary line between things corporeal and incorporeal, inasmuch as it is an incorporeal substance and at the same time the form of a body."[3]

Second, connected to the idea that humans inhabit a special position at the very top of the natural order, just shy of divinity, is the notion of a firm ontological divide between human and nonhuman nature (metaphysical dualism). This divide is expressed by such familiar dualisms as culture/nature and mind/body or soul/body. Anthropocentrists often cite the possession of an immaterial soul lodged in a material body as evidence of dualism (as does French philosopher René Descartes).

Third, aligned with this dualism is the idea of nature-as-machine (mechanism) – nature as a system of inanimate particles rather than as inherent Aristotelian forces.[4] This system operates deterministically according to the mathematical laws of physics. According to Descartes and English mathematician and physicist Isaac Newton, even biota are mechanistic.[5] Human beings, graced with free will, are exempt from these laws.

Fourth, anthropocentrists hold the position that human beings alone are intrinsically valuable (good in and of ourselves) and that nonhuman nature is valuable only insofar as it has use-value for humans (good instrumentally for our ends). This instrumental valuation of nature is epitomized by the view of nature as economic resource (resourcism), articulated most prominently by the English philosopher John Locke.[6]

Fifth, anthropocentrists maintain that human beings constitute, solely and exclusively, the moral community. This position is founded on the two foregoing points: the class of entities worthy of moral considerability is separate from nature, and only humans are intrinsically valuable and hence worthy of moral consideration.

In the first reading in this section, from *The Summa Contra Gentiles*,[7] Aquinas develops the ethical implications of the Great Chain of Being. In the Great Chain of Being, humans are closest to the likeness of God. Rational creatures exercise free will (that is, have dominion over their actions). God bestows on such creatures (namely, human beings) intrinsic value. The actions of other organisms are causally determined by the environment, making them "slaves" to their surroundings. Because beings higher in the hierarchy manifest more fully the work and glory of God than beings lower down, and humans are at the top of the natural order, human beings alone are morally considerable. Moreover, human beings have the right to subjugate beings below. Animals who do not exercise free will (dumb animals) can be used and killed for human ends in accordance with the will of God. Anticipating Kant, Aquinas argues that the only danger in killing dumb animals is that such behavior might lead to cruelty to other human beings.

For English philosopher Francis Bacon (1561–1626 CE), the focus of knowledge should not be abstract, immaterial, Platonic Forms, but the material improvement of the human condition. As he writes in the selection from *The Great Instauration*, this focus enjoins the mastery (command) of nature. The value of nature is as resource for human purposes. The method of manipulating the operations of nature for human ends is to carve nature at its joints in order to see what parts nature is made of and how they are put together (reductionism).

French philosopher René Descartes (1596–1650 CE) gave an honest application of the mechanical view of nature to biota. In the estimation of American biologist Ernst Mayr, perhaps no one "contributed more to the spread of the mechanistic world picture than … Descartes."[8] In the *Discourse* and in personal correspondence, Descartes argues that (1) either nonhuman animals are utterly devoid of sentience or they have human-like sentience; (2) nonhuman animals do not have human-like sentience; (3) therefore nonhuman animals are utterly devoid of sentience. Nonhuman animals are, in a word, machines – albeit incredibly complex biological machines, the handiwork of God, but machines nonetheless. If nonhuman organisms are mere machines, then they cannot be the object of moral consideration any more than can a clock or an engine. Kant would take up the issue of moral duties to nonhumans more than a century later, and arrive at a slightly different conclusion.

Bacon and Descartes were part of a trend during the modern period in championing the mechanical view of nature. Nature, on this metaphysics, operates according to mathematical and deterministic laws of physics. This includes *all* natural motions (including those of living things). English mathematician and physicist Isaac Newton (1642–1727 CE) elaborates the mechanical view in the *Principia*:

> For the basic problem of philosophy seems to be to discover the forces of nature from the phenomena of motions and then to demonstrate the other phenomena from these forces … by means of propositions demonstrated mathematically[.] [W]e derive from celestial phenomena the gravitational forces by which bodies tend toward the sun and toward the individual planets. Then the motions of the planets, the comets, the moon, and the sea are deduced from these forces by propositions that are also mathematical. If only we could derive the other phenomena of nature from mechanical principles by the same kind of reasoning! For many things lead me to have a suspicion that all phenomena may depend on certain forces by which the particles of bodies, by causes not yet known, either are impelled toward one another and cohere in regular figures, or are repelled from one another and recede. Since these forces are unknown, philosophers have hitherto made trial of nature in vain. But I hope that the principles set down here will shed some light on either this mode of philosophizing or some other truer one.[9]

If we knew the details of the initial conditions and vectors of all natural motion (organic things included) as we do celestial bodies, then we ought to be able to calculate their motions (organic growth included) with mathematical certainty based on mechanical principles.

In the selection from the *Opticks* presented here, Newton derides two of Aristotle's four causes[10] – formal and final causation – as "occult qualities." By "occult" Newton means that those causes have no place in the natural order, and that all natural phenomena can be understood in terms of Aristotle's two other causes – material and efficient causation. The study of material and efficient causation is the methodology of the mechanical view. Newton claims that God operates all parts of nature by mechanical principles, just as humans move parts of our bodies.

In his essay "Nature," English philosopher John Stuart Mill (1806–73 CE) considers the multiple meanings of the word "nature," a topic taken up in the introductory essay of this volume, "What is Environmental Ethics?" Mill observes that "nature" might mean "aggregate … sum of all phenomena" and "everything which happens … without the agency of man" – that is, natural as opposed to the artificial. There is a third teleological meaning, the inner essence of a thing, which Mill casts in a normative light as per natural law theory. In this third sense, "nature" provides a prescriptive standard for human conduct, and in this third sense Mill finds fault. Nature is destructive and ought not to be used as a standard for human conduct. Rather, as Bacon argued, humans should ameliorate the flaws of nature by tinkering with its workings.

It is worth noting that Holmes Rolston echoes Mill in his environmental ethics of hierarchical (anthropometric) biocentrism. Rolston contends that nature itself is amoral:

> Nature proceeds with a recklessness that is indifferent to life; this results in senseless cruelty and is repugnant to our moral sensitivities. Life is wrested from her creatures by continual struggle, usually soon lost; those few who survive to maturity only face eventual collapse in disease and death. With what indifference nature casts forth her creatures to slaughter! Everything is condemned to live by attacking or competing with other life. There is no altruistic consideration of others, no justice.[11]

For Mill, as for Rolston, nature will not suffice as a template for intra-human ethics.

If you believe that there is no formal and final causation outside of nature and that natural process consists wholly of material and efficient causation, that nature is a colossal Machine ticking according to the deterministic laws of physics (mechanism), then you are likely to see no value in nature besides resource value. This view is "resourcism," influentially summarized by English philosopher John Locke (1632–1704 CE) in his essay "Of Property." Locke conjectures that God gave humankind the Earth in common for use as a natural resource.[12] God also gave humans rationality so that we can make the "best advantage" of this gift.[13] Each individual "owns" his or her body, and labor is a function of the body. By extension, the fruits of labor are also owned by the working individual. Once one exerts one's labor on the inert pool of natural resources to make them advantageous to human well-being – by clearing forest, moving rocks, plowing soil, planting crops – one is entitled to the products of that labor: "Whatsoever, then, he removes out of the state that Nature hath provided and left it in, he hath mixed his labour with it, and joined to it something that is his own, and thereby makes it his property."[14]

This is the essence of the Western notion of private property. It is based on the fundamental assumption that the value of natural resources is latent in that the resources must be actualized by human labor to become valuable, but only of instrumental value. Natural resources have no intrinsic value. Human beings, through labor, transform the latent resource value into useful products.

Gifford Pinchot (1865–1946), the first chief of the US Forest Service and later Governor of Pennsylvania, would apply Lockean resourcism to twentieth-century American land-use policy. He saw "just two things on this material earth – people and natural resources."[15] From this ontology, Pinchot adduced the environmental policy of conservationism:

> The first great fact about conservation is that it stands for development. … Conservation does mean provision for the future, but it means also and first of all the recognition of the right of the present generation to the fullest necessary use of all the resources with which this country is so abundantly blessed. Conservation demands the welfare of this generation first, and afterward the welfare of the generations to follow. … In the second place conservation stands for the prevention of waste.[16]

It is wrong to let natural resources lie fallow, their latent value unactualized. The thinking of Pinchot and Locke is behind an argument heard against wilderness designation throughout the western United States: developers should "release" as much value from the land as possible through development and not let those resources remain unutilized, locked away in "wilderness."[17]

In our selection from *Lectures on Ethics*, Immanuel Kant (1724–1804 CE) takes up the issue of moral duties to nonhuman nature addressed previously by Aquinas and Descartes. Kant agrees with both predecessors that humans have no *direct* duties to nonhumans. Only rational beings are worthy of moral considerability (ratiocentrism) and only human beings are rational.[18] Kant, however, thought that there is an anthropocentric rationale for *indirect* duties to both inanimate and animate nonhuman nature.

Kant thinks there is a behavioral connection between habits regarding the treatment of human beings and nonhuman nature. The way one treats nonhuman animals, for example, will likely affect the way one treats fellow humans, "for he who is cruel to animals becomes hard also in his dealing with men."[19] So if you sizzle ants under a magnifying glass using the rays of the sun for fun, if you shoot squirrels hopping along branches from your porch while drinking whisky for evening entertainment, if you take cats out in the middle of a lake and throw them overboard to watch them panic, flail, and drown, or if you wire a coyote to a fence to let it die slowly of starvation and dehydration and exposure in retribution for killing sheep,[20] a Kantian ethicist would say that these actions are not morally repugnant in-and-of themselves because these nonhuman animals lack rationality and hence cannot be the proper objects of moral considerability. But these actions could help foster habits of cruelty which ultimately might result in you hurting a human being for which you *would* be morally culpable. Take the example of the 7-year-old boy in Australia who broke into a zoo before opening hours. Caught on video cameras sporting a big grin, the boy tossed live reptiles into the jaws of a huge crocodile and bludgeoned three lizards to death in their pens.[21] It does not require a big stretch of the imagination to think that this is the kind of kid who later in life would be an assailant or murderer.

In the final selection of this section, Wilfred Beckerman (an economist) and Joanna Pasek (a philosopher) give a contemporary defense of anthropocentrism, which in many ways parallels the anthropocentric environmental philosophy of Bryan Norton. Beckerman and Pasek argue that, despite the most energetic exertions of nonanthropocentrists intent upon outlining an objectivist axiology of intrinsic value in nature, anthropocentrism is inevitable because all interpretations of nature will always be rooted in a human-centered perspective. Therefore, even "nonanthropocentrism" is anthropocentric.

Environmental ethics must be understood within the context of the Western intellectual tradition. As illustrated in these readings, most great philosophers advanced an anthropocentric agenda by touching on one or more of the five defining features of anthropocentrism. Environmental ethics is to be understood as a set of critiques, some commendatory but most condemnatory, of the anthropocentric worldview.

Notes

1 See Lovejoy's classic work on this subject, *The Great Chain of Being*.

2 Aquinas, *Summa Contra Gentiles*, Carroll Press edn., p. 133.

3 Ibid.

4 See Merchant, *The Death of Nature*, p. 193. (See this volume, p. 299.)

5 Descartes, February 5, 1649, letter to More, *The Philosophical Writings of Descartes*, vol. 3, pp. 365–6; Newton, The *Principia*, pp. 382–3.

6 "Of Property," *Second Treatise of Government*, in Laslett, ed., *Two Treatises of Government*, pp. 285–302.

7 This reading selection is taken from the Burns, Oates & Washbourne edition.

8 Mayr, *The Growth of Biological Thought*, p. 97.

9 Newton, *The Principia*, pp. 382–3.

10 *Metaphysics* Book V, in McKeon, ed., *The Basic Works of Aristotle*, p. 752.

11 Rolston, *Environmental Ethics*, p. 39.

12 "Of Property," *Second Treatise of Government*, in Laslett, ed., *Two Treatises of Government*, §25, p. 286. (See this volume, p. 77.)

13 Ibid., §26, p. 286. (See this volume, p. 77.)

14 Ibid., §27, p. 288. (See this volume, p. 78.)

15 Pinchot, *Breaking New Ground*, p. 325.

16 *The Fight for Conservation*, pp. 42, 44.

17 See e.g. Baum, "Wise Guise."

18 Kant's ratiocentrism implies that nonrational human beings are not worthy of moral consideration – a problem latched onto by animal welfare theorists. See, e.g., Regan, "An Examination and Defense of One Argument Concerning Animal Rights." Cf. also p. 10.

19 Kant, *Lectures on Ethics*, Century edn., p. 240. (See this volume, p. 82.)

20 Evidence suggests that each one of these things has actually occurred.

21 Cavanagh, "Boy, 7, Feeds Live Zoo Animals to Croc."

1   Humans as Moral Ends

Thomas Aquinas

THAT RATIONAL CREATURES ARE GOVERNED FOR THEIR OWN
SAKE, AND OTHER CREATURES, AS DIRECTED TO THEM

In the first place then, the very condition of the rational creature, in that it has dominion over its actions, requires that the care of providence should be bestowed on it for its own sake: whereas the condition of other things that have not dominion over their actions shows that they are cared for, not for their own sake, but as being directed to other things. Because that which acts only when moved by another, is like an instrument; whereas that which acts by itself, is like a principal agent. Now an instrument is required, not for its own sake, but that the principal agent may use it. Hence whatever is done for the care of the instruments must be referred to the principal agent as its end: whereas any such action directed to the principal agent as such, either by the agent itself or by another, is for the sake of the same principal agent. Accordingly intellectual creatures are ruled by God, as though He cared for them for their own sake, while other creatures are ruled as being directed to rational creatures.

Again. That which has dominion over its own act, is free in its action, because *he is free who is cause of himself:* whereas that which by some kind of necessity is moved by another to act, is subject to slavery. Therefore every other creature is naturally under slavery; the intellectual nature alone is free. Now, in every government provision is made for the free for their own sake; but for slaves that they may be useful to the free. Accordingly divine providence makes provision for the intellectual creature for its own sake, but for other creatures for the sake of the intellectual creature.

✓ Moreover. Whenever certain things are directed to a certain end, if any of them are unable of themselves to attain to the end, they must needs be directed to those that attain to the end, which are directed to the end for their own sake. Thus the end of the army is victory, which the soldiers obtain by their own action in fighting, and they alone in the army are required for their own sake; whereas all others, to whom other duties are assigned, such as the care of horses, the preparing of arms, are requisite for the sake of the soldiers of the army. Now, it is clear from what has been said, that God is the last end of the universe, whom the intellectual nature alone obtains in Himself, namely by knowing and loving Him, as was proved above. Therefore the intellectual nature alone is requisite for its own sake in the universe, and all others for its sake.

Further. In every whole, the principal parts are requisite on their own account for the completion of the whole, while others are required for the preservation or betterment of the former. Now, of all the parts of the universe, intellectual creatures hold the highest place, because they approach nearest to the divine likeness. Therefore divine providence provides for the intellectual nature for its own sake, and for all others for its sake.

Besides. It is clear that all the parts are directed to the perfection of the whole: since the whole is not on account of the parts, but the parts on account of the whole. Now, intellectual natures are more akin to the whole than other natures: because, in a sense, the intellectual substance is all things, inasmuch as by its intellect it is able to comprehend all things; whereas every other substance has only a particular participation of being. Consequently God cares for other things for the sake of intellectual substances.

Besides. Whatever happens to a thing in the course of nature happens to it naturally. Now, we see that in the course of nature the intellectual substance uses all others for its own sake; either for the perfection of the intellect, which sees the truth in them as in a mirror; or for the execution of its power and development of its knowledge, in the same way as a craftsman develops the conception of his art in corporeal matter; or again to sustain the body that is united to an intellectual soul, as is the case in man. It is clear, therefore, that God cares for all things for the sake of intellectual substances.

From *The Summa Contra Gentiles*, Part II, Book 3, Chapter CXII (London: Burns, Oates & Washbourne Ltd., 1928), pp. 88–92.

Moreover. If a man seek something for its own sake, he seeks it always, because *what is per se, is always:* whereas if he seek a thing on account of something else, he does not of necessity seek it always but only in reference to that for the sake of which he seeks it. Now, as we proved above, things derive their being from the divine will. Therefore whatever is always is willed by God for its own sake; and what is not always is willed by God, not for its own sake, but for another's. Now, intellectual substances approach nearest to being always, since they are incorruptible. They are, moreover, unchangeable, except in their choice. Therefore intellectual substances are governed for their own sake, as it were; and others for the sake of intellectual substances.

The fact that all the parts of the universe are directed to the perfection of the whole is not in contradiction with the foregoing conclusion: since all the parts are directed to the perfection of the whole, in so far as one part serves another. Thus in the human body it is clear that the lungs belong to the body's perfection, in that they serve the heart: wherefore there is no contradiction in the lungs being for the sake of the heart, and for the sake of the whole animal. In like manner that other natures are on account of the intellectual is not contrary to their being for the perfection of the universe: for without the things required for the perfection of the intellectual substance, the universe would not be complete.

Nor again does the fact that individuals are for the sake of the species militate against what has been said. Because through being directed to their species, they are directed also to the intellectual nature. For a corruptible thing is directed to man, not on account of only one individual man, but on account of the whole human species. Yet a corruptible thing could not serve the whole human species, except as regards its own entire species. Hence the order whereby corruptible things are directed to man, requires that individuals be directed to the species.

When we assert that intellectual substances are directed by divine providence for their own sake, we do not mean that they are not also referred to God

and for the perfection of the universe. Accordingly they are said to be provided for on their own account, and others on account of them, because the goods bestowed on them by divine providence are not given them for another's profit: whereas those bestowed on others are in the divine plan intended for the use of intellectual substances. Hence it is said (Deut. iv. 19): *Lest thou see the sun and the moon and the other stars, and being deceived by error, thou adore and serve them, which the Lord thy God created for the service of all the nations that are under heaven:* and (Ps. viii. 8): *Thou hast subjected all things under his feet, all sheep and oxen: moreover, the beasts also of the field:* and (Wis. xii. 18): *Thou, being master of power, judgest with tranquillity, and with great favour disposest of us.*

Hereby is refuted the error of those who said it is sinful for a man to kill dumb animals: for by divine providence they are intended for man's use in the natural order. Hence it is no wrong for man to make use of them, either by killing or in any other way whatever. For this reason the Lord said to Noe (Gen. ix. 3): *As the green herbs I have delivered all flesh to you.*

And if any passages of Holy Writ seem to forbid us to be cruel to dumb animals, for instance to kill a bird with its young:[2] this is either to remove man's thoughts from being cruel to other men, and lest through being cruel to animals one become cruel to human beings: or because injury to an animal leads to the temporal hurt of man, either of the doer of the deed, or of another: or on account of some signification: thus the Apostle expounds[3] the prohibition against *muzzling the ox that treadeth the corn.*[4]

Notes

1 Aristotle, *Metaphysics*, Bk I, ch. 2 [982b25].
2 Deuteronomy xxii. 6.
3 I Corinthians ix. 9.
4 Deuteronomy xxv. 4.

2   The Mastery of Nature

Francis Bacon

i

On a given body to generate and superinduce a new nature or new natures, is the work and aim of *human power*. Of a given nature to discover the form, or true specific difference, or nature-engendering nature, or source of emanation (for these are the terms which come nearest to a description of the thing), is the work and aim of *human knowledge*. Subordinate to these primary works are two others that are secondary and of inferior mark: to the former, the transformation of concrete bodies, so far as this is possible; to the latter, the discovery, in every case of generation and motion, of the Latent Process carried on from the manifest efficient and the manifest material to the form which is engendered; and in like manner the discovery of the Latent Configuration of bodies at rest and not in motion.

ii

In what an ill condition human knowledge is at the present time, is apparent even from the commonly received maxims. It is a correct position that "true knowledge is knowledge by causes." And causes again are not improperly distributed into four kinds: the material, the formal, the efficient, and the final. But of these the final cause rather corrupts than advances the sciences, except such as have to do with human action. The discovery of the formal is despaired of. The efficient and the material (as they are investigated and received, that is, as remote causes, without reference to the latent process leading to the form) are but slight and superficial, and contribute little, if anything, to true and active science. Nor have I forgotten that in a former passage I noted and corrected as an error of the human mind the opinion that Forms give existence. For though in nature nothing really exists beside individual bodies, performing pure individual acts according to a fixed law, yet in philosophy this very law, and the investigation, discovery, and explanation of it, is the foundation as well of knowledge as of operation. And it is this law, with its clauses, that I mean when I speak of *Forms;* a name which I the rather adopt because it has grown into use and become familiar.

iii

If a man be acquainted with the cause of any nature (as whiteness or heat) in certain subjects only, his knowledge is imperfect; and if he be able to superinduce an effect on certain substances only (of those susceptible of such effect), his power is in like manner imperfect. Now if a man's knowledge be confined to the efficient and material causes (which are unstable causes, and merely vehicles, or causes which convey the form in certain cases), he may arrive at new discoveries in reference to substances in some degree similar to one another, and selected beforehand; but he does not touch the deeper boundaries of things. But whosoever is acquainted with Forms, embraces the unity of nature in substances the most unlike; and is able therefore to detect and bring to light things never yet done, and such as neither the vicissitudes of nature, nor industry in experimenting, nor accident itself, would ever have brought into act, and which would never have occurred to the thought of man. From the discovery of Forms therefore results truth in speculation and freedom in operation.

iv

Although the roads to human power and to human knowledge lie close together, and are nearly the same, nevertheless on account of the pernicious and inveterate habit of dwelling on abstractions, it is safer to begin and raise the sciences from those foundations which have relation to practice, and to

From *The Great Instauration*. In James Spedding, Robert Leslie Ellis, and Douglas Denon Heath, eds., *The Works*, vol VIII. Boston: Taggard and Thompson, 1863, pp. 84–93.

let the active part itself be as the seal which prints and determines the contemplative counterpart. We must therefore consider, if a man wanted to generate and superinduce any nature upon a given body, what kind of rule or direction or guidance he would most wish for, and express the same in the simplest and least abstruse language. For instance, if a man wishes to superinduce upon silver the yellow color of gold, or an increase of weight (observing the laws of matter), or transparency on an opaque stone, or tenacity on glass, or vegetation on some substance that is not vegetable, – we must consider, I say, what kind of rule or guidance he would most desire. And in the first place, he will undoubtedly wish to be directed to something which will not deceive him in the result, nor fail him in the trial. Secondly, he will wish for such a rule as shall not tie him down to certain means and particular modes of operation. For perhaps he may not have those means, nor be able conveniently to procure them. And if there be other means and other methods for producing the required nature (beside the one prescribed) these may perhaps be within his reach; and yet he shall be excluded by the narrowness of the rule, and get no good from them. Thirdly, he will desire something to be shown him which is not as difficult as the thing proposed to be done, but comes nearer to practice.

For a true and perfect rule of operation then the direction will be *that it be certain, free, and disposing or leading to action.* And this is the same thing with the discovery of the true Form. For the Form of a nature is such that, given the Form, the nature infallibly follows. Therefore it is always present when the nature is present, and universally implies it, and is constantly inherent in it. Again, the Form is such that if it be taken away, the nature infallibly vanishes. Therefore it is always absent when the nature is absent, and implies its absence, and inheres in nothing else. Lastly, the true Form is such that it deduces the given nature from some source of being which is inherent in more natures, and which is better known in the natural order of things than the Form itself. For a true and perfect axiom of knowledge then the direction and precept will be, *that another nature be discovered which is convertible with the given nature, and yet is a limitation of a more general nature, as of a true and real genus.* Now these two directions, the one active the other contemplative, are one and the same thing; and what in operation is most useful, that in knowledge is most true.

V

The rule or axiom for the transformation of bodies is of two kinds. The first regards a body as a troop or collection of simple natures. In gold, for example, the following properties meet. It is yellow in color; heavy up to a certain weight; malleable or ductile to a certain degree of extension; it is not volatile, and loses none of its substance by the action of fire; it turns into a liquid with a certain degree of fluidity; it is separated and dissolved by particular means; and so on for the other natures which meet in gold. This kind of axiom, therefore, deduces the thing from the forms of simple natures. For he who knows the forms of yellow, weight, ductility, fixity, fluidity, solution, and so on, and the methods for superinducing them, and their gradations and modes, will make it his care to have them joined together in some body, whence may follow the transformation of that body into gold. And this kind of operation pertains to the first kind of action. For the principle of generating some one simple nature is the same as that of generating many; only that a man is more fettered and tied down in operation if more are required, by reason of the difficulty of combining into one so many natures, which do not readily meet except in the beaten and ordinary paths of nature. It must be said however that this mode of operation (which looks to simple natures though in a compound body) proceeds from what in nature is constant and eternal and universal, and opens broad roads to human power, such as (in the present state of things) human thought can scarcely comprehend or anticipate.

The second kind of axiom, which is concerned with the discovery of the Latent Process, proceeds not by simple natures, but by compound bodies, as they are found in nature in its ordinary course. As, for instance, when inquiry is made, from what beginnings, and by what method and by what process, gold or any other metal or stone is generated, from its first menstrua and rudiments up to the perfect mineral; or in like manner by what process herbs are generated, from the first concretion of juices in the ground or from seeds up to the formed plant, with all the successive motions and diverse and continued efforts of nature. So also in the inquiry concerning the process of development in the generation of animals, from coition to birth; and in like manner of other bodies.

It is not however only to the generations of bodies that this investigation extends, but also to other motions and operations of nature. As, for instance, when inquiry is made concerning the whole course and continued action of nutrition, from the first reception of the food to its complete assimilation; or again, concerning the voluntary motion of animals, from the first impression on the imagination and the continued efforts of the spirit up to the bendings and movements of the limbs; or concerning the motion of the tongue and lips and other instruments, and the changes through which it passes till it comes to the utterance of articulate sounds. For these inquiries also relate to natures concrete or combined into one structure, and have regard to what may be called particular and special habits of nature, not to her fundamental and universal laws which constitute Forms. And yet it must be confessed that this plan appears to be readier and to lie nearer at hand and to give more ground for hope than the primary one.

In like manner the operative which answers to this speculative part, starting from the ordinary incidents of nature, extends its operation to things immediately adjoining, or at least not far removed. But as for any profound and radical operations on nature, they depend entirely on the primary axioms. And in those things too where man has no means of operating, but only of knowing, as in the heavenly bodies (for these he cannot operate upon or change or transform), the investigation of the fact itself or truth of the thing, no less than the knowledge of the causes and consents, must come from those primary and catholic axioms concerning simple natures; such as the nature of spontaneous rotation, of attraction or magnetism, and of many others which are of a more general form than the heavenly bodies themselves. For let no one hope to decide the question whether it is the earth or heaven that really revolves in the diurnal motion, until he has first comprehended the nature of spontaneous rotation.

vi

But this Latent Process, of which I speak, is quite another thing than men, preoccupied as their minds now are, will easily conceive. For what I understand by it is not certain measures or signs or successive steps of process in bodies, which can be seen; but a process perfectly continuous, which for the most part escapes the sense.

For instance: in all generation and transformation of bodies, we must inquire what is lost and escapes; what remains, what is added; what is expanded, what contracted; what is united, what separated; what is continued, what cut off; what propels, what hinders; what predominates, what yields; and a variety of other particulars.

Again, not only in the generation or transformation of bodies are these points to be ascertained, but also in all other alterations and motions it should in like manner be inquired what goes before, what comes after; what is quicker, what more tardy; what produces, what governs motion; and like points; all which nevertheless in the present state of the sciences (the texture of which is as rude as possible and good for nothing) are unknown and unhandled. For seeing that every natural action depends on things infinitely small, or at least too small to strike the sense, no one can hope to govern or change nature until he has duly comprehended and observed them.

vii

In like manner the investigation and discovery of the Latent Configuration in bodies is a new thing, no less than the discovery of the Latent Process and of the Form. For as yet we are but lingering in the outer courts of nature, nor are we preparing ourselves a way into her inner chambers. Yet no one can endow a given body with a new nature, or successfully and aptly transmute it into a new body, unless he has attained a competent knowledge of the body so to be altered or transformed. Otherwise he will run into methods which, if not useless, are at any rate difficult and perverse and unsuitable to the nature of the body on which he is operating. It is clear therefore that to this also a way must be opened and laid out.

And it is true that upon the anatomy of organised bodies (as of man and animals) some pains have been well bestowed and with good effect; and a subtle thing it seems to be, and a good scrutiny of nature. Yet this kind of anatomy is subject to sight and sense, and has place only in organised bodies. And besides it is a thing obvious and easy, when compared with the true anatomy of the Latent Configuration in bodies which are thought to be of uniform structure: especially in things that have a specific character and their parts, as iron, stone; and again in parts of uniform structure in plants and animals, as the root, the leaf, the flower, flesh, blood, and bones. But even in this kind, human industry has not been altogether wanting; for this is the very thing aimed at in the separation of bodies of uniform structure by means of distillations and other modes of analysis, – that the complex structure of the compound may be made apparent by bringing together its several homogeneous parts. And this is of use too, and conduces to the object we are seeking; although too often fallacious in its results, because many natures which are in fact newly brought out and superinduced by fire and heat and other modes of solution are taken to be the effect of separation merely, and to have subsisted in the compound before. And after all, this is but a small part of the work of discovering the true configuration in the compound body; which configuration is a thing far more subtle and exact, and such as the operation of fire rather confounds than brings out and makes distinct.

Therefore a separation and solution of bodies must be effected, not by fire indeed, but by reasoning and true induction, with experiments to aid; and by a comparison with other bodies, and a reduction to simple natures and their Forms, which meet and mix in the compound. In a word we must pass from Vulcan to Minerva, if we intend to bring to light the true textures and configurations of bodies; on which all the occult and, as they are called, specific properties and virtues in things depend; and from which too the rule of every powerful alteration and transformation is derived.

For example, we must inquire what amount of spirit there is in every body, what of tangible essence; and of the spirit, whether it be copious and turgid, or meagre and scarce; whether it be fine or coarse, akin to air or to fire, brisk or sluggish, weak or strong, progressive or retrograde, interrupted or continuous, agreeing with external and surrounding objects or disagreeing, etc. In like manner we must inquire into the tangible essence (which admits of no fewer differences than the spirit), – into its coats, its fibres, its kinds of texture. Moreover the disposition of the spirit throughout the corporeal frame, with its pores, passages, veins and cells, and the rudiments or first essays of the organised body, fall under the same investigation. But on these inquiries also, and I may say on all the discovery of the Latent Configuration, a true and clear light is shed by the primary axioms, which entirely dispels all darkness and subtlety.

viii

Nor shall we thus be led to the doctrine of atoms, which implies the hypothesis of a vacuum and that of the unchangeableness of matter (both false assumptions); we shall be led only to real particles, such as really exist. Nor again is there any reason to be alarmed at the subtlety of the investigation, as if it could not be disentangled: on the contrary, the nearer it approaches to simple natures, the easier and plainer will everything become; the business being transferred from the complicated to the simple, from the incommensurable to the commensurable, from surds to rational quantities, from the infinite and vague to the finite and certain, – as in the case of the letters of the alphabet and the notes of music. And inquiries into nature have the best result when they begin with physics and end in mathematics. Again, let no one be afraid of high numbers or minute fractions. For in dealing with numbers it is as easy to set down or conceive a thousand as one, or the thousandth part of an integer as an integer itself.

ix

From the two kinds of axioms which have been spoken of, arises a just division of philosophy and the sciences; taking the received terms (which come nearest to express the thing) in a sense agreeable to my own views. Thus, let the investigation of Forms, which are (in the eye of reason at least, and in their essential law) eternal and immutable, constitute *metaphysics;* and let the investigation of the Efficient Cause, and of Matter, and of the Latent Process, and the Latent Configuration (all of which have reference to the common and ordinary course of nature, not to her eternal and fundamental laws) constitute *physics*. And to these let there be subordinate two practical divisions: to physics, *mechanics;* to metaphysics, what (in a purer sense of the word) I call *magic,* on account of the broadness of the ways it moves in, and its greater command over nature.

3 Nonhumans as Machines

René Descartes

I specially dwelt on showing that if there were machines with the organs and appearance of a monkey, or some other irrational animal, we should have no means of telling that they were not altogether of the same nature as those animals; whereas if there were machines resembling our bodies, and imitating our actions as far as is morally possible, we should still have two means of telling that, all the same, they were not real men. First, they could never use words or other constructed signs, as we do to declare our thoughts to others. It is quite conceivable that a machine should be so made as to utter words, and even utter them in connexion with physical events that cause a change in one of its organs; so that e.g. if it is touched in one part, it asks what you want to say to it, and if touched in another, it cries out that it is hurt; but not that it should be so made as to arrange words variously in response to the meaning of what is said in its presence, as even the dullest men can do. Secondly, while they might do many things as well as any of us or better, they would infallibly fail in others, revealing that they acted not from knowledge but only from the disposition of their organs. For while reason is a universal tool that may serve in all kinds of circumstances, these organs need a special arrangement for each special action; so it is morally impossible that a machine should contain so many varied arrangements as to act in all the events of life in the way reason enables us to act.

Now in just these two ways we can also recognise the difference between men and brutes. For it is a very remarkable thing that there are no men so dull and stupid, not even lunatics, that they cannot arrange various words and form a sentence to make their thoughts (*pensées*) understood; but no other animal, however perfect or well bred, can do the like. This does not come from their lacking the organs; for magpies and parrots can utter words like ourselves, and yet they cannot talk like us, that is, with any sign of being aware of (*qu'ils pensent*) what they say. Whereas men born deaf-mutes, and thus devoid of the organs that others use for speech, as much as brutes are or more so, usually invent for themselves signs by which they make themselves understood to those who are normally with them, and who thus have a chance to learn their language. This is evidence that brutes not only have a smaller degree of reason than men, but are wholly lacking in it. For it may be seen that a very small degree of reason is needed in order to be able to talk; and in view of the inequality that occurs among animals of the same species, as among men, and of the fact that some are easier to train than others, it is incredible that a monkey or parrot who was one of the most perfect members of his species should not be comparable in this regard to one of the stupidest children or at least to a child with a diseased brain, if their souls were not wholly different in nature from ours. And we must not confuse words with natural movements, the expressions of emotion, which can be imitated by machines as well as by animals. Nor must we think, like some of the ancients, that brutes talk but we cannot understand their language; for if that were true, since many of their organs are analogous to ours, they could make themselves understood to us, as well as to their fellows. It is another very remarkable thing that although several brutes exhibit more skill than we in some of their actions, they show none at all in many other circumstances; so their excelling us is no proof that they have a mind (*de l'esprit*), for in that case they would have a better one than any of us and would excel us all round; it rather shows that they have none, and that it is nature that acts in them according to the arrangements of their organs; just as

From "Discourse on the Method Part V" and "Correspondence," excerpted from John Cottingham, Robert Stoothoff, and Dugald Murdoch, ed. and trans., *The Philosophical Writings of Descartes*, vol. I (Cambridge: Cambridge University Press, 1985). © 1985 by Cambridge University Press. Reproduced with permission of the translators and Cambridge University Press. And from John Cottingham, Robert Stoothoff, Dugald Murdoch, and Anthony Kenny, ed. and trans., *The Philosophical Writings of Descartes*, vol. III: *The Correspondence* (Cambridge: Cambridge University Press, 1991), pp. 302–4, 365–7. © 1991 by Cambridge University Press. Reproduced with permission of the translators and Cambridge University Press.

we see how a clock, composed merely of wheels and springs, can reckon the hours and measure time more correctly than we can with all our wisdom.

I went on to describe the rational soul, and showed that, unlike the other things I had spoken of, it cannot be extracted from the potentiality of matter, but must be specially created; and how it is not enough for it to dwell in the human body like a pilot in his ship, which would only account for its moving the limbs of the body; in order to have in addition feelings and appetites like ours, and so make up a true man, it must be joined and united to the body more closely. Here I dwelt a little on the subject of the soul, as among the most important; for, after the error of denying God, (of which I think I have already given a sufficient refutation), there is none more likely to turn weak characters from the strait way of virtue than the supposition that the soul of brutes must be of the same nature as ours, so that after this life we have no more to hope or fear than flies or ants. Whereas, when we realise how much they really differ from us, we understand much better the arguments proving that our soul is of a nature entirely independent of the body, and thus not liable to die with it; and since we can discern no other causes that should destroy it, we are naturally led to decide that it is immortal.

[…]

I cannot share the opinion of Montaigne and others who attribute understanding or thought to animals. I am not worried that people say that human beings have absolute dominion over all the other animals; for I agree that some of them are stronger than us, and I believe that there may also be some animals which have a natural cunning capable of deceiving the shrewdest human beings. But I consider that they imitate or surpass us only in those of our actions which are not guided by our thought. It often happens that we walk or eat without thinking at all about what we are doing; and similarly, without using our reason, we reject things which are harmful for us, and parry the blows aimed at us. Indeed, even if we expressly willed not to put our hands in front of our head when we fall, we could not prevent ourselves. I consider also that if we had no thought then we would walk, as the animals do, without having learnt to; and it is said that those who walk in their sleep sometimes swim across streams in which they would drown if they were awake. As for the movements of our passions, even though in us they are accompanied by thought because we have the faculty of thinking, it is nevertheless very clear that they do not depend on thought, because they often occur in spite of us. Consequently they can also occur in animals, even more violently than they do in human beings, without our being able to conclude from that that animals have thoughts.

In fact, none of our external actions can show anyone who examines them that our body is not just a self-moving machine but contains a soul with thoughts, with the exception of spoken words, or other signs that have reference to particular topics without expressing any passion. I say 'spoken words or other signs', because deaf-mutes use signs as we use spoken words; and I say that these signs must have reference, to exclude the speech of parrots, without excluding the speech of madmen, which has reference to particular topics even though it does not follow reason. I add also that these words or signs must not express any passion, to rule out not only cries of joy or sadness and the like, but also whatever can be taught by training to animals. If you teach a magpie to say good-day to its mistress when it sees her approach, this can only be by making the utterance of this word the expression of one of its passions. For instance it will be an expression of the hope of eating, if it has always been given a titbit when it says it. Similarly, all the things which dogs, horses and monkeys are taught to perform are only expressions of their fear, their hope or their joy; and consequently they can be performed without any thought. Now it seems to me very striking that the use of words, so defined, is something peculiar to human beings. Montaigne and Charron may have said that there is a greater difference between one human being and another than between a human being and an animal; yet there has never been known an animal so perfect as to use a sign to make other animals understand something which bore no relation to its passions; and there is no human being so imperfect as not to do so, since even deaf-mutes invent special signs to express their thoughts. This seems to me a very strong argument to prove that the reason why animals do not speak as we do is not that they lack the organs but that they have no thoughts. It cannot be said that they speak to each other but we cannot understand them; for since dogs and some other animals express their passions to us, they would express their thoughts also if they had any.

I know that animals do many things better than we do, but this does not surprise me. It can even be used to prove that they act naturally and mechanically, like a clock which tells the time better than our judgement does. Doubtless when the swallows come in spring, they operate like clocks. The actions of honeybees are of the same nature; so also is the discipline of cranes in flight, and of apes in fighting, if it is true that they keep discipline. Their instinct to bury their dead is no stranger than that of dogs and cats which scratch the earth for the purpose of burying their excrement; they hardly ever actually bury it, which shows that they act only by instinct and without thinking. The most that one can say is that though the animals do not perform any action which shows us that they think, still, since the organs of their bodies are not very different from ours, it may be conjectured that there is attached to these organs some thought such as we experience in ourselves, but of a very much less perfect kind. To this I have nothing to reply except that if they thought as we do, they would have an immortal soul like us. This is unlikely, because there is no reason to believe it of some animals without believing it of all, and many of them such as oysters and sponges are too imperfect for this to be credible. But I am afraid of boring you with this discussion, and my only desire is to show you that I am, etc.

[…]

But there is no preconceived opinion to which we are all more accustomed from our earliest years than the belief that dumb animals think. Our only reason for this belief is the fact that we see that many of the organs of animals are not very different from ours in shape and movements. Since we believe that there is a single principle within us which causes these movements – namely the soul, which both moves the body and thinks – we do not doubt that some such soul is to be found in animals also. I came to realize, however, that there are two different principles causing our movements. The first is purely mechanical and corporeal, and depends solely on the force of the spirits and the structure of our organs, and can be called the corporeal soul. The other, an incorporeal principle, is the mind or that soul which I have defined as a thinking substance. Thereupon I investigated very carefully whether the movements of animals originated from both these principles or from one only. I soon perceived clearly that they could all originate from the corporeal and mechanical principle, and I regarded it as certain and demonstrated that we cannot at all prove the presence of a thinking soul in animals. I am not disturbed by the astuteness and cunning of dogs and foxes, or by all the things which animals do for the sake of food, sex and fear; I claim that I can easily explain all of them as originating from the structure of their bodily parts.

But though I regard it as established that we cannot prove there is any thought in animals, I do not think it can be proved that there is none, since the human mind does not reach into their hearts. But when I investigate what is most probable in this matter, I see no argument for animals having thoughts except this one: since they have eyes, ears, tongues and other sense-organs like ours, it seems likely that they have sensation like us; and since thought is included in our mode of sensation, similar thought seems to be attributable to them. This argument, which is very obvious, has taken possession of the minds of all men from their earliest age. But there are other arguments, stronger and more numerous, but not so obvious to everyone, which strongly urge the opposite. One is that it is more probable that worms, flies, caterpillars and other animals move like machines than that they all have immortal souls.

In the first place, it is certain that in the bodies of animals, as in ours, there are bones, nerves, muscles, animal spirits and other organs so arranged that they can by themselves, without any thought, give rise to all the movements we observe in animals. This is very clear in convulsions, when the mechanism of the body moves despite the mind, and often moves more violently and in a more varied manner than usually happens when it is moved by the will.

Second, since art copies nature, and people can make various automatons which move without thought, it seems reasonable that nature should even produce its own automatons, which are much more splendid than artificial ones – namely the animals. This is especially likely since we know no reason why thought should always accompany the sort of arrangement of organs that we find in animals. It is much more wonderful that a mind should be found in every human body than that one should be lacking in every animal.

But in my opinion the main reason for holding that animals lack thought is the following. Within a single species some of them are more perfect than others, as humans are too. This can be seen in horses and dogs, some of which learn what they are taught much better than others; and all animals easily communicate to us, by voice or bodily movement, their natural impulses of anger, fear, hunger, and so on. Yet in spite of all these facts, it has never been observed that any brute animal has attained the perfection of using real speech, that is to say, of indicating by word or sign something relating to thought alone and not to natural impulse. Such speech is the only certain sign of thought hidden in a body. All human beings use it, however stupid and insane they may be, even though they may have no tongue and organs of voice; but no animals do. Consequently this can be taken as a real specific difference between humans and animals.

For brevity's sake I here omit the other reasons for denying thought to animals. Please note that I am speaking of thought, and not of life or sensation. I do not deny life to animals, since I regard it as consisting simply in the heat of the heart; and I do not even deny sensation, in so far as it depends on a bodily organ. Thus my opinion is not so much cruel to animals as indulgent to human beings – at least to those who are not given to the superstitions of Pythagoras – since it absolves them from the suspicion of crime when they eat or kill animals.

Perhaps I have written at greater length than the sharpness of your intelligence requires; but I wished to show you that very few people have yet sent me objections which were as agreeable as yours. Your kindness and candour have made you a friend of that most respectful admirer of all who seek true wisdom.

---

4   Mechanistic Metaphysics

Isaac Newton

Particles have not only a *Vis inertiæ*, accompanied with such passive Laws of Motion as naturally result from that Force, but also that they are moved by certain active Principles, such as is that of Gravity, and that which causes Fermentation, and the Cohesion of Bodies. These Principles I consider, not as occult Qualities, supposed to result from the specifick Forms of Things, but as general Laws of Nature, by which the Things themselves are form'd; their Truth appearing to us by Phænomena, though their Causes be not yet discover'd. For these are manifest Qualities, and their Causes only are occult. And the *Aristotelians* gave the Name of occult Qualities, not to manifest Qualities, but to such Qualities only as they supposed to lie hid in Bodies, and to be the unknown Causes of manifest Effects: Such as would be the Causes of Gravity, and of magnetick and electrick Attractions, and of Fermentations, if we should suppose that these Forces or Actions arose from Qualities unknown to us, and uncapable of being discovered and made manifest. Such occult Qualities put a stop to the Improvement of natural Philosophy, and therefore of late Years have been rejected. To tell us that every Species of Things is endow'd with an occult specifick

Quality by which it acts and produces manifest Effects, is to tell us nothing: But to derive two or three general Principles of Motion from Phænomena, and afterwards to tell us how the Properties and Actions of all corporeal Things follow from those manifest Principles, would be a very great step in Philosophy, though the Causes of those Principles were not yet discover'd: And therefore I scruple not to propose the Principles of Motion above-mention'd, they being of very general Extent, and leave their Causes to be found out.

Now by the help of these Principles, all material Things seem to have been composed of the hard and solid Particles above-mention'd, variously associated in the first Creation by the Counsel of an intelligent Agent. For it became him who created them to set them in order. And if he did so, it's unphilosophical to seek for any other Origin of the World, or to pretend that it might arise out of a Chaos by the mere Laws of Nature; though being once form'd, it may continue by those Laws for many Ages. For while Comets move in very excentrick Orbs in all manner of Positions, blind Fate could never make all the Planets move one and the same way in Orbs concentrick, some inconsiderable Irregularities excepted, which may have risen from

From *Opticks* (G. Bell & Sons, Ltd., London, 1931), pp. 401–4.

the mutual Actions of Comets and Planets upon one another, and which will be apt to increase, till this System wants a Reformation. Such a wonderful Uniformity in the Planetary System must be allowed the Effect of Choice. And so must the Uniformity in the Bodies of Animals, they having generally a right and a left side shaped alike, and on either side of their Bodies two Legs behind, and either two Arms, or two Legs, or two Wings before upon their Shoulders, and between their Shoulders a Neck running down into a Back-bone, and a Head upon it; and in the Head two Ears, two Eyes, a Nose, a Mouth, and a Tongue, alike situated. Also the first Contrivance of those very artificial Parts of Animals, the Eyes, Ears, Brain, Muscles, Heart, Lungs, Midriff, Glands, Larynx, Hands, Wings, swimming Bladders, natural Spectacles, and other Organs of Sense and Motion; and the Instinct of Brutes and Insects, can be the effect of nothing else than the Wisdom and Skill of a powerful ever-living Agent, who being in all Places, is more able by his Will to move the Bodies within his boundless uniform Sensorium, and thereby to form and reform the Parts of the Universe, than we are by our Will to move the Parts of our own Bodies. And yet we are not to consider the World as the Body of God, or the several Parts thereof, as the Parts of God. He is an uniform Being, void of Organs, Members or Parts, and they are his Creatures subordinate to him, and subservient to his Will; and he is no more the Soul of them, than the Soul of Man is the Soul of the Species of Things carried through the Organs of Sense into the place of its Sensation, where it perceives them by means of its immediate Presence, without the Intervention of any third thing. The Organs of Sense are not for enabling the Soul to perceive the Species of Things in its Sensorium, but only for conveying them thither; and God has no need of such Organs, he being every where present to the Things themselves. And since Space is divisible *in infinitum*, and Matter is not necessarily in all places, it may be also allow'd that God is able to create Particles of Matter of several Sizes and Figures, and in several Proportions to Space, and perhaps of different Densities and Forces, and thereby to vary the Laws of Nature, and make Worlds of several sorts in several Parts of the Universe. At least, I see nothing of Contradiction in all this.

5   The Amoral Status of Nature

John Stuart Mill

Nature, natural, and the group of words derived from them, or allied to them in etymology, have at all times filled a great place in the thoughts and taken a strong hold on the feelings of mankind. That they should have done so is not surprising, when we consider what the words, in their primitive and most obvious signification, represent; but it is unfortunate that a set of terms which play so great a part in moral and metaphysical speculation, should have acquired many meanings different from the primary one, yet sufficiently allied to it to admit of confusion. The words have thus become entangled in so many foreign associations, mostly of a very powerful and tenacious character, that they have come to excite, and to be the symbols of, feelings which their original meaning will by no means justify; and which have made them one of the most copious sources of false taste, false philosophy, false morality, and even bad law.

[...]

As the nature of any given thing is the aggregate of its powers and properties, so Nature in the abstract is the aggregate of the powers and properties of all things. Nature means the sum of all phenomena, together with the causes which produce them; including not only all that happens, but all that is capable of happening; the unused capabilities of causes being as much a part of the idea of Nature, as those which

From *Nature* (New York: AMS Press, Inc., 1970), pp. 1, 5–9, 12–13, 15–18, 19–23.

take effect. Since all phenomena which have been sufficiently examined are found to take place with regularity, each having certain fixed conditions, positive and negative, on the occurrence of which it invariably happens; mankind have been able to ascertain, either by direct observation or by reasoning processes grounded on it, the conditions of the occurrence of many phenomena; and the progress of science mainly consists in ascertaining those conditions. When discovered they can be expressed in general propositions, which are called laws of the particular phenomenon, and also, more generally, Laws of Nature. Thus, the truth that all material objects tend towards one another with a force directly as their masses and inversely as the square of their distance, is a law of Nature. The proposition that air and food are necessary to animal life, if it be as we have good reason to believe, true without exception, is also a law of nature, though the phenomenon of which it is the law is special, and not, like gravitation, universal.

Nature, then, in this its simplest acceptation, is a collective name for all facts, actual and possible: or (to speak more accurately) a name for the mode, partly known to us and partly unknown, in which all things take place. For the word suggests, not so much the multitudinous detail of the phenomena, as the conception which might be formed of their manner of existence as a mental whole, by a mind possessing a complete knowledge of them: to which conception it is the aim of science to raise itself, by successive steps of generalization from experience.

Such, then, is a correct definition of the word Nature. But this definition corresponds only to one of the senses of that ambiguous term. It is evidently inapplicable to some of the modes in which the word is familiarly employed. For example, it entirely conflicts with the common form of speech by which Nature is opposed to Art, and natural to artificial. For in the sense of the word Nature which has just been defined, and which is the true scientific sense, Art is as much Nature as anything else; and everything which is artificial is natural – Art has no independent powers of its own: Art is but the employment of the powers of Nature for an end. Phenomena produced by human agency, no less than those which as far as we are concerned are spontaneous, depend on the properties of the elementary forces, or of the elementary substances and their compounds. The united powers of the whole human race could not create a new property of matter in general, or of any one of its species. We can only take advantage for our purposes of the properties which we find. A ship floats by the same laws of specific gravity and equilibrium, as a tree uprooted by the wind and blown into the water. The corn which men raise for food, grows and produces its grain by the same laws of vegetation by which the wild rose and the mountain strawberry bring forth their flowers and fruit. A house stands and holds together by the natural properties, the weight and cohesion of the materials which compose it: a steam engine works by the natural expansive force of steam, exerting a pressure upon one part of a system of arrangements, which pressure, by the mechanical properties of the lever, is transferred from that to another part where it raises the weight or removes the obstacle brought into connexion with it. In these and all other artificial operations the office of man is, as has often been remarked, a very limited one; it consists in moving things into certain places. We move objects, and by doing this, bring some things into contact which were separate, or separate others which were in contact: and by this simple change of place, natural forces previously dormant are called into action, and produce the desired effect. Even the volition which designs, the intelligence which contrives, and the muscular force which executes these movements, are themselves powers of Nature.

✓ It thus appears that we must recognize at least two principal meanings in the word Nature. In one sense, it means all the powers existing in either the outer or the inner world and everything which takes place by means of those powers. In another sense, it means, not everything which happens, but only what takes place without the agency, or without the voluntary and intentional agency, of man. This distinction is far from exhausting the ambiguities of the word; but it is the key to most of those on which important consequences depend.

[…]

Is it necessary to recognize in these forms of speech, another distinct meaning of the word Nature? Or can they be connected, by any rational bond of union, with either of the two meanings already treated of? At first it may seem that we have no option but to admit another ambiguity in the term. All inquiries are either into what is, or into what ought to be: science and history belonging to the first division, art, morals and politics to the second. But the two senses of the word Nature first pointed out, agree in referring only to what is. In the first meaning, Nature is a collective name for everything which is. In the second, it is a name for everything which is of itself, without voluntary human intervention. But the employment of the word Nature as a term of ethics seems to disclose a third meaning, in which Nature does not stand for what is, but for what ought to be; or for the rule or standard of what ought to be. A little consideration, however, will show that this is not a case of ambiguity; there is not here a third sense of the word. Those who set up Nature as a standard of action do not intend a merely verbal proposition; they do not mean that the standard, whatever it be, should be *called* Nature; they think they are giving some information as to what the standard of action really is. Those who say that we ought to act according to Nature do not mean the mere identical proposition that we ought to do what we ought to do. They think that the word Nature affords some external criterion of what we should do; and if they lay down as a rule for what ought to be, a word which in its proper signification denotes what is, they do so because they have a notion, either clearly or confusedly, that what is, constitutes the rule and standard of what ought to be.

[…]

The conception which the ethical use of the word Nature implies, of a close relation if not absolute identity between what is and what ought to be, certainly derives part of its hold on the mind from the custom of designating what is, by the expression "laws of nature," while the same word Law is also used, and even more familiarly and emphatically, to express what ought to be.

When it is asserted, or implied, that Nature, or the laws of Nature, should be conformed to, is the Nature which is meant, Nature in the first sense of the term, meaning all which is – the powers and properties of all things? But in this signification, there is no need of a recommendation to act according to nature, since it is what nobody can possibly help doing, and equally whether he acts well or ill. There is no mode of acting which is not conformable to Nature in this sense of the term, and all modes of acting are so in exactly the same degree. Every action is the exertion of some natural power, and its effects of all sorts are so many phenomena of nature, produced by the powers and properties of some of the objects of nature, in exact obedience to some law or laws of nature. When I voluntarily use my organs to take in food, the act, and its consequences, take place according to laws of nature: if instead of food I swallow poison, the case is exactly the same.

To bid people conform to the laws of nature when they have no power but what the laws of nature give them – when it is a physical impossibility for them to do the smallest thing otherwise than through some law of nature, is an absurdity. The thing they need to be told is, what particular law of nature they should make use of in a particular case. When, for example, a person is crossing a river by a narrow bridge to which there is no parapet, he will do well to regulate his proceedings by the laws of equilibrium in moving bodies, instead of conforming only to the law of gravitation, and falling into the river.

Yet, idle as it is to exhort people to do what they cannot avoid doing, and absurd as it is to prescribe as a rule of right conduct what agrees exactly as well with wrong; nevertheless a rational rule of conduct *may* be constructed out of the relation which it ought to bear to the laws of nature in this widest acceptation of the term. Man necessarily obeys the laws of nature, or in other words the properties of things, but he does not necessarily *guide* himself by them. Though all conduct is in conformity to laws of nature, all conduct is not grounded on knowledge of them, and intelligently directed to the attainment of purposes by means of them. Though we cannot emancipate ourselves from the laws of nature as a whole, we can escape from any particular law of nature, if we are able to withdraw ourselves from the circumstances in which it acts. Though we can do nothing except through laws of nature, we can use one law to counteract another.

According to Bacon's maxim, we can obey nature in such a manner as to command it. Every alteration of circumstances alters more or less the laws of nature under which we act; and by every choice which we make either of ends or of means, we place ourselves to a greater or less extent under one set of laws of nature instead of another. If, therefore, the useless precept to follow nature were changed into a precept to study nature; to know and take heed of the properties of the things we have to deal with, so far as these properties are capable of forwarding or obstructing any given purpose; we should have arrived at the first principle of all intelligent action, or rather at the definition of intelligent action itself. And a confused notion of this true principle, is, I doubt not, in the minds of many of those who set up the unmeaning doctrine which superficially resembles it. They perceive that the essential difference between wise and foolish conduct consists in attending, or not attending, to the particular laws of nature on which some important result depends. And they think, that a person who attends to a law of nature in order to shape his conduct by it, may be said to obey it, while a person who practically disregards it, and acts as if no such law existed, may be said to disobey it: the circumstance being overlooked, that what is thus called disobedience to a law of nature is obedience to some other or perhaps to the very law itself. For example, a person who goes into a powder magazine either not knowing, or carelessly omitting to think of, the explosive force of gunpowder, is likely to do some act which will cause him to be blown to atoms in obedience to the very law which he has disregarded.

[…]

Right action, must mean something more and other than merely intelligent action: yet no precept beyond this last, can be connected with the word Nature in the wider and more philosophical of its acceptations. We must try it therefore in the other sense, that in which Nature stands distinguished from Art, and denotes, not the whole course of the phenomena which come under our observation, but only their spontaneous course.

Let us then consider whether we can attach any meaning to the supposed practical maxim of following Nature, in this second sense of the word, in which Nature stands for that which takes place without human intervention. In Nature as thus understood, is the spontaneous course of things when left to themselves, the rule to be followed in endeavouring to adapt things to our use? But it is evident at once that the maxim, taken in this sense, is not merely, as it is in the other sense, superfluous and unmeaning, but palpably absurd and self-contradictory. For while human action cannot help conforming to Nature in the one meaning of the term, the very aim and object of action is to alter and improve Nature in the other meaning. If the natural course of things were perfectly right and satisfactory, to act at all would be a gratuitous meddling, which as it could not make things better, must make them worse. Or if action at all could be justified, it would only be when in direct obedience to instincts, since these might perhaps be accounted part of the spontaneous order of Nature; but to do anything with forethought and purpose, would be a violation of that perfect order. If the artificial is not better than the natural, to what end are all the arts of life? To dig, to plough, to build, to wear clothes, are direct infringements of the injunction to follow nature.

Accordingly it would be said by every one, even of those most under the influence of the feelings which prompt the injunction, that to apply it to such cases as those just spoken of, would be to push it too far. Everybody professes to approve and admire many great triumphs of Art over Nature: the junction by bridges of shores which Nature had made separate, the draining of Nature's marshes, the excavation of her wells, the dragging to light of what she has buried at immense depths in the earth; the turning away of her thunderbolts by lightning rods, of her inundations by embankments, of her ocean by breakwaters. But to commend these and similar feats, is to acknowledge that the ways of Nature are to be conquered, not obeyed: that her powers are often towards man in the position of enemies, from whom he must wrest, by force and ingenuity, what little he can for his own use, and deserves to be applauded when that little is rather more than might be expected from his physical weakness in comparison to those gigantic powers. All praise of Civilization, or Art, or Contrivance, is so much dispraise of Nature; an admission of imperfection, which it is man's business, and merit, to be always endeavouring to correct or mitigate.

The consciousness that whatever man does to improve his condition is in so much a censure and a thwarting of the spontaneous order of Nature, has in all ages caused new and unprecedented attempts at improvement to be generally at first under a shade of religious suspicion; as being in any case uncomplimentary, and very probably offensive to the powerful beings (or, when polytheism gave place to monotheism, to the all-powerful Being) supposed to govern the various phenomena of the universe, and of whose will the course of nature was conceived to be the expression. Any attempt to mould natural phenomena to the convenience of mankind might easily appear an interference with the government of those superior beings: and though life could not have been maintained, much less made pleasant, without perpetual interferences of the kind, each new one was doubtless made with fear and trembling, until experience had shown that it could be ventured on without drawing down the vengeance of the Gods. The sagacity of priests showed them a way to reconcile the impunity of particular infringements with the maintenance of the general dread of encroaching on the divine administration. This was effected by representing each of the principal human inventions as the gift and favour of some God. The old religions also afforded many resources for consulting the Gods, and obtaining their express permission for what would otherwise have appeared a breach of their prerogative. When oracles had ceased, any religion which recognized a revelation afforded expedients for the same purpose. The Catholic religion had the resource of an infallible Church, authorized to declare what exertions of human spontaneity were permitted or forbidden; and in default of this, the case was always open to argument from the Bible whether any particular practice had expressly or by implication been sanctioned. The notion remained that this liberty to control Nature was conceded to man only by special indulgence, and as far as required by his necessities; and there was always a tendency, though a diminishing one, to regard any attempt to exercise power over nature, beyond a certain degree, and a certain admitted range, as an impious effort to usurp divine power, and dare more than was permitted to man. The lines of Horace in which the familiar

arts of shipbuilding and navigation are reprobated as *vetitum nefas*, indicate even in that sceptical age a still unexhausted vein of the old sentiment. The intensity of the corresponding feeling in the middle ages is not a precise parallel, on account of the superstition about dealing with evil spirits with which it was complicated: but the imputation of prying into the secrets of the Almighty long remained a powerful weapon of attack against unpopular inquirers into nature; and the charge of presumptuously attempting to defeat the designs of Providence, still retains enough of its original force to be thrown in as a make-weight along with other objections when there is a desire to find fault with any new exertion of human forethought and contrivance. No one, indeed, asserts it to be the intention of the Creator that the spontaneous order of the creation should not be altered, or even that it should not be altered in any new way.

6 Nature as Economic Resource

John Locke

25. Whether we consider natural reason, which tells us that men, being once born, have a right to their preservation, and consequently to meat and drink and such other things as Nature affords for their subsistence, or "revelation," which gives us an account of those grants God made of the world to Adam, and to Noah and his sons, it is very clear that God, as King David says (Psalm cxv. 16), "has given the earth to the children of men," given it to mankind in common. But, this being supposed, it seems to some a very great difficulty how any one should ever come to have a property in anything, I will not content myself to answer, that, if it be difficult to make out "property" upon a supposition that God gave the world to Adam and his posterity in common, it is impossible that any man but one universal monarch should have any "property" upon a supposition that God gave the world to Adam and his

heirs in succession, exclusive of all the rest of his posterity; but I shall endeavour to show how men might come to have a property in several parts of that which God gave to mankind in common, and that without any express compact of all the commoners.

26. God, who hath given the world to men in common, hath also given them reason to make use of it to the best advantage of life and convenience. The earth and all that is therein is given to men for the support and comfort of their being. And though all the fruits it naturally produces, and beasts it feeds, belong to mankind in common, as they are produced by the spontaneous hand of Nature, and nobody has originally a private dominion exclusive of the rest of mankind in any of them, as they are thus in their natural state, yet being given for the use of men, there must of necessity be a means to appropriate them some way or other before they can be of any

From *Two Treatises of Civil Government*: Chapter V: "Of Property" (London: J. M. Dent & Sons Ltd., 1970), pp. 129–36, 137–9, 141.

use, or at all beneficial, to any particular men. The fruit or venison which nourishes the wild Indian, who knows no enclosure, and is still a tenant in common, must be his, and so his – *i.e.*, a part of him, that another can no longer have any right to it before it can do him any good for the support of his life.

27. Though the earth and all inferior creatures be common to all men, yet every man has a "property" in his own "person." This nobody has any right to but himself. The "labour" of his body and the "work" of his hands, we may say, are properly his. Whatsoever, then, he removes out of the state that Nature hath provided and left it in, he hath mixed his labour with it, and joined to it something that is his own, and thereby makes it his property. It being by him removed from the common state Nature placed it in, it hath by this labour something annexed to it that excludes the common right of other men. For this "labour" being the unquestionable property of the labourer, no man but he can have a right to what that is once joined to, at least where there is enough, and as good left in common for others.

28. He that is nourished by the acorns he picked up under an oak, or the apples he gathered from the trees in the wood, has certainly appropriated them to himself. Nobody can deny but the nourishment is his. I ask, then, when did they begin to be his? when he digested? or when he ate? or when he boiled? or when he brought them home? or when he picked them up? And it is plain, if the first gathering made them not his, nothing else could. That labour put a distinction between them and common. That added something to them more than Nature, the common mother of all, had done, and so they became his private right. And will any one say he had no right to those acorns or apples he thus appropriated because he had not the consent of all mankind to make them his? Was it a robbery thus to assume to himself what belonged to all in common? If such a consent as that was necessary, man had starved, notwithstanding the plenty God had given him. We see in commons, which remain so by compact, that it is the taking any part of what is common, and removing it out of the state Nature leaves it in, which begins the property, without which the common is of no use. And the taking of this or that part does not depend on the express consent of all the commoners. Thus, the grass my horse has bit, the turfs my servant has cut, and the ore I have digged in any place, where I have a right to them in common with others, become my property without the assignation or consent of any-

body. The labour that was mine, removing them out of that common state they were in, hath fixed my property in them.

29. By making an explicit consent of every commoner necessary to any one's appropriating to himself any part of what is given in common. Children or servants could not cut the meat which their father or master had provided for them in common without assigning to every one his peculiar part. Though the water running in the fountain be every one's, yet who can doubt but that in the pitcher is his only who drew it out? His labour hath taken it out of the hands of Nature where it was common, and belonged equally to all her children, and hath thereby appropriated it to himself.

30. Thus this law of reason makes the deer that Indian's who hath killed it; it is allowed to be his goods who hath bestowed his labour upon it, though, before, it was the common right of every one. And amongst those who are counted the civilised part of mankind, who have made and multiplied positive laws to determine property, this original law of Nature for the beginning of property, in what was before common, still takes place, and by virtue thereof, what fish any one catches in the ocean, that great and still remaining common of mankind; or what ambergris any one takes up here is by the labour that removes it out of that common state Nature left it in, made his property who takes that pains about it. And even amongst us, the hare that any one is hunting is thought his who pursues her during the chase. For being a beast that is still looked upon as common, and no man's private possession, whoever has employed so much labour about any of that kind as to find and pursue her has thereby removed her from the state of Nature wherein she was common, and hath begun a property.

31. It will, perhaps, be objected to this, that if gathering the acorns or other fruits of the earth, etc., makes a right to them, then any one may engross as much as he will. To which I answer, Not so. The same law of Nature that does by this means give us property, does also bound that property too. "God has given us all things richly." Is the voice of reason confirmed by inspiration? But how far has He given it us – "to enjoy"? As much as any one can make use of to any advantage of life before it spoils, so much he may by his labour fix a property in. Whatever is beyond this is more than his share, and belongs to others. Nothing was made by God for man to spoil or destroy. And thus considering the plenty of

natural provisions there was a long time in the world, and the few spenders, and to how small a part of that provision the industry of one man could extend itself and engross it to the prejudice of others, especially keeping within the bounds set by reason of what might serve for his use, there could be then little room for quarrels or contentions about property so established.

32. ⌐But the chief matter of property being now not the fruits of the earth and the beasts that subsist on it, but the earth itself, as that which takes in and carries with it all the rest, I think it is plain that property in that too is acquired as the former. As much land as a man tills, plants, improves, cultivates, and can use the product of, so much is his property.⌐ He by his labour does, as it were, enclose it from the common. Nor will it invalidate his right to say everybody else has an equal title to it, and therefore he cannot appropriate, he cannot enclose, without the consent of all his fellow-commoners, all mankind. God, when He gave the world in common to all mankind, commanded man also to labour, and the penury of his condition required it of him.⌐God and his reason commanded him to subdue the earth – i.e., improve it for the benefit of life and therein lay out something upon it that was his own, his labour. He that, in obedience to this command of God, subdued, tilled, and sowed any part of it, thereby annexed to it something that was his property, which another had no title to, nor could without injury take from him.⌐

33. Nor was this appropriation of any parcel of land, by improving it, any prejudice to any other man, since there was still enough and as good left, and more than the yet unprovided could use. So that, in effect, there was never the less left for others because of his enclosure for himself. For he that leaves as much as another can make use of does as good as take nothing at all. Nobody could think himself injured by the drinking of another man, though he took a good draught, who had a whole river of the same water left him to quench his thirst. And the case of land and water, where there is enough of both, is perfectly the same.

34. God gave the world to men in common, but since He gave it them for their benefit and the greatest conveniencies of life they were capable to draw from it, it cannot be supposed He meant it should always remain common and uncultivated. He gave it to the use of the industrious and rational (and labour was to be his title to it); not to the fancy or covetousness of the quarrelsome and contentious. He that had as good left for his improvement as was already taken up needed not complain, ought not to meddle with what was already improved by another's labour; if he did it is plain he desired the benefit of another's pains, which he had no right to, and not the ground which God had given him, in common with others, to labour on, and whereof there was as good left as that already possessed, and more than he knew what to do with, or his industry could reach to.

35. ⌐It is true, in land that is common in England or any other country, where there are plenty of people under government who have money and commerce, no one can enclose or appropriate any part without the consent of all his fellow-commoners; because this is left common by compact – i.e., by the law of the land, which is not to be violated. ⌐And, though it be common in respect of some men, it is not so to all mankind, but is the joint propriety of this country, or this parish. Besides, the remainder, after such enclosure, would not be as good to the rest of the commoners as the whole was, when they could all make use of the whole; whereas in the beginning and first peopling of the great common of the world it was quite otherwise. The law man was under was rather for appropriating. ⌐God commanded, and his wants forced him to labour. That was his property, which could not be taken from him wherever he had fixed it. And hence subduing or cultivating the earth and having dominion, we see, are joined together. The one gave title to the other. So that God, by commanding to subdue, gave authority so far to appropriate. And the condition of human life, which requires labour and materials to work on, necessarily introduces private possessions.⌐

36. The measure of property Nature well set, by the extent of men's labour and the conveniency of life. No man's labour could subdue or appropriate all, nor could his enjoyment consume more than a small part; so that it was impossible for any man, this way, to entrench upon the right of another or acquire to himself a property to the prejudice of his neighbour, who would still have room for as good and as large a possession (after the other had taken out his) as before it was appropriated. Which measure did confine every man's possession to a very moderate proportion, and such as he might appropriate to himself without injury to anybody in the first ages of the world, when men were more in danger to be lost, by wandering from their company, in the then vast wilderness of the earth then to be straitened for

want of room to plant in. And the same measure may be allowed still, without prejudice to anybody, full as the world seems. For, supposing a man or family, in the state they were at first, peopling of the world by the children of Adam or Noah, let him plant in some inland vacant places of America. We shall find that the possessions he could make himself, upon the measures we have given, would not be very large, nor, even to this day, prejudice the rest of mankind or give them reason to complain or think themselves injured by this man's encroachment, though the race of men have now spread themselves to all the corners of the world, and do infinitely exceed the small number was at the beginning. Nay, the extent of ground is of so little value without labour that I have heard it affirmed that in Spain itself a man may be permitted to plough, sow, and reap, without being disturbed, upon land he has no other title to, but only his making use of it. But, on the contrary, the inhabitants think themselves beholden to him who, by his industry on neglected, and consequently waste land, has increased the stock of corn, which they wanted. But be this as it will, which I lay no stress on, this I dare boldly affirm, that the same rule of propriety – viz., that every man should have as much as he could make use of, would hold still in the world, without straitening anybody, since there is land enough in the world to suffice double the inhabitants, had not the invention of money, and the tacit agreement of men to put a value on it, introduced (by consent) larger possession and a right to them; which, how it has done, I shall by and by show more at large.

37.   This is certain, that in the beginning, before the desire of having more than men needed had altered the intrinsic value of things, which depends only on their usefulness to the life of man, or had agreed that a little piece of yellow metal, which would keep without wasting or decay, should be worth a great piece of flesh or a whole heap of corn, though men had a right to appropriate by their labour, each one to himself, as much of the things of Nature as he could use, yet this could not be much, nor to the prejudice of others, where the same plenty was still left, to those who would use the same industry.

Before the appropriation of land, he who gathered as much of the wild fruit, killed, caught, or tamed as many of the beasts as he could – he that so employed his pains about any of the spontaneous products of Nature as any way to alter them from the state Nature put them in, by placing any of his labour on them, did thereby acquire a propriety in them; but if they perished in his possession without their due use – if the fruits rotted or the venison putrefied before he could spend it, he offended against the common law of Nature, and was liable to be punished: he invaded his neighbour's share, for he had no right farther than his use called for any of them, and they might serve to afford him conveniencies of life.

38.   The same measures governed the possession of land, too. Whatsoever he tilled and reaped, laid up and made use of before it spoiled, that was his peculiar right; whatsoever he enclosed, and could feed and make use of, the cattle and product was also his. But if either the grass of his enclosure rotted on the ground, or the fruit of his planting perished without gathering and laying up, this part of the earth, notwithstanding his enclosure, was still to be looked on as waste, and might be the possession of any other. Thus, at the beginning, Cain might take as much ground as he could till and make it his own land, and yet leave enough to Abel's sheep to feed on: a few acres would serve for both their possessions. But as families increased and industry enlarged their stocks, their possessions enlarged with the need of them; but yet it was commonly without any fixed property in the ground they made use of till they incorporated, settled themselves together, and built cities, and then, by consent, they came in time to set out the bounds of their distinct territories and agree on limits between them and their neighbours, and by laws within themselves settled the properties of those of the same society. For we see that in that part of the world which was first inhabited, and therefore like to be best peopled, even as low down as Abraham's time, they wandered with their flocks and their herds, which was their substance, freely up and down – and this Abraham did in a country where he was a stranger; whence it is plain that, at least, a great part of the land lay in common, that the inhabitants valued it not, nor claimed property in any more than they made use of; but when there was not room enough in the same place for their herds to feed together, they, by consent, as Abraham and Lot did (Gen. xiii. 5), separated and enlarged their pasture where it best liked them. And for the same reason, Esau went from his father and his brother, and planted in Mount Seir (Gen. xxxvi. 6).

[…]

43.   An acre of land that bears here twenty bushels of wheat, and another in America, which, with the same husbandry, would do the like, are, without

doubt, of the same natural, intrinsic value. But yet the benefit mankind receives from one in a year is worth five pounds, and the other possibly not worth a penny; if all the profit an Indian received from it were to be valued and sold here, at least I may truly say, not one thousandth. It is labour, then, which puts the greatest part of value upon land, without which it would scarcely be worth anything; it is to that we owe the greatest part of all its useful products; for all that the straw, bran, bread, of that acre of wheat, is more worth than the product of an acre of as good land which lies waste is all the effect of labour. For it is not barely the ploughman's pains, the reaper's and thresher's toil, and the baker's sweat, is to be counted into the bread we eat; the labour of those who broke the oxen, who digged and wrought the iron and stones, who felled and framed the timber employed about the plough, mill, oven, or any other utensils, which are a vast number, requisite to this corn, from its sowing to its being made bread, must all be charged on the account of labour, and received as an effect of that; Nature and the earth furnished only the almost worthless materials as in themselves. It would be a strange catalogue of things that industry provided and made use of about every loaf of bread before it came to our use if we could trace them; iron, wood, leather, bark, timber, stone, bricks, coals, lime, cloth, dyeing-drugs, pitch, tar, masts, ropes, and all the materials made use of in the ship that brought any of the commodities made use of by any of the workmen, to any part of the work, all which it would be almost impossible, at least too long, to reckon up.

44.   From all which it is evident, that though the things of Nature are given in common, man (by being master of himself, and proprietor of his own person, and the actions or labour of it) had still in himself the great foundation of property; and that which made up the great part of what he applied to the support or comfort of his being, when invention and arts had improved the conveniences of life, was perfectly his own, and did not belong in common to others.

45.   Thus labour, in the beginning, gave a right of property, wherever any one was pleased to employ it, upon what was common, which remained a long while, the far greater part, and is yet more than mankind makes use of. Men at first, for the most part, contented themselves with what unassisted Nature offered to their necessities; and though afterwards, in some parts of the world, where the increase of people and stock, with the use of money, had made land scarce, and so of some value, the several communities settled the bounds of their distinct territories, and, by laws, within themselves, regulated the properties of the private men of their society, and so, by compact and agreement, settled the property which labour and industry began. And the leagues that have been made between several states and kingdoms, either expressly or tacitly disowning all claim and right to the land in the other's possession, have, by common consent, given up their pretences to their natural common right, which originally they had to those countries; and so have, by positive agreement, settled a property amongst themselves, in distinct parts of the world; yet there are still great tracts of ground to be found, which the inhabitants thereof, not having joined with the rest of mankind in the consent of the use of their common money, lie waste, and are more than the people who dwell on it, do, or can make use of, and so still lie in common; though this can scarce happen amongst that part of mankind that have consented to the use of money.

[...]

51.   And thus, I think, it is very easy to conceive, without any difficulty, how labour could at first begin a title of property in the common things of Nature, and how the spending it upon our uses bounded it; so that there could then be no reason of quarrelling about title, nor any doubt about the largeness of possession it gave. Right and conveniency went together. For as a man had a right to all he could employ his labour upon, so he had no temptation to labour for more than he could make use of. This left no room for controversy about the title, nor for encroachment on the right of others. What portion a man carved to himself was easily seen; and it was useless, as well as dishonest, to carve himself too much, or take more than he needed.

7   Indirect Duties to Nonhumans

Immanuel Kant

Duties Towards Animals and Spirits

So far as animals are concerned, we have no direct duties. Animals are not self-conscious and are there merely as a means to an end. That end is man. We can ask, 'Why do animals exist?' But to ask, 'Why does man exist?' is a meaningless question. Our duties towards animals are merely indirect duties towards humanity. Animal nature has analogies to human nature, and by doing our duties to animals in respect of manifestations which correspond to manifestations of human nature, we indirectly do our duty towards humanity. Thus, if a dog has served his master long and faithfully, his service, on the analogy of human service, deserves reward, and when the dog has grown too old to serve, his master ought to keep him until he dies. Such action helps to support us in our duties towards human beings, where they are bounden duties. If then any acts of animals are analogous to human acts and spring from the same principles, we have duties towards the animals because thus we cultivate the corresponding duties towards human beings. If a man shoots his dog because the animal is no longer capable of service, he does not fail in his duty to the dog, for the dog cannot judge, but his act is inhuman and damages in himself that humanity which it is his duty to show towards mankind. If he is not to stifle his human feelings, he must practise kindness towards animals, for he who is cruel to animals becomes hard also in his dealings with men. We can judge the heart of a man by his treatment of animals. Hogarth[1] depicts this in his engravings. He shows how cruelty grows and develops. He shows the child's cruelty to animals, pinching the tail of a dog or a cat; he then depicts the grown man in his cart running over a child; and lastly, the culmination of cruelty in murder. He thus brings home to us in a terrible fashion the rewards of cruelty, and this should be an impressive lesson to children. The more we come in contact with animals and observe their behaviour, the more we love them, for we see how great is their care for their young. It is then difficult for us to be cruel in thought even to a wolf. Leibnitz used a tiny worm for purposes of observation, and then carefully replaced it with its leaf on the tree so that it should not come to harm through any act of his. He would have been sorry – a natural feeling for a humane man – to destroy such a creature for no reason. Tender feelings towards dumb animals develop humane feelings towards mankind. In England butchers and doctors do not sit on a jury because they are accustomed to the sight of death and hardened. Vivisectionists, who use living animals for their experiments, certainly act cruelly, although their aim is praiseworthy, and they can justify their cruelty, since animals must be regarded as man's instruments; but any such cruelty for sport cannot be justified. A master who turns out his ass or his dog because the animal can no longer earn its keep manifests a small mind. The Greeks' ideas in this respect were high-minded, as can be seen from the fable of the ass and the bell of ingratitude.[2] Our duties towards animals, then, are indirect duties towards mankind.

Our duties towards immaterial beings are purely negative. Any course of conduct which involves dealings with spirits is wrong. Conduct of this kind makes men visionaries and fanatics, renders them superstitious, and is not in keeping with the dignity of mankind; for human dignity cannot subsist without a healthy use of reason, which is impossible for those who have commerce with spirits. Spirits may exist or they may not; all that is said of them may be true; but we know them not and can have no intercourse with them. This applies to good and to evil spirits alike. Our Ideas of good and evil are coordinate, and as we refer all evil to hell so we refer all good to heaven. If we personify the perfection of evil, we have the Idea of the devil. If we believe that evil spirits can have an influence upon us, can appear

From Louis Infield, trans., *Lectures on Ethics* (The Century Co., London, 1930), pp. 239–41. © 1930. Reprinted with permission from Taylor and Francis Books UK.

and haunt us at night, we become a prey to phantoms and incapable of using our powers in a reasonable way. Our duties towards such beings must, therefore, be negative.

Duties Towards Inanimate Objects

[Consider also] duties towards inanimate objects. These duties are also indirectly duties towards mankind. Destructiveness is immoral; we ought not to destroy things which can still be put to some use. No man ought to mar the beauty of nature; for what he has no use for may still be of use to some one else. He need, of course, pay no heed to the thing itself, but he ought to consider his neighbour. Thus we see that all duties towards animals, towards immaterial beings and towards inanimate objects are aimed indirectly at our duties towards mankind.

Notes

1 Hogarth's four engravings, 'The Stages of Cruelty', 1751.
2 Philipp Camerarius, *Operae horarum subcisivarum centuria prima*, 1644, cap. XXI.

---

8   In Defense of Anthropocentrism

Wilfred Beckerman and Joanna Pasek

The Concept of 'Intrinsic Values'

The attempt to attribute 'intrinsic' value to the environment has probably been one of the central and the most recalcitrant problems of environmental ethics.[1] But one prominent contributor to the debate believes that it would be better to abandon the attempt altogether (Regan 1992). He may well be right, since the term 'intrinsic' value means different things to different people. So we shall simply state here how we shall interpret it before going on to consider its applicability to the environment in general or nature in particular. We use the term 'intrinsic' value [...] to indicate merely one part of a twofold classification of values as being either 'intrinsic' or 'instrumental'.[2] By that we mean that objects of value are, respectively, either valued for their own sake or valued for the sake of the contribution that they make to some other objective.

Some objects may have both kinds of value. For example, beautiful music may be valued for its own sake and may also possess the instrumental therapeutic value of soothing the savage breast. Flowers may have intrinsic aesthetic value and also have the instrumental value of providing important sources of food for insects or medicinal beverages for herbalists. Similarly, a primeval forest would be *instrumentally* valuable insofar as it contains scientifically valuable information that can be potentially useful for, say, medicinal purposes. But some people would claim that it is also valuable in itself over and above its usefulness: that it is *intrinsically* valuable.

There are two main routes by which one can arrive at the conclusion that certain values are intrinsic. One is the 'objectivist' approach. On this approach, a valued object is valuable objectively, *independently of any human valuations*. It would be argued that some objects, such as nature, are valuable on account of some objective characteristics that they possess, such as beauty, integrity, or harmony, and not on account of the value that outside valuers may attach to them.

In 1903 the philosopher G. E. Moore, who is usually regarded as a strong advocate of this objectivist view, invited us to make a famous thought-experiment concerning beauty. He asked us to imagine two worlds,

From *Justice, Posterity, and the Environment* (Oxford: Oxford University Press, 2001), pp. 129–35. © 2001 by Wilfred Beckerman and Joanna Pasek. Reprinted with permission from Oxford University Press.

one in which all imaginable natural beauty exists: 'put into it whatever on this earth you most admire – mountains, rivers, the sea, trees, and sunsets, stars and the moon … And then imagine the ugliest world you can possibly conceive We then have to assume that neither of these worlds can ever possibly be seen by any human being.' Moore goes on to ask 'is it irrational to hold that it is better that the beautiful world should exist, than the one which is ugly' (Moore 1978: 83–4). The subjectivist would say that such a comparison would, indeed, be irrational. Moore, however, took the opposite view. If the choice was between the sheer existence of beauty and the sheer existence of ugliness, then, according to him, 'beauty must *in itself*, be regarded as a greater good than ugliness' and we must prefer its existence to that of ugliness (Moore 1978: 84; emphasis added).[3]

But Brian Barry (1999: 114) is surely right in saying that 'I have to say that the whole question [that is, Moore's question] strikes me as ridiculous. In what possible sense could the universe be a better or a worse place on one supposition rather than the other? It seems to me an abuse of our language to assume that the word "good" still has application when applied to such a context'.

In other words, it is difficult to imagine what beauty would be if it were not beauty as it presents itself to some consciousness. Thus Moore's experiment is fundamentally flawed. Imagining the world without humans is really imagining the world without their sense of beauty and other values. If, in Moore's experiments, we were allowed to be 'spectators', so to speak, but not 'actors' on the stage of the world, then of course it is plausible that as spectators we would choose a beautiful world rather than an ugly one. But if we are not allowed to be spectators either, then 'beauty' and 'ugliness' are terms that seem to be devoid of any significance.

The alternative route, which is the 'subjective' route, and which is the one that we followed in our discussion of intergenerational egalitarianism, is that values cannot exist without a valuer. In the example of Moore's two worlds, it does not make sense to talk about a beautiful world unless there is some valuer who perceives it as beautiful. But the subjectivist view of value by no means implies that the mere fact that something is valued by somebody means that it must be valuable to everybody.[4]

Furthermore, this so-called '*subjectivist*' approach to valuation, that is, requiring the existence of a valuer, does not prejudge the issue of which sort of value the valuer would ascribe to the valued object. One can subjectively attribute either instrumental or intrinsic value to the object in question. For example, […] some people may believe that greater equality between people is intrinsically valuable, and others may believe that it is only instrumentally valuable, for example, as a means of increasing social harmony. But both ways of valuing equality will be values held by people and neither need rest on a claim that the values in question are 'objective' values that exist independently of valuers. Thus, the subjectivist approach to valuation still allows the valuer to attribute *intrinsic* value to something.

How far values can be objective or subjective has been the subject of extensive speculation among philosophers for centuries. One classic discussion of this issue, by the late J. L. Mackie, began with the blunt statement: 'There are no objective values'. But, as he went on to explain, to some people this proposition appears outrageous while to others it appears as a trivial truth (Mackie 1988). Thus the problem of the objectivity or otherwise of values in general is a vast and complex problem to which we would not presume to attempt to contribute. Here we are concerned chiefly with the question of whether the environment or some parts of it can be the bearer of intrinsic values, and, if so, in what sense. This is a question for subjectivists as much as for those who subscribe to objective values. For where the value comes from and what possesses value are two different questions. As John O'Neill has pointed out, some of the confusion in the debate about intrinsic values arises out of a failure to distinguish between the *source* of value, for example human valuers, and the *object* of value – O'Neill's terminology, or *locus* of value in other people's terminology (J. O'Neill 1993: 11). For instance a common mistake is to assume that if we follow the subjectivist path, we are committed to the view that is despised by preservationists, namely, that nature can have only instrumental value to us. But, in fact, nothing prevents a subjectivist from attributing intrinsic value to nature or the preservation of the environment.

However, many environmentalists would not be satisfied with, let alone welcome, a subjectivist defence of the intrinsic value of nature. They believe it is unduly anthropocentric, and hence sells a crucial pass in the struggle to justify the intrinsic value of nature. It makes the status of nature too dependent on changes in human tastes and fashions or on differences in cultural norms. As is well-known, one of the dangers in the subjectivist approach to valuation is that it can slip into moral relativism, that is, that what is morally 'good' may depend too much on the particular society or epoch with which we are concerned.

The same could apply to the valuation of nature. If all that matters is human appreciation of nature then one day our cultural ideals may change. The human race could become so culturally depraved that whereas it had previously regarded magnificent trees or forests as intrinsically valuable it now denied them intrinsic value and regarded plastic trees as more beautiful than real ones. All real trees would then be cut down except those required to satisfy minority tastes for quaint, old-fashioned wooden furniture or other useful purposes. Many environmentalists also share the view that 'In our enlightened times, when most forms of chauvinism have been abandoned, at least in theory, by those who consider themselves progressive, Western ethics still appears to retain a fundamental form of chauvinism, namely human chauvinism' (Routley and Routley 1979: 36).

The Objectivist Defence of Nature's Intrinsic Value

A widely-used argument that brings out the character of the objectivist case for attaching objective intrinsic value to nature is the 'last man argument', which closely resembles Moore's famous thought-experiment discussed above.[5] This takes a form such as 'Suppose you were the last man on earth and knew that you were about to die as well, but you had it in your power to press a button that would destroy all the beautiful things that would otherwise be left behind – the mountains, the forests, the beautiful scenery, the animals, and so on. Would you do so?' Those who claim that the items in question have *objective* intrinsic value would argue that it would be immoral to do so even in the absence of human beings. It is not a question of whether such an act of wilful and pointless vandalism would be stupid and contemptible, about which we can all agree. The question is whether the beautiful things that would be left behind if the last person to leave did not destroy them would be valuable on account of their beauty or integrity or whatever.

A clear illustration of the weakness of the 'last man' argument is exposed if one pushes the thought-experiment a bit further. Suppose that after the last man has departed, leaving behind the mountains and trees, and so on, perhaps in due deference to their intrinsic value and beauty, some aliens from outer space arrive on earth one day who have very different tastes from ours. They much prefer flat surfaces and find all these mountains and trees sticking up all over the place to be very ugly. Any philosophers among them who had previously espoused the 'last man' argument would be looking rather silly.[6]

Other arguments put up in defence of the objective view as applied to nature are equally unconvincing. For example, some environmental philosophers have argued that value is a concept that is applicable to any being that has a good of its own – for example, bamboo is 'good' for pandas, mild winters are 'good' for greenfly.[7] But this is a glaring example of the fallacy of equivocation: the word 'good' is being used in two entirely different senses. For even if certain inputs may be instrumentally 'good' for certain animals or inanimate objects in the sense that they may be necessary or sufficient conditions for them to flourish, this is a sense of the term 'good' that has nothing to do with being intrinsically morally 'good'. The mere fact that some living organism, like the tse tse fly or the HIV virus, or a more complex entity like an ecosystem, may flourish in particular conditions does not impose any moral obligation on humans to protect and promote those conditions.

There are other prominent avowedly objectivist defences of the intrinsic value of nature, but when it comes to the crunch they seem to sell crucial passes in that human interests and valuations enter by the back door. For example, Arne Naess, the founder of deep ecology, states that 'Richness and diversity of life forms … are also values in themselves. Humans have no right to reduce this richness and diversity *except to satisfy vital needs*' (emphasis added).[8] But the 'vital needs' to which reference is made are, presumably, the vital needs of humans.

Similarly, 'deep green' theory adopts the principle that 'there should be no substantially differential treatment of items outside any favoured class or species of a discriminatory sort that *lacks sufficient justification*' (Sylvan and Bennett 1994: 142, emphasis added). Again, it is presumably humans who are to decide what is 'sufficient justification' and to weigh this against the value of the environment. Thus the qualifications about the moral legitimacy of sacrificing nature in the interests of satisfying vital human needs, or when there is sufficient justification, means that, in the end, humans are entitled to weigh up the claims of the natural environment against any other claims that they think are vital. So we are once again relying on humans to weigh up competing claims on resources. In that case the concept of objective values outside the valuations made by humans can have no place.

All in all, therefore, the common environmentalist claim that nature is the bearer of some objectively intrinsic values seems difficult to defend. Indeed, the difficulty seems so great that those environmentalists who want to claim a privileged status for the environment would probably be on firmer ground if they defended the intrinsic value to the environment from a subjectivist point of view (O. O'Neill 1997: 128). In the end, objectivism may prove to be a liability to them rather than an asset, and some other, less metaphysically demanding view, such as that set out here [...], may better serve the cause of environmental protection.

The Inevitability of Human-Centred Values

The objectivist case for regarding the environment, or parts of it, as the bearer of intrinsic value is closely linked, as already indicated, to the belief that the value of nature should not be seen from a purely anthropocentric viewpoint. But, in some fundamental sense, even objectivists are no less anthropocentric than those who believe that nature has purely instrumental value. For it is simply inevitable that, to whatever view we subscribe about the value of nature, it will always be our human view. There is no other perspective available to us and there is no other perspective that can be adopted in our treatment of the non-human world. Since 'anthropocentric' simply means 'seen from the standpoint of a human being', then all views about the status and value of nature are equally anthropocentric.[9]

There is also a certain tension between notions like 'biological egalitarianism' or 'eco-impartiality' and insistence on treating the human species on an equal footing with the other species. For if all species are to be treated equally why is the human species not allowed to act in the way that other species do, namely, in their self-interest? No other species respects the 'intrinsic' value of other forms of life. But we are expected to be different and, instead of safeguarding our own interests by displaying natural 'human chauvinism' in the way that lions display 'leo

chauvinism', we are expected to overcome this natural inclination of all species, and adopt what might be called 'species impartiality'.

Now the demand that human beings should cultivate sensibilities such that they treat 'nature' with due respect – but not more – seems to be perfectly legitimate. But it is so because of a clear affirmation of human superiority. No other species would be capable of conceiving of such a grand idea as the equality of species which requires it to rise above the natural limitations of its own species. As Bernard Williams points out, it is one of the stranger paradoxes in many people's attitudes to nature that

> while they supposedly reject traditional pictures of human beings as discontinuous from nature in virtue of reason, they remind us all the time that other species share the same world with us on (so to speak) equal terms, and they unhesitatingly carry over into their picture of human beings a moral transcendence over the rest of nature, which makes us uniquely able and therefore uniquely obliged, to detach ourselves from any natural determination of our behaviour. Such views in fact firmly preserve the traditional doctrine of our transcendence of nature, and with it our proper monarchy of the earth; they merely ask us to exercise it in a more benevolent manner. (Williams 1992: 65)

As Bernard Williams (1992: 65) writes, 'a self-conscious concern for nature is not itself a piece of nature: it is an expression of culture'. And he goes on to explain that 'nature which is preserved by us is no longer a nature that is simply not controlled. A natural park is not nature, but a park; a wilderness that is preserved is a definite, delimited, wilderness. The paradox is that we have to use our power to preserve a sense of what is not in our power. Anything we leave untouched we have already touched'. And finally Williams warns us that in order to avoid self-deception we must not forget 'the inescapable truth that our refusal of the anthropocentric must itself be a human refusal' (1992: 68).

But being anthropocentric does not necessarily mean that we are 'human chauvinists', as is suggested in much environmentalist literature. For the term 'chauvinism', as usually employed in connection with attitudes to national or racial differences, suggests narrowness of sympathy, ruthlessness, and a callous indifference to the feelings of people of different national or racial affiliation. However, the philosophical position represented by, say, Passmore, which is commonly described as anthropocentric, can hardly be accused of narrowness of sympathy. Passmore (1974: 187) openly admits that 'I treat human "interests" as paramount. I do not apologise for that fact'. But he strongly defends the need for the preservation of nature.

His humanism is of the hospitable, friendly type, as opposed to what Mary Midgley (1999: 111) calls 'exclusive humanism', or 'human chauvinism', which would be characterized by narrowness of sympathy. Her support for the friendly kind of humanism is unequivocal: '… there is a sense in which it is right for us to feel that we are at the centre of our own lives. Attempts to get rid of that sense would be doomed in the same way as stoical attempts to tell people not to care especially about themselves, or about those dear to them' (1999: 110). But, she adds, 'We need, then, to recognise that people do right, not wrong, to have a particular regard for their own kin and their own species' (1999: 111).

Thus, a concern with non-human components of the natural world – for example, other animal species, and plants – or with environmental preservation is by no means incompatible with an anthropocentric approach. Indeed, it may well be that an anthropocentric approach in terms of human obligations provides a stronger basis for environmental protection than does the ecocentric appeal to objective intrinsic values in the environment or the rights of the non-human world. For since obligations can be only human obligations, the anthropocentric approach seems to be unavoidable. Hence, it is argued, the benefits of diversity of species, as distinct from concern with individual animals or insects on the basis of other considerations, such as simple 'compassion', must be evaluated from a basically anthropocentric point of view.

3 At other points in the book, however, Moore appears to express doubts about this view. For example, he writes (1978: 28), without indicating any dissent, that 'It seems to be true that to be conscious of a beautiful object is a thing of great intrinsic value; whereas the same object, if no one be conscious of it, has certainly comparatively little value, and is commonly held to have none at all'. And he displays a certain amount of equivocation in writing 'I have myself urged in Chap. III that the mere existence of what is beautiful does appear to have *some* intrinsic value; but I regard it as indubitable that Prof. Sidgwick was so far right, in the view there discussed, that such mere existence of what is beautiful has value, so small as to be negligible, in comparison with that which attaches to the consciousness of beauty' (1978: 189). It is only the distinction between 'negligible' value in the absence of any consciousness and zero value that protects Moore from the charge of blatant inconsistency, and the distinction is very difficult to justify in the context.

4 Many people value things that most of us would regard as abhorrent, but it is probably true that such people would probably prefer to keep their 'values' quiet or deny that they had them, and this is probably largely because they know that the things that they value do not really have any moral value.

5 This was set out very forcefully by Richard and Val Routley (1980).

6 See also Elliott Sober's (1986: 190–1) powerful critique of the 'last man' argument.

7 See a useful discussion of this assertion and its advocates in J. O'Neill (1993: Ch. 2).

8 See Naess and Session's 'platform' quoted in Sikora and Barry (1978: 95).

9 As Luc Ferry (1995: 131) puts it in his criticism of deep ecologists, 'imagining that good is inscribed within the very being of things they forget that all valorization, including that of nature, is the deed of man and that, consequently, all normative ethic is in some sense humanistic and anthropocentrist'.

Notes

1 Callicott (1985: 271). See an excellent discussion of this feature of environmentalism in Sober (1986).

2 For example, Nozick (1981: 414) writes, 'The notion of value I wish to investigate is not the value of something for some other purpose or further effects or consequences (assumed to be valuable). It is not its instrumental value, but rather its value in itself, apart from these further consequences and connections. Philosophers have termed this type of value intrinsic value'. Sometimes, in the context of this sort of classification, 'instrumental values' are referred to as 'extrinsic values'.

References

Barry, B. (1999). 'Sustainability and Intergenerational Justice', in A. Dobson (ed.), *Fairness and Futurity*. Oxford: Oxford University Press.

Callicott, J. (1985). 'Intrinsic Value, Quantum Theory and Environmental Ethics'. *Environmental Ethics*, 7/3: 257–75.

Ferry, L. (1995). *The New Ecological Order*. Chicago: Chicago University Press.

Mackie, J. L. (1988). 'The Subjectivity of Values', in G. Sayre–McCord (ed.), *Essays on Moral Realism*. Ithaca, NY: Cornell University Press.

Midgley, M. (1999). 'The End of Anthropocentrism?', in R. Attfield and A. Belsey (eds), *Philosophy and the Natural Environment*. Cambridge: Cambridge University Press.

Moore, G. E. (1978). *Principia Ethica*. Cambridge: Cambridge University Press.

Nozick, R. (1981). *Philosophical Explanations*. Oxford: Clarendon Press.

O'Neill, J. (1993). *Ecology, Policy and Politics*. London and New York: Routledge.

O'Neill, O. (1997). 'Environmental Values, Anthropocentrism and Speciesism'. *Environmental Values*, 6/2: 127–42.

Passmore, J. (1974). *Man's Responsibility for Nature*. London: Duckworth.

Regan, T. (1992). 'Does Environmental Ethics Rest on a Mistake?'. *The Monist*, 75: 161–82.

Routley, R. and Routley, V. (1979). 'Against the Inevitability of Human Chauvinism', in K. Goodpaster and K. Sayre (eds), *Ethics and Problems of the 21ˢᵗ Century*. Notre Dame: University of Notre Dame Press.

Routley, R. and Routley, V. (1980). 'Human Chauvinism and Environmental Ethics', in D. Mannison, M. McRobbie, and R. Routley (eds), *Environmental Philosophy*. Canberra: Australian National University.

Sikora, R. and Barry, B. (eds) (1978). *Obligations to Future Generations*. Philadelphia: Temple University Press.

Sober, E. (1986). 'Philosophical Problems for Environmentalism', in B. Norton (ed.), *The Preservation of Species: The Intrinsic Value of Nonhuman Species*. Princeton: Princeton University Press.

Sylvan, R. and Bennett, D. (1994). *The Greening of Ethics*. Cambridge: The White Horse Press.

Williams, B. (1992). 'Must a Concern for the Environment be Centred on Human Beings?', in C. Taylor (ed.), *Ethics and the Environment*. Oxford: Corpus Christi College.

PART III

WHAT IS NONANTHROPOCENTRISM?

9   Walking
    Henry David Thoreau

10 The Wild Parks and Forest Reservations of the West and Hetch Hetchy Valley
    John Muir

11 Is There a Need for a New, an Environmental, Ethic?
    Richard (Routley) Sylvan

12 Attitudes to Nature
    John Passmore

13 Should Trees Have Standing? Toward Legal Rights for Natural Objects
    Christopher D. Stone

14 The Varieties of Intrinsic Value
    John O'Neill

15 Value in Nature and the Nature of Value
    Holmes Rolston III

16 The End of Anthropocentrism?
    Mary Midgley

17 Is the Crown of Creation a Dunce Cap?
    Chip Ward

Introduction

The powerful alliance of Cartesian-Newtonian mechanism and Baconian-Lockean resourcism became evident with the Industrial Revolution. Economically, nature came to be viewed less as valuable for its own sake, as a source for inspiration and wonder, and more as brute material substance good for economic ends. The graphic result was an exploitation of natural resources never before seen in the history of human civilization.

Although anthropocentrism is the dominant worldview of Western culture, it is countered by a vigorous minority tradition, appropriately known as *nonanthropocentrism*. With Kant's publication of *Observations on the Feeling of the Beautiful and Sublime* in 1764, nonanthropocentrists tended to express value of nature mainly in aesthetic terms. Following Kant's lead, Romantic writers provided the first line of resistance against the depreciation and deprecation of nature as mere economic resource.

In revolt to the depreciation and deprecation of nature, Henry David Thoreau (1817–62 CE) had begun questioning the ontological divide between culture and nature. In "Walking," Thoreau regards humans "as an inhabitant, or part and parcel of Nature, rather than a member of society."[1] Thoreau recognized the psychological necessity of wildness – of wilderness – that would become prominent in American environmental thinking a century later.[2]

Another clarion call for the revaluation of nature was that of John Muir (1838–1914 CE). In the selection from "The Wild Parks and Forest Reservations of the West," Muir argues that we need unspoiled wilderness as a sanctuary from the neuroses of modern industrial civilization[3] – echoing Thoreau and anticipating Wallace Stegner. The psychic necessity of wilderness can be said to be anthropocentric, and was a main reason for establishing the Sierra Club. But for the most part Muir seems avowedly nonanthropocentric, a pantheist who equates nature with divinity.[4] For Muir, nature was *living* God, not *dead* Machine. God suffuses nature; God is nature. As he fulminates in the selection from "Hetch Hetchy Valley," destroying wilderness is nothing short of sacrilege. During his 1867 trek across the southeastern United States, Muir deplored the hollow instrumentalism of resourcism:

The World, we are told, was made especially for man – a presumption not supported by the facts. A numerous class of men are painfully astonished whenever they find anything, living or dead, in all God's universe, which they cannot eat or render in some way what they call useful to themselves.[5]

In "Is There a Need for a New, an Environmental, Ethic?," Australian philosopher Richard Sylvan (Routley) (1935–96 CE) outlines his original thought-experiment for nonanthropocentric intrinsic valuation of nature. If the last human (or people) in existence were to destroy as many living things as possible before perishing, would something valuable be lost even if there were no sentient beings around to do the valuing? Sylvan thinks so. Nonhuman nature has objective intrinsic value absolutely independent of human valuation.

In "Attitudes to Nature," fellow Australian philosopher John Passmore (1914–2004 CE) contextualizes the anthropocentric worldview historically in the Western tradition. Since Passmore claims this essay is "an attempt to bring together and to reformulate some of the basic philosophical themes" in his book *Man's Responsibility for Nature*, a case could be made that this selection should be placed in the preceding section, "What is Anthropocentrism?" Yet a careful reading of both texts reveals that in "Attitudes to Nature" Passmore strays significantly from his resolutely anthropocentric perspective in *Man's Responsibility for Nature*: "Western metaphysics and Western ethics have certainly done nothing to discourage, have done a great deal to encourage, the ruthless exploitation of nature."[6] If one lesson is to be gleaned from Passmore's well-crafted essay, it is that in the West the history of ideas and the history of environmental abuses are complex and multifactorial.

American law professor Christopher D. Stone outlines his novel argument for giving natural objects legal standing in "Should Trees Have Standing?" Stone surmises that "It is not inevitable, nor is it wise, that natural objects should have no rights to seek redress in their own behalf." To make this argument, he draws an analogy between natural objects and human incompetents. Human incompetents cannot speak intelligibly on their own behalf in court; lawyers speak for them. By parity of logic, Stone says, the same should go for natural objects, such as ecosystems. Stone contrasts the Liberalized Standing Approach with his more radical alternative, the Guardianship Approach. The former – based on defending the rights of human persons being aggrieved by the denigration of an ecological system (an anthropocentric justification) – is already in practice. The latter involves a court-appointed guardian to represent the interests of an ecological system under threat (a nonanthropocentric justification), which Stone argues is a much more straightforward and efficient use of judicial resources.

English philosopher John O'Neill, in "The Varieties of Intrinsic Value," makes clear the logically independent tasks of environmental normative ethics and environmental metaethics. O'Neill defends the thesis that nature has objective intrinsic value independent of human valuation (nonanthropocentrism), but also asserts that this axiology does not automatically mandate human moral obligations. Rather, environmental normative ethics requires an additional move, one that demonstrates that the integrity of ecological systems is beneficial to human flourishing, and only then do moral obligations to nonhuman nature ensue.

American philosopher Holmes Rolston is the most well-known proponent of the autonomous, objective intrinsic value of nonhuman nature. Like Sylvan, Rolston believes nature has value independently of being valued by valuers (the position held by Callicott). In "Value in Nature and the Nature of Value," Rolston confers objective intrinsic value to all living things (biocentrism). At the same time, he recognizes an indispensable instrumental value of ecological systems in providing the necessary framework for life to flourish (holism). Such "systemic" value is based in the creative capacity of natural processes to generate life. Systemic value is instrumentally valuable for human beings. It is in this recognition of the systemic value of ecological wholes that Rolston attempts an intriguing synthesis of individualism and holism, as Callicott notes.[7]

In "The End of Anthropocentrism?," English philosopher Mary Midgley points out that being "anthropocentric" is not necessarily bad. As Beckerman and Pasek insisted in the previous section, humans are, by default, at the center of our universe, perspectively speaking. Midgley observes that being "centered" might lead to care and compassion for those beings around us, for if we do not first love ourselves, how

may we be expected to love more-than-human others? Commonly understood, "anthropocentrism" means a diminished capacity for empathy, comparable to jingoism, racism, or sexism. Anthropocentrism in this sense is "human chauvinism" (the phrase used by Sylvan and Plumwood[8]), and, according to Midgley, no more rationally defensible than other forms of chauvinism centered around nation, race, or sex.

Independent Utah author Chip Ward wonders, in "Is the Crown of Creation a Dunce Cap?," if the anthropocentric model of intelligence ("brain chauvinism") deserves the kudos we have given it – and ourselves. Ward notes that, on the one hand, human beings do some pretty unintelligent things (unmitigated consumption, for example), and, on the other, that organisms exhibit community, or group, intelligence in surprising ways.

The sections on anthropocentrism and nonanthropocentrism set the historical context for the development of environmental ethics. The Western intellectual tradition consists of a constructive dissonance between the antipodes of anthropocentrism and nonanthropocentrism for rethinking the human place in nature. As Passmore observes, the "modern West . . . leaves more options open than most other societies; its traditions, intellectual, political, moral, are complex, diversified and fruitfully discordant."[9] This constructive dissonance is what made the precipitation of environmental ethics out of the medium of the Western intellectual tradition utterly inevitable.

Notes

1   "Walking," *The Works of Thoreau*, pp. 659–60. (See this volume, p. 93.)
2   Ibid., pp. 673–5. (See this volume, p. 94.)
3   "The Wild Parks and Forest Reservations of the West," in *Our National Parks*, p. 1. (See this volume, p. 96.)
4   See Cohen, *The Pathless Way*, particularly p. 125.
5   *A Thousand Mile Walk to the Gulf*, p. 136.
6   "Attitudes to Nature," in Peters, ed., *Nature and Conduct*, p. 259. (See this volume, p. 107.)
7   See Callicott's "Introduction," in Zimmerman et al., eds., *Environmental Philosophy*, 4th edn., p. 10.
8   Sylvan (Routley), "Is There a Need for a New, an Environmental, Ethic?," p. 207 (see this volume, p. 100); Sylvan (Routley) and Plumwood (Routley), "Against the Inevitability of Human Chauvinism," in Goodpaster and Sayre, eds., *Ethics and Problems of the 21st Century*, pp. 36–59.
9   *Man's Responsibility for Nature*, p. 195.

9 Walking

Henry David Thoreau

I wish to speak a word for Nature, for absolute freedom and wildness, as contrasted with a freedom and culture merely civil, – to regard man as an inhabitant, or a part and parcel of Nature, rather than a member of society. I wish to make an extreme statement, if so I may make an emphatic one, for there are enough champions of civilization: the minister and the school-committee and every one of you will take care of that.

[. . .]

The West of which I speak is but another name for the Wild; and what I have been preparing to say is, that in Wildness is the preservation of the World. Every tree sends its fibres forth in search of the Wild. The cities import it at any price. Men plough and sail for it. From the forest and wilderness come the tonics and barks which brace mankind. Our ancestors were savages. The story of Romulus and Remus being suckled by a wolf is not a meaningless fable. The founders of every State which has risen to eminence have drawn their nourishment and vigor from a similar wild source. It was because the children of the Empire were not suckled by the wolf that they were conquered and displaced by the children of the Northern forests who were.

I believe in the forest, and in the meadow, and in the night in which the corn grows. We require an infusion of hemlock-spruce or arbor vitæ in our tea. There is a difference between eating and drinking for strength and from mere gluttony. The Hottentots eagerly devour the marrow of the koodoo and other antelopes raw, as a matter of course. Some of our Northern Indians eat raw the marrow of the Arctic reindeer, as well as various other parts, including the summits of the antlers, as long as they are soft. And herein, perchance, they have stolen a march on the cooks of Paris. They get what usually goes to feed the fire. This is probably better than stall-fed beef and slaughter-house pork to make a man of. Give me a wildness whose glance no civilization can endure – as if we lived on the marrow of koodoos devoured raw.

There are some intervals which border the strain of the wood-thrush, to which I would migrate – wild lands where no settler has squatted; to which, methinks, I am already acclimated.

The African hunter Cummings tells us that the skin of the eland, as well as that of most other antelopes just killed, emits the most delicious perfume of trees and grass. I would have every man so much like a wild antelope, so much a part and parcel of Nature, that his very person should thus sweetly advertise our senses of his presence, and remind us of those parts of Nature which he most haunts. I feel no disposition to be satirical, when the trapper's coat emits the odor of musquash even; it is a sweeter scent to me than that which commonly exhales from the merchant's or the scholar's garments. When I go into their wardrobes and handle their vestments, I am reminded of no grassy plains and flowery meads which they have frequented, but of dusty merchants' exchanges and libraries rather.

A tanned skin is something more than respectable, and perhaps olive is a fitter color than white for a man – a denizen of the woods. "The pale white man!" I do not wonder that the African pitied him. Darwin the naturalist says, "A white man bathing by the side of a Tahitian was like a plant bleached by the gardener's art, compared with a fine, dark green one, growing vigorously in the open fields."

Ben Jonson exclaims –

"How near to good is what is fair!"

So I would say –

How near to good is what is *wild!*

Life consists with wildness. The most alive is the wildest. Not yet subdued to man, its presence refreshes him. One who pressed forward incessantly and never rested from his labors, who grew fast and made infinite demands on life, would always find himself in a new country or wilderness, and surrounded by the

From *Excursions* (Boston: Houghton, Mifflin & Co., 1883), pp. 260, 275–83, 287–9.

raw material of life. He would be climbing over the prostrate stems of primitive forest-trees.

Hope and the future for me are not in lawns and cultivated fields, not in towns and cities, but in the impervious and quaking swamps. When, formerly, I have analyzed my partiality for some farm which I had contemplated purchasing, I have frequently found that I was attracted solely by a few square rods of impermeable and unfathomable bog – a natural sink in one corner of it. That was the jewel which dazzled me. I derive more of my subsistence from the swamps which surround my native town than from the cultivated gardens in the village. There are no richer parterres to my eyes than the dense beds of dwarf andromeda (*Cassandra calyculata*) which cover these tender places on the earth's surface. Botany cannot go farther than tell me the names of the shrubs which grow there – the high-blueberry, panicled andromeda, lamb-kill, azalea, and rhodora – all standing in the quaking sphagnum. I often think that I should like to have my house front on this mass of dull red bushes omitting other flower plots and borders, transplanted spruce and trim box, even gravelled walks – to have this fertile spot under my windows, not a few imported barrow-fulls of soil only to cover the sand which was thrown out in digging the cellar. Why not put my house, my parlor, behind this plot, instead of behind that meagre assemblage of curiosities, that poor apology for a Nature and Art, which I call my front-yard? It is an effort to clear up and make a decent appearance when the carpenter and mason have departed, though done as much for the passer-by as the dweller within. The most tasteful front-yard fence was never an agreeable object of study to me; the most elaborate ornaments, acorn-tops, or what not, soon wearied and disgusted me. Bring your sills up to the very edge of the swamp, then, (though it may not be the best place for a dry cellar,) so that there be no access on that side to citizens. Front-yards are not made to walk in, but, at most, through, and you could go in the back way.

Yes, though you may think me perverse, if it were proposed to me to dwell in the neighborhood of the most beautiful garden that ever human art contrived, or else of a Dismal swamp, I should certainly decide for the swamp. How vain, then, have been all your labors, citizens, for me!

My spirits infallibly rise in proportion to the outward dreariness. Give me the ocean, the desert or the wilderness! In the desert, pure air and solitude compensate for want of moisture and fertility. The traveller Burton says of it – "Your *morale* improves; you become frank and cordial, hospitable and single-minded. . . . In the desert, spirituous liquors excite only disgust. There is a keen enjoyment in a mere animal existence." They who have been travelling long on the steppes of Tartary say – "On reëntering cultivated lands, the agitation, perplexity, and turmoil of civilization oppressed and suffocated us; the air seemed to fail us, and we felt every moment as if about to die of asphyxia." When I would recreate myself, I seek the darkest wood, the thickest and most interminable, and, to the citizen, most dismal swamp. I enter a swamp as a sacred place – a *sanctum sanctorum*. There is the strength, the marrow of Nature. The wild-wood covers the virgin mould – and the same soil is good for men and for trees. A man's health requires as many acres of meadow to his prospect as his farm does loads of muck. There are the strong meats on which he feeds. A town is saved, not more by the righteous men in it than by the woods and swamps that surround it. A township where one primitive forest waves above, while another primitive forest rots below – such a town is fitted to raise not only corn and potatoes, but poets and philosophers for the coming ages. In such a soil grew Homer and Confucius and the rest, and out of such a wilderness comes the Reformer eating locusts and wild honey.

To preserve wild animals implies generally the creation of a forest for them to dwell in or resort to. So it is with man. A hundred years ago they sold bark in our streets peeled from our own woods. In the very aspect of those primitive and rugged trees, there was, methinks, a tanning principle which hardened and consolidated the fibres of men's thoughts. Ah! already I shudder for these comparatively degenerate days of my native village, when you cannot collect a load of bark of good thickness – and we no longer produce tar and turpentine.

The civilized nations – Greece, Rome, England – have been sustained by the primitive forests which anciently rotted where they stand. They survive as long as the soil is not exhausted. Alas for human culture! little is to be expected of a nation, when the vegetable mould is exhausted, and it is compelled to make manure of the bones of its fathers. There the poet sustains himself merely by his own superfluous fat, and the philosopher comes down on his marrow-bones.

It is said to be the task of the American "to work the virgin soil," and that "agriculture here already assumes proportions unknown everywhere else." I think that the farmer displaces the Indian even because he redeems the meadow, and so makes himself stronger and in some respects more natural. I was surveying for a man the other day a single straight line one hundred and thirty-two rods long, through a swamp, at whose entrance might have been written the words which Dante read over the entrance to the infernal regions – "Leave all hope, ye that enter," – that is, of ever getting out again; where at one time I saw my employer actually up to his neck and swimming for his life in his property, though it was still winter. He had another similar swamp which I could not survey at all, because it was completely under water, and nevertheless, with regard to a third swamp, which I did *survey* from a distance, he remarked to me, true to his instincts, that he would not part with it for any consideration, on account of the mud which it contained. And that man intends to put a girdling ditch round the whole in the course of forty months, and so redeem it by the magic of his spade. I refer to him only as the type of a class.

✓ The weapons with which we have gained our most important victories, which should be handed down as heirlooms from father to son are not the sword and the lance, but the bush whack, the turf-cutter, the spade, and the bog-hoe rusted with the blood of many a meadow, and begrimed with the dust of many a hard-fought field. The very winds blew the Indian's cornfield into the meadow, and pointed out the way which he had not the skill to follow. He had no better implement with which to intrench himself in the land than a clam-shell. But the farmer is armed with plough and spade.

[. . .]

✓ In short, all good things are wild and free. There is something in a strain of music, whether produced by an instrument or by the human voice – take the sound of a bugle in a summer night, for instance – which by its wildness, to speak without satire, reminds me of the cries emitted by wild beasts in their native forests. It is so much of their wildness as I can understand. Give me for my friends and neighbors wild men, not tame ones. The wildness of the savage is but a faint symbol of the awful ferity with which good men and lovers meet.

I love even to see the domestic animals reassert their native rights – any evidence that they have not wholly lost their original wild habits and vigor; as when my neighbor's cow breaks out of her pasture early in the spring and boldly swims the river, a cold, gray tide, twenty-five or thirty rods wide, swollen by the melted snow. It is the buffalo crossing the Mississippi. This exploit confers some dignity on the herd in my eyes – already dignified. The seeds of instinct are preserved under the thick hides of cattle and horses, like seeds in the bowels of the earth, an indefinite period.

Any sportiveness in cattle is unexpected. I saw one day a herd of a dozen bullocks and cows running about and frisking in unwieldly sport, like huge rats, even like kittens. They shook their heads, raised their tails, and rushed up and down a hill, and I perceived by their horns, as well as by their activity, their relation to the deer tribe. But, alas! a sudden loud *Whoa!* would have damped their ardor at once, reduced them from venison to beef, and stiffened their sides and sinews like the locomotive. Who but the Evil One has cried, "Whoa!" to mankind? Indeed, the life of cattle, like that of many men, is but a sort of locomotiveness; they move a side at a time, and man, by his machinery, is meeting the horse and the ox half-way. Whatever part the whip has touched is thenceforth palsied. Who would ever think of a *side* of any of the supple cat tribe, as we speak of a *side* of beef?

I rejoice that horses and steers have to be broken before they can be made the slaves of men, and that men themselves have some wild oats still left to sow before they become submissive members of society. Undoubtedly, all men are not equally fit subjects for civilization; and because the majority, like dogs and sheep, are tame by inherited disposition, this is no reason why the others should have their natures broken that they may be reduced to the same level. Men are in the main alike, but they were made several in order that they might be various. If a low use is to be served, one man will do nearly or quite as well as another; if a high one, individual excellence is to be regarded. Any man can stop a hole to keep the wind away, but no other man could serve so rare a use as the author of this illustration did. Confucius says – "The skins of the tiger and the leopard, when they are tanned, are as the skins of the dog and the sheep tanned." But it is not the part of a true culture to tame tigers, any more than it is to make sheep ferocious; and tanning their skins for shoes is not the best use to which they can be put.

10   The Wild Parks and Forest Reservations of the West and Hetch Hetchy Valley

John Muir

The tendency nowadays to wander in wildernesses is delightful to see. Thousands of tired, nerve-shaken, over-civilized people are beginning to find out that going to the mountains is going home; that wildness is a necessity; and that mountain parks and reservations are useful not only as fountains of timber and irrigating rivers, but as fountains of life. Awakening from the stupefying effects of the vice of over-industry and the deadly apathy of luxury, they are trying as best they can to mix and enrich their own little ongoings with those of Nature, and to get rid of rust and disease. Briskly venturing and roaming, some are washing off sins and cobweb cares of the devil's spinning in all-day storms on mountains; sauntering in rosiny pinewoods or in gentian meadows, brushing through chaparral, bending down and parting sweet, flowery sprays; tracing rivers to their sources, getting in touch with the nerves of Mother Earth; jumping from rock to rock, feeling the life of them, learning the songs of them, panting in whole-souled exercise, and rejoicing in deep, long-drawn breaths of pure wildness. This is fine and natural and full of promise. So also is the growing interest in the care and preservation of forests and wild places in general, and in the half wild parks and gardens of towns. Even the scenery habit in its most artificial forms, mixed with spectacles, silliness, and kodaks; its devotees arrayed more gorgeously than scarlet tanagers, frightening the wild game with red umbrellas – even this is encouraging, and may well be regarded as a hopeful sign of the times.

All the Western mountains are still rich in wildness, and by means of good roads are being brought nearer civilization every year. To the sane and free it will hardly seem necessary to cross the continent in search of wild beauty, however easy the way, for they find it in abundance wherever they chance to be. Like Thoreau they see forests in orchards and patches of huckleberry brush, and oceans in ponds and drops of dew. Few in these hot, dim, strenuous times are quite sane or free; choked with care like clocks full of dust, laboriously doing so much good and making so much money – or so little – they are no longer good for themselves.

When, like a merchant taking a list of his goods, we take stock of our wildness, we are glad to see how much of even the most destructible kind is still unspoiled. Looking at our continent as scenery when it was all wild, lying between beautiful seas, the starry sky above it, the starry rocks beneath it, to compare its sides, the East and the West, would be like comparing the sides of a rainbow. But it is no longer equally beautiful. The rainbows of to-day are, I suppose, as bright as those that first spanned the sky; and some of our landscapes are growing more beautiful from year to year, notwithstanding the clearing, trampling work of civilization. New plants and animals are enriching woods and gardens, and many landscapes wholly new, with divine sculpture and architecture, are just now coming to the light of day as the mantling folds of creative glaciers are being withdrawn, and life in a thousand cheerful, beautiful forms is pushing into them, and new-born rivers are beginning to sing and shine in them. The old rivers, too, are growing longer, like healthy trees, gaining new branches and lakes as the residual glaciers at their highest sources on the mountains recede, while the rootlike branches in their flat deltas are at the same time spreading farther and wider into the seas and making new lands.

Under the control of the vast mysterious forces of the interior of the earth all the continents and islands are slowly rising or sinking. Most of the mountains are diminishing in size under the wearing action of the weather, though a few are increasing in height and girth, especially the volcanic ones, as fresh floods of molten rocks are piled on their summits and spread in successive layers, like the wood-rings of

From *Our National Parks* (Boston: Houghton, Mifflin & Co., 1901), pp. 1–5, and *The Yosemite* (The Century Co., 1912), pp. 255–7, 261–2.

trees, on their sides. New mountains, also, are being created from time to time as islands in lakes and seas, or as subordinate cones on the slopes of old ones, thus in some measure balancing the waste of old beauty with new. Man, too, is making many far-reaching changes. This most influential half animal, half angel is rapidly multiplying and spreading, covering the seas and lakes with ships, the land with huts, hotels, cathedrals, and clustered city shops and homes, so that soon, it would seem, we may have to go farther than Nansen to find a good sound solitude. None of Nature's landscapes are ugly so long as they are wild; and much, we can say comfortingly, must always be in great part wild, particularly the sea and the sky, the floods of light from the stars, and the warm, unspoilable heart of the earth, infinitely beautiful, though only dimly visible to the eye of imagination. The geysers, too, spouting from the hot underworld; the steady, long-lasting glaciers on the mountains, obedient only to the sun; Yosemite domes and the tremendous grandeur of rocky cañons and mountains in general – these must always be wild, for man can change them and mar them hardly more than can the butterflies that hover above them. But the continent's outer beauty is fast passing away, especially the plant part of it, the most destructible and most universally charming of all.

[. . .]

Hetch Hetchy Valley, far from being a plain, common, rock-bound meadow, as many who have not seen it seem to suppose, is a grand landscape garden, one of Nature's rarest and most precious mountain temples. As in Yosemite, the sublime rocks of its walls seem to glow with life, whether leaning back in repose or standing erect in thoughtful attitudes, giving welcome to storms and calms alike, their brows in the sky, their feet set in the groves and gay flowery meadows, while birds, bees, and butterflies help the river and waterfalls to stir all the air into music – things frail and fleeting and types of permanence meeting here and blending, just as they do in Yosemite, to draw her lovers into close and confiding communion with her.

Sad to say, this most precious and sublime feature of the Yosemite National Park, one of the greatest of all our natural resources for the uplifting joy and peace and health of the people, is in danger of being dammed and made into a reservoir to help supply San Francisco with water and light, thus flooding it from wall to wall and burying its gardens and groves one or two hundred feet deep. This grossly destructive commercial scheme has long been planned and urged (though water as pure and abundant can be got from sources outside of the people's park, in a dozen different places), because of the comparative cheapness of the dam and of the territory which it is sought to divert from the great uses to which it was dedicated in the Act of 1890 establishing the Yosemite National Park.

The making of gardens and parks goes on with civilization all over the world, and they increase both in size and number as their value is recognized. Everybody needs beauty as well as bread, places to play in and pray in, where Nature may heal and cheer and give strength to body and soul alike. This natural beauty-hunger is made manifest in the little window-sill gardens of the poor, though perhaps only a geranium slip in a broken cup, as well as in the carefully tended rose and lily gardens of the rich, the thousands of spacious city parks and botanical gardens, and in our magnificent National parks – the Yellowstone, Yosemite, Sequoia, etc. – Nature's sublime wonderlands, the admiration and joy of the world. Nevertheless, like anything else worth while, from the very beginning, however well guarded, they have always been subject to attack by despoiling gainseekers and mischief-makers of every degree from Satan to Senators, eagerly trying to make everything immediately and selfishly commercial, with schemes disguised in smug-smiling philanthropy, industriously, shampiously crying, "Conservation, conservation, panutilization," that man and beast may be fed and the dear Nation made great. Thus long ago a few enterprising merchants utilized the Jerusalem temple as a place of business instead of a place of prayer, changing money, buying and selling cattle and sheep and doves; and earlier still, the first forest reservation, including only one tree, was likewise despoiled. Ever since the establishment of the Yosemite National Park, strife has been going on around its borders and I suppose this will go on as part of the universal battle between right and wrong, however much its boundaries may be shorn, or its wild beauty destroyed.

[. . .]

These temple destroyers, devotees of ravaging commercialism, seem to have a perfect contempt for Nature, and, instead of lifting their eyes to the God of the mountains, lift them to the Almighty Dollar.

Dam Hetch Hetchy! As well dam for water-tanks the people's cathedrals and churches, for no holier temple has ever been consecrated by the heart of man.

11   Is There a Need for a New, an Environmental, Ethic?

Richard (Routley) Sylvan

§ 1. It is increasingly said that civilization, Western civilization at least, stands in need of a new ethic (and derivatively of a new economics) setting out people's relations to the natural environment, in Leopold's words 'an ethic dealing with man's relation to land and to the animals and plants which grow upon it' ([1], p. 238). It is not of course that old and prevailing ethics do not deal with man's relation to nature: they do, and on the prevailing view man is free to deal with nature as he pleases, i.e. his relations with nature, insofar at least as they do not affect others, are not subject to moral censure. Thus assertions such as 'Crusoe ought not to be mutilating those trees' are significant and morally determinate but, inasmuch at least as Crusoe's actions do not interfere with others, they are false or do not hold – and trees are not, in a good sense, moral objects.[1] It is to this, to the values and evaluations of the prevailing ethics, that Leopold and others in fact take exception. Leopold regards as subject to moral criticism, as wrong, behaviour that on prevailing views is morally permissible. But it is not, as Leopold seems to think, that such behaviour is beyond the scope of the prevailing ethics and that an *extension* of traditional morality is required to cover such cases, to fill a moral void. If Leopold is right in his criticism of prevailing conduct what is required is a *change* in the ethics, in attitudes, values and evaluations. For as matters stand, as he himself explains, men do not feel morally ashamed if they interfere with a wilderness, if they maltreat the land, extract from it whatever it will yield, and then move on; and such conduct is not taken to interfere with and does not rouse the moral indignation of others. 'A farmer who clears the woods off a 75% slope, turns his cows into the clearing, and dumps its rainfall, rocks, and soil into the community creek, is still (if otherwise decent) a respected member of society' ([1], p. 245). Under what we shall call *an environmental ethic* such traditionally permissible conduct would be accounted morally wrong, and the farmer subject to proper moral criticism.

Let us grant such evaluations for the purpose of the argument. What is not so clear is that a *new* ethic is required even for such radical judgements. For one thing it is none too clear what is going to count as a new ethic, much as it is often unclear whether a new development in physics counts as a new physics or just as a modification or extension of the old. For, notoriously, ethics are not clearly articulated or at all well worked out, so that the application of identity criteria for ethics may remain obscure.[2] Furthermore we tend to cluster a family of ethical systems which do not differ on core or fundamental principles together as the one ethic; e.g. the Christian ethic, which is an umbrella notion covering a cluster of differing and even competing systems. In fact then there are two other possibilities, apart from a new environmental ethic, which might cater for the evaluations, namely that of an extension or modification of the prevailing ethics or that of the development of principles that are already encompassed or latent within the prevailing ethic. The second possibility, that environmental evaluations can be incorporated within (and ecological problems solved within) the framework of prevailing Western ethics, is open because there isn't a single ethical system uniquely assumed in Western civilization: on many issues, and especially on controversial issues such as infanticide, women's rights and drugs, there are competing sets of principles. Talk of a new ethic and prevailing ethics tends to suggest a sort of monolithic structure, a uniformity, that prevailing ethics, and even a single ethic, need not have.

Indeed Passmore (in [2]) has mapped out three important traditions in Western ethical views concerning man's relation to nature; a dominant tradition, the despotic position, with man as despot (or tyrant), and two lesser traditions, the stewardship position, with man as custodian, and the co-operative

From *Proceedings of the XVth World Congress of Philosophy* (September 17–22, 1973, Varna, Bulgaria), Sofia Press, 1975. © 1973 by Richard Routley.

position with man as perfector. Nor are these the only traditions; primitivism is another, and both romanticism and mysticism have influenced Western views.

The dominant Western view is simply inconsistent with an environmental ethic; for according to it nature is the dominion of man and he is free to deal with it as he pleases (since – at least on the mainstream Stoic – Augustine view – it exists only for his sake), whereas on an environmental ethic man is not so free to do as he pleases. But it is not quite so obvious that an environmental ethic cannot be coupled with one of the lesser traditions. Part of the problem is that the lesser traditions are by no means adequately characterised anywhere, especially when the religious backdrop is removed, e.g. *who* is man steward for and responsible to? However both traditions are inconsistent with an environmental ethic because they imply policies of complete interference, whereas on an environmental ethic some worthwhile parts of the earth's surface should be preserved from substantial human interference, whether of the "improving" sort or not. Both traditions would in fact prefer to see the earth's land surfaces reshaped along the lines of the tame and comfortable north-European small farm and village landscape. According to the co-operative position man's proper role is to develop, cultivate and perfect nature – all nature eventually – by bringing out its potentialities, the test of perfection being primarily usefulness for human purposes; while on the stewardship view man's role, like that of a farm manager, is to make nature productive by his efforts though not by means that will deliberately degrade its resources. Although these positions both depart from the dominant position in a way which enables the incorporation of some evaluations of an environmental ethic, e.g. some of those concerning the irresponsible farmer, they do not go far enough: for in the present situation of expanding populations confined to finite natural areas, they will lead to, and enjoin, the perfecting, farming and utilizing of all natural areas. Indeed these lesser traditions lead to, what a thoroughgoing environmental ethic would reject, a principle of total use, implying that every natural area should be cultivated or otherwise used[3] for human ends, "humanized".

As the important Western traditions exclude an environmental ethic, it would appear that such an ethic, not primitive, mystical or romantic, would be new alright. The matter is not so straightforward; for the dominant ethic has been substantially qualified by the rider that one is not always entitled to do as one pleases where this physically interferes with others. Maybe some such proviso was implicit all along (despite evidence to the contrary), and it was simply assumed that doing what one pleased with natural items would not affect others (the non-interference assumption). Be this as it may, the *modified* dominant position appears, at least for many thinkers, to have supplanted the dominant position; and the modified position can undoubtedly go much further towards an environmental ethic. For example, the farmer's polluting of a community stream may be ruled immoral on the grounds that it physically interferes with others who use or would use the stream. Likewise business enterprises which destroy the natural environment for no satisfactory returns or which cause pollution deleterious to the health of future humans, can be criticised on the sort of welfare basis (e.g. that of [3]) that blends with the modified position; and so on. The position may even serve to restrict the sort of family size one is entitled to have since in a finite situation excessive population levels will interfere with future people. Nonetheless neither the modified dominant position nor its Western variants, obtained by combining it with the lesser traditions, is adequate as an environmental ethic, as I shall try to show. A new ethic *is* wanted.

§ 2. As we noticed (an) *ethic* is ambiguous, as between a specific ethical system, a *specific* ethic, and a more generic notion, a super ethic, under which specific ethics cluster.[4] An ethical system S is, near enough, a propositional system (i.e. a structured set of propositions) or theory which includes (like individuals of a theory) a set of values and (like postulates of a theory) a set of general evaluative judgements concerning conduct, typically of what is obligatory, permissible and wrong, of what are rights, what is valued, and so forth. A general or lawlike proposition of a system is a principle; and certainly if systems S_1 and S_2 contain different principles, then they are different systems. It follows that any environmental ethic differs from the important traditional ethics outlined. Moreover if environmental ethics differ from Western ethical systems on some *core* principle embedded in Western systems, then these systems differ from the Western super ethic (assuming, what seems to be so, that it can be uniquely characterised) – in which case if an environmental ethic *is* needed then a new ethic is wanted. It suffices then to locate a core principle and to provide environmental counter examples to it.

It is commonly assumed that there are, what amount to, core principles of Western ethical systems, principles that will accordingly belong to the super ethic. The fairness principle inscribed in the Golden Rule provides one example. Directly relevant here, as a good stab at a core principle, is the commonly formulated liberal principle of the modified dominance position. A recent formulation[5] runs as follows ([3], p. 58): 'The liberal philosophy of the Western world holds that one should be able to do what he wishes, providing (1) that he does not harm others and (2) that he is not likely to harm himself irreparably.'

Let us call this principle *basic (human) chauvinism* – because under it humans, or people, come first and everything else a bad last – though sometimes the principle is hailed as a *freedom* principle because it gives permission to perform a wide range of actions (including actions which mess up the environment and natural things) providing they do not harm others. In fact it tends to cunningly shift the onus of proof to others. It is worth remarking that *harming others* in the restriction is narrower than a restriction to the (usual) interests of others; it is not enough that it is in my interests, because I detest you, that you stop breathing; you are free to breathe, for the time being anyway, because it does not harm me. There remains a problem however as to exactly what counts as harm or interference. Moreover the width of the principle is so far obscure because 'other' may be filled out in significantly different ways: it makes a difference to the extent, and privilege, of the chauvinism whether 'other' expands to 'other human' – which is too restrictive – or to 'other person' or to 'other sentient being'; and it makes a difference to the adequacy of the principle, and inversely to its economic applicability, to which class of others it is intended to apply, whether to future as well as to present others, whether to remote future others or only to non-discountable future others, and whether to possible others. The latter would make the principle completely unworkable, and it is generally assumed that it applies at most to present and future others.

It is taken for granted in designing counter examples to basic chauvinist principles, that a semantical analysis of permissibility and obligation statements stretches out over ideal situations (which may be incomplete or even inconsistent), so that what is permissible holds in some ideal situation, what is obligatory in every ideal situation, and what is wrong is excluded in every ideal situation. But the main point to grasp for the counter examples that follow, is that ethical principles if correct are universal and are assessed over the class of ideal situations.

(i) The *last man* example. The last man (or person) surviving the collapse of the world system lays about him, eliminating, as far as he can, every living thing, animal or plant (but painlessly if you like, as at the best abattoirs). What he does is quite permissible according to basic chauvinism, but on environmental grounds what he does is wrong. Moreover one does not have to be committed to esoteric values to regard Mr. Last Man as behaving badly (the reason being perhaps that radical thinking and values have shifted in an environmental direction in advance of corresponding shifts in the formulation of fundamental evaluative principles).

(ii) The *last people* example. The last man example can be broadened to the last people example. We can assume that they know they are the last people, e.g. because they are aware that radiation effects have blocked any chance of reproduction. One considers the last people in order to rule out the possibility that what these people do harms or somehow physically interferes with later people. Otherwise one could as well consider science fiction cases where people arrive at a new planet and destroy its ecosystems, whether with good intentions such as perfecting the planet for their ends and making it more fruitful or, forgetting the lesser traditions, just for the hell of it.

Let us assume that the last people are very numerous. They humanely exterminate every wild animal and they eliminate the fish of the seas, they put all arable land under intensive cultivation, and all remaining forests disappear in favour of quarries or plantations, and so on. They may give various familiar reasons for this, e.g. they believe it is the way to salvation or to perfection, or they are simply satisfying reasonable needs, or even that it is needed to keep the last people employed or occupied so that they do not worry too much about their impending extinctions. On an environmental ethic the last people have behaved badly; they have simplified and largely destroyed all the natural ecosystems, and with their demise the world will soon be an ugly and largely wrecked place. But this conduct may conform with the basic chauvinist principle, and as well with the principles enjoined by the lesser traditions. Indeed the main point of elaborating this example is because, as the last man example reveals, basic chauvinism may conflict with stewardship or cooperation principles. The conflict may be removed it seems by conjoining a further proviso to the basic principle, to the effect (3) that he does not wilfully destroy natural resources. But as the last people do not destroy resources wilfully, but perhaps "for the best of reasons", the variant is still environmentally inadequate.

(iii) The *great entrepreneur* example. The last man example can be adjusted so as to not fall foul of clause (3). The last man is an industrialist; he runs a giant complex of automated factories and farms which he proceeds to extend. He produces automobiles among other things, from renewable and recyclable resources of course, only he dumps and recycles these shortly after manufacture and sale to a dummy buyer instead of putting them on the road for a short time as we do. Of course he has the best of reasons for his activity, e.g. he is increasing gross world product, or he is improving output to fulfil some plan, and he will be increasing his own and general welfare since he much prefers increased output and productivity. The entrepreneur's behaviour is on the Western ethic quite permissible; indeed his conduct is commonly thought to be quite fine and may even meet Pareto optimality requirements given prevailing notions of being "better off".

Just as we can extend the last man example to a class of last people, so we can extend this example to the *industrial society* example: the society looks rather like ours.

(iv) The *vanishing species* example. Consider the blue whale, a mixed good on the economic picture. The blue whale is on the verge of extinction because of his qualities as a private good, as a source of valuable oil and meat. The catching and marketing of blue whales does not harm the whalers; it does not harm or physically interfere with others in any good sense, though it may upset them and they may be prepared to compensate the whalers if they desist; nor need whale hunting be wilful destruction. (Slightly different examples which eliminate the hunting aspect of the blue whale example are provided by cases where a species is eliminated or threatened through destruction of its habitat by man's activity or the activities of animals he has introduced, e.g. many plains-dwelling Australian marsupials and the Arabian oryx.) The behaviour of the whalers in elimi-

nating this magnificent species of whale is accordingly quite permissible – at least according to basic chauvinism. But on an environmental ethic it is not. However the free-market mechanism will not cease allocating whalers to commercial uses, as a satisfactory environmental economics would; instead the market model will grind inexorably[6] along the private demand curve until the blue whale population is no longer viable – if that point has not already been passed.

In sum, the class of permissible actions that rebound on the environment is more narrowly circumscribed on an environmental ethic than it is in the Western super ethic. But aren't environmentalists going too far in claiming that these people, those of the examples and respected industrialists, fishermen and farmers are behaving, when engaging in environmentally degrading activities of the sort described, in a morally impermissible way? No, what these people do is to a greater or lesser extent evil, and hence in serious cases morally impermissible. For example, insofar as the killing or forced displacement of primitive peoples who stand in the way of an industrial development is morally indefensible and impermissible, so also is the slaughter of the last remaining blue whales for private profit. But how to reformulate basic chauvinism as a satisfactory freedom principle is a more difficult matter. A tentative, but none too adequate beginning might be made by extending (2) to include harm to or interference with others who would be so affected by the action in question were they placed in the environment and (3) to exclude specieside. It may be preferable, in view of the way the freedom principle sets the onus of proof, simply to scrap it altogether, and instead to specify classes of rights and permissible conduct, as in a bill of rights.

§ 3. A radical change in a theory sometimes forces changes in the meta-theory; e.g. a logic which rejects the Reference Theory in a thoroughgoing way requires a modification of the usual meta-theory which also accepts the Reference Theory and indeed which is tailored to cater only for logics which do conform. A somewhat similar phenomenon seems to occur in the case of a meta-ethic adequate for an environmental ethic. Quite apart from introducing several environmentally important notions, such as *conservation, pollution, growth* and *preservation*, for meta-ethical analysis, an environmental ethic compels re-examination and modified analyses of such characteristic actions as *natural right, ground* of right, and of the relations of obligation and permissibility to rights; it may well require re-assessment of traditional analyses of such notions as *value* and *right,* especially where these are based on chauvinist assumptions; and it forces the rejection of many of the more prominent meta-ethical positions. These points are illustrated by a very brief examination of accounts of *natural right* and then by a sketch of the species bias of some major positions.[7]

Hart (in [5]) accepts, subject to defeating conditions which are here irrelevant, the classical doctrine of natural rights according to which, among other things, 'any adult human . . . capable of choice is at liberty to do (i.e. is under no obligation to abstain from) any action which is not one coercing or restraining or designed to injure other persons'. But this sufficient condition for a human natural right depends on accepting the very human chauvinist principle an environmental ethic rejects, since if a person has a natural right he has a right; so too the *definition* of a natural right adopted by classical theorists and accepted with minor qualifications by Hart presupposes the same defective principle. Accordingly an environmental ethic would have to amend the classical notion of a natural right, a far from straightforward matter now that human rights with respect to animals and the natural environment are, like those with respect to slaves not all that long ago, undergoing major re-evaluation.

An environmental ethic does not commit one to the view that natural objects such as trees have rights (though such a view is occasionally held, e.g. by pantheists. But pantheism is false since artefacts are not alive). For moral prohibitions forbidding certain actions with respect to an object do not award that object a correlative right. That it would be wrong to mutilate a given tree or piece of property does not entail that the tree or piece of property has a correlative right not to be mutilated (without seriously stretching the notion of a right). Environmental views can stick with mainstream theses according to which rights are coupled with corresponding responsibilities and so with bearing obligations, and with corresponding interests and concern; i.e., at least, whatever has a right also has responsibilities and therefore obligations, and whatever has a right has interests. Thus although any person may have a right by no means every living thing can (significantly) have rights, and arguably most sentient objects other than persons cannot have rights. But persons can relate morally, through obligations, prohibitions and so forth, to practically anything at all.

The species bias of certain ethical and economic positions which aim to make principles of conduct or reasonable economic behaviour calculable is easily brought out. These positions typically employ a single criterion p, such as preference or happiness, as a *summum bonum;* characteristically each individual of some *base* class, almost always humans, but perhaps including future humans, is supposed to have an ordinal p ranking of the states in question (e.g. of affairs, of the economy); then some principle is supplied to determine a collective p ranking of these states in terms of individual p rankings, and what is best or ought to be done is determined either directly, as in act-utilitarianism under the Greatest Happiness principle, or indirectly, as in rule-utilitarianism, in terms of some optimization principle applied to the collective ranking. The species bias is transparent from the selection of the base class. And even if the base class is extended to embrace persons, or even some animals (at the cost, like that of including remotely future humans, of losing testability), the positions are open to familiar criticism, namely that the whole of the base class may be prejudiced in a way which leads to unjust principles. For example if every member of the base class detests dingoes, on the basis of mistaken data as to dingoes' behaviour, then by the Pareto ranking test the collective ranking will rank states where dingoes are exterminated very highly, from which it will generally be concluded that dingoes ought to be exterminated (the evaluation of most Australian farmers anyway). Likewise it would just be a happy accident, it seems, if collective demand (horizontally summed from individual demand) for a state of the economy with blue whales as a mixed good were to succeed in outweighing private whaling demands; for if no one in the base class happened to know that blue whales exist or cared a jot that they do then "rational" economic decision-making would do nothing to prevent their extinction. Whether the blue whale survives should not have to depend on what humans know or what they see on television. Human interests and preferences are far too parochial to provide a satisfactory basis for deciding on what is environmentally desirable.

These ethical and economic theories are not alone in their species chauvinism; much the same applies to most going meta-ethical theories which, unlike intuitionistic theories, try to offer some rationale for their basic principles. For instance, on social contract positions obligations are a matter of mutual agreements between individuals of the base class; on a social justice picture rights and obligations spring from the application of symmetrical fairness principles to members of the base class, usually a rather special class of persons, while on a Kantian position which has some vague obligations they somehow arise from respect for members of the base class persons. In each case if members of the base class happen to be ill-disposed to items outside the base class then that is too bad for them: that is (rough) justice.

Notes

1   A view occasionally tempered by the idea that trees house spirits.
2   To the consternation no doubt of Quineans. But the fact is that we can talk perfectly well about inchoate and fragmentary systems the identity of which may be indeterminate.
3   If 'use' is extended, somewhat illicitly, to include use for preservation, this total use principle is rendered innocuous at least as regards its actual effects. Note that the total use principle is tied to the resource view of nature.

4   A *meta-ethic* is, as usual, a theory about ethics, super ethics, their features and fundamental notions.
5   A related principle is that (modified) free enterprise can operate within similar limits.
6   For the tragedy-of-the-commons type reasons well explained in [3].
7   Some of these points are developed by those protesting about human maltreatment of animals; see especially the essays collected in [4].

References

[1]   A. Leopold, *A Sand County Almanac with Other Essays on Conservation*. New York (1966).
[2]   J. Passmore, *Ecological Problems and Western Traditions* (unpublished).
[3]   P. W. Barkley and D. W. Seckler, *Economic Growth and Environmental Decay. The Solution Becomes the Problem*. New York (1972).
[4]   S. and R. Godlovitch and J. Harris (eds.), *Animals, Men and Morals. An Enquiry into the Maltreatment of Non-humans*. London (1971).
[5]   H. L. A. Hart, 'Are there any natural rights?', reprinted in A. Quinton (ed.), *Political Philosophy*. Oxford (1967).

12   Attitudes to Nature[1]

John Passmore

The ambiguity of the word 'nature' is so remarkable that I need not remark upon it. Except perhaps to emphasise that this ambiguity – scarcely less apparent, as Aristotle long ago pointed out, in its Greek near-equivalent *physis* – is by no means a merely accidental product of etymological confusions or conflations: it faithfully reflects the hesitancies, the doubts and the uncertainties, with which men have confronted the world around them. For my special purposes, it is enough to say, I shall be using the word 'nature' in one of its narrower senses – so as to include only that which, setting aside the supernatural, is human neither in itself nor in its origins. This is the sense in which neither Sir Christopher Wren nor St Paul's Cathedral

forms part of 'nature' and it may be hard to decide whether an oddly shaped flint or a landscape where the trees are evenly spaced is or is not 'natural'. The question I am raising, then, is what our attitudes have been, and ought to be, to nature in this narrow sense of the word, in which it excludes both the human and the artificial. And more narrowly still, I shall be devoting most of my attention to our attitudes towards that part of nature which it lies within man's power to modify and, in particular, towards what Karl Barth calls 'the strange life of beasts and plants which lies around us', a life we can by our actions destroy.

In what respect is animal and plant life 'strange'? The attitudes of human beings to other human

From R. S. Peters, ed., *Nature and Conduct* (London: Macmillan Press, 1975), pp. 251–64. © 1975 by Royal Institute of Philosophy. Reprinted with permission from Palgrave Macmillan.

beings are themselves variable and complicated; our fellow human beings often act in ways which are, in our eyes, strange. But there are ways of dealing with human beings which fail us when we confront nature. We can argue with human beings, expostulate with them, try to alter their courses by remonstration or by entreaty. No doubt there are human beings of whom this is not true: the hopelessly insane. And just for that reason there has been a tendency to exclude them from humanity, in some societies as supernatural beings, in others as mere animals: old Bedlam was, indeed, a kind of zoo. The psychopath, immune to argument or entreaty, arouses in us a quite peculiar fear and horror. As for artefacts, these admittedly we cannot modify in the ways in which we modify human beings; it is pointless to entreat a building to move out of the way of our car. But we understand them as playing a designed part in a form of human behaviour which we might, in principle, attempt to modify; we look through them to their human makers. When this is not so, when we encounter what clearly seems to be an artefact but cannot guess in what way of life it played a part, we find it, like Stonehenge, 'uncanny'.

'Strange', as Karl Barth uses the word, connotes not only unfamiliar but foreign, alien. (The uneducated find any foreigner 'uncanny' because they cannot communicate with him – to get him to act they have to *push* him like a natural object rather than speak to him.) That nature is thus alien, men have, of course, by no means always recognised. During most of their history they have thought of natural processes as having intentions and as capable of being influenced, exactly in the manner of human beings, by prayer and entreaty – not by way of an anthropomorphically-conceived God but directly, immediately.

For the last two thousand years, however, the Graeco-Christian Western world has entirely rejected this conception of nature. At least, it has done so in its *official* science, technology and philosophy: the ordinary countryman was harder to convince that natural processes cannot have intentions, even when they are not so much as animal. As late as the nineteenth century German foresters thought it only prudent to explain to a tree they were about to fell exactly why it had to be cut down. In Ibsen's *Wild Duck*, Old Ekdal is convinced that the forest will 'seek revenge' for having been too ruthlessly thinned; in Büchner's *Woyzeck* a countryman explains the drowning of a man in a river by telling his companion

the river had been seeking a victim for a long time past. (Recall the familiar newspaper metaphor: a dangerous stretch of coast 'claims another victim'.)

Such attitudes, I believe, still exert an influence; in some of the recent ecological literature, the view that nature 'will have its revenge' on mankind for their misdeeds operates as something more than a metaphor, just as old ideas of pollution, sacrilege, *hubris*, are still, in such writings, potent concepts.

The fact remains that the Stoic-Christian tradition has insisted on the absolute uniqueness of man, a uniqueness particularly manifest, according to Christianity, in the fact that he alone, in Karl Barth's words, has been 'addressed by God' and can therefore be saved or damned but also, in the Stoic-Christian tradition as a whole, apparent in his capacity for rational communication. If nature, on that view, is not wholly strange, this is only because it has been created by God for men to use. Animals and plants can for that reason be assimilated, at least in certain respects, to the class of tools, dumb beasts but none the less obedient to men's will. Peter Lombard summed up the traditional Christian view in his *Sentences*: 'As man is made for the sake of God, namely that he may serve him, so is the world made for the sake of man, that it may serve him.' So although nature is 'alien' in so far as it is not rational, it is for orthodoxy neither hostile nor indifferent, appearances to the contrary notwithstanding. Every natural process exists either as an aid to men materially or as a spiritual guide, recalling, as flood or volcano or tempest, their corrupt state.

In this doctrine, which they trace back to the Old Testament, the ecologically-minded critics of Western culture discern the roots of its destructiveness. This is a mistake on two accounts. First, that everything exists to serve man is certainly not the regular teaching of the Old Testament, which constantly insists that, in the words of the Book of Job, God 'causes it to rain on the earth, where no man is; on the wilderness, wherein there is no man; to satisfy the desolate and the waste ground; and to cause the bud of the tender herb to spring forth'. To Paul's rhetorical question: 'Doth God care for oxen?' an Old Testament Jew would have answered 'Yes, of course.' It was the Stoics who took the contrary view. And it is they, under the pretence that it was the Old Testament, who were followed by such influential Christian intellectuals as Origen. Secondly, the doctrine that 'everything is made for man' does not at once entail that man should go forth and transform the world. On the contrary, it was for centuries interpreted in a conservative fashion: God knows best what we need. To attempt to reshape what God has created is a form of presumption, of *hubris*. Sinful corrupt men ought not to attempt to reshape the world in their own image.

After the Crusades, Europe witnessed the development of the 'mechanical arts', as exemplified in the water-wheel, windmills, the compass, clocks. But these inventions were in many quarters condemned as diabolical. In a wonderful example of Heideggerian etymology, 'mechanical' was derived from 'moecha', an adulteress. God, so it was argued, had provided ready-made on earth all it was proper for men to desire. For them to seek to make their labours less onerous was to go directly against God's will, by attempting to construct a world which was as if Adam had never sinned.

Yet there is this much truth in the ecological diagnosis: the view that everything exists to serve man encouraged the development of a particular way of looking at nature, not as something to respect, but rather as something to utilise. Nature is in no sense sacred; this was a point on which Christian theology and Greek cosmology agreed. God, no doubt, could make particular places or objects sacred by choosing to take up residence in them, as in Roman Christianity he made sacred the sacrificial bread and wine. But no natural object was sacred in itself; there was no risk of sacrilege in felling a tree, or killing an animal. When Bacon set up as his ideal the transformation of nature – or, more accurately, the re-creation of the Garden of Eden – he had to fight the view that man was too corrupt to undertake any such task but not the view that nature was too sacred to be touched. It was man, he pointed out, whom God made in his own image, not nature.

When Christian apologists see in science and technology the product of a distinctively Christian civilisation, they are so far right: Christianity taught men that there was nothing sacrilegious either in analysing or in modifying nature. But only when Christianity modified its belief in original sin, only when it became, in practice, Pelagian could it witness without disapproval, let alone positively encourage, the attempt to create on earth a new nature, more suitable to human needs. Locke's vigorous attack on original sin – explicit in his theological writings, implicit in the *Essay* – formed part of his task as an under-labourer, clearing away obstacles to the transformation of nature – and man – by man.

Associated with the Christian concept of nature was a particular ethical thesis: that no moral considerations bear upon man's relationship to natural objects, except where they happen to be someone else's property or except where to treat them cruelly or destructively might encourage corresponding attitudes towards other human beings. This thesis the Stoics had strongly maintained and it was no less warmly advocated by Augustine. Jesus, Augustine argues, drove the devils into swine – innocent though the swine were of any crime – instead of destroying them, as a lesson to men that they may do as they like with animals. Not even cruelty to animals, so Aquinas tells us, is wrong in itself. 'If any passage in Holy Scripture seems to forbid us to be cruel to brute animals that is either . . . lest through being cruel to animals one becomes cruel to human beings or because injury to animals leads to the temporal hurt of man.' In other words, cruelty to animals is wrong only in virtue of its effects on human beings, as Kant, in this same tradition, still maintained in the final decades of the eighteenth century. And what is true of cruelty to animals applies, on this view, even more obviously to our dealings with other members of the non-human world. Only in Jewish, or Jewish-inspired, speculation, was the opposite view at all widespread. The Talmud in several places advocates a more considerate attitude to nature and when Kant reaffirms the traditional position it is in opposition to Baumgarten, who had on this question followed the Talmud.

The question whether it is intrinsically wrong to be cruel to animals has an importance much greater than at first sight appears: it is precisely for that reason that philosophers like Kant, humane though they certainly were, insist that cruelty to animals is wrong only on the – in fact very dubious – empirical hypothesis that it encourages cruelty to human beings. For if cruelty to animals is intrinsically wrong, then it is *not* morally indifferent how men behave towards nature; in at least one case – and then perhaps in others – man's relationship with nature ought to be governed by moral considerations which are not reducible to a concern for purely human interests, to a duty either to others or, as Kant thought, to oneself.

There is one simple and decisive way of denying that it is wrong unnecessarily to cause suffering to animals, namely by denying that animals can in fact suffer. This is the step Descartes took. The philosophy of Descartes represents, in certain respects, the culmination of the tendency of Graeco-Christian thought to differentiate man from his fellow-animals. For Descartes denies that animals can so much as feel, let alone exercise intelligence. (One is forcibly reminded at this point of the Ciceronian dictum, to which he subscribes, that there is no doctrine so absurd but that some philosopher has held it.) All suffering, so his follower Malebranche tells us, is the result of Adam's sin: animals, as not implicated in that sin, cannot suffer. As a result of our actions animals do not *really* suffer, they only behave exactly as if they suffered – a doctrine that some of the Stoics had also managed to believe. So it is not only wrong to suppose that we can reason with animals but wrong to suppose, even, that we can sympathise with them. It is true that this conclusion was reached at the cost of placing the human body itself within nature, as something not sacred; what was left outside nature was only consciousness. Yet at the same time the human body was for Descartes unique in being in some way 'united' with consciousness; the human person, conjoining mind and body, could thus be set in total opposition to the non-human world it encounters.

So the Cartesian dualism could be used, and was used, to justify the view that, in his relationships with nature, man was not subject to any moral curbs. Yet at the same time Descartes broke this doctrine loose from its historical association with the view that everything is made for man's use – a view he characterised as 'childish and absurd'. It was, he thought, *obvious* that 'an infinitude of things exist, or did exist, which have never been beheld or comprehended by any man and which have never been of any use to him'. No doubt, man could in fact make use of what he found in nature, and he ought indeed to do so, but nature did not exist as something ready-made for him. Effectively to use it, he had first to transform it. One is not surprised, then, to find Descartes proclaiming that it is man's task 'to make himself master and possessor of nature'; the proper attitude to the world, in his eyes, is exploitative. The paradigmatic case of a material substance is, for Descartes, a piece of wax, the traditional symbol of malleability.

Like Bacon before him he also suggests a particular method of exploitation, what he calls a 'practical philosophy', what we should call a 'science-based technology'. So far as we can make natural processes less 'strange', the assumption is, this is only by first bringing them under concepts which are either inherent in or created by human reason and then using this conceptual grasp to make them work in a manner more conformable with human interests. This is the attitude to nature which has dominated Western science: understanding through laws, transformation through technology.

The philosophy of science associated with this enterprise has been, in certain important respects, Platonic. 'Understanding' has been identified with the discovery of mathematically expressible functional relationships between abstractly-conceived processes and objects. Science, so it is then said, is not about the particular things we see and attempt to cope with in the world around us, except in a rather indirect way. The physics textbook talks about everyday natural objects only in its description of experimental set-ups. And physics is presumed to be science in its ideal form. Rutherford's notorious description of science as 'physics and stamp-collecting' expresses this attitude very precisely; natural history, the direct investigation of nature in a manner which is content to describe qualitative relationships between everyday natural objects and processes, is condemned as mere 'stamp-collecting'. Only a third-rate mind, the presumption is, could devote itself to studying, let us say, the life-history of the whale. To be what Plato calls 'a lover of sights and sounds', to take delight in the flight of birds as such as distinct from the mathematical problems set by that flight, is at once to show oneself an inferior, sensual, being.

Of course, this attitude to nature has always had its critics. Poets like Blake protested against it; painting, before painters, too, were beguiled into pure geometry, drew attention, sensually, to the forms and colours in the world around us. Biologists like John Ray emphasised against Descartes the importance of the multiplicity and diversity of forms of life. But the mainstream of science has been Cartesian-Platonic.

Philosophers, however, were generally unhappy with Cartesian dualism, for reasons which practising scientists found, and still find, it difficult to understand. Descartes, so philosophers argued, had separated consciousness from nature so absolutely that the two could no longer be brought into any relationship with one another. In general, if in very different ways, they reacted against Descartes by trying to maintain that nature was a great deal more human-like than Descartes had been prepared to admit. But they did so, in many cases, at the cost of denying to nature a wholly independent existence, or, at best, by treating independent nature as a sort of 'thing in itself', not as the nature we encounter and try to deal with in our everyday life.

[. . .]

Associated with this attitude to nature is a depreciation of natural beauty as vastly inferior to works of art: the feeling one finds in classical literature and which is still enunciated by Hegel that nature deserves appreciation only when it has been transformed into a farm, a garden, and so has lost its wildness, its strangeness. It was a common theme in Christian thought that the world had been created a perfect globe; nature as we now see it with its mountains and its valleys is a dismal ruin, a melancholy reminder of Adam's sin. [. . .]

[. . .]

It is easy to see from this brief historical excursus why the ecological critics of Western civilization are now pleading for a new religion, a new ethics, a new aesthetics, a new metaphysics. One could readily imagine a sardonic history of Western philosophy which would depict it as a long attempt to allay men's fears, their insecurities, by persuading them that natural processes do not represent any real threat, either because they are completely malleable to human pressures, or because men are ultimately safe in a universe designed to secure their interests – an enterprise which issued in wilder and wilder absurdities in a desperate attempt to deny the obvious facts. This would not be a wholly accurate history of philosophy; even phenomenalism has its merits as the *reductio ad absurdum* of the plausible-looking theory of perception. Philosophy, as we have already suggested, had good reasons for rejecting the Cartesian dualism even if its reasons are less good for replacing it with a new version of anthropocentrism. At the same time, to think of philosophy thus is not an entirely monstrous interpretation; it is quite understandable that philosophy should look like an apologia for anthropocentrism to those who now so urgently emphasise man's responsibility for nature. Western metaphysics and Western ethics have certainly done nothing to discourage, have done a great deal to encourage, the ruthless exploitation of nature, whether they have seen in that exploitation the rightful manipulation of a nature which is wax in man's hands or the humanising of it in a manner which somehow accords with nature's real interests.

As philosophers, of course, we cannot merely acquiesce in the demand for a new metaphysics or a new ethics on the simple ground that the widespread acceptance of the older metaphysics, the older ethics, has encouraged the exploitation of nature – any more than a biologist would acquiesce in the demand for a new biology if that demand were grounded merely on the fact, or alleged fact, that men would be less inclined to act in ecologically destructive ways if they were persuaded that all living things possessed a developed brain. The philosopher is unlikely to be at all satisfied, in particular, with the demand of the primitivist wing of the ecological movement that he should encourage man to revert to the belief that nature is sacred. We are in fact *right* in condemning as superstitious the belief that trees, rivers, volcanoes, can be swayed by arguments; we are *right* in believing that we have found in science ways of understanding their behaviour; we are *right* in regarding civilisation as important and thus far in attempting to transform nature. It is not by abandoning our hard-won tradition of rationality that we shall save ourselves.

We can, however, properly ask ourselves what general conditions any philosophy of nature must fulfil if it is to do justice to the scientific themes of the ecological movement, as distinct from its reactionary, mystical, overtones. Any satisfactory philosophy of nature, we can then say, must recognise:

1 That natural processes go on in their own way, in a manner indifferent to human interests and by no means incompatible with man's total disappearance from the face of the earth.

2 When men act on nature, they do not simply modify a particular quality of a particular substance. What they do, rather, is to interact with a system of interactions, setting in process new interactions. Just for that reason, there is always a risk that their actions will have consequences which they did not predict.

3 In our attempt to understand nature the discovery of physics-type general laws is often of very limited importance. The complaint that biology and sociology are inferior because they know no such laws can be reversed, formulated as an argument against an undue emphasis on a Platonic-Cartesian analysis of 'understanding'. When it comes to understanding either biological or social structures, we can then say, what is important is a detailed understanding of very specific circumstances rather than a knowledge of high-level functional relationships. The 'laws' involved are often trite and ill-formulated, serving only as boundaries to what is possible. Whales, to revert

to my previous example, must like every other animal, eat and breed; we can describe it, if we like, as a 'biological law' that every animal must ingest food and must have a way of reproducing itself. But these 'laws' leave almost everything of interest about whales still to be discovered.

One could put the general conditions I have laid down by saying that in an important sense the philosopher has to learn to live with the 'strangeness' of nature, with the fact that natural processes are entirely indifferent to our existence and welfare – not *positively* indifferent, of course, but *incapable* of caring about us – and are complex in a way that rules out the possibility of our wholly mastering and transforming them. So expressed, these conclusions sound so trite and obvious that one is almost ashamed to set them out. But, from what has already been said, it will be obvious that they have not been satisfied in most of the traditional philosophies of nature. To that degree it is true, I think, that we do need a 'new metaphysics' which is genuinely not anthropocentric and which takes change and complexity with the seriousness they deserve. It must certainly not think of natural processes either as being dependent upon man for their existence, as infinitely malleable, or as being so constructed as to guarantee the continued survival of human beings and their civilisation.

Such a philosophy of nature, of course, would be by no means entirely new. Its foundations have been laid in the various forms of naturalism. Naturalistic philosophies, however, like the Darwinian biology which lends them support, often attempt to reduce the 'strangeness' of nature – even if they do this by naturalising man rather than by spiritualising nature. That way of using the word 'nature' which I have so far employed is, so many naturalistic philosophers would say, wholly misleading; we should think of 'nature' only as something of which man forms part, not alien to him because he is a full member of it. And, of course, I should agree with the naturalistic philosophers that, in a very important sense of the word 'nature', both man and human artefacts form part of nature: they are subject to natural laws. Nature does not have that *metaphysical* 'strangeness' which Descartes ascribed to it. Both senses of 'nature', however, have a particular role to play; they are important in different types of discussion. Naturalistic philosophers are sometimes tempted into reductionism, tempted into denying that our dealings with our fellow-men differ in any important respect from our dealings with other things, that nature is any 'stranger' than those of our fellow human beings with whom we are not fully acquainted. This is a temptation which has to be resisted. It is not anthropocentric to think of human beings and what they create as having a peculiar value and importance, or to suggest that human beings have unique ways of relating to one another – most notably through their capacity for asserting and denying, but also because, as the existentialists argue, they are unique in their concern for, and about, the future. For many purposes, it is not arbitrary, but essential, to contrast the human with what is not human – with the 'natural' in the limited special sense of the word.

So it will not do to argue, for example, that what has happened in the world is just that man as the dominant species is destroying, in normal biological competition, competitive species, and that to repine at the disappearance of these species is as absurd as it would be to complain that the world no longer contains dinosaurs. It is perfectly true that like any other species men can survive only at the cost of other species. But men can see what is happening: they can observe the disappearance of competing species; they can consider what the effects of that disappearance will be; they can – at least in principle – preserve a species and modify their own behaviour so that it will be less destructive. That in many ways, fundamental ways, men are *not* unique is the starting point for any satisfactory metaphysics. But in other ways they are. A 'new metaphysics', if it is not to falsify the facts, will have to be naturalistic, but not reductionist. The working out of such a metaphysics is, in my judgement, the most important task which lies ahead of philosophy.

What of the contention that the West now needs a new ethics, with responsibility for nature lying at its centre? This, too, is often carried further than I am prepared to follow it. Men need to recognise, it is then suggested, that they 'form a community' with plants, animals, the biosphere, and that every member of that community has rights – including the right to live and the right to be treated with respect. In opposition to any such doctrine, the Stoics long ago argued that civilization would be quite impossible, that indeed human beings could not even survive, if men were bound to act justly in relation to nature. Primitivists would reverse this argument; since civilization depends upon men acting unjustly towards nature, civilization ought, they would argue, to be abandoned. Men, so Porphyry for one maintained, ought to reduce their claims to the barest minimum, surviving, under these minimal circumstances, on nothing but the fruits which plants do not need for *their* survival.

Even the fruits a plant does not need, however, may be needed by a variety of micro-organisms; men cannot survive, as I have already suggested, except by being in some degree a predator. As Hume said, it is one thing to maintain that men ought to act *humanely* towards animals, quite another to maintain that they ought to act *justly* towards them. The first of these doctrines rests on no more elaborate assumption than that animals suffer; the second doctrine rests on the much less plausible assumption that animals have claims or interests in a sense which makes the notion of justice applicable to them. Some moral philosophers [. . .] have taken this view. But I am not convinced that it is appropriate to speak of animals as having 'interests' unless 'interests' are identified with *needs* – and to have needs, as a plant, too, has needs, is by no means the same thing as to have rights. It is one thing to say that it is wrong to treat plants and animals in a certain manner, quite another thing to say that they have a *right* to be treated differently.

No doubt, men, plants, animals, the biosphere, form parts of a single community in the ecological sense of the word; each is dependent upon the others for its continued existence. But this is not the sense of community which generates rights, duties, obligations; men and animals are not involved in a network of responsibilities or a network of mutual concessions. That is why nature, even within a naturalistic philosophy, is still 'strange', alien.

To a not inconsiderable degree, it can be added, very familiar ethical principles are quite strong enough to justify action against ecological despoilers. We do not need the help of a 'new ethics' in order to justify our blaming those who make our rivers into sewers and our air unbreathable, who give birth to children in an over-populated world or – this is a little more disputable – who waste resources which posterity will need. Only where specifically human interests are not so obviously involved does the question of a 'new ethics' so much as arise. Even the preservation of wild species and of wildernesses can largely be defended in a familiar utilitarian fashion.

What has certainly to be dropped, nevertheless, is the Augustinian doctrine that in his dealings with nature man is simply not subject to moral censure, except where specifically human interests arise. Few moral philosophers would now accept that view in its original unrestricted form. It is, indeed, very striking with what unanimity they condemn the older doctrine that cruelty to animals is morally wrong only when it does direct harm to human beings. Their predecessors, they say, were guilty of moral blindness, a blindness with theological origins, in not seeing that it was wrong to cause animals unnecessarily to suffer. The question remains, however, whether moral philosophers are not still to some extent 'morally blind' in their attitudes to nature and especially to those parts of nature which are not sentient and therefore do not suffer.

Certainly, they – and we – have a tendency to restrict such condemnatory moral epithets as vandalism and philistinism to the destruction of property and indifference to works of art. On the face of it, however, the condemnation of vandalism is as applicable to those who damage or destroy the natural as it is to those who damage or destroy artefacts. When, for example, Baumgarten condemns what he calls 'the spirit of destruction' this has as much application to the wilful destruction of natural objects as it does to the wilful destruction of property, or of things likely to be useful to our fellow human beings. The last man on earth would for that reason be blameable were he to end his days in an orgy of destruction, even though his actions could not adversely affect any other human being.

Similarly, a failure to appreciate the natural scene is as serious a human weakness as a failure to appreciate works of art. Once we fully free ourselves from the Augustinian doctrine that nature exists only as something to be used, not enjoyed, the extension of such moral notions as vandalism and philistinism to man's relationship with trees and landscapes will seem as obvious as the extension of the idea of cruelty to man's relationships with animals. It is the great importance of Romanticism that it partly saw this and encouraged us to *look* at nature, to see it otherwise than as a mere instrument. But we do not need to accept the Romantic identification of God with nature in order to accept this way of looking at the world. Indeed, the divinisation of nature, even apart from the philosophical problems it raises, dangerously underestimates the *fragility* of so many natural processes and relationships, a fragility to which the ecological movement has drawn such forcible attention.

In general, if we can bring ourselves fully to admit the independence of nature, the fact that things go on in their own complex ways, we are likely to feel more respect for the ways in which they go on. We are prepared to contemplate them with admiration, to enjoy them sensuously, to study them in their complexity as distinct from looking for simple methods of manipulating them. The suggestion that we *cannot* do this, that, inevitably, so long as we think of nature as 'strange', we cannot, as Hegel thought, take any interest in it or feel any concern for it underestimates the degree to which we can overcome egoism and achieve disinterestedness. The emergence of new moral attitudes to nature is bound up, then, with the emergence of a more realistic philosophy of nature. That is the only adequate foundation for effective ecological concern.

Note

1   This paper is an attempt to bring together and to reformulate some of the basic philosophical themes in my *Man's Responsibility for Nature* (Duckworth and Charles Scribner, 1974). It should properly be pockmarked with references. Those who are interested will find most of the historical references fully annotated in my book.

---

13   Should Trees Have Standing? Toward Legal Rights for Natural Objects

---

Christopher D. Stone

Introduction: The Unthinkable

In *Descent of Man*, Darwin observes that the history of man's moral development has been a continual extension in the objects of his "social instincts and sympathies." Originally each man had regard only for himself and those of a very narrow circle about him; later, he came to regard more and more "not only the welfare, but the happiness of all his fellowmen"; then "his sympathies became more tender and widely diffused, extending to men of all races, to the imbecile, maimed, and other useless members of society, and finally to the lower animals. . . ."[1] The history of the law suggests a parallel development. Perhaps there never was a pure Hobbesian state of nature, in which no "rights" existed except in the vacant sense of each man's "right to self-defense." But it is not unlikely that so far as the earliest "families" (including extended kinship groups and clans) were concerned, everyone outside the family was suspect, alien, rightless. And even within the family, persons we presently regard as the natural holders of at least some rights had none. Take, for example, children. We know something of the early rights-status of children from the widespread practice of infanticide – especially of the deformed and female.[3] (Senicide,[4] as among the North American Indians, was the corresponding rightlessness of the aged).[5] Maine tells us that as late as the Patria Potestas of the Romans, the father had *jus vitae necisque* – the power of life and death – over his children. A fortiori, Maine writes, he had power of "uncontrolled corporal chastisement; he can modify their personal condition at pleasure; he can give a wife to his son; he can give his daughter in marriage; he can divorce his children of either sex; he can transfer them to another family by adoption; and he can sell them." The child was less than a person: an object, a thing.[6]

The legal rights of children have long since been recognized in principle, and are still expanding in practice. Witness, just within recent time, *In re Gault*,[7] guaranteeing basic constitutional protections to juvenile defendants, and the Voting Rights Act of 1970.[8] We have been making persons of children although they were not, in law, always so. And we have done the same, albeit imperfectly some would say, with prisoners,[9] aliens, women

From *Southern California Law Review*, vol. 45 (1972), extracts from pp. 450–87. © 1972 by *Southern California Law Review*. Reprinted with permission of the *Southern California Law Review*.

(especially of the married variety), the insane,[10] Blacks, foetuses,[11] and Indians.

Nor is it only matter in human form that has come to be recognized as the possessor of rights. The world of the lawyer is peopled with inanimate right-holders: trusts, corporations, joint ventures, municipalities, Subchapter R partnerships,[12] and nation-states, to mention just a few. Ships, still referred to by courts in the feminine gender, have long had an independent jural life, often with striking consequences.[13] We have become so accustomed to the idea of a corporation having "its" own rights, and being a "person" and "citizen" for so many statutory and constitutional purposes, that we forget how jarring the notion was to early jurists. "That invisible, intangible and artificial being, that mere legal entity" Chief Justice Marshall wrote of the corporation in *Bank of the United States v. Deveaux*[14] – could a suit be brought in *its* name? Ten years later, in the *Dartmouth College* case,[15] he was still refusing to let pass unnoticed the wonder of an entity "existing only in contemplation of law."[16] Yet, long before Marshall worried over the personifying of the modern corporation, the best medieval legal scholars had spent hundreds of years struggling with the notion of the legal nature of those great public "corporate bodies," the Church and the State. How could they exist in law, as entities transcending the living Pope and King? It was clear how a king could bind *himself* – on his honor – by a treaty. But when the king died, what was it that was burdened with the obligations of, and claimed the rights under, the treaty *his* tangible hand had signed? The medieval mind saw (what we have lost our capacity to see)[17] how *unthinkable* it was, and worked out the most elaborate conceits and fallacies to serve as anthropomorphic flesh for the Universal Church and the Universal Empire.[18]

It is this note of the *unthinkable* that I want to dwell upon for a moment. Throughout legal history, each successive extension of rights to some new entity has been, theretofore, a bit unthinkable. We are inclined to suppose the rightlessness of rightless "things" to be a decree of Nature, not a legal convention acting in support of some status quo. It is thus that we defer considering the choices involved in all their moral, social, and economic dimensions. And so the United States Supreme Court could straight-facedly tell us in *Dred Scott* that Blacks had been denied the rights of citizenship "as a subordinate and inferior class of beings, who had been subjugated by the dominant race. . .."[19]

[. . .]

The fact is, that each time there is a movement to confer rights onto some new "entity," the proposal is bound to sound odd or frightening or laughable.[20] This is partly because until the rightless thing receives its rights, we cannot see it as anything but a *thing* for the use of "us" – those who are holding rights at the time.[21] [. . .]

The reason for this little discourse on the unthinkable, the reader must know by now, if only from the title of the paper. I am quite seriously proposing that we give legal rights to forests, oceans, rivers and other so-called "natural objects" in the environment – indeed, to the natural environment as a whole.[22]

[. . .]

Toward Having Standing in its Own Right

It is not inevitable, nor is it wise, that natural objects should have no rights to seek redress in their own behalf. It is no answer to say that streams and forests cannot have standing because streams and forests cannot speak. Corporations cannot speak either; nor can states, estates, infants, incompetents, municipalities or universities. Lawyers speak for them, as they customarily do for the ordinary citizen with legal problems. One ought, I think, to handle the legal problems of natural objects as one does the problems of legal incompetents – human beings who have become vegetable. If a human being shows signs of becoming senile and has affairs that he is de jure incompetent to manage, those concerned with his well being make such a showing to the court, and someone is designated by the court with the authority to manage the incompetent's affairs. The guardian[23] (or "conservator"[24] or "committee"[25] – the terminology varies) then represents the incompetent in his legal affairs. Courts make similar appointments when a corporation has become "incompetent" – they appoint a trustee in bankruptcy or reorganization to oversee its affairs and speak for it in court when that becomes necessary.

On a parity of reasoning, we should have a system in which, when a friend of a natural object perceives it to be endangered, he can apply to a court for the creation of a guardianship.[26] Perhaps we already have the machinery to do so. California law, for example, defines an incompetent as "any person, whether insane or not, who by reason of old age, disease, weakness of mind, or other cause, is unable, unassisted, properly to manage and take care of himself or his property, and by reason thereof is likely to be deceived or imposed upon by artful or designing persons."[27] Of course, to urge a court that an endangered river is "a person" under this provision will call for lawyers as bold and imaginative as those who convinced the Supreme Court that a railroad corporation was a "person" under the fourteenth amendment, a constitutional provision theretofore generally thought of as designed to secure the rights of freedmen.[28] (As this article was going to press, Professor Byrn of Fordham petitioned the New York Supreme Court to appoint him legal guardian for an unrelated foetus scheduled for abortion so as to enable him to bring a class action on behalf of all foetuses similarly situated in New York City's 18 municipal hospitals. Judge Holtzman granted the petition of guardianship.[29]) If such an argument based on present statutes should fail, special environmental legislation could be enacted along traditional guardianship lines. Such provisions could provide for guardianship both in the instance of public natural objects and also, perhaps with slightly different standards, in the instance of natural objects on "private" land.[30]

The potential "friends" that such a statutory scheme would require will hardly be lacking. The Sierra Club, Environmental Defense Fund, Friends of the Earth, Natural Resources Defense Counsel, and the Izaak Walton League are just some of the many groups which have manifested unflagging dedication to the environment and which are becoming increasingly capable of marshalling the requisite technical experts and lawyers. If, for example, the Environmental Defense Fund should have reason to believe that some company's strip mining operations might be irreparably destroying the ecological balance of large tracts of land, it could, under this procedure, apply to the court in which the lands were situated to be appointed guardian.[31] As guardian, it might be given rights of inspection (or visitation) to determine and bring to the court's attention a fuller finding on the land's condition. If there were indications that under the substantive law some redress might be available on the land's behalf, then the guardian would be entitled to raise the land's rights in the land's name, i.e., without having to make the roundabout and often unavailing demonstration, discussed below, that the "rights" of the club's members were being invaded. Guardians would also be

looked to for a host of other protective tasks, e.g., monitoring effluents (and/or monitoring the monitors), and representing their "wards" at legislative and administrative hearings on such matters as the setting of state water quality standards. Procedures exist, and can be strengthened, to move a court for the removal and substitution of guardians, for conflicts of interest or for other reasons,[32] as well as for the termination of the guardianship.[33]

In point of fact, there is a movement in the law toward giving the environment the benefits of standing, although not in a manner as satisfactory as the guardianship approach. What I am referring to is the marked liberalization of traditional standing requirements in recent cases in which environmental action groups have challenged federal government action. Scenic Hudson Preservation Conference v. FPC[34] is a good example of this development. There, the Federal Power Commission had granted New York's Consolidated Edison a license to construct a hydroelectric project on the Hudson River at Storm King Mountain. The grant of license had been opposed by conservation interests on the grounds that the transmission lines would be unsightly, fish would be destroyed, and nature trails would be inundated. Two of these conservation groups, united under the name Scenic Hudson Preservation Conference, petitioned the Second Circuit to set aside the grant. Despite the claim that Scenic Hudson had no standing because it had not made the traditional claim "of any personal economic injury resulting from the Commission's actions,"[35] the petitions were heard, and the case sent back to the Commission. On the standing point, the court noted that Section 313(b) of the Federal Power Act gave a right of instituting review to any party "aggrieved by an order issued by the Commission";[36] it thereupon read "aggrieved by" as not limited to those alleging the traditional personal economic injury, but as broad enough to include "those who by their activities and conduct have exhibited a special interest" in "the aesthetic, conservational, and recreational aspects of power development."[37]

[. . .]

Unlike the liberalized standing approach, the guardianship approach would secure an effective voice for the environment even where federal administrative action and public-lands and waters were not involved. It would also allay one of the fears courts – such as the Ninth Circuit – have about the extended standing concept: if any ad hoc group can spring up overnight, invoke some "right" as universally claimable as the esthetic and recreational interests of its members and thereby get into court, how can a flood of litigation be prevented?[38] If an ad hoc committee loses a suit brought *sub nom.* Committee to Preserve our Trees, what happens when its very same members reorganize two years later and sue *sub nom.* The Massapequa Sylvan Protection League? Is the new group bound by res judicata? Class action law may be capable of ameliorating some of the more obvious problems. But even so, court economy might be better served by simply designating the guardian de jure representative of the natural object, with rights of discretionary intervention by others, but with the understanding that the natural object is "bound" by an adverse judgment.[39] The guardian concept, too, would provide the endangered natural object with what the trustee in bankruptcy provides the endangered corporation: a continuous supervision over a period of time, with a consequent deeper understanding of a broad range of the ward's problems, not just the problems present in one particular piece of litigation. It would thus assure the courts that the plaintiff has the expertise and genuine adversity in pressing a claim which are the prerequisites of a true "case or controversy."

The guardianship approach, however, is apt to raise two objections, neither of which seems to me to have much force. The first is that a committee or guardian could not judge the needs of the river or forest in its charge; indeed, the very concept of "needs," it might be said, could be used here only in the most metaphorical way. The second objection is that such a system would not be much different from what we now have: is not the Department of Interior already such a guardian for public lands, and do not most states have legislation empowering their attorneys general to seek relief – in a sort of *parens patriae* way – for such injuries as a guardian might concern himself with?

As for the first objection, natural objects *can* communicate their wants (needs) to us, and in ways that are not terribly ambiguous. I am sure I can judge with more certainty and meaningfulness whether and when my lawn wants (needs) water, than the Attorney General can judge whether and when the United States wants (needs) to take an appeal from an adverse judgment by a lower court. The lawn tells me that it wants water by a certain dryness of the blades and soil – immediately obvious to the touch – the appearance of bald spots, yellowing, and a lack of

springiness after being walked on; how does "the United States" communicate to the Attorney General? For similar reasons, the guardian-attorney for a smog-endangered stand of pines could venture with more confidence that his client wants the smog stopped, than the directors of a corporation can assert that "the corporation" wants dividends declared. We make decisions on behalf of, and in the purported interests of, others every day; these "others" are often creatures whose wants are far less verifiable, and even far more metaphysical in conception, than the wants of rivers, trees, and land.[40]

As for the second objection, one can indeed find evidence that the Department of Interior was conceived as a sort of guardian of the public lands.[41] But there are two points to keep in mind. First, insofar as the Department already is an adequate guardian it is only with respect to the federal public lands as per Article IV, section 3 of the Constitution.[42] Its guardianship includes neither local public lands nor private lands. Second, to judge from the environmentalist literature and from the cases environmental action groups have been bringing, the Department is itself one of the bogeys of the environmental movement. (One thinks of the uneasy peace between the Indians and the Bureau of Indian Affairs.) Whether the various charges be right or wrong, one cannot help but observe that the Department has been charged with several institutional goals (never an easy burden), and is currently looked to for action by quite a variety of interest groups, only one of which is the environmentalists. In this context, a guardian outside the institution becomes especially valuable. Besides, what a person wants, fully to secure his rights, is the ability to retain independent counsel even when, and perhaps especially when, the government is acting "for him" in a beneficent way. I have no reason to doubt, for example, that the Social Security System is being managed "for me"; but I would not want to abdicate my right to challenge its actions as they affect me, should the need arise.[43] I would not ask more trust of national forests, vis-à-vis the Department of Interior. The same considerations apply in the instance of local agencies, such as regional water pollution boards, whose members' expertise in pollution matters is often all too credible.[44]

The objection regarding the availability of attorneys-general as protectors of the environment within the existing structure is somewhat the same. Their statutory powers are limited and sometimes unclear. As political creatures, they must exercise the discretion they have with an eye toward advancing and reconciling a broad variety of important social goals, from preserving morality to increasing their jurisdiction's tax base. The present state of our environment, and the history of cautious application and development of environmental protection laws long on the books,[45] testifies that the burdens of an attorney-general's broad responsibility have apparently not left much manpower for the protection of nature. No doubt, strengthening interest in the environment will increase the zest of public attorneys even where, as will often be the case, well-represented corporate pollutors are the quarry. Indeed, the United States Attorney-General has stepped up anti-pollution activity, and ought to be further encouraged in this direction.[46] The statutory powers of the attorneys-general should be enlarged, and they should be armed with criminal penalties made at least commensurate with the likely economic benefits of violating the law.[47] On the other hand, one cannot ignore the fact that there is increased pressure on public law-enforcement offices to give more attention to a host of other problems, from crime "on the streets" (why don't we say "in the rivers"?) to consumerism and school bussing. If the environment is not to get lost in the shuffle, we would do well, I think, to adopt the guardianship approach as an additional safeguard, conceptualizing major natural objects as holders of their own rights, raisable by the court-appointed guardian.

[. . .]

The Psychic and Socio-Psychic Aspects

There are, as we have seen, a number of developments in the law that may reflect a shift from the view that nature exists *for men*. These range from increasingly favorable procedural rulings for environmental action groups – as regards standing and burden of proof requirements, for example – to the enactment of comprehensive legislation such as the National Environmental Policy Act and the thoughtful Michigan Environmental Protection Act of 1970. Of such developments one may say, however, that it is not the environment *per se* that we are prepared to take into account, but that man's increased awareness of possible long range effects on himself militate in the direction of stopping environmental harm in its incipiency. And this is part of the truth, of course.

Even the far-reaching National Environmental Policy Act, in its preambulatory "Declaration of National Environmental Policy," comes out both for "restoring and maintaining environmental quality *to the overall welfare and development of man*" as well as for creating and maintaining "conditions under which *man and nature can exist in productive harmony.*"[48] Because the health and well-being of mankind depend upon the health of the environment, these goals will often be so mutually supportive that one can avoid deciding whether our rationale is to advance "us" or a new "us" that includes the environment. For example, consider the Federal Insecticide, Fungicide, and Rodenticide Act (FIFRA) which insists that, *e.g.*, pesticides, include a warning "adequate to prevent injury to living man and other vertebrate animals, vegetation, and useful invertebrate animals." Such a provision undoubtedly reflects the sensible notion that the protection of humans is best accomplished by preventing dangerous accumulations in the food chain. Its enactment does not necessarily augur far-reaching changes in, nor even call into question, fundamental matters of consciousness.

[. . .] For my part, I would prefer a frank avowal that even making adjustments for esthetic improvements, what I am proposing is going to cost "us," *i.e.*, reduce our standard of living as measured in terms of our present values.

Yet, this frankness breeds a frank response – one which I hear from my colleagues and which must occur to many a reader. Insofar as the proposal is not just an elaborate legal fiction, but really comes down in the last analysis to a compromise of *our* interests for *theirs*, why should we adopt it? "What is in it for 'us'?"

This is a question I am prepared to answer, but only after permitting myself some observations about how *odd* the question is. It asks for me to justify my position in the very anthropocentric hedonist terms that I am proposing we modify. One is inclined to respond by a counter: "couldn't you (as a white) raise the same questions about compromising your preferred rights-status with Blacks?"; or "couldn't you (as a man) raise the same question about compromising your preferred rights-status with women?" Such counters, unfortunately, seem no more responsive than the question itself. (They have a nagging ring of "yours too" about them.) What the exchange actually points up is a fundamental problem regarding the nature of philosophical argument. Recall that Socrates, whom we remember as an opponent of hedonistic thought, confutes Thrasymachus by arguing that immorality makes one miserably unhappy! Kant, whose moral philosophy was based upon the categorical imperative ("Woe to him who creeps through the serpent windings of Utilitarianism"[49]) finds himself justifying, *e.g.*, promise keeping and truth telling, on the most prudential – one might almost say, commercial – grounds.[50] This "philosophic irony" (as Professor Engel calls it) may owe to there being something unique about ethical argument.[51] "Ethics cannot be put into words", Wittgenstein puts it; such matters "make themselves manifest."[52] On the other hand, perhaps the truth is that in any argument which aims at persuading a human being to action (on ethical or any other bases), "logic" is only an instrument for illuminating positions, at best, and in the last analysis it is psychological appeals to the listener's self-interest that hold sway, however "principled" the rhetoric may be.

With this reservation as to the peculiar task of the argument that follows, let me stress that the strongest case can be made from the perspective of human advantage for conferring rights on the environment. Scientists have been warning of the crises the earth and all humans on it face if we do not change our ways – radically – and these crises make the lost "recreational use" of rivers seem absolutely trivial. The earth's very atmosphere is threatened with frightening possibilities: absorption of sunlight, upon which the entire life cycle depends, may be diminished; the oceans may warm (increasing the "greenhouse effect" of the atmosphere), melting the polar ice caps, and destroying our great coastal cities; the portion of the atmosphere that shields us from dangerous radiation may be destroyed. Testifying before Congress, sea explorer Jacques Cousteau predicted that the oceans (to which we dreamily look to feed our booming populations) are headed toward their own death: "The cycle of life is intricately tied up with the cycle of water . . . the water system has to remain alive if we are to remain alive on earth."[53] We are depleting our energy and our food sources at a rate that takes little account of the needs even of humans now living.

These problems will not be solved easily; they very likely can be solved, if at all, only through a willingness to suspend the rate of increase in the standard of living (by present values) of the earth's "advanced" nations, and by stabilizing the total human population. For some of us this will involve forfeiting material comforts; for others it will involve abandoning the hope someday to obtain comforts long envied. For all of us it will involve giving up the right to have as many offspring as we might wish. Such a program is not impossible of realization, however. Many of our so-called "material comforts" are not only in excess of, but are probably in opposition to, basic biological needs. Further, the "costs" to the advanced nations is not as large as would appear from Gross National Product figures. GNP reflects social gain (of a sort) without discounting for the social *cost* of that gain, *e.g.*, the losses through depletion of resources, pollution, and so forth. As has well been shown, as societies become more and more "advanced," their real marginal gains become less and less for each additional dollar of GNP.[54] Thus, to give up "human progress" would not be as costly as might appear on first blush.

Notes

1 C. Darwin, *Descent of Man*, 119, 120–1 (2nd edn. 1874). See also R. Waelder, *Progress and Revolution*, 39 *et seq.* (1967).

2 See Darwin, *supra* note 1, at 113–14:

   . . . No tribe could hold together if murder, robbery, treachery, etc., were common; consequently such crimes within the limits of the same tribe "are branded with everlasting infamy"; but excite no such sentiment beyond these limits. A North-American Indian is well pleased with himself, and is honored by others, when he scalps a man of another tribe; and a Dyak cuts off the head of an unoffending person, and dries it as a trophy . . . It has been recorded that an Indian Thug conscientiously regretted that he had not robbed and strangled as many travelers as did his father before him. In a rude state of civilization the robbery of strangers is, indeed, generally considered as honorable.

   See also Service, "Forms of Kinship" in *Man in Adaptation*, 112 (Y. Cohen ed., 1968).

3 See Darwin, *supra* note 1, at 113. See also E. Westermarck, 1 *The Origin and Development of the Moral Ideas*, 406–12 (1912).

   The practice of allowing sickly children to die has not been entirely abandoned, apparently, even at our most distinguished hospitals. See "Hospital Let Retarded Baby Die, Film Shows," *LA Times*, Oct. 17, 1971, §A, at 9, col. 1.

4 There does not appear to be a word "gericide" or "geronticide" to designate the killing of the aged. "Senicide" is as close as the Oxford English Dictionary

comes, although, as it indicates, the word is rare. 9 *Oxford English Dictionary*, 454 (1933).

5   See Darwin, *supra* note 1, at 386–93. Westermarck, *supra* note 3, at 387–9, observes that where the killing of the aged and infirm is practiced, it is often supported by humanitarian justification; this, however, is a far cry from saying that the killing is *requested* by the victim as his right.

6   H. Maine, *Ancient Law*, 153 (Pollock ed. 1930). Maine claimed that these powers of the father extended to all regions of private law, although not to the Jus Publicum, under which a son, notwithstanding his subjection in private life, might vote alongside his father. Id. at 152. Westermarck, *supra* note 3, at 393–4, was skeptical that the arbitrary power of the father over the children extended as late as into early Roman law.

7   387 U.S. 1 (1967).

8   42 U.S.C. §§1973 *et seq.* (1970).

9   See *Landman v. Royster*, 40 *U.S.L.W.* 2256 (E.D. Va., Oct. 30, 1971) (eighth amendment and due process clause of the fourteenth amendment require federal injunctive relief, including compelling the drafting of new prison rules, for Virginia prisoners against prison conduct prohibited by vague rules or no rules, without disciplinary proceedings embodying rudiments of procedural due process, and by various penalties that constitute cruel and unusual punishment). See Note, "Courts, Corrections and the Eighth Amendment: Encouraging Prison Reform by Releasing Inmates," 44 *S. Cal. L. Rev.* 1060 (1971).

10 But see T. Szasz, *Law, Liberty and Psychiatry* (1963).

11 See notes 22, 52 and accompanying text *infra*. The trend toward liberalized abortion can be seen either as a legislative tendency back in the direction of rightlessness for the foetus – or toward increasing rights of women. This inconsistency is not unique in the law of course; it is simply support for Hohfeld's scheme that the "jural opposite" of someone's right is someone else's "no-right." W. Hohfeld, *Fundamental Legal Conceptions* (1923).

Consider in this regard a New York case in which a settlor *S* established a trust on behalf of a number of named beneficiaries and "lives in being." Desiring to amend the deed of trust, the grantor took steps pursuant to statute to obtain "the written consent of all persons beneficially interested in [the] trust." At the time the grantor was pregnant and the trustee Chase Bank advised it would not recognize the proposed amendment because the child *en ventre sa mère* might be deemed a person beneficially interested in the trust. The court allowed the amendment to stand, holding that birth rather than conception is the controlling factor in ascertaining whether a person is beneficially interested in the trust which the grantor seeks

to amend. *In re Peabody*, 5 N.Y.2d 541, 158 N.E.2d 841 (1959).

The California Supreme Court has recently refused to allow the deliberate killing of a foetus (in a non-abortion situation) to support a murder prosecution. The court ruled foetuses not to be denoted by the words "human being" within the statute defining murder. *Keeler v. Superior Court*, 2 Cal. 3d 619, 87 Cal. Rptr. 481, 470 P.2d 617 (1970). But see note 52 and accompanying text *infra*.

Some jurisdictions have statutes defining a crime of "feticide" – deliberately causing the death of an unborn child. The absence of such a specific feticide provision in the California case was one basis for the ruling in *Keeler*. See 2 Cal. 3d at 633 n.16, 87 Cal. Rptr. at 489 n.16, 470 P.2d at 625 n.16.

12 Int. Rev. Code of 1954, §1361 (repealed by Pub. L. No. 89-389, effective Jan. 1, 1969).

13 For example, see *United States v. Cargo of the Brig Malek Adhel*, 43 U.S. (2 How.) 210 (1844). There, a ship had been seized and used by pirates. All this was done without the knowledge or consent of the owners of the ship. After the ship had been captured, the United States condemned and sold the "offending vessel." The owners objected. In denying release to the owners, Justice Story cited Chief Justice Marshall from an earlier case: "This is not a proceeding against the owner; it is a proceeding against the vessel for an offense committed by the vessel; which is not the less an offense . . . because it was committed without the authority and against the will of the owner." 43 U.S. at 234, quoting from *United States v. Schooner Little Charles*, 26 F. Cas. 979 (No. 15,612) (C.C.D. Va. 1818).

14 9 U.S. (5 Cranch) 61, 86 (1809).

15 *Trustees of Dartmouth College v. Woodward*, 17 U.S. (4 Wheat.) 518 (1819).

16 Id. at 636.

17 Consider, for example, that the claim of the United States to the naval station at Guantanamo Bay, at $2,000-a-year rental, is based upon a treaty signed in 1903 by José Montes for the President of Cuba and a minister representing Theodore Roosevelt; it was subsequently ratified by two-thirds of a Senate no member of which is living today. Lease [from Cuba] of Certain Areas for Naval or Coaling Stations, July 2, 1903, T.S. No. 426; C. Bevans, 6 *Treaties and Other International Agreements of the United States 1776–1949*, at 1120 (U.S. Dep't of State Pub. 8549, 1971).

18 O. Gierke, *Political Theories of the Middle Age* (Maitland transl. 1927), especially at 22–30. The reader may be tempted to suggest that the "corporate" examples in the text are distinguishable from environmental objects in that the former are comprised by and serve humans.

On the contrary, I think that the more we learn about the sociology of the firm – and the realpolitik of our society – the more we discover the ultimate reality of these institutions, and the increasingly legal fictiveness of the individual human being. See note 125 and accompanying text *infra*.

19 *Dred Scott v. Sandford*, 60 U.S. (19 How.) 396, 404–5 (1856). In *Bailey v. Poindexter's Ex'r*, 56 Va. (14 Gratt.) 132, 142–3 (1858) a provision in a will that testator's slaves could choose between emancipation and public sale was held void on the ground that slaves have no legal capacity to choose:

These decisions are legal conclusions flowing naturally and necessarily from the one clear, simple, fundamental idea of chattel slavery. That fundamental idea is, that, in the eye of the law, so far certainly as civil rights and relations are concerned, the slave is not a person, but a thing. The investiture of a chattel with civil rights or legal capacity is indeed a legal solecism and absurdity. The attribution of legal personality to a chattel slave, – legal conscience, legal intellect, legal freedom, or liberty and power of free choice and action, and corresponding legal obligations growing out of such qualities, faculties and action – implies a palpable contradiction in terms.

20 Recently, a group of prison inmates in Suffolk County tamed a mouse that they discovered, giving him the name Morris. Discovering Morris, a jailer flushed him down the toilet. The prisoners brought a proceeding against the Warden complaining, *inter alia*, that Morris was subjected to discriminatory discharge and was otherwise unequally treated. The action was unsuccessful, on grounds that the inmates themselves were "guilty of imprisoning Morris without a charge, without a trial, and without bail," and that other mice at the prison were not treated more favorably. "As to the true victim the Court can only offer again the sympathy first proffered to his ancestors by Robert Burns. . . ." The Judge proceeded to quote from Burns' "To a Mouse." *Morabito v. Cyrta*, 9 *Crim. L. Rep.* 2472 (NY Sup. Ct. Suffolk Co. Aug. 26, 1971).

The whole matter seems humorous, of course. But what we need to know more of is the function of humor in the unfolding of a culture, and the ways in which it is involved with the social growing pains to which it is testimony. Why do people make jokes about the Women's Liberation Movement? Is it not on account of – rather than in spite of – the underlying validity of the protests, and the uneasy awareness that a recognition of them is inevitable? A. Koestler rightly begins his study of the human mind, *Act of Creation* (1964), with an analysis of humor, entitled "The Logic of Laughter." And *cf.* Freud, "Jokes and the Unconscious," 8 *Standard Edition of the Complete Psychological Works of Sigmund Freud* (J. Strachey transl. 1905). (Query too: what is the relationship between the conferring of proper *names*, e.g., Morris, and the conferring of social and legal *rights*?)

21 Thus it was that the Founding Fathers could speak of the inalienable rights of all men, and yet maintain a society that was, by modern standards, without the most basic rights for Blacks, Indians, children and women. There was no hypocrisy; emotionally, no one *felt* that these other things were men.

22 In this article I essentially limit myself to a discussion of non-animal but natural objects. I trust that the reader will be able to discern where the analysis is appropriate to advancing our understanding of what would be involved in giving "rights" to other objects not presently endowed with rights – for example, not only animals (some of which already have rights in some senses) but also humanoids, computers, and so forth. *Cf.* the National Register for Historic Places, 16 U.S.C. § 470 (1970), discussed in *Ely v. Velde*, 321 F. Supp. 1088 (E.D. Va. 1971).

23 See, e.g., *Cal. Prob. Code* §§1460–2 (West Supp. 1971).

24 *Cal. Prob. Code* §1751 (West Supp. 1971) provides for the appointment of a "conservator."

25 In New York the Supreme Court and county courts outside New York City have jurisdiction to appoint a committee of the person and/or a committee of the property for a person "incompetent to manage himself or his affairs." *NY Mental Hygiene Law* §100 (McKinney 1971).

26 This is a situation in which the ontological problems discussed in note 22 *supra* become acute. One can conceive a situation in which a guardian would be appointed by a county court with respect to a stream, bring a suit against alleged polluters, and lose. Suppose now that a federal court were to appoint a guardian with respect to the larger river system of which the stream were a part, and that the federally appointed guardian subsequently were to bring suit against the same defendants in state court, now on behalf of the river, rather than the stream. (Is it possible to bring a still subsequent suit, if the one above fails, on behalf of the entire hydrologic cycle, by a guardian appointed by an international court?)

While such problems are difficult, they are not impossible to solve. For one thing, pre-trial hearings and rights of intervention can go far toward their amelioration. Further, courts have been dealing with the matter of potentially inconsistent judgments for years, as when one state appears on the verge of handing down a divorce decree inconsistent with the judgment of another state's courts. *Kempson v. Kempson*, 58 N.J. Eg. 94, 43 A. 97 (Ch. Ct. 1899). Courts could, and of course would, retain some natural objects in the res nullius classification to help stave off the problem. Then, too, where (as is always the case) several "objects" are interrelated, several guardians could all be involved, with procedures for removal to the appropriate court – probably that of the guardian of the most encompassing "ward" to be acutely threatened. And in some cases subsequent suit by the guardian of a more encompassing ward, not guilty of laches, might be appropriate. The problems are at least no more complex than the corresponding problems that the law has dealt with for years in the class action area.

27 *Cal. Prob. Code* § 1460 (West Supp. 1971). The *NY Mental Hygiene Law* (McKinney 1971) provides for jurisdiction "over the custody of a person and his property if he is incompetent to manage himself or his affairs by reason of age, drunkenness, mental illness or other cause. . . ."

28 *Santa Clara County v. Southern Pac. R.R.*, 118 U.S. 394 (1886). Justice Black would have denied corporations the rights of "persons" under the fourteenth amendment. See *Connecticut Gen. Life Ins. Co. v. Johnson*, 303 U.S. 77, 87 (1938) (Black, J. dissenting): "Corporations have neither race nor color."

29 *In re Byrn*, LA Times, Dec. 5, 1971, §1, at 16, col. I. A preliminary injunction was subsequently granted, and defendant's cross-motion to vacate the guardianship was denied. Civ. 13113/71 (Sup. Ct. Queens Co., Jan. 4, 1972) (Smith, J.). Appeals are pending. Granting a guardianship in these circumstances would seem to be a more radical advance in the law than granting a guardianship over communal natural objects like lakes. In the former case there is a traditionally recognized guardian for the object – the mother – and her decision has been in favor of aborting the foetus.

30 The laws regarding the various communal resources had to develop along their own lines, not only because so many different persons' "rights" to consumption and usage were continually and contemporaneously involved, but also because no one had to bear the costs of his consumption of public resources in the way in which the owner of resources on private land has to bear the costs of what he does. For example, if the landowner strips his land of trees, and puts nothing in their stead, he confronts the costs of what he has done in the form of reduced value of his land; but the river polluter's actions are costless, so far as he is concerned – except insofar as the legal system can somehow force him to internalize them. The result has been that the private landowner's power over natural objects on his land is far less restrained by law (as opposed to economics) than his power over the public resources that he can get his hands on. If this state of affairs is to be changed, the standard for interceding

in the interests of natural objects on traditionally recognized "private" land might well parallel the rules that guide courts in the matter of people's children whose upbringing (or lack thereof) poses social threat. The courts can, for example, make a child "a dependent of the court" where the child's "home is an unfit place for him by reason of neglect, cruelty, or depravity of either of his parents. . . ." *Cal. Welf. & Inst. Code* §600(b) (West 1966). See also *id* at §601: any child "who from any cause is in danger of leading an idle, dissolute, lewd, or immoral life [may be adjudged] a ward of the court."

31 See note 30 *supra*. The present way of handling such problems on "private" property is to try to enact legislation of general application under the police power, see *Pennsylvania Coal Co. v. Mahon*, 260 U.S. 393 (1922), rather than to institute civil litigation which, though a piecemeal process, can be tailored to individual situations.

32 *Cal. Prob. Code* §1580 (West Supp. 1971) lists specific causes for which a guardian may, after notice and a hearing, be removed.

Despite these protections, the problem of overseeing the guardian is particularly acute where, as here, there are no immediately identifiable human beneficiaries whose self-interests will encourage them to keep a close watch on the guardian. To ameliorate this problem, a page might well be borrowed from the law of ordinary charitable trusts, which are commonly placed under the supervision of the Attorney General. See *Cal. Corp. Code* §§9505, 10207 (West 1955).

33 See *Cal. Prob. Code* §§1472, 1590 (West 1956 and Supp. 1971).

34 354 F.2d 608 (2d Cir. 1965), *cert. denied, Consolidated Edison Co. v. Scenic Hudson Preservation Conf.*, 384 U.S. 941 (1966).

35 354 F.2d 608, 615 (2d Cir. 1965).

36 Act of Aug. 26, 1935, ch. 687, Title II, §213, 49 Stat. 860 (codified in 16 U.S.C. §8251(b) (1970)).

37 354 F.2d 608, 616 (2d Cir. 1965). The court might have felt that because the New York-New Jersey Trial Conference, one of the two conservation groups that organized Scenic Hudson, had some 17 miles of trailways in the area of Storm King Mountain, it therefore had sufficient economic interest to establish standing; Judge Hays' opinion does not seem to so rely, however.

38 Concern over an anticipated flood of litigation initiated by environmental organizations is evident in Judge Trask's opinion in *Alameda Conservation Ass'n v. California*, 437 F.2d 1087 (9th Cir.), *cert. denied, Leslie Salt Co. v. Alameda Conservation Ass'n*, 402 U.S. 908 (1971), where a non-profit corporation having as a primary purpose protection of the public's interest in San Francisco Bay was denied standing to seek an injunction prohibiting a land exchange that

would allegedly destroy wildlife, fisheries and the Bay's unique flushing characteristics:

> Standing is not established by suit initiated by this association simply because it has as one of its purposes the protection of the "public interest" in the waters of the San Francisco Bay. However well intentioned the members may be, they may not by uniting create for themselves a super-administrative agency or a *parens patriae* official status with the capability of over-seeing and of challenging the action of the appointed and elected officials of the state government. Although recent decisions have considerably broadened the concept of standing, we do not find that they go this far. [Citation.]
>
> Were it otherwise the various clubs, political, economic and social now or yet to be organized, could wreak havoc with the administration of government, both federal and state. There are other forums where their voices and their views may be effectively presented, but to have standing to submit a "case or controversy" to a federal court, something more must be shown.
> (437 F.2d at 1090)

39 See note 26 *supra*.

40 Here, too, we are dogged by the ontological problem discussed in note 22 *supra*. It is easier to say that the smog-endangered stand of pines "wants" the smog stopped (assuming that to be a jurally significant entity) than it is to venture that the mountain, or the planet earth, or the cosmos, is concerned about whether the pines stand or fall. The more encompassing the entity of concern, the less certain we can be in venturing judgments as to the "wants" of any particular substance, quality, or species within the universe. Does the cosmos care if we humans persist or not? "Heaven and earth . . . regard all things as insignificant, as though they were playthings made of straw." *Lao-Tzu, Tao Teh King* 13 (D. Goddard transl. 1919).

41 See *Knight v. United States Land Ass'n*, 142 U.S. 161, 181 (1891).

42 Clause 2 gives Congress the power "to dispose of and make all needful Rules and Regulations respecting the Territory or other Property belonging to the United States."

43 See *Flemming v. Nestor*, 363 U.S. 603 (1960).

44 See the *LA Times* editorial "Water: Public vs. Polluters" criticizing: ". . . the ridiculous built-in conflict of interests on Regional Water Quality Control Board. By law, five of the seven seats are given to spokesmen for industrial, governmental, agricultural or utility users. Only one representative of the public at large is authorized, along with a delegate from fish and game interests." Feb. 12, 1969, Part II, at 8, cols. 1–2.

45 The Federal Refuse Act is over 70 years old. Refuse Act of 1899, 33 U.S.C. §407 (1970).

46 See Hall, "Refuse Act of 1899 and the Permit Program," 1 *Nat'l Res. Defense Council Newsletter* i (1971).

47 To be effective as a deterrent, the sanction ought to be high enough to bring about an internal reorganization of the corporate structure which minimizes the chances of future violations. Because the corporation is not necessarily a profit-maximizing "rationally economic man," there is no reason to believe that setting the fine as high as – but no higher than – anticipated profits from the violation of the law, will bring the illegal behavior to an end.

48 National Environmental Policy Act, 42 U.S.C. §§4321–47 (1970).

49 I. Kant, *Philosophy of Law* 195 (Hastie transl. 1887).

50 I. Kant, "The Metaphysics of Morality," in *The Philosophy of Kant* §1 at 230–1 (J. Watson transl. 1908).

51 Engel, "Reasons, Morals and Philosophic Irony," in *Language and Illumination* 60 (1969).

52 L. Wittgenstein, *Tractatus Logico-Philosophicus* §§6.421, 6.522 (D. Pears & B. McGuinness transl. 1961).

53 Cousteau, "The Oceans: No Time to Lose," *LA Times*, Oct. 24, 1971, § (opinion), at 1, col. 4.

54 See J. Harte & R. Socolow, *Patient Earth* (1971).

14   The Varieties of Intrinsic Value

John O'Neill

To hold an environmental ethic is to hold that non-human beings and states of affairs in the natural world have intrinsic value. This seemingly straight-forward claim has been the focus of much recent philosophical discussion of environmental issues. Its clarity is, however, illusory. The term 'intrinsic value' has a variety of senses and many arguments on environmental ethics suffer from a conflation of these different senses: specimen hunters for the fallacy of equivocation will find rich pickings in the area. This paper is largely the work of the underlabourer. I distinguish different senses of the concept of intrinsic value, and, relatedly, of the claim that non-human beings in the natural world have intrinsic value; I exhibit the logical relations between these claims and examine the distinct motivations for holding them. The paper is not, however, merely an exercise in conceptual underlabouring. It also defends one substantive thesis: that while it is the case that natural entities have intrinsic value in the strongest sense of the term, i.e., in the sense of value that exists independently of human valuations, such value does not as such entail any obligations on the part of human beings. The defender of nature's intrinsic value still needs to show that such value contributes to the well-being of human agents.

I

The term 'intrinsic value' is used in at least three different basic senses:

(1)   *Intrinsic value₁* Intrinsic value is used as a synonym for non-instrumental value. An object has instrumental value insofar as it is a means to some other end. An object has intrinsic value if it is an end in itself. Intrinsic goods are goods that other goods are good for the sake of. It is a well rehearsed point that, under pain of an infinite regress, not everything can have only instrumental value. There must be some objects that have intrinsic value. The defender

of an environmental ethic argues that among the entities that have such non-instrumental value are non-human beings and states. It is this claim that Naess makes in defending deep ecology:

> The well-being of non-human life on Earth has value in itself. This value is independent of any instrumental usefulness for limited human purposes.[1]

(2)   *Intrinsic value₂* Intrinsic value is used to refer to the value an object has solely in virtue of its 'intrinsic properties'. The concept is thus employed by G. E. Moore:

> To say a kind of value is 'intrinsic' means merely that the question whether a thing possesses it, and in what degree it possesses it, depends solely on the intrinsic nature of the thing in question.[2]

This account is in need of some further clarification concerning what is meant by the 'intrinsic nature' of an object or its 'intrinsic properties'. I discuss this further below. However, as a first approximation, I will assume the intrinsic properties of an object to be its non-relational properties, and leave that concept for the moment unanalysed. To hold that non-human beings have intrinsic value given this use is to hold that the value they have depends solely on their non-relational properties.

(3)   *Intrinsic value₃* Intrinsic value is used as a synonym for 'objective value', i.e., value that an object possesses independently of the valuations of valuers. As I show below, this sense itself has sub-varieties, depending on the interpretation that is put on the term 'independently'. Here I simply note that if intrinsic value is used in this sense, to claim that non-human beings have intrinsic value is not to make an ethical but a meta-ethical claim. It is to deny the subjectivist view that the source of all value lies in valuers – in their attitudes, preferences and so on. Which sense of 'intrinsic value' is the proponent of an environmental ethic employing? To hold

From *The Monist*, vol. 75, no. 2 (April): 119–38. © 1992, *The Monist: An International Quarterly Journal of General Philosophical Inquiry*. Peru, Illinois, USA. Reprinted by permission.

an environmental ethic is to hold that non-human beings have intrinsic value in the first sense: it is to hold that non-human beings are not simply of value as a means to human ends. However, it might be that to hold a defensible ethical position about the environment, one needs to be committed to the view that they also have intrinsic value in the second or third senses. Whether this is the case is the central concern of this paper.

II

In much of the literature on environmental ethics the different senses of 'intrinsic value' are used interchangeably. In particular senses 1 and 3 are often conflated. Typical is the following passage from Worster's *Nature's Economy*:

> One of the most important ethical issues raised anywhere in the past few decades has been whether nature has an order, a pattern, that we humans are bound to understand and respect and preserve. It is the essential question prompting the environmentalist movement in many countries. Generally, those who have answered 'yes' to the question have also believed that such an order has an intrinsic value, which is to say that not all value comes from humans, that value can exist independently of us: it is not something we bestow. On the other hand those who have answered 'no' have tended to be in an instrumentalist camp. They look on nature as a storehouse of 'resources' to be organised and used by people, as having no other value than the value some human gives it.[3]

In describing the 'yes' camp Worster characterises the term in sense 3. However, in characterising the 'no's' he presupposes an understanding of the term in both senses 1 and 3. The passage assumes that to deny that natural patterns have value independently of the evaluations of humans is to grant them only instrumental value: a subjectivist meta-ethics entails that non-humans can have only instrumental value. This assumption is widespread.[4] It also underlies the claims of some critics of an environmental ethic who reject it on meta-ethical grounds thus: To claim that items in the non-human world have intrinsic values commits one to an objectivist view of values; an objectivist view of values is indefensible; hence the non-human world contains nothing of intrinsic value.[5]

The assumption that a subjectivist meta-ethics commits one to the view that non-humans have only instrumental value is false. Its apparent plausibility is founded on a confusion of claims about the source of values with claims about their object.[6] The subjectivist claims that the only sources of value are the evaluative attitudes of humans. But this does not entail that the only ultimate objects of value are the states of human beings. Likewise, to be an objectivist about the source of value, i.e., to claim that whether or not something has value does not depend on the attitudes of valuers, is compatible with a thoroughly anthropocentric view of the object of value – that the only things which do in fact have value are humans and their states, such that a world without humans would have no value whatsoever.

To enlarge, consider the emotivist as a standard example of a subjectivist. Evaluative utterances merely evince the speaker's attitudes with the purpose of changing the attitudes of the hearer. They state no facts. Within the emotivist tradition Stevenson provides an admirably clear account of intrinsic value. Intrinsic value is defined as non-instrumental value: ' "intrinsically good" is roughly synonymous with "good for its own sake, as an end, as distinct from good as a means to something else" '.[7] Stevenson then offers the following account of what it is to say something has intrinsic value:

> 'X is intrinsically good' asserts that the speaker approves of X intrinsically, and acts emotively to make the hearer or hearers likewise approve of X intrinsically.[8]

There are no reasons why the emotivist should not fill the X place by entities and states of the non-human world. There is nothing in the emotivist's meta-ethical position that precludes her holding basic attitudes that are biocentric. Thus let the H! operator express hurrah attitudes and B! express boo attitudes.[9] Her ultimate values might for example include the following:

> H! (The existence of natural ecosystems)
> B! (The destruction of natural ecosystems by humans)

There is no reason why the emotivist must assume that either egoism or humanism is true, that is that she must assign non-instrumental value only to her own or other humans' states.[10]

It might be objected, however, that there are other difficulties in holding an emotivist meta-ethics and an environmental ethic. In making humans the source of all value, the emotivist is committed to the view that a world without humans contains nothing of value. Hence, while nothing logically precludes the emotivists assigning non-instrumental value to objects in a world which contains humans, it undermines some of the considerations that have led to the belief in the need to assign such value. For example, the standard last man arguments[11] in defence of an environmental ethic fail: the last man whose last act is to destroy a rain forest could on a subjectivist account of value do no wrong, since a world without humans is without value.

✓ This objection fails for just the same reason as did the original assumption that subjectivism entails non-humans have only instrumental value. It confuses the source and object of value. There is nothing in emotivism that forces the emotivist to confine the objects of her attitudes to those that exist at the time at which she expresses them. Her moral utterances might evince attitudes towards events and states of affairs that might happen after her death, for example,

> H! (My great-grand-children live in a world without poverty)

Likewise her basic moral attitudes can range over periods in which humans no longer exist, for example,

> H! (Rain forests exist after the extinction of the human species)

Like the rest of us she can deplore the vandalism of the last man. Her moral utterances might evince attitudes not only to other times but also to other possible worlds. Nothing in her meta-ethics stops her asserting with Leibniz that this world is the best of all possible worlds, or, in her despair at the destructiveness of humans, expressing the attitude that it would have been better had humans never existed:

> H! (the possible world in which humans never came into existence)

That humans are the source of value is not incompatible with their assigning value to a world in which they do not exist. To conclude, nothing in

the emotivist's meta-ethics dictates the content of her attitudes.

Finally it needs to be stressed that while subjectivism does not rule out non-humans having non-instrumental value, objectivism does not rule it in. To claim that moral utterances have a truth value is not to specify which utterances are true. The objectivist can hold that the moral facts are such that only the states of humans possess value in themselves: everything else has only instrumental value. Ross, for example, held that only states of conscious beings have intrinsic value:

> Contemplate any imaginary universe from which you suppose mind entirely absent, and you will fail to find anything in it you can call good in itself.[12]

Moore allowed that without humans the world might have some, but only very insignificant, value.[13] It does not follow from the claim that values do not have their source in humans that they do not have humans as their sole ultimate object.

The upshot of this discussion is a very traditional one, that meta-ethical commitments are logically independent of ethical ones. However, in the realm of environmental ethics it is one that needs to be re-affirmed. No meta-ethical position is required by an environmental ethic in its basic sense, i.e., an ethic which holds that non-human entities should not be treated merely as a means to the satisfaction of human wants. In particular, one can hold such an ethic and deny objectivism. However, this is not to say that there might not be other reasons for holding an objectivist account of ethics and that some of these reasons might appear particularly pertinent when considering evaluative statements about non-humans. It has not been my purpose in this section of the paper to defend ethical subjectivism and in section IV I defend a version of objectivism about environmental values. First, however, I discuss briefly intrinsic value in its Moorean sense, intrinsic value$_2$ – for this sense of the term is again often confused with intrinsic value$_1$.

III

In its second sense intrinsic value refers to the value an object has solely in virtue of its 'intrinsic properties': it is value that 'depends solely on the intrinsic nature of the thing in question'.[14] I suggested earlier that the intrinsic properties of an object are its non-relational properties. What is meant by 'non-relational properties'? There are two interpretations that might be placed on the phrase:

(i) The non-relational properties of an object are those that persist regardless of the existence or non-existence of other objects (weak interpretation).

(ii) The non-relational properties of an object are those that can be characterised without reference to other objects (strong interpretation).[15]

The distinction between the two senses will not concern me further here, although a similar distinction will take on greater significance in the following section. If any property is irreducibly relational then rarity is. The rarity of an object depends on the non-existence of other objects, and the property cannot be characterised without reference to other objects. In practical concern about the environment a special status is ascribed to rare entities. The preservation of endangered species of flora and fauna and of unusual habitats and ecological systems is a major practical environmental problem. Rarity appears to confer a special value to an object. This value is related to that of another irreducibly relational property of environmental significance, i.e., diversity. However, it has been argued that such value can have no place in an environmental ethic which places intrinsic value on natural items. The argument runs something as follows:

1 To hold an environmental ethic is to hold that natural objects have intrinsic value.
2 The values objects have in virtue of their relational properties, e.g., their rarity, cannot be intrinsic values.

Hence:

3 The value objects have in virtue of their relational properties have no place in an environmental ethic.[16]

This argument commits a fallacy of equivocation. The term 'intrinsic value' is being used in its Moorean sense, intrinsic value₂ in the second premise, but as synonym for non-instrumental value, intrinsic valuer, in the first. The senses are distinct. Thus, while it may be true that if an object has only instrumental value it cannot have intrinsic value in the Moorean sense, it is false that an object of non-instrumental value is necessarily also of intrinsic value in the Moorean sense. We might value an object in virtue of its relational properties, for example its rarity, without thereby seeing it as having only instrumental value for human satisfactions.

This point can be stated with greater generality. We need to distinguish:

(1) values objects can have in virtue of their relations to other objects; and
(2) values objects can have in virtue of their relations to human beings.[17]

The second set of values is a proper subset of the first. Moreover, the second set of values is still not co-extensive with

(3) values objects can have in virtue of being instrumental for human satisfaction.

An object might have value in virtue of its relation with human beings without thereby being of only instrumental value for humans. Thus, for example, one might value wilderness in virtue of its not bearing the imprint of human activity, as when John Muir opposed the damming of the Hetch Hetchy valley on the grounds that wild mountain parks should lack 'all . . . marks of man's work'.[18] To say 'x has value because it is untouched by humans' is to say that it has value in virtue of a relation it has to humans and their activities. Wilderness has such value in virtue of our absence. However, the value is not possessed by wilderness in virtue of its instrumental usefulness for the satisfaction of human desires. The third set of values is a proper subset of both the second and the first. Intrinsic value in the sense of non-instrumental value need not then be intrinsic in the Moorean sense.

What of the relation between Moorean intrinsic value and objective value? Is it the case that if there is value that 'depends solely on the intrinsic nature of the thing in question' then subjectivism about values must be rejected? If an object has value only in virtue of its intrinsic nature, does it follow that it has value independently of human valuations? The answer depends on the interpretation given to the phrases 'depends solely on' and 'only in virtue of'. If these are interpreted to exclude the activity of human evaluation, as I take it Moore intended, then the answer to both questions is immediately 'yes'. However, there is a natural subjectivist reading to the phrases. The subjectivist can talk of the valuing agent assigning value to objects solely in virtue of their intrinsic natures. Given a liberal interpretation of the phrases, a subjectivist can hold that some objects have intrinsic value in the Moorean sense.

IV

In section III I argued that the claim that nature has non-instrumental value does not commit one to an objectivist meta-ethics. However, I left open the question as to whether there might be other reasons particularly pertinent in the field of environmental ethics that would lead us to hold an objectivist account of value. I will show in this section that there are.

The ethical objectivist holds that the evaluative properties of objects are real properties of objects, that is, that they are properties that objects possess independently of the valuations of valuers. What is meant by 'independently of the valuations of valuers'? There are two readings of the phrase which parallel the two senses of 'non-relational property' outlined in the last section:

(1) The evaluative properties of objects are properties that exist in the absence of evaluating agents. (Weak interpretation)
(2) The evaluative properties of objects can be characterised without reference to evaluating agents. (Strong interpretation)

The distinction is a particular instance of a more general distinction between two senses in which we can talk of a property being a real property of an object:

(1) A real property is one that exists in the absence of any being experiencing that object. (Weak interpretation)
(2) A real property is one that can be characterised without reference to the experiences of a being who might experience the object. (Strong interpretation)

Is there anything about evaluations of the environment that make the case for objectivism especially compelling? I begin by considering the case for the weak version of objectivism. For the purpose of the rest of the discussion I will assume that only human persons are evaluating agents.

1. Weak objectivity

A popular move in recent work on environmental ethics has been to establish the objectivity of values by invoking an analogy between secondary qualities and evaluative properties in the following manner:

(1) The evaluative properties of objects are analogous to secondary qualities. Both sets of properties are observer dependent.
(2) The Copenhagen interpretation of quantum mechanics has shown the distinction between primary qualities and secondary qualities to be untenable. All the properties of objects are observer dependent.

Hence,

(3) The evaluative properties of objects are as real as their primary qualities.[19]

The argument fails at every stage. In the first place the conclusion itself is too weak to support objectivism about values: it is no argument for an objectivist theory of values to show that all properties of objects are observer dependent. The second premise should in any case be rejected. Not only is it the case that the Copenhagen interpretation of quantum theory is but one amongst many,[20] it is far from clear that the Copenhagen interpretation is committed to the ontological extravagance that all properties are observer dependent. Rather it can be understood as a straightforward instrumentalist interpretation of quantum theory. As such it involves no ontological commitments about the quantum domain.[21]

More pertinent to the present discussion, there are also good grounds for rejecting the first premise. The analogy between secondary qualities and values has often been used to show that values are not real properties of objects. Thus Hume remarks:

Vice and virtue . . . may be compared to sounds, heat and cold, which according to modern philosophy, are not qualities in objects, but perceptions in the mind.[22]

For the Humean, both secondary qualities and evaluative properties are not real properties of objects, but, rather, illustrate the mind's 'propensity to spread itself on external objects': as Mackie puts it, moral qualities are the 'projection or objectification of moral attitudes'.[23] The first premise of the argument assumes this Humean view of the analogy between secondary qualities and values. However, there are good grounds for inverting the analogy and that inversion promises to provide a more satisfactory argument for objectivism than that outlined above.

On the weak interpretation of the concept of a real property, secondary qualities are real properties of objects. They persist in the absence of observers. Objects do not lose their colours when we no longer perceive them. In the kingdom of the blind the grass is still green. Secondary qualities are dispositional properties of objects to appear in a certain way to ideal observers in ideal conditions. So, for example, an object is green if and only if it would appear green to a perceptually ideal observer in perceptually ideal conditions.[24] It is consistent with this characterisation of secondary qualities that an object possesses that quality even though it may never actually be perceived by an observer. Thus, while in the strong sense of the term secondary qualities are not real properties of objects – one cannot characterise the properties without referring to the experiences of possible observers – in the weak sense of the term they are.[25]

This point opens up the possibility of an inversion of the Humean analogy between secondary and evaluative qualities [. . .]. Like the secondary qualities, evaluative qualities are real properties of objects. An object's evaluative properties are similarly dispositional properties that it has to produce certain attitudes and reactions in ideal observers in ideal conditions. Thus, we might tentatively characterise goodness thus: x is good if and only if x would produce feelings of moral approval in an ideal observer in ideal conditions. Likewise, beauty might be characterised thus: x is beautiful if and only if x would produce feelings of aesthetic delight in ideal observers in ideal conditions. Given this characterisation, an object is beautiful or good even if it never actually appears as such to an observer. The evaluative properties of objects are real in just the same sense that secondary qualities are. Both sets of properties are independent of observers in the sense that they persist in the absence of observers. The first premise of the argument outlined above should therefore be rejected. Furthermore, in rejecting this premise, one arrives at a far more convincing case for the reality of evaluative properties than that provided by excursions into quantum mechanics.

However, the promise of this line of argument for environmental ethics is, I believe, limited. There are a variety of particular arguments that might be raised against it. For example, the Humean might respond by suggesting that the analogy between secondary and evaluative properties is imperfect. The arguments for and against the analogy I will not rehearse here.[27] For even if the analogy is a good one, it is not clear to me that any point of substance about the nature of values divides the Humean and his opponent. The debate is one about preferred modes of speech, specifically about how the term 'real property' is to be read. For the Humean such as Mackie, the term 'real property' is understood in its strong sense. It is a property that can be characterised without reference to the experiences of an observer. Hence neither secondary qualities nor values are real properties of objects. The opponent of the Humean in employing the analogy to establish the reality of evaluative properties merely substitutes a weak interpretation of 'real property' for the strong interpretation. There may be good reasons for doing this, but nothing about the nature of values turns on this move.[28] Moreover, there seems to be nothing about evaluative utterances concerning the natural environment which adds anything to this debate. Nothing about specifically environmental values tells for or against this argument for objectivism.

2. Strong objectivity

A more interesting question is whether there are good reasons for believing that there are objective values in the strong sense: are there evaluative properties that can be characterised without reference to the experiences of human observers? I will now argue that there are and that uses of evaluative utterances about the natural world provide the clearest examples of such values.

Consider the gardener's use of the phrase 'x is good for greenfly'. The term 'good for' can be understood in two distinct ways. It might refer to what is conducive to the destruction of greenfly, as in 'detergent sprays are good for greenfly', or it can be used to describe what causes greenfly to flourish, as in 'mild winters are good for greenfly'. The term 'good for' in the first use describes what is instrumentally good for the gardener: given the ordinary gardener's interest in the flourishing of her rosebushes, detergent sprays satisfy that interest. The second use describes what is instrumentally good for the greenfly, quite independently of the gardener's interests. This instrumental goodness is possible in virtue of the fact that greenflies are the sorts of things that can flourish or be injured. In consequence they have their own goods that are independent of both human interests and any tendency they might have to produce in human observers feelings of approval or disapproval.[29] Such goods I will follow Von Wright in terming the 'goods of X'.[30]

What is the class of entities that can be said to possess such goods? Von Wright in an influential passage offers the following account:

A being, of whose good it is meaningful to talk, is one who can meaningfully be said to be well or ill, to thrive, to flourish, be happy or miserable . . . the attributes, which go along with the meaningful use of the phrase 'the good of X', may be called *biological* in a broad sense. By this I do not mean that they were terms, of which biologists make frequent use. 'Happiness' and 'welfare' cannot be said to belong to the professional vocabulary of biologists. What I mean by calling the terms 'biological' is that they are used as attributes of beings, of whom it is meaningful to say they have a *life*. The question 'What kinds or species of being have a good?' is therefore broadly identical with the question 'What kinds or species of being have a life?'.[31]

This biological use of the terms 'good for' and 'good of' is at the centre of Aristotelian ethics. The distinction between 'good for' and 'good of' itself corresponds to the Aristotelian distinction between goods externally instrumental to a being's flourishing and those that are constitutive of a being's flourishing.[32] And the central strategy of Aristotle's ethics is to found ethical argument on the basis of this broadly biological use of the term 'good'. I discuss this further below.

The terms 'good' and 'goods' in this biological context characterise items which are real in the strong interpretation of the term. In order to characterise the conditions which are constitutive of the flourishing of a living thing one need make no reference to the experiences of human observers. The goods of an entity are given rather by the characteristic features of the kind or species of being it is. A living thing can be said to flourish if it develops those characteristics which are normal to the species to which it belongs in the normal conditions for that species. If it fails to realise such characteristics then it will be described by terms such as 'defective', 'stunted', 'abnormal' and the like. Correspondingly, the truth of statements about what is good for a living thing, what is conducive to its flourishing, depends on no essential reference to human observers. The use of the evaluative terms in the biological context does then provide good reasons for holding that some evaluative properties are real properties on the strong interpretation of the phrase. Hence, evaluative utterances about living things do have a particular relevance to the debate about the objectivity of values. Specifically biological values tell for objectivism.

[. . .]

It makes sense to talk of the goods of collective biological entities – colonies, ecosystems and so on – in a way that is irreducible to that of its members. The realisation of the good of a colony of ants might in certain circumstances involve the death of most of its members. It is not a condition for the flourishing of an individual animal that it be eaten: it often is a condition for the flourishing of the ecosystem of which it is a part. Relatedly, a point central to Darwin's development of the theory of evolution was that living beings have a capacity to reproduce that outstrips the capacity of the environment to support them. Most members of a species die in early life. This is clearly bad for the individuals involved. But it is again essential to the flourishing of the ecosystems of which they are a part. Collective entities have their own goods. In defending this claim one need not show that they have their own life.[35]

Both individual living things and the collective entities of which they are members can be said, then, to have their own goods. These goods are quite independent of human interests and can be characterised without reference to the experiences of human observers. It is a standard at this juncture of the argument to assume that possession of goods entails moral considerability: 'moral standing or considerability belongs to whatever has a good of its own'.[36] This is mistaken. It is possible to talk in an objective sense of what constitutes the goods of entities, without making any claims that these ought to be realised. We can know what is 'good for X' and relatedly what constitutes 'flourishing for X' and yet believe that X is the sort of thing that ought not to exist and hence that the flourishing of X is just the sort of thing we ought to inhibit. The case of the gardener noted earlier is typical in this regard.

The gardener knows what it is for greenfly to flourish, recognises they have their own goods, and has a practical knowledge of what is good for them. No moral injunction follows. She can quite consistently believe they ought to be done harm. Likewise one can state the conditions for the flourishing of dictatorship and bureaucracy. The anarchist can claim that 'war is the health of the state'. One can discover what is good both for rain forests and the AIDS virus. One can recognise that something has its own goods, and quite consistently be morally indifferent to these goods or believe one has a moral duty to inhibit their development.[37] That Y is a good of X does not entail that Y should be realised unless we have a prior reason for believing that X is the sort of thing whose good ought to be promoted. While there is not a logical gap between facts and values, in that some value statements are factual, there is a logical gap between facts and oughts. 'Y is a good' does not entail 'Y ought to be realised'.[38]

This gap clearly raises problems for environmental ethics. The existence of objective goods was promising precisely because it appeared to show that items in the non-human world were objects of proper moral concern. The gap outlined threatens to undermine such concern. Can the gap be bridged? There are two ways one might attempt to construct such a bridge. The first is to invoke some general moral claim that linked objective goods and moral duties. One might for example invoke an objectivist version of utilitarianism: we have a moral duty to maximise the total amount of objective good in the world.[39] There are a number of problems of detail with such an approach: What are the units for comparing objective goods? How are different goods to be weighed? However, it also has a more general problem that it shares with hedonistic utilitarianism. Thus, the hedonistic utilitarian must include within his calculus pleasures that ought not to count at all, e.g., those of a sadist who gets pleasure from needless suffering. The hedonistic utilitarian fails to allow that pleasures themselves are the direct objects of ethical appraisal. Similarly, there are some entities whose flourishing simply should not enter into any calculations – the flourishing of dictatorships and viruses for example. It is not the case that the goods of viruses should count, even just a very small amount. There is no reason why these goods should count at all as ends in themselves (although there are of course good instrumental reasons why some viruses should flourish, in that many are indispensable to the ecosystems of

which they are a part). The flourishing of such entities is itself a direct object of ethical appraisal. The quasi-utilitarian approach is unpromising.

A second possible bridge between objective goods and oughts is an Aristotelian one. Human beings like other entities have goods constitutive of their flourishing, and correspondingly other goods instrumental to that flourishing. The flourishing of many other living things ought to be promoted because they are constitutive of our own flourishing. This approach might seem a depressingly familiar one. It looks as if we have taken a long journey into objective value only to arrive back at a narrowly anthropocentric ethic. This, however, would be mistaken. It is compatible with an Aristotelian ethic that we value items in the natural world for their own sake, not simply as an external means to our own satisfaction. Consider Aristotle's account of the relationship of friendship to human flourishing.[40] It is constitutive of friendship of the best kind that we care for friends for their own sake and not merely for the pleasures or profits they might bring. To do good for a friend purely because one thought they might later return the compliment not for their own sake is to have an ill-formed friendship. Friendship in turn is a constitutive component of a flourishing life. Given the kind of beings we are, to lack friends is to lack part of what makes for a flourishing human existence. Thus the egoist who asks 'why have friends?' or 'why should I do good for my friends?' has assumed a narrow range of goods – 'the biggest share of money, honours and bodily pleasures'[41] – and asked how friends can bring such goods. The appropriate response is to point out that he has simply misidentified what the goods of a human life are.

The best case for an environmental ethic should proceed on similar lines. For a large number of, although not all, individual living things and biological collectives, we should recognise and promote their flourishing as an end in itself.[42] Such care for the natural world is constitutive of a flourishing human life. The best human life is one that includes an awareness of and practical concern with the goods of entities in the nonhuman world. On this view, the last man's act of vandalism reveals the man to be leading an existence below that which is best for a human being, for it exhibits a failure to recognise the goods of nonhumans. To outline such an approach is, however, only to provide a promissory note. The claim that care for the natural world for its own sake is a part of the best life for humans requires detailed defence. The most promising general strategy would be to appeal to the claim that a good human life requires a breadth of goods. Part of the problem with egoism is the very narrowness of the goods it involves. The ethical life is one that incorporates a far richer set of goods and relationships than egoism would allow. This form of argument can be made for a connection of care for the natural world with human flourishing: the recognition and promotion of natural goods as ends in themselves involves just such an enrichment.[43]

Notes

1 A. Naess, 'A Defence of the Deep Ecology Movement', *Environmental Ethics*, 6 (1984), 266. However, Naess's use of the term is unstable and he sometimes uses the phrase 'intrinsic value' to refer to objective value. See n. 4, below.

2 G. E. Moore, 'The Conception of Intrinsic Value', in *Philosophical Studies* (London: Routledge and Kegan Paul, 1922), p. 260.

3 D. Worster, *Nature's Economy* (Cambridge: Cambridge University Press, 1985), p. xi.

4 Thus, for example, Naess and Rothenberg in *Ecology, Community and Lifestyle* (Cambridge: Cambridge University Press, 1989) initially define 'intrinsic value' as value which is 'independent of our valuation' (ibid., p. 11) but then in the text characterise it in terms of a contrast with instrumental value (ibid., pp. 74–5). In his own account of deep ecology Naess employs the term in the sense of non-instrumental value (see n. 2 and A. Naess, 'The Shallow and the Deep: Long Range Ecology Movement', *Inquiry*, 16, 1973). Others are more careful. Thus, while Attfield is committed to both an objectivist meta-ethics and the view that the states of some non-humans have intrinsic value, in *A Theory of Value and Obligation* (London: Croom Helm, 1987) ch. 2, he defines intrinsic value as non-instrumental value and distinguishes this from his 'objectivist understanding of it'. Callicott, in 'Intrinsic Value, Quantum Theory, and Environmental Ethics', *Environmental Ethics*, 7 (1989), 257–75, distinguishes non-instrumental value from objective value, using the term 'inherent value' for the former and 'intrinsic value' for the latter. However, the use of these terms raises its own problems since there is little agreement in the literature as to how they are to be employed. For example, P. Taylor, *Respect for Nature* (Princeton, NJ: Princeton University Press, 1986), pp. 68–77 makes the same distinction but uses 'inherent value' to describe Callicott's 'intrinsic value' and 'intrinsic value' to describe his 'inherent value', while R. Attfield in *The*

Ethics of Environmental Concern (Oxford: Blackwell, 1983), ch. 8, uses the term 'inherent value' to refer to something quite different. Another exceptionally clear discussion of the meta-ethical issues surrounding environmental ethics is R. and V. Routley, 'Human Chauvinism and Environmental Ethics', in D. Mannison, M. McRobbie and R. Routley (eds.), *Environmental Philosophy* (Canberra: Australian National University, 1980).

5 This kind of argument is to be found in particular in the work of McCloskey. See H. J. McCloskey, 'Ecological Ethics and its Justification', in Mannison et al., *Environmental Philosophy*, and *Ecological Ethics and Politics* (Totowa, NJ: Rowman and Littlefield, 1983).

6 Cf. D. Gauthier, *Morals by Agreement* (Oxford: Oxford University Press, 1986), pp. 46–9 and Callicott, 'Intrinsic Value, Quantum Theory, and Environmental Ethics', who make this point quite emphatically.

7 C. L. Stevenson, *Ethics and Language* (New Haven, CT: Yale University Press, 1944).

8 Ibid., p. 178.

9 I take the operators from S. Blackburn, *Spreading the Word* (Oxford: Clarendon Press, 1984), p. 193ff.

10 Cf. R. and V. Routley, 'Human Chauvinism and Environmental Ethics'.

11 See ibid., pp. 121–3.

12 W. D. Ross, *The Right and the Good* (Oxford: Clarendon Press, 1930), p. 140. Ross held four things to have intrinsic value – 'virtue, pleasure, the allocation of pleasure to the virtuous, and knowledge' (ibid., p. 140).

13 G. E. Moore, *Principia Ethica* (Cambridge: Cambridge University Press, 1903), pp. 28, 83ff and 188ff.

14 G. E. Moore, 'The Conception of Intrinsic Value', in *Philosophical Studies* (London: Routledge and Kegan Paul, 1922), p. 260.

15 I do not follow Moore's own discussion here. Moore's own use of the term is closer to the weaker than the stronger interpretation. Thus, for example, the method of isolation as a test of intrinsic value proceeds by considering if objects keep their value 'if they existed by themselves, in absolute isolation': Moore, *Principia Ethica*, p. 187.

16 A similar argument is to be found in A. Gunn, 'Why Should We Care about Rare Species?', *Environmental Ethics*, 2, 1980, pp. 17–37, especially pp. 29–34.

17 J. Thompson partially defines intrinsic value and hence an environmental ethic in terms of a contrast with such values: 'those who find intrinsic value in nature are claiming . . . that things and states which are of value are valuable for what they are in themselves and not because of their relation to us . . . ' (J. Thompson, 'A Refutation of Environmental

Ethics', p. 148, *Environmental Ethics*, 12 (1990), 147–60). This characterisation is inadequate, in that it rules out of an environmental ethic positions such as that of Muir who values certain parts of nature because of the absence of the marks of humans. I take it that Thompson intends a contrast to the third set of values – values objects can have in virtue of being instrumental for human satisfaction.

18 Cited in R. Dubos, *The Wooing of Earth* (London: The Athlone Press, 1980), p. 135.

19 A relatively sophisticated version of the argument is to be found in Holmes Rolston, III, 'Are Values in Nature Subjective or Objective?', in *Philosophy Gone Wild* (Buffalo, NY: Prometheus Books, 1989), pp. 92–5. Cf. Callicott, 'Intrinsic Value, Quantum Theory, and Environmental Ethics'.

20 M. Jammer, *The Philosophy of Quantum Mechanics* (New York: John Wiley, 1974) remains a good survey of the basic different interpretations of quantum theory.

21 It should also be noted that the view, popular among some Green thinkers (see, for example, F. Capra, *The Tao of Physics* (London: Wildwood House, 1975)), that the Copenhagen interpretation entails a radically new world view that undermines the old classical Newtonian picture of the world is false. The Copenhagen interpretation is conceptually conservative and denies the possibility that we could replace the concepts of classical physics by any others (see N. Bohr, *Atomic Theory and the Description of Nature* (Cambridge: Cambridge University Press, 1934), p. 94). Cf. W. Heisenberg, *Physics and Philosophy* (London: Allen and Unwin, 1959), p. 46. I discuss this conservativism in J. O'Neill, *Worlds Without Content* (London: Routledge, 1992), ch. 6.

22 D. Hume, *A Treatise of Human Nature* (London: Fontana, 1972), Book III, Section 1, p. 203.

23 J. Mackie, *Ethics* (Harmondsworth, England: Penguin, 1977), p. 42.

24 Cf. J. McDowell, 'Values and Secondary Qualities', p. 111 in T. Honderich (ed.), *Morality and Objectivity* (London: Routledge, 1985).

25 Cf. ibid., p. 113 and J. Dancy, 'Two Conceptions of Moral Realism', *Proceedings of the Aristotelian Society*, supp. vol. 60, 1986.
[. . .]

27 For such a Humean response, see Blackburn, 'Errors and the Phenomenology of Value', in Honderich (ed.), *Morality and Objectivity*.

28 Cf. C. Hookway's reply to Dancy, 'Two Conceptions of Moral Realism', *Proceedings of the Aristotelian Society*, supp. vol. 60, 1986, p. 202.

29 Hence I also reject Feinberg's claim that the goods of plants are reducible to those of humans with an interest in their thriving: 'The Rights of Animals and Unborn Generations', in *Rights, Justice and the Bounds*

of Liberty* (Princeton, NJ: Princeton University Press, 1980), pp. 10–71. For a similar argument against Feinberg see Taylor, *Respect for Nature*, p. 68.

30 G. H. von Wright, *The Varieties of Goodness* (London: Routledge and Kegan Paul, 1963), ch. 3.

31 Ibid., p. 50. Cf. Taylor, *Respect for Nature*, pp. 60–71.

32 See J. Cooper, *Reason and Human Good in Aristotle* (Cambridge, MA: Harvard University Press, 1975), p. 19ff.
[. . .]

35 Hence, there is no need to invoke scientific hypotheses such as the Gaia hypothesis to defend the existence of such goods, as for example Goodpaster does (K. Goodpaster, 'On Being Morally Considerable', p. 323, *Journal of Philosophy*, 75, 1978, pp. 308–25).

36 R. Attfield, *A Theory of Value and Obligation* (Beckenham: Croom Helm, 1987), p. 21. Cf. Rolston, *Environmental Ethics*; Goodpaster, 'On Being Morally Considerable'; and Taylor, *Respect for Nature*.

37 This point undermines a common objection to objectivism, i.e., that objectivists cannot explain why value statements necessarily motivate actions. If values were objective then 'someone might be indifferent to things which he regards as good or actively hostile to them' (Blackburn, *Spreading the Word*, p. 188). The proper reply to this is that not all value statements do motivate actions, as the example in the text reveals.

38 Compare Wiggins's point that we need to discriminate between 'the (spurious) fact-value distinction and the (real) is-ought distinction' (D. Wiggins, 'Truth, Invention, and the Meaning of Life', in *Needs, Values, Truth: Essays in the Philosophy of Value* (Oxford: Blackwell, 1987), p. 96). Cf. Taylor, *Respect for Nature*, pp. 71–2.

39 See Attfield, *A Theory of Value and Obligation*, for this kind of position. For a different attempt to bridge the gap between objective goods and moral oughts, see Taylor, *Respect for Nature*, chs. 2–4.

40 Aristotle, *Nicomachean Ethics*, trans. T. Irwin (Indianapolis, IN: Hackett, 1985), Books viii–ix.

41 Ibid., 1168b.

42 This would clearly involve a rejection of Aristotle's own view that animals are made for the sake of humans. Aristotle, *Politics*, trans. J. Warrington (London: J. A. Dent and Sons, 1959), 1265b.

43 This line of argument has the virtue of fitting well with Aristotle's own account of happiness, given an inclusive interpretation of his views. Happiness on this account is inclusive of all goods that are ends in themselves: a happy life is self-sufficient in that nothing is lacking. It is a maximally consistent set of goods. Aristotle, *Nicomachean Ethics*, 1097b14-20; see J. L. Ackrill, 'Aristotle on Eudaimonia', in A. O. Rorty (ed.), *Essays on Aristotle's Ethics* (Berkeley, CA: University of California Press, 1980) for a presentation of this interpretation.

15   Value in Nature and the Nature of Value

Holmes Rolston III

I offer myself as a nature guide, exploring for values. Many before us have got lost and we must look the world over. The unexamined life is not worth living; life in an unexamined world is not worth living either. We miss too much of value.

Valuable Humans

Let us start from well-mapped ground: humans are able to value. Descartes's *cogito* is as well an indubitable *valeo*. I cannot doubt that I value. Humans are able to value nature instrumentally, to value their own experiential states both intrinsically and instrumentally. Objective natural things and events may contribute to these subjective interest satisfactions, a tree supplies firewood, a sunny day makes a picnic possible.

Taking the first step on our journey into non-human nature, some travellers notice that we must take along this indubitable valuing self; afterwards, along the way, finding these selves always present, they deny any value outside our own minds. Wilhelm Windelband insists: 'Value . . . is never found in the object itself as a property. It consists in a relation to an appreciating mind. . . . Take away will and feeling and there is no such thing as value' (Windelband, 1921, p. 215). Bryan Norton concludes: 'Moralists among environmental ethicists have erred in looking for a value in living things that is *independent* of human valuing. They have therefore forgotten a most elementary point about valuing anything. Valuing always occurs from the viewpoint of a conscious valuer. . . . Only the humans are valuing agents' (Norton, 1991, p. 251).

Taking an interest in an object gives humans a value-ability. Additionally to valuing nature instrumentally, humans can sometimes value nature intrinsically. When we value a giant sequoia tree, our valuing stops in the tree itself, without further contributory reference. What then is going on? Philosophical travellers, after taking a look at the tree, will want to take a look at their language. 'Intrinsic' means without instrumental reference, but that leaves unsettled whether the value is located in the tree independently, autonomously intrinsic, or placed on the tree upon our arrival. We cannot just take it as elementary that there is no such thing as non-human value. Is this intrinsic value discovered or conferred? There is excitement in the beholder; but what is valued is what is beheld.

If the value-ability of humans is the source of this valued excitement, then value is anthropogenic even though it is not anthropocentric (Callicott, 1984; 1986). Tourists in Yosemite do not value the sequoias as timber but as natural classics, for their age, strength, size, beauty, resilience and majesty. This viewing constitutes the trees' value, which is not present independent of the human valuing. Value thus requires subjectivity to coagulate it in the world. But the value so coagulated, it will be claimed, is placed objectively on the tree. Such value is not self-regarding, or even human-regarding, merely, though it is human-generated. It is not centred on human well-being. That '*n* is valuable' does mean that a human, *H*, takes an interest in *n*, a natural object, but it need not mean '*n* satisfies *H*'s desire', since *H* may take an interest in the trees for what they are in themselves, and not merely to satisfy *H*'s desires. Meanwhile, there is no value until consciousness comes on scene.

Visiting the Grand Canyon, we intrinsically value the rock strata with their colour bands. Visiting Kentucky, we value Mammoth Cave, with its stalactites. Taking any interest whatever constitutes value *ipso facto*. An otherwise valueless object can thus come to have intrinsic value. As travellers we will wonder what was here before, what will remain after. The obvious answer is that there will be whatever properties these trees, canyons, and caves have. Even

From Robin Attfield and Andrew Belsey, eds., *Philosophy and the Natural Environment*, Royal Institute of Philosophy Supplement 36 (Cambridge: Cambridge University Press, 1994), pp. 13–17, 20–30. © 1994 by The Royal Institute of Philosophy and the contributors. Reproduced with permission from Cambridge University Press.

Descartes found himself unable to doubt the exist-ence of external nature, and no philosopher who doubts that the world exists bothers to take a trip through it.

What account do we give when, excited by a sense of deep time at the Grand Canyon, we realize that humans have rarely been there? At that point, we may wish to give a dispositional twist to value. To say that *n* is valuable means that *n* is able to be val-ued, if and when human valuers, *H*s, come along, but *n* has these properties whether or not humans arrive. Faced with trilobite fossils, we conclude that the trilobites were potentially intrinsically valuable. By this account there is no actual value ownership autonomous to the valued and valuable trees, can-yons, trilobites; there is a value ignition when humans arrive. Intrinsic value in the realized sense emerges relationally with the appearance of the subject-generator.

Despite the language of value conferral, if we try to take the term *intrinsic* seriously, this cannot refer to anything the object gains, to something *within* ('intra') the present tree or the past trilobite, for the human subject does not really place anything on or in the natural object. We have only a 'truncated sense' of *intrinsic* (Callicott, 1986, p. 143). The *attributes* under consideration are objectively there before humans come, but the *attribution* of value is subjec-tive. The object causally affects the subject, who is excited by the incoming data and translates this as value, after which the object, the tree, appears as hav-ing value, rather like it appears to have green colour. But nothing is really added *intrinsically*; everything in the object remains what it was before. Despite the language that humans are the *source* of value which they *locate* in the natural object, no value is really located there at all.

The term *intrinsic*, even when truncated, is mis-leading. What is meant is better specified by the term *extrinsic*, the *ex* indicating the external, anthropo-genic ignition of the value, which is not *in, intrinsic*, internal to the nonsentient organism, even though this value, once generated, is apparently conferred on the organism. In the *H-n* encounter, value is conferred by *H* on *n*, and that is really an extrinsic value for *n*, since it comes to *n* from *H*, and likewise it is an extrinsic value for *H*, since it is conferred from *H* to *n*. Neither *H* nor *n*, standing alone, have such value.

We humans carry the lamp that lights up value, although we require the fuel that nature provides.

Actual value is an event in our consciousness, though natural items while still in the dark of value have potential intrinsic value. Man is the measure of things, said Protagoras. Humans are the measurers, the valuers of things, even when we measure what they are in themselves.

Valuable Animals

A mother free-tail bat, a mammal like ourselves, can, using sonar, wend her way out of Bracken Cave, in Texas, in total darkness, catch 500–1000 insects each hour on the wing, and return to find and nurse her own young. That gives evidence of bat-valuing; she values the insects and the pup. Now, it seems absurd to say that there are no valuers until humans arrive. Animals do not make humans the measure of things at all. There is no better evidence of non-human values and valuers than spontaneous wildlife, born free and on its own. Animals hunt and howl, find shelter, seek out their habitats and mates, care for their young, flee from threats, grow hungry, thirsty, hot, tired, excited, sleepy. They suffer injury and lick their wounds. Here we are quite convinced that value is non-anthropogenic, to say nothing of anthropocentric.

These wild animals defend their own lives because they have a good of their own. There is somebody there behind the fur or feathers. Our gaze is returned by an animal that itself has a concerned outlook. Here is value right before our eyes, right behind those eyes. Animals are value-able, able to value things in their world. But we may still want to say that value exists only where a subject has an object of interest. David Prall writes: 'The being liked or dis-liked of the object is its value. . . . Some sort of a subject is always requisite to there being value at all' (Prall, 1921, p. 227). So at least the higher animals can value too, because they are experiencing subjects and can take an interest in things.

Do animals value anything intrinsically? We may not think that animals have the capacity, earlier claimed for humans, of conferring intrinsic value on anything else. Mostly they seek their own basic needs, food and shelter, and care for their young. But then why not say that an animal values its own life for what it is in itself, intrinsically, without fur-ther contributory reference? Else we have an ani-mal world replete with instrumental values and devoid of intrinsic values, everything valuing the resources it needs, nothing valuing itself. That is implausible. Animals maintain a valued self-identity as they cope through the world. Valuing is intrinsic to animal life.]

Valuable Organisms

Outdoors it is difficult to get out of sight of plants. It is also difficult for philosophers to 'see' plants philosophically. Few are botanists. Also, it is easy to overlook the insects. Even fewer philosophers are entomologists.

A plant is not a subject, but neither is it an inanimate object, like a stone. Plants, quite alive, are unified entities of the botanical though not of the zoological kind, that is, they are not unitary organisms highly integrated with centred neural control, but they are modular organisms, with a meristem that can repeatedly and indefinitely produce new vegetative modules, additional stem nodes and leaves when there is available space and resources, as well as new reproductive modules, fruits and seeds.

Plants make themselves; they repair injuries; they move water, nutrients, and photosynthate from cell to cell; they store sugars; they make tannin and other toxins and regulate their levels in defence against grazers; they make nectars and emit pheromones to influence the behaviour of pollinating insects and the responses of other plants; they emit allelopathic agents to suppress invaders; they make thorns, trap insects. They can reject genetically incompatible grafts.

A plant, like any other organism, sentient or not, is a spontaneous, self-maintaining system, sustaining and reproducing itself, executing its program, making a way through the world, checking against performance by means of responsive capacities with which to measure success. Something more than physical causes, even when less than sentience, is operating; there is *information* superintending the causes; without it the organism would collapse into a sand heap. The information is used to preserve the plant identity.

All this cargo is carried by the DNA, essentially a *linguistic* molecule. The genetic set is really a *propositional* set – to choose a provocative term – recalling how the Latin *propositum* is an assertion, a set task, a theme, a plan, a proposal, a project, as well as a cognitive statement. These molecules are set to drive the movement from genotypic potential to phenotypic

expression. Given a chance, these molecules seek organic self-expression. An organism, unlike an inert rock, claims the environment as source and sink, from which to abstract energy and materials and into which to excrete them. It 'takes advantage' of its environment.]

We pass to value when we recognize that the genetic set is a *normative set*; it distinguishes between what *is* and what *ought to be*. The organism is an axiological system, though not a moral system. So the tree grows, reproduces, repairs its wounds, and resists death. The physical state that the organism defends is a valued state. A life is defended for what it is in itself, without necessary further contributory reference. Every organism has a *good-of-its-kind*; it defends its own kind as a *good kind*. In this sense, the genome is a set of conservation molecules.]

Does not that mean that the plant is valuable (able to value) itself? If not, we will have to ask, as an open question: Well, the plant has a good of its own, but is there anything of value to it?[1] Possibly, even though plants have a good of their own, they are not able to value because they are not able to feel anything. Nothing matters to a plant. Hence, says Peter Singer, 'there is nothing to be taken into account' (Singer, 1976, p. 154). There is plant good, but not plant value. There is no valuer evaluating anything. Plants can do things that interest us, but the plants are not interested in what they are doing. They do not have any options among which they are choosing. They have only their merely functional goods.

[. . .]

Valuable Ecosystems

Exploring, we will see different ecosystems: an oak-hickory forest, a tall grass prairie. At least we see trees and grasses. But do we see ecosystems? Maybe we immerse ourselves in them, for an ecosystem is not so much an object in the focus of vision as an enveloping community, a place in space, a process in time, a set of vital relationships. This can mean that philosophers have difficulty seeing, and valuing, ecosystems. Yet, really, the ecosystem is the fundamental unit of development and survival.

Humans can value whatever they wish in nature. This can include ecosystems. 'A thing is right,' concluded Aldo Leopold, 'when it tends to preserve the integrity, stability, and beauty of the biotic community. It is wrong when it tends otherwise' (Leopold, 1966,

p. 240). Leopold wanted a 'land ethic'. So humans can value ecosystem communities intrinsically – for what they are in themselves – as well as instrumentally. But can ecosystems be valuable all by themselves?

Actually, there is a deeper worry again, partly scientific and partly philosophical. Perhaps ecosystems do not exist – or exist in too loose a way to be valuers. They are nothing but aggregations of their more real members, like a forest is (some say) nothing more than a collection of trees. Even a human will have trouble valuing what does not really exist. We can value collections, as of stamps, but this is just the aggregated value of individual stamps. Still, an ecosystem, if it exists, is rather different. Nothing in the stamp collection is alive; the collection is neither self-generating nor self-maintaining. Neither stamp nor collection is valuable on its own. But perhaps ecosystems are both valuable to humans and, if they exist, value-able as systems in themselves.

We need ecology to discover what biotic community means as an organisational mode. Then we can reflect philosophically to discover the values there. Ecosystems can seem little more than stochastic processes. A sea-shore, a tundra, is a loose collection of externally related parts. Much of the environment is not organic at all (rain, groundwater, rocks, nonbiotic soil particles, air). Some is dead and decaying debris (fallen trees, scat, humus). These things have no organized needs; the collection of them is a jumble. The fortuitous interplay between organisms is simply a matter of the distribution and abundance of organisms, how they get dispersed, birth rates and death rates, population densities, moisture regimes, parasitism and predation, checks and balances. There is really not enough centred process to call community.

An ecosystem has no brain, no genome, no skin, no self-identification, no *telos*, no unified program. It does not defend itself against injury or death. It is not irritable. The parts (foxes, sedges) are more complex than the wholes (forests, grasslands). So it can begin to seem as if an ecosystem is too low a level of organisation to be the direct focus of concern. Ecosystems do not and cannot care; they have no interests about which they or we can care.

But this is to misunderstand ecosystems, to make a category mistake. To fault *communities* as though they ought to be organismic *individuals* is to look at one level for what is appropriate at another. One should look for a matrix of interconnections between centres, for creative stimulus and open-ended potential. Everything will be connected to many other things, sometimes by obligate associations, more often by partial and pliable dependencies; and, among other components, there will be no significant interactions. There will be shunts and criss-crossing pathways, cybernetic subsystems and feedback loops. One looks for selection pressures and adaptive fit, not for irritability or repair of injury, for speciation and life support, not for resisting death. We must think more systemically, and less organismically.

An ecosystem generates a spontaneous order that envelops and produces the richness, beauty, integrity and dynamic stability of the component parts. Though these organized interdependencies are loose in comparison with the tight connections within an organism, all these metabolisms are as vitally linked as are liver and heart. The equilibrating ecosystem is not merely push-pull forces. It is an equilibrating of values.

We do not want in an undiscriminating way to extrapolate criteria of value from organism to biotic community, any more than from person to animal or from animal to plant. Rather, we want to discriminate the criteria appropriate to this level. The selective forces in ecosystems at once transcend and produce the lives of individual plants and animals. Evolutionary ecosystems over geological time have increased the numbers of species on Earth from zero to five million or more. R. H. Whittaker found that on continental scales and for most groups 'increase of species diversity . . . is a self-augmenting evolutionary process without any evident limit'. There is a tendency toward what he called 'species packing' (Whittaker, 1972, p. 214).

Superimposed on this, the quality of individual lives in the upper trophic rungs of ecological pyramids has risen. One-celled organisms evolved into many-celled, highly integrated organisms. Photosynthesis evolved and came to support locomotion – swimming, walking, running, flight. Stimulus-response mechanisms became complex instructive acts. Warm-blooded animals followed cold-blooded ones. Neural complexity, conditioned behaviour, and learning emerged. Sentience appeared – sight, smell, hearing, taste, pleasure, pain. Brains evolved, coupled with hands. Consciousness and self-consciousness arose. Persons appeared with intense concentrated unity. The products are valuable, able to be valued by these humans; but why not say that the process is what is really value-able, able to produce these values?

Ecosystems are selective systems, as surely as organisms are selective systems. The system selects over the long ranges for individuality, for diversity, for adapted fitness, for quantity and quality of life. Organisms defend only their own selves or kinds, but the system spins a bigger story. Organisms defend their continuing survival; ecosystems promote new arrivals. Species increase their kinds, but ecosystems increase kinds, and increase the integration of kinds. The system is a kind of field with characteristics as vital for life as any property contained within particular organisms. The ecosystem is the depth source of individual and species alike.

In the current debate among biologists about the levels at which selection takes place – individual organisms, populations, species, genes – the recent tendency to move selective pressures down to the genetic level forgets that a gene is always emplaced in an organism that is emplaced in an ecosystem. The molecular configurations of DNA are what they are because they record the story of a particular form of life in the macroscopic, historical ecosystem. What is generated arises from molecular mutations, but what survives is selected for adaptive fit in an ecosystem. We cannot make sense of biomolecular life without understanding ecosystemic life, the one level as vital as the other.

Philosophers, sometimes encouraged by biologists, may think ecosystems are just epiphenomenal aggregations. This is a confusion. Any level is real if there is significant downward causation. Thus the atom is real because that pattern shapes the behaviour of electrons; the cell because that pattern shapes the behaviour of amino acids; the organism because that pattern co-ordinates the behaviour of hearts and lungs; the community because the niche shapes the morphology and behaviour of the foxes within it. Being real requires an organisation that shapes the existence and the behaviour of members or parts.

Axiologically, in the more comprehensive levels, the terms 'instrumental' and 'intrinsic' do not work very well. Ecosystems have 'systemic value'. But if we want to know what is value-able, able to create value, why not say that it is the productivity of such ecosystems, bringing into existence these phenomena that, when we arrive, the human consciousness is also able to value? What is incredible is not the existence of ecosystems. What is really incredible is that we humans, arriving late on the evolutionary scene, ourselves products of it, bring all the value into the world, when and as we turn our attention to our sources. That claim has too much subjective bias. It values a late product of the system, psychological life, and subordinates everything else to this. It mistakes a fruit for the whole plant, the last chapter for the whole story.

All value does not end in either human or non-human intrinsic value, to which everything else is contributory. Values are intrinsic, instrumental, and systemic, and all three are interwoven, no one with priority over the others in significance, although systemic value is foundational. Each locus of intrinsic value gets folded into instrumental value by the system, and vice versa. There are no intrinsic values, nor instrumental ones either, without the encompassing systemic creativity. It would be foolish to value the golden eggs and disvalue the goose that lays them. It would be a mistake to value the goose only instrumentally. A goose that lays golden eggs is systemically valuable. How much more so is an ecosystem that generates myriads of species, or even, as we next see, an Earth that produces billions of species, ourselves included.

Valuable Earth

I promised to explore the whole world; so let's get the planet in focus. Viewing Earthrise, Edgar Mitchell, was entranced: 'Suddenly from behind the rim of the moon, in long-slow motion moments of immense majesty, there emerges a sparkling blue and white jewel, a light, delicate sky-blue sphere laced with slowly swirling veils of white, rising gradually like a small pearl in a thick sea of black mystery. It takes more than a moment to fully realize this is Earth . . . home' (Kelley, 1988, at photographs 42–5). Michael Collins was Earthstruck: 'When I travelled to the moon, it wasn't my proximity to that battered rockpile I remember so vividly, but rather what I saw when I looked back at my fragile home – a glistening, inviting beacon, delicate blue and white, a tiny outpost suspended in the black infinity. Earth is to be treasured and nurtured, something precious that *must* endure' (Gallant, 1980, p. 6).

Pearls are, a philosopher might object, valuable only when humans come around. But this mysterious Earth-pearl, a biologist will reply, is a home long before we humans come. This is the only biosphere, the only planet with an ecology. Earth may not be the only planet where anything is valuable – able to be valued by humans intrinsically or instrumentally – but it is the only place able to produce vitality before humans come. The view from space symbolizes all this.

Earlier the challenge was to evaluate persons, animals, plants, species, ecosystems; but environmental valuing is not over until we have risen to the planetary level. Earth is really the relevant survival unit. But valuing the whole Earth is unfamiliar and needs philosophical analysis. We may seem to be going to extremes. Earth is, after all, just earth. The belief that dirt could have intrinsic value is sometimes taken as a *reductio ad absurdum* in environmental philosophy. Dirt is not the sort of thing that has value by itself. Put like that, we agree. An isolated clod defends no intrinsic value and it is difficult to say that it has much value in itself. But that is not the end of the matter, because a clod of dirt is integrated into an ecosystem; earth is a part, Earth the whole. Dirt is product and process in a systemic nature. We should try to get the global picture, and switch from a lump of dirt to the Earth system in which it has been created.

Earth is, some will insist, a big rockpile like the moon, only one on which the rocks are watered and illuminated in such way that they support life. So maybe it is really the life we value and not the Earth, except as instrumental to life. We do not have duties to rocks, air, ocean, dirt, or Earth; we have duties to people, or living things. We must not confuse duties to the home with duties to the inhabitants. We do not praise so much the dirt as what is in the dirt, not earth so much as what is on Earth. But this is not a systemic view of what is going on. We need some systematic account of the valuable Earth we now behold, before we beheld it, not just some value that is generated in the eye of the beholder. Finding that value will generate a global sense of obligation.

The evolution of rocks into dirt into fauna and flora is one of the great surprises of natural history, one of the rarest events in the astronomical universe. Earth is all dirt, we humans too arise up from the humus, and we find revealed what dirt can do when it is self-organizing under suitable conditions. This is pretty spectacular dirt. Really, the story is little short of a series of 'miracles', wondrous, fortuitous events, unfolding of potential; and when Earth's most complex product, *Homo sapiens*, becomes intelligent enough to reflect over this cosmic wonderland, everyone is left stuttering about the mixtures of accident and necessity out of which we have evolved. For some the black mystery will be numinous and signal transcendence; for some the mystery may be impenetrable. Perhaps we do not have to have all the cosmological answers. Nobody has

much doubt that this is a precious place, a pearl in a sea of black mystery.

The elemental chemicals of life – carbon, oxygen, hydrogen, nitrogen – are common enough throughout the universe. They are made in the stars. But life, rare elsewhere, is common on Earth, and the explanation lies in the ordinary elements in an extraordinary setting, the super-special circumstances in which these common chemicals find themselves arranged on Earth, that is, in the self-organizing system. On an everyday scale, earth, dirt, seems to be passive, inert, an unsuitable object of moral concern. But on a global scale?

The scale changes nothing, a critic may protest, the changes are only quantitative. Earth is no doubt precious as life support, but it is not precious in itself. There is nobody there in a planet. There is not even the objective vitality of an organism, or the genetic transmission of a species line. Earth is not even an ecosystem, strictly speaking; it is a loose collection of myriads of ecosystems. So we must be talking loosely, perhaps poetically or romantically, of valuing Earth. Earth is a mere thing, a big thing, a special thing for those who happen to live on it, but still a thing, and not appropriate as an object of intrinsic or systemic valuation. We can, if we insist on being anthropocentrists, say that it is all valueless except as our human resource.

But we will not be valuing Earth objectively until we appreciate this marvellous natural history. This really is a superb planet, the most valuable entity of all, because it is the entity able to produce all the Earthbound values. At this scale of vision, if we ask what is principally to be valued, the value of life arising as a creative process on Earth seems a better description and a more comprehensive category.

Perhaps you think that species are unreal. Perhaps you still insist that ecosystems are unreal, only aggregations, but how about Earth? Will you say that Earth too, being a higher level entity, is unreal? Only an aggregation, and not a systemic whole? There is no such thing as a biosphere? Surely, Earth has some rather clear boundaries, does it not? Will you say that this is a planet where nothing matters? Nothing matters to Earth, perhaps, but everything matters on Earth, for Earth.

Do not humans sometimes value Earth's life-supporting systems because they are valuable, and not always the other way round? Is this value just a matter of late-coming human interests? Or is Earth not historically a remarkable, valuable place, a place able to produce value prior to the human arrival, and even now valuable antecedently to the human uses of it? It seems parochial to say that our part alone in the drama establishes all its worth. The production of value over the millennia of natural history is not something subjective that goes on in the human mind. In that sense, a valuable Earth is not the *reductio ad absurdum* of valuing dirt. It is not even locating the most valuable thing in the world; it is locating the ultimate value of the world itself. The creativity within the natural system we inherit, and the values this generates, are the ground of our being, not just the ground under our feet. Earth could be the ultimate object of duty, short of God, if God exists.

Valuable Nature

William James, toward the beginning of our century, starkly portrayed the utterly valueless world, transfigured as a gift of the human coming:

> Conceive yourself, if possible, suddenly stripped of all the emotion with which your world now inspires you, and try to imagine it *as it exists*, purely by itself, without your favorable or unfavorable, hopeful or apprehensive comment. It will be almost impossible for you to realize such a condition of negativity and deadness. No one portion of the universe would then have importance beyond another; and the whole collection of its things and series of its events would be without significance, character, expression, or perspective. Whatever of value, interest, or meaning our respective worlds may appear endued with are thus pure gifts of the spectator's mind. (James, 1925, p. 150)

At the end of this century, this is not what the astronauts think at all. They do not see Earth as negativity and deadness, nor do they think that this portion of the universe has no significance beyond any other part, except by gift of our spectating minds. They did not say that the world was valuable only because they took along an indubitable self into space and projected value onto Earth. They rather see that human life arises in a spectacular place, in a nature of whose creative patterns they are part.

According to the old paradigm, so long dominant that to some it now seems elementary, there is no value without an experiencing valuer, just as there are no thoughts without a thinker, no percepts without a perceiver, no deeds without a doer, no targets without an aimer. Valuing is felt preferring by human choosers. Possibly, extending this paradigm, sentient animals may also value. But plants cannot value; they have no options and make no choices. *A fortiori*, Earth and nature cannot be bona fide valuers. One can always hang on to the claim that value, like a tickle or remorse, must be felt to be there. Its *esse* is *percipi*. Nonsensed value is nonsense. It is only beings with 'insides' to them that have value.

But the problem with the 'no value without a valuer' axiom is that it is too individualistic; it looks for some centre of value located in a subjective self. And we nowhere wish to deny that such valuers are sufficient for value. But that is not the whole account of value in a more holistic, systemic, ecological, global account. Perhaps there can be no doing science without a scientist, no religion without a believer, no tickle without somebody tickled. But there can be law without a lawgiver, history without a historian; there is biology without biologists, physics without physicists, creativity without creators, story without story-tellers, achievement without achievers – and value without valuers. A sentient valuer is not necessary for value. Another way is for there to be a value-generating system able to generate value. If you like, that is another meaning of value-er; any *x* is a valuer if *x* is value-able, able to produce values.

It is true that humans are the only evaluators who can reflect about what is going on at this global scale, who can deliberate about what they ought to do about conserving it. When humans do this, they must set up the scales; and humans are the measurers of things. Animals, organisms, species, ecosystems, Earth, cannot teach us how to do this evaluating. But they can display what it is that is to be valued. The axiological scales we construct do not constitute the value, any more than the scientific scales we erect create what we thereby measure.

Humans are not so much lighting up value in a merely potentially valuable world, as they are psychologically joining ongoing planetary natural history in which there is value wherever there is positive creativity. While such creativity can be present in subjects with their interests and preferences, it can also be present objectively in living organisms with their lives defended, and in species that defend an identity over time, and in systems that are self-organizing and that project storied achievements. The valuing subject in an otherwise valueless world is an insufficient premise for the experienced conclusions of those who value natural history.

Conversion to a biological and geological view seems truer to world experience and more logically compelling. This too is a perspective, but ecologically better informed; we know our place on a home planet. From this more objective viewpoint, there is something subjective, something philosophically naive, and even something hazardous in a time of ecological crisis, about living in a reference frame where one species takes itself as absolute and values everything else in nature relative to its potential to produce value for itself. Such philosophers live in an unexamined world, and, in result, they and those they guide live unworthy lives, because they cannot see their valuable world.

Note

1 Robin Attfield remarks that 'even if trees have needs and a good of their own, they may still have no value of their own' (Attfield, 1981, p. 35).

References

Attfield, Robin 1981. 'The good of trees', *Journal of Value Inquiry* 15, 35–54.
Callicott, J. Baird 1984. 'Non-anthropocentric value theory and environmental ethics', *American Philosophical Quarterly* 21, 299–309.
Callicott, J. Baird 1986. 'On the intrinsic value of nonhuman species', in Bryan G. Norton (ed.), *The Preservation of Species*. Princeton, NJ: Princeton University Press, 138–72.
Gallant, Roy A. 1980. *Our Universe*. Washington, DC: National Geographic Society.
James, William 1925. *The Varieties of Religious Experience*. New York: Longmans, Green.
Kelley, Kevin W. (ed.) 1988. *The Home Planet*. Reading, MA: Addison-Wesley.
Leopold, Aldo 1966. *A Sand County Almanac*. New York: Oxford University Press.
Norton, Bryan G. 1991. *Toward Unity Among Environmentalists*. New York: Oxford University Press.
Prall, David 1921. *A Study in the Theory of Value*. Berkeley, CA: University of California Press.
Singer, Peter 1976. 'All animals are equal', in Tom Regan and Peter Singer (eds.), *Animal Rights and Human Obligations*. Englewood Cliffs, NJ: Prentice-Hall.
Whittaker, R. 1972. 'Evolution and measurement of species diversity', *Taxon* 21, 213–51.
Windelband, Wilhelm 1921. *An Introduction to Philosophy*. London: T. Fisher Unwin.

16   The End of Anthropocentrism?

Mary Midgley

What Is It To Be Central?

Are human beings in some sense central to the cosmos? It used to seem obvious that they were. It seems less obvious now. But the idea is still powerful in our thinking, and it may be worth while asking just what it has meant.

There is of course a minor point of view from which we really are central – for our own lives, our own species do provide the natural focus. Our starting-point, the angle from which we look at things, is bound to be our own region. In the same way, if we think about *self*-centredness, each of us does unavoidably see our own self as in some sense the centre of the world.

This parallel is surely helpful. In neither case can we spread our consciousness impartially over the whole scene. We do have powers of sympathy, but since we are finite beings, those powers are necessarily limited. We have no choice but to be specially interested in ourselves and those close to us. As Bishop Butler

From Robin Attfield and Andrew Belsey, eds., *Philosophy and the Natural Environment*, Royal Institute of Philosophy Supplement 36 (Cambridge: Cambridge University Press, 1994), pp. 103–12. © 1994 by The Royal Institute of Philosophy and the contributors. Reproduced with permission from Cambridge University Press.

pointed out, this kind of priority is not necessarily a bad thing. Indeed it is vital that we do love and care for ourselves properly. If we have not enough self-love, if we despise or hate ourselves, we cannot love other people. The trouble with human beings (he said) is not really that they love themselves too much; they ought to love themselves more. The trouble is simply that they don't love others enough (Butler, 1969, p. 24).

In that sense, then, the self *must* be the centre of each person's world and accordingly the word 'self-centred' seems at first to have had quite a good meaning. It was coined to describe the balanced state of heavenly bodies like the sun, spinning securely on their own axes, rather than shooting off at an angle like badly made tops. Figuratively, then, it was used to describe well-organized, balanced people. Thus the *Oxford English Dictionary* quotes from a novel in 1895: 'He would be fixed at last, swinging steadily on a pivot of happiness. . . . Now at last he would be self-centred'.

Interestingly, however, this image of independence soon began to show a darker side. Thus the Dictionary gives a remark by one Norris, writing *Practical Discourses* in 1693: 'The self-ending, self-centring man does in a very true sense idolise himself'. Again, it quotes from Dr Johnson's letters (1783): 'A stubborn sufficiency self-centred', and from Coleridge (1809): 'They pursue the interests of freedom steadily, but with narrow and self-centring views'. In short, the natural balance of the independent spinning top cannot be relied on for human social life. If there is too much ego in your cosmos, other people are likely to go short. Charity may indeed begin at home, but it had better not end there.

This is now a commonly accepted moral principle, indeed, something of a platitude, not just for individual selves, but also for the various human groups into which they cluster – families, classes, professions, races, nations. Group chauvinism, as well as individual selfishness, is understood to be a serious fault. So far, indeed, we are on ground common to our whole moral tradition.

Species Politics During the Enlightenment

If, however, we turn from self to species, things have not been so simple. Here people have seen themselves as placed, not just at the relative centre of a particular life, but at the absolute, objective centre of everything. The centrality of MAN (*sic*) has been pretty steadily conceived, both in the West and in many other traditions, not as an illusion of perspective imposed by our starting-point, but as an objective fact, and indeed an essential fact, about the whole universe.

Christian thought grounded this status firmly on creation by a humanoid God who had made man in his (*sic*) own image in order to mark a quite special status among the ruck of ordinary, non-Godlike creatures. But this Christian account has not stood alone. Enlightenment thinkers who reckoned to be emancipated from such imagery were no less confident on the matter. Thus Kant: 'As the single being upon earth that possesses understanding, [man] is certainly titular lord of nature and, supposing we regard nature as a teleological system, he is born to be its ultimate end' (Kant, 1928, pp. 93–4).

Kant states here three themes which often recur and need a great deal of attention: the claim to dominance, the emphasis on intellect as its ground, and the reference to cosmic teleology. As for dominance, man is 'titular lord'. For beings who think hierarchically, this is no doubt a natural way to interpret centrality. What is alarming about it, however, is how easily the imagery of dominance escalates to that of exploitation and even warfare.

Thus Marx observed that capitalism had been right to reject 'the deification of nature': 'thus nature becomes for the first time simply an object for mankind, purely a matter of utility' (Marx, 1971, p. 94). More sharply still, Freud suggested that the right way to sublimate human aggression was to direct it away from other people against the rest of the biosphere, by 'becoming a member of the human community, and, with the help of a technique guided by science, going over to the attack against nature and subjecting her to the human will' (Freud, 1985, p. 265). William James proposed the same solution to that problem in his famous essay on 'The Moral Equivalent of War'. In fact, the idea that human beings should use the intellectual power of science to conquer nature by war or suppression seems to have looked perfectly normal to many thinkers, at least up till the middle of [the twentieth] century, both in the capitalist world and, if anything, still more so in the communist one. Thus John Passmore quotes (along with many other fascinating examples) M. N. Pokrovskiy, writing in a *Brief History of Russia* in 1931: 'It is easy to foresee that in the future, when science and technique have attained to a perfection which we are as yet unable to visualise, nature will become soft wax in his [man's] hands which he will be able to cast into whatever form he chooses' (Passmore, 1980, p. 25).

Doubt Seeps In

We can understand how people had reached this curious view. Starting from the already ambitious biblical position, human beings had for some centuries been performing many increasingly dazzling technological and scientific feats. At the same time, and partly as a result of these changes, various doctrines of historical progress had been developed, focusing attention still more strongly on the rising curve of human achievement, glorifying humans yet further and making the gap between them and the rest of the biosphere look still wider.

At this same time, however, a whole string of other intellectual developments were moving thought away from this cheerful pattern. The effect has been to leave that pattern now strangely isolated and conceptually unsupported, though still emotionally very strong. I think that a sizeable part of our present confusion may flow from our sense of anomaly here – from the Gestalt-shift between a wildly exaggerated, euphoric idea of human standing and a despairing nihilism about it which may be equally wild ('people are pollution'). Today, though we still often hear very flattering accounts of ourselves, we just as often come across much less flattering ones, and on the whole these are pronounced with more conviction.

Thus early in this century William James (writing in the *Atlantic Monthly* in 1904) remarked that 'man, biologically considered, and whatever else he may be into the bargain, is simply the most formidable of all the beasts of prey, and, indeed, the only one that preys systematically on its own species'. Or again, Arthur Koestler observed that 'The most persistent sound that reverberates through man's history is the beating of war-drums. . . . Man can leave the earth and land on the moon, but cannot cross from East to West Berlin. Prometheus reaches for the stars with an insane grin on his face and a totem-symbol in his hand' (Koestler, 1978, Prologue).

Of course, dark remarks of this sort are not new. There was always an ambivalence within Christian thought that called for humility and penitence and reminded us that our righteousness was as filthy rags.

But certain changes in the modern age have given this kind of thinking so much more force that they might, at a glance, be seen as heralding the end of anthropocentrism.

The Paradox of Science

What, then, have been these eroding changes? In the first place, of course, scientific progress itself began to cast doubts on the whole euphoric way of thinking. The universe has turned out to be both so much larger and so much less tidily organized than it used to seem that the idea of its having any centre, in a literal physical sense, no longer makes sense. And though we might think that it should be easy to accept these new factual beliefs without losing what the older ones used to symbolize, it turns out that this imagery is in fact quite hard to shift. Symbols that persist in this way always deserve attention.

Several different sciences have converged to alarm us here. Astronomy now tells us that there is no physical centre and no absolute up and down. There surrounds us, instead, a formless stage so vast, both in time and space, that even the most splendid human actors are almost imperceptible as they move upon it – insects or bacteria, at best. Biology adds that, even among the living things which have lately entered on this scene, human beings are particularly late and perhaps accidental arrivals. Their shape, too, does not appear to be so much a direct imprint from God as a slight variation on an existing primate pattern. Xenophanes, in fact, was right – if horses and cattle had gods, they would make them in the shape of horses and cattle. Man has made God in his own image. Geography adds that the continents which we have usually thought of as at least a firm grounding for our part of the stage are themselves on the move. Most recently, too, ecology has told us that we are by no means securely moulding wax-like nature to suit our needs and are never likely to do so. On the contrary, we are busily sawing off the branches we sit on, and can only cease to do that if we attend respectfully to the internal guiding principles of nature instead of trying to distort it through ones invented by ourselves.

More generally still, however, there is a metaphysical change in the scientific perspective. The teleological assumptions that seemed to hold the symbolic core of 'anthropocentrism' in place are themselves no longer deemed scientific. The idea of a central cosmic purpose is as foreign to modern science as the idea of a central location is. The word 'anthropocentric' itself seems to have been invented to make just this point. Thus the *Oxford English Dictionary* quotes Haeckel (or his translator into English) writing in 1876 of 'the anthropocentric error, that man is the premeditated aim of the creation of the earth'.

The paradox here – comic or tragic, as you choose to look at it – is that science, which has always seemed a particularly bright jewel in the crown of the titular lord, turns out also, paradoxically, to be an axe cutting away the floor under his throne. Nor is science alone in this destructive work; political theory plays an equally double part. After the Enlightenment, what are we doing with the notion of a titular lord anyway? If we are proud of science, we are surely still more proud of discovering that government should always be by consent. Its authority comes from below, from those who accept it, not from an outside ruler, as in the Divine Right of Kings. The idea of being a lord arbitrarily appointed from outside, more particularly a violent lord, liable at the drop of a hat to make war on his disobedient subjects, doesn't suit our self-image at all. Yet, if we keep the traditional reasoning and imagery, that is how we are supposed to see ourselves.

Anthropic Escapism

What is to be done about all this? It is quite interesting that some desperate efforts have been made to extend modern science so as to make it endorse the traditional picture, most strikingly through the Strong Anthropic Principle. This rules that 'The Universe must have those properties which allow life to develop within it at some stage in its history' (Barrow and Tipler, 1986, p. 21). This is considered necessary because matter cannot really function unless it is observed, and observed in the special way in which physicists observe quantum events. (A confused memory of Berkeleian idealism is evidently at work here.) Human perception, and indeed the perception of contemporary scientists, is thus absolutely indispensable to the existence of the cosmos.

Officially, this quasi-idealist approach is not supposed to imply that the cosmos works with the aim of producing the observer who will save it. But it is usually combined with the thought that the constitution of the existing universe is so extraordinarily improbable that the fact of its development can only

be accounted for by the need to produce just one of its existing artefacts. And by a remarkable coincidence, this selected artefact turns out to be not a set of giraffes or redwood trees or colonial jellyfish, but the species *Homo sapiens* – especially, of course, in its current manifestation as *Homo sapiens physicus*.

In effect, this can only be an attempt to bring back teleology – to renew the notion of a cosmic drama with a central role for MAN, not in the context of religion, nor with any explicitly defended philosophical assumptions, but nominally as a simple, objective part of physics. This principle teaches that the universe has indeed had the production of MAN as its central business, but that MAN is needed simply as a physicist, able to collapse certain wave-functions by observing quantum events, and thereby to make the universe itself at last fully and properly real. Until then it was not thus real, for, as John Wheeler explains, 'Acts of observer-participancy – via the mechanism of the delayed-choice experiment – in turn give tangible "reality" to the universe not only now but back to the beginning' (Wheeler, 1983, pp. 209, 194; cf. Barrow and Tipler, 1986, p. 464). Professors Barrow and Tipler add that MAN, having performed this feat, will then proceed to computerize himself and to occupy the whole of space by colonization, arriving finally at the Omega Point in possession of all the information that there is, and thereby in some sense apparently becoming God. (Their most startling claims about this may be found at the end of their book, and especially in its concluding sentences.)

I have discussed this amazing project elsewhere (see Midgley, 1992, pp. 21–7 and ch. 17). Here, I can only suggest that this sort of thing is in no sense science, but simply a piece of wild metaphysics, made possible by the weird metaphorical language already in use on the topics of quantum mechanics, time and probability theory. Ignorance about how metaphors work is widespread among modern English-speaking physicists, and is particularly deep among British ones. They very much need to read the chapter on science in Janet Martin Soskice's sharp little book *Metaphor and Religious Language*, and also Graham Richards's *On Psychological Language*.

Why All or Nothing?

What matters here, however, is not the muddles but the point of the project. The Anthropic Principle seems aimed, somewhat desperately, at bridging the gap just mentioned – the gap that yawns in our current thinking between our immense sense of our own importance on the local scene and our apparent total insignificance in the objective universe.

We cannot bridge that gap if we insist on an all-or-nothing solution. The anthropicists are making a desperate effort to keep *all*. They are in fact setting up by far the highest claims ever made for the importance of our species, because they do not even have the background figure of God to moderate our status. While God is present, MAN can be reduced to the figure of a responsible steward, even if he remains, in some sense, central among earthly creatures. But for the anthropicists, MAN replaces God as creator, not just of earth, but of everything. In effect, they are offering us anthropolatry. As Norris puts it: 'The self-ending, self-centring man does in a very true sense idolise himself'.

⌈I suggest that the reason why cosmologists do this is not necessarily that they are more conceited than the rest of us, but that the fear of total insignificance produces a violent reaction, leading people to claim immense, inconceivable kinds of significance. Exactly as happens over individual paranoia, frightened subjects react against being down-graded by grading themselves up – if necessary, indefinitely, and becoming gods. The trouble starts, surely, with the fact that, when our traditional symbols are attacked, we do not stop thinking symbolically, we just change the symbol.⌋

When the cosmic stage on which we used to figure becomes larger, we do not drop the idea of any such stage. Instead, we see ourselves as shrinking puppets, and eventually as ants or bacteria, still performing on this same expanding stage. Because this is unbearable, people look for a counter-symbol, a story which can somehow be taken as scientifically literal, and which yet gives us back our key part in the drama.

What we need to do instead, I suggest, is to change the symbolism in a deeper and more discriminating way. We never needed that vast cosmic stage in the first place, and only very lately have we had it. Our business has never been with anything outside our own planet.

⌈We do indeed need a sense of destiny – a sense of a larger background, a context within which our own lives make sense. We need the idea of a drama in which we are acting. We have to have a sense of the sort of role that is expected of us. We need that sense whether or no we believe in God, whether or no we are important and influential people, whether or no we understand where it comes from. All cultures supply this sort of background framework – indeed, doing so is one of their most basic functions. We need it both for ourselves individually and for all the groups with which we seriously identify. That is what it is for life to have a meaning.⌋ But nothing fixes in advance the range of beings that must figure in our drama. Nothing forces us to take the vast extra-terrestrial background into our theatre. And certainly nothing commits us to swallowing or conquering all figures in the drama who are outside our own group.

At every level – both for the individual and for various kinds of group – there is a temptation to supply this drama simply by drawing a firm line between ourselves and a range of opponents. That is always the quickest way to give life a meaning. Individuals can set themselves against the whole world; Ajax defies the lightning. Similarly group members can set their group against everybody outside it, and life so organized can go on charmingly for the inside circle. All disasters, even death, are more easily faced in this pugnacious context which so readily gets the adrenalin flowing. This is the tendency which has again and again fixed people in mutually destructive, confrontational groups, and it is surely the one that has accounted for the exclusive, pugnacious glorification of our own species in earlier thinking.

What Should We Call It?

I do not think Anthropocentrism is the best name for this habit. It is, no doubt, a word that can be used at the everyday level, and at that level I am not trying to get rid of it. But if we try to put much weight on it, it can lead us into trouble. In the first place, as I said at the outset, there is a sense in which it is right for us to feel that we are at the centre of our own lives. Attempts to get rid of that sense would be doomed in the same way as stoical attempts to tell people not to care specially about themselves, or about those dear to them. As Bishop Butler (again) pointed out in his 'Sermon upon Compassion', puritanism of this sort can only be destructive. It may succeed in damaging the particular affections it attacks, but it has no power to produce nobler, more universal affections to replace them. And, in controversy, such unrealistic puritanism is always damaging to one's own cause.

We need, then, to recognize that people do right, not wrong, to have a particular regard for their own kin and their own species. From a practical angle, this recognition does not harm green causes, because the measures needed today to save the human race are, by and large, the same measures that are needed to save the rest of the biosphere. There simply is no lifeboat option by which human beings can save themselves alone, either as a whole or in particular areas. If there were, this issue of emotional centrality might be a serious one, but there isn't. There are indeed local conflicts of interests over things like culling. But in general, in the kind of major emergency we have at present, the interests of different species coincide so widely that really enlightened self-interest would not dictate seriously different policies from species-altruism. I don't, therefore, see much point in disputing hotly about the rightness of 'anthropocentrism' in this very limited sense.

When, however, we leave that intelligible ground – when 'anthropocentrism' is taken to mean an absolute claim to be at the centre of the universe – I simply do not know what this metaphor is supposed to mean at all. The Anthropicists are probably doing us a service by sketching out a possible meaning for it, since that meaning is so ludicrous as to reduce the whole idea to absurdity. What is commonly *meant* by the word 'anthropocentric' today, however, is something much more ordinary and much less intellectually ambitious. It is simple *human chauvinism, narrowness of sympathy*, comparable to national or race or gender chauvinism. It could also be called *exclusive humanism*, as opposed to the hospitable, friendly, inclusive kind.

That chauvinism is surely as indefensible rationally as the chauvinism of smaller human groups. Enlightenment thinking has certainly built protective barriers round it by devices like defining the idea of 'rights' in a way that confines it to articulate humans who can speak in law-courts, and ruling that rights can only belong to those who have, in a recognized human sense, duties. These constructions seem to me evidently artificial and unconvincing once the spotlight of attention actually reaches them. (I have discussed them elsewhere (Midgley, 1983, ch. 5).) As tools of admirable campaigning for the Rights of Man, these ideas were originally aimed at extending concern to the whole human race, not at shutting it off from dogs and horses. Some of the major Enlightenment sages, such as Tom Paine, Montaigne and Voltaire, were in fact much concerned about the sufferings of animals, and Bentham surely spoke for the deeper spirit of Enlightenment humanitarianism when he said: 'The question is not, Can they reason? nor Can they talk? but, Can they suffer?'.

Certainly this wider perspective leaves us with some hard problems. We have to arbitrate all sorts of local inter-species conflicts; we do not have a tidy system of Rights and Duties that will always tell us how to do so. But then, did anybody ever suppose that we did have one, even on the human scene? Such a project would be still less plausible if it were applied, as human chauvinists might still like to apply it, to all conflicts of interests between species in the fast-changing, distracted world that we have today. The kind of anthropolatry that would always set immediate human interests above those of other life-forms is surely no longer defensible. Enlightenment individualism incorporated strong contributions from egoism, which, in their own time, had their uses. But today we need less, not more, ego in our cosmos, both individually and collectively. What we, as philosophers, have to do next is to work hard on forging the ways of thinking that will help to make this need clear and understandable.

References

Barrow, John D. and Tipler, Frank J. 1986. *The Anthropic Cosmological Principle*. Oxford: Oxford University Press.

Butler, Joseph 1969. *Butler's Sermons*, ed. W. R. Matthews. London: Bell.

Freud, Sigmund 1985. *Civilization and its Discontents*, in *Civilization, Society and Religion* (Pelican Freud Library, vol. 12). London: Penguin.

Kant, Immanuel 1928. *Critique of Teleological Judgment*, trans. J. C. Meredith. Oxford: Clarendon Press.

Koestler, Arthur 1978. *Janus*. London: Hutchinson.

Marx, Karl 1971. *Marx's Grundrisse*, ed. David McLellan. London: Macmillan.

Midgley, Mary 1983. *Animals and Why they Matter*. Athens, GA: University of Georgia Press.

Midgley, Mary 1992. *Science as Salvation*. London: Routledge.

Passmore, John 1980. *Man's Responsibility for Nature* (2nd ed.). London: Duckworth.

Richards, Graham 1989. *On Psychological Language*. London: Routledge.

Soskice, Janet Martin 1985. *Metaphor and Religious Language*. Oxford: Clarendon Press.

Wheeler, John A. 1983. 'Law without law', in John A. Wheeler and W. H. Zurek (eds.), *Quantum Theory and Measurement*. Princeton, NJ: Princeton University Press.

17 Is the Crown of Creation a Dunce Cap?

Chip Ward

The evidence of human intelligence has always been mixed. On the one hand, we have traveled to the moon. On the other hand, it took us a couple of hundred years to figure out we needed wheels on our luggage. We have created astonishing computers and the Internet that we use to look up Britney Spears's skirt. Some of us can do brain surgery but most of us can't locate Iraq on a map and think H_2O is a cable channel. And if humans express the epitome of intelligence, as opposed to, say, the intelligence of migrating birds or even underground networks of mushroom spores, then how do you explain that hundreds of years after the "Enlightenment" we are still slaughtering each other in serial warfare; that we poison our own bloodstreams with toxic pollution; and that we have so altered the climate that harbors our proud civilization that it may collapse around our ears? Our intelligence encompasses both Mozart and suicide bombers. Perhaps it's time to take a second look.

The Brain Chauvinist Menu and the Limits of Doing the Math

What is intelligence? No doubt most humans will answer, it's what I've got that animals don't have: language, reasoning, problem-solving skills, and the ability to make and use tools. After all, monkeys and parrots might learn a few words but they can't do crossword puzzles and when was the last time you saw a dolphin on a pimped-out street bike?

The difference between our way of thinking and that of our fellow creatures is a key to how we treat them. We are brain chauvinists.[1] We believe, for instance, that it is okay to consume without a second thought any brainless creature – oyster mistreatment is not on PETA's radar. For those with brains, the degree of intelligence that we acknowledge governs our relationship. We have no qualms about eating a stupid tuna but we'll pay big bucks to swim with dolphins and want our tuna "dolphin-free." You can

be jailed and shunned for torturing a cat or dog, but the routine and massive abuse of chickens in factory farms is largely ignored as if they are merely vegetables with feathers. Our attitude toward animals is basically "If you're smart, you're safe and if you're dumb, you're dead."

Our kind of intelligence is undeniable. Humans are very sharp when it comes to all those aspects of the world that are fixed, measurable, happen in a linear progression, and are predictable. That is how, after all, we put a man on the moon. The moon is pretty predictable – it doesn't take last-minute vacations or sleep in. So if we are dealing with the mechanical realm of physics, our airplanes, dams, chemical finesse, and nuclear machines are wonders to behold.

What we are not good at are all those phenomena that are nonlinear and have emergent behaviors, where, in other words, the whole tends to be greater than the sum of its parts but not predictably so – things like the climate, ecosystems, fetal development, immune systems, brain function, and crowd behavior. We are only beginning to understand the dynamics of our chaotic world – feedback loops, thresholds, and basins of attraction. We have a rather myopic view of scales, seeing well what is happening now and predicting what's right around the corner, but missing the slow variables that can be more important in the long run. This is why we deplete soils, turn grasslands into deserts, and use up ancient aquifers and oil deposits in a geological instant.

Virgin Births and Cultural Amnesiacs

Our intelligence is also tempered by the human condition. Although we can boast about the scientific prowess we express through our technology and medicine, we are easily distracted by emotional needs for validation, approval, and identity. Our persistent

An earlier version of this paper appeared in *Catalyst: Healthy Living, Healthy Planet*, vol. 26, no. 1 (January 2008) (Salt Lake City: New Moon Press, Inc.).

belief in religious doctrines has us accepting as true phenomena that contradict our otherwise proud powers of reasoning – how else do you explain virgin births and angels with gold plates? We compete as much as we compute, greed still drives us, and we can rationalize any destructive behavior. We are easily addicted and not easily satiated. There is reason to believe we have been traumatized by our recent history of global war, genocide, environmental dislocation, and fear.

Because we have short memories and a tendency toward denial, collectively we act like amnesiacs, as if every other past civilization or previous empire didn't also think it was smarter than all the others that had preceded it and, unlike them, was immune to failure. Consider that almost everything an intellectual in the sixteenth century knew for certain has since been proved wrong, and almost everything we know for sure today will be radically revised 100 years hence. Today's genius is tomorrow's fool.

Stink Think, Bee Dancing, and the Mushroom Internet

For a moment, then, let's concede the field to our nonhuman fellow creatures and redefine intelligence simply as the capacity to learn from experience and apply that learning to future challenges. Even moths can do that. Ohio State University entomologists implanted electrodes into the brains of sphinx moths. The researchers monitored the moths' nervous systems while presenting them with different odors – including sugar water, a favorite moth treat. They saw a dramatic restructuring of the neural networks that convert scent into a code that the rest of the brain can understand, and concluded that, like humans, moths learn.[2] Even the lowly slime mold can find the shortest route through a maze to get to nutritious food sources.

Learning involves pattern recognition and communication. We've all heard about the complicated messages that dolphins, elephants, and prairie dogs can convey through their various vocalizations. But nonvocal communication is also common. Insects use pheromones to communicate a wide range of messages that are, like human messages, mostly about food and sex. Bees perch at the door of the hive and do a little dance that indicates to the other bees where the flowers are in relation to the sun. Because we humans cannot understand the language nonhumans are speaking doesn't mean communication is either absent or inferior to ours. If computers can communicate with nothing more than series of ones and zeroes, creatures that can emit endless variations of notes, clicks, and tones might be up to more than we suspect.

Mushroom visionary Paul Stamets argues that mycelium fungi function as the neurological network of the soil. Layering the ground with interwoven microbial mats that share information, mycelium fungi react to changes that threaten soil health by devising diverse enzymatic and chemical responses to the complex challenges they detect. We are not sure how they do this, but Stamets claims they are the sentient membrane of the earth, a biomolecular matrix that is in constant dialogue with the environment, responding to and governing the flow of essential nutrients. "I believe," he writes in *Mycelium Running*, "mycelium operate at a level of complexity that exceeds our most advanced computers. I see mycelium as the Earth's natural Internet."[3]

Drop for a moment our brain chauvinism and it is clear that there is such a thing as non-centralized intelligence. Immune systems learn or you wouldn't make it through the next flu season. Microbes learn, too, or there wouldn't *be* a next flu season. An entire pharmaceutical infrastructure, peopled by the best human brains Big Pharma can pay, works constantly to outwit the viruses that would consume us and lately the antibiotics side is losing.

Lizard Avoidance and the Wisdom of the Hive

Then there is "swarm intelligence." How is it that an individual ant cannot survive alone and is downright clueless about the big picture he is in, but an ant colony makes complicated decisions daily and can thrive for decades? How do the actions of individual ants, undirected by leaders, add up to the complex behaviors of the group?

Swarm intelligence depends on simple creatures following simple rules and acting on local information. Ants communicate by touch and smell. Patroller ants leave the colony and don't return until they find food. When they return they touch other ants. If the patrollers are successful, they return quickly and often. When the colony's forager ants are touched by enough patrollers in a short time, they leave the colony to harvest the food, following scent trails left by the patrollers. If, on the other hand, the patrollers encounter bad weather or a hungry lizard, they don't return and they don't touch their fellow foragers, who stay put. A variety of critical decisions about life in the ant colony are made in a similar way.[4]

Bees also show how swarm intelligence works. When a hive becomes too large, about half the population splits off and clusters on a nearby tree branch. Scout bees search for a new home. When they find a likely location, they return and communicate to the other scouts via that tiny dance. The other scouts then visit the various locations that have been identified. At some point, enough scouts coalesce in a particular location that a kind of consensus is reached and then communicated to the cluster that it's time to move. Researchers have learned that the bees' method always picks the most ideal habitat to rebuild the hive.[5]

Bee behavior could be characterized as unconscious democracy where diverse options are examined openly and choices made on the basis of the information as it freely emerges. Give humans a similar challenge of moving and reconstituting an entire community and, long after the bees have resumed constructive relationships, we'd still be arguing, vying for power, dividing into factions, hiding our agendas, spreading rumors, suing each other, and speaking in tongues.

Swarm intelligence is also expressed by schools of fish, flocks of birds, and herds of caribou to confound predators. Again, coordination is based on individuals following simple rules and responding to local information and the cues of others in the group. These distributed behaviors become a whole that is greater than the sum of the individual parts. What we have learned about swarm intelligence is now being used by computer programmers to solve traffic problems, distribute goods, and route telephone calls. Google and Wikipedia use the principles of swarm intelligence to gather and select information. The anti-globalization protestors who challenged international capitalists in Seattle in 1999 used mobile communication to become "smart mobs" and the Pentagon is developing fleets of "swarmanoid" robots to find bombs planted by terrorists.[6]

Perhaps the most profound example of such self-organizing intelligence is Gaia herself. The planet's various natural operating systems – its climate, oceans, biosphere, soils, minerals, and nutrients – are integrated into complex feedback loops that prompt constant adjustments to keep life viable.

If Gaia is smart enough to keep life as a whole going, humans should worry, since we are behaving collectively like a persistent rash on the planetary skin.

What if the Crown of Creation is a Dunce Cap?

The intelligence revealed in such self-organizing behaviors might give us second thoughts about the prevalent notion that we humans, the crown of creation, should second-guess the natural processes that we have re-engineered. For instance, we suppressed forest fires until the build-up of unburned fuels within forests guarantees that future wild fires will be catastrophic. We skewed whole ecosystems by eliminating the key role that predators played within them. We drained wetlands and dammed and channeled watersheds with mixed results.

As far as we know, of course, microbes and insects do not act with conscious intent, at least outside of Gary Larsen cartoons. But if conscious intent is the criterion for "learning," then we can't claim we understand the consciousness and intent of nonhuman creatures any better than they understand our consciousness. Your cat and you sit on opposite sides of a cognitive wall, you thinking "he loves me" and him thinking . . . well, we don't know what he is thinking, though chances are it has more to do with food and amusement than filial affection. If you drop dead in your house tomorrow and remain undiscovered, chances are your supposedly loyal cat will eat your eyeballs by the end of the week. Our notion of what and how our pets think says more about how we project our own needs and notions on them and less about the nature of their consciousness or lack thereof.

No Stupid Survivors

Certainly, human learning often involves a motive, like wanting to learn Chinese so you can be a buyer for WalMart, whereas brainless life forms may simply adapt to changing conditions through an algorithmic process linked to random mutations and the consequent improvements in viability that result from those changes. But why would the existence of an introspective motive be so important? Wouldn't it make more sense to define intelligence as the ability to solve problems related to survival? If a species' ability to remain viable – to fit its environmental conditions – is used as a criterion for intelligence, then turtles were here long before us and are likely to be here when we leave. What's so smart about self-destructive behavior, no matter how sophisticated the motives?

Indigenous cultures that lived close enough to nature's processes and actors to admire the unique characteristics of nonhuman species to thrive in the wild acknowledge and honor the intelligence of wild creatures. In America, for example, many indigenous cultures paid tribute in story and song to ravens and coyotes. The coyote is perceived as the clever trickster who always manages to face adversity, often of his own making, but comes back. And ravens share carcasses with wolves and bears without becoming lunch themselves – a tricky, teeth-defying act that humans admired.

Yeah, but can ravens do this! (Imagine here some kind of technological back-flip, cultural sleight-of-hand, or problem-solving cartwheel.) Well no, ravens, like all creatures, have limits. But ravens are thriving on the detritus of our crisis – those troubling gas-guzzling cars we drive that are pushing our climate toward tipping points also leave behind lots of tasty roadkills. They are not at war for oil. They will not suffer the calamities of disruption when our fossil-fuel-loaded infrastructure runs out of gas. When climate change forces us all to adapt quickly to survive, we may yet admire the ability of the raven and coyote to change habits and strategies to fit new circumstances.

I Shop, Therefore I Am

Again, if we're so much smarter than nonhuman creatures, why do we engage in such self-destructive and confusing behaviors? The purpose of mycelium communication is to heal and cleanse, not to inundate the soil with spam emails. Elephants are not tricking each other into adjustable-rate mortgages. In one of my favorite movies, *Forest Gump*, Forest answers those who question his own innate intelligence with a quote from his mother: "Stupid is as stupid does." If human intelligence isn't a means to survive, then maybe it's just the way evolution's eventual losers – humans – rationalize their self-destructive addictions to going faster and getting more stuff. But I refuse to believe that WalMart and NASCAR are what it is all about.

All I'm suggesting is a little humility. Creation's other beings have much to show us that we need to learn if we would only shut up, drop the mirror, and listen. When we recognize the self-organizing genius of nature, we realize that the natural world may not only be more complex than we thought; it may be more complex than we *can* think. Appreciating nonhuman intelligence might even be humbling and awesome enough to make us rethink our "crown of creation" attitudes and enjoy a new sense of kinship with the rest of life on the planet. That new attitude would be healthy for them and, in the long run, be better for us too.

We need the uniquely human intellectual skills we have acquired to survive. Clearly, far-reaching innovations in technology – like alternative energy technologies and green designs – are required to meet the challenges of global climate chaos. But new infrastructures alone will not heal the wounds we have inflicted on the earthly nest that holds us, nor will it get us over the ecological abyss we now face. We will not solve the critical challenges we face with the same assumptions and methods that created those crises in the first place. Command and control thinking has brought us to the brink of catastrophe. We need to rethink and re-feel our relationship to the rest of the living world. To do that, we must wipe off that smirk and pay attention to the evidence of intelligence all around us. When we perceive and respect the self-organizing intelligence at work in the natural world, we try to dance with nature, not drive it. Now that's smart!

Notes

1   Frank T. Vertosick Jr., *The Genius Within: Discovering The Intelligence of Every Living Thing*. New York: Harcourt, Inc., 2002, pp. 5–11.
2   Kevin Daley, Michele Durtschi, and Brian Smith, "Olfactory-based Discrimination Learning in Moth, Manduca Sexta," *Journal of Insect Physiology* 47/4–5 (April 2001): 375–84.
3   Paul Stamets, *Mycelium Running: How Mushrooms Can Help Save the World*. Berkeley, CA: Ten Speed Press, 2005, p. 4.
4   Peter Miller, "Swarm Theory," *National Geographic Magazine* 212/1 (July 2007): 131.
5   Ibid., p. 135.
6   Ibid., pp. 139–42.

PART IV

WHAT IS THE SCOPE OF MORAL CONSIDERABILITY?

A   Individualism (Polycentrism)

Hierarchical Biocentrism

18   Persons in Nature: Toward an Applicable and Unified Environmental Ethics
     Frederick Ferré

Psychocentrism

19   Animals as Subjects-of-a-Life
     Tom Regan

20   All Animals are Equal
     Peter Singer

Egalitarian Biocentrism

21   The Ethics of Respect for Nature
     Paul W. Taylor

22   Kantians and Utilitarians and the Moral Status of Nonhuman Life
     James P. Sterba

B   Holism (Ecocentrism)

23   The Land Ethic
     Aldo Leopold

24   The Conceptual Foundations of the Land Ethic
     J. Baird Callicott

25   Gaia As Seen Through the Atmosphere
     James E. Lovelock

C   General Ethics

26   Developing a General Ethics (with Particular Reference to the Built,
     or Human-Constructed, Environment)
     Warwick Fox

Introduction

All ethical theories presuppose a set, or class, of beings which are worthy of moral consideration. The class of beings worthy of moral consideration and the class of moral agents need not be coextensive: there might be beings worthy of moral consideration who are themselves not moral agents.

The identification of this class is preparatory to the construction of the actual ethical theory, and is thus a *metaethical* task. Environmental ethics can be seen as the project of widening the scope of the class of beings worthy of moral consideration (directly or indirectly) beyond humans.

Picture the various theories of environmental ethics as a series of widening concentric spheres, radiating out from a core of the class of human beings (see figure I.1 in my introduction to this volume, p. 11). Just beyond that we have the hierarchical biocentrism of Rolston and Ferré, the psychocentric animal welfare ethics of Regan and Singer, the egalitarian biocentrism of Goodpaster and Taylor, the ecocentrism of Leopold and Callicott, and the general ethics, which includes the human built environment, of Fox.

Hierarchical biocentrism gives value to intensity of sentience, as does psychocentrism, whereas egalitarian biocentrism does not. Hierarchical biocentrism is represented by the Whiteheadian-inspired environmental ethic of Frederick Ferré, outlined in "Persons in Nature."[1] As this article is in large part a response to the normative dualism of Rolston's anthropometric biocentrism, a brief look at Rolston's environmental ethic is needed.

As I outline in the introductory essay, Rolston sees fundamental ontological differences between humans and nonhumans. These differences underlay the need of two ethical systems, one exclusively for human beings (social ethics) and one inclusively for ecological systems (environmental ethics). Contra sociobiology, social ethics is in no way either translatable or reducible to biology. Social ethics and environmental ethics are discrete normativities.[2]

As discrete normativities, humans cannot apply the tenets of social ethics to environmental ethics (Mill makes this same point in "Nature"): while it may be compulsory that human beings take action to eliminate suffering of innocent human life, it is not the case that human beings must take action to eliminate suffering of innocent nonhuman life, such as the killing of a doe by a cougar. Predation is integral to natural selection. Environmental ethics is thus a "painful good" – we ought not to interfere with normal ecological processes for the good of those processes.[3]

Ferré asserts that Rolston's normative dualism results in metaethical incoherence. When human interest conflicts with nonhuman interest, "By what higher ethics shall we 'adjudicate' between the two incoherent ethics in conflict?" he asks.[4] Rolston says only that "humans ought to preserve so far as they can the richness of the biological community,"[5] but as long as reasons are given why human interests trump nonhuman interests, there is no binding moral duty to the nonhuman biocommunity.

But if we really do believe that there are instances in which moral duties to nonhumans override duties to humans (a fundamental assumption for many environmental philosophers), then, as Ferré writes, it follows "that on the really tough questions, when genuine obligations to the environment or to humanity conflict, we have no guidance."[6] In order to have substantive normative guidance, Ferré argues that Rolston needs to provide a *third* normative system to help evaluate incommensurable social and ecological obligations, and provide serviceable action-guiding principles which coordinate social and environmental ethics. The lack of such a system leaves Rolston's environmental ethic incomplete. Like Rolston, Ferré constructs a hierarchical ontology which values intensity of subjectivity, but, unlike Rolston, adduces from this ontology just one ethical system.

Regan and Singer find rationality and discursive language no more ethically relevant than skin color or degree of hairiness. For Regan, the scope of beings worthy of moral consideration are animals that are sentient and self-aware (animal rights). For Singer, the scope of beings worthy of moral consideration are animals capable of suffering (animal liberation).

In the two selections on animal rights, Regan denounces the use of nonhuman animals as resources. He outlines his theory by initially surveying three alternative theories which he finds insufficient: Kantianism, the "cruelty-kindness view," and utilitarianism.[7] Kantian-based ethics makes the right move by recognizing some duties to nonhuman animals. Nonetheless, it falls short of making those duties indirect rather than direct. If, for example, I kick a dog, I have done something wrong to that dog above and beyond the danger that my actions may be a harbinger to harming a human. The "cruelty-kindness view" purports to provide the rationale for direct moral duties. On this view there is a necessary connection between kindness and moral strength, on the one hand, and cruelty and moral turpitude on the other. But Regan argues that this line of reasoning is fallacious: there is no necessary connection between kindness and virtue or cruelty and turpitude. One might do the right thing for the wrong reasons.[8] Or one might not be cruel but still be unethical.[9] Utilitarian-based animal welfare ethics makes the right move by recognizing nonhuman interests; nonetheless, it remains possible that the consequences of factory farming may still be justified if human interests outweigh nonhuman suffering.[10]

The correct view, by Regan's lights, is direct moral duties to all sentient beings who are self-aware "subjects-of-a-life." Subjects-of-a-life are aware of themselves both spatially and temporally; that is, they are aware of being subjects in relation to other subjects in a world around them, and a subject with a future. When the aspirations of subjects are frustrated or terminated, something unethical has happened to them. Subjects have the right to live, and moral agents have the duty to respect those rights. Regan's instantiation of animal welfare ethics is deontological.

In "All Animals are Equal," Singer grants moral consideration to all beings capable of suffering. The innovation of Singer was not to invent some entirely new ethical system – as ecocentrists have attempted – but to consistently apply the principle of utility to all sentient beings. Singer's instantiation of animal welfare ethics is consequentialistic and utilitarian.

The class of beings worthy of moral considerability consists of, most obviously, the higher mammals included in Regan's theory, but also other vertebrates. This class includes animals that may not exhibit much in the way of self-awareness but can experience pain, such as poultry. Singer ventures to guess, based on the assumption that invertebrates, whose animal behavior is more reflexive than volitional, that the cut-off point in the Great Chain of Being for moral considerability is "somewhere between a shrimp and an oyster."[11] It is morally wrong, for example, to kill mice using mousetraps.

Egalitarian biocentrism is represented by Paul Taylor and Jim Sterba, developing an ethic (consciously or unconsciously) in the spirit of Goodpaster in his "On Being Morally Considerable." Taylor, like Regan, Singer, and Goodpaster, is an ethical extensionist. Singer adapts utilitarianism to meet the problem of assuaging nonhuman animal suffering; Regan adapts deontology to meet the problem of respecting the rights of self-aware animals. In "The Ethics of Respect for Nature," Taylor adapts deontology to meet the demand of respect for all living things. Taylor extends Kant's Kingdom of Ends to all living things by exchanging rationality with vitality as the criterion of moral considerability. As Taylor writes in his book-length elaboration of biocentrism:

> In addition to and independently of whatever moral obligations we might have toward our fellow humans, we also have duties that are owed to wild living things in their own right. . . . Our duties toward the Earth's non-human forms of life are grounded on their status as entities possessing inherent worth. They have a kind of value that belongs to them by their very nature, and it is this value that makes it wrong to treat them as if they existed as mere means to human ends. It is for *their* sake that their good should be promoted or protected. Just as humans should be treated with respect, so should they.[12]

Taylor is keenly aware that biocentrism needs to be augmented with some kind of principle which reconciles inevitable conflicting interests of individual organisms in ecological systems. Parasitic microorganisms, for example, are living things, so the biocentrist must provide a method for arbitrating mutually exclusive interests of parasites and their hosts. (For example, the eradication of *Plasmodium falciparum*, a protozoan which causes malaria – and the mosquitoes such as *Anopheles quadrimaculatus* which transmit malarial parasites – is vital for the flourishing of some Asians, Africans, Americans, and others.) Taylor solves this conflict of biotic interests with the Principle of Self-Defense. This principle makes it "permissible for moral agents to protect themselves against dangerous or harmful organisms by destroying them" (such as killing *Plasmodium falciparum* and even the more complex organisms such as *Anopheles quadrimaculatus*).[13]

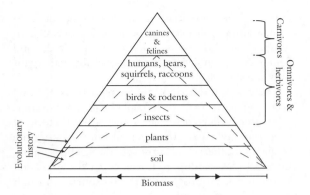

Figure IV. 1   The Land Pyramid.

Sterba, like Taylor, is aware of the difficulties of conflicting moral claims between living beings in ecological systems, and he draws an analogy between the libertarian call for equality between humans and the call for equality between living things of biocentrism.[14] In "Kantians and Utilitarians and the Moral Status of Nonhuman Life," building on his biocentric position, Sterba lays down several principles which allow anthropocentric interests to trump in some situations and nonanthropocentric interests to trump in others. In the first case, principles of human preservation and human defense allow for humans to kill nonhuman animals and plants. In the second case, a principle of disproportionality bars humans from exploiting nonhuman animals and plants for elective luxury.

"The Land Ethic," by Aldo Leopold, is the pioneering ecocentric classic. It marks the rejection of ethical extensionism for ethical holism. Leopold argues that the foci of moral considerability should be entire ecosystems. He describes a biological community as a pyramid composed of layers configured in feeding relationships (see figure IV.1):

> The species of a layer are alike not in where they come from, or in what they look like, but rather in what they eat. Each successive layer depends on those below it for food and often for other services, and each in turn furnishes food and services to those above. Proceeding upward, each successive layer decreases in numerical abundance. Thus, for every carnivore there are hundreds of his prey, thousands of their prey, millions of insects, uncountable plants. The pyramidal form of the system reflects this numerical progression from apex to base.[15]

At the bottom is the soil, where detritivores break down dead organic matter to form humus. Members of this layer are the most numerous in the community, forming the soil layer at the base. Next are plants, which depend upon the soil, and insects, which feed on plants. Above that are herbivores and omnivores. Humans share this niche with squirrels, bears, and raccoons. At the top are the large carnivores. Each ascending layer contains fewer individuals, represented by narrowing breadth of layers from base to apex.

Human beings are citizens of not only human communities but also biotic communities. If a biotic community is pictured as a pyramid, human beings occupy a specific layer in the pyramid, and depend on the biota forming layers below for survival. If one layer disintegrates, so do all the layers above it. Consequently, ecologically speaking, humans are much less important to the biosphere than termites and ants. As entomologist Edward Wilson remarks, if *Homo sapiens* were suddenly to disappear, the biosphere would continue functioning just fine (or even better?), but if invertebrates were suddenly to disappear, the human species would not persist for more than a few months.[16] The Land Ethic is thus resolutely nonanthropocentric.

Leopold insists that resourcism is the major obstacle to achieving a Land Ethic. Currently, our relations with biotic communities are guided only by human economic interest. Resourcism is not equipped to recognize non-economic (that is, ecological) types of value: "[A] system of conservation based solely on economic self-interest is hopelessly lopsided. It tends to ignore, and thus eventually to eliminate, many elements in the land community that lack commercial value, but that are (as far as we know) essential to its healthy functioning."[17]

Biocommunities possess intrinsic (what Leopold calls "philosophical") value.[18] This value eclipses mere economic worth. The triumph of achieving an ethical relationship to the land requires the recognition of inherent ecological value. And as an aesthetic insight, the recognition of this value is not merely rational but also emotional: "The ecological conscience, then, is an affair of the mind as well as the heart. It implies a capacity to study and learn, as well as to emote about the problems of conservation."[19]

Poignant ethical theories are often condensed to one memorable maxim: Aristotle's Doctrine of the Mean, Christianity's Golden Rule, Kant's Categorical Imperative, Mill's Principle of Utility. Leopold provides a similar summarization of the Land Ethic: "A thing is right when it tends to preserve the integrity, stability, and beauty of the biotic community. It is wrong when it tends otherwise."[20]

Seminal as it is, "The Land Ethic" is rather philosophically unsystematic. J. Baird Callicott brings the holistic repudiation of ethical extensionism to the fore. He contends that the standard polycentric (individualistic) paradigms of moral philosophy, despite the good work of pychocentrists and biocentrists, are simply not up to the task of grappling with the holistic ontology of ecological systems. In "The Conceptual Foundations of the Land Ethic," Callicott ferrets out the abundant nuances of the Leopoldian revolution in ethics. Callicottian Land Ethics rests on two principles: bioempathy (outlined in my introductory essay "What is Environmental Ethics?") and ecological literacy. The two principles are tightly connected. Although action springs from emotion rather than from reason, as David Hume maintains, the tools of reason can help us achieve what we desire. Ecological knowledge can help us achieve one thing we desire – survival. Because ecological science has taught us that the limit of the human community is not civilization but the biosphere at large, this wisdom should stir bioempathy. For this reason Callicott speaks of the need for ecological education: "the key to the emergence of a land ethic is, simply, universal ecological literacy."[21]

Ecological literacy and bioempathy entail the Land Ethic:[22]

1   Ecological science shows that ecological systems are biotic communities to which we belong (ecological literacy).
2   We are generally predisposed to have positive attitudes toward the individuals of communities to which we belong (bioempathy).
3   Humans ought to preserve the integrity, stability, and beauty of biotic communities (the Land Ethic).

The positive attitude toward life and survival which is part of our very make-up surmounts the is/ought or fact/value gaps: (2) bridges (3) with (1). Descriptions of ecological systems entail prescriptions about how those systems ought to be treated by moral agents (us). What must be affirmed – the protection and preservation of biotic communities – follows directly from descriptions of healthy ecosystemic function.

Environmental ethics for Callicott is the activity of ecologically enlightened and bioempathetically motivated persons making judgments about individuals and populations of species using overall ecosystemic health as a normative standard, and adjudicating conflicting interests of individual organisms accordingly.

There is a more rigorous form of holism, however – one that treats the biosphere as one ontologically interconnected whole. Some of the rhetoric of deep ecology evokes biospherical unity, as does the "Gaia Hypothesis" of atmospheric scientist James Lovelock.[23] According to Lovelock, in "Gaia As Seen Through the Atmosphere," the biosphere, through the activity of the atmosphere, has created conditions favorable to life. The normative implication is that the entire biosphere, as one unitary system, should be the focus of environmental ethics.

As numerous philosophers have noticed,[24] environmental philosophers have tended to focus almost exclusively on the natural (that is, the nonhuman) environment. Recently, philosophers have begun to call this focus into question and suggest a need to reintroduce human-constructed environments as a legitimate subject-matter for ethics of the environment. If cities and even farms are human-constructed ecosystems, then to exclude them from the purview of environmental ethics is myopic – especially if the goal of environmental ethics is to improve the biospherical condition.

An Australian now living in England, philosopher Warwick Fox, brings us to the outer plenum of the class of moral considerability in "Developing a General Ethics." For Fox, "just as traditional, anthropocentrically focused forms of ethics have exhibited a major blind spot in their theorizing with respect to the non-human world, so the development of environmental ethics has thus far exhibited a major blind spot of its own," namely, the human-built environment.[25] Figuring out how best to live our lives involves figuring out how best to build our cities and homes, how best to move ourselves and products around the globe from one place to another. This recognition, in a profound sense, brings ethics full circle from the Greeks' initial human-centered focus through the nonanthropocentrism of psychocentrism, biocentrism, and ecocentrism, back to the human.

The story of ethics in the West is a story about widening the aperture of the lens of moral consideration. The narrative began with human beings as the only characters on stage, and the play continued that way, with minor exceptions, well beyond 2,000 years. Eventually, nonhuman animals entered the scene, followed by all living things, the entire ecosystems. Most recently, the stage has been set with the props of the human-built environment, bringing our investigation back to where we began: if human beings are biota and integral parts of ecological systems, then the human-built environment (farms, cities, reservoirs) ought to be included in the purview of environmental ethics.

Notes

1 Ferré also elaborates his theory of hierarchical biocentrism in "Personalistic Organicism."

2 See Rolston, *Environmental Ethics*, p. 57.

3 Ibid., p. 59.

4 Ferré, "Persons in Nature," p. 20. (See this volume, p. 157.)

5 Rolston, *Environmental Ethics*, p. 230.

6 Ferré, "Persons in Nature," p. 21. (See this volume, p. 159.)

7 In "The Case for Animal Rights" (pp. 16–17), Regan frames the problems of indirect moral duties toward nonhuman animals in terms of "contractarianism" rather than Kantianism, though the fundamentals of the argument are comparable.

8 Kant makes this brilliantly clear in *Grounding for the Metaphysics of Morals*, p. 10.

9 Regan, "The Case for Animal Rights," p. 18.

10 Regan, "Animal Rights, Human Wrongs," p. 112.

11 Singer, *Animal Liberation*, p. 174.

12 Taylor, *Respect for Nature*, p. 13.

13 Ibid., pp. 264–5.

14 Sterba, "A Biocentrist Strikes Back," p. 363.

15 Leopold, *A Sand County Almanac*, p. 215. (See this volume, p. 197.)

16 Wilson, "The Little Things that Run the World," p. 345.

17 Leopold, *A Sand County Almanac*, p. 214. (See this volume, p. 197.)

18 Ibid., p. 223. (See this volume, p. 200.)

19 Leopold, "The Ecological Conscience," p. 111.

20 *A Sand County Almanac*, pp. 224–5. (See this volume, p. 200.)

21 "The Conceptual Foundations of the Land Ethic," in *In Defense of the Land Ethic*, p. 82. (See this volume, p. 205.)

22 "Hume's *Is/Ought* Dichotomy," in *In Defense of the Land Ethic*, p. 127.

23 *Gaia: A New Look at Life on Earth*.

24 Sylvan, "A Critique of Deep Ecology," Part II, p. 13; King, "Environmental Ethics and the Built Environment"; Light, "The Urban Blindspot in Environmental Ethics"; Jamieson, *Ethics and the Environment*, p. 1.

25 Fox, ed., *Ethics and the Built Environment*, p. 2.

A Individualism (Polycentrism)

Hierarchical Biocentrism

18   Persons in Nature: Toward an Applicable and Unified Environmental Ethics
     Frederick Ferré

Psychocentrism

19   Animals as Subjects-of-a-Life
     Tom Regan

20   All Animals are Equal
     Peter Singer

Egalitarian Biocentrism

21   The Ethics of Respect for Nature
     Paul W. Taylor

22   Kantians and Utilitarians and the Moral Status of Nonhuman Life
     James P. Sterba

HIERARCHICAL BIOCENTRISM

18   Persons in Nature: Toward an Applicable and Unified Environmental Ethics

Frederick Ferré

I take it for granted, speaking to a seminar program of the Environmental Ethics faculty and students within the distinguished Institute of Ecology at the University of Georgia, that we here need no preachments against the heedless abuse of the earth nor even against an anthropocentric, "shallow" ecology. That gets us a long way, at least if the initial standard is set low enough, but it does not get us to our destination. This because it is my reluctant conclusion that the main candidates, even for a "robust" environmental ethics, fumble – or worse – when it comes to providing applicable guidance for resolving that really tough problems show why I have come to this unhappy position and to say what I think would be necessary to change the situation.

From *Ethics in the Environment*, vol. 1, no. 1 (1996): 15–25. © 1996 by JAI Press, Inc. Reprinted with permission from Springer Science & Business Media.

The two prominent candidates I plan to discuss are, first, Aldo Leopold's Land Ethic as interpreted by Baird Callicott; and, second, what I will call the "Painful Good" Ethic, as formulated by Holmes Rolston, III. The first frustrates our need for guidance by flunking the applicability/adequacy test; the second undermines the demand for ethical coherence.

The first two parts of my discussion will be critical, spelling out why I find little real guidance from either of these important sources. My final constructive part will point to a way forward; I shall advocate a revision in worldview, a frank embrace of a theory of value and reality that puts persons into continuity with – but not "on all fours" with – the rest of the natural order. It is what I have been calling Personalistic Organicism. I shall not try in addition to apply Personalistic Organicism to complex problems in any detail, but I hope it will be clear, when I finish, that this is a "vision," such as our program calls for, that can in principle "provide guidance," since it avoids the problems that handicap the others.

The Land Ethic: Problems of Adequacy

Aldo Leopold's *A Sand County Almanac* is a wonderful book, and one of its later chapters, "The Land Ethic," contains perhaps the most stirring and influential statement ever made on environmental responsibility.[1] Leopold is in many ways the founder-patron of what I called "robust" environmental ethics. His influence has been immensely constructive. His evocation of the morally appalling image of Odysseus, hanging "all on one rope a dozen slave-girls of his household whom he suspected of misbehavior during his absence,"[2] required many people to think for the first time about the rightness of doing "whatever they wish with their property," even when that property is land rather than ladies. In this way he forced the issue of what philosophers call "moral considerability" and required us to notice that the range of recipients of our moral attention has slowly but steadily grown. To members of other tribes or language-groups, to prisoners of war, to men with differently colored skins, even (!) to women – the circle of those to whom moral obligations are in principle due has expanded; and nothing but habit, Leopold implies, prevents us from making the evolutionary move toward incorporating in our ethics the land and animals and plants live on it.

He writes, "The extension of ethics to this . . . element in human environments is, if I read the evidence correctly, an evolutionary possibility and an ecological necessity."[3]

But Leopold urged more than a simple "extension" of ethics; he was proposing a genuine revolution. In the same essay he formulated a new *standard* for ethics. In judging the very meaning of "right" and "wrong," he said, we should put the living land at the center: "A thing is right when it tends to preserve the integrity, stability, and beauty of the biotic community. It is wrong when it tends otherwise."[4]

Baird Callicott is right, therefore, when he maintains that this is not evolutionary at all, but rather a revolutionary contribution of the Land Ethic.[5] It shifts concern from collections of "atomistic" individuals, as was the central consideration for both Kantianism and Utilitarianism (the two main branches of modern ethical theory), and places it squarely on the health of the *biotic system*. Thus Leopold offers a holistic, biocentric ethics, in contrast to the mainly atomistic, anthropocentric ethics familiar in all the Western traditions.

This is immensely important. Exclusive, short-sighted attention to what is good for *Homo sapiens* has proven ruinous, and promises to inflict even worse environmental damage in the future. By default, because there is hardly a hint of any alternative to anthropocentrism among our mainstream ethical resources, it seems that a Land Ethic of holistic biocentrism might be the life-affirming guide we are seeking.

Unfortunately, for three reasons, it is not. The first of these reasons, although not an obstacle in principle, reminds us of a serious current practical difficulty of application. Frankly, at this stage of biological and ecological knowledge we simply *do not know enough* about the web of life to be confident which actions will or will not enhance the "integrity, stability, and beauty" of the biotic community. That ignorance, insisted on not only by Leopold himself but also – often even more warmly – by contemporary ecologists, is a profound block to confident policy-making, if our ethical success depends on our getting it right. It is a further sub-obstacle, that the words Leopold chose by which to define his standard of biocentric ethics are notoriously hard to understand with precision. Even aside from the notorious problems of defining "beauty," what is the operational meaning of "integrity" in a living community? How "stable" should "stability" be in a constantly evolving world?

Even the term "community" has been replaced with "ecosystem," but not exactly replaced, since "community" was never an exactly defined term to begin with. If the Land Ethic is asked to be a clear guide for resolving problems, it lets us down on this first, cognitive level. It expresses, perhaps, a wholesome general attitude, a way of getting beyond a purely economic relationship to the land and its inhabitants; but when pressed to show, in concrete cases, one specific course of action as "better" than another, it passes the ball to the ecologists – who punt.

✔ There is a second reason that the Land Ethic does not satisfy our needs. It simply *leaves out of account* huge dimensions of ethical life which we would be wrong to ignore. Ought I to keep all my promises, or only some? Is it ever right to lie, perhaps in a good cause? Is slavery right or wrong? Should torture be used to extract confessions from suspected witches? These are examples of questions that demand ethical answers, but for the Land Ethic they are neither right nor wrong unless they can be shown to have bearing on the "integrity, stability, and beauty" of the biotic community. If we are looking for guidance on many of the central issues of human life, even intuitively obvious questions like whether it is right to murder one's mother for her piggy bank, we shall not find it here. Most of human culture is simply marginalized by the biocentric shift.

✔ The third reason for my complaint of inadequacy against an unsupplemented Land Ethic relates to this marginalization. Holistic biocentrism can do much worse than merely fail to give guidance in crucial ethical situations; rather, it can be expected to *guide in terrible directions*. One of the earth's great problems, both today and as far as we can see into the future, is human overpopulation. However vaguely we may define the "integrity, stability, and beauty of the biotic community," it almost certainly would be enhanced by many fewer people burdening the land. Therefore . . . (and here is a consequence from which Leopold and followers like Callicott, rightly heeding fundamental moral intuitions, would recoil), anything we could do to exterminate excess people – especially where they are congregated in large, unsanitary, destabilizing slums – would be morally "right"! To refrain from such extermination would be "wrong"! "Culling" individuals, if held short of extinction, is a good thing, biologically, as long as the species is plentiful; and the human species is obviously too plentiful and getting more so. We have here what could be used as a justification for mass murder, in particular to support policies of deliberate extermination by the wealthy few in the global North against the teeming global South. Is this an ethic, or a potential excuse for ruthless genocide? No purported ethic can do such violence to fundamental moral intuitions and still offer itself as guide.

Short of genocide, but still ethically disturbing, another problem requires our notice. For thoroughgoing holism, of the sort we are considering, *individual* organisms matter only for the sake of the *system* in which they play parts. Tadpoles, that is, matter only for the persistence of their own species and for the predators that depend on them for food. Shall human beings be reevaluated in the same holistic terms? Taken as a guide for human culture, the Land Ethic – despite the best intentions of its supporters – would lead us toward classical fascism, the submergence of the individual person in the glorification of the collectivity, race, tribe, or nation.

Although a truly needed and refreshing change from anthropocentrism, Leopold's vision could easily swing to the opposite extreme and become an excuse for radical misanthropy. As Callicott himself observes, "The extent of misanthropy in modern environmentalism . . . may be taken as a measure of the degree to which it is biocentric."[6] Can such self-hating biocentrism be a guide for human policy-making? Have we other choices?

The "Painful Good" Ethic: Problems of Coherence

Holmes Rolston sees very clearly that the tender-heartedness we cultivate for dealings among human beings is unsupported and unsupportable in nature. He is, however, keenly aware that the predacious standards of biotic health in nature are morally outrageous when imported into human culture. Early in his book, *Environmental Ethics*, he states the contrast very clearly:

> Nature proceeds with a recklessness that is indifferent to life; this results in senseless cruelty and is repugnant to our moral sensitivities. Life is wrested from her creatures by continual struggle, usually soon lost; those few who survive to maturity only face eventual collapse in disease and death. With what indifference nature casts forth her creatures to slaughter! Everything is condemned to live by

attacking or competing with other life. There is no altruistic consideration of others, no justice.[7]

Since this is so, "right" and its opposite cannot be simply equated with what enhances or hinders biotic flourishing. Thus, drawing on widely shared ethical intuitions, Rolston concludes that there are "elements in nature which, if we were to transfer them to interhuman conduct in culture, would be immoral and therefore ought not to be imitated."[8]

Rolston's realism about what goes on in ecosystems forms the foundation of his environmental ethics. Despite our tender human sympathies for an innocent fawn, for example, we must accept that a hungry cougar will make a meal of it, if it can; and even if we have a chance to intervene to save the fawn, we should not. This follows from one of Rolston's major principles: "There is no human duty to eradicate the sufferings of creation."[9] Here we catch a familiar echo from the Land Ethic, as when Rolston writes that "environmental ethics has no duty to deny ecology but rather to affirm it."[10] But this ethic, Rolston insists, should not be used for inter-human guidance. On the basis of sheerly biological principles, there would be little or no difference whether a hungry predator were to eat a wandering fawn or a lost child. We should *not*, on Rolston's principles, save the fawn; but our ethical intuitions strongly urge us that we *should* save the child. Rolston accepts this difference and explains:

> The fawn lives only in an ecosystem, in nature; the child lives also in culture. Environmental ethics is not social ethics. . . . We would not want to take predation out of the system if we could (though we take humans out of the predation system), because pain and pleasure are not the only criteria of value, not even the principal ones.[11]

The more important criterion, for Rolston, is "satisfactory fitness" in nature. Fitness rests on predation, which makes for suffering; and since animals are morally innocent, this results in enormous quantities of innocent suffering. Is this a problem? Yes and no, for Rolston:

> It may seem unsatisfactory that innocent life has to suffer, and we may first wish for an ethical principle that protects innocent life. This principle is persuasive in culture, and we do all we can to eliminate human suffering. But ought suffering to continue when humans do or can intervene in nature? That it

ought not to continue is a tender sentiment but so remote from the way the world *is* that we must ask whether this is the way the world *ought* to be in a tougher, realistic environmental ethic. A morally satisfactory fit must be a biologically satisfactory fit. What *ought to be* is derived from what *is*. . . . Nature is not a moral agent; we do not imitate nature for interhuman conduct. But nature is a place of satisfactory fitness, and we take that as a criterion for some moral judgments. We endorse a painful good.[12]

In Rolston's sharp separation (here and throughout his book) of environmental ethics from social ethics, we encounter what I call ethical incoherence. Incoherence, in general, is an obstacle for thought when principles are "just different" and out of connection. In Rolston's case, we are given, in effect, two ethics. *Social* ethics urges us to do whatever we can to prevent innocent suffering (when a human life is at stake); *environmental* ethics assures us that "we are wrongheaded to meddle."[13] *Social* ethics condemns predatory activity in culture; *environmental* ethics praises predation as enhancing "satisfactory fitness." Rolston uses the strongest moral disparagements to urge against humans contributing to the extinction of species; at the same time he contemplates pre-human periods of even catastrophic extinctions with unruffled approval.

Incoherence is always theoretically uncomfortable, but matters get worse. Discomforts become practical, too. Conflicts between domains arise. Which ethics should we follow? As Rolston acknowledges, "Our duties to persons in culture will at times bring us into conflict with this land ethic, and we will have to adjudicate such conflicts."[14] For one example, half the world's deforestation, annually, is caused by subsistence needs of poor people in the global South. But the preservation of forests is high on the agenda of those who would save biodiversity, minimize extinctions, counter global warming, and somehow atone for destructive anthropogenic encroachments. Which ethics do we use? Shall we protect the forests at the expense of our obligations to the needy? What if we cannot have both? By what higher ethics shall we "adjudicate" between the two incoherent ethics in conflict?

Rolston's answer is not much help. He acknowledges that there is nothing unusual in "higher trophic levels" (including human cultures) "eating up" lower ones.

> But we have also been saying that there is, and should be, systems-wide interdependence, stability,

cohesiveness. These have been achieved amorally in nature, where the community is found, not made. But when humans, who are moral agents, enter such a scene and make their communities, rebuilding those found naturally, they may and should capture such values in their own behalf, but they also have an obligation to do so with a view over the whole (which also, derivatively, involves considering individual pains, pleasures, and welfares). The obligation remains a prima facie one: humans ought to preserve so far as they can the richness of the biological community. This too is among human obligations. It is not the only one. In a capstone sense it is not the ultimate one, since the cultural values supervening on nature are more eminent. But in a foundational sense it is ultimate, since it is out of projective nature that everything is created and maintained. Such duty must be heeded or reasons given why not.[15]

Reasons given why not? Which reasons will trump other reasons? Do "capstone" reasons trump "foundational" reasons, or *vice versa*? Have we come all this way only to be told that our prima facie obligations to environmental ethics can be overridden by "giving reasons" if we decide that cultural values are more "eminent"? On our quest to "provide guidance for resolving problems," we have come to a dead end. Rolston's two scales – one for culture, one for nature; one "capstone," one "foundational" – have turned out to be incommensurable. This means that on the really tough questions, when genuine obligations to the environment or to humanity conflict, we have no guidance.

Personalistic Organicism: Continuity Without Reduction

At the start of this final section let me affirm boldly what will be necessary in general for a "guiding vision" of the sort we need. Such a vision must reveal a single, continuous worldscape in which human culture is situated fully within nature. It must offer conceptual clarity on what constitutes value, intrinsic and instrumental. It must show how genuine values of both sorts in nature can extend beyond (and can sometimes conflict with) human values. It must offer a way to make distinctions between different degrees of value on a common scale, so that discriminating moral choices can be made, not always or automatically in favor of human interests. It need not come with quantitative value-tags affixed, to

remove the need for qualitative judgments, but it should be able to indicate areas where additional knowledge would be relevant for morally responsible decision making. In other words, it should be neither anthropocentric nor value-leveling; it should be organismic, but able to appreciate the precious values of individual personhood.

First, on the relation of culture to nature, some conceptual analysis of the slippery term "nature" is overdue. Callicott and Rolston recently gave each other some needless lumps in a debate over wilderness policy, partially because of un-analyzed terms.[16] Callicott assumes that "nature" simply means "*everything that is* (except the supernatural, if such there be)," and has a harder time, in consequence, seeing why Rolston persists in saying that human beings should just leave some parts of "nature" alone. If human culture is (necessarily) part of nature, as Callicott takes for granted, then Rolston's advice is logically impossible. But Rolston tends to use "nature" to mean, instead, "*whatever has not been changed, caused, intruded upon, or spoiled by human purpose.*"

Interestingly, Rolston is aware that different meanings of "nature" are possible, commenting parenthetically: "There is another meaning of 'natural' by which even deliberated human actions break no laws of nature. Everything, better or worse, is natural in this sense, unless there is the supernatural."[17]

But he prefers to insist instead on the sense of the word that separates and divides, by definition, as follows: "On the meaning of 'natural' at issue here, that of nature proceeding by evolutionary and ecological processes, any deliberated human agency, however well intended, is intention nevertheless and interrupts these spontaneous processes and is inevitably artificial, unnatural."[18]

This terminological stipulation seems to suggest, however, that "evolutionary and ecological processes" themselves lose out or disappear once "deliberated human agency" comes on the scene. But this is obviously false. Ecological processes – tough ones, coming back to haunt us for human folly – are exactly what worry us these days! Evolutionary and ecological processes are not suspended, though they are influenced, by the emergence of human purpose and intelligence. Does Rolston want to say that ecological processes, once "intruded upon" by human agency, are not "really" ecological any more? It would be *possible* for him, since we may stipulate our meanings as we please; it might even be *tempting* for him, since it would parallel his saying that "nature," once affected by human intention, is no longer "really" nature; but it would not be *useful*. It fragments thought without necessity. Would ecologists, on his proposed definition, need to change fields, from ecology (proper) to some other field, to do research on acidified lakes or forests – on which human purposes have obviously intruded?

Therefore I opt against Rolston on this matter, since it is much harder to think coherently with terms designed to bifurcate; and we have already seen the ethical consequences of disconnection and incommensurability. The best solution is to recognize that words like "natural" and "artificial" are not all-or-nothing terms. "Artificiality" comes in degrees. An apple orchard is more artificial than a forest, but a plastic apple is more artificial yet. "Natural," by inversion, is also a relative term – and nature, containing many degrees of naturalness, from penguins to people and even plastics, is none the less still natural, for all that.

Human beings, granted, are strange, awkward members of the natural order. We do not fall spontaneously into our behaviors. Not only are we not like rocks rolling down hill, we differ, too, in obvious ways from living things like chipmunks or sea gulls. We plan longer ahead. We consider many more alternatives. We employ tools to help us gain our distant ends. We take responsibility. We feel pangs of conscience.

I do not claim, please note, that all this repertoire is absolutely unique in human beings. But if there are analogues of tool use, strategy sessions, or guilt trips elsewhere in nature, they are very significantly less prominent compared to us. What does not seem to distinguish us so much, at least in living nature, is the tendency to *prefer*. Preference need not be conscious, as it is with human beings; preference, positive or negative, may be expressed by engulfing a speck of food, by fleeing from an attacking lion, by buzzing into sweet-smelling blossoms, or even by unfolding leaves and petals toward the sun. Here, at the level of organism, is the behavioral equivalent of value judgments. The organismic world is full of valuers; therefore the world – emphatically including the world outside the human realm – is full of value.

For conceptual clarity it is essential that we recognize that values entail valuers, just as thoughts entail thinkers and experiences entail experiencers. Without thinkers, no thoughts; without valuers, no values.[19] But in fact this is a world rich in valuers and values. Among these values are those, the intrinsic values, that are enjoyed for their own sakes, and those, the instrumental values, that are valued because they contribute to or make possible the intrinsic values. To be able to enjoy an intrinsic value, a valuer must be a center of experience of some sort. This need not be self-conscious experience; but intrinsically satisfying experiences of a wide range of sharpness and complexity are not hard to imagine. Consider the saying, "As happy as a clam at high tide." We need not be talking in metaphors when we speak of contented cows and happy clams.

It is no metaphor, either, to speak of a pond as valuable. But if the pond is not the sort of thing that can experience anything at all, if it is not itself a valuer, it confuses matters to say that it is *intrinsically* valuable. Rather, the pond is of very high *instrumental* value to the many varieties of valuers who flourish in and around it, who depend on it as a necessary condition for their continued valuing. In like manner, it obfuscates to say that collective nouns like "species" and "systems" refer to things of intrinsic value. A species does not value, experience, prefer – or even exist apart from the actual, individual entities which exemplify "it" at any given time. When we work hard to preserve an endangered species, what we are valuing (in that shorthand expression) is the *set of possible organisms which might enjoy their own existence, and contribute to the well-being of other organisms, into the indefinite future*. For this we defend "habitat," which is a collective name including both instrumentally necessary inorganic features of the species' environment and other intrinsically and instrumentally valuable organisms.

Two additional points emerge from this. First, all organisms can be both instrumentally and intrinsically valuable. To the extent that they value their own inherently satisfactory experiences, they constitute intrinsic value, apart from any use they may have; and to the extent that they contribute to or make possible the inherently satisfactory experiences of other organisms, they are instrumentally valuable, apart from any intrinsic value they may represent for themselves. Second, though individual valuers are the only possible centers of intrinsic value, organisms are not isolated, atomic phenomena. In fact, even atoms are no longer conceived as "atomic" in that old-fashioned sense! Organisms and atoms, alike, are what they are because of their environments. An organismic worldview means, above all, that every entity contributes to and is in turn shaped by an entity-network that makes a real difference.

This is holism that retains the individual as the indispensable center of intrinsic value. Its affirmation of the deep *connectedness* of things bars selfish individualism and provides the basis for real community; but its recognition of the character of value as dependent on *actual valuers* resists the lure of collectivisms that would submerge individuals for the sake of some mythic supervening "good of the whole." Here is the basis for a new Land Ethic which can stand, with Leopold and Callicott, for ethical interconnections with flora and fauna, but oppose in principle the potential dangers of ecofascism.

Such organicism is not, however, undiscriminatingly "biocentric" or merely egalitarian as between, say, clams and clam-diggers. The locus of intrinsic value is in inherently satisfactory experience which can be a focus of preference for the experiencer. Clams, we noted, may be capable of a certain level of value for themselves. For people, clams are of significant instrumental value as a means toward obtaining other inherently satisfying experiences: their own gustatory pleasures. The two conflict. Is there no ethically principled way to choose? If clams and clammers simply inhabited different worlds, the world of nature and the world of culture, the problem of adjudication is in principle insoluble. But the organismic world I have been propounding is a world of continuities rather than bifurcations. Experience and preference are common features, but these features come in many different qualities and intensities. There is a huge difference in the neural complexity, the behavioral repertoire, the creative potential, the "culture" of clam and clam-cooker. It is reasonable to hold that the intensity, complexity, intrinsic satisfactoriness of the clam-eating person's gustatory experience is immensely richer than the general glow of organic well-being that may pervade the interior psychological life of the undisturbed clam. All other things being equal, of course, in the absence of any higher intrinsic value to be realized, the clam should not be wantonly upset by moral agents. It should be left alone to enjoy its own torpid satisfaction – at least until some sea gull expresses a preference for the clam's instrumental value and puts an end to its dream.

Philosophers have supposed for a long time that the very highest levels of intrinsic value on earth are the exclusive preserve of human personhood. This may or may not be true. We are learning amazing things about cetacean capacities, including communication and sociality, that may make us change our minds. This is the sort of scientific research that will make a moral difference in determining policies for inter-species relations. Metaphysical theorizing, responsibly conducted in contact with scientific findings, will also make a difference. Though I have offered a general theory of value and reality, I have not attempted any elaborate metaphysical system. There is good reason to go on from here to ask how widespread in our universe inherently satisfactory experience may be. That is a matter to be decided on the basis of the best evidence and the most coherent, comprehensive, and adequate arguments. We may find ourselves drawn to some form of thoroughgoing panpsychism, in which every entity in the universe has at least a rudimentary capacity for preference and interior feeling. Since the only reality we know first-hand from inside is our own, it would be odd to scoff at the notion that all reality has the same basic architecture of inside and outside, agent and patient, end and means. But what I have said here does not depend on going so far with an organismic metaphysics. All it requires is acknowledgment of the relatively obvious continuities between organisms as far "down," toward unawareness and toward the "means" end of the means-ends continuum, as one cares to go. Below that, where intrinsic values become negligible, if they do, our inorganic environment can and should still be cherished for its wondrous instrumental values: not just for its abilities to sustain the huge community of valuers who constitute our interconnected biosphere, but also for its miraculous capacities to refresh and renew – both in us and, I believe, in myriad other centers of appreciation – the aesthetic delights we perpetually value in and for themselves.

Notes

1 Aldo Leopold. 1966. *A Sand County Almanac: With Essays on Conservation from Round River*. New York: Ballentine Books.
2 Ibid., p. 237.
3 Ibid., p. 239.
4 Ibid., p. 262.
5 J. Baird Callicott. 1980. "Animal Liberation: A Triangular Affair," *Environmental Ethics*, 2(4): 318–24.
6 Ibid., p. 326.
7 Holmes Rolston, III. 1988. *Environmental Ethics: Duties to and Values in the Natural World*. Philadelphia, PA: Temple University Press, p. 39.
8 Ibid.
9 Ibid., p. 56.
10 Ibid.

11 Ibid., p. 57.
12 Ibid., pp. 58–9.
13 Ibid., p. 56.
14 Ibid., p. 229.
15 Ibid., pp. 229–30.
16 J. Baird Callicott. 1991. "The Wilderness Idea Revisited: The Sustainable Development Alternative," *The Environmental Professional*, 13: 235–47; Holmes Rolston, III. 1991. "The Wilderness Idea Reaffirmed,"

ibid.: 370–7; J. Baird Callicott. 1991. "That Good Old-Time Wilderness Religion," ibid.: 378–9.
17 Rolston, *The Environmental Professional*, 13: 371.
18 Ibid.
19 Callicott (1980) comes close to this position when he affirms "that there can be no value apart from an evaluator." In Callicott, *Environmental Ethics*, p. 325. But he pays too little attention to the importance of nonhuman evaluators.

PSYCHOCENTRISM

19 Animals as Subjects-of-a-Life

Tom Regan

I regard myself as an advocate of animal rights – as a part of the animal rights movement. That movement, as I conceive it, is committed to a number of goals, including:

- the total abolition of the use of animals in science;
- the total dissolution of commercial animal agriculture;
- the total elimination of commercial and sport hunting and trapping.

There are, I know, people who profess to believe in animal rights but do not avow these goals. Factory farming, they say, is wrong – it violates animals' rights – but traditional animal agriculture is all right. Toxicity tests of cosmetics on animals violates their rights, but important medical research – cancer research, for example – does not. The clubbing of baby seals is abhorrent, but not the harvesting of adult seals. I used to think I understood this reasoning. Not any more. You don't change unjust institutions by tidying them up.

What's wrong – fundamentally wrong – with the way animals are treated isn't the details that vary from case to case. It's the whole system. The for-lornness of the veal calf is pathetic, heart wrenching; the pulsing pain of the chimp with electrodes planted deep in her brain is repulsive; the slow, tortuous death of the racoon caught in the leg-hold trap is agonizing. But what is wrong isn't the pain, isn't the suffering, isn't the deprivation. These compound what's wrong. Sometimes – often – they make it much, much worse. But they are not the fundamental wrong.

The fundamental wrong is the system that allows us to view animals as *our resources*, here for *us* – to be eaten, or surgically manipulated, or exploited for sport or money. Once we accept this view of animals – as our resources – the rest is as predictable as it is regrettable. [. . .]

[. . .] I believe the idea of animal rights has reason, not just emotion, on its side.

[. . .]

The Kantian Account

It is a commonplace to say that morality places some limits on how animals may be treated. We are not to kick dogs, set fire to cats' tails, torment hamsters or parakeets⌐Philosophically, the issue is not so much *whether* but *why* these acts are wrong.⌐

⌐ An answer favored by many philosophers, including Thomas Aquinas and Immanuel Kant, is that people who treat animals in these ways develop a habit which, in time, inclines them to treat humans similarly.[1] People who torment animals will, or are likely to, torment people. It is this spillover effect that makes mistreating animals wrong. We are not concerned directly with the ill-treatment that the animals themselves receive. Rather, our concern is that this bodes ill for humankind. So, on this Kantian account, the moral principle runs something like this: don't treat animals in ways that will lead you to mistreat human beings.

One need have no quarrel with this principle itself. The real quarrel lies with the grounds on which this principle is allegedly based. Peter Singer argues that there is a close parallel between this view and those of the racist and sexist, a view which, following Richard Ryder, he denominates speciesism.[2] The racist believes that the interests of others matter only if they happen to be members of his own race. The speciesist believes that the interests of others matter only if they happen to be members of his own species. Racism has been unmasked for the prejudice that it is. The color of one's skin cannot be used to determine the relevance of an individual's interests. Singer and Ryder both argue that neither can the number of one's legs, whether one walks upright or on all fours, lives in the trees, the sea or the suburbs. Here they recall Bentham.[3] There is, they argue forcefully, no rational, unprejudiced way to exclude the interests of nonhuman animals just because they are not the interests of human beings. Because the Kantian account would have us think otherwise, we are right to reject it.

The Cruelty Account

A second view about constraints on how animals may be treated involves the idea of cruelty. The reason we are not to kick dogs is that we are not to be cruel to animals and kicking dogs is cruel. It is the prohibition against cruelty which covers and conveniently sums up our negative duties to animals, duties concerning how animals are *not* to be treated.

The prohibition against cruelty can be given a distinctively Kantian twist. This happens when the grounds given are that cruelty to animals leads people to be cruel to other people. John Locke suggests, but does not clearly endorse, this view:

> One thing I have frequently observed in Children, that when they have got possession of any poor Creature, they are apt to use it ill: They often *torment*, and treat very roughly, young Birds, Butterflies, and such other poor Animals, which fall into their Hands, and that with a seeming kind of Pleasure. This I think should be watched in them, and if they incline to any such *Cruelty*, they should be taught the contrary Usage. For the Custom of Tormenting and Killing of Beasts, will, by Degrees, harden their Minds even towards Men; and they who delight in the Suffering and Destruction of Inferior Creatures, will not be apt to be very compassionate, or benign to those of their own kind.[4]

Locke's position suggests the speciesism which characterizes the Kantian account and will not do for the same reasons. However, Locke's understanding of what cruelty is – tormenting a sentient creature or causing it to suffer, "with a seeming kind of Pleasure" – seems correct and has important implications. Many thinkers, including many persons active in the humane movement, champion the prohibition against cruelty to animals because it is wrong to be cruel to the animals themselves. This way of grounding the prohibition against cruelty, which I call "the cruelty account," deserves our critical attention.

It is difficult to overestimate the importance the idea of preventing cruelty has played, and continues to play, in the movement to secure better treatment for animals. Entire societies are devoted to this cause, the Society for the Prevention of Cruelty to Animals (SPCA) in the United States and the Royal Society for the Prevention of Cruelty to Animals (RSPCA) in Great Britain being perhaps the best known examples. I do not wish to deny the importance of preventing cruelty nor to deprecate the crusading work done by these organizations, but I must conclude that to stake so much on the prevention of cruelty both clouds the fundamental moral issues and runs a serious risk of being counterproductive.

Cruel is a term of moral appraisal used to refer either to the character of a person or to an individual action. Persons are cruel who are inclined to delight in or, in Locke's phrase, to take "a seeming kind of Pleasure" in causing pain. An individual action is cruel if one takes pleasure in making another suffer. It is clear that someone's being cruel is distinct from someone's causing pain. Surgeons cause pain. Dentists cause pain.

Wrestlers, boxers, football players cause pain. But it does not follow that they are cruel people or that their individual actions are cruel. To establish cruelty we need to know more than that someone caused pain; we also need to know the state of mind of the agent, whether he/she took "a seeming kind of Pleasure" in the pain inflicted. It is faulty to reason in this way:

> Those who cause pain are cruel. Surgeons (football players, etc.) cause pain.
>
> Therefore, surgeons (football players, etc.) are cruel.

But just as clearly, it is faulty to reason in the following way:

> Those who cause pain are cruel. Those who experiment on animals (or kill whales, or raise veal calves in isolation, etc.) cause pain. Therefore, those who treat animals in these ways are cruel.

Those who are inclined to march under the banner of anti-cruelty must soon recognize the speciousness of this line of reasoning, if their thought, however well intentioned, is not to cloud the issues.

Once cruelty is understood in the way Locke saw that it should be, we can understand why more is needed. Take the case of the use of animals in the Draize test. Increasingly people want to object morally to this, to say it is wrong. However, if this required establishing cruelty, the weight of the evidence would be on the side of the experimenters and against the objectors, for there is no adequate evidence for believing that people who administer the Draize test are cruel people or that they are cruel when they administer this test. Do they take "a seeming kind of Pleasure" in causing the animals pain? That they cause *pain* to the animals is certain. But causing pain does not establish cruelty. Except for a few sadists in the scientific community, there is good reason to believe that researchers are no more cruel than are most persons.

Does this mean that using animals in the Draize test is right? Precisely not. Rather, to ask whether this is right is logically distinct from, and should not be confused with, asking whether someone is cruel. Cruelty has to do with a person's state of mind. The moral rightness or wrongness of a person's actions is different. Persons can do what is right or wrong whatever their state of mind. Researchers using the Draize test can be doing what is wrong, whether or not they enjoy causing animals to suffer. If they do

enjoy this, we shall certainly think less of them as persons. But even if they enjoy the pain it will not follow that the pain is unjustified, any more than it will follow that the pain is justified if they feel sorry for the animals or feel nothing at all. The more we are able to keep in view how the morality of what a person does is distinct from his/her state of mind, distinct from the presence or absence of taking pleasure in pain; the better the chances will be for significant dialogue between vivisectors and anti-vivisectionists.

To charge vivisectors with cruelty *can* only serve to call forth all their defenses, because the charge will be taken as a denunciation of *what they are* (evil people) rather than of *what they do*. It will also give them an easy way out. After all, *they* are in privileged position to know their own mental states; *they* can take a sober moment and see whether in fact they do take a "seeming kind of Pleasure" in causing pain. If, as will usually be the case, they find that they honestly do not, then they can reply that they are not cruel (evil) people. So we see now where the well-intentioned efforts of those defending animals can be and often are counterproductive. If it's cruelty they are charged with, and they are not cruel, then they can come away with a feeling that their hands are clean. They win, and the litany of accusations about cruelty is so much water off their backs. It is no good trying to improve the lot of animals by trying to convince persons who are not cruel that they are.

Some will complain that my argument is "too picky." They might say that cruelty has been interpreted too narrowly: what is meant is treating animals badly in ways they don't deserve, harming or wronging them. In practice this is what anti-cruelty charges often come to. But then this is the way the charges should be made, lest they be misunderstood or be counterproductive. To ask for more care in the charges leveled is not to strain at gnats. It is to begin to make the charges more difficult to answer. Perhaps a name like "The Society for the Prevention of Maltreatment of Animals" is not as euphonious as "The Anti-Cruelty Society," but a lack of euphony is a price those laboring for animal welfare should gladly pay.

The Utilitarian Account

Utilitarians give a different account of the constraints regarding how animals ought to be treated. The utilitarian account, or one version of it, involves two principles.[5] The first is a principle of equality.

This principle declares that the desires, needs, hopes, etc. of different individuals, when these are of equal importance *to* these individuals, *are* of equal importance or value no matter who the individuals are, prince or pauper, genius or moron, white or black, male or female, *human or animal*. This equality of interests principle seems to provide a philosophical basis for avoiding the grossest forms of prejudice, including racism, sexism and, following Ryder and Singer, speciesism. Whether it succeeds is an issue which we shall take up below.

The second principle is that of utility itself. Roughly speaking, according to this principle, we are to act so as to bring about the greatest possible balance of good over evil, for example, the greatest possible balance of satisfaction over dissatisfaction, taking the interests of everyone affected into account *and* counting equal interests equally. Now, since animals have interests, *their* interests must be taken into account, and because their interests are frequently as important to them as comparable interests are to human beings, *their* interests must be given the same weight as comparable human interests. It is because kicking dogs and setting fire to cats' tails run counter to the principles of equality and utility that, on this utilitarian account, they are wrong.

[. . .]

On the face of it, utilitarianism seems to be the fairest, least prejudicial view available. Everyone's interests count, and no one's counts for more or less than the equal interests of anyone else. The trouble is [. . .] that there is no necessary connection, no preestablished harmony between respect for the equality of interests principle *and* promoting the utilitarian objective of maximizing the balance of good over bad. On the contrary, the principle of utility might be used to justify the most radical kinds of differential treatment between individuals or groups of individuals, and thus it might justify forms of racism and sexism, for these prejudices can take different forms and find expression in different ways. One form consists in not even taking the interests of a given race or sex into account at all; another takes these interests into account but does not count them equally with those of the equal interests of the favored group. Another does take their interests into account equally, but adopts laws and policies, engages in practices and customs which give greater opportunities to the members of the favored group, because doing so promotes the greatest balance of good over evil, all considered.

Thus, forms of racism or sexism, which seem to be eliminated by the utilitarian principle of equality of interests, could well be resurrected and justified by the principle of utility. If a utilitarian here replies that denying certain humans an equal opportunity to satisfy or promote their equal interests on racial or sexual grounds must violate the equality of interests principle and so, on his position, is wrong, we must remind him that differential treatment is not the same as, and does not entail, violating the equality of interests principle. It is quite possible, for example, to count the equal interests of blacks and whites the same (and thus to honor the equality principle) and still discriminate between races when it comes to what members of each race are permitted to do to pursue those interests, on the grounds that such discrimination promotes the utilitarian objective. So, utilitarianism, despite initial appearances, does not provide us with solid grounds on which to exclude all forms of racism or sexism.

Similarly with speciesism. The same kind of argument can show a possible utilitarian justification of an analogous speciesism. We count the equal interests of animals and humans equally; it just so happens that the consequences of treating animals in ways that humans are not treated, such as intensively raising animals, but not humans, are better, all considered, than are other arrangements. Thus, utilitarianism might provide a basis for speciesist practices. Whether it *actually* does depends on whether the consequences are better, all considered, if animals continue to be treated as they are. Since Singer fails to provide us with empirical data showing that the consequences would be better if we changed, it follows that, for all we know, the present speciesist way of treating animals might actually be justified, given his version of utilitarianism.

Animal Rights

Our results to this point are mainly negative. I have thus far argued (1) that the moral principles we seek cannot refer to the agent's state of mind, to whether the agent takes a "seeming kind of Pleasure" in causing animal suffering. (2) These principles cannot refer only to consequences that harm or benefit human beings, since this prejudicially leaves out of account the harms and benefits to the animals themselves. (3) These principles cannot refer only to the utilitarian objective of maximizing the balance of good over evil, even if animal harms and benefits are taken into account. What is wanted, then, is an account which avoids each of these shortcomings. This account is to be found, I believe, by postulating the existence of animal rights. Indeed, I believe that only if we postulate human rights can we provide a theory which adequately guards humans against the abuses which utilitarianism might permit.

Various analyses of the concept of a right have been proposed. We will bypass the nooks and crannies of these competing analyses so as to focus attention on the role that moral rights play in our thinking about the status of the individual, relative to the interests of the group. Here the truth seems to lie where Ronald Dworkin sees it: the rights of the individual trump the goals of the group.⁶

What does this mean? It means that the moral rights of the individual place a justifiable limit on what the group can do to the individual. Suppose a group of people stand to gain enjoyment by arranging for others to be harmed. Imagine, for example, the Romans enjoying how the Christians go up against lions. Such a group does wrong because they allow their interests to override the individual's moral rights. This does not mean that there are no circumstances in which an individual's rights must give way to the collective interest. Imagine that Bert has inadvertently swallowed the microfilmed code which we must have in order to prevent a massive nuclear explosion in New Zealand. Bert sits safely in Tucson, Arizona. We explain the situation but Bert refuses to consent to our request that we operate, retrieve the code, and prevent the explosion. He cites his right to determine what is to be done to his body. In such a case it is not implausible to say that Bert's right must give way to the collective interests of others.

Individual rights then normally, but not always, trump collective interests. To give a precise statement of the conditions which determine which ought to prevail is very difficult indeed, but the following conditions, which deal only with the right not to be harmed, at least seem to incorporate necessary conditions for overriding this right.⁷

An individual's right not to be harmed can justifiably be overridden only if

(a)   we have very good reason to believe that overriding the individual's right by itself will prevent, and is the only realistic way to prevent, vastly greater harm to other innocent individuals; or

(b)   we have very good reason to believe that allowing the individual to be harmed is a necessary link in a chain of events which collectively will prevent vastly greater harm to innocent individuals, *and* we have very good reason to believe that this chain of events is the only realistic way to prevent this vastly greater harm; or

(c)   we have very good reason to believe that it is only if we override the individual's right that we can have a reasonable hope of preventing vastly greater harm to other innocent individuals.

[. . .]

These conditions share an extremely important feature. Each specifies what we must know or have good reason to believe if we are justified in overriding an individual's right not to be harmed. Each requires anyone who would harm an individual to show that this does not involve violating the individual's right. Part of the importance of the question, whether animals have rights, specifically, the right not to be harmed, now comes into clear focus. *If* they have this right, then it will be violated whenever animals are harmed and condition (a), (b), (c) is not satisfied. Moreover, the onus of justification is always on those who harm animals to explain how they are not violating the right of animals not to be harmed, if animals have this right. So, the question continues to press itself upon us. Do animals have the right not to be harmed?

This is not an easy question to answer. One is reminded of Bentham's observation that the idea of moral rights is "nonsense on stilts." Bentham meant this in the case of *human* moral rights. One can only speculate regarding what he might have thought concerning the moral rights of *animals*! So, how is one to proceed? The circuitous path we must cautiously travel, I think, is in broad outline as follows.⁸

We begin by asking about our reasons for thinking that human beings have the moral right not to be harmed; then we go on to ask whether, given these reasons, a case can be made for saying that animals have this right as well. Let us go back to the idea that individual human beings have this right and that, except in extreme cases, this right trumps collective interest. Why? What is there about being a human being to which we can point and say, "*That's* why you must not harm the individual even if the group benefits?"

The heart of the answer lies, I believe, in thinking that human beings have a certain kind of value, inherent value. By this I mean that each human being has value logically independently of whether he/she is valued by anyone else (or, what perhaps comes to the same thing, whether he/she is the object of anyone else's interest).[9] The view that human beings have inherent value implies that the kind of value properly attributable to them is not exclusively instrumental. Humans have value not just because, and not just so long as, they are good for something. They have value distinct from their utility and skill.

If this is true, we can explain, in general terms reminiscent of Kant, what is involved in mistreating human beings. Humans are mistreated if they are treated as valuable only if they forward the interests of other beings. To treat a human being thus is to show a lack of proper respect for the sort of value humans have. In Kant's terms, what has value in itself must always be treated as an end, never merely as a means. However, this is precisely what we are doing if we harm an individual so that others might gain pleasure or profit; we are treating the individual merely as a means, as valuable only to the extent he/she contributes to the collective interest.

Now, *if* we accept the postulate that human beings have inherent value, we can press on and ask how rights enter the picture. They enter in being grounded in inherent value. In other words, it is individuals who have inherent value who have moral rights, and it is *because* they have value of this kind that they have a moral right not to be treated in ways that deny their having this kind of value. Rather than rights being connected with *the value of consequences* which affect individuals for good or ill, rather than rights being justified by the utility of recognizing them, rights are based on *the value of individuals*. In the case of the right not to be harmed, then, what we can say is that individuals who have inherent value have the right not to be harmed, which precludes treating them merely as a means. This would fail to treat these individuals with that respect to which, because of the kind of value they have, they are entitled.

Now, certainly the foregoing is not a definitive account of the view that individuals having inherent value have basic moral rights, in particular the right not to be harmed. One omission is especially conspicuous. What is there about being a human being that underlies this inherent value? Any answer is controversial, and a sustained defense of the answer proposed here is not possible.[10] But here is the answer

I would give: human beings not only are alive; *they have a life*.[11] What is more, we are the subjects of a life that is better or worse for us, logically independently of anyone else's valuing us or finding us useful.

[. . .]

Conclusion

Two final philosophical points are in order, before I bring the results of my argument to bear on how animals are treated in the world at large. First, it is important to realize that I have not *proven* that animals have rights, or even that *human* beings have rights. Rather, I have argued that if humans have rights, so do many animals. More particularly, I have argued for what appears to be the most promising line of argument for explaining human rights, the view that we have inherent value, and that this can rationally be extended to animals of some kinds. So, while I admit that I have not proven that animals (or humans) have rights, I hope at least to have made clear the direction in which future argument ought to proceed. Erecting pointers, to be sure, is not the same as constructing proofs, but pointers are the best I can do here.

Second, the history of moral philosophy teaches us that utilitarianism dies hard. Just when one thinks it has been forced off the stage for good, one finds it loitering in the wings, awaiting yet another curtain call. The utilitarian can be counted on to say that there is nothing introduced by the idea of rights for which he cannot account.[12] One has only to see that the utilitarian objective is promoted if we recognize a strict obligation not to harm individuals except in extreme cases, *and* that, furthermore, utility is promoted by saying that individuals have the right not to be harmed, this invocation of a right functioning as an especially forceful way of conveying the idea that we ought not to harm individuals.

I am not convinced by this attempt to resurrect utilitarianism, and here I raise my final and most fundamental objection to it. The utilitarian is in no position to say that he knows that the utilitarian objective is promoted by talk of individuals having rights. But even if it is true that talk of rights helps promote the utilitarian objective, and for this reason such talk ought to be encouraged and honored, there can only be a *contingent* connection between any right, such as the right not to be harmed, and the fact that respecting this right forwards the utilitarian objective. The most that the utilitarian can say is that recognizing the right not to be harmed *as a matter of fact* fits in with forwarding his goal of maximizing the balance of good over evil.[13] The utilitarian must also accept that things could have been (and could become) otherwise. He must accept the possibility that it could have been or might become all right to harm individuals if this ever happened to forward the utilitarian objective. But neither the wrongness of harming individuals nor the right not to be harmed can change in the ways utilitarian theory implies they can. They are not contingent upon *utility*. Neither depends on the value of consequences. Instead, each depends on *the value of individuals.*

Let us put this in perspective before applying it. Earlier we said that before making an informed judgment about the morality of whaling or the use of the Draize test we must know both facts and moral principles. Otherwise, we cannot know which facts are morally relevant; and without this preliminary knowledge, we do not know what moral judgments to make. To determine what these principles are, we said, is one of the distinctive tasks of moral philosophy. Three positions were examined and found wanting: the Kantian account, the cruelty account, and the utilitarian account. We then considered an account ascribing rights to animals, a position which meets the objections which were fatal to the views examined earlier. Unlike the Kantian account, the rights account insists upon the moral status of animals in their own right; unlike the cruelty account, the rights account does not confuse the morality of acts with the mental states of agents; and unlike utilitarianism, this account closes the door to the justification of prejudices which merely happen to bring about the best consequences and emphasizes the value of individuals as distinct from the value of consequences. This emphasis on the value of individuals becomes prominent now as we turn at last to the task of applying the rights account to the whale, the veal calf, and the others.

[. . .]

We allow then that it is *possible* that harming animals might be justified; but we also maintain that those harming animals typically fail to show that the harm caused is *actually* justified. A further question we must ask ourselves is what, morally speaking, we ought to do in such a situation? Reflection on comparable situations involving human beings will help make the answer clear.

Consider racism and sexism. Imagine that slavery is an institution of the day and that it is built on racist or sexist lines. Blacks or women are assigned the rank of slave. Suppose we are told that in extreme circumstances even slavery might conceivably be justified, and that we ought not to object to it or try to bring it down, even though no one has shown that it is actually justified in the present case. Well, I do not believe for a moment that we would accept such an attempt to dissuade us from toppling the institution of slavery. Not for a moment would we accept the general principle involved here, that an institution actually is justified because it might conceivably be justified. We would accept the quite different principle that we are morally obligated to oppose any practice which appears to violate rights unless we are shown that it really does not do so. To be satisfied with anything less is to cheapen the value attributable to the victims of the practice.

Exactly the same line of reasoning applies in the case where animals are regarded as so many dispensible commodities, models, subjects, etc. We ought not to back away from bringing these industries and related practices to a halt just because it is *possible* that the harm caused to the animals *might* be justified. If we do, we fail to mean it when we say that animals are not mere things, that they are the subjects of a life that is better or worse for them, that they have inherent value. As in the comparable case involving harm to human beings, our duty is to act, to do all that we can to put an end to the harm animals are made to endure. The fact that the animals themselves cannot speak out on their own behalf, the fact that they cannot organize, petition, march, exert political pressure, or raise our level of consciousness – all this does not weaken our obligation to act on their behalf. If anything, their impotence makes our obligation the greater.[14]

Notes

1 Relevant selections from both St Thomas and Kant are included in T. Regan and P. Singer, *Animal Rights and Human Obligations* (Englewood Cliffs, NJ: Prentice-Hall, 1989). What I call the Kantian account is criticized further in my "Exploring the Idea of Animal Rights," in D. Paterson and R. Ryder, eds., *Animal*

Rights: A Symposium (London: Centaur Press, 1979). Kant's views are criticized at length by Elizabeth Pybus and Alexander Broadie, "Kant's Treatment of Animals," *Philosophy* 49 (1974): 375–83. I defend Kant against their objections in my "Broadie and Pybus on Kant," *Philosophy* 51 (1976): 471–2. Broadie and Pybus reply in their "Kant on the Maltreatment of Animals," *Philosophy* 53 (1978): 560–1. At present I am persuaded that Broadie and Pybus are correct in arguing that Kant cannot account for the idea that animals themselves can be maltreated.

2 P. Singer, *Animal Liberation*, 2nd edn. (London: Pimlico, 1995); T. Ryder, *Victims of Science*, 2nd edn. (London: National Anti-Vivisection Society, 1983).

3 The famous passage from Bentham reads as follows (from *The Principles of Morals and Legislation* (1789), chap. 17, Sect. 1, reprinted in Regan and Singer, *Animal Rights and Human Obligations*): "The day has been, I grieve to say in many places it is not yet past, in which the greater part of the species, under the denomination of slaves, have been treated by the law exactly upon the same footing as, in England for example, the inferior races of animals are still. The day may come, when the rest of the animal creation may acquire those rights which never could have been withholden from them but by the hand of tyranny. The French have already discovered that the blackness of the skin is no reason why a human being should be abandoned without redress to the caprice of a tormentor. It may come one day to be recognized, that the number of the legs, the villosity of the skin, or the termination of the os sacrum, are reasons equally insufficient for abandoning a sensitive being to the same fate. What else is it that should trace the insuperable line? Is it the faculty of reason, or, perhaps, the faculty of discourse? But a full-grown horse or dog is beyond comparison a more rational, as well as a more conversable animal, than an infant of a day, or a week, or even a month, old. But suppose the case were otherwise, what would it avail? The question is not, Can they reason? not, Can they talk? but, Can they suffer?"

4 John Locke, *Some Thoughts Concerning Education*, 5th edn. (London, 1905). See also James Antell, ed., *The Educational Writings of John Locke* (Cambridge: Cambridge University Press, 1968), sec. 116, pp. 225–6.

5 The utilitarian position I consider is the one associated with Bentham and forcefully presented by Peter Singer. That Singer is a utilitarian is made unmistakably clear in his "The Fable of the Fox and the Unliberated Animals," *Ethics* 88 (1978): 119–25.

6 Ronald Dworkin, *Taking Rights Seriously* (Cambridge: Harvard University Press, 1977).

7 The present statement of these conditions deviates somewhat from my earlier effort in "The Moral Basis of Vegetarianism," *Canadian Journal of Philosophy* 5 (1975): 181–214. I believe the inclusion of conditions (b) and (c) marks an improvement over the earlier formulation. However, a fuller statement has to include more than simply the idea of *preventing* vastly greater harm: for example, *reducing* already existing harm also has a place.

8 See my "An Examination and Defense of One Argument Concerning Animal Rights," *Inquiry* 22 (1979): 189–219.

9 Whether sense can be made of including irreversibly comatose human beings in the class of beings having inherent value is a troublesome question indeed. I consider this issue, perhaps not very adequately, in the essay referred to in note 8.

10 I do not believe it is absurd to think of natural objects which lack consciousness, or collections of such objects, as having inherent value, in the sense in which I use this expression. An *X* has inherent value if it has value logically independently of anyone's valuing *X*. I do not say this is easy to clarify or to defend, and it may be wrongheaded. At present, however, I believe it is a view that must be held, if we are to develop an environmental ethic, as distinct from an ethic for the use of the environment.

11 The distinction between being alive and having a life is one James Rachels frequently makes. See, for example, his "Euthanasia," in Tom Regan, ed., *Matters of Life and Death* (New York: Random House, 1980). Rachels does not, so far as I am aware, relate this distinction to the idea of inherent value.

12 It is possible that Mill meant to give rights a utilitarian basis. On this see David Lyons, "Human Rights and the General Welfare," *Philosophy and Public Affairs* 6 (1977): 113–29, reprinted in David Lyons, ed., *Rights* (Belmont, California: Wadsworth Publishing Co., 1979). The principal objection to this enterprise is the third objection I raise against utilitarianism here.

13 I do not believe utilitarianism is alone in implying that the duty not to harm an individual (or the individual's right not to be harmed) are *contingent* moral truths, which *might* have been otherwise (or *might* become otherwise). Certain aspects of Kant's theory as well as ethical egoism arguably imply this as well. This is absolutely fatal to these theories, a point I argue in my "Utilitarianism, Vegetarianism, and Animal Rights," *Philosophy and Public Affairs* 9 (1980): 305–24.

14 For a more complete list of recent philosophical work relating to the topics discussed in the present essay, see Charles Magel and Tom Regan, "Animal Rights and Human Obligations: A Select Bibliography," *Inquiry* 22 (1979): 243–7.

20   All Animals are Equal

Peter Singer

In recent years a number of oppressed groups have campaigned vigorously for equality. The classic instance is the black liberation movement, which demands an end to the prejudice and discrimination that has made blacks second-class citizens. The immediate appeal of the black liberation movement and its initial, if limited, success made it a model for other oppressed groups to follow. We became familiar with liberation movements for Spanish-Americans, gay people, and a variety of other minorities. When a majority group – women – began their campaign, some thought we had come to the end of the road. Discrimination on the basis of sex, it has been said, is the last universally accepted form of discrimination, practiced without secrecy or pretense even in those liberal circles that have long prided themselves on their freedom from prejudice against racial minorities.

One should always be wary of talking of "the last remaining form of discrimination." If we have learnt anything from the liberation movements, we should have learnt how difficult it is to be aware of latent prejudice in our attitudes to particular groups until this prejudice is forcefully pointed out.

A liberation movement demands an expansion of our moral horizons and an extension or reinterpretation of the basic moral principle of equality. Practices that were previously regarded as natural and inevitable come to be seen as the result of an unjustifiable prejudice. Who can say with confidence that all his or her attitudes and practices are beyond criticism? If we wish to avoid being numbered amongst the oppressors, we must be prepared to rethink even our most fundamental attitudes. We need to consider them from the point of view of those most disadvantaged by our attitudes, and the practices that follow from these attitudes. If we can make this unaccustomed mental switch we may discover a pattern in our attitudes and practices that consistently operates so as to benefit one group – usually the one to which we ourselves belong – at the expense of another. In this way we may come to see that there is a case for a new liberation movement. My aim is to advocate that we make this mental switch in respect of our attitudes and practices towards a very large group of beings: members of species other than our own – or, as we popularly though misleadingly call them, animals. In other words, I am urging that we extend to other species the basic principle of equality that most of us recognize should be extended to all members of our own species.

All this may sound a little far-fetched, more like a parody of other liberation movements than a serious objective. In fact, in the past the idea of "The Rights of Animals" really has been used to parody the case for women's rights. When Mary Wollstonecraft, a forerunner of later feminists, published her *Vindication of the Rights of Women* in 1792, her ideas were widely regarded as absurd, and they were satirized in an anonymous publication entitled *A Vindication of the Rights of Brutes*. The author of this satire (actually Thomas Taylor, a distinguished Cambridge philosopher) tried to refute Wollstonecraft's reasonings by showing that they could be carried one stage further. If sound when applied to women, why should the arguments not be applied to dogs, cats, and horses? They seemed to hold equally well for these "brutes"; yet to hold that brutes had rights was manifestly absurd; therefore the reasoning by which this conclusion had been reached must be unsound, and if unsound when applied to brutes, it must also be unsound when applied to women, since the very same arguments had been used in each case.

One way in which we might reply to this argument is by saying that the case for equality between men and women cannot validly be extended to nonhuman animals. Women have a right to vote, for instance, because they are just as capable of making rational decisions as men are; dogs, on the other hand, are incapable of understanding the significance of voting, so they cannot have the right to vote.

From *Philosophical Exchange*, vol. 1, no. 5 (1974): 103–16. © 1974 by Peter Singer. Reprinted by permission of the author.

There are many other obvious ways in which men and women resemble each other closely, while humans and other animals differ greatly. So, it might be said, men and women are similar beings and should have equal rights, while humans and nonhumans are different and should not have equal rights.

The thought behind this reply to Taylor's analogy is correct up to a point, but it does not go far enough. There are important differences between humans and other animals, and these differences must give rise to some differences in the rights that each have. Recognizing this obvious fact, however, is no barrier to the case for extending the basic principle of equality to nonhuman animals. The differences that exist between men and women are equally undeniable, and the supporters of Women's Liberation are aware that these differences may give rise to different rights. Many feminists hold that women have the right to an abortion on request. It does not follow that since these same people are campaigning for equality between men and women they must support the right of men to have abortions too. Since a man cannot have an abortion, it is meaningless to talk of his right to have one. Since a pig can't vote, it is meaningless to talk of its right to vote. There is no reason why either Women's Liberation or Animal Liberation should get involved in such nonsense. The extension of the basic principle of equality from one group to another does not imply that we must treat both groups in exactly the same way, or grant exactly the same rights to both groups. Whether we should do so will depend on the nature of the members of the two groups. The basic principle of equality, I shall argue, is equality of consideration; and equal consideration for different beings may lead to different treatment and different rights.

So there is a different way of replying to Taylor's attempt to parody Wollstonecraft's arguments, a way which does not deny the differences between humans and nonhumans, but goes more deeply into the question of equality and concludes by finding nothing absurd in the idea that the basic principle of equality applies to so-called "brutes." I believe that we reach this conclusion if we examine the basis on which our opposition to discrimination on grounds of race or sex ultimately rests. We will then see that we would be on shaky ground if we were to demand equality for blacks, women, and other groups of oppressed humans while denying equal consideration to nonhumans.

When we say that all human beings, whatever their race, creed, or sex, are equal, what is it that we are asserting? Those who wish to defend a hierarchical, inegalitarian society have often pointed out that by whatever test we choose, it simply is not true that all humans are equal. Like it or not, we must face the fact that humans come in different shapes and sizes; they come with differing moral capacities, differing intellectual abilities, differing amounts of benevolent feeling and sensitivity to the needs of others, differing abilities to communicate effectively, and differing capacities to experience pleasure and pain. In short, if the demand for equality were based on the actual equality of all human beings, we would have to stop demanding equality. It would be an unjustifiable demand.

Still, one might cling to the view that the demand for equality among human beings is based on the actual equality of the different races and sexes. Although humans differ as individuals in various ways, there are no differences between the races and sexes as such. From the mere fact that a person is black, or a woman, we cannot infer anything else about that person. This, it may be said, is what is wrong with racism and sexism. The white racist claims that whites are superior to blacks, but this is false – although there are differences between individuals, some blacks are superior to some whites in all of the capacities and abilities that could conceivably be relevant. The opponent of sexism would say the same: a person's sex is no guide to his or her abilities, and this is why it is unjustifiable to discriminate on the basis of sex.

This is a possible line of objection to racial and sexual discrimination. It is not, however, the way that someone really concerned about equality would choose, because taking this line could, in some circumstances, force one to accept a most inegalitarian society. The fact that humans differ as individuals, rather than as races or sexes, is a valid reply to someone who defends a hierarchical society like, say, South Africa, in which all whites are superior in status to all blacks. The existence of individual variations that cut across the lines of race or sex, however, provides us with no defense at all against a more sophisticated opponent of equality, one who proposes that, say, the interests of those with IQ ratings above 100 be preferred to the interests of those with IQs below 100. Would a hierarchical society of this sort really be so much better than one based on race or sex? I think not. But if we tie the moral principle of equality to the factual equality of the different races or sexes, taken as a whole, our opposition to racism and sexism does not provide us with any basis for objecting to this kind of inegalitarianism.

There is a second important reason why we ought not to base our opposition to racism and sexism on any kind of factual equality, even the limited kind which asserts that variations in capacities and abilities are spread evenly between the different races and sexes: we can have no absolute guarantee that these abilities and capacities really are distributed evenly, without regard to race or sex, among human beings. So far as actual abilities are concerned, there do seem to be certain measurable differences between both races and sexes. These differences do not, of course, appear in each case, but only when averages are taken. More important still, we do not yet know how much of these differences is really due to the different genetic endowments of the various races and sexes, and how much is due to environmental differences that are the result of past and continuing discrimination. Perhaps all of the important differences will eventually prove to be environmental rather than genetic. Anyone opposed to racism and sexism will certainly hope that this will be so, for it will make the task of ending discrimination a lot easier; nevertheless it would be dangerous to rest the case against racism and sexism on the belief that all significant differences are environmental in origin. The opponent of, say, racism who takes this line will be unable to avoid conceding that if differences in ability did after all prove to have some genetic connection with race, racism would in some way be defensible.

It would be folly for the opponent of racism to stake his whole case on a dogmatic commitment to one particular outcome of a difficult scientific issue which is still a long way from being settled. While attempts to prove that differences in certain selected abilities between races and sexes are primarily genetic in origin have certainly not been conclusive, the same must be said of attempts to prove that these differences are largely the result of environment. At this stage of the investigation we cannot be certain which view is correct, however much we may hope it is the latter.

Fortunately, there is no need to pin the case for equality to one particular outcome of this scientific investigation. The appropriate response to those who claim to have found evidence of genetically-based differences in ability between the races or sexes is not to stick to the belief that the genetic explanation

must be wrong, whatever evidence to the contrary may turn up: instead we should make it quite clear that the claim to equality does not depend on intelligence, moral capacity, physical strength, or similar matters of fact. Equality is a moral ideal, not a simple assertion of fact. There is no logically compelling reason for assuming that a factual difference in ability between two people justifies any difference in the amount of consideration we give to satisfying their needs and interests. The principle of the equality of human beings is not a description of an alleged actual equality among humans: it is a prescription of how we should treat humans.

Jeremy Bentham incorporated the essential basis of moral equality into his utilitarian system of ethics in the formula: "Each to count for one and none for more than one." In other words, the interests of every being affected by an action are to be taken into account and given the same weight as the like interests of any other being. A later utilitarian, Henry Sidgwick, put the point in this way: "The good of any one individual is of no more importance, from the point of view (if I may say so) of the Universe, than the good of any other."[1] More recently, the leading figures in contemporary moral philosophy have shown a great deal of agreement in specifying as a fundamental presupposition of their moral theories some similar requirement which operates so as to give everyone's interests equal consideration – although they cannot agree on how this requirement is best formulated.[2]

It is an implication of this principle of equality that our concern for others ought not to depend on what they are like, or what abilities they possess – although precisely what this concern requires us to do may vary according to the characteristics of those affected by what we do. It is on this basis that the case against racism and the case against sexism must both ultimately rest; and it is in accordance with this principle that speciesism is also to be condemned. If possessing a higher degree of intelligence does not entitle one human to use another for his own ends, how can it entitle humans to exploit nonhumans?

Many philosophers have proposed the principle of equal consideration of interests, in some form or other, as a basic moral principle; but, as we shall see in more detail shortly, not many of them have recognized that this principle applies to members of other species as well as to our own. Bentham was one of the few who did realize this. In a forward-looking passage, written at a time when black slaves in the

British dominions were still being treated much as we now treat nonhuman animals, Bentham wrote:

> The day may come when the rest of the animal creation may acquire those rights which never could have been withholden from them but by the hand of tyranny. The French have already discovered that the blackness of the skin is no reason why a human being should be abandoned without redress to the caprice of a tormentor. It may one day come to be recognized that the number of the legs, the villosity of the skin, or the termination of the *os sacrum*, are reasons equally insufficient for abandoning a sensitive being to the same fate. What else is it that should trace the insuperable line? Is it the faculty of reason, or perhaps the faculty of discourse? But a full-grown horse or dog is beyond comparison a more rational, as well as a more conversable animal, than an infant of a day, or a week, or even a month, old. But suppose they were otherwise, what would it avail? The question is not, Can they *reason*? nor, Can they *talk*? but, Can they *suffer*?[3]

In this passage Bentham points to the capacity for suffering as the vital characteristic that gives a being the right to equal consideration. The capacity for suffering – or more strictly, for suffering and/or enjoyment or happiness – is not just another characteristic like the capacity for language, or for higher mathematics. Bentham is not saying that those who try to mark "the insuperable line" that determines whether the interests of a being should be considered happen to have selected the wrong characteristic. The capacity for suffering and enjoying things is a prerequisite for having interests at all, a condition that must be satisfied before we can speak of interests in any meaningful way. It would be nonsense to say that it was not in the interests of a stone to be kicked along the road by a schoolboy. A stone does not have interests because it cannot suffer. Nothing that we can do to it could possibly make any difference to its welfare. A mouse, on the other hand, does have an interest in not being tormented, because it will suffer if it is. If a being suffers, there can be no moral justification for refusing to take that suffering into consideration. No matter what the nature of the being, the principle of equality requires that its suffering be counted equally with the like suffering – in so far as rough comparisons can be made – of any other being. If a being is not capable of suffering, or of experiencing enjoyment or happiness, there is nothing to be taken into account. This is why the limit of sentience (using the term as a convenient, if not

strictly accurate, shorthand for the capacity to suffer or experience enjoyment or happiness) is the only defensible boundary of concern for the interests of others. To mark this boundary by some characteristic like intelligence or rationality would be to mark it in an arbitrary way. Why not choose some other characteristic, like skin color?

The racist violates the principle of equality by giving greater weight to the interests of members of his own race, when there is a clash between their interests and the interests of those of another race. Similarly the speciesist allows the interests of his own species to override the greater interests of members of other species.[4] The pattern is the same in each case. Most human beings are speciesists. I shall now very briefly describe some of the practices that show this.

For the great majority of human beings, especially in urban, industrialized societies, the most direct form of contact with members of other species is at mealtimes: we eat them. In doing so we treat them purely as means to our ends. We regard their life and well-being as subordinate to our taste for a particular kind of dish. I say "taste" deliberately – this is purely a matter of pleasing our palate. There can be no defense of eating flesh in terms of satisfying nutritional needs, since it has been established beyond doubt that we could satisfy our need for protein and other essential nutrients far more efficiently with a diet that replaced animal flesh by soy beans, or products derived from soy beans, and other high-protein vegetable products.[5]

It is not merely the act of killing that indicates what we are ready to do to other species in order to gratify our tastes. The suffering we inflict on the animals while they are alive is perhaps an even clearer indication of our speciesism than the fact that we are prepared to kill them.[6] In order to have meat on the table at a price that people can afford, our society tolerates methods of meat production that confine sentient animals in cramped, unsuitable conditions for the entire durations of their lives. Animals are treated like machines that convert fodder into flesh, and any innovation that results in a higher "conversion ratio" is liable to be adopted. As one authority on the subject has said, "cruelty is acknowledged only when profitability ceases."[7]

Since, as I have said, none of these practices cater for anything more than our pleasures of taste, our practice of rearing and killing other animals in order to eat them is a clear instance of the sacrifice of the most important interests of other beings in order to satisfy trivial interests of our own. To avoid speciesism we must stop this practice, and each of us has a moral obligation to cease supporting the practice. Our custom is all the support that the meat industry needs. The decision to cease giving it that support may be difficult, but it is no more difficult than it would have been for a white Southerner to go against the traditions of his society and free his slaves: if we do not change our dietary habits, how can we censure those slaveholders who would not change their own way of living?

The same form of discrimination may be observed in the widespread practice of experimenting on other species in order to see if certain substances are safe for human beings, or to test some psychological theory about the effect of severe punishment on learning, or to try out various new compounds just in case something turns up . . .

In the past, argument about vivisection has often missed the point, because it has been put in absolutist terms: Would the abolitionist be prepared to let thousands die if they could be saved by experimenting on a single animal? The way to reply to this purely hypothetical question is to pose another: Would the experimenter be prepared to perform his experiment on an orphaned human infant, if that were the only way to save many lives? (I say "orphan" to avoid the complication of parental feelings, although in doing so I am being overfair to the experimenter, since the nonhuman subjects of experiments are not orphans.) If the experimenter is not prepared to use an orphaned human infant, then his readiness to use nonhumans is simple discrimination, since adult apes, cats, mice, and other mammals are more aware of what is happening to them, more self-directing and, so far as we can tell, at least as sensitive to pain, as any human infant. There seems to be no relevant characteristic that human infants possess that adult mammals do not have to the same or a higher degree. (Someone might try to argue that what makes it wrong to experiment on a human infant is that the infant will, in time and if left alone, develop into more than the nonhuman, but one would then, to be consistent, have to oppose abortion, since the fetus has the same potential as the infant – indeed, even contraception and abstinence might be wrong on this ground, since the egg and sperm, considered jointly, also have the same potential. In any case, this argument still gives us no reason for selecting a nonhuman, rather than a human with severe and irreversible brain damage, as the subject for our experiments).

The experimenter, then, shows a bias in favor of his own species whenever he carries out an experiment on a nonhuman for a purpose that he would not think justified him in using a human being at an equal or lower level of sentience, awareness, ability to be self-directing, etc. No one familiar with the kind of results yielded by most experiments on animals can have the slightest doubt that if this bias were eliminated the number of experiments performed would be a minute fraction of the number performed today.

Experimenting on animals, and eating their flesh, are perhaps the two major forms of speciesism in our society. By comparison, the third and last form of speciesism is so minor as to be insignificant, but it is perhaps of some special interest to those for whom this article was written. I am referring to speciesism in contemporary philosophy.

Philosophy ought to question the basic assumptions of the age. Thinking through, critically and carefully, what most people take for granted is, I believe, the chief task of philosophy, and it is this task that makes philosophy a worthwhile activity. Regrettably, philosophy does not always live up to its historic role. Philosophers are human beings, and they are subject to all the preconceptions of the society to which they belong. Sometimes they succeed in breaking free of the prevailing ideology: more often they become its most sophisticated defenders. So, in this case, philosophy as practiced in the universities today does not challenge anyone's preconceptions about our relations with other species. By their writings, those philosophers who tackle problems that touch upon the issue reveal that they make the same unquestioned assumptions as most other humans, and what they say tends to confirm the reader in his or her comfortable speciesist habits.

I could illustrate this claim by referring to the writings of philosophers in various fields – for instance, the attempts that have been made by those interested in rights to draw the boundary of the sphere of rights so that it runs parallel to the biological boundaries of the species *Homo sapiens*, including infants and even mental defectives, but excluding those other beings of equal or greater capacity who are so useful to us at mealtimes and in our laboratories. I think it would be a more appropriate conclusion to this article, however, if I concentrated on the problem with which we have been centrally concerned, the problem of equality.

It is significant that the problem of equality, in moral and political philosophy, is invariably formulated in terms of human equality. The effect of this is that the question of the equality of other animals does not confront the philosopher, or student, as an issue itself – and this is already an indication of the failure of philosophy to challenge accepted beliefs. Still, philosophers have found it difficult to discuss the issue of human equality without raising, in a paragraph or two, the question of the status of other animals. The reason for this, which should be apparent from what I have said already, is that if humans are to be regarded as equal to one another, we need some sense of "equal" that does not require any actual, descriptive equality of capacities, talents or other qualities. If equality is to be related to any actual characteristics of humans, these characteristics must be some lowest common denominator, pitched so low that no human lacks them – but then the philosopher comes up against the catch that any such set of characteristics which covers all humans will not be possessed only by humans. In other words, it turns out that in the only sense in which we can truly say, as an assertion of fact, that all humans are equal, at least some members of other species are also equal – equal, that is, to each other and to humans. If, on the other hand, we regard the statement "All humans are equal" in some non-factual way, perhaps as a prescription, then, as I have already argued, it is even more difficult to exclude nonhumans from the sphere of equality.

[. . .]

[The] idea of a distinctive human dignity and worth has a long history; it can be traced back directly to the Renaissance humanists, for instance to Pico della Mirandola's *Oration on the Dignity of Man*. Pico and other humanists based their estimate of human dignity on the idea that man possessed the central, pivotal position in the "Great Chain of Being" that led from the lowliest forms of matter to God himself; this view of the universe, in turn, goes back to both classical and Judeo-Christian doctrines. Contemporary philosophers have cast off these metaphysical and religious shackles and freely invoke the dignity of mankind without needing to justify the idea at all. Why should we not attribute "intrinsic dignity" or "intrinsic worth" to ourselves? Fellow-humans are unlikely to reject the accolades we so generously bestow on them, and those to whom we deny the honor are unable to object. Indeed, when one thinks only of humans, it can be very liberal, very progressive, to talk of the dignity of all human

beings. In so doing, we implicitly condemn slavery, racism, and other violations of human rights. We admit that we ourselves are in some fundamental sense on a par with the poorest, most ignorant members of our own species. It is only when we think of humans as no more than a small sub-group of all the beings that inhabit our planet that we may realize that in elevating our own species we are at the same time lowering the relative status of all other species.

The truth is that the appeal to the intrinsic dignity of human beings appears to solve the egalitarian's problems only as long as it goes unchallenged. Once we ask why it should be that all humans – including infants, mental defectives, psychopaths, Hitler, Stalin, and the rest – have some kind of dignity or worth that no elephant, pig, or chimpanzee can ever achieve, we see that this question is as difficult to answer as our original request for some relevant fact that justifies the inequality of humans and other animals. In fact, these two questions are really one: talk of intrinsic dignity or moral worth only takes the problem back one step, because any satisfactory defense of the claim that all and only humans have intrinsic dignity would need to refer to some relevant capacities or characteristics that all and only humans possess. Philosophers frequently introduce ideas of dignity, respect, and worth at the point at which other reasons appear to be lacking, but this is hardly good enough. Fine phrases are the last resource of those who have run out of arguments.

In case there are those who still think it may be possible to find some relevant characteristic that distinguishes all humans from all members of other species, I shall refer again, before I conclude, to the existence of some humans who quite clearly are below the level of awareness, self-consciousness, intelligence, and sentience, of many nonhumans. I am thinking of humans with severe and irreparable brain damage, and also of infant humans. To avoid the complication of the relevance of a being's potential, however, I shall henceforth concentrate on permanently retarded humans.

Philosophers who set out to find a characteristic that will distinguish humans from other animals rarely take the course of abandoning these groups of humans by lumping them in with the other animals. It is easy to see why they do not. To take this line without re-thinking our attitudes to other animals would entail that we have the right to perform painful experiments on retarded humans for trivial reasons; similarly it would follow that we had the right to rear and kill these humans for food. To most philosophers these consequences are as unacceptable as the view that we should stop treating nonhumans in this way.

Of course, when discussing the problem of equality it is possible to ignore the problem of mental defectives, or brush it aside as if somehow insignificant.[8] This is the easiest way out. What else remains? [. . .]

An imbecile [. . .] may have no characteristics superior to those of a dog; nevertheless this does not make the imbecile a member of "a different species" as the dog is. Therefore it would be "unfair" to use the imbecile for medical research as we use the dog. But why? That the imbecile is not rational is just the way things have worked out, and the same is true of the dog – neither is any more responsible for their mental level. If it is unfair to take advantage of an isolated defect, why is it fair to take advantage of a more general limitation? I find it hard to see anything in this argument except a defense of preferring the interests of members of our own species because they are members of our own species.

Notes

1   *The Methods of Ethics*, 7th edn. (Bristol: Thoemmes, 1996), p. 382.

2   For example, R. M. Hare, *Freedom and Reason* (Oxford, 1963) and J. Rawls, *A Theory of Justice* (Harvard, 1972); for a brief account of the essential agreement on this issue between these and other positions, see R. M. Hare, "Rules of War and Moral Reasoning," *Philosophy and Public Affairs*, vol. 1, no. 2 (1972).

3   *Introduction to the Principles of Morals and Legislation*, ch. XVII.

4   I owe the term speciesism to Richard Ryder.

5   In order to produce 1lb. of protein in the form of beef or veal, we must feed 21lbs of protein to the animal. Other forms of livestock are slightly less inefficient, but the average ratio in the United States is still 1:8. It has been estimated that the amount of protein lost to humans in this way is equivalent to 90 percent of the annual world protein deficit. For a brief account, see Frances Moore Lappe, *Diet for a Small Planet* (Friends of The Earth/Ballantine, New York, 1971), pp. 4–11.

6   Although one might think that killing a being is obviously the ultimate wrong one can do to it, I think that the infliction of suffering is a clearer indication of speciesism because it might be argued that at least part of what is wrong with killing a human is that most humans are conscious of their existence over time and have desires and purposes that extend into the future; see, for instance, M. Tooley, "Abortion and Infanticide," *Philosophy and Public Affairs*, vol. 2, no. 1 (1972). Of course, if one took this view one would have to hold – as Tooley does – that killing a human infant or mental defective is not in itself wrong and is less serious than killing certain higher mammals that probably do have a sense of their own existence over time.

7   Ruth Harrison, *Animal Machines* (London: Stuart, 1964). For an account of farming conditions, see my *Animal Liberation* (New York: New York Review, 1975).

8   For example, Bernard Williams, "The Idea of Equality," in *Philosophy, Politics, and Society* (second series), ed. P. Laslett and W. Rundman (Oxford: Blackwell, 1962), p. 118; Rawls, *A Theory of Justice*, pp. 509–10.

EGALITARIAN BIOCENTRISM

21   The Ethics of Respect for Nature

Paul W. Taylor

Human-Centered and Life-Centered Systems of Environmental Ethics

In this paper I show how the taking of a certain ultimate moral attitude toward nature, which I call "respect for nature," has a central place in the foundations of a life-centered system of environmental ethics. I hold that a set of moral norms (both standards of character and rules of conduct) governing human treatment of the natural world is a rationally grounded set if and only if, first, commitment to

From *Environmental Ethics*, vol. 3 (1981): 197–200, 205–7, 210–11, 213–18. © 1981 by Paul W. Taylor. Reprinted with permission from the author.

those norms is a practical entailment of adopting the attitude of respect for nature as an ultimate moral attitude, and second, the adopting of that attitude on the part of all rational agents can itself be justified.

When the basic characteristics of the attitude of respect for nature are made clear, it will be seen that a life-centered system of environmental ethics need not be holistic or organicist in its conception of the kinds of entities that are deemed the appropriate objects of moral concern and consideration. Nor does such a system require that the concepts of ecological homeostasis, equilibrium, and integrity provide us with normative principles from which could be derived (with the addition of factual knowledge) our obligations with regard to natural ecosystems. The "balance of nature" is not itself a moral norm, however important may be the role it plays in our general outlook on the natural world that underlies the attitude of respect for nature. I argue that finally it is the good (well-being, welfare) of individual organisms, considered as entities having inherent worth, that determines our moral relations with the Earth's wild communities of life.

In designating the theory to be set forth as life-centered, I intend to contrast it with all anthropocentric views. According to the latter, human actions affecting the natural environment and its nonhuman inhabitants are right (or wrong) by either of two criteria: they have consequences which are favorable (or unfavorable) to human well-being, or they are consistent (or inconsistent) with the system of norms that protect and implement human rights. From this human-centered standpoint it is to humans and only to humans that all duties are ultimately owed. We may have responsibilities *with regard to* the natural ecosystems and biotic communities of our planet, but these responsibilities are in every case based on the contingent fact that our treatment of those ecosystems and communities of life can further the realization of human values and/or human rights. We have no obligation to promote or protect the good of nonhuman living things, independently of this contingent fact.

A life-centered system of environmental ethics is opposed to human-centered ones precisely on this point. From the perspective of a life-centered theory, we have prima facie moral obligations that are owed to wild plants and animals themselves as members of the Earth's biotic community. We are morally bound (other things being equal) to protect or promote their good for *their* sake. Our duties to respect the integrity of natural ecosystems, to preserve endangered species, and to avoid environmental pollution stem from the fact that these are ways in which we can help make it possible for wild species populations to achieve and maintain a healthy existence in a natural state. Such obligations are due those living things out of recognition of their inherent worth. They are entirely additional to and independent of the obligations we owe to our fellow humans. Although many of the actions that fulfill one set of obligations will also fulfill the other, two different grounds of obligation are involved. Their well-being, as well as human well-being, is something to be realized *as an end in itself*.

[. . .]

The Good of a Being and the Concept of Inherent Worth

[. . .]

We can think of the good of an individual nonhuman organism as consisting in the full development of its biological powers. Its good is realized to the extent that it is strong and healthy. It possesses whatever capacities it needs for successfully coping with its environment and so preserving its existence throughout the various stages of the normal life cycle of its species. The good of a population or community of such individuals consists in the population or community maintaining itself from generation to generation as a coherent system of genetically and ecologically related organisms whose average good is at an optimum level for the given environment. (Here *average good* means that the degree of realization of the good of *individual organisms* in the population or community is, on average, greater than would be the case under any other ecologically functioning order of interrelations among those species populations in the given ecosystem.)

The idea of a being having a good of its own, as I understand it, does not entail that the being must have interests or take an interest in what affects its life for better or for worse. We can act in a being's interest or contrary to its interest without its being interested in what we are doing to it in the sense of wanting or not wanting us to do it. It may, indeed, be wholly unaware that favorable and unfavorable events are taking place in its life. I take it that trees, for example, have no knowledge or desires or feelings.

Yet it is undoubtedly the case that trees can be harmed or benefited by our actions. We can crush their roots by running a bulldozer too close to them. We can see to it that they get adequate nourishment and moisture by fertilizing and watering the soil around them. Thus we can help or hinder them in the realization of their good. It is the good of trees themselves that is thereby affected. [. . .]

When construed in this way, the concept of a being's good is not coextensive with sentience or the capacity for feeling pain. William Frankena has argued for a general theory of environmental ethics in which the ground of a creature's being worthy of moral consideration is its sentience. I have offered some criticisms of this view elsewhere, but the full refutation of such a position, it seems to me, finally depends on the positive reasons for accepting a life-centered theory of the kind I am defending in this essay.[1]

[. . .]

The Justifiability of the Attitude of Respect for Nature

I return to the question posed earlier, which has not yet been answered: why *should* moral agents regard wild living things as possessing inherent worth? [. . .] To be disposed to further, as an end in itself, the good of any entity in nature just because it is that kind of entity, is to be disposed to give consideration to *every* such entity and to place intrinsic value on the realization of its good. Insofar as we subscribe to these two principles we regard living things as possessing inherent worth. Subscribing to the principles is what it *means* to so regard them. To justify the attitude of respect for nature, then, is to justify commitment to these principles and thereby to justify regarding wild creatures as possessing inherent worth.

[. . .]

This belief system underlying the attitude of respect for nature I call (for want of a better name) "the biocentric outlook on nature." Since it is not wholly analyzable into empirically confirmable assertions, it should not be thought of as simply a compendium of the biological sciences concerning our planet's ecosystems. It might best be described as a philosophical world view, to distinguish it from a scientific theory or explanatory system. However, one of its major tenets is the great lesson we have learned from the science of ecology: the interdependence of all living things in an organically unified order whose balance and stability are necessary conditions for the realization of the good of its constituent biotic communities.

Before turning to an account of the main components of the biocentric outlook, it is convenient here to set forth the overall structure of my theory of environmental ethics as it has now emerged. The ethics of respect for nature is made up of three basic elements: a belief system, an ultimate moral attitude, and a set of rules of duty and standards of character. These elements are connected with each other in the following manner. The belief system provides a certain outlook on nature which supports and makes intelligible an autonomous agent's adopting, as an ultimate moral attitude, the attitude of respect for nature. It supports and makes intelligible the attitude in the sense that, when an autonomous agent understands its moral relations to the natural world in terms of this outlook, it recognizes the attitude of respect to be the only *suitable* or *fitting* attitude to take toward all wild forms of life in the Earth's biosphere. Living things are now viewed as *the appropriate objects of the attitude of respect* and are accordingly regarded as entities possessing inherent worth. One then places intrinsic value on the promotion and protection of their good. As a consequence of this, one makes a moral commitment to abide by a set of rules of duty and to fulfill (as far as one can by one's own efforts) certain standards of good character. Given one's adoption of the attitude of respect, one makes that moral commitment because one considers those rules and standards to be validly binding on all moral agents. They are seen as embodying forms of conduct and character structures in which the attitude of respect for nature is manifested.

This three-part complex which internally orders the ethics of respect for nature is symmetrical with a theory of human ethics grounded on respect for persons. Such a theory includes, first, a conception of oneself and others as persons, that is, as centers of autonomous choice. Second, there is the attitude of respect for persons as persons. When this is adopted as an ultimate moral attitude it involves the disposition to treat every person as having inherent worth or "human dignity." Every human being, just in virtue of her or his humanity, is understood to be worthy of moral consideration, and intrinsic value is placed on the autonomy and well-being of each. This is what Kant meant by conceiving of persons as ends in themselves. Third, there is an ethical system of duties which are acknowledged to be owed by everyone to everyone. These duties are forms of conduct in which public recognition is given to each individual's inherent worth as a person.

This structural framework for a theory of human ethics is meant to leave open the issue of consequentialism (utilitarianism) versus nonconsequentialism (deontology). That issue concerns the particular kind of system of rules defining the duties of moral agents toward persons. Similarly, I am leaving open in this paper the question of what particular kind of system of rules defines our duties with respect to the natural world.

The Biocentric Outlook on Nature

The biocentric outlook on nature has four main components. (1) Humans are thought of as members of the Earth's community of life, holding that membership on the same terms as apply to all the nonhuman members. (2) The Earth's natural ecosystems as a totality are seen as a complex web of interconnected elements, with the sound biological functioning of each being dependent on the sound biological functioning of the others. (This is the component referred to above as the great lesson that the science of ecology has taught us.) (3) Each individual organism is conceived of as a teleological center of life, pursuing its own good in its own way. (4) Whether we are concerned with standards of merit or with the concept of inherent worth, the claim that humans by their very nature are superior to other species is a groundless claim and, in the light of elements (1), (2), and (3) above, must be rejected as nothing more than an irrational bias in our own favor.

The conjunction of these four ideas constitutes the biocentric outlook on nature.

[. . .]

Individual Organisms as Teleological Centers of Life

As our knowledge of living things increases, as we come to a deeper understanding of their life cycles, their interactions with other organisms, and the manifold ways in which they adjust to the environment, we become more fully aware of how each of them is carrying out its biological functions according to the laws of its species-specific nature. But besides this, our increasing knowledge and understanding also develop in us a sharpened awareness of the uniqueness of each individual organism. Scientists who have made careful studies of particular plants and animals, whether in the field or in laboratories, have often acquired a knowledge of their subjects as identifiable individuals. Close observation over extended periods of time has led them to an appreciation of the unique "personalities" of their subjects. Sometimes a scientist may come to take a special interest in a particular animal or plant, all the while remaining strictly objective in the gathering and recording of data. Nonscientists may likewise experience this development of interest when, as amateur naturalists, they make accurate observations over sustained periods of close acquaintance with an individual organism. As one becomes more and more familiar with the organism and its behavior, one becomes fully sensitive to the particular way it is living out its life cycle. One may become fascinated by it and even experience some involvement with its good and bad fortunes (that is, with the occurrence of environmental conditions favorable or unfavorable to the realization of its good). The organism comes to mean something to one as a unique, irreplaceable individual. The final culmination of this process is the achievement of a genuine understanding of its point of view and, with that understanding, an ability to "take" that point of view. *Conceiving of it as a center of life, one is able to look at the world from its perspective.*

This development from objective knowledge to the recognition of individuality, and from the recognition of individuality to full awareness of an organism's standpoint, is a process of heightening our consciousness of what it means to be an individual living thing. We grasp the particularity of the organism as a teleological center of life, striving to preserve itself and to realize its own good in its own unique way.

It is to be noted that we need not be falsely anthropomorphizing when we conceive of individual plants and animals in this manner. Understanding them as teleological centers of life does not necessitate "reading into" them human characteristics. We need not, for example, consider them to have consciousness. Some of them may be aware of the world around them and others may not. Nor need we deny that different kinds and levels of awareness are exemplified when consciousness in some form is present. But conscious or not, all are equally teleological centers of life in the sense that each is a unified system of goal-oriented activities directed toward their preservation and well-being.

When considered from an ethical point of view, a teleological center of life is an entity whose "world" can be viewed from the perspective of *its* life. In looking at the world from that perspective we recognize objects and events occurring in its life as being beneficent, maleficent, or indifferent. The first are occurrences which increase its powers to preserve its existence and realize its good. The second decrease or destroy those powers. The third have neither of these effects on the entity. With regard to our human role as moral agents, we can conceive of a teleological center of life as a being whose standpoint we can take in making judgments about what events in the world are good or evil, desirable or undesirable. In making those judgments it is what promotes or protects the being's own good, not what benefits moral agents themselves, that sets the standard of evaluation. Such judgments can be made about anything that happens to the entity which is favorable or unfavorable in relation to its good. As was pointed out earlier, the entity itself need not have any (conscious) *interest* in what is happening to it for such judgments to be meaningful and true.

It is precisely judgments of this sort that we are disposed to make when we take the attitude of respect for nature. In adopting that attitude those judgments are given weight as reasons for action in our practical deliberation. They become morally relevant facts in the guidance of our conduct.

The Denial of Human Superiority

[. . .] [T]he biocentric outlook on nature is the single most important idea in establishing the justifiability of the attitude of respect for nature. Its central role is due to the special relationship it bears to the first three components of the outlook. This relationship will be brought out after the concept of human superiority is examined and analyzed.[2]

[. . .]

The inherent worth of an entity does not depend on its merits.[3] To consider something as possessing inherent worth, we have seen, is to place intrinsic value on the realization of its good. This is done regardless of whatever particular merits it might have or might lack, as judged by a set of grading or ranking standards. In human affairs, we are all familiar with the principle that one's worth as a person does

not vary with one's merits or lack of merits. The same can hold true of animals and plants. To regard such entities as possessing inherent worth entails disregarding their merits and deficiencies, whether they are being judged from a human standpoint or from the standpoint of their own species.

The idea of one entity having more merit than another, and so being superior to it in merit, makes perfectly good sense. Merit is a grading or ranking concept, and judgments of comparative merit are based on the different degrees to which things satisfy a given standard. But what can it mean to talk about one thing being superior to another in inherent worth? In order to get at what is being asserted in such a claim it is helpful first to look at the social origin of the concept of degrees of inherent worth.

The idea that humans can possess different degrees of inherent worth originated in societies having rigid class structures. Before the rise of modern democracies with their egalitarian outlook, one's membership in a hereditary class determined one's social status. People in the upper classes were looked up to, while those in the lower classes were looked down upon. In such a society one's social superiors and social inferiors were clearly defined and easily recognized.

Two aspects of these class-structured societies are especially relevant to the idea of degrees of inherent worth. First, those born into the upper classes were deemed more worthy of respect than those born into the lower orders. Second, the superior worth of upper class people had nothing to do with their merits nor did the inferior worth of those in the lower classes rest on their lack of merits. One's superiority or inferiority entirely derived from a social position one was born into. The modern concept of a meritocracy simply did not apply. One could not advance into a higher class by any sort of moral or nonmoral achievement. Similarly, an aristocrat held his title and all the privileges that went with it just because he was the eldest son of a titled nobleman. Unlike the bestowing of knighthood in contemporary Great Britain, one did not earn membership in the nobility by meritorious conduct.

We who live in modern democracies no longer believe in such hereditary social distinctions. Indeed, we would wholeheartedly condemn them on moral grounds as being fundamentally unjust. We have come to think of class systems as a paradigm of social injustice, it being a central principle of the democratic way of life that among humans there are no superiors and no inferiors. Thus we have rejected the whole conceptual framework in which people are judged to have different degrees of inherent worth. That idea is incompatible with our notion of human equality based on the doctrine that all humans, simply in virtue of their humanity, have the same inherent worth. (The belief in universal human rights is one form that this egalitarianism takes.)

The vast majority of people in modern democracies, however, do not maintain an egalitarian outlook when it comes to comparing human beings with other living things. Most people consider our own species to be superior to all other species and this superiority is understood to be a matter of inherent worth, not merit. There may exist thoroughly vicious and depraved humans who lack all merit. Yet because they are human they are thought to belong to a higher class of entities than any plant or animal. That one is born into the species *Homo sapiens* entitles one to have lordship over those who are one's inferiors, namely, those born into other species. The parallel with hereditary social classes is very close. Implicit in this view is a hierarchical conception of nature according to which an organism has a position of superiority or inferiority in the Earth's community of life simply on the basis of its genetic background. The "lower" orders of life are looked down upon and it is considered perfectly proper that they serve the interests of those belonging to the highest order, namely humans. The intrinsic value we place on the well-being of our fellow humans reflects our recognition of their rightful position as our equals. No such intrinsic value is to be placed on the good of other animals, unless we choose to do so out of fondness or affection for them. But their well-being imposes no moral requirement on us. In this respect there is an absolute difference in moral status between ourselves and them.

This is the structure of concepts and beliefs that people are committed to insofar as they regard humans to be superior in inherent worth to all other species. I now wish to argue that this structure of concepts and beliefs is completely groundless. If we accept the first three components of the biocentric outlook and from that perspective look at the major philosophical traditions which have supported that structure, we find it to be at bottom nothing more than the expression of an irrational bias in our own favor. The philosophical traditions themselves rest on very questionable assumptions or else simply beg the question. I briefly consider three of the main

traditions to substantiate the point. These are classical Greek humanism, Cartesian dualism, and the Judeo-Christian concept of the Great Chain of Being.

The inherent superiority of humans over other species was implicit in the Greek definition of man as a rational animal. Our animal nature was identified with "brute" desires that need the order and restraint of reason to rule them (just as reason is the special virtue of those who rule in the ideal state). Rationality was then seen to be the key to our superiority over animals. It enables us to live on a higher plane and endows us with a nobility and worth that other creatures lack. This familiar way of comparing humans with other species is deeply ingrained in our Western philosophical outlook. The point to consider here is that this view does not actually provide an argument *for* human superiority but rather makes explicit the framework of thought that is implicitly used by those who think of humans as inherently superior to nonhumans. The Greeks who held that humans, in virtue of their rational capacities, have a kind of worth greater than that of any nonrational being, never looked at rationality as but one capacity of living things among many others. But when we consider rationality from the standpoint of the first three elements of the ecological outlook, we see that its value lies in its importance for *human* life. Other creatures achieve their species-specific good without the need of rationality, although they often make use of capacities that humans lack. So the humanistic outlook of classical Greek thought does not give us a neutral (nonquestion-begging) ground on which to construct a scale of degrees of inherent worth possessed by different species of living things.

The second tradition, centering on the Cartesian dualism of soul and body, also fails to justify the claim to human superiority. That superiority is supposed to derive from the fact that we have souls while animals do not. Animals are mere automata and lack the divine element that makes us spiritual beings. I won't go into the now familiar criticisms of this two-substance view. I only add the point that, even if humans are composed of an immaterial, unextended soul and a material, extended body, this in itself is not a reason to deem them of greater worth than entities that are only bodies. Why is a soul substance a thing that adds value to its possessor? Unless some theological reasoning is offered here (which many, including myself, would find unacceptable on epistemological grounds), no logical connection is evident. An immaterial something which thinks is better than a material something which does not think only if thinking itself has value, either intrinsically or instrumentally. Now it is intrinsically valuable to humans alone, who value it as an end in itself, and it is instrumentally valuable to those who benefit from it, namely humans.

For animals that neither enjoy thinking for its own sake nor need it for living the kind of life for which they are best adapted, it has no value. Even if "thinking" is broadened to include all forms of consciousness, there are still many living things that can do without it and yet live what is for their species a good life. The anthropocentricity underlying the claim to human superiority runs throughout Cartesian dualism.

A third major source of the idea of human superiority is the Judeo-Christian concept of the Great Chain of Being. Humans are superior to animals and plants because their Creator has given them a higher place on the chain. It begins with God at the top, and then moves to the angels, who are lower than God but higher than humans, then to humans, positioned between the angels and the beasts (partaking of the nature of both), and then on down to the lower levels occupied by nonhuman animals, plants, and finally inanimate objects. Humans, being "made in God's image," are inherently superior to animals and plants by virtue of their being closer (in their essential nature) to God.

The metaphysical and epistemological difficulties with this conception of a hierarchy of entities are, in my mind, insuperable. Without entering into this matter here, I only point out that if we are unwilling to accept the metaphysics of traditional Judaism and Christianity, we are again left without good reasons for holding to the claim of inherent human superiority.

The foregoing considerations (and others like them) leave us with but one ground for the assertion that a human being, regardless of merit, is a higher kind of entity than any other living thing. This is the mere fact of the genetic makeup of the species *Homo sapiens*. But this is surely irrational and arbitrary. Why should the arrangement of genes of a certain type be a mark of superior value, especially when this fact about an organism is taken by itself, unrelated to any other aspect of its life? We might just as well refer to any other genetic makeup as a ground of superior value. Clearly we are confronted here with a wholly arbitrary claim that can only be explained as an irrational bias in our own favor.

That the claim is nothing more than a deep-seated prejudice is brought home to us when we look at our relation to other species in the light of the first three elements of the biocentric outlook. Those elements taken conjointly give us a certain overall view of the natural world and of the place of humans in it. When we take this view we come to understand other living things, their environmental conditions, and their ecological relationships in such a way as to awake in us a deep sense of our kinship with them as fellow members of the Earth's community of life. Humans and nonhumans alike are viewed together as integral parts of one unified whole in which all living things are functionally interrelated. Finally, when our awareness focuses on the individual lives of plants and animals, each is seen to share with us the characteristic of being a teleological center of life striving to realize its own good in its own unique way.

As this entire belief system becomes part of the conceptual framework through which we understand and perceive the world, we come to see ourselves as bearing a certain moral relation to nonhuman forms of life. Our ethical role in nature takes on a new significance. We begin to look at other species as we look at ourselves, seeing them as beings which have a good they are striving to realize just as we have a good we are striving to realize. We accordingly develop the disposition to view the world from the standpoint of their good as well as from the standpoint of our own good. Now if the groundlessness of the claim that humans are inherently superior to other species were brought clearly before our minds, we would not remain intellectually neutral toward that claim but would reject it as being fundamentally at variance with our total world outlook. In the absence of any good reasons for holding it, the assertion of human superiority would then appear simply as the expression of an irrational and self-serving prejudice that favors one particular species over several million others.

Rejecting the notion of human superiority entails its positive counterpart: the doctrine of species impartiality. One who accepts that doctrine regards all living things as possessing inherent worth – the *same* inherent worth, since no one species has been shown to be either "higher" or "lower" than any other. Now we saw earlier that, insofar as one thinks of a living thing as possessing inherent worth, one considers it to be the appropriate object of the attitude of respect and believes that attitude to be the only fitting or suitable one for all moral agents to take toward it.

[. . .]

Moral Rights and the Matter of Competing Claims

I have not asserted anywhere in the foregoing account that animals or plants have moral rights. This omission was deliberate. I do not think that the reference class of the concept, bearer of moral rights, should be extended to include nonhuman living things. My reasons for taking this position, however, go beyond the scope of this paper. I believe I have been able to accomplish many of the same ends which those who ascribe rights to animals or plants wish to accomplish. There is no reason, moreover, why plants and animals, including whole species populations and life communities, cannot be accorded *legal* rights under my theory. To grant them legal protection could be interpreted as giving them legal entitlement to be protected, and this, in fact, would be a means by which a society that subscribed to the ethics of respect for nature could give public recognition to their inherent worth.

There remains the problem of competing claims, even when wild plants and animals are not thought of as bearers of moral rights. If we accept the biocentric outlook and accordingly adopt the attitude of respect for nature as our ultimate moral attitude, how do we resolve conflicts that arise from our respect for persons in the domain of human ethics and our respect for nature in the domain of environmental ethics? This is a question that cannot adequately be dealt with here. My main purpose in this paper has been to try to establish a base point from which we can start working toward a solution to the problem. I have shown why we cannot just begin with an initial presumption in favor of the interests of our own species. It is after all within our power as moral beings to place limits on human population and technology with the deliberate intention of sharing the Earth's bounty with other species. That such sharing is an ideal difficult to realize even in an approximate way does not take away its claim to our deepest moral commitment.

Notes

1   See W. K. Frankena, "Ethics and the Environment," in K. E. Goodpaster and K. M. Sayre, eds., *Ethics and Problems of the 21st Century* (Notre Dame: University of Notre Dame Press, 1979), pp. 3–20. I critically examine Frankena's views in "Frankena on Environmental Ethics," *Monist*, 64 (1981): 313–24.

2   My criticisms of the dogma of human superiority gain independent support from a carefully reasoned essay by R. and V. Routley showing the many logical weaknesses in arguments for human-centered theories of environmental ethics. R. and V. Routley, "Against the Inevitability of Human Chauvinism," in K. E. Goodpaster and K. M. Sayre, eds., *Ethics and Problems of the 21st Century* (Notre Dame: University of Notre Dame Press, 1979), pp. 36–59.

3   For this way of distinguishing between merit and inherent worth, I am indebted to Gregory Vlastos, "Justice and Equality," in R. Brandt, ed., *Social Justice* (Englewood Cliffs, NJ: Prentice-Hall, 1962), pp. 31–72.

---

22   Kantians and Utilitarians and the Moral Status of Nonhuman Life

James P. Sterba

If Kantian and utilitarian ethics can be reconciled at the practical level, [. . .] it should then be possible to reach agreement on the moral status of nonhuman life. Indeed, in recent years both Kantian and utilitarian moral philosophers have surely tried to provide a defense of the moral status of at least some forms of nonhuman life. For example, Peter Singer has attempted to provide a utilitarian defense of the moral status of all sentient beings.[1] Tom Regan has proposed a Kantian defense of the moral status of all

From *The Triumph of Practice Over Theory in Ethics* (Oxford: Oxford University Press, 2005), pp. 58–73. © 2005 by Oxford University Press, Inc. Reprinted with permission from Oxford University Press.

experiencing subjects of life.[2] An alternative Kantian defense of the moral status of all individual living beings has been proposed by Paul Taylor.[3] And I have extended Taylor's account to include species and ecosystems as well.[4] All of these views are versions of nonanthropocentrism because they all hold that at least some nonhuman living beings have moral status. As such, they are opposed to anthropocentrism in all its forms which holds that all or only human beings have moral status. What I propose to do in this chapter is first to try to show why my particular version of nonanthropocentrism is morally preferable to anthropocentrism, and then to try to show why it is also morally preferable to other forms of nonanthropocentrism as well. Throughout I will be looking for a defense of nonanthropocentrism that should be acceptable to both Kantians and utilitarians alike.

The Moral Status of All Living Beings

Clearly what we need to defend nonanthropocentrism is a really good argument that nonhuman living beings have moral status. A really good argument, by definition, must be a non-question-begging argument. So what we need is a non-question-begging argument that nonhuman living beings have moral status, which is to say that they should count morally. Is there such an argument?

Consider: We clearly have the capacity of entertaining and acting upon both anthropocentric reasons that take only the interests of humans into account and nonanthropocentric reasons that also take the interests of nonhuman living beings into account. Given that capacity, the question we seek to answer is what sort of reasons are rational for us to accept.

Now right off, we might think that we have non-question-begging grounds for only taking the interests of humans into account, namely, the possession by human beings of the distinctive traits of rationality and moral agency. But while human beings clearly do have such distinctive traits, members of nonhuman species also have distinctive traits that humans lack, like the homing ability of pigeons, the speed of the cheetah, and the ruminative ability of sheep and cattle. Nor will it do to claim that the distinctive traits that humans possess are more valuable than the distinctive traits that members of other species possess because there is

no non-question-begging standpoint from which to justify this claim. From a human standpoint, rationality and moral agency are more valuable than any of the distinctive traits found in nonhuman species, since, as humans, we would not be better off if we were to trade in those traits for the distinctive traits found in nonhuman species. Yet the same holds true of nonhuman species. Generally, pigeons, cheetahs, sheep, and cattle would not be better off if they were to trade in their distinctive traits for the distinctive traits of other species.[5]

Of course, the members of some species might be better off if they could retain the distinctive traits of their species while acquiring one or another of the distinctive traits possessed by some other species. For example, we humans might be better off if we could retain our distinctive traits while acquiring the ruminative ability of sheep and cattle.[6] But many of the distinctive traits of species cannot be even imaginatively added to the members of other species without substantially altering the original species. For example, in order for the cheetah to acquire the distinctive traits possessed by humans, presumably it would have to be so transformed that its paws became something like hands to accommodate its humanlike mental capabilities, thereby losing its distinctive speed, and ceasing to be a cheetah. So possessing distinctively human traits would not be good for the cheetah.[7] And with the possible exception of our nearest evolutionary relatives, the same holds true for the members of other species: they would not be better off having distinctively human traits. Only in fairy tales and in the world of Disney can the members of nonhuman species enjoy a full array of distinctively human traits.[8] So there appears to be no non-question-begging perspective from which to judge that distinctively human traits are more valuable than the distinctive traits possessed by other species, and so no non-question-begging justification for only taking anthropocentric reasons into account. Judged from a non-question-begging perspective, we would seemingly have to grant the prima facie relevance of both anthropocentric and nonanthropocentric reasons to rational choice and then try to determine which reasons we would be rationally required to act upon, all things considered.

In this regard, there are two kinds of cases that must be considered. First, there are cases in which there is a conflict between the relevant anthropocentric and nonanthropocentric reasons. Second, there are cases in which there is no such conflict.

It seems obvious that where there is no conflict and both reasons are conclusive reasons of their kind, both reasons should be acted upon. In such contexts, we should do what is favored both by anthropocentrism and by nonanthropocentrism.

Now when we turn to rationally assess the relevant reasons in conflict cases, three solutions are possible. First, we can say that anthropocentric reasons always have priority over conflicting nonanthropocentric ones. Second, we can say, just the opposite, that nonanthropocentric reasons always have priority over conflicting anthropocentric ones. Third, we can say that some kind of compromise is rationally required. In this compromise, sometimes anthropocentric reasons will have priority over nonanthropocentric reasons, and sometimes nonanthropocentric reasons will have priority over anthropocentric reasons.

Once the conflict is described in this manner, the third solution can be seen as the one that is rationally required. This is because the first and second solutions give exclusive priority to one class of relevant reasons over the other, and only a question-begging justification can be given for such an exclusive priority. Only by employing the third solution, and sometimes giving priority to anthropocentric reasons, and sometimes giving priority to nonanthropocentric reasons, can we avoid a question-begging resolution.[9] What we need, therefore, are conflict resolution principles that specify these priorities.

Conflict Resolution Principles

But how are these priorities to be specified? Now surely, even if we hold that all living beings should count morally, we can justify a preference for humans on grounds of preservation.[10] Accordingly, we have:

- A PRINCIPLE OF HUMAN PRESERVATION. Actions that are necessary for meeting one's basic needs or the basic needs of other human beings are permissible even when they require aggressing against the basic needs of individual animals and plants, or even of whole species or ecosystems.[11]

Needs, in general, if not satisfied, lead to lacks or deficiencies with respect to various standards. The basic needs of humans, if not satisfied, lead to lacks or deficiencies with respect to a standard of a decent life. The basic needs of animals and plants, if not satisfied, lead to lacks or deficiencies with respect to

a standard of a healthy life. The basic needs of species and ecosystems, if not satisfied, lead to lacks or deficiencies with respect to a standard of a healthy living system. The means necessary for meeting the basic needs of humans can vary widely from society to society. By contrast, the means necessary for meeting the basic needs of particular species of animals and plants tend to be invariant.[12] Of course, while only some needs can be clearly classified as basic, and others clearly classified as nonbasic, there still are other needs that are more or less difficult to classify. Yet the fact that not every need can be clearly classified as either basic or nonbasic, as similarly holds for a whole range of dichotomous concepts like moral/immoral, legal/illegal, living/nonliving, human/nonhuman, should not immobilize us from acting at least with respect to clear cases.[13]

In human ethics, there is no principle that is strictly analogous to this Principle of Human Preservation.[14] There is a principle of self-preservation in human ethics that permits actions that are necessary for meeting one's own basic needs or the basic needs of other people, even if this requires *failing to meet* (through an act of omission) the basic needs of still other people. For example, we can use our resources to feed ourselves and our families, even if this necessitates failing to meet the basic needs of people in underdeveloped countries. But, in general, we don't have a principle that allows us to *aggress against* (through an act of commission) the basic needs of some people in order to meet our own basic needs or the basic needs of other people to whom we are committed or happen to care about. One place where we do permit aggressing against the basic needs of other people in order to meet our own basic needs or the basic needs of people to whom we are committed or happen to care about is our acceptance of the outcome of life and death struggles in lifeboat cases, where no one has an antecedent right to the available resources. For example, if you had to fight off others in order to secure the last place in a lifeboat for yourself or for a member of your family, we might say that you justifiably aggressed against the basic needs of those you fought to meet your own basic needs or the basic needs of the members of your family.[15]

Now the Principle of Human Preservation does not permit aggressing against the basic needs of humans even if it is the only way to meet our own basic needs or the basic needs of other human beings.[16] Rather this principle is directed at a different range of cases with respect to which we can meet our own basic needs and the basic needs of other humans simply by aggressing against the basic needs of nonhuman living beings. With respect to those cases, the Principle of Human Preservation permits actions that are necessary for meeting one's own basic needs or the basic needs of other human beings, even when they require aggressing against the basic needs of individual animals and plants, or even of whole species or ecosystems.

Of course, we can envision an even more permissive Principle of Human Preservation, one that would permit us to aggress against the basic needs of both humans and nonhumans to meet our own basic needs or the basic needs of other human beings. But while adopting such a principle, by permitting cannibalism, would clearly reduce the degree of predation of humans on other species, and thus be of some benefit to other species, it would clearly be counterproductive with respect to meeting basic human needs. This is because implicit nonaggression pacts based on a reasonable expectation of a comparable degree of altruistic forbearance from fellow humans have been enormously beneficial and probably were necessary for the survival of the human species. So it is difficult to see how humans could be justifiably required to forgo such benefits.

Moreover, beyond the prudential value of such implicit nonaggression pacts against fellow humans, there appears to be no morally defensible way to exclude some humans from their protection. This is because any exclusion would fail to satisfy that most basic principle of morality, the "ought" implies "can" principle, given that it would impose a sacrifice on at least some humans that is unreasonable to ask and/or require them to accept.[17]

But what about the interests of nonhuman living beings? Doesn't the Principle of Human Preservation impose a sacrifice on nonhumans that it would be unreasonable to ask and/or require any would-be human guardian of their interests to accept? Surely, we expect the animals and plants to fight us however they can to prevent being used in this fashion. Why then is it not reasonable for would-be human guardians of the interests of nonhuman living beings to also try to prevent their being used in this fashion? But this would mean that it is morally permissible for would-be human guardians of the interest of nonhumans to prevent other humans from meeting their own basic needs, or the basic needs of still other humans, when this requires aggressing against the basic needs of nonhumans. Understood as "strong

permissibility," it implies that other humans are *prohibited* from interfering with such preventive actions, even if it means that their own basic needs are not met as a result. But surely, this is an unreasonable requirement for humans to impose on other humans – one that does not accord with the "ought" implies "can" principle.

But suppose we understand the permissibility involved to be that of weak permissibility according to which virtually everything is permissible and virtually nothing is morally required or prohibited. Then the Principle of Human Preservation would imply that it is permissible, in this weak sense, for humans to aggress against the basic needs of nonhumans when this was necessary for meeting their own basic needs, and at the same time imply that it is permissible, in this same weak sense, for would-be human guardians of the interests of nonhumans to prevent humans from meeting their basic needs by aggressing against the basic needs of nonhumans. Since under this interpretation of moral permissibility, virtually nothing is morally required or prohibited, what gets done will tend to depend on the relative power of the contending parties. The purpose of morality, however, is to provide resolutions in just such severe conflict-of-interest situations. Assuming then that a moral resolution must satisfy the "ought" implies "can" principle, it cannot impose moral requirements on humans that are unreasonable for them to accept.[18] This seems to suggest that the permissibility in the Principle of Human Preservation must be that of strong permissibility, which means that would-be human guardians of the interests of nonhumans are prohibited from interfering with humans who are taking the necessary action to meet their basic needs, even when this requires them to aggress against the basic needs of nonhumans.

But are there no exceptions to the Principle of Human Preservation? Consider, for example, the following real-life case.[19] Thousands of Nepalese have cleared forests, cultivated crops, and raised cattle and buffalo on land surrounding the Royal Chitwan National Park in Nepal, but they have also made incursions into the park to meet their own basic needs. In so doing, they have threatened the rhino, the Bengal tiger, and other endangered species in the park. Assume that the basic needs of no other humans are at stake.[20] For this case, then, are would-be human guardians of these nonhuman endangered species justified in preventing the

Nepalese from meeting their basic needs in order to preserve these endangered species? It seems to me that before the basic needs of disadvantaged Nepalese can be sacrificed, the would-be human guardians of these endangered species are first required to use whatever surplus is available to them and to other humans to meet the basic needs of the Nepalese they propose to restrict. Yet clearly it is very difficult to have first used up all the surplus available to the whole human population for meeting basic human needs. Under present conditions, this requirement has certainly not been met. Moreover, insofar as rich people are unwilling to make the necessary transfers of resources so that poor people are not led to prey on endangered species in order to survive, then, the appropriate means of preserving endangered species should be to use force against such rich people rather than against poor people, like the Nepalese near Royal Chitwan National Park.[21] So for all present purposes, the moral permissibility in the Principle of Human Preservation remains that of strong permissibility, which means that other humans are prohibited from interfering with the aggression against nonhumans that is permitted by the principle.[22]

Nevertheless, preference for humans can still go beyond bounds, and the bounds that are required are captured by the following:

● A Principle of Disproportionality. Actions that meet nonbasic or luxury needs of humans are prohibited when they aggress against the basic needs of individual animals and plants or even of whole species or ecosystems.

This principle is strictly analogous to the principle in human ethics that similarly prohibits meeting some people's nonbasic or luxury needs by aggressing against the basic needs of other people. Without a doubt, the adoption of such a principle with respect to nonhumans would significantly change the way we live our lives. Such a principle is required, however, if there is to be any substance to the claim that the members of all species count morally. We can no more consistently claim that the members of all species count morally and yet aggress against the basic needs of some animals or plants whenever this serves our own nonbasic or luxury needs than we can consistently claim that all humans count morally and then aggress against the basic needs of other human beings whenever this serves our nonbasic or luxury needs. Consequently, if saying that species count

morally is to mean anything, it must be the case that the basic needs of the members of nonhuman species are protected against aggressive actions that only serve to meet the nonbasic needs of humans, as required by the Principle of Disproportionality.[23] Another way to put the central claim here is to hold that counting morally rules out domination, where domination means aggressing against the basic needs of some for the sake of satisfying the nonbasic needs of others.

To see why these limits on preference for the members of the human species are what is required for recognizing that other species and their members count morally, we need to understand the nondomination of species by analogy with the nondomination of humans. We need to see that just as we claim that humans should not be dominated but treat them differently, so too we can claim that species should not be dominated but also treat them differently. In human ethics, there are various interpretations given to human nondomination that allow for different treatment of humans. In ethical egoism, everyone is *equally at liberty* to pursue his or her own interests, but this allows us to always prefer ourselves to others, who are understood to be like opponents in a competitive game. In libertarianism, everyone has an *equal right to liberty*, but although this imposes some limits on the pursuit of self-interest, it is said to allow us to refrain from helping others in severe need.[24] In welfare liberalism, everyone has an *equal right to welfare and opportunity*, but this need not commit us to providing everyone with exactly the same resources. In socialism, everyone has an *equal right to self-development*, and although this may commit us to providing everyone with the same resources, it still sanctions some degree of self-preference. So just as there are these various ways to interpret the nondomination of humans that still allow us to treat humans differently, there are various ways that we can interpret the nondomination of species that allow us to treat species differently.

Now one might interpret the nondomination of species in a very strong sense, analogous to the interpretation of nondomination found in socialism. But the kind of nondomination of species that I have defended here is more akin to the nondomination found in welfare liberalism or in libertarianism than it is to the nondomination found in socialism.[25] In brief, this form of nondomination requires that we not aggress against the basic needs of the members of other species for the sake of the nonbasic needs of the members of our own species (the Principle of Disproportionality), but it permits us to aggress against the basic needs of the members of other species for the sake of the basic needs of the members of our own species (the Principle of Human Preservation). In this way, I have argued that we can endorse the nondomination of species, while avoiding imposing an unreasonable sacrifice on the members of our own species.

It is important to note here that the Principle of Disproportionality also imposes a limit on human reproduction. There is little doubt that the currently expanding population of six billion humans threatens the survival of many nonhuman species and possibly human survival as well, in part, simply because of its size. Consequently, human reproduction needs to be limited to the legitimate exercise of the basic human need to procreate, which means roughly one child per family.

Later, after the human population has been significantly reduced, this policy should be relaxed to one that simply serves the long-term survivability of the human species, consistent with maintaining humans within their environmental niche, where, unlike today, they would be in balance with the rest of the biotic community. This is the human reproduction policy that the Principle of Disproportionality requires. It permits human reproduction when it serves existing basic human needs and the long-term survivability of the human species, but not when it simply serves nonbasic or luxury needs at the expense of nonhuman nature. Any less restrictive policy would impose an unacceptable sacrifice on nonhuman species.

Nevertheless, in order to avoid imposing an unacceptable sacrifice on the members of our own species, we can also justify a preference for humans on grounds of defense. Thus, we have:

- A PRINCIPLE OF HUMAN DEFENSE. Actions that defend oneself and other human beings against harmful aggression are permissible even when they necessitate killing or harming individual animals or plants, or even destroying whole species or ecosystems.

This Principle of Human Defense allows us to defend ourselves and other human beings from harmful aggression first against our persons and the persons of other human beings we are committed to or happen to care about and second against our justifiably held property and the justifiably held property of other human beings that we are committed to or happen to care about.[26]

Here there are two sorts of cases. First, there are cases where humans are defending their own basic needs against harmful aggression from nonhumans. In cases of this sort, not only are the human defenders perfectly justified in defending themselves against aggression but also no would-be human guardians of nonhuman interests are justified on grounds of what we could reasonably require of humans in opposing that defense.

Second, there are cases where humans are defending their nonbasic needs against harmful aggression from nonhumans who, let's assume, are trying to meet their basic needs. In cases of this sort, is it justified for would-be human guardians of the interests of nonhuman living beings to assist them in their aggression against humans? In analogous cases in human ethics, we can see how just this type of aggression can be justified when the poor, who have exhausted all the other means that are legitimately available to them, take from the surplus possessions of the rich just what they require to meet their basic needs. Expressed in terms of an ideal of negative liberty endorsed by libertarians, the justification for this aggression is the priority of the liberty of the poor not to be interfered with when taking from the surplus possessions of the rich what they require to meet their basic needs over the liberty of the rich not to be interfered with when using their surplus for luxury purposes.[27] Expressed in terms of an ideal of fairness endorsed by welfare liberals, the justification for this aggression is the right to welfare that the needy have against those with a surplus. And expressed in terms of an ideal of equality endorsed by socialists, the justification for this aggression is the right that everyone has to equal self-development. Under each of these justifications, would-be guardians of the poor (for example, real or idealized Robin Hoods) are certainly justified in assisting the poor in their aggression against the rich. Are then would-be human guardians of nonhuman living beings (for example, real or idealized Earth Firsters) similarly justified in assisting plants and animals in their aggression against the nonbasic needs of humans in order to meet the basic needs of nonhumans?

There are two reasons why this is unlikely to be the case. First, as the above justifications from human ethics suggest, achieving either libertarian, welfare liberal, or socialist justice for humans requires a considerable redistribution of resources in order to meet the basic needs of humans in both existing and future generations.[28] So if justice is done in this regard, it will significantly constrain the availability of resources for legitimately meeting nonbasic human needs, and thereby limit the possibilities where humans can justifiably defend their nonbasic needs against aggression from nonhumans. Second, the Principle of Disproportionality further constrains those possibilities where humans can justifiably defend their nonbasic needs against aggression from nonhumans. This is because the principle prohibits humans from aggressing against the basic needs of nonhumans in order to meet their own nonbasic needs, and thereby significantly constrains the ways that humans can legitimately acquire resources that are used simply for meeting nonbasic human needs. For these two reasons, therefore, the possibilities for legitimately exercising the Principle of Human Defense for the sake of nonbasic needs are drastically limited, thus providing few occasions where would-be human guardians of the interests of nonhumans can have any role with regard to its exercise. Of course, some nonbasic human needs can still be legitimately met indirectly through meeting basic human needs. But any attempt by would-be human guardians of the interests of nonhumans to help nonhumans aggress against the nonbasic needs of other humans in such contexts would most likely result in aggressing against the basic needs of those humans as well, and thus would not be justified. Of course, in the nonideal societies in which we live, many humans still have access to a surplus for meeting nonbasic needs. But in these circumstances, other humans surely have a claim to a significant part of that surplus, and much of what remains has been illegitimately acquired in violation of the Principle of Disproportionality. In any case, the Principle of Defense will rarely apply because it presupposes for its application that the means for meeting the nonbasic needs of humans have been legitimately acquired.

Lastly, we need one more principle to deal with violations of the above three principles. Accordingly, we have:

A PRINCIPLE OF RECTIFICATION. Compensation and reparation are required when the other principles have been violated.

Obviously, this principle is somewhat vague, but for those who are willing to abide by the other three principles, it should be possible to remedy that vagueness in practice. Here too would-be human guardians of the interests of nonhumans could have a useful role figuring out what is appropriate compensation or reparation for violations of the Principle of Disproportionality, and, even more importantly, designing ways to get that compensation or reparation enacted.

Taken altogether, these four principles, I claim, constitute a defensible set of principles for resolving conflicts between human and nonhuman living beings. Of course, some may find it intuitively implausible that we should have to inconvenience ourselves at all for the sake of nonsentient living things. That some of us feel this way is certainly understandable given that virtually all of us have been socialized in the dominant anthropocentrism of our culture. But a different reaction is available to us if we begin to reflect on what we should do from a non-question-begging standpoint, as I attempted to do in this chapter. By such reflection, we can come to recognize that our dominating attitudes toward nonhuman nature cannot be given a non-question-begging justification, and we then should seek to adjust our conduct accordingly.

Individualism and Holism

It might be objected, however, that I have not yet taken into account the conflict between holists and individualists. According to holists, the good of a species, or the good of an ecosystem, or the good of the whole biotic community can trump the good of individual living things.[29] According to individualists, the good of each individual living thing must be respected.[30]

Now one might think that holists would require us to abandon my Principle of Human Preservation. Yet consider: Assuming that people's basic needs are at stake, how can it be morally objectionable for them to try to meet these needs, even if this were to harm nonhuman individuals, or species, or whole ecosystems, or even, to some degree, the whole biotic community? Of course, we can *ask* people in such conflict cases not to meet their basic needs in order to prevent harm to nonhuman individuals or species, ecosystems, or the whole biotic community. But if people's basic needs are at stake, it will be a very unusual case where we can reasonably demand that they make such a sacrifice.

We can demand, of course, that people do all that they reasonably can to keep such conflicts from arising in the first place, for, just as in human ethics, many severe conflicts of interest can be avoided simply by doing what is morally required early on. Nevertheless, when lives or basic needs are at stake, the individualist perspective seems generally incontrovertible. We cannot normally require people to be saints.

At the same time, when people's basic needs are not at stake, we are justified in acting on holistic grounds to prevent serious harm to nonhuman individuals, or species, or ecosystems, or the whole biotic community. Obviously, it is difficult to know when our interventions will have this effect, but when we are reasonably sure that they will, such interventions (for example, culling elk herds in wolf-free ranges or preserving the habitat of endangered species) are morally permissible, and even morally required when the Principle of Rectification applies. This shows that it is possible to agree with individualists when the basic needs of human beings are at stake, and to agree with holists when they are not.[31]

Yet this combination of individualism and holism appears to conflict with recognizing that all species count morally by imposing greater sacrifices on the members of nonhuman species than it imposes on the members of the human species. Fortunately, appearances are deceiving here. Although the proposed resolution only justifies imposing holism when people's basic needs are not at stake, it does not justify imposing individualism at all. Rather, it simply permits individualism when people's basic needs *are* at stake. Of course, we could impose holism under all conditions. But given that this would, in effect, involve going to war against people who are simply striving to meet their own basic needs in the only way they can, as permitted by the Principle of Human Preservation, intervention in such cases is generally not justified.[32] It would involve taking away the means of survival from people, even when these means are not required for one's own survival.

Nevertheless, this combination of individualism and holism may leave animal liberationists wondering about the further implications of this resolution for the treatment of animals. Obviously, a good deal of work has already been done on this topic. Initially, philosophers thought that humanism could be extended to include animal liberation and eventually environmental concern.[33] Then Baird Callicott argued that animal liberation and environmental concern were as opposed to each other as they were to humanism.[34] The resulting conflict Callicott called "a triangular affair." Agreeing with Callicott, Mark Sagoff contended that any attempt to link together animal liberation and environmental concern would lead to "a bad marriage and a quick divorce."[35] Yet more recently, other philosophers, such as Mary Ann Warren, have tended to play down the opposition between animal liberation and environmental concern, and even Callicott now thinks he can bring the two back together again.[36] There are good reasons for thinking that such reconciliation is possible.

Right off, it would be good for the environment if people generally, especially people in the developed world, adopted a more vegetarian diet of the sort that animal liberationists recommend. This is because a good portion of livestock production today consumes grains that could be more effectively used for direct human consumption. For example, 90 percent of the protein, 99 percent of the carbohydrate, and 100 percent of the fiber value of grain is wasted by cycling it through livestock, and currently 64 percent of the US grain crop is fed to livestock.[37] So by adopting a more vegetarian diet, people generally, and especially people in the developed world, could significantly reduce the amount of farmland that has to be kept in production to feed the human population. This, in turn, could have beneficial effects on the whole biotic community by eliminating the amount of soil erosion and environmental pollutants that result from raising livestock. For example, it has been estimated that 85 percent of US topsoil lost from cropland, pasture, range land, and forest land is directly associated with raising livestock.[38] So, in addition to preventing animal suffering, there are these additional reasons to favor a more vegetarian diet.

But even though a more vegetarian diet seems in order, it is not clear that the interests of farm animals would be well served if all of us became complete vegetarians. Sagoff assumes that in a completely vegetarian human world people will continue to feed farm animals as before.[39] But it is not clear that we would have any obligation to do so. Moreover, in a completely vegetarian human world, we would probably need about half of the grain we now feed livestock to meet people's nutritional needs, particularly in underdeveloped countries. There simply would not be enough grain to go around. And then there would be the need to conserve cropland for future generations. So in a completely vegetarian human world, it seems likely that the population of farm animals would be decimated, relegating many of the farm animals that remain to zoos. But raising farm animals can be seen as mutually beneficial for humans and the farm animals involved. Surely, it would benefit farm animals to be brought into existence, maintained under healthy conditions, and hence not in the numbers sustainable only with factory farms, but then killed relatively painlessly and eaten, rather than that they not be brought into existence or maintained at all.[40] So a completely vegetarian human world would not be in the interest of farm animals.[41] Of course, no one would be morally required to bring farm animals into existence and maintain them in this manner. Morally, it would suffice just to maintain representative members of the various subspecies in zoos. Nevertheless, many will find it difficult to pass up an arrangement that is morally permissible and mutually beneficial for both humans and farm animals.

It also seems in the interest of wild species that no longer have their natural predators to be at least therapeutically hunted by humans.[42] Of course, where possible, it may be preferable to reintroduce natural predators. But this may not always be possible because of the unavoidable proximity of farm animals and human populations, and then if action is not taken to control the populations of wild species, disaster could result for the species and their environments. For example, in the absence of predators ungulates (hooved mammals such as white-tailed and mule deer, elk, and bison) as well as elephants regularly tend to exceed the carrying capacity of their environments.[43] So it may be in the interest of these wild species and their environments that humans intervene periodically to maintain a balance. Of course, there are many natural environments where it is in the interest of the environment and the wild animals that inhabit it to be left alone. But here too animal liberation and environmental concern are not in conflict. For these reasons, animal liberationists might seem to have little reason to object in this regard to the proposed combination of individualism and holism that is captured by these conflict resolution principles.

Notes

1 Peter Singer, *Animal Liberation*, rev. edn. (New York: Avon Books, 1992).

2 Most recently in Tom Regan, *Animal Rights, Human Wrongs* (Lanham, MD: Rowman & Littlefield, 2004).

3 Paul Taylor, *Respect for Nature* (Princeton, NJ: Princeton University Press, 1987).

4 James P. Sterba, "Taylor's Biocentrism and Beyond," in *Environmental Ethics*, 17 (1995): 191–208. Taylor now accepts my development of his view. See his new preface to the Chinese translation of *Respect for Nature* (Institute of Philosophy at the Chinese Academy of Social Sciences, 2004).

5 See Taylor, *Respect for Nature*, 129–35, and R. and V. Routley, "Against the Inevitability of Human Chauvinism," in *Ethics and Problems of the 21st Century*, ed. by K. E. Goodpaster and K. M. Sayre (Notre Dame: University of Notre Dame Press, 1979).

6 Assuming God exists, humans might also be better off if they could retain their distinctive traits while acquiring one or another of God's qualities, but consideration of this possibility would take us too far afield. Nonhuman animals might also be better off if they could retain their distinctive traits and acquire one or another of the distinctive traits possessed by other nonhuman animals.

7 This assumes that there is an environmental niche that cheetahs can fill.

8 Since some things that are good for some (like rationality) are not good for others, there are no universal standards of excellence that apply to all living beings, even though there are some basic goods that all living beings need (like water).

9 So far the argument for taking nonanthropocentric reasons into account parallels the argument for taking altruistic reasons into account [outlined in my *The Triumph of Practice Over Theory in Ethics* (New York: Oxford University Press, 2005), chapter 2]. Here I go on to specify the practical consequences of the argument in terms of conflict resolution principles with respect to human and nonhuman living beings.

10 We can make this assumption here because the net effect of giving priority to high-ranking anthropocentric reasons over low-ranking nonanthropocentric reasons and giving priority to high-ranking nonanthropocentric reasons over low-ranking anthropocentric reasons, other things being equal, is to count all living beings morally.

11 For the purposes of this chapter, I will follow the convention of excluding humans from the denotation of "animals."

12 For further discussion of basic needs, see my *How to Make People Just* (Totowa, NJ: Rowman & Littlefield, 1988), 45ff.

13 Moreover, this kind of fuzziness in the application of the distinction between basic and nonbasic needs is characteristic of the application of virtually all our classificatory concepts, and so is not an objection to its usefulness.

14 By "human ethics" I mean "an ethics that assumes without argument that only humans count morally."

It should also be pointed out that the Principle of Human Preservation must be implemented in a way that causes the least harm possible, which means that, other things being equal, basic needs should be met by aggressing against nonsentient rather than against sentient living beings so as to avoid the pain and suffering that would otherwise be inflicted on sentient beings.

15   It is important to recognize here that we also have a strong obligation to prevent lifeboat cases from arising in the first place.

16   The principle just does not speak to the issue, although I do discuss in the text what is permissible and impermissible in this regard.

17   For a discussion of the "ought" implies "can" principle, see [*The Triumph of Practice Over Theory*, chapter 3].

18   Nevertheless, as I shall argue, this assumption does not always hold. Moral resolutions can also permit actions that they cannot require, as, for example, in lifeboat cases.

19   See Holmes Rolston III, "Enforcing Environmental Ethics: Civil Law and Natural Value," in *Social and Political Philosophy: Contemporary Perspectives*, ed. James P. Sterba (London: Routledge, 2001), where Rolston uses this example to object to my Principle of Human Preservation and I respond. Rolston has also raised a further objection (email 1/27/04) to which I now respond in the text.

20   This did not hold in the real-life case that Rolston actually presented. See my response in *Social and Political Philosophy*.

21   Of course, we may be required to meet our basic needs and the basic needs of other humans by aggressing against the basic needs of the members of some nonhuman species rather than others, for example, in order to protect, in this way, certain endangered species. But clearly this requirement would not undermine the present and prevailing moral acceptability of the Principle of Human Preservation understood as involving strong permissibility.

22   In the nonideal world in which we live, the Nepalese and their human allies should press rich people to acquire the available surplus to meet the basic needs of the Nepalese until their own lives are threatened. At that point, regrettably, the Nepalese would be justified in preying on endangered species as the only way for them to survive.

23   It should be pointed out that, although the Principle of Disproportionality prohibits aggressing against basic needs of nonhumans to serve nonbasic needs of humans, the Principle of Human Defense permits defense of nonbasic needs of humans against aggression of nonhumans. So while we cannot legitimately aggress against nonhumans to meet our nonbasic needs, we can legitimately defend our nonbasic needs against the aggression of nonhumans seeking to meet their basic needs, although this will rarely happen for the reasons given in the text.

24   Of course, this is just how libertarians present their view. However, I have argued [elsewhere] that the view actually does entail a right to welfare, which would lead to something like the equality that socialists favor.

25   Actually, a slogan for my view could be: Welfare Liberalism or Socialism for Humans, Libertarianism for Nonhumans! Of course, in my view, there is not a lot of difference between these perspectives.

26   For an account of what constitutes justifiably held property within human ethics, see my *Justice for Here and Now*, especially chapter 3.

27   For a detailed discussion of this argument, see my article "From Liberty to Welfare," *Ethics* (1994): 64–98, and chapter 3 of *Justice for Here and Now*.

28   For further argument of this conclusion, see [my *The Triumph of Practice Over Theory*], chapter 3. See also *Justice for Here and Now*, chapter 3, and *How to Make People Just*, chapters 2–10.

29   Aldo Leopold's view is usually interpreted as holistic in this sense. Leopold wrote "A thing is right when it tends to preserve the integrity, stability and beauty of the biotic community. It is wrong when it tends otherwise." See his *A Sand County Almanac* (New York: Oxford University Press, 1949).

30   For a defender of this view, see Paul Taylor, *Respect for Nature* (Princeton, NJ: Princeton University Press, 1987).

31   Of course, actions justified on holist grounds may sometimes preclude the satisfaction of nonbasic human needs (for example, by restricting urban sprawl), but they will only rarely involve aggressing against nonbasic human needs for the reasons given earlier, except when compensation and reparation is required.

32   See, however, the last section of [chapter 4 in my *The Triumph of Practice Over Theory*].

33   Peter Singer's *Animal Liberation* (New York: Avon Books, 1975) inspired this view.

34   Baird Callicott, "Animal Liberation: A Triangular Affair," *Environmental Ethics* (1980): 311–28.

35   Mark Sagoff, "Animal Liberation and Environmental Ethics: Bad Marriage, Quick Divorce," *Osgood Hall Law Journal* (1984): 297–307.

36   Mary Ann Warren, "The Rights of the Nonhuman World," in *Environmental Philosophy*, ed. by Robert Elliot and Arran Gare (New York: University of Queensland Press, 1983), 109–34, and Baird Callicott, *In Defense of the Land Ethic* (Albany: State University of New York Press, 1989), chapter 3.

37   *Realities for the 90's* (Santa Cruz, Calif.: Earth Save Foundation, 1991), 4.

38   Ibid., 5.

39   Sagoff, "Animal Liberation and Environmental Ethics," 301–5.

40 There is an analogous story to tell here about "domesticated" plants, but hopefully there is no analogous story about "extra humans" who are raised for food. Given the knowledge these "extra humans" would have of their fate, a similar use of humans would not be mutually beneficial and would most likely make their lives not worth living. But even assuming that this were not the case, with the consequence that this particular justification for domestication is ruled out because of its implications for a similar use of humans, it still would be the case that domestication is justified in a sustainable agriculture to provide fertilizer for crops to meet basic human needs.

41 To say that the proposed arrangement is in the interest of farm animals implies that the farm animals brought into existence by means of this arrangement will benefit overall, not that there are some preexistent farm animals who will benefit from the arrangement. However, the arrangement can be in the interest of some existing animals as well.

42 For a valuable discussion of this issue, see Gary Varner, *In Nature's Interests?* (New York: Oxford University Press, 1998), 100–18.

43 There are other species, such as mourning doves, cottontail rabbits, gray squirrels, bobwhite and blue quail, that each year produce more young than their habitat can support through the winter, but they usually do not degrade their environment. With respect to such species, it might be argued that hunting is morally permissible. Nevertheless, unless such hunting is either therapeutic or required to meet basic human needs, it is difficult to see how it could be permissible.

B Holism (Ecocentrism)

23 The Land Ethic
    Aldo Leopold

24 The Conceptual Foundations of the Land Ethic
    J. Baird Callicott

25 Gaia As Seen Through the Atmosphere
    James E. Lovelock

23 The Land Ethic

Aldo Leopold

When god-like Odysseus returned from the wars in Troy, he hanged all on one rope a dozen slave-girls of his household whom he suspected of misbehavior during his absence.

This hanging involved no question of propriety. The girls were property. The disposal of property was then, as now, a matter of expediency, not of right and wrong.

Concepts of right and wrong were not lacking from Odysseus' Greece: witness the fidelity of his wife through the long years before at last his black-prowed galleys clove the wine-dark seas for home. The ethical structure of that day covered wives, but had not yet been extended to human chattels. During the three thousand years which have since elapsed, ethical criteria have been extended to many fields of conduct, with corresponding shrinkages in those judged by expediency only.

The Ethical Sequence

This extension of ethics, so far studied only by philosophers, is actually a process in ecological evolution. Its sequences may be described in ecological as well as in philosophical terms. An ethic, ecologically, is a limitation on freedom of action in the struggle for existence. An ethic, philosophically, is a differentiation of social from anti-social conduct. These are two definitions of one thing. The thing has its origin in the tendency of interdependent individuals or groups to evolve modes of co-operation. The ecologist calls these symbioses. Politics and economics are advanced symbioses in which the original free-for-all competition has been replaced, in part, by co-operative mechanisms with an ethical content.

The complexity of co-operative mechanisms has increased with population density, and with the

From *A Sand County Almanac* (New York: Oxford University Press, 1960), pp. 201–11, 213–19, 220–6. © 1949 by Oxford University Press, Inc. Reprinted with permission from Oxford University Press.

efficiency of tools. It was simpler, for example, to define the anti-social uses of sticks and stones in the days of the mastodons than of bullets and billboards in the age of motors.

The first ethics dealt with the relation between individuals; the Mosaic Decalogue is an example. Later accretions dealt with the relation between the individual and society. The Golden Rule tries to integrate the individual to society; democracy to integrate social organization to the individual.

There is as yet no ethic dealing with man's relation to land and to the animals and plants which grow upon it. Land, like Odysseus' slave-girls, is still property. The land-relation is still strictly economic, entailing privileges but not obligations.

The extension of ethics to this third element in human environment is, if I read the evidence correctly, an evolutionary possibility and an ecological necessity. It is the third step in a sequence. The first two have already been taken. Individual thinkers since the days of Ezekiel and Isaiah have asserted that the despoliation of land is not only inexpedient but wrong. Society, however, has not yet affirmed their belief. I regard the present conservation movement as the embryo of such an affirmation.

An ethic may be regarded as a mode of guidance for meeting ecological situations so new or intricate, or involving such deferred reactions, that the path of social expediency is not discernible to the average individual. Animal instincts are modes of guidance for the individual in meeting such situations. Ethics are possibly a kind of community instinct in-the-making.

The Community Concept

All ethics so far evolved rest upon a single premise: that the individual is a member of a community of interdependent parts. His instincts prompt him to compete for his place in that community, but his ethics prompt him also to co-operate (perhaps in order that there may be a place to compete for).

The land ethic simply enlarges the boundaries of the community to include soils, waters, plants, and animals, or collectively: the land.

This sounds simple: do we not already sing our love for and obligation to the land of the free and the home of the brave? Yes, but just what and whom do we love? Certainly not the soil, which we are sending helter-skelter downriver. Certainly not the

waters, which we assume have no function except to turn turbines, float barges, and carry off sewage. Certainly not the plants, of which we exterminate whole communities without batting an eye. Certainly not the animals, of which we have already extirpated many of the largest and most beautiful species. A land ethic of course cannot prevent the alteration, management, and use of these 'resources,' but it does affirm their right to continued existence, and, at least in spots, their continued existence in a natural state.

In short, a land ethic changes the role of *Homo sapiens* from conqueror of the land-community to plain member and citizen of it. It implies respect for his fellow-members, and also respect for the community as such.

In human history, we have learned (I hope) that the conqueror role is eventually self-defeating. Why? Because it is implicit in such a role that the conqueror knows, *ex cathedra*, just what makes the community clock tick, and just what and who is valuable, and what and who is worthless, in community life. It always turns out that he knows neither, and this is why his conquests eventually defeat themselves.

In the biotic community, a parallel situation exists. Abraham knew exactly what the land was for: it was to drip milk and honey into Abraham's mouth. At the present moment, the assurance with which we regard this assumption is inverse to the degree of our education.

The ordinary citizen today assumes that science knows what makes the community clock tick; the scientist is equally sure that he does not. He knows that the biotic mechanism is so complex that its workings may never be fully understood.

That man is, in fact, only a member of a biotic team is shown by an ecological interpretation of history. Many historical events, hitherto explained solely in terms of human enterprise, were actually biotic interactions between people and land. The characteristics of the land determined the facts quite as potently as the characteristics of the men who lived on it.

Consider, for example, the settlement of the Mississippi valley. In the years following the Revolution, three groups were contending for its control: the native Indian, the French and English traders, and the American settlers. Historians wonder what would have happened if the English at Detroit had thrown a little more weight into the Indian side of those tipsy scales which decided the outcome of the colonial migration into the cane-lands of Kentucky. It is time now to ponder the fact that the cane-lands, when subjected to the particular mixture of forces represented by the cow, plow, fire, and axe of the pioneer, became bluegrass. What if the plant succession inherent in this dark and bloody ground had, under the impact of these forces, given us some worthless sedge, shrub, or weed? Would Boone and Kenton have held out? Would there have been any overflow into Ohio, Indiana, Illinois, and Missouri? Any Louisiana Purchase? Any transcontinental union of new states? Any Civil War?

Kentucky was one sentence in the drama of history. We are commonly told what the human actors in this drama tried to do, but we are seldom told that their success, or the lack of it, hung in large degree on the reaction of particular soils to the impact of the particular forces exerted by their occupancy. In the case of Kentucky, we do not even know where the bluegrass came from – whether it is a native species, or a stowaway from Europe.

Contrast the cane-lands with what hindsight tells us about the Southwest, where the pioneers were equally brave, resourceful, and persevering. The impact of occupancy here brought no bluegrass, or other plant fitted to withstand the bumps and buffetings of hard use. This region, when grazed by livestock, reverted through a series of more and more worthless grasses, shrubs, and weeds to a condition of unstable equilibrium. Each recession of plant types bred erosion; each increment to erosion bred a further recession of plants. The result today is a progressive and mutual deterioration, not only of plants and soils, but of the animal community subsisting thereon. The early settlers did not expect this: on the ciénegas of New Mexico some even cut ditches to hasten it. So subtle has been its progress that few residents of the region are aware of it. It is quite invisible to the tourist who finds this wrecked landscape colorful and charming (as indeed it is, but it bears scant resemblance to what it was in 1848).

This same landscape was 'developed' once before, but with quite different results. The Pueblo Indians settled the Southwest in pre-Columbian times, but they happened *not* to be equipped with range livestock. Their civilization expired, but not because their land expired.

In India, regions devoid of any sod-forming grass have been settled, apparently without wrecking the land, by the simple expedient of carrying the grass to the cow, rather than vice versa. (Was this the result of

some deep wisdom, or was it just good luck? I do not know.)

In short, the plant succession steered the course of history; the pioneer simply demonstrated, for good or ill, what successions inhered in the land. Is history taught in this spirit? It will be, once the concept of land as a community really penetrates our intellectual life.

The Ecological Conscience

Conservation is a state of harmony between men and land. Despite nearly a century of propaganda, conservation still proceeds at a snail's pace; progress still consists largely of letterhead pieties and convention oratory. On the back forty we still slip two steps backward for each forward stride.

The usual answer to this dilemma is 'more conservation education.' No one will debate this, but is it certain that only the *volume* of education needs stepping up? Is something lacking in the *content* as well?

It is difficult to give a fair summary of its content in brief form, but, as I understand it, the content is substantially this: obey the law, vote right, join some organizations, and practice what conservation is profitable on your own land; the government will do the rest.

Is not this formula too easy to accomplish anything worth-while? It defines no right or wrong, assigns no obligation, calls for no sacrifice, implies no change in the current philosophy of values. In respect of land-use, it urges only enlightened self-interest. Just how far will such education take us? An example will perhaps yield a partial answer.

By 1930 it had become clear to all except the ecologically blind that southwestern Wisconsin's topsoil was slipping seaward. In 1933 the farmers were told that if they would adopt certain remedial practices for five years, the public would donate CCC labor to install them, plus the necessary machinery and materials. The offer was widely accepted, but the practices were widely forgotten when the five-year contract period was up. The farmers continued only those practices that yielded an immediate and visible economic gain for themselves.

This led to the idea that maybe farmers would learn more quickly if they themselves wrote the rules. Accordingly the Wisconsin Legislature in 1937 passed the Soil Conservation District Law. This said to farmers, in effect: *We, the public, will furnish you free technical service and loan you specialized machinery, if you will write your own rules for land-use. Each county may write its own rules, and these will have the force of law.* Nearly all the counties promptly organized to accept the proffered help, but after a decade of operation, *no county has yet written a single rule.* There has been visible progress in such practices as strip-cropping, pasture renovation, and soil liming, but none in fencing woodlots against grazing, and none in excluding plow and cow from steep slopes. The farmers, in short, have selected those remedial practices which were profitable anyhow, and ignored those which were profitable to the community, but not clearly profitable to themselves.

When one asks why no rules have been written, one is told that the community is not yet ready to support them; education must precede rules. But the education actually in progress makes no mention of obligations to land over and above those dictated by self-interest. The net result is that we have more education but less soil, fewer healthy woods, and as many floods as in 1937.

The puzzling aspect of such situations is that the existence of obligations over and above self-interest is taken for granted in such rural community enterprises as the betterment of roads, schools, churches, and baseball teams. Their existence is not taken for granted, nor as yet seriously discussed, in bettering the behavior of the water that falls on the land, or in the preserving of the beauty or diversity of the farm landscape. Land-use ethics are still governed wholly by economic self-interest, just as social ethics were a century ago.

To sum up: we asked the farmer to do what he conveniently could to save his soil, and he has done just that, and only that. The farmer who clears the woods off a 75 percent slope, turns his cows into the clearing, and dumps its rainfall, rocks, and soil into the community creek, is still (if otherwise decent) a respected member of society. If he puts lime on his fields and plants his crops on contour, he is still entitled to all the privileges and emoluments of his Soil Conservation District. The District is a beautiful piece of social machinery, but it is coughing along on two cylinders because we have been too timid, and too anxious for quick success, to tell the farmer the true magnitude of his obligations. Obligations have no meaning without conscience, and the problem we face is the extension of the social conscience from people to land.

No important change in ethics was ever accomplished without an internal change in our intellectual emphasis, loyalties, affections, and convictions. The proof that conservation has not yet touched these foundations of conduct lies in the fact that philosophy and religion have not yet heard of it. In our attempt to make conservation easy, we have made it trivial.

Substitutes for a Land Ethic

When the logic of history hungers for bread and we hand out a stone, we are at pains to explain how much the stone resembles bread. I now describe some of the stones which serve in lieu of a land ethic.

One basic weakness in a conservation system based wholly on economic motives is that most members of the land community have no economic value. Wildflowers and songbirds are examples. Of the 22,000 higher plants and animals native to Wisconsin, it is doubtful whether more than 5 percent can be sold, fed, eaten, or otherwise put to economic use. Yet these creatures are members of the biotic community, and if (as I believe) its stability depends on its integrity, they are entitled to continuance.

When one of these non-economic categories is threatened, and if we happen to love it, we invent subterfuges to give it economic importance. At the beginning of the century songbirds were supposed to be disappearing. Ornithologists jumped to the rescue with some distinctly shaky evidence to the effect that insects would eat us up if birds failed to control them. The evidence had to be economic in order to be valid.

It is painful to read these circumlocutions today. We have no land ethic yet, but we have at least drawn nearer the point of admitting that birds should continue as a matter of biotic right, regardless of the presence or absence of economic advantage to us.

[. . .]

There is a clear tendency in American conservation to relegate to government all necessary jobs that private landowners fail to perform. Government ownership, operation, subsidy, or regulation is now widely prevalent in forestry, range management, soil and watershed management, park and wilderness conservation, fisheries management, and migratory bird management, with more to come. Most of this growth in governmental conservation is proper and logical, some of it is inevitable. That I imply no disapproval of it is implicit in the fact that I have spent most of my life working for it. Nevertheless the question arises: What is the ultimate magnitude of the enterprise? Will the tax base carry its eventual ramifications? At what point will governmental conservation, like the mastodon, become handicapped by its own dimensions? The answer, if there is any, seems to be in a land ethic, or some other force which assigns more obligation to the private landowner.

Industrial landowners and users, especially lumbermen and stockmen, are inclined to wail long and loudly about the extension of government ownership and regulation to land, but (with notable exceptions) they show little disposition to develop the only visible alternative: the voluntary practice of conservation on their own lands.

When the private landowner is asked to perform some unprofitable act for the good of the community, he today assents only with outstretched palm. If the act costs him cash this is fair and proper, but when it costs only forethought, open-mindedness, or time, the issue is at least debatable. The overwhelming growth of land-use subsidies in recent years must be ascribed, in large part, to the government's own agencies for conservation education: the land bureaus, the agricultural colleges, and the extension services. As far as I can detect, no ethical obligation toward land is taught in these institutions.

To sum up: a system of conservation based solely on economic self-interest is hopelessly lopsided. It tends to ignore, and thus eventually to eliminate, many elements in the land community that lack commercial value, but that are (as far as we know) essential to its healthy functioning. It assumes, falsely, I think, that the economic parts of the biotic clock will function without the uneconomic parts. It tends to relegate to government many functions eventually too large, too complex, or too widely dispersed to be performed by government.

An ethical obligation on the part of the private owner is the only visible remedy for these situations.

The Land Pyramid

An ethic to supplement and guide the economic relation to land presupposes the existence of some mental image of land as a biotic mechanism. We can be ethical only in relation to something we can see, feel, understand, love, or otherwise have faith in.

The image commonly employed in conservation education is 'the balance of nature.' For reasons too lengthy to detail here, this figure of speech fails to describe accurately what little we know about the land mechanism. A much truer image is the one employed in ecology: the biotic pyramid. I shall first sketch the pyramid as a symbol of land, and later develop some of its implications in terms of land-use.

Plants absorb energy from the sun. This energy flows through a circuit called the biota, which may be represented by a pyramid consisting of layers. The bottom layer is the soil. A plant layer rests on the soil, an insect layer on the plants, a bird and rodent layer on the insects, and so on up through various animal groups to the apex layer, which consists of the larger carnivores.

The species of a layer are alike not in where they came from, or in what they look like, but rather in what they eat. Each successive layer depends on those below it for food and often for other services, and each in turn furnishes food and services to those above. Proceeding upward, each successive layer decreases in numerical abundance. Thus, for every carnivore there are hundreds of his prey, thousands of their prey, millions of insects, uncountable plants. The pyramidal form of the system reflects this numerical progression from apex to base. Man shares an intermediate layer with the bears, raccoons, and squirrels which eat both meat and vegetables.

The lines of dependency for food and other services are called food chains. Thus soil-oak-deer-Indian is a chain that has now been largely converted to soil-corn-cow-farmer. Each species, including ourselves, is a link in many chains. The deer eats a hundred plants other than oak, and the cow a hundred plants other than corn. Both, then, are links in a hundred chains. The pyramid is a tangle of chains so complex as to seem disorderly, yet the stability of the system proves it to be a highly organized structure. Its functioning depends on the co-operation and competition of its diverse parts.

In the beginning, the pyramid of life was low and squat; the food chains short and simple. Evolution has added layer after layer, link after link. Man is one of thousands of accretions to the height and complexity of the pyramid. Science has given us many doubts, but it has given us at least one certainty: the trend of evolution is to elaborate and diversify the biota.

Land, then, is not merely soil; it is a fountain of energy flowing through a circuit of soils, plants, and animals. Food chains are the living channels which conduct energy upward; death and decay return it to the soil. The circuit is not closed; some energy is dissipated in decay, some is added by absorption from the air, some is stored in soils, peats, and long-lived forests; but it is a sustained circuit, like a slowly augmented revolving fund of life. There is always a net loss by downhill wash, but this is normally small and offset by the decay of rocks. It is deposited in the ocean and, in the course of geological time, raised to form new lands and new pyramids.

The velocity and character of the upward flow of energy depend on the complex structure of the plant and animal community, much as the upward flow of sap in a tree depends on its complex cellular organization. Without this complexity, normal circulation would presumably not occur. Structure means the characteristic numbers, as well as the characteristic kinds and functions, of the component species. This interdependence between the complex structure of the land and its smooth functioning as an energy unit is one of its basic attributes.

When a change occurs in one part of the circuit, many other parts must adjust themselves to it. Change does not necessarily obstruct or divert the flow of energy; evolution is a long series of self-induced changes, the net result of which has been to elaborate the flow mechanism and to lengthen the circuit. Evolutionary changes, however, are usually slow and local. Man's invention of tools has enabled him to make changes of unprecedented violence, rapidity, and scope.

One change is in the composition of floras and faunas. The larger predators are lopped off the apex of the pyramid; food chains, for the first time in history, become shorter rather than longer. Domesticated species from other lands are substituted for wild ones, and wild ones are moved to new habitats. In this world-wide pooling of faunas and floras, some species get out of bounds as pests and diseases, others are extinguished. Such effects are seldom intended or foreseen; they represent unpredicted and often untraceable readjustments in the structure. Agricultural science is largely a race between the emergence of new pests and the emergence of new techniques for their control.

Another change touches the flow of energy through plants and animals and its return to the soil. Fertility is the ability of soil to receive, store, and release energy. Agriculture, by overdrafts on the soil, or by too radical a substitution of domestic for native species in the superstructure, may derange the channels of flow or deplete storage. Soils depleted of their storage, or of the organic matter which anchors it, wash away faster than they form. This is erosion.

Waters, like soil, are part of the energy circuit. Industry, by polluting waters or obstructing them with dams, may exclude the plants and animals necessary to keep energy in circulation.

Transportation brings about another basic change: the plants or animals grown in one region are now consumed and returned to the soil in another. Transportation taps the energy stored in rocks, and in the air, and uses it elsewhere; thus we fertilize the garden with nitrogen gleaned by the guano birds from the fishes of seas on the other side of the Equator. Thus the formerly localized and self-contained circuits are pooled on a world-wide scale.

The process of altering the pyramid for human occupation releases stored energy, and this often gives rise, during the pioneering period, to a deceptive exuberance of plant and animal life, both wild and tame. These releases of biotic capital tend to becloud or postpone the penalties of violence.

* * *

This thumbnail sketch of land as an energy circuit conveys three basic ideas:

(1) That land is not merely soil.
(2) That the native plants and animals kept the energy circuit open; others may or may not.
(3) That man-made changes are of a different order than evolutionary changes, and have effects more comprehensive than is intended or foreseen.

These ideas, collectively, raise two basic issues: Can the land adjust itself to the new order? Can the desired alterations be accomplished with less violence?

Biotas seem to differ in their capacity to sustain violent conversion. Western Europe, for example, carries a far different pyramid than Caesar found there. Some large animals are lost; swampy forests have become meadows or plowland; many new plants and animals are introduced, some of which escape as pests; the remaining natives are greatly changed in distribution and abundance. Yet the soil is still there and, with the help of imported nutrients, still fertile; the waters flow normally; the new structure seems to function and to persist. There is no visible stoppage or derangement of the circuit.

[. . .]

The combined evidence of history and ecology seems to support one general deduction: the less violent the man-made changes, the greater the probability of successful readjustment in the pyramid. Violence, in turn, varies with human population density; a dense population requires a more violent conversion. In this respect, North America has a better chance for permanence than Europe, if she can contrive to limit her density.

This deduction runs counter to our current philosophy, which assumes that because a small increase in density enriched human life, that an indefinite increase will enrich it indefinitely. Ecology knows of no density relationship that holds for indefinitely wide limits. All gains from density are subject to a law of diminishing returns.

Whatever may be the equation for men and land, it is improbable that we as yet know all its terms. Recent discoveries in mineral and vitamin nutrition reveal unsuspected dependencies in the up-circuit: incredibly minute quantities of certain substances determine the value of soils to plants, of plants to animals. What of the down-circuit? What of the vanishing species, the preservation of which we now regard as an esthetic luxury? They helped build the soil; in what unsuspected ways may they be essential to its maintenance? Professor Weaver proposes that we use prairie flowers to reflocculate the wasting soils of the dust bowl; who knows for what purpose cranes and condors, otters and grizzlies may some day be used?

Land Health and the A-B Cleavage

A land ethic, then, reflects the existence of an ecological conscience, and this in turn reflects a conviction of individual responsibility for the health of the land. Health is the capacity of the land for self-renewal. Conservation is our effort to understand and preserve this capacity.

Conservationists are notorious for their dissensions. Superficially these seem to add up to mere confusion, but a more careful scrutiny reveals a single plane of cleavage common to many specialized fields. In each field one group (A) regards the land as soil, and its function as commodity-production; another group (B) regards the land as a biota, and its function as something broader. How much broader is admittedly in a state of doubt and confusion.

In my own field, forestry, group A is quite content to grow trees like cabbages, with cellulose as the basic forest commodity. It feels no inhibition against violence; its ideology is agronomic. Group B, on the other hand, sees forestry as fundamentally different from agronomy because it employs natural species, and manages a natural environment rather than creating an artificial one. Group B prefers natural reproduction on principle. It worries on biotic as well as economic grounds about the loss of species like chestnut, and the threatened loss of the white pines. It worries about a whole series of secondary forest functions: wildlife, recreation, watersheds, wilderness areas. To my mind, Group B feels the stirrings of an ecological conscience.

In the wildlife field, a parallel cleavage exists. For Group A the basic commodities are sport and meat; the yardsticks of production are ciphers of take in pheasants and trout. Artificial propagation is acceptable as a permanent as well as a temporary recourse – if its unit costs permit. Group B, on the other hand, worries about a whole series of biotic side-issues. What is the cost in predators of producing a game crop? Should we have further recourse to exotics? How can management restore the shrinking species, like prairie grouse, already hopeless as shootable game? How can management restore the threatened rarities, like trumpeter swan and whooping crane? Can management principles be extended to wild-flowers? Here again it is clear to me that we have the same A-B cleavage as in forestry.

In the larger field of agriculture I am less competent to speak, but there seem to be somewhat parallel cleavages. Scientific agriculture was actively developing before ecology was born, hence a slower penetration of ecological concepts might be expected. Moreover the farmer, by the very nature of his techniques, must modify the biota more radically than the forester or the wildlife manager. Nevertheless, there are many discontents in agriculture which seem to add up to a new vision of 'biotic farming.'

Perhaps the most important of these is the new evidence that poundage or tonnage is no measure of the food-value of farm crops; the products of fertile soil may be qualitatively as well as quantitatively superior. We can bolster poundage from depleted soils by pouring on imported fertility, but we are not necessarily bolstering food-value. The possible ultimate ramifications of this idea are so immense that I must leave their exposition to abler pens.

The discontent that labels itself 'organic farming,' while bearing some of the earmarks of a cult, is nevertheless biotic in its direction, particularly in its insistence on the importance of soil flora and fauna.

The ecological fundamentals of agriculture are just as poorly known to the public as in other fields of land-use. For example, few educated people realize that the marvelous advances in technique made during recent decades are improvements in the pump, rather than the well. Acre for acre, they have barely sufficed to offset the sinking level of fertility.

In all of these cleavages, we see repeated the same basic paradoxes: man the conqueror *versus* man the biotic citizen; science the sharpener of his sword *versus* science the searchlight on his universe; land the slave and servant *versus* land the collective organism. Robinson's injunction to Tristram may well be applied, at this juncture, to *Homo sapiens* as a species in geological time:

> Whether you will or not
> You are a King, Tristram, for you are one
> Of the time-tested few that leave the world,
> When they are gone, not the same place it was.
> Mark what you leave.

The Outlook

It is inconceivable to me that an ethical relation to land can exist without love, respect, and admiration for land, and a high regard for its value. By value, I of course mean something far broader than mere economic value; I mean value in the philosophical sense.

Perhaps the most serious obstacle impeding the evolution of a land ethic is the fact that our educational and economic system is headed away from, rather than toward, an intense consciousness of land. Your true modern is separated from the land by many middlemen, and by innumerable physical gadgets. He has no vital relation to it; to him it is the space between cities on which crops grow. Turn him loose for a day on the land, and if the spot does not happen to be a golf links or a 'scenic' area, he is bored stiff. If crops could be raised by hydroponics instead of farming, it would suit him very well. Synthetic substitutes for wood, leather, wool, and other natural land products suit him better than the originals. In short, land is something he has 'outgrown.'

Almost equally serious as an obstacle to a land ethic is the attitude of the farmer for whom the land is still an adversary, or a taskmaster that keeps him in slavery. Theoretically, the mechanization of farming ought to cut the farmer's chains, but whether it really does is debatable.

One of the requisites for an ecological comprehension of land is an understanding of ecology, and this is by no means co-extensive with 'education'; in fact, much higher education seems deliberately to avoid ecological concepts. An understanding of ecology does not necessarily originate in courses bearing ecological labels; it is quite as likely to be labeled geography, botany, agronomy, history, or economics. This is as it should be, but whatever the label, ecological training is scarce.

The case for a land ethic would appear hopeless but for the minority which is in obvious revolt against these 'modern' trends.

The 'key-log' which must be moved to release the evolutionary process for an ethic is simply this: quit thinking about decent land-use as solely an economic problem. Examine each question in terms of what is ethically and esthetically right, as well as what is economically expedient. A thing is right when it tends to preserve the integrity, stability, and beauty of the biotic community. It is wrong when it tends otherwise.

It of course goes without saying that economic feasibility limits the tether of what can or cannot be done for land. It always has and it always will. The fallacy the economic determinists have tied around our collective neck, and which we now need to cast off, is the belief that economics determines *all* land-use. This is simply not true. An innumerable host of actions and attitudes, comprising perhaps the bulk of all land relations, is determined by the land-users' tastes and predilections, rather than by his purse. The bulk of all land relations hinges on investments of time, forethought, skill, and faith rather than on investments of cash. As a land-user thinketh, so is he.

I have purposely presented the land ethic as a product of social evolution because nothing so important as an ethic is ever 'written.' Only the most superficial student of history supposes that Moses 'wrote' the Decalogue; it evolved in the minds of a thinking community, and Moses wrote a tentative summary of it for a 'seminar.' I say tentative because evolution never stops.

The evolution of a land ethic is an intellectual as well as emotional process. Conservation is paved with good intentions which prove to be futile, or even dangerous, because they are devoid of critical understanding either of the land, or of economic land-use. I think it is a truism that as the ethical frontier advances from the individual to the community, its intellectual content increases.

The mechanism of operation is the same for any ethic: social approbation for right actions: social disapproval for wrong actions.

By and large, our present problem is one of attitudes and implements. We are remodeling the Alhambra with a steam-shovel, and we are proud of our yardage. We shall hardly relinquish the shovel, which after all has many good points, but we are in need of gentler and more objective criteria for its successful use.

---

24   The Conceptual Foundations of the Land Ethic

J. Baird Callicott

I

As Wallace Stegner observes, *A Sand County Almanac* is considered "almost a holy book in conservation circles," and Aldo Leopold a prophet, "an American Isaiah." And as Curt Meine points out, "The Land Ethic" is the climatic essay of *Sand County*, "the upshot of 'The Upshot.'"[1] One might, therefore, fairly say that the recommendation and justification of moral obligations on the part of people to nature is what the prophetic *A Sand County Almanac* is all about.

But, with few exceptions, "The Land Ethic" has not been favorably received by contemporary academic philosophers. Most have ignored it. Of those who have not, most have been either nonplussed or hostile. Distinguished Australian philosopher John Passmore dismissed it out of hand, in the first book-length academic discussion of the new philosophical subdiscipline called "environmental ethics."[2] In a more recent and more deliberate discussion, the equally distinguished Australian philosopher H. J. McCloskey patronized Aldo Leopold and saddled "The Land Ethic" with various far-fetched "interpretations." He concludes that "there is a real problem in attributing a coherent meaning to Leopold's statements, one that exhibits his land ethic as representing a major advance in ethics rather than a retrogression to a morality of a kind held by various primitive peoples."[3] Echoing McCloskey, English philosopher Robin Attfield went out of his way to impugn the philosophical respectability of "The Land Ethic."

And Canadian philosopher L. W. Sumner has called it "dangerous nonsense."[4] Among those philosophers more favorably disposed, "The Land Ethic" has usually been simply quoted, as if it were little more than a noble, but naive, moral plea, altogether lacking a supporting theoretical framework – that is, foundational principles and premises which lead, by compelling argument, to ethical precepts.

The professional neglect, confusion, and (in some cases) contempt for "The Land Ethic" may, in my judgment, be attributed to three things: (1) Leopold's extremely condensed prose style in which an entire conceptual complex may be conveyed in a few sentences, or even in a phrase or two; (2) his departure from the assumptions and paradigms of contemporary philosophical ethics; and (3) the unsettling practical implications to which a land ethic appears to lead. "The Land Ethic," in short, is, from a philosophical point of view, abbreviated, unfamiliar, and radical.

Here I first examine and elaborate the compactly expressed abstract elements of the land ethic and expose the "logic" which binds them into a proper, but revolutionary, moral theory. I then discuss the controversial features of the land ethic and defend them against actual and potential criticism. I hope to show that the land ethic cannot be ignored as merely the groundless emotive exhortations of a moonstruck conservationist or dismissed as entailing wildly untoward practical consequences. It poses, rather, a serious intellectual challenge to business-as-usual moral philosophy.

From *In Defense of the Land Ethic* (Albany, NY: State University of New York Press, 1989), pp. 75–91. © 1989 State University of New York. Reprinted with permission from SUNY Press.

II

"The Land Ethic" opens with a charming and poetic evocation of Homer's Greece, the point of which is to suggest that today land is just as routinely and remorselessly enslaved as human beings then were. A panoramic glance backward to our most distant cultural origins, Leopold suggests, reveals a slow but steady moral development over three millennia. More of our relationships and activities ("fields of conduct") have fallen under the aegis of moral principles ("ethical criteria") as civilization has grown and matured. If moral growth and development continue, as not only a synoptic review of history, but recent past experience suggest that it will, future generations will censure today's casual and universal environmental bondage as today we censure the casual and universal human bondage of three thousand years ago.[5]

A cynically inclined critic might scoff at Leopold's sanguine portrayal of human history. Slavery survived as an institution in the "civilized" West, more particularly in the morally self-congratulatory United States, until a mere generation before Leopold's own birth. And Western history from imperial Athens and Rome to the Spanish Inquisition and the Third Reich has been a disgraceful series of wars, persecutions, tyrannies, pogroms, and other atrocities.

The history of moral practice, however, is not identical with the history of moral consciousness. Morality is not descriptive; it is prescriptive or normative. In light of this distinction, it is clear that today, despite rising rates of violent crime in the United States and institutional abuses of human rights in Iran, Chile, Ethiopia, Guatemala, South Africa, and many other places, and despite persistent organized social injustice and oppression in still others, moral consciousness is expanding more rapidly now than ever before. Civil rights, human rights, women's liberation, children's liberation, animal liberation, and so forth, all indicate, as expressions of newly emergent moral ideals, that ethical consciousness (as distinct from practice) has if anything recently accelerated – thus confirming Leopold's historical observation.

III

Leopold next points out that "this extension of ethics, so far studied only by philosophers" – and therefore, the implication is clear, not very satisfactorily studied – "is actually a process in ecological evolution" (p. 202). What Leopold is saying here, simply, is that we may understand the history of ethics, fancifully alluded to by means of the Odysseus vignette, in biological as well as philosophical terms. From a biological point of view, an ethic is "a limitation on freedom of action in the struggle for existence" (p. 202).

I had this passage in mind when I remarked that Leopold manages to convey a whole network of ideas in a couple of phrases. The phrase "struggle for existence" unmistakably calls to mind Darwinian evolution as the conceptual context in which a biological account of the origin and development of ethics must ultimately be located. And at once it points up a paradox: Given the unremitting competitive "struggle for existence" how could "limitations of freedom of action" ever have been conserved and spread through a population of *Homo sapiens* or their evolutionary progenitors?

For a biological account of ethics, as Harvard social entomologist Edward O. Wilson has recently written, "the central theoretical problem . . . [is] how can altruism [elaborately articulated as morality or ethics in the human species], which by definition reduces personal fitness, possibly evolve by natural selection?"[6] According to modern sociobiology, the answer lies in kinship. But according to Darwin – who had tackled this problem himself "exclusively from the side of natural history" in *The Descent of Man* – the answer lies in society.[7] And it was Darwin's classical account (and its diverse variations), from the side of natural history, which informed Leopold's thinking in the late 1940s.

Let me put the problem in perspective. How, we are asking, did ethics originate and, once in existence, grow in scope and complexity?

The oldest answer in living human memory is theological. God (or the gods) imposes morality on people. And God (or the gods) sanctions it. A most vivid and graphic example of this kind of account occurs in the Bible when Moses goes up on Mount Sinai to receive the Ten Commandments directly from God. That text also clearly illustrates the divine sanctions (plagues, pestilences, droughts, military defeats, and so forth) for moral disobedience. Ongoing revelation of the divine will, of course, as handily and as simply explains subsequent moral growth and development.

Western philosophy, on the other hand, is almost unanimous in the opinion that the origin of ethics in human experience has somehow to do with human reason. Reason figures centrally and pivotally in the "social contract theory" of the origin and nature of morals in all its ancient, modern, and contemporary expressions from Protagoras, to Hobbes, to Rawls. Reason is the wellspring of virtue, according to both Plato and Aristotle, and of categorical imperatives, according to Kant. In short, the weight of Western philosophy inclines to the view that we are moral beings because we are rational beings. The ongoing sophistication of reason and the progressive illumination it sheds upon the good and the right explain "the ethical sequence," the historical growth and development of morality, noticed by Leopold.

An evolutionary natural historian, however, cannot be satisfied with either of these general accounts of the origin and development of ethics. The idea that God gave morals to man is ruled out in principle – as any supernatural explanation of a natural phenomenon is ruled out in principle in natural science. And while morality might *in principle* be a function of human reason (as, say, mathematical calculation clearly is), to suppose that it is so *in fact* would be to put the cart before the horse. Reason appears to be a delicate, variable, and recently emerged faculty. It cannot, under any circumstances, be supposed to have evolved in the absence of complex linguistic capabilities which depend, in turn, for their evolution upon a highly developed social matrix. But we cannot have become social beings unless we assumed limitations on freedom of action in the struggle for existence. Hence we must have become ethical before we became rational.

Darwin, probably in consequence of reflections somewhat like these, turned to a minority tradition of modern philosophy for a moral psychology consistent with and useful to a general evolutionary account of ethical phenomena. A century earlier, Scottish philosophers David Hume and Adam Smith had argued that ethics rest upon feelings or "sentiments" – which, to be sure, may be both amplified and informed by reason.[8] And since in the animal kingdom feelings or sentiments are arguably far more common or widespread than reason, they would be a far more likely starting point for an evolutionary account of the origin and growth of ethics.

Darwin's account, to which Leopold unmistakably (if elliptically) alludes in "The Land Ethic," begins with the parental and filial affections common, perhaps, to all mammals.[9] Bonds of affection and sympathy between parents and offspring permitted the formation of small, closely kin social groups, Darwin argued. Should the parental and filial affections bonding family members chance to extend to less closely related individuals, that would permit an enlargement of the family group. And should the newly extended community more successfully defend itself and/or more efficiently provision itself, the inclusive fitness of its members severally would be increased, Darwin reasoned. Thus the more diffuse familial affections, which Darwin (echoing Hume and Smith) calls the "social sentiments," would be spread throughout a population.[10]

Morality, properly speaking – that is, morality as opposed to mere altruistic instinct – requires, in Darwin's terms, "intellectual powers" sufficient to recall the past and imagine the future, "the power of language" sufficient to express "common opinion," and "habituation" to patterns of behavior deemed, by common opinion, to be socially acceptable and beneficial.[11] Even so, ethics proper, in Darwin's account, remains firmly rooted in moral feelings or social sentiments which were – no less than physical faculties, he expressly avers – naturally selected, by the advantages for survival and especially for successful reproduction, afforded by society.[12]

The protosociobiological perspective on ethical phenomena, to which Leopold as a natural historian was heir, leads him to a generalization which is remarkably explicit in his condensed and often merely resonant rendering of Darwin's more deliberate and extended paradigm: Since "the thing [ethics] has its origin in the tendency of interdependent individuals or groups to evolve modes of co-operation, . . . all ethics so far evolved rest upon a single premise: that the individual is a member of a community of interdependent parts" (pp. 202–3).

Hence, we may expect to find that the scope and specific content of ethics will reflect both the perceived boundaries and actual structure or organization of a cooperative community or society. *Ethics and society or community are correlative.* This single, simple principle constitutes a powerful tool for the analysis of moral natural history, for the anticipation of future moral development (including, ultimately, the land ethic), and for systematically deriving the specific precepts, the prescriptions and proscriptions, of an emergent and culturally unprecedented ethic like a land or environmental ethic.

IV

Anthropological studies of ethics reveal that in fact the boundaries of the moral community are generally coextensive with the perceived boundaries of society.[13] And the peculiar (and, from the urbane point of view, sometimes inverted) representation of virtue and vice in tribal society – the virtue, for example, of sharing to the point of personal destitution and the vice of privacy and private property – reflects and fosters the life way of tribal peoples.[14] Darwin, in his leisurely, anecdotal discussion, paints a vivid picture of the intensity, peculiarity, and sharp circumscription of "savage" mores: "A savage will risk his life to save that of a member of the same community, but will be wholly indifferent about a stranger."[15] As Darwin portrays them, tribespeople are at once paragons of virtue "within the limits of the same tribe" and enthusiastic thieves, manslaughterers, and torturers without.[16]

For purposes of more effective defense against common enemies, or because of increased population density, or in response to innovations in subsistence methods and technologies, or for some mix of these or other forces, human societies have grown in extent or scope and changed in form or structure. Nations – like the Iroquois nation or the Sioux nation – came into being upon the merger of previously separate and mutually hostile tribes. Animals and plants were domesticated and erstwhile hunter-gatherers became herders and farmers. Permanent habitations were established. Trade, craft, and (later) industry flourished. With each change in society came corresponding and correlative changes in ethics. The moral community expanded to become co-extensive with the newly drawn boundaries of societies and the representation of virtue and vice, right and wrong, good and evil, changed to accommodate, foster, and preserve the economic and institutional organization of emergent social orders.

Today we are witnessing the painful birth of a human supercommunity, global in scope. Modern transportation and communication technologies, international economic interdependencies, international economic entities, and nuclear arms have brought into being a "global village." It has not yet become fully formed and it is at tension – a very dangerous tension – with its predecessor, the nation-state. Its eventual institutional structure, a global federalism or whatever it may turn out to be, is at this point completely unpredictable. Interestingly, however, a corresponding global human ethic – the "human rights" ethic, as it is popularly called – has been more definitely articulated.

Most educated people today pay lip service at least to the ethical precept that all members of the human species, regardless of race, creed, or national origin, are endowed with certain fundamental rights which it is wrong not to respect. According to the evolutionary scenario set out by Darwin, the contemporary moral ideal of human rights is a response to a perception – however vague and indefinite – that mankind worldwide is united into one society, one community, however indeterminate or yet institutionally unorganized. As Darwin presciently wrote:

> As man advances in civilization, and small tribes are united into larger communities, the simplest reason would tell each individual that he ought to extend his social instincts and sympathies to all the members of the same nation, though personally unknown to him. This point being once reached, there is only an artificial barrier to prevent his sympathies extending to the men of all nations and races. If, indeed, such men are separated from him by great differences of appearance or habits, experience unfortunately shows us how long it is, before we look at them as our fellow-creatures.[17]

According to Leopold, the next step in this sequence beyond the still incomplete ethic of universal humanity, a step that is clearly discernible on the horizon, is the land ethic. The "community concept" has, so far, propelled the development of ethics from the savage clan to the family of man. "The land ethic simply enlarges the boundary of the community to include soils, waters, plants, and animals, or collectively: the land" (p. 204).

As the foreword to *Sand County* makes plain, the overarching thematic principle of the book is the inculcation of the idea – through narrative description, discursive exposition, abstractive generalization, and occasional preachment – "that land is a community" (viii). The community concept is "the basic concept of ecology" (viii). Once land is popularly perceived as a biotic community – as it is professionally perceived in ecology – a correlative land ethic will emerge in the collective cultural consciousness.

V

Although anticipated as far back as the mid-eighteenth century – in the notion of an "economy of nature" – the concept of the biotic community was more fully and deliberately developed as a working model or paradigm for ecology by Charles Elton in the 1920s.[18] The natural world is organized as an intricate corporate society in which plants and animals occupy "niches," or as Elton alternatively called them, "roles" or "professions," in the economy of nature.[19] As in a feudal community, little or no socio-economic mobility (upward or otherwise) exists in the biotic community. One is born to one's trade.

Human society, Leopold argues, is founded, in large part, upon mutual security and economic inter-dependency and preserved only by limitations on freedom of action in the struggle for existence – that is, by ethical constraints. Since the biotic community exhibits, as modern ecology reveals, an analogous structure, it too can be preserved, given the newly amplified impact of "mechanized man," only by analogous limitations on freedom of action – that is, by a land ethic (viii). A land ethic, furthermore, is not only "an ecological necessity," but an "evolutionary possibility" because a moral response to the natural environment – Darwin's social sympathies, sentiments, and instincts translated and codified into a body of principles and precepts – would be automatically triggered in human beings by ecology's social representation of nature (p. 203).

Therefore, the key to the emergence of a land ethic is, simply, universal ecological literacy.

VI

The land ethic rests upon three scientific corner-stones: (1) evolutionary and (2) ecological biology set in a background of (3) Copernican astronomy. Evolutionary theory provides the conceptual link between ethics and social organization and development. It provides a sense of "kinship with fellow-creatures" as well, "fellow-voyagers" with us in the "odyssey of evolution" (p. 109). It establishes a dia-chronic link between people and nonhuman nature. Ecological theory provides a synchronic link – the community concept – a sense of social integration of human and nonhuman nature. Human beings, plants, animals, soils, and waters are "all interlocked in one humming community of cooperations and competitions, one biota."[20] The simplest reason, to paraphrase Darwin, should, therefore, tell each individual that he or she ought to extend his or her social instincts and sympathies to all the members of the biotic community though different from him or her in appearance or habits.

And although Leopold never directly mentions it in *A Sand County Almanac*, the Copernican perspective, the perception of the earth as "a small planet" in an immense and utterly hostile universe beyond, contributes, perhaps subconsciously, but nevertheless very powerfully, to our sense of kinship, community, and interdependence with fellow denizens of the earth household. It scales the earth down to something like a cozy island paradise in a desert ocean.

Here in outline, then, are the conceptual and logical foundations of the land ethic: Its conceptual elements are a Copernican cosmology, a Darwinian protosociobiological natural history of ethics, Darwinian ties of kinship among all forms of life on earth, and an Eltonian model of the structure of bio-cenoses all overlaid on a Humean-Smithian moral psychology. Its logic is that natural selection has endowed human beings with an affective moral response to perceived bonds of kinship and commu-nity membership and identity; that today the natural environment, the land, is represented as a commu-nity, the biotic community; and that, therefore, an environmental or land ethic is both possible – the biopsychological and cognitive conditions are in place – and necessary, since human beings collec-tively have acquired the power to destroy the integ-rity, diversity, and stability of the environing and supporting economy of nature. In the remainder of this essay I discuss special features and problems of the land ethic germane to moral philosophy.

The most salient feature of Leopold's land ethic is its provision of what Kenneth Goodpaster has care-fully called "moral considerability" for the biotic community per se, not just for fellow members of the biotic community:[21]

> In short, a land ethic changes the role of *Homo sapi-ens* from conqueror of the land-community to plain member and citizen of it. It implies respect for his fellow-members, *and also respect for the community as such*. (p. 204, emphasis added)

The land ethic, thus, has a holistic as well as an indi-vidualistic cast.

Indeed, as "The Land Ethic" develops, the focus of moral concern shifts gradually away from plants, animals, soils, and waters severally to the biotic community collectively. Toward the middle, in the subsection called 'Substitutes for a Land Ethic,' Leopold invokes the "biotic rights" of *species* – as the context indicates – of wildflowers, songbirds, and predators. In 'The Outlook,' the climactic section of "The Land Ethic," nonhuman natural entities, first appearing as fellow members, then considered in profile as species, are not so much as mentioned in what might be called the "summary moral maxim" of the land ethic: "A thing is right when it tends to preserve the integrity, stability, and beauty of the biotic community. It is wrong when it tends otherwise" (pp. 224–5).

By this measure of right and wrong, not only would it be wrong for a farmer, in the interest of higher profits, to clear the woods off a 75 percent slope, turn his cows into the clearing and dump its rainfall, rocks, and soil into the community creek, it would also be wrong for the federal fish and wildlife agency, in the interest of individual animal welfare, to permit populations of deer, rabbits, feral burros, or whatever to increase unchecked and thus to threaten the integrity, stability, and beauty of the biotic communities of which they are members. The land ethic not only provides moral considerability for the biotic community per se, but ethical consideration of its individual members is preempted by concern for the preservation of the integrity, stability, and beauty of the biotic community. The land ethic, thus, not only has a holistic aspect; it is holistic with a vengeance.

The holism of the land ethic, more than any other feature, sets it apart from the predominant paradigm of modern moral philosophy. It is, therefore, the feature of the land ethic which requires the most patient theoretical analysis and the most sensitive practical interpretation.

VII

As Kenneth Goodpaster pointed out, mainstream modern ethical philosophy has taken egoism as its point of departure and reached a wider circle of moral entitlement by a process of generalization:[22] I am sure that *I*, the enveloped ego, am intrinsically or inherently valuable and thus that *my* interests ought to be considered, taken into account, by "others" when their actions may substantively affect *me*. My own claim to moral consideration, according to

the conventional wisdom, ultimately rests upon a psychological capacity – rationality or sentiency were the classical candidates of Kant and Bentham, respectively – which is arguably valuable in itself and which thus qualifies *me* for moral standing.[23] However, then I am forced grudgingly to grant the same moral consideration I demand from others, on this basis, to those others who can also claim to possess the same general psychological characteristic.

A criterion of moral value and consideration is thus identified. Goodpaster convincingly argues that mainstream modern moral theory is based, when all the learned dust has settled, on this simple paradigm of ethical justification and logic exemplified by the Benthamic and Kantian prototypes.[24] If the criterion of moral values and consideration is pitched low enough – as it is in Bentham's criterion of sentiency – a wide variety of animals are admitted to moral entitlement.[25] If the criterion of moral value and consideration is pushed lower still – as it is in Albert Schweitzer's reverence-for-life ethic – all minimally conative things (plants as well as animals) would be extended moral considerability.[26] The contemporary animal liberation/rights, and reverence-for-life/life-principle ethics are, at bottom, simply direct applications of the modern classical paradigm of moral argument. But this standard modern model of ethical theory provides no possibility whatever for the moral consideration of wholes – of threatened population of animals and plants, or of endemic, rare, or endangered species, or of biotic communities, or most expansively, of the biosphere in its totality – since wholes per se have no psychological experience of any kind.[27] Because mainstream modern moral theory has been "psychocentric," it has been radically and intractably individualistic or "atomistic" in its fundamental theoretical orientation.

Hume, Smith, and Darwin diverged from the prevailing theoretical model by recognizing that altruism is as fundamental and autochthonous in human nature as is egoism. According to their analysis, moral value is not identified with a natural quality objectively present in morally considerable beings – as reason and/or sentiency is objectively present in people and/or animals – it is, as it were, projected by valuing subjects.[28]

Hume and Darwin, furthermore, recognize inborn moral sentiments which have society as such as their natural object. Hume insists that "we must renounce the theory which accounts for every moral sentiment by the principle of self-love. We must adopt a more *publick affection* and allow that the *interests of society* are not, *even on their own account*, entirely indifferent to us."[29] And Darwin, somewhat ironically (since "Darwinian evolution" very often means natural selection operating exclusively with respect to individuals), sometimes writes as if morality had no other object than the commonweal, the welfare of the community as a corporate entity:

> We have now seen that actions are regarded by savages, and were probably so regarded by primeval man, as good or bad, solely as they obviously affect the welfare of the tribe, – not that of the species, nor that of the individual member of the tribe. This conclusion agrees well with the belief that the so-called moral sense is aboriginally derived from social instincts, for both relate at first exclusively to the community.[30]

Theoretically then, the biotic community owns what Leopold, in the lead paragraph of 'The Outlook,' calls "value in the philosophical sense" – that is, direct moral considerability – because it is a newly discovered proper object of a specially evolved "publick affection" or "moral sense" which all psychologically normal human beings have inherited from a long line of ancestral social primates (p. 223).[31]

VIII

In the land ethic, as in all earlier stages of social-ethical evolution, there exists a tension between the good of the community as a whole and the "rights" of its individual members considered severally. While 'The Ethical Sequence' section of "The Land Ethic" clearly evokes Darwin's classical biosocial account of the origin and extension of morals, Leopold is actually more explicitly concerned, in that section, with the interplay between the holistic and individualistic moral sentiments – between sympathy and fellow-feeling on the one hand, and public affection for the commonweal on the other:

> The first ethics dealt with the relation between individuals; the Mosaic Decalogue is an example. Later accretions dealt with the relation between the individual and society. The Golden Rule tries to integrate the individual to society; democracy to integrate social organization to the individual. (pp. 202–3)

Actually, it is doubtful that the first ethics dealt with the relation between individuals and not at all with the relation between the individual and society. (This, along with the remark that ethics replaced an "original free-for-all competition," suggests that Leopold's Darwinian line of thought has been uncritically tainted with Hobbesean elements (p. 202). Of course, Hobbes's "state of nature," in which there prevailed a war of each against all, is absurd from an evolutionary point of view.) A century of ethnographic studies seems to confirm, rather, Darwin's conjecture that the relative weight of the holistic component is greater in tribal ethics – the tribal ethic of the Hebrews recorded in the Old Testament constitutes a vivid case in point – than in more recent accretions. The Golden Rule, on the other hand, does not mention, in any of its formulations, society per se. Rather, its primary concern seems to be "others," that is, other human individuals. Democracy, with its stress on individual liberties and rights, seems to further rather than countervail the individualistic thrust of the Golden Rule.

In any case, the conceptual foundations of the land ethic provide a well-informed, self-consistent theoretical basis for including both fellow members of the biotic community and the biotic community itself (considered as a corporate entity) within the purview of morals. The pre-emptive emphasis, however, on the welfare of the community as a whole, in Leopold's articulation of the land ethic, while certainly consistent with its Humean-Darwinian theoretical foundations, is not determined by them alone. The overriding holism of the land ethic results, rather, more from the way our moral sensibilities are informed by ecology.

IX

Ecological thought, historically, has tended to be holistic in outlook.[32] Ecology is the study of the relationships of organisms to one another and to the elemental environment. These relationships bind the *relata* – plants, animals, soils, and waters – into a seamless fabric. The ontological primacy of objects and the ontological subordination of relationships characteristic of classical Western science is, in fact, reversed in ecology.[33] Ecological relationships determine the nature of organisms rather than the other way around. A species is what it is because it has adapted to a niche in the ecosystem. The whole, the system itself, thus, literally and quite straightforwardly shapes and forms its component species.

Antedating Charles Elton's community model of ecology was F. E. Clements and S. A. Forbes's organism model.[34] Plants and animals, soils and waters, according to this paradigm, are integrated into one superorganism. Species are, as it were, its organs; specimens its cells. Although Elton's community paradigm (later modified, as we shall see, by Arthur Tansley's ecosystem idea) is the principal and morally fertile ecological concept of "The Land Ethic," the more radically holistic superorganism paradigm of Clements and Forbes resonates in "The Land Ethic" as an audible overtone. In the peroration of 'Land Health and the A–B Cleavage,' for example, which immediately precedes 'The Outlook,' Leopold insists that

> in all these cleavages, we see repeated the same basic paradoxes: man the conqueror *versus* man the biotic citizen; science the sharpener of his sword *versus* science the searchlight on his universe; land the slave and servant *versus* land the collective organism. (p. 223)

And on more than one occasion Leopold, in the latter quarter of "The Land Ethic," talks about the "health" and "disease" of the land – terms which are at once descriptive and normative and which, taken literally, characterize only organisms proper.

In an early essay, "Some Fundamentals of Conservation in the Southwest," Leopold speculatively flirted with the intensely holistic superorganism model of the environment as a paradigm pregnant with moral implications:

> It is at least not impossible to regard the earth's parts – soil, mountains, rivers, atmosphere, etc. – as organs or parts of organs, of *a coordinated whole,* each part with a definite function. And if we could see *this whole, as a whole,* through a great period of time, we might perceive not only organs with coordinated functions, but possibly also that process of consumption and replacement which in biology we call metabolism, or growth. In such a case we would have all the visible attributes of a living thing, which we do not realize to be such because it is too big, and its life processes too slow. And there would also follow that invisible attribute – a soul or consciousness – which . . . many philosophers of all ages

ascribe to all living things and aggregates thereof, including the "dead" earth.

> Possibly in our intuitive perceptions, which may be truer than our science and less impeded by words than our philosophies, we realize the indivisibility of the earth – its soil, mountains, rivers, forests, climate, plants, and animals – and *respect it collectively* not only as a useful servant but as a living being, vastly less alive than ourselves, but vastly greater than ourselves in time and space. . . . Philosophy, then, suggests one reason why we cannot destroy the earth with moral impunity; namely, that the "dead" earth is an organism possessing a certain kind and degree of life, which we intuitively respect as such.[35]

Had Leopold retained this overall theoretical approach in "The Land Ethic," the land ethic would doubtless have enjoyed more critical attention from philosophers. The moral foundations of a land or, as he might then have called it, "earth" ethic, would rest upon the hypothesis that the Earth is alive and ensouled – possessing inherent psychological characteristics, logically parallel to reason and sentiency. This notion of a conative whole earth could plausibly have served as a general criterion of intrinsic worth and moral considerability, in the familiar format of mainstream moral thought.

Part of the reason, therefore, that "The Land Ethic" emphasizes more and more the integrity, stability, and beauty of the environment as a whole, and less and less the biotic right of individual plants and animals to life, liberty, and the pursuit of happiness, is that the superorganism ecological paradigm invites one, much more than does the community paradigm, to hypostatize, to reify the whole, and to subordinate its individual members.

In any case, as we see, rereading "The Land Ethic" in light of "Some Fundamentals," the whole Earth organism image of nature is vestigially present in Leopold's later thinking. Leopold may have abandoned the "earth ethic" because ecology had abandoned the organism analogy in favor of the community analogy as a working theoretical paradigm. And the community model was more suitably given moral implications by the social/sentimental ethical natural history of Hume and Darwin.

Meanwhile, the biotic community ecological paradigm itself had acquired, by the late thirties and forties, a more holistic cast of its own. In 1935 British ecologist Arthur Tansley pointed out that from the perspective of physics the "currency" of the "economy of nature" is energy.[36] Tansley suggested that Elton's qualitative and descriptive food chains, food webs, trophic niches, and biosocial professions could be quantitatively expressed by means of a thermodynamic flow model. It is Tansley's state-of-the-art thermodynamic paradigm of the environment that Leopold explicitly sets out as a "mental image of land" in relation to which "we can be ethical" (p. 214). And it is the ecosystemic model of land which informs the cardinal practical precepts of the land ethic.

'The Land Pyramid' is the pivotal section of "The Land Ethic" – the section which effects a complete transition from concern for "fellow-members" to the "community as such." It is also its longest and most technical section. A description of the "ecosystem" (Tansley's deliberately nonmetaphorical term) begins with the sun. Solar energy "flows through a circuit called the biota" (p. 215). It enters the biota through the leaves of green plants and courses through plant-eating animals, and then on to omnivores and carnivores. At last the tiny fraction of solar energy converted to biomass by green plants remaining in the corpse of a predator, animal feces, plant detritus, or other dead organic material is garnered by decomposers – worms, fungi, and bacteria. They recycle the participating elements and degrade into entropic equilibrium any remaining energy. According to this paradigm

> land, then, is not merely soil; it is a fountain of energy flowing through a circuit of soils, plants, and animals. Food chains are the living channels which conduct energy upward; death and decay return it to the soil. The circuit is not closed; . . . but it is a sustained circuit, like a slowly augmented revolving fund of life. (p. 216)

In this exceedingly abstract (albeit poetically expressed) model of nature, process precedes substance and energy is more fundamental than matter. Individual plants and animals become less autonomous beings than ephemeral structures in a patterned flux of energy. According to Yale biophysicist Harold Morowitz,

> viewed from the point of view of modern [ecology], each living thing . . . is a dissipative structure, that is it does not endure in and of itself but only as a result of the continual flow of energy in the system. [. . .] From this point of view the reality of individuals is

problematic because they do not exist per se but only as local perturbations in this universal flow.[37]

Though less bluntly stated and made more palatable by the unfailing charm of his prose, Leopold's proffered mental image of land is just as expansive, systemic, and distanced as Morowitz's. The maintenance of "the complex structure of the land and its smooth functioning as an energy unit" emerges in 'The Land Pyramid' as the *summum bonum* of the land ethic (p. 216).

Notes

1 Wallace Stegner, "The Legacy of Aldo Leopold"; Curt Meine, "Building 'The Land Ethic'"; both in J. Baird Callicott, ed., *Companion to A Sand County Almanac: Interpretive and Critical Essays* (Madison, Wis.: University of Wisconsin Press, 1987). The oft-repeated characterization of Leopold as a prophet appears traceable to Roberts Mann, "Aldo Leopold: Priest and Prophet," *American Forests* 60, no. 8 (August 1954): 23, 42–3; it was picked up, apparently, by Ernest Swift, "Aldo Leopold: Wisconsin's Conservationist Prophet," *Wisconsin Tales and Trails* 2, no. 2 (September 1961): 2–5; Roderick Nash institutionalized it in his chapter, "Aldo Leopold: Prophet," in *Wilderness and the American Mind* (New Haven: Yale University Press, 1967).

2 John Passmore, *Man's Responsibility for* [significantly not *"to"*] *Nature: Ecological Problems and Western Traditions* (New York: Charles Scribner's Sons, 1974).

3 H. J. McCloskey, *Ecological Ethics and Politics* (Totowa, NJ: Rowman and Littlefield, 1983), p. 56.

4 Robin Attfield, in "Value in the Wilderness," *Metaphilosophy* 15 (1984), writes, "Leopold the philosopher is something of a disaster, and I dread the thought of the student whose concept of philosophy is modeled principally on these extracts. (Can value 'in the philosophical sense' be contrasted with instrumental value? If concepts of right and wrong did not apply to slaves in Homeric Greece, how could Odysseus suspect the slavegirls of 'misbehavior'? If all ethics rest on interdependence how are obligations to infants and small children possible? And how can 'obligations have no meaning without conscience,' granted that the notion of conscience is conceptually dependent on that of obligation?)" (p. 294). L. W. Sumner, "Review of Robin Attfield, *The Ethics of Environmental Concern*," *Environmental Ethics* 8 (1986): 77.

5 Aldo Leopold, *A Sand County Almanac* (New York: Oxford University Press, 1949). Quotations from *Sand County* are cited in the text of this essay by page numbers in parentheses.

6 Edward O. Wilson, *Sociobiology: The New Synthesis* (Cambridge: Harvard University Press, 1975), p. 3. See also W. D. Hamilton, "The Genetical Theory of Social Behavior," *Journal of Theoretical Biology* 7 (1964): 1–52.

7 Charles R. Darwin, *The Descent of Man and Selection in Relation to Sex* (New York: J. A. Hill and Company, 1904). The quoted phrase occurs on p. 97.

8 See Adam Smith, *The Theory of the Moral Sentiments* (London and Edinburgh: A. Millar, A. Kinkaid, and J. Bell, 1759) and David Hume, *An Enquiry Concerning the Principles of Morals* (Oxford: The Clarendon Press, 1777; first published in 1751). Darwin cites both works in the key fourth chapter of *Descent* (pp. 106 and 109, respectively).

9 Darwin, *Descent*, pp. 98ff.

10 Ibid., pp. 105ff.

11 Ibid., pp. 113ff.

12 Ibid., p. 105.

13 See, for example, Elman R. Service, *Primitive Social Organization: An Evolutionary Perspective* (New York: Random House, 1962).

14 See Marshall Sahlins, *Stone Age Economics* (Chicago: Aldine Atherton, 1972).

15 Darwin, *Descent*, p. 111.

16 Ibid., pp. 117ff. The quoted phrase occurs on p. 118.

17 Ibid., p. 124.

18 See Donald Worster, *Nature's Economy: The Roots of Ecology* (San Francisco: Sierra Club Books, 1977).

19 Charles Elton, *Animal Ecology* (New York: Macmillan, 1927).

20 Aldo Leopold, *Round River* (New York: Oxford University Press, 1953), p. 148.

21 Kenneth Goodpaster, "On Being Morally Considerable," *Journal of Philosophy* 22 (1978): 308–25. Goodpaster wisely avoids the term *rights*, defined so strictly albeit so variously by philosophers, and used so loosely by nonphilosophers.

22 Kenneth Goodpaster, "From Egoism to Environmentalism" in *Ethics and Problems of the 21st Century*, ed. K. E. Goodpaster and K. M. Sayre (Notre Dame, Ind.: University of Notre Dame Press, 1979), pp. 21–35.

23 See Immanuel Kant, *Foundations of the Metaphysics of Morals* (New York: Bobbs-Merrill, 1959; first published in 1785); and Jeremy Bentham, *An Introduction to the Principles of Morals and Legislation*, new edition (Oxford: The Clarendon Press, 1823).

24 Goodpaster, "Egoism to Environmentalism." Actually Goodpaster regards *Hume* and Kant as the cofountainheads of this sort of moral philosophy. But Hume does not reason in this way. For Hume, the other-oriented sentiments are as primitive as self-love.

25 See Peter Singer, *Animal Liberation: A New Ethics for Our Treatment of Animals* (New York: Avon Books, 1975) for animal liberation; and see Tom Regan, *All That Dwell Therein: Animal Rights and Environmental Ethics* (Berkeley: University of California Press, 1982) for animal rights.

26 See Albert Schweitzer, *Philosophy of Civilization: Civilization and Ethics*, trans. John Naish (London: A. & C. Black, 1923). For a fuller discussion see J. Baird Callicott, "On the Intrinsic Value of Nonhuman Species," in *The Preservation of Species*, ed. Bryan Norton (Princeton: Princeton University Press, 1986), pp. 138–72.

27 Peter Singer and Tom Regan are both proud of this circumstance and consider it a virtue. See Peter Singer, "Not for Humans Only: The Place of Nonhumans in Environmental Issues" in *Ethics and Problems of the 21st Century*, pp. 191–206; and Tom Regan, "Ethical Vegetarianism and Commercial Animal Farming" in *Contemporary Moral Problems*, ed. James E. White (St Paul, Minn.: West Publishing Co., 1985), pp. 279–94.

28 See J. Baird Callicott, "Hume's *Is/Ought* Dichotomy and the Relation of Ecology to Leopold's Land Ethic," *Environmental Ethics* 4 (1982): 163–74; and "Non-anthropocentric Value Theory and Environmental Ethics," *American Philosophical Quarterly* 21 (1984): 299–309, for an elaboration.

29 Hume, *Enquiry*, p. 219, emphasis added.

30 Darwin, *Descent*, p. 120.

31 I have elsewhere argued that "value in the philosophical sense" means "intrinsic" or "inherent" value. See J. Baird Callicott, "The Philosophical Value of Wildlife," in *Valuing Wildlife: Economic and Social Values of Wildlife*, ed. Daniel J. Decker and Gary Goff (Boulder, Col.: Westview Press, 1986), pp. 214–21.

32 See Worster, *Nature's Economy*.

33 See J. Baird Callicott, "The Metaphysical Implications of Ecology," *Environmental Ethics* 8 (1986): 300–15, for an elaboration of this point.

34 Robert P. McIntosh, *The Background of Ecology: Concept and Theory* (Cambridge: Cambridge University Press, 1985).

35 Aldo Leopold, "Some Fundamentals of Conservation in the Southwest," *Environmental Ethics* 1 (1979): 139–40, emphasis added.

36 Arthur Tansley, "The Use and Abuse of Vegetational Concepts and Terms," *Ecology* 16 (1935): 292–303.

37 Harold J. Morowitz, "Biology as a Cosmological Science," *Main Currents in Modern Thought* 28 (1972): 156.

25   Gaia As Seen Through the Atmosphere

James E. Lovelock

The climate and the chemical composition of the Earth is usually said to be uniquely favourable for life; indeed, it is not commonly known how small are the changes which might render the planet unsuited for the contemporary biota. An increase in oxygen concentration to 25 per cent would so increase the probability of fires that even tropical rain forests might be in hazard. A change in atmospheric pressure of 10 per cent, assuming that the composition remained unchanged, would cause a change of 4°C in the mean surface temperature; enough to set the world on an unfavourable climatic course. These are but two examples chosen from many which might show just how well suited is the environment of Earth for life. Or is it more probable that the biosphere interacts actively with the environment so as to hold it at an optimum of its choosing?

The purpose of this letter is to suggest that life at an early stage of its evolution acquired the capacity to control the global environment to suit its needs and that this capacity has persisted and is still in active use. In this view the sum total of species is more than just a catalogue, "The Biosphere", and like other associations in biology is an entity with properties greater than the simple sum of its parts. Such a large creature, even if only hypothetical, with the powerful capacity to homeostat the planetary environment needs a name; I am indebted to Mr. William Golding for suggesting the use of the Greek personification of mother Earth, "Gaia".

As yet there exists no formal physical statement of life from which an exclusive test could be designed to prove the presence of "Gaia" as a living entity. Fortunately such rigour is not usually expected in biology and it may be that the statistical nature of life processes would render such an approach a sterile one. At present most biologists can be convinced that a creature is alive by arguments drawn from phenomenological evidence. The persistent ability to maintain a constant temperature and a compatible chemical composition in an environment which is changing or is perturbed if shown by a biological system would usually be accepted as evidence that it was alive. Let us consider the evidence of this nature which would point to the existence of Gaia.

During the period that life has existed on Earth, at least 3 giga-years, there have been profound changes in the chemical and physical environment: Rubey (1951), Cloud (1968), Holland (1964). The pE has gone from less than −5 to +13 and the output of radiant energy from the sun will have increased by approximately one astronomical order, if it is a typical star moving along the main sequence. The change from reducing to oxidizing conditions carried the atmosphere through a sequence of quite different chemical compositions and at the same time the solar output was steadily increasing; yet the geological record and the fact of the persistence of life shows that the surface temperature did not vary by more than a few degrees from its current levels. These changes in the Earth's environment probably, although not certainly, occurred slowly enough for life to adapt. Even so, it would have been a remarkable coincidence for these environmental changes always to have followed that narrow path whose bounds are the conditions permitting the continued existence of life. It is even more improbable that this could have happened in a system where the energy received from the sun was also changing by a substantial amount. In the face of these improbabilities the presence of a biological cybernetic system able to homeostat the planet for an optimum physical and chemical state appropriate to its current biosphere becomes a possibility.

Another body of evidence which favours the existence of Gaia comes from a consideration of the contemporary atmospheres of the Earth and of Mars. It has frequently been stated, Lewis and Randall (1923), Hutchinson (1954), Sillen (1966), that the presence of nitrogen in the present atmosphere is a chemical anomaly, for the stable form of the element nitrogen at the present state of oxidation of the Earth is the

From *Atmospheric Environment*, vol. 6, no. 8 (1972): 579–80.© 1972 by Elsevier Ltd. Reprinted with permission from Elsevier.

nitrate ion in solution in the oceans. An even greater chemical disparity is the simultaneous presence of oxygen and of methane in the air. In fact a close examination of the composition of the atmosphere reveals that it has departed so far from any conceivable abiological steady state equilibrium that it is more consistent in composition with a mixture of gases contrived for some specific purpose. Such an examination was used to prove that the presence of life on Earth could be inferred simply from a knowledge of the chemical composition of the atmosphere (Hitchcock and Lovelock, 1967). The cratered moonlike appearance of Mars revealed by the television experiment aboard the 1965 Mariner space craft (Leighton et al., 1965) suggested that Mars was unlikely to bear life. This evidence together with the arguments above were used (Lovelock and Giffen, 1969) to predict that Mars would have little or no nitrogen in its atmosphere.

Finally it can be shown that if life on Earth were to cease, the oxygen and the nitrogen would decline in concentration until they were both trace components in an atmosphere of water vapour, carbon dioxide and noble gases. Earth without life would have an atmosphere whose chemical composition was a reasonable interpolation between those of Mars and Venus and appropriate to its station in the solar system. Life is abundant on Earth and the chemically reactive gases almost all have their principal sources and sinks in the biosphere. This taken with the evidence above is sufficient to justify the probability that the atmosphere is a biological contrivance, a part and a property of Gaia. If this is assumed to be true then it follows that she who controls the atmospheric composition must also be able to control the climate. In this hypothesis the air is not to be thought of as a living part of Gaia but rather as an essential but non-living component which can be changed or adapted as the needs require. Like the fur of a mink or the shell of a snail.

The concept of Gaia has been intuitively familiar throughout history and perhaps only recently has it been distorted by anthropocentric rationalizations. One of these, fashionable in discourse upon the "Environment", is that we are travellers within the "Space Ship Earth" and that the biosphere is there as a "Life Support System", presumably for our special benefit. Analogies of this form are used in considerations of the possible consequences of species deletions, destructive changes of the land surfaces by farming and pollution. They are both misleading and unnecessary as a replacement for the older concept of the Earth as a very large living creature, Gaia, several giga-years old who has moulded the surface, the oceans, and the air to suit her and for the very brief time we have been part of her, our needs.

References

Cloud P. E. (1968) Atmospheric and hydrospheric evolution of the primitive earth. *Science* **160**, 729–36.

Holland H. D. (1964) On the chemical evolution of the terrestrial and cytherean atmospheres. In *The Origin and Evolution of the Atmospheres and Oceans* (edited by Brancazio P. J. and Cameron A. G. W.) 86–91. Wiley, New York.

Hitchcock D. R. and Lovelock J. E. (1967) Life detection by atmospheric analysis. *Icarus* 7, 149–59.

Hutchinson G. E. (1954) The biochemistry of the terrestrial atmosphere. In *The Earth as a Planet* (edited by Kuiper G. P.) pp. 371–433. Chicago Univ. Press.

Leighton R. B., Murray B. C., Sharp R. P., Denton Allen J. and Sloan R. K. (1965) Mariner IV. Photography of Mars; initial results. *Science* **169**, 627–30.

Lewis G. N. and Randall M. (1923) *Thermodynamics and the Free Energy of Chemical Substrates*, Chapter 39, McGraw-Hill, New York.

Lovelock J. E. and Giffen C. E. (1969) In *Advanced Space Experiments* (edited by Tiffany O. L. and Zaiteff E.) p. 179. American Astronautical Society, Washington, DC.

Rubey W. W. (1951) Geolic history of sea water. *Geol. Soc. Am. Bull.* **62**, 1111–47.

C General Ethics

26 Developing a General Ethics (with Particular Reference to the Built, or Human-Constructed, Environment)

Warwick Fox

The Ethical Challenge Posed by the Built (or Human-Constructed) Environment

If (for us) a basic way of dividing the world up is between humans and everything else, which we assign to the general category of "the environment," then surely interhuman ethics taken together with environmental ethics just about wraps things up in terms of the possible range of ethical concerns, doesn't it? What else is there besides humans on the one hand and everything else on the other hand? What else *could* we give ethical attention to?

The problem inherent in this line of thinking lies in the fact that the term *environmental ethics*, as it has been used to date at least, is either a misnomer or else the field of inquiry it describes has not lived up to its own name. The reason is this: when we look around the world – our "environment" – we see people, other animals, trees and plants, rain clouds (evidence of ecospherical hydrological cycles) and so on, but we also see buildings, roads, cars, and so on. The world around us – our "environment" – consists not only of a self-organizing, natural environment but also of an intentionally organized, artificial, built, or human-constructed environment (as well as all manner of combinations of these two kinds of environments). Indeed, many of us in the modern world seem to have even more day-to-day contact with intentionally organized, human-constructed environments

than self-organizing, natural environments. And yet the main approaches to environmental ethics to date have been overwhelmingly concerned with the *natural* environment (or various members or aspects of it) – sentient beings, living things, ecological integrity – and have had very little to say about the intentionally organized, artificial, built, or human-constructed environment.[1] Thus, the term *environmental ethics* has effectively meant the *ethics of the natural environment* (or some subset of it such as individual animals and plants).

But the natural environment and the human-constructed environment are quite different kinds of environments and they can prompt quite different kinds of ethical questions. Even if we set aside the profound implications that questions concerning how we build and live in human-constructed environments have for the natural environment (which is a lot to set aside, since the fate of the natural, "green bits" of the planet is now completely bound up with how we build and live in the human-constructed, "brown bits" of the planet), there remain a multitude of important ethically related questions that we can ask about human-constructed environments themselves.

Consider this example: suppose we take two buildings and, for argument's sake, specify the following about them: (i) both have the same overall environmental impact; neither detracts from whatever value we might assign to ecological integrity any more than the other (and we'll also assume here that neither

From *A Theory of General Ethics: Human Relationships, Nature, and the Built Environment* (Cambridge, MA: The MIT Press, 2006), 2,500-word extract from pp. 9–15 (with minor modifications). © 2006 by Massachusetts Institute of Technology. By permission of The MIT Press.

contributes to harming individual sentient beings or living things in general any more than the other); (ii) one of these buildings, to your and my discerning eyes, is "as ugly as sin," "sticks out like a sore thumb," is a "blot upon the landscape," and so on, while the other fits in beautifully with its surrounding landscape – "the line of its roof echoes those hills over there," and so on; and (iii) notwithstanding the previous point, it turns out that people in general "don't mind" the contextually ill-fitting building when their preferences are considered overall – in fact, maybe they even prefer it overall – because, whatever its faults, it is "just so convenient," or offers easier parking, or has stores that offer cheaper prices. Who knows, perhaps other people "don't mind" or even come to "really like" the contextually ill-fitting building out of some kind of perverse pride in the fact that it has helped to "put the place on the map." Whatever the reasons, suppose that these reasons get all mixed together with whatever preferences people might (or, alas, might not) have in terms of architectural design such that the users of the contextually ill-fitting building come to see it as not even being particularly ugly or ill-fitting – or perhaps just come not to *see* it in various ways, such as in terms of any wider contextual understanding.

Surely there are ethically related questions that we can ask about these buildings, and foremost among them is this: Should we build in the contextually ill-fitting way described in (ii) even if it's no worse, ecologically speaking, than building in more landscape-fitting ways, and even if people "don't mind" – or even come to prefer – the contextually ill-fitting building to the landscape-fitting building when their preferences are considered overall? Is doing this consistent with the values we should live by? Or should people prioritize their preferences such that cheaper prices or more parking or "putting the place on the map" is simply not a good enough reason to accept contextually ill-fitting buildings – especially since there is no reason in principle why these features cannot also be offered by a contextually fitting building. If we think that building in the contextually ill-fitting way is consistent with the values we should live by, then we would probably feel that we ought to describe any personal preference that we might have for the landscape-fitting building as just that – as "just a personal preference," or as "just an aesthetic preference." But what if we think that we should take our spontaneous expression upon seeing this building that "there ought to be a law against it"

seriously? What if we think that there is something wrong *in principle* with building in the contextually ill-fitting way? What if we think that we should not live by the kinds of values that would sanction this kind of building (a building that seems to exemplify a disconnection from and even a sense of contempt for its surroundings)? Under these circumstances, we do not consider ourselves to be talking about a merely "personal" or "aesthetic" preference. Rather, we consider ourselves to be talking about an ethically based objection to building in the contextually ill-fitting way – an objection that obtains regardless of points (i) and (iii) in the above example.

But on what grounds can we make such an ethically based objection? The older forms of interhuman ethics can't help us here in any direct way because these older forms of ethics value people and people alone, and we've already seen in the example given that people either don't have much of a preference either way in regard to these buildings or else actually prefer the contextually ill-fitting building overall. The newer forms of environmental ethics can't help us in any direct way either. As specified in the example, neither of the buildings is any worse than the other in terms of detracting from ecological integrity (and we also assumed here that neither contributes to harming individual sentient beings or living things in general any more than the other). How, then, can these newer approaches hope to get any purchase on the issue – an issue that resides at the intangible and ephemeral level of contextually related design?

This example highlights a profoundly important problem. Quite apart from their ecological implications, there are many serious, ethically based problems – problems relating directly to the values we should live by – that we ought to be able to explore in regard to our (too often thoroughly dispiriting) human-constructed environments. Yet we have no language, no framework, for approaching these problems as *ethical* problems. We spontaneously say "There ought to be a law against it" when we see certain kinds of buildings – which is a strongly formulated normatively loaded reaction – yet we then back down when challenged on our view by describing our reaction as a merely "personal preference" or "aesthetic preference." I think we do this because we don't know how to say in *ethically* weighted terms what we really want to be able to say.

If this is right, then we ultimately need an approach to ethics that goes beyond even the newer, natural-environment- (and natural entities-) oriented approaches that have been developed to date, since, like interhuman ethics, these approaches cannot offer us any direct help when we start to consider certain kinds of problems relating to how we should proceed in regard to our intentionally organized, human-constructed environment. If we think of the world as consisting of a biophysical realm (which includes ecosystems and the plants and animals that live in them), a realm of symbolic culture (which is constituted by language-using human moral agents), and a realm of material culture (which includes all the "stuff" that humans make), then we can see that whereas the older forms of interhuman ethics were concerned only with those entities that exist in the second of these realms (i.e., humans), the newer forms of (so-called) "environmental" ethics – the animal welfare, life-based, and ecosystem integrity approaches – have been concerned with both the first and the second of these realms (since any argument for the value of nonhuman biophysical entities either builds on or automatically incorporates an argument for the value of humans). This is an improvement: giving ethical attention to two out of these three realms is better than giving it to just one of them. But a *comprehensive* approach to ethics would provide a unified framework for directly addressing ethical problems in all three realms.

The Idea of a General Ethics

I refer to such a comprehensive approach to ethics – an approach that is concerned with giving ethical attention to all three realms, and doing so within an integrated theoretical framework – as a *General Ethics*. (I capitalize this term to mark it out as the name of a field of inquiry and to distinguish it from coincidental or haphazard references to "general ethics" or "ethics in general," by which an author may well mean something much more limited.) In the light of what I've explained here, we can set out this conception of General Ethics almost as a kind of simple equation:

> General Ethics = {interhuman ethics + animal welfare ethics + life-based ethics + ecosystem integrity ethics + ethics of the human-constructed environment}

It should immediately be noted here, however, that I have placed curly brackets around this sum specifically to suggest that General Ethics is not concerned simply with adding together different "bits" of the ethical approaches that are listed – as if that could be done coherently! – but rather with the development of an *integrated approach* that covers all these areas. Thus, "{}" does not mean "simply add together what is inside the brackets," but rather "replace what is inside the brackets with a single integrated approach that both covers all the areas referred to inside the brackets *and* irons out the wrinkles between them." Developing an "{}" approach to any area amounts to theoretical progress in that area. It is good work if you can get it!

With this understanding in mind, we can simplify the above "equation" as follows:

> General Ethics = {interhuman ethics + ethics of the natural environment + ethics of the human-constructed environment}

Or even:

> General Ethics = {the older forms of ethics + the newer forms of ethics + some even newer form of ethics}

Having now explained what I mean by a General Ethics, it is relatively straightforward to explain why we need such an ethics. First, as we have just seen in regard to the example of the two buildings, we cannot adequately deal with all the ethical problems that we ought to be able to deal with *as* ethical problems if we do not have an ethical framework that can incorporate but also go beyond both interhuman ethical concerns and ethical concerns relating to the natural environment (including natural entities). Second, anyone who works in either the older or newer fields of ethics that I have referred to knows that "they do not add up"; they simply cannot be "glued together" in their present forms in order to produce some seamless "super-theory" of ethics that would constitute, say, two-thirds of a truly General Ethics. Not only are there spectacular conflicts between the claims endorsed by the older, anthropocentric forms of ethics and the newer, nonanthropocentric approaches to ethics, but there are likewise spectacular conflicts between the claims endorsed by the newer forms of ethics themselves – especially between the more individualistic approaches and the more holistic approaches.[2]

In my view, then, we badly need two things. First, we need an ethics that will allow us directly to address ethical problems (i.e., problems regarding the values we should live by) across the broadest possible range of domains of interest (i.e., including all three realms outlined above). Second, we need this ethics in a unified or integrated form; we need an ethics that can account in its own way for all the points that are worthwhile in the various "smaller" ethical approaches that have been developed to date, and yet one that can do this in the context of an over-arching theory that offers clear priority rules when different kinds or levels of value come into tension or outright conflict. To have these two things – to have a unified theoretical framework that allows us directly to address ethical problems across the broadest possible range of domains of interest – is to have a General Ethics.

The Theory of Responsive Cohesion

I refer to my own approach to General Ethics as the *theory of responsive cohesion*. In order to understand this theory properly, it is necessary to understand four things about it: (i) the theory's proposal that things – anything at all – can potentially assume one of three basic forms of organization (we can also refer to these as three basic kinds of *relational qualities*); (ii) the argument for the superiority of one of these forms of organization – one of these relational qualities – over the other two and, indeed, for the claim that this superior form of organization represents the *foundational value*, by which I mean the most basic value we can find; (iii) the development of this idea regarding the best form of organization into a full-blown *theory of contexts*; and (iv) the development of ideas relating to the previous two points into a *differentiated model of our obligations in respect of all beings*. Here, however, I must confine my attention to a brief summary of the first three points only since to enter into the fourth point would take us well beyond what can sensibly be summarized in an article of this length. Even so, doing this much will enable us to see how the theory of responsive cohesion is able to address the kind of two buildings problem – and, more generally, the kind of contextual fit problem – that I outlined above. This represents an important focus of interest for present purposes because if an ethical approach cannot directly address this kind of two buildings problem (which represents a paradigmatic example of a problem that applies to the human-constructed realm as

such), then it is not even a candidate for an approach that could be developed into a General Ethics as I have defined that above.[3]

The theory of responsive cohesion proceeds from the claim that things can be organized in any of three basic ways (and it is important to note at the outset that these categories can be applied literally or meta-phorically to anything at all, whether physical or non-physical). The most basic distinction we can make about things in terms of their organization is simply to note whether they can be characterized as organized or as "holding together" or cohering in some way or whether they can't (bearing in mind that there are all manner of gradations between these contrasts). This is a fundamental distinction that we make all the time. Within the category of organization (as opposed to disorganization), we can make a further basic distinction between those things that can be characterized as organized, "holding together," or cohering in a relatively fixed or regimented way and those that can be characterized as organized, "holding together," or cohering by virtue of the mutual responsiveness of their constituent elements. Note that this notion of responsiveness – of elements answering to each other – can be understood not only in *literal* terms but also in *metaphorical* terms (e.g., the compositional elements of a good painting can be said to answer or be responsive to each other in metaphorical terms) and not only in *intentional* terms but also in *functional* terms (e.g., none of the elements of a living system such as a plant consciously intends anything but they are nevertheless exquisitely responsive to each other in functional terms).

This gives us three basic ways in which things can be organized: they can be organized in a way that is fixed or regimented; they can be organized in such a way that they hold together by virtue of the mutual responsiveness of (or mutual interdependencies between) their constituent elements; or they can be disorganized. I refer to these three categories as *fixed cohesion*, *responsive cohesion*, and *discohesion*, respectively. Examples of fixed cohesion tend to be described in terms of being locked into a fixed, regimented, rigid, frozen, forced, mechanical, or formulaic pattern; examples of discohesion as being chaotic, anarchic, or "all over the place"; and examples of responsive cohesion as having a fluid, adaptive, creative, organic, "alive" quality about them.

The theory of responsive cohesion advances the claim that in any genuinely open consideration of the matter – that is, a situation in which consideration of one of these forms of organization is not defined out of the picture from the outset – it is always the example that exemplifies the most responsively cohesive form of organization that is typically judged to be the best example of its kind by informed judges – or that (for reasons that I simply cannot pursue here for reasons of space) ought to be judged to be the best example of its kind.[4]

The first substantive thing to note about this claim is that it is not just a claim about what we find *when* we bring informed judgment to bear upon a problem situation, as if the notion of informed judgment were a tool that floats free of the theory of responsive cohesion itself. Rather, this claim is intended to apply even to our most informed judgments about what constitutes an informed judgment. Let me illustrate this. Even if a view holds together internally (i.e., is internally cohesive), we do not think that it represents an informed judgment if it is a fixed and dogmatic view (i.e., if it is *unresponsive* to or does not *cohere* with relevant reasons and evidence). Rather, such a view represents an example of *fixed cohesion* in the domain of ideas or judgments. On the other hand, we do not think that a view that is internally inconsistent, that "doesn't hold together," or "doesn't add up" (i.e., a view that is discohesive) represents an informed judgment either. Rather, such a view represents an example of *discohesion* in the domain of ideas or judgments. Instead, our most informed judgments *about* what constitutes an informed judgment suggest that an informed judgment is a view that is based on and remains open to reasons and evidence (i.e., a view that *answers to* or is *responsive to* relevant reasons and evidence) while also "holding together" internally. And a view of this kind is clearly an example of *responsive cohesion* in the domain of ideas or judgments. Thus, the relational quality of responsive cohesion lies at the heart of the mode of reasoning we consider to be involved in making any genuinely informed judgment.

But the theory of responsive cohesion does not just advance the view that responsive cohesion is the most valuable form of organization at the level of our most informed judgments about what constitutes an informed judgment. Rather, to repeat, the theory of responsive cohesion advances the claim that our most informed judgments suggest that responsive cohesion is the most valuable form of organization in *any* area we care to consider. Let's therefore quickly consider some other examples across realms as broad as science, ethics, psychology, and politics.

In the realms of both science and ethics, informed judges typically consider both rigid adherence to a theory in the face of significantly differing reasons and evidence *and* the complete lack of a theory (such that one lives in a "wilderness of single instances") to represent bad examples of science and ethics. These two ways of proceeding represent examples of *fixed cohesion* and *discohesion*, respectively, at the level of theory. In contrast, good procedure in both science and ethics consists in there being a *responsive cohesion* between theory and observations in the case of science and between theory and particular moral judgments (sometimes referred to, albeit often misleadingly, as "moral intuitions") in the case of ethics.

In the realm of psychology, informed judges typically consider a person to be in "good (psychological) shape" when there is a *responsive cohesion* between their thoughts, emotions, and desires (i.e., when the various elements of their psyche "answer" to each other). In contrast, we consider a person to be in "bad (psychological) shape" when they feel compelled to do the same things in the same ways (we say that they are "stuck in a rut" or "acting like a zombie") or when they seem to be (psychologically) "all over the place," "a mess," "crazy," and so on. The latter two ways of being represent examples of *fixed cohesion* and *discohesion*, respectively, at the level of psychological organization.

In the realm of politics, informed judges typically consider that the best forms of politics are those in which there is a *responsive cohesion* between a government and the population it governs, that is, where there are mechanisms in place to ensure that the government answers to the people (e.g., through democratic elections, an independent judiciary, and a free press) and that people answer to the government (e.g., through the rule of law). In contrast, informed judges typically consider that the worst forms of politics consist in situations in which rulers dictate to the people but are not answerable to them (as in dictatorships) or in which there is no government and everyone is a "law unto themselves" (anarchy). Again, the latter two ways of proceeding represent examples of *fixed cohesion* and *discohesion*, respectively, at the level of political organization.

We can extend this kind of analysis to as many other domains of interest as we like, but the point I'm trying to convey very briefly here is the idea that *whatever* domain of interest we wish to consider – whether it be scientific theories, ethics, psychology, politics, or others such as conversations, personal relationships generally, economics, organizational management, skills (including sports) and the arts, the natural environment, and the human-constructed environment – we will find that it is always the example that most exemplifies the relational quality of responsive cohesion that is typically judged to be the best example of its kind. But note the full implications of this conclusion. We are not saying merely that valuable things have this feature of responsive cohesion *in common*, but something much deeper. This is because this conclusion is based on a level of analysis that concerns the most basic distinctions that we can make in regard to the very organization of things. Thus, if we find that one of these fundamental forms of organization – responsive cohesion – is consistently found to underpin our most informed judgments of value, then we have reached rock bottom in our search for the basis of value. I therefore refer to responsive cohesion as the *foundational value*.

If we are persuaded by the idea that responsive cohesion is the foundational value – the most fundamental value there is – then it follows that we should live or be guided by this foundational value to the extent that we reasonably can because the best answer to the question "What value or values should we live by?" is not, say, the 26th most fundamental value we can find, or even the 3rd most fundamental value we can find, but rather *the* most fundamental value we can find. (Indeed, it is worth noting here that the relational quality of responsive cohesion is, in my view, not only the most fundamental *value* we can find but that it even underpins the process of *valuing*. This is because the brain itself is organized in a responsively cohesive way – there's no central organizing factor or feature in the brain that dictates what all the other parts will do; rather, the brain is constituted by an astonishingly rich network of neurons and neuronal connections that are exquisitely responsive to each other – so even the brain and, thus, consciousness and, thus, the very possibility of valuing is underpinned by this feature of responsive cohesion.)

What would it mean to live by the foundational value of responsive cohesion? One important implication is that it would lead us to think about things much more in terms of how they fit with their contexts. This follows from the fact that when we think about the idea of responsive cohesion further, we can see that it becomes necessary to distinguish between *internal* responsive cohesion and *contextual*

responsive cohesion. Consider the following. Suppose you've just put a tremendous amount of work into composing a beautiful symphony and that this symphony has a very responsively cohesive structure; its various elements play into and play off each other in a way that makes them seem like they all belong together; the composition "works." But suppose you then introduce some new bars of music into this symphony that have this characteristic: even though they fit together very well when considered in their own right, they simply don't fit with the overall structure of the symphony you've composed (they are metaphorically and perhaps also literally off key relative to the rest of the symphony). This means that although the new bars of music exhibit an *internal* form of responsive cohesion, they don't fit with the *contextual* responsive cohesion that is represented by the overall symphony. What are you going to do? If you live by the foundational value of responsive cohesion, then the obvious thing to do is to substantially modify or else reject the smaller ill-fitting new part of the symphony because if you tried to turn the whole symphony into something that would fit with this smaller ill-fitting new part, then you'd be undoing lots of responsive cohesion (namely, the rest of the symphony) to fit in with just a small bit of responsive cohesion (namely, the smaller ill-fitting part). Moreover, if you modified the whole to fit with the part every time you introduced some new part that didn't fit (imagine some builders doing this in your house!), then you'd be remaking the whole on an ongoing basis. This would represent the functional equivalent of discohesion rather than responsive cohesion.

The message here is that although any *individual* example of responsive cohesion is a *good* thing, the widest *context* in which we can find or realize this form of organization is the *best* thing. This means that, on the whole, internal forms of responsive cohesion need to be modified to fit with contextual forms of responsive cohesion rather than the other way around. Note, however, that none of these comments regarding the most appropriate *direction of fit* between contextual and internal forms of responsive cohesion should be taken to imply that contextual forms of responsive cohesion should ride roughshod over internal forms of responsive cohesion. Rather, responsively cohesive modification can occur in both directions; it is just that living by the foundational value of responsive cohesion necessarily commits us to the view that contextual forms of responsive cohesion should always be given proportionately more weight in our deliberations than internal forms of responsive cohesion since this is the best way in which we can create and preserve examples of responsive cohesion. However, if this kind of (proportionately weighted) mutual modification is simply not possible because there is an outright clash between contextual and internal forms of responsive cohesion, then, clearly, contextual responsive cohesion should prevail over internal responsive cohesion.

These considerations bring us to a crucial question, namely: What is the widest responsively cohesive context that we can think of for all earthly purposes? The answer is the Earth itself: the largest example of responsive cohesion we can think of for all earthly purposes is the way in which the ecosphere – sometimes referred to these days as *Gaia* (after the Greek goddess of the earth; from Greek *gaia* earth) – maintains its integrity over time through the mutual responsiveness of its component parts. Thus, if we accept the point that, on the whole, internal forms of responsive cohesion need to be modified to fit with contextual forms of responsive cohesion rather than the other way around, then it follows that the internal aspects of our Gaian context, including our social, political, and economic arrangements as well as the *human-created built environment* need to be modified to fit with that context, rather than the other way around.

This enables us to see how the theory of responsive cohesion can respond to the kind of two buildings problem – and, more generally, the kind of contextual fit problem – that I introduced earlier. In brief, the advice that the theory has for architects, designers, builders, and planners can be summarized as follows.

> When you make material things, make them so that they exemplify both contextual and internal responsive cohesion. If tough choices have to be made between these two forms of responsive cohesion, then give priority to contextual responsive cohesion over internal responsive cohesion. And if tough choices have to be made between contextual forms of responsive cohesion themselves, then give priority to contextual responsive cohesion with (i) the natural realm over the human social realm (since the natural realm provides the wider, generative and sustaining context of the human social realm) and (ii) the human social realm over the human-constructed realm (since the human social realm provides the wider, generative and sustaining context of the human-constructed realm). But on no account

engage in prioritizing things in any of these ways unless you are confronted with a genuinely forced choice. The thing to aim for is responsive cohesion at all levels. To settle for less is actually to settle for a failure of design.

The theory of responsive cohesion clearly provides us with a basis for objecting to a building not only in terms of its failure to be responsive to the physical ecological integrity of its surroundings but also – and this was the point of my two buildings example – in terms of its failure to be responsive to its biophysical, social, and built contexts (in that order of priority) at the more intangible level of its design. Moreover, the basis of this objection is fundamentally an ethical one rather than "merely" an aesthetic one because ethics is concerned with the values we should live by and this response proceeds from us living by the deepest value we can find, namely, the foundational value of responsive cohesion.

Now some of what I've said here has been fairly abstract but I've tried to point you in the direction of a fundamental and deep idea, the kind of idea we're going to need to adopt as a society if we are to get beyond individualistic thinking and begin to think in terms of contexts and the value of certain kinds of contexts relative to others. My own view is that we will not as a society be sufficiently motivated to organize how we live and what we make in contextually sensitive ways (including, but not only, ecologically sensitive ways) until we come to see that the relational quality of responsive cohesion actually represents the deepest value there is. If we collectively come to see this, then we will find ourselves far more motivated to engage in the kind of *context saturated thinking* that the adoption of this foundational value brings in its wake and that is clearly crucial to the future of life on Earth – both human and nonhuman.

If there is a "take-home message" of the theory of responsive cohesion, it is this:

> In being responsive to your own goals and desires – that is, in living *your* life – do what you reasonably can to *preserve* examples of the relational quality of responsive cohesion where you find them, *regenerate or create* examples of it in and through your chosen undertakings, *reflect and reinforce* it in your judgments and ways of proceeding, and so on.

If sufficient people and sufficient powers-that-be took the framework offered by the theory of responsive cohesion seriously, then we would live in a world that was more ecologically coherent, more demo-cratic, and in which human institutions and the human-constructed features of the world were designed so as to be responsively cohesive with the natural world and the needs and desires of people (in that order of priority if necessary). A world that was more responsively cohesive along these lines would, according to the theory of responsive cohesion, be a better world because it would exemplify the founda-tional value of responsive cohesion far more than our world presently does.

Notes

1   For further elaboration of this point by myself and others see Warwick Fox, "Introduction: Ethics and the Built Environment," in Warwick Fox, ed., *Ethics and the Built Environment* (London: Routledge, 2000), pp. 1–12. This introduction also contains references to the few previous contributions to the ethics of the human-constructed environment.

2   Recent research suggests that the second leading cause of loss of biodiversity in the world today is that of intro-duced species that have become invasive and out-com-peted the indigenous species: see Bob Holmes, "Day of the Sparrow," *New Scientist* (June 27, 1998): 32–5; Chris Bright, *Life Out of Bounds: Bioinvasion in a Borderless World* (London: Earthscan, 1999). What to do? In the case of invasive (nonhuman) animals (e.g., feral cats and foxes in Australia), the animal liberation-ist – and certainly the animal rights – advocate is com-mitted to saying, in effect, "Leave the invasive animals alone; they have as much right to live as any other ani-mals," whereas the ecocentrist is committed to saying "Do whatever is necessary to get rid of the invasive ani-mals; we have a duty to preserve the characteristic diversity of this region." (There are real-world examples

of precisely this sort of confrontation.) This kind of situation therefore presents us with an argument, at minimum, between human-centered concerns, animal welfare concerns, and ecological concerns – and this is before we even begin to explore the differences between different kinds of anthropocentric approaches them-selves, different kinds of animal welfare approaches, and different kinds of ecocentric approaches. For more on this general theme see J. Baird Callicott, "Animal Liberation: A Triangular Affair," *Environmental Ethics* 2 (1980): 311–38; Mark Sagoff, "Animal Liberation and Environmental Ethics: Bad Marriage, Quick Divorce," reprinted in Michael Zimmerman, gen. ed., *Environmental Philosophy: From Animal Rights to Radical Ecology*, 3rd edn. (Upper Saddle River, NJ: Prentice Hall, 2001), pp. 87–96.

3   For the full development of the theory of responsive cohesion see Warwick Fox, *A Theory of General Ethics: Human Relationships, Nature, and the Built Environment* (Cambridge, MA: The MIT Press, 2006). Note that in addition to developing the theory of responsive cohe-sion in this book I also apply it to eighteen central prob-lems that any General Ethics must be able to address. The first seventeen of these problems consist of central problems relating to interhuman ethics, animal welfare ethics, life-based ethics, and ecological integrity ethics. Here, however, I am simply confining my attention to an outline of some (but, as noted, not all) of the basics of the theory and to the application of the theory to what I refer to in *A Theory of General Ethics* as "Problem 18: The Human-Constructed Environment Problem or the Comprehensiveness Problem." (I give this "Human-Constructed Environment Problem" a dual name because it represents a test for the comprehensiveness of any approach that is already able to address central prob-lems relating to interhuman ethics and the ethics of the natural environment.)

4   See *A Theory of General Ethics*, pp. 86–7, for more on this caveat.

PART V

WHAT ARE THE PROMINENT ALTERNATIVES TO GROUNDING ENVIRONMENTAL ETHICS IN AXIOLOGY?

A   Environmental Psychologism

27   The Shallow and the Deep Ecology Movement
     Arne Naess

28   The Heart of Deep Ecology
     Andrew McLaughlin

29   The Deep Ecological Movement: Some Philosophical Aspects
     Arne Naess

30   Transpersonal Ecology
     Warwick Fox

B   Environmental Virtue Ethics

31   Environmental Virtue Ethics
     Ronald Sandler

C   Continental Environmental Ethics

32   On Environmental Philosophy and Continental Thought
     Steven Vogel

D   Political Environmental Ethics

Social Ecology

33   What Is Social Ecology?
     Murray Bookchin

34   Socialism and Ecology
     James O'Connor

Ecological Feminism

35 The Power and the Promise of Ecological Feminism
    Karen J. Warren

36 Feminism and the Philosophy of Nature
    Carolyn Merchant

37 Nature, Self, and Gender: Feminism, Environmental Philosophy,
    and the Critique of Rationalism
    Val Plumwood

E   Environmental Pragmatism

38 Beyond Intrinsic Value: Pragmatism in
    Environmental Ethics
    Anthony Weston

39 Methodological Pragmatism, Pluralism, and
    Environmental Ethics
    Andrew Light

F   Direct Action

40 Earth First!
    Dave Foreman

The Ethics of Ecological Sabotage: An Exchange

41 Ecological Sabotage: Pranks or Terrorism?
    Eugene Hargrove

42 Earth First! and *The Monkey Wrench Gang*
    Edward Abbey

43 More on Earth First! and *The Monkey Wrench Gang*
    Dave Foreman

44 Editor's Response
    Eugene Hargrove

Introduction

The story of environmental ethics during its watershed period of the 1970s and on into the early '80s is mostly a narrative about reassessing the proper class of entities worthy of moral considerability in light of the critique of anthropocentrism. If human beings are not the sole class of beings worthy of moral consideration, what is the class? What beings, besides humans, are intrinsically valuable? Subjects-of-a-life? Sentient vertebrates? All living things? Entire ecological systems?

Grounding ethics in ontology via axiology is habit for philosophers trained in the Anglo-American analytical tradition. While this approach predominated during the gestational phase of the field, six important alternatives have also emerged:

1 Environmental psychologism
2 Environmental virtue ethics
3 Continental environmental ethics
4 Political environmental ethics (social ecology and ecological feminism)
5 Environmental pragmatism
6 Direct action.[1]

Environmental Psychologism

Outside academe, environmental activists have enthusiastically adopted the deep ecology movement as an ideological platform. Acolytes of "deep ecology" range from bedraggled Earth First!ers dancing around campfires in satyr choruses to bespectacled philosophy professors clad in Harris Tweed traversing the quads of elite east coast colleges. This popularity makes it difficult to define "deep ecology" with precision.

Narrowly, academically, deep ecology is the psychologization of environmental ethics.[2] According to both Naess and Sessions, the norms of deep ecology precipitate directly from psychological awakening. Naess has maintained that deep ecology is essentially *descriptive*. Deep ecology is simply an enumeration of general principles that persons open to the direct apprehension of nature agree upon.

Three selections are stitched together at the start of this section (Naess's "The Shallow and the Deep Ecology Movement," Andrew McLaughlin's "The Heart of Deep Ecology," and excerpts from Naess's "The Deep Ecological Movement") to outline deep ecology as an environmental ethic. Deep ecology rests upon two principles: an axiology of egalitarian biocentrism and an ontology of metaphysical holism. Regarding the first, in the words of Naess, "*the equal right to live and blossom* is an intuitively clear and obvious value axiom."[3] The target of egalitarian biocentrism is any value hierarchy, evident in anthropocentrism (Descartes and Kant), hierarchical biocentrism (VanDeVeer, Rolston, and Ferré) and psychocentrism (Singer and Regan), which gives preference to certain kinds of organisms over others. Naess and Sessions, with Taylor, take egalitarianism seriously.[4]

Awareness of metaphysical holism is apprehended through a phenomenological process of enlightenment or "self-realization."[5] In this psychic process of awakening, the ontological boundaries of the self are pressed outward. More and more of the lifeworld is incorporated in the "self." This insight discloses that there is in reality only one big Self, the lifeworld. To mark the difference in conceptions of atomistic and ecological selfhood, the latter is capitalized: *Self-realization*. Once one awakens to the fact that ontological boundaries are illusory, one understands that biospherical interests are the same as one's own interests. (This is a sort of enlightened self-interest that reminds us of Callicott's Land Ethic.)

Australian philosopher Warwick Fox rejects the egalitarian biocentrism of orthodox deep ecology outright. Orthodox deep ecology, Fox contends, "does itself a disservice by employing a definition of anthropocentrism which is so overly exclusive that it condemns more or less *any* theory of value that attempts to guide 'realistic praxis.'"[6] Instead, Fox persuasively argues for a position which abandons egalitarian biocentrism and alternatively asserts that all biota *have* intrinsic value, but are not *equal* in intrinsic value because "richness of experience" differs.[7] On this point Fox aligns himself with the Whiteheadian-inspired environmental ethics of Frederick Ferré.

Yet Fox finds sage wisdom in the psychological approach to environmental ethics. Environmental psychologism discloses profound truths about the essence of ontological interconnectedness of the biosphere. Once ontological boundaries between living beings are recognized as illusory, one realizes that biospherical interests are one's own interests. To mark the difference between his sophisticated reformulation of deep ecological thinking from orthodox deep ecology, Fox renamed his theory transpersonal ecology, detailed in "Transpersonal Ecology as a Distinctive Approach to Ecophilosophy."

Environmental Virtue Ethics

Ethics, in the tradition set by ancient Greek philosophers, concerns how we ought best to live our lives.[8] Identifying rules may help, or, alternately, identifying the personality traits – the *character* – of the morally good person and then trying to model one's life on those character traits, or virtues. This difference of emphasis, which is woven throughout the history of moral philosophy, has also surfaced in environmental ethics.

The environmentally virtuous person is the person who has the disposition to live his or her life as best as possible in the webwork of ecological relationships that structure the biosphere. While rule ethics emphasizes adherence to guidelines of conduct, such as Leopold's maxim, environmental virtue ethicists emphasize the disposition of the type of person who treats nonhuman nature with the respect it deserves. As in mainstream moral philosophy, typically a role model is held up as an exemplar of environmental virtue – Henry David Thoreau or Aldo Leopold or Rachel Carson,[9] or activists who dedicate their lives to the preservation and protection of nonhuman nature, or the person who lives life sustainably by gauging the effects her actions will have seven generations in the future.[10]

Actions may be condemned on account of environmental vice. In Salt Lake City, Utah, burglars severely beat a two-and-a-half-year-old cocker spaniel-poodle mix, causing intracranial hemorrhaging and brain damage, because he barked. On their arrival home, the owners found their pet having a seizure.[11] What kind of morally repugnant person would cause this kind of suffering to a sentient being? The environmental virtue ethicist, joining Singer, Regan, and Kant, would argue that this person is an archetype of moral turpitude.

American philosopher Ronald Sandler, in "Environmental Virtue Ethics," identifies four strategies for formulating a virtue-based environmental ethic. First, one might extrapolate standard interpersonal virtues of human relationships, such as temperance and generosity, to relationships with the natural environment. Second, one might identify virtues that benefit its possessor (Sandler does not mention Socrates' final answer to Thrasymachus regarding the virtue of justice, but this seems to the point). Third, one might identify virtues which promote flourishing – in this case, not just human social flourishing, but also biocommunity flourishing. Fourth, one might identify role models of environmental sensitivity – Sandler mentions Rachel Carson, Aldo Leopold, John Muir, and Julia Butterfly Hill, the indefatigable tree-sitter – as examples. Taken together, Sandler concludes, collectively these four strategies provide a rich resource for outlining an environmental virtue ethic.

Continental Environmental Ethics

We have seen how the development of environmental ethics through its formative years of the 1970s and '80s occurred primarily in the spirit of the Anglo-American analytic tradition. This involved the axiological analysis of the proper sphere of moral considerability, and then the application of normative categories to the entities fortunate enough to fall within those limits.

In the late 1980s, philosophers schooled in the continental tradition became interested in environmental ethics and the tenor of the publications that emerged as a result was very different from what had come before. Rather than analyze moral categories and extend conventional moral paradigms to nonhuman nature, these philosophers instead focused on the experiential dimensions of the human/nonhuman dynamic. Not surprisingly, they have found inspiration in the continental European phenomenological tradition which tends to emphasize ontology over ethics.[12]

As American philosopher Steven Vogel describes in "Nature as Origin and Difference," instead of grounding environmental ethics in the analysis of axiology, continental environmental ethicists began to look to German and French philosophers for clues about how humans experience nonhuman nature and how these experiences inform the way in which we should live given our ontological place in the wider horizon of the lifeworld. These philosophers have found valuable resources in the phenomenology of G. W. F. Hegel, Edmund Husserl, and Maurice

Merleau-Ponty, the hermeneutics of Martin Heidegger and Hans-Georg Gadamer, and the post-modernism of Jacques Derrida and Michel Foucault.

To give voice to these new approaches, in the mid-1990s the International Association for Environmental Philosophy (IAEP) was formed by members of the Society for Phenomenology and Existential Philosophy (SPEP), to better promote continental environmental ethics than the International Society for Environmental Ethics (ISEE) had done. The formation of these two different associations reflects different styles of doing environmental ethics, but is also an unfortunate polarization in the field. As American philosopher Anthony Weston observes, both approaches are needed: "We need to think more wildly and widely, and *also* more critically and carefully. We need to think globally *and* locally, and act globally *and* locally. We need to take heed of scientific and continental and Eastern and indigenous voices, but without just appropriating them."[13]

Many of the most creative talents in the field of environmental ethics traverse the analytic/continental divide, at times dropping into the Anglo-American watershed to analyze moral categories, and at other times descending into the continental basin to describe the ways in which nonhuman nature is experienced and what can be learned from that experience. I tried to meld the two approaches in an essay about being caught in a tornado, which in earlier drafts I entitled "The Physics and Phenomenology of a Tornado" to make explicit the appropriation of the two schools of twentieth-century philosophy.[14]

Political Environmental Ethics

For a number of environmental philosophers, a just social framework is a necessary precondition of a just ecological framework. Expanding the scope of moral considerability by way of axiology is one metaethical route to establishing a normative environmental ethic. However, a significant number of environmental philosophers have rejected this route altogether, instead focusing on critiques of hierarchies in human social structures which prop up anthropocentrism. For these philosophers, such hierarchies must be dismantled before ethical relationships to nonhuman nature can be realized. Social ecologists and ecological feminists have taken this route.

Over several decades, American political theorist Murray Bookchin has outlined an ethic which draws

parallels between social systems and ecological systems in a body of theory called social ecology and profiled in "What is Social Ecology?" According to Bookchin – and reminiscent of the organismic metaphysics of Bergson and Whitehead – the universe is striving, developing, and growing. Metaphysically, ecological systems and social systems are organically connected, both evolving, as parts of the biosphere, to ever-increasing complexity and diversity. Human consciousness is a gift from an inherent creative integrant (*telos*) of nature. Natural process is *good*:

> [F]rom the ever-greater complexity and variety that raises subatomic particles through the course of evolution to those conscious, self-reflexive life forms we call human beings, we cannot help but speculate about the existence of a broadly conceived *telos* and a latent subjectivity in substance itself that eventually yields mind and intellectuality. . . . Hence our study of nature . . . exhibits a self-evolving, patterning, a 'grain,' so to speak, that is implicitly ethical. Mutualism, freedom, and subjectivity are not strictly human values or concerns.[15]

Mutualism, freedom, and subjectivity are integral components of natural process. They indicate the intersection of ecological and social systems.

Social problems cause ecological problems because social systems and ecological systems are organically connected. These problems are problems of domination, socially by one group of humans over other groups (in class hierarchies), and ecologically by humans over nonhuman nature (in anthropocentric hierarchies). Unjust social frameworks of domination of one class over another class are inextricably linked to unjust ecological frameworks of domination of humans over nonhuman nature. This points to the central thesis of social ecology: ecological problems are rooted in class hierarchy. Social domination prefigures ecological domination, and, consequently, solving social problems is a necessary precondition to solving ecological problems.

Like Hegel and also Marx (whom he denounces, not without irony[16]), Bookchin has an acute sense of history. Bookchin argues that in primitive, preliterate societies, internal social relations were non-oppressive and mutualistic. These social relations paralleled external relations with the environment which were also non-oppressive and mutualistic. But, in time, elites sought to oppress and control plebeians through the creation of class divisions based on the valorization of human differences.[17] This led to the misguided idea of the human domination of nature and the destruction of nature.[18] In our time, the primary culprit in erecting hierarchies of domination is capitalism.

Bookchin is notorious for his denunciation of those whom he sees as guilty of misanthropy – the misanthropy of reducing humans from complex social beings to a scourge "overpopulating" the planet and "devouring" its resources.[19] Those guilty? Malthusians, deep ecologists, and Earth First!ers. The transgression of Malthus and neo-Malthusians such as Paul Erhlich and Garrett Hardin is to lay the blame of environmental degradation on a certain class of people – the overpopulating underclasses. As a humanistic thinker of the European Enlightenment tradition, Bookchin is sensitive to social injustice. Environmental problems must not be "solved" at the expense of the well-being of people. Neo-Malthusians, according to Bookchin, fail to realize the organic unity of social and environmental problems, and forsake social justice for biodiversity in misguided attempts to address the environmental degradation caused by capitalism.

Ecological feminists (or ecofeminists) also find political linkages between the social and ecological. As propounded by American philosopher Karen Warren in "The Power and the Promise of Ecological Feminism," ecological feminism reconceives feminism in a way that makes feminism environmental; and symmetrically, ecological feminism reconceives environmental ethics in a way that makes environmental ethics feminist. This reciprocal reconception is possible because patriarchy (the male domination of women) and anthropocentrism (the human domination of nonhuman nature) are based on the same *logic of domination*: bifurcation and prioritization. The logic of domination validates oppressive conceptual frameworks. An oppressive conceptual framework "explains, justifies, and maintains relationships of domination and subordination."[20]

In all forms, the logic of domination works in the same way: a category is bifurcated (man/woman, human/nature), and one category is prioritized over the other (man over woman, human over nonhuman). The logic of domination is used in other forms of domination besides patriarchy and humanism (racism, heteronormativity, ageism, classism, etc.). All of these oppressive conceptual frameworks are framed in terms of a value hierarchy.[21]

Ecological feminism starts with the project of dismantling the logic of domination which supports the oppressive conceptual framework of patriarchy. But because all oppressive conceptual frameworks are logically linked through the ubiquitous logic of domination, this project entails ending anthropocentrism (Warren uses the word "naturism" to describe the project[22]). Environmental ethics, in fact, is innately feminist because "failure to notice the connections between the twin oppressions of women and nature *is* male-gender bias."[23]

In "Ecofeminism and Feminist Theory," American ecofeminist philosopher and historian of science Carolyn Merchant compares and contrasts ecofeminism with liberal feminism, Marxist feminism, radical feminism, and socialist feminism. This is followed by a lucid and influential critique of the view of nature-as-machine (mechanism). In excerpts from *The Death of Nature*, Merchant depicts the pre-modern conception of nature as organic. Nature, as organic, was associated with the feminine (as in the notion of Mother Earth). The modern conception of nature is mechanistic. This conception furthers the project of the domination of nature, which is a masculine impulse. The domination of nature is to be achieved through science.

Ecological feminism can also be understood as virtue ethics. As American psychologist Carol Gilligan describes the manner in which women tend to make moral judgments based on relationships, rather than through the rational, detached, adherence to rigid and abstract principles,[24] Australian philosopher Val Plumwood argues in "Nature, Self, and Gender" that the same notions of care, which are constitutive of virtuous character, ought also to be accorded to nonhuman nature. Plumwood writes in her book on the same topic:

> Special relationships with, care or empathy with particular aspects of nature as experienced, rather than with nature as abstraction, are essential to provide a depth of concern. Under appropriate conditions, experience of and care and reasonability for particular animals, trees, rivers, places and ecosystems which are known well, are loved and are appropriately connected to the self, enhance rather than hinder a wider, more generalized concern for the global environment.[25]

Both social ecology and ecological feminism are built around the central thesis that social domination (class hierarchy or patriarchy) lays the foundation for the human domination of nature; the solution to the ecological crisis is the dismantling of repressive social frameworks. And in this central thesis we glimpse the main criticisms of both political approaches to environmental ethics: dismantling repressive social frameworks may not necessarily and automatically result in a harmonious human relationship to non-human nature.

Environmental Pragmatism

Not all philosophers are enamored with environmental axiology and the obsession with grounding environmental ethics in ontology. A group which can be categorized as environmental pragmatists have argued that discussions of intrinsic value are unproductive because they distract us from paying attention to practical solutions.[26]

The need for normative pluralism – as opposed to "hegemonic" nonanthropocentrism[27] – is a central point of consensus amongst environmental pragmatists. Environmental pragmatists embrace moral pluralism for the end of finding theories that work most effectively in practice. In the estimation of Australian philosopher Andrew Brennan, pluralism provides for a normative "overdetermination" for environmental policy: "[W]e have to recognize that there is not just one moral framework within which to articulate our thinking about the rights and wrongs of our dealings with nature."[28] There are likely to be both anthropocentric and nonanthropocentric arguments leading to the same conclusions.

Bryan Norton calls this the Convergence Hypothesis: anthropocentric and nonanthropocentric arguments are likely to converge in roughly the same conclusion about sound environmental policy.[29] In most cases, different axiological arguments (whether anthropocentric or nonanthropocentric) will end up with roughly the same conclusions regarding the importance of biodiversity, the value of ecosystemic stability and integrity, the bane of pollution, etc. Since humans are embedded in ecological systems and human flourishing is contingent upon the flourishing of those ecological systems, Norton morphs Callicott's triangulation of anthropocentric individualism (orthodox anthropocentrism), nonanthropocentric individualism

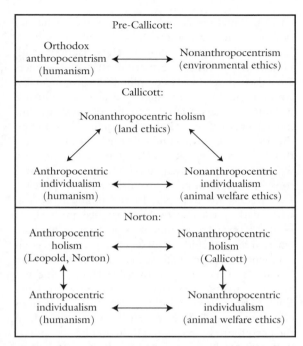

Figure V.1   Callicott's Triangulation and Norton's Quadrilateralization.

(animal welfare ethics), and nonanthropocentric holism (land ethics) into a quadrilateral anthropocentric individualism (orthodox anthropocentrism), nonanthropocentric individualism (animal welfare ethics), nonanthropocentric holism (land ethics), and anthropocentric holism (Norton's view – and the view he claims Leopold *really* had).[30] (See figure V.1.)

Historically, the first article on environmental ethics to take an explicitly pragmatic approach is Anthony Weston's "Beyond Intrinsic Value." Weston argues that environmental pragmatists foreswear the search for objective intrinsic axiology for such a search is futile: there will always be the extremist who sees no such value in nature. Rather than seeing the project of environmental ethics as the search for the endpoint of objective value in nature, the project of environmental pragmatism is ongoing, the search for ever better arguments that *work*.

In "Methodological Pragmatism, Pluralism, and Environmental Ethics," Andrew Light wonders why environmental philosophers have not influenced environmental public policy in the way their history (Cronon) and sociology (Bullard) colleagues have. Light attributes this failure to the "fixation" with nonanthropocentrism. Environmental philosophers are also part of large plural environmentalist communities, and just might be able to influence non-philosophers through "methodological environmental pragmatism." But this requires abandoning the dogma that environmental ethics must be nonanthropocentric, and acknowledging that there very well might be extremely good anthropocentric reasons for setting sound environmental public policy.

Consider this example. In the political process, what works most effectively in practice are likely to be anthropocentric arguments. For example, in Utah, where free-market ideology reigns supreme and environmentalism is generally seen as a form of socialism in danger of fettering the Invisible Hand, logic and evidence matter less than the persons speaking. Environmentalists pointing out the deleterious effects of air pollution, especially for children, and the need for fewer roads and more public transportation are quickly dismissed as anti-market leftists. Utah Moms for Clean Air make the same argument and are praised for their "values." From the perspective of environmental pragmatism, arguments need to be couched in terms which will be most likely to achieve the end result (think of the Sophists) – protection of the environment. Indeed, standing in front of the Utah State Legislature and arguing that some plant, such as the endangered Dwarf Bearclaw Poppy (*Arctomecon humilis*), has "intrinsic value" and ought to be protected from all-terrain vehicle use is unlikely to get very far. But to argue that the Bearclaw Poppy is a unique feature of Washington County, and that protecting it and the ecosystem it inhabits increases the quality of human life by providing recreational opportunities, and will increase property values by drawing California retirees to St George, is much more likely to be taken seriously.

Environmental philosophers who are adamant that the anthropocentrism of the Western tradition is the fundamental root cause of ecological degradation find such defenses of human-centeredness, even if it aims to secure the integrity, stability, and beauty of ecological systems, treasonous. Critics of environmental pragmatism, like Callicott, express suspicion of a "hidden agenda" – that it is really a foil for the same old worn-out anthropocentrism that environmental ethicists have been working so hard to vanquish.[31]

Direct Action

Environmental pragmatists are not the only ones impatient with the apparent impotence of environmental ethics in the political process. For Earth First! co-founder Dave Foreman, philosophical rumination leads to political impotence.[32]

The solution is not more environmental ethics publications on library shelves, but direct action: action aimed directly at staving off the incessant destruction of wilderness and diminution of biodiversity for economic ends. Theories don't physically impede development; direct action does. Groups well known for direct action include Greenpeace and Earth First!.[33]

In the first reading selection Dave Foreman describes the origins and purpose of founding Earth First!. While lobbyists for mainstream environmental groups such as the Sierra Club and the Wilderness Society haunt the hallowed halls of power back in Washington, DC, donned in suits and ties, Foreman recognizes the need for grassroots activism to protect and preserve biodiversity by whatever means necessary. This includes publicity stunts, nonviolent civil disobedience, or, more controversially, sabotage for ecological ends (ecological sabotage).

Eugene Hargrove, in "Ecological Sabotage: Pranks or Terrorism?", questions the philosophical legitimacy of ecological sabotage, portrayed fictionally and humorously in Edward Abbey's novel *The Monkey Wrench Gang*.[34] Hargrove disputes the identification of ecological sabotage with civil disobedience. Civil disobedience is usually carried out in public in order to bring attention to some unjust law. In contrast, ecological sabotage is closer to terrorism in that it is carried out in secret. The paramilitarism of ecological sabotage makes it more criminal than civil.

Against Hargrove, Abbey defends ecotage by distinguishing it from terrorism. As Abbey says in "Earth First! and *The Monkey Wrench Gang*," ecological sabotage is the use of the tools of industry against itself. Though violent, sabotage is not terrorism. Terrorism aims at mutilation and murder; sabotage, in the spirit of English activist Ned Ludd, destroys machinery. Foreman also berates Hargrove for claiming that the environmental movement has been successful. In the final reading in this section, Hargrove remains dissuaded with regard to the ethical legitimacy of the extralegal tactics of ecotage.

Notes

1 Clare Palmer identifies another category, omitted in my essay, but worth noting: "Revivalism." This category contains environmental philosophers who rediscover, or revive, the work of great past philosophers and find insights for environmental ethics: John Cobb, Charles Birch, Charles Hartshorne, and Frederick Ferré reappropriate Whitehead; Naess and Sessions reappropriate Spinoza; Zimmerman reappropriates Heidegger; Bryant reappropriates Leibniz; Abram reappropriates Merleau-Ponty; and environmental pragmatists reappropriate Dewey. See Palmer, "A Bibliographic Essay on Environmental Ethics," pp. 92–5. As a doctoral student at the University of Georgia, I intended for a time to apply Derrida's deconstruction of binary oppositions to the anthropocentric/nonanthropocentric dualism in order to argue that anthropocentrism has no justifiable ontological priority over nonanthropocentrism.

2 See Keller, "Deep Ecology," in Callicott and Frodeman, eds., *Encyclopedia of Environmental Ethics and Philosophy*, vol. 1, pp. 206–11.

3 Naess, "The Shallow and the Deep, Long-Range Ecology Movement: A Summary," p. 96. Emphasis in original.

4 Sessions has steadfastly remained true and faithful to egalitarian biocentrism. For Sessions, value hierarchies (such as preferencing sentience) lay the groundwork for claims of moral superiority. In an unpublished manuscript, he writes: "The point is not whether humans in fact do have the greatest degree of sentience on this planet (although dolphins and whales might provide a counterinstance), deep ecologists argue that the degree of sentience is *irrelevant* in terms of how humans relate to the rest of Nature" ("Spinoza, Perennial Philosophy and Deep Ecology," p. 18). Naess, for his part, had apparently backed away from doctrinaire egalitarian biocentrism by 1992 and was open to the notion of hierarchies of value in nature (Palmer, "A Bibliographic Essay on Environmental Ethics," p. 91).

5 Devall and Sessions, *Deep Ecology: Living as if Nature Mattered*, pp. 67–9. Sessions later disputed the centrality of the process of Self-realization to deep ecology, claiming it to be a feature of Naess's *personal* ecological philosophy, Ecosophy T, but *not* a deep ecology proper (see Sessions, "Introduction: Deep Ecology," in Zimmerman et al. (eds.), *Environmental Philosophy*, 2nd edn., p. 173). This claim, however, is inconsistent with the fact that Naess's 1987 article, "Self-Realization: An Ecological Approach to Being in the World," is a treatment of general philosophical principles of that process rather than a personal testimony.

6 "Deep Ecology: A New Philosophy of Our Time?," pp. 198–9.

7 Ibid., p. 198.

8 See Socrates' remarks to Thrasymachus, *Republic* line 352d, in Hamilton and Cairns, eds., *Plato: The Collected Dialogues*, p. 603.

9 See, e.g., Cafaro, "Thoreau, Leopold, and Carson."

10 Newton, *Ethics and Sustainability*, p. 1.

11 Breton, "Dog Found Badly Beaten After Apparent Burglary."

12 See Irene Klaver's comments in the Introduction to the section on Continental Environmental Philosophy in Zimmerman et al. (eds.), *Environmental Philosophy*, 4th edn., p. 289.

13 Weston, "Introduction," in *An Invitation to Environmental Philosophy*, p. 12.

14 The essay was published as "The Fallacy of Safe Space," in Rothenberg and Pryor, eds., *Writing on Air*, pp. 287–93.

15 Bookchin, *The Ecology of Freedom*, pp. 466–7.

16 See Joel Kovel, "Negating Bookchin," in Light, ed., *Social Ecology After Bookchin*, pp. 37–40.

17 Crist, "Social Ecology," in Callicott and Frodeman, eds., *Encyclopedia of Environmental Ethics and Philosophy*, vol. 2, p. 254.

18 Light, "Bookchin as/and Social Ecology," in Light, ed., *Social Ecology After Bookchin*, p. 6.

19 Bookchin, "Social Ecology Versus Deep Ecology," p. 13.

20 "The Power and the Promise of Ecological Feminism," p. 127. (See this volume, p. 282.)

21 Ibid., p. 128. (See this volume, p. 282.)

22 Ibid., p. 133. (See this volume, p. 285.)

23 Ibid., p. 144.

24 See *In a Different Voice*, ch. 1.

25 *Feminism and the Mastery of Nature*, p. 187.

26 Light and Katz, in Light and Katz, eds., *Environmental Pragmatism*, p. 1.

27 Light, "Environmental Pragmatism as Philosophy or Metaphilosophy?," in Light and Katz, eds., *Environmental Pragmatism*, p. 327.

28 *Thinking about Nature*, p. 30.

29 *Toward Unity Among Environmentalists*, pp. 237–43.

30 *Sustainability*, p. 216.

31 "Introduction," in Zimmerman et al., eds., *Environmental Philosophy*, 4th edn., p. 15.

32 Foreman, "More on Earth First! and *The Monkey Wrench Gang*," p. 95. (See this volume, p. 335.)

33 See Keller, "Earth First!," in Callicott and Frodeman, eds., *Encyclopedia of Environmental Ethics and Philosophy*, vol. 1, pp. 221–3.

34 See Keller, "Abbey, Edward," in Callicott and Frodeman, eds., *Encyclopedia of Environmental Ethics and Philosophy*, vol. 1, pp. 1–3.

A Environmental Psychologism

27 The Shallow and the Deep Ecology Movement
Arne Naess

28 The Heart of Deep Ecology
Andrew McLaughlin

29 The Deep Ecological Movement: Some Philosophical Aspects
Arne Naess

30 Transpersonal Ecology
Warwick Fox

27   The Shallow and the Deep Ecology Movement

Arne Naess

Theoretical Frame

"Ecology" is a key term in today's research of the future. On the one hand, however, we find a restricted movement which has many friends among the power elite, while on the other hand, we find a deeper and wider movement with less numerous but powerful allies, and which enjoys a large following of people who question the policy of the big industrial nations. Both movements use the term "ecology" as a kind of slogan, but only the latter movement deserves our full attention and sympathy, as well as our collaboration. At the same time, this movement is directly inspired by the new scientific elite of researchers in the domain of ecology.

This article maintains that while the restricted movement concentrates on pollution and the deple-

tion of natural resources in our contemporary world, the deep movement deals with causes and large-scale effects, and consists of at least seven themes: The system of thinking inspired by biology; universal egalitarianism; principles of diversity and symbiosis; the struggle against the ecologically relevant social domination inside and between nations; the struggle against pollution and depletion of natural resources; the struggle for local autonomy and the decentralization of cultural and economic life.

The term "ecology" has become a most powerful slogan. No wonder that numerous pressure groups of various kinds as well as power constellations seek to adopt it into their own policy.

We need to remind ourselves of the message of those who patiently study the ecosystems, the field researchers in the domain of ecology. They have inspired the deep ecology movement. At present,

From Peder Anker, "Deep Ecology in Bucharest," The *Trumpeter*, vol. 24, no. 1 (2008): 59–67. © 2008 by Arne Naess. Reprinted by permission of Kit-Fai Naess.

a shallower movement is supported by many governmental and non-governmental centres of power, while the deeper movement finds itself in danger of being deceived through smart manoeuvres.

Let us try to characterize the two movements.

The shallow ecology movement has just two objectives: Combating pollution and combating the depletion of natural resources. The objectives are isolated from the broader problems concerning ways of life, economic systems, power structures and the differences between and inside nations.

The deep ecology movement has the two key objectives of the shallow movement, but uses them in a wider and deeper frame. The realization of these implies a change in the concept of life amongst the majority groups of the world's population. Such a change cannot materialize without reforms that will have consequences for all aspects of human life.

We could try to characterize the deep ecology movement through some basic principles and notions. To elaborate on these, we will, needless to say, have to turn to the already very rich ecological literature.

The Deep Ecology Movement

1. *The systemic orientation.* If we think in terms of biological systems where "the whole is greater than the sum of its parts," we are led to reject the concept of things, and parts of isolated things. Let us take an example: Economic policy has been inspired by abstract mechanics where the parts are assembled into a whole, and the behaviour of the latter always can be deduced with certainty through our knowledge of the isolated parts. Man is conceived as an object or as part of a greater object: The human environment.

Ecologists who are profoundly engaged in systemic thinking reject the concept of "man in environment" and declare themselves in favour of a *"man-in-environment" picture, in relation to the totality of the field.* The organisms meet in the biospherical network or in the field of intrinsic relations. An intrinsic relation between two objects *A* and *B* implies that it is bound by the definitions or basic constitutions of both *A* and *B*. Without this relation, *A* and *B* are no longer the same objects. They lose their identity. This does not mean that *A* and *B* are independent entities. The total-domain model does not only dissolve the "man in environment" model, but also every "*A* in *B*" image – except when talking at a superficial or preliminary level of communication. In exchange, we obtain *AB* models, totalities with properties that cannot be deduced from the properties of *A* and *B*. The deduction does not give any results because *A* and *B* do not exist as separate entities.

The above succinct and condensed presentation of the relational concept, as opposed to the objectified concept, cannot feign to adequately express systemic ecological thought.

2. *Biospherical egalitarianism – in principle.* The "in principle" clause is inserted here because any realistic praxis today implies a degree of exploitation and repression.

The ecological field-worker cultivates a deep-rooted respect, a real veneration, for the ways and forms of life. He seeks an understanding from within, an understanding which most others reserve for a small group of people and for a limited set of ways and forms of life. To the ecological field-worker, the *equal right to live and to blossom* constitutes an evident and intuitively clear axiomatic value. Restricting this right to human beings is an anthropocentrism with detrimental effects upon the quality of life of humans themselves. This quality depends in part upon the deep satisfaction we receive from the close partnership, the symbiosis, with other forms of life. The attempt to ignore our dependence and to establish a master–slave role has contributed to the alienation of man from himself.

Ecological egalitarianism implies – to limit ourselves to one sole example – the reinterpretation of the future-research variable, "level of crowding," in such a way that not only *human crowding*, but also mammalian crowding *in general*, as well as the deterioration of their quality of life will be taken seriously. Incidentally, research on the high requirements for free space of certain mammals has disclosed that theorists of human urbanism to a large degree have underestimated people's need for life-space. Behavioural crowding symptoms (neuroses, aggressiveness, loss of traditions . . .) are probably, to a large degree, the same in mammals.

3. *Principles of diversity and of symbiosis.* Diversity enhances the potentialities of survival, the chances of new modes of life, the richness of life forms, but the so-called struggle for life and survival of the fittest should be interpreted in the sense of ability to coexist and cooperate in a system of complex relationships, rather than the ability to kill, exploit,

and suppress. "Live and let live" is a more powerful ecological principle than "Either you or me."

The latter principle tends to reduce the multiplicity of forms of life and lead to destruction within the communities of the same species. Hence, ecologically inspired attitudes favour the diversity of ways of life, of cultures, of occupations, of economies. They support the fight against economic, cultural, and military domination, and they are opposed to the annihilation of seals and whales to the same degree that they are opposed to the annihilation of human tribes or cultures.

Social Darwinism and kindred concepts have misinterpreted the function of the predators within the framework of ecosystems. There exists a kind of harmony between the predators and those who "suffer" from their attacks. (Let us remind ourselves of the symbiosis between wolves and elk.) Man, as predator, has sometimes annihilated other animals of prey although this annihilation did not serve anybody.

4. *Anti-class posture*. The diversity of human ways of life has been mentioned above, and it is realized in many places without exploitation or suppression on the part of certain groups. This is the conclusion of a social anthropological inquiry and of other materials in the centre of human ecology with respect to class status and differences. Exploitation and suppression exist, however. Sometimes they are maintained deliberately by way of brutal force, but mostly there is no underlying intention, they are supported by ignorance and passivity. The domination exercised by the industrialized and centralized countries all over the world generates exploitation and suppression, especially of the second type. The exploiter lives in another way than the exploited, but the master/slave relationship adversely affects the potentialities of self-realization of them both. The principle of diversity does not cover differences between ways of life. They are due only to the fact that certain attitudes or behaviours are forcibly prevented or blocked. The principles of ecological egalitarianism and of symbiosis support the hostile attitude to class dominance. The ecological attitude is in favour of the extension of all three principles to any group conflict, including today's conflicts between developing and developed nations. The three principles also favour taking extreme caution in any comprehensive plans for the future, except those consistent with a wide diversity, free from any class distinction.

The principal aspect may be presented as follows: Let there be an ecosystem in which two groups of organisms manifest themselves through activities A, B and C. If a group by domination succeeds in manifesting itself through activities A, B, C and D, and the other group is constrained to reduce itself only to activities A and B, the natural diversity postulated by the principle of diversity and by the principle of symbiosis does *not* increase. The self-realization of the first group is prevented. The mere cessation or inhibition of activity C does not create a new variety of life. Group domination might develop a new variety of way of life, but if a strong master/slave interaction exists, the necessity of maintaining the positions of domination in relation to the subjugated party paralyzes, overcomes, and narrows the range of activities (and of other life manifestations). This feedback relation cannot be symbolized as long as we only consider the differences between the series of activities A, B; A, B, C and A, B, C, D.

5. *Combating pollution and depletion of the natural resources*. In this struggle ecologists have found powerful supporters, sometimes, however, even to the detriment of their overall position. This happens when too little attention is paid to the deeper causes, to the effects with a large action radius, and to the differences between the poor and rich countries. Thus, if the price of life necessities increases because of the installation of anti-pollution devices, the class differences between nations deepen as well. If the purity standards which such countries as the German Federal Republic and the USA can permit themselves should be imposed on poor nations, their competitive capacity on the world industrial market would remain limited.

In general, the direct struggle against pollution and depletion of natural resources will lead to no solution of the problems if it is not seen in close correlation with the other aspects of the ecosystem, especially with the other six problems mentioned here.

An ethics of responsibility demands that ecologists not serve the shallow, but the deep ecology movement. This means that item 5 must not be seen separately; on the contrary, we must consider all seven points.

6. *Complexity, not complication*. The theory of ecosystems contains an important distinction between what is complicated without any "Gestalt" or unifying principles and what is complex, in the sense of

being multilateral and having different causes and effects. A multiplicity of more or less legitimate, interacting factors may operate together to form a unity, a system. The ways of life and the interactions in the biosphere, in general, exhibit such a high level of complexity as to darken the general outlook of ecologists. This makes thinking in terms of vast systems inevitable and from this there originates a keen, steady perception of our present-day *profound human ignorance* of the biospherical relationships, including our ignorance of the effects of the deliberate, ever-increasing disturbances which take place all over the world.

The way in which we have used the models in physics, from Newton onwards, has given us a feeling of competence or even domination over the relevant physical problems we confront. Physical science and society have developed without acute crises of confidence: there has been no race whatsoever for theoretically justified questions (within the framework of fundamental models) which could have created in us a feeling of profound ignorance. The models of special ecosystems and the immense system of the biosphere have created in us a feeling of ignorance which is completely new in Western culture and which makes the "buyers" of scientific knowledge feel frustrated and confused. And now we see *the scientists* pleading for restraints because of what they call our abysmal ignorance!

Applied to humans, the complexity-not-complication principle favours *division of labour, not fragmentation of labour*. It favours integrated actions, and due to this the human personality is integrally active and does not confine itself to mere reactions. It favours complex economies, the integrated diversity of means of living. (Combinations of industrial and agricultural activity, of intellectual and manual work, of specialized and non-specialized occupations, of urban and non-urban activities, of work in the city and recreation in nature, of recreation in the city and work in nature, etc.)

It supports an elastic technique and an "elastic-future research," less prognosis, more clarification of possibilities. More sensitivity towards continuity and live traditions, and most importantly – towards our state of ignorance. This suggests a combination of conservative and radical principles in a competent ecological politics.

7. *Local autonomy and decentralization*. The vulnerability of a form of life is roughly proportional to the weight of accidental influences from afar, from outside the region in which that form has obtained an ecological equilibrium. This lends support to efforts to strengthen local self-government and material and mental self-sufficiency.

The development of world trade, one of the values less questioned in the non-socialist industrialized countries, is becoming an extremely problematic issue.

The division of labour is beneficial when we consider the small communities, but when it comes to bigger entities, the ecological considerations become much more relevant and to a large extent arrive at negative conclusions. The principal argument in favour of world trade, i.e., that commodities must be produced where they can be manufactured in the most inexpensive way, was based on an economic science which until lately was not influenced by ecology.

Developing local self-government and self-sufficiency implies a decentralization effort. On the other hand, the struggle against pollution and depletion of the natural resources requires centralized authorities.

Local autonomy is consolidated when the connections between the hierarchal, "vertical," decision-making chain links are reduced. Even if a decision is taken on the basis of the majority principle at every stage, many local interests may be overlooked along the chain. Horizontal cooperation at the lower level is urgent.

In summary, then, it should, first of all, be borne in mind that the norms and tendencies of the deep ecology movement are not derived from ecology by means of logic or induction. Ecological insight and the life style of the ecological field-worker have *suggested, inspired, and reinforced* the perspectives of the deep ecology movement.

Many of the formulations in this seven-item study are rather vague generalizations, only tenable if they are stated more precisely in certain senses. All over the world, however, ecological field-workers have inspired remarkable convergences. The above survey does not pretend to be anything more than one of the possible condensed codifications of these convergences.

The most important points of dissension between the outstanding personalities of the ecology movement stem from priorities of value and from the theories and hypotheses about the consequences of certain political decisions within the domain of ecology. However, these disagreements seldom refer to the above mentioned convergences.

Secondly, it should be fully appreciated that the significant tenets of the deep ecology movement are clearly *normative*. They express a value priority system which is based only in part upon the results of scientific research (or upon the lack of results, cf. item 6). Today, the ecologists try to influence the policy-making bodies largely through threats, through predictions concerning pollutants and resource depletion, knowing that policy-makers accept at least certain *minimum standards* concerning health and a fair distribution. But it is clear that a vast number of people in all countries, including many persons of consequence, accept as valid the wider norms and values characteristic of the deep ecology movement. There is political potential in this movement which should not be overlooked and which has little to do with pollution and resource depletion. In plotting possible futures, the standards should be freely elaborated on and utilized.

The ecologists serve as irreplaceable sources of information in all societies no matter what the political colour of the society in question. If the ecologists are well organized, they should be able to refuse posts which would subject them to institutions or society planners with limited ecological perspectives. In today's situation, the ecologists sometimes serve masters who deliberately ignore wider perspectives.

Thirdly, in so far as the ecology movement deserves our attention, its concepts are *ecophilosophical* rather than ecological. Ecology is a limited science which makes use of scientific methods. Philosophy is the highest forum for debating fundamental problems, descriptive as well as prescriptive, and political philosophy is one of its subsections. By an ecosophy I mean a philosophy of ecological harmony or equilibrium. A philosophy as a kind of *sofia*, wisdom, is openly normative, it contains norms, rules, postu-lates, value priority pronouncements, and hypotheses on the state of affairs in our universe. Wisdom is political wisdom, prescription, not only mere scientific description and prediction.

The details of an ecosophy will vary quite a lot due to significant differences as to the "facts" of pollution, resources, population, etc., but also as to value priorities. Today, however, the seven items listed above provide a framework for a diversity of ecosophical systems.

In general system theory, "systems" are mostly conceived in terms of causally or functionally interacting items. An ecosophy, however, is more like a system of the kind constructed by Aristotle or Spinoza. It is expressed verbally as a set of sentences with a variety of functions, descriptive and prescriptive. The basic relation is one between subsets of premises and subsets of conclusions, that is: a relation of derivability. The relevant notions of derivability may be classified in accordance with the logical and mathematical deductions of first rank, but also in accordance with the degree to which they are acknowledged implicitly to be good.

An exposition of an ecosophy must of necessity be only moderately precise considering the vast scope of the relevant ecological and normative (social, political, ethical) material. Presently, ecosophy might use models of systems, approximations of global systems. It is the global nature, not preciseness in detail, which distinguishes an ecosophy. It forms and integrates the efforts of a real ecological team, a team comprising not only scientists from an extreme variety of disciplines, but also students of politics and active policy-makers.

It would be wrong to claim here that the perspective of the deep ecology movement only depends on modifications of the structures of the political powers that be. A clear and informed international debate, normative and descriptive, constitutes in itself a central part of politics.

28   The Heart of Deep Ecology

Andrew McLaughlin

In the last few hundred years, industrial society has encircled the earth and, in requiring massive disruptions of ecological processes for its ordinary functioning, threatens all forms of life on this planet. Both capitalist and socialist variants of expansionary industrialism routinely require the destruction of species and ecosystems. Industrialism now threatens to disrupt atmospheric conditions fundamental to the whole biosphere. If ecological problems have roots in industrialism, then a perspective which takes industrialism itself as part of the problem is needed.[1]

The transformation of industrialism will, I believe, involve a multifaceted struggle over several generations. The changes required are of the magnitude of the agricultural and industrial revolutions.

Deep Ecology is one perspective which beckons us in the right direction. In just two decades, Deep Ecology as a theory – as distinct from Deep Ecology as a social movement – has become a benchmark in defining varieties of environmental philosophies.[2] In the course of its relatively short history, there has been considerable controversy surrounding Deep Ecology, but most of it has been misdirected. One reason for this has been the failure of critics to notice that the "logic" of Deep Ecology differs fundamentally in form from many other philosophical positions.

The heart of Deep Ecology is its platform, which consists of a number of inter-related factual and normative claims about humans and their relations with the rest of nature. The platform was intended as a description of a Deep Ecology social movement and as a basis for a larger unity among all those who accept the importance of nonanthropocentrism and understand that this entails *radical* social change.

The platform, articulated by Arne Naess and George Sessions while they were camping in Death Valley in 1984, is a nontechnical statement of principles around which, it is hoped, people with differing *ultimate* understandings of themselves, society, and nonhuman nature, could unite. Thus, from the start, the platform was meant to be a terrain of commonality which allowed, recognized, and even encouraged differences in more logically ultimate philosophies.

The Deep Ecology Platform

The platform itself consists of eight points.

1. *The well-being and flourishing of human and non-human Life on Earth have value in themselves (synonyms: intrinsic value, inherent value). These values are independent of the usefulness of the nonhuman world for human purposes.*

Essentially, this is a rejection of anthropocentrism. It is an assertion that human *and* nonhuman life should flourish. "Life," in this context, is understood broadly to include, for example, rivers, landscapes, and ecosystems. Accepting the idea that humans are not the *only* valuable part of nature is the watershed perception from which Deep Ecology flows.

This plank should not be taken as implying a commitment to any philosophically precise theory about intrinsic or inherent value. When Deep Ecologists use the language of moral discourse they are not usually trying to construct a formal ethical theory. If one wishes to speak outside the academy, one must use language which communicates in popular contexts. That language right now uses concepts of intrinsic or inherent value and rights. To take Devall and Sessions literally, when they ascribe an "equal right" to all things and claim they are "equal in intrinsic worth," is interpreting them out of context.[3] In the passage in which those phrases appear, they are writing with the intent of having practical effect within the environmental movement. They are not writing with philosophical precision, and for them to do so would counter their main purpose.[4]

Perhaps the search for some sort of value *in* nonhuman nature, be it inherent, intrinsic, or some

From George Sessions, ed., *Deep Ecology for the Twenty-First Century* (Boston: Shambhala Publications, Inc., 1995), pp. 85–93. © 1995 by Andrew McLaughlin.

other sort of nonanthropocentric value seems necessary because we cannot now fully imagine an adequate environmental ethic. Often an ethic is supposed to constrain people from doing what they otherwise would do. As both Warwick Fox and Val Plumwood point out, many ethical theorists implicitly assume that we would care about nonhuman nature "for itself" *only* if it has intrinsic value.[5] This assumption motivates the search for the elusive intrinsic value, but it may be overly constraining in the search for an environmental ethic. Simply put, we *can* care for the rest of nature for reasons which have nothing to do with whether or not it has intrinsic, inherent, or whatever sort of value. Such a caring can spring, for example, from a felt sense of relatedness to the rest of nature or a love of existence.

2. *Richness and diversity of life forms contribute to the realization of these values and are also values in themselves.*

This, along with the first point, is intended to counter the often-held image of evolution as resulting in "higher" forms of life. It involves a re-visioning of life and evolution, changing from understanding evolution as "progress" from "lower" to "higher" forms to understanding evolution as a magnificent expression of a multitude of forms of life. Cherishing diversity appreciates differences and rejects any single standard of excellence.

Valuing diversity means freeing large areas of the earth from domination by industrial economy and culture. Expand wilderness! But in interpreting this injunction, it should be remembered that "wilderness" is an outsider's construct. Most of what appears to industrial peoples as wilderness has been steadily occupied or traversed by indigenous peoples for eons. Thus, preserving such areas from industrial regimes is not only protecting wilderness, but is, in some cases, also preserving indigenous peoples. The struggle for wilderness is both for biological and human diversity.

3. *Humans have no right to reduce this richness and diversity except to satisfy vital needs.*

The key point in this claim is the implied distinction between "vital" and other needs. This distinction is denied by the consumerism inherent in industrialism. To lose sight of it is to become trapped within an endlessly repeating cycle of deprivation and temporary satiation. Making the distinction opens to the possibility of more enduring forms of

happiness and joy. Of course, the distinction cannot be drawn precisely, since what is a vital need in one context may be a trivial want in another. There is a real difference between an Eskimo's wearing the skin of a seal and one worn for social status in an affluent society.

4. *The flourishing of human life and cultures is compatible with a substantial decrease in human population. The flourishing of nonhuman life requires such a decrease.*

Once recognition is given to other forms of life, then it is clear that we humans are too many already. We have already jostled many species out of existence and the near future promises an expansion of such extinctions. Recent projections by the United Nations indicate that current trends in population growth will involve converting about 80 percent of current nature reserves to human use.[6] This would drastically accelerate the already alarming trends towards the extinction of myriad species of life.[7]

The continuing increase in human numbers also condemns many humans to a life of suffering. Parents within industrial societies easily recognize that many children means fewer life prospects for each and limit themselves to fewer children, hoping to give them each a better life. We should collectively recognize that an increase in human numbers is not in the best interest of humans, much less the rest of life.

It is to the credit of the Deep Ecology movement that it clearly gives priority to human population as a problem and calls for a gradual decrease.[8] This does not imply misanthropy or cruelty to presently existing humans. In fact, it implies the reverse for there is considerable evidence indicating that the best way of moderating and then reversing the growth of human population is to find ways of providing a decent life for all.[9]

There is, of course, much more that might be said about the problem of overpopulation and the ways the human population might decline. In this regard, alliances between Deep Ecologists and Ecofeminists may be very helpful. The problem of coerced motherhood exists in all societies to some degree, but it is most acute in poorer countries where population growth is most rapid. Current evidence indicates that there has been a global increase in coerced pregnancy and motherhood and this trend must be reversed for there to be much hope in slowing population growth.[10] The worldwide struggle for the rights of women to choose the number of children they will bear will help in at least slowing the growth of human populations. Such a right includes the right to choose sexual partners and manage fertility in safe ways, which includes the right to access to safe abortions. Ecofeminists have much to contribute both theoretically and practically to success in this struggle.

5. *Present human interference with the nonhuman world is excessive, and the situation is rapidly worsening.*

This directs attention to current trends and claims that current levels of "interference" with the rest of nature are excessive. There are at least two sorts of such interference which need to be addressed. One sort is the destruction of existing areas of wilderness, such as old growth forests. This is irreparable within any moderate time scale and is wrong. In fact, the guiding principle should probably be the continuation of biological history, creating large enough wilderness areas to allow for the continued speciation of plants and animals. This does not involve dispossessing indigenous peoples who have found ways of living within those ecosystems without destroying them.

Another sort of interference is based on particular forms of technology. Many technologies disrupt natural cycles far more than is necessary. For example, agricultural practices involving large scale monocropping create expanding needs for fertilizer and pesticides. Multicropping, integrated pest management, and a variety of organic farming techniques interfere less with natural cycles and can enhance the fertility of soils.

6. *Policies must therefore be changed. These policies affect basic economic, technological, and ideological structures. The resulting state of affairs will be deeply different from the present.*

The scope of the changes needed is great. However, significant work is being done in trying to create adequate models for change. Although the concept remains obscure and controversial, "sustainability" is becoming a slogan in thinking about how economies should be restructured, even among those who remain within an anthropocentric perspective. We need to be clear about precisely "what" is to be sustained. For Deep Ecology, at least, we need to sustain the very conditions for the diversity of the myriad forms of life, including the cultural diversity of human life.

7. *The ideological change is mainly that of appreciating life quality (dwelling in situations of inherent value) rather than adhering to an increasingly higher standard of living. There will be a profound awareness of the difference between big and great.*

This point is especially important for industrial peoples enmeshed within an ultimately unsatisfying consumerism.[11] With a focus on quality, people can see that existing patterns of labor and consumption are not satisfying, but rather involve chronic dissatisfaction. Moving towards an appreciation of the *quality* of life, instead of quantities of things, leads to an *increase* in happiness, not a decrease. This is fundamental, since people are more apt to change when they experience change as improvement, rather than a grudging submission to necessity. As long as environmentalism seems to require only denial and sacrifice, its political effectiveness will be lessened. Deep Ecology seeks a more satisfactory way of living, an increase in vitality and joy.

8. *Those who subscribe to the foregoing points have an obligation directly or indirectly to try to implement the necessary changes.*

Although this is clear in claiming that we must begin to act now, it is vague in not indicating *particular* priorities. At this point in history, priorities cannot be made more specific. No one now knows *exactly* what positive changes are necessary. The problems with economic growth and the emptiness of consumerism are clear enough, but they do not show just what needs to be done now. People who accept the Deep Ecology platform may disagree about what is most urgent now, and there are many ways to attempt the needed changes. In the light of the value of diversity, such differences should be respected and not become occasions for sectarian squabble.

The Logic of Deep Ecology

The eight-point platform is not "ultimate" or "basic" in a logical sense. That is, it is not put forward as requiring or allowing no further justification. Rather, it is basic in being the most general view that supporters of Deep Ecology hold in common. There is no expectation nor need for wide agreement on logically more ultimate premises which might be used to render a deductive justification of the platform. In fact, disagreement on such ultimate premises is to be expected.

From a *historical* perspective, the platform as articulated by Naess and Sessions is unique to Deep

Ecology. However, were it to become grounds for widespread unity within a movement directed toward transforming industrial society and creating a non-anthropocentric society, it might no longer be called a specifically "Deep Ecology" position. The platform is part of a program for what Robyn Eckersley calls an "ecocentric" Green political movement, a movement which will encompass many who might not identify themselves as "Deep Ecologists."[12] Thus, while it is now a specifically "Deep Ecology" platform, should it achieve its intended end, it might no longer be identified *as* a "Deep Ecology" platform. If it is successful in its intent, it might dissolve as a distinct position.

If one seeks a *justification* for the Deep Ecology platform, then discussion might proceed to more ultimate premises characteristically espoused by some deep ecologists. But other justifications might depend on "ultimate premises" of some other ecocentric perspective, such as ecofeminism or some variant of social ecology. The central point is that there is not only one possible justification for the platform.

The *platform* is the heart of Deep Ecology, and it is this platform, not the various justifications of it, which should be the focus of argument about the value of Deep Ecology.[13]

The development of a radical ecology movement must start its collective discussion somewhere, and the Deep Ecology platform is a good beginning. People may come to adopt this platform from quite diverse directions and for differing reasons. Those who start from social concerns and come to believe that an ecological perspective must be taken very seriously may come to the Deep Ecology position through an understanding of the ecological inadequacy of more traditional social ideologies. On the other hand, those who start with a concern about nonhuman nature are likely to arrive at the Deep Ecology platform more directly by reflecting on what follows from a rejection of anthropocentrism and a recognition of the worth of the flourishing of *all* of nature.

Although some Deep Ecologists have emphasized the process of expanding one's sense of self towards a larger identification with all of nature to arrive at a denial of anthropocentrism, this is surely not the only path. The Ecofeminist Marti Kheel argues persuasively that the differences in the ways men and women now typically form their identities makes *any* gender neutral concept of the self suspect. This

means that different genders now may find different paths toward the Deep Ecology platform. Ecofeminism, in speaking to this historically conditioned difference between men and women, offers other routes to a justification of the platform. But, as Kheel argues, this unique strength of Ecofeminism does not entail any fundamental opposition between Ecofeminism and Deep Ecology.[14]

Even the *kinds* of reasons which might persuade a person to adopt a version of the platform may range from rational to nonrational to irrational. For example, acceptance might be based on philosophical reflection, religious conviction, personal experience, intuitions, mystical experience, aesthetic perception, or some other basis. *Allowing for a variety of paths to the same position is precisely the intent of the Deep Ecology platform.* It is not intended to be, nor is it, a systematic philosophical position; it proposes a common ground for defining an ecocentric movement for radical social change. Even the particular formulation of the platform is not final or the only acceptable expression.[15] The point of these principles is to define the Deep Ecology movement, create clarity within the movement, and make clear where real disagreement might exist.[16]

When the structure of Deep Ecology is understood this way, much of the controversy surrounding Deep Ecology can be seen as irrelevant. While argument directed against one, some, or all of the eight points is of great importance, criticism directed to one of the underlying philosophical positions used to justify the Deep Ecology platform is far less relevant. Clearly, one could reject a particular philosophical or religious justification of the platform, yet still believe that the platform is correct at this point in history. I think it has been a failure to appreciate this aspect of the structure of the Deep Ecology position which has led to much heated but fruitless controversy. Focusing on the platform may help us find the basis for unity among those who may disagree on more philosophically ultimate issues.

This approach to Deep Ecology does not make clear what is philosophically distinctive in the writings of deep ecologists. Although this question may be of great interest to theorists of Deep Ecology, it may be of less importance to movement activists. The platform is a proposal for us now, in this particular historical context. When that context changes, the platform may change. Perhaps Deep Ecology would even disappear as a distinctive position.

Without understanding the platform as the heart of Deep Ecology, attempts to justify the platform tend to create needless schisms. For example, the most exhaustive attempt to define what is distinctive about Deep Ecology is Warwick Fox's *Toward a Transpersonal Ecology*. He focuses on the nature of the self and explains Deep Ecology as involving an identification of self with all that is. But his specification of Deep Ecology, *unless* it is understood as one among many alternative justifications for the platform, creates unneeded friction. It leaves out others who accept the platform, but do not agree with Fox's notion of identification. Richard Sylvan and Jim Cheney, for example, both accept the platform, but are critics of Fox's Transpersonal Ecology.[17] Which is more important – finding differences or realizing unity?

If Deep Ecology is understood primarily as the attempt to spark profound social change, then the question of who is and who isn't a Deep Ecologist can be settled by referring to the platform. But disputes over possible justifications are of pressing importance only if they lead to differences over the platform.

The platform, then, is a proposal for a set of general agreements among radical ecocentrists, a common ground for those who value *all* nature. Deep ecologists have done a valuable service in bringing such a platform to the fore. Our urgent task is social change.

Notes

1   I have argued at length that industrialism *is* the core problem which we must confront. See Andrew McLaughlin, *Regarding Nature: Industrialism and Deep Ecology* (Albany: SUNY Press, 1993).

2   See Warwick Fox, *Toward a Transpersonal Ecology: Developing New Foundations for Environmentalism* (Boston: Shambhala Publications, 1990), 44–5 and the works referenced there. Deep Ecology as a social *movement* has origins which predate Naess's formulation of deep ecology as a *theory*.

3   Bill Devall and George Sessions, *Deep Ecology: Living as if Nature Mattered* (Salt Lake City: Gibbs Smith, 1985), 67.

4   See Warwick Fox's "Approaching Deep Ecology: A Response to Richard Sylvan's Critique of Deep Ecology," *Environmental Studies Occasional Paper 20* (Hobart: University of Tasmania, 1986), 37ff, and

Fox's *Toward a Transpersonal Ecology* for extended discussions as to why it is an error to interpret Deep Ecology as an alternative axiology. For further discussion, see note 25 of chap. 9 in *Regarding Nature*.

5   Fox, "Approaching Deep Ecology," p. 79. Val Plumwood, "Nature, Self, and Gender: Feminism, Environmental Philosophy, and the Critique of Rationalism," *Hypatia* 6 (1991): 10. See also Anthony Weston, "Beyond Intrinsic Value: Pragmatism in Environmental Ethics," *Environmental Ethics* 7, no. 4 (Winter 1985): 321–39.

6   Nafis Sadik, *The State of World Population: 1992* (New York: United Nations Population Fund, 1992), ii.

7   See Edward O. Wilson, *The Diversity of Life* (Cambridge: Harvard University Press, 1992), for a sobering discussion of this problem.

8   "Population reduction towards decent levels might incidentally require a thousand years." Arne Naess, *Ecology, Community and Lifestyle: Outline of an Ecosophy*, translated by David Rothenberg (New York: Cambridge University Press, 1989), 127.

9   See Sadik, *The State of World Population: 1992*.

10 See Jodi L. Jacobson, "Coerced Motherhood Increasing," in Lester R. Brown et al., *Vital Signs: 1992* (New York: Norton & Co., 1992), 114–15.

11 See chap. 4 of my *Regarding Nature* for a fuller discussion of consumerism.

12 See Robyn Eckersley, *Environmentalism and Political Theory: Toward an Ecocentric Approach* (Albany: SUNY Press, 1992), especially chap. 3.

13 The centrality of the platform has been claimed by a number of Deep Ecology writers. See, for example, Arne Naess, "The Deep Ecological Movement," *Philosophical Inquiry* 8, nos. 1–2 (1986): 23–6; Arne Naess, *Ecology, Community, and Lifestyle*, 27–32; Bill Devall, *Simple in Means, Rich in Ends: Practicing Deep Ecology* (Salt Lake City: Gibbs Smith, 1988), 12–18.

14 Marti Kheel, "Ecofeminism and Deep Ecology: Reflections on Identity and Difference," *The Trumpeter* 8, no. 2 (Spring 1991).

15 Other sketches are possible, even encouraged. Naess regards his own formulation as tentative. (See Naess, *Ecology, Community, and Lifestyle*, 31.) He expects that others who identify with the Deep Ecology movement "will work out their own alternative formulations" (*Ecology*, 28). Bill Devall, one founder of Deep Ecology, prefers the concept of "worth" to "value." (See Devall, *Simple in Means*, 14.)

16 Naess, *Ecology*, 32.

17 See Richard Sylvan, "A Critique of (Wild) Western Deep Ecology," unpublished manuscript, 2; Jim Cheney, "The Neo-Stoicism of Radical Environmentalism," *Environmental Ethics* 11, no. 4 (Winter 1989): 295.

29 The Deep Ecological Movement: Some Philosophical Aspects

Arne Naess

Deep Ecology on the Defensive

Increasing pressures for growth have placed the vast majority of ecologists and other environmental professionals into a defensive position. Let me illustrate.

The field ecologist K, who both professionally and personally vigorously advocated deep ecological principles in the late sixties, encountered considerable resistance. Colleagues in the university said he should keep to his science and not meddle in philosophical and political matters. He should resist the temptation to become a prominent "popularizer" through exposure in the mass media. Nevertheless, he continued and influenced thousands (including myself). He became a recognized professional 'expert' in assessing the damage done when bears killed or maimed sheep or other domestic animals in Norway. According to the law, their owners are to be paid damages. Licensed hunters can get permission to shoot a bear if its misdeeds become considerable.[1] Growth pressures required consolidating the sheep industry, and sheepowners became fewer, richer, and more prone to live in towns. Due to wage increases, they could not afford to hire shepherds to watch the flock, so the sheep were left alone even more than before. And growth now required placing sheep on what were traditionally "bear territories." In spite of this invasion, bear populations grew, and troubles multiplied.

What was K's reaction? Setting limits to human encroachments on bear territory? Direct application of his deep ecology perspective? Quite the contrary. He adopted a shallow wildlife management perspective which defended the sheepowners: more money in compensation for losses, quicker compensation, and immediate hiring of hunters to reduce the bear population. Other deep ecologists noted with concern the change of his public "image;" had K really abandoned his former value priorities? Privately he insisted: No. But, in public, he was silent.

The reason for K's unexpected actions was not difficult to find: the force of economic growth was so strong that the laws protecting bears would be changed in a direction highly unfavorable to the bears if the sheepowners were not soon pacified by accepting some of their demands. And some of their demands seemed reasonable. After all, it did cost a lot of money to hire and equip rescuers to locate a flock of sheep which had been harassed by a bear and, further, to prove the bear's guilt. And the bureaucratic procedures involved were time consuming. In short, K had not changed his basic value priorities at all. Rather, he had adopted a purely defensive compromise. He stopped promoting his deep ecological philosophy publicly in order to retain credibility and standing among opponents of his principles.

And what is true of K is true of thousands more. These people often hold responsible positions in society, where they might strengthen responsible environmental policy, but, given the exponential forces of growth, their publications are limited to narrowly professional and specialized concerns. Their writings are surely competent, but lack a deeper and more comprehensive perspective (although I admit that there are some brilliant exceptions). If professional ecologists persist in voicing their value priorities, their jobs are often in peril, or they tend to lose influence and status among those who are in charge of general policies. Privately, they may admit the necessity for deep and far-reaching changes, but they remain silent in public. As a result, their positive impact on the public has largely vanished. Deeply concerned people feel abandoned by the 'experts'.

In ecological debate many participants know a lot about particular conservation policies in particular places, and many others have strong opinions regarding fundamental philosophical questions of environmental ethics, but only a few have both qualities. When they are silent, the loss is formidable.

[. . .]

From *Inquiry*, vol. 5 (1986): 10–12, 23–31.

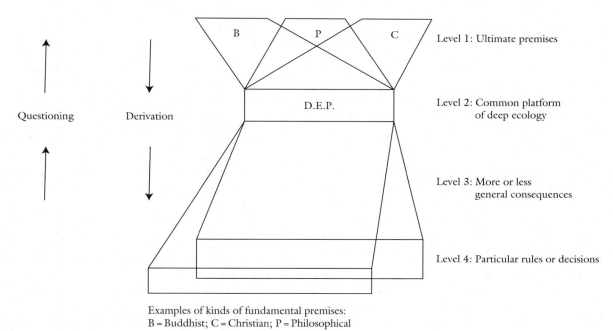

Questioning   Derivation

Level 1: Ultimate premises

Level 2: Common platform
of deep ecology

Level 3: More or less
general consequences

Level 4: Particular rules or decisions

Examples of kinds of fundamental premises:
B = Buddhist; C = Christian; P = Philosophical

Figure 29.1

The complicated question of how industrial societies can increase energy production with the least undesirable consequences is of the same kind: a waste of time if the increase is pointless in relation to ultimate ends. When thousands of experts hired by government and other big institutions devote their time to this complicated problem, it is difficult for the public to learn that many of them judge the problem pointless and irrelevant. What is relevant, according to them, are the problems of how to stabilize and eventually decrease consumption without loss of life quality.

A Call to Speak Out

What I advocate and argue for is this: even those who completely subsume ecological policies under the narrow ends of human health and well-being cannot attain their more modest aims, at least not fully and easily, without being joined by supporters of deep ecology. They need what these people have to contribute, as this will work for them more often than it works against them. Those in charge of environmental policies, even if they are resource-oriented (and growth tolerating?) decision makers, will increasingly welcome, if only for tactical and not fundamental reasons, what deep ecologists have to say. Even though

the more radical ethic may seem nonsensical or untenable to them, they know that its advocates are doing in practice conservation work that sooner or later must be done. They concur with the practice, although they operate from diverging theories. If I am right, the time is ripe for professional deep ecologists to break their silence and freely express their deepest concerns. A bolder advocacy of deep ecology by those who are working within the shallow, resource-oriented 'environmental' sphere is the best strategy for regaining some of the strength of this movement among the general public, and thereby to contribute, however modestly, toward a turning of the tide.

[. . .]

Deep Ecology Illustrated as a Derivational System

Underlying the eight tenets or principles presented [by McLaughlin in this volume, chapter 28], there are still more basic positions and norms which reside in philosophical systems and various world religions. Schematically we may represent the total views implied in the movement by streams of derivation from the most fundamental norms and descriptive assumptions to particular decisions in actual life situations. See figure 29.1.

This pyramidal model has some features in common with hypothetico-deductive systems. The main difference, however, is that some sentences at the top (= deepest) level are normative, and are preferably expressed by imperatives. This makes it possible to arrive at imperatives at the lowest derivational level, the crucial level in terms of decisions. Thus, there are oughts in our premises, as well as in our conclusions. We do not move from an is to an ought.

Just as in a hypothetico-deductive system in physics, where only the two upper levels of the pyramid are thought of as forming physics as a system, so also in normative systems, only the upper levels are considered to be part of the total system. The sentences in the lowest part are changing from day to day as life situations change.

The above derivational structure of a total view must not be taken too seriously. It is not meant in any restrictive way to characterize creative thinking within the deep ecological movement. That thinking moves freely in any direction. But some of us with a professional background in science and analytical philosophy find it helpful.[2]

Answers to ultimate questions, i.e., the highest normative principles and basic assumptions about the world, occur in the upper part of the derivational pyramid. The first three basic principles of deep ecology [see chapter 28] belong to the upper level of the pyramid because they assert, in a general way, life in its diversity as a value in itself, thus forming a norm against undue human interference. The next four (4–7) tenets belong to the middle region because they are more local, they view what is going on at the present. This involves factual claims and projections about the consequences of present policies in industrial and nonindustrial countries. An application of the last tenet (8) is at the lowest derivational level because it imposes an obligation to take part in actions to change policies. Such an obligation must be derivable from principles higher up in the pyramid.

There are few propositions at the top of the pyramid, a great variety at the middle level, and innumerable recommendations at the bottom.

Multiple Roots of the Deep Ecology Principles

The deep ecological movement seriously questions the presuppositions of shallow argumentation. Even what counts as a rational decision is challenged, because "rational" is always defined in relation to specific aims and goals. If a decision is rational in relation to the lower level aims and goals of our pyramid but not in relation to the highest level, then the decision should not be judged to be rational. If an environmentally oriented policy decision is not linked to intrinsic values, its rationality is yet undetermined. The deep movement connects rationality with a set of philosophical and religious foundations. One cannot expect the ultimate premises to constitute rational conclusions. There are no "deeper" premises available.

The deep ecological questioning reveals the fundamental normative orientations. Shallow argumentation stops before reaching fundamentals or jumps from the ultimate to the particular, that is, from level 1 to level 4.

It is not only normative claims that are at stake. Most (perhaps all) norms presuppose ideas about how the world functions. Typically the vast majority of propositions needed in normative systems are descriptive. This holds of all levels.

Notice, however, that it does not follow that supporters of deep ecology must have, on ultimate issues, identical beliefs. They do have common attitudes about intrinsic values in nature, but these can, in turn (at a still deeper level), be derived from different, mutually incompatible sets of ultimate beliefs.

Thus, while a specific decision may be judged as rational from within the derivational system (if there is such) of shallow ecology, it might be judged irrational from within the derivational system of deep ecology. What is rational within the deep ecology derivational pyramid does not require unanimity in ontology and fundamental ethics. Deep ecology as a conviction, with its subsequently derived practical recommendations, can follow from several more comprehensive worldviews.

Those engaged in the deep movement have so far revealed their philosophical or religious homes mainly to be in Christianity, Buddhism, Taoism, or philosophy. The top level of the derivational pyramid can therefore be made up of normative and descriptive principles which belong to forms of Christianity, Buddhism, Taoism, and various philosophical creeds.

Since the late seventies, numerous Christians in Europe and America, some of them teachers of theology, have taken part actively in the deep ecological movement. Their interpretations of the Bible and their theological positions in general have been reformed from what was, until recently, a dominating crudely anthropocentric emphasis within Christianity.

There is an intimate relation between some forms of Buddhism and the deep ecological movement. The history of Buddhist thought and practice, especially the principles of non-violence, non-injury and reverence for life, sometimes makes it easier for Buddhists to understand and appreciate that movement than it is for Christians, despite a (sometimes overlooked) blessedness which Jesus recommended in peace-making. I mention Taoism chiefly because there is some basis for calling John Muir a Taoist.[3]

Ecosophies are not religions in the classical sense, but are general philosophies inspired by ecology. In the next section I will further introduce Ecosophy T.

The adherents of different religions and philosophies disagree and may not even ultimately understand each other at the foundational levels of conviction and experience. But they can have important derived views in common, and these, though themselves derived, are nevertheless deep enough to form what I wish to call the upper level of the deep ecology derivational pyramid.

Some have worried that the mixture of religion and environmentalism could prove a source of dogmatism, intolerance, and "mysticism" (in the sense of obscurantism). So far, there is no evidence that this is happening. Nature mysticism has little to do with obscurantism.[4]

Ecosophy T

The main theoretical complaint against shallow ecology is not that it is based on a well-articulated but incorrect philosophical or religious foundation. It is, rather, that there is a lack of depth – or complete absence – of guiding philosophical or religious foundations.

In his excellent book on how to "live in the environment," G. Tyler Miller writes: "The American attitude (and presumably that of most industrialized nations) toward nature can be expressed as eight basic beliefs [four of which are reproduced here]."

1 Humans are the source of all value.
2 Nature exists only for our use.
3 Our primary purpose is to produce and consume. Success is based on material wealth.

4 Production and consumption must rise endlessly because we have a right to an ever increasing material level of living.

But he adds an important reservation: "Although most of us probably would not accept all of these statements, we act individually, corporately, and governmentally as if we did – and this is what counts."[5]

When they are so baldly exposed, we might find that very few persons would actually subscribe to what Miller characterizes as "the American attitude." Nevertheless, as Miller notices, most modern people (and not only Americans!) behave as if they believed such a creed. There is no articulated philosophical or religious view from which "the American attitude" is carefully justified.

Referring back to the illustration, the shallow movement has not offered examples of total views comprising the four levels. I am tempted to say that there will be no examples. Serious attempts to find a deep justification of the way life on the planet is treated today (including the threats of using nuclear "weapons") are doomed to failure. What I say is meant as a challenge: is there a philosopher somewhere who would like to try?

My main purpose in announcing that I feel at home in "Ecosophy T" is didactic and dialectic. I hope to get others to announce their philosophy. If they say they have none, I maintain that they have, but perhaps don't know their own views, or are too modest or inhibited to proclaim what they believe. Following Socrates I want to provoke questioning until others know where they stand on basic matters of life and death. This is done using ecological issues, and also by using Ecosophy T as a foil. But Socrates pretended in debate that he knew nothing. My posture seems to be the opposite. I may seem to know everything and to derive it magically from a small set of hypotheses about the world. But both interpretations are misleading! Socrates did not consistently claim to know nothing, nor do I in my Ecosophy T pretend to have all that comprehensive a knowledge. He claimed to know, for instance, about the fallibility of humans' claims to know.

So, here is Ecosophy T!

Its fundamental norm is 'Self-realization!' But I do not use this expression in any narrow, individualistic sense. I want to give it an expanded meaning based on the distinction between Self and self conceived in certain Eastern traditions of âtman, comprising all the life forms, and selves (jivas) as usually interpreted in social and personal life. Using five words: maximum (long range, universal) Self realization![6] If I had to give up the term fearing its inevitable misunderstanding, I would use the term 'symbiosis'. "Maximize Self-realization!" could be interpreted in the direction of colossal egotrips. But "Maximize symbiosis!" could be interpreted in the opposite direction, that of the elimination of individuality in favor of collectivity.

Viewed systematically, not individually, maximum Self-realization implies maximizing the manifestations of life. So I next derive the second term, "Maximize (long range, universal) diversity!" A corollary is that the higher the levels of Self-realization which are attained by a person, the more any further increase depends upon the Self-realization of others. Increased self-identification is increased identification with others. "Altruism" is a natural consequence of this identification.

This leads to a hypothesis about an inescapable increase of identification with other beings when one's own self-realization increases. We increasingly see ourselves in others, and others in ourselves. The self is extended and deepened as a natural process of the realization of its potentialities in others.

Universalizing, we can derive the norm, "Self-realization for every being!" From "Diversity!" and a hypothesis that maximum diversity implies a maximum of symbiosis, is derived the norm "Maximum symbiosis!" Further, we work for life conditions such that there is a minimum of coercion in the life of others. And so on![7]

A philosophy as a world view inevitably has implications in practical situations. Ecosophy T therefore without apology moves on to concrete questions of life style. These will obviously show great variation because of differences in hypotheses about the world in which each of us is living, and in the 'factual' statements about the concrete situation in which we make a decision. I shall limit myself to a couple of areas where my "style" of thinking and behaving seem somewhat strange to friends and others who know a little about my philosophy. Firstly, a somewhat extreme appreciation of diversity; positive appreciation of the existence of styles and behaviors which I personally detest or find nonsensical (but not clearly incompatible with symbiosis); enthusiasm for "the mere" diversity of species or varieties within a genus of plants or animals; support, as the head of a department of philosophy, of doctrinal theses completely at odds with my own inclinations, with only

the requirement that the authors are able to understand fairly adequately some basic features of the kind of philosophy I myself feel at home with; combination of **seemingly** incompatible interests and behaviors, which makes for an increase of subcultures within industrial states and might to some extent help future cultural diversity. So much about "diversity!"

Secondly, I have a somewhat extreme appreciation of what Kant calls beautiful actions (good actions based on inclination), in contrast to dutiful ones. The choice of the formulation 'Self-realization!' is in part motivated by the belief that maturity in humans can be measured along a scale from selfishness to Selfishness, that is, broadening and deepening the self, rather than measures of dutiful altruism. I see joyful sharing and caring as a natural process (which, I regret, is somewhat retarded in myself).

Thirdly, I believe that many-sided, high level Self-realization is more easily reached through a "spartan" life style than through the material standard of average citizens of industrial states.

The simple formulations of the deep ecology platform and Ecosophy T are not meant primarily to be used among philosophers, but in dialogues with "the experts." When I wrote to them personally, asking whether they accept the 8 points of the platform, many answered positively in relation to most or all points. And this includes top people in ministries of oil and energy! But it is still an open question to what extent they are willing to let their written answers be widely published. It is also an open question to what extent they try to influence their colleagues who use only shallow argumentation. The main conclusion is moderately encouraging: there is a philosophy of the man/nature relationship widely accepted among established experts responsible for environmental decisions which requires a pervasive, substantial change of present policies – in favor of our "living" planet, and not only for shortsighted human interests.

Notes

1 For more about interspecific community relationships, see Arne Naess, "Self-realization in Mixed Communities of Humans, Bears, Sheep, and Wolves," *Inquiry* 22 (1979): 321–41.

2 Many authors take some steps towards derivational structures, offering mild systematizations. The chapter

on "environmental ethics and hope" in G. Tyler Miller, *Living in the Environment*, 3rd edn. (Belmont: Wadsworth, 1983) is a valuable start, but the derivational relations are unclear. The logic and semantics of simple models of normative systems is briefly discussed in my "Notes on the Methodology of Normative Systems," *Methodology and Science* 10 (1977): 64–79. For defense of the thesis that as soon as persons assert anything at all we assume a total view, implicit with ontology, methodology, epistemology and ethics, see my "Reflections about Total Views," *Philosophy and Phenomenological Research* 25 (1964–5): 16–29. The best and wittiest warning against taking systematizations too seriously is to be found in Soren Kierkegaard, "Concluding Unscientific Postscript."

3 Trusting Bill Devall, one may say that "Muir is now understood as the first Taoist of American ecology." Devall, "John Muir as Deep Ecologist," *Environmental Review* 6 (1982); see also Michael Cohen, *The Pathless Way: John Muir and American Wilderness* (Madison: Univ. of Wisconsin Press, 1984).

4 For empirical studies of attitudes of "Wilderness-users," see the survey by Chris R. Kent (16438 Clymer St., Granada Hills, CA 91344) in his thesis "The Experiential Process of Nature Mysticism . . .," Humboldt State Univ., 1981.

5 *Living in the Environment*, 489.

6 The term *âtman* is not taken in its absolutistic senses, not as a permanent indestructible "soul." This makes it consistent with those Buddhist denials (the *avâtman doctrine*) that the *âtman* is to be taken in absolutist senses. Within the Christian tradition some theologians distinguish "ego" and "true self" in ways similar to these distinctions in Eastern religion. See the ecophilosophical interpretation of the gospel of Luke in Stephen Verney's *Onto the New Age* (Glasgow: Collins, 1976), 33–41.

7 For criticism and defence of this fundamental norm, and my answer, see *In Sceptical Wonder, Essays in Honor of Arne Naess* (Oslo: University Press, 1982). My main exposition of Ecosophy T was originally offered in the Norwegian work *Okologi, samfunn og livsstil* (Oslo: University Press, 5th edn. 1976). Even there, the exposition is sketchy.

---

30   Transpersonal Ecology

Warwick Fox

Transpersonal Ecology and Transpersonal Psychology

Naess's philosophical sense of deep ecology refers to the this-worldly realization of as expansive a sense of self as possible in a world in which selves and things-in-the-world are conceived as processes. Since this approach is one that involves the realization of a sense of self that extends beyond (or that is *trans-*) one's egoic, biographical, or personal sense of self, the clearest, most accurate, and most informative term for this sense of deep ecology is, in my view, *transpersonal ecology*.

The fact that the term *transpersonal* derives from recent work in psychology is appropriate since Naess's philosophical sense of deep ecology obviously refers to a psychologically based approach to the question of our relationship with the rest of nature as opposed to an axiologically based (i.e., a value theory based) approach. [. . .]

There are two main points that should immediately be noted in connection with my introduction of the term *transpersonal*. First, there is one point that I want to make absolutely clear (if it isn't already) in regard to the use of the prefix *trans-*. It is possible that some people who hear the term *transpersonal ecology* for the first time but who are aware neither of the context

From *Toward a Transpersonal Ecology: Developing New Foundations for Environmentalism* (Boston: Shambhala Publications, Inc., 1990), pp. 197–206, 213–15, 242–7. © 1990 by Warwick Fox. Reprinted with permission from the author.

(and, hence, the intended meaning) of this term as discussed herein nor of the emerging field of transpersonal *psychology* might interpret the prefix *trans-* in *transpersonal* to mean "across," as in *transcontinental*. Thus, *transpersonal* might be taken to suggest something like "across persons," and this in turn could suggest that *transpersonal ecology* refers in some way to an *anthropocentric* approach to ecology. However, the prefix *trans-* also means, *inter alia*, "beyond," as in *transcend*; "changing thoroughly," as in *transfigure*, *transform*, or *transliterate*; and "transcending," as in *transubstantiation*.[1] And it is these meanings of extending "beyond," "changing thoroughly," and "transcending" one's egoic, biographical, or personal sense of self that the originators of the term *transpersonal* (i.e., Stanislav Grof, Abraham Maslow, and Anthony Sutich), and others influenced by them, have always intended by this term. In general, the most convenient way of capturing these senses of *trans-* is simply to employ the word *beyond*. Thus, Maslow employs this word when he speaks of transpersonal as meaning "beyond individuality, beyond the development of the individual person into something which is more inclusive than the individual person"; [. . .]

A transpersonal approach to ecology is, then, precisely *not* an anthropocentric approach to ecology. [. . .] Rather, a transpersonal approach to ecology is concerned precisely with *opening* to ecological awareness; with realizing one's ecological, wider, or big Self; or, as I have already expressed it, with the this-worldly realization of as expansive a sense of self as possible.

Having said that, however, it is important to add that a transpersonal approach to ecology does not *deny* the existence of the egoic, biographical, or personal sense of self. This can be seen if we consider transpersonal psychologists' use of the word *beyond*. Although this word can mean either *to* the far side of something or *at* the far side of something, it is axiomatic in transpersonal uses of this word that it is intended in the first sense of *extending beyond* the limits of one's egoic, biographical, or personal sense of self, rather than in the second sense of *lying beyond*, that is, existing wholly *outside* those limits. Thus, when transpersonal psychologists employ the word *beyond* in a transpersonal sense, they mean to *include* the egoic, biographical, or personal sense of self while also pointing, as Maslow says, to "something which is *more inclusive* than the individual person" (emphasis added).

The second main point to be noted in this introduction of the term *transpersonal ecology* is this: the fact that this term implies the existence of a relationship with those recent developments in psychology that go under the heading of transpersonal psychology is in no way intended to suggest that theorizing in transpersonal ecology should be subordinated to theorizing in transpersonal psychology. Rather, transpersonal ecology has as much to do with "ecologizing" transpersonal psychology (which is by *no means* free from anthropocentric theorizing) as it has to do with "psychologizing" our ways of approaching ecophilosophical issues and of arguing for the views advocated by the ecocentric ecology movement. [. . .]

Many people who are attracted to spiritual views (including transpersonal theorists) see God, the Absolute, or the Ultimate as "pure consciousness," or something similar; and see humans as participating more in this ideal than other beings and, consequently, as superior to them. [. . .] (This gnosticized Darwinism – "we are God-in-the-process-of-becoming" – sort of view is associated with many New Age/traditional wisdom adherents.) Thus, one will find transpersonal theorists as respected as Ken Wilber saying things that are radically anthropocentric (not to mention scientifically bankrupt) like "cosmic evolution . . . is completed in and as human evolution, which itself reaches ultimate unity consciousness and so completes that absolute gestalt toward which all manifestation moves," and referring to "the very lowest levels of being" as "the levels that are *sub*human, such as matter, plant, reptile, and mammal" (emphasis added).[2] Transpersonal ecologists reject such views outright. They point out that it shows a total lack of evolutionary (and, hence, ecological) understanding to think of viruses, eucalyptus trees, flies, salmon, frogs, eagles, dolphins, and humans as members of a series that can meaningfully be compared along some linear scale (or Great Chain of Being) of developmental perfection. Rather, evolution has to be thought of as a luxuriously branching bush, not as a linear scale that is filled in by greater and lesser examples of some ideal end point. The fact that all life forms are the products of *distinct* evolutionary pathways and ecological relationships means that, at any given point in time, they should be thought of as more or less perfect (complete) examples *of their own kind*. In evolutionary terms, it simply makes no sense to say that evolution is "completed in and as human evolution" or to refer to other entities or life forms as "subhuman" – never mind Wilber's suggestion that humans are not mammals!

As with a considerable number of other theorists in transpersonal psychology, anthropocentric assumptions are built into Wilber's approach at the theoretical level by virtue of his subscription to a hierarchical ontology of a kind that is generally associated, in the West, with the Renaissance and medieval idea of the Great Chain of Being and with Gnosticism. In contrast, a number of other theorists in transpersonal psychology have avoided anthropocentrism at the theoretical level but then failed to draw out the nonanthropocentric implications of their own theorizing. Thus, Abraham Maslow, for example, seems explicitly to have precluded anthropocentric theorizing in transpersonal psychology when he wrote in regard to this emerging "fourth force" in psychology that it was to be "transpersonal, transhuman, centered in the cosmos rather than in human needs and interest, going beyond humanness, identity, self-actualization, and the like," and that the reason we need such a psychology is because "without the transcendent and the transpersonal, we get sick, violent, and nihilistic, or else hopeless and apathetic. We need something 'bigger than we are' to be awed by and to commit ourselves to in a new, naturalistic, empirical, non-churchly sense, perhaps as Thoreau and Whitman, William James and John Dewey did."[3]

Maslow's endorsement of a "naturalistic, empirical, non-churchly" (or what we might call a thoroughly "this-worldly") approach to the question of our ultimate concerns is consistent with other basic features of his work. For example, Maslow was always concerned to point out that his theorizing was grounded in empirical reality and that his proposals were open to empirical investigation; he had a profound respect for "the *biological* rooting of the value life"; and he continually pointed to Spinozist and Taoist attitudes as characterizing those individuals whom he described as "transcending self-actualizers" (i.e., he continually pointed to those attitudes that are associated with living "under the aspect of eternity" in this world as opposed to some "next" or "hidden" world that is presumed to be superior to or more real than this world).[4]

Yet despite having originally pointed transpersonal psychology in both a nonanthropocentric and a naturalistic direction (as opposed to the anthropocentric and transcendental direction that has been pursued by Wilber and some other transpersonal theorists), Maslow still proceeded to describe the attributes of transpersonal modes of being in terms like this: "Identification-love . . . means transcendence of the selfish Self. It implies also a wider circle of identifications, i.e., with more and more and more people approaching *the limit of identification with all human beings*. This can also be phrased as the more and more inclusive Self. *The limit here is identification with the human species*" (emphases added).[5]

The general thrust of these comments is, as we will see, "pure Naess" – *except* for the fact that Maslow limits the maximum extent of human identifications (or the limits of "the more and more inclusive Self") to the rest of the human species. Although Maslow does occasionally speak of "behaving and relating, as ends rather than as means, to oneself, to significant others, to human beings in general, to other species, to nature, and to the cosmos,"[6] anthropocentric formulations are the norm in Maslow's writings. For example, the anthropocentric limit that he sets on identification in the "identification-love" quotation above is suggested both implicitly and explicitly at many points in the paper from which the quotation is taken. Yet there is absolutely no theoretical or empirical reason for Maslow to set such anthropocentric limits.

[. . .]

These observations on the relationship between transpersonal ecology and transpersonal psychology should be enough, then, to suggest two things. First, it should be clear that there is no *inherent* reason why theorizing in transpersonal psychology should be anthropocentric. And second, it should be equally clear that much theorizing in transpersonal psychology nevertheless *is* anthropocentric and, hence, that there is much work to be done in ecologizing transpersonal psychology.

[. . .]

Psychologizing Ecophilosophy

The fact that transpersonal ecology – the idea of the this-worldly realization of as expansive a sense of self as possible – refers to a psychologically based approach to ecophilosophical problems raises the interesting question of how we might conceive of the most widely recognized approaches to ecophilosophy (i.e., instrumental and intrinsic value theory approaches) in psychological rather than axiological (i.e., value theory) terms. It is illuminating to approach this question by considering a well-known and apparently widely accepted way of conceiving of human psychology or the *self*.

There is much theoretical and popular support for a dynamic, tripartite conception of the self. Specifically, most of us recognize a *desiring-impulsive* aspect of the self, a *rationalizing-deciding* aspect, and a *normative-judgmental* aspect. In fact, unless we are exceptionally well integrated, it is often more appropriate to speak not so much of three aspects of *the* self but rather of three selves. Thus, we can speak of a desiring-impulsive self, a rationalizing-deciding self, and a normative-judgmental self. It should of course be noted that these labels simply refer to hypothetical constructs. The validity of these constructs rests upon their usefulness in both describing certain recognizable systems of thought and behavior and illuminating the dynamics between these systems.[7]

The desiring-impulsive self wants much (the desiring aspect) and wants it *now* (the impulsive aspect). This means that it functions without particular regard for others, the future, or the constraints that are imposed by reality in general. The normative-judgmental self sets standards or expectations on our behavior, whether in the moral sphere, where it decrees what *ought* to be and demands conformance with a certain code of conduct, or in other spheres of activity, where it also expects the attainment of certain standards of performance. It judges "us" (the other aspects of our self – or our other selves) critically if we fall short of its standards or expectations. The rationalizing-deciding self sees itself as the decision maker or the locus of control with respect to the three selves. This means that it mediates between the competing demands of the desiring-impulsive self, the normative-judgmental self, and the constraints that are imposed by reality.

This general kind of dynamic, tripartite conception of the self finds popular support in the pre-Darwinian and pre-Freudian distinctions that people commonly used to make (and to some extent still do make) between their *lower* – also called *animal* or *primitive* – nature (i.e., their desiring-impulsive self), their *rational* nature (i.e., their rationalizing-deciding self), and their *higher* nature or conscience (i.e., their normative-judgmental self). This tripartite conception also finds theoretical support in more rigorous, psychological analyses of the self, which (in the West) is to say in Freudian and post-Freudian psychology. For example, the tripartite conception I have outlined has strong parallels with Freud's

division of the personality into *id*, *ego*, and *superego*. Indeed, my characterization of the rationalizing-deciding self as the self that mediates between the competing demands of the desiring-impulsive self, the normative-judgmental self, and the constraints that are imposed by reality represents a more or less textbook definition of the Freudian ego. In terms of more recent psychotherapeutic approaches, this tripartite conception also has strong parallels, for example, with the division that is made in transactional analysis – not to be confused with transpersonal approaches – between childlike, adultlike, and parentlike aspects of the personality (transactional analysts refer to these aspects of the personality simply as *child*, *adult*, and *parent*).

When we attempt to conceptualize the instrumental and intrinsic value theory approaches [...] in psychological rather than axiological terms we find a compelling correspondence between these approaches and the well-known and obviously useful tripartite conception of the self that I have just outlined. Specifically, the kind of self that is emphasized *in regard to our relations with the nonhuman world* in the unrestrained exploitation and expansionism approach is the desiring-impulsive, "primitive," id-like, or childlike self, which functions without particular regard for others, the future, or the constraints that are imposed by reality in general; the kind of self that is emphasized *in regard to our relations with the nonhuman world* in the resource conservation and development and resource preservation approaches is the rationalizing-deciding, "rational," (Freudian) ego-like, or adultlike self, which mediates between the competing demands of the desiring-impulsive self, the normative-judgmental self, and the constraints that are imposed by reality; and the kind of self that is emphasized *in regard to our relations with the nonhuman world* in intrinsic value theory approaches in general is the normative-judgmental, "higher," superego-like, or parentlike self, which, *inter alia*, decrees what *ought* to be and demands conformance with a certain code of conduct.

[. . .]

When we [. . .] consider those approaches that break with our anthropocentric traditions and argue for the moral considerability of the nonhuman world (i.e., intrinsic value theory approaches), we see that, however much these approaches may play upon one's feelings and inspire one to feel a certain way toward certain members or aspects of the nonhuman world, the end that such approaches serve is, finally, that of showing that certain members or aspects of the nonhuman world are morally considerable *irre-spective* of how one personally happens to feel about them. Objectivist intrinsic value theory approaches, in other words, are ultimately normative-judgmental in character. They attempt to show that it is morally wrong to do some things to certain members or aspects of the nonhuman world and morally right to do other things; that one's personal likes and dislikes – one's personal prejudices – are neither here nor there with respect to the validity of these judgments; and that, where conflict occurs between intrinsic value based concerns (i.e., moral concerns) and either appetitive, desiring-impulsive concerns or anthropocentric, "responsible management" concerns, it is the intrinsic value based concerns that should be given overriding priority.

These observations clearly suggest that the kind of self that is emphasized in intrinsic value theory approaches is the superego-like, normative-judgmental self, which, *inter alia*, decrees what *ought* to be and demands conformance with a certain code of conduct. This point can be illustrated further by comparing the ways in which the rationalizing-deciding self and the normative-judgmental self deal with particular intrinsic value theory claims. Take the ethical sentientism approach as an example. Ethical sentientists claim that it is always morally wrong to cause unnecessary suffering and that this implies that we should all be vegetarian (in view of this, Singer's already classic statement *Animal Liberation* concludes with an appendix entitled "Cooking for Liberated People," which provides a helpful guide to vegetarian cooking and an annotated list of vegetarian cookbooks). The approach of the rationalizing-deciding self to such normative-judgmental claims is to weigh them against the desiring-impulsive self's desire to eat meat, which may be strong, and to consider these competing demands within the context of the general availability of meat, which, these days, usually means its price. For the rationalizing-deciding self, each of these factors simply represents one factor that must be taken into account among others. Thus, the rationalizing-deciding self's mini-max solution to these competing psychic demands and reality-based constraints or opportunities is, in general, not to stop eating meat altogether but rather to eat somewhat less meat than was eaten prior to registering the normative-judgmental claims of ethical sentientism.

In contrast, the normative-judgmental self gives overriding priority to moral claims and so demands that one should stop eating meat altogether. The normative-judgmental self, in other words, is the psychological face of intrinsic value theory approaches since these approaches demand that intrinsic values should, in principle, be accorded overriding priority in deciding how to act as opposed to being regarded as "just another" factor that needs to be taken into account.

The overriding nature of moral claims is most obvious to us in the human realm. Here, for example, claims regarding the intrinsic worth of people mean that, in principle, it is always wrong to torture another person. It is no defense to say that you took their desire not to be tortured "into account" but nevertheless reached a decision that, "on balance," your desire to torture them, along with the likelihood that your crime would not be discovered (i.e., the lack of reality-based constraints), outweighed this "other factor." In respect of interactions between humans, it is *expected* that the interests of the normative-judgmental self should override any contrary decisions that the rationalizing-deciding self may make. Ecophilosophical intrinsic value theorists simply attempt to extend the domain of activities in which this expectation holds.

[. . .]

Proof, Moral Injunctions, and Experiential Invitations

As we have seen, deep ecologists – or transpersonal ecologists – sometimes reject approaches that issue in moral "oughts" without offering any explanation; at other times they offer any of a number of different reasons (e.g., they may hold such approaches to constitute a superficial approach to the issues concerned or to be repressive or ineffective). However, my analysis of the kind of self that is emphasized by approaches that issue in moral "oughts" suggests that the most fundamental reason for the fact that transpersonal ecologists reject these approaches is that these thinkers explicitly emphasize a wide, expansive, or field-like conception of self whereas advocates of approaches that issue in moral "oughts" necessarily emphasize a narrow, atomistic, or particle-like conception of self – whether they intend to do this or not. If this view is correct then transpersonal ecologists consider these approaches to be superficial, repressive, or ineffective precisely *because* they emphasize a limited and limiting conception of self.

This rejection of approaches that issue in moral "oughts" explains a peculiar and, for many, a particularly frustrating fact about the transpersonal ecology approach. Specifically, the fact that transpersonal ecologists are not in the business of wanting to claim that their conclusions are *morally binding* on others means that they do not attempt to *prove* the correctness of their approach. They present their approach as a realistic, positive option (i.e., as an approach that one *can* take and that one might *want* to take) rather than as a logically or morally established obligation (i.e., as an approach with which one ought to *comply*). [. . .]

Rather than dealing with moral *injunctions*, transpersonal ecologists are therefore inclined far more to what might be referred to as experiential *invitations*: readers or listeners are invited to experience themselves as intimately bound up with the world around them, bound up to such an extent that it becomes more or less impossible to *refrain* from wider identification (i.e., impossible to refrain from the this-worldly realization of a more expansive sense of self).

[. . .]

Transpersonal ecologists claim that ecology, and modern science in general, provides a compelling account of our interconnectedness with the world. However, they are not in the business of attempting to claim that this fact *logically* implies that we ought to care about the world. The fact of our interconnectedness with the world does not *logically* imply either that we ought to care about the world of which we are a part or that we ought *not* to care about it. Logic, in other words, is of no help to us either way in proceeding from the fact of our interconnectedness with the world to the practical question of how we should live. Accordingly, transpersonal ecologists are not concerned with the question of the *logical* connection between the fact that we are intimately bound up with the world and the question of how we should behave but rather with the *psychological* connection between this fact and our behavior. Their analysis of the self is such that they consider that if one has a deep understanding of the way things *are* (i.e., if one empathically incorporates the fact that we and all other entities are aspects of a single unfolding reality) then one *will* (as opposed to should) naturally be inclined to care for the unfolding of the world in all its aspects. For transpersonal ecologists, this kind of response to the fact of our interconnectedness with the world represents a natural (i.e., spontaneous) unfolding of human potentialities. Indeed, given a deep enough understanding of this fact, we can scarcely *refrain* from responding in this way. This is why one finds transpersonal ecologists making statements to the effect that they are more concerned with ontology or cosmology (i.e., with the general question of the way the world is) than with ethics.

[. . .] Transpersonal ecology constitutes a distinctive approach to ecophilosophy in that it emphasizes a fundamentally different kind of self to the kinds of self that are emphasized by instrumental and intrinsic value theory approaches. Understanding this fact enables us to see why transpersonal ecologists reject approaches that issue in moral "oughts" [. . .] and why they do not attempt to prove the correctness of their views in such a way that their conclusions are morally binding on others. In both cases, the reason is that they are not interested in supporting approaches that serve to reinforce the primary reality of the narrow, atomistic, or particle-like volitional self. For transpersonal ecologists, given a deep enough understanding of the way things are, the response of being inclined to care for the unfolding of the world in all its aspects follows "naturally" – not as a *logical* consequence but as a *psychological* consequence; as an expression of the spontaneous unfolding (development, maturing) of the self.

Notes

1 *Collins English Dictionary.*
2 Ken Wilber, *Eye to Eye: The Quest for the New Paradigm* (Garden City, NY: Anchor Books, 1983), p. 100; and Ken Wilber, "Odyssey: A Personal Inquiry into Humanistic and Transpersonal Psychology," *Journal of Humanistic Psychology* 22(1) (1982): 57–90, p. 72. See also Ken Wilber, *Up from Eden: A Transpersonal View of Human Evolution* (New York: Doubleday, 1981).
3 Abraham H. Maslow, *Toward a Psychology of Being*, 2nd edn. (Princeton: D. Van Nostrand, 1968), p. iv.
4 The phrase "the biological rooting of the value life" is taken from the title of Maslow's paper "A Theory of Metamotivation: The Biological Rooting of the Value-Life," contained in his book *The Farther Reaches of Human Nature* (New York: The Viking Press, 1971), pp. 299–342; reprinted in part in Walsh and Vaughan,

eds., *Beyond Ego: Transpersonal Dimensions in Psychology*, pp. 122–31. On the Spinozist/Taoist point see, for example, the chapters entitled "Various Meanings of Transcendence" and "Theory Z" in *The Farther Reaches of Human Nature*, pp. 269–79 and 280–95 respectively.

5 Maslow, *The Farther Reaches of Human Nature*, p. 272.
6 Ibid., p. 279.
7 In regard to this general point, see John Rowan, "The Self: One or Many," *The Psychologist*, July 1989, pp. 279–81.

B Environmental Virtue Ethics

31 Environmental Virtue Ethics

Ronald Sandler

There is at least one certainty regarding the human relationship with nature: there is no getting away from it. One simply cannot opt out of a relationship with the natural world. On some accounts this is because humans are themselves a part of nature. On others it is because we must breathe, eat, drink, and decompose, each of which involves an exchange with the natural world. But whereas a relationship with nature is given, the nature of that relationship is not. Both human history and the contemporary world are replete with diverse and contradictory ways of conceiving of and interacting with the natural environment. Environmental ethics as a field of inquiry is the attempt to understand the human relationship with the environment (including natural ecosystems, agricultural ecosystems, urban ecosystems, and the individuals that populate and constitute those systems) and determine the norms that should govern our interactions with it. These norms can be either norms of action or norms of character. The project of specifying the latter is *environmental virtue ethics*, and a particular account of the character dispositions that we ought to have regarding the environment is an *environmental virtue ethic*.

Why Is There a Need for an Environmental Virtue Ethic?

The central ethical question is, "How should one live?" Answering this question of course requires providing an account of what actions we ought and ought not to perform. But an account of right action – whether a set of rules, a general principle, or a decision-making procedure – does not answer it entirely. A complete answer will inform not only what we ought to do but also what kind of person we ought to be. An adequate ethical theory must provide an ethic of character, and our lived ethical experience belies the claim that one's character is merely the sum of one's actions. Environmental ethics is simply ethics as it pertains to human–environment interactions and relationships. So an adequate environmental ethic likewise requires not only an ethic of action – one that provides guidance regarding what we ought and ought not to do to the environment – but also an ethic of character – one that provides guidance on what attitudes and dispositions we ought and ought not to have regarding the environment.

Consider four widely regarded environmental heroes: Rachel Carson (naturalist and author of *Silent Spring*), John Muir (naturalist and founder of the Sierra Club), Aldo Leopold (wildlife ecologist and author of *A Sand County Almanac*), and Julia Butterfly Hill (activist who lived two years atop a threatened redwood). Why do we admire these individuals? Is it their accomplishments in defense of the environment? Yes. The sacrifices they made for those accomplishments? Of course. Their capacity to motivate others to take action? To be sure. But it is not only what they have done and the legacy they have left that we admire. It is also them – the individuals who managed those accomplishments, made those sacrifices, and have left those legacies. That is, we admire them also for their character – their fortitude, compassion, wonder, sensitivity, respectfulness, courage, love, appreciation, tenacity, and gratitude.

It is not always easy to keep this dimension of environmentalism in mind. Public discourse regarding the environment tends to be framed almost exclusively in legislative and legal terms, so it is tempting to become fixated on what activities and behaviors regarding the environment are or ought to be legal. After all, we might restrict the use of off-road vehicles in an ecologically sensitive area and take legal action against those who fail to adhere to that boundary; but we will not legislate against ecological insensitivity or indifference itself, and no one will be called to court merely for possessing those attitudes. We legislate regarding behavior, not character; policy concerns actions, not attitudes; and the courts apply the standards accordingly.

But as our environmental heroes remind us – both by example and by word – we must not take so narrow a perspective of our relationship with the environment. It is always *people* – with character traits, attitudes, and dispositions – who perform actions, promote policies, and lobby for laws. So while we decry removing mountaintops, filling wetlands, and poisoning wolves and we make our case against these practices before lawmakers, the courts, and the public, we must also consider the character of persons responsible for them. Indeed, how one interacts with the environment is largely determined by one's disposition toward it, and it seems to many that the enabling cause of reckless environmental exploitation is the attitude that nature is merely a boundless resource for satisfying human wants and needs. In Muir's words, "No dogma taught by the present civilization seems to form so insuperable an obstacle in the way of a right understanding of the relations which culture sustains to wildness as that which regards the world as made especially for the uses of man." So it would seem that any significant change in our environmental practices and policies is going to require a substantial shift in our dispositions toward the environment. In this way proper character is indispensable for facilitating right action and behavior.

But as our environmental heroes also remind us – again, by example and by word – environmental virtue is not merely instrumentally valuable as the disposition to identify and then perform proper actions; it is also valuable in itself. It is life-affirming and life-enhancing. Those who possess it are better off than those who do not, for they are able to find reward, satisfaction, and comfort from their relationship with nature; and it is their character – their capacity to appreciate, respect, and love nature – that opens them to these benefits. "Those who dwell, as scientists or laymen, among the beauties and mysteries of the earth are never alone or weary of life," writes Carson; and according to Muir, "Everybody needs beauty as well as bread, places to play in and pray in, where nature may heal and give strength to body and soul alike." To those who are receptive to it, nature is a source of joy, peace, renewal, and self-knowledge.

Once the need for an environmental virtue ethic is recognized two questions immediately present themselves. First, what are the attitudes and dispositions that constitute environmental virtue? Second, what is the proper role of an ethic of character in an environmental ethic? These two issues – specifying environmental virtue and identifying the appropriate role of virtue in an environmental ethic – are central to environmental virtue ethics and largely orient the philosophical work that appears in this collection. The remainder of this introduction is intended to serve as a primer on these issues and to locate the contributions in this collection within these philosophical themes.

Specifying Environmental Virtue

The environmental virtues are the proper dispositions or character traits for human beings to have regarding their interactions and relationships with the environment. The environmentally virtuous person is disposed to respond – both emotionally and through action – to the environment and the non-human individuals (whether inanimate, living, or conscious) that populate it in an excellent or fine way. But although this formal account may be accurate, it does not provide any substantive description of what the environmentally virtuous person will actually be like. So how does one establish which dispositions regarding the environment are constitutive of virtue and which are constitutive of vice (and which are neither)? That is, how does one go about providing a substantive account of the environmental virtues and vices?

Perhaps the most common strategy for specifying environmental virtue is to argue by extension from standard interpersonal virtues, that is, from virtues that are typically applied to relationships among humans. Each interpersonal virtue is normative for a particular range of items, activities, or interactions, and that range is its sphere or field of applicability. For example, the field of honesty is the revealing or withholding of truth; the field of temperance is bodily pleasures and pains; and the field of generosity is the giving and withholding of material goods. Extensionists attempt to expand the range of certain interpersonal virtues to include nonhuman entities by arguing that the features that characterize their fields in interpersonal interaction or relationships also obtain in (at least some) environmental contexts. The virtues, they conclude, should therefore be normative in those environmental contexts as well. For example, if compassion is the appropriate disposition to have toward the suffering of other human beings and there is no relevant moral difference between human suffering and the suffering of nonhuman animals, then one should be compassionate toward the suffering of nonhuman animals. Or if gratitude is the appropriate disposition toward other human beings from whom one has benefited and one has similarly benefited from the natural environment, then gratitude is also an appropriate disposition to have toward the natural environment. Extension from the substance of the interpersonal virtues is thus one strategy for specifying the environmentally virtuous person.

A second strategy is to appeal to agent benefit. On this approach, what establishes a particular character trait as constitutive of environmental virtue is that it typically benefits its possessor. This is a wide-ranging approach bounded only by the limit to the ways in which the environment benefits moral agents. The environment provides not only material goods – such as clean water and air – but also aesthetic goods, recreational goods, and a location to exercise and develop physically, intellectually, morally, and aesthetically. That the environment can benefit individuals in such ways straightforwardly justifies a disposition to preserve these opportunities and goods. But it does not only justify a disposition toward conservation and preservation. It justifies cultivating the kind of character traits that allow one to enjoy those goods. The natural environment provides the opportunity for aesthetic experience, but that benefit accrues only to those who possess the disposition to appreciate the natural environment in that way. It provides the opportunity for intellectual challenge and reward, but those benefits come only to those who are disposed first to wonder and then to try to understand nature. The natural environment provides plentiful opportunities for meaning-

ful relationships with its denizens, but those relationships are only possible for those who are open to having them. So considerations of which environmental dispositions benefit their possessor (and allow their possessor to be benefited by the natural environment) are relevant to the substantive specification of environmental virtue. In this way environmental virtue ethics emphasizes the role that enlightened self-interest can play in promoting or motivating environmental consciousness and its corresponding behavior in a way that reinforces rather than undermines the other-regarding aspects of environmental ethics. It allows for environmental ethics to be self-interested without being egoistic.

A third strategy for the specification of environmental virtue is to argue from considerations of human excellence. On this approach what establishes a particular character trait as constitutive of environmental virtue is that it makes its possessor a good human being. What it means to be a good human being – to flourish as a human being – is typically understood naturalistically. That is, it is understood in terms of the characteristic features of the life of members of the human species. Human beings are, for example, social beings. Excellence as a human being therefore involves character dispositions that promote the good functioning of social groups and encourage one to maintain healthy relationships with members in the group. A human being who is disposed to undermine social cohesion, disrupt the conditions that make cooperation among individuals possible, and sour relationships with others is properly described as deviant. Such a person fails to be a good human being precisely in virtue of his or her antisocial disposition. Many environmental philosophers have argued that a proper naturalistic understanding of human beings will locate them not only socially (as members of the human community) but also ecologically (as members of the broader biotic community). If this is correct, then excellence as a human being would include dispositions to maintain and promote the well-being of the larger ecological community. Given that the well-being of the ecological community is threatened by further habitat fragmentation and biodiversity loss, a disposition to oppose these would thereby be constitutive of environmental virtue. A human being who lacked these dispositions would, from the perspective of human beings as members of the biotic community, be properly described as deviant. Considerations of human excellence need not, however, be confined to secular or naturalistic accounts of environmental virtue. Human excellence is often understood by religious traditions in a way that transcends the natural by connecting it with divine or cosmic purposes. For example, if it is the divinely proscribed role of human beings that they be stewards of the land, then the environmental virtues will be those character traits or dispositions that make human beings reliable and effective stewards.

A fourth strategy for specifying environmental virtue is to study the character traits of individuals who are recognized as environmental role models. By examining the life, work, and character of exemplars of environmental excellence we may be able to identify particular traits that are conducive to, or constitutive of, that excellence. The lives of John Muir, Rachel Carson, and Aldo Leopold, for example, are not just compelling narratives; they also instruct us on how to improve ourselves and our approach to the natural world. Environmental role models of course need not be such public or renowned figures as Carson, Muir, and Leopold. Exemplars of environmental excellence can be found in local communities and in many organizations working for environmental protection and improvement. No doubt many of us have been benefited by such people, not only by their accomplishments but also by the guidance, inspiration, and example they provide.

These four approaches to the specification of environmental virtue – extensionism, considerations of benefit to agent, considerations of human excellence, and the study of role models – are not mutually exclusive. A particular disposition might draw support from all four approaches. Indeed, in the contributions in this collection one often finds them working in concert. Collectively they provide a rich variety of resources for thinking about the substance of environmental virtue.

The Role of Environmental Virtue in Environmental Ethics

A complete environmental ethic will include both an account of how one ought to interact with the natural environment and an account of the character dispositions that one ought to have regarding the natural environment. But what is the proper relationship between these two? This is an instance of the more general (and very much live) question in moral philosophy: What is the appropriate role of virtue in ethical theory?

Some moral philosophers believe that the virtues are simply dispositions to do the right thing. In the context of environmental ethics this would imply that environmental virtue is merely the disposition to act according to the rules, principles, or norms of action of the correct environmental ethic. On this account the environmental virtues are strictly instrumental and subordinate to right action. First one determines what the right ways to act or behave regarding the environment are, and then one determines which character dispositions tend to produce that behavior. Those dispositions are the environmental virtues.

I argued earlier that environmental virtue is instrumental to promoting proper action. The environmentally virtuous person – precisely because of his or her virtue – will be disposed both to recognize the right thing and to do it for the right reasons. However, there is more to how one ought to be in the world than the rules, principles, or guidelines of moral action. For example, it might not be morally required that one appreciate the beauty or complexity of the natural environment, but those who are disposed to do so are benefited and so better off than those who are not. So although it is undoubtedly true that the environmental virtues are dispositions to act well regarding the environment, they are not only that. As we have seen, they can be excellences or beneficial to their possessor in their own right, not merely insofar as they tend to produce right action.

Moreover, environmental virtue might provide the sensitivity or wisdom necessary for the application of action-guiding rules and principles to concrete situations. At a minimum, this sensitivity is required to determine which rules or principles are applicable to which situations, as well as for determining what course of action they recommend in those situations where they are operative. But it may also be indispensable in adjudicating between conflicting demands of morality or resolving moral dilemmas that arise from a plurality of sources of value and justification. Indeed, many moral philosophers have argued that it is implausible and unreasonable to believe that there is some finite set of rules or principles that can be applied by any human moral agent in any situation to determine what the proper course of action is in that situation. If they are correct – if action guidance cannot always be accomplished by moral rules and principles alone – then the wisdom and sensitivity that are part of virtue (including environmental virtue) are in some situations indispensable for determining or identifying right action (including environmentally right action).

Some moral philosophers believe that virtue should play an even more prominent or fundamental role within ethical theory than it is afforded in the previous account. These virtue ethicists consider an ethic of character to be theoretically prior to an ethic of action. On this approach to moral philosophy an action is right if and only if it is the virtuous thing to do, it hits the target of virtue, or it is what the virtuous person would do under the circumstances. So a substantive account of the virtues and the virtuous person informs what actions one ought or ought not to perform. In the context of environmental ethics this would imply that reflections on the content of the virtues and studying the character traits and behavior of environmentally virtuous people are what ultimately inform how we ought to behave regarding the environment.

There is thus a range of roles – from instrumental to foundational – that environmental virtue might play within a complete environmental ethic. This is not, however, to claim that each position is equally defensible. I have, for example, argued that a merely instrumental role for environmental virtue is too narrow. But those arguments notwithstanding, it is very much an unsettled issue what the proper role (or roles) of virtue is in an adequate environmental ethic.

C Continental Environmental Ethics

32 On Environmental Philosophy and Continental Thought

Steven Vogel

Recently the question of what insights and conceptual resources the traditions of continental philosophy might provide to contemporary environmental thought has received much attention; in this essay I would like to consider this issue, focusing in particular on the traditions associated with poststructuralism. To some extent, interest in this question among environmental philosophers has been marked by a fair degree of anxiety – a vague sense that "postmodernism," by turning the whole world into a text, denies the very existence of nature and therefore the significance of attempts either to understand the dangers to which it is currently exposed or to argue for the need to protect it.[1] Others, of course, have argued on the contrary that contemporary continental thought is not only compatible with but indispensable for an environmental philosophy capable of grasping the character and origin of our current environmental crisis.[2] I want in this essay to ask the question of the relation between the "postmodern turn" and environmental theory not so much in terms of the particular debates it has already engendered, but rather at a more abstract level.[3] I will identify four accounts of nature that might be distinguished in contemporary continental thought, and try to point out both the connections among them and also the difficulties they each face, asking in turn of each what it might provide in terms of a philosophically adequate environmental theory. The second and third of these are familiar ones deriving from contemporary poststructuralism. The first is probably familiar too, but is older, and is presented

here as a contrast, while the fourth, which I will end up defending, is perhaps less well known and hearkens back to an earlier continental tradition associated with certain forms of Hegelian Marxism. The accounts here will be sketchy ones, for which I apologize in advance; what I am interested in developing is a kind of typology of views of nature, and thus what I present will have something of the character of ideal types.

Nature as Origin

Some of those who worry about the supposedly pernicious influence of poststructuralism on environmental philosophy do so in the name of a view of nature that has its own (often unacknowledged) pedigree in the history of continental thought, originating in traditions of Romanticism, vitalism, and neo-Kantianism. The view is certainly a familiar one, and holds a powerful grasp on the contemporary environmental imagination, especially that associated with "deep ecology" and similarly radical views. Nature on this account functions as an immense and complex organic whole, a massive order in which humans are embedded and out of which they emerged. This order has its own logic and teleology that transcend human understanding and even in a certain sense the human world. The "natural" here, indeed, is contrasted with the human-made or "artificial": what is natural is that which occurs through the workings of that massive whole independently of

From *Philosophy Today*, vol. 42 (SPEP Supplement, 1998): 169–81. © 1998 by Steven Vogel. Reprinted with permission from the author.

human will or action. Humans have a strange (and in fact paradoxical) role in this account, since they too are part of nature and hence are subject to this higher teleological order, yet in applying "calculative" or "instrumental" rationality in a doomed attempt to achieve control over it they forget their own rootedness in the natural, with dangerous consequences. Similarly, the natural is contrasted in this sort of view with the social, via a set of dichotomies whose tenor we recognize well from Rousseau. Natural impulses are reminders of our animal selves, which is to say our real selves; on top of those are imposed social rules and conventions which serve to transform (and thereby to corrupt) those impulses, producing a social world whose artificial character shows it to be a locus of distortion and deception. Thus humans behave naturally when they act in accordance with "natural processes" (i.e., those that would take place anyway in their absence) while their actions are harmful and unnatural (and immoral) when they act in ways indifferent or worse at cross-purposes to those processes. It is the hubristic human dream that our actions could fundamentally transform (indeed, master) nature that leads ultimately to a series of technological and other acts whose ultimate consequence is environmental disaster. I take it that the general contours of this kind of account are well-known.

"Nature" on this view stands for a stable world that precedes humans, ontologically prior to human activity and to the social structures (and the language) within which that activity takes place. It is what the world, including the social world, is made of. The practical processes in which human beings engage – the practices through which they provide for themselves shelter, food, and the prerequisites for communal existence – are ones that may transform the pre-given natural reality but do not in any serious sense generate a new one. The hubris of technology is the hubris of a culture that has forgotten this, believing that we can transform the world *essentially*. The utopian dreams of a technological mastery of nature forget that nature is both prior to and more powerful than anything humans can do, and so the "new world" of automobiles and nuclear power and genetic engineering and deodorized underarms they promise produces instead – and inevitably – a world of global warming, toxic wastes, dangerous genetic experimentation, and ozone holes.

The Critique of Nature

Nature on this first account is where we come from; it is the origin or foundation on which everything else is built, and we ignore this at our peril. It is this very notion of *nature as origin* that one significant strain in recent continental philosophy calls radically into question. Poststructuralism's celebrated antifoundationalism turns in this context into what might be called a "critique of nature": to the extent that "nature" is the term we use to stand for the original or foundational or immediate, it is precisely something whose existence various forms of poststructuralism tend to deny. The project of deconstruction, on one reading, is a project of taking that which appears to be original, foundational – in a word: natural – and revealing the complex processes of linguistic and social construction required to produce that appearance. The origin turns out, in this project, always to be constructed, and hence to be no origin at all; that which was supposed to be foundational is always discovered not to be what it claimed to be, what it was "meant" to be, and so the arrival of the origin is always, as Derrida famously puts it, deferred. With this, the promise that indeed there *is* something original, something out of which everything else is built but that was not itself built, becomes harder and harder to believe.

The unmistakable implication of this line of argument is thus that nature doesn't exist. The familiar view of nature as something prior to humans on which they work but which they cannot fundamentally transform is thereby rejected; a strongly antinaturalist impulse now expresses itself in the form of scholarly interest in something like a "cultural studies of nature" devoted to discovering the myriad ways in which the concept of nature is culturally produced and reproduced.[4] Views of nature turn out to be historically and socially contingent: what counts as natural in the post-industrial world today, for instance, is very much a function of the ambivalence with which that world views itself and what it has wrought. Furthermore, so-called "natural" landscapes turn out upon inspection frequently to require significant expenditures of human work to maintain them in the condition tourists looking for respite from the human world have come to expect.[5]

The concept of "wilderness" has come to play an important role in this debate. As has been noted by several authors, it is an idiosyncrasy specifically of

American environmental thought to emphasize the significance of wilderness and wilderness preservation as central to a progressive environmental program.[6] The idea of the untouched natural world, of areas where no human footprint can be found – and of the importance of preserving them – seems to play a role here that it does not, say, in Europe or the third world; and the social and historical reasons for this are not hard to imagine, whether these be the existence here of an enormous and for many centuries relatively unpopulated landmass or (more likely) the stupendous historical amnesia whereby a North America that before the seventeenth century was not *so* unpopulated is still viewed as somehow having been entirely empty of human beings.[7] In any case wilderness even here, if this is defined strictly as land absolutely untouched by human action, is awfully hard to find; instead the definition gets stretched and transformed in a way that provides ripe pickings for a strategy of deconstruction. What is held up as wilderness to be preserved from human intervention always turns out on examination to reveal, somewhere, the mark of the human, and so appears next as only "relatively" wild; the discovery of true wilderness, as always, is deferred, and all we have before us is wilderness's signifier.[8]

The "trouble with wilderness," as William Cronon calls it, reveals the antinomies that bedevil the naturalist views I associated earlier with vitalism and romanticism. Bill McKibben wrote a book some years ago that received much attention called *The End of Nature*, in which he argued that the widespread climate or atmospheric changes caused by greenhouse gases or chlorofluorocarbon use meant that nature in the sense of untouched wilderness no longer existed; his claim was that *this* was the environmental catastrophe – that there will never again be a "nature." Yet there was little recognition in his book that in fact such a catastrophe has always already taken place. The trees out his window in the Adirondacks, he complains, will never again be natural ones, responding as they now do to a climate transformed by human action – and yet he concedes elsewhere that the landscape surrounding him, including the (relatively young) forest, is itself the result of failed early colonial attempts at farming, as well as who knows what activities by pre-colonial inhabitants.[9] Which is to say, the nature whose end he bemoans really ended a while ago – and to answer the question of when requires a constant deferral as

the moment of origin gets pushed farther and farther into some mythic past. It is the Heideggerian *immer schon* one has to appeal to here: the human hand is always already on the earth, and to pine for the days when it was not is to pine for the sort of foundation we wish we had but must learn to live without.

If nature is that which is prior to the human, of course, then humans are not natural. There is a curious inconsistency within the view I am sketching between the claim that the natural excludes the artificial and the claim that humans are part of nature.[10] Humans are not the only organisms to have produced significant atmospheric change; but when we read of how the invention of oxygen-generating photosynthesis by the early cyanobacteria increased the oxygen concentration in the earth's atmosphere from one part in a million to one part in five (and wiped out a significant proportion of life on earth), we don't think of these bacteria as having ended nature.[11] They were themselves natural – but isn't the same true of humans? If nature gave rise to everything, then nature gave rise to us too, and to everything we produce, including superhighways and strip mines – and so pure nature turns out not to be so hard to find, nor so difficult to protect, nor (for that matter) so charming. On the other hand, if "unnatural" means "artificial" then all human action turns out to violate nature. The only way out of this antinomy is to introduce a dualism of a very traditional sort, whereby certain human functions (typically bodily ones) are treated as still natural whereas others (involving will and reason) are not. Such a dualism does not move an inch beyond Descartes, of course, except that the signs attached to the two sides are inverted; more to the point, however, with it the vaunted "holism" of nature is radically ruptured.

The deconstructive "critique of nature," then, is above all a critique of this impossible and antinomical dualism, pointing us towards the ways in which humans are always already entangled in the natural, and reminding us that while we are doubtless nature's product at the same time nature is always already our product too. This is so both in the sense that the way we see it and think of it never reveals to us a nature-*an-sich* but always a nature from our particular social and historical perspective, and also in the more direct and practical sense that we are active creatures, always building and rebuilding the world we inhabit, always (and always already) making it into our own. *There is no nature*, in the sense anyway of an origin or a world somehow beyond or underneath the human one; the single world in which we live is one in which we are always already active, and which we are further always already in the process of changing.

But then there is no world or thing to be "saved" from our changes, to be "preserved." If all worlds are equally human worlds – the precolonial Adirondacks inhabited by Algonquins and Iroquois, the not-quite-wilderness where McKibben today makes his home, and some future one where his beloved forests have been clear-cut to put up massive indoor malls air-conditioned against global warming – then we can no longer find in nature the standard by which our environmentally consequential actions can be judged. This is the source of the fear that the deconstructive critique of nature engenders in environmental philosophers – the fear that anything goes, that there is no longer any basis for preferring one kind of environment over another. In the claim that nature is a "social construct" they hear once more the hubris of the technological dream that the world could somehow be made (or remade) by us, and that we get to choose what world to make – a utopian dream whose potentially (and often enough, actually) dystopian consequences we are all too familiar with nowadays.

But for those who defend something like the "constructionist" position – and here I must acknowledge that I am one such – what appears as a dangerous weakness in the view is in fact a strength. The naturalistic fallacy is a fallacy; the political and social questions about what technologies to build and what transformations of the landscape to countenance are political and social questions, it seems to us, and we want to reject the naturalism that thinks it can find the answer to such questions by an appeal to an asocial, pre-historical, apolitical nature – by appeal, that is, to an origin from which we have strayed and to which we are called to return. This is what anti-foundationalism means: we cannot answer the practical question about how we are to act except from where we are now; and where we are now, for better or worse, is in a world where the human touch is everywhere and where a principled refusal to act is both a practical and a conceptual impossibility. Indeed, the deconstructive turn in the discussion of nature shows us why the naturalistic fallacy is a fallacy: because each appeal to nature as independent of the social turns out upon analysis to possess its own social meaning and its own historical pedigree, and hence cannot in truth achieve the origin it claims to know.

Nature as Difference

Yet there is another role that nature plays in post-structuralist theory – not simply the negative role of a concept to be deconstructed but also a more positive one, which some environmental thinkers find more congenial. Nature in this other version comes to stand not for the origin that is to be rejected but rather for *difference*. It appears now as the name we might give to the otherness of the world, to that which is always left out of any attempt to grasp the world as a whole and bring it entirely into the light. This is the radical form a postmodern anti-foundationalism takes: it calls us to attend, in every language or conceptual scheme, to what that scheme occludes, excludes, inhibits – more, it calls us to attend to the crucial fact that every such scheme does occlude, exclude, inhibit something, and does so essentially, because this is what such a scheme *is*. The idea here is not, however, that there is some single reality that, could we only see it without the scheme, would appear to us whole and unhidden, as if the scheme were simply a kind of latticework that always conceals something or other and that one could imagine removing. Instead the claim is that "reality" is subject to what's here being called a scheme; there's nothing hidden by the scheme that can be imagined as unhidden except in the context of another one. The point simply is that there always is another one, that no worldview or vocabulary can call itself final and complete, that in showing the world to us in some particular way it also at the same time (and necessarily) does not show it to us in some other way, and so that it always both reveals and conceals.

Again, I assume the general outlines of this view are familiar.[12] It is certainly connected to what I have called the critique of nature as origin, since its denial that one can meaningfully speak of a world independent of a particular social and linguistic framework means in particular that there can be no original, pre-social, nature in the sense discussed above. And yet in another sense "nature" now can still stand for difference, simply that is for the finitude and limitation of every such framework, without any longer standing for an impossible reality before or behind them. It can stand for the gap between frameworks, for that which is left out – without this being thought of as some particular present Thing. Such a view of nature as difference, further, draws attention to the incompleteness not just of theoretical structures but also importantly of technological practices. Thus while rejecting the naturalistic dream of speaking for, and protecting, a pure world of nature independent of the human, this kind of postmodern environmental theory nonetheless goes on to say that just as no human understanding of "the world" could ever be complete, neither could any technological "remaking" of it – and so every humanized world we inhabit will always also already have something of the non-human within it. Every making is also an unmaking, which is to say that to build the world in one way is again always also not to build it in another, and no matter how smart and masterful we are in our building still those non-buildings or un-makings are processes over which we have no mastery at all. In all our actions to transform the world, that is, there is an inescapable moment of otherness, of resistance, of unexpected consequences and unimagined side-effects – and we could call that moment "nature," which now comes to stand precisely for our inevitable failure, and to appear as the intractable Other of the modernist attempt to understand and control everything there is. Nature for such a view is no longer opposed to freedom in the way that distinction has traditionally been drawn, but instead comes rather to stand for freedom; except that the word "freedom" no longer bears an implicit reference to the autonomy and self-control of a unified subject, but rather precisely to that which escapes that subject's claims to mastery. Thus it refers instead to the chaotic, the unpredictable, the unthinkable, the different.

As I say, many environmental thinkers find this approach to nature more compatible with their own concerns, with its clear implication of the need for modesty in our claims to understand nature and its clear critique of the technological desire to put it fully under our control. Nature by its very nature, so to speak, escapes that control; indeed, as I have suggested, it becomes the name we give to our inability to remake the world exactly the way we want. It teaches us a lesson about humility, about limits and the need for care. This view of nature calls us to something like a *Gelassenheit*, a recognition that we are not the world and that its concrete reality and

thereness, its Otherness from us, are irreducible and irremediable. The world resists us, and always has more to it than we think is there, and so to think and act in it is at the same time to call into being forces that go far beyond what we know and intend. This is built into what it is to be a world and to be an agent within it; it is not a contingent fact or a limitation to be overcome by the victorious historical march of science or technology or any other form of "enlightenment." The notion of a "revenge of nature" that punishes technological attempts at domination, which in its romantic version always seemed to depend too much on a fairy-tale anthropomorphizing of natural forces, on this account becomes clearer and more justifiable: all practical transformations of the world must produce "unanticipated" side-effects, just as all attempts by thought to grasp the world always leave something left over and ungrasped, and nature is the name we give to this very fact – and so its "vengeance" turns out to be central to what it is.

Yet there are difficulties with this view. If "nature" is to stand for the difference between thought and thing it cannot itself be a Thing, present and available for inspection and fully open to conceptual understanding. Thus we will have to avoid the strong temptation to re-reify it, to turn it into some particular object we need to honor, respect, protect, preserve – and whose nature we can know. This was McKibben's mistake, for example: he too wanted to think of nature as Otherness, but he understood this so literally and flatfootedly that for him as soon as humans put their dirty fossil-fuel burning paws anywhere near it, it immediately lost its otherness and so met its "end." He couldn't see that human transformative activity does not rob nature of its otherness, because the otherness remains within the activity itself, is indeed characteristic of it; he buys, that is to say, the modernist utopian dream that there could be pure activity (or pure knowledge) without otherness or limitation, and simply bemoans this fact, not realizing that actually it's not a fact at all.

If nature is to stand for the inevitable gap between what we intend and what we produce, or between the world and what we think we know of the world, then we have to be careful: nature itself cannot be known, cannot be grasped or understood. Claims that nature is thus-and-such have to be eschewed; the holism characteristic of deep ecology and much other popular environmental radicalism, for example, is certainly unacceptable from this point of view, as are the claims for this or that as nature's "inherent telos." So too are things like the Gaia hypothesis as a basis for environmental theorizing of an ontological sort. Nature is no longer a thing, but rather simply a way to refer to the concreteness and thereness of the world that no amount of theorizing or of technologizing can ever start to overcome. But if it's not a thing, then it's also not some thing we need to "defend"; even talk of "letting nature be" becomes suspect here, because nature in this sense isn't anything at all. If nature is what is left out, it will be left out too of any attempts we make to protect or support it, or even to talk about it.

But with that the danger arises that the very subject matter of environmental thinking and the concrete motivations that lead people into that thinking start to dissolve. The result of this line of reasoning threatens a kind of quietism with respect to any large-scale attempts to "save" the environment or "solve" environmental problems; they appear like the same old dreams of mastery, subject to the same humbling dialectic of unanticipated side-effects and inevitable yet also unexpected failures. This comes close to being explicit in late Heidegger, with his counseling of *Gelassenheit* and his call for a patient anticipation of a god who may or may not arrive; but it's implicit, too, as I'm not the first to point out, in Nietzschean levity or Derridean irony.[13] Furthermore, if nature is simply the fact of an otherness to the world, one so ultimate that no technological attempt at mastery can even begin to touch it, then in a certain sense it is in no real danger at all. There is just as much "otherness" in the urban world as in the world of what we used to call "nature."[14] Why, then, is the latter an appropriate object of our environmental concern and not the former?

More serious from a philosophical point of view, perhaps, is the logical problem produced when one tries to speak at all about that which by definition cannot be spoken of. The difficulty is well-known, and forms a central theme in the work of postmodern lovers of paradox from Adorno to Derrida. After all, if the term "nature" is supposed to remind us of the way our terms never fully capture that which they are intended to describe, then this term too must fail in the same way – which means that nature itself must differ from our account of it as difference, and in a way that cannot be said or even thought. "Difference," after all, is not a thing, nor is it a name of a thing; that's why Derrida brilliantly uses a name for it that is no name but a simple spelling error. "There is no name for it," he writes, adding that this

is "a proposition to be read in its *platitude*," and not a reference to some "ineffable Being" like God, or we might add, like the Nature radical environmentalists typically want to save.[15] But the paradox here – that "nature" is supposed to be the name of something that cannot be named and that assertions about it are assertions about something about which nothing can be asserted – is a paradox; there's no getting around it, except to take seriously the last sentence of Wittgenstein's *Tractatus*. If what nature "is" – and it doesn't matter here what techniques one uses to put the "is" under erasure – cannot be said, then the right thing for philosophy to say about nature is: nothing. And that doesn't seem to leave much room for environmental theorizing.

The trouble with interpreting nature as difference is that it falls prey to something like Hegel's critique of the Kantian notion of things-in-themselves, to wit that it just isn't clear why it's so important to insist on the existence of something (or worse, some un-thing) about which there is absolutely nothing to be said. What difference does it make whether it exists or not? The only way one can get mileage out of the notion is by playing a kind of shell game, trading on various ambiguities (including, here, various meanings of the word "nature") so as to be able to make assertions about the noumenal realm on the one hand while just as quickly taking them back and conceding their meaninglessness on the other. Adorno is a master at this sort of thing; Heidegger does it too. (Derrida is much better at avoiding it, which may be why he actually has very little to say about nature at all.) "Nature" – ordinary nature: mountains, forests, rural landscapes – gets described as somehow "pointing at" or otherwise "indicating" the noumenal world of utter otherness or difference that the term ought in the strict sense to denote, but there's no real account of how this is possible, or of why such landscapes are better able to do this than, say, urban ones, or indeed even of what "indicating" or "pointing" in this sense could possibly mean – or, finally, how any of this could come to be known.[16]

Better here would be Wittgensteinian reticence, which would direct us back to what we can say, what we can speak about – which is the ordinary world we inhabit, the one in which and on which we work and which we come to know through our practices. This world, the world of our real environment, is as I have already suggested one where the human and the natural are inextricably intertwined, not (simply) because we are natural beings but rather because we are always already actively involved in the natural environment – we act on it, transform it, rethink and reshape it, although doubtless we do not do so any way we want. In this sense it is not "other" than us, not something that "goes beyond" or "escapes" us: rather it is right here, the very world we inhabit now, a world which everywhere shows the mark of our activity and yet of course is never identical to us or to that activity either.

Nature and Practice

I want to propose at this juncture a fourth way of thinking of "nature" that might represent an improvement upon those I have already examined. It would be a throwback of sorts, to a tradition in continental thought that in recent years suffered a decline – a tradition in which human practice plays a central role. My reference to Hegel's critique of Kant was not adventitious, for in this tradition Hegel has a significant founding place, above all because of his insistence on the active character of knowledge. His radicalization of the Kantian "answer" to skepticism – and his rejection of the doctrine of noumena – implied that we know the real world because we are involved in constituting it; the Marxist inversion of his doctrine, which stands behind early twentieth century philosophers of practice such as Lukács and Korsch, in turn suggested that the act of constitution had to be understood materialistically, as concrete human labor. Thus this view will emphasize, just as the deconstructive critique of nature as origin does, the constructed character of the environment we inhabit, insisting however on taking the idea of "construction" literally. It is through our practices, which are in the first instance above all laboring practices, that the world around us is shaped into the world it is; our first access to that world is through such practices and indeed there is no access to it that does not involve them.

Part of the point of such a view will be to deny the dualist distinction between the physical world of nature and the "artificial" social world that bedevils too much environmental thinking. For if we take seriously that practice means something like labor – by which here I mean a set of physical, bodily, activities – that distinction starts to collapse. The social world is perfectly real and physical; social institutions are produced and reproduced through concrete activities, and are instantiated in concrete objects every one of which has to be built, while on the other hand the practical processes of building through which those institutions and objects come to be are themselves always socially organized ones. The social world is a physical world, and vice versa; practice doesn't constitute some social part of the world – it constitutes the environing world as such, the world of real objects that surround us, a world that is quite literally "socially constructed."

A philosophy of practice, then, directs our attention to the built environment, which for most of us is the environment – and it is with this environment, I would argue, that "environmental theory" ought to begin.[17] This is the significance of the "problem of wilderness" discussed earlier; to question the concept of wilderness, if by this term is meant a world absolutely untouched by humans, is to point out that the whole environment in a certain sense is a built environment, and to draw our attention even in so-called wilderness to the complex social practices that make it possible – practices of trail-blazing, of boundary-drawing, of policing, of ecological planning, not to speak of course of the political practices needed to bring "National Wilderness Areas" into being at all.[18] The point here isn't that everything in the world is Manhattan; there are differences among practices, certainly, including differences in the kinds of effects they have on what was there "before" (but we must always remember that the world "before" was itself not untouched either). The point is that there is no deep ontological difference between cities and national parks, as though the one represented human activity and change while the other represented that timeless Origin away from which the change occurred.

Or as though, more simply, one represented the human and the other nature. Practice, for the kind of view I am describing, is not something ontologically secondary, taking place between two pre-existing poles of actor and nature, subject and world. Rather this view tries to hold to the strange idea of practice as prior to those poles, arguing that both the world and the subject come to be what they are through practical action. Such an approach avoids the problems associated with positing nature – or, for that matter, the subject – as an absolute origin, as well as those connected with the fallacies of naturalism. Rather it takes its cue from the *immer schon*: as a subject engaging in practice, I am always *in media res*, finding both myself and the world in which I act to be the products in turn of earlier practices. I can no longer explain or justify my practices in terms of what the world "in itself" requires, any more than I can explain or justify them in terms of my own sovereign desires or thoughts. What I know of nature, and what I know of myself as well, I come to know only through my practices; and thus it makes no sense to appeal to a nature independent of those practices in order to guide them.

The deconstructive moment in the poststructuralist critique of nature as origin here takes the form of something like a theory of alienation, thereby revealing once again the debt to Hegel and to Marx. While the world we inhabit is in fact something that we build, have built, are building through our practices, still under current conditions it does not appear to us as such. Rather we are surrounded by objects and institutions – markets, gender roles, character structures, but also commodities, landscapes, the distinction between city and country, etc. – that seem to have dropped from the sky, seem that is perfectly "natural"; the role of critical social theory is to deconstruct that apparent naturalness and to reveal the concrete processes of construction that generate it. The call then is for a recognition and reappropriation by social subjects (socially and practically constituted as they doubtless are) of the world they have in fact produced. The motive for the deconstruction is clearer here than it is in the case of the ironic deconstructions associated with the other view: it is driven by a kind of ethical imperative towards self-knowledge. Without such an imperative, it becomes impossible to explain why the loss of nature as origin doesn't leave one in a relativistic quandary.[19] If all views of nature are socially constructed, why should one sort of view be privileged over another? Why prefer the construction of nature as Gaia or wilderness over the construction of it as matter for instrumental manipulation or resource for human enjoyment? Neo-Hegelian theories can answer this question in a way Derridean ones cannot: because processes of construction that know themselves as such are to be preferred over those that remain systematically deluded about what they are and what they produce. The problem of providing a standard by which to judge environmental actions without falling into the naturalistic fallacy – which is to say, without attempting to read this standard off from some account of what nature in itself "is" – is here solved in a non-relativistic, and I would argue an environmentally sensitive, fashion, by finding the standard in practice itself. World-constituting practices that acknowledge themselves

as such, that know their implications and take their responsibilities seriously, are to be preferred over those that do not.

In this sense the deconstructive critiques that show the "constructed" character of what we call nature have a liberatory function; they are supposed to call us to acknowledge our own entanglement in and indeed responsibility for the world we inhabit. Far from reconfirming in humans the hubristic dream of a total domination of nature, though, I think such an acknowledgment can evoke in us a startled humility, and with it potentially a change for the better not just in the level of our "ecological awareness" but in our lives and in our social structures. The world we inhabit, this view insists, is a world that for better or worse comes to be what it is through our practices; to recognize, however, that nowadays it's mostly for worse – that the world surrounding us is in the deep trouble it is, ugly, toxic, warming too quickly, with a torn ozone hole, undergoing apparently massive extinctions, with all the other signs of poor ecological health – is implicitly to call for us to find new practices, ones that will do a better job of "constructing" an environment that is healthier, more sustainable, more beautiful, more able to support life of all kinds.

There is, of course, an anthropocentrism lurking in that last sentence, and many environmental philosophers will note it immediately and perhaps reject it on that basis. It's true that what counts as "healthy", "beautiful," "sustainable," etc. can only be decided by us. It is our practices that make the world what it is, and so the question "what practices should we engage in?" is also the question "what ought the environing world be like?" and many will find the same old hubris in the suggestion that the latter is a question for us to answer. The trouble is that there is no one else who can answer it. It won't do to try to answer it by asking nature or studying nature or in some other way coming to know what nature really *is*; indeed the whole line of argument I have been developing here – and that I find in contemporary continental thought – is that this makes no sense, because there is no way nature really is, and so naturalistic attempts to find the solution to environmental problems by reading them off from nature are doomed to fail. Those who claim to be able to solve them this way are still subject to alienation: they do not see that what they claim to find "in" nature is really something that has already been put there by previous social practices – which in this case also means by previous social ideologies. A non-alienated approach would acknowledge that the environmental question is fundamentally a social question, a question about the sorts of practices we want to engage in, and that it therefore ought to be answered only through the democratic processes in which those sorts of questions legitimately find their answers. There is no escape from that task.⌋

How does this account of nature fare compared to the view of nature as difference discussed above? It would be easy to interpret the philosophy of practice being outlined here (especially given its Hegelian provenance) as a form of unabashed idealism of just the sort that the other account wants to condemn. Doesn't the claim that "the world comes to be what it is through our practices" involve a failure to acknowledge the otherness and thereness of the world, the way it inevitably escapes our attempts to grasp it? I do not think so; to say we construct the world that surrounds us in our practices is not to say that we dream up some way we want the world to be and then find it magically transformed accordingly; it is to say that we try to build it in a quite literal and physical way. ⌈Practice is real; it involves work and difficulty and sweat and, quite possibly, failure.⌋ It's the Marxist inversion of Hegel that's relevant here – this is materialism, not idealism. We don't imagine a world, or theorize it, we build it, and the world we build is never the same as any world we might have imagined or theorized before we started work. The "otherness" of the world, that is, is part of the notion of "practice," and indeed it is just this that distinguishes practice from theory, action from thought.

Thus the claim that the environing world is socially constructed does not mean that somehow we build it *ex nihilo*. Of course we don't; building requires materials – everybody knows that. We build the world that surrounds us out of real objects that pre-date our (current) building processes – but they too, of course, are objects that were themselves (at some earlier point) built. We're back to the always already: my home was built of wood, but the wood was in the form of 2 × 4's which had first to be built at the lumber yard in processes that employed timber that had been felled in some forest; the timber too needed tools to fell it, which tools were produced in a factory somewhere else, out of steel that had been smelted in yet another factory, and so on and so on. ⌈It won't do, for the reasons the critique of nature as origin made clear, to look for some ultimate Thing out of which and on which all building takes place.

We can assert that every act of building requires some "substrate" or other, meaning material which gets transformed in the building, without asserting that some particular privileged Substrate is itself unbuilt and deserves the honorific name "nature."⌋

But then rather than talking of a substrate, with its (to philosophers) dangerously tempting metaphysical connotations, it might be better to talk simply of practice and of its difference from theory. In our practices we build the environing world, but what we build is always other than what we "thought" we would build; our ideas about the world always fail to grasp what's really in it, which is to say what we really put there. Thus our practices never match our expectations or our plans, and that they do not is part of what it means to say that they are practices (and not dreams or theories). Marxist versions of the philosophy of practice sometimes failed to understand this point and its implications, believing that the plan was identical to the achievement. Insisting on it is one of the important services performed by poststructuralist ideas of nature as difference, not least as a way of correcting for a tendency towards utopianizing among certain "social constructionists" about nature. The realness and resistance of the world, the difficulty of labor, call us towards a modesty with respect to our practices, deriving from a sober and even chastened recognition of the inevitable limits to planning and of the essential unpredictability of the consequences of our actions. We are even called here, too, I think, to a modesty with respect to the possibility of the kind of democratic control over our practices that I spoke of above. ⌈As indicated, the question of what the environing world ought to be can't be separated from the questions of what practices will help to build that world and how they are to be engaged in – and those are things that indeed can never be known for certain, nor ever be entirely planned. The history of the unanticipated ecological damage caused by new practices, even those supposed to be ecologically beneficial, is too familiar.⌋

⌈Thus to understand that "difference," otherness, is part of what a practice *is*, is to insist upon the importance of modesty and caution in our practices, of considering ahead of time what their consequences might be, of paying attention to worst-case scenarios and "normal accidents," of making risk analyses and recognizing too the risks involved in believing them, of building in redundancy and error-checking and all the other tools needed to provide some additional security that things will more or less go the way that we expect (knowing nonetheless that they never will). What is not to be concluded here, however, is that we should therefore attempt to abstain from any transformative practices whatsoever – not merely because such an attempt would be a bad idea but rather because it is an impossibility. The call for modesty in those practices ought not to be misinterpreted as a call to try to return nostalgically to the way the world was before we engaged in them – to return, that is, to nature as origin. Nor should it be taken as a call to avoid the attempt to bring them under the sway of democratic social processes, or to give up the attempt to understand them and consciously to choose which ones we engage in, leaving them to the "natural" processes of the market, as some environmental thinkers have begun to do.[20] Consciousness is still better than unconsciousness, even if full consciousness is impossible. Rather it should simply make us more careful and more humble about what we can and cannot achieve, but no less mindful of the responsibility for the environment that our transformative role within it imposes upon us.

What I have been suggesting, then, is that the two "postmodern" views of nature with which I began – the critique of nature as origin and the identification of nature with difference – despite the real insights they have to offer about fundamental issues in environmental philosophy, each lack an appreciation for the crucial role in such a philosophy that ought to be played by the notion of practice. As a result they fail to grasp the *active* character of the relation between humans and their environment, a failure which threatens to lead environmental theory back first of all towards a pernicious dualism that identifies the natural with the non-human, and secondly towards a naturalism that thinks it can find in a nature so purified of human action the source of an appropriate set of standards for human interactions with the environment. I have tried to suggest instead an alternative approach, one that sees nature neither as origin nor as what is left out, but rather as connected to practice. The "social constructions" through which the environment we inhabit comes to be what it is are above all practical ones: the world is made through our activities in it, which is not to say we can make it any way we want or that it is entirely us, or ours. What distinguishes practice from theory is that the former is real, difficult, concrete (and unpredictable by theory in its results): and nature might be the name we give to that very concreteness.[21]

Notes

1   See, for example, the anthology edited by Michael Soulé and Gary Lease entitled *Reinventing Nature? Responses to Postmodern Deconstruction* (Washington, DC: Island Press, 1995); Holmes Rolston, III, "Nature for Real: Is Nature a Social Construct?" in T. D. J. Chappell, ed., *The Philosophy of the Environment* (New York: Columbia University Press, 1997); Robert Frodeman, "Radical Environmentalism and the Political Roots of Postmodernism: Differences That Make a Difference," in Max Oelschlaeger, ed., *Postmodern Environmental Ethics* (Albany: SUNY Press, 1995), pp. 121–35.

2   Heidegger is the figure most often cited here, claimed by many to be the most important of twentieth-century environmental thinkers. Michael Zimmerman has played a significant part in making this argument – ambivalent though he now is about Heidegger's legacy – and his recent book *Contesting Earth's Future: Radical Ecology and Postmodernity* (Berkeley: University of California Press, 1994) is an important text for anyone concerned with the relation between poststructuralist thought and the environment. For Zimmerman's earlier views on Heidegger, see his "Toward A Heideggerean *Ethos* for Radical Environmentalism," *Environmental Ethics* 5 (Summer 1983): 99–131.

3   Other texts worth mentioning here are Verena Andermatt Conley, *Ecopolitics: The Environment in Poststructuralist Thought* (London: Routledge, 1997); Arran E. Gare, *Postmodernism and the Environmental Crisis* (London: Routledge, 1995); and Peter C. van Wyck, *Primitives in the Wilderness: Deep Ecology and the Missing Human Subject* (Albany: State University of New York Press, 1997). Max Oelschlaeger's anthology *Postmodern Environmental Ethics* includes a number of important essays on the issue, including Jim Cheney's "Postmodern Environmental Ethics: Ethics as Bioregional Narrative," pp. 23–42.

4   For three different versions of this sort of thing see, e.g., William Cronon, ed., *Uncommon Ground: Toward Reinventing Nature* (New York: W.W. Norton and Company, 1995); Donna Haraway, *Simians, Cyborgs, and Women: The Reinvention of Nature* (New York: Routledge, 1991); Simon Schama, *Landscape and Memory* (New York: Alfred A. Knopf, 1995).

5   There are an awful lot of pipes and other equipment at work to keep Niagara Falls looking terrific; apparently indeed on occasion the Falls are simply turned off for routine maintenance – late at night, of course, when no tourists are around. And the important and ongoing debates about fire and predator suppression in the national parks similarly show how much work is needed to keep them in their natural state – or, more precisely, to define (socially!) what that natural state is. See David M. Graber, "Resolute Biocentrism: The

Dilemma of Wilderness in National Parks," in Soulé and Lease, eds., *Reinventing Nature*, pp. 123–35. Cf. also Alston Chase, *Playing God in Yellowstone: The Destruction of America's First National Park* (San Diego: Harcourt, Brace, Jovanovich, 1987). Stephen J. Pyne, in his recent book *How the Canyon Became Grand* (New York: Viking Press, 1998), writes: "The Grand Canyon was not so much revealed as it was created" (p. xiii).

6   An excellent collection of essays on the question of wilderness is J. Baird Callicott and Michael P. Nelson, eds., *The Great New Wilderness Debate* (Athens, Ga.: University of Georgia Press, 1998). On the peculiar role of wilderness in American environmentalism, see (in that collection) especially Ramachandra Guha, "Radical American Environmentalism and Wilderness Preservation: A Third World Critique," J. Baird Callicott, "The Wilderness Idea Revisited: The Sustainable Development Alternative," and William Cronon, "The Trouble With Wilderness, or, Getting Back to the Wrong Nature."

7   See William M. Denevan, "The Pristine Myth: The Landscape of the Americas in 1492" in Callicott and Nelson, *The Great New Wilderness Debate*, pp. 414–42; also Gary Paul Nabhan, "Cultural Parallax in Viewing North American Habitats," in Soulé and Lease, *Reinventing Nature*, pp. 87–101. Susanna Hecht and Alexander Cockburn have made a similar point with respect to the Amazon forests; see their *The Fate of the Forest: Developers, Destroyers and Defenders of the Amazon* (London: Verso, 1989).

8   For an interesting case study of this sort of phenomenon, see Jan Dizard, *Going Wild: Hunting, Animal Rights, and the Contested Meaning of Nature* (Amherst: University of Massachusetts Press, 1994). See also John Rodman, "Restoring Nature: Natives and Exotics" in Jane Bennett and William Chaloupka, eds., *In the Nature of Things: Language, Politics, and the Environment* (Minneapolis: University of Minnesota Press, 1993), pp. 139–53.

9   Bill McKibben, *The End of Nature* (New York: Anchor Books, 1989), pp. 47–9, 32. Cf. Albert Borgmann's discussion of McKibben in "The Nature of Reality and the Reality of Nature" in Soulé and Lease, *Reinventing Nature*, pp. 31–45.

10 John Stuart Mill pointed this out in his essay "Nature," in *Collected Works*, vol. 10 (Toronto: University of Toronto Press, 1963), pp. 373–403; cf. Holmes Rolston III, "Can and Ought We to Follow Nature?" in his *Philosophy Gone Wild: Essays in Environmental Ethics* (Buffalo: Prometheus Books, 1986), pp. 30–52.

11 Lynn Margulis and Dorion Sagan call this "the greatest pollution crisis the earth has ever endured." See their *Microcosmos* (New York: Summit Books, 1986), p. 108.

12 Of course I am abstracting here from real differences among the Heideggerian, Derridean, Adornoian, Foucauldian, etc. versions in which this kind of position appears.

13 Cf. Jürgen Habermas, *The Philosophical Discourse of Modernity*, Frederick Lawrence, transl. (Cambridge, Mass.: MIT Press, 1987), lectures 4 and 6; also Thomas McCarthy, "The Politics of the Ineffable: Derrida's Deconstructionism," in *Ideals and Illusions: On Reconstruction and Deconstruction in Contemporary Critical Theory* (Cambridge, Mass.: MIT Press, 1991), pp. 97–119.

14 Indeed, this is one way of understanding Heidegger's claim that "the essence of technology must harbor in itself the growth of the saving power": that Being, and its difference from beings, is at play within the world-disclosure characteristic of technology, too. See "The Question Concerning Technology" in Martin Heidegger, *Basic Writings*, David Farrell Krell, ed. (San Francisco: Harper Collins, 1993), p. 334. But of course it is just to this extent that some might question Heidegger's relevance as a specifically *environmental* thinker.

15 Jacques Derrida, "Différance," in *Margins of Philosophy*, trans. Alan Bass (Chicago: University of Chicago Press, 1982), p. 26.

16 Sometimes, in a more sophisticated version – and again both Adorno and Heidegger do this – the locus is moved from nature to art. In Heidegger's case, anyway, this isn't much of a move: it's telling that his example is Van Gogh's painting of the peasant shoes, not (say) Leger or the Italian Futurists.

17 Thus Andrew Ross opens a discussion of environmentalism by writing: "Why not begin, as ecology has ordained, with a local environment? As a city dweller who does not regard himself as much of a nature-lover, it is important to start with the stores in my neighborhood. Living in Manhattan's SoHo . . ." and etc. (*The Chicago Gangster Theory of Life* [London: Verso, 1994], p. 1). We need more, I would argue, of this kind of "bioregionalism."

18 Cf. Mark Woods, "Federal Wilderness Preservation in the United States: The Preservation of Wilderness?" in Callicott and Nelson, eds., *The Great New Wilderness Debate*, pp. 131–53.

19 Cf. Gare, *Postmodernism and the Environmental Crisis*, pp. 96–102.

20 Zimmerman flirts with this idea – see *Contesting Earth's Future*, pp. 332–8. See also Gus diZerega, "Social Ecology, Deep Ecology, and Liberalism," *Critical Review* 6 (1993): 305–70.

21 I am grateful to Jonathan Maskit for suggestions and conversations that were very helpful in the writing of this essay.

D Political Environmental Ethics

Social Ecology

33 What Is Social Ecology?
    Murray Bookchin

34 Socialism and Ecology
    James O'Connor

Ecological Feminism

35 The Power and the Promise of Ecological Feminism
    Karen J. Warren

36 Feminism and the Philosophy of Nature
    Carolyn Merchant

37 Nature, Self, and Gender: Feminism, Environmental Philosophy,
    and the Critique of Rationalism
    Val Plumwood

SOCIAL ECOLOGY

33 What Is Social Ecology?

Murray Bookchin

What literally defines social ecology as "social" is its recognition of the often overlooked fact that nearly all our present ecological problems arise from deep-seated social problems. Conversely, present ecological problems cannot be clearly understood, much less resolved, without resolutely dealing with problems within society. To make this point more concrete: economic, ethnic, cultural, and gender conflicts, among many others, lie at the core of the most serious ecological dislocations we face today – apart, to be sure, from those that are produced by natural catastrophes.

If this approach seems a bit too "sociological" for those environmentalists who identify ecological problems with the preservation of wildlife, wilderness, or more broadly, with "Gaia" and planetary

From Michael E. Zimmerman, J. Baird Callicott, Karen J. Warren, Irene Klaver, and John Clark, eds., *Environmental Philosophy: From Animal Rights to Radical Ecology*, 4th edn. (Upper Saddle River, NJ: Pearson Education, Inc., 1993), pp. 462–3, 466–78. © 2005, 2001, 1998, 1993 by Pearson Education, Inc. Reprinted by permission of Pearson Education, Inc., Upper Saddle River, NJ.

"Oneness," it might be sobering to consider certain recent facts. The massive oil spill by an Exxon tanker at Prince William Sound, the extensive deforestation of redwood trees by the Maxxam Corporation, and the proposed James Bay hydroelectric project that would flood vast areas of northern Quebec's forests, to cite only a few problems, should remind us that the real battleground on which the ecological future of the planet will be decided is clearly a social one.

Indeed, to separate ecological problems from social problems – or even to play down or give token recognition to this crucial relationship – would be to grossly misconstrue the sources of the growing environmental crisis. The way human beings deal with each other as social beings is crucial to addressing the ecological crisis. Unless we clearly recognize this, we will surely fail to see that the hierarchical mentality and class relationships that so thoroughly permeate society give rise to the very idea of dominating the natural world.

Unless we realize that the present market society, structured around the brutally competitive imperative of "grow or die," is a thoroughly impersonal, self-operating mechanism, we will falsely tend to blame technology as such or population growth as such for environmental problems. We will ignore their root causes, such as trade for profit, industrial expansion, and the identification of "progress" with corporate self-interest. In short, we will tend to focus on the symptoms of a grim social pathology rather than on the pathology itself, and our efforts will be directed toward limited goals whose attainment is more cosmetic than curative.

[. . .]

Nature and Society

[. . .]

Human beings always remain rooted in their biological evolutionary history, which we may call "first nature," but they produce a characteristically human social nature of their own, which we may call "second nature." And far from being "unnatural," human second nature is eminently a creation of organic evolution's first nature. To write the second nature created by human beings out of nature as a whole, or indeed, to minimize it, is to ignore the creativity of natural evolution itself and to view it onesidedly. If "true" evolution embodies itself simply in creatures like grizzly bears, wolves, and

whales – generally, animals that *people* find aesthetically pleasing or relatively intelligent – then human beings are literally *de*-natured. In such views, whether seen as "aliens" or as "fleas," humans are essentially placed outside the self-organizing thrust of natural evolution toward increasing subjectivity and flexibility. The more enthusiastic proponents of this de-naturing of humanity may see human beings as existing apart from nonhuman evolution, thereby dealing with people as a "freaking," as Paul Shepard puts it, of the evolutionary process. Others simply avoid the problem of humanity's unique place in natural evolution by promiscuously putting human beings on a par with beetles in terms of their "intrinsic worth." In this "either/or" propositional thinking, the social is either separated from the organic, or flippantly reduced to the organic, resulting in an inexplicable dualism at one extreme or a naive reductionism at the other. The dualistic approach, with its quasi-theological premise that the world was "made" for human use is saddled with the name of "anthropocentricity," while the reductionist approach, with its almost meaningless notion of a "biocentric democracy," is saddled with the name of "biocentricity."

The bifurcation of the human from the nonhuman reveals a failure to think organically, and to approach evolutionary phenomena with an evolutionary way of thought. Needless to say, if we are content to regard nature as no more than a scenic vista, mere metaphoric and poetic description of it might suffice to replace systematic thinking about it. But if we regard nature as the history of nature, as an evolutionary process that is going on to one degree or another under our very eyes, we dishonor this process by thinking of it in anything but a processual way. That is to say, we require a way of thinking that recognizes that "what-is" as it seems to lie before our eyes is always developing into "what-it-is-not," that it is engaged in a continual self-organizing process in which past and present, seen as a richly differentiated but shared continuum, give rise to a new potentiality for a future, ever-richer degree of *wholeness*. Accordingly, the human and the nonhuman can be seen as aspects of an evolutionary continuum, and the emergence of the human can be located in the evolution of the nonhuman, without advancing naive claims that one is either "superior to" or "made for" the other.

By the same token, in a processual, organic, and dialectical way of thinking, we would have little difficulty in locating and explaining the emergence of the social out of the biological, of second nature out of first nature. It seems more fashionable these days to deal with ecologically significant social issues like a bookkeeper. One simply juxtaposes two columns – labeled "old paradigm" and "new paradigm" – as though one were dealing with debits and credits. Obviously distasteful terms like "centralization" are placed under "old paradigm," while more appealing ones like "decentralization" are regarded as "new paradigm." The result is an inventory of bumper-sticker slogans whose "bottom line" is patently a form of "absolute good versus absolute evil." All of this may be deliciously synoptic and easy for the eyes, but it is singularly lacking as food for the brain. To truly *know* and be able to give interpretative *meaning* to the social issues so arranged, we should want to know how each idea derived from others and is part of an overall development. What, in fact, do we mean by the notion of "decentralization," and how does it derive from or give rise in the history of human society to "centralization"? Again: processual thinking is needed to deal with processual realities so that we can gain some sense of *direction* – practical as well as theoretical – in dealing with our ecological problems.

Social ecology seems to stand alone, at present, in calling for the use of organic, developmental, and derivative ways of thinking out problems that are basically organic and developmental in character. The very definition of the natural world as a development indicates the need for an organic way of thinking, as does the derivation of human from nonhuman nature – a derivation that has the most far-reaching consequences for an ecological ethics that can offer serious guidelines for the solution of our ecological problems.

Social ecology calls upon us to see that nature and society are interlinked by evolution into one nature that consists of two differentiations: first or biotic nature, and second or human nature. Human nature and biotic nature share an evolutionary potential for greater subjectivity and flexibility. Second nature is the way in which human beings as flexible, highly intelligent primates *inhabit* the natural world. That is to say, people create an environment that is most suitable for their mode of existence. In this respect, second nature is no different from the environment that *every* animal, depending upon its abilities, creates as well as adapts

to, the biophysical circumstances – or ecocommunity – in which it must live. On this very simple level, human beings are, in principle, doing nothing that differs from the survival activities of nonhuman beings – be it building beaver dams or gopher holes.

But the environmental changes that human beings produce are significantly different from those produced by nonhuman beings. Humans act upon their environments with considerable technical foresight, however lacking that foresight may be in ecological respects. Their cultures are rich in knowledge, experience, cooperation, and conceptual intellectuality; however, they may be sharply divided against themselves at certain points of their development, through conflicts between groups, classes, nation-states, and even city-states. Nonhuman beings generally live in ecological niches, their behavior guided primarily by instinctive drives and conditioned reflexes. Human societies are "bonded" together by institutions that change radically over centuries. Nonhuman communities are notable for their fixity in general terms or by clearly preset, often genetically imprinted, rhythms. Human communities are guided in part by ideological factors and are subject to changes conditioned by those factors.

Hence human beings, emerging from an organic evolutionary process, initiate, by the sheer force of their biology and survival needs, a social evolutionary development that profoundly involves their organic evolutionary process. Owing to their naturally endowed intelligence, powers of communication, capacity for institutional organization, and relative freedom from instinctive behavior, they refashion their environment – as do nonhuman beings – to the full extent of their biological equipment. This equipment now makes it possible for them to engage in social development. It is not so much that human beings, in principle, behave differently from animals or are inherently more problematical in a strictly ecological sense, but that the social development by which they grade out of their biological development often becomes more problematical for themselves and nonhuman life. How these problems emerge, the ideologies they produce, the extent to which they contribute to biotic evolution or abort it, and the damage they inflict on the planet as a whole lie at the very heart of the modern ecological crisis. Second nature, far from marking the fulfillment of human potentialities, is riddled by contradictions, antagonisms, and conflicting interests that have distorted humanity's unique capacities for development. It contains both the danger of tearing down the biosphere and, given a further development of humanity toward an ecological society, the capacity to provide an entirely new ecological dispensation.

Social Hierarchy and Domination

How, then, did the social – eventually structured around status groups, class formations, and cultural phenomena – emerge from the biological? We have reason to speculate that as biological facts such as lineage, gender distribution, and age differences were slowly institutionalized, their uniquely social dimension was initially quite egalitarian. Later it acquired an oppressive hierarchical and then an exploitative class form. The lineage or blood tie in early prehistory obviously formed the organic basis of the family. Indeed, it joined together groups of families into bands, clans, and tribes, through either intermarriage or fictive forms of descent, thereby forming the earliest social horizon of our ancestors. More than in other mammals, the simple biological facts of human reproduction and protracted maternal care of the infant tended to knit siblings together and produced a strong sense of solidarity and group inwardness. Men, women, and their children were brought into a condition of a fairly stable family life, based on mutual obligation and an expressed sense of affinity that was often sanctified by marital vows of one kind or another.

Outside the family and all its elaborations into bands, clans, tribes and the like, other human beings were regarded as "strangers," who could alternatively be welcomed hospitably or enslaved or put to death. What mores existed were based on an unreflected body of *customs* that seemed to have been inherited from time immemorial. What we call *morality* began as the commandments of a deity, in that they required some kind of supernatural or mystical reinforcement to be accepted by the community. Only later, beginning with the ancient Greeks, did *ethical* behavior emerge, based on rational discourse and reflection. The shift from blind custom to a commanding morality, and finally, to a rational ethics occurred with the rise of cities and urban cosmopolitanism. Humanity, gradually disengaging itself from the biological facts of blood ties, began to admit the "stranger" and increasingly recognize

itself as a shared community of human beings rather than an ethnic folk – a community of citizens rather than of kinsmen.

[. . .]

"Why" hierarchy emerges is transparent enough: the infirmities of age, increasing population, natural disasters, certain technological changes that privilege male activities of hunting and caring for animals over the horticultural functions of females, the growth of civil society, the spread of warfare. All serve to enhance the male's responsibilities at the expense of the female's. Marxist theorists tend to single out technological advances and the presumed material surpluses they produce to explain the emergence of elite strata – indeed, of exploiting ruling classes. However, this does not tell us why many societies whose environments were abundantly rich in food never produced such strata. That surpluses are necessary to support elites and classes is obvious, as Aristotle pointed out more than two millennia ago. But too many communities that had such resources at their disposal remained quite egalitarian and never "advanced" to hierarchical or class societies.

It is worth emphasizing that hierarchical domination, however coercive it may be, is not to be confused with class exploitation. Often the role of high status individuals is very well-meaning, as in the case of commands given by caring parents to their children, of concerned husbands and wives to each other, or of elderly people to younger ones. In tribal societies, even where a considerable measure of authority accrues to a chief – and most chiefs are advisers rather than rulers – he usually must earn the esteem of the community by interacting with the people, and he can easily be ignored or removed from his position by them. Many chiefs earn their prestige, so essential to their authority, by disposing of gifts, and even by a considerable disaccumulation of their personal goods. The respect accorded to many chiefs is earned, not by hoarding surpluses as a means to power but by disposing of them as evidence of generosity.

Classes tend to operate along different lines. Power is usually gained by the acquisition of wealth, not by its disposal; rulership is guaranteed by outright physical coercion, not simply by persuasion; and the state is the ultimate guarantor of authority. That hierarchy is more entrenched than class can perhaps be verified by the fact that women have been dominated for millennia, despite sweeping changes in class societies. By the same token, the abolition of class rule and economic exploitation offers no guarantee whatever that elaborate hierarchies and systems of domination will disappear.

In nonhierarchical and even some hierarchical societies, certain customs guide human behavior along basically decent lines. Of primary importance in early customs was the "law of the irreducible minimum" (to use Radin's expression), the shared notion that all members of a community are entitled to the means of life, irrespective of the amount of work they perform. To deny anyone food, shelter, and the basic means of life because of infirmities or even frivolous behavior would have been seen as a heinous denial of the very right to live. Nor were the resources and things needed to sustain the community ever completely privately owned: overriding individualistic control was the broader principle of usufruct – the notion that the means of life that were not being used by one group could be used, as need be, by another. Thus unused land, orchards, and even tools and weapons, if left idle, were at the disposition of anyone in the community who needed them. Lastly, custom fostered the practice of mutual aid, the rather sensible cooperative behavior of sharing things and labor, so that an individual or family in fairly good circumstances could expect to be helped by others if their fortunes should change for the worse. Taken as a whole, these customs became so sedimented into society that they persisted long after hierarchy became oppressive and class society became prodominant.

The Idea of Dominating Nature

"Nature," in the broad sense of a biotic environment from which humans take the simple things they need for survival, often has no meaning to preliterate peoples. Immersed in nature as the very universe of their lives, it has no special meaning, even when they celebrate animistic rituals and view the world around them as a nexus of life, often imputing their own social institutions to the behavior of various species, as in the case of "beaver lodges" and human-like spirits. Words that express our conventional notions of nature are not easy to find, if they exist at all, in the languages of aboriginal peoples.

With the rise of hierarchy and human domination, however, the seeds are planted for a belief that nature not only exists as a world apart, but that it is hierarchically organized and can be dominated. The study of magic reveals this shift clearly. Early forms of magic did not view nature as a world apart. Its worldview tended to be such that a practitioner essentially pleaded with the "chief spirit" of the game to coax an animal in the direction of an arrow or a spear. Later, magic becomes almost entirely instrumental; the game is coerced by magical techniques to become the hunter's prey. While the earliest forms of magic may be regarded as the practices of a generally nonhierarchical and egalitarian community, the later forms of animistic beliefs betray a more or less hierarchical view of the natural world and of latent human powers of domination.

We must emphasize, here, that the *idea* of dominating nature has its primary source in the domination of human by human and the structuring of the natural world into a hierarchical Chain of Being (a static conception, incidentally, that has no relationship to the evolution of life into increasingly advanced forms of subjectivity and flexibility). The biblical injunction that gave to Adam and Noah command of the living world was above all an expression of a *social* dispensation. Its idea of dominating nature can be overcome only through the creation of a society without those class and hierarchical structures that make for rule and obedience in private as well as public life. That this new dispensation involves changes in attitudes and values should go without saying. But these attitudes and values remain vaporous if they are not given substance through objective institutions, the ways in which humans concretely interact with each other, and in the realities of everyday life from childrearing to work and play. Until human beings cease to live in societies that are structured around hierarchies as well as economic classes, we shall never be free of domination, however much we try to dispel it with rituals, incantations, ecotheologies, and the adoption of seemingly "natural" ways of life.

[. . .]

"Grow or Die!"

But just as hierarchies and class structures tend to acquire a momentum of their own and permeate much of society, so too the market began to acquire a life of its own and extended its reach beyond limited regions into the depths of vast continents. Exchange ceased to be primarily a means to provide for modest needs, subverting the limits imposed upon it by guilds or by moral and religious restrictions. Not only did it place a high premium on techniques for increasing production; it also became the procreator of needs, many of which are simply useless, and gave an explosive impetus to consumption and technology. First in northern Italy and the European lowlands, later – and most effectively – in England during the seventeenth and eighteenth centuries, the production of goods exclusively for sale and profit (the capitalistic commodity) rapidly swept aside all cultural and social barriers to market growth.

By the late eighteenth and early nineteenth centuries, the new industrial capitalist class with its factory system and commitment to limitless expansion began to colonize the entire world, and finally, most aspects of personal life. Unlike the feudal nobility, which had its cherished lands and castles, the bourgeoisie had no home but the marketplace and its bank vaults. As a class, they turned more and more of the world into an ever-expanding domain of factories. Entrepreneurs of the ancient and medieval worlds had normally gathered their profits together to invest in land and live like country gentry – given the prejudices of their times against "ill-gotten" gains from trade. On the other hand, the industrial capitalists of the modern world spawned a bitterly competitive marketplace that placed a high premium on industrial expansion and the commercial power it conferred, and functioned as though growth were an end in itself.

It is crucially important, in social ecology, to recognize that industrial growth does not result from a change in a cultural outlook alone – and least of all, from the impact of scientific rationality on society. It stems above all from *harshly objective factors* churned up by the expansion of the market itself, *factors that are largely impervious to moral considerations and efforts at ethical persuasion*. Indeed, despite the close association between capitalist development and technological innovation, the most driving imperative of the capitalist market, given the dehumanizing competition that defines it, is the need to grow, and to avoid dying at the hands of savage rivals. Important as greed or the power conferred by wealth may be, sheer survival requires that an entrepreneur must expand his or her productive apparatus to remain ahead of other entrepreneurs and try, in fact, to devour them. The key to this law of life – to survival – is expansion, and greater profit, to be invested in still further expansion. Indeed, the notion of progress, once identified by our ancestors as a faith in the evolution of greater human cooperation and care, is now identified with economic growth.

The effort by many well-intentioned ecology theorists and their admirers to reduce the ecological crisis to a cultural rather than a social problem can easily become obfuscatory. However ecologically concerned an entrepreneur may be, the harsh fact is that his or her very survival in the marketplace precludes a meaningful ecological orientation. To engage in ecologically sound practices places a morally concerned entrepreneur at a striking, and indeed, fatal disadvantage in a competitive relationship with a rival – notably one who lacks any ecological concerns and thus produces at lower costs and reaps higher profits for further capital expansion.

Indeed, to the extent that environmental movements and ideologies merely moralize about the "wickedness" of our anti-ecological society, and emphasize change in personal life and attitudes, they obscure the need for social action. Corporations are skilled at manipulating this desire to be present as an ecological image. Mercedes-Benz, for example, declaims in a two-page ad, decorated with a bison painting from a Paleolithic cave wall, that "we must work to make more environmentally sustainable progress by including the theme of the environment in the planning of new products."[1] Such deceptive messages are commonplace in Germany, one of western Europe's worst polluters. Advertising is equally self-serving in the United States, where leading polluters piously declare that for them, "Every day is Earth Day."

The point social ecology emphasizes is not that moral and spiritual change is meaningless or unnecessary, but that modern capitalism is *structurally* amoral and hence impervious to any moral appeals. The modern marketplace has imperatives of its own, irrespective of who sits in the driver's seat or grabs on to its handlebars. The direction it follows depends not upon ethical factors but rather on the mindless "laws" of supply and demand, grow or die, eat or be eaten. Maxims like "business is business" explicitly tell us that ethical, religious, psychological, and emotional factors have absolutely no place in the impersonal world of production, profit, and growth. It is grossly misleading to think that we can divest this brutally materialistic, indeed, mechanistic, world of its objective character, that we can vaporize its hard facts rather than transforming it.

A society based on "grow or die" as its all-pervasive imperative must necessarily have a devastating ecological impact. Given the growth imperative generated by market competition, it would mean little or nothing if the present-day population were reduced to a fraction of what it is today. Insofar as entrepreneurs must always expand if they are to survive, the media that have fostered mindless consumption would be mobilized to increase the purchase of goods, irrespective of the need for them. Hence it would become "indispensable" in the public mind to own two or three of every appliance, motor vehicle, electronic gadget, or the like, where one would more than suffice. In addition, the military would continue to demand new, more lethal instruments of death, of which new models would be required annually.

[. . .]

An Ecological Society

Social ecology is an appeal not only for moral regeneration but also, and above all, for social reconstruction along ecological lines. It emphasizes that an ethical appeal to the powers that be (that embody blind market forces and competitive relationships), taken by itself, is likely to be futile. Indeed, taken by itself, it often obscures the real power relationships that prevail today by making the attainment of an ecological society seem merely a matter of "attitude," of "spiritual change," or of quasi-religious redemption.

Although always mindful of the need for spiritual change, social ecology seeks to redress the ecological abuses that society has inflicted on the natural world by going to the structural as well as the subjective sources of notions like the "domination of nature." That is, it challenges the entire system of domination itself and seeks to eliminate the hierarchical and class edifice that has imposed itself on humanity and defined the relationship between nonhuman and human nature. It advances an ethics of complementarity in which human beings must play a supportive role in perpetuating the integrity of the biosphere, as potentially, at least, the most conscious products of natural evolution. Indeed humans are seen to have a moral responsibility to function creatively in the unfolding of that evolution. Social ecology thus stresses the need for embodying its ethics of complementarity in palpable social institutions that will give active meaning to its goal of wholeness, and of

human involvement as conscious and moral agents in the interplay of species. It seeks the enrichment of the evolutionary process by diversification of life-forms. Notwithstanding romantic views, "Mother Nature" does not necessarily "know best." To oppose activities of the corporate world does not mean that one has to become naively romantic and "biocentric." By the same token, to applaud humanity's potential for foresight and rationality, and its technological achievements, does not mean that one is "anthropocentric." The loose usage of such buzzwords, so commonplace in the ecology movement, must be brought to an end by reflective discussion.

Social ecology, in effect, recognizes that – like it or not – the future of life on this planet pivots on the future of society. It contends that evolution, whether in first nature or in second, is not yet complete. Nor are the two realms so separated from each other that we must choose one or the other – either natural evolution with its "biocentric" halo, or social evolution, as we have known it up to now, with its "anthropocentric" halo – as the basis for a creative biosphere. We must go beyond both the natural and the social toward a new synthesis that contains the best of both. Such a synthesis will transcend them in the form of a creative, self-conscious, and therefore "free nature," in which human beings intervene in natural evolution with their best capacities – their moral sense, their unprecedented degree of conceptual thought, and their remarkable powers of communication.

[. . .]

Power will always belong to elite strata if it is not diffused, in face-to-face democracies, among the people, who are *empowered* as partly autonomous, partly social beings – that is to say, as free individuals, but as individuals responsible to popular institutions. Empowerment of the people in this sense will constitute a challenge to the nation-state – the principal source of nationalism, a regressive ideology, and of statism, the principal source of coercion. Diversity of cultures is obviously a desideratum, the source of cultural creativity, but never can it be celebrated in a nationalistic "apartness" from the general interests of humanity as a whole, without a regression into folkdom and tribalism.

The full reality of citizenship has begun to wane, and its disappearance would mark an irrevocable loss in human development. Citizenship, in the classical sense of the term, meant a lifelong, ethically oriented education to participation in public affairs, not the empty form of national legitimation that it so often indicates today. It meant the cultivation of an affiliation with the interests of the community, one in which the communal interest was placed above personal interest, or, more properly, in which the personal interest was congruent with and realized through the common.

Property, in this ethical constellation, would be shared and, in the best of circumstances, belong to the community as a whole, not to producers ("workers") or owners ("capitalists"). In an ecological society composed of a "Commune of communes," property would belong, ultimately, neither to private producers nor to a nation-state. The Soviet Union gave rise to an overbearing bureaucracy; the anarcho-syndicalist vision to competing "worker-controlled" factories that ultimately had to be knitted together by a labor bureaucracy. From the standpoint of social ecology, property "interests" would become generalized, not reconstituted in different conflicting or unmanageable forms. They would be *municipalized*, rather than nationalized or privatized. Workers, farmers, professionals, and the like would thus deal with municipalized property as citizens, not as members of a vocational or social group. Leaving aside any discussion of such visions as the rotation of work, the citizen who engages in both industrial and agricultural activity, and the professional who also does manual labor, the communal ideas advanced by social ecology would give rise to

individuals for whom the collective interest is inseparable from the personal, the public interest from the private, the political interest from the social.

The step-by-step reorganization of municipalities, their confederation into ever-larger networks that form a dual power in opposition to the nation-state, the remaking of the constituents of republican representatives into citizens who participate in a direct democracy – all may take a considerable period of time to achieve. But in the end, they alone can potentially eliminate the domination of human by human and thereby deal with those ecological problems whose growing magnitude threatens the existence of a biosphere that can support advanced forms of life. To ignore the need for these sweeping but eminently practical changes would be to let our ecological problems fester and spread to a point where there would no longer be any opportunity to resolve them. Any attempt to ignore their impact on the biosphere or deal with them singly would be a recipe for disaster, a guarantee that the anti-ecological society that prevails in most of the world today would blindly hurtle the biosphere as we know it to certain destruction.

Note

1   See *Der Spiegel* (Sept. 16, 1991), pp. 144–5.

---

34   Socialism and Ecology

James O'Connor

The premise of red green political action is that there is a global ecological and economic crisis; that the ecological crisis cannot be resolved without a radical transformation of capitalist production relationships; and that the economic crisis cannot be resolved without an equally radical transformation of capitalist productive forces. This means that solutions to the ecological crisis presuppose solutions to the economic crisis and vice versa. Another *a priori* of red

green politics is that both sets of solutions presuppose an ecological socialism.

The problem is that socialism in theory and practise has been declared "dead on arrival." In theory, post-Marxist theorists of radical democracy are completing what they think is the final autopsy of socialism. In practise, in the North, socialism has been banalized into a species of welfare capitalism. In Eastern Europe, the moment for democratic socialism

From *Capitalism, Nature, Socialism*, vol. 2, no. 3 (1991): 1–13. © 1991. Reprinted by permission of the publisher, Taylor and Francis Ltd.

seems to have been missed over 20 years ago and socialism is being overthrown. In the South, most socialist countries are introducing market incentives, reforming their tax structures, and taking other measures that they hope will enable them to find their niches in the world market. Everywhere market economy and liberal democratic ideas on the right, and radical democratic ideas on the left, seem to be defeating socialism and socialist ideas.

Meanwhile, a powerful new force in world politics has appeared, an ecology or green movement that puts the earth first and takes the preservation of the ecological integrity of the planet as the primary issue. The simultaneous rise of the free market and the greens together with the decline of socialism suggests that capitalism has an ally in its war against socialism. This turns out to be the case. Many or most greens dismiss socialism as irrelevant. Some or many greens attack it as dangerous. Especially are they quick to condemn those who they accuse of trying to appropriate ecology for Marxism.[1] The famous green slogan, "neither left nor right, but out front," speaks for itself.[2]

But most greens are not friends of capitalism, either, as the green slogan makes clear. The question then arises, who or what are the greens allied with? The crude answer is, the small farmers and independent business, i.e., those who used to be called the "peasantry" and "petty bourgeoisie;" "liveable cities" visionaries and planners; "small is beautiful" technocrats; and artisans, cooperatives, and others engaged in ecologically friendly production. In the South, greens typically support decentralized production organized within village communal politics; in the North, greens are identified with municipal and local politics of all types.

By the way of contrast, mainstream environmentalists might be called "fictitious greens."[3] These environmentalists support environmental regulations consistent with profitability and the expansion of global capitalism, e.g., resource conservation for long-run profitability and profit-oriented regulation or abolition of pollution. They are typically allied with national and international interests. In the U.S., they are environmental reformers, lobbyists, lawyers, and others associated with the famous "Group of Ten."

As for ecology, everywhere it is at least tinged with populism, a politics of resentment against not only big corporations and the national state and central planning but also against environmentalism.

Ecology (in the present usage) is thus associated with "localism," which has always been opposed to the centralizing powers of capitalism. If we put two and two together, we can conclude that ecology and localism in all of their rich varieties have combined to oppose both capitalism and socialism. Localism uses the medium or vehicle of ecology and vice versa. They are both the content and context of one another. Decentralism is an expression of a certain type of social relationship, a certain social relation of production historically associated with small-scale enterprise. Ecology is an expression of a certain type of relationship between human beings and nature – a relationship which stresses the integrity of local and regional eco-systems. Together ecology and localism constitute the most visible political and economic critique of capitalism (and state socialism) today.

Besides the fact that both ecology and localism oppose capital and the national state, there are two main reasons why they appear to be natural allies. First, ecology stresses the site specificity of the interchange between human material activity and nature, hence opposes both the abstract valuation of nature made by capital and also the idea of central planning of production, and centralist approaches to global issues generally.[4] The concepts of site specificity of ecology, local subsistence or semi-autarkic economy, communal self-help principles, and direct forms of democracy all seem to be highly congruent.

Second, the socialist concept of the "masses" has been deconstructed and replaced by a new "politics of identity" in which cultural factors are given the place of honor. The idea of the specificity of cultural identities seems to meld easily with the site specificity of ecology in the context of a concept of social labor defined in narrow, geographic terms. The most dramatic examples today are the struggles of indigenous peoples to keep both their cultures and subsistence type economies intact. In this case, the struggle to save local cultures and local eco-systems turns out to be two different sides of the same fight.

For their part, most of the traditional left, as well as the unions, remain focused on enhanced productivity, growth, and international competitiveness, i.e., jobs and wages, or more wage labor – not to abolish exploitation but to be exploited less. This part of the left does not want to be caught any more defending any policies which can be identified with "economic austerity" or policies which labor leaders and others think would endanger past economic gains won by the working class (although union and worker struggles for healthy and safe conditions inside and outside of the workplace obviously connect in positive ways with broader ecological struggles). Most of those who oppose more growth and development are mainstream environmentalists from the urban middle classes who have the consumer goods that they want and also have the time and knowledge to oppose ecologically dangerous policies and practises. It would appear, therefore, that any effort to find a place for the working class in this equation, i.e., any attempt to marry socialism and ecology, is doomed from the start.

But just because something has never happened does not mean that it cannot happen. Or that it is not happening in various ways right now. In the developed capitalist countries, one can mention the green caucuses within Canada's NDP; the work of Barry Commoner, who calls for source reduction, the "social governance of technology," and economic planning based on a "deep scientific understanding of nature;" the antitoxic and worker and community health and safety movements which bring together labor, community, and ecological issues; various red-green Third World solidarity movements, such as the Third World Network and Environmental Project on Central America; and the new emphasis on fighting ecological racism. One thinks of the Socialist Party's struggle for control of the Upper House of the Diet against the long-entrenched Liberal Democrats, which reflects rising concern about both ecological and social issues in Japan. In Europe, we can see the greening of Labor, Social Democratic, and Communist Parties, even if reluctantly and hesitatingly, as well as the rise of the Green Parties, some of which (as in Germany) are to the left of these parties with respect to some traditional demands of the labor movement. And in the sub-imperialist powers, which are taking the brunt of the world capitalist crisis, e.g., Brazil, Mexico, and Argentina in Latin America, and India and perhaps Nigeria, Korea, and Taiwan, there are new ecological movements in which the traditional working class is engaged. And we cannot forget the Nicaraguan experiment which combined policies aimed at deep environmental reforms with socialism and populism.

There are good reasons to believe that these and other eco-socialist tendencies are no flash in the pan, which permits us to propose that ecology and socialism is not a contradiction in terms. Or, to put the point differently, there are good reasons to believe that world capitalism itself has created the conditions for an ecological socialist movement. These reasons can be collected under two general headings. The first pertains to the causes and effects of the world economic and ecological crisis from the mid-1970s to the present. The second pertains to the nature of the key ecological issues, most of which are national and international, as well as local, issues.

First, the vitality of Western capitalism since World War II has been based on the massive externalization of social and ecological costs of production. Since the slow-down of world economic growth in the mid-1970s, the concerns of both socialism and ecology have become more pressing than ever before in history. The accumulation of global capital through the modern crisis has produced even more devastating effects not only on wealth and income distribution, norms of social justice, and treatment of minorities, but also on the environment. An "accelerated imbalance of (humanized) nature" is a phrase that neatly sums this up. Socially, the crisis has led to more wrenching poverty and violence, rising misery in all parts of the world, especially the South, and, environmentally, to toxification of whole regions, the production of drought, the thinning of the ozone layer, the greenhouse effect, and the withering away of rain forests and wildlife. The issues of economic and social justice and ecological justice have surfaced as in no other period in history. It is increasingly clear that they are, in fact, two sides of the same historical process.

Given the relatively slow rate of growth of worldwide market demand since the mid-1970s, capitalist enterprises have been less able to defend or restore profits by expanding their markets and selling more commodities in booming markets. Instead, global capitalism has attempted to rescue itself from its deepening crisis by cutting costs, by raising the rate of exploitation of labor, and by depleting and exhausting resources. This "economic restructuring" is a two-sided process.

Cost cutting has led big and small capitals alike to externalize more social and environmental costs, or to pay less attention to the global environment, pollution, depletion of resources, worker health and safety, and product safety (meanwhile, increasing efficiency in energy and raw material use in the factories). The modern ecological crisis is aggravated and deepened as a result of the way that capitalism has reorganized itself to get through its latest economic crisis.

In addition, new and deeper inequalities in the distribution of wealth and income are the result of a worldwide increase in the rate of exploitation of labor. In the United States during the 1980s, for example, property income increased three times as fast as wage and salary income. Higher rates of exploitation have also depended upon the ability to abuse undocumented workers and set back labor unions, social democratic parties, and struggles for social justice generally, especially in the South. It is no accident that in those parts of the world where ecological degradation is greatest – Central America, for example – there is greater poverty and heightened class struggles. The feminization of poverty is also a part of this trend of ecological destruction. It is the working class, oppressed minorities, women, and the rural and urban poor worldwide who suffer most from both economic and ecological exploitation. The burden of ecological destruction falls disproportionately on these groups.

Crisis-ridden and crisis-dependent capitalism has forced the traditional issues of socialism and the relatively new issues ("new" in terms of public awareness) of ecology to the top of the political agenda. Capitalism itself turns out to be a kind of marriage broker between socialism and ecology, or, to be more cautious, if there is not yet a prospect for marriage, there are at least openings for an engagement.

Second, the vast majority of economic and social and ecological problems worldwide cannot be adequately addressed at the local level. It is true that the degradation of local ecological systems often does have local solutions in terms of prevention and delinking (although less so in terms of social transformation). Hence it comes as no surprise to find strong connections between the revival of municipal and village politics and local ecological destruction. But most ecological problems, as well as the economic problems which are both cause and effect of the ecological problems, cannot be solved at the local level alone. Regional, national, and international planning are also necessary. The heart of ecology is, after all, the inter-dependence of specific sites and the need to situate local responses in regional, national, and international contexts, i.e., to sublate the "local" and the "central" into new political forms.

National and international priorities are needed to deal with the problem of energy supplies, and supplies of nonrenewal resources in general, not just for the present generation but especially for future generations. The availability of other natural resources, e.g., water, is mainly a regional issue, but in many parts of the globe it is a national or international issue. The same is true of the destruction of forests. Or take the problem of soil depletion, which seems to be local or site specific. Insofar as there are problems of soil quantity and quality, or water quantity or quality, in the big food exporting countries, e.g., the US, the food importing countries are also affected. Further, industrial and agricultural pollution of all kinds spills over local, regional and national boundaries. North Sea pollution, acid rain, ozone depletion, and global warming are obvious examples.

Furthermore, if we broaden the concept of ecology to include urban environments, or what Marx called "general, communal conditions of production," problems of urban transport and congestion, high rents and housing, and drugs, which appear to be local issues amenable to local solutions, turn out to be global issues pertaining to the way that money capital is allocated worldwide; the loss of foreign markets for raw materials and foodstuffs in drug-producing countries; and the absence of regional, national and international planning of infrastructures.

If we broaden the concept of ecology even more to include the relationship between human health and well-being and environmental factors (or what Marx called the "personal condition of production"), given the increased mobility of labor nationally and internationally, and greater emigration and immigration, partly thanks to the way capital has restructured itself to pull out of the economic crisis, we are also talking about problems with only or mainly national and international solutions.

Finally, if we address the question of technology and its transfer, and the relationship between new technologies and local, regional, and global ecologies, given that technology and its transfer are more or less monopolized by international corporations and nation states, we have another national and international issue.

In sum, we have good reasons to believe that both the causes and consequences of, and also the solutions to, most ecological problems are national and international, hence that far from being incompatible, socialism and ecology presuppose one another. Socialism needs ecology because the latter stresses site specificity and reciprocity, as well as the central importance of the material interchanges within nature and between society and nature. Ecology needs socialism because the latter stresses democratic planning, and the key role of the social interchanges between human beings. By contrast, popular movements confined to the community, municipality or village cannot by themselves deal effectively with most of both the economic and ecological aspects of the general destructiveness of global capitalism, not to speak of the destructive dialectic between economic and ecological crisis.

If we assume that ecology and socialism presuppose one another, the logical question is, why haven't they gotten together before now? Why is Marxism especially regarded as unfriendly to ecology and vice versa? To put the question another way, where did socialism go wrong, ecologically speaking?

The standard, and in my opinion correct, view is that socialism defined itself as a movement which would complete the historical tasks of fulfilling the promises of capitalism. This meant two things: first, socialism would put real social and political content into the formal claims of capitalism of equality, liberty, and fraternity. Second, socialism would realize the promise of material abundance which crisis-ridden capitalism was incapable of doing. The first pertains to the ethical and political meanings of socialism; the second, to the economic meaning.

It has been clear for a long time to almost everyone that this construction of socialism failed on two counts. First, instead of an ethical, political society, in which the state is subordinated to civil society, we have the Party bureaucratic state; and thus the post-Marxist attempt to reconcile social justice demands with liberalism.

Second, and related to the first point, in place of material abundance, we have the economic crisis of socialism; and thus the post-Marxist attempt to reconcile not only social justice demands and liberalism but also both of these with markets and market incentives.

However, putting the focus on these obvious failures obscures two other issues that have moved into the center of political debates in the past decade or two. The first is that the ethical and political construction of socialism borrowed from bourgeois society ruled out any ethical or political practise that is not more or less thoroughly human-centered, as well as downplaying or ignoring reciprocity and "discursive truth." The second is that the economic construction of abundance borrowed with only small modifications from capitalism ruled out any material practise that did not advance the productive forces, even when these practises were blind to nature's economy. Stalin's plan to green Siberia, which fortunately was never implemented, is perhaps the most grotesque example.

These two issues, or failures, one pertaining to politics and ethics, the other to the relationship between human economy and nature's economy, are connected to the failure of historical materialism itself. Hence they need to be addressed in methodological as well as theoretical and practical terms.

Historical materialism is flawed in two big ways. Marx tended to abstract his discussions of social labor, i.e., the divisions of labor, from both culture and nature. A rich concept of social labor which includes both society's culture and nature's economy cannot be found in Marx or traditional historical materialism.

The first flaw is that the traditional conception of the productive forces ignores or plays down the fact that these forces are social in nature, and include the mode of cooperation, which is deeply inscribed by particular cultural norms and values.

The second flaw is that the traditional conception of the productive forces also plays down or ignores the fact that these forces are natural as well as social in character.

It is worth recalling that Engels himself called Marxism the "materialist conception of history," where "history" is the noun and "materialist" is the modifier. Marxists know the expression "in material life social relations between people are produced and reproduced" by heart, and much less well the expression "in social life the material relations between people and nature are produced and reproduced." Marxists are very familiar with the "labor process" in which human beings are active agents, and much less familiar with the "waiting process" or "tending process" characteristic of agriculture, forestry, and other nature-based activities in which human beings are more passive partners and, more generally, where both parties are "active" in complex, interactive ways.

Marx constantly hammered away on the theme that the material activity of human beings is two-sided, i.e., a social relationship as well as a material relationship; in other words, that capitalist production produced and reproduced a specific mode of cooperation and exploitation and a particular class structure as well as the material basis of society. But in his determination to show that material life is also social life, Marx tended to neglect the opposite and equally important fact that social life is also material life. To put the same point differently, in the formulation "material life determines consciousness," Marx stressed that since material life is socially organized, the social relationships of production determine consciousness. He played down the equally true fact that since material life is also the interchange between human beings and nature, that these material or natural relationships also determine consciousness. These points have been made in weak and strong ways by a number of people, although they have never been integrated and developed into a revised version of the materialist conception of history.

It has also been suggested *why* Marx played up history (albeit to the exclusion of culture) and played down nature. The reason is that the problem facing Marx in his time was to show that capitalist property relationships were historical not natural. But so intent was Marx to criticize those who naturalized hence reified capitalist production relationships, competition, the world market, etc., that he forgot or downplayed the fact that the development of human-made forms of "second nature" does not make nature any less natural. This was the price he paid for inverting Feuerbach's passive materialism and Hegel's active idealism into his own brand of active materialism. As Kate Soper has written, "the fact is that in its zeal to escape the charge of biological reductionism, Marxism has tended to fall prey to an antiethical form of reductionism, which in arguing the dominance of social over natural factors literally spirits the biological out of existence altogether."[5] Soper then calls for a "social biology." We can equally call for a "social chemistry," "social hydrology," and so on, that is, a "social ecology," which for socialists means "socialist ecology."

The greens are forcing the reds to pay close attention to the material interchanges between people and nature and to the general issue of biological exploitation, including the biological exploitation of labor, and also to adopt an ecological sensibility. Some reds have been trying to teach the greens to pay closer attention to capitalist production relationships, competition, the world market, etc. – to sensitize the greens to the exploitation of labor and the themes of economic crisis and social labor. And feminists have been teaching both greens and reds to pay attention to the sphere of reproduction and women's labor.

What does a green socialism mean politically? Green consciousness would have us put "earth first," which can mean anything you want it to mean politically. As mentioned earlier, what most greens mean in practise most of the time is the politics of localism. By contrast, pure red theory and practise historically has privileged the "central."

To sublate socialism and ecology does not mean in the first instance defining a new category which contains elements of both socialism and ecology but which is in fact neither. What needs to be sublated politically is localism (or decentralism) and centralism, i.e., self-determination and the overall planning, coordination, and control of production. To circle back to the main theme, localism per se won't work politically and centralism has self-destructed. To abolish the state will not work; to rely on the liberal democratic state in which "democracy" has merely a procedural or formal meaning will not work, either. The only political form that might work, that might be eminently suited to both ecological problems of site specificity and global issues, is a democratic state – a state in which the administration of the division of social labor is democratically organized.[6]

Finally, the only *ecological* form that might work is a sublation of two kinds of ecology, the "social biology" of the coastal plain, the plateau, the local hydrological cycle, etc., and the energy economics, the regional and international "social climatology," etc., of the globe – that is, in general, the sublation of nature's economy defined in local, regional and international terms. To put the conclusion somewhat differently, we need "socialism" *at least* to make the social relations of production transparent, to end the rule of the market and commodity fetishism, to end the exploitation of human beings by other human beings; we need "ecology" *at least* to make the social productive forces transparent, to end the degradation and destruction of the earth.

Notes

1 This is a crude simplification of green thought and politics, which varies from country to country, and which are also undergoing internal changes. In the US, for example, where Marxism historically has been

relatively hostile to ecology, "left green" is associated with anarchism or libertarian socialism.

2 This slogan was coined by a conservative co-founder of the German Greens and was popularized in the US by anti-socialist "New Age" greens, F. Capra and C. Spretnak. Needless to say, it was never accepted by left greens of any variety.

3 "Mainstream environmentalists" is used to identify those who are trying to save capitalism from its eco-logically self-destructive tendencies. Many individuals who call themselves "environmentalists" are alienated by, and hostile to, global capitalism, and also do not necessarily identify with the "local" (see below).

4 Martin O'Connor writes, "One of the striking ambiva-lencies of many writers on 'environmental' issues is their tendency to make recourse to authoritarian solutions, e.g., based on ethical elitism. An example is the uneasy posturings found in the collection by Herman Daly in 1973 on *Steady-State Economics*."

5 Quoted by Ken Post, "In Defense of Materialistic History," *Socialism in the World*, 74/75, 1989, p. 67.

6 I realize that the idea of a "democratic state" seems to be a contradiction in terms, or at least immediately raises difficult questions about the desirability of the separation of powers; the problem of scale inherent in any coherent description of substantive democracy; and also the question of how to organize much less plan a nationally and internationally regulated divi-sion of social labor without a universal equivalent for measuring costs and productivity (however "costs" and "productivity" are defined) (courtesy of John Ely).

ECOLOGICAL FEMINISM

35   The Power and the Promise of Ecological Feminism

Karen J. Warren

Introduction

Ecological feminism (ecofeminism) has begun to receive a fair amount of attention lately as an alterna-tive feminism and environmental ethic.[1] Since Françoise d'Eaubonne introduced the term *ecofemi-nisme* in 1974 to bring attention to women's poten-tial for bringing about an ecological revolution,[2] the term has been used in a variety of ways. As I use the term in this paper, ecological feminism is the posi-tion that there are important connections – histori-cal, experiential, symbolic, theoretical – between the domination of women and the domination of nature, an understanding of which is crucial to both femi-nism and environmental ethics. I argue that the promise and power of ecological feminism is that *it provides a distinctive framework both for reconceiving feminism and for developing an environmental ethic which takes seriously connections between the domina-tion of women and the domination of nature*. I do so

by discussing the nature of a feminist ethic and the ways in which ecofeminism provides a feminist and environmental ethic. I conclude that any feminist theory *and* any environmental ethic which fails to take seriously the twin and interconnected domina-tions of women and nature is at best incomplete and at worst simply inadequate.

Feminism, Ecological Feminism, and Conceptual Frameworks

Whatever else it is, feminism is at least the movement to end sexist oppression. It involves the elimination of any and all factors that contribute to the contin-ued and systematic domination or subordination of women. While feminists disagree about the nature of and solutions to the subordination of women, all feminists agree that sexist oppression exists, is wrong, and must be abolished.

From *Environmental Ethics*, vol. 12 (1990): 125–33, 138–44, 145–6. © 1990 by Karen J. Warren. Reprinted with permission from the author.

A "feminist issue" is any issue that contributes in some way to understanding the oppression of women. Equal rights, comparable pay for comparable work, and food production are feminist issues wherever and whenever an understanding of them contributes to an understanding of the continued exploitation or subjugation of women. Carrying water and searching for firewood are feminist issues wherever and whenever women's primary responsibility for these tasks contributes to their lack of full participation in decision making, income producing, or high status positions engaged in by men. What counts as a feminist issue, then, depends largely on context, particularly the historical and material conditions of women's lives.

Environmental degradation and exploitation are feminist issues because an understanding of them contributes to an understanding of the oppression of women. In India, for example, both deforestation and reforestation through the introduction of a monoculture species tree (e.g., eucalyptus) intended for commercial production are feminist issues because the loss of indigenous forests and multiple species of trees has drastically affected rural Indian women's ability to maintain a subsistence household. Indigenous forests provide a variety of trees for food, fuel, fodder, household utensils, dyes, medicines, and income-generating uses, while monoculture-species forests do not.[3] Although I do not argue for this claim here, a look at the global impact of environmental degradation on women's lives suggests important respects in which environmental degradation is a feminist issue.

Feminist philosophers claim that some of the most important feminist issues are *conceptual* ones: these issues concern how one conceptualizes such mainstay philosophical notions as reason and rationality, ethics, and what it is to be human. Ecofeminists extend this feminist philosophical concern to nature. They argue that, ultimately, some of the most important connections between the domination of women and the domination of nature are conceptual. To see this, consider the nature of conceptual frameworks.

A *conceptual framework* is a set of *basic* beliefs, values, attitudes, and assumptions which shape and reflect how one views oneself and one's world. It is a socially constructed lens through which we perceive ourselves and others. It is affected by such factors as gender, race, class, age, affectional orientation, nationality, and religious background.

Some conceptual frameworks are oppressive. An *oppressive conceptual framework* is one that explains, justifies, and maintains relationships of domination and subordination. When an oppressive conceptual framework is *patriarchal*, it explains, justifies, and maintains the subordination of women by men.

I have argued elsewhere that there are three significant features of oppressive conceptual frameworks: (1) value-hierarchical thinking, i.e., "up-down" thinking which places higher value, status, or prestige on what is "up" rather than on what is "down"; (2) value dualisms, i.e., disjunctive pairs in which the disjuncts are seen as oppositional (rather than as complementary) and exclusive (rather than as inclusive), and which place higher value (status, prestige) on one disjunct rather than the other (e.g., dualisms which give higher value or status to that which has historically been identified as "mind," "reason," and "male" than to that which has historically been identified as "body," "emotion," and "female"); and (3) logic of domination, i.e., a structure of argumentation which leads to a justification of subordination.[4]

The third feature of oppressive conceptual frameworks is the most significant. A logic of domination is not *just* a logical structure. It also involves a substantive value system, since an ethical premise is needed to permit or sanction the "just" subordination of that which is subordinate. This justification typically is given on grounds of some alleged characteristic (e.g., rationality) which the dominant (e.g., men) have and the subordinate (e.g., women) lack.

Contrary to what many feminists and ecofeminists have said or suggested, there may be nothing *inherently* problematic about "hierarchical thinking" or even "value-hierarchical thinking" in contexts other than contexts of oppression. Hierarchical thinking is important in daily living for classifying data, comparing information, and organizing material. Taxonomies (e.g., plant taxonomies) and biological nomenclature seem to require *some* form of "hierarchical thinking." Even "value-hierarchical thinking" may be quite acceptable in certain contexts. (The same may be said of "value dualisms" in non-oppressive contexts.) For example, suppose it is true that what is unique about humans is our conscious capacity to radically reshape our social environments (or "societies"), as Murray Bookchin suggests.[5] Then one could truthfully say that humans are better equipped to radically reshape their environments than are rocks or plants – a "value-hierarchical" way of speaking.

The problem is not simply *that* value-hierarchical thinking and value dualisms are used, but *the way* in which each has been used *in oppressive conceptual frameworks* to establish inferiority and to justify subordination.[6] It is the logic of domination, *coupled with* value-hierarchical thinking and value dualisms, which "justifies" subordination. What is explanatorily basic, then, about the nature of oppressive conceptual frameworks is the logic of domination.

For ecofeminism, that a logic of domination is explanatorily basic is important for at least three reasons. First, without a logic of domination, a description of similarities and differences would be just that – a description of similarities and differences. Consider the claim, "Humans are different from plants and rocks in that humans can (and plants and rocks cannot) consciously and radically reshape the communities in which they live; humans are similar to plants and rocks in that they are both members of an ecological community." Even if humans are "better" than plants and rocks with respect to the conscious ability of humans to radically transform communities, one does not *thereby* get any *morally* relevant distinction between humans and nonhumans, or an argument for the domination of plants and rocks by humans. To get *those* conclusions one needs to add at least two powerful assumptions, viz., (A2) and (A4) in argument A below:

(A1) Humans do, and plants and rocks do not, have the capacity to consciously and radically change the community in which they live.

(A2) Whatever has the capacity to consciously and radically change the community in which it lives is morally superior to whatever lacks this capacity.

(A3) Thus, humans are morally superior to plants and rocks.

(A4) For any X and Y, if X is morally superior to Y, then X is morally justified in subordinating Y.

(A5) Thus, humans are morally justified in subordinating plants and rocks.

Without the two assumptions that *humans are morally superior* to (at least some) nonhumans, (A2), and that *superiority justifies subordination*, (A4), all one has is some difference between humans and some nonhumans. This is true *even if* that difference is given in terms of superiority. Thus, it is the logic of domination, (A4), which is the bottom line in ecofeminist discussions of oppression.

Second, ecofeminists argue that, at least in Western societies, the oppressive conceptual framework which sanctions the twin dominations of women and nature is a patriarchal one characterized by all three features of an oppressive conceptual framework. Many ecofeminists claim that, historically, within at least the dominant Western culture, a patriarchal conceptual framework has sanctioned the following argument B:

(B1) Women are identified with nature and the realm of the physical; men are identified with the "human" and the realm of the mental.

(B2) Whatever is identified with nature and the realm of the physical is inferior to ("below") whatever is identified with the "human" and the realm of the mental; or, conversely, the latter is superior to ("above") the former.

(B3) Thus, women are inferior to ("below") men; or, conversely, men are superior to ("above") women.

(B4) For any X and Y, if X is superior to Y, then X is justified in subordinating Y.

(B5) Thus, men are justified in subordinating women.

If sound, argument B establishes *patriarchy*, i.e., the conclusion given at (B5) that the systematic domination of women by men is justified. But according to ecofeminists, (B5) is justified by just those three features of an oppressive conceptual framework identified earlier: value-hierarchical thinking, the assumption at (B2); value dualisms, the assumed dualism of the mental and the physical at (B1) and the assumed inferiority of the physical vis-à-vis the mental at (B2); and a logic of domination, the assumption at (B4), the same as the previous premise (A4). Hence, according to ecofeminists, insofar as an oppressive patriarchal conceptual framework has functioned historically (within at least dominant Western culture) to sanction the twin dominations of women and nature (argument B), both argument B and the patriarchal conceptual framework, from whence it comes, ought to be rejected.

Of course, the preceding does not identify which premises of B are false. What is the status of premises (B1) and (B2)? Most, if not all, feminists claim that (B1), and many ecofeminists claim that (B2), have been assumed or asserted within the dominant Western philosophical and intellectual tradition.[7] As such, these feminists assert, as a matter of historical fact, that the dominant Western philosophical tradition has assumed the truth of (B1) and (B2). Ecofeminists, however, either deny (B2) or do not affirm (B2). Furthermore, because some ecofeminists are anxious to deny any ahistorical identification of women with nature, some ecofeminists deny (B1) when (B1) is used to support anything other than a strictly historical claim about what has been asserted or assumed to be true within patriarchal culture – e.g., when (B1) is used to assert that women properly are identified with the realm of nature and the physical.[8] Thus, from an ecofeminist perspective, (B1) and (B2) are properly viewed as problematic though historically sanctioned claims; they are problematic precisely because of the way they have functioned historically in a patriarchal conceptual framework and culture to sanction the dominations of women and nature.

What *all* ecofeminists agree about, then, is the way in which *the logic of domination* has functioned historically within patriarchy to sustain and justify the twin dominations of women and nature.[9] Since *all* feminists (and not just ecofeminists) oppose patriarchy, the conclusion given at (B5), all feminists (including ecofeminists) must oppose at least the logic of domination, premise (B4), on which argument B rests – whatever the truth-value status of (B1) and (B2) *outside of* a patriarchal context.

That *all* feminists must oppose the logic of domination shows the breadth and depth of the ecofeminist critique of B: it is a critique not only of the three assumptions on which this argument for the domination of women and nature rests, viz., the assumptions at (B1), (B2), and (B4); it is also a critique of patriarchal conceptual frameworks generally, i.e., of those oppressive conceptual frameworks which put men "up" and women "down," allege some way in which women are morally inferior to men, and use that alleged difference to justify the subordination of women by men. Therefore, ecofeminism is necessary to *any* feminist critique of patriarchy, and, hence, necessary to feminism (a point I discuss again later).

Third, ecofeminism clarifies why the logic of domination, and any conceptual framework which gives rise to it, must be abolished in order both to make possible a meaningful notion of difference which does not breed domination and to prevent feminism from becoming a "support" movement based primarily on shared experiences. In contemporary society, there is no one "woman's voice," no *woman* (or *human*) *simpliciter:* every woman (or human) is a woman (or human) of some race, class, age, affectional orientation, marital status, regional or national background, and so forth. Because there are no "monolithic experiences" that all women share, feminism must be a "solidarity movement" based on shared beliefs and interests rather than a "unity in sameness" movement based on shared experiences and shared victimization.[10] In the words of Maria Lugones, "Unity – not to be confused with solidarity – is understood as conceptually tied to domination."[11]

Ecofeminists insist that the sort of logic of domination used to justify the domination of humans by gender, racial or ethnic, or class status is also used to justify the domination of nature. Because eliminating a logic of domination is part of a feminist critique – whether a critique of patriarchy, white supremacist culture, or imperialism – ecofeminists insist that *naturism* is properly viewed as an integral part of any feminist solidarity movement to end sexist oppression and the logic of domination which conceptually grounds it.

Ecofeminism Reconceives Feminism

The discussion so far has focused on some of the oppressive conceptual features of patriarchy. As I use the phrase, the "logic of traditional feminism" refers to the location of the conceptual roots of sexist oppression, at least in Western societies, in an oppressive patriarchal conceptual framework characterized by a logic of domination. Insofar as other systems of oppression (e.g., racism, classism, ageism, heterosexism) are also conceptually maintained by a logic of domination, appeal to the logic of traditional feminism ultimately locates the basic conceptual interconnections among *all* systems of oppression in the logic of domination. It thereby explains at a *conceptual* level why the eradication of sexist oppression requires the eradication of the other forms of oppression.[12] It is by clarifying this conceptual connection between systems of oppression that a movement to end sexist oppression – traditionally the special turf of feminist theory and practice – leads to a reconceiving of feminism as *a movement to end all forms of oppression.*

Suppose one agrees that the logic of traditional feminism requires the expansion of feminism to include other social systems of domination (e.g., racism and classism). What warrants the inclusion of nature in these "social systems of domination"? Why must the logic of traditional feminism include the abolition of "naturism" (i.e., the domination or oppression of nonhuman nature) among the "isms" feminism must confront? The conceptual justification for expanding feminism to include ecofeminism is twofold. One basis has already been suggested: by showing that the conceptual connections between the dual dominations of women and nature are located in an oppressive and, at least in Western societies, patriarchal conceptual framework characterized by a logic of domination, ecofeminism explains how and why feminism, conceived as a movement to end sexist oppression, must be expanded and reconceived as also a movement to end naturism. This is made explicit by the following argument C:

(C1) Feminism is a movement to end Sexism.
(C2) But Sexism is conceptually linked with naturism (through an oppressive conceptual framework characterized by a logic of domination).
(C3) Thus, Feminism is (also) a movement to end naturism.

Because, ultimately, these connections between sexism and naturism are conceptual – embedded in an oppressive conceptual framework – the logic of traditional feminism leads to the embracement of ecological feminism.[13]

The other justification for reconceiving feminism to include ecofeminism has to do with the concepts of gender and nature. Just as conceptions of gender are socially constructed, so are conceptions of nature. Of course, the claim that women and nature are social constructions does not require anyone to deny that there are actual humans and actual trees, rivers, and plants. It simply implies that *how* women and nature are conceived is a matter of historical and social reality. These conceptions vary cross-culturally and by historical time period. As a result, any discussion of the "oppression or domination of nature" involves reference to historically specific forms of social domination of nonhuman nature by humans, just as discussion of the "domination of women" refers to historically specific forms of social domination of women by men. Although I do not argue for it here, an ecofeminist defense of the historical connections between the dominations of women and of nature, claims (B1) and (B2) in argument B, involves showing that within patriarchy the feminization of nature and the naturalization of women have been

crucial to the historically successful subordinations of both.[14]

If ecofeminism promises to reconceive traditional feminism in ways which include naturism as a legitimate feminist issue, does ecofeminism also promise to reconceive environmental ethics in ways which are feminist? I think so. This is the subject of the remainder of the paper.

[. . .]

Ecofeminism as a Feminist and Environmental Ethic

A feminist ethic involves a twofold commitment to critique male bias in ethics wherever it occurs, and to develop ethics which are not male-biased. Sometimes this involves articulation of values (e.g., values of care, appropriate trust, kinship, friendship) often lost or underplayed in mainstream ethics.[15] Sometimes it involves engaging in theory building by pioneering in new directions or by revamping old theories in gender sensitive ways. What makes the critiques of old theories or conceptualizations of new ones "feminist" is that they emerge out of sex-gender analyses and reflect whatever those analyses reveal about gendered experience and gendered social reality.

As I conceive feminist ethics in the pre-feminist present, it rejects attempts to conceive of ethical theory in terms of necessary and sufficient conditions, because it assumes that there is no essence (in the sense of some transhistorical, universal, absolute abstraction) of feminist ethics. While attempts to formulate joint necessary and sufficient conditions of a feminist ethic are unfruitful, nonetheless, there are some necessary conditions, what I prefer to call "boundary conditions," of a feminist ethic. These boundary conditions clarify some of the minimal conditions of a feminist ethic without suggesting that feminist ethics has some ahistorical essence. They are like the boundaries of a quilt or collage. They delimit the territory of the piece without dictating what the interior, the design, the actual pattern of the piece looks like. Because the actual design of the quilt emerges from the multiplicity of voices of women in a cross-cultural context, the design will change over time. It is not something static.

What are some of the boundary conditions of a feminist ethic? First, nothing can become part of a feminist ethic – can be part of the quilt – that promotes sexism, racism, classism, or any other "isms" of social domination. Of course, people may disagree about what counts as a sexist act, racist attitude, classist behavior. What counts as sexism, racism, or classism may vary cross-culturally. Still, because a feminist ethic aims at eliminating sexism and sexist bias, and (as I have already shown) sexism is intimately connected in conceptualization and in practice to racism, classism, and naturism, a feminist ethic must be anti-sexist, anti-racist, anti-classist, anti-naturist and opposed to any "ism" which presupposes or advances a logic of domination.

Second, a feminist ethic is a *contextualist* ethic. A contextualist ethic is one which sees ethical discourse and practice as emerging from the voices of people located in different historical circumstances. A contextualist ethic is properly viewed as a *collage* or *mosaic*, a *tapestry* of voices that emerges out of felt experiences. Like any collage or mosaic, the point is not to have *one picture* based on a unity of voices, but a *pattern* which emerges out of the very different voices of people located in different circumstances. When a contextualist ethic is *feminist*, it gives central place to the voices of women.

Third, since a feminist ethic gives central significance to the diversity of women's voices, a feminist ethic must be structurally pluralistic rather than unitary or reductionistic. It rejects the assumption that there is "one voice" in terms of which ethical values, beliefs, attitudes, and conduct can be assessed.

Fourth, a feminist ethic reconceives ethical theory as theory in process which will change over time. Like all theory, a feminist ethic is based on some generalizations.[16] Nevertheless, the generalizations associated with it are themselves a pattern of voices within which the different voices emerging out of concrete and alternative descriptions of ethical situations have meaning. The coherence of a feminist theory so conceived is given within a historical and conceptual context, i.e., within a set of historical, socioeconomic circumstances, including circumstances of race, class, age, and affectional orientation) and within a set of basic beliefs, values, attitudes, and assumptions about the world.

Fifth, because a feminist ethic is contextualist, structurally pluralistic, and "in-process," one way to evaluate the claims of a feminist ethic is in terms of their *inclusiveness;* those claims (voices, patterns of voices) are morally and epistemologically favored (preferred, better, less partial, less biased) which are more inclusive of the felt experiences and perspectives of oppressed persons. The condition of inclusiveness requires and ensures that the diverse voices of women (as oppressed persons) will be given legitimacy in ethical theory building. It hereby helps to minimize empirical bias, e.g., bias rising from faulty or false generalizations based on stereotyping, too small a sample size, or a skewed sample. It does so by ensuring that any generalizations which are made about ethics and ethical decision making include – indeed cohere with – the patterned voices of women.[17]

Sixth, a feminist ethic makes no attempt to provide an "objective" point of view, since it assumes that in contemporary culture there really is no such point of view. As such, it does not claim to be "unbiased" in the sense of "value-neutral" or "objective." However, it does assume that whatever bias it has as an ethic centralizing the voices of oppressed persons is a *better bias* – "better" because it is more inclusive and therefore less partial – than those which exclude those voices.[18]

Seventh, a feminist ethic provides a central place for values typically unnoticed, underplayed, or misrepresented in traditional ethics, e.g., values of care, love, friendship, and appropriate trust.[19] Again, it need not do this at the exclusion of considerations of rights, rules, or utility. There may be many contexts in which talk of rights or of utility is useful or appropriate. For instance, in contracts or property relationships, talk of rights may be useful and appropriate. In deciding what is cost-effective or advantageous to the most people, talk of utility may be useful and appropriate. In a feminist *qua* contextualist ethic, whether or not such talk is useful or appropriate depends on the context; *other values* (e.g., values of care, trust, friendship) are *not* viewed as reducible to or captured solely in terms of such talk.[20]

Eighth, a feminist ethic also involves a reconception of what it is to be human and what it is for humans to engage in ethical decision making, since it rejects as either meaningless or currently untenable any gender-free or gender-neutral description of humans, ethics, and ethical decision making. It thereby rejects what Alison Jaggar calls "abstract individualism," i.e., the position that it is possible to identify a human essence or human nature that exists independently of any particular historical context.[21] Humans and human moral conduct are properly understood essentially (and not merely accidentally) in terms of networks or webs of historical and concrete relationships.

All the props are now in place for seeing how ecofeminism provides the framework for a distinctively feminist and environmental ethic. It is a feminism that critiques male bias wherever it occurs in ethics (including environmental ethics) and aims at providing an ethic (including an environmental ethic) which is not male biased – and it does so in a way that satisfies the preliminary boundary conditions of a feminist ethic.

First, ecofeminism is quintessentially anti-naturist. Its anti-naturism consists in the rejection of any way of thinking about or acting toward nonhuman nature that reflects a logic, values, or attitude of domination. Its anti-naturist, anti-sexist, anti-racist, anti-classist (and so forth, for all other "isms" of social domination) stance forms the outer boundary of the quilt: nothing gets on the quilt which is naturist, sexist, racist, classist, and so forth.

Second, ecofeminism is a contextualist ethic. It involves a shift *from* a conception of ethics as primarily a matter of rights, rules, or principles predetermined and applied in specific cases to entities viewed as competitors in the contest of moral standing, *to* a conception of ethics as growing out of what Jim Cheney calls "defining relationships," i.e., relationships conceived in some sense as defining who one is.[22] As a contextualist ethic, it is not that rights, or rules, or principles are *not* relevant or important. Clearly they are in certain contexts and for certain purposes.[23] It is just that what *makes* them relevant or important is that those to whom they apply are entities *in relationship with* others.

Ecofeminism also involves an ethical shift *from* granting moral consideration to nonhumans *exclusively* on the grounds of some similarity they share with humans (e.g., rationality, interests, moral agency, sentiency, right-holder status) *to* "a highly contextual account to see clearly what a human being is and what the nonhuman world might be, morally speaking, *for* human beings."[24] For an ecofeminist, *how* a moral agent is in relationship to another becomes of central significance, not simply *that* a moral agent is a moral agent or is bound by rights, duties, virtue, or utility to act in a certain way.

Third, ecofeminism is structurally pluralistic in that it presupposes and maintains difference – difference among humans as well as between humans and at least some elements of nonhuman nature. Thus, while ecofeminism denies the "nature/culture" split, it affirms that humans are both members of an ecological community (in some respects) and different from it (in other respects). Ecofeminism's attention to relationships and community is not, therefore, an erasure of difference but a respectful acknowledgement of it.

Fourth, ecofeminism reconceives theory as theory in process. It focuses on patterns of meaning which emerge, for instance, from the storytelling and first-person narratives of women (and others) who deplore the twin dominations of women and nature. The use of narrative is one way to ensure that the content of the ethic – the pattern of the quilt – may/will change over time, as the historical and material realities of women's lives change and as more is learned about women–nature connections and the destruction of the nonhuman world.[25]

Fifth, ecofeminism is inclusivist. It emerges from the voices of women who experience the harmful domination of nature and the way that domination is tied to their domination as women. It emerges from listening to the voices of indigenous peoples such as Native Americans who have been dislocated from their land and have witnessed the attendant undermining of such values as appropriate reciprocity, sharing, and kinship that characterize traditional Indian culture. It emerges from listening to voices of those who, like Nathan Hare, critique traditional approaches to environmental ethics as white and bourgeois, and as failing to address issues of "black ecology" and the "ecology" of the inner city and urban spaces.[26] It also emerges out of the voices of Chipko women who see the destruction of "earth, soil, and water" as intimately connected with their own inability to survive economically.[27] With its emphasis on inclusivity and difference, ecofeminism provides a framework for recognizing that what counts as ecology and what counts as appropriate conduct toward both human and nonhuman environments is largely a matter of context.

Sixth, as a feminism, ecofeminism makes no attempt to provide an "objective" point of view. It is a social ecology. It recognizes the twin dominations of women and nature as social problems rooted both in very concrete, historical, socioeconomic circumstances and in oppressive patriarchal conceptual frameworks which maintain and sanction these circumstances.

Seventh, ecofeminism makes a central place for values of care, love, friendship, trust, and appropriate reciprocity – values that presuppose that our relationships to others are central to our understanding of who we are.[28] It thereby gives voice to the sensitivity that in climbing a mountain, one is doing something in relationship with an "other," an "other" whom one can come to care about and treat respectfully.

Lastly, an ecofeminist ethic involves a reconception of what it means to be human, and in what human ethical behavior consists. Ecofeminism denies abstract individualism. Humans are who we are in large part by virtue of the historical and social contexts and the relationships we are in, including our relationships with nonhuman nature. Relationships are not something extrinsic to who we are, not an "add on" feature of human nature; they play an essential role in shaping what it is to be human. Relationships of humans to the nonhuman environment are, in part, constitutive of what it is to be a human.

By making visible the interconnections among the dominations of women and nature, ecofeminism shows that both are feminist issues and that explicit acknowledgement of both is vital to any responsible environmental ethic. Feminism *must* embrace ecological feminism if it is to end the domination of women because the domination of women is tied conceptually and historically to the domination of nature.

A responsible environmental ethic also *must* embrace feminism. Otherwise, even the seemingly most revolutionary, liberational, and holistic ecological ethic will fail to take seriously the interconnected dominations of nature and women that are so much a part of the historical legacy and conceptual framework that sanctions the exploitation of nonhuman nature. Failure to make visible these interconnected, twin dominations results in an inaccurate account of how it is that nature has been and continues to be dominated and exploited and produces an environmental ethic that lacks the depth necessary to be truly *inclusive* of the realities of persons who at least in dominant Western culture have been intimately tied with that exploitation, viz., women. Whatever else can be said in favor of such holistic ethics, a failure to make visible ecofeminist insights into the common denominators of the twin oppressions of women and nature is to perpetuate, rather than overcome, the source of that oppression.

[. . .]

Conclusion

I have argued in this paper that ecofeminism provides a framework for a distinctively feminist and environmental ethic. Ecofeminism grows out of the felt and theorized about connections between the domination of women and the domination of nature. As a contextualist ethic, ecofeminism refocuses environmental ethics on what nature might mean, morally speaking, *for* humans, and on how the relational attitudes of humans to others – humans as well as nonhumans – sculpt both what it is to be human and the nature and ground of human responsibilities to the nonhuman environment. Part of what this refocusing does is to take seriously the voices of women and other oppressed persons in the construction of that ethic.

A Sioux elder once told me a story about his son. He sent his seven-year-old son to live with the child's grandparents on a Sioux reservation so that he could "learn the Indian ways." Part of what the grandparents taught the son was how to hunt the four-leggeds of the forest. As I heard the story, the boy was taught, "to shoot your four-legged brother in his hind area, slowing it down but not killing it. Then, take the four-legged's head in your hands, and look into his eyes. The eyes are where all the suffering is. Look into your brother's eyes and feel his pain. Then, take your knife and cut the four-legged under his chin, here, on his neck, so that he dies quickly. And as you do, ask your brother, the four-legged, for forgiveness for what you do. Offer also a prayer of thanks to your four-legged kin for offering his body to you just now, when you need food to eat and clothing to wear. And promise the four-legged that you will put yourself back into the earth when you die, to become nourishment for the earth, and for the sister flowers, and for the brother deer. It is appropriate that you should offer this blessing for the four-legged and, in due time, reciprocate in turn with your body in this way, as the four-legged gives life to you for your survival." As I reflect upon that story, I am struck by the power of the environmental ethic that grows out of and takes seriously narrative, context, and such values and relational attitudes as care, loving perception, and appropriate reciprocity, and doing what is appropriate in a given situation – however that notion of appropriateness eventually gets filled out. I am also struck by what one is able to see, once one begins to explore some of the historical and conceptual connections between the dominations of women and of nature. A *re-conceiving* and *re-visioning* of both feminism and environmental ethics is, I think, the power and promise of ecofeminism.

Notes

1 Explicit ecological feminist literature includes works from a variety of scholarly perspectives and sources. Some of these works are Leonie Caldecott and Stephanie Leland, eds., *Reclaim the Earth; Women Speak Out for Life on Earth* (London: The Women's Press, 1983); Jim Cheney, "Eco-Feminism and Deep Ecology," *Environmental Ethics* 9 (1987): 115–45; Andree Collard with Joyce Contrucci, *Rape of the Wild: Man's Violence against Animals and the Earth* (Bloomington: Indiana University Press, 1988); Katherine Davies, "Historical Associations: Women and the Natural World," *Women & Environments* 9, no. 2 (Spring 1987): 4–6; Sharon Doubiago, "Deeper than Deep Ecology: Men Must Become Feminists," in *The New Catalyst Quarterly*, no. 10 (Winter 1987/88): 10–11; Brian Easlea, *Science and Sexual Oppression: Patriarchy's Confrontation with Women and Nature* (London: Weidenfeld & Nicholson, 1981); Elizabeth Dodson Gray, *Green Paradise Lost* (Wellesley, Mass.: Roundtable Press, 1979); Susan Griffin, *Women and Nature: The Roaring Inside Her* (San Francisco: Harper and Row, 1978); Joan L. Griscom, "On Healing the Nature/History Split in Feminist Thought," in *Heresies #13: Feminism and Ecology* 4, no. 1 (1981): 4–9; Ynestra King, "The Ecology of Feminism and the Feminism of Ecology," in *Healing Our Wounds: The Power of Ecological Feminism*, ed. Judith Plant (Boston: New Society Publishers, 1989), pp. 18–28; "The Eco-feminist Imperative," in *Reclaim the Earth*, ed. Caldecott and Leland (London: The Women's Press, 1983), pp. 12–16. "Feminism and the Revolt of Nature," in *Heresies #13: Feminism and Ecology* 4, no. 1 (1981): 12–16, and "What is Ecofeminism?" *The Nation*, 12 December 1987; Marti Kheel, "Animal Liberation Is A Feminist Issue," *The New Catalyst Quarterly*, no. 10 (Winter 1987–8): 8–9; Carolyn Merchant, *The Death of Nature: Women, Ecology and the Scientific Revolution* (San Francisco: Harper and Row, 1980); Patrick Murphy, ed., "Feminism, Ecology, and the Future of the Humanities," special issue of *Studies in the Humanities* 15, no. 2 (December 1988); Abby Peterson and Carolyn Merchant, "Peace with the Earth: Women and the Environmental Movement in Sweden," *Women's Studies International Forum* 9, no. 5–6 (1986): 465–79; Judith Plant, "Searching for Common Ground: Ecofeminism and Bioregionalism," in *The New Catalyst Quarterly*, no. 10 (Winter 1987/8): 6–7; Judith Plant, ed., *Healing Our Wounds: The Power of Ecological Feminism* (Boston: New Society Publishers, 1989); Val Plumwood, "Ecofeminism: An Overview and Discussion of Positions and Arguments," *Australasian Journal of Philosophy*, Supplement to vol. 64 (June 1986): 120–37; Rosemary Radford Ruether, *New Woman/New Earth: Sexist Ideologies & Human Liberation* (New York: Seabury Press, 1975); Kirkpatrick Sale, "Ecofeminism – A New Perspective," *The Nation* (26 September 1987): 302–5; Ariel Kay Salleh, "Deeper than Deep Ecology: The Eco-Feminist Connection," *Environmental Ethics* 6 (1984): 339–45, and "Epistemology and the Metaphors of Production: An Eco-Feminist Reading of Critical Theory," in *Studies in the Humanities* 15 (1988): 130–9; Vandana Shiva, *Staying Alive: Women. Ecology and Development* (London: Zed Books, 1988); Charlene Spretnak, "Ecofeminism: Our Roots and Flowering," *The Elmswood Newsletter*, Winter Solstice 1988; Karen J. Warren, "Feminism and Ecology: Making Connections," *Environmental Ethics* 9 (1987): 3–21; "Toward an Ecofeminist Ethic," *Studies in the Humanities* 15 (1988): 140–56; Miriam Wyman, "Explorations of Ecofeminism," *Women & Environments* (Spring 1987): 6–7; Iris Young, " 'Feminism and Ecology' and 'Women and Life on Earth: Eco-Feminism in the 80's'," *Environmental Ethics* 5 (1983): 173–80; Michael Zimmerman, "Feminism, Deep Ecology, and Environmental Ethics," *Environmental Ethics* 9 (1987): 21–44.

2 Françoise d'Eaubonne, *Le Feminisme ou la Mort* (Paris: Pierre Horay, 1974), pp. 213–52.

3 I discuss this in my paper, "Toward An Ecofeminist Ethic."

4 The account offered here is a revision of the account given earlier in my paper "Feminism and Ecology: Making Connections." I have changed the account to be about "oppressive" rather than strictly "patriarchal" conceptual frameworks in order to leave open the possibility that there may be some patriarchal conceptual frameworks (e.g., in non-Western cultures) which are *not* properly characterized as based on value dualisms.

5 Murray Bookchin, "Social Ecology versus 'Deep Ecology'," in *Green Perspectives: Newsletter of the Green Program* Project no. 4–5 (Summer 1987): 9.

6 It may be that in contemporary Western society, which is so thoroughly structured by categories of gender, race, class, age, and affectional orientation, that there simply is no meaningful notion of "value-hierarchical thinking" which does not function in an oppressive context. For purposes of this paper, I leave that question open.

7 Many feminists who argue for the historical point that claims (B1) and (B2) have been asserted or assumed to be true within the dominant Western philosophical tradition do so by discussion of that tradition's conceptions of reason, rationality, and science. For a sampling of the sorts of claims made within that context, see "Reason, Rationality, and Gender," ed. Nancy Tuana and Karen J. Warren, a special issue of the American Philosophical Association's *Newsletter on Feminism and*

Philosophy 88, no. 2 (March 1989): 17–71. Ecofeminists who claim that (B2) has been assumed to be true within the dominant Western philosophical tradition include: Gray, *Green Paradise Lost*; Griffin, *Woman and Nature: The Roaring Inside Her*; Merchant, *The Death of Nature*; Ruether, *New Woman/New Earth*. For a discussion of some of these ecofeminist historical accounts, see Plumwood, "Ecofeminism." While I agree that the historical connections between the domination of women and the domination of nature is a crucial one, I do not argue for that claim here.

8   Ecofeminists who deny (B1) when (B1) is offered as anything other than a true, descriptive, historical claim about patriarchal culture often do so on grounds that an objectionable sort of biological determinism, or at least harmful female sex-gender stereotypes, underlie (B1). For a discussion of this "split" among those ecofeminists ("nature feminists") who assert and those ecofeminists ("social feminists") who deny (B1) as anything other than a true historical claim about how women are described in patriarchal culture, see Griscom, "On Healing the Nature/History Split."

9   I make no attempt here to defend the historically sanctioned truth of these premises.

10 See, e.g., Bell Hooks, *Feminist Theory From Margin to Center* (Boston: South End Press, 1984), pp. 51–2.

11 Maria Lugones, "Playfulness, 'World-Travelling,' and Loving Perception," *Hypatia* 2, no. 2 (Summer 1987): 3.

12 At an *experiential* level, some women are "women of color," poor, old, lesbian, Jewish, and physically challenged. Thus, if feminism is going to liberate these women, it also needs to end the racism, classism, heterosexism, anti-Semitism, and discrimination against the handicapped that is constitutive of their oppression as black, or Latina, or poor, or older, or lesbian, or Jewish, or physically challenged women.

13 This same sort of reasoning shows that feminism is also a movement to end racism, classism, age-ism, heterosexism and other "isms," which are based in oppressive conceptual frameworks characterized by a logic of domination. However, there is an important caveat: ecofeminism is *not* compatible with all feminisms and all environmentalisms. For a discussion of this point, see my article, "Feminism and Ecology: Making Connections." What it *is* compatible with is the minimal condition characterization of feminism as a movement to end sexism that is accepted by all contemporary feminisms (liberal, traditional Marxist, radical, socialist, Blacks and non-Western).

14 See, e.g., Gray, *Green Paradise Lost*; Griffin, *Woman and Nature*; Merchant, *The Death of Nature*; and Ruether, *New Woman/New Earth*.

15 This account of a feminist ethic draws on my paper "Toward an Ecofeminist Ethic."

16 Marilyn Frye makes this point in her illuminating paper, "The Possibility of Feminist Theory," read at the American Philosophical Association Central Division Meetings in Chicago, 29 April–1 May 1986. My discussion of feminist theory is inspired largely by that paper and by Kathryn Addelson's paper "Moral Revolution," in *Women and Values: Readings in Recent Feminist Philosophy*, ed. Marilyn Pearsall (Belmont, Calif.: Wadsworth Publishing Co., 1986), pp. 291–309.

17 Notice that the standard of inclusiveness does not exclude the voices of men. It is just that those voices must cohere with the voices of women.

18 For a more in-depth discussion of the notions of impartiality and bias, see my paper, "Critical Thinking and Feminism," *Informal Logic* 10, no. 1 (Winter 1988): 31–44.

19 The burgeoning literature on these values is noteworthy. See, e.g., Carol Gilligan, *In a Different Voice: Psychological Theories and Women's Development* (Cambridge: Harvard University Press, 1982); *Mapping the Moral Domain: A Contribution of Women's Thinking to Psychological Theory and Education*, ed. Carol Gilligan, Janie Victoria Ward, and Jill McLean Taylor, with Betty Bardige (Cambridge: Harvard University Press, 1988); Nel Noddings, *Caring: A Feminine Approach to Ethics and Moral Education* (Berkeley: University of California Press, 1984); Maria Lugones and Elizabeth V. Spelman, "Have We Got a Theory for You! Feminist Theory, Cultural Imperialism, and 'the Women's Voice,'" *Women's Studies International Forum* 6 (1983): 573–81; Maria Lugones, "Playfulness"; Annette C. Baier, "What Do Women Want In A Moral Theory?" *Nous* 19 (1985): 53–63.

20 Jim Cheney would claim that our fundamental relationships to one another as moral agents are not as moral agents to rights holders, and that whatever rights a person properly may be said to have are relationally defined rights, not rights possessed by atomistic individuals conceived as Robinson Crusoes who do not exist essentially in relation to others. On this view, even rights talk itself is properly conceived as growing out of a relational ethic, not vice versa.

21 Alison Jaggar, *Feminist Politics and Human Nature* (Totowa, NJ: Rowman and Allanheld, 1980), pp. 42–4.

22 Henry West has pointed out that the expression "defining relations" is ambiguous. According to West, "the 'defining' as Cheney uses it is an adjective, not a principle – it is not that ethics defines relationships: it is that ethics grows out of conceiving of the relationships that one is in as defining what the individual is."

23 For example, in relationships involving contracts or promises, those relationships might be correctly

described as that of moral agent to rights holders. In relationships involving mere property, those relationships might be correctly described as that of moral agent to objects having only instrumental value, "relationships of instrumentality." In comments on an earlier draft of this paper, West suggested that possessive individualism, for instance, might be recast in such a way that an individual is defined by his or her property relationships.

24 Cheney, "Eco-Feminism and Deep Ecology," p. 144.
25 One might object that such permission for change opens the door for environmental exploitation. This is not the case. An ecofeminist ethic is anti-naturist. Hence, the unjust domination and exploitation of nature is a "boundary condition" of the ethic; no such

actions are sanctioned or justified on ecofeminist grounds. What it *does* leave open is some leeway about what counts as domination and exploitation. This, I think, is a strength of the ethic, not a weakness, since it acknowledges that *that* issue cannot be resolved in any practical way in the abstract, independent of a historical and social context.

26 Nathan Hare, "Black Ecology," in *Environmental Ethics*, ed. K. S. Shrader-Frechette (Pacific Grove, Calif.: Boxwood Press, 1981), pp. 229–36.
27 For an ecofeminist discussion of the Chipko movement, see my "Toward an Ecofeminist Ethic," and Shiva's *Staying Alive*.
28 See Cheney, "Eco-Feminism and Deep Ecology," p. 122.

---

36   Feminism and the Philosophy of Nature

Carolyn Merchant

Ecofeminism and Feminist Theory

The term *ecofeminisme* was coined by the French writer Françoise d'Eaubonne in 1974 to represent women's potential for bringing about an ecological revolution to ensure human survival on the planet.[1] Such an ecological revolution would entail new gender relations between women and men and between humans and nature. Liberal, radical, and socialist feminism have all been concerned with improving the human/nature relationship, and each has contributed to an ecofeminist perspective in different ways.[2] Liberal feminism is consistent with the objectives of reform environmentalism to alter human relations with nature through the passage of new laws and regulations. Radical ecofeminism analyzes environmental problems from within its critique of patriarchy and offers alternatives that could liberate both women and nature. Socialist ecofeminism grounds its analysis in capitalist patriarchy and would totally restructure, through a socialist revolution, the domination of

women and nature inherent in the market economy's use of both as resources. While radical feminism has delved more deeply into the woman/nature connection, I believe that socialist feminism has the potential for a more thorough critique of the domination issue.

Liberal feminism characterized the history of feminism from its beginnings in the seventeenth century until the 1960s. Its roots are liberalism, the political theory that incorporates the scientific analysis that nature is composed of atoms moved by external forces with a theory of human nature that views humans as individual rational agents who maximize their own self-interest and capitalism as the optimal economic structure for human progress. Historically, liberal feminists have argued that women do not differ from men as rational agents and that exclusion from educational and economic opportunities have prevented them from realizing their own potential for creativity in all spheres of human life.[3]

For liberal feminists (as for liberalism generally), environmental problems result from the overly rapid

Table 36.1 Feminism and the Environment

	Nature	Human nature	Feminist critique of environmentalism	Image of a feminist environmentalism
Liberal feminism	Atoms Mind/body dualism Domination of nature	Rational agents Individualism Maximization of self-interest	"Man and his environment" leaves out women	Women participate in natural resources and environmental sciences
Marxist feminism	Transformation of nature by science and technology for human use Domination of nature as a means to human freedom Nature is material basis of life: food, clothing, shelter, energy	Creation of human nature through mode of production, praxis Historically specific – not fixed Species nature of humans	Critique of capitalist control of resources and accumulation of goods and profits	Socialist/communist society will use resources for good of all men and women Resources will be controlled by workers Environmental pollution will be minimal since no surpluses will be produced Environmental research by men and women
Radical feminism	Nature is spiritual and personal Conventional science and technology problematic because of their emphasis on domination	Biology is basic Humans are sexually reproducing bodies Sexed by biology/Gendered by society	Unaware of interconnectedness of male domination of nature and women Male environmentalism retains hierarchies Insufficient attention to environmental threats to women's reproduction (chemicals, nuclear war)	Woman/nature both valued and celebrated Reproductive freedom Against pornographic depictions of both women and nature Radical ecofeminism
Socialist feminism	Nature is material basis of life: food, clothing, shelter, energy Nature is socially and historically constructed Transformation of nature by production	Human nature created through biology and praxis (sex, race, class, age) Historically specific and socially constructed	Leaves out nature as active and responsive Leaves out women's role in reproduction and reproduction as a category Systems approach is mechanistic not dialectical	Both nature and human production are active Centrality of biological and social reproduction Dialectic between production and reproduction Multileveled structural analysis Dialectical (not mechanical) systems Socialist ecofeminism

development of natural resources and the failure to regulate environmental pollutants. Better science, conservation, and laws are the proper approaches to resolving resource problems. Given equal educational opportunities to become scientists, natural resource managers, regulators, lawyers, and legislators, women like men can contribute to the improvement of the environment, the conservation of natural resources, and the higher quality of human life. Women, therefore, can transcend the social stigma of their biology and join men in the cultural project of environmental conservation.

Radical feminism developed in the late 1960s and 1970s with the second wave of feminism. The radical form of ecofeminism is a response to the perception that women and nature have been mutually associated and devalued in Western culture and that both can be elevated and liberated through direct political action. In prehistory an emerging patriarchal culture dethroned the mother Goddesses and replaced them with male gods to whom the female deities became subservient.[4] The scientific revolution of the seventeenth century further degraded nature by replacing Renaissance organicism and a nurturing earth with the metaphor of a machine to be controlled and repaired from the outside. The Earth is to be dominated by male-developed and -controlled technology, science, and industry.

Radical feminism instead celebrates the relationship between women and nature through the revival of ancient rituals centered on Goddess worship, the moon, animals, and the female reproductive system. A vision in which nature is held in esteem as mother and Goddess is a source of inspiration and empowerment for many ecofeminists. Spirituality is seen as a source of both personal and social change. Goddess worship and rituals centered around the lunar and female menstrual cycles, lectures, concerts, art exhibitions, street and theater productions, and direct political action (web weaving in antinuclear protests) are all examples of the re-visioning of nature and women as powerful forces. Radical ecofeminist philosophy embraces intuition, an ethic of caring, and weblike human/nature relationships.

For radical feminists, human nature is grounded in human biology. Humans are biologically sexed and socially gendered. Sex/gender relations give men and women different power bases. Hence the personal is political. Radical feminists object to the dominant society's perception that women are limited by being closer to nature because of their ability to bear children. The dominant view is that menstruation, pregnancy, nursing, and nurturing of infants and young children should tie women to the home, decreasing their mobility and inhibiting their ability to remain in the work force. Radical feminists argue that the perception that women are totally oriented toward biological reproduction degrades them by association with a nature that is itself devalued in Western culture. Women's biology and nature should instead be celebrated as sources of female power.

Turning the perceived connection between women and biological reproduction upside down becomes the source of women's empowerment and ecological activism. Women argue that male-designed and -produced technologies neglect the effects of nuclear radiation, pesticides, hazardous wastes, and household chemicals on women's reproductive organs and on the ecosystem. They argue that radioactivity from nuclear wastes, power plants, and bombs is a potential cause of birth defects, cancers, and the elimination of life on Earth.[5] They expose hazardous waste sites near schools and homes as permeating soil and drinking water and contributing to miscarriage, birth defects, and leukemia. They object to pesticides and herbicides being sprayed on crops and forests as potentially affecting children and the childbearing women living near them. Women frequently spearhead local actions against spraying and power plant siting and organize others to demand toxic cleanups. When coupled with an environmental ethic that values rather than degrades nature, such actions have the potential both for raising women's consciousness of their own oppression and for the liberation of nature from the polluting effects of industrialization. For example, many lower-middle-class women who became politicized through protests over toxic chemical wastes at Love Canal in New York simultaneously became feminists when their activism spilled over into their home lives.[6]

Yet in emphasizing the female, body, and nature components of the dualities male/female, mind/body, and culture/nature, radical ecofeminism runs the risk of perpetuating the very hierarchies it seeks to overthrow. Critics point to the problem of women's own reinforcement of their identification with a nature that Western culture degrades.[7] If "female is to male as nature is to culture," as anthropologist Sherry Ortner argues,[8] then women's hopes for liberation are set back by association with nature. Any analysis that makes women's essence and qualities special ties them to a biological destiny that thwarts the possibility of liberation. A politics grounded in women's culture, experience, and values can be seen as reactionary.

To date, socialist feminists have had little to say about the problem of the domination of nature. To them, the source of male domination of women is the complex of social patterns called capitalist patriarchy, in which men bear the responsibility for labor in the marketplace and women for labor in the home. Yet the potential exists for a socialist ecofeminism that would push for an ecological, economic, and social revolution that would simultaneously liberate women, working-class people, and nature.

For socialist ecofeminism, environmental problems are rooted in the rise of capitalist patriarchy and the ideology that the Earth and nature can be exploited for human progress through technology. Historically, the rise of capitalism eroded the subsistence-based farm and city workshop in which production was oriented toward use values and men and women were economic partners. The result was a capitalist economy dominated by men and a domestic sphere in which women's labor in the home was unpaid and subordinate to men's labor in the marketplace. Both women and nature are exploited by men as part of the progressive liberation of humans from the constraints imposed by nature. The consequence is the alienation of women and men from each other and both from nature.

Socialist feminism incorporates many of the insights of radical feminism, but views both nature and human nature as historically and socially constructed. Human nature is seen as the product of historically changing interactions between humans and nature, men and women, classes, and races. Any meaningful analysis must be grounded in an understanding of power not only in the personal but also in the political sphere. Like radical feminism, socialist feminism is critical of mechanistic science's treatment of nature as passive and of its male-dominated power structures. Similarly, it deplores the lack of a gender analysis in history and the omission of any treatment of women's reproductive and nurturing roles. But rather than grounding its analysis in biological reproduction alone, it also incorporates social reproduction. Biological reproduction includes the reproduction of the species and the reproduction of daily life through food, clothing, and shelter; social reproduction includes socialization and the legal/political reproduction of the social order.[9]

Like Marxist feminists, socialist feminists see nonhuman nature as the material basis of human life, supplying the necessities of food, clothing, shelter, and energy. Materialism, not spiritualism, is the driving force of social change. Nature is transformed by human science and technology for use by all humans for survival. Socialist feminism views change as dynamic, interactive, and dialectical, rather than as mechanistic, linear, and incremental. Nonhuman nature is dynamic and alive. As a historical actor, nature interacts with human beings through mutual ecological relations. Socialist feminist environmental theory gives both reproduction and production central places. A socialist feminist environmental ethic involves developing sustainable, nondominating relations with nature and supplying all peoples with a high quality of life.

In politics, socialist feminists participate in many of the same environmental actions as radical feminists. The goals, however, are to direct change toward some form of an egalitarian socialist state, in addition to resocializing men and women into nonsexist, nonracist, nonviolent, anti-imperialist forms of life. Socialist ecofeminism deals explicitly with environmental issues that affect working-class women, Third World women, and women of color. Examples include support for the women's *Chipco* (tree-hugging) movement in India that protects fuel resources from lumber interests, for the women's Green Belt movement in Kenya that has planted more than 2 million trees in 10 years, and for Native-American women and children exposed to radioactivity from uranium mining.[10]

Although the ultimate goals of liberal, radical, and socialist feminists may differ as to whether capitalism, women's culture, or socialism should be the ultimate objective of political action, shorter-term objectives overlap. In this sense there is perhaps more unity than diversity in women's common goal of restoring the natural environment and quality of life for people and other living and nonliving inhabitants of the planet.

Women and Ecology

Women and nature have an age-old association – an affiliation that has persisted throughout culture, language, and history. Their ancient interconnections have been dramatized by the simultaneity of two recent social movements – women's liberation, symbolized in its controversial infancy by Betty Friedan's *Feminine Mystique* (1963), and the ecology movement, which built up during the 1960s and finally captured national attention on Earth Day, 1970. Common to both is an egalitarian perspective. Women are struggling to free themselves from cultural and economic constraints that have kept them subordinate to men in American society. Environmentalists, warning us of the irreversible consequences of continuing environmental exploitation, are developing an ecological ethic emphasizing the interconnectedness between people and nature. Juxtaposing the goals of the two movements can suggest new values and social structures, based not on the domination of women and nature as resources but on the full expression of both male and female talent and on the maintenance of environmental integrity.

New social concerns generate new intellectual and historical problems. Conversely, new interpretations of the past provide perspectives on the present and hence the power to change it. Today's feminist and ecological consciousness can be used to examine the historical interconnections between women and nature that developed as the modern scientific and economic world took form in the sixteenth and seventeenth centuries – a transformation that shaped and pervades today's mainstream values and perceptions.

Feminist history in the broadest sense requires that we look at history with egalitarian eyes, seeing it anew from the viewpoint not only of women but also of social and racial groups and the natural environment, previously ignored as the underlying resources on which Western culture and its progress have been built. To write history from a feminist perspective is to turn it upside down – to see social structure from the bottom up and to flip-flop mainstream values. An egalitarian perspective accords both women and men their place in history and delineates their ideas and roles. The impact of sexual differences and sex-linked language on cultural ideology and the use of male, female, and androgynous imagery will have important places in the new history.

The ancient identity of nature as a nurturing mother links women's history with the history of the environment and ecological change. The female earth was central to the organic cosmology that was undermined by the Scientific Revolution and the rise of a market-oriented culture in early modern Europe. The ecology movement has reawakened interest in the values and concepts associated historically with the premodern organic world. The ecological model and its associated ethics make possible a fresh and critical interpretation of the rise of modern science in the crucial period when our cosmos ceased to be viewed as an organism and became instead a machine.

[. . .]

In investigating the roots of our current environmental dilemma and its connections to science, technology, and the economy, we must reexamine the formation of a world view and a science that, by reconceptualizing reality as a machine rather than a living organism, sanctioned the domination of both nature and women. The contributions of such founding "fathers" of modern science as Francis Bacon, William Harvey, René Descartes, Thomas Hobbes, and Isaac Newton must be reevaluated. The fate of other options, alternative philosophies, and social groups shaped by the organic world view and resistant to the growing exploitative mentality needs reappraisal. To understand why one road rather than the other was taken requires a broad synthesis of both the natural and cultural environments of Western society at the historical turning point. [. . .]

Nature as Female

The world we have lost was organic. From the obscure origins of our species, human beings have lived in daily, immediate, organic relation with the natural order for their sustenance. In 1500, the daily interaction with nature was still structured for most Europeans, as it was for other peoples, by close-knit, cooperative, organic communities.

Thus it is not surprising that for sixteenth-century Europeans the root metaphor binding together the self, society, and the cosmos was that of an organism. As a projection of the way people experienced daily life, organismic theory emphasized interdependence among the parts of the human body, subordination of individual to communal purposes in family, community, and state, and vital life permeating the cosmos to the lowliest stone.

The idea of nature as a living organism had philosophical antecedents in ancient systems of thought, variations of which formed the prevailing ideological framework of the sixteenth century. The organismic metaphor, however, was immensely flexible and adaptable to varying contexts, depending on which of its presuppositions was emphasized. A spectrum of philosophical and political possibilities existed, all of which could be subsumed under the general rubric of *organic*.

Nature as Nurture: Controlling Imagery

Central to the organic theory was the identification of nature, especially the earth, with a nurturing mother: a kindly beneficent female who provided for the needs of mankind in an ordered, planned universe. But another opposing image of nature as female was also prevalent: wild and uncontrollable nature that could render violence, storms, droughts, and general chaos. Both were identified with the female sex and were projections of human perceptions onto the external world. The metaphor of the earth as a nurturing mother was gradually to vanish as a dominant image as the Scientific Revolution proceeded to mechanize and to rationalize the world view. The second image, nature as disorder, called forth an important modern idea, that of power over nature. Two new ideas, those of mechanism and of the domination and mastery of nature, became core concepts of the modern world. An organically oriented mentality in which female principles played an important role was undermined and replaced by a mechanically oriented mentality that either eliminated or used female principles in an exploitative manner. As Western culture became increasingly mechanized in the 1600s, the female earth and virgin earth spirit were subdued by the machine.[11]

The change in controlling imagery was directly related to changes in human attitudes and behavior toward the earth. Whereas the nurturing earth image can be viewed as a cultural constraint restricting the types of socially and morally sanctioned human actions allowable with respect to the earth, the new images of mastery and domination functioned as cultural sanctions for the denudation of nature. Society needed these new images as it continued the processes of commercialism and industrialization, which depended on activities directly altering the earth – mining, drainage, deforestation, and assarting (grubbing up stumps to clear fields). The new activities utilized new technologies – lift and force pumps, cranes, windmills, geared wheels, flap valves, chains, pistons, treadmills, under- and overshot watermills, fulling mills, flywheels, bellows, excavators, bucket chains, rollers, geared and wheeled bridges, cranks, elaborate block and tackle systems, worm, spur, crown, and lantern gears, cams and eccentrics, ratchets, wrenches, presses, and screws in magnificent variation and combination.

These technological and commercial changes did not take place quickly; they developed gradually over the ancient and medieval eras, as did the accompanying environmental deterioration. Slowly over many centuries early Mediterranean and Greek civilization had mined and quarried the mountainsides, altered the forested landscape, and overgrazed the hills. Nevertheless, technologies were low level, people considered themselves parts of a finite cosmos, and animism and fertility cults that treated nature as sacred were numerous. Roman civilization was more pragmatic, secular, and commercial and its environmental impact more intense. Yet Roman writers such as Ovid, Seneca, Pliny, and the Stoic philosophers openly deplored mining as an abuse of their mother, the earth. With the disintegration of feudalism and the expansion of Europeans into new worlds and markets, commercial society began to have an accelerated impact on the natural environment. By the sixteenth and seventeenth centuries, the tension between technological development in the world of action and the controlling organic images in the world of the mind had become too great. The old structures were incompatible with the new activities.

Both the nurturing and domination metaphors had existed in philosophy, religion, and literature. The idea of dominion over the earth existed in Greek philosophy and Christian religion; that of the nurturing earth, in Greek and other pagan philosophies. But, as the economy became modernized and the Scientific Revolution proceeded, the dominion metaphor spread beyond the religious sphere and assumed ascendancy in the social and political spheres as well. These two competing images and their normative associations can be found in sixteenth-century literature, art, philosophy, and science.

The image of the earth as a living organism and nurturing mother had served as a cultural constraint restricting the actions of human beings. One does not readily slay a mother, dig into her entrails for gold or mutilate her body, although commercial mining would soon require that. As long as the earth was considered to be alive and sensitive, it could be considered a breach of human ethical behavior to carry out destructive acts against it. For most traditional cultures, minerals and metals ripened in the uterus of the Earth Mother, mines were compared to her vagina, and metallurgy was the human hastening of the birth of the living metal in the artificial womb of the furnace – an abortion of the metal's natural growth cycle before its time. Miners offered propitiation to the deities of the soil and subterranean world, performed ceremonial sacrifices, and observed strict cleanliness, sexual abstinence, and fasting before violating the sacredness of the living earth by sinking a mine. Smiths assumed an awesome responsibility in precipitating the metal's birth through smelting, fusing, and beating it with hammer and anvil; they were often accorded the status of shaman in tribal rituals and their tools were thought to hold special powers.

The Renaissance image of the nurturing earth still carried with it subtle ethical controls and restraints. Such imagery found in a culture's literature can play a normative role within the culture. Controlling images operate as ethical restraints or as ethical sanctions – as subtle "oughts" or "ought-nots." Thus as the descriptive metaphors and images of nature change, a behavioral restraint can be changed into a sanction. Such a change in the image and description of nature was occurring during the course of the Scientific Revolution.

[. . .]

Dominion over Nature: Bacon's Mechanistic Philosophy of Nature

[. . .] Francis Bacon (1561–1626), a celebrated "father of modern science," transformed tendencies already extant in his own society into a total program advocating the control of nature for human benefit. Melding together a new philosophy based on natural magic as a technique for manipulating nature, the technologies of mining and metallurgy, the emerging concept of progress and a patriarchal structure of family and state, Bacon fashioned a new ethic sanctioning the exploitation of nature.

[. . .]

Scientific method, combined with mechanical technology, would create a "new organon," a new system of investigation, that unified knowledge with material power. The technological discoveries of printing, gunpowder, and the magnet in the fields of learning, warfare, and navigation "help us to think about the secrets still locked in nature's bosom." "They do not, like the old, merely exert a gentle guidance over nature's course; they have the power to conquer and subdue her, to shake her to her foundations." Under the mechanical arts, "nature betrays her secrets more fully . . . than when in enjoyment of her natural liberty."[12]

Mechanics, which gave man power over nature, consisted in motion; that is, in "the uniting or disuniting of natural bodies." Most useful were the arts that altered the materials of things – "agriculture, cookery, chemistry, dying, the manufacture of glass, enamel, sugar, gunpowder, artificial fires, paper, and the like." But in performing these operations, one was constrained to operate within the chain of causal connections; nature could "not be commanded except by being obeyed." Only by the study, interpretation, and observation of nature could these possibilities be uncovered; only by acting as the interpreter of nature could knowledge be turned into power. Of the three grades of human ambition, the most wholesome and noble was "to endeavor to establish and extend the power and dominion of the human race itself over the universe." In this way "the human race [could] recover that right over nature which belongs to it by divine bequest."[13]

[. . .]

Human dominion over nature, an integral element of the Baconian program, was to be achieved through the experimental "disclosure of nature's secrets." Seventeenth-century scientists, reinforcing aggressive attitudes toward nature, spoke out in favor of "mastering" and "managing" the earth. Descartes wrote in his *Discourse on Method* (1636) that through knowing the crafts of the artisans and the forces of bodies we could "render ourselves the masters and possessors of nature."[14] Joseph Glanvill, the English philosopher who defended the Baconian program in his *Plus Ultra* of 1668, asserted that the objective of natural philosophy was to "enlarge knowledge by observation and experiment . . . so that nature being known, it may be mastered, managed, and used in the services of humane life." To achieve this objective, arts and instruments should be developed for "searching out the beginnings and depths of things and discovering the intrigues of remoter nature."[15] The most useful of the arts were chemistry, anatomy, and mathematics; the best instruments included the microscope, telescope, thermometer, barometer, and air pump.

[. . .]

The new image of nature as a female to be controlled and dissected through experiment legitimated the exploitation of natural resources. Although the

Figure 36.1 *Nature Reveals Herself*, sculpture by Louis-Ernest Barrias (French, 1841–1905), Musée d'Orsay, Paris. This sculpture suggests the sexuality of nature in revealing her secrets to science. A similar statue by the same sculptor in the Ecole de Médecine, Paris, bears the inscription, "La Nature se dévoilant devant la Science" ("Nature Revealing Herself to Science").
Source: Réunion des Musées Nationaux/Art Resource, NY.

image of the nurturing earth popular in the Renaissance did not vanish, it was superseded by new controlling imagery. The constraints against penetration associated with the earth-mother image were transformed into sanctions for denudation. After the Scientific Revolution, *Natura* no longer complains that her garments of modesty are being torn by the wrongful thrusts of man. She is portrayed in statues by the French sculptor Louis-Ernest Barrias (1841–1905) coyly removing her own veil and exposing herself to science [see fig. 36.1]. From an active teacher and parent, she has become a mindless, submissive body. Not only did this new

image function as a sanction, but the new conceptual framework of the Scientific Revolution – mechanism – carried with it norms quite different from the norms of organicism. The new mechanical order and its associated values of power and control would mandate the death of nature.

The Mechanical Order

The fundamental social and intellectual problem for the seventeenth century was the problem of order. The perception of disorder, so important to the Baconian doctrine of dominion over nature, was also crucial to the rise of mechanism as a rational antidote to the disintegration of the organic cosmos. The new mechanical philosophy of the mid-seventeenth century achieved a reunification of the cosmos, society, and the self in terms of a new metaphor – the machine. Developed by the French thinkers Mersenne, Gassendi, and Descartes in the 1620s and 1630s and elaborated by a group of English emigrés to Paris in the 1640s and 1650s, the new mechanical theories emphasized and reinforced elements in human experience developing slowly since the late Middle Ages, but accelerating in the sixteenth century.

New forms of order and power provided a remedy for the disorder perceived to be spreading throughout culture. In the organic world, order meant the function of each part within the larger whole, as determined by its nature, while power was diffused from the top downward through the social or cosmic hierarchies. In the mechanical world, order was redefined to mean the predictable behavior of each part within a rationally determined system of laws, while power derived from active and immediate intervention in a secularized world. Order and power together constituted control. Rational control over nature, society, and the self was achieved by redefining reality itself through the new machine metaphor.

As the unifying model for science and society, the machine has permeated and reconstructed human consciousness so totally that today we scarcely question its validity. Nature, society, and the human body are composed of interchangeable atomized parts that can be repaired or replaced from outside. The "technological fix" mends an ecological malfunction, new human beings replace the old to maintain the smooth functioning of industry and bureaucracy, and interventionist medicine exchanges a fresh heart for a worn-out, diseased one.

The mechanical view of nature now taught in most Western schools is accepted without question as our everyday, common sense reality – matter is made up of atoms, colors occur by the reflection of light waves of differing lengths, bodies obey the law of inertia, and the sun is in the center of our solar system. None of this was common sense to our seventeenth-century counterparts. The replacement of the older, "natural" ways of thinking by a new and "unnatural" form of life – seeing, thinking, and behaving – did not occur without struggle. The submergence of the organism by the machine engaged the best minds of the times during a period fraught with anxiety, confusion, and instability in both the intellectual and social spheres.

The removal of animistic, organic assumptions about the cosmos constituted the death of nature – the most far-reaching effect of the Scientific Revolution. Because nature was now viewed as a system of dead, inert particles moved by external, rather than inherent forces, the mechanical framework itself could legitimate the manipulation of nature. Moreover, as a conceptual framework, the mechanical order had associated with it a framework of values based on power, fully compatible with the directions taken by commercial capitalism.

Concluding Remarks

The mechanistic view of nature, developed by the seventeenth-century natural philosophers and based on a Western mathematical tradition going back to Plato, is still dominant in science today. This view assumes that nature can be divided into parts and that the parts can be rearranged to create other species of being. "Facts" or information bits can be extracted from the environmental context and rearranged according to a set of rules based on logical and mathematical operations. The results can then be tested and verified by resubmitting them to nature, the ultimate judge of their validity. Mathematical formalism provides the criterion for rationality and certainty, nature the criterion for empirical validity and acceptance or rejection of the theory.

The work of historians and philosophers of science notwithstanding, it is widely assumed by the scientific community that modern science is objective, value-free, and context-free knowledge of the external world. To the extent to which the sciences can be reduced to this mechanistic mathematical model, the more legitimate they become as sciences. [. . .]

The mechanistic approach to nature is as fundamental to the twentieth-century revolution in physics as it was to classical Newtonian science, culminating in the nineteenth-century unification of mechanics, thermodynamics, and electromagnetic theory. Twentieth-century physics still views the world in terms of fundamental particles – electrons, protons, neutrons, mesons, muons, pions, taus, thetas, sigmas, pis, and so on. The search for the ultimate unifying particle, the quark, continues to engage the efforts of the best theoretical physicists.

Mathematical formalism isolates the elements of a given quantum mechanical problem, places them in a latticelike matrix, and rearranges them through a mathematical function called an *operator*. Systems theory extracts possibly relevant information bits from the environmental context and stores them in a computer memory for later use. But since it cannot store an infinite number of "facts," it must select a finite number of potentially relevant pieces of data according to a theory or set of rules governing the selection process. For any given solution, this mechanistic approach very likely excludes some potentially relevant factors.

Systems theorists claim for themselves a holistic outlook, because they believe that they are taking into account the ways in which all the parts in a given system affect the whole. Yet the formalism of the calculus of probabilities excludes the possibility of mathematizing the gestalt – that is, the ways in which each part at any given instant takes its meaning from the whole. The more open, adaptive, organic, and complex the system, the less successful is the formalism. It is most successful when applied to closed, artificial, precisely defined, relatively simple systems. Mechanistic assumptions about nature push us increasingly in the direction of artificial environments, mechanized control over more and more aspects of human life, and a loss of the quality of life itself.

Notes

1   Françoise d'Eaubonne, "Feminism or Death," in Elaine Marks and Isabelle de Courtivron (eds.), *New French Feminisms: An Anthology* (Amherst: University of Massachusetts Press, 1980).

2 See Karen Warren, "Feminism and Ecology: Making Connections," *Environmental Ethics* 9 (no. 1: 1981): 3–20.

3 See Alison M. Jaggar, *Feminist Politics and Human Nature* (Totowa, NJ: Rowman and Allanheld, 1983).

4 Merlin Stone, *When God Was a Woman* (New York: Harcourt Brace Jovanovich, 1976).

5 See Dorothy Nelkin, "Nuclear Power as a Feminist Issue," *Environment* 23 (no. 1: 1981): 14–20, 38–9.

6 Carolyn Merchant, "Earthcare: Women and the Environmental Movement," *Environment* 22 (June 1970): 7–13, 38–40.

7 Donna Haraway, "A Manifesto for Cyborgs," *Socialist Review* 15 (no. 80: 1985): 65–107.

8 Sherry Ortner, "Is Female to Male as Nature Is to Culture?" in Michelle Rosaldo and Louise Lamphere (eds.), *Woman, Culture, and Society* (Stanford, CA: Stanford University Press, 1974), pp. 67–87.

9 Carolyn Merchant, "The Theoretical Structure of Ecological Revolutions," *Environmental Review* 11 (no. 4: Winter 1987): 265–74.

10 See Jeanne Henn, "Female Farmers – The Doubly Ignored," *Development Forum* 14 (nos. 7 and 8: 1986); and Gillian Goslinga, "Kenya's Women of the Trees," *Development Forum* 14 (no. 8: 1986): 15.

11 On the tensions between technology and the pastoral ideal in American culture, see Leo Marx, *The Machine in the Garden* (New York: Oxford University Press, 1964). On the domination of nature as female, see Annette Kolodny, *The Lay of the Land* (Chapel Hill: University of North Carolina Press, 1975); Rosemary Radford Ruether, "Women, Ecology, and the Domination of Nature," *The Ecumenist* 14 (1975): 1–5; William Leiss, *The Domination of Nature* (New York: Braziller, 1972). On the roots of the ecological crisis, see Donald Hughes, *Ecology in Ancient Civilizations* (Albuquerque: University of New Mexico Press, 1976); Lynn White, Jr., *Medieval Technology and Social Change* (New York: Oxford University Press, 1966); and L. White, Jr., "Historical Roots of Our Ecologic Crisis," in White, Jr., *Machina ex Deo* (Cambridge, MA: MIT Press, 1968), pp. 75–94; Reijer Hooykaas, *Religion and the Rise of Modern Science* (Grand Rapids, MI: Eerdmans, 1972); Christopher Derrick, *The Delicate Creation: Towards a Theology of the Environment* (Old Greenwich, CT: Devin-Adair, 1972). On traditional rituals in the mining of ores and in metallurgy, see Mircea Eliade, *The Forge and the Crucible*, trans. Stephan Corrin (New York: Harper & Row, 1962), pp. 42, 53–70, 74, 79–96. On the divergence between attitudes and practices toward the environment, see Yi-Fu Tuan, "Our Treatment of the Environment in Ideal and Actuality," *American Scientist* (May–June 1970): 246–9.

12 Bacon, "Thoughts and Conclusions on the Interpretation of Nature or A Science of Productive Works," trans. Farrington, *The Philosophy of Francis Bacon* (Liverpool: Liverpool University Press, 1964), pp. 96, 93, 99.

13 Bacon, "De Augmentis," *Works*, vol. 4, p. 294; "Parasceve," *Works*, vol. 4, p. 257; "Plan of the Work," vol. 4, p. 32; "Novum Organum," *Works*, ed. James Spedding, Robert Leslie Ellis, Douglas Heath, 14 vols. (London: Longmans Green, 1870), vol. 4, pp. 114, 115.

14 René Descartes, "Discourse on Method," Part 4, in E. S. Haldane and G. R. T. Ross, eds., *Philosophical Works of Descartes* (New York: Dover, 1955), vol. 1, p. 119.

15 Joseph Glanvill, *Plus Ultra* (Gainesville, Fla.: Scholar's Facsimile Reprints, 1958; first published 1668), quotations on pp. 9, 10, 13, 56, 87, 104.

37 Nature, Self, and Gender: Feminism, Environmental Philosophy, and the Critique of Rationalism

Val Plumwood

Environmental philosophy has recently been criticized on a number of counts by feminist philosophers. I want to develop further some of this critique and to suggest that much of the issue turns on the failure of environmental philosophy to engage properly with the rationalist tradition, which has been inimical to both women and nature. Damaging assumptions from this tradition have been employed in attempting to formulate a new environmental philosophy that often makes use of or embeds itself

From *Hypatia*, vol. 6, no. 1 (1991): 3–18, 22–7. © 1991 by Val Plumwood. Reprinted with permission from Blackwell Publishing Ltd.

within rationalist philosophical frameworks that are not only biased from a gender perspective, but have claimed a negative role for nature as well.

In sections I through IV I argue that current mainstream brands of environmental philosophy, both those based in ethics and those based in deep ecology, suffer from this problem, that neither has an adequate historical analysis, and that both continue to rely implicitly upon rationalist-inspired accounts of the self that have been a large part of the problem. In section V [. . .] I show how the critique of rationalism offers an understanding of a range of key broader issues that environmental philosophy has tended to neglect or treat in too narrow a way. Among these issues are those connected with concepts of the human self and with instrumentalism.

I. Rationalism and the Ethical Approach

The ethical approach aims to center a new view of nature in ethics, especially universalizing ethics or in some extension of human ethics. This approach has been criticized from a feminist perspective by a number of recent authors (especially Cheney 1987, 1989). I partly agree with and partly disagree with these criticisms; that is, I think that the emphasis on ethics as the central part (or even the whole) of the problem is misplaced, and that although ethics (and especially the ethics of non-instrumental value) has a role, the particular ethical approaches that have been adopted are problematic and unsuitable. I shall illustrate this claim by a brief discussion of two recent books: Paul Taylor's *Respect for Nature* (1986) and Tom Regan's *The Case for Animal Rights* (1986). Both works are significant, and indeed impressive, contributions to their respective areas.

Paul Taylor's book is a detailed working out of an ethical position that rejects the standard and widespread Western treatment of nature as instrumental to human interests and instead takes living things, as teleological centers of life, to be worthy of respect in their own right. Taylor aims to defend a biocentric (life-centered) ethical theory in which a person's true human self includes his or her biological nature (Taylor 1986, 44), but he attempts to embed this within a Kantian ethical framework that makes strong use of the reason/emotion dichotomy. Thus we are assured that the attitude of respect is a moral one because it is universalizing and disinterested, "that

is, each moral agent who sincerely has the attitude advocates its universal adoption by all other agents, regardless of whether they are so inclined and regardless of their fondness or lack of fondness for particular individuals" (41). The essential features of morality having been established as distance from emotion and "particular fondness," morality is then seen as the domain of reason and its touchstone, belief. Having carefully distinguished the "valuational, conative, practical and affective dimensions of the attitude of respect," Taylor goes on to pick out the essentially cognitive "valuational" aspect as central and basic to all the others: "It is *because* moral agents look at animals and plants in this way that they are disposed to pursue the aforementioned ends and purposes" (82) and, similarly, to have the relevant emotions and affective attitudes. The latter must be held at an appropriate distance and not allowed to get the upper hand at any point. Taylor claims that actions do not express moral respect unless they are done as a matter of moral principle conceived as ethically obligatory and pursued disinterestedly and not through inclination, solely or even primarily:

> If one seeks that end solely or primarily from incli-
> nation, the attitude being expressed is not moral
> respect but personal affection or love. . . . It is not
> that respect for nature *precludes* feelings of care and
> concern for living things. One may, as a matter of
> simple kindness, not want to harm them. But the
> fact that one is so motivated does not itself indicate
> the presence of a moral attitude of respect. Having
> the desire to preserve or protect the good of wild
> animals and plants for their sake is neither contrary
> to, nor evidence of, respect for nature. It is only if
> the person who has the desire understands that the
> actions fulfilling it would be obligatory even in the
> absence of the desire, that the person has genuine
> respect for nature. (85–6)

There is good reason to reject as self-indulgent the "kindness" approach that reduces respect and morality in the protection of animals to the satisfaction of the carer's own feelings. Respect for others involves treating them as worthy of consideration for their own sake and not just as an instrument for the carer's satisfaction, and there is a sense in which such "kindness" is not genuine care or respect for the other. But Taylor is doing much more than this – he is treating care, viewed as "inclination" or "desire," as irrelevant to morality. Respect for nature on this account becomes an essentially *cognitive* matter (that of a person believing something to have "inherent worth" and then acting from an understanding of ethical principles as universal).

The account draws on the familiar view of reason and emotion as sharply separated and opposed, and of "desire," caring, and love as merely "personal" and "particular" as opposed to the universality and impartiality of understanding and of "feminine" emotions as essentially unreliable, untrustworthy, and morally irrelevant, an inferior domain to be dominated by a superior, disinterested (and of course masculine) reason. This sort of rationalist account of the place of emotions has come in for a great deal of well-deserved criticism recently, both for its implicit gender bias and its philosophical inadequacy, especially its dualism and its construal of public reason as sharply differentiated from and controlling private emotion (see, for example, Benhabib 1987; Blum 1980; Gilligan 1982, 1987; Lloyd 1983a and 1983b).

A further major problem in its use in this context is the inconsistency of employing, in the service of constructing an allegedly biocentric ethical theory, a framework that has itself played such a major role in creating a dualistic account of the genuine human self as essentially rational and as sharply discontinuous from the merely emotional, the merely bodily, and the merely animal elements. For emotions and the private sphere with which they are associated have been treated as sharply differentiated and inferior as part of a pattern in which they are seen as linked to the sphere of nature, not the realm of reason.

And it is not only women but also the earth's wild living things that have been denied possession of a reason thus construed along masculine and oppositional lines and which contrasts not only with the "feminine" emotions but also with the physical and the animal. Much of the problem (both for women and nature) lies in rationalist or rationalist-derived conceptions of the self and of what is essential and valuable in the human makeup. It is in the name of such a reason that these other things – the feminine, the emotional, the merely bodily or the merely animal, and the natural world itself – have most often been denied their virtue and been accorded an inferior and merely instrumental position. Thomas Aquinas states this problematic positions succinctly: "the intellectual nature is alone requisite for its own sake in the universe, and all others for its sake" (Thomas Aquinas 1976, 56). And it is precisely

reason so construed that is usually taken to characterize the authentically human and to create the supposedly sharp separation, cleavage, or discontinuity between all humans and the nonhuman world, and the similar cleavage within the human self. The supremacy accorded an oppositionally construed reason is the key to the anthropocentrism of the Western tradition. The Kantian-rationalist framework, then, is hardly the area in which to search for a solution. Its use, in a way that perpetuates the supremacy of reason and its opposition to contrast areas, in the service of constructing a supposedly biocentric ethic is a matter for astonishment.

Ethical universalization and abstraction are both closely associated with accounts of the self in terms of rational egoism. Universalization is explicitly seen in both the Kantian and the Rawlsian framework as needed to hold in check natural self-interest; it is the moral complement to the account of the self as "disembodied and disembedded," as the autonomous self of liberal theory, the rational egoist of market theory, the falsely differentiated self of object-relations theory (Benhabib 1987; Poole 1984, 1985). In the same vein, the broadening of the scope of moral concern along with the according of rights to the natural world has been seen by influential environmental philosophers (Leopold 1949, 201–2) as the final step in a process of increasing moral abstraction and generalization, part of the move away from the merely particular – *my* self, *my* family, *my* tribe – the discarding of the merely personal and, by implication, the merely selfish. This is viewed as moral progress, increasingly civilized as it moves further away from primitive selfishness. Nature is the last area to be included in this march away from the unbridled natural egoism of the particular and its close ally, the emotional. Moral progress is marked by increasing adherence to moral rules and a movement away from the supposedly natural (in human nature), and the completion of its empire is, paradoxically, the extension of its domain of adherence to abstract moral rules to nature itself.

[. . .]

Concern for nature [. . .] should not be viewed as the completion of a process of (masculine) universalization, moral abstraction, and disconnection, discarding the self, emotions, and special ties (all, of course, associated with the private sphere and femininity). Environmental ethics has for the most part placed itself uncritically in such a framework, although it is one that is extended with particular difficulty to the natural world. Perhaps the kindest thing that can be said about the framework of ethical universalization is that it is seriously incomplete and fails to capture the most important elements of respect, which are not reducible to or based on duty or obligation any more than the most important elements of friendship are, but which are rather an expression of a certain kind of selfhood and a certain kind of relation between self and other.

II. Rationalism, Rights, and Ethics

An extension to nature of the standard concepts of morality is also the aim of Tom Regan's *The Case for Animal Rights* (1986). This is the most impressive, thorough, and solidly argued book in the area of animal ethics, with excellent chapters on topics such as animal intentionality. But the key concept upon which this account of moral concern for animals is based is that of rights, which requires strong individual separation of rights-holders and is set in a framework of human community and legality. Its extension to the natural world raises a host of problems (Midgley 1983, 61–4). Even in the case of individual higher animals for which Regan uses this concept of rights, the approach is problematic. His concept of rights is based on Mill's notion that, if a being has a right to something not only should he or she (or it) have that thing but others are obliged to intervene to secure it. The application of this concept of rights to individual wild living animals appears to give humans almost limitless obligations to intervene massively in all sorts of far reaching and conflicting ways in natural cycles to secure the rights of a bewildering variety of beings. In the case of the wolf and the sheep, an example discussed by Regan, it is unclear whether humans should intervene to protect the sheep's rights or to avoid doing so in order not to violate the wolf's right to its natural food.

Regan attempts to meet this objection by claiming that since the wolf is not itself a moral agent (although it is a moral patient), it cannot violate the sheep's rights not to suffer a painful and violent death (Regan 1986, 285). But the defense is unconvincing, because even if we concede that the wolf is not a moral agent, it still does not follow that on a rights view we are not obliged to intervene. From the fact that the wolf is not a moral agent it only follows that it is not *responsible* for violating the sheep's rights, not that they are not violated or that others

do not have an obligation (according to the rights view) to intervene. If the wolf were attacking a human baby, it would hardly do as a defense in that case to claim that one did not have a duty to intervene because the wolf was not a moral agent. But on Regan's view the baby and the sheep do have something like the same rights. So we do have a duty, it seems, (on the rights view) to intervene to protect the sheep – leaving us where with the wolf?

The concept of rights seems to produce absurd consequences and is impossible to apply in the context of predators in a natural ecosystem, as opposed to a particular human social context in which claimants are part of a reciprocal social community and conflict cases either few or settleable according to some agreed-on principles. All this seems to me to tell against the concept of rights as the correct one for the general task of dealing with animals in the natural environment (as opposed, of course, to domestic animals in a basically humanized environment).[1]

Rights seem to have acquired an exaggerated importance as part of the prestige of the public sphere and the masculine, and the emphasis on separation and autonomy, on reason and abstraction. A more promising approach for an ethics of nature, and also one much more in line with the current directions in feminism, would be to remove rights from the center of the moral stage and pay more attention to some other, less dualistic, moral concepts such as respect, sympathy, care, concern, compassion, gratitude, friendship, and responsibility (Cook 1977, 118–19). These concepts, because of their dualistic construal as feminine and their consignment to the private sphere as subjective and emotional, have been treated as peripheral and given far less importance than they deserve for several reasons. First, rationalism and the prestige of reason and the public sphere have influenced not only the concept of what morality is (as Taylor explicates it, for example, as essentially a rational and cognitive act of understanding that certain actions are ethically obligatory) but of what is *central* to it or what count as moral concepts. Second, concepts such as respect, care, concern, and so on are resistant to analysis along lines of a dualistic reason/emotion dichotomy, and their construal along these lines has involved confusion and distortion (Blum 1980). They *are* moral "feelings" but they involve reason, behavior and emotion in ways that do not seem separable. Rationalist-inspired ethical concepts are highly ethnocentric and cannot account adequately for the views of many indigenous peoples, and the attempted application of these rationalist concepts to their positions tends to lead to the view that they lack a real ethical framework (Plumwood 1990). These alternative concepts seem better able to apply to the views of such peoples, whose ethic of respect, care and responsibility for land is often based on special relationships with particular areas of land via links to kin (Neidjie 1985, 1989). Finally these concepts, which allow for particularity and mostly do not require reciprocity, are precisely the sorts of concepts feminist philosophers have argued should have a more significant place in ethics at the expense of abstract, malestream concepts from the public sphere such as rights and justice (Gilligan 1982, 1987, Benhabib 1987). The ethic of care and responsibility they have articulated seems to extend much less problematically to the nonhuman world than do the impersonal concepts which are currently seen as central, and it also seems capable of providing an excellent basis for the noninstrumental treatment of nature many environmental philosophers have now called for. Such an approach treats ethical relations as an expression of self-in-relationship (Gilligan 1987, 24) rather than as the discarding, containment, or generalization of a self viewed as self-interested and non-relational, as in the conventional ethics of universalization.[2] As I argue later, there are important connections between this relational account of the self and the rejection of instrumentalism.

It is not that we need to abandon ethics or dispense with the universalized ethical approach entirely, although we do need to reassess the centrality of ethics in environmental philosophy.[3] What is needed is not so much the abandonment of ethics as a different and richer understanding of it (and, as I argue later, a richer understanding of environmental philosophy generally than is provided by ethics), one that gives an important place to ethical concepts owing to emotionality and particularity and that abandons the exclusive focus on the universal and the abstract associated with the nonrelational self and the dualistic and oppositional accounts of the reason/emotion and universal/particular contrasts as given in rationalist accounts of ethics.

III. The Discontinuity Problem

The problem is not just one of restriction *in* ethics but also of restriction *to* ethics. Most mainstream environmental philosophers continue to view environmental philosophy as mainly concerned with ethics. For example, instrumentalism is generally viewed by mainstream environmental philosophers as a problem in ethics, and its solution is seen as setting up some sort of theory of intrinsic value. This neglects a key aspect of the overall problem that is concerned with the definition of the human self as separate from nature, the connection between this and the instrumental view of nature, and broader *political* aspects of the critique of instrumentalism.

One key aspect of the Western view of nature, which the ethical stance neglects completely, is the view of nature as sharply discontinuous or ontologically divided from the human sphere. This leads to a view of humans as apart from or "outside of" nature, usually as masters or external controllers of it. Attempts to reject this view often speak alternatively of humans as "part of nature" but rarely distinguish this position from the obvious claim that human fate is interconnected with that of the biosphere, that humans are subject to natural laws. But on the divided-self theory it is the essentially or authentically human part of the self, and in that sense the human realm proper, that is outside nature, not the human as a physical phenomenon. The view of humans as outside of and alien to nature seems to be especially strongly a Western one, although not confined to the West. There are many other cultures which do not hold it, which stress what connects us to nature as genuinely human virtues, which emphasize continuity and not dissimilarity.[4]

As ecofeminism points out, Western thought has given us a strong human/nature dualism that is part of the set of interrelated dualisms of mind/body, reason/nature, reason/emotion, masculine/feminine and has important interconnected features with these other dualisms.[5] This dualism has been especially stressed in the rationalist tradition. In this dualism what is characteristically and authentically human is defined against or in opposition to what is taken to be natural, nature, or the physical or biological realm. This takes various forms. For example, the characterization of the genuinely, properly, characteristically, or authentically human, or of human virtue, in polarized terms to exclude what is taken to be characteristic of the natural is what John Rodman (1980) has called "the Differential Imperative" in which what is virtuous in the human is taken to be what maximizes distance from the merely natural. The maintenance of sharp dichotomy and polarization is achieved by the rejection and denial of what links humans to the animal. What is taken to be authentically and characteristically human, defining of the human, as well as the ideal for which humans should strive is *not* to be found in what is shared with the natural and animal (e.g., the body, sexuality, reproduction, emotionality, the senses, agency) but in what is thought to separate and distinguish them – especially reason and its offshoots. Hence humanity is defined not as part of nature (perhaps a special part) but as separate from and in opposition to it. Thus the relation of humans to nature is treated as an oppositional and value dualism.

The process closely parallels the formation of other dualisms, such as masculine/feminine, reason/emotion, and spirit/body criticized in feminist thought (see, for example, Ruether 1975, Griffin 1978, Griscom 1981, King 1981, Lloyd 1983, Jaggar 1983) but this parallel logic is not the only connection between human/nature dualism and masculine/feminine dualism. [. . .] Humanity is defined oppositionally to both nature and the feminine.

The upshot is a deeply entrenched view of the genuine or ideal human self as not including features shared with nature, and as defined *against* or in *opposition to* the nonhuman realm, so that the human sphere and that of nature cannot significantly overlap. Nature is sharply divided off from the human, is alien and usually hostile and inferior. Furthermore, this kind of human self can only have certain kinds of accidental or contingent connections to the realm of nature. I shall call this the discontinuity problem or thesis and I argue later that it plays a key role with respect to other elements of the problem.

IV. Rationalism and Deep Ecology

Although the discontinuity problem is generally neglected by the ethical stance, a significant exception to its neglect within environmental philosophy seems to be found in deep ecology, which is also critical of the location of the problem within ethics.[6] Furthermore, deep ecology also seems initially to be more likely to be compatible with a feminist philosophical framework, emphasizing as it does connections with the self, connectedness, and merger. Nevertheless, there are severe tensions between deep ecology and a feminist perspective. Deep ecology has not satisfactorily identified the key elements in the traditional framework or observed their connections to rationalism. As a result, it fails to reject adequately rationalist assumptions and indeed often seems to provide its own versions of universalization, the discarding of particular connections, and rationalist accounts of self.

Deep ecology locates the key problem area in human-nature relations in the separation of humans and nature, and it provides a solution for this in terms of the "identification" of self with nature. "Identification" is usually left deliberately vague, and corresponding accounts of self are various and shifting and not always compatible.[7] There seem to be at least three different accounts of self involved – indistinguishability, expansion of self, and transcendence of self – and practitioners appear to feel free to move among them at will. As I shall show, all are unsatisfactory from both a feminist perpective and from that of obtaining a satisfactory environmental philosophy, and the appeal of deep ecology rests largely on the failure to distinguish them.

A. The Indistinguishability Account

The indistinguishability account rejects boundaries between self and nature. Humans are said to be just one strand in the biotic web, not the source and ground of all value and the discontinuity thesis is, it seems, firmly rejected. Warwick Fox describes the central intuition of deep ecology as follows: "We can make no firm ontological divide in the field of existence . . . there is no bifurcation in reality between the human and nonhuman realms. . . . to the extent that we perceive boundaries, we fall short of deep ecological consciousness" (Fox 1984, 7). But much more is involved here than the rejection of discontinuity, for deep ecology goes on to replace the human-in-environment image by a holistic or gestalt view that "dissolves not only the human-in-environment concept, but every compact-thing-in-milieu concept" – except when talking at a superficial level of communication (Fox 1984, 1). Deep ecology involves a cosmology of "unbroken wholeness which denies the classical idea of the analyzability of the world into separately and independently existing parts."[8] It is strongly attracted to a variety of mystical traditions and to the Perennial Philosophy, in which the self is merged with the other – "the other is none other than yourself." As John Seed puts it: "I am protecting the rain forest" develops into "I am part of the rain forest protecting myself. I am that part of the rain forest recently emerged into thinking" (Seed et al. 1988, 36).

There are severe problems with these claims, arising not so much from the orientation to the concept of self (which seems to me important and correct) or from the mystical character of the insights themselves as from the indistinguishability metaphysics which is proposed as their basis. It is not merely that the identification process of which deep ecologists speak seems to stand in need of much more clarification, but that it does the wrong thing. The problem, in the sort of account I have given, is the discontinuity between humans and nature that emerges as part of the overall set of Western dualisms. Deep ecology proposes to heal this division by a "unifying process," a metaphysics that insists that everything is really part of and indistinguishable from everything else. This is not only to employ overly powerful tools but ones that do the wrong job, for the origins of the particular opposition involved in the human/nature dualism remain unaddressed and unanalyzed. The real basis of the discontinuity lies in the concept of an authentic human being, in what is taken to be valuable in human character, society, and culture, as what is distinct from what is taken to be natural. The sources of and remedies for this remain unaddressed in deep ecology. Deep ecology has confused dualism and atomism and then mistakenly taken indistinguishability to follow from the rejection of atomism. The confusion is clear in Fox, who proceeds immediately from the ambiguous claim that there is no "bifurcation in reality between the human and nonhuman realms" (which could be taken as a rejection of human discontinuity from nature) to the conclusion that what is needed is that we embrace an indistinguishability metaphysics of unbroken wholeness in the whole of reality. But the problem must be addressed in terms of this specific dualism and its connections. Instead deep ecology proposes the obliteration of all distinction.

Thus deep ecology's solution to removing this discontinuity by obliterating *all* division is far too powerful. In its overgenerality it fails to provide a genuine basis for an environmental ethics of the kind sought, for the view of humans as metaphysically unified with the cosmic whole will be equally true whatever relation humans stand in with nature – the situation of exploitation of nature exemplifies such unity equally as well as a conserver situation and the human self is just as indistinguishable from the bulldozer and Coca-Cola bottle as the rocks or the rain forest. What John Seed seems to have in mind here is that once one has realized that one is indistinguishable from the rain forest, its needs would become one's own. But there is nothing to guarantee this – one could equally well take one's own needs for its.

This points to a further problem with the indistinguishability thesis, that we need to recognize not only our human continuity with the natural world but also its distinctness and independence from us and the distinctness of the needs of things in nature from ours. The indistinguishability account does not allow for this, although it is a very important part of respect for nature and of conservation strategy.

[. . .]

To the extent that deep ecology is identified with the indistinguishability thesis, it does not provide an adequate basis for a philosophy of nature.

B. The Expanded Self

In fairness to deep ecology it should be noted that it tends to vacillate between mystical indistinguishability and the other accounts of self, between the holistic self and the expanded self. Vacillation occurs often by way of slipperiness as to what is meant by identification of self with the other, a key notion in deep ecology. This slipperiness reflects the confusion of dualism and atomism previously noted but also seems to reflect a desire to retain the mystical appeal of indistinguishability while avoiding its many difficulties. Where "identification" means not "identity" but something more like "empathy," identification with other beings can lead to an expanded self. According to Arne Naess, "The self is as comprehensive as the totality of our identifications. . . . Our Self is that with which we identify."[9] This larger self (or Self, to deep ecologists) is something for which we should strive "insofar as it is in our power to do so" (Fox 1986, 13–19), and according to Fox we should also strive to make it as large as possible. But this expanded self is not the result of a critique of egoism; rather, it is an enlargement and an extension of egoism.[10] It does not question the structures of possessive egoism and self-interest; rather, it tries to allow for a wider set of interests by an expansion of self. The motivation for the expansion of self is to allow for a wider set of concerns while continuing to allow the self to operate on the fuel of self-interest (or Self-interest). This is apparent from the claim that "in this light . . . ecological resistance is simply another name for self defense" (Fox 1986, 60). Fox quotes with approval John Livingstone's statement: "When I say that the fate of the sea tuttle or the tiger or the gibbon is mine, I mean it. All that is in my universe is not merely mine; it is *me*. And I shall defend myself. I shall defend myself not only against overt aggression but also against gratuitous insult" (Fox 1986, 60).

Deep ecology does not question the structures of rational egoism and continues to subscribe to two of the main tenets of the egoist framework – that human nature is egoistic and that the alternative to egoism is self-sacrifice.[11] Given these assumptions about egoism, the obvious way to obtain some sort of human interest in defending nature is through the expanded Self operating in the interests of nature but also along the familiar lines of self-interest.[12] The expanded-self strategy might initially seem to be just another pretentious and obscure way of saying that humans empathize with nature. But the strategy of transfering the structures of egoism is highly problematic, for the widening of interest is obtained at the expense of failing to recognise unambiguously the distinctness and independence of the other.[13] Others are recognized morally only to the extent that they are incorporated into the self, and their difference denied (Warren 1990). And the failure to critique egoism and the disembedded, nonrelational self means a failure to draw connections with other contemporary critiques.

[. . .]

V. The Problem in Terms of the Critique of Rationalism

I now show how the problem of the inferiorization of nature appears if it is viewed from the perspective of the critique of rationalism and seen as part of the general problem of revaluing and reintegrating what rationalist culture has split apart, denied, and devalued. Such an account shifts the focus away from the preoccupations of both mainstream ethical approaches and deep ecology, and although it does retain an emphasis on the account of the self as central, it gives a different account from that offered by deep ecology. [. . .]

First, what is missing from the accounts of both the ethical philosophers and the deep ecologists is an understanding of the problem of discontinuity as created by a dualism linked to a network of related dualisms. Here I believe a good deal can be learned from the critique of dualism feminist philosophy has developed and from the understanding of the mechanisms of dualisms ecofeminists have produced. A dualistically construed dichotomy typically polarizes difference and minimizes shared characteristics, construes difference along lines of superiority/inferiority, and views the inferior side as a means to the higher ends of the superior side (the instrumental thesis). Because its nature is defined oppositionally, the task of the superior side, that in which it realizes itself and expresses its true nature, is to separate from, dominate, and control the lower side. This has happened both with the human/nature division and with other related dualisms such as masculine/feminine, reason/body, and reason/emotion. Challenging these dualisms involves not just a reevaluation of superiority/inferiority and a higher status for the underside of the dualisms (in this case nature) but also a reexamination and reconceptualizing of the dualistically construed categories themselves. So in the case of the human/nature dualism it is not just a question of improving the status of nature, moral or otherwise, while everything else remains the same, but of reexamining and reconceptualizing the concept of the human, and also the concept of the contrasting class of nature. For the concept of the human, of what it is to be fully and authentically human, and of what is genuinely human in the set of characteristics typical humans possess, has been defined oppositionally, by *exclusion* of what is associated with the inferior natural sphere in very much the way that Lloyd (1983), for example, has shown in the case of the categories of masculine and feminine, and of reason and its contrasts. Humans have both biological and mental characteristics, but the mental rather than the biological have been taken to be characteristic of the human and to give what is "fully and authentically" human. The term "human" is, of course, not merely descriptive here but very much an evaluative term setting out an ideal: it is what is essential or worthwhile in the human that excludes the natural. It is not necessarily denied that humans have some material or animal component – rather, it is seen in this framework as alien or inessential to them, not part of their fully or truly human nature. The human essence is often seen as lying in maximizing control over the natural sphere (both within and without) and in qualities such as rationality, freedom, and transcendence of the material sphere. These qualities are also identified as masculine, and hence the *oppositional* model of the human coincides or converges with a masculine model, in which the characteristics attributed are those of the masculine ideal.

Part of a strategy for challenging this human/ nature dualism, then, would involve recognition of these excluded qualities – split off, denied, or construed as alien, or comprehended as the sphere of supposedly *inferior* humans such as women and blacks – as equally and fully human. This would provide a basis for the recognition of *continuities* with the natural world. Thus reproductivity, sensuality, emotionality would be taken to be as fully and authentically human qualities as the capacity for abstract planning and calculation. This proceeds from the assumption that one basis for discontinuity and alienation from nature is alienation from those qualities which provide continuity with nature in ourselves.

This connection between the rationalist account of nature within and nature without has powerful repercussions. So part of what is involved is a challenge to the centrality and dominance of the rational in the account of the human self. Such a challenge would have far-reaching implications for what is valuable in human society and culture, and it connects with the challenge to the cultural legacy of rationalism made by other critiques of rationalism such as feminism, and by critiques of technocracy, bureaucracy, and instrumentalism.

What is involved here is a reconceptualization of the human side of the human/nature dualism, to free it from the legacy of rationalism. Also in need of reconceptualization is the underside of this dualism, the concept of nature, which is construed in polarized terms as bereft of qualities appropriated to the human side, as passive and lacking in agency and teleology, as pure materiality, pure body, or pure mechanism. So what is called for here is the development of alternatives to mechanistic ways of viewing the world, which are also part of the legacy of rationalism.

Notes

1   Regan, of course, as part of the animal rights movement, is mainly concerned not with wild animals but with domestic animals as they appear in the context and support of human society and culture, although he does not indicate any qualification in moral treatment. Nevertheless, there may be an important moral boundary here, for natural ecosystems cannot be organized along the lines of justice, fairness and rights, and it would be absurd to try to impose such a social order upon them via intervention in these systems. This does not mean, of course, that humans can do anything in such a situation, just that certain kinds of intervention are not in order. But these kinds of intervention may be in order in the case of human social systems and in the case of animals that have already been brought into these social systems through human intervention, and the concept of rights and of social responsibility may have far more application here. This would mean that the domestic/wild distinction would demarcate an important moral boundary in terms of duties of intervention, although neither Regan (1986) nor Taylor (1986) comes to grips with this problem. In the case of Taylor's "wild living things" rights seem less important than respect for independence and autonomy, and the prima facie obligation may be nonintervention.

2   If the Kantian universalizing perspective is based on self-containment, its major contemporary alternative, that of John Rawls, is based on a "definitional identity" in which the "other" can be considered to the extent that it is not recognized as truly different, as genuinely other (Benhabib 1987, 165).

3   Contra Cheney, who appears to advocate the abandonment of all general ethical concepts and the adoption of a "contextual" ethics based in pure particularity and emotionality. We do need both to reintegrate the personal and particular and reevaluate more positively its role, but overcoming moral dualism will not simply amount to an affirmation of the personal in the moral sphere. To embrace pure particularity and emotionality is implicitly to accept the dualistic construction of these as oppositional to a rationalist ethics and to attempt to reverse value. In general this reactive response is an inadequate way to deal with such dualisms. And rules themselves, as Grimshaw (1986, 209) points out, are not incompatible with recognition of special relationships and responsibility to particular others. Rules themselves are not the problem, and hence it is not necessary to move to a ruleless ethics; rather it is rules that demand the discarding of the personal, the emotional, and the particular and which aim at self-containment.

4   For example, Bill Neidjie's words "This ground and this earth/like brother and mother" (Neidjie 1985, 46) may be interpreted as an affirmation of such kinship or continuity. (See also Neidjie 1985, 53, 61, 62, 77, 81, 82, 88).

5   The logic of dualism and the masculinity of the concept of humanity are discussed in Plumwood (1986, 1988) and Warren (1987, 1990).

6   Nonetheless, deep ecology's approach to ethics is, like much else, doubtfully consistent, variable and shifting.

Thus although Arne Naess (1973, 1986, 1988) calls for recognition of the intrinsic value of nature, he also tends to treat "the maxim of self-realization" as *substituting for* and obviating an ethical account of care and respect for nature (Naess 1988, 20, 86), placing the entire emphasis on phenomenology. In more recent work, however, the emphasis seems to have quietly shifted back again from holistic intuition to a broad and extremely vague "biocentric egalitarianism" which places the center once again in ethics and enjoins an ethic of maximum expansion of Self (Fox 1990).

7   Other critics of deep ecology, such as Sylvan (1985) and Cheney (1987), have also suggested that it shifts between different and incompatible versions. Ecofeminist critics of deep ecology have included Salleh (1984), Kheel (1985), Biehl (1987), and Warren (1990).

8   Arne Naess, quoted in Fox (1982, 3, 10).

9   Arne Naess, quoted in Fox (1986, 54).

10   As noted by Cheney (1989, 293–325).

11   Thus John Seed says: "Naess wrote that when most people think about conservation, they think about sacrifice. This is a treacherous basis for conservation, because most people aren't capable of working for anything except their own self-interest. . . . Naess argued that we need to find ways to extend our identity into nature. Once that happens, being out in front of bulldozers or whatever becomes no more of a sacrifice than moving your foot if you notice that someone's just about to strike it with an axe" (Seed 1989).

12   This denial of the alterity of the other is also the route taken by J. Baird Callicott, who indeed asserts that "The principle of axiological complementarity posits an essential unity between self and world and establishes the problematic intrinsic value of nature in relation to the axiologically privileged value of self" (1985, 275). Given the impoverishment of Humean theory in the area of relations (and hence its inability to conceive a self-in-relationship whose connections to others are not merely contingent but essential), Callicott has little alternative to this direction of development.

13   Grimshaw (1986, 182). See also the excellent discussion in Warren (1990, 136–8) of the importance of recognition and respect for the other's difference; Blum (1980, 75); and Benhabib (1987, 166).

References

Benhabib, Seyla. 1987. The generalised and the concrete other. In *Women and Moral Theory*, 154–77. E. Kittay and D. Meyers, eds. Totowa, NJ: Rowman and Allenheld.

Biehl, Janet. 1987. It's deep, but is it broad? An ecofeminist looks at deep ecology. *Kick It Over*, special supplement (Winter).

Blum, Lawrence A. 1980. *Friendship, Altruism and Morality*. Boston and London: Routledge & Kegan Paul.

Callicott, J. Baird. 1985. Intrinsic value, quantum theory, and environmental ethics. *Environmental Ethics* 7: 261–2.

Cheney, Jim. 1987. Ecofeminism and deep ecology. *Environmental Ethics* 9: 115–45.

Cheney, Jim. 1989. The neo-stoicism of radical environmentalism. *Environmental Ethics* 11: 293–325.

Fox, Warwick. 1982. The intuition of deep ecology. Paper presented at Environment, Ethics and Ecology Conference, Canberra. Also published under the title Deep ecology: A new philosophy of our time? *The Ecologist* 14 (1984): 194–200.

Fox, Warwick. 1986. Approaching deep ecology: A response to Richard Sylvan's critique of deep ecology. Environmental Studies Occasional Paper 20. Hobart: University of Tasmania Centre for Environmental Studies.

Fox, Warwick. 1990. *Towards a Transpersonal Ecology: Developing New Foundations for Environmentalism*. Boston: Shambala.

Gilligan, Carol. 1982. *In a Different Voice*. Cambridge: Harvard University Press.

Gilligan, Carol. 1987. Moral orientation and moral development. In *Women and Moral Theory*, 19–33. E. Kittay and D. Meyers, eds. Totowa, NJ: Rowman and Allenheld.

Griffin, Susan. 1978. *Woman and Nature: The Roaring Inside Her*. New York: Harper and Row.

Grimshaw, Jean. 1986. *Philosophy and Feminist Thinking*. Minneapolis: University of Minnesota Press. Also published as *Feminist Philosophers*. Brighton: Wheatsheaf.

Griscom, Joan L. 1981. On healing the nature/history split in feminist thought. *Heresies* 4(1): 4–9.

Jaggar, Alison. 1983. *Feminist Politics and Human Nature*. Totowa, NJ: Rowman & Allenheld; Brighton: Harvester.

Kheel, Marti. 1985. The liberation of nature: A circular affair. *Environmental Ethics* 7: 135–49.

King, Ynestra. 1981. Feminism and revolt. *Heresies* 4(1): 12–16.

Leopold, Aldo. 1949. *A Sand County Almanac*, 201–2. Oxford and New York: Oxford University Press.

Lloyd, Genevieve. 1983a. Public reason and private passion. *Metaphilosophy* 14: 308–26.

Lloyd, Genevieve. 1983b. Reason, gender and morality in the history of philosophy. *Social Research* 50(3): 490–513.

Midgley, Mary. 1983. *Animals and Why They Matter*. Athens: University of Georgia Press; London: Penguin.

Naess, Arne. 1973. The shallow and the deep, long-range ecology movement: A summary. *Inquiry* 16: 95–100.

Naess, Arne. 1986. Intrinsic value: Will the defenders of nature please rise. In *Conservation Biology*. M. Soule, ed. Sunderland, MA: Sinauer Associates.

Naess, Arne. 1988. *Ecology, Community and Lifestyle.* Cambridge: Cambridge University Press.

Neidjie, Bill. 1985. *Kakadu Man.* With S. Davis and A. Fox. Canberra: Mybrood P/L.

Plumwood, Val. 1986. Ecofeminism: an overview and discussion of positions and arguments. In *Women and Philosophy*, Supplement to vol. 64. *Australasian Journal of Philosophy* (June 1986): 120–38.

Plumwood, Val. 1988, 1990. Women, humanity and nature. *Radical Philosophy* 48: 6–24. Reprinted in *Feminism, Socialism and Philosophy: A Radical Philosophy Reader*. S. Sayers, ed. London: Routledge.

Poole, Ross. 1984. Reason, self-interest and "commercial society": The social content of Kantian morality. *Critical Philosophy* 1: 24–46.

Poole, Ross. 1985. Morality, masculinity and the market. *Radical Philosophy* 39: 16–23.

Regan, Tom. 1986. *The Case for Animal Rights.* Berkeley: University of California Press.

Rodman, John. 1980. Paradigm change in political science. *American Behavioural Scientist* 24(1): 54–5.

Ruether, Rosemary Radford. 1975. *New Woman New Earth.* Minneapolis: Seabury Press.

Salleh, Ariel. 1984. Deeper than deep ecology. *Environmental Ethics* 6: 339–45.

Seed, John. 1989. Interviewed by Pat Stone. *Mother Earth News* (May/June).

Seed, John, Joanna Macy, Pat Fleming, and Arne Naess. 1988. *Thinking Like a Mountain: Towards a Council of All Beings.* Philadelphia and Santa Cruz: New Society Publishers.

Sylvan, Richard. 1985. A critique of deep ecology. *Radical Philosophy* 40 and 41.

Taylor, Paul. 1986. *Respect For Nature.* Princeton: Princeton University Press.

Thomas Aquinas. 1976. *Summa contra Gentiles.* Bk. 3, Pt. 2, chap. 62. Quoted in *Animal Rights and Human Obligations*, 56. T. Regan and P. Singer, eds. Englewood Cliffs, NJ: Prentice Hall.

Warren, Karen J. 1987. Feminism and ecology: Making connections. *Environmental Ethics* 9: 17–18.

Warren, Karen J. 1990. The power and promise of ecological feminism. *Environmental Ethics* 12(2): 121–46.

E Environmental Pragmatism

38 Beyond Intrinsic Value: Pragmatism in Environmental Ethics
Anthony Weston

39 Methodological Pragmatism, Pluralism, and Environmental Ethics
Andrew Light

38 Beyond Intrinsic Value: Pragmatism in Environmental Ethics

Anthony Weston

"Pragmatism" sounds like just what environmental ethics is against: shortsighted, human-centered instrumentalism. In popular usage that connotation is certainly common. *Philosophical* pragmatism, however, offers a theory of values which is by no means committed to that crude anthropocentrism, or indeed to any anthropocentrism at all. True, pragmatism rejects the means-ends distinction, and consequently rejects the notion of fixed, final ends objectively grounding the entire field of human striving. True, pragmatism takes valuing to be a certain kind of desiring, and possibly only human beings desire in this way. But neither of these starting points rules out a genuine environmental ethic. I argue that the truth is closer to the reverse: only these starting points may make a workable environmental ethic possible.

One charge of anthropocentrism should not detain us. Pragmatism is a form of subjectivism – it makes valuing an activity of subjects, possibly only of human subjects – but subjectivism is not necessarily anthropocentric. Even if only human beings value in this sense, it does not follow that only human beings *have* value; it does not follow that human beings must be the sole or final objects of valuation. Subjectivism does not imply, so to say, subject-*centrism:* our actual values can be much more complex and world-directed.

Pragmatism insists most centrally on the *interrelatedness* of our values. The notion of fixed ends is replaced by a picture of values dynamically interdepending with other values and with beliefs, choices, and exemplars; pragmatism offers, metaphorically at least, a kind of "ecology" of values. Values so conceived are resilient under stress, because, when put to question, a value can draw upon those other values, beliefs, etc., which hold it in place in the larger system. At the same time, though, every value is open to critical challenge and change, because each value is also *at stake* precisely with those related values, beliefs, etc. which on other occasions reinforce it. We are thus left with a plurality of concrete values, in which many different kinds of value, and many different sources of value, can be recognized as serious and deep without requiring further reduction to some single end in itself. And there is every reason to think that respect for other life forms and concern for natural environments are among those values. The problem is not to

From *Environmental Ethics*, vol. 7 (1985): 321–3, 328–9, 331–9. © 1985 by Anthony Weston. Reprinted with permission from the author.

devise still more imaginative or exotic justifications for environmental values. We do not need to *ground* these values, pragmatists would say, but rather to situate them in their supporting contexts and to adjudicate their conflicts with others – a subtle enough difference at first glance, perhaps, but in fact a radical shift in philosophical perspective.

Intrinsic Value and Contemporary Environmental Ethics

We seem to be compelled to distinguish means and ends almost as soon as we begin thinking about environmental values. Nature has certain obvious appeals: recreational and aesthetic satisfactions, "ecosystem stabilization" values (seemingly useless species may play a role in controlling pests, or fixing nitrogen), research and teaching uses, the attraction of natural objects and lifeforms simply as exemplars of survival, and so on.[2] In making these appeals, however, we value nature not "for its own sake," but for a further end: because it is necessary, useful, or satisfying to *us*. Even aesthetic appreciation does not necessarily require valuing nature for itself, since we might be tempted to say that only aesthetic *experience* is valued intrinsically. Beauty is in the mind of the beholder: aesthetic objects are only means to it.

The familiar next step is to ask whether nature could also be valuable in its own right. Could nature have *intrinsic* value, could it have worth as an end in itself, and not just because it serves human ends?[3] This question, of course, frames much of the debate in contemporary environmental ethics. If human beings, or some particular and unique human characteristics (e.g., a certain kind of conscious experience), are the only ends in themselves, then we have, for better or worse, "anthropocentrism." If some broader, but not universal class of beings has intrinsic value, and if, as usual, this class is taken to be the class of sentient or (even more broadly) living beings, then we have what might be called "sentientism" or (more broadly) "biocentrism." If *all* ("natural"?) beings, living or not, have intrinsic value and must not be treated merely as means, then we have what might be called "universalism." There is a continuum of possible ethical relations to nature, then, ranging from views which limit the bearers of intrinsic value strictly to human beings through views which progressively extend the franchise until finally it is (nearly?) universal.[4]

This much seems perfectly innocent. No views are actually endorsed, after all: only a range of possibilities is set out. In fact, however, I think that this "frame" is far from innocent. This seemingly uncommitted range of possibilities is in fact narrowly restricted by the underlying notion of intrinsic value itself.

Consider, after all, how that range of possibilities is determined in the first place: each option is defined precisely by the set of beings to which it attributes intrinsic value. Richard and Val Routley, for instance, argue that anthropocentrism represents a kind of moral "chauvinism," as egregious as the egoist's blindness to values beyond his or her self or the racist's failure to look beyond his or her race;[5] they insist upon the existence of *other* intrinsic values besides conscious human experience, values which deserve similar respect. Tom Regan *defines* an environmental ethic as a view which attributes "inherent goodness" to at least some nonhuman natural objects, where "inherent goodness" is an "objective property" of objects which compels us to respect its bearers.[6] That notion of intrinsic or "inherent" value, however, is itself extremely specific and demanding. A great deal of philosophical baggage comes with it. Regan already weighs in with some of it, as Evelyn Pluhar points out, by construing inherent value as a "supervenient," "nonnatural" property, notions whose Moorean ancestry and problematic metaphysical commitments are plain to see.[7] [. . .]

Against Intrinsic Value

Moore argues that some notion of "valuable for its own sake" or "valuable in itself" is required simply to *understand* the notion of "valuable for the sake of something else," the everyday notion of instrumental value which we usually take for granted. If we speak of means, then logically we must also be able to conceive of ends, since an end seems to be implicated in the very concept of a means. Thus, Moore reads the phrase "good as a means" as equivalent to "a means to good," where the "good" in the second case seems to be intrinsic.[8]

This rationale fails, however, for a simple reason. We can also understand the notion of instrumental value by reference to further, but nonintrinsic values. Values may refer beyond themselves without ever necessitating a value which must be self-explanatory. The value of a day's hike in the woods need not be explained either by the intrinsic value of my appreciation of the woods or by the intrinsic value of the woods themselves; instead, both the appreciation and the woods may be valuable for further reasons, the same may be true of *those* reasons, and so forth. Appreciation may be valued, as Hill points out, partly because it can lead to greater sensitivity to others; but greater sensitivity to others may in turn make us better watchers of animals and storms, and so on. The woods may be valued not only as an expression of freedom and nobility, but also as a refuge for wildlife, and both of these values may in turn be explained by still other, not necessarily human-centered values.

Someone may respond that explanations such as these must still have stopping points somewhere. If *X* is valuable because it leads to or enhances Y, we might seem to be required to say that *X*'s value is "passed on" from Y. Y's value in turn may be passed on from Z. But – the argument goes – there must be some origin to the value which is thus "passed on." Like a bucket of water in a fire chain, it must have started in some reservoir which is not merely another bucket. Monroe Beardsley likens this argument to the first cause argument for the existence of God; ". . . the existence of any instrumental value [is supposed to] prove the existence of some intrinsic value just as the occurrence of any event is said to prove the existence of a First Cause."[9]

Beardsley's analogy, however, suggests an initial objection. The "first value" argument may beg the very question it is trying to answer. Just as the first cause argument must assume that the chain of causes it invokes cannot be infinite, so the "first value" argument assumes that the long process of tracing means back to ends must have a final stopping point. But actually this is just what it was supposed to *show*.

[. . .]

It may be urged that, intrinsic values *can* be concrete, plural, and possibly even inconsistent. This is Holmes Rolston's view, and a version of it has been held even by some pragmatists, such as C. I. Lewis. There are times, Rolston or Lewis would say, when we apprehend value concretely and directly, without having to look farther afield or into the future in order to recognize it. Lewis echoes Moore by comparing this recognition to the way we see redness or hear shrillness.[10] Rolston speaks of the intrinsic value of "point experiences," like the warmth of the spring sun, calling it "as fleeting and plural as any other kind of value."[11] Rolston's intrinsic values need not be abstract, then, and they need no justification at all, let alone "special" justification. A day's hike in

the woods is worthwhile even if it does not contribute to peace of mind or animal-watching ability or job performance: the experience, as well as the woods itself considered even apart from my experience, is simply good "for what it is in itself."[12]

Undeniably, Lewis and Rolston are pointing to a real kind of experience; the question is what this kind of experience shows. It is, at least, an experience of what we might call *immediate* value. John Dewey argued, however, that "to pass from immediacy of enjoyment to something called 'intrinsic value' is a leap for which there is no ground."[13] When we do endorse something in an immediate and non-inferential way, according to Dewey, we do not usually make a judgment of value at all, and so *a fortiori* do not make a judgment of intrinsic value. Instead, that endorsement is a "statement to the effect that no judgment is required, because there is no conflict of values, no occasion for deliberation and choice. . . ."[14] Even obviously instrumental activities – doing the dishes, driving the highways – are sometimes appreciated in this immediate and non-referential way. Even something that destroys, a virus or a tornado, can sometimes be arrestingly beautiful. *Arresting* is the right word, too: our response to them precisely *disconnects* the frame of reference in which value questions even arise.

When values do become problematic, when choice is required, then they need articulation and defense. But to call them "intrinsic," in Rolston's sense, now offers no help. Since we have to disconnect objects and actions from their contexts in order to value them just "for what they are in themselves," what they are in relation to everything else is pushed out of focus. If I lose myself in the beauty of the tornado, I may not reach shelter in time. Rolston insists that immediate values must be put in context, like any others, and that they are sometimes ambiguous or even downright bad when contextualized. The upshot, however, is that the attribution of intrinsic value, in his sense, carries no special force in the real world. A thousand other "point experiences" of values press in upon us from every side, just as ordinary values have always pressed in upon us, and what we *do* will and should be determined, just as it has always been determined, by the balances and synergies and tradeoffs between them. By all means let us remember that this is a world lavish with its moments of beauty and preciousness – but let us honor those moments without cutting them off from the practical living of our lives.

Earlier I called into question the traditional demands for self-sufficiency and abstractness in intrinsic values. Here, finally, the task of justification too is reconceived. It is not the task of "grounding" values: what Rolston's defense of the notion of intrinsic values may finally illustrate, in fact, is the way in which the project of "grounding" natural values (or, perhaps, any values) finally cuts itself off from the real-life task of assessment and choice. For assessment and choice we must learn, again, to *relate* values. Any adequate theory of valuation must recognize that valuation involves desires with a complex internal structure, desires interlinked, and mutually dependent with a large number of other desires, beliefs, exemplars, and choices.[15] Love, for example, interlinks with a wide range of desires and beliefs, from the tenderness of "being with" to sexual desires, from one's complex understanding of the other person to the culture's images and exemplars of love, and so on. Justification draws on these interdependencies. We justify a value by articulating the supporting role it plays with respect to other values, which in turn play a supporting role with respect to it by referring to the beliefs which make it natural, and which it in turn makes natural by reaffirming those choices and models which link it to the living of our lives. Precisely this is Beardsley's "wider context of things."

Interdependent values are not closed to criticism: it may actually be this sort of interdependence, indeed, which makes the most effective criticism *possible*. Criticism becomes an attempt to alter certain desires by altering something in the constellation of other desires, beliefs, choices, etc. to which they are linked.[16] Some of the beliefs in question may be false, desires artificial or shallow, and so forth. Norton is right to point out that "felt preferences" exploitative of nature can often be criticized on the basis of "considered preferences." Too often we are simply thoughtless, or not thoughtful enough. But the power of this sort of criticism goes far beyond the dialectic of "ideals"; only Norton's wish to set up shop on the edge of the concept of intrinsic value, I think, leads him to conceive considered preferences on the model of ideals, thus making them seem far more marginal than they are.[17] As Pluhar writes:

> It is amazing how much prejudice and ignorance fuel ethical disputes, not to mention bad reasoning. . . . How much lack of impartiality and empathy underlie common attitudes toward animals . . .? How much greed (a prime source of partiality),

ignorance, and muddled thinking fuel common attitudes about ecosystems and natural objects?[18]

As she points out, visiting a meat factory makes many vegetarians! Although Pluhar, oddly, regards this pragmatic sort of criticism as an alternative way of defending Regan's "inherent values," she offers no argument that the values which might emerge from this procedure are in any sense "inherent" or intrinsic.[19] I suspect that no such arguments can be found. It is time to abandon the old preoccupation with intrinsic values entirely: let practical criticism be practical.

Not even radical criticism is excluded. The culture to which we owe so many of our explicit desires and their interlinkings also includes an attic full of latent ideals, inconsistent perhaps with its main tendencies, but still there waiting to be drawn out. God may have given us dominion over land and sea, but He also gave us St. Francis; against the swashbuckling exploitation of the Industrial Revolution we have the romantic poets, landscape painting, Rousseau, Emerson, Thoreau; against factory farms we have the still compelling image of the solitary farmer close to the soil. The wide-ranging recent debates about Christian and Judaic attitudes toward nature underscore this fundamental dissonance.[20] It is a mistake to try to find *the* Christian (or *the* American, etc.) attitude toward nature: there are many. Our traditions, I want to suggest (I have tried to argue this general point elsewhere[21]), contain their dialectical opposites within themselves. Even our biologically rooted desires are far from monolithic and static. Sometimes criticism simply needs the time and the patience to draw these latent elements out.

Pragmatism in Environmental Ethics

The real power of the pragmatic approach lies in what it does *not* say, in what it has removed the need to say. Thus, my concern here is emphatically not to devise new arguments for environmental values, but instead to show that the familiar ones are laboring under needless constraints. Still, this may be a modest, if unexotic, bit of progress, and I expect that it will be controversial all the same. I think that if values are conceived along the lines just sketched, then the case we can already make for environmental values – and in quite simple terms – is far stronger than most environmental ethicists themselves seem to believe.

We know that the experience of nature can awaken respect and concern for it. We know indeed that these feelings can become deep and synergistic desires in some lives, and we have before us exemplars of such lives in Muir, Thoreau, Leopold, and others. Most of us are not so single-minded, but we, nevertheless, know how essential a return to nature can be, how Thoreau felt returning to Walden Pond from town, and why Yeats yearned for the bee-loud glade. While there are varied motives behind the recent boom in backpacking, cross-country skiing, canoeing, camping, and the like, at least part of the cause is surely a growing appreciation of nature, not just as another frame for our exercise and relaxation, but for its own unique voices, from the silence of the winter woods to the roar of waterfalls in spring.

These feelings are essential starting points for a pragmatic defense of environmental values. They are *not* "second best," "weak" anthropocentric substitutes for the intrinsic values philosophers want but cannot find. They do not need a philosophical "grounding." The questions that arise for us are of quite a different sort. Again, we need to know how to articulate, to ourselves and to others, the *relation* of these values to other parts of our system of desires, to other things that are important, and to the solution of concrete problems. For ourselves we want to understand and strengthen these values; in others we want to nourish and extend them. Nor, finally, need we start by trying to assimilate environmental values to our other values. Even our respect and concern for each other may be of quite a different type, and have entirely different sources, from our respect and concern for the environment.

The articulation of these values is not the province of philosophy alone. Poetry and biography are just as vital. Think of Wordsworth:

> And I have felt
> A presence that disturbs me with the joy
> Of elevated thoughts; a sense sublime
> Of something far more deeply interfused.
> Whose dwelling is the light of setting suns,
> And the round ocean and the living air . . .
>   Therefore let the moon
> Shine on thee in thy solitary walk;
> And let the misty mountain winds be free
> To blow against thee. . . .[22]

We must not read this as an incomplete statement of pantheism, in need of philosophical clarification. Maybe Wordsworth was a closet metaphysician, but the possible linkage to Spinoza is not what makes us ache to feel those winds. Wordsworth offers a way to begin to describe a kind of experience which for our purposes may not need a stricter formulation. It is not a "grounding": it is a kind of *portrait*. Likewise, what is finally important in *Walden* is not Thoreau's misanthropic philosophizing, but the way in which he shows us, in his own person, how a human being can meet the evening, between the squirrels and the shadows, or how to look at a lake:

> A lake is the landscape's most . . . expressive feature. It is earth's eye, looking into which the beholder measures the depth of his own nature. The fluviate trees next to the shore are the slender eyelashes which fringe it, and the wooded hills and cliffs around are its overhanging brows. . . .[23]

Nietzsche suggests more than once that philosophers are too clumsy to handle real values. He may exaggerate, but all the same we do know that philosophy has too long failed to take seriously what it cannot itself fully articulate. By rejecting the demand to "ground" these values, then, pragmatism also begins to undercut the demand that we articulate them in philosophy's peculiar, epistemically oriented way.

Still, on the whole, many philosophical arguments fare well in terms of the new set of questions I am advancing. Indeed many of them fare *better* when measured against this new set of questions than against the set of questions that they are actually trying to answer. Let us first return to Rolston's "Values Gone Wild." Rolston begins with a critique of the idea of nature as a "resource." The idea that "everything is a resource," he argues, like the idea that "everybody is selfish," becomes simply trivial at the extremes, "eating up everything, as if humans had no other operating mode vis-à-vis wilderness." In fact, we must enter wilderness "on its own terms" – not, or not primarily, as a means to "high quality experience." In this way, he argues, "one is not so much looking to *resources* as to *sources*, seeking relationships in an elemental stream of being with transcending integrities."[24] At this point, however, Rolston goes on to suggest that nature is intrinsically valuable because it is a source, in this sense, of whatever (else) we intrinsically value. This seems to me to add nothing: it only *weakens* the evocative force of the notion of "sourcehood." Although "elemental . . . transcending integrities" make a certain ecosystemic sense, trying to make their *value* transcendental either introduces an extremely problematic ontology, [. . .]

or represents only one way of talking, [...] with no special force in actual moral thinking. "Sourcehood" is a perfectly understandable and powerful model of value in its own right: why force it into the mold of intrinsic values?

Consider one other example. Rolston writes of "sympathetically turning to value what does not stand directly in our lineage or underpinning" – our "kin" and "neighbors" in the animal world.[25] This too is genuinely perceptive: we do have a latent sense of community with animals which close acquaintance may bring out. But here too Rolston tries to wring intrinsic values out of facts which are better left alone. He argues, for instance, that the similarity between our reactions and those of animals suggests that we should take their reactions to express imperatives – values – as well, presumably including intrinsic values. Why these imperatives also bear on *us*, however, is not clear, and the claim that they do bear on us involves analogic arguments problematic in both philosophy of mind and moral theory. Once again Rolston's concrete notions, here of "kinship" and of being "neighbors," capture the values at stake much more freshly and directly than the philosophically problematic analogies necessary to make them over into intrinsic values. Moreover, as Rolston also points out, even within the animate world the notion of kinship eventually stretches beyond the breaking point: certainly we have little kinship with spiders. If another kind of value must be invoked for such "aliens," then it is not clear why this should not be so even for "neighbors." There is no need to fit all values into a single model.

Even more standard philosophical arguments – or at least their basic intentions – fit naturally into this framework. Recall Sagoff's argument that we may value in nature expressions of things that we value intrinsically in our lives: freedom, nobility, etc. Critics have pointed out that this cannot demonstrate the intrinsic value of nature itself.[26] Pragmatists, however, want to know simply how this value relates to others and can form an organic part of our lives. This is exactly what Sagoff helps to show us, locating it partly in the orbit of the desire for freedom. Or again, the persistent inclination to attribute "rights" directly to nature might now be reapproached and understood. In part, certainly, that attribution is a straightforward political attempt to state environmental values with enough force that others will take them seriously. But it is also an attempt to articulate a specific and familiar attitude toward nature. Alone in

the woods we find ourselves feeling a sense of gratefulness, of "awe," finally almost of intrusion, a feeling which probably has its closest parallel in those responses to other *people* which make us want to attribute *them* rights. But how closely these feelings are actually parallel remains an open question. Here we first need a careful phenomenology. This may be true even of human rights: real respect for others comes only through the concrete experience and finally "awe" of the other. It is the conditions and nature of this feeling which we really need to understand. Reversing the usual deduction entirely, we might even take rights talk itself as a first and rather crude attempt at just such a phenomenology – but surely we can do better.

Let me conclude by returning to the level of practical problems in environmental ethics. Why, for instance, should we value wilderness? What sort of justification can we give for keeping exploitable land and resources in their natural state? Not surprisingly, it is necessary to begin with a reorientation. Notice that this question is already posed in abstraction from any specific situation. This may itself give rise to absurdities. If we answer that wilderness indeed has intrinsic value, then presumably we are required to go to any lengths to support as much of it as possible, and wherever possible, at least consistent with other intrinsic values. But too many other things of equal or greater importance in the *situation* will not be captured by a hierarchical scheme of intrinsic values. Of course, there are other ways out, perhaps invoking intrinsic principles of such generality that they can be used to justify anything. The response I am urging, however, is the abandonment of these very ways of posing the question. The important questions for pragmatism are the ones posed by specific situations, and while the answers across different situations will probably bear a strong family resemblance, they will not always be the same.

Why should we protect the new Alaskan national parks, for example? Now the answers are much easier: because the new parks are both exceptionally wild and exceptionally fragile: because the non-preservationist pressures in at least this case are exceptionally unworthy, tied largely to the exploitation of energy resources to which there are any number of more intelligent alternatives; perhaps because their protection is still possible. These arguments do indeed seem to dodge the original question. They do not say why wilderness as such should be protected. On the other hand, one certainly does not have to be an anthropocentrist to doubt whether it *should* be protected "as such." This is why the *exceptional* nature of the Alaskan wilderness makes that particular case so powerful. These "practical" arguments are precisely the kinds offered by the Sierra Club, the Nature Conservancy, and most of the other environmentally oriented organizations. Are these arguments offered merely for lack of better (philosophical?) ones? Or might those organizations actually have a more reasonable position after all?

"What about those people, though, who simply could not care less about wilderness? What about the many cases in which such values simply cannot be assumed? Tame rivers are much nicer than wild ones if one owns a motorboat; exploitation in Alaska might lower our fuel bills and make America more self-sufficient in some vital resources; and so on." Let me respond in several ways. First, even these cases may not be real cases of "could not care less." Nearly everyone recognizes *some* value in nature; think of how often natural scenes turn up on wall calendars and church bulletins. Even motorboaters like to see woods. Wilderness values may just seem to them less significant than other values at stake in the particular situation. Common ground remains. If we begin by treating others as absolutists, we run the risk of turning them into just what we fear. But this is only a caricature, and we can instead approach them from a standpoint of complex mutuality. Then, though, if some shared values can indeed be agreed upon, the real issue shifts to the question of alternatives, and this is a recognizably factual issue on both sides, and also negotiable. Motorboats don't have to go everywhere.

The pragmatic approach defended here forswears the search for knockdown arguments that will convince absolutely everyone that natural values are important. We cannot defeat the occasional extremist who sees no value at all in nature. But if this is a defect, it is certainly not unique to pragmatism. No other approach has knockdown arguments to offer either; otherwise, environmental ethics would not be a *problem*. The real difference is that pragmatists are not looking for knockdown arguments; we propose to concern ourselves with defending environmental values in other ways. It is striking, actually, that the search for a proof of the intrinsic value of nature is almost always *post hoc*. Even if someone were finally to discover a knockdown proof, it would not be the reason that most of us who are in search of such a proof do in fact value nature, since our

present accounts of natural values differ so markedly. *We* learned the values of nature through experience and effort, through mistakes and mishaps, through poetry and stargazing, and, if we were lucky, a few inspired friends. What guarantees that there is a shortcut? It is wiser to accept the fact that many of our contemporaries, even our most thoughtful contemporaries, hold deeply different, probably irreconcilable, visions of the ideal world.[27] Pragmatism, indeed, celebrates a wide-open and diverse culture: it is the prerequisite of all the central Deweyan virtues: intelligence, freedom, autonomy, growth. What we have yet to accept is its inconclusiveness and open-endedness, its demand that we struggle for our own values without being closed to the values and the hopes of others. The search for intrinsic values substitutes a kind of shadowboxing for what must always be a good fight.

Notes

1   The confusion of subjectivism with "subject-centrism" is dissected, though not in these terms, by Richard and Val Routley in "Against the Inevitability of Human Chauvinism," in K. E. Goodpaster and K. M. Sayre, eds., *Ethics and the Problems of the 21st Century* (Notre Dame: University of Notre Dame Press, 1979), pp. 42–7.

2   For an extensive list, see David Ehrenfeld, *The Arrogance of Humanism* (Oxford: Oxford University Press, 1978), chap. 5; or Holmes Rolston, III, "Valuing Wildlands," *Environmental Ethics* 7(1985): 24–30.

3   I am equating intrinsic values with ends in themselves, instrumental values with means to ends. For present purposes I think that subtle distinctions between these concepts can be ignored.

4   See W. K. Frankena, "Ethics and the Environment," in Goodpaster and Sayre, *Ethics*, pp. 5–6 and pp. 18–19; and J. Baird Callicott, "Non-anthropocentric Value Theory and Environmental Ethics," *American Philosophical Quarterly* 21 (1984), pp. 299–309.

5   Routley and Routley, "Against the Inevitability," pp. 36–62.

6   Tom Regan, "The Nature and Possibility of an Environmental Ethic," *Environmental Ethics* 3 (1981): 30–4. Frankena, C. I. Lewis, and others use *inherent value* to refer to objects or actions the contemplation of which leads to intrinsically valuable experience. Regan, however, clearly means by *inherent* what Frankena and Lewis mean by *intrinsic*. "If an object is inherently good," he tells us, "its value must *inhere* in the object itself" (p. 30). Its value does not depend upon experience at all.

7   Evelyn Pluhar, "The Justification of an Environmental Ethic," *Environmental Ethics* 5 (1983): 55–8.

8   G. E. Moore, *Principia Ethica* (Cambridge: Cambridge University Press, 1903), p. 24.

9   Monroe Beardsley, "Intrinsic Value," *Philosophy and Phenomenological Research* 26 (1965): 6. The critique offered here is indebted to Beardsley's first article.

10 C. I. Lewis, *An Analysis of Knowledge and Valuation* (LaSalle, Ill.: Open Court, 1946), pp. 374–5.

11 Rolston was generous enough to comment extensively on an earlier draft of this paper, and I am quoting from his comments. Obviously he should not be held to these exact words, though I think his position here is a natural completion of what he has said in print. See Holmes Rolston, III, "Values Gone Wild," Inquiry 26 (1983); and Holmes Rolston, III, "Are Values in Nature Objective or Subjective?," *Environmental Ethics* 4 (1982): 125–52; reprinted in Robert Eliot and Arran Gare, eds., *Environmental Philosophy* (University Park: Pennsylvania State Press, 1983), pp. 135–65.

12 Rolston, "Are Values in Nature Objective or Subjective?" in Eliot and Gare, *Environmental Philosophy*, p. 158.

13 John Dewey, *Theory of Valuation* (Chicago: International Encyclopedia of Unified Science, 1939), p. 41.

14 Beardsley, "Intrinsic Value," p. 16.

15 See Anthony Weston, "Toward the Reconstruction of Subjectivism: Love as a Paradigm of Values," *Journal of Value Inquiry* 18 (1984): 181–94.

16 Ibid. and R. B. Brandt, *Theory of the Good and the Right* (Oxford: Clarendon Press, 1979), part I.

17 Norton ends up arguing that having ideals need not presuppose the intrinsic value of the things or states of affairs idealized; see Bryan Norton, "Environmental Ethics and Weak Anthropocentrism," *Environmental Ethics* 6 (1984): 137.

18 Pluhar, "Justification," p. 60.

19 Ibid., p. 58. This curious inference also mars J. Baird Callicott's otherwise fine survey; see Callicott, "Non-anthropocentric Value Theory," p. 305.

20 See Robin Attfield, "Western Traditions and Environmental Ethics," in Eliot and Gare, *Environmental Philosophy*, pp. 201–30.

21 See Anthony Weston, "Subjectivism and the Question of Social Criticism," *Metaphilosophy* 16 (1985): 57–65.

22 William Wordsworth, "Lines Composed a Few Miles above Tintern Abbey," lines 93–8 and 134–7.

23 H. D. Thoreau, *Walden* (New York: Signet, 1960), p. 128.

24 Rolston, "Values Gone Wild," pp. 181–3.

25 Ibid., pp. 188, 191.

26 For instance, Louis Lombardi, "Inherent Worth, Respect, and Rights," *Environmental Ethics* 5 (1983): 260.

27 A particularly striking example is Steven S. Schwarzschild, "The Unnatural Jew," *Environmental Ethics* 6 (1984): 347–62.

39 Methodological Pragmatism, Pluralism, and Environmental Ethics

Andrew Light

In 1992 I began developing a pluralist position in environmental ethics which I called "environmental pragmatism" (Light 1993). My attempt was to try to come up with normative arguments for why environmental ethics should be done in a more pragmatic way in order to move it outside the walls of the ivory tower and the seldom-read pages of philosophy journals, into the public sphere where it could contribute to the vibrant conversations taking place on how to mend the world and our relationship to it.[1]

This argument was in part a reaction to the frustration that some of us were feeling that environmental ethics, as a field, was not making the

contribution that it could be making to the resolution of environmental problems, contributions which we saw other disciplines, such as environmental history and sociology, making in abundance and to great effect. For just two examples, consider the enormous influence of William Cronon (a historian) and Robert Bullard (a sociologist) on environmental debates and movements of the late 1980s and early 1990s. Cronon's essay "The Trouble with Wilderness" (1995) was absolutely critical in shaping debates over the future of US national park and wilderness management following the Yellowstone fires of 1988. Robert Bullard's body of work, starting

Specially written for this volume.

with *Dumping in Dixie* (1990), not only described the early environmental justice movement, but actively helped to shape it, resulting in US President Bill Clinton's February 1994 executive order mandating consideration of the effects of environmental policies on minority and low-income populations. While there are some truly talented people working in environmental ethics today, I believe that we can point to no comparable achievement in our ranks, at least in the US.[2]

Is this gap between the achievements of environmental ethicists and other environmental professionals reflective of something about the nature of philosophy in general, or this field of philosophy in particular? My view is that it has more to do with the particular fixations of environmental ethicists, which may have been partially influenced by broader trends in academic philosophy in general. Regardless of the explanation for how environmental ethics got where it is today, while there are many purely theoretical questions about the environment that are interesting and well worth teaching and pursuing, if, in the end, at least some of those working in the field cannot contribute to the actual resolution of environmental problems, then it is not fulfilling what I believe to be its inherent promise. That promise is to do what other areas of applied ethics do – improve the moral quality of the decisions, actions, policies, and priorities relevant to the realm with which it is concerned.

The importance of that promise can be understood by merely recognizing the fact that most, if not all, environmental problems have moral dimensions that can be described in a variety of ways. If our public discussion of those problems did not include attention to these moral dimensions, then they would be lacking in the same respect as if we were ignoring their ecological dimensions. The latter would be clearly unacceptable, but the former is possible unless environmental ethicists do a better job of demonstrating their relevance to the broader environmental community. To strike an analogy, if environmental ethicists had nothing to offer the policy or advocacy process, it would be like an alternative history of medical ethics which had nothing of use to offer medical practitioners, policy-makers, or patients. Given that the realm of human health clearly contains substantial, pressing, and critical moral issues, a medical ethics without a robust capacity to engage on the ground issues would mark some kind of intellectual or moral failure.

Many of the most important first generation of thinkers in this field do not, however, share the view that environmental ethics is failing to live up to its potential. J. Baird Callicott (1995, 2002) argues that environmental ethics fulfills its promise as a field of philosophy and environmental activity if it concentrates on the project of either offering an alternative human worldview toward the environment or refining theories of why nature (either ecosystems, species, or writ large) has some kind of non-instrumental or intrinsic value that warrants moral recognition or obligation. But while figures like Callicott can point to examples of how environmental ethicists have used such work to influence both activist environmental organizations and the public policy process, there are ample reasons to believe that either this approach to environmental ethics is too limited (see the arguments in Light and de-Shalit 2003) or that the results are largely inconsequential for the work of environmental advocates. For the fact remains that most work in environmental ethics is aimed at engagement in intramural debates between and among professional environmental ethicists over issues such as the moral foundations for a nonanthropocentric intrinsic value of nature. While there have been some significant advances of late, traditionally, little in this literature has been of much direct use to those resource managers in the field or those policy-makers, given that the social realm of law and policy must of necessity be aimed at appeals to human interests which are usually not considered in such debates (as will be explained below).[3]

I call my position "methodological environmental pragmatism." I believe this view is one that is open to other environmental ethicists who share my pluralist inclinations but who otherwise would not embrace the label "pragmatist." What I wish to do here is make a brief case for the version of environmental pragmatism that I have developed, clarify what I take to be its particularly pluralist virtues, and then explore two possible problems with its further development against the backdrop of showing it to be a tool that even a non-pragmatist could use.

Methodological Environmental Pragmatism

To understand the place of methodological environmental pragmatism in environmental ethics, we must first understand where it enters the ongoing debates in environmental ethics. What, then, is environmental ethics? As this volume demonstrates, there are many ways of understanding what environmental ethics is and the aspirations of environmental ethicists. I see it this way, however: environmental ethics is that branch of applied ethics, or applied philosophy, directed at the central issue of ascertaining and articulating the moral grounds for protection, preservation, or restoration of the nonhuman environment and improving the relationship between humans and the nonhuman natural world, preferably, for the benefit of both.

The first interesting thing about environmental ethics is that, unlike other areas of applied ethics – for example, medical ethics – it has by and large not developed as a form of ethical "extensionism." Extensionism in this sense just means different philosophers starting with different traditions in the history of ethics – utilitarianism, Kantian deontological ethics, virtue theories, different versions of principalism, feminism, etc. – and applying the resources of one of these traditions to an ethical problem involving medicine, physical health, or the relationship between patients and doctors or other professionals in the medical establishment. In contrast, environmental ethics has evolved more as an attempt to establish a new and philosophically unique foundation for the direct moral consideration of nonhuman natural entities, especially those which are at the center of environmental controversies – endangered species, ecosystems, and other large-scale environmental processes. Overwhelmingly, the basis for this new foundation for moral recognition is based in arguments that such collective natural entities have some form of intrinsic, inherent, or otherwise non-instrumental value which warrants some level of moral consideration. As a result, the field has not been dominated by debates between utilitarians and Kantians, or the like, but, rather, along a very different set of divides from what we normally see in other areas of applied ethics, including, it is interesting to note, the field of animal welfare (see Light and McKenna 2004).

The first and most important of these divides involves the rejection of "anthropocentrism." Tim Hayward defines ethical anthropocentrism as the view that prioritizes those attitudes, values, or practices which give "exclusive or arbitrarily preferential consideration to human interests as opposed to the interests of other beings" or the environment (1997: 51). Many early environmental ethicists were adamant that if environmental ethics was going to be a distinctive field of ethics, it must necessarily involve a rejection of the prevalence for anthropocentrism in the history of ethics. Using Hayward's definition,

this amounted to a rejection of the claim that ethics should be restricted only to the provision of obligations, duties, and rights among and between humans, thereby prioritizing in moral terms all human interests over whatever could be arguably determined as the interests of nonhumans, species or ecosystems.

Among the first papers published by professional philosophers in the field (e.g., landmark papers in the early 1970s by Arne Naess, Holmes Rolston III, Richard Routley (later Sylvan), Val Routley (later Plumwood), and Peter Singer), some version of anthropocentrism was often the target even if it was not explicitly labeled as such by that name. Regardless of the terminology, the assumption that anthropocentric moral views were antithetical to the agenda of environmentalists, and to the development of environmental ethics, was largely assumed to be the natural starting point for any environmental ethic. So pervasive was this assumption that it was often not adequately defended. It became one of what Gary Varner calls the "two dogmas of environmental ethics" (1998: 142). This position is largely still accepted by most environmental ethicists today. Furthermore, the notion of what anthropocentrism meant, and consequently what overcoming anthropocentrism entailed, often relied on very narrow, strawman definitions of this position. Anthropocentrism was equated with forms of valuing which easily, or even necessarily, led to nature's destruction.

The first divide, then, among environmental ethicists is between those who accept the rejection of anthropocentrism as a necessary prerequisite for establishing a unique field of environmental ethics and those who do not accept this position, arguing that "weaker" forms of anthropocentrism – for example, those which admit humanly based values to nature other than mere resource value – are sufficient to generate an adequate ethic of the environment (see, for example, Norton 1984 for an early description of this debate). If environmental ethics was to start with a rejection of anthropocentrism, then the next step was to come up with a description of the value of nonhumans, or the nonhuman natural world, in nonanthropocentric terms. As just mentioned, the preferred description of this form of value has generally been as some form of intrinsic value, or at least non-instrumental value, thought to imply that nonhumans or ecosystems possessed some sort of value in and of themselves which demands recognition.

As was suggested earlier, however, the form of value preferred in many of these accounts was a form of monism rather than pluralism. Monists in environmental ethics generally argue that a single scheme of valuation is required to anchor our various duties and obligations in an environmental ethic (see, for example, Callicott 1990). This would mean that one ethical framework would have to cover the range of diverse objects of moral concern included under a complete environmental ethics: other humans, other animals, living organisms, ecosystems, species, and perhaps even the Earth itself. Such a view would have the advantage of generating a cleaner methodology for resolving disputes over conflicting obligations to and among these objects, itself a very worrisome problem, as a nonanthropocentric environmental ethic has as a mandate covering many more competing claims for moral consideration than a traditional ethic which only grants direct moral considerability to humans. With a nonanthropocentric environmental ethics, one can have conflicts between obligations not only between humans but between humans and nonhumans, humans and species, ecosystems, etc.

Pluralists counter that it cannot be the case that we could have one ethical theory that covered this range of objects, either because the sources of value in nature are too diverse to account for in any single theory, or because the multitude of contexts in which we find ourselves in different kinds of ethical relationships with both humans and nature demand a plurality of approaches for fulfilling our moral obligations (see, for example, Brennan 1988 and 1992). Accordingly, for Andrew Brennan, there is "no one set of principles concerning just one form of value that provides ultimate government for our actions" (1992: 6).[4]

While less a dogma than nonanthropocentrism, arguments over moral monism continue to push the evolution of the field, particularly over the issue of the relationship between theory and practice in environmental ethics. For example, the debate over pluralism raises the question of how appeals concerning the welfare of the environment cohere with other issues in moral philosophy in particular situations. Many, if not most, cases of potential harm to the value of ecosystems are also cases of moral harm to human communities which can be objected to for independent anthropocentric moral reasons. The literature on environmental justice, especially the concern that minority communities often bear a disproportionate burden of environmental harms, such as exposure to toxic waste, is based on linking concerns about human health and well-being to environmental protection. A truly pluralist environmental ethic would not be terribly concerned with whether the claims to harm to the interests of a minority community by a toxic waste dump could or could not be based on the same scheme of value that would describe the harm done to the ecosystem by the dump. A pluralist ethic would be open to describing the harm to the ecosystem and to the human community in different though compatible terms for the purposes of forming a broader coalition for fighting the dump.

There are many problems with contemporary environmental ethics that could be mentioned at this point considering its tendency toward both nonanthropocentrism and monism. But I find that these problems are arguably more practical than philosophical at the present time. For even though there are several dissenters to the dominant nonanthropocentric tradition in the field, the more important consideration is that it is widely acknowledged that the world of natural resource management takes a predominantly anthropocentric and pluralist approach to assessing natural value, as do most other humans. After all, if this were not true, why would environmentalists be so concerned about anthropocentrism? Because many previous environmental ethicists are not interested in elucidating reasons for protection of the environment which stem from such anthropocentric considerations, the field as a whole has unfortunately found itself unable to make a substantial impact on the actual debates over environmental policy.

In this context I began developing my methodological form of environmental pragmatism. My start on this question has been to remind environmental ethicists that, in addition to being part of a philosophical community, they are also part of another community, namely, the environmental community. While this connection has never been clear, the field continues to be part of at least an ongoing conversation about environmental issues, if not an outright intentional community of environmentalists. The drive to create a more pragmatic environmental ethics is motivated by a desire not only to actively participate in the resolution of environmental problems, but to hold up our philosophical end, as it were, among the community of environmentalists.

How could environmental ethicists better serve the environmental community? The answer for the methodological pragmatist begins in a recognition that if philosophy is to serve a larger community, then it must allow the plural interests of the community to help to determine the philosophical problems which the theorist addresses. This does not mean that the pragmatic philosopher, in my sense of this term, necessarily finds all the problems that a given community is concerned with as the problems for her own work. Nor does it mean that she assumes her conclusions before analyzing a problem, like a hired legal counsel who doesn't inquire as to the guilt or innocence of her client. It only means that a fair description of the work of the pragmatic philosopher is to investigate the problems of interest to their community and then articulate the policy recommendations of that community on these problems to those outside of their community – that is, to the public at large. Articulation of these issues from a more limited community to a broader public should be done in terms closer to the moral intuitions of the broader public for the strategic reasons of being in a better position to persuade that public. This requires a form of "moral translation" whereby the interests of the smaller community of environmentalists is translated into a range of appeals corresponding to the various moral intuitions which are represented in the broader public arena. We can think of this work of translation as the "public task" of a methodologically pragmatist environmental ethics. It is necessarily a pluralist project, attempting to articulate the considered interests of the environmental community in as broad a set of moral appeals as is possible (see Light 2003).

A pluralist and pragmatic environmental ethics would not rest with a mere description of or series of debates on the value of nature (even a description that justified a secure foundation for something as strong as a claim for the rights of nature). A public environmental ethics would further question whether the nonanthropocentric description of the value of nature which dominates the philosophical work of most environmental ethicists today is likely to succeed in motivating most people to change their moral attitudes about nature taking into account the overwhelming ethical anthropocentrism of most humans (amply demonstrated by studies like that of Kempton et al. 1997, which shows that most people take obligations to future human generations as the most compelling reason to protect the environ-ment). As such, a public environmental ethics would have either to embrace a weak or enlightened anthropocentrism about natural value (for example, arguing that nature had value either for aesthetic reasons or as a way of fulfilling our obligations to future generations), or endorse a pluralism which admitted the possibility, indeed the necessity, of sometimes describing natural value in human-centered terms rather than always in nonanthropocentric terms in order to help to achieve wider public support for a more morally responsible environmental policy.

The appeal to pragmatism here, however, is only methodological. So, this approach does not insist that environmental ethicists should give up their various philosophical debates over the existence of nonanthropocentric natural value, nor their position on these debates. Such work should continue as another more purely philosophical task for environmental ethicists. But ethicists who choose to follow this methodology must accept the public task as well, which requires that they be willing to morally translate their philosophical views about the value of nature, when necessary, in terms which will more likely morally motivate policy-makers and the general public even when they have come to their views about the value of nature through a nonanthropocentric approach.

In other work (Light 2002), I have provided more detail on how such a "two task" approach would look. Here, I will only note that this strategy, asking that ethicists sometimes translate their views to a language that resonates more with the public, is only warranted where convergence on the ends of environmental policy has been reached. That is, where the preponderance of views among environmentalists of various camps, as well as among environmental ethicists themselves, has converged on the same end – such as the necessity of forging an international agreement limiting the emission of greenhouse gases which are causing global warming – then the public task of the philosopher is to articulate the moral arguments that would most effectively motivate non-environmentalists to accept that end (for a good account of why such convergence does often occur, see Norton 1991). Empirically, for many issues, this will involve making weak anthropocentric arguments. But one can imagine that in some cases nonanthropocentric claims would be more appealing as well. What appeals best is an empirical question. Where convergence has not been achieved, however, this public task of moral translation is not warranted.

Under those circumstances, we must continue with the more traditional philosophical task of environmental ethicists, our version of an environmental "first philosophy," attempting to hammer out the most plausible and defensible moral foundations for the ethical consideration of nonhuman nature.

There are many other details to fill in to this approach; I trust charitable readers will allow for its full defense and explication elsewhere. But, to provide just one recent example, when a coalition of British evangelicals and American scientists recently set out to convince their American evangelical counterparts to support efforts to push the Bush administration in the US to take climate change more seriously, at least some of these figures were engaging in a kind of methodological pragmatism. First, they recognized the convergence of views on the necessity of an international convention on regulation of greenhouse gases (and, of course, the science behind those views); second, they took this convergence as a warrant for action; third, they translated the reasons for such an agreement into the language of Christian fundamentalism; and, finally, they found compelling ways of articulating those reasons to their target audience (American evangelicals). The method worked. There grew up a substantial community of American evangelicals who lobbied the Bush administration to do something about global warming and also change their personal consumptive practices (see Eilperin 2007). It is not that all those involved in this campaign believe the claims, for example, that a Christian God commands us to be good stewards of the Earth and that this has implications for how we should think about the threat of global warming. It is the case, though, that these figures saw that their core task was to open up the toolbox of ethical reasons for environmental protection (of necessity a pluralist toolbox of many reasons which can appeal to a diverse audience) and translate the end of a comprehensive agreement on climate change into the moral language of an audience which they believed to be particularly important to moving the Bush administration to take this issue more seriously. The strategy has proven correct. Even though the Bush administration did not agree to sign the Kyoto Protocol in its waning days, it at least acknowledged the scientific consensus on anthropogenic global warming, and, perhaps more importantly, the Republican Party in general has acknowledged that it cannot ignore this issue any longer, nor can it cling to climate change skepticism. We now have the opening, at least, to move forward in the US with a much more productive debate on this critical issue than we have been able to have so far.

In what remains, I will take up two issues that may hinder the acceptance of this view by those starting from the more traditional nonanthropocentric starting points in the field, especially those who cling to the hope of finding a single moral foundation for assessing environmental value.

Can We Always Get What We Want?

The first issue I wish to take up is what might be called the problem of "incrementalism." My version of pragmatism for environmental ethics is not amenable to "all or nothing" approaches to the application of philosophical ideals to problems of public policy. The methodological pragmatist does not insist that a full acceptance of a single nonanthropocentric moral value of nature must be recognized in order to achieve the best ends of environmental policy. For example, it should be perfectly fine on this view that people endorse stronger laws for the protection of endangered species based on reasons which involve human self-interest (such as some version of the precautionary principle applied to this issue) and that we must accept trade-offs in terms of achieving these ends in some cases so long as the trade-offs do not necessarily lead to a loss of a species.

Those who take a more strident nonanthropocentric position may at first disagree with this position. Since the beginning of the field, many important theorists have argued that long-term environmental protection will only be achieved through a more widespread change in environmental consciousness generally achieved through some particular kinds of experiences in nature. For example, one of the first nonanthropocentric theories, deep ecology, was spread by some of its American adherents as requiring a conversion experience of sublime proportions:

> Most people in Deep Ecology have had the feelings – usually, but not always in nature – that they are connected with something greater than their ego, greater than their home, their family, their special attributes as an individual – a feeling that is often called oceanic because many have it on the ocean. Without that identification, one is not easily drawn to become involved in Deep Ecology. (Devall and Session 1985: 76)

One implication of such a view is that a necessary condition for achieving environmental sustainability is a critical mass of people achieving some kind of fundamental change in how they order their experiences of the world and thus value the world. Would insistence on such a view be compatible with my pluralist and pragmatist methodology?

Clearly not. But as the view I am trying to articulate is only a methodological form of pragmatism, rather than a view that adheres to a particular historical school of pragmatism, then perhaps committed deep ecologists could simultaneously hold onto their core principles and adhere to this pragmatist methodology when confronting issues of public policy. Even if deep ecologists had a longer-term end in view about changes they would like to see in terms of a change in environmental consciousness, they could, and should, at the same time have at the ready viable immediate policy solutions which are compatible with current political or economic systems. This is not to say that the pragmatic environmental ethicist gives up on the task of defending alternatives to current structures and the pursuit of those alternatives in debates on the reallocation of resources. It only means that the position requires, for consistency's sake to our pragmatic intentions at least, that we not rely on such fundamental changes in articulating our preferred long-term, more ambitious ends, in order to advocate better public policies consistent with current worldviews.

Let me make just one suggestion for how an environmental ethicist could go about reconciling her desire to change fundamental worldviews with the need to make achievable policy recommendations. As is suggested by my approach, my view is that if a pragmatic philosophy in the end is in the service of an argument to create better policies, then in our democratic society it must be prepared to argue its case before the public and, perhaps, sometimes only before policy-makers. This raises the critical issue of how such appeals to the public are to be made, which in turn brings up the question of how important persuasion is to the creation of pragmatic arguments.

All philosophy is in some sense about persuasion, though to differentiate ourselves from rhetoricians (if we are interested in making such distinctions, which I still am), we must restrict ourselves to persuasion through some form of argument given more or less agreed-upon (and revisable) standards for what counts as a good argument. But the pragmatic philosopher is not simply concerned with persuading other philosophers. She is also interested in persuading the public either directly (in hopes that they will in turn influence policy-makers) or indirectly, by appealing to policy-makers who in turn help to shape public opinion. The work of a public philosophy is not solely for intramural philosophical discussion; it is aimed at larger forums. But, as I suggested before, such a task requires some attention to the question of what motivates either the public, the policy-makers, or both, to act. Our bar is set higher than traditional philosophical standards of validity and soundness abstractly conceived. For if we are to direct our philosophy at policies in a context other than a hypothetical philosophical framework, we must also make arguments which will motivate our audiences to act. Since we are dealing in ethical and political matters here, the question for pragmatic philosophers like myself is how much we must attend to the issue of moral motivation in forming our pragmatic arguments.

If we agree that the issue of moral motivation is always crucial for a pragmatic philosophy then, again, we must be prepared to embrace a form of pluralism which allows us to pick and choose from a range of conceptual frameworks in making our arguments, without committing to the theoretical monism which may be assumed in some versions of these frameworks. The reason is that we need to be able to make arguments that will appeal to the conceptual frameworks of our audiences while recognizing that these frameworks can change from audience to audience as was hopefully illustrated in the climate change example offered above.

Who Are We Speaking For?

This problem of incrementalism leads me to a second issue involving this pragmatic and pluralist form of environmental ethics. Let us call this one the problem of "inclusion." By this, I don't mean the general question of making sure that all voices are taken into account in some social, political, or cultural institution, but, rather, how we are to define the community which our pragmatic form of public philosophy is supposed to serve. Recall that earlier I said that one warrant for my version of methodological pragmatism in environmental ethics was some kind of agreement among the diverse voices in the environmental community on the ends of environmental public policy, even if they disagreed about the reasons for pursuing those ends. But even if such a view has merit, it suffers from the obvious critique that the boundaries of the "environmental community" are ill-defined. Who, after all, counts as an environmentalist?

Unfortunately, such a question appears to have only one answer, which doesn't seem fairly easy to reject: someone is an environmentalist who calls themselves an environmentalist. Though unsatisfying on the face of it, the alternatives are worse. One could argue that environmentalists are only those who have a specific kind of appreciation for the natural world. But clearly, as the pluralist recognizes, there are not only many ways to appreciate the natural world but also many ways to express that appreciation and no single one seems to be satisfactory. If we tried to characterize environmental appreciation as "spiritual," for example, would we be willing to endorse the claim that those people who do not acknowledge this term as meaningful in their lives are not really environmentalists? One could argue that environmentalists are only those who rank the environment as the first or second most important priority in their lives. But how would we measure such priorities? Is it the case that those who commit to lying down in front of bulldozers or sitting in trees for years to keep them from being cut down are the only ones who are really environmentalists? If this is true, then I'm not an environmentalist, or I haven't yet fulfilled my true environmental responsibilities. Alternatively, one could argue that adherence to one particular environmental policy, or range of policies, is what makes someone an environmentalist. But certainly, adherence to policies can be a matter of disagreement, and policies change over time. One might as well then stick to the answer that you are an environmentalist if you say that you are.

For the pragmatic philosopher, the upshot of such considerations seems to be that the community of environmentalists to which one is responding will have to be effectively limited to those who organize themselves in self-described environmental organizations, or otherwise make their environmentalism known through some public process. Would a more mainstream environmental ethicist accept such a view as a condition of using my form of methodological pragmatism when engaging in the more public task of environmental philosophy?

Here we could again encounter some problems. For example, it should be predictable from the discussion above that some environmental ethicists would argue that no long-term environmental sustainability is possible in a world where most humans think in anthropocentric terms. But there is actually quite a lot of empirical evidence to suggest that beneficial environmental policies have in fact been based on human-centered notions of natural value, such as the ample appeals in environmental policies to a stewardship ethic. So, while we can be cautious about the utility of basing environmental policies exclusively on anthropocentric grounds, the empirical evidence alone would suggest that there are good reasons not to engage in a wholesale rejection of anthropocentric arguments, or to assume that we can ever achieve a more publicly engaged environmental ethics, by only producing a form of nonanthropocentric holism.

In considering the problem of incrementalism and the problem of inclusion, I hope to have shown how a publicly engaged pluralist and pragmatic philosophy could work, as well as how some of the problems of my methodological pragmatism could be solved. I certainly would never suggest that all those engaging in the moral dimensions of environmental problems must follow this pragmatic model. I believe that it is only warranted in specific circumstances when a philosophical response is needed to a particular problem of public policy. Where that response is needed, we would well consider changing our philosophical practice to better serve the larger plural communities in which we could have a significant public role.

Notes

1 At the time, no one else was using the term "environmental pragmatism" to describe the infusion of pragmatist ideas into environmental philosophy but, rather, figures like Bryan Norton were describing their views as "broadly pragmatic" (Norton 1991: x), or, like Anthony Weston, were describing a role for the insertion of the thought of canonical pragmatist figures, such as John Dewey, into environmental ethics (Weston 1985). By 1996, with Eric Katz, I had brought together the work of these figures and others in an edited volume titled *Environmental Pragmatism* to try to roll out what looked like an emerging school of thought in the field.

2 While it may seem to some an arbitrary distinction, we can point to a comparatively much greater level of influence on regulatory institutions and advocacy organizations by those working in animal welfare and agricultural ethics. The work of Peter Singer, Tom Regan, Bernard Rollin, and Paul Thompson stand out in particular. It

should be noted, however, that those working in these fields generally are not working from the same starting points as most environmental ethicists.

3 While I will not go into the issue here there is another way of understanding what is meant by "environmental pragmatism," namely the extension of views originating with the canonical historical pragmatists, such as John Dewey, William James, and Charles Pierce, to environmental problems. For reasons I discuss elsewhere (Light 2004) I do not see this as a helpful path to reorienting the field of environmental ethics.

4 Such claims lead Callicott to charge pluralists with moral relativism. I answer this worry in Light 2003.

References

Brennan, A. 1988. *Thinking about Nature* (Athens, GA: University of Georgia Press).

Brennan, A. 1992. "Moral pluralism and the environment." *Environmental Values* 1: 15–33.

Bullard, R. 1990. *Dumping in Dixie* (Boulder, CO: Westview Press).

Callicott, J. B. 1990. "The case against moral pluralism." *Environmental Ethics* 12: 99–124.

Callicott, J. B. 1995. "Environmental philosophy is environmental activism: The most radical and effective kind." In D. Marietta and L. Embree (eds.), *Environmental Philosophy and Environmental Activism* (Lanham, MD: Rowman and Littlefield Publishers), pp. 19–36.

Callicott, J. B. 2002. "The pragmatic power and promise of theoretical environmental ethics." *Environmental Values* 11: 3–26.

Cronon, W. 1995. "The Trouble with Wilderness." In Cronon (ed.), *Uncommon Ground: Toward Reinventing Nature* (New York: W. W. Norton and Company).

Devall, B. and G. Sessions. 1985. *Deep Ecology: Living as if Nature Mattered* (Salt Lake City: Peregrine Smith Books).

Eilperin, J. 2007. "Warming draws evangelicals into environmentalists' fold." *Washington Post* (August 8): A1.

de-Shalit, A. 1995. *Why Posterity Matters* (London: Routledge).

Hayward, T. 1997. "Anthropocentrism: A misunderstood problem." *Environmental Values* 6: 49–63.

Kempton, W., J. Boster and J. Hartley. 1997. *Environmental Values in American Culture* (Cambridge, MA: The MIT Press).

Light, A. 1993. "Environmental pragmatism and valuation in nature." In S. Wright (ed.), *Human Ecology: Crossing Boundaries* (Fort Collins: Society for Human Ecology), pp. 23–30.

Light, A. 2002. "Taking environmental ethics public." In D. Schmidtz and E. Willott (eds.), *Environmental Ethics: What Really Matters? What Really Works?* (Oxford: Oxford University Press), pp. 556–66.

Light, A. 2003. "The case for a practical pluralism." In A. Light and H. Rolston, III (eds.), *Environmental Ethics: An Anthology* (Cambridge, MA: Blackwell Publishers), pp. 229–47.

Light, A. 2004. "Methodological pragmatism, animal welfare, and hunting." In E. McKenna and A. Light (eds.), *Animal Pragmatism* (Bloomington: Indiana University Press), pp. 119–39.

Light, A. and A. de-Shalit. 2003. "Environmental Ethics: Whose Philosophy? Which Practice?" In A. Light and A. de Shalit (eds.), *Moral and Political Reasoning in Environmental Practice* (Cambridge, MA: The MIT Press), pp. 1–27.

Light, A. and E. McKenna. 2004. "Pragmatism and the Future of Human-Nonhuman Relationships." In E. McKenna and A. Light (eds.), *Animal Pragmatism* (Bloomington: Indiana University Press), pp. 1–18.

Norton, B. G. 1984. "Environmental ethics and weak anthropocentrism." *Environmental Ethics* 6: 131–48.

Norton, B. G. 1991. *Toward Unity Among Environmentalists* (Oxford: Oxford University Press).

Varner, G. 1998. *In Nature's Interests* (Oxford: Oxford University Press).

Weston, A. 1985. "Beyond intrinsic value: Pragmatism in environmental ethics." *Environmental Ethics* 7: 321–39.

F Direct Action

40 Earth First!
    Dave Foreman

The Ethics of Ecological Sabotage: An Exchange

41 Ecological Sabotage: Pranks or Terrorism?
    Eugene Hargrove

42 Earth First! and *The Monkey Wrench Gang*
    Edward Abbey

43 More on Earth First! and *The Monkey Wrench Gang*
    Dave Foreman

44 Editor's Response
    Eugene Hargrove

---

40   Earth First!

Dave Foreman

The early conservation movement in the United States was a child – and no bastard child – of the Establishment. The founders of the Sierra Club, the Audubon Society, the Wilderness Society, and the wildlife conservation groups were, as a rule, wealthy pillars of American society. They were an elite band – sportsmen of the Teddy Roosevelt variety, naturalists like John Burroughs, outdoorsmen in the mold of John Muir, pioneer foresters and ecologists on the order of Aldo Leopold, and wealthy social visionaries like Robert Marshall. No anarchistic Luddites these.

When such groups as the Sierra Club grew into the politically effective force that blocked Echo Park Dam in 1956 and got the Wilderness Act passed in 1964, their members were likely to be physicians, mathematicians, and nuclear physicists. To be sure, in the 1950s and 1960s a few oddball refugees from the American mainstream joined the conservation outfits. But it was not until Earth Day in 1970 that the environmental movement received its first influx of real anti-establishment radicals as anti-war protesters found a new cause – the environment. Suddenly, in environmental meetings beards appeared alongside crewcuts – and the rhetoric quickened.

The militancy was short-lived. Along with dozens of other products of the 1960s who went to work for conservation groups in the early 1970s, I discovered that a suit and tie gained access to regional foresters and members of Congress. We learned to

From *The Progressive*, vol. 45, no. 10 (1981): 39–42. © 1981. Reprinted by permission from *The Progressive*, 409 E Main St, Madison, WI 53703, USA.

moderate our opinions along with our dress. We heard that extremists were ignored in the councils of government, that the way to get a Senator to put his arm around your shoulders and drop a wilderness bill in the hopper was to consider the conflicts – mining, timber, grazing – and pare back the offending acreage. Of course we were good patriotic Americans. Of course we were concerned with the production of red meat, timber, and minerals. We tried to demonstrate that preserving wilderness did not conflict all that much with the gross national product and that clean air actually helped the economy. We argued that we could have our booming industry and still sink oil wells in pristine areas.

Our moderate stance appeared to pay off when the first avowed conservationist since Teddy Roosevelt took the helm at the White House in 1977. Suddenly our colleagues – self-professed conservationists – occupied important and decisive positions in the Carter Administration. Editorials proclaimed that environmentalism had been enshrined in the Establishment, that conservation was here to stay. A new environmental ethic was at hand: Environmental Quality and Continued Economic Progress.

But although we had access – indeed, influence – in high places, something seemed amiss. When the chips were down, conservation still lost out to industry. But these were our *friends* turning us down. We tried to understand the problems they faced in the real political world. We gave them the benefit of the doubt. We failed to sue when we should have. . . .

I wondered about all this on a gray day in January 1979, as I sat in my private office in the headquarters of the Wilderness Society, only three blocks from the White House in Washington, DC. I had just returned from a news conference at the South Agriculture Building, where the Forest Service had announced a disappointing decision on RARE II – the second Roadless Area Review and Evaluation (a twenty-month exercise by the Forest Service to determine which National Forest lands should be protected in their natural condition).

As I loosened my tie, propped my cowboy boots up on my desk, and popped the top to another Stroh's, I thought about RARE II and why it had gone so wrong. Jimmy Carter, supposedly a great friend of wilderness, was President. Dr M. Rupert Cutler, a former assistant executive director of the Wilderness Society, was assistant secretary of agriculture over the Forest Service and had conceived the

RARE II program. But we had lost to the timber, mining, and cattle interests on every point. Of sixty million acres still roadless and undeveloped in the 220 million acres of National Forests, the Department of Agriculture was recommending only fifteen million for wilderness protection from road building and timber cutting.

Moreover, damn it, we – the conservationists – had been moderate. The anti-environmental side had been extreme, radical, emotional. Their arguments had been easily shot full of holes. We had been factual, rational. We had provided more – and better – serious public comment. But we had lost. And now we were worried that some local wilderness group might go off the reservation and sue the Forest Service over the clearly inadequate environmental impact statement for RARE II. We didn't want a suit – because we knew we could win and were afraid of the political consequences of such a victory. We might make some powerful Senators and Representatives angry. So those of us in Washington were plotting on how to keep the grass roots in line. But, vaguely, something seemed wrong to me.

After RARE II, I left my position as issues coordinator for the Wilderness Society in Washington to return to New Mexico and my old job as the Society's Southwest representative. I was particularly concerned with the overgrazing on the 180 million acres of public lands in the West managed by the Department of Interior's Bureau of Land Management (BLM). For years, these lands – rich in wildlife, scenic, recreational, and wilderness values – had been the private preserve of stockgrowers in the West. BLM had done little to manage national lands or to control the serious overgrazing that was sending millions of tons of topsoil down the Colorado, Rio Grande, and other rivers; wiping out wildlife habitat, and generally beating the land to hell.

Prodded by a Natural Resources Defense Council suit, BLM began to try to get a handle on the overgrazing problem through a series of environmental impact statements. These confirmed that most BLM lands were seriously overgrazed and recommended cuts in animal numbers. But after the expected outcry from the few thousand ranchers leasing BLM land and their political cronies in Congress and state capitals, BLM backtracked so quickly that a fair number of knees must have been dislocated. Why were BLM and the Department of Interior so gutless?

While that question gnawed at my innards, I was growing increasingly disturbed about the trends in the conservation organizations themselves. When I had originally gone to work for the Wilderness Society in 1973, the way to get a job with a conservation group was to prove yourself first as a volunteer. It helped to have the right academic background, but experience as a capable grass-roots conservation activist was more important.

We realized that we would not receive the salary we could earn in government or private industry but we didn't expect it. We were working for nonprofit groups funded by the contributions of concerned people. Give us enough to keep food on the table, pay rent, buy a six-pack – we didn't want to get rich. But a change occurred after the mid-1970s. Now young people seeking to work for conservation groups were career-oriented, they had relevant degrees (science, law – not history or English), they saw jobs in environmental organizations in the same light as jobs in government or industry. One was a stepping stone to another, more powerful position later on. They were less part of a cause and more part of a profession.

A gulf began to grow between staff and volunteers. We also began to squabble over salaries. We were no longer content to be paid subsistence, and the figures in our salaries chalked up our status in the movement. Perrier and brie replaced Bud and beans.

Within the Wilderness Society, Celia Hunter, prominent Alaskan conservationist and outfitter, World War II pilot, and feminist, had been executive director while I was in Washington. Celia instituted staff discussions, democratic decision-making, more equitable salaries, and emphasis on results instead of flash. But the governing council of the Society, controlled by retired Federal bureaucrats, was not sympathetic; the council preferred a hierarchy dominated by a strong male figure (there was a definite undercurrent of sexism in the struggle).

The council found this strong male figure in Bill Turnage, an eager young businessman who had made his mark by marketing Ansel Adams. Turnage took over as executive director late in 1978, and within two years he had replaced virtually all those on the staff under Celia with professional organization people. The clique running things on the governing council also moved to bring millionaires with a vague environmental interest onto the council. We were, it seemed to some of us, becoming indistinguishable from those we were ostensibly fighting.

I resigned my position in June 1980.

But what of the rest of the movement? Were there any radicals anywhere? Anyone to take the hard stands? Sadly, no. The national groups – Sierra Club, Friends of the Earth, Audubon Society, Wilderness Society, and the rest – took almost identical middle-of-the-road positions on most issues. And then those half-a-loaf demands were readily compromised further. The top conservation staffs of these groups fretted about keeping local conservationists (and some of their field staffs) in line, keeping them from becoming extreme or unreasonable, keeping them from blowing moderate national strategy on a variety of issues.

For years I was a strong advocate of this approach. We could, I believed, gain more wilderness by a moderate tack, we would stir up less opposition by keeping a low profile. We could inculcate conservation in the Establishment by using rational, economic arguments. The last thing we needed was somebody running amok. We needed to present a solid front. We all had to be on the same bandwagon. Even Friends of the Earth, which had started out to be the radical among us back in the heady Earth Day era, had gravitated to the center and, as a rule, was a comfortable member of the informal coalition of environmental organizations.

A major crack in my personal moderation appeared early in 1979, when I returned from Washington to the small ranching community of Glenwood, New Mexico. I had lived there earlier for six years and, although a known conservationist, was fairly well accepted. Shortly after my return, *The New York Times* published an article on RARE II, with the Gila National Forest around Glenwood as chief exhibit. To my amazement, the article included a quote from a rancher, whom I considered to be a friend, threatening *my* life because of wilderness lockups! A couple of days later I was accosted on the street by four men, one of whom ran the town cafe at which I had eaten many a fried steak. They threatened my life because of RARE II.

I was not afraid, but I was irritated – and surprised. I had been a leading moderate among New Mexico conservationists. I had successfully convinced them to propose fewer RARE II areas on the Gila National Forest as wilderness. What had backfired? I thought again about the different approaches to RARE II: the moderate, subdued one advanced by the major conservation groups; the howling, impassioned, extreme stand set forth by off-road-vehicle zealots, many ranchers, local boosters, loggers, and miners.

They looked like fools. We looked like statesmen. Who won? They did.

The last straw fell last Fourth of July in Moab, Utah. There the local county commission sent a flag-flying bulldozer into an area the Bureau of Land Management had identified as a possible study area for wilderness review. The bulldozer incursion was to be an opening salvo for the so-called Sagebrush Rebellion, a move by chambers of commerce, ranchers, and right-wing fanatics in the West to claim all Federal public lands for the states and eventual transfer to private hands. The Rebellion was clearly an extremist effort, lacking the support of even many conservative members of Congress in the West. But BLM was afraid to stop the county commission.

"What have we really accomplished?" I thought. "Are we any better off as far as saving the Earth now than we were ten years ago?" I ticked off the real problems: world population growth, destruction of tropical forests, expanding slaughter of African wildlife, oil pollution of the ocean, acid rain, carbon dioxide buildup in the atmosphere, spreading deserts on every continent, destruction of native peoples and the imposition of one world culture (European), plans to carve up Antarctica, deep seabed mining, nuclear proliferation, recombinant DNA research, toxic wastes. . . . It was staggering. And I feared we had done nothing to reverse the tide. Indeed, it had accelerated.

And then: Ronald Reagan. James "Rape'n'Ruin" Watt is Secretary of the Interior. The Forest Service is Louisiana-Pacific's. Interior is Exxon's. The Environmental Protection Agency is Dow's. Already, the Reagan Administration and the Republican Senate talk of gutting the gutless Alaska Lands Bill. The Clean Air Act, up for renewal, faces a Government more interested in corporate black ink than human lungs. The lands of the Bureau of Land Management appear to our Interior Department obscenely naked without the garb of oil wells. Meanwhile, the Agriculture Department will direct the Forest Service in ridding the National Forests of those disgustingly decadent and diseased old-growth trees. The cowboys have the grazing lands and God help the hiker, coyote, or blade of grass that gets in their way.

Maybe – some of us began to feel, even before Reagan's election – it was time for a new joker in the deck: a militant, uncompromising group unafraid to say what needed to be said or to back it up with stronger actions than the established organizations were willing to take. This idea had been kicking around for a couple of years; finally last year several

of us (including, among others, Susan Morgan, formerly educational director for the Wilderness Society; Howie Wolke, former Wyoming representative for Friends of the Earth; Bart Koehler, former Wyoming representative for the Wilderness Society, and myself) decided that the time for talk was past. We formed a new national group, EARTH FIRST! We set out to be radical in style, positions, philosophy, and organization in order to be effective and to avoid the pitfalls of co-option and moderation which we had already experienced.

What, we asked ourselves as we sat around a campfire in the Wyoming mountains, were the advantages, the reasons for environmental radicalism?

- To state honestly the views held by many conservationists.
- To demonstrate that the Sierra Club and its allies were raging moderates, believers in the system, and to refute the Reagan/Watt contention that they were "extremist environmentalists."
- To balance such anti-environmental radicals as the Grand County commission and provide a broader spectrum of viewpoints.
- To return some vigor, joy, and enthusiasm to the allegedly tired environmental movement.
- To keep the established groups honest. By stating a pure, non-compromise pro-Earth position, we felt EARTH FIRST! could help keep the other groups from straying too far from their philosophical base.
- To give an outlet to many hard-line conservationists who were no longer active because of disenchantment with compromise politics and the co-option of environmental organizations.
- To provide a productive fringe since it seems that ideas, creativity, and energy spring up on the fringe and later spread into the middle.
- To inspire others to carry out activities straight from the pages of *The Monkey Wrench Gang* even though EARTH FIRST!, we agreed, would itself be ostensibly law-abiding.
- To question the system; to help develop a new world view, a biocentric paradigm, an Earth philosophy. To fight, with uncompromising passion, for Mother Earth.

The name – EARTH FIRST! – was chosen deliberately because it succinctly summed up the one thing on which we could all agree: That in *any* decision, consideration for the health of the Earth must come first, or, as Aldo Leopold said, "A thing is right when it tends to preserve the integrity, stability, and beauty of the biotic community. It is wrong when it tends otherwise."

In a true Earth-radical group, concern for wilderness preservation must be the keystone. The idea of wilderness, after all, is the most radical in human thought – more radical than Paine, than Marx, than Mao. Wilderness says: Human beings are not dominant, Earth is not for *Homo sapiens* alone, human life is but one life form on the planet and has no right to take exclusive possession. Yes, wilderness for its own sake, without any need to justify it for human benefit. Wilderness for wilderness. For grizzlies and whales and titmice and rattlesnakes and stink bugs. And . . . wilderness for human beings. Because it is the laboratory of three million years of human evolution – and because it is home.

It is not enough to protect our few remaining bits of wilderness. The only hope for Earth (and humanity for that matter) is to withdraw huge areas as inviolate natural sanctuaries from the depredations of modern industry and technology. Keep Cleveland, Los Angeles. Contain them. Try to make them habitable. But identify areas – big areas – that can be restored to a semblance of natural conditions, reintroduce the griz and wolf and prairie grasses, and declare them off limits to modern civilization.

In the United States pick an area for each of our major ecosystems and recreate the American wilderness – not in little pieces of a thousand acres but in chunks of a million or ten million. Move out the people and cars. Reclaim the roads and plowed land. It is not enough any longer to say no more dams on our wild rivers. We must begin tearing down some dams already built – beginning with Glen Canyon, Hetch Hetchy, Tellico, and New Melones – and freeing shackled rivers.

This emphasis on wilderness is not to ignore other enviromental issues or to abandon the people who suffer because of them. In the United States blacks and Chicanos of the inner cities are the ones most affected by air and water pollution, the ones most trapped by the unnatural confines of urbanity. So we decided that not only should ecomilitants be concerned with these human environmental problems; we should also make common ground with other progressive elements of society whenever possible.

Obviously, for a group more committed to Gila monsters and mountain lions than to people, there will not be a total alliance with the other social movements. But there are issues where Earth radicals can cooperate with feminist, Indian rights, anti-nuke, peace, civil rights, and civil liberties groups. The inherent conservatism of the conservation community has made it wary of snuggling too close to these questionable (in their minds) leftist organizations. We hoped that the way might be paved for better cooperation from the entire conservation movement.

We believed that new tactics were needed – something more than commenting on dreary environmental impact statements and writing letters to members of Congress. Politics in the streets. Civil disobedience. Media stunts. Holding the villains up to ridicule. Using music to charge the cause.

Action is the key. Action is more important than philosophical hair-splitting or endless refining of dogma (for which radicals are so well known). Let our actions set the finer points of our philosophy. And let us recognize that diversity is not only the spice of life, it is also the strength. All that would be required to join us, we decided, was a belief in Earth first. Apart from that, EARTH FIRST! would be big enough to contain street poets and cowboy bar bouncers, agnostics and pagans; vegetarians and raw steak eaters, pacifists and those who think that turning the other cheek is a good way to get a sore face.

Radicals frequently verge toward a righteous seriousness. But we felt that if we couldn't laugh at ourselves we would be merely another bunch of dangerous fanatics who should be locked up (like the oil companies). Not only does humor preserve individual and group sanity, it retards hubris, a major cause of environmental rape, and it is also an effective weapon. Additionally, fire, passion, courage, and emotionalism are called for. We have been too reasonable, too calm, too understanding. It's time to get angry, to cry, to let rage flow at what the human cancer is doing to Mother Earth, to be uncompromising. For EARTH FIRST! it is all or nothing. Win or lose. No truce or cease fire. No surrender. No partitioning of the territory.

Ever since the Earth goddesses of ancient Greece were supplanted by the macho Olympians, repression of women and Earth has gone hand in hand with imperial organization. EARTH FIRST! decided to be non-organizational: no officers, no bylaws or constitution, no incorporation, no tax status; just a collection of women and men committed to the Earth. At the turn of the century William Graham

Sumner wrote a famous essay entitled "The Conquest of the United States by Spain." His thesis was that Spain had ultimately won the Spanish-American War because the United States took on the imperialism and totalitarianism of Spain as a result. We felt that if we took on the organization of the industrial state, we would soon accept their anthropocentric paradigm (much as Audubon and the Sierra Club already had).

In keeping with that view, EARTH FIRST! took the shape of a circle, a group of thirteen women and men around the country who more or less direct the movement, and a collection of regional contacts. We also have local affiliates (so far in Alaska, Montana, Wyoming, Colorado, Arizona, New Mexico, Utah, Arkansas, Maine, and Virginia). We publish a newsletter eight times a year and are developing position papers on a range of issues from automobiles to overgrazing. We also send out press releases. Membership is free, although we do encourage members to kick in ten bucks or more, if they can afford it, to help with expenses. We have not sought any grants or funding with strings attached, nor do we plan to have paid staff (although we hope to have field organizers receiving expenses in the tradition of the Wobblies).

And, when we are inspired, we *act*.

Massive, powerful, like some creation of Darth Vader's, Glen Canyon Dam squats in the canyon of the Colorado River on the Arizona-Utah border and backs the cold dead waters of Lake Powell some 180 miles upstream, drowning the most awesome and magical canyon on Earth. More than any other single entity, Glen Canyon Dam is the symbol of the destruction of wilderness, of the technological rape of the West. The finest fantasy of eco-warriors in the West is the destruction of the dam and the liberation of the Colorado. So it was only proper that on March 21, 1981 – on the Spring Equinox, the traditional time of rebirth – EARTH FIRST! held its first national gathering at Glen Canyon Dam.

On that morning, seventy-five members of EARTH FIRST! lined the walkway of the Colorado River Bridge 700 feet above the once free river and watched five compatriots busy at work with an awkward black bundle on the massive dam just upstream. Those on the bridge carried placards reading "Damn Watt, Not Rivers," "Free the Colorado," and "Let It Flow." The four men and one woman on the dam attached ropes to a grill on the dam, shouted out "Earth first!" and let 300 feet of black plastic unfurl down the side of the dam, creating the impression of a growing crack. Those on the bridge returned the cheer.

A few minutes later, Edward Abbey, author of *The Monkey Wrench Gang*, a novel of environmental sabotage in the Southwest, told the protesters of the "green and living wilderness" that was Glen Canyon only nineteen years ago:

"And they took it away from us. The politicians of Arizona, Utah, New Mexico, and Colorado, in cahoots with the land developers, city developers, industrial developers of the Southwest, stole this treasure from us in order to pursue and promote their crackpot ideology of growth, profit, and power – growth for the sake of power, power for the sake of growth."

Speaking toward the future, Abbey offered this advice: "Oppose. Oppose the destruction of our homeland by these alien forces from Houston, Tokyo, Manhattan, Washington, D.C., and the Pentagon. And if opposition is not enough, we must resist. And if resistance is not enough, then subvert."

Abbey then launched a nationwide petition campaign demanding the dismantling of Glen Canyon Dam. Hardly had he finished speaking when Park Service police and Coconino County sheriff's deputies arrived on the scene. While they questioned the organizers of the illegal assembly and tried to disperse it, outlaw country singer Johnny Sagebrush led the demonstrators in song for another twenty minutes.

The Glen Canyon Dam caper brought EARTH FIRST! an unexpected degree of media attention. Membership in our group has spiraled to more than a thousand with members from Maine to Hawaii. Even the Government is interested – according to reliable reports, the FBI dusted the entire Glen Canyon Dam crack for fingerprints!

Last Fourth of July more than 200 EARTH FIRST!ers gathered in Moab, Utah, for the first Sagebrush Patriot Rally to express support for Federal public lands and to send a message to anti-Earth fanatics that there are Americans who are patriotic about *their* wilderness.

When a few of us kicked off EARTH FIRST! we sensed a growing environmental radicalism in the country but we did not expect the response we have received. Maybe EARTH FIRST! is in the right place at the right time. Tom Turner, editor of Friends of the Earth's *Not Man Apart*, recently wrote to us to say:

"Russ Train once said, 'Thank God for Dave Brower – he makes it so easy for the rest of us to appear reasonable.' Youze guys are about to make Dave Brower look reasonable, and more power to you!"

The cynical may smirk. "But what can you really accomplish? How can you fight Exxon, Coors, David Rockefeller, Japan, and the other great corporate giants of the Earth? How, indeed, can you fight the dominant dogmas of Western Civilization?"

Perhaps it *is* a hopeless quest. But is that relevant? Is that important? No, what is important is that one who loves Earth can do no less. Maybe a species will be saved or a forest will go uncut or a dam will be torn down. Maybe not. A monkey wrench thrown into the gears of the machine may not stop it. But it might delay it. Make it cost more. And it feels good to put it there.

THE ETHICS OF ECOLOGICAL SABOTAGE: AN EXCHANGE

41   Ecological Sabotage: Pranks or Terrorism?

Eugene Hargrove

In 1975 Edward Abbey wrote a novel called *The Monkey Wrench Gang* which recounts the adventures of three men and one woman filled with "healthy hatred" who decide to sabotage construction projects which they find environmentally distasteful. Meeting accidentally near the Glen Canyon Dam, casual conversation about the possibility of blowing up the dam turns to serious plans for ecological sabotage on a smaller scale. Passing reference is made to the Luddite movement of the nineteenth century and *sabotage* is defined as the destruction of machinery using wooden shoes. No underlying philosophy, set of principles, or ideology is developed, however, then or at any time later in the book:

"Do we know what we are doing and why?"
"No."
"Do we care?"
"We'll work it out as we go along. Let our practice form our doctrine, thus assuring precise theoretical coherence."

The group agrees to stop short of murdering people – planning to murder machines instead – but such niceties fall by the wayside as the police close in after an abortive attempt to blow up a bridge. Two surrender. One is captured without a fight. The

fourth, the Vietnam veteran, chooses to fight it out to the end, an end in which his "riddled body hung on the rimrock for a final moment before the impact of the hail of steel, like hammer blows, literally pushed it over the edge," and it "fell like a sack of garbage into the foaming gulf of the canyon, vanishing forever from men's eyes."

Now, seven years later, this book is the inspiration for a new environmental group, Earth First! which, according to *Newsweek* (19 July 1982, pp. 26–7), is "pledged to 'ecological sabotage' and other forms of civil disobedience," and is endorsed by Abbey himself who is quoted as telling the organization: "Oppose, resist and if necessary subvert. Of course, I never advocate illegal action at any time. Except at night. . . ."

Perhaps if the group is really able to engage in civil disobedience (pranks, according to *Newsweek*), there will be no cause for alarm – but the activities in Abbey's book, as acknowledged by the characters themselves, are criminal, not civil, in nature, and it is hard to imagine a group of people enthusiastically inspired by Abbey's book foregoing the acts described in it indefinitely. Indeed, it seems hard to imagine the ecological sabotage of the book having anything to do with civil disobedience at all. Persons who engage in civil disobedience normally participate in some legally unacceptable activity in order to get

From *Environmental Ethics*, vol. 4 (1983): 291–2. © 1983 by Eugene Hargrove. Reprinted with permission from the author.

arrested and thereby publicize their cause. The book, however, is filled with paramilitary operations for the purpose of destroying equipment and bridges. The participants try to keep their identities a secret and avoid capture. These activities seem closer to terrorism than civil disobedience, and seem to differ from them only in the preference for killing machines, rather than humans, a preference abandoned easily by the most militant member of the gang once the police arrive.

Although presumably the organization, like the book, has no clear philosophy, there does seem to be something there implicitly and it is more radical than any position put forward in the field of environmental ethics to date. In the past, environmental ethicists have talked about *extending* moral considerability in some way to include nature (Leopold and his followers, for example), but here nature, rather than being included, is given priority. This nature chauvinism is a nonhumanistic, indeed an antihumanistic, position, and probably has much to do with Abbey's earlier attitudes in *Desert Solitaire:* "I'm a humanist; I'd rather kill a *man* than a snake."

I would doubt that many members of Earth First! would be ready at this time to put Abbey's sentiments into action; however, as their practice forms their doctrine, who knows where their theory will lead them? We live in a society socially and politically dedicated to the protection of property (including construction equipment and bridges). As Locke put it long ago, a man who destroys property declares a state of war with society and in that state, society has the right to destroy the offender "as a *Lyon* or a *Tyger*, one with whom Men can have no Society nor Security." This right was invoked when the Vietnam veteran took his stand in the book, and it is what will inevitably happen in real life if authentic ecological sabotage begins. From there, it should be a small step for the surviving and uncaptured saboteurs to begin protecting the snake by killing the man.

In the twentieth century, terrorism (the use of force as a political weapon to demoralize, intimidate, and subjugate) has been the last resort when normal political action was frustrated and improvement through peaceful means was absolutely impossible. The environmental movement, however, with its beginnings in the nineteenth century with Yosemite and Yellowstone and culminating in the 1960s and 1970s with the wilderness, endangered species, and clean air and water acts, to name a few, has been an immensely successful political movement. In this context, what could be the practical, ethical, or political justification for acts which could easily create a terrible backlash undoing all the good that has been done and preventing future accomplishments?

---

42 Earth First! and *The Monkey Wrench Gang*

Edward Abbey

Thank you for inviting me to respond to your editorial regarding Earth First! and *The Monkey Wrench Gang* [see *Environmental Ethics* 4 (1982): 291].

So far as I know, Earth First! as an organization – though it's more a spontaneous grouping than an organization, having neither officers nor bylaws – is *not* "pledged to ecological sabotage." If *Newsweek* said that, *Newsweek* is hallucinating (again). We *are* considering acts of civil disobedience, in the usual sense of that term, when and where they might be useful. For example, if the Getty Oil Co. attempts to invade Gros Ventre wilderness (Wyoming) with bulldozers, we intend to peaceably assemble and block the invasion with guitars, American flags, live human bodies, and maybe an opposing D-9 tractor. If arrested, we shall go to jail, pay the fines, and try again. We invite your readers to join us. A good time will be had by all.

As for the book, please note that *The Monkey Wrench Gang* is a novel, a work of fiction, and – I like

From *Environmental Ethics*, vol. 5 (1983): 94–6.

to think – a work of art. It would be naive to read it as a tract, a program for action, or a manifesto. The book is a comedy, with a happy ending. It was written to entertain, to inspire tears and laughter, to amuse my friends and to aggravate our enemies. (Aggravate their ulcers.) So far about a million readers seem to have found that approach appealing.

The book does not condone terrorism in any form. Let's have some precision in language here: terrorism means deadly violence – for a political and/or economic purpose – carried out against people and other living things, and is usually conducted by governments against their own citizens (as at Kent State, or in Vietnam, or in Poland, or in most of Latin America right now) or by corporate entities such as J. Paul Getty, Exxon, Mobil Oil, etc., etc., against the land and all creatures that depend upon the land for life and livelihood. A bulldozer ripping up a hillside to strip-mine for coal is committing terrorism; the damnation of a flowing river followed by the drowning of Cherokee graves, of forest and farmland, is an act of terrorism.

Sabotage, on the other hand, means the application of force against inanimate property, such as machinery, which is being used, for example, to deprive human beings of their rightful work, as in the case of Ned Ludd and his mates; sabotage – for whatever purpose – has never meant and has never implied the use of violence against living creatures. The characters in *Monkey Wrench* engage in industrial sabotage in order to defend a land they love against industrial terrorism. They do this only when it appears that in certain cases and places all other means of defense of land and life have failed and that force – the final resort – becomes morally justified. Not only justified but a moral obligation, as in the defense of one's own life, one's own family, one's own home, one's own *nature*, against a violent assault.

Such is the basis of my characters' rationale in *The Monkey Wrench Gang*. How the reader chooses to interpret all this is the reader's business. And if the reader is impelled to act out in real life the exploits of Doc, Bonnie, Slim, & Hayduke, that too is a matter for decision by the individual conscience. But first and last it should be remembered that the book is a fiction, make-believe, a story, and no more than a story.

As for my own views on environmental ethics, I prefer to state them in the essay form: see *The Journey Home* (1977), *Abbeys Road* (1979), and *Down to the River* (1982).

---

43   More on Earth First! and *The Monkey Wrench Gang*

Dave Foreman

I certainly agree that the question of monkeywrenching is an important one and deserves discussion. I am currently preparing an essay justifying such action which I'll send to you for later consideration in *Environmental Ethics*.

I am sorry that you wrote your editorial [*Environmental Ethics* 4 (1983): 291] based on such sketchy knowledge of Earth First! [. . .]

It is important to point out that Earth First! is a movement and not a formally organized group. There is a wide variety of opinion within EF! over monkeywrenching. As editor of the *Earth First!*

Journal, I do not advocate it nor do I *not* advocate it. It is a personal decision.

I would like to touch on two points in your editorial. You charge that there is no underlying philosophy in *The Monkey Wrench Gang* and therefore none in Earth First! I have written, "Let our actions set the finer points of our philosophy." Too often, philosophers are rendered impotent by their ability to act without analyzing everything to an absurd detail. To act, to trust your instincts, to go with the flow of natural forces, *is* an underlying philosophy. Talk is cheap. Action is dear.

You say the environmental movement has been immensely successful. Only on the surface, I think. It appears to be successful because it asks for so little and actually threatens the corporate state to such a minor extent. The great ecologist Paul Sears suggested preserving twenty-five percent of our land in a wilderness condition. We've protected only one and one-half percent. The Sierra Club has asked for only three percent. That's success? The California condor faces imminent extinction. The grizzly may soon be eliminated from the lower forty-eight states. That's success? Thousands die each year because of toxic substances in our air, our water, our soil, our food, our mother's milk – that's success?

44 Editor's Response

Eugene Hargrove

Although I now have a deeper understanding of Earth First! thanks to the two letters above and the material supplied by Dave Foreman, my concern over the ethical or moral implications of the nonorganization remains unchanged. In an article called "Earth First!" (published in *The Progressive*, 1981, and reprinted in the February 1982 issue of *Earth First!*), Foreman writes that one of the original purposes of Earth First! was "to inspire others to carry out activities straight from the pages of *The Monkey Wrench Gang* even though EARTH FIRST!, we agreed, would itself be ostensibly law-abiding." A sample of this approach seems to be the following statement by Foreman from the August 1982 issue of *Earth First!*: "While we don't advocate illegal acts in defense of Mother Earth, we admire those who have the guts to fight." The group's admiration of monkeywrenching seems to be a legal euphemism intended to encourage ("inspire") others to commit acts of sabotage while evading legal responsibility for those acts. Even if this tactic is successful, it is hard to imagine how the group can avoid moral responsibility for acts which are both criminal and morally reprehensible by normal moral or ethical standards. While I can understand the frustration of the nonleaders of the nonorganization that so little was accomplished by environmentalist administrators during the Carter Administration (the reason Earth First! was started), there are still legal and moral alternatives which could be pursued. An environmentalist political party like the Green party in Germany, for instance, might provide the support that environmentalist administrators need to accomplish their goals – without the legal and moral difficulties Earth First!ers may face in the near future. I am amused by Foreman's characterization of philosophy as cheap talk, since the nonphilosophy of the nonorganization, in order for the group to avoid criminal prosecution, also has to be all talk and no action.

PART VI

WHAT ARE THE CONNECTIONS BETWEEN REALISM, RELATIVISM, TECHNOLOGY, AND ENVIRONMENTAL ETHICS?

A   Subjectivist Environmental Ethics

45   Meta-Ethics and Environmental Ethics
     Robert Elliot

B   The Social Construction of Nature

46   How to Construe Nature: Environmental Ethics
     and the Interpretation of Nature
     Roger J. H. King

47   The Trouble With Wilderness
     William Cronon

C   Ecological Realism

48   Virtually Hunting Reality in the Forests of Simulacra
     Paul Shepard

D   Environmental Ethics and the Philosophy of Technology

49   Technology and the Limits of Nature
     David Rothenberg

Introduction

Whether the value in nature upon which normative standards rest is independent of or dependent on human consciousness is the pre-eminent metaethical question in environmental ethics. Realism in environmental ethics is the position that value in nature exists independently, or objectively, of human consciousness. Relativism in environmental ethics is the position that value in nature exists dependently, or subjectively, upon human consciousness.

As Australian philosopher Robert Elliot points out in "Meta-Ethics and Environmental Ethics," it has been assumed by many environmental philosophers that metaethical objectivism is necessary for founding an environmental ethic. Avoiding the radical subjectivism of emotivism, Elliot argues for a more normatively robust inter-subjective metaethics in which shared valuational frameworks allow for prescriptive claims to be judged as empirically true or false. Certain claims, such as damming a river or relaxing fly-ash containment standards, should be able to be evaluated within the valuational frameworks of persons expressing opinions about such issues.

Elliot's subjectivist metaethics points toward another large and looming issue in environmental ethics, that of *social constructivism*. Social constructivism holds that the value of nature is relative to culture. On this account, "nature" is like a cosmic JumboTron onto which the human mind projects various socially constructed images of a great enveloping "other." Social constructivist themes have been elaborated by Arthur Lovejoy in *The Great Chain of Being*, Robin Collingwood in *The Idea of Nature*, Clarence Glacken in *Traces on the Rhodian Shore*, and Max Oelschlaeger in *The Idea of Wilderness* (all must-reads for the student of environmental ethics!).

Social constructivists, such as American philosopher Roger King in "How to Construe Nature," argue that the words "nature" and "wilderness" have no absolute, extra-social referent (in other words, that there really is no nature$_1$); rather, "nature" and "wilderness" are concepts resulting from complex constellations of social influences. What appear to be "truths" of nature are really truths about the cultural lens through which nature is perceived. Social constructivists do not necessarily deny that something material exists outside of our ideas, as Irish philosopher George Berkeley did, but that the *meanings* of "nature" and "wilderness" are relative to culture.

For example, the "nature" of Alfred Tennyson – "red in tooth and claw"[1] and Thomas Hobbes, where human life is "solitary, poore, nasty, brutish, and short"[2] – bears no resemblance to the "nature" of Shakespeare's pastoral plays or Thoreau's meditations. For Hobbes, the best thing for humans is to get *out* of the state of nature. In direct opposition, for Thoreau, the best thing for humans is to become immersed *in* the state of nature:

> [I]n Wildness is the preservation of the World. Every tree sends its fibres forth in search of the Wild. The cities import it at any price. Men plough and sail for it. From the forest and wilderness come the tonics and barks which brace mankind. Our ancestors were savages. The story of Romulus and Remus being suckled by a wolf is not a meaningless fable. The founders of every state which has risen to eminence have drawn their nourishment and vigor from a similar wild source.[3]

"In short, all good things are wild and free"[4] – certainly not the life in the wilderness Hobbes had in mind.

In my own life, Zion Canyon of the Virgin River and environs has provided a place of solace, a place I'd live if I could, a welcome escape from my hectic life in urban Salt Lake City. Imagine my shock when I read the description of Zion Canyon as a "stone box," a sort of prison:

> I found it to be a remarkable valley with high, vertical cliffs, towering upward from two to three thousand feet, and so completely locked that there was no outlet other than the way of entrance. From a picturesque point of view, it was grand, sublime, and majestic, but as a place of residence, lonely and unattractive, reminding one of living in a stone box; the landscape, a skyscraper; a good place to visit, and a nice place to leave.[5]

One person's refuge is another's jail cell.

Canadian environmental studies scholar Neil Evernden offers a useful explanation of how social constructivism affects environmental ethics. Evernden points out that there are two distinct meanings of the word "nature": (1) objective otherness and (2) culturally-constructed otherness which is either benign or threatening depending on the context. Evernden denotes the former usage with uppercase "Nature" and the common latter usage with the lowercase "nature."[6]

The problem, Evernden asserts, is that "nature" ≠ "Nature," yet pundits of opposing political agendas each assert that their "nature" = Nature: "The environmentalist and the industrialist possess differing ideas about the proper order of things."[7] Different concepts of nature are discernible even in the science of ecology, although ecology is supposed to be the foundational science when it comes to the description of natural systems.[8] The "hard" objective data of ecology is open to interpretation:[9] "Nature is, therefore, nowhere near as independent or as 'given' as we like to suppose."[10]

Worse: real nature, as supposedly described by scientific ecology, is mistaken for plastic nature, and enlisted to support competing political agendas.[11] In fact, Nature can be enlisted in defense of both environmentalism and industrialism:[12] "nature justifies nothing, or everything. Ecology is today's official voice on natural matters, an institutional shaman that can be induced to pronounce natural whatever we wish to espouse. Ecology is, in this sense, simply being used as a blunt instrument to help implement particular life-styles of social goals."[13] Thus all use of the allegedly "scientific" wisdom of ecology is nothing more than political posturing. For metaethical subjectivists in environmental philosophy, the essence of "nature" is dependent upon, and relative to, culture. For metaethical objectivists in environmental philosophy, the essence of "nature" is independent of culture.

American historian William Cronon popularized the notion of the social construction of nature in the widely read essay "The Trouble with Wilderness" in *The New York Times Magazine* (reprinted herein) and the longer lead essay in *Uncommon Ground*. Cronon assails the millennia-old dichotomy in the Western tradition between culture and nature: "Far from being the one place on earth that stands apart from humanity, it is quite profoundly a human creation."[14] With Evernden, Cronon argues that the "objective" nonhuman nature evoked to support normative positions is itself a product of culture. And by obsessively focusing on wild nature, as opposed to the non-wild nature of cities and suburbia and exurbia, Cronon argues that environmental-

ists have unwittingly allowed political forces hostile to conservation to gain credibility: "Considered as a cultural construct, wilderness does not even sustain the ground on which it itself can be defended. And so we have the ultimate irony: by not adequately defending and celebrating *non*-wild nature we have helped create a political coalition that threatens wild and non-wild nature alike."[15]

American interdisciplinarian Paul Shepard refutes the relativism of constructivism in "Virtually Hunting Reality in the Forests of Simulacra." Shepard targets social constructivists who argue that the ontological essence of an external world – nature – is beyond the reach of humans who argue that we humans are entangled in webworks of words, prisons of discursive language, whose representations of this external world are mere "interpretations." Shepard argues that this is little more than solipsism. A million nonhuman animal species prove the postmodern constructivists wrong. Nonhuman animals, who are not disoriented by the fog of language, are connected directly to the environment moment by moment. The naturalist has the advantage over the linguist in studying these concrete, tangible, ecological connections.

In an excerpt from *Hand's End*, American philosopher David Rothenberg weaves the variable meanings of "culture" and "nature" in the fabric of technology. Rothenberg argues that, in contrast to the Aristotelian separation of inventions and their uses, technology is never separate from the intentions that prompt us into action: "Technology does not exist without the human intent that drives it."[16] According to Rothenberg, technology defines the scope of human possibility within the context of nature. In this sense, through the practice of technology, we carve out a realm from nature which we can control but which was once beyond our control. This realm is the "environment."

This last point strikes at the core of the first question about the subject of environmental ethics mentioned in the introductory essay of this textbook: What are human beings? Humankind transforms itself through transforming nature. The process begins with the intention of transforming wild nature into something manipulable – transforming nature into artifice. To accomplish this, a tool is devised. Once the tool is implemented, the range of possible human activity is expanded, and in so doing human identity itself is redefined. This redefinition leads to new intentions, and the process begins anew (see figure 49.1 on p. 374). In Rothenberg's words,

"Our desires and intentions to act upon the world are themselves altered through the tools that we create to realize them. This is the essence of the philosophy of technology as human extension."[17]

Notes

1 "In Memoriam A. H. H," *The Poems of Tennyson*, p. 373.
2 *Leviathan*, p. 186.
3 Thoreau, "Walking," *Excursions*, p. 275. (See this volume, p. 93.)
4 Ibid., p. 287. (See this volume, p. 95.)
5 1870 description of Zion Canyon, Zion National Park, near Springdale, Utah, by photographer Charles Savage. In Richards, *The Savage View*, p. 66.
6 *The Social Creation of Nature*, p. xi.
7 Ibid., p. 6.
8 Ibid., p. 8.
9 Ibid., p. 4.
10 Ibid., p. xii.
11 Ibid.
12 Ibid., pp. 10, 16.
13 Ibid., p. 15.
14 *Uncommon Ground*, p. 69.
15 "The Trouble with Wilderness: A Response," p. 53.
16 *Hand's End*, p. xiii.
17 Ibid., p. 14.

A Subjectivist Environmental Ethics

---

45 Meta-Ethics and Environmental Ethics

Robert Elliot

I

There is an important distinction to be borne in mind between (i) theories about what has value and (ii) theories about what it is for a thing to have value. The first kind of theory is a normative theory, at least in the sense that it endeavours to specify just what values there are. The second kind of theory is a meta-ethical theory; loosely, it attempts to explain the nature of value. Quite obviously (i) and (ii) are connected. If someone claims that X is a value, or that 0 has value, and if X could not be a value, or 0 could not have value, then he or she would be mistaken. Theories of the second kind constrain theories of the first kind; they may be thought of as demarcating an area of possible normative theories.

This provides the basis for a cluster of closely related arguments against the possibility of an environmental ethic. If successful, such arguments are decisive since they do not show merely that an environmental ethic is at odds with entrenched normative moral theories; in fact it probably is. What the arguments would show is that an environmental ethic is impossible, self-contradictory, inconsistent, incoherent or the like. Such arguments attempt to connect an environmental ethic with meta-ethical objectivism of some kind or other and then to argue that objectivism is false or inconsistent. A variant is to argue that subjectivism is the correct meta-ethic and

then to attempt to demonstrate that subjectivism cannot sustain an environmental ethic. The appropriate environmentalist response to these moves is to argue for one of: (A) objectivism has not been shown false, incoherent, inconsistent, or the like; or (B) an environmental ethic does not require an objectivist meta-ethic since a subjectivist meta-ethic is adequate to the task. I shall argue for (B), having first spelt out the reasons why (A) is not an attractive option.

II

Meta-ethical objectivism is seen by some, for example McCloskey 1980, Godfrey-Smith 1980, Mannison 1980, and Regan 1981, to be necessary to provide the required support for an environmental ethic. Certainly an objectivist meta-ethic would leave open the possibility that the objects of concern for deep ecologists are indeed appropriate objects of value. If an object's value is determined solely by the presence or absence of some non-natural property objectively possessed, then it is at least possible that rocks, trees, lakes, mountains or whole ecosystems should possess this property. If this possibility turned out to obtain, then many of the claims made by advocates of an environmental ethic would find theorietical support. For example, support would be given to the claim that the natural environment has intrinsic

From *Metaphilosophy*, vol. 16, nos. 2 & 3 (April/July 1985): 103–17.

value independently of any actual, or even possible, assignments of value to it by valuers. In other words, some theoretical basis would be given to the claim that possible worlds that are devoid of valuers nevertheless possess intrinsic value.

Perhaps most importantly, an objectivist meta-ethic would give sense to the injunction that human chauvinism should be rejected. One thing that characterises one variety of human chauvinism is its identification of value with valuings by human beings. Things are said to be of value insofar as they answer back to, satisfy or serve the interests, attitudes, desires or preferences of human beings. An objectivist meta-ethic does leave open a way for tackling this normative position. It provides a theoretical base for the creation of a competing normative ethic. However, it does not provide normative support for the ethic over and above providing the logical space for it. This can be seen once it is noted that many meta-ethical objectivists adopt a human chauvinist normative position (or some extension thereof). Thus it might be insisted that the objects of deep, ecological concern do not possess the requisite non-natural property, as McCloskey insists.

This is not to denigrate the strategic value of winning acceptance for an objectivist meta-ethic. For instance, if opposition to environmental ethics centred on a refusal to accept them as starters in the normative stakes, then, if someone who initially thought this way could be convinced of an objectivist theory of value, he or she would be rationally compelled to reconsider his or her initial response. In other words such a theory of value could be used as a lever; first, to persuade someone that an environmental ethic is a possible ethic and, second, to persuade someone to give serious consideration to the normative content of such an ethic. However, it is not clear just how much help an objectivist account of value is going to be beyond this. It is certainly not going to compel acceptance of an environmental ethic, since, as I have said, there is room for argument concerning the objects, states of affairs and so forth, to which objective value attaches.

Regan has some points to make about the connection between environmental ethics and an objectivist meta-ethic which are worth considering. He introduces the notion of *inherent goodness*, which, as far as I can understand it, is a species of intrinsic value. He makes some clarificatory remarks about the notion: (i) *inherent goodness* is independent of the attitudinal states of all conscious beings; (ii) inherent goodness is a supervenient property; (iii) inherent goodness is an objective property; (iv) the fitting attitude to objects possessing inherent goodness is admiring respect (Regan 1981, pp. 30–1). Regan appears to be suggesting that an object has inherent goodness utterly independently of any valuer. For instance, he contrasts his view with the view Wittgenstein espouses in the *Tractatus* to the effect that there is no value *in* the world. Regan claims that there is value in the world and that it can be discovered. He is not merely claiming that objects which have intrinsic value are valued for their own sakes and because of properties that they objectively possess. That view is compatible with the subjectivist claim that it is an evaluation by a valuer that brings value into the world. For example, it might be said that my positive valuation of temperate rain forest, because of the objective (non-moral) properties it possesses, confers value on it. Regan's claim is significantly stronger. Referring to the question of the value of wild stretches of the Colorado River, Regan says that '*the value of the river's being free* . . . is an objective property of the river' (Regan 1981, p. 31). He suggests that the value of the river is something it has completely independently of how it was, is, will be or could be regarded.

If Regan's view of inherent goodness is correct (and I should point out that he does not advance it with confidence) then the possibility of an environmental ethic is open. However, there is a catalogue of problems associated with meta-ethical objectivism which makes it decidedly unattractive. First, meta-ethical objectivists face the problem of explaining the kind of thing that non-natural intrinsic value is. Regan says it is an objective property which is supervenient on, or a consequence of, other objective properties of things. He also makes it clear that value is in no sense relational; it is supposed to inhere in the object itself. There is a certain mysterious flavour about values so construed. My complaint here is not exactly that which J. L. Mackie labels 'The argument from queerness' (Mackie 1977, pp. 28–9). I concede that the argument from queerness is in many ways an argument from ignorance. There are many kinds of things, for example transfinite ordinals, neutrinos, black holes and various other entities, from the more esoteric reaches of mathematics and physics, that strike me as mysterious. Learning the appropriate theory may render them much less so. However, it is not clear to me how the similar demystification is to proceed with the non-natural, non-relational properties that are identified with values. Moreover, Regan himself admits to a certain bafflement. He says that he is not sure which are the properties upon which inherent goodness (intrinsic value) supervenes and he is not clear about how we come to perceive the presence of the supervenient property. Given this, there would be some theoretical advantage in dispensing with objective intrinsic value.

The question of how we become aware of objective values is difficult. The usual claim is that we come to know them by means of intuition. And indeed modern, normative, moral philosophy plays fast and loose with this notion. Appeals to intuition are made to compel acceptance of normative claims, to defeat normative principles and so on. Understood as appeals to the details of commonsense moral theory or to the details of our moral pyschology such appeals are innocuous. They can be integrated into a thoroughly subjectivist meta-ethical theory. However, meta-ethical objectivism typically posits a faculty of moral intuition which somehow delivers insights into the value structure of the world. This is where the argument from weirdness gains a foothold once more. It is not clear what the moral sense is like. It is a theoretical anomaly.

Part of the reason that it is a theoretical anomaly is that it does not reveal the connection between the (presumably, cognitive) moral sense and the affective and the volitional. Regan, for example, says that there is an appropriate attitude which goes with the realisation that an object has inherent value. One might well ask why this is so. He remarks:

Respect is appropriate because this is a fitting attitude to have toward that which has value in its own right. One must realise that its being valuable is not contingent on one's happening to value it, so that to treat it *merely* as a means to human ends is to mistreat it. (Regan 1981, p. 31)

There is, here, at least a suggestion of a link between the cognitive and the affective and the volitional, since the realisation of inherent value is supposed to 'give rise to' the preservation principle. However, there is no obvious connection provided by the meta-ethic. I might note the presence of inherent goodness but simply be indifferent to it or even sneer. Perhaps the suggestion is that the moral sense is built into us as part of a larger unit which includes appropriately linked affective and volitional elements as well. In other words, in most of us the recognition of inherent goodness triggers certain emotions and

motivates us to act so as to preserve what has intrinsic value. But filling out the story this way shifts the meta-ethic back towards subjectivism.

There are also well known problems with the epistemology of non-natural objective values. For example, it is a possibility that all of a person's judgments about what is good and right turn out to be false. As Richard Brandt reports, 'one of the most eminent non-naturalists has remarked that, in complex situations, whether we apprehend our duty aright is very largely a matter of good fortune' (Brandt 1959, pp. 188–9).

If intrinsic value is literally an objective property of objects, states of affairs, actions and so on, then it is surprising that it should just now be discovered in wild nature. One reply is to argue that present environmental ethics have historical antecedents which likewise attribute intrinsic value to wild nature. Nevertheless the appeal of such ethics seems to be dramatically increasing and I do not think the objectivist can explain this as easily as the subjectivist. Have the shutters only just dropped from our moral sense that we may apprehend now what we previously could not? Are there more morally mature people around now than there used to be? Have we only recently succeeded in throwing off the distorting prejudices that made human chauvinism compelling? The phenomenon of environmentalism seems more easily explained in terms of attitudinal changes that have their source in such things as social, political and economic movements. Again the objection amounts to a difficulty rather than anything like a knockdown argument.

There are also problems in offering an account of how we come to learn to use the moral terms if their meanings are only explicable in terms of elusive, non-natural properties. It may be that clever meta-ethical objectivists are able to meet the various objections and solve the various problems to which I have alluded. However, their way forward does not appear either straight or easy. To this extent the existence of any dependency relation between an objectivist meta-ethic and an environmental ethic renders the possibility of the latter more remote.

Debates about which normative theory is correct would, irrespective of whether objectivism or subjectivism is correct, take the form of presenting a variety of situations, states of affairs etc. which are deemed to be valuable, in an attempt to derive general principles that systematise our valuations. Thus the environmental ethicist may forcefully direct the attention of the disputants to situations that he or she thinks clearly show that the objects of his or her special concern do have value. He or she might then suggest general principles that offer an explanation of this and which may highlight similarities between such situations and others that are more widely accorded value. Such effects might be challenged by the production of counter-examples to the general claims, by pointing to inconsistencies and contradictions, and by the production of alternative explanations of why the situations which the environmentalist erroneously thinks have value merely seem to have value. In short, the dispute between environmental ethicists and their opponents will take a form with which we are quite familiar in the context of disputes between competing normative ethics or narrower scope. Acceptance of meta-ethical objectivism as against subjectivism does not alter the structure, the dynamic of normative disputes about environmental ethics. Such disputes do not become possible only within the framework of an objectivist meta-ethic. I turn now to a discussion of meta-ethical subjectivism.

III

A subjectivist might claim that an object or state of affairs has value if and only if it is valued by some valuer. The 'is' is to be read in a way that allows an object to have value even though it is not presently valued by any valuer. For example, it may be that no one presently existing values to any degree whatsoever the continued existence of the snaildarter. However, a subjectivist might claim that it has value if it will be valued at some future time by some valuer. I shall suggest presently that this is not in fact a theory about value so much as a theory about what has value. For the moment though, let us try to think of it as the former, and trace the consequences for an environmental ethic.

There are two things an environmental ethicist might want to say that are precluded by this version of subjectivism. First, it does not allow him to claim that there are future states of affairs that have value even though there is no one around, and never will be anyone around, who places any value on them whatsoever. This can be stated somewhat more formally:

Claim$_1$: Possibly there is some X at time$_a$ which has value and which is not valued by any valuer at time$_a$.

This falls foul of the first version of subjectivism because that version says:

Principle$_1$: If X has value then X is valued by some valuer contemporaneous with X.

It is here claimed that an object or a state of affairs has value if and only if it is valued by some valuer, and only if it affects such a valuer's state of mind. The point of the second clause is to rule out the following kinds of case. P claims that he values the continued existence of the Amazon rain forests even after he is no longer around to think about them, enjoy them, perceive them and the like. No-one else shares P's valuation, and so some might suggest that the rain forests would no longer have value. They have, however, been valued at some time by someone so without the additional clause they would continue to be bearers of value.

Strictly speaking, it is not objects which have value on this view, rather it is objects at a time which have value. The basic idea is that values cease to exist when valuers cease to exist. Value may attach to objects for a while and then fail to attach and then attach once more. Values will vary as valuations vary.

The second thing that this version of subjectivism prohibits is the claim that even if there had never been any valuer, the objects of his special concern would nevertheless have value. We can imagine a world in which there are complex forest eco-systems that do not include valuers. The environmentalist might want to claim that such a world has value and that, from a value point of view, it is preferable to other worlds (maybe even the actual world). Clearly this violates Principle$_1$. It may be more formally rendered as:

Claim$_2$: In a world other than the actual world and in which there are no valuers there is possibly some X which has value.

Claim$_1$ and Claim$_2$ are certainly prominent elements in various environmental ethics that have been advocated and there is a tension between them on the one hand and the first version of subjectivism on the other.

There are, however, numerous ways in which some of the concerns of an environmental ethic can be fitted to this first version of subjectivism. To begin with there is no restriction on the kind of thing that can have value: anything can, provided that it is actually, or will be, valued. On this view forests, lakes, mountains, complex eco-systems and so forth can all have value. Environmentalist policies such as the preservation of wilderness areas, the conservation of resources, the maintenance of species diversity can all be supported within the framework provided by this theory of value. Certain reasons cannot be advanced in defense of these policies of course. Thus it is out of court to argue that national parks should be created so as to ensure that pieces of wilderness will exist long after human, even animal, life is extinct.

I maintained earlier that this first version of subjectivism is a normative theory in disguise. It is this in two ways at least. First, as I stated it, it embodied the following normative value: whatever is valued by anyone has value (restricted in the way appropriate to the first version of subjectivism). Indeed some philosophers, notably R. M. Hare, have attempted to devise a full normative position, embodying such a principle, from purely conceptual considerations. However, such attempts do not succeed. Conceptual reasons alone cannot compel one to accept the valuations of others and somehow to accommodate them (e.g. by adopting a Harean preference utilitarianism) within one's own valuations. (See, for example, Robinson 1981.)

Second, there is a tendency to turn this kind of subjectivism into a strange kind of objectivism. Thus my valuing a particular stand of mountain ash is somehow conceived of as generating a property which independently, but additively, attaches to the stand of mountain ash. The picture that emerges is one of the stand of mountain ash acquiring value independently of my valuations but not independently of valuations. Despite the connection that is posited between the value of the object and the valuers who place some value on it, what we end up with is a kind of objectivism in which the value is somehow 'out there in the world'. My saying that an object has value is, so far as subjectivism is concerned, ultimately analysable in terms of my attitudes. One thing to which I might not have a favourable attitude is the anti-environmental attitude of someone else. The mere fact that someone else attributes negative value to the stand of mountain ash need not impress me. It only need impress me if my normative moral theory requires that I take account of the preferences of others. Claiming that it is my attitudes, in some suitably broad sense, that determine the normative theory on the basis of which I make evaluations, does not in the least compel me to give the same weight, or any weight, to the attitudes of others.

Subjectivism is a meta-ethical theory and normative elements need to be disentangled from any attempt at articulating it. Part of what went wrong with the version of subjectivism discussed above is that it failed to take sufficient notice of what is central to a subjectivist meta-ethic. What is distinctive of subjectivism is that it insists that valuations are made from, and are only answerable to, particular valuational points of view. Taking subjectivism seriously involves relating valuations to particular points of view, that is to the points of view of individual valuers. Co-incidence of valuational points of view is not ruled out. Quite the opposite would seem to be the case, since it is presumably the existence of shared, or partially shared, points of view that makes reasoned moral disputes possible and which gives point to moral arguments for and against policies, courses of action and such like.

Consider the case of P who attributes intrinsic value to rain forests. The question we need to ask ourselves is not how P's absence from a state of affairs which includes the rain forests affects our valuation of them. Rather the question is how it bears on P's valuation of them. Taking P at his word, he has implied that his valuation of the rain forests is not dependent upon his perceiving them, enjoying them, contemplating them or even on the possibility of his doing things of this kind. P has claimed that from his valuational point of view the continued existence of Amazon rain forests is preferable, other things being equal, to their destruction at any time whatsoever. All this is just to admit what subjectivism minimally requires, namely that the arbiter of questions about the values of objects, states of affairs, and so on, is a valuational viewpoint. If P asks Q whether the forests have value that is a question about what is true of forests given Q's valuational point of view. We can, in a general way, which makes reference to Q's preferences, desires, wants, and so on, specify the conditions in which Q would assert 'The continued existence of the forest is of value'. And P, of course, need not be swayed by how Q sees things from Q's valuational point of view.

Imagine that P and Q disagree over a preservationist policy. P supports it. Q objects to it. The dispute hinges on P's preparedness to assent to 'The continued existence of the forest is of value', whereas Q refuses to assent to it. P can be taken as claiming that given his valuational point of view (which presumably includes environmentalist values) it is a good thing that the policy be carried out. (Q, of course, can agree that this is correct from P's point of view.) Q, on the other hand, can be taken as saying that given her valuational point of view the policy ought not to be pursued. The dispute is a normative one: it is a dispute about items viewed from valuational points of view. The dispute is not one which can be resolved by an appeal to meta-ethical considerations. Thus if Q attempts to counter P by pointing out that the state of affairs which he claims to value is one which does not include him, it is open to P to respond that the relevant element in P's valuational point of view is represented by (i) rain forests have value, not by (ii) rain forests have value only if they are contemporaneous with me or some other valuer. That is sufficient to deflect Q's criticism. Thus subjectivism, properly understood and properly represented, allows for at least one of the distinctive claims of an environmentalist normative theory, namely Claim$_1$.

I have said that subjectivism does not necessitate, although it does permit, that valuational points of view other than one's own be taken into account when assessing intrinsic value. And when others do get a look in it is by courtesy of an aspect (for example, a commitment to tolerance) of one's own point of view. This relativisation of value to points of view is not just the relativisation of values to valuers. Quite obviously valuers are subject to moral development and even moral conversion, the result of which is either modest, or dramatic, change in valuational point of view. As those attitudes, desires, preferences and the like which are relevant to moral valuation change, so too do the frameworks with reference to which particular claims about value are judged. This suggests that the proper relativisation which subjectivism demands is to valuers at a time. And of course subjectivism does not require that the points of view of the one changing valuer count, in some sense or other, equally in determinations of value. There is nothing amiss with the claim that P at t_1 assents to 'Rain forests have value' and at t_2 dissents, provided there has been a change or shift in the relevant valuational elements in P's point of view between t_1 and t_2. One complaint that might be made about this relativisation of value to temporal stages of valuers is that it provides an insubstantial base upon which to ground any normative moral theory. I shall reply to this presently. It is useful, first of all, to see how this version of subjectivism handles Claim$_2$.

As I have noted, environmentalists make claims about the respective value of possible worlds even where some of those worlds are devoid of valuers. They may even claim that the value of certain worlds devoid of valuers is greater than that of the actual world. Are such judgments and comparisons incoherent? Two ways of showing that they are suggest themselves. First, one could argue that they are incoherent because they involve judgments about states of affairs which do not include valuers. This line of argument is not open for the kinds of reasons offered above. In other words Principle$_1$ is to be rejected. Second, one could concede that the absence of valuers does not by itself preclude value but maintain, nevertheless, that valuations cannot extend beyond the actual world.

This second option can be given two distinct glosses. To begin with, one could argue that it is practically impossible to have valuations which extend beyond the actual world (or, more liberally, beyond worlds close to the actual world). The claim then is that we do not know exactly what our valuations of these worlds are. I say 'are' rather than 'would be' for a reason that will be made clear in a moment. An appropriate response at this point is to refer to the large number of valuers who behave as if, speak as if, and act as if they do make exactly these kinds of valuations. In the face of this it seems highhanded to claim that such valuers are not making genuine, real valuations. It is simply a fact that people have preferences concerning worlds other than the actual world and that they are prepared to rank possible worlds in accordance with preferences which must really count as of the moral kind if any do. Even if this reply is inadequate the environmentalist does not lose out altogether, since the point of this first gloss is not that there is a logical bar to inter-world valuations. Rather there are alleged practical difficulties involved, for example ones to do with imaginative capacities.

It is important to realise that subjectivism does not suppose that valuers be able to estimate what valuations they would make if they were in different possible worlds. That might be an interesting enterprise in itself, and it might even be necessary given certain normative moral premises, but it is not required by meta-ethical subjectivism. Maybe if P were in a world quite different from this, he might turn out to have very different attitudes, desires, preferences, etc., to those he has in this world right now. That is no more relevant to questions about value than is the fact that P may be surprised by the attitudes etc. that he turns out to have in the future in the actual world. We should add one more element to the value-relativisation matrix. Along with point of view and time we should include world.

The second gloss that can be given of the second option does not rely on practical, empirical barriers to making inter-world preference rankings. The argument would instead be that such rankings are impossible for logical reasons. How the case for this would be made out I am at a loss to say. Once again it seems appropriate to posit the apparent counter-examples to the claim. People do make such preference rankings, for example there are possible worlds in which the Gordon River is not dammed that I rank higher than the actual world. The only possible constraint on logical grounds would seem to be that what is valued to degree X must be logically possible.[1] This said, there is no obvious reason why subjectivism cannot accommodate both of the environmentalist's distinctive claims. I do not have to be in other worlds in order to rank them value-wise. Inter-world valuations like intra-world valuations are made from the point of view of a valuer in the actual world.

Several paragraphs back I foreshadowed an objection to the subjectivism that relativised valuations to a valuer, a time, and a world. The suggestion was that such a meta-ethic would be insufficiently stable to ground a normative, moral theory. It is true that the value-related attitudes do change over time both at the individual and societal level. This is a fact about morality which a meta-ethic must accommodate and subjectivism does this very well. I suppose that objectivism may explain it also, in terms of increasing moral enlightenment, in terms of discoveries of new values and in terms of the realisation that previously held moral beliefs resulted from failure of the moral sense. On this view the development of normative moral theories is like the development of a science. However, I find the idea of a moral science, that is more than just the attempt to articulate and systematise (changing) elements in our moral psychology, difficult to swallow. What is clear is that subjectivism can tell a story about moral development which is at least as plausible as the story objectivism tells. I agree that subjectivism does introduce potential instability but, since it is unlikely that this potential will be realised, this is not a real worry. As a matter of fact changes in moral systems take place slowly, hence the widespread normative resistance to an environmental ethic despite local instances of rapid moral conversion. If valuational points of view changed both frequently and rapidly then normative moral philosophy might be impossible. The data base with which it worked would be too volatile.

A related worry that the environmental ethicist might have about subjectivism is that it leaves valuers as the source of, or at least essential to, values. While it does admit that Claim$_1$ and Claim$_2$ are perfectly coherent, it may not seem to secure the independence of values from valuers which was initially hoped for. The complaint then, is not that subjectivism renders environmental ethics anthropocentric. Clearly nonhumans can be valuers. Nor does subjectivism restrict the intrinsically valuable to whatever answers back to the interests of valuers, since forests, rivers, mountains may be counted as valuable even though they serve no one's interest at all. I think that the core of the worry is that if there had never been any valuers at any time then nothing would have intrinsic value. If complex eco-systems had developed on the earth without sentient animal life emerging, then those eco-systems would have contained nothing of value. This is true. It is simply to say what subjectivism admits, namely valuers are essential in order for value to be introduced into the world. And of course objectivism does not require this. However, given that I, for example, exist and given that I accept an environmental ethic, it is possible for me to evaluate the possibility described in the previous paragraph. If that other possible world had been the actual world, then it would have contained intrinsic value. It may even have contained more intrinsic value than the actual world. This is a judgment I may make given my valuational point of view at this time in this world. What more could the environmental ethicist require?

Perhaps what really worries the critic of subjectivism is that I might have turned out to have had a thoroughly human chauvinist valuational point of view. If I were the only valuer in the world, then it might be thought that the forests, and so on, would have no intrinsic value. In other words whether or not the forests have intrinsic value is going to depend on whether I happen to have the appropriate moral psychology. This problem can be handled in the same fashion as the previous one. If the world had been different and if I had, in that world, a human chauvinist ethic, then I would have been wrong in my valuations. Again this is a judgment which I make from my present valuational point of view. The case is analogous to one in which I review my past valuations. I once thought that forests did not have intrinsic value. Now I think that they do. From my present valuational point of view I may condemn my earlier one.

There are two things a critic might say at this point. First, he or she could observe that from my earlier evaluational point of view the later one may be concerned. Agreed. Second, he or she could observe that my present evaluational point of view might not be a lasting one: I might, for instance, revert to human chauvinism. Agreed. If these possibilities constitute problems which cannot but perturb the environmental ethicist, then there is nothing more I can say. However, I do not think that they should perturb him or her for two reasons. First, it is only while a particular normative ethic seems to us to represent and express our moral psychology that we are likely to want to elevate it to theoretical permanency. I admit to feeling this way. I am convinced that an environmental ethic is correct and its widespread violation does more than sadden me. However, if my moral psychology dramatically changed, then my attachment to an environmental ethic would dissolve. It should be remembered though, that the permanency of the environmental ethic, expressed in my valuational point of view, is tied inextricably to my commitment to it. Commitment to it is its guarantee. Now I think that this removes the critic's worry. The upshot of this is that the ethic will be around for as long as it matters to me that it is around and for as long as its rejection strikes me as unthinkable. Second, even if the worry remains it is not clear that it is removed by the step to meta-ethical objectivism. What should matter to an objectivist is that his or her moral beliefs mirror the moral truth. He or she must admit that there are many instances in which we are mistaken in our moral beliefs. We used to think X was right, but realise that we were mistaken. Leastways we think we were mistaken. However, we might later come to believe that our original judgment was correct; that we did not step from error into truth but slid from truth into error. In other words, objectivism offers no guarantee of permanency for normative ethics which goes further than the present constitution of our moral psychology. Subjectivism accepts that there are transformations in valuational points of view. By the same token, objectivism must accept that views (theories) about the moral facts change from time to time. Unless it can be shown that meta-ethical objectivism carries with it an epistemology that more or less guarantees the moral truth, it is difficult to see why it should be preferred to subjectivism. As far as I have established no such guarantee is provided. One person's self-evident moral truth may be another's self-evident moral falsehood; one person's rational insight may be another's intellectual error.

IV

The subjectivism that I have described allows for talk about the truth and falsity of moral judgments. Crude subjectivisms, such as emotivism, do not allow for this, and this places them at a disadvantage with respect to objectivism. To see how subjectivism can admit the truth or falsity of moral judgments, it is useful to give some attention to the meta-ethical theory developed by D. H. Monro (see Monro 1967).

Monro describes a view which might be called subjective naturalism. On this view moral judgments are held to be the kinds of things that are true or false and their truth or falsity is empirically determinable. To say that actions of kind K are good is to say that they are actions of which the individual making the claim approves. One way of understanding Monro is to take him to be offering a reductive analysis of moral judgments. Thus moral judgments turn out to be judgments about states of mind. To claim that abortion is wrong is simply to claim that one has a negative attitude towards acts of aborting human foetuses. When one's opponent claims that abortion is permissible he or she is to be understood as reporting that he or she has no such negative attitudes to acts of that kind.

An obvious objection to this view is that it fails to explain how conflicting moral judgments engage one another. On the subjective naturalist view conflicting judgments will pass each other by; they will simply be reports about the states of mind of their respective utterers.

A first response to this objection is to avoid the reduction of moral judgments to judgments about states of mind and to recast the theory in terms of the reduction of moral judgments to verbal *expressions* of states of mind. It follows from this view that moral judgments are not the kind of thing that can be true or false. At best they are either appropriate or inappropriate. (Still, in some reasonably clear sense they may be used to deceive, mislead, distort, tell lies. Certainly I can cause someone to hold false beliefs about my states of mind by expressing approval when I disapprove. This would be especially useful in combatting an extremely contrary adversary. However, one thing that this new reductive account has going for it is that it affords some explanation of the engagement of conflicting moral claims. The engagement is supposed to reside in the different attitudinal responses to the things under moral scrutiny.

It is not clear, however, that subjective naturalism cannot be built on in such a way to capture conflict of this kind. What is more, emotivism, in throwing cognitive content out of moral judgments, appears to throw out too much. If subjective naturalism may be objected to on the grounds that it fails to capture a salient element we tend to think is present, viz. disagreement, emotivism can be objected to on the grounds that it fails to capture another element we tend to think is present, viz. *cognitive* disagreement. It is at least as fair to say that moral dispute has elements of more straightforwardly empirical dispute, as it is to say that it involves emotive conflict. A subjectivism can be developed which does justice to both claims.

Even though, on Monro's view, moral judgments do not obviously conflict they have as their objects motivational structures which do. What I report on when I judge an action to be bad is my attitude to it (as an action of a certain kind). The attitude I have is going to have motivational force. Thus it might cause me to frustrate the action, to persuade the agent to desist, to express my attitude, to evince similar attitudes in others. The emotive conflict we notice in moral disputes might be attributed to the motivational or affective context in which the judgment is made. This involves admitting that the judgments themselves do not conflict but it does suggest that the judgment immediately generates emotive conflict which may manifest itself in conflicting or potentially conflicting actions. Given this, the advocacy of emotivism (or prescriptivism) over subjective naturalism loses some of its justification.

On a more sophisticated version of Monro's view, the judgment that an action is good reduces to the judgment that the action stands in a certain relationship to an additional set which may include, as well as attitudes, preferences and desires. We might call this the approval relationship. It should not be taken to be a relationship which holds between a valuer and an action, rather it holds between an action and an attitudinal set which may be formally represented as an hierarchical preference structure, a set of general principles, a system of norms or something of that ilk. Moral judgments are thus not straightforwardly reports about their utterers' states of mind. Instead they are judgments, the truth-conditions for which can be specified in terms of the approval relation. Cognitive content is returned to moral judgments without reducing that content to first-person avowals. My claim that A is right will be true, relative to a given valuational framework, if A stands in the approval relation to that framework. Moreover the judgment turns out to be about the action as much as about my current mental states.

Importantly, valuational frameworks may be shared; for example, by the one person at different times and by different people at the same time. If we share a valuational framework then when I claim that A is wrong and you claim that it is not, one of us must be mistaken. This is real cognitive disagreement. Similarly, when we agree that A is right the agreement is real. It is not a case, as it is with subjective naturalism, of two people making announcements concerning their respective mental states; rather both are asserting the very same thing.

Valuational frameworks will not always be shared of course. When they are not totally shared there will frequently be a partial sharing, an overlap, and so there will be scope for some cognitive disagreement. In those cases where there is no overlap at all there will still be the kind of disagreement which I suggested was present in the case of subjective naturalism. Valuational frameworks presumably are embedded in a motivational context. What is more, what is distinctive of those values, preferences, desires and the like which fall into the category of the morally relevant, is that they are (usually) values which we want others to share and adopt. At least they are values to which we would wish others' actions, and states of affairs, to conform; and they are values to which we may want all *our* future actions to conform. (There are problems here about moral development that need to be taken into account. Thus I might accept that a future time-slice of me will have altered values and allow, from my present valuational point of view, that this represents moral progress. This possibility is difficult to fit into the scheme I have described. One solution is to say that it is a possibility about which we are deceived. I shall not pursue the issue here.) It should be clear that the subjectivist meta-ethic I have described leaves logical space for an environmental ethic.

Note

1   Even this might be too strong since it is not obviously logically impossible that there be coherent valuations of logically impossible states of affairs.

References

Brandt, Richard. *Ethical Theory*. Englewood Cliffs: Prentice Hall, 1959.

Godfrey-Smith, William. "The Rights of Nonhumans and Intrinsic Values", in D. Mannison, M. McRobbie, R. Routley (eds), *Environmental Philosophy*. Canberra: Research School of Social Sciences, Australian National University, 1980, pp. 30–47.

Mackie, J. L. *Ethics: Inventing Right and Wrong*. Harmondsworth: Penguin, 1977.

Mannison, Don. "A Critique of a Proposal for an Environmental Ethic", in Mannison, McRobbie, Routley, *op. cit.*, pp. 52–64.

McCloskey, J. J. "Ecological Ethics and Its Justification: A Critical Appraisal", in Mannison, McRobbie, Routley, *op. cit.*, pp. 65–87.

Monro, D. H. *Empiricism and Ethics*. Cambridge: Cambridge University Press, 1967.

Regan, Tom. "The Nature and Possibility of an Environmental Ethic", *Environmental Ethics*, 3 (1981), pp. 16–31.

Robinson, H. M. "Imagination, Prescription and Desire", *Analysis*, 41, 2 (1981), pp. 55–9.

B The Social Construction of Nature

46 How to Construe Nature: Environmental Ethics and the Interpretation of Nature
Roger J. H. King

47 The Trouble With Wilderness
William Cronon

46 How To Construe Nature: Environmental Ethics and the Interpretation of Nature

Roger J. H. King

I

Does Nature have moral value? The belief that it does lies at the heart of environmental ethics. Yet two very different conceptions of environmental ethics reveal themselves when we consider how an answer to such a question might be justified. The most common approach would have us investigate the properties which natural beings possess. The assumption here is that when we know what these properties are, we will be in a position to deduce the value of Nature from a determination of the moral relevance of these properties. Appeals to sentience, self-consciousness, or life as criteria of moral considerability are examples resulting from this type of inquiry.

An alternative approach to environmental ethics, which I shall call "contextualist," would have us investigate the processes whereby Nature is construed as something which either possesses or fails to possess moral value. On this view, the value we should place on Nature cannot be deduced from the way Nature is itself; it depends on the place which Nature has acquired in our discourses with one another. In other words, the moral status of Nature is determined by the contexts within which non-human entities are incorporated into human cultural understanding. Since our ability to value the non-human world is mediated by this understanding of what Nature is, a contextualist environmental ethics would direct our attention to the social and political matrices within which human beings become cognizant of that world.

At a time when contemporary philosophy increasingly turns toward contextualist strategies of inquiry, writers in environmental ethics still seem to prefer the direct investigation of Nature itself. The strategy of contemporary environmental ethics remains predominately foundationalist. By this I mean that it defends its criticisms of human intervention in Nature by an appeal to a standard of conduct which lies outside human thought and culture. It is supposed that if we construe Nature as it *really* is in itself, then it will be possible to apprehend the obligations which Nature imposes upon human beings with the necessary philosophical certainty. The foundationalist strategy presupposes timeless criteria of moral relevance which forever remain free of the vicissitudes of cultural interpretation.

From *Between the Species*, vol. 6 (Summer 1990): 101–8. © 1990. Reprinted by permission of *Between the Species*.

But this strategy no longer seems philosophically plausible. Lying at the heart of this enterprise is the assumption that we can be clear about what Nature requires of us, since Nature is a determinate something, independent of our culturally based interpretation and understanding of what it is. Nature is not something in itself, but rather an artifact of human cultural life.

In order to pose the moral question of our obligations to Nature, we necessarily call before us a particular conception of what Nature is. It is to Nature as it is conceptualized and interpreted by historically situated human beings that we relate, not the brute and uninterpreted data of biological forces. To say that Nature is an artifact is to say that we have no access to a Nature in itself; our interpretation of Nature can never be independent of the intellectual, artistic, emotional, and technological resources available to us. These resources constitute the matrix, or context, within which what we call Nature appears to us and within which we interpret our experiences of the world.

Moral reflection necessarily poses the question of Nature's value from a standpoint that is contextualized within this matrix. Thus, the inquiry into Nature's moral status proceeds against the background of a prior interpretation and understanding of just what Nature is. But this understanding itself presupposes the historically specific matrix from within which we begin our interpretive effort. It follows from this that we cannot answer the question concerning Nature's moral value abstractly, that is, without first specifying a particular way of knowing Nature and the concrete results of that way of knowing. That the moral value of the environment depends upon a conception of Nature which in turn is relative to a particular way of knowing the world, is the contextualist premise for practicing environmental ethics.

As an example of the force of this contextualist premise, consider how beliefs about the value of wilderness areas depend upon the cultural context from within which it is perceived. When the Puritans first settled the wilderness of New England, they found it to be the grim and forbidding domain of Satan. Through the lenses of Puritan religious convictions, wild Nature possessed only negative value; religious duty demanded that it be cut down, cultivated, and domesticated.[1]

Following the advent of Romanticism, however, landscape painting helped to form a more benign relationship with those wilderness areas which fit the criteria of the picturesque and the sublime. Wild Nature took on an aesthetic value which could then be used to develop conservationist arguments of a moral kind.[2]

But in contemporary society, the aesthetic value of Nature as a spectacle must compete with economic constructions of the wilderness. Not only do wilderness areas contain valuable timber resources, but they offer economic opportunities for hunting, fishing, and other recreational uses with significant economic importance. These uses often lead to a degradation of the aesthetic values of wild areas.

These three perspectives construe Nature differently; for one, Nature is a religious entity – the domain of Satan – for another, it is an aesthetic entity – a picturesque or sublime view – and for a third, it is an economic entity – a commercially profitable resource. Any answer to the question of Nature's moral value, then, will necessarily be guided and informed by our conception of the Nature which is intended. Thus, inquiry into the moral status of Nature must inevitably return to a moral and political investigation of the social context within which Nature is constructed.

The view that Nature is constructed within particular cultural contexts conflicts with the usual practice of environmental ethics. Philosophers engaged in environmental ethics tend to presuppose the existence of a stable Nature that is both the victim of human wrong-doing and the source of guidance on the proper path of redemption.[3] Despite the internal differences between them, most of the competing views about environmental ethics agree on two things: first, the way in which we ought to treat nonhuman entities follows from the properties which those entities possess, so that Nature's admittance to participant status in the moral community depends upon its objective possession of the relevant qualifying characteristics. And second, the function of an environmental ethic is to help us to return from our alienation from Nature so that we may live more closely in harmony with it. This will happen when we recognize that Nature qualifies for moral consideration and act accordingly. But these two points only make sense if we also agree that our understanding of Nature and its moral law comes from unmediated access to the way that Nature is in itself. If this is not possible, then appeals to follow the dictates of Nature reduce to appeals to do what is right, as that is defined by the environmental ethic in question. Nature, therefore, is unable to play the independent justificatory role which foundationalist ethics requires of it.

II

The idea that Nature should be our moral guide appears in a number of different guises, depending on the moral theory in question. It informs the arguments of those who deny that we have moral obligations to Nature as well as those who affirm them. Let me clarify what I mean by this.

In his *Lectures on Ethics*, Immanuel Kant denies that we can have direct duties to animals because they lack certain features necessary to participate in the moral community.[4] In particular, they lack the capacity of reason and free will. Since animals do not possess these properties, we can have no moral relations with them directly, although we may have obligations *regarding* animals. For example, if other human beings will be adversely affected by our mistreatment of animals, then our direct obligations to other human beings require us not to mistreat animals. In any case, the question of the moral standing of animals depends, for Kant, on the objective properties which beings do or do not possess independently of how we think about them. It follows that Nature is disqualified from playing the role of victim or of moral guide from the Kantian standpoint.

The animal liberation movement attacks the Kantian perspective but retains its foundationalist framework.[5] Peter Singer argues, for example, that to be a member of the moral community a being must possess sentience, that is, the capacity to feel either pleasure or pain. Any being which has this property qualifies for moral respect, those which do not, remain outside the protection of moral strictures. Using this criterion, Singer extends the moral community to include certain species of animals which clearly can feel pleasure and pain.

Proponents of the "land ethic" articulated by Aldo Leopold in *A Sand County Almanac* criticize animal liberation theories because they focus too narrowly on the individual animal, with the result that they ignore the ecological wholes of which individual animals are a part.[6] While animal liberationists are primarily concerned with our treatment of domestic animals, the "land ethic" starts from a concern for wild biotic communities. Our moral concern should not be to avoid pain and suffering but, rather, to maintain the stability, integrity, and beauty of the biotic community as a whole. That is what has moral value. Thus, all aspects of Nature come to have moral value, from this perspective, insofar as they contribute to the stability, integrity, and beauty of the ecosystem.

The "land ethic" thereby greatly extends the scope of the moral community. Nonetheless, the argument supposes that Nature can only make a moral claim on human beings to the extent that it satisfies an objective demand, namely, that the natural entity in question be significant for the health of the ecosystem. If it does not have that property, or if it in some way is a threat to the health of the ecosystem, then that natural entity is excluded from moral protection. Thus, some proponents of the "land ethic" suppose that hunting is compatible with their moral concern for the stability, integrity, and beauty of the biotic community.[7]

Some members of the eco-feminist movement also follow the same sort of strategy.[8] The common commitment to foundationalism manifests itself differently in eco-feminism, however. The significance of the eco-feminist contribution to environmental ethics lies in its recognition that the environmental crisis is not merely a product of human relations to Nature. Rather, it is a symptom of oppressive relations between human beings as well. They draw a connection, then, between the culture's willingness to ignore the interests of nonhuman beings and the culture's willingness to ignore and suppress the interests and needs of women. Western philosophy has consistently drawn a distinction between culture and nature and associated men with culture and women with nature.[9] Patriarchal control of Nature is seen, therefore, as intimately bound up with patriarchal control of women.

For more radical members of the eco-feminist movement these parallels suggest the possibility that women are in fact "closer to Nature" than men. While men are fundamentally alienated from natural processes, women have managed to retain closer ties to Nature, and are thus in a privileged position to care for Nature and to guide the culture in its return to a way of life more in harmony with Nature. But this position also evinces the commitment to a Nature which exists independently of human culture. If we are to make sense of the notion that women are "closer to Nature" than men, we must first make sense of the notion that there is an objective Nature there to be "closer to" in the first place. We must agree, in other words, that these dualisms which separate men from women and culture from Nature are not merely patriarchal constructs, but reflections of the way in which Nature truly is.

The positions which I have just identified all share allegiance to the two points I mentioned earlier. They agree that our moral obligations depend upon what properties the object actually has and that a proper understanding of these properties will allow us to return to a close and harmonious moral relationship with the natural world. In the rest of this paper I shall indicate some aspects of the alternative position I am proposing.

III

In order to make Nature our guide in matters of morality we have to understand what Nature is. This, it seems to me, is more problematic an undertaking than many in environmental ethics suppose. Our understanding of Nature is the product of cultural institutions and the plurality of interpretations of the natural world which they make available. Before we can make Nature our moral guide, we must ask how our present understanding of Nature was constructed and how it has led us onto the particular path of environmental destruction we currently follow. From that standpoint we should ask *not*, how is Nature *really* constructed? Rather, we should ask, what understanding of Nature would support and sustain a life which is morally responsible both towards the environment and towards other human beings?

Several interpretive frameworks exist for approaching the question of how to construe Nature, although the cultural origins of these frameworks are often obscured by their proponents. For members of the Deep Ecology movement, for example, our problems with the environment stem from our one-sided anthropocentrism and concern with ever-increasing material consumption.[10] The anthropocentric tradition, which Deep Ecology attacks, perceives Nature as inferior to human nature because it lacks the properties of rationality and freedom which are essential to human moral status. Nature is thus perceived as out there to satisfy human needs and purposes, perhaps "given" by God for these ends.

For eco-feminism, on the other hand, it is the exploitive impulse inherent in men, or in the male principle as it is manifested in patriarchal institutions, which explains how it is possible for our culture to marginalize Nature as a force in moral deliberation. Patriarchal culture perceives Nature as an antagonist, an opponent to be conquered, subdued, and overcome. It perceives natural entities as competitors and threats which must be neutralized. Such a culture is symbolized by the male hunter who supposes that the life which is most in harmony with Nature is one given to the pursuit and killing of wild animals.[11]

And for Marxists and anarchists, a certain blindness towards the environment appears to be inherent in the capitalist mode of production.[12] Profit and efficiency have not motivated ecologically responsible productive practices. For the capitalist, Nature is perceived as a source of raw materials for mass production. Drained of moral value, it is a material universe to be used for the increase of private profit and advantage in the most economically efficient manner possible.

When I say that these are interpretive frameworks, I mean that these explanations of the environmental crisis do not just attack particular forms of human action, but also critique the particular ways of construing Nature which appear to justify the unwanted human action. Deep Ecology, eco-feminism, Marxism, and anarchism provide examples of the sort of frameworks without which defining what is morally problematic about human relations with the environment would be impossible.

Once we recognize the presence of interpretive frameworks such as those I have just identified, it becomes clear that without such frameworks, 'Nature' remains an empty term and the relevance of ethics to Nature becomes completely undecidable. If this is so, then Nature can only guide us if we accept the framework within which some particular Nature has already acquired a meaning and a value for us. And if we oppose specific human practices because of their effects on the environment, then our critique cannot simply appeal to Nature as foundation and legitimation, but, rather, must first seem to uncover the process of construing Nature which buttresses those practices and the habits of thought which motivate them. We might then try to articulate new interpretations of Nature that would motivate alternative practices.

IV

Let me say something briefly about two ways in which how we construe Nature in our present culture is a reflection of thought patterns intrinsic to cultural categories quite separate from any notion of a Nature in itself. First, we live in a society whose economic health depends upon expanding commodity production. We should expect, therefore, that Nature will have been enlisted to support this project. Second, we live in a society which has gradually objectified human beings in the process of transforming them into participants in capitalist processes of production. We might expect, therefore, to find that Nature, too, has been objectified as a consequence of this process.[13] In order to see this, we might ask, what interpretation of Nature would support the demands for economic growth which are part of the capitalist economy? Certainly, a view of nonhuman entities as containing spirits, needs, interests, or rights runs contrary to the desire to treat nature as a mere source of raw materials. Rather than following animistic constructions of Nature, our culture tends to give priority to a vision of Nature constructed by the natural sciences. This is true despite the fact that most people are ill-equipped to comprehend the world which is so constructed.[14] The dominance of the natural scientific view of Nature as the site of merely physical relations and forces does not just advance a particular cognitive project. It also gives legitimacy to the economic and political interests of those engaged in commodity production under present conditions by undermining alternative construals of Nature which would invest it with moral and aesthetic values capable of justifying a moral critique of the prevailing social system.[15]

Mass production can proceed most efficiently if Nature becomes invisible to human beings or is visible only as a commodity in the production process itself. It becomes invisible when the majority of the population no longer live in direct contact with the land nor make their livelihood from an understanding of the physical objects and processes of the environment.[16] For urban culture, Nature regains its visibility in the visual images of landscape painting, travel posters, television documentaries, and advertising photographs. These images have two significant features. First, they construe Nature as a spectacle that has value to the extent that it possesses certain aesthetic visual qualities. Nature is understood to be external to the everyday life of a person, a place to visit for relaxation or edification, like a museum or zoo, but not a place in which to live. As such, Nature is understood in terms of the masks held up by the artist and the leisure industry.

The second feature of these images is that they construct Nature as a commodity to be purchased by an otherwise passive consumer. One buys the leisure weekend, or the vacation package, in order to recuperate from the everyday life of work. But this purchase promotes only an external relation to what is purchased. It is not a living interaction but a passive appreciation of the spectacle, which one buys. And in the name of this purchase the economy is licensed to continue to destroy Nature through "business-as-usual" – to make the leisure industry both possible and necessary – while at the same time preserving selected bits of it for selective enjoyment.

To say that our culture seeks to render Nature invisible and to translate it into a human commodity does not entail that it has been fully successful. The unwillingness of people to move from economically depressed rural areas on account of the "way of life" that is possible there, reveals the extent to which economic rationality has failed to uniformly dominate the deliberations of individuals. People do not, in fact, think solely in terms of their economic advantage. However, within the framework of a capitalist society, such individuals expose themselves to the suspicion that they must then be responsible for any consequent economic harm which they suffer, since they have failed to act in a fully rational manner. But that is precisely the problem. What it is reasonable to do, and what we can truly and literally say about the natural world depend upon the discourses of the dominant mode of thinking, in this case on capitalist economics and the natural sciences. Alternative patterns of thought and action inevitably appear marginal and eccentric. As such they are more easily ignored.

At this point, we must resist asking whether economic and natural scientific discourses *correctly* characterize Nature as it *really* is. Since what Nature is a function of a particular way of knowing and thinking about it, we might instead ask, who is empowered and who is subjugated by construing Nature in economic and natural scientific terms?[17] Putting the question this way side-steps our impulse to engage a definition of Nature as if all that were at stake was a question of fact. It acknowledges the pragmatic or performative dimension of any understanding of Nature. We are led, that is, to evaluate the merits of a view of Nature not simply according to the canons of scientific method or economic efficiency, but also with regard to its practical moral and political implications for our lives and what we value. And this is no small matter. It is clear that the dominant construal of Nature ignores and marginalizes other forms of understanding and living in the world. This makes it difficult for us to perceive other ways in which Nature exists or to take seriously those who do perceive the world in ways which deviate from the mainstream perspective.

V

I am suggesting, then, that inquiry into Nature's moral value cannot be separated from inquiry into the ways in which we construe Nature to defend or attack the economic, social, and political practices and institutions of our society. It is no accident that the environmentalist movement has an uphill struggle trying to argue that Nature has intrinsic moral value or moral standing independent of human self-interest. Such conclusions require that we understand and perceive Nature in ways that are different from those which currently sustain the mainstream activities of Western industrial cultures.

But what alternative do we really have, it might be asked, given that we cannot simply decide to believe that trees and animals have spirits or that they are gods, just because that might be a view of Nature which would limit our aggression against it? I am not sure that a clear, socially meaningful alternative does exist at the present time. Nonetheless, there is a model for what we might do if we take seriously the need to re-construe Nature as a part of re-valuing it. This model may be found in the writings of literary naturalists.

It is significant that most of the great figures in the environmentalist tradition are literary not philosophical writers. Thoreau, Burroughs, Muir, Leopold, Abbe, and Lopez, to name a few, all stand out as proponents of a moral relationship with Nature, yet are best known for their narrative depictions of particular settings, not for their abstract, theoretical arguments. What this literary tradition makes possible is a moral and philosophical association with place which is not narrowly economic, self-interested, or political. It re-introduces subjectivity and moral connectedness into the landscape. Walden Pond – to take the best known example – is no longer just a small lake near Concord, Massachusetts.[18] It functions as a sign of Thoreau's ideas about the way one should live life. As such, Walden Pond has become a symbol which serves to recall Thoreau's writing and the respect and admiration for natural beings which he helped to promote.[19]

In the language of rhetoric, naturalist literature empowers the landscape through the figure of metonymy.[20] That is, the landscape acquires agency through this literature because it creates a close connection between places and particular ideas, values and experiences. To say that the landscape can speak to us is no more mystical and obscure than to say that the White House denied all knowledge, or that the Church announced its disapproval; all three are metonymic statements. Thus the association of particular ideas and narratives with landmarks in Nature provides one avenue by which Nature can be re-invested with a subjectivity denied to it by current exploitive interpretations. The broader task implied here is to incorporate physical into social and moral geography in such a way that Nature ceases to function invisibly, external to the everyday life of human beings.[21]

At a time when philosophers are acknowledging that the pursuit of philosophical absolutes and indubitable certainties is a bankrupt project, it is unfortunate to find the tradition of environmental ethics looking to Nature to find just such treasures.[22] Appeals to "follow Nature" or to live in "harmony with Nature" mask the contexts which have given birth to the image of Nature one is to follow or harmonize with. If environmental ethics is to be critical, then it must participate in the discourses which construe Nature and reflect on the desires, needs, and motivations which constitute those discourses. Only from within this participation does it make sense to ask the normative question, how ought we to relate to Nature from the moral point of view?

Notes

1   Cf. Peter N. Carroll, *Puritanism and the Wilderness: The Intellectual Significance of the New England Frontier* (New York: Columbia University Press, 1969).

2   One example of an argument using aesthetic value as the basis for a moral argument can be found in Mark Sagoff, "On Preserving the Natural Environment," *Yale Law Review* 84 (1974): 245–52, 264–7.

3   An exception to this way of seeing the problem can be found in Steven Vogel's "Nature, Science, and the Bomb," *Tikkun* 3 (4): 19–21, 86–8; and "Marx and Alienation from Nature," *Social Theory and Practice* 14 (Fall 1988): 367–87.

4   Immanuel Kant, *Lectures on Ethics*, trans. by Louis Infield (Indianapolis: Hackett Publishing Company, 1930), pp. 239–41.

5   Statements of the animal liberation position include: Tom Regan, *All that Dwell Therein: Animal Rights and Environmental Ethics* (Berkeley: University of California Press, 1982); *The Case for Animal Rights* (Berkeley: University of California Press, 1983); Peter Singer, *Animal Liberation: A New Ethics for Our Treatment of Animals* (New York: Random House, 1975); Singer, ed., *In Defense of Animals* (Oxford: Basil Blackwell, 1985); and Regan and Singer, eds., *Animal Rights and Human Obligations* (Englewood Cliffs, NJ: Prentice-Hall, 1976).

6   Aldo Leopold, *A Sand County Almanac* (Oxford University Press, 1966); see also, J. Baird Callicott, *In Defense of the Land Ethic: Essays in Environmental Philosophy* (Albany: State University of New York Press, 1989), and Callicott, ed., *A Companion to A Sand County Almanac: Interpretive and Critical Essays* (Madison: The University of Wisconsin Press, 1987).

7   Cf. J. Baird Callicott, "Animal Liberation: A Triangular Affair," in Callicott, *In Defense of the Land Ethic*, pp. 15–37.

8   Leonie Caldecott, Stephanie Leland, eds., *Reclaim the Earth: Women Speak Out for Life on Earth* (London: The Women's Press, 1983); Andree Collard, with Joyce Contrucci, *Rape of the Wild: Man's Violence against Animals and the Earth* (Bloomington: Indiana University Press, 1989); Mary Daly, *Gyn/Ecology: The Metaethics of Radical Feminism* (Boston: Beacon Press, 1978); Susan Griffin, *Woman and Nature: The Roaring Inside Her* (New York: Harper and Row, 1978); Marti Kheel, "The Liberation of Nature: A Circular Affair," *Environmental Ethics* 7 (1985): 138–63; Carolyn Merchant, *The Death of Nature: Woman, Ecology, and the Scientific Revolution* (San Francisco: Harper and Row, 1980); Ariel Kay Salleh, "Deeper than Deep Ecology: The Eco-Feminist Connection," *Environmental Ethics* 6 (1984): 339–46.

9   Cf. Karen Warren, "Feminism and Ecology: Making Connections," *Environmental Ethics* 9 (1987).

10 For significant statements of the Deep Ecology position, see Bill Devall, George Sessions, *Deep Ecology: Living as if Nature Mattered* (Salt Lake City: Peregrine Smith Books, 1985); Arne Naess, "The Shallow and the Deep, Long Range Ecology Movement: A Summary," *Inquiry* 16 (1973): 95–100; Michael Tobias, ed., *Deep Ecology* (Avant Books, 1988).

11 This view is found in Callicott, *In Defense of the Land Ethic*; Jose Ortega y Gassett, *Meditations on Hunting*, trans. by Howard B. Wescott (New York: Charles Scribner's Sons, 1972); Paul Shepard, *The Tender Carnivore and the Sacred Game* (New York: Scribner's, 1973).

12 Important statements of the anarchist position can be found in Murray Bookchin, *The Ecology of Freedom: The Emergence and Dissolution of Hierarchy* (Cheshire Books, 1982), and *Post-Scarcity Anarchism* (Montreal: Black Rose Books, 1971); Andre Gorz, *Ecology as Politics* (Boston: South End Press, 1980).

13 Stuart Ewen's book, *Captains of Consciousness: Advertising and the Social Roots of the Consumer Culture* (New York: McGraw Hill, 1976), offers useful insights into the important role which advertising has played in bringing about the objectification of workers within capitalism as a part of the strategy of neutralizing opposition to capitalist work conditions. This is useful because advertising is one of the significant sources of our present understanding of what Nature is.

14 George Steiner underlines the extent to which mathematical and scientific languages are not translatable into the natural languages of everyday discourse in "The Retreat from the Word" in *George Steiner; A Reader* (New York: Oxford University Press, 1984), pp. 283–304.

15 Cf. William Leiss, *The Domination of Nature* (Boston: Beacon Press, 1974), especially Part Two, "Science, Technology, and the Domination of Nature."

16 See Ewen, *Captains of Consciousness*.

17 This question is inspired by Michel Foucault's conception of power as expressed in "Two Lectures" and "Truth and Power" in *Power/Knowledge; Selected Interviews and Other Writings, 1972–1977*, ed. by Colin Gordon, trans. by Colin Gordon, Leo Marshall, John Mepham, Kate Soper (New York: Pantheon Books, 1980), pp. 78–133.

18 Henry David Thoreau, *Walden* (Thomas Y. Crowell Company, 1961).

19 A "symbol" is a particular kind of sign. According to C. S. Peirce, a symbol signifies its object because of a conventional use of the sign to signify that particular object. The conventionality of the signification differentiates symbols from other signs such as icons or indexes. Cf. Peirce, "Logic as Semiotic: The Theory of Signs," in *Philosophical Writings of Peirce*, ed. by Justus Buchler (New York: Dover Publications, 1955), pp. 98–119.

20 The connection between symbols and metonymy is made by Chaim Perelman in *The Realm of Rhetoric*, trans. by William Kluback (Notre Dame, London: University of Notre Dame Press, 1982), p. 102.

21 These remarks are derived from Keith H. Basso's essay on the use of geographical landmarks in the historical/moral narratives of the Apache Indians to bind the moral narrative to specific locations in the physical world of the community. Cf. "'Stalking with Stories': Names, Places, and Moral Narratives Among the

Western Apaches," in *On Nature: Nature, Landscape, and Natural History*, ed. by Daniel Halpern (San Francisco: North Point Press, 1987), pp. 95–116.

22 In Anglo-American philosophy, one of the most influential figures in this attack on foundationalism has been Richard Rorty. Cf. *Consequences of Pragmatism: Essays 1972–1980* (Minneapolis: University of Minnesota Press, 1982), and *Philosophy and the Mirror of Nature* (Princeton: Princeton University Press, 1979).

47 The Trouble With Wilderness

William Cronon

Preserving wilderness has for decades been a fundamental tenet – indeed, a passion – of the environmental movement, especially in the United States. For many Americans, wilderness stands as the last place where civilization, that all-too-human disease, has not fully infected the earth. It is an island in the polluted sea of urban-industrial modernity, a refuge we must somehow recover to save the planet. As Henry David Thoreau famously declared, "In Wildness is the preservation of the World."

But is it? The more one knows of its peculiar history, the more one realizes that wilderness is not quite what it seems. Far from being the one place on earth that stands apart from humanity, it is quite profoundly a human creation – indeed, the creation of very particular human cultures at very particular moments in human history. It is not a pristine sanctuary where the last remnant of an endangered but still transcendent nature can be encountered without the contaminating taint of civilization. Instead, it is a product of that civilization. As we gaze into the mirror it holds up for us, we too easily imagine that what we behold is nature when in fact we see the reflection of our own longings and desires. Wilderness can hardly be the solution to our culture's problematic relationship with the nonhuman world, for wilderness is itself a part of the problem.

To assert the unnaturalness of so natural a place may seem perverse: we can all conjure up images and sensations that seem all the more hauntingly real for having engraved themselves so indelibly on our memories. Remember this? The torrents of mist shooting out from the base of a great waterfall in the depths of a Sierra Nevada canyon, the droplets cooling your face as you listen to the roar of the water and gaze toward the sky through a rainbow that hovers just out of reach. Or this: Looking out across a desert canyon in the evening air, the only sound a lone raven calling in the distance, the rock walls dropping away into a chasm so deep that its bottom all but vanishes as you squint into the amber light of the setting sun. Remember the feelings of such moments, and you will know as well as I do that you were in the presence of something irreducibly nonhuman, something profoundly Other than yourself. Wilderness is made of that too.

And yet: what brought each of us to the places where such memories became possible is entirely a cultural invention.

For the Americans who first celebrated it, wilderness was tied to the myth of the frontier. The historian Frederick Jackson Turner wrote the classic academic statement of this myth in 1893, but it had been part of American thought for well over a century. As Turner described the process, Easterners and European immigrants, in moving to the wild lands of the frontier, shed the trappings of civilization and thereby gained an energy, an independence and a creativity that were the sources of American democracy and national character. Seen this way, wilderness became a place of religious redemption and national renewal, the quintessential location for experiencing what it meant to be an American.

Adapted from *Uncommon Ground* (New York: W. W. Norton, 1995), pp. 69–90. © 1995 by William Cronon. Used by permission of W. W. Norton & Company, Inc.

Those who celebrate the frontier almost always look backward, mourning an older, simpler world that has disappeared forever. That world and all its attractions, Turner said, depended on free land – on wilderness. It is no accident that the movement to set aside national parks and wilderness areas gained real momentum just as laments about the vanishing frontier reached their peak. To protect wilderness was to protect the nation's most sacred myth of origin.

The decades following the civil war saw more and more of the nation's wealthiest citizens seeking out wilderness for themselves. The passion for wild land took many forms: enormous estates in the Adirondacks and elsewhere (disingenuously called "camps" despite their many servants and amenities); cattle ranches for would-be roughriders on the Great Plains; guided big-game hunting trips in the Rockies. Wilderness suddenly emerged as the landscape of choice for elite tourists. For them, it was a place of recreation.

In just this way, wilderness came to embody the frontier myth, standing for the wild freedom of America's past and seeming to represent a highly attractive natural alternative to the ugly artificiality of modern civilization. The irony, of course, was that in the process wilderness came to reflect the very civilization its devotees sought to escape. Ever since the 19th century, celebrating wilderness has been an activity mainly for well-to-do city folks. Country people generally know far too much about working the land to regard unworked land as their ideal.

There were other ironies as well. The movement to set aside national parks and wilderness areas followed hard on the heels of the final Indian wars in which the prior human inhabitants of these regions were rounded up and moved onto reservations so that tourists could safely enjoy the illusion that they were seeing their nation in its pristine, original state – in the new morning of God's own creation. Meanwhile, its original inhabitants were kept out by dint of force, their earlier uses of the land redefined as inappropriate or even illegal. To this day, for instance, the Blackfeet continue to be accused of "poaching" on the lands of Glacier National Park, in Montana, that originally belonged to them and that were ceded by treaty only with the proviso that they be permitted to hunt there.

The removal of Indians to create an "uninhabited wilderness" reminds us just how invented and how constructed the American wilderness really is. One of the most striking proofs of the cultural invention of wilderness is its thoroughgoing erasure of the history from which it sprang. In virtually all its manifestations, wilderness represents a flight from history. Seen as the original garden, it is a place outside time, from which human beings had to be ejected before the fallen world of history could properly begin. Seen as the frontier, it is a savage world at the dawn of civilization, whose transformation represents the very beginning of the national historical epic. Seen as sacred nature, it is the home of a God who transcends history, untouched by time's arrow. No matter what the angle from which we regard it, wilderness offers us the illusion that we can escape the cares and troubles of the world in which our past has ensnared us. It is the natural, unfallen antithesis of an unnatural civilization that has lost its soul, the place where we can see the world as it really is, and so know ourselves as we really are – or ought to be.

The trouble with wilderness is that it reproduces the very values its devotees seek to reject. It offers the illusion that we can somehow wipe clean the slate of our past and return to the tabula rasa that supposedly existed before we began to leave our marks on the world. The dream of an unworked natural landscape is very much the fantasy of people who have never themselves had to work the land to make a living – urban folk for whom food comes from a supermarket or a restaurant instead of a field, and for whom the wooden houses in which they live and work apparently have no meaningful connection to the forests in which trees grow and die. Only people whose relation to the land was already alienated could hold up wilderness as a model for human life in nature, for the romantic ideology of wilderness leaves no place in which human beings can actually make their living from the land.

We live in an urban-industrial civilization, but too often pretend to ourselves that our real home is in the wilderness. We work our nine-to-five jobs, we drive our cars (not least to reach the wilderness), we benefit from the intricate and all too invisible networks with which society shelters us, all the while pretending that these things are not an essential part of who we are. By imagining that our true home is in the wilderness, we forgive ourselves for the homes we actually inhabit. In its flight from history, in its siren song of escape, in its reproduction of the dangerous dualism that sets human beings somehow outside nature – in all these ways, wilderness poses a threat to responsible environmentalism at the end of the 20th century.

Do not misunderstand me. What I criticize here is not wild nature, but the alienated way we often think of ourselves in relation to it. Wilderness can still teach lessons that are hard to learn anywhere else. When we visit wild places, we find ourselves surrounded by plants and animals and landscapes whose otherness compels our attention. In forcing us to acknowledge that they are not of our making, that they have little or no need for humanity, they recall for us a creation far greater than our own. In wilderness, we need no reminder that a tree has its own reasons for being, quite apart from us – proof that ours is not the only presence in the universe.

We get into trouble only if we see the tree in the garden as wholly artificial and the tree in the wilderness as wholly natural. Both trees in some ultimate sense are wild; both in a practical sense now require our care. We need to reconcile them, to see a natural landscape that is also cultural, in which city, suburb, countryside and wilderness each has its own place. We need to discover a middle ground in which all these things, from city to wilderness, can somehow be encompassed in the word "home." Home, after all, is the place where we live. It is the place for which we take responsibility, the place we try to sustain so we can pass on what is best in it (and in ourselves) to our children.

Learning to honor the wild – learning to acknowledge the autonomy of the other – means striving for critical self-consciousness in all our actions. It means that reflection and respect must accompany each act of use, and means we must always consider the possibility of nonuse. It means looking at the part of nature we intend to turn toward our own ends and asking whether we can use it again and again and again – sustainably – without diminishing it in the process. Most of all, it means practicing remembrance and gratitude for the nature, culture and history that have come together to make the world as we know it. If wildness can stop being (just) out there and start being (also) in here, if it can start being as humane as it is natural, then perhaps we can get on with the unending task of struggling to live rightly in the world – not just in the garden, not just in the wilderness, but in the home that encompasses them both.

C Ecological Realism

48 Virtually Hunting Reality in the Forests of Simulacra

Paul Shepard

It would be difficult to argue with the assertions that our representations of the world are always "interpretations," that concepts shape our perceptions, that the human organism is its own shuttered window. Here I wish to explore the conclusion that reality is therefore invented by words, much the way Benjamin Whorf claimed seventy years ago that colors are a consequence of their differentiation by names. In its current form this idea further argues that such inventions are motivated by a struggle for power and that there is no Grand Truth beyond texts which are "allusions to the conceivable which cannot be presented."[1] I am also interested in the relationship of this inaccessibility of reality to "virtual reality."

According to the postmodern view, what most of us think of as simulations are only focused chatter about an unknowable external world. Even though they use living materials, the practitioners of "restoration ecology" may now find themselves, in this deconstructionist view, in the same boat with the museum curators making dioramas or habitat groups, who claim to be making artificial reproductions of the past or present world – and who are, therefore, merely engaged unconsciously in a sort of paranoid babble, lost in the vapors of their own imaginations without a compass or a satellite.

A 1973 essay in *Science* asks: "What's Wrong with Plastic Trees?"[2] The essay hardly deals with the question it poses; primarily it is the last gasp of a spurious "argument" between "preservation" and "conservation." But the question is important. More recently the curator of the Devonian Botanical Garden, writing in *The Futurist*, points to fabricated lawns and polyester Christmas trees which do not wilt in polluted environments or have to be watered, giving his blessing to the wonderful world of "artificial nature."[3] For years I have bedeviled my students with the issue of the validity of surrogates for living organisms and the enigma of the mindset in which this kind of ambiguity arises, wherein the nature of authenticity and the authenticity of nature are riddled with qualification.[4] For a time I thought the issue could be clarified by examining the megaphysiology of exchange by natural trees with their environment, health-giving to the soil, air, and other organisms, as contrasted to poisoning the surroundings by the industrial pollution from making plastic trees. Now I see that such comparisons no longer matter, since what I said to them, my own psychobabble, is itself the subject.

Reality – You Can't Get There from Here

Looking behind the facades of grafted signification was the intent in 1949 of Marshall McLuhan's brilliant book *The Mechanical Bride*, which dissolved the rhetoric of magazine advertisements to expose the tacit messages concealed in the hypocrisy, presumptions, and deceit of the corporate purveyors of consumerism and our own lust to be seduced.[5] According to the current literary fashion, however, McLuhan himself can now be deconstructed and his own agenda shown to be just another level of presumption and the struggle for power.

If McLuhan still lived in the ocean of positivist naïveté, David Lowenthal, the geographer, appeared on the new, dry shore of equivocal reality only thirteen years later. In an essay called "Is Wilderness Paradise Enow?" he argues that the substantive reality of wilderness exists solely in the romantic ideas of it. Even its inhabitants are fictions, the noble savage having been the first victim of the "new criticism." Even the buffalo, Lowenthal says, "is only a congeries of feelings."[6] The buffalo is not some *thing* among other things – the cowbirds, Indians, pioneers, and you and I. It exists only as the feelings that arise from our respective descriptions.

Lowenthal's argument is reminiscent of the psychological conception of life as being locked inside a series of boxes and therefore precluding us from knowing anything but our own internal pulsations: coded patterns of electrochemical stimuli. At the level of cerebral axons, nuclei, and their glial cohorts the assertion that my world is more real than yours seems ridiculous. And suddenly we are back in Psychology 101, where we realize that all contact with "reality" is translated to the brain as neural drumbeats, nothing more, and in Psych 102, where the instructor titillates the class with the sensational observation that no old tree crashes down on an island if there is no ear to hear it. A thrill runs through the class, who will go on to Literature 101 to learn that the other impulses arise in words, a barrier behind which is a vast, unknowable enigma – or, perhaps, nothing at all.

Many of us – including myself – may think of a photograph as the visual evidence of a past reality, so that certain events may then be recalled or better understood. But we are now confronted with the assertion that there is nothing "in" a picture but light and dark patches or bits of pigment – that the events to which we supposed such photographs refer are not themselves in the blobs. If something actually occurred it cannot be known. The result, in the case of photographs of starving people, is insensitivity to human suffering. This callous aesthetic is the object of Susan Sontag's anathema, identifying her as grounded – like McLuhan – rather than detached with the postmodern solipsists.[7]

Reflected light from actual events, focused through a lens onto a chemically sensitized plate, inscribing images that can be transferred by means of more light, lens, and photochemicals onto paper, does not, however, neutralize the "subject matter" even if it is a century old. The assay of such a photograph on formal grounds is a form of aesthetic distancing. This surreality of pictures which denies the terms of their origin reminds us that, according to the fashion, such a picture is a text, an impenetrable facade, whose truth is hidden.

Likewise, Hal Foster observes that recent abstract painting is only about abstract painting. Paintings are no more than the simulation of modes of abstraction, he says, made "as if to demonstrate that they are no longer critically reflexive or historically necessary forms with direct access to unconscious truths or a transcendental realm beyond the world – that they are simply styles among others."[8] As painting becomes a sign of painting, the simulacra become images without resemblances except to other images. Like the events which occasioned the photographs, the original configurations to which abstractions refer no longer have currency. Reality has dissolved in a connoisseurship of structural principles. A twentieth-century doubt has interposed itself between us and the world. "We have paid a high enough price for the nostalgia of the whole and the one," says Lyotard, and so allusion of any kind is suspect.

In my view this denial of a prior event is an example of what Alfred North Whitehead calls "misplaced concreteness." Paradoxically, the postmodern rejection of Enlightenment positivism has about it a grander sweep of presumption than the metaphysics of being and truth that it rejects. There is an armchair or coffeehouse smell about it. Lyotard and his fellows have about them no glimmer of earth, of leaves or soil. They seem to live entirely in a made rather than a grown world; to think that "making" language is analogous to making plastic trees, to be always on the edge of supposing that the words for things are more real than the things they stand for.[9] Reacting against the abuses of modernism, they assert that life consists of a struggle for verbal authority just as their predecessors in the eighteenth century knew that life was a social struggle for status or a technological war against nature. Misconstruing the dynamics of language, they are the final spokesmen of a world of forms as opposed to process, for whom existence is a mix of an infinite number of possible variations making up the linguistic elements of a "text."

Under all narrative we find merely more layers of intent until we realize with Derrida, Rorty, Lacan, Lyotard, and critics of visual arts that our role as human organisms is to replace the world with webs of words, sounds, and signs that refer only to other such constructions. Intellectuals seem caught up in the dizzy spectacle and brilliant subjectivity of a kind of deconstructionist fireworks in which origins and truth have become meaningless. Nothing can be traced further than the semiotic in which everything is trapped. The chain of relationships that orders a functional fish market, the cycle of the tree's growth, breath, decay, and death, the underlying physiological connections that link people in communities and organisms in ecosystems or in temporal continuity – all are subordinate to the arguments for or against their existence. The text – the only reality – is comparable only to other texts. Nothing is true, says Michel Foucault, except "regimes of truth and power." It is not that simulacra are good or bad replicas – indeed, they are not replicas at all; they are all there is! In a recent essay, Richard Lee characterizes this attitude as a "cool detachment and ironic distanciation," an eruption of cynicism caused by our daily bombardment of media fantasy, assaults on the "real," and consequent debasement of the currency of reality.[10] But I think it is not, as he concludes, simply a final relativism. There is no room even for relative truth in a nihilistic ecology.

The deconstructionist points with glee to the hidden motivations in these "falsifications" of a past and perhaps inadvertently opens the door to the reconfiguration of places as the setting of entertainment and consumption. This posture is not only a Sartrean game or artistic denial. It spreads throughout the ordinary world, where pictorial, electronic, and holographic creations, architectural facades for ethnic, economic, and historical systems, pets as signifiers of the animal kingdom, and arranged news are the floating reality that constitutes our experience. We seem to be engaged in demonstrating the inaccessibility of reality.

In the past half century we have invented alternative worlds that give physical expression to the denial of disaster. Following the lead and iconography of *The National Geographic* magazine with its blue-bird landscapes, and then the architecture of Disneyland happiness, a thousand Old Waterfronts, Frontier Towns, Victorian Streets, Nineteenth-Century Mining Communities, Ethnic Villages, and Wildlife Parks have appeared. One now travels not only in space while sitting still but "back" to a time that never was. As fast as the relics of the past, whether old-growth forests or downtown Santa Fe, are demolished they are reincarnated in idealized form.

As the outer edges of cities expand, the centers are left in shambles, the habitation of the poor, or they are transformed into corporate wastelands which administer distant desolation as if by magic. To console the middle-class inhabitants and tourists, a spuriously appropriated history and cityscape replace the lost center with "Oldtown." In 1879 Thomas Sargeant Perry, having looked at Ludwig Friedlander's book on romanticism, wrote: "In the complexity of civilization we have grown accustomed to finding whatever we please in the landscape, and read in it what we have in our own hearts."[11] An example would be the "monumental architecture" of the rocky bluffs of the North Platte River as reported by the emigrants on the Oregon Trail in the 1840s.[12] Were Perry present today he could say that we make "whatever we please" out there and then announce it as found.

Michael Sorkin speaks of this architectural "game of grafted signification . . . [and] urbanism inflected by applique" and the "caricaturing of places." Theme parks succeed the random decline of the city with their nongeography, their surveillance systems, the simulation of public space, the programmed uniformity sold as diversity. Condensed, they become the mall.[13] It is as though a junta of deconstructionist body-snatchers had invaded the skins of the planners, architects, and tour businessmen who are selling fantasy as history, creating a million Disneylands and everbigger "events" for television along with electronic playsuits and simulated places in three-dimensional "virtual reality." Apart from the rarefied discourse and intimidating intellectualism of the French philosophes, their streetwise equivalents are already at work turning everyday life into a Universal Studios tour. It is not just that here and there in malls are cafés representing the different national cuisines but that the referent does not exist. Who cares about authenticity with respect to an imaginary origin?

The point at which the architectural fantasists and virtual realists intersect with intellectual postmoderns and deconstructionists is in the shared belief that a world beyond our control is so terrifying that we can – indeed, must – believe only in the landscapes of our imagination.

Amid the erosion of true relicts from our past, can we not turn to the museum? What are the custodians of the portable physical relicts doing? According to

Kevin Walsh, museums now show that all trails lead to ourselves, create displays equating change with progress, and reprogram the past not so much as unlike ourselves but as trajectory toward the present.[14] The effect is like those representations of biological evolution with humankind at the top instead of the tip of one of many branches. In effect the museum dispenses with the past in the guise of its simulation, "sequestering the past from those to whom it belongs." Its contents are "no longer contingent upon our experiences in the world" but become a patchwork or bricolage "contributing to historical amnesia." Roots in this sense are not the sustaining and original structure but something adventitious, like banyan tree "suckers" dropped from the ends of its limbs. "Generations to come," Walsh predicts, "will inherit a heritage of heritage – an environment of past plu-perfects which will ensure the death of the past."

Not long ago I was in the Zoological Museum at St Petersburg, Russia, an institution which has not reorganized its exhibits according to the new fashion of diorama art – those "habitat groups," simulated swamps, seacoasts, prairies, or woodlands, each with its typical association of plants and animals against a background designed to give the illusion of space. There in Russia, among the great, old-fashioned glass cases with their stuffed animals in family groups, with no effort at naturalistic surroundings, I felt a rare pleasure. I realized that the individual animal's beauty and identity remain our principal source of satisfaction. When all members of the cat family, or the woodpeckers, are placed together, instead of feeling that I am being asked to pretend that I am looking through a window at a natural scene, I am free to compare closely related forms. Instead of an ersatz view I have the undiluted joy of those comparisons that constitute and rehabilitate the cognitive processes of identification. Nor does the museum display in St Petersburg insidiously invade my thoughts as a replacement for vanishing woodlands and swamps by substituting an aesthetic image for noetics, the voyeur's super-real for the actuality.

New Dress for the Fear of Nature

Plastic trees? They are more than a practical simulation. They are the message that the trees which they represent are themselves but surfaces. Their principal defect is that one can still recognize plastic, but it is only a matter of time and technology until they achieve virtual reality, indistinguishable from the older retinal and tactile sensa. They are becoming *acceptable configurations.* No doubt we can invent electronic hats and suits into which we may put our heads or crawl, which will reduce the need even for an ersatz mock-up like the diorama. These gadgets trick our nervous systems somewhat in the way certain substances can fool our body chemistry – as, for example, the body fails to discriminate radioactive strontium 90 from calcium. (Strontium was part of the downwind fallout of atomic bomb testing which entered the soil from the sky, the grass from the soil, the cows from the grass, the milk from the cows, children from the milk, and finally their growing bones, where it caused cancer.) As the art of simulacrum becomes more convincing, its fallout enters our bodies and heads with unknown consequences. As the postmodern high fashion of deconstruction declares that the text – or bits cobbled into a picture – is all there is, all identity and taxonomy cease to be keys to relations, to origins, or to essentials, all of which become mere phantoms. As Richard Lee says of the search for origins in anthropology, any serious quest for evolutionary antecedents, social, linguistic, or cultural ur-forms, has become simply an embarrassment.

But is this really new or is it a continuation of an old, antinatural position that David Ehrenfeld has called "the arrogance of humanism"?[15] Mainstream Western philosophy, together with the Renaissance liberation of Art as a separate domain and its Neoclassical thesis of human eminence, were like successive cultural wedges driven between humans and nature, hyperboles of separateness, autonomy, and control. It may be time, as the voices of deconstruction say, for much of this ideological accretion to be pulled down. But as downpullers trapped in the ideology of Art as High Culture, of nothing beyond words, they can find nothing beneath "text." Life is indistinguishable from a video game, one of the alternatives to the physical wasteland that the Enlightenment produced around us. As the tourists flock to their pseudo history villages and fantasy-lands, the cynics take refuge from overwhelming problems by announcing all lands to be illusory. Deconstructionist postmodernism rationalizes the final step away from connection: beyond relativism to denial. It seems more like the capstone to an old story than a revolutionary perspective.

Alternatively, the genuinely innovative direction of our time is not the final surrender to the anomie of meaninglessness or the escape to fantasylands but in the opposite direction – toward affirmation and continuity with something beyond representation. The new humanism is not really radical. As Charlene Spretnak says: "The ecologizing of consciousness is far more radical than ideologues and strategists of the existing political forms . . . seem to have realized."[16]

Life – or Its Absence – on the *Enterprise*

The question about plastic trees assumes that nature is mainly of interest as spectacle. The tree is no longer in process with the rest of its organic and inorganic surroundings: it is a form – like the images in old photographs. As the plastic trees are made to appear more like natural trees, they lose their value as a replacement and cause us to surrender perception of all plants to the abstract eye. Place and function are exhausted in their appearance. The philosophy of disengagement certifies whatever meanings we attach to these treelike forms – and to trees themselves. The vacuum of essential meaning implies that there really is no meaning. A highbrow wrecking crew confirms this from their own observations of reality – that is, of conflicting texts.

There is a certain bizarre consequence of all this which narrows our attention from a larger, interspecies whole to a kind of bedrock ethnos. For example, in each episode of the television series "Star Trek" we are given a rhetorical log date and place, but in fact the starship *Enterprise* is neither here nor there, now or then. Its stated mission to "contact other civilizations and peoples" drives it frantically nowhere at "warp speed" (speed that transcends our ordinary sense of transit), its "contacts" with other beings so abbreviated that the substance of each story rests finally on the play of interpersonal dynamics, like that which energizes most drama from Shakespeare to soap opera.

This dynamics is *essentially* primate – their own physicality is the only connecting thread to organic life left to the fictional crew and its vicarious companions, the audience. For all of its fancy hardware, software, and bombastic rhetoric, the story depends on projections of primatoid foundations, a shifting equilibrium like any healthy baboon social dynamic – the swirl of intimidation, greed, affection, dominance, status, and groupthink that make the social primates look like caricatures of an overwrought humanity.

The story implies that we may regress through an ecological floor – the lack of place and time and the nonhuman continuum – to farcical substitutes and a saving anthropoid grace. Should such a vehicle as the *Enterprise* ever come into existence, I doubt that their primatehood will save its occupants from the madness of deprivation – the absence of sky, earth, seasons, nonhuman life, and, finally, their own identities as individuals and species, all necessary to our life as organisms.

In the later series, "Star Trek: The Next Generation," the spacecraft has a special room for recreation, the "holo-deck," in which computers re-create the holographic ambience and inhabitants of any place and any time. The difference between this deck and H. G. Wells's time-travel machine is that the *Enterprise* crew is intellectually autistic, knowing that other places and times are their own inventions. The holo-decks that we now create everywhere, from Disneyworld to Old Town Mainstreets, may relieve us briefly from the desperate situations we face on the Flight Deck as we struggle in "the material and psychic waste accumulating everywhere in the wake of what some of us still call 'progress.'" The raucous cries of post-Pleistocene apes on the *Enterprise* are outside the ken of the ship's cyborg second mate, just as the technophiles on earth will witness without comprehension the psychopathology of High Culture and literary dissociation, with its "giddy, regressive carnival of desire," rhetoric of excess, "orgies of subjectivity, randomness," and "willful playing of games."[17]

What, then, is the final reply to the subjective and aesthetic dandyism of our time? Given our immersion in text, who can claim to know reality?

As for "truth," "origins," or "essentials" beyond the "metanarratives," the naturalist has a peculiar advantage – by attending to species who have no words and no text other than context and yet among whom there is an unspoken consensus about the contingency of life and real substructures. A million species constantly make "assumptions" in their body language, indicating a common ground and the validity of their responses. A thousand million pairs of eyes, antennas, and other sense organs are fixed on something beyond themselves that sustains their being, in a relationship that works. To argue that because we interpose talk or pictures between us and this shared immanence, and that it therefore is meaningless, contradicts the testimony of life itself. The nonhuman realm, acting as if in common knowledge of a shared quiddity, of unlike but congruent representations, tests its reality billions of times every hour. It is the same world in which we ourselves live, experiencing it as process, structures, and meanings, interacting with the same events that the plants and other animals do.

Notes

1   Jean-François Lyotard, *The Post-Modern Condition*, quoted in Jane Flax, *Thinking Fragments: Psychoanalysis, Feminism and Postmodernism in the Contemporary West* (Berkeley: University of California Press, 1990).

2   Martin H. Krieger, "What's Wrong with Plastic Trees?" *Science* 179(1973): 446–54.

3   Roger Vick, "Artificial Nature, the Synthetic Landscape of the Future," *Futurist* (July–August 1989).

4   See Umberto Eco, "The Original and the Copy," in Francisco J. Varella and Jean-Pierre Dupuy Crea (eds.), *Understanding Origins* (Boston: Kluwer, 1992).

5   Marshall McLuhan, *The Mechanical Bride: Folklore of Industrial Man* (New York: Vanguard Press, 1951).

6   David Lowenthal, "Is Wilderness Paradise Enow?" *Columbia University Forum* (Spring 1964). See also my reply, "The Wilderness as Nature," *Atlantic Naturalist* (January–March 1965).

7   Susan Sontag, *On Photography* (New York: Dell, 1977).

8   Hal Foster, "Signs Taken for Wonders," *Art in America* (June 1986).

9   I used to think of this attitude as the "Marjorie Nicolson Syndrome." It was from her book *Mountain Gloom and Mountain Glory* that I first got the sense there were those who seemed to think the test of nature was whether it lived up to the literary descriptions of it. Clearly, Nicolson neither invented nor bears the full responsibility for this peculiar notion.

10   Richard B. Lee, "Art, Science, or Politics? The Crisis in Hunter-Gatherer Studies," *American Anthropologist* 94(1993): 31–54.

11   Thomas Sargeant Perry, "Mountains in Literature," *Atlantic Monthly* 44 (September 1879): 302.

12   An account appears in Paul Shepard, "The American West," in *Man in the Landscape* (College Station: Texas A&M University Press, 1991).

13   Michael Sorkin, "See You in Disneyland," in Michael Sorkin (ed.), *Variations on a Theme Park* (New York: Hill & Wang, 1992).

14   Kevin Walsh, *The Representation of the Past: Museums and Heritage in the Post-Modern World* (London: Routledge, 1992).

15   David Ehrenfeld, *The Arrogance of Humanism* (New York: Oxford University Press, 1981).

16   Charlene Spretnak, *States of Grace* (San Francisco: Harper, 1991), p. 229.

17   Klaus Poenicke, "The Invisible Hand," in Gunter H. Lenz and Kurt L. Shell (eds.), *Crisis of Modernity* (Boulder: Westview Press, 1986).

D Environmental Ethics and the Philosophy of Technology

---

49 Technology and the Limits of Nature

David Rothenberg

Technology. *Techne + Logos*: order imposed upon skill. When we organize our abilities, they become a structure which determines our world. We are accustomed to using the word *technology* in a total sense, symbolizing all that is mechanical in our society and thus opposed to a personal level of understanding: essential, constantly encountered, yet somehow out of reach. Our sense of technology could not have started out that way, and it cannot be penetrated if conceived as an impasse. No, technology is meaningful only as individuals use it, developing as it flows from the transformation of skill into idea. [Here I] trace the history of attempts to weave practical knowledge of how to construct and to make things with the ineffable sense of an overriding order. Technology stretches human presence further outward, making the world tangible by enveloping it in the web of our actions.

Knowing Through Making

People discovered early on that they could manipulate the world to fit their purposes. Philosophy wants to compare these purposes with the order and purpose of the world as a whole. It is thus often opposed to technology: tools show a definite progress through history, while the same philosophical questions always seem to remain. Yet each tool brings with it the imposition of ideas. The merger of *techne* and *logos* is the logic of action, the order of art. It shows how our dreams are constrained by what we are able to do. The bond linking what we know to what we can accomplish is evident in some of the earliest recorded reflections on human place in the universe – the few surviving fragments of the writings of Heraclitus. The world, he suggests, does follow some elusive kind of order, but it is continually beyond our grasp:

> Of *this account which holds forever* men prove uncomprehending, both before hearing it and after they have heard it. For although all things come about in accordance with this account, they are like tyros as they try the words and the deeds which I expound as I divide up each thing according to its nature and say how it is. . . . For that reason you must follow *what is universal*. But although *the account is common*, most men live as though they had an understanding of their own.[1]

The italicized words[2] in this translation of portions of the first two fragments are attempts to render the elusive term *logos* into English. This Heraclitean *logos*

From David Rothenberg, *Hand's End* (Berkeley: University of California Press, 1993), pp. 1–9, 14–19. © 1993 by The Regents of the University of California. Reprinted by permission of the University of California Press.

is eternal, universal, common to all of us and everything around us, yet we are most often deaf to its presence. It's as if we live in perpetual slumber. To "wake up," we should learn to follow the order which guides the world, inclusive of our role in it. This is the *logos* of Heraclitus, the notion of order from which all Western attempts to claim systematic knowledge of anything are descended.

When we speak of techno-logy, are we asking for a systematic theory of practical action and artifice, or are we groping for a technique that is worthy of the order of the universe? The two are intertwined from the outset: practical knowledge and the ability to make give a certain sense of security and control that speculation will never warrant. A piece of the *logos* becomes tangible when it is tamed – when we work with it and are no longer terrified by it. When sure of a technique, we soon imagine what it implies about nature. Fire is a strange and terrible demon until we can light it and extinguish it. Once it becomes a tool, we wonder: perhaps this is what forms the universe? Or water, or air: these are not only sensed in the surrounding world, they are things which we *use*.

The wonder that engenders philosophy is *not* born out of times of rest, moments when we had leisure to spare in the struggle for survival. No, it comes hand in hand with the human way of living in the world by changing it. It is thus difficult to separate our explanation of the world from our transformation of it. Heraclitus is wise enough to know that human language itself is strained and stretched when it is made to tackle such vast and vaporous concepts as the *logos*. But to bring this abstract omnipresence within our reach, he analogizes from the realm of familiar tools which do not scare us. What can he say to help us to contemplate the one and the many, the universal and the particular, the ambiguous and the definite? He needs images from the world of *techne*, of artifacts which we may literally touch, pull, and *grasp*. Here is why people are frustrated by the apparent indecisiveness of the world's rule:

> They do not comprehend how, in differing, it agrees with itself – a backward-turning connection, like that of *a bow and a lyre*.[3]

What could this analogy mean? Both instruments – one of music, one of war – function through harnessing the potential energy within a drawn and taut string. So the universe seems built around a tension held and supported. We pull on the string firmly and

gently, and either the arrow or the tone is released. These devices *work*: is it folly to suggest that the universe might work in a similar way? How might the bow and the lyre be *like* the order of the universe? Octavio Paz suggests that the lyre "consecrates man and thus gives him a place in the cosmos," while the bow "shoots him beyond himself."[4] For Lewis Mumford, the bow is an archetypal example of art and technics together, as it is both part of a musical instrument and a device that extends our aim by transforming the energy in the pull into the arrow's path.[5] Remember also Fragment 48: "The name of the bow is *bios*, its function death." In other words, the word *bios* can mean either "bow" or "life" in common usage; so the tool which kills is the equivalent of what lives. Once again opposites confront the truth through each other, in action and in speech. The question is an open one: we stop shooting, stop singing, and imagine a vast universe doing these same things, just like us.

This is but an early trace of a recurring kind of reasoning [...]. We see the progression of technical metaphor as the universe and its subset of inhabitants are successively seen through history to be *like* different types of machines – wheels, clocks, engines, arrays of digital on/off memory chips. The explanatory power of what we can construct should not be underestimated, though few have interpolated artifact into nature as subtly as Heraclitus. He has introduced the *logos* as an order which humanity ignores, but when he strives to make it accessible, he reveals its presence in the forces at work in the tools which we use all the time. The grand logic is explained through everyday things.

So from the outset, technology is essential to explanation of the world. Later, even such a skeptic as Socrates recognizes the exemplary value of technical knowledge: he mines it as the clearest vein of examples of how we progress from the particular towards the general – from specific skill to elusive truth. *Techne* is the clearest and most definite type of knowledge, because we immediately understand what it is for. "What result," asks Socrates, "does the art of the shipbuilders produce?" "Obviously," replies Euthyphro, "the making of ships." "Now tell me, best of friends, about the service of the gods. What result will this art serve to produce?"[6] With this second question, Socrates has analogized from the technical to the spiritual, forcing his accomplice to strain the term *art* towards the limit of what can be known. Art, the most common translation of *techne*, signifies the human ability to make and produce, and as *homo faber* we grasp its power at once. Knowledge which can create something useful to us may be justified by its end, and need not be questioned or mystified.

But it is not to be so easy – the virtue which Socrates so strives for will not stand to be encompassed by any learnable technique. No, the simple recognition of its presence comes only through ceaseless questioning of what can be accomplished, and doubt detaches one from the certainty of a sensible tool. A technique shows us how to make and control things, but it does not tell us why anything should be done. It soon becomes subsumed as a mere step on the road toward higher knowledge in the hierarchy of the philosopher: with Plato, technical knowledge is demoted in status, separated out from pure contemplation. Though he does recognize how good tools are internalized and accepted, he chooses to emphasize the gaping hole revealed when we admit that we cannot explain *why* we use them so readily without pause to reflect. If we cannot present any higher purpose for ourselves, why do anything? Plato instead looks for some certainty in detached, descriptive knowledge of the world, *episteme*, which might suggest an equally normative knowledge of the Good, the Virtuous, or the Beautiful.

Though technical knowledge might be an adequate analogy to suggest the kind of questions we need to ask, it gives no glimmer of the absolute to justify any hope. So Plato chooses to be inspired by geometry, a human discovery that seems to eclipse human limitations: a perfect circle is something we can never draw, but only approximate with our pens and compasses. Still, it exists as a tangible idea that transcends technique but may be easily grasped by the human mind. Quickly reason transcends prowess – our quest for the right way to live need no longer be limited by the approximate means we are able to master.

In his later work, the analogical power of technology returns, as Plato realizes that the idea of the technical end justifying the technical means is by no means as obvious as Socrates thought it was. The *Philebus* is a dialogue concerned with attempts to divide and conquer various types of knowledge. They are split up so that those based on random conjecture and guesswork may be weeded out from the exact, orderly, and "common" (in the Heraclitean sense) parts which could be universally called "true." Plato distinguishes the "element of numbering,

measuring, and weighing" which constitutes the order inherent in any craft from that part based on "rule of thumb," enabling the practitioner to make the "lucky shots"[7] necessary to excel in the craft. Here, as usual with Plato's attempt at categorical knowledge, we are not exactly sure how he is relating the relative merits of each category to the single noble purpose of pursuit of the Good. Though the argument seems to demote once more this nonsystematic side of all actual techniques, there is a kind of latent respect for the *ability* to make those lucky strikes:

> Well, now, we find plenty of it, to take one instance, in music when it adjusts its concords not by measurement but by *lucky shots of a practiced finger* – in the whole of music, flute playing and lyre playing alike, for this latter hunts for the proper length of each string as it gives its note, making a shot for the note, and attaining a most unreliable result with a large element of uncertainty.[8]

Unreliable, yes, but still of the essence of art. It's not really so bad, as any musician will tell you how remarkable it is to be able to play passages quicker than one can imagine or plan them.

This section of the dialogue concludes with the stated aim that it has *not* been trying to discover "which art or which form of knowledge is superior to all others in respect of being the greatest or the best or the most serviceable, *but* which devotes its attention to precision, exactness, *and the fullest truth*."[9] Now does technology offer an order for machines, or new chances for surprise?

If we want to find order for the universe and human purpose within it, then we may be inspired by those aspects of technical knowledge which are organized, systematically and definitely arranged, possessing a *logos* of their own. Precision is recognized in the things we are able to master and direct before we can imagine it in the world outside us. The next question is whether or not we need to shun this penchant for "lucky strikes" which allows human improvisation to show through even the most codified of technical situations. As Plato's subtle way of embellishing distinctions suggests, one choice should never negate the other. He finds a place in his ideas and his rhetoric for both the comprehensible and the magical sides of technology, as stages on life's way, and as a profound analogy for a knotted duality in the rigging which ties all strands together, tangled between the random and the planned.

But such a wisplike, indefinite way of dividing and uniting ideas in disparate ways one after the other is frustrating to anyone who wants a quick-and-dirty answer. The students of Plato were aware of this, and they learned the value of taking a stand. Aristotle would never waft around the question, but state the simple and necessary truth of the matter: *techne* is a finite means, separated from the *logos*. Why and what it is used for is a separate matter. He takes his distinctions seriously, and when a concept is defined it is sharply delineated from related concepts: "*techne* is identical with a state of capacity to make, involving a true course of reasoning."[10] It is thus sharply distinguished from acting, which is governed by a separate faculty of practical wisdom, a virtue and not an art. This schism between the tool and the use may be seen as the root of so many problems engendered by technology. Most of us today, so influenced by Aristotle that we find many of his conclusions banal and obvious, tend implicitly to agree with his view of technology as a means to an end: it is the "true course of reasoning" necessary to keep machines and tools running.

By what criteria might this reason be called true? It is certainly not true in the sense in which the virtuous is true. Aristotle must be suggesting something akin to the precision which Plato seeks above, but in his characteristic manner he has sketched its edges more succinctly – the course is true if the technique works as expected, if it does what it is told to do, reliably and consistently, so that we may forget about it and concentrate on why we picked up the tool in the first place. Correct technology often works transparently as a means to realize the ends dictated by practical wisdom. [...]

But this invisibility is not to be carried too far: instruments do *not* accomplish their work without human guidance, like those oft-cited statues of Dædalus, which moved by themselves once completed, so perfectly did they resemble the living forms of which they were the image.[11] Yet they are an apt image for technology as well; *techne* imitates nature in its manner of operation, but completes what nature alone has only hinted at. Within the activity of art, all material is seen in terms of the purpose we are trying to realize, "and we use everything *as if* it was there for our sake."[12] This implies that the technical stance changes our sense of what the world can be *for us*. Attribute is perceived as resource; meaning develops out of the potential for use. According to Aristotle, since we too follow the laws of nature, what we make and build teaches us as much about the world as it extends ourselves:

> Now intelligent action is for the sake of an end; therefore the nature of things also is so. Thus if a house . . . had been a thing made by nature, it would have been made in the same way as it is now by art. . . . [which] *partly completes what nature cannot bring to a finish, and partly imitates her. . . .* It is plain that nature is a cause, a cause that operates for a purpose.[13]

Just what kind of cause is nature, within Aristotle's famous fourfold scheme? To the extent that nature is to mean the matter we may shape into our artifacts, it is the *material* cause. If nature includes the ideal schemata that make the building of things like houses possible, it could be conceived to be the *formal* cause. Nature as the prime mover is the original *efficient* cause for everything if neither God nor human free will are invoked. And if nature includes rules that determine how things grow, change, and reach their ends, it needs to encompass the *final* cause as well.

Aristotle's discernment of the varieties of cause is enough to encompass a wide range of colorations of the omnipresent concept "nature" in its most total form. But the imperfect analogy between the natural and the technical reveals an uneasiness always present in any attempt to spread nature too wide as an enveloping idea. Within technical process, the material cause still remains nature: we start with natural materials and refine them successively to suit our needs. Since we are the ones instigating a change in the order of things, realigning the world with our purposes, *we* are the efficient cause of any technology.

The two remaining categories are the ones open to the greatest range of interpretations. Presumably, if we imitate with our tools the manner of nature's operation, we apply existing natural formal causes to new materials, abstracting the laws of nature from their original context and realizing new potentials by applying them out of place. Need we say that those technical solutions which work are just those *permitted* by the laws of nature, included within its forms and essences? Under this conception, nature is the final arbiter of any technical stab at modification of our world. Or, if we abandon this view, we can name technology to be the *logos* of changing the world, specifically providing those forms which go against nature, perfecting it where alone it has been unable to succeed. It remains to be seen whether our attempts to alter the world are at all possible without some kind of *consent* from nature as the thing which precedes and guides all process.

Is nature a *sufficient* cause for technical innovation? Is nature strong enough to guide technology? [...] [A]lignment with nature has always been part of theories that hope to direct technical development. [...] [N]ature itself changes as a result of different techniques that both extend human reach and offer new metaphors for the description of the surrounding, enveloping, present world and the forces which underlie it.

The final cause of a technical process can be considered natural only if human purpose is completely subsumed by nature. This would require either a broadening of the meaning of the word *nature* into a synonym for everything which could be created *or* a redirecting of the term so that it refers not only to what is, but to what will be, as we shape the world towards some goal which it was always meant to realize. Some of the dynamic sense of this process is beyond the scope of Aristotle's time, when explanation was more appropriate than prognosis for change. (It was not so dynamic a society as ours, in which tools seem to be evolving so much quicker than our capacity to make sense of them.) But he was still wont to justify nearly all his conclusions with the maxim that they are simply true "by nature." And this is a nature that includes morality as well as physical law, containing the ethics to guide technology as well as the materials and their relationships which make it possible.

In Aristotle, nature is an all-knowing concept that may be a synonym for the totality of the world as well as all the causal processes that operate within it. But *techne* represents the human penchant to go beyond nature, thereby completing our place in the natural world.

This concept contributes to the deemphasis on practical action within philosophy itself. *Episteme* takes over as the central human pursuit of pure wisdom: knowledge of what is unchangeable and fundamental, not what we can do to the world. Aristotle is important here not because he elegantly severs the concept of *techne* from the world it acts upon, but because he so subtly blurs humanity with nature when he hypothesizes how they work together: both follow almost identical principles, but automatically in the latter and voluntarily in the former. We choose what to do, while nature never worries. Yet the conflation of *techne* with *logos* imagines more order and

design than Aristotle might care to admit. As we refine its compound meaning, we need to retain Plato's inquisitive stance while building on the deep roots of the metaphor of Heraclitus, which shows so poignantly how what is made may serve to explain what is thought to precede it. Unfolding a vision of technology as an extension of human essentials toward the limits of nature, these ancient historical views continue to cast a shadow on the great, unforeseen material changes wrought in our time and in the future.

[...]

The Circle of Intent and Result

Technology seems to make us larger than life. Just as powerful is the basic idea that the world exists to be bent toward our purposes. This world is revealed to the extent that we can turn it toward our designs. Technology as a topic for philosophical speculation quickly veers toward the all-encompassing, emerging either as a total metaphor for our whole machine-guided civilization or as a neutral means in the mess of clouded, shaky goals and ends. Here I want to shy away from abstract, global pronouncements and to investigate how the tool specifically influences the range and direction of our thoughts and aspirations.

The more we learn about how to use an instrument, the less we think about it as we use it. It becomes like an extra limb, a new way to reach out and change the world. But what is it precisely that is extended? Not simply an internal human idea, but an idea to act, a thought that engages the world, making the possible actual. The more we understand of the tool, the more ways we conceive of how it may be put into practice. Our desires and intentions to act upon the world are themselves altered through the tools that we create to realize them. This is the essence of the philosophy of technology as human extension.

Joseph Weizenbaum describes it well in his book on the limits of the computer as an accessory to human reason:

> We must, in order to operate our instruments skillfully, internalize aspects of them in the form of kinesthetic and perceptual habits. In that sense at least, our instruments become literally part of us and modify us, and thus alter the basis of our affective relationship to ourselves.[14]

Like our own arms, legs, eyes, and ears, instruments which we internalize can never be purely transparent extensions of any premeditated intention, since the successful application of tools modifies our desire to use them. Technology does not extend an essential human nature outward to successively inscribe an external nonhuman nature, but alters the meaning of humanity by turning our own intention increasingly towards those aspects outside us which may be shaped in greater accord with our ideas. We see the world as we make the world, and we make the world into what we have seen and imagined through the tangible construction of technical possibilities.

First, a stab at more precise definitions of terms which I have thrown about more or less as they are found in common usage.[15] I am not ready to lose the rich possibilities inherent in the ambiguities of "ordinary" language, but some specifics must now be stated.

Technology is the entire logic of artifice, the order of art. It has been demonstrated above to emerge as a historical concept once rules about the way we create and transform things can be identified. The *technique, tool, device, instrument, implement, technology* (in the singular form), or *machine*[16] will be the objects within the overall field of technology, those constructed things which enable humanity to make and shape the world in an ordered way.

What guides our action towards transformation of the world? First, the *desire* to do so. A human want, never easy to distinguish from a need. In its general form, emanating from us, outwardly directed, human *intention* focuses our attention toward the world as something to be made through our actions. This usage of the term *intention* is very different from that characteristic of phenomenology, as Husserl and Brentano speak primarily of intended *perception*, where human gaze is always directed to something, never abstract, always oriented to an object in the context of a universal horizon. The intention I am speaking of is more active, more akin to the common usage of *want*. It implies an attention to action. Any human act that makes a mark on any "outside" world also makes that world an extension of the human being who guides the change. In other words, the world that we make through technology is *humanity extended*, the hand's end.

What is meant by *extension* here? It is certainly not the metaphysical attribute of an entity which spreads out in space and time. Rather, the word is used to explain how intention operates in a dynamic, territory-expanding manner. It reaches out from the deciding being to leave a tangible record of the decision in the thing which is done. A part of human essence is evident in the things which we build, create, and design to make the Earth into *our* place. Techniques can extend all those human aspects for which we possess a mechanical understanding. Telescopes and microscopes can extend the acuity of our vision, because we know something about how our eyes perceive the world optically. But we cannot technically extend our sense of what is right, because we do not systematically understand how this judgment operates. And if we did, could we envision a machine to improve it? Only if morality could be conceived as a faculty, appendable by a device.

Technology as extension means that when we make something, we thrust our intentions upon the world. The result of an extended intention through technology is the *realization* of the intention. Sometimes this is something perceptible in the landscape, like a strip mine that has denuded a hillside upon the idea that the significance of the site is the coal which the trees and grasses kept hidden before. We intend the Earth to be a resource, and we drive our idea of resource into the ground itself. With technology, we turn the scenery into whatever we wish it to be: material for our sustenance, formerly invisible, now unassailable before us. What we saw in it it has become.

Other examples may be more subtle, as the realization of a technology turns back toward our intentions, showing us more of ourselves. We dream of a regular temporal pattern in the universe and observe its passage in the shadows and the stars. We conjure the clock as an image of time. It does not make or break any physical part of our surrounding world, but returns to us as a recurrent and regular reminder of a consistency that we hope is real [...]. We come to rely on it to organize our lives, to fall into precise patterns from morning until night. The universe may possess light and dark, but without our penchant for meticulous division [...], can we say there is such a thing as a nonhuman second, or even a millennium? Only *we* care about time, and extend it out to all things we believe to exist.

There is a variant of the concept of extension which serves to explain how a human idea spreads out to cover all we may perceive. *Expression* is the process by which a human idea is made into something else. Because it is a tangible manifestation of our thoughts, the tool and its outcome also exist apart from us – we can point to them while the idea remains unseen. The clock is an expression of our obsession with time. A skyscraper is an expression of our faith in gravity and our belief in the strength of rectilinear construction. The road is an expression of our desire to travel. These and all human-made things appear as expressions when we consider them in themselves, apart from the human need to cause them in some way. Perhaps the idea of expression is best understood aesthetically, as when we say that a particular poem or painting is an expression of sadness, loss, time, gravity, or the need to travel. When we assess the technique as an object, we examine what it expresses about its creators and their purposes. When we focus on these purposes and try to envision the technique as a means, we see it as an extension of what we intend to do. But it is never merely a means: loaded down with the baggage of our desires, the device turns back upon us and suggests new intentions, propelling its usage forward in time and towards more complex applications. This is what we like to call progress.

It is useful to speak of a technology as an extension of desires because this does not innocently detach the tool from its stated purpose. Following Dewey, they are bound together within the seamless web of experience. Why do we have telephones? Because we believe it is useful to be able to contact people all over the world by summoning their voices without leaving the house. It is an ancient dream, envisioned in countless myths in many cultures. Long ago there were drums that could beat out messages audible miles away. Then a technique is first developed to send messages by wire. All that the telegraph manages is a simple dash and a dot, the digital yes and no of the computer world. Soon voices too course through the wires, and finally they travel through the air without wires at all. Magic? Only if there is no systematic *logos* to explain it. With a global network of waves and satellites we may speak to anyone without stepping out the door.

But why speak? What is the intention which drives the device? Speech, as the basis for most human attempts at immediate communication, gains new powers as it is further disembodied. The telephone was initially a curiosity – who knew what to do with this sudden closeness? Everyone was like the child making her first phone call, not sure if the other end of the line was real. Now phoning is a fact of our lives. There is business by phone, love by phone, all kinds of feelings and thoughts coursing through the

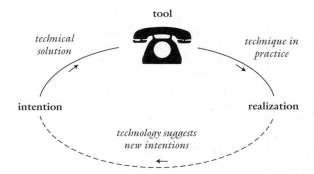

Figure 49.1   The circle of technology in action.

air at any given moment. Knowing we can reach almost all of the persons we care about by dialing a number radically alters the way we relate to people throughout the world. We speak of those whom we know not as friends, but as contacts; not as a community, but as a network.

A tool realizes a human inventor's intention, and the realization of this technique suggests new intentions. Those who use the tool begin with their own intentions, and the more they accept the technology, the more their desires are changed. The technique alters its user's grasp on the world. It is a circle of technological practice and technical innovation, a cybernetic relationship between predicted use and discovered use, a situation something like [that shown in figure 49.1].

When we consent to apply a technique, we agree to let our desires themselves be manipulated and tested. One needs to do a lot of business on a telephone before conceiving the need for a fax machine. One needs to drive a lot and simultaneously to call many people before needing a car phone. And these gadgets need to be technically and economically feasible before they gain wide currency. Already their proliferation changes the way communication is conducted. The stranger thing is that we cannot now imagine life without them, even though they were impractical just several years ago.

What does the telephone express? As a working, designed object, the twofold nature of basic human communication coupled with a component to address anyone in the world by number. Microphone and receiver, one talks, the other listens. A society that did not value individual conversation so highly would not have any use for this ringing thing. Expressing the kind of communication we are most comfortable with, it transforms the extent of this need into the kind of talk it can handle: one to another, all aural, without body language or the effect of a mutually shared real space.[17]

Expression may seem here to blur with extension, but the two concepts need to be kept apart to remind us that technology is not equivalent to humanity, neither subservient to us nor prefacing us. Instruments never play just what we expect them to. Sophocles knew this, in the ode in *Antigone*, where humanity finds,

> in *techne*'s ingenuity,
> unexpected guile.[18]

The tool solves a problem, and then creates new and more thorny issues not dreamable before. Technology, unlike science, does not even claim to reveal larger truths about what exists, but hints at more ways for humanity to change the world. Born of simple need and want, it emerges as an agent of human evolution.

Notes

1 Translation by Jonathan Barnes in *Early Greek Philosophy* (London, 1987), p. 101.
2 Italics within quotations will generally indicate *my* emphasis.
3 Heraclitus, Fragment B51; *Early Greek Philosophy*, p. 102.
4 Octavio Paz, *The Bow and the Lyre*, trans. R. Simms (Austin, TX, 1973), p. 262.
5 Lewis Mumford, *The Myth of the Machine* (New York, 1967), p. 115.
6 Plato, *Euthyphro*, 13e–14b; *Collected Dialogues,* ed. Edith Hamilton and Huntington Cairns (Princeton, 1961), p. 183.
7 Plato, *Philebus*, 55e; *Collected Dialogues*, p. 1137.
8 Ibid., 56a; *Collected Dialogues*, p. 1137.
9 Ibid., 58c; *Collected Dialogues*, p. 1140.
10 Aristotle, *Nicomachean Ethics*, VI, 4, 1140a; *Introduction to Aristotle*, ed. Richard McKeon (New York, 1947), p. 427.
11 Plato, *Meno*, 97d; *Collected Dialogues*, p. 381.
12 Aristotle, *Physics*, II, 2, 194b; *Introduction to Aristotle*, p. 121.
13 Aristotle, *Physics*, II, 8, 199a–b; *Introduction to Aristotle*, pp. 134–5.
14 Joseph Weizenbaum, *Computer Power and Human Reason* (San Francisco, 1976), p. 9.
15 Philosophical application of terminology always risks comparison with common usage of the terms it employs. When one is concerned with sharpening the edges of concepts so that they will be better understood by all, it is appropriate to remember the inherent fluidity of the meaning of words within natural languages, and not to supplant this flexibility with overdetermination. Hence, definitions should not be too exclusive or narrow in philosophy, else it will be impossible to write clearly on general, foundational topics in an interesting way. This has led some philosophers to forego such an enterprise, but I think that just begs the question. Definitions in this work will, as in the most durable of philosophies, suggest clarified uses of familiar concepts without forgetting their original ambiguity.
16 Is a machine the same as a tool? As we use it, yes. As metaphors, machines suggest some autonomous intricacy, something more self-contained than a hammer. Ramelli has drawn "ingenious machines," true, but when it comes time to piloting them, they too serve as tools. At this point I wish to emphasize the similarities, not the differences.
17 For a thoroughly eccentric look at how the telephone underlies all of modern communication and philosophy, see Avital Ronell, *The Telephone Book*.
18 Sophocles, *Antigone*, 365–6 (Cambridge, MA, 1912), p. 342. Literally: "having, in the inventiveness of *techne*, something cunning beyond expectation." My translation.

PART VII

WHAT ARE THE CONNECTIONS BETWEEN ECOLOGICAL SCIENCE AND ENVIRONMENTAL ETHICS?

50 Ecology – A Subversive Subject
    Paul B. Sears

51 What is Conservation Biology?
    Michael E. Soulé

52 Environmental Ethics and Ecological Science
    Mark Sagoff

53 The Metaphysical Implications of Ecology
    J. Baird Callicott

54 The Ends of the World as We Know Them
    Jared Diamond

Introduction

For most of the twentieth century, philosophers of the Anglo-American school have argued whether it is or is not possible to derive normative statements from descriptive statements.[1] This interesting debate leads back to the great David Hume. In *A Treatise of Human Nature*, Hume recalls his reaction on reading the majority of moral philosophy:

> I am surpriz'd to find, that instead of the usual copulations of propositions, *is*, and *is not*, I meet with no proposition that is not connected with an *ought*, or an *ought not*. This change is imperceptible; but is, however, of the last consequence. For as this *ought*, or *ought not*, expresses some new relation or affirmation, 'tis necessary that it shou'd be observ'd and explain'd.[2]

Interpreters have not been unanimous about what Hume meant. Some believe he is asserting the existence of an unbridgeable chasm between normative and descriptive propositions; others believe that he is not saying it is impossible to derive an *ought* from an *is*, only that if such an inference is to be made, the connection needs to be explicated.

Numerous metaethicists have taken the former position. According to this line of reasoning, what Hume meant is that it is logically impossible to derive value-laden statements, such as ethical statements, from value-free statements, such as factual statements. There is, in effect, a stultifying *is–ought* or *fact–value* gap. Inferring a *moral prescription* from a *nonmoral description* is forbidden. The only way to move from the observation that the lawn is brown to the imperative WATER THE LAWN! is another normative assumption that a brown lawn is bad. In other words, upholders of the taboo say, there is no way to get from descriptions to prescriptions. Any prescription presupposes some other prescription. Values are not facts because values are not embedded in the essence of things – that is, values are not objectively real. As Bertrand Russell says, "questions as to 'values' lie wholly outside the domain of knowledge. That is to say, when we assert that this or that has 'value,' we are giving expression to our own emotions, not to a fact."[3]

The fact/value gap underlies the distinction between science and ethics, between fact and value. If there is a gap, then ethics cannot be connected with science. On the mechanistic model, values are not embedded in nature; values are products of human emotion and desire. Each individual scientist, if she or he successfully brackets personal prejudices, is able to agree about the facts of nature – the way things really work. The role of the scientist is not to ask whether splitting atoms or cloning animals ought or ought not to be done, and the achievement of splitting atoms or cloning sheep does not itself say anything about ethics. Ethics plays no role in scientific investigation, and the knowledge of science yields no moral injunctions. This assumption underlies the status quo position in modern Western science: scientists describe the world, and must leave the making of moral injunctions about the state of the world up to theologians, philosophers, and politicians.

All contributors to Part VII reject the notion that an is/ought or fact/value gap estranges ethics from ecology. Ecologist Paul Sears, in "Ecology – A Subversive Subject," brings attention to the fact that, as far as the history of Western science goes, ecology is a renegade discipline. In the main, Western science has been focused on descriptive rigor and has shied away from prescriptive pronouncements. Yet the study of ecosystems must include an assessment of the human impact on them: "ecology affords a continuing critique of man's operations within the ecosystem." Ecology is thus inherently political. This has made ecology, in the phraseology of Sears, a "subversive science."

In "What is Conservation Biology?," biologist Michael Soulé unabashedly rejects the self-imposed taboo of modernity barring scientists from making value judgments and taking ethical stands in their work. According to the model of the scientific method that Soulé rejects, the proficient scientist achieves objectivity by isolating or "bracketing" any subjective and socially inculcated biases. In this way, different scientists in different places, studying the same subject, should be able to reach similar conclusions. Bracketing biases is only possible if the essence of the self is absolutely ontologically independent of spatiotemporality.

Against this modern ideal of objectivity in science and unfazed by the taboo against making ethical claims, Soulé asserts that knowledge of the natural world – in his case, the value of biodiversity – ought to lead to normative prescriptions, such as *Biodiversity is good! Protect and preserve biodiversity!*

In "Environmental Ethics and Ecological Science," American philosopher Mark Sagoff argues that, despite the disparate character and aims of ecological science and environmental ethics, the two disciplines share fundamental assumptions. Most prominent is the assumption that nature has design – illustrated, for example, in the ontology of the Great Chain of Being – and to corrupt this design is bad. Yet Sagoff argues that, as an empirical truth, design and balance in nature is baseless. It is better, Sagoff recommends, to think of the spontaneous processes of nature as the norm for both ecological science and environmental ethics.

J. Baird Callicott, in "The Metaphysical Implications of Ecology," finds direct links between the lessons of the science of ecology and environmental ethics. Against the reductionism of atomism, which holds that relations between constituent parts of natural systems are external, the metaphysical implication of ecology is that the relations between constituent parts of natural systems are internal (an assertion also made by Naess[4]). Internal relations provide the framework for a relational view of the self, a view which asserts that the essence or identity of a self is dependent upon how that self is related to the environment. And herein lies the connection with ethics: the health of human selves depends upon the health of the ecological systems within which we are embedded. Environmental ethics, if nothing else, is "enlightened self-interest."

Geographer Jared Diamond casts the issue of ethics and ecological science in terms of the survival or collapse of entire civilizations. "The Ends of the World as We Know Them" consists of a brief summary – detailed in greater length in his popular book *Collapse* – of the history of several civilizations that essentially committed collective suicide by ruining their environments. Evidence suggests that contemporary industrialized civilizations are making the same mistakes. While one could be pessimistic or even fatalistic about such parallels, Diamond draws a positive conclusion. The largest and most looming of humanity's problems are of our own making; consequently, if we take environmental problems seriously, we have the power to avoid disaster. We have knowledge of ecology and an awareness of history that other failed civilizations did not have. The question is whether we will put ecological knowledge to ethical use.

Notes

1   For an excellent overview of the debate, see Hudson, *The Is–Ought Question*, pp. 11–31.
2   *A Treatise of Human Nature*, p. 469.
3   *Religion and Science*, pp. 230–1.
4   Naess, "The Shallow and the Deep Ecology Movement," in Anker, "Deep Ecology in Bucharest," p. 60. (See this volume, p. 231.)

---

50   Ecology – A Subversive Subject

Paul B. Sears

My choice of title is not facetious. I wish to explore a question of growing concern. Is ecology a phase of science of limited interest and utility? Or, if taken seriously as an instrument for the long-run welfare of mankind, would it endanger the assumptions and practices accepted by modern societies, whatever their doctrinal commitments? To this end, I propose to consider its position in the world of science, the field of education, and the arena of practical life.

Disregarding for a moment the judgments of ecologists themselves, I have encountered two criticisms. The first is that ecology is merely a matter of

From *Bioscience*, vol. 14, no. 17 (1964): 11–13. © 1964 by American Institute of Biological Sciences (AIBS). Reproduced with permission of the American Institute of Biological Sciences in the format Textbook via Copyright Clearance Center.

emphasizing the obvious. It merely assembles matters of common knowledge and attempts to invest them with status by means of a special and not very winning vocabulary. The second represents an opposite extreme. Conceding the ultimate importance of understanding the great pattern of life and environment, sound logic and practice dictate that we must *first* get on with the infinitely detailed analysis of the many factors involved. In other words, we do not yet know enough about the bricks and mortar to get on with the building. I am certain these attitudes have been reflected in the appointment programs of influential schools.

Furthermore, we should not neglect the mutual scourging of ecologists themselves – not the self-flagellation of Penitentes, but a lusty swinging of the whip on the other fellows' backs. The most recent and vigorous example is by Egler (1). Although the editor informs us that a considerable part of the original manuscript has been deleted, presumably as too hot to handle, this remains: ". . . it seems reasonable to question and consider whether 'ecology' exists as an effective social strand in this ecosystem. The answer quite simply is 'no' for more reasons than the immaturity of the science . . . this time I would say it is the social immaturity of the ecologists."

Whatever the justice of criticisms, without and within, the present position of ecology in education is an eloquent fact. I have lectured on more than six-score campuses, generally under circumstances that permitted a look around, thanks to the hospitality encountered. Almost without exception, I have found audiences of students, faculty, and citizens responsive to discussion of the nature and significance of ecology. Yet, with too few exceptions, I have found the instructional juggernaut creaking along in conventional paths so far as this subject is concerned.

The several introductory science courses which should here if anywhere have a common intellectual bond continue to go their separate, insulated ways, each with a reverent eye upon the minority – its future 'majors.' Incidentally, but by no means trivially, I know of cases where potential recruits of high scientific promise have been lost by this frozen practice. Even the millions spent on course improvement, fruitful as they may have been, have done more to intensify teaching of the individual sciences than to integrate them.

It is also my observation that the majority of biological curricula have been unable to wriggle free from the trap of convention. In the typical introductory course, ecology tends to come in as a chapter along the way rather than as a unifying philosophical point of view. With few exceptions, the builders of textbooks follow this pattern, thereby perpetuating it. Since their publishers must keep a shrewd eye on the buyer's market, it is hard to assess final responsibility.

I have no recent figures on the number of departments that offer formal courses in ecology, nor do I have time to get them before the deadline of this paper. A number of years ago, I found many instances in which the subject was not taught. I judge that the situation is improving, but, in almost every instance, ecology is reserved until toward the end of a major program and so exists largely for the elite. Since, as I shall show later, the benefits of ecology must come largely through wide popular understanding, this is a serious matter.

Now training and education form a continuum whose charter derives from the needs of the culture. The group must survive under satisfying conditions and, to that end, so must the individual. Thus the elements of necessity and satisfaction, of advantage and delight, are intertwined. As in a crude handmade rope, one strand may at times conceal or suppress the others. Military and civic necessity led the Romans to foster the military arts, lucid communication, engineering, and medicine. Aristocratic delight was a large element in the brilliant science of 18th century France and lingered on to inspire Darwin.

What we call higher education is compounded of all these factors. It reenforces the training needed for social and individual advantage by intellectual challenge or respectability. Does ecology qualify under these latter rubrics? Genetics, its twin, certainly has done so. To answer this question fairly, we must lay aside any arrogance with respect to the simple pioneer work of the early ecologists, or even its relevance to certain steps in the present learning process. Astronomers do not laugh off Kepler or Copernicus or even Ptolemy, and, if chemists were to speak too lightly of the Greek elements – earth, air, fire, and water – their students would miss the very basis of the analytical process.

It is worth noting that, in the early meetings of the Study Committee of the Ecological Society of America, one of the first points of agreement was that the subject had to command intellectual respect to be recognized. Equally important, to me at least, was the evidence that one could be an ecologist regardless of what he called himself or what techniques of investigation he used. The true test is the breadth of his perspective – whether he knows what he is up to in terms of the great pattern of life and environment. On that basis, some physicists might come out with better credentials than some of the brotherhood.

A look at recent volumes of *Ecology* or its British counterpart, the *Journal of Ecology*, should dispel any doubts about the quality of cerebration or scientific workmanship now going on in the profession. One will see increasing use of sophisticated methods and instrumentation, increasing concern with such fundamental concepts as energetics, material recycling, productivity, and community function. Not to be overlooked is the growing activity in fields such as forestry, range management, oceanography, limnology, and climatology, all basically ecological. Yet, in honesty, it must be recorded that some effort has been required to assure that biological (i.e., *ecological*) oceanography was duly provided for in the designing of floating laboratories.

This list of ancillary fields is enough to suggest that ecology has important applications. Discoveries in these fields, however, are not likely to be patentable. Their benefits arise when they are placed in the public domain rather than by sale over the counter. This is even more true of advances within the narrower field of ecology proper, whose findings generally must become a matter of wide public understanding to be effective.

As Frank Darling (2) has demonstrated, ecology, despite its fragmentary progress beginning with the environmental relations of plant life, is a study of the entire ecosystem. Of this system, man is not just an observer and irresponsible exploiter but an integral part, now the world's dominant organism. He has come into the system and survived thus far by the bounty of that system plus his own marvelous power of adjustment. Even so, the historical record is replete with his failures.

By its very nature, ecology affords a continuing critique of man's operations within the ecosystem. The applications of other sciences are particulate, specialized, based on the solution of individual problems with little if any attention to side effects and practically uncontrolled by any thought of the larger whole.

The problems to which scientific technology has addressed itself are real enough. No farm boy who has forked manure, milked many cows by hand, or trudged a long distance to school would question this. No parent who has seen his family suffer the ills of overcrowding, poverty, and hunger would question it – and neither would the producer who has been able to substitute power machinery for slow and laborious hand labor, nor the householder who recalls the days before telephones and modern plumbing. The handicaps of distance, disease, hard muscular labor, and insufficient food cannot be ignored.

But technical improvements on the farm have driven millions off the land and into the city where the progress of invention has made the profitable use of manpower less and less necessary. Within the cities themselves, the penalties of overcrowding daily become more obvious as the maintenance of order, education, and health become increasingly difficult. Mass production, with its steadily increasing drains upon energy and materials, is now so efficient that industry has to exert itself to create demand, while government is enmeshed in legerdemain to increase purchasing power through devices that were old when kings diluted the gold in their coins. Meanwhile our efficient industry and domestic sanitation push their wastes into air and water – painful mockery of the quiet recycling of materials in the ancient pattern of nature.

I know of no more eloquent presentation of the situation than that by the great humanitarian Dr Alan Gregg (3) shortly before his death. After a lifetime spent in bringing the benefits of modern hygiene and medicine to the edges of the habitable planet, thereby mightily helping to reduce the death rate and prolong life, he reviewed the resulting ecological imbalance with grim dismay. Drawing upon his professional knowledge, he could only compare the uncontrolled increase in human numbers and the resulting disorder with the spread of cancer cells within an organism.

To me, at least, it is disturbing to hear the current glib emphasis on economic "growth" as the solution of all ills. Growth, in all biological experience, is a determinate process. Out of control, say by pituitary imbalance, it becomes pathological gigantism and by no means the same thing as health. With the concept of a healthy economy there can be no quarrel, but to equate this with an ever-expanding, ever-rising spiral is to relapse into the folly of perpetual motion, long since discredited by a sane understanding of energetics.

I have no wish to continue a depressing recital, even when I recall that the value of stored farm surplus is exceeded by that of military matériel designed and manufactured since the end of World War II but already obsolete. Honorable men are now wondering whether it has been ethical to introduce modern death-control into areas where there is no control of human numbers. I have not yet heard them justify the continuance of suspicion and the multiplication of armaments with the double objective of keeping industry prosperous and eventually reducing global population, but this may be a short step. I hope not.

One could quarrel with the profit motive or political philosophy as a source of present troubles, but the trouble lies deeper. The individual must see a reasonable advantage to himself to do his best. The leader of world Communism saw the great ears of Iowa corn but not the results of exploiting our dry steppes, and so he needlessly repeated that folly. The British Labour party, when in power, spent treasure on the ground-nut adventure when any ecologist worth his salt (and Britain has some of the best) knew it would not work. Likewise he could have warned the industries and housing developments that suffered great damage during the New England flood of 1955 of the hazards of their disastrous choice of sites.

My fellow ecologists are insistent on the need for more study of ecosystems, and they are correct. The planet is so vast and varied that our knowledge of it is quite imperfect. Blanket solutions from distant centers of power can seldom be trusted. It was this fact, combined with my belief that, as a matter of political health, the citizen must face the facts where he lives, that led me in 1935 (4) to suggest the need for ecologists at the local level. I have lately been heartened to hear this suggestion rise anew from others. Let me repeat that the benefits of applied ecology can be realized only through widespread general understanding rather than through ordinary commercial channels. Closely related to this are, in my judgment, some fundamental reforms in the educational process, suggested in earlier paragraphs and in a recent booklet. (5)

Withal I am mindful of the complaint of a Congressman who said that every scientist who appeared before his committee believes that his cat is blackest. Viewing, as I do, science as it should be, a seamless fabric, this is not my point. Granting the need for continuing advances along the entire front, I am trying to say that we are not using vital knowledge we now have. And, because this kind of knowledge affords perspective to a peculiar degree, we cannot safely continue to neglect it, however much it may threaten some of our cherished practices in the interest of our long-time welfare.

Postscript

Lest my estimate of the impact which the rules of ecological experience might have on our present ideas and practices seem ill-judged, I submit the following questions:

What conclusion would you draw if you observed a population curve, similar to that of man, in any other organism?

What are the effects upon the ecosystem where profit to the developer is the sole check upon urban expansion?

What are the patterns of material and energy flow consequent upon modern technology?

What is known of the cumulative effects on human beings of the wastes and byproducts of our present culture?

What is known of the long-range effects of monoculture and heavy machinery upon fertile agricultural land?

What will be the consequences of locating highways and other permanent public works on strictly engineering considerations, without regard to long-range use potential?

References

1. Egler, Frank E. 1964. Pesticides – in our ecosystem. *American Scientist*, 52(1): 110–36.
2. Darling, F. Fraser. 1960. The unity of ecology. *Advancement of Science*, 297–306 (Nov.). (Presidential address to Section D, British Association.)
3. Gregg, Alan. 1955. A medical aspect of the population problem. *Science*, 121(3150): 681–2.
4. Sears, Paul B. 1935. *Deserts On The March*. Univ. of Oklahoma Press.
5. Sears, Paul B. 1962. *Where There Is Life*. Dell Publ. Co., NY.

51   What is Conservation Biology?

Michael E. Soulé

Conservation biology, a new stage in the application of science to conservation problems, addresses the biology of species, communities, and ecosystems that are perturbed, either directly or indirectly, by human activities or other agents. Its goal is to provide principles and tools for preserving biological diversity. In this article I describe conservation biology, define its fundamental propositions, and note a few of its contributions. I also point out that ethical norms are a genuine part of conservation biology, as they are in all mission- or crisis-oriented disciplines.

Crisis Disciplines

Conservation biology differs from most other biological sciences in one important way: it is often a crisis discipline. Its relation to biology, particularly ecology, is analogous to that of surgery to physiology and war to political science. In crisis disciplines, one must act before knowing all the facts; crisis disciplines are thus a mixture of science and art, and their pursuit requires intuition as well as information. A conservation biologist may have to make decisions or recommendations about design and management before he or she is completely comfortable with the theoretical and empirical bases of the analysis (May 1984, Soulé and Wilcox 1980, chap. 1). Tolerating uncertainty is often necessary.

Conservation biologists are being asked for advice by government agencies and private organizations on such problems as the ecological and health consequences of chemical pollution, the introduction of exotic species and artificially produced strains of existing organisms, the sites and sizes of national parks, the definition of minimum conditions for viable populations of particular target species, the frequencies and kinds of management practices in existing refuges and managed wildlands, and the ecological effects of development. For political reasons, such decisions must often be made in haste.

For example, the rapidity and irreversibility of logging and human resettlement in Western New Guinea (Irian Jaya) prompted the Indonesian government to establish a system of national parks. Two of the largest areas recommended had never been visited by biologists, but it appeared likely that these areas harbored endemic biotas.[1] Reconnaissance later confirmed this. The park boundaries were established in 1981, and subsequent development has already precluded all but minor adjustments. Similar crises are now facing managers of endangered habitats and species in the United States – for example, grizzly bears in the Yellowstone region, black-footed ferrets in Wyoming, old-growth Douglas-fir forests in the Pacific Northwest, red-cockaded woodpeckers in the Southeast, and condors in California.

Other Characteristics of Conservation Biology

As illustrated in figure 51.1, conservation biology shares certain characteristics with other crisis-oriented disciplines. A comparison with cancer biology illustrates some of these characteristics, including conservation biology's synthetic, eclectic, multidisciplinary structure. Furthermore, both fields take many of their questions, techniques, and methods from a broad range of fields, not all biological. This illustration is also intended to show the artificiality of the dichotomy between pure and applied disciplines.

Finally, this figure illustrates the dependence of the biological sciences on social science disciplines. Today, for example, any recommendations about the location and size of national parks should consider the impact of the park on indigenous peoples and their cultures, on the local economy, and on opportunity costs such as forfeited logging profits.

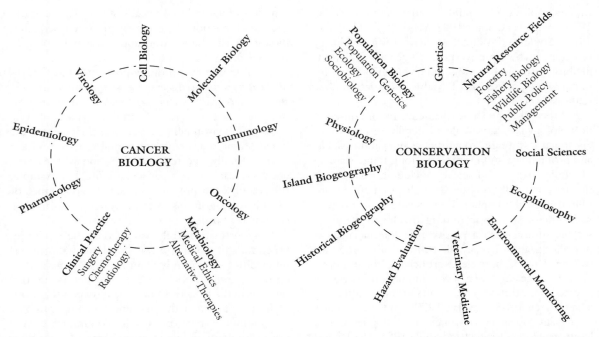

Figure 51.1 Cancer biology and conservation biology are both synthetic, multidisciplinary sciences. The dashed line indicates the artificial nature of the borders between disciplines and between "basic" and "applied" research. See text.

There is much overlap between conservation biology and the natural resource fields, especially fisheries biology, forestry, and wildlife management. Nevertheless, two characteristics of these fields often distinguish them from conservation biology. The first is the dominance in the resource fields of utilitarian, economic objectives. Even though individual wildlife biologists honor Aldo Leopold's land ethic and the intrinsic value of nature, most of the financial resources for management must go to enhancing commercial and recreational values for humans. The emphasis is on *our* natural *resources*.

The second distinguishing characteristic is the nature of these resources. For the most part, they are a small number of particularly valuable target species (e.g., trees, fishes, deer, and waterfowl) – a tiny fraction of the total biota. This distinction is beginning to disappear, however, as some natural resource agencies become more "ecological" and because conservation biologists frequently focus on individual endangered, critical, or keystone species.

Conservation biology tends to be holistic, in two senses of the word. First, many conservation biologists, including many wildlife specialists, assume that

ecological and evolutionary processes must be studied at their own macroscopic levels and that reductionism alone cannot lead to explanations of community and ecosystem processes such as body-size differences among species in guilds (Cody and Diamond 1975), pollinator-plant coevolution (Gilbert and Raven 1975), succession, speciation, and species-area relationships. Even ecological reductionists, however, agree that the proper objective of conservation is the protection and continuity of entire communities and ecosystems. The holistic assumption of conservation biology should not be confused with romantic notions that one can grasp the functional intricacies of complex systems without conducting scientific and technological studies of individual components (Levins and Lewontin 1985, chap. 6). Holism is not mysticism.

The second implication of the term *holistic* is the assumption that multidisciplinary approaches will ultimately be the most fruitful. Conservation biology is certainly holistic in this sense. Modern biogeographic analysis is now being integrated into the conservation movement (Diamond 1975, Simberloff and Abele 1976, Terborgh 1974, Wilcox 1980). Population genetics, too, is now being applied to the technology of wildlife management (Frankel 1974, Frankel and Soulé 1981, Schonewald-Cox et al. 1983, Soulé and Wilcox 1980). Multidisciplinary research, involving government agencies and wildlife biologists, is also evident in recent efforts to illuminate the question of viable population size (Salwasser et al. 1984).

Another distinguishing characteristic of conservation biology is its time scale. Generally, its practitioners attach less weight to aesthetics, maximum yields, and profitability, and more to the long-range viability of whole systems and species, including their evolutionary potential. Long-term viability of natural communities usually implies the persistence of diversity, with little or no help from humans. But for the foreseeable future, such a passive role for managers is unrealistic, and virtually all conservation programs will need to be buttressed artificially. For example, even the largest nature reserves and national parks are affected by anthropogenic factors in the surrounding area (Janzen 1983, Kushlan 1979), and such refuges are usually too small to contain viable populations of large carnivores (Frankel and Soulé 1981, Shaffer and Samson 1985). In addition, poaching, habitat fragmentation, and the influx of feral animals and exotic plants require extraordinary practices such as culling, eradication, wildlife immunization, habitat protection, and artificial transfers. Until benign neglect is again a possibility, conservation biology can complement natural resource fields in providing some of the theoretical and empirical foundations for coping with such management conundrums.

Postulates of Conservation Biology

Conservation biology, like many of its parent sciences, is very young. Therefore, it is not surprising that its assumptions about the structure and function of natural systems, and about the role of humans in nature, have not been systematized. What are these postulates? I propose two sets: a functional, or mechanistic, set and an ethical, or normative, set.

The functional postulates

These are working propositions based partly on evidence, partly on theory, and partly on intuition. In essence, they are a set of fundamental axioms, derived from ecology, biogeography, and population genetics, about the maintenance of both the form and function of natural biological systems. They suggest the rules for action. A necessary goal of conservation biology is the elaboration and refinement of such principles.

The first, the evolutionary postulate states: *Many of the species that constitute natural communities are the products of coevolutionary processes.* In most communities, species are a significant part of one another's environment. Therefore, their genetically based physiological and behavioral repertoires have been naturally selected to accommodate the existence and reactions of a particular biota. For example, the responses of prey to a predator's appearance or of a phytophagous insect to potential host plants are continually "tuned" by natural selection.

This postulate merely asserts that the structure, function, and stability of coevolved, natural communities differ significantly from those of unnatural or synthetic communities. It does not necessarily rely on deterministic factors like density-dependent population dynamics or the molding by competition of morphological relationships in communities over both ecological and evolutionary time. In addition, this postulate is neutral on the issue of holistic versus reductionistic analysis of community structure. (In practice, a reductionistic methodology, including autecological research, may be the best way to establish the holistic structure of communities.)

There are many "corollaries" of this postulate. Strictly speaking, most of them are empirically based generalizations. The following all assume the existence of community processes as well as a coevolutionary component in community structure.

Species are interdependent. Not only have species in communities evolved unique ways of avoiding predators, locating food, and capturing and handling prey, but mutualistic relationships are frequent (Janzen 1975, Seifert and Seifert 1979). This is not to say that every species is essential for community function, but that there is always uncertainty about the interactions of species and about the biological consequences of an extinction. Partly for this reason, Aldo Leopold (1953) admonished conservationists to save all of the parts (species) of a community.

Many species are highly specialized. Perhaps the majority of animal species, including phytophagous insects, parasites, and parasitoids, depend on a particular host (Price 1980). This means that the coattails of endangered host species can be very long, taking with them dozens (Raven 1976) or hundreds (Erwin 1983) of small consumer species when they go.

Extinctions of keystone species can have long-range consequences. The extinction of major predators, large herbivores, or plants that are important as breeding or feeding sites for animals may initiate sequences of causally linked events that ultimately lead to further extinctions (Frankel and Soulé 1981, Gilbert 1980, Terborgh and Winter 1980).

Introductions of generalists may reduce diversity. The introduction of exotic plant and animal species may reduce diversity, especially if they are large or generalist species (Diamond 1984, Elton 1958). Apparently, the larger the land mass, the less the impact of exotics (e.g., Simberloff 1980).

The evolutionary postulate and its corollaries formalize the evidence that natural communities comprise species whose genetic makeups have been mutually affected by their coexistence (Futuyma and Slatkin 1983, Gilbert and Raven 1975). An alternative theory, the null hypothesis that communities are randomly assembled, is usually restricted to "horizontal" subcommunities such as guilds, specific taxa, or trophic levels (e.g., James and Boecklen 1984). In general, this latter thesis lacks empirical support, except that competitive structuring within guilds or trophic levels is often absent or difficult to demonstrate (Strong et al. 1984), and that harsh environments or the vagaries of dispersal may often be more important than biological interactions in determining local community composition (e.g., Underwood and Denley 1984).

The second functional postulate concerns the scale of ecological processes: *Many, if not all, ecological processes have thresholds below and above which they become discontinuous, chaotic, or suspended.* This postulate states that many ecological processes and patterns (including succession, nutrient cycling, and density-dependent phenomena) are interrupted or fail altogether where the system is too small. Smallness and randomness are inseparable.

Nonecological processes may also dominate at the other end of the spatial and temporal scale, in very large or very old systems. In very large systems, such as continents, climatic and physiographic phenomena often determine the major patterns of the landscape, including species distribution. In very old systems, ecological processes give way to geological and historical ones or to infrequent catastrophic events, such as inundation, volcanism, and glaciation. In other words, ecological processes belong to an intermediate scale of physical size and time (MacArthur 1972), and these processes begin to fail or are overwhelmed near the extremities of these ranges.

Two major assumptions, or generalizations, underlie this postulate. First, *the temporal continuity of habitats and successional stages depends on size.* The random disappearance of resources or habitats will occur frequently in small sites but rarely, if ever, in large ones. The reasons include the inherent randomness of such processes as patch dynamics, larval settlement, or catastrophic events, as well as the dynamics of contagious phenomena such as disease, windstorm destruction, and fire. The larger an area, the less likely that all patches of a particular habitat will disappear simultaneously. Species will disappear if their habitats disappear.

Second, *outbursts reduce diversity.* If population densities of ecologically dominant species rise above sustainable levels, they can destroy local prey populations and other species sharing a resource with such species. Outbursts are most probable in small sites that lack a full array of population buffering mechanisms, including habitat sinks for dispersing individuals, sufficient predators, and alternative feeding grounds during inclement weather. The unusually high population densities that often occur in nature reserves can also increase the rate of disease transmission, frequently leading to epidemics that may affect every individual.

Taken together, the corollaries of this postulate lead to the conclusion that survival rates of species in reserves are proportional to reserve size. Even though there is now a consensus that several small sites can contain as many species as one large site (when barriers to dispersal are absent), the species extinction rate is generally higher in small sites (Soulé and Simberloff 1986).

The third functional postulate concerns the scale of population phenomena: *Genetic and demographic processes have thresholds below which nonadaptive, random forces begin to prevail over adaptive, deterministic forces within populations.* The stochastic factors in population extinction have been discussed extensively (Shaffer 1981, Soulé 1983, Terborgh 1974) in the context of the minimum conditions for population viability. The main implication of this postulate for conservation is that the probability of survival of a local population is a positive function of its size. One of the corollaries of this postulate is that below a certain population size (between 10 and 30), the probability of extinction from random demographic events increases steeply (Shaffer 1981).

The next three corollaries are genetic. First, populations of outbreeding organisms will suffer a chronic loss of fitness from inbreeding depression at effective population sizes of less than 50 to 100 (Franklin 1980, Soulé 1980). Second, genetic drift in small populations (less than a few hundred individuals) will cause a progressive loss of genetic variation; in turn, such genetic erosion will reduce immediate fitness because multilocus heterozygosity is generally advantageous in outbreeding species (Beardmore 1983, Soulé 1980, and references cited below). (The genetic bases of these two corollaries may be the same: homozygosity for deleterious, recessive alleles.) Finally, natural selection will be less effective in small populations because of genetic drift and the loss of potentially adaptive genetic variation (Franklin 1980).

The fourth functional postulate is that *nature reserves are inherently disequilibrial for large, rare organisms*. There are two reasons for this. First, extinctions are inevitable in habitat islands the size of nature reserves (MacArthur and Wilson 1967); species diversity must be artificially maintained for many taxa because natural colonization (reestablishment) from outside sources is highly unlikely. Second, speciation, the only other nonartificial means of replacing species, will not operate for rare or large organisms in nature reserves because reserves are nearly always too small to keep large or rare organisms isolated within them for long periods, and populations isolated in different reserves will have to be maintained by artificial gene flow if they are to persist. Such gene flow would preclude genetic differentiation among the colonies (Soulé 1980).

The normative postulates

The normative postulates are value statements that make up the basis of an ethic of appropriate attitudes toward other forms of life – an ecosophy (Naess 1973). They provide standards by which our actions can be measured. They are shared, I believe, by most conservationists and many biologists, although ideological purity is not my reason for proposing them.

Diversity of organisms is good. Such a statement cannot be tested or proven. The mechanisms by which such value judgments arise in consciousness are unknown. The conceptual mind may accept or reject the idea as somehow valid or appropriate. If accepted, the idea becomes part of an individual's philosophy.

We could speculate about the subconscious roots of the norm, "diversity is good." In general, humans enjoy variety. We can never know with certainty whether this is based on avoiding tedium and boredom or something else, but it may be as close to a universal norm as we can come. This is probably one of the reasons for the great popularity of zoos and national parks, which in recent years have had, respectively, over 100 million and 200 million visitors annually in the United States. Perhaps there is a genetic basis in humans for the appeal of biotic diversity (Orians 1980, Wilson 1984). After all, humans have been hunter-gatherers, depending on a wide array of habitats and resources, for virtually all of the past several million years.

A corollary of this postulate is that the untimely extinction of populations and species is bad. Conservation biology does not abhor extinction per se. Natural extinction is thought to be either value free or good because it is part of the process of replacing less well-adapted gene pools with better adapted ones. Ultimately, natural extinction, unless it is catastrophic, does not reduce biological diversity, for it is offset by speciation. Natural extinctions, however, are rare events on a human time scale. Of the hundreds of vertebrate extinctions that have occurred during the last few centuries, few, if any, have been natural (Diamond 1984, Frankel and Soulé 1981), whereas the rate of anthropogenic extinctions appears to be growing exponentially.

It may seem logical to extend the aversion of anthropogenic extinction of populations to the suffering and untimely deaths of individuals because populations are composed of individuals. I do not believe this step is necessary or desirable for conservation biology. Although disease and suffering in animals are unpleasant and, perhaps, regrettable, biologists recognize that conservation is engaged in the protection of the integrity and continuity of natural processes, not the welfare of individuals. At the population level, the important processes are ultimately genetic and evolutionary because these maintain the potential for continued existence. Evolution, as it occurs in nature, could not proceed without the suffering inseparable from hunger, disease, and predation.

For this reason, biologists often overcome their emotional identification with individual victims. For example, the biologist sees the abandoned fledgling or the wounded rabbit as part of the process of natural selection and is not deceived that "rescuing" sick, abandoned, or maimed individuals is serving the species or the cause of conservation. (Salvaging a debilitated individual from a very small population would be an exception, assuming it might eventually contribute to the gene pool.) Therefore, the ethical imperative to conserve species diversity is distinct from any societal norms about the value or the welfare of individual animals or plants. This does not in any way detract from ethical systems that provide behavioral guidance for humans on appropriate relationships with individuals from other species, especially when the callous behavior of humans causes animals to suffer unnecessarily. Conservation and animal welfare, however, are conceptually distinct, and they should remain politically separate.

Returning to the population issue, we might ask if all populations of a given species have equal value. I think not. The value of a population, I believe, depends on its genetic uniqueness, its ecological position, and the number of extant populations. A large, genetically polymorphic population containing unique alleles or genetic combinations has greater value, for example, than a small, genetically depauperate population of the same species. Also, the fewer the populations that remain, the greater the probability of the simultaneous extinction (random or not) of *all* populations, and thus of the species. Hence, how precious a population is, is a function of how many such populations exist.

Ecological complexity is good. This postulate parallels the first one, but assumes the value of habitat diversity and complex ecological processes. Arriving at this judgment may require considerable sophistication, training, and thought. Someone familiar with descriptive plant and animal biogeography, trophic levels, nutrient cycling, edaphic heterogeneity, and other aspects of ecological classification is in a better position to fully appreciate the complexity in a tide-pool or forest.

Like the first one, this postulate expresses a preference for nature over artifice, for wilderness over gardens (cf. Dubos 1980). When pressed, however, ecologists cannot prove that their preference for natural diversity should be the standard for managing habitats. For example, even if it could be shown that a decrease in species diversity led to desertification, eutrophication, or the piling up of organic material, it is still not a logical conclusion that such consequences are bad. For example, such events in the past created fossil fuels (although not everyone would argue that this was good).

Ecological diversity can be enhanced artificially, but the increase in diversity can be more apparent than real (especially if cryptic taxa and associations are considered, such as soil biotas and microbial communities). In addition, humans tend to sacrifice ecological and geographic heterogeneity for an artificially maintained, energy-intensive, local species diversity. Take, for example, the large numbers of plant taxa maintained in the warm-temperate and subtropical cities of the world. Most of these species are horticultural varieties that do well in landscaped gardens and parks. One sees a great variety of such plants in Sydney, Buenos Aires, Cape Town, Athens, Mexico City, Miami, and San Diego. But the roses, citrus, camellias, bougainvilleas, daffodils, eucalyptus, and begonias are everywhere similar.

This combination of local variety and geographic homogeneity produces several pleasant benefits for humans. Not only are the exotic species more spectacular, but the world traveler can always feel botanically at home. In addition, many cities now have a greater diversity of plant families and tree species than did the original habitat destroyed to make way for the city. But these aesthetic benefits are costly. The price is low geographic diversity and ecological complexity. Botanical gardens, zoos, urban parks, and aquaria satisfy, to a degree, my desire to be with other species, but not my need to see wild and free creatures or my craving for solitude or for a variety of landscapes and vistas.

Evolution is good. Implicit in the third and fourth functional postulates is the assumption that the continuity of evolutionary potential is good. Assuming that life itself is good, how can one maintain an ethical neutrality about evolution? Life itself owes its existence and present diversity to the evolutionary process. Evolution is the machine, and life is its product. One possible corollary of this axiom is an ethical imperative to provide for the continuation of evolutionary processes in as many undisturbed natural habitats as possible.

Biotic diversity has intrinsic value, irrespective of its instrumental or utilitarian value. This normative postulate is the most fundamental. In emphasizing the inherent value of nonhuman life, it distinguishes the dualistic, exploitive world view from a more unitary perspective: Species have value in themselves, a value neither conferred nor revocable, but springing from a species' long evolutionary heritage and potential or even from the mere fact of its existence.[2] A large literature exists on this subject (Devall and Sessions 1985; Ehrenfeld 1981; Passmore 1974; Rolston 1985; Tobias 1985; and the journal *Environmental Ethics*).

Endless scholarly debate will probably take place about the religious, ethical, and scientific sources of this postulate and about its implications for policy and management. For example, does intrinsic value imply egalitarianism and equal rights among species? A more profitable discussion would be about the rules to be used when two or more species have conflicting interests (Naess 1985).

[...]

Conclusions

Conservation biology is a young field, but its roots antedate science itself. Each civilization and each human generation responds differently to the forces that weaken the biological infrastructure on which society depends and from which it derives much of its spiritual, aesthetic, and intellectual life. In the past, the responses to environmental degradation were often literary, as in the Babylonian Talmud (Vol. I, Shabbath 129a, chap. xviii, p. 644), Marsh (1864), Leopold (1966), Carson (1962) and others (see Passmore 1974). More recently, legal and regulatory responses have been noticeable, especially in highly industrialized and democratized societies. Examples include the establishment of national parks and government policies on human population and family planning, pollution, forest management, and trade in endangered species. At this point in history, a major threat to society and nature is technology, so it is appropriate that this generation look to science and technology to complement literary and legislative responses.

Our environmental and ethical problems, however, dwarf those faced by our ancestors. The current frenzy of environmental degradation is unprecedented (Ehrlich and Ehrlich 1981), with deforestation, desertification, and destruction of wetlands and coral reefs occurring at rates rivaling the major catastrophes in the fossil record and threatening to eliminate most tropical forests and millions of species in our lifetimes. The response, therefore, must also be unprecedented. It is fortunate, therefore, that conservation biology, and parallel approaches in the social sciences, provides academics and other professionals with constructive outlets for their concern.

Conservation biology and the conservation movement cannot reverse history and return the biosphere to its prelapsarian majesty. The momentum of the human population explosion, entrenched political and economic behavior, and withering technologies are propelling humankind in the opposite direction. It is, however, within our capacity to modify significantly the *rate* at which biotic diversity is destroyed, and small changes in rates can produce large effects over long periods of time. Biologists can help increase the efficacy of wildland management; biologists can improve the survival odds of species in jeopardy; biologists can help mitigate technological impacts. The intellectual challenges are fascinating, the opportunities plentiful, and the results can be personally gratifying.

References

Beardmore, J. A. 1983. Extinction, survival, and genetic variation. Pages 125–51 in C. M. Schonewald-Cox, S. M. Chambers, B. MacBryde, and W. L. Thomas, eds. *Genetics and Conservation*. Benjamin-Cummings Publishing, Menlo Park, CA.

Carson, R. 1962. *Silent Spring*. Houghton Mifflin, Boston.

Cody, M. L., and J. M. Diamond, eds. 1975. *Ecology and Evolution of Communities*. Harvard University Press, Cambridge, MA.

Devall, B., and G. Sessions. 1985. *Deep Ecology: Living as if Nature Mattered*. Peregrine Smith Books, Layton, UT.

Diamond, J. M. 1975. The island dilemma: lessons of modern biogeographic studies for the design of natural reserves. *Biol. Conserv.* 7: 129–46.

Diamond, J. M. 1984. Historic extinctions: their mechanisms, and their lessons for understanding prehistoric extinctions. Pages 824–62 in P. S. Martin and R. Klein, eds. *Quarternary Extinctions*, University of Arizona Press, Tucson.

Dubos, R. 1980. *The Wooing of the Earth*. Charles Scribner's Sons, New York.

Ehrenfeld, D. 1981. *The Arrogance of Humanism*. Oxford University Press, London.

Ehrlich, P. R., and A. H. Ehrlich. 1981. *Extinction*. Random House, New York.

Elton, C. S. 1958. *The Ecology of Invasions by Animals and Plants*. Methuen, London.

Erwin, T. L. 1983. Tropical forest canopies: the last biotic frontier. *Bull. Entomol. Soc. Am.* 29: 14–19.

Frankel, O. H., and M. E. Soulé, 1981. *Conservation and Evolution*. Cambridge University Press, Cambridge, UK.

Franklin, I. A. 1980. Evolutionary change in small populations. Pages 135–49 in M. E. Soulé and B. A. Wilcox, eds. *Conservation Biology*. Sinauer Associates, Sunderland, MA.

Futuyma, D. J., and M. Slatkin, eds. 1983. *Coevolution.* Sinauer Associates, Sunderland, MA.

Gilbert, L. E. 1980. Food web organization and the conservation of neotropical diversity. Pages 11–33 in M. E. Soulé and B. A. Wilcox, eds. *Conservation Biology.* Sinauer Associates, Sunderland, MA.

Gilbert, L. E., and P. H. Raven, eds. 1975. *Coevolution of Plants and Animals.* University of Texas Press, Austin.

James, F. C., and W. J. Boecklen. 1984. Interspecific morphological relationships and the densities of birds. Pages 458–77 in D. R. Strong, Jr., D. S. Simberloff, L. G. Abele, and A. B. Thistle, eds. *Ecological Communities.* Princeton University Press, Princeton, NJ.

Janzen, D. H. 1975. *Ecology of Plants in the Tropics.* Edward Arnold, London.

Janzen, D. H. 1983. No park is an island. *Oikos* 41: 402–10.

Kushlan, J. A. 1979. Design and management of continental wildlife reserves: lessons from the Everglades. *Biol. Conserv.* 15: 281–90.

Leopold, A. 1953. *The Round River.* Oxford University Press, New York.

Leopold, A. 1966. *A Sand County Almanac.* Oxford University Press, New York.

Levins, R., and R. Lewontin. 1985. *The Dialectical Biologist.* Harvard University Press, Cambridge, MA.

MacArthur, R. H. 1972. *Geographical Ecology.* Harper & Row, New York.

MacArthur, R. H., and E. O. Wilson. 1967. *The Theory of Island Biogeography.* Princeton University Press, Princeton, NJ.

Marsh, G. P. 1864. *Man and Nature.* Scribners, New York.

May, R. M. 1984. An overview: real and apparent patterns in community structure. Pages 3–16 in D. R. Strong, Jr., D. S. Simberloff, L. G. Abele, and A. B. Thistle, eds. *Ecological Communities.* Princeton University Press, Princeton, NJ.

Naess, A. 1973. The shallow and the deep, long-range ecology movement. *Inquiry* 16: 95–100.

Naess, A. 1985. Identification as a source of deep ecological attitudes. Pages 256–70 in M. Tobias, ed. *Deep Ecology.* Avant Books, San Diego, CA.

Orians, G. H. 1980. Habitat selection: general theory and applications to human behavior. Pages 49–66 in J. S. Lockard, ed. *The Evolution of Human Social Behavior.* Elsevier North Holland, New York.

Passmore, J. 1974. *Man's Responsibility for Nature.* Duckworth, London.

Price, P. W. 1980. *Evolutionary Biology of Parasites.* Princeton University Press, Princeton, NJ.

Raven, P. R. 1976. Ethics and attitudes. Pages 155–79 in J. B. Simmons, R. I. Bayer, P. E. Branham, G. LI. Lucas, and W. T. H. Parry, eds. *Conservation of Threatened Plants.* Plenum Press, New York.

Rolston, H. 1985. Duties to endangered species. *BioScience* 35: 718–26.

Salwasser, H., S. P. Mealey, and K. Johnson. 1984. Wildlife population viability: a question of risk. *Trans. N. Am. Wildl. Nat. Resource Conf.* 49.

Seifert, R. P., and F. H. Seifert. 1979. A *Heliconia* insect community in a Venezuelan cloud forest. *Ecology* 60: 462–7.

Shaffer, M. L. 1981. Minimum population sizes for species conservation. *BioScience* 31: 131–4.

Shaffer, M. L., and F. B. Samson. 1985. Population size and extinction: a note on determining critical population sizes. *Am. Nat.* 125: 144–51.

Simberloff, D. S. 1980. Community effects of introduced species. Pages 53–83 in M. H. Nitecki, ed. *Biotic Crises in Ecological and Evolutionary Time.* Academic Press, New York.

Simberloff, D. S., and L. G. Abele. 1976. Island biogeography theory and conservation practice. *Science* 191: 285–6.

Soulé, M. E. 1980. Thresholds for survival: maintaining fitness and evolutionary potential. Pages 151–69 in M. E. Soulé and B. A. Wilcox, eds. *Conservation Biology.* Sinauer Associates, Sunderland, MA.

Soulé, M. E. 1983. What do we really know about extinction? Pages 111–25 in C. M. Schonewald-Cox, S. M. Chambers, B. MacBryde, and W. L. Thomas, eds. *Genetics and Conservation.* Benjamin-Cummings Publishing, Menlo Park, CA.

Soulé, M. E., and D. S. Simberloff. 1986. What do genetics and ecology tell us about the design of nature reserves? *Biol. Conserv.*

Soulé, M. E., and B. A. Wilcox, eds. 1980. *Conservation Biology: An Ecological-Evolutionary Perspective.* Sinauer Associates, Sunderland, MA.

Strong, D. R., Jr., D. S. Simberloff, L. G. Abele, and A. B. Thistle, eds. 1984. *Ecological Communities.* Princeton University Press, Princeton, NJ.

Terborgh, J. 1974. Preservation of natural diversity: the problem of extinction-prone species. *BioScience* 24: 715–22.

Terborgh, J., and B. Winter. 1980. Some causes of extinction. Pages 119–34 in M. E. Soulé and B. A. Wilcox, eds. *Conservation Biology.* Sinauer Associates, Sunderland, MA.

Tobias, M. 1985. *Deep Ecology.* Avant Books, San Diego, CA.

Underwood, A. J., and E. J. Denley. 1984. Paradigms, explanations, and generalizations in models for the structure of intertidal communities on rocky shores. Pages 151–80 in D. R. Strong, Jr., D. S. Simberloff, L. G. Abele, and A. B. Thistle, eds. *Ecological Communities.* Princeton University Press, Princeton, NJ.

Wilcox, B. A. 1980. Insular ecology and conservation. Pages 95–117 in M. E. Soulé and B. A. Wilcox, eds. *Conservation Biology.* Sinauer Associates, Sunderland, MA.

Wilson, E. O. 1984. *Biophilia.* Harvard University Press, Cambridge, MA.

52   Environmental Ethics and Ecological Science

Mark Sagoff

At first impression, environmental ethics and environmental science appear to serve different objectives and to rely on different arguments and evidence. The field of environmental ethics addresses moral concerns such as intergenerational justice, fairness in the distribution of risk, respect for nature and compassion for other animals, and the preservation of the intrinsic and aesthetic value of wild places. As importantly, environmental ethics draws on a long spiritual tradition that regards the beauty and complexity of nature as divine – that sees Creation as so majestic and mysterious that it seems sinful to alter it more than necessary, especially if what we do causes the extinction of species in order to increase consumption beyond modest to conspicuous levels.

On the other hand, the environmental sciences might seem to rely primarily on observation and experiment to determine patterns of causality, in other words, what causes what. Normative concerns, such as the rights and duties we should respect toward nature and toward each other in relation to the environment would seem to be beyond the reach of an empirical science such as ecology. Ecologists can tell us what may cause the extinction of a species and, therefore, recommend methods to avoid it. Biologists may not say, however, whether we *ought* to protect that or any creature. Ecologist Michael Rosenzweig has written, "The words 'good' and 'bad' constitute value judgments and so lie beyond the bounds of science. Were exotic species to reduce diversity by 30%, no ecologist could test whether that loss of species would be a bad thing."[1]

The Great Chain of Being

Despite the apparent disparity of environmental ethics and science, these fields of research share basic concepts, values, and assumptions. They take fundamentally the same view of nature as a hierarchy of nested levels of organization. Ethicist Holmes Rolston describes the ascending levels of nature from its geological substrate to individual organisms such as plants and animals, then to ecosystems, and to the human societies that depend on them. Rolston writes, "Life takes place in community. So our inquiry into the value of life must take place at the scale of the ecosystem."[2]

Environmental ethicists as a rule support the belief that the natural or biotic communities – and not just the individuals within them – possess an intrinsic value or "moral considerability" and therefore require protection and respect. That the natural community or ecosystem has an organization, structure, or function to protect, moreover, is a standard assumption not only of environmental ethics but also environmental science. According to standard ecological theory, "there is a reality to community structure . . . There is a highly significant underlying element of organization and constancy, and this has existed with overall and local changes here and there, and now and then, over hundreds of thousands or millions of years."[3]

This view of life reflects a long cultural tradition that sees nature in terms of a Great Chain of Being which, according to historian of ideas A. O. Lovejoy, was "chiefly derivative from philosophical and theological premises" rather than from empirical or observational evidence.[4] The image of the "Great Chain of Being" epitomizes the moral and religious attention people within the Western tradition, among many other cultural groups, have long paid to the diversity of life. The British poet Alexander Pope ably expressed the underlying metaphor in his "Essay on Man" (1751):

Vast chain of being! which from God began,
Natures aethereal, human, angel, man,
Beast, bird, fish, insect, what no eye can see . . .
Where, one step broken, the great scale destroyed
From Nature's chain whatever link you strike,
Tenth, or ten thousandth, breaks the chain alike.

Specially adapted for this volume by the author. An earlier version appeared as "Environmental Science and Environmental Ethics," in Henk A. M. J. ten Have (ed.), *Environmental Ethics and International Policy* (UNESCO Publishing, France, 2006), pp. 145–63. Reprinted with permission from UNESCO Publishing.

Central to this view is the belief that the living world – from organisms to ecosystems – displays an intelligible order or design in which each creature has a reason for being – a "niche" as we might now say. In the twelfth century, the French theologian Abelard, following Plato's *Timaeus*, wrote, "Whatever is generated is generated by some necessary cause, for nothing comes into being except there be some due cause and reason antecedent to it." This principle of sufficient reason explains the properties of the Great Chain, such as plenitude (the idea that every niche is filled), continuity and gradation (that all life from the least creature, such as a microbe, to the greatest, ourselves, belongs to a hierarchy), and the interconnection of life in systems nested in systems.

Traditionally, theologians attributed the organization of nature to divine causes. Today, environmental scientists generally refer to random mutation and natural selection to explain the design of organisms, and they prefer to say that ecosystems are self-organizing – that the "ecosystem generates a spontaneous order that envelops and produces the richness, beauty, integrity, and dynamic stability of the component parts," as Rolston has written.[5] Ecologists James J. Kay and Eric Schneider have endorsed this view: "We must always remember that left alone, living systems are self-organizing, that is they will look after themselves. Our responsibility is not to interfere with this self-organizing process."[6]

Until the middle of the nineteenth century, the idea that nature is organized in ascending scales from the microbe to the ecosystem was associated with natural theology. The same God who designed the tiniest organism, so it was thought, also organized the communities in which each species found its niche or place. After Darwin, however, biologists substituted the force of evolution or natural selection for that of divine intervention to explain the organization of natural ecosystems or communities. Stephen Forbes, in his classic study of 1887, "The Lake as a Microcosm," argued that in a natural community, "equilibrium has been reached and is steadily maintained that actually accomplishes for all the parties involved the greatest good which the circumstances will at all permit." To explain this equilibrium, he cited "the beneficent power of natural selection which compels such adjustments of the rates of destruction and of multiplication of the various species as shall best promote this common interest."[7]

The assumption that principles of organization – sufficient reason, continuity, plenitude, hierarchy, interconnectedness – characterize the living world runs from the *Timaeus* through Plotinus, medieval philosophy, Spinoza and Leibniz, to modern ecologists in the tradition of Aldo Leopold, such as Eugene Odum and G. E. Hutchinson. By the middle of the twentieth century, ecologists, particularly in the United States, taught that natural communities, such as forests, if left alone progressed or developed to a stable state of homeostasis, equilibrium, or climax. As E. P. Odum presented this teaching of science in his popular text, "Much has been written about this 'balance of nature' but only with the recent development of good methods for measuring rates of function of whole systems has a beginning been made in the understanding of the mechanisms involved."[8]

The commitment of both environmental ethics and ecological science to the thesis that natural ecosystems or communities if left undisturbed reached a desirable "balance" or equilibrium lent academic support to the environmental movement of the 1970s. The "balance of nature" paradigm gave scientific credibility to environmental laws, such as the Endangered Species Act, enacted in the United States at the time. According to law professor Dan Tarlock, "Legislators and lawyers enthusiastically embraced this paradigm because it seemed to be a neutral, universal public policy principle applicable to the use and management of all natural resources. The contributions of modern environmental resource management to the legal system are premised on this paradigm."[9]

Are Ecosystems Organized?

In the early 1970s, at the first flood of the environmental movement, which avidly embraced the idea of the balance of nature, environmental scientists and ethicists shared the assumption that natural communities or ecosystems possess enough order or organization to justify attempts to protect them. Starting in the 1970s and through the 1990s, however, many ecologists began to lose faith in the "balance of nature" or equilibrium paradigm of ecosystem development. In fact, they were unable to find any empirical or observational support for any general principles or rules of ecosystem structure or function. "Certainly the idea that species live in integrated communities is a myth," conservation biologist Michael Soulé wrote during this questioning period. "So-called biotic communities, a misleading term, are constantly changing in membership." Soulé noted, "The science of ecology has been hoist on its own petard by maintaining, as many did during the middle of this century, that natural communities tend toward equilibrium. Current ecological thinking argues that nature at the level of local biotic assemblages has never been homeostatic. Therefore, any serious attempt to define the original state of a community or ecosystem leads to a logical and scientific maze."[10]

Among the reasons that have led many ecologists to doubt the assumption that "there is a reality to community structure," six are most important. The first is the lack of empirical evidence that ecosystems possess an element of organization – a complete lack of observational support for any rule or principle, not just equilibrium principles, that could describe or explain the sense in which communities possess a structure or function. "Wherever we seek to find constancy, we discover change," Daniel Botkin has observed. We find "that nature undisturbed is not constant in form, structure, or proportion, but changes at every scale of time and space."[11] Donald Worster summarized the view many ecologists have now come to accept. "Nature should be regarded as a landscape of patches, big and little, patches of all textures and colors, a patchwork quilt of living things, changing continually through time and space, responding to an unceasing barrage of perturbations. The stitches in that quilt never hold for long."[12]

Second, if ecological communities or systems possessed a function or structure, it must have a cause, but no one has identified what it is. The idea that natural selection accounts for the design of ecosystems has been a recurring theme of theoretical ecology since the time of Forbes. One can see why. What could substitute for divine will as the cause of ecosystem structure or function besides the "beneficent power of natural selection?" Yet no one has been able to explain how natural selection can structure ecosystems which, after all, have no genomes and do not compete for relative reproductive success. Ecosystems are not units of selection. Drake and co-authors caution that "the relationships between self-organization, natural selection, and the mechanisms and assembly operators of ecology are simply unknown despite a growing theoretical effort."[13]

Third, most ecologists agree that in spite of nearly a century of theoretical and mathematical research, they have not arrived at a consensus concerning the principles or rules that may explain and thus allow us to observe how ecosystems are organized. It seems that every theoretical ecologist has his or her own view of the structure and function of ecosystems but no one is able to show that his or her vision is better than the next. As long as no one is embarrassed about the absence of empirical evidence, a thousand paradigms will flourish, and this is called "pluralism" in ecology. Anyone with a metaphor and some mathematics can model the ecosystem.

Fourth, ecologists have yet to agree upon definitions that allow them to tell what kinds of places constitute ecosystems or communities and to determine whether they remain the "same" systems or communities through time and change. In philosophical terms, ecologists have not worked out the identity conditions of the objects they study. Is an impoundment behind a dam a "lake," a large Christmas tree farm a "forest," a bay consisting mostly of non-native species an "estuary," a rotting carcass of a beached whale an "ecosystem" for purposes of ecological theory? Concepts such as "community" and "ecosystem" are accepted uncritically as if they meant something; to be meaningful, however, they must be defined and the definitions tested by the logical method of suggesting counter-examples that meet the definition but plainly defeat its intention.

Fifth, because the concept *ecosystem* lacks an agreed-upon definition, there is no way to distinguish the essential or defining properties of a system from the accidental and contingent ones. There is no logical basis to say, then, whether a given system, as a result of a given alteration, retains its "organizational mode" and thus remains the same system – whether it displays "resiliency" – or whether it collapses and segues into a different system or into a mere collection. We have no criterion for determining what kinds of changes destroy the system and what changes are consistent with its preservation.

Sixth, if one looks out of one's window over a period of years or decades, one sees enormous changes in the landscape caused by human beings. A forest once burnt and hunted by native tribes becomes a farm; this is planted with tract homes and turns into a suburb; the housing "bubble" bursts and the area becomes an urban slum; then it may be developed for some other use. Are these changes – which are typical – representative of evolving ecosystems? If one considers human activity to be natural, the answer has to be "yes," since human beings are just one more factor in evolution. If one separates between humanity and nature – as an idea of self-organizing ecosystems requires – one faces a metaphysical conundrum. What are the scientific grounds for exempting humanity from the rest of the natural world?

In spite of these problems theoretical ecologists keep faith with environmental ethicists that ecosystems are integrated, interconnected systems that conform to organizational principles. In other words, ecosystems are unified enough to give us something definite to protect. Whatever empirical or observational evidence may suggest, ethicists and scientists are generally not willing to concede that what are called communities or ecosystems lack organization, structure, or function but are each idiosyncratic, each a law unto itself, each a blooming, buzzing confusion of contingency, an ephemeral accident of history, a Heraclitean flux without purpose or form. The lack of empirical evidence to support the view that ecosystems possess an organizational mode serves not as a caution but as a challenge to many ecologists and ethicists to redouble their theoretical and mathematical efforts to show that communities and ecosystems exist as structured, organized entities. Ethicists depend on ecologists to vindicate their view of the ecosystem as existing in a form that can possess value. "We need ecology to discover what biotic community means as an organizational mode," Rolston has written.[14]

The Ethical and Aesthetic Basis of Ecosystem Organization

Research in both environmental ethics and environmental science takes as a premise the presupposition that principles of self-organization govern ecosystems or natural communities. Even if this assumption is not yet supported by non-question-begging definitions and crucial experiments, it nevertheless draws intuitive support from the aesthetic judgments that accompany our perception of the natural world, in particular, of its most magnificent and glorious productions, such as old growth forests, heirloom lakes, wild savannahs, estuaries, and the like. Few of us experience these kinds of places without becoming convinced that they possess an intrinsic form or unity or an "organizational mode." It might be misleading

to suggest, however, that the scientific assumption that ecosystems are self-organized or otherwise structured as systems justifies the aesthetic judgment and moral intuition that ecosystems have a good worth protecting or that demands respect. In fact, the inference may go the other way. Ecosystem scientists may adopt as a research program a commitment to understanding through mathematical modeling the organizational mode of ecosystems because moral intuitions and aesthetic judgments convince them and us that such a design is there to be discovered.

One way to understand the free lawfulness or dynamic unity of an ecosystem may be to invoke the concept of an aesthetic idea, which the eighteenth-century German philosopher Immanuel Kant introduced in the *Critique of Judgment* (Sec. 49). An aesthetic idea in the perception of an object is a unity recognized by the imagination for which no cognitive concept is adequate. One can say that an aesthetic idea exhibits an order that is always straining after a rational, cognitive, or causal explanation, even if no such empirical principle of organization can be found. The unity of ecosystems as they appear to us – or the beauty of places in the natural world – on this view exists but cannot be reduced to rational concepts of the sort sought by empirical science.

It is widely understood that ecosystems are not organized or formed to serve a purpose and, therefore, that their arrangement cannot be explained in teleological terms. Kant famously argued, however, that the objects in nature we find beautiful display a "free lawfulness . . . which has also been called purposiveness-without-a-purpose."[15] Because the natural phenomena as represented by the imagination seem suitable for conceptual or cognitive understanding, the result is a "mental state in which imagination and understanding are in free play."[16] This play of the imagination and understanding "points" to a concept but reveals none; it compels ethicists and scientists to believe that ecological communities possess an organizational mode, yet it denies them any way to vindicate or confirm this belief by objective observation or experiment.

Kant offered a metaphysical explanation of the tension between (1) our common belief or sense that natural objects (including ecosystems as we would call them today) present an organizational mode suitable for understanding and (2) our inability to bring this organization under concepts of the sort that can be tested by empirical science. He thought that in aesthetic judgments our faculties of feeling and our associated moral intuitions pierce through the conditions of causal determinism that govern all phenomena to the noumenal world that makes freedom possible. This intuition of the possibility of freedom combined with lawfulness accompanies all aesthetic judgment. For Kant and for many philosophers who followed him, the beauty and magnificence of nature is a kind of revelation of the hidden order of things that also makes human freedom possible – an order that we can only capture in aesthetic judgment since it defies the organizational principles that can be applied by scientific understanding.

If we suppose that the organizational mode of what we call natural communities is initially aesthetic in this way, we can understand that ethicists and scientists are drawn to the idea that the ecosystem is organized even though their research fails to discover empirical principles that govern its behavior. The principles or laws that explain how ecosystems are organized do not lie, as it were, on this side of the phenomena. Theoretical ecologists may multiply mathematical models of the structure and function of the ecosystem, but they cannot discover anything. Yet their aesthetic and moral sense tells them – and us – that communities possess a unity that is valuable and is worth protecting.

Biodiversity: A Systematically Ambiguous Concept

"If one values life at all," Rolston has written, "one must value it generically, collectively, as with the term 'biodiversity.' Every individual organism is a distributive increment in a collective good – at least presumably."[17] While this proposition appears fundamental to environmental ethics, it has to be understood in the context of an important change in the course of natural history. In the very distant past, nature's spontaneous course (whether one ascribes it to evolution or Creation) determined the abundance and distribution of plants and animals. More recently, human activity, whether intentional or inadvertent, has come to influence and then determine both the abundance and distribution of organisms. Thus, when one values biodiversity one values all kinds of human effects from non-native species to genetically engineered crops.

In the past, ecologists may have believed that a given environment contains only a limited number of niches so that when a newcomer arrives, it is likely to expropriate a native creature. Today ecologists are more likely to regard the "niche" as an epiphenomenon, i.e., an inference from the presence of a species at a place. The number of species that can reach a site may be the principal factor that determines how many coexist there – and in that sense how many niches exist. There appears to be no upper limit to the number of coexisting species at any sizeable site; the number that flourishes may represent the number that human beings introduce either intentionally or inadvertently. The biodiversity at any place, therefore, may be largely an effect or result of human activity.

Human activity also increases the richness or variety of species globally by creating through centuries of conventional breeding and more recently through advanced biotechnology huge inventories of novel organisms. Artificial selection has fabricated from a few ancestral plants thousands of distinct landraces or cultivars of rice, many of which now grow wild. Landraces of maize – about 60 in current use in Mexico – descend from an ancient Mexican teosinte which they hardly resemble. Economic plants that result from conventional breeding, such as tomato and canola, may be regarded as artifacts, since they bear so little similarity to their ancestral stock. The maintenance of genetic diversity may not require the preservation of wild types. For example, the beef and dairy industries, which no one thinks are in jeopardy, maintain all sorts of germplasm even though the last wild ancestor of cattle went extinct in the 1700s. Similarly, the demise of the Atwater Prairie Chicken has not affected the genetic viability of the poultry trade.

Advances in genetic engineering make the potential contribution of industry – particularly the laboratories of multinational life-sciences corporations such as Monsanto and Novartis – practically unlimited. The recently marketed "Glofish" suggests that industry might design the greatest and weirdest variety of creatures first for gardens and the pet trade but inevitably for inadvertent or intentional introduction into natural ecosystems. These may add to the exotic organisms already there further to increase the species richness of places. By designing species for introduction into particular lakes and other island-like environments, genetic engineers could add to the genetic variety between and among ecosystems. On any definition of "biodiversity" that does not exclude human-made or arranged organisms and ecosystems a priori, the potential of biotechnology to increase biodiversity and thus the good environmentalists cherish appears infinite.

The Intrinsic Value of Nature

The appealing ethical principle that attaches intrinsic value to biodiversity leads on to ask whether it applies (1) on an equal basis to all species, habitats, and ecosystems or (2) primarily to those species, habitats, and ecosystems the qualities of which arise as a result of nature's spontaneous course rather than as a consequence of human intention, intervention, and activity. The question is particularly important because human-dominated systems do not appear to be less rich in biological diversity than do more "pristine" ones; indeed, empirical research constantly finds that because species adapt to, invade, or otherwise find opportunities to flourish in areas human beings have opened up and tamed, human-dominated systems may often possess greater species richness than do the forests or savannahs they may have replaced. Do species, ecosystems, and habitats found, say, in suburban backyards possess the same intrinsic value – and therefore make the same demand for respect and protection – as those found in more "natural" or "pristine" environments? If we value the ecosystem is it the heirloom pristine ecosystem or the suburban backyard? What if "backyard" biodiversity includes but is far more extensive than the biodiversity found in the same place a thousand years before?

One could answer that the species, habitats, and ecosystems that characterize suburban sprawl carry the same intrinsic value and make the same moral and aesthetic demand for protection as those that inhabit places in which human influence is far less apparent. This line of reply has three advantages. First, it acknowledges the empirical finding that suburban landscapes are often bastions of biological diversity attracting not only the species of the original forest (deer, raccoon, possum, beaver, muskrat, etc.) but also far greater numbers of invasive species that flourish there as well. The open and variegated ecosystems of suburbs, indeed, can harbor an amount of biological diversity that may rival the species richness of rainforests, the structure of many of which, according to some accounts, has also resulted from human activity, although by millions of indigenous peoples who flourished many centuries ago.

Second, this reply recognizes that the distinction between human-dominated and natural systems, while logically meaningful, may by now lack a significant empirical difference. One can imagine examples to illustrate the difference between more or less "natural" systems. The San Francisco Bay, in which the majority of species by number or by biomass are present as a result of human activity, may be said to be less "natural" than a similarly sized bay in some less frequented part of the world. Introduced species and other anthropogenic changes, however, are likely to have thoroughly altered the "pristine" estuary as well. The Amazon rainforest, long thought to exemplify nature's spontaneous course, is now recognized in many or most of its ecological properties to be an artifact of human engineering, in this instance, by earlier civilizations.[18] As early as 1854, George Perkins Marsh observed that humanity had long since completely altered and interfered with the spontaneous arrangements of the organic and inorganic world.

Third, the belief that no difference in intrinsic value separates more from less "natural" species, habitats, and ecosystems corresponds with the finding that no biological difference distinguishes them. For example, suppose that a group of ecologists, on the basis of historical evidence and research, lists those species established in an ecosystem that are native and those that are exotic, i.e., that arrived as a result of human activity or assistance, including those contrived and introduced by genetic engineers. A second group of ecologists, who might observe everything about the behavior, morphology, and other characteristics of these organisms, could not tell which list was which.

The same problem affects ecosystems. There is no evidence that ecosystems possess an organization or design that gives them form, structure, or function. There is certainly no evidence that "natural," pristine, or heirloom ecosystems exhibit properties of structure, function, or design which differ from those of less "natural" ones. To test this assertion, one might identify a measurable property, such as productivity or species richness, that is thought to correlate with the "naturalness" of a system. One group of ecologists might then rank a random sample of ecosystems in terms of this property. Another group of ecologists would then rank the same sample in terms of an independent criterion of "naturalness." There is no reason to believe that a significant correlation would hold between these rankings, although the experiment has not been done.

These advantages support the supposition that the species, habitats, and communities associated with areas dominated by human beings have an intrinsic value – they make a demand for protection and respect – equal to or the same as heirloom, pristine, or more "natural" systems. This supposition, however, presents disadvantages. Ecologists are probably unwilling to accept the idea that human-dominated places, such as suburban lots, even if they are species-rich, operate under the same assembly rules or self-organizing principles as pristine ecosystems. It is hard to see what rules organize the suburban lawn, for example, that can be of interest to theoretical ecologists rather than lawn service firms, such as Chemlawn, for example. If ecologists concede that artifactual environments, such as factory farms, operate under the same rules or principles as pristine ecosystems, it would be hard for them to argue that they know anything more than do agronomists, veterinarians, and genetic engineers.

Aesthetic and moral intuitions, moreover, rebel at the idea that alien organisms – much less those contrived by genetic engineering – deserve the same degree of respect and protection for the same reasons as endemic or native species. Probably no one believes that all ecosystems, habitats, and species are equal in intrinsic value. Yet more could be done to assure that the idea of intrinsic value does not lose plausibility because it applies too broadly. If we try to protect every living thing equally, we can protect nothing.

The Normative Commitment of Ecological Science

The environmental and ecological sciences tend to agree with environmental ethics in distinguishing between the natural and the artificial and thus between species, habitats, and ecosystems insofar as they are free of or affected by human influence and activity. While environmental ethics distinguishes the natural from the artificial as a basis for valuation, however, the conservation sciences, such as conservation biology, ecosystem science, and theoretical ecology adopt the same distinction as a fundamental methodological commitment. According to ecologist R. V. O'Neill: "The ecosystem concept typically considers human activities as external disturbances . . . *Homo sapiens* is the only important species that is considered external from its ecosystem, deriving goods and services rather than participating in ecosystem dynamics."[19] Other ecologists agree. "Ecologists traditionally have sought to study pristine ecosystems to try to get at the workings of nature without the confounding influences of human activity."[20]

In separating humanity from nature, ecologists must rely on conceptual strategies to "save" the phenomena, that is, to explain away conundrums and paradoxes. Consider, for example, the relationship between biodiversity and ecosystem integrity. Many ecologists have argued that biodiversity supports ecosystem structure, function, stability, productivity, and other valuable emergent properties. According to one study, for example, "diversity can be expected, on average, to give rise to ecosystem stability."[21]

A paradox arises because introduced species vastly increase species richness for virtually every kind of taxon in every kind of place. These alien species, since their presence results from human activity, could only disrupt ecosystem structure and function as, indeed, the literature of invasion biology insists they often do. Yet, by increasing the number of organisms available in the ecosystem, exotic species would seem to enhance its structure and function. To solve such a paradox, many biologists define biodiversity in a system to exclude non-native species. Thus, Sala and others write, "Our definition [of biodiversity] excludes exotic organisms that have been introduced."[22] Ecosystem integrity, organization, and related concepts are generally defined in a way that makes the presence of non-native species a per se indicator of ecosystem decline.[23] Thus, the basic theses of conservation biology and related sciences have become tautologies.

What is crucial for both environmental science and environmental ethics is that nature is the norm. Whatever arises as a result of nature's spontaneous course represents ecosystem integrity and health and has intrinsic value; whatever results from human activity represents corruption and sin and thus is potentially harmful to the natural system. "Our ability to protect biological resources depends on our ability to identify and predict the effects of human actions on biological systems, especially our ability to distinguish between natural and human-induced variability in biological condition."[24] That nature's spontaneous course endows species, habitats, and ecosystems with both ecological organization and intrinsic value remains the assumption of both environmental ethics and the conservation sciences.

Policy Recommendations

The conceptual and normative confluence of environmental ethics and science both strengthens and supports the policy work of environmentalists. By assuming that ecological communities are organized, ethicists are able to find in them a subject of intrinsic value and scientists locate an object of mathematical study. This assumption, because it is based on a priori commitment and not on empirical evidence or argument, cannot be dislodged. The tradition in environmental science which goes back to the *Timaeus* and matured with Great Chain of Being cosmology is here to stay. Historian William Glacken has written, "I am convinced that modern ecological theory, so important in our attitudes towards nature and man's interference with it, owes its origin to the design argument. The wisdom of the creator is self-evident . . . no living thing is useless, and all are related one to the other."[25]

The philosophical approach that separates humanity from nature and finds in the economic activity of the former a threat to the organizational integrity of the latter has brushed off every opposing view, from the mechanistic materialism of Lucretius and Hobbes to the animadversions of many Darwinians. The conservation sciences hardly blinked as they replaced conceptions of the balance of nature, systems in equilibrium, and the like with stochastic models of community assembly, matrices of interaction coefficients, interspecific tradeoff curves, theories of self-organized criticality, languages of ecosystem ontogeny, hierarchical path-dependent complex dynamical computational representations with multiple basins of attraction, and so on. From these conceptual constructs ecologists without moving from their computer screens can infer the mathematical pattern, process, structure, or function that characterizes the original and properly formed ecosystem policy-makers are to protect. Let the mathematicians work it out. If anyone raises questions, throw equations at them. As an empirical proposition, the belief that the ecosystem or natural community has an "organizational mode" has no merit. As the basis of a scientific consensus, however, it is not going to change.

Agencies charged with environmental policy-making must confront the stunning lack of empirical evidence of any non-tautological, i.e., testable, principles of organization in natural communities or ecosystems. They may also find themselves stymied by the absence of any useful definition of "community" or "ecosystem" which can identify these things as continuous objects through time and change. (Philosophers might say that ecologists have not yet worked out or even worried about the identity conditions of communities or ecosystems.) As a result, these agencies, while paying lip service to the rhetoric of intrinsic value, ecosystem services, and sustainable communities, may lack a basis for understanding these concepts. These agencies may revert to promoting standard economic goals, such as the protection of yields from fisheries and the control of damaging environmental externalities such as pollution, since they have no idea what concepts such as *ecosystem* and *community* mean. At the same time, mathematicians who study ecosystem structure and function will always enjoy great academic reputations and financial support because there is no resource limit to the number and complexity of theories and mathematical models that can coexist in ecology.

Both environmental ethics and theoretical ecology are securely founded on the aesthetic idea that the living world, as it unfolds itself, exhibits purposiveness without a purpose, a meaningfulness without a definite meaning, and a unity or organizational mode that has not been and perhaps cannot be reduced to empirical concepts. As such, the living world commands our deepest respect but also excites our greatest curiosity. This aesthetic and moral commitment to the flourishing of nature may unite all humanity in the goal of protecting it – even if, when confronted with hard facts or difficult cases, no one really has a clue what that means.

Both environmental ethicists and scientists tend to assume that ecological communities and systems possess or present an organizational element or mode that academic researchers can identify and policy-makers may protect. In the absence of empirical evidence that this organizational element or mode exists in a way science can describe, it is hard to see how policy-makers can apply concepts such as the *community* or the *ecosystem* in any but the most metaphorical and rhetorical sense. The problem for both environmental science and ethics is to provide a vocabulary that can provide an effective guide – not just a hortatory and aspirational rhetoric – for environmental policy. There has not been very much progress on this front.

Notes

1   M. L. Rosenzweig, The four questions: what does the introduction of exotic species do to diversity? *Evol. Ecol. Res.* 3 (2001): 361–7.
2   Holmes Rolston III, Intrinsic values on Earth: nature and the nations. In Henk ten Have, ed., *Environmental*

Ethics and International Policy (Paris: UNESCO, 2006), pp. 47–68; quotation at p. 59.

3   W. H. Wagner, Problems with biotic invasives. In B. N. McKnight, eds., *Biological Pollution: The Control and Impact of Invasive Exotic Species* (Indianapolis: Indiana Academy of Science, 1993), pp. 1–8.

4   Arthur O. Lovejoy, *The Great Chain of Being* (Cambridge, Mass.: Harvard University Press, 1971; first published 1936).

5   Holmes Rolston III, Value in nature and the nature of value. In Andrew Light and Holmes Rolston III, eds., *Environmental Ethics: An Anthology* (New York: Wiley-Blackwell, 2002), ch. 11 (pp. 143–53); quotation at p. 149.

6   J. J. Kay and E. Schneider, Embracing complexity: The challenge of the ecosystem approach. In L. Westra and J. Lemons, eds., *Perspectives on Ecological Integrity* (Kluwer: Dordrecht, 1995), pp. 49–59.

7   S. I. Forbes, The lake as a microcosm. *Bulletin of the Illinois State Natural History Survey* 15 (1925): 537–50.

8   E. P. Odum and H. T. Odum, *Fundamentals of Ecology*, 2nd edn. (Philadelphia, PA: W. B. Saunders Co., 1959).

9   A. D. Tarlock, Environmental law: Ethics or science? In *Beyond the Balance of Nature: Environmental Law Faces the New Ecology*. First annual Cummings Colloquium on Environmental Law. Duke Environmental Law and Policy Forum 7 (1996): 193–223.

10   M. Soulé, The social siege of nature. In M. Soulé and G. Lease, eds., *Reinventing Nature: Responses to Postmodern Deconstruction* (Washington, DC: Island Press, 1995), pp. 137–70.

11   D. B. Botkin, *Discordant Harmonies: A New Ecology for the Twenty-First Century* (New York: Oxford University Press, 1990).

12   D. Worster, The ecology of order and chaos. *Environmental History Review* 14/1–2 (1990): 1–13.

13   J. A. Drake, C. R. Zimmerman, T. Purucker, and C. Rojo, On the nature of the assembly trajectory. In E. Weiher and P. Keddy, eds., *Ecological Assembly Rules: Perspectives, Advances, Retreats* (Cambridge: Cambridge University Press, 1999), pp. 233–50.

14   Rolston, Intrinsic values on Earth, p. 59.

15   Immanuel Kant, *Kritik der Urtheilskraft* (Ak. V). In English translation, *Critique of Judgment*, trans. Werner S. Pluhar (Indianapolis: Hackett, 1987), p. 241.

16   Ibid., p. 217.

17   Rolston, Intrinsic values on Earth, p. 55.

18   Charles Mann, 1491. *The Atlantic Monthly* (March 2000): 41–53.

19   R. V. O'Neill, Is it time to bury the ecosystem concept? (with full military honors, of course!). *Ecology* 82 (2001): 3275–84.

20   R. Gallagher and B. Carpenter, Human-dominated ecosystems. *Science* 277 (1997): 485–6.

21   K. McCann, The diversity-stability debate. *Nature* 405 (2000): 228–33.

22   O. E. Sala et al., Global biodiversity scenarios for the year 2100. *Science* 287 (2000): 1770–4.

23   P. L. Angermeier and J. R. Karr, Biological integrity versus biological diversity as policy directives: Protecting biotic resources. *BioScience* 44/10 (1994): 690–7.

24   J. R. Karr and E. W. Chu, *Restoring Life in Running Waters: Better Biological Monitoring* (Washington, DC: Island Press, 1998).

25   C. J. Glacken, *Traces on the Rhodian Shore* (Berkeley: University of California Press, 1967), p. 243.

53   The Metaphysical Implications of Ecology

J. Baird Callicott

I

The subject of this paper is the metaphysical implications of ecology. From an orthodox philosophical point of view, not only is value segregated from fact, but philosophy is substantively informed only by the universal and foundational sciences.[1] The idea, therefore, that ecology – a scientific newcomer and a science remote from the more fundamental natural sciences – might have *metaphysical implications* may appear, on the face of it, ridiculous. So here at the beginning let me enter a couple of apologetic caveats.

From *Environmental Ethics*, vol. 8 (1986): 301–16. © 1986 by J. Baird Callicott. Reprinted with permission from the author.

⌐Although it is not a foundational science like physics or a universal science like astronomy, ecology has profoundly altered our understanding of the proximate terrestrial environment in which we live, move, and have our being. And by "implications" I do not mean to suggest that there are logical relationships between ecological premises and metaphysical conclusions such that if the former are true the latter must also be true. *Imply, implicate*, and *implication* have a wider meaning evolved from the Latin root, *implicare* – to enfold, involve, or engage – which I wish to evoke. Ecology has made plain to us the fact that we are enfolded, involved, and engaged within the living, terrestrial, environment – i.e., implicated in and implied by it. (This proposition is itself among the metaphysical implications of ecology.) Therefore, ecology also necessarily profoundly alters our understanding of ourselves, severally, and human nature, collectively.⌐From this altered representation of the environment, people (personally and collectively), and the relationships in it and between it and ourselves, we may *abstract* certain general conceptual notions. These abstractive distillates are the metaphysical implications of ecology to which I draw attention in this discussion.

Ecology and contemporary physics, interestingly, complement one another conceptually and converge toward the same metaphysical notions. Hence, the sciences at the apex of the hierarchy of the natural sciences and those at the base, the "New Ecology" and the "New Physics," respectively, draw mutually consistent and mutually supporting abstract pictures of nature in its most elementary and universal and in its most complex and local manifestations.[2] A consolidated metaphysical consensus, thus, appears to be presently emerging from twentieth-century science which may at last supplant the metaphysical consensus distilled from the scientific paradigm of the seventeenth century.

II

To bring dramatically to light the metaphysical implications of ecology, let me begin with a foil: the metaphysical ideas, just mentioned, implicated in modern classical science including pre-ecological natural history. Modern classical science adopted and adapted an ontology first set out in Western thought by Leucippus and Democritus in the fifth century BC – atomic materialism.[3]

The classical atom is essentially a mathematical entity and its so-called primary qualities may be precisely and quantitatively expressed as aspects or "modes" of geometrical space. An atom's solid mass was thus understood, mathematically, as a positive or "full" portion of negative or "empty" Euclidean space, shape its plane limits in a three-dimensional continuum, size its cubic volume, and motion its linear translation from one location (point) to another.[4]

The void and the simple bodies (or atoms) it contains were conceived by Democritus to be uncreated and indestructible. The theistic moderns conceived space, time, and the atoms to have been uniquely created by God as the permanent theater and immutable constituents of the universe.[5]

Composite bodies, the macroscopic things composed of atoms, however, routinely come into being and pass away. The "generation" and "corruption" (or "coming into being" and "passing away") of composite bodies were understood as the temporary association and dissociation of the atoms in the course of their ceaseless jostling and shuffling.[6]

Atomism, thus, is reductive. A composite body is ontologically reducible to its simple constituents. And the career of a composite body – its generation, growth, corruption, and disintegration – is reducible to the local motions of its several constituents.

⌐And atomism, thus, is mechanical. All causal relations are reducible to the motion or translation from point to point of simple bodies or the composite bodies made up of them. The mysterious causal efficacy of fire, disease, light, or anything else is explicable, in the last analysis, as the motion, bump, and grind of the implacable particles. Putative causal relations which could not be so conceived – those postulated in astrology, magic, witchcraft, priestcraft, Newton's gravitational theory, the Faraday-Maxwell representation of magnetism, etc., etc. – were either dismissed as superstitions and their existence denied or regarded as physical problems awaiting a mechanical solution.[7] Only a mechanical solution could be satisfactory, since only a mechanical solution implicated exclusively the fundamental ontology of atomic materialism.[8]⌐

This material, reductive, particulate, aggregative, mechanical, geometric, and quantitative paradigm in physics governed thought in other areas of philosophical interest, for example in moral psychology and biology.

Although Democritus, Lucretius, and Hobbes were thoroughgoing materialists and attempted to treat mind in exactly the same mechanical terms as, say, fire, light, and heat, dualism as espoused by Pythagoras, Plato, and Descartes became more characteristic of the dominant psychology of modern classical science.[9]

Mind, nevertheless, was derivatively and analogously conceived by the dualists in atomistic terms – as a psychic monad. Each mind, in other words, was a discrete psychic substance insulated within an alien (to its own nature) material cladding.[10] The mind was passively bedazzled and deluded by the bodily senses which were mechanically excited by the local "external" world. But minds were not otherwise informed by interaction with matter. That is, the rational structure of the human mind together with its passions and volitions was regarded as an independent given. By carefully sifting and sorting the raw, confused data afforded by sensation, disciplined rational minds could figure out the mechanical laws of the foreign material world and apply that knowledge to practical problem solving.

Given a monadic moral psychology, there are two fundamental options for ethics. For example, as represented most clearly by Hobbes, ethics might consist in finding the most felicitous rules to harmonize the inertia-like appetites of individual egos (or social atoms).[11] Or, a conceptual talisman to overcome the appetitive egoism of the discrete psychic monads might be posited. The concept of reason functions as such a transcendental principle in Kant's ethic.[12]

In biology, an even more subtle "conceptual atomism" prevailed. To explain the existence of natural kinds or species had been a major burden of Plato's theory of forms.[13] For each species or natural kind there was a corresponding eternal form or idea. Individuals acquired their "essences," their specific, discrete natures, by "participation" in the forms. Thus, lions were lions and differed from panthers because lions participated in the form lion, and panthers in the form panther. And so for horses, cows, and all other living specimens, each acquired the specific characteristics they to one degree or another possessed through their association as token to type with specific forms.

Although Aristotle (whose relationship to subsequent Western biology is comparable to Pythagoras' relationship to subsequent Western mathematics) rejected Plato's theory of independently existing forms, he retained the more insidious Platonic doctrine of essences. According to Aristotle, a thing's essence was its definition, given in terms of a classificatory hierarchy.[14] The universals of this hierarchy (later modified and refined by Carl Linnaeus) – species, genes, family, order, class, phylum, and kingdom – were not real or actual; only individual organisms fully existed. Nevertheless, for Aristotle, a species acquires its peculiar characteristics, not through interaction with other species, but through the place it occupies in a logically determined classificatory schematism.

Aristotle's teleological conception of nature introduced into biology a hierarchy of another sort. Some species were "lower," others "higher" on the scale of ends. Lower organisms existed for the sake of higher ones.[15] This habit of calling evolutionarily more venerable beings "lower organisms" persists today as an Aristotelian residue in modern biology much as the habit of referring to certain numbers as "square" or "cubic" persists as a Pythagorean residue in modern mathematics. The former, however, seems, somehow, more than a quaint and harmless terminological legacy of classical antiquity; it seems to impute a distinct pecking order to nature.

In sum, then, the endemic Western picture of living nature prior to its transformation by ecology might be characterized (or caricatured) as follows. The terrestrial natural environment consists of a collection of bodies composed of molecular aggregates of atoms. A living natural body is in principle a very elaborate machine. That is, its generation, gestation, development, decay, and death can be exhaustively explained reductively and mechanically. Some of these natural machines are mysteriously inhabited by a conscious monad, a "ghost-in-the-machine." Living natural bodies come in a wide variety of types or species, which are determined by a logico-conceptual order, and have, otherwise, no essential connection to one another. They are, as it were, loosed upon the landscape, each outfitted with its (literally God-given) Platonic or Aristotelian essence, to interact catch-as-catch-can.

[. . .]

III

Ecology was given its name in 1866 by Ernst Haeckel, but the concept of an "economy of nature" had been current in natural history since Linnaeus had devoted a treatise to it a century earlier.[16] Although the idea of an orderly economy of nature was an improvement over the Hobbesian picture of nature as a chaotic free-for-all, Linnaeus and his exponents explicitly represented it in mechanical terms. Living nature is, as it were, a mechanical Leviathan, a vast machine which is itself composed of machines. "Like a planet in its orbit or a gear in its box, each species exists to perform some function in the grand apparatus."[17] The grand apparatus and its functions, to which each species is fitted, were, like the component species, believed to be designed by God. So, all natural relations and interactions remain external.

The subsequent Arcadian and Romantic intellectual countercurrents to eighteenth-century rationalism and mechanism, however, gave the proto-ecological notion of a natural economy a more integrative and holistic cast. Ecology as it eventually emerged as a distinct subdiscipline of natural history was shaped by a complex of governing metaphors derived from these minority traditions. Natural relations among species were portrayed, for example, by Gilbert White in the late eighteenth century, as a "harmony" and as a felicitous "balance" – balance both in the physical sense of a dynamic equilibrium and in the distinctly aesthetic sense of a tension and resolution of opposites, as in beautiful painting, poetry, and music.[18]

In contrast to the Linnaean designed, reductive, mechanical Leviathan, John Burroughs in the late nineteenth century posited an evolving and animated organic Leviathan, an idea later given theoretical definition and articulation by William Morton Wheeler.[19] Wheeler's exemplar was a beehive, a superorganism composed of multicelled organisms – the bees – which were in turn composed of single-cell organic units. Populations of bees, other insects, plants, avifauna, mammals, and so on are to biocoenoses as cells to multicelled organisms and bees to hives. The whole Earth's living mantle might similarly be represented as a vast "comprehensive" organic being. In Wheeler's representation, each higher level of organization is "emergent"; thus, the whole cannot be reduced to the sum of the parts.

The original notion of an economy of nature was itself a metaphor which at the turn of the century ecologists began to unpack to construct an important theoretical model. Plant and animal associations might be studied as "biotic communities." Phytographers Eugenius Warming and Frederick Clements introduced the idea of competitive dynamic "succession" in plant communities which typically evolved from "pioneer" to "climax" stages.[20] In the 1920s and 1930s, zoologist Charles Elton developed the

community analogy further, with a greater emphasis on structure than process. Each species occupies a "trophic *niche*" in the biotic community which is, as it were, a "profession" in the economy of nature.[21] There are three great guilds – producers (the green plants), first and second-order consumers (herbivorous and carnivorous animals respectively), and decomposers (fungi and bacteria). In biotic communities the myriad specialists in each great group are linked in "food chains" which when considered together constitute tangled "food webs." Certain common structures characterized all biotic communities, however different their component species, and peculiar professions. For example, the producers must be many times more numerous than the consumers and the prey many times more numerous than predators; nor might any two species share precisely the same ecological niche.

Oxford University ecologist Arthur Tansley coined the term *ecosystem* in 1935 deliberately to supplant the more metaphorical characterizations of biocoenoses as "communities" of plants and animals or as "super-organismic" entities.[22] Tansley's ecosystem model of biotic processes was intended to bring ecology as a science out of a qualitative, descriptive stage, with anthropomorphic and mystic overtones, and transform it into a value-free, exact quantitative science. Hence, Tansley suggested that measurable "energy" contained in food coursed through the ecosystem and was at the foundation of its structure.

The scientific exemplar to which Tansley looked was physics. Of the so-called "New Ecology," for which Tansley's ecosystem model was the critical ingredient, Donald Worster writes:

> It owed nothing to any of its forebears in the history of science. . . . It was born of entirely different parentage: that is, modern thermodynamic physics, not biology.[23]

Hence, it is no wonder that the New Physics and the New Ecology should be conceptually complementary and convergent. Tansley's exemplar for a new paradigm in ecology was, it turns out, the new paradigm emerging in physics. The ecosystem model was expressly designed to be the "field theory" of modern biology.

However, as Worster emphatically points out, the quantitative, thermodynamic, biophysical model of nature which is the hallmark of the New Ecology was immediately turned to economic advantage as a powerful new weapon in mankind's age-old campaign to conquer nature. With the quantitative precision of which Tansley's energy circuit model was capable, ecosystems could be made more "productive" and "efficient" so as to "yield" a higher caloric "crop." But just as the philosophical interpretation of the New Physics, the Copenhagen Interpretation and its variations and alternatives, is quite another thing from its economic and military applications – from TV to laser weaponry – so the philosophical interpretation of the new ecology is quite another thing from its agronomic and managerial applications – from Ducks Unlimited to the green revolution. As Worster prophetically remarks: "Organicism has a way of gaining a foothold on even the most unpromising surface."[24]

IV

At mid-century ecologist and conservationist Aldo Leopold strove to erect a secular environmental ethic on evolutionary and ecological foundations.[25] In his land ethic one finds traces of Burroughs' organic image of nature, although Leopold himself seems to have gotten the idea from the Russian philosopher P. D. Ouspensky.[26] And certainly crucial to the conceptual foundations of the land ethic is Elton's community concept. However, when Leopold turns more deliberately to the construction of a "mental image" of the natural environment in relation to which he urged new ethical sensibilities he sketches, in poetic terms, the physics-born ecosystem model. According to Leopold, *land*, his shorthand term for the natural environment

> is a fountain of energy flowing through a circuit of soils, plants, and animals. Food chains are the living channels conducting energy upward [*sc.*, to the apex of the trophic pyramid]. . . . The velocity and character of the upward flow of energy depend on the complex structure of the plant and animal community. . . . Without this complexity normal circulation would presumably not occur.[27]

Ecologist Paul Shepard, a decade or so later, developed more consciously the metaphysical overtones of this field theory of living nature adumbrated by Leopold. According to Shepard, from the modern classical perspective

> nature is epitomized by living objects rather than the complex flow patterns of which objects are temporary formations. . . . [T]he landscape [from the classical point of view] is a room-like collection of animated furniture. . . . [B]ut it should be noted that it is best describable in terms of events which constitute a field pattern.[28]

Shepard, thus, more abstractively than Leopold, suggested that an object ontology is inappropriate to an ecological description of the natural environment. Living natural objects should be regarded as ontologically subordinate to "events" and/or "flow patterns" and/or "field patterns." As reflectively represented at mid-century, from the point of view of a mature ecological science, the biological reality seems to be, at the very least, more fluid and integrally patterned and less substantive and discrete than it had been previously represented.

Let me sum up and attempt to express more precisely the abstractive general concept of nature distilled from the New Ecology. First, in the "organic" concept of nature implied by the New Ecology as in that implied by the New Physics, energy seems to be a more fundamental and primitive reality than material objects or discrete entities – elementary particles and organisms respectively.[29] An individual organism, like an elementary particle is, as it were, a momentary configuration, a local perturbation, in an energy flux or "field."

The metaphysical ecologists here quoted, however, if pressed, would seem hardly prepared to deny outright a primary reality to atomic and molecular matter per se in addition to energy and its "flow." Organisms, though conduits of and configured by energy, remain *composed* of molecules – solid material substances. Rather, ecological interactions, primarily and especially trophic relationships, constitute a macrocosmic network or pattern through which solar energy, fixed by photosynthesis, is transferred from organism to organism until it is dissipated. Organisms are moments in this network, knots in this web of life.

However, if we combine quantum theory with ecology, as well as compare them, and resolve the erstwhile solid and immutable atoms of matter which compose the molecules, which in turn compose the cells of organic bodies, into the ephemeral, energetic quanta, then we may say quite literally and unambiguously that organisms are, in their entire structure – from subatomic microcosm to ecosystemic macrocosm – patterns, perturbations, or configurations of energy.

[. . .]

Second, the concept of nature emergent from the New Ecology, as that emergent from the New Physics, is holistic. It is impossible to conceive of organisms – if they are, as it were, knots in the web of life, or temporary formations or perturbations in complex flow patterns – apart from the field, the matrix of which they are modes. Contrary to the object ontology of classical physics and biology in which it was possible to conceive of an entity in isolation from its milieu – hanging alone in the void or catalogued in a specimen museum – the conception of one thing in the New Physics and New Ecology necessarily involves the conception of others and so on, until the entire system is, in principle, implicated.

Naess points out another sense in which ecology implies a holistic conception of the organic world, the import of which only an academic philosopher would be likely to notice. He claims, in effect, that ecology revives the metaphysical doctrine of internal relations.[30] This suggestion, remarkably, had been advanced even earlier by comparative philosopher Eliot Deutsch who also connected it with the Vedantic concept of *karma*.[31]

The doctrine of internal relations is, of course, associated with nineteenth and early twentieth-century German and English idealism – with the philosophies of Hegel, Fichte, Bradley, Royce, and Bosanquet. The basic idea is that a thing's essence is exhaustively determined by its relationships, that it cannot be conceived apart from its relationships with other things. Whatever the motives of the idealists (coherency theories of truth, the omniscience and omnipresence of spirit or whatever) and notwithstanding the inevitable entanglement of the doctrine of internal relations with other concurrently fashionable topics by mid-century neo-scholastic, academic philosophers (with "bare particulars," nominalism, the analytic-synthetic distinction, and so on) internal relations are straightforwardly implicated in ecology.

From the perspective of modern biology, species adapt to a *niche* in an ecosystem. Their actual relationships to other organisms (to predators, to prey, to parasites and disease organisms, etc.) and to physical and chemical conditions (to temperature, radiation, salinity, wind, soil and water pH, and so on) literally sculpt their outward forms, their metabolic, physiological, and reproductive processes, and even their psychological and mental capacities.

A specimen is, in effect, a summation of its species' historical, adaptive relationship to the environment. This observation led Shepard to claim that "relationships of things are as real as the things."[32] Indeed, I would be inclined to go even further. To convey an anti-Aristotelian thought in an Aristotelian manner of speech one might say that from an ecological perspective, relations are "prior" to the things related, and the systemic wholes woven from these relations are "prior" to their component parts. Ecosystemic wholes are "logically prior" to their component species because the nature of the part is determined by its relationship to the whole. That is, more simply and concretely expressed, a species has the particular characteristics that it has because those characteristics result from its adaptation to a *niche* in an eco*system*.

[. . .]

V

Ecology has rather signal implications for moral psychology which we may treat here for convenience as part of metaphysics. Since individual organisms, from an ecological point of view, are less discrete objects than modes of a continuous, albeit differentiated whole, the distinction between self and other is blurred. Hence, the central problem of modern classical moral philosophy as elegantly exposed by Kenneth Goodpaster in a recent discussion – the problem of either managing or overcoming egoism – is not solved by the moral psychology implicated in ecology so much as outflanked.[33]

Paul Shepard has remarked that

> In one aspect the self is an arrangement of organs, feelings, and thoughts – a "me" – surrounded by a hard body boundary: skin, clothes, and insular habits. . . . The alternative [aspect] is a self as a center of organization, constantly drawing on and influencing the surroundings. . . . Ecological thinking . . . requires a kind of vision across boundaries. The epidermis of the skin is ecologically like a pond surface or a forest soil, not a shell so much as a delicate interpenetration. It reveals the self ennobled and extended . . . as part of the landscape and the ecosystem.[34]

He then goes on to endorse a notion earlier crystallized by Alan Watts (whose inspiration came from oriental philosophies) – that "the world is your body."[35]

Environmental philosopher Holmes Rolston has alluded to and extended Shepard's notion of the "relational self" as implied by ecology. Meditating by the shores of a Rocky Mountain wilderness lake, Rolston asks:

Does not my skin resemble this lake surface? Neither lake nor self has independent being. . . . Inlet waters have crossed this interface and are now embodied within me. . . . The waters of North Inlet are part of my circulatory system; and the more literally we take this truth the more nearly we understand it. I incarnate the solar energies that flow through this lake. No one is free-living . . . *Bios* is intrinsically symbiosis.[36]

As one moves, in imagination, outwardly from the core of one's organism, it is impossible to find a clear demarcation between oneself and one's environment. The environing gases and fluids flow continuously in and out. The organisms outside (and inside!) one's osmotic envelope continually, albeit selectively, are transubstantiated into and through oneself. In the time-lapse cinematography of imagination one can see oneself arising from the earth, as it were, a pulsating structure in a vast sea of other patterns large and small – some of them mysteriously translating through oneself – finally to be transmitted into the others. The world is, indeed, one's extended body and one's body is the precipitation, the focus of the world in a particular space-time locale.

This idea is very old, even in the West, expressed abstractly and philosophically by Heraclitus in the Greek tradition and concretely and poetically – with the phrase, "for dust thou art, and unto dust shalt thou return" – by the author(s) of Genesis-J. In the West, however, there still lingers the image of the substantive *nephesh*, *psyche*, soul, or conscious mind – the more vulnerable and self-pitying, the more diaphanous and insubstantial its organic cladding is perceived to be. Paul Shepard, however, has pointed out that the relational concept of self extends to consciousness as well as organism, to mind as well as matter. According to Shepard:

Internal complexity, as the mind of a primate, is an extension of natural complexity, measured by the variety of plants and animals and the variety of nerve cells – organic extensions of each other.

The exuberance of kinds [is] the setting in which a good mind could evolve (to deal with a complex world). . . . The idea of natural complexity as a counterpart to human intricacy is essential to an ecology of man.[37]

In a subsequent discussion Shepard elaborates this insight.[38] The more primitive elements of animal consciousness – palpable hunger and thirst, fear and rage, pleasure and pain – are as clearly evolutionary adaptations to an ever more elaborate ecosystem as fur and feathers, toes and digits, eyes and ears. The distinctive mark of human consciousness and the material of human reason are the systems of concepts embodied by human languages. Shepard has suggested that conceptual thought evolved as the taxonomical array of animals and plants was mapped by the emergent consciousness of primate hunter-gatherers. In a very direct way, therefore, human consciousness, including abstract rational thought, is an extension of the environment, just as the "environment" becomes fully actual in the mind-body unity of the New Physics, only as it interacts with consciousness.[39]

Shepard has constructed on this basis an interesting argument for species conservation: if we simplify and impoverish the Earth's ecosystems, we risk rendering future generations of human beings mentally degenerate. Lacking a rich and complex natural environment to support – as correspondent, analogue, and stimulus – a rich and complex intelligence, human intelligence may atrophy.

The relational view of self – both self as bodily organism and self as conscious, thinking thing – transforms egoism into environmentalism, to borrow Kenneth Goodpaster's felicitous phrase. As I have elsewhere pointed out, egoism has been regarded as axiologically privileged.[40] The intrinsic value of oneself is taken as a given. How to account for the value of "others" – human others and now nonhuman natural others – has been the principal problematic of non-egoistic ethics.[41]

However, if the world is one's body and one's consciousness not only images in its specific content the world around, but the very structure of one's psyche and rational faculties are formed through adaptive interaction with the ecological organization of nature, then one's self, both physically and psychologically, gradiently merges from its central core outwardly to the environment. One cannot, thus, draw hard and fast boundaries between oneself, either physically or spiritually, and the environment.

For me this realization took concrete form, as I stood two decades and an ecological education later, on the banks of the Mississippi River where I had roamed as a boy. As I gazed at the brown silt-choked waters absorbing a black plume of industrial and municipal sewage from Memphis and followed bits of some unknown beige froth floating continually down from Cincinnati, Louisville, or St. Louis, I experienced a palpable pain. It was not distinctly located in any of my extremities, nor was it like a headache or nausea. Still, it was very real. I had no plans to swim in the river, no need to drink from it, no intention of buying real estate on its shores. My narrowly personal interests were not affected, and yet somehow I was personally injured. It occurred to me then, in a flash of self-discovery, that the river was a part of me. And I recalled a line from Leopold's *Sand County Almanac*: "One of the penalties of an ecological education is that one lives alone in a world of wounds."[42]

Australian conservationist John Seed, musing on his efforts on behalf of rain forest preservation in Queensland, has come to a similar conclusion:

> [A]s the implications of evolution and ecology are internalized . . . there is an identification with all life. . . . Alienation subsides. . . . "I am protecting the rain forest" develops to "I am part of the rain forest protecting myself. I am that part of the rain forest recently emerged into thinking."[43]

Ecology, thus, gives a new meaning as well as new substance to the phrase, "enlightened self-interest."

Notes

1   See for example, E. A. Burtt, *The Metaphysical Foundations of Modern Science* (Garden City, NY: Anchor Books, 1954) and Ernest Nagel, *The Structure of Science* (New York: Harcourt, Brace and World, 1961).

2   The term *New Ecology* was first used in H. G. Wells, with Julian Huxley and G. P. Wells, *The Science of Life* (New York: Garden City Publishing Co., 1939), p. 961, to characterize ecology after the quantifiable "ecosystem" model was developed by Arthur Tansley in 1935. See Warwick Fox, "Deep Ecology: A New Philosophy of Our Time?" *The Ecologist* 14 (1984): 194–200, and J. Baird Callicott, "Intrinsic Value, Quantum Theory, and Environmental Ethics," *Environmental Ethics* 7 (1985): 257–75, for a discussion of the convergence and complementary characteristics of the New Physics and New Ecology.

3   John Gribbin, *In Search of Schrodinger's Cat: Quantum Physics and Reality* (New York: Bantam, 1984), claims that while "Newton had [atomism] in mind in his work on physics and optics, atoms only really became a

part of scientific thought in the latter part of the eighteenth century when the French chemist Antoine Lavoisier investigated why things burn" (p. 19). But, according to Thomas Kuhn, *The Copernican Revolution: Planetary Astronomy and the Development of Western Thought* (Cambridge, Mass.: Harvard University Press, 1957), whose historical point of view is somewhat broader than Gribbin's, "early in the seventeenth century atomism experienced an immense revival. . . . Atomism was firmly merged with Copernicanism as a fundamental tenet of the 'new philosophy' which directed the scientific imagination" (p. 237).

4   "Primary" and "secondary" qualities were terms given to the distinction between putative actual and nonactual qualities of the elements by John Locke, *Essay Concerning Human Understanding* (New York: E. P. Dutton and Co., 1961). Locke attempted to ground the distinction empirically rather than theoretically, the futility of which was subsequently demonstrated by Berkeley. The revealing terms, "the full" and "the empty," are attributed to the fifth-century atomists by Aristotle, *Metaphysics* 985b4.

5   See G. S. Kirk and J. E. Raven, *The Presocratic Philosophers: A Critical History with a Selection of Texts* (Cambridge: Cambridge University Press, 1962), and Burtt, *Metaphysical Foundations of Modern Science*.

6   Ibid.

7   See Ernst Nagel, *Structure of Science*.

8   Ibid.

9   For Democritus' materialistic psychology see W. K. C. Guthrie, *A History of Greek Philosophy* (Cambridge: Cambridge University Press, 1965), vol. 2; for Lucretius' position see Titus Lucretius Carus, *De Rerum Natura*, trans. Robert Latham (Harmondsworth: Penguin, 1951); and for Hobbes' views see Thomas Hobbes, *Leviathan* (New York: Collier Books, 1962). For Pythagoras' dualism see W. K. C. Guthrie, *A History of Greek Philosophy* (Cambridge: Cambridge University Press, 1962), vol. 1; for Plato's see especially the *Phaedo*; and for Descartes' see *Meditations on First Philosophy*, in E. S. Haldane and G. R. T. Ross, trans., *The Philosophical Works of Descartes* (Cambridge: Cambridge University Press, 1911), vol. 1.

10   There is remarkable unanimity of thought on this head among Pythagoras, Plato, and Descartes, the West's most influential dualists.

11   See Hobbes, *Leviathan*.

12   See Immanuel Kant, *Foundations of the Metaphysics of Morals* (New York: Bobbs-Merrill Co., 1959).

13   See especially Plato, *Parmenides and Phaedo*.

14   See Aristotle, *De Partibus Animalium and Politicus*.

15   Ibid.

16   See Ernst Haeckel, *Generelle Morphologie der Organismen*, 2 vols. (Berlin: Reimer, 1966); and

Carl Linnaeus, "Specimen Academicum de Oeconomia Naturae," *Amoenitates Academicae. II: Holmae* (Lugdoni Batavorum. Apud Cotnelium Haak, 1751).

17 Donald Worster, *Nature's Economy: The Roots of Ecology* (Garden City, NY: Anchor Books, 1979).

18 See Gilbert White, *The Natural History of Selborne* (New York: Harper, 1842).

19 See John Burroughs, "The Noon of Science," in *The Writings of John Burroughs*, vol. 17; *The Summit of the Years* (Boston: Houghton Mifflin and Company, 1913); and William Morton Wheeler, *Essays in Philosophical Biology* (New York: Russell and Russell, 1939).

20 See Eugenius Warming, *The Oecology of Plants*, rev. ed. (Oxford: Clarendon Press, 1909); and Frederick Clements, *Plant Succession: An Analysis of the Development of Vegetation* (Washington, DC: Carnegie Institution of Washington, 1916).

21 See Charles Elton, *Animal Ecology* (New York: Macmillan, 1927).

22 See Arthur G. Tansley, "The Use and Abuse of Vegetational Concepts and Terms," *Ecology* 16 (1935): 292–303.

23 Worster, *Nature's Economy*, p. 300.

24 Ibid., p. 332.

25 See Aldo Leopold, *A Sand County Almanac and Sketches Here and There* (New York: Oxford University Press, 1949).

26 See Aldo Leopold, "Some Fundamentals of Conservation," *Environmental Ethics* 1 (1979): 131–48.

27 Aldo Leopold, *A Sand County Almanac*, p. 216.

28 Paul Shepard, "A Theory of the Value of Hunting." *Twenty-Fourth North American Wildlife Conference* (1957), pp. 505–6.

29 Werner Haisenberg, *Physics and Philosophy: The Revolution in Modern Science* (New York: Harper and Row, 1958), remarked "[W]e may say that all elementary particles consist of energy. This could be interpreted as defining energy as the primary substance of the world. . . . The elementary particles are certainly not eternal and indestructible units of matter, they can actually be transformed into each other. . . . Such events have been frequently observed and offer the best proof that all particles are made of the same substance: energy" (pp. 70–1).

30 See Naess, "The Shallow and the Deep, Long-Range Ecology Movement."

31 Eliot Deutsch, "Vedanta and Ecology," in T. M. P. Mehederan, ed., *Indian Philosophical Annual 7* (Madras Center for Advanced Study in Philosophy, 1970): 1–10.

32 Paul Shepard, "Ecology and Man: A Viewpoint," in Paul Shepard and Daniel McKinley, eds., *The Subversive Science: Essays Toward an Ecology of Man* (Boston: Houghton Mifflin, 1967), p. 3.

33 See Kenneth Goodpaster, "From Egoism to Environmentalism," in Kenneth Goodpaster and Kenneth Sayre, eds., *Ethics and Problems of the 21st Century* (Notre Dame: University of Notre Dame Press, 1979), pp. 21–35.

34 Paul Shepard, "Ecology and Man: A Viewpoint," p. 2.

35 See Alan Watts, *The Book on the Taboo Against Knowing Who You Are* (New York: Pantheon Books, 1966).

36 Holmes Rolston, III, "Lake Solitude: The Individual in Wildness," *Main Currents in Modern Thought* 31 (1975): 122.

37 Paul Shepard, "Ecology and Man: A Viewpoint," p. 4.

38 See Paul Shepard, *Thinking Animals: Animals and the Development of Human Intelligence* (New York: Viking Press, 1978).

39 See Jonathan Powers, *Philosophy and the New Physics* (London: Methuen, 1982).

40 See Callicott, "Intrinsic Value, Quantum Theory and Environmental Ethics."

41 See Goodpaster, "From Egoism to Environmentalism."

42 Aldo Leopold, *A Sand County Almanac with Essays on Conservation from Round River* (New York: Ballantine Books, 1966), p. 197.

43 John Seed, "Anthropocentrism," Appendix E, in Bill Devall and George Sessions, *Deep Ecology*, p. 243.

54   The Ends of the World as We Know Them

Jared Diamond

When it comes to historical collapses, five groups of interacting factors have been especially important: the damage that people have inflicted on their environment; climate change; enemies; changes in friendly trading partners; and the society's political, economic and social responses to these shifts. That's not to say that all five causes play a role in every case. Instead, think of this as a useful checklist of factors that should be examined, but whose relative importance varies from case to case.

For instance, in the collapse of the Polynesian society on Easter Island three centuries ago, environmental problems were dominant, and climate change, enemies and trade were insignificant; however, the latter three factors played big roles in the disappearance of the medieval Norse colonies on Greenland. Let's consider two examples of declines stemming from different mixes of causes: the falls of classic Maya civilization and of Polynesian settlements on the Pitcairn Islands.

Maya Native Americans of the Yucatan Peninsula and adjacent parts of Central America developed the New World's most advanced civilization before Columbus. They were innovators in writing, astronomy, architecture and art. From local origins around 2,500 years ago, Maya societies rose especially after the year A.D. 250, reaching peaks of population and sophistication in the late 8th century.

Thereafter, societies in the most densely populated areas of the southern Yucatan underwent a steep political and cultural collapse: between 760 and 910, kings were overthrown, large areas were abandoned, and at least 90 percent of the population disappeared, leaving cities to become overgrown by jungle. The last known date recorded on a Maya monument by their so-called Long Count calendar corresponds to the year 909. What happened?

A major factor was environmental degradation by people: deforestation, soil erosion and water management problems, all of which resulted in less food.

Those problems were exacerbated by droughts, which may have been partly caused by humans themselves through deforestation. Chronic warfare made matters worse, as more and more people fought over less and less land and resources.

Why weren't these problems obvious to the Maya kings, who could surely see their forests vanishing and their hills becoming eroded? Part of the reason was that the kings were able to insulate themselves from problems afflicting the rest of society. By extracting wealth from commoners, they could remain well fed while everyone else was slowly starving.

What's more, the kings were preoccupied with their own power struggles. They had to concentrate on fighting one another and keeping up their images through ostentatious displays of wealth. By insulating themselves in the short run from the problems of society, the elite merely bought themselves the privilege of being among the last to starve.

Whereas Maya societies were undone by problems of their own making, Polynesian societies on Pitcairn and Henderson Islands in the tropical Pacific Ocean were undone largely by other people's mistakes. Pitcairn, the uninhabited island settled in 1790 by the H.M.S. Bounty mutineers, had actually been populated by Polynesians 800 years earlier. That society, which left behind temple platforms, stone and shell tools and huge garbage piles of fish and bird and turtle bones as evidence of its existence, survived for several centuries and then vanished. Why?

In many respects, Pitcairn and Henderson are tropical paradises, rich in some food sources and essential raw materials. Pitcairn is home to Southeast Polynesia's largest quarry of stone suited for making adzes, while Henderson has the region's largest breeding seabird colony and its only nesting beach for sea turtles. Yet the islanders depended on imports from Mangareva Island, hundreds of miles away, for canoes, crops, livestock and oyster shells for making tools.

Unfortunately for the inhabitants of Pitcairn and Henderson, their Mangarevan trading partner collapsed for reasons similar to those underlying the Maya decline: deforestation, erosion and warfare. Deprived of essential imports in a Polynesian equivalent of the 1973 oil crisis, the Pitcairn and Henderson societies declined until everybody had died or fled.

The Maya and the Henderson and Pitcairn Islanders are not alone, of course. Over the centuries, many other societies have declined, collapsed or died out. Famous victims include the Anasazi in the American Southwest, who abandoned their cities in the 12th century because of environmental problems and climate change, and the Greenland Norse, who disappeared in the 15th century because of all five interacting factors on the checklist. There were also the ancient Fertile Crescent societies, the Khmer at Angkor Wat, the Moche society of Peru – the list goes on.

But before we let ourselves get depressed, we should also remember that there is another long list of cultures that have managed to prosper for lengthy periods of time. Societies in Japan, Tonga, Tikopia, the New Guinea Highlands and Central and Northwest Europe, for example, have all found ways to sustain themselves. What separates the lost cultures from those that survived? Why did the Maya fail and the shogun succeed?

Half of the answer involves environmental differences: geography deals worse cards to some societies than to others. Many of the societies that collapsed had the misfortune to occupy dry, cold or otherwise fragile environments, while many of the long-term survivors enjoyed more robust and fertile surroundings. But it's not the case that a congenial environment guarantees success: some societies (like the Maya) managed to ruin lush environments, while other societies – like the Incas, the Inuit, Icelanders and desert Australian Aborigines – have managed to carry on in some of the earth's most daunting environments.

The other half of the answer involves differences in a society's responses to problems. Ninth-century New Guinea Highland villagers, 16th-century German landowners, and the Tokugawa shoguns of 17th-century Japan all recognized the deforestation spreading around them and solved the problem, either by developing scientific reforestation (Japan and Germany) or by transplanting tree seedlings (New Guinea). Conversely, the Maya, Mangarevans

and Easter Islanders failed to address their forestry problems and so collapsed.

Consider Japan. In the 1600s, the country faced its own crisis of deforestation, paradoxically brought on by the peace and prosperity following the Tokugawa shoguns' military triumph that ended 150 years of civil war. The subsequent explosion of Japan's population and economy set off rampant logging for construction of palaces and cities, and for fuel and fertilizer.

The shoguns responded with both negative and positive measures. They reduced wood consumption by turning to light-timbered construction, to fuel-efficient stoves and heaters, and to coal as a source of energy. At the same time, they increased wood production by developing and carefully managing plantation forests. Both the shoguns and the Japanese peasants took a long-term view: the former expected to pass on their power to their children, and the latter expected to pass on their land. In addition, Japan's isolation at the time made it obvious that the country would have to depend on its own resources and couldn't meet its needs by pillaging other countries. Today, despite having the highest human population density of any large developed country, Japan is more than 70 percent forested.

There is a similar story from Iceland. When the island was first settled by the Norse around 870, its light volcanic soils presented colonists with unfamiliar challenges. They proceeded to cut down trees and stock sheep as if they were still in Norway, with its robust soils. Significant erosion ensued, carrying half of Iceland's topsoil into the ocean within a century or two. Icelanders became the poorest people in Europe. But they gradually learned from their mistakes, over time instituting stocking limits on sheep and other strict controls, and establishing an entire government department charged with landscape management. Today, Iceland boasts the sixth-highest per-capita income in the world.

What lessons can we draw from history? The most straightforward: take environmental problems seriously. They destroyed societies in the past, and they are even more likely to do so now. If 6,000 Polynesians with stone tools were able to destroy Mangareva Island, consider what six billion people with metal tools and bulldozers are doing today. Moreover, while the Maya collapse affected just a few neighboring societies in Central America, globalization now means that any society's problems have the potential to affect anyone else. Just think how crises in Somalia, Afghanistan and Iraq have shaped the United States today.

Other lessons involve failures of group decision-making. There are many reasons why past societies made bad decisions, and thereby failed to solve or even to perceive the problems that would eventually destroy them. One reason involves conflicts of interest, whereby one group within a society (for instance, the pig farmers who caused the worst erosion in medieval Greenland and Iceland) can profit by engaging in practices that damage the rest of society. Another is the pursuit of short-term gains at the expense of long-term survival, as when fishermen overfish the stocks on which their livelihoods ultimately depend.

History also teaches us two deeper lessons about what separates successful societies from those heading toward failure. A society contains a built-in blueprint for failure if the elite insulates itself from the consequences of its actions. That's why Maya kings, Norse Greenlanders and Easter Island chiefs made choices that eventually undermined their societies. They themselves did not begin to feel deprived until they had irreversibly destroyed their landscape.

Could this happen in the United States? It's a thought that often occurs to me here in Los Angeles, when I drive by gated communities, guarded by private security patrols, and filled with people who drink bottled water, depend on private pensions, and send their children to private schools. By doing these things, they lose the motivation to support the police force, the municipal water supply, Social Security and public schools. If conditions deteriorate too much for poorer people, gates will not keep the rioters out. Rioters eventually burned the palaces of Maya kings and tore down the statues of Easter Island chiefs; they have also already threatened wealthy districts in Los Angeles twice in recent decades.

In contrast, the elite in 17th-century Japan, as in modern Scandinavia and the Netherlands, could not ignore or insulate themselves from broad societal problems. For instance, the Dutch upper class for hundreds of years has been unable to insulate itself from the Netherlands' water management problems for a simple reason: the rich live in the same drained lands below sea level as the poor. If the dikes and pumps keeping out the sea fail, the well-off Dutch know that they will drown along with everybody else, which is precisely what happened during the floods of 1953.

The other deep lesson involves a willingness to re-examine long-held core values, when conditions change and those values no longer make sense. The medieval Greenland Norse lacked such a willingness: they continued to view themselves as transplanted Norwegian pastoralists, and to despise the Inuit as pagan hunters, even after Norway stopped sending trading ships and the climate had grown too cold for a pastoral existence. They died off as a result, leaving Greenland to the Inuit. On the other hand, the British in the 1950s faced up to the need for a painful reappraisal of their former status as rulers of a world empire set apart from Europe. They are now finding a different avenue to wealth and power, as part of a united Europe.

In this New Year, we Americans have our own painful reappraisals to face. Historically, we viewed the United States as a land of unlimited plenty, and so we practiced unrestrained consumerism, but that's no longer viable in a world of finite resources. We can't continue to deplete our own resources as well as those of much of the rest of the world.

Historically, oceans protected us from external threats; we stepped back from our isolationism only temporarily during the crises of two world wars. Now, technology and global interconnectedness have robbed us of our protection. In recent years, we have responded to foreign threats largely by seeking short-term military solutions at the last minute.

But how long can we keep this up? Though we are the richest nation on earth, there's simply no way we can afford (or muster the troops) to intervene in the dozens of countries where emerging threats lurk – particularly when each intervention these days can cost more than $100 billion and require more than 100,000 troops.

A genuine reappraisal would require us to recognize that it will be far less expensive and far more effective to address the underlying problems of public health, population and environment that ultimately cause threats to us to emerge in poor countries. In the past, we have regarded foreign aid as either charity or as buying support; now, it's an act of self-interest to preserve our own economy and protect American lives.

Do we have cause for hope? Many of my friends are pessimistic when they contemplate the world's growing population and human demands colliding with shrinking resources. But I draw hope from the knowledge that humanity's biggest problems today are ones entirely of our own making. Asteroids hurtling at us beyond our control don't figure high on our list of imminent dangers. To save ourselves, we don't need new technology: we just need the political will to face up to our problems of population and the environment.

I also draw hope from a unique advantage that we enjoy. Unlike any previous society in history, our global society today is the first with the opportunity to learn from the mistakes of societies remote from us in space and in time. When the Maya and Mangarevans were cutting down their trees, there were no historians or archaeologists, no newspapers or television, to warn them of the consequences of their actions. We, on the other hand, have a detailed chronicle of human successes and failures at our disposal. Will we choose to use it?

PART VIII

WHAT ARE SOME ETHICAL DIMENSIONS OF ENVIRONMENTAL PUBLIC POLICY?

A   The Population/Poverty Debate

55   An Essay on the Principle of Population
Thomas Robert Malthus

56   Impact of Population Growth
Paul R. Ehrlich and John P. Holdren

57   The Ecological Necessity of Confronting the Problem of Human Overpopulation
Garrett Hardin

58   How Poverty Breeds Overpopulation
Barry Commoner

59   More People, Greater Wealth, More Resources, Healthier Environment
Julian L. Simon

60   Population: Delusion and Reality
Amartya Sen

61   A Special Moment in History
Bill McKibben

B   Industrial Agriculture

62   Nature as the Measure for a Sustainable Agriculture
Wes Jackson

63   Putting Food Production in Context: Toward a Postmechanistic Agricultural Ethic
David R. Keller and E. Charles Brummer

C   Socioeconomic Environmental Justice

64   Environmental Justice for All
Robert D. Bullard

65   Just Garbage
Peter S. Wenz

D   Environmental Ethics and Economic Policy

66   A Declaration of Sustainability
     Paul Hawken

67   The Steady-State Economy
     Herman E. Daly

68   Making Capitalism Sustainable
     John Elkington

69   The Ignorance Argument: What Must We Know to be Fair to the Future?
     Bryan Norton

70   Environmental Justice and Intergenerational Debt
     Clark Wolf

E   Globalization

71   The Environmental Limits to Globalization
     David Ehrenfeld

Introduction

A primary goal of environmental ethics, as practical ethics, is the formulation of reasoned and informed public policy on the environment. The range of issues of environmental public policy is staggering: global climate change, land-use planning, biodiversity, genetic engineering, agriculture, the infiltration of synthetic chemicals into ecological systems, and so on. Let's take a closer look at five of these issues which are certain to loom large in the decades to come: (1) the population debate; (2) industrial agriculture; (3) environmental justice; (4) environmental economic policy; and (5) globalization.

The Population Debate

This debate goes back to the English demographer Thomas Malthus, became heated during the late 1960s and '70s, and continues unabated. For the reason that this issue is perhaps the single greatest challenge humans face in terms of public policy (and is connected with global climate change), it demands the attention of students of environmental ethics.

The population debate is an intensely emotional one, in part because it has overtones of antagonism to religion and elements of misanthropy. The most famous early position on population is stated in Genesis 1:28: "Be fruitful and multiply, and fill the earth and subdue it."[1] Although some ancient Greek thinkers addressed the issue of population (for Plato and Aristotle, the ideal *polis* has a limited size, as too many citizens destabilize the social structure[2]), the biblical injunction remained essentially unquestioned until Thomas Malthus's impolite 1798 *An Essay on the Principle of Population*. Economists reacted no more favorably then than today: Karl Marx dismissed the essay as nothing more than the "school-boyish, superficial plagiary of other dilettantes,"[3] a "lampoon on the human race!"[4] For Marx, "overpopulation" is the result of the bourgeoisie investing in machinery, creating a surplus of laborers. Contra Malthus, overpopulation is not naturally occurring but is a symptom of capitalism.

In his *Essay*, Malthus argues that natural populations have the potential to increase rapidly, while resource utilization, under the best conditions, increases slowly:

> Taking the whole earth instead of this island, emigration would of course be excluded; and supposing the present population equal to a thousand millions, the human species would increase as the numbers 1, 2, 4, 8, 16, 32, 64, 128, 256, and subsistence as 1, 2, 3, 4, 5, 6, 7, 8, 9. In two centuries the population would be to the means of subsistence as 256 to 9; in three centuries as 4096 to 13, and in two thousand years the difference would be almost incalculable.[5]

Malthus concludes, in the wording of the first edition:

> [T]he power of population is infinitely greater than the power in the earth to produce subsistence for man. Population, when unchecked, increases in a geometric ratio. Subsistence increases only in an arithmetic ratio . . . This implies a strong and constantly operating check on population from the difficulty of subsistence.[6]

What Malthus has in mind by using the mathematical words "geometric" and "arithmetic" is that populations have the *potential* to increase exponentially (if two parents have four offspring, and the offspring breed at the same rate, the population could grow from 2 to 2,048 in only 10 generations), while food production's potential to increase is linear (the amount of cultivated land can be increased only one acre at a time). The main point is that reproductive rates always outstrip agricultural carrying capacity of the land (see figure VIII.1).

In the early 1970s an acrimonious debate flared up among life scientists about the primary cause of environmental degradation, which was essentially a Malthusian/anti-Malthusian exchange (*Time* magazine called it "A Clash of Gloomy Prophets"[7]). On one hand, some biologists asserted that human overpopulation was mainly to blame for environmental degradation. Others asserted that it is not human population growth but industrialization that is the culprit.

In "Impact of Population Growth," lepidopterist Paul Ehrlich and physicist John Holdren argue in a neo-Malthusian vein that the most direct and

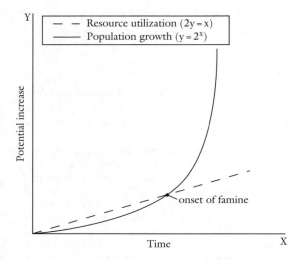

Figure VIII.1   Malthus's Population Principle.

effective way to deal with the negative human impact on the biosphere is population control. This article follows on the heels of Ehrlich's well-known 1968 book *The Population Bomb*, a controversial work which asserts that human population growth is the main cause of environmental degradation: "Too many cars, too many factories, too much detergent, too much pesticide, multiplying contrails, inadequate sewage treatment plants, too little water, too much carbon dioxide – all can be traced easily to *too many people*."[8] Crowding not only affects the human condition, but impacts the entire biosphere: "It is fair to say that the environment of every organism, human and nonhuman, on the face of the Earth has been influenced by the population explosion of *Homo sapiens*."[9] The solution is zero – or better yet, negative – population growth.[10] If voluntary methods fail, compulsory measures should be implemented.[11] After dealing with the problem of overpopulation in the United States, we must then "adopt some very tough foreign policy positions."[12] Providing food aid to countries whose populations have outstripped the carrying capacity of the land only makes a tragic situation worse; people who would have died due to starvation live to reproduce, further increasing the population level and consequently exacerbating the next famine. Along this line of reasoning, wealthy nations should withhold aid to countries suffering from famine.[13]

American biologist Garrett Hardin agrees. As he points out in "The Tragedy of the Commons," since the Earth is finite, population growth must at some point fall below the rate of replaceability.[14] The tragedy of the commons is the situation in which individuals overexploit natural resources and thus outstrip the carrying capacity of ecological systems. The ethical implication, outlined in Hardin's "The Ecological Necessity of Confronting the Problem of Human Overpopulation," is that governments ought to be "selfish" and protect ecological systems from being overexploited by foreigners. It also means that humanitarian interventions are unwarranted from a biological point of view. In "The Immorality of Being Softhearted," Hardin asks and answers (controversially): "How can we help a foreign country to escape overpopulation? Clearly the worst thing we can do is send food . . . Atomic bombs would be kinder. For a few moments the misery would be acute, but it would soon come to an end for most of the people, leaving a very few survivors to suffer thereafter."[15]

In "How Poverty Breeds Overpopulation" and his best-selling 1972 book *The Closing Circle*, plant physiologist Barry Commoner identifies the main cause of environmental degradation as industrialization.[16] Dubbed the "Paul Revere of Ecology" by *Time* magazine for alerting the country to the danger of pollution,[17] Commoner argues that in the case of the United States, the sharp increase in pollution levels (from 200 to 2,000 percent) since the end of World War II cannot be explained by the much smaller increases in population and affluence.[18] Rather, technologies that have replaced organic material with synthetics (plastics, synthetic fibers, DDT and other biocides, fertilizers, detergents, drugs, and so on) are to blame.[19]

By emphasizing pollution, Commoner disputes Ehrlich and Hardin's claim that human population growth is the leading cause of environmental degradation. Despite the popularity of claims to the contrary, "population growth in the United States has only a minor influence on the intensification of environmental pollution."[20] There is no ecological evidence to believe that the US is "overpopulated."[21] Commoner points out that scientific predictions about future population levels are ambiguous: vastly different predictions can be inferred from the same data.[22]

In developing countries, poverty is the cause of population growth, not unrestrained fertility. In agrarian societies with high infant mortality rates, children are essential to the improvement of a family's economic condition, so parents typically have many children. As affluence rises, so does the quality of medical care, and large numbers of children become a liability rather than an asset. Unfortunately, many countries remain locked in poverty due to exploitation by colonial powers. For example, in Indonesia, the Dutch promoted population growth to provide labor for the rubber industry, yet the wealth generated did not remain in Oceania but went back to the Netherlands.[23] As Commoner states: "The poor countries have high birthrates because they are extremely poor, and they are extremely poor because other countries are extremely rich."[24]

For these reasons, Commoner makes the exact opposite recommendation of Ehrlich and Hardin: provide aid for the developing countries in order to increase affluence and decrease the birth rate: "[I]f the root cause of the world population crisis is poverty, then to end it we must abolish poverty."[25] The act of withholding aid is tantamount to imperialism.[26] Commoner's own moral conviction is that coercion is an affront to human dignity. Consequently the only ethically acceptable method regarding reproductive choices is personal, voluntary birth control.[27] The alternative, population control, is tantamount to political repression.[28]

Enter the economists. In "More People, Greater Wealth, More Resources, Healthier Environment," American economist Julian Simon not only rejects Ehrlich's hypothesis that human population growth poses a serious ecological threat; he argues the *more* people, the *better*! Human population growth assuages the human impact on the environment through technological innovation. Simon argues that while *certain* resources are limited, substitutes are not.[29] For instance, copper used to make wire for telephone lines is finite, but copper wire can be substituted with fiber optic cable, and so on. As resources become scarce, the impetus to find replacements through a technological innovation is redoubled. Simon writes: "[T]he more people there are, the more minds that are working to discover new sources, and increase productivity, with raw materials as with all other goods."[30]

Economist Amartya Sen argues, in "Population: Delusion and Reality," that just because Malthus's predictions have not yet come to pass does not mean that they will not come to pass. It is also too simplistic to worry that ballooning populations of impoverished southern nations will overwhelm richer northern nations, since immigration is not fueled by differential population densities. Moreover, the negative environmental impact of one American equals that of dozens of Madagascarians and Zimbabweans. But as the standard of living of citizens of developing nations increases, so will their environmental impact begin to approach that of Europeans and Americans. So the population problem is a complex intermixture of demographic and economic factors.

The issue of the differential impact of the wealthy and poor is writer Bill McKibben's point of departure in "A Special Moment in History." McKibben points out, as does Sen, that human beings are not the same "size" ecologically: the average American uses approximately 75 times the energy (mostly in the form of fossil fuel) as an ancient hunter-gatherer: as much as a pilot whale.[31] Similarly, individuals in developing countries impact the biosphere far less than individuals in developed countries. For example, one-quarter of the world's population consumes three-quarters of the energy,[32] burdening individuals living in industrialized nations with a larger share of the responsibility for global climate change caused by increasing levels of carbon dioxide emission.[33] In the United States, this is evidenced by the widespread use of industrial-sized vehicles (e.g. Chevy Suburbans and Ford Expeditions) for domestic chores, and the attitude that it is hard to have fun if one's recreational appliance does not have an engine in it (motor boats, motor homes, all-terrain vehicles, jet skis, snowmobiles, motocross bikes, etc.).

Industrial Agriculture

Agriculture is a defining characteristic of human civilization: its invention marks the transition from nomadic to sedentary life. And no other human activity has transformed so much of the Earth's surface as farming. Oddly, the attention given to agriculture by environmental philosophers seems inversely proportional to its environmental effects.[34]

Industrial agriculture involves farming with heavy machinery, which disturbs topsoil and exacerbates erosion, and chemicals, which substitute the energy input to agroecosystems from sunlight to petrochemicals. Because uniformity of agroecosystems enables the use of industrial techniques, industrial agriculture is usually monoculture farming (cultivating uniform single-species crops).

In "Nature as the Measure for a Sustainable Agriculture," agronomist Wes Jackson argues that research at the Land Institute in Kansas points to distinct advantages of perennial polyculture over annual monoculture. Perennial polyculture, the natural state of the prairie, does not entail the extraction of the root system annually and consequently mitigates unsustainable topsoil erosion. Also, perennial polyculture does not require the input of energy-intensive chemicals.

Philosopher David Keller and agronomist Charles Brummer consider the metaphysical underpinnings of industrial agriculture in "Putting Food Production in Context," which they identify as the mechanical view of nature. The mechanical view of nature, a defining feature of modernity, underlies the production paradigm where agroecosystems are manipulated through external interventions based on universal laws. Keller and Brummer argue that agriculture ought not to be premised on the idea that agroecosystems are deterministic and predictable, and consequently that the activity of farming be gauged in terms of the unique ecological conditions of each locale.

Environmental Justice

Environmental justice means an equitable distribution of environmental risks across the population. Environmental injustice is the inequitable exposure to deleterious environmental conditions based on socioeconomic status. Environmental injustice is a complex issue involving demography, geography, epidemiology, economics, and politics. Factors which cause or aggravate environmental injustice include zoning policies which permit residential and industrial areas in close proximity,[35] the intentional targeting by corporations of minority communities as sites for hazardous materials facilities,[36] and the political weakness of minority communities to resist exploitation.[37]

In the United States, sources of pollution, such as manufacturing plants, toxic waste dumps, incinerators, and other industrial facilities, are typically located in low-income neighborhoods, often African American, Latino, and Native American, and less frequently in Caucasian areas.[38] Why? Consultants to the California Waste Management Board observe: "All socioeconomic groupings tend to resent the nearby siting of major [toxic waste] facilities, but middle and upper socioeconomic strata possess better resources to effectuate their opposition. Middle and higher socioeconomic strata neighborhoods

should not fall within the one-mile and five-mile radius of the proposed site."[39] Even the effectiveness of the use of bribery and corruption has been identified as considerations in hazardous waste siting.[40]

As sociologist Robert Bullard points out in "Environmental Justice for All," there is considerable demographic evidence of socioeconomic differentials in the exposure to noxious pollution: the affluent are not exposed to industrial effluents at nearly the same rates as the impoverished. Noxious facility siting often occurs in low-income and minority areas. In Chicago, 92 percent of the city's approximately one million African Americans live in racially segregated areas. One segregated area, the Altgeld Gardens housing project in southeast Chicago, is 70 percent African American and 11 percent Hispanic.[41] Altgeld Gardens is encircled by municipal and hazardous waste landfills, sewage treatment plants, toxic waste incinerators, smelters, steel mills, chemical plants, and a paint factory. The co-location of Altgeld Gardens and industry can be traced to racist zoning decisions dating back to the 1920s in which homes preceded the construction of hazardous waste facilities.[42] Collectively, the industrial facilities around Altgeld Gardens emit pollutants which are deleterious to health, particularly respiratory health.[43] Across the US, asthma is more prevalent amongst minority groups such as Hispanics and Blacks, and area of residence has been identified by public health researchers as a factor in this difference.[44]

In "Just Garbage," philosopher Peter Wenz applies a Principle of Commensurate Burdens and Benefits to the issue of environmental justice. According to this principle, if a community benefits from industrialization with a high standard of living, it should also share some of the burdens from that industrialization. Environmental injustice is the situation in which wealthy communities enjoy benefits of industrialization without shouldering costs, and poor communities shoulder costs without enjoying benefits. Wenz suggests that a calculation of relative benefits and burdens could be made using LULU (locally undesirable land uses) points.

Environmental Ethics and Economic Policy

"Economics" shares the same root (*oikos*) as ecology, and means, roughly, "management of the home." Recognizing this family resemblance, one could well conclude that in order to manage our earthly home well, we must know how it works. Informed economics presupposes ecological wisdom. Ethics is the art of systemically weighing the relative merits of mutually exclusive values, such as between ecological sustainability and robust economic growth. Ethically speaking, the goal for environmental economic policy is living well within the bounds of our earthly home.

In "A Declaration of Sustainability," which is a synopsis of *The Ecology of Commerce*, business writer Paul Hawken identifies 12 strategies for sustainability. Among his suggestions is that the public should have the authority to revoke the charters of corporations that wrongly abuse the environment. Hawken also argues that the true costs of the production of goods must be reflected in the price, such as pollution, worker health, and other costs which at present are "externalized" (in the language of economics). Connected to this strategy is Hawken's call to scrap the entire tax code and replace it with "green fees" which represent the environmental impact of the production of goods on ecological systems. Hawken also points out that manufacturing processes are linear (products are made, used, and discarded), whereas natural systems are cyclical, and that manufacturing processes must be brought in harmony with natural processes through the recycling of waste.

For American economist Herman Daly, steady-state (what Mill called "stationary-state"[45]) economics is the attempt to give concreteness to the vague notion of "sustainable development."[46] Traditional neoclassical-Keynesian growth macroeconomics has focused on allocation and distribution of goods at the expense of the scale of economic activity. The issue of scale has been overlooked, or ignored, due to a presumption that natural resources and sinks are functionally inexhaustible.[47] On the orthodox model, natural systems are but one variable in making decisions about the larger, all-encompassing economy. This has been the case for both communist and capitalist societies.[48] In contrast, on the steady-state model "the ecosystem contains the economy."[49] Steady-state economics is consistent with the biological view of organisms and the biosphere as open, steady-state systems.[50] Two categories of physical objects – artifacts and people – exist within the larger natural system.[51] As Daly outlines in "The Steady-State Economy,"[52] steady-state economics holds that the magnitudes of artifacts of

production and human population levels should be kept as constant as possible, in direct opposition to the Keynesian "growthmania synthesis."

In "Making Capitalism Sustainable" – selections from *Cannibals with Forks* – business writer John Elkington provides a framework of internalizing externalities with his notion of the "triple bottom line." In addition to the traditional bottom line of profit, Elkington argues that business decisions must be made with consideration to two other "bottom lines": social justice and environmental quality. Using the procedure of triple bottom line analysis, business decisions will be different from the traditional single bottom line of profit, since more factors are weighed. As has been clear since Marx and Engels brought attention to the plight of the working poor in Britain and elsewhere – see for example Engels's description of Manchester[53] – profit is often generated at the expense of social justice. For example, a garment manufacturer may be able to avoid adhering to US labor law by moving operations from Manhattan to Matamoras and exploiting Mexican children. However, the triple bottom line mandates that if the company decides to move, it should limit working hours, buy safe equipment, and provide health and medical benefits, even if Mexican law does not require it. The environmental bottom line may also impact the economic bottom line. Or the environmental bottom line may impact the social justice bottom line.

Bryan Norton maintains, in "The Ignorance Argument," that the attempt by mainstream economists to cast the issue of intergenerational environmental justice in terms of individualistic preference satisfaction is seriously misguided. On the argument Norton rejects, we (the present generation) do not know exactly what the individuals of future generations will and will not prefer, so there is no concrete reason to preserve natural resources at the expense of the creation of wealth. Against this, Norton argues that human beings are "cultural beings who have evolved culturally within a particular natural setting."[54] Therefore, against the economic reductionism of mainstream critiques of intergenerational environmental justice, there are non-economic goods which present generations are obliged to leave future generations. One of these non-economic goods is ecological integrity and the preservation of natural history.

In "Environmental Justice and Intergenerational Debt," American philosopher Clark Wolf acknowledges the danger of utopian thinking by assuming that we know what will be good for future generations, since our decisions may actually limit their range of possibilities. But this does not mean that there is also no danger in saddling them with environmental debt, such as denuded farmland or collapsed fisheries. While we may not necessarily know what will be good for future generations (welfare), ecological knowledge can give us a pretty good idea of what will be bad for them (illfare). If we live unsustainably, we are morally culpable for causing the latter.

Globalization

We close this section with an essay on globalization. As is obvious from a brief survey of history, globalization – or globalism – is nothing new. Global interaction between cultures has been going on at least since the time of the great European seafarers of the fifteenth century and before. But with the advent of air travel, containerized shipping, and the electronic transmission of money, the late twentieth and early twenty-first centuries represent an intensification of globalization heretofore unseen in the history of human civilization.

Conservation biologist David Ehrenfeld attends to the ecological consequences in "The Environmental Limits to Globalization." Much discussion has been given to the economic dynamics of globalization. As Ehrenfeld makes clear, there are also severe ecological repercussions. One is the exhaustion of cheap energy – the petroleum that pours out of the ground on the Arabian Peninsula and a few other places around the world. Another is the loss of agricultural biodiversity caused by the homogenizing effects of industrialized farming. A third is the diminution of wild species through habitat loss and extinction by invasive species. Ehrenfeld argues that globalization must occur within environmental limits, and awareness of the need for the economy to function within ecological constraints is a mandate that can unite conservatives and liberals in our common goal of securing a healthy future.

Notes

1 *Oxford Annotated Bible*, Revised Standard Edition, p. 2.
2 See Plato, *Republic* 460 ff. and *Laws* 740 ff., in Hamilton and Cairns, eds., *Plato: The Collected Dialogues*, pp. 699 and 1325 respectively; and Aristotle,

Politics 1326a, in McKeon, ed., *The Basic Works of Aristotle*, p. 1283.
3 *Capital*, p. 629, n.3.
4 Letter to J. B. Schweitzer, January 24, 1865. In Marx and Engels, *Collected Works*, vol. 20, p. 27; italics omitted.
5 *An Essay on the Principle of Population*, ed. James, vol. I, p. 15.
6 1798 edition, pp. 13–14. (See this volume, pp. 422–5.)
7 "A Clash of Gloomy Prophets," *Time* 97 (January 11, 1971), p. 56. See also "Ehrlich vs. Commoner," *Commonweal* 96 (August 11, 1972), p. 418.
8 *The Population Bomb*, p. 57; emphasis in original. Indeed, the copy I obtained from the University of Utah library is sprinkled with derisive commentary, probably a manifestation that readers who are members of the Church of Jesus Christ of Latter-day Saints (Mormons) who, like Catholics, value large families, do not take kindly to Ehrlich's argument.
9 Ibid., p. 39.
10 Ibid., p. 118.
11 Ibid., p. 6.
12 Ibid., p. 121.
13 Ibid., p. 143.
14 "The Tragedy of the Commons," p. 1243. (See this volume, p. 434.)
15 "The Immorality of Being Softhearted," p. 18. (See this volume, p. 440.)
16 *The Closing Circle*, pp. 246–7.
17 *Time* (February 2, 1970), p. 58.
18 *The Closing Circle*, pp. 130ff, 140.
19 Ibid., pp. 140–77.
20 Ibid., p. 233.
21 Ibid.
22 Ibid., p. 239.
23 Ibid., p. 245.
24 "How Poverty Breeds Overpopulation," p. 25.
25 Ibid., p. 59.
26 *The Closing Circle*, p. 214.
27 Ibid., p. 242.
28 Commoner, "Response to 'One Dimensional Ecology,'" *Bulletin of the Atomic Scientists*, vol. 28 (May 1972), p. 56.
29 *The Ultimate Resource*, pp. 62–7.
30 Ibid., pp. 407–8.
31 In *Atlantic Monthly* (May 1998), p. 57. See also the book-length version of this essay, *Maybe One*. (See this volume, p. 469.)
32 Parikh, ed., *Sustainable Development in Agriculture*.
33 Meyer, *Human Impact on the Earth*.
34 Thompson, *The Spirit of the Soil*, p. 3.
35 See Richardson, "It Takes a Movement to Secure Environmental Justice."
36 Pellow, "The Politics of Illegal Dumping," p. 523.
37 See Pastor et al., "Which Came First?"
38 Poor whites have also been subjected to potentially hazardous environmental conditions. In Bhopal,

India, a leak at a Union Carbide plant killed 4,000 people in 1984. The only plant in the US that produces methyl isocyanate, the deadly gas that caused the Bhopal tragedy, was produced at Union Carbide's sister plant in Kanawha Valley, West Virginia (see Murphy, "Could It Happen in West Virginia?"), where residents are predominantly Caucasian and low socioeconomic status. For this reason "Environmental Injustice" is preferable over "Environmental Racism."

39 Cerrell Associates, "Political Difficulties Facing Waste-to-Energy Conversion Plant Siting," p. 26.

40 Pellow, "The Politics of Illegal Dumping," p. 521.

41 Bullard, "Overcoming Racism in Environmental Decision-Making," p. 13.

42 Grossman, "Environmental Racism."

43 Summerhays and Croke, *Air Toxics Emissions Inventory for the Southeast Chicago Area.*

44 Litonjua et al., "Race, Socioeconomic Factors, and Area of Residence are Associated with Asthma Prevalence."

45 See Mill, *Principles of Political Economy.*

46 Personal communication with Daly, email, June 10, 2003.

47 Daly and Townsend, *Valuing the Earth*, pp. 2–3.

48 Ibid., p. 7.

49 Ibid., p. 3.

50 Ibid., p. 17.

51 Daly, *Steady-State Economics*, p. 15.

52 In Daly and Townsend, eds., *Valuing the Earth*, pp. 325–63.

53 Engels, "The Condition of the Working Class in England," in Marx and Engels, *Collected Works*, vol. 4, pp. 350–4.

54 "The Ignorance Argument," p. 45.

A The Population/Poverty Debate

55   An Essay on the Principle of Population
     Thomas Robert Malthus

56   Impact of Population Growth
     Paul R. Ehrlich and John P. Holdren

57   The Ecological Necessity of Confronting the Problem of Human Overpopulation
     Garrett Hardin

58   How Poverty Breeds Overpopulation
     Barry Commoner

59   More People, Greater Wealth, More Resources, Healthier Environment
     Julian L. Simon

60   Population: Delusion and Reality
     Amartya Sen

61   A Special Moment in History
     Bill McKibben

---

55   An Essay on the Principle of Population

Thomas Robert Malthus

I think I may fairly make two postulata.

First, That food is necessary to the existence of man.

Secondly, That the passion between the sexes is necessary, and will remain nearly in its present state.

These two laws ever since we have had any knowledge of mankind, appear to have been fixed laws of our nature; and, as we have not hitherto seen any alteration in them, we have no right to conclude that they will ever cease to be what they now are, without an immediate act of power in that Being who first arranged the system of the universe; and for the advantage of his creatures, still executes, according to fixed laws, all its various operations.

[. . .]

Assuming then, my postulata as granted, I say, that the power of population is indefinitely greater than the power in the earth to produce subsistence for man.

Population, when unchecked, increases in a geometrical ratio. Subsistence increases only in an arithmetical ratio. A slight acquaintance with numbers will shew the immensity of the first power in comparison of the second.

From *An Essay on the Principle of Population as it Affects the Future Improvement of Society with Remarks on the Speculations of Mr. Godwin, M. Condorcet, and Other Writers* (London: J. Johnson, St Paul's Churchyard, 1798), pp. 11–12, 13–17, 18–38.

By that law of our nature which makes food necessary to the life of man, the effects of these two unequal powers must be kept equal.

This implies a strong and constantly operating check on population from the difficulty of subsistence. This difficulty must fall some where; and must necessarily be severely felt by a large portion of mankind.

Through the animal and vegetable kingdoms, nature has scattered the seeds of life abroad with the most profuse and liberal hand. She has been comparatively sparing in the room, and the nourishment necessary to rear them. The germs of existence contained in this spot of earth, with ample food, and ample room to expand in, would fill millions of worlds in the course of a few thousand years. Necessity, that imperious all pervading law of nature, restrains them within the prescribed bounds. The race of plants, and the race of animals shrink under this great restrictive law. And the race of man cannot, by any efforts of reason, escape from it. Among plants and animals its effects are waste of seed, sickness, and premature death. Among mankind, misery and vice. The former, misery, is an absolutely necessary consequence of it. Vice is a highly probable consequence, and we therefore see it abundantly prevail; but it ought not, perhaps, to be called an absolutely necessary consequence. The ordeal of virtue is to resist all temptation to evil.

This natural inequality of the two powers of population, and of production in the earth, and that great law of our nature which must constantly keep their effects equal, form the great difficulty that to me appears insurmountable in the way to the perfectibility of society. All other arguments are of slight and subordinate consideration in comparison of this. I see no way by which man can escape from the weight of this law which pervades all animated nature. No fancied equality, no agrarian regulations in their utmost extent, could remove the pressure of it even for a single century. And it appears, therefore, to be decisive against the possible existence of a society, all the members of which, should live in ease, happiness, and comparative leisure; and feel no anxiety about providing the means of subsistence for themselves and families.

[. . .]

I said that population, when unchecked, increased in a geometrical ratio; and subsistence for man in an arithmetical ratio.

Let us examine whether this position be just.

I think it will be allowed, that no state has hitherto existed (at least that we have any account of) where the manners were so pure and simple, and the means of subsistence so abundant, that no check whatever has existed to early marriages; among the lower classes, from a fear of not providing well for their families; or among the higher classes, from a fear of lowering their condition in life. Consequently in no state that we have yet known, has the power of population been left to exert itself with perfect freedom.

Whether the law of marriage be instituted, or not, the dictate of nature and virtue, seems to be an early attachment to one woman. Supposing a liberty of changing in the case of an unfortunate choice, this liberty would not affect population till it arose to a height greatly vicious; and we are now supposing the existence of a society where vice is scarcely known.

In a state therefore of great equality and virtue, where pure and simple manners prevailed, and where the means of subsistence were so abundant, that no part of the society could have any fears about providing amply for a family, the power of population being left to exert itself unchecked, the increase of the human species would evidently be much greater than any increase that has been hitherto known.

In the United States of America, where the means of subsistence have been more ample, the manners of the people more pure, and consequently the checks to early marriages fewer, than in any of the modern states of Europe, the population has been found to double itself in twenty-five years.

This ratio of increase, though short of the utmost power of population, yet as the result of actual experience, we will take as our rule; and say, That population, when unchecked, goes on doubling itself every twenty-five years, or increases in a geometrical ratio.

Let us now take any spot of earth, this Island for instance, and see in what ratio the subsistence it affords can be supposed to increase. We will begin with it under its present state of cultivation.

If I allow that by the best possible policy, by breaking up more land, and by great encouragements to agriculture, the produce of this Island may be doubled in the first twenty-five years, I think it will be allowing as much as any person can well demand.

In the next twenty-five years, it is impossible to suppose that the produce could be quadrupled. It would be contrary to all our knowledge of the qualities of land. The very utmost that we can conceive, is, that the increase in the second twenty-five years might equal the present produce. Let us then take this for our rule, though certainly far beyond the truth; and allow that by great exertion, the whole produce of the Island might be increased every twenty-five years, by a quantity of subsistence equal to what it at present produces. The most enthusiastic speculator cannot suppose a greater increase than this. In a few centuries it would make every acre of land in the Island like a garden.

Yet this ratio of increase is evidently arithmetical.

It may be fairly said, therefore, that the means of subsistence increase in an arithmetical ratio.

Let us now bring the effects of these two ratios together.

The population of the Island is computed to be about seven millions; and we will suppose the present produce equal to the support of such a number. In the first twenty-five years the population would be fourteen millions; and the food being also doubled, the means of subsistence would be equal to this increase. In the next twenty-five years the population would be twenty-eight millions; and the means of subsistence only equal to the support of twenty-one millions. In the next period, the population would be fifty-six millions, and the means of subsistence just sufficient for half that number. And at the conclusion of the first century, the population would be one hundred and twelve millions, and the means of subsistence only equal to the support of thirty-five millions; which would leave a population of seventy-seven millions totally unprovided for.

A great emigration necessarily implies unhappiness of some kind or other in the country that is deserted. For few persons will leave their families, connections, friends, and native land, to seek a settlement in untried foreign climes, without some strong subsisting causes of uneasiness where they are, or the hope of some great advantages in the place to which they are going.

But to make the argument more general, and less interrupted by the partial views of emigration, let us take the whole earth, instead of one spot, and suppose that the restraints to population were universally removed. If the subsistence for man that the earth affords was to be increased every twenty-five years by a quantity equal to what the whole world at present produces; this would allow the power of production in the earth to be absolutely unlimited, and its ratio of increase much greater than we can conceive that any possible exertions of mankind could make it.

Taking the population of the world at any number, a thousand millions, for instance, the human species would increase in the ratio of 1, 2, 4, 8, 16, 32, 64, 128, 256, 512, &c. and subsistence as 1, 2, 3, 4, 5,

6, 7, 8, 9, 10, &c. In two centuries and a quarter, the population would be to the means of subsistence as 512 to 10: in three centuries as 4096 to 13; and in two thousand years the difference would be almost incalculable, though the produce in that time would have increased to an immense extent.

No limits whatever are placed to the productions of the earth; they may increase for ever and be greater than any assignable quantity; yet still the power of population being a power of a superior order, the increase of the human species can only be kept commensurate to the increase of the means of subsistence, by the constant operation of the strong law of necessity acting as a check upon the greater power.

The effects of this check remain now to be considered.

Among plants and animals the view of the subject is simple. They are all impelled by a powerful instinct to the increase of their species; and this instinct is interrupted by no reasoning, or doubts about providing for their offspring. Wherever therefore there is liberty, the power of increase is exerted; and the superabundant effects are repressed afterwards by want of room and nourishment, which is common to animals and plants; and among animals, by becoming the prey of others.

The effects of this check on man are more complicated.

Impelled to the increase of his species by an equally powerful instinct, reason interrupts his career, and asks him whether he may not bring beings into the world, for whom he cannot provide the means of subsistence. In a state of equality, this would be the simple question. In the present state of society, other considerations occur. Will he not lower his rank in life? Will he not subject himself to greater difficulties than he at present feels? Will he not be obliged to labour harder? and if he has a large family, will his utmost exertions enable him to support them? May he not see his offspring in rags and misery, and clamouring for bread that he cannot give them? And may he not be reduced to the grating necessity of forfeiting his independence, and of being obliged to the sparing hand of charity for support?

These considerations are calculated to prevent, and certainly do prevent, a very great number in all civilized nations from pursuing the dictate of nature in an early attachment to one woman. And this restraint almost necessarily, though not absolutely so, produces vice. Yet in all societies, even those that are most vicious, the tendency to a virtuous attachment is so strong, that there is a constant effort towards an increase of population. This constant effort as constantly tends to subject the lower classes of the society to distress, and to prevent any great permanent amelioration of their condition.

The way in which these effects are produced seems to be this.

We will suppose the means of subsistence in any country just equal to the easy support of its inhabitants. The constant effort towards population, which is found to act even in the most vicious societies, increases the number of people before the means of subsistence are increased. The food therefore which before supported seven millions, must now be divided among seven millions and a half or eight millions. The poor consequently must live much worse, and many of them be reduced to severe distress. The number of labourers also being above the proportion of the work in the market, the price of labour must tend toward a decrease; while the price of provisions would at the same time tend to rise. The labourer therefore must work harder to earn the same as he did before. During this season of distress, the discouragements to marriage, and the difficulty of rearing a family are so great, that population is at a stand. In the mean time the cheapness of labour, the plenty of labourers, and the necessity of an increased industry amongst them, encourage cultivators to employ more labour upon their land; to turn up fresh soil, and to manure and improve more completely what is already in tillage; till ultimately the means of subsistence become in the same proportion to the population as at the period from which we set out. The situation of the labourer being then again tolerably comfortable, the restraints to population are in some degree loosened; and the same retrograde and progressive movements with respect to happiness are repeated.

This sort of oscillation will not be remarked by superficial observers; and it may be difficult even for the most penetrating mind to calculate its periods. Yet that in all old states some such vibration does exist; though from various transverse causes, in a much less marked, and in a much more irregular manner than I have described it, no reflecting man who considers the subject deeply can well doubt.

Many reasons occur why this oscillation has been less obvious, and less decidedly confirmed by experience, than might naturally be expected.

One principal reason is, that the histories of mankind that we possess, are histories only of the higher classes. We have but few accounts that can be depended upon of the manners and customs of that part of mankind, where these retrograde and progressive movements chiefly take place. A satisfactory history of this kind, of one people, and of one period, would require the constant and minute attention of an observing mind during a long life. Some of the objects of enquiry would be, in what proportion to the number of adults was the number of marriages: to what extent vicious customs prevailed in consequence of the restraints upon matrimony: what was the comparative mortality among the children of the most distressed part of the community, and those who lived rather more at their ease: what were the variations in the real price of labour: and what were the observable differences in the state of the lower classes of society, with respect to ease and happiness, at different times during a certain period.

Such a history would tend greatly to elucidate the manner in which the constant check upon population acts; and would probably prove the existence of the retrograde and progressive movements that have been mentioned; though the times of their vibration must necessarily be rendered irregular, from the operation of many interrupting causes; such as, the introduction or failure of certain manufactures: a greater or less prevalent spirit of agricultural enterprize: years of plenty, or years of scarcity: wars and pestilence: poor laws: the invention of processes for shortening labour without the proportional extension of the market for the commodity: and, particularly, the difference between the nominal and real price of labour; a circumstance, which has perhaps more than any other, contributed to conceal this oscillation from common view.

It very rarely happens that the nominal price of labour universally falls; but we well know that it frequently remains the same, while the nominal price of provisions has been gradually increasing. This is, in effect, a real fall in the price of labour; and during this period, the condition of the lower orders of the community must gradually grow worse and worse. But the farmers and capitalists are growing rich from the real cheapness of labour. Their increased capitals enable them to employ a greater number of men. Work therefore may be plentiful; and the price of labour would consequently rise. But the want of freedom in the market of labour, which occurs more or less in all communities, either from parish laws, or the more general cause of the facility of combination among the rich, and its difficulty among the poor, operates to prevent the price of labour from rising at the natural period, and keeps it down some time longer; perhaps, till a year of scarcity, when the clamour is too loud, and the necessity too apparent to be resisted.

The true cause of the advance in the price of labour is thus concealed; and the rich affect to grant it as an act of compassion and favour to the poor, in consideration of a year of scarcity; and when plenty returns, indulge themselves in the most unreasonable of all complaints, that the price does not again fall; when a little reflection would shew them, that it must have risen long before, but from an unjust conspiracy of their own.

But though the rich by unfair combinations, contribute frequently to prolong a season of distress among the poor; yet no possible form of society could prevent the almost constant action of misery, upon a great part of mankind, if in a state of inequality, and upon all, if all were equal.

The theory, on which the truth of this position depends, appears to me so extremely clear; that I feel at a loss to conjecture what part of it can be denied.

That population cannot increase without the means of subsistence, is a proposition so evident, that it needs no illustration.

That population does invariably increase, where there are the means of subsistence, the history of every people that have ever existed will abundantly prove.

And, that the superior power of population cannot be checked, without producing misery or vice, the ample portion of these too bitter ingredients in the cup of human life, and the continuance of the physical causes that seem to have produced them, bear too convincing a testimony.

---

56   Impact of Population Growth

Paul R. Ehrlich and John P. Holdren

The interlocking crises in population, resources, and environment have been the focus of countless papers, dozens of prestigious symposia, and a growing avalanche of books. In this wealth of material, several questionable assertions have been appearing with increasing frequency. Perhaps the most serious of these is the notion that the size and growth rate of the US population are only minor contributors to this country's adverse impact on local and global environments (*1*, *2*). We propose to deal with this and several related misconceptions here, before persistent and unrebutted repetition entrenches them in the public mind – if not the scientific literature. Our discussion centers around five theorems which we believe are demonstrably true and which provide a framework for realistic analysis:

1 Population growth causes a *disproportionate* negative impact on the environment.

2 Problems of population size and growth, resource utilization and depletion, and environmental deterioration must be considered jointly and on a global basis. In this context, population control is obviously not a panacea – it is necessary but not alone sufficient to see us through the crisis.

3 Population density is a poor measure of population pressure, and redistributing population would be a dangerous pseudosolution to the population problem.

4 "Environment" must be broadly construed to include such things as the physical environment of urban ghettos, the human behavioral environment, and the epidemiological environment.

5 Theoretical solutions to our problems are often not operational and sometimes are not solutions.

We now examine these theorems in some detail.

From *Science*, vol. 171 (1971): 1212–17. © 1971. Reprinted with permission from AAAS.

Population Size and Per Capita Impact

In an agricultural or technological society, each human individual has a negative impact on his environment. He is responsible for some of the simplification (and resulting destabilization) of ecological systems which results from the practice of agriculture (*3*). He also participates in the utilization of renewable and nonrenewable resources. The total negative impact of such a society on the environment can be expressed, in the simplest terms, by the relation

$$I = P \cdot F$$

where P is the population, and F is a function which measures the per capita impact. A great deal of complexity is subsumed in this simple relation, however. For example, F increases with per capita consumption if technology is held constant, but may decrease in some cases if more benign technologies are introduced in the provision of a constant level of consumption. (We shall see in connection with theorem 5 that there are limits to the improvements one should anticipate from such "technological fixes.")

Pitfalls abound in the interpretation of manifest increases in the total impact I. For instance, it is easy to mistake changes in the composition of resource demand or environmental impact for absolute per capita increases, and thus to underestimate the role of the population multiplier. Moreover, it is often assumed that population size and per capita impact are independent variables, when in fact they are not. Consider, for example, the recent article by Coale (*1*), in which he disparages the role of US population growth in environmental problems by noting that since 1940 "population has increased by 50 percent, but per capita use of electricity has been multiplied several times." This argument contains both the fallacies to which we have just referred.

First, a closer examination of very rapid increases in many kinds of consumption shows that these changes reflect a shift among alternatives within a larger (and much more slowly growing) category. Thus the 760 percent increase in electricity consumption from 1940 to 1969 (*4*) occurred in large part because the electrical *component* of the energy budget was (and is) increasing much faster than the budget itself. (Electricity comprised 12 percent of the US energy consumption in 1940 versus 22 percent today.) The total energy use, a more important figure than its electrical component in terms of resources and the environment, increased much less dramatically – 140 percent from 1940 to 1969. Under the simplest assumption (that is, that a given increase in population size accounts for an exactly proportional increase in consumption), this would mean that 38 percent of the increase in energy use during this period is explained by population growth (the actual population increase from 1940 to 1969 was 53 percent). Similar considerations reveal the imprudence of citing, say, aluminum consumption to show that population growth is an "unimportant" factor in resource use. Certainly, aluminum consumption has swelled by over 1400 percent since 1940, but much of the increase has been due to the substitution of aluminum for steel in many applications. Thus a fairer measure is combined consumption of aluminum and steel, which has risen only 117 percent since 1940. Again, under the simplest assumption, population growth accounts for 45 percent of the increase.

The "simplest assumption" is not valid, however, and this is the second flaw in Coale's example (and in his thesis). In short, he has failed to recognize that per capita consumption of energy and resources, and the associated per capita impact on the environment, are themselves functions of the population size. Our previous equation is more accurately written

$$I = P \cdot F(P)$$

displaying the fact that impact can increase faster than linearly with population. Of course, whether $F(P)$ is an increasing or decreasing function of P depends in part on whether diminishing returns or economies of scale are dominant in the activities of importance. In populous, industrial nations such as the United States, most economies of scale are already being exploited; we are on the diminishing returns part of most of the important curves.

As one example of diminishing returns, consider the problem of providing nonrenewable resources such as minerals and fossil fuels to a growing population, even at fixed levels of per capita consumption. As the richest supplies of these resources and those nearest to centers of use are consumed, we are obliged to use lower-grade ores, drill deeper, and extend our supply networks. All these activities increase our per capita use of energy and our per capita impact on the environment. In the case of partly renewable resources such as water (which is effectively nonrenewable when groundwater supplies are mined at rates far exceeding natural recharge), per capita costs and environmental impact escalate dramatically when the human population demands more than is locally available. Here the loss of free-flowing rivers and other economic, esthetic, and ecological costs of massive water-movement projects represent increased per capita diseconomies directly stimulated by population growth.

Diminishing returns are also operative in increasing food production to meet the needs of growing populations. Typically, attempts are made both to overproduce on land already farmed and to extend agriculture to marginal land. The former requires disproportionate energy use in obtaining and distributing water, fertilizer, and pesticides. The latter also increases per capita energy use, since the amount of energy invested per unit yield increases as less desirable land is cultivated. Similarly, as the richest fisheries stocks are depleted, the yield per unit effort drops, and more and more energy per capita is required to maintain the supply (5). Once a stock is depleted it may not recover – it may be nonrenewable.

Population size influences per capita impact in ways other than diminishing returns. As one example, consider the oversimplified but instructive situation in which each person in the population has links with every other person – roads, telephone lines, and so forth. These links involve energy and materials in their construction and use. Since the number of links increases much more rapidly than the number of people (6), so does the per capita consumption associated with the links.

Other factors may cause much steeper positive slopes in the per capita impact function, $F(P)$. One such phenomenon is the *threshold effect*. Below a certain level of pollution trees will survive in smog. But, at some point, when a small increment in population produces a small increment in smog, living trees become dead trees. Five hundred people may be able to live around a lake and dump their raw sewage into the lake, and the natural systems of the lake will be able to break down the sewage and keep the lake from undergoing rapid ecological change. Five hundred and five people may overload the system and result in a "polluted" or eutrophic lake. Another phenomenon capable of causing near-discontinuities is the *synergism*. For instance, as cities push out into farmland, air pollution increasingly becomes a mixture of agricultural chemicals with power plant and automobile effluents. Sulfur dioxide from the city paralyzes the cleaning mechanisms

of the lungs, thus increasing the residence time of potential carcinogens in the agricultural chemicals. The joint effect may be much more than the sum of the individual effects. Investigation of synergistic effects is one of the most neglected areas of environmental evaluation.

Not only is there a connection between population size and per capita damage to the environment, but the cost of maintaining environmental quality at a given level escalates disproportionately as population size increases. This effect occurs in part because costs increase very rapidly as one tries to reduce contaminants per unit volume of effluent to lower and lower levels (diminishing returns again!). Consider municipal sewage, for example. The cost of removing 80 to 90 percent of the biochemical and chemical oxygen demand, 90 percent of the suspended solids, and 60 percent of the resistant organic material by means of secondary treatment is about 8 cents per 1000 gallons (3785 liters) in a large plant (7). But if the volume of sewage is such that its nutrient content creates a serious eutrophication problem (as is the case in the United States today), or if supply considerations dictate the reuse of sewage water for industry, agriculture, or groundwater recharge, advanced treatment is necessary. The cost ranges from two to four times as much as for secondary treatment (17 cents per 1000 gallons for carbon absorption; 34 cents per 1000 gallons for disinfection to yield a potable supply). This dramatic example of diminishing returns in pollution control could be repeated for stack gases, automobile exhausts, and so forth.

Now consider a situation in which the limited capacity of the environment to absorb abuse requires that we hold man's impact in some sector constant as population doubles. This means *per capita effectiveness* of pollution control in this sector must double (that is, effluent per person must be halved). In a typical situation, this would yield doubled per capita costs, or quadrupled total costs (and probably energy consumption) in this sector for a doubling of population. Of course, diminishing returns and threshold effects may be still more serious: we may easily have an eightfold increase in control costs for a doubling of population. Such arguments leave little ground for the assumption, popularized by Barry Commoner (2, 8) and others, that a 1 percent rate of population growth spawns only 1 percent effects.

It is to be emphasized that the possible existence of "economies of scale" does not invalidate these arguments. Such savings, if available at all, would apply in the case of our sewage example to a change in the amount of effluent to be handled at an installation of a given type. For most technologies, the United States is already more than populous enough to achieve such economies and is doing so. They are accounted for in our example by citing figures for the largest treatment plants of each type. Population growth, on the other hand, forces us into quantitative *and* qualitative changes in how we handle each unit volume of effluent – what fraction and what kinds of material we remove. Here economies of scale do not apply at all, and diminishing returns are the rule.

Global Context

We will not deal in detail with the best example of the global nature and interconnections of population resource and environmental problems – namely, the problems involved in feeding a world in which 10 to 20 million people starve to death annually (*9*), and in which the population is growing by some 70 million people per year. The ecological problems created by high-yield agriculture are awesome (*3, 10*) and are bound to have a negative feedback on food production. Indeed, the Food and Agriculture Organization of the United Nations has reported that in 1969 the world suffered its first absolute decline in fisheries yield since 1950. It seems likely that part of this decline is attributable to pollution originating in terrestrial agriculture.

A second source of the fisheries decline is, of course, overexploitation of fisheries by the developed countries. This problem, in turn, is illustrative of the situation in regard to many other resources, where similarly rapacious and shortsighted behavior by the developed nations is compromising the aspirations of the bulk of humanity to a decent existence. It is now becoming more widely comprehended that the United States alone accounts for perhaps 30 percent of the nonrenewable resources consumed in the world each year (for example, 37 percent of the energy, 25 percent of the steel, 28 percent of the tin, and 33 percent of the synthetic rubber) (*11*). This behavior is in large part inconsistent with American rhetoric about "developing" the countries of the Third World. *We* may be able to afford the technology to mine lower grade deposits when we have squandered the world's rich ores, but the underdeveloped countries, as their needs grow and their means remain meager, will not be able to do so.

Some observers argue that the poor countries are today economically dependent on our use of their resources, and indeed that economists in these countries complain that world demand for their raw materials is too low (*1*). This proves only that their economists are as shortsighted as ours.

It is abundantly clear that the entire context in which we view the world resource pool and the relationships between developed and underdeveloped countries must be changed, if we are to have any hope of achieving a stable and prosperous existence for all human beings. It cannot be stated too forcefully that the developed countries (or, more accurately, the overdeveloped countries) are the principal culprits in the consumption and dispersion of the world's nonrenewable resources (*12*) as well as in appropriating much more than their share of the world's protein. Because of this consumption, and because of the enormous negative impact on the global environment accompanying it, the population growth in these countries must be regarded as the most serious in the world today.

In relation to theorem 2 we must emphasize that, even if population growth were halted, the present population of the world could easily destroy civilization as we know it. There is a wide choice of weapons – from unstable plant monocultures and agricultural hazes to DDT, mercury, and thermonuclear bombs. If population size were reduced and per capita consumption remained the same (or increased), we would still quickly run out of vital, high-grade resources or generate conflicts over diminishing supplies. Racism, economic exploitation, and war will not be eliminated by population control (of course, they are unlikely to be eliminated without it).

Population Density and Distribution

Theorem 3 deals with a problem related to the inequitable utilization of world resources. One of the commonest errors made by the uninitiated is to assume that population density (people per square mile) is the critical measure of overpopulation or underpopulation. For instance, Wattenberg states that the United States is not very crowded by "international standards" because Holland has 18 times the population density (*13*). We call this notion "the Netherlands fallacy." The Netherlands actually requires large chunks of the earth's resources and vast areas of land not within its borders to maintain itself. For example, it is the second largest per capita importer of protein in the world, and it imports 63 percent of its cereals, including 100 percent of its corn and rice. It also imports all of its cotton, 77 percent of its wool, and all of its iron ore, antimony, bauxite, chromium, copper, gold, lead, magnesite, manganese, mercury, molybdenum, nickel, silver, tin, tungsten, vanadium, zinc, phosphate rock (fertilizer), potash (fertilizer), asbestos, and diamonds. It produces energy equivalent to some 20 million metric tons of coal and consumes the equivalent of over 47 million metric tons (*14*).

A certain preoccupation with density as a useful measure of overpopulation is apparent in the article by Coale (*1*). He points to the existence of urban problems such as smog in Sydney, Australia, "even though the total population of Australia is about 12 million in an area 80 percent as big as the United States," as evidence that environmental problems are unrelated to population size. His argument would be more persuasive if problems of population *distribution* were the only ones with environmental consequences, and if population distribution were unrelated to resource distribution and population size. Actually, since the carrying capacity of the Australian continent is far below that of the United States, one would *expect* distribution problems – of which Sydney's smog is one symptom – to be encountered at a much lower total population there. Resources, such as water, are in very short supply, and people cluster where resources are available. (Evidently, it cannot be emphasized enough that carrying capacity includes the availability of a wide variety of resources in addition to space itself, and that population pressure is measured relative to the carrying capacity. One would expect water, soils, or the ability of the environment to absorb wastes to be the limiting resource in far more instances than land area.)

In addition, of course, many of the most serious environmental problems are essentially independent of the way in which population is distributed. These include the global problems of weather modification by carbon dioxide and particulate pollution, and the threats to the biosphere posed by man's massive inputs of pesticides, heavy metals, and oil (*15*). Similarly, the problems of resource depletion and ecosystem simplification by agriculture depend on how many people there are and their patterns of consumption, but not in any major way on how they are distributed.

Naturally, we do not dispute that smog and most other familiar urban ills are serious problems, or that they are related to population distribution. Like many of the difficulties we face, these problems will not be cured simply by stopping population growth; direct and well-conceived assaults on the problems themselves will also be required. Such measures may occasionally include the redistribution of population, but the considerable difficulties and costs of this approach should not be underestimated. People live where they do not because of a perverse intention to add to the problems of their society but for reasons of economic necessity, convenience, and desire for agreeable surroundings. Areas that are uninhabited or sparsely populated today are presumably that way because they are deficient in some of the requisite factors. In many cases, the remedy for such deficiencies – for example, the provision of water and power to the wastelands of central Nevada – would be extraordinarily expensive in dollars, energy, and resources and would probably create environmental havoc. (Will we justify the rape of Canada's rivers to "colonize" more of our western deserts?)

Moving people to more "habitable" areas, such as the central valley of California or, indeed, most suburbs, exacerbates another serious problem – the paving-over of prime farmland. This is already so serious in California that, if current trends continue, about 50 percent of the best acreage in the nation's leading agricultural state will be destroyed by the year 2020 (*16*). Encouraging that trend hardly seems wise.

Whatever attempts may be made to solve distribution-related problems, they will be undermined if population growth continues, for two reasons. First, population growth and the aggravation of distribution problems are correlated – part of the increase will surely be absorbed in urban areas that can least afford the growth. Indeed, barring the unlikely prompt reversal of present trends, most of it will be absorbed there. Second, population growth puts a disproportionate drain on the very financial resources needed to combat its symptoms. Economist Joseph Spengler has estimated that 4 percent of national income goes to support our 1 percent per year rate of population growth in the United States (*17*). The 4 percent figure now amounts to about $30 billion per year. It seems safe to conclude that the faster we grow the less likely it is that we will find the funds either to alter population distribution patterns or to deal more comprehensively and realistically with our problems.

Meaning of Environment

Theorem 4 emphasizes the comprehensiveness of the environment crisis. All too many people think in terms of national parks and trout streams when they say "environment." For this reason many of the suppressed people of our nation consider ecology to be just one more "racist shuck" (*18*). They are apathetic or even hostile toward efforts to avert further environmental and sociological deterioration, because they have no reason to believe they will share the fruits of success (*19*). Slums, cockroaches, and rats are ecological problems, too. The correction of ghetto conditions in Detroit is neither more nor less important than saving the Great Lakes – both are imperative.

We must pay careful attention to sources of conflict both within the United States and between nations. Conflict within the United States blocks progress toward solving our problems; conflict among nations can easily "solve" them once and for all. Recent laboratory studies on human beings support the anecdotal evidence that crowding may increase aggressiveness in human males (*20*). These results underscore long-standing suspicions that population growth, translated through the inevitable uneven distribution into physical crowding, will tend to make the solution of all of our problems more difficult.

As a final example of the need to view "environment" broadly, note that human beings live in an epidemiological environment which deteriorates with crowding and malnutrition – both of which increase with population growth. The hazard posed by the prevalence of these conditions in the world today is compounded by man's unprecedented mobility: potential carriers of diseases of every description move routinely and in substantial numbers from continent to continent in a matter of hours. Nor is there any reason to believe that modern medicine has made widespread plague impossible (*21*). The Asian influenza epidemic of 1968 killed relatively few people only because the virus *happened* to be nonfatal to people in otherwise good health, not because of public health measures. Far deadlier viruses, which easily could be scourges without precedent in the population at large, have on more than one occasion been confined to research workers largely by good luck [for example, the Marburgvirus incident of 1967 (*22*) and the Lassa fever incident of 1970 (*21*, *23*)].

Solutions: Theoretical and Practical

Theorem 5 states that theoretical solutions to our problems are often not operational, and sometimes are not solutions. In terms of the problem of feeding the world, for example, technological fixes suffer from limitations in scale, lead time, and cost (*24*). Thus potentially attractive theoretical approaches – such as desalting seawater for agriculture, new irrigation systems, high-protein diet supplements – prove inadequate in practice. They are too little, too late, and too expensive, or they have sociological costs which hobble their effectiveness (*25*). Moreover, many aspects of our technological fixes, such as synthetic organic pesticides and inorganic nitrogen fertilizers, have created vast environmental problems which seem certain to erode global productivity and ecosystem stability (*26*). This is not to say that important gains have not been made through the application of technology to agriculture in the poor countries, or that further technological advances are not worth seeking. But it must be stressed that even the most enlightened technology cannot relieve the necessity of grappling forthrightly and promptly with population growth [as Norman Borlaug aptly observed on being notified of his Nobel Prize for development of the new wheats (*27*)].

Technological attempts to ameliorate the environmental impact of population growth and rising per capita affluence in the developed countries suffer from practical limitations similar to those just mentioned. Not only do such measures tend to be slow, costly, and insufficient in scale, but in addition they most often *shift* our impact rather than remove it. For example, our first generation of smog-control devices increased emissions of oxides of nitrogen while reducing those of hydrocarbons and carbon monoxide. Our unhappiness about eutrophication has led to the replacement of phosphates in detergents with compounds like NTA – nitrilotriacetic acid – which has carcinogenic breakdown products and apparently enhances teratogenic effects of heavy metals (*28*). And our distaste for lung diseases apparently induced by sulfur dioxide inclines us to accept the hazards of radioactive waste disposal, fuel reprocessing, routine low-level emissions of radiation, and an apparently small but finite risk of catastrophic accidents associated with nuclear fission power plants. Similarly, electric automobiles would simply shift part of the environmental burden of personal transportation from the vicinity of highways to the vicinity of power plants.

We are not suggesting here that electric cars, or nuclear power plants, or substitutes for phosphates are inherently bad. We argue rather that they, too, pose environmental costs which must be weighed against those they eliminate. In many cases the choice is not obvious, and in *all* cases there will be some environmental impact. The residual per capita impact, after all the best choices have been made, must then be multiplied by the population engaging in the activity. If there are too many people, even the most wisely managed technology will not keep the environment from being overstressed.

In contending that a change in the way we use technology will invalidate these arguments, Commoner (*2, 8*) claims that our important environmental problems began in the 1940s with the introduction and rapid spread of certain "synthetic" technologies: pesticides and herbicides, inorganic fertilizers, plastics, nuclear energy, and high-compression gasoline engines. In so arguing, he appears to make two unfounded assumptions. The first is that man's pre-1940 environmental impact was innocuous and, without changes for the worse in technology, would have remained innocuous even at a much larger population size. The second assumption is that the advent of the new technologies was independent of the attempt to meet human needs and desires in a growing population. Actually, man's record as a simplifier of ecosystems and plunderer of resources can be traced from his probable role in the extinction of many Pleistocene mammals (*29*), through the destruction of the soils of Mesopotamia by salination and erosion, to the deforestation of Europe in the Middle Ages and the American dust-bowls of the 1930s, to cite only some highlights. Man's contemporary arsenal of synthetic technological bludgeons indisputably magnifies the potential for disaster, but these were evolved in some measure to *cope* with population pressures, not independently of them. Moreover, it is worth noting that, of the four environmental threats viewed by the prestigious Williamstown study (*15*) as globally significant, three are associated with pre-1940 technologies which have simply increased in scale [heavy metals, oil in the seas, and carbon dioxide and particulates in the atmosphere, the latter probably due in considerable part to agriculture (*30*)]. Surely, then, we can anticipate that supplying food, fiber, and metals for a population even larger than today's will have a profound (and destabilizing) effect on the global ecosystem under *any* set of technological assumptions.

Conclusion

John Platt has aptly described man's present predicament as "a storm of crisis problems" (*31*). Complacency concerning any component of these problems – sociological, technological, economic, ecological – is unjustified and counterproductive. It is time to admit that there are no monolithic solutions to the problems we face. Indeed, population control, the redirection of technology, the transition from open to closed resource cycles, the equitable distribution of opportunity and the ingredients of prosperity must *all* be accomplished if there is to be a future worth having. Failure in any of these areas will surely sabotage the entire enterprise.

In connection with the five theorems elaborated here, we have dealt at length with the notion that population growth in industrial nations such as the United States is a minor factor, safely ignored. Those who so argue often add that, anyway, population control would be the slowest to take effect of all possible attacks on our various problems, since the inertia in attitudes and in the age structure of the population is so considerable. To conclude that this means population control should be assigned low priority strikes us as curious logic. Precisely because population is the most difficult and slowest to yield among the components of environmental deterioration, we must start on it at once. To ignore population today because the problem is a tough one is to commit ourselves to even gloomier prospects 20 years hence, when most of the "easy" means to reduce per capita impact on the environment will have been exhausted. The desperate and repressive measures for population control which might be contemplated then are reason in themselves to proceed with foresight, alacrity, and compassion today.

References and Notes

1   A. J. Coale, *Science* 170, 132 (1970).

2   B. Commoner, *Saturday Rev.* 53, 50 (1970); *Humanist* 30, 10 (1970).

3   For a general discussion, see P. R. Ehrlich and A. H. Ehrlich, *Population, Resources, Environment* (Freeman, San Francisco, 1970), chap. 7. More technical treatments

of the relationship between complexity and stability may be found in R. H. MacArthur, *Ecology* 36, 533 (1955); D. R. Margalef, *Gen. Syst.* 3, 3671 (1958); E. G. Leigh, Jr., *Proc. Nat. Acad. Sci. U.S.* 53, 777 (1965); and O. T. Loucks, "Evolution of diversity, efficiency, and stability of a community," paper delivered at AAAS meeting, Dallas, Texas, 30 Dec. 1968.

4   The figures used in this paragraph are all based on data in *Statistical Abstract of the United States 1970* (US Department of Commerce) (Government Printing Office, Washington, DC, 1970).

5   A dramatic example of this effect is given in R. Payne's analysis of the whale fisheries [*NY Zool. Soc. Newsl.* (Nov. 1968)]. The graphs in Payne's paper are reproduced in Ehrlich and Ehrlich (*3*).

6   If N is the number of people, then the number of links is $N(N-1)/2$, and the number of links per capita is $(N-1)/2$.

7   These figures and the others in this paragraph are from *Cleaning Our Environment: The Chemical Basis for Action* (American Chemical Society, Washington, DC, 1969), pp. 95–162.

8   In his unpublished testimony before the President's Commission on Population Growth and the American Future (17 Nov. 1970), Commoner acknowledged the operation of diminishing returns, threshold effects, and so on. Since such factors apparently do not account for *all* of the increase in per capita impact on the environment in recent decades, however, Commoner drew the unwarranted conclusion that they are negligible.

9   R. Dumont and B. Rosier, *The Hungry Future* (Praeger, New York, 1969), pp. 34–5.

10 L. Brown, *Sci. Amer.* 223, 160 (1970); P. R. Ehrlich, *War on Hunger* 4, 1 (1970).

11 These figures are based on data from the *United Nations Statistical Yearbook 1969* (United Nations, New York, 1969), with estimates added for the consumption by Mainland China when none were included.

12 The notion that dispersed resources, because they have not left the planet, are still available to us, and the hope that mineral supplies can be extended indefinitely by the application of vast amounts of energy to common rock have been the subject of lively debate elsewhere. See, for example, the articles by P. Cloud, T. Lovering, A. Weinberg, *Texas Quart.* 11, 103, 127, 90 (Summer 1968); and *Resources and Man* (National Academy of Sciences) (Freeman, San Francisco,

1969). While the pessimists seem to have had the better of this argument, the entire matter is academic in the context of the rate problem we face in the next 30 years. Over that time period, at least, cost, lead time, and logistics will see to it that industrial economies and dreams of development stand or fall with the availability of high-grade resources.

13 B. Wattenberg, *New Republic* 162, 18 (4 Apr. and 11 Apr. 1970).

14 These figures are from (*11*), from the *FAO Trade Yearbook*, the *FAO Production Yearbook* (United Nations, New York, 1968), and from G. Borgstrom, *Too Many* (Collier-Macmillan, Toronto, Ont., 1969).

15 *Man's Impact on the Global Environment, Report of the Study of Critical Environmental Problems* (MIT Press, Cambridge, Mass., 1970).

16 *A Model of Society, Progress Report of the Environmental Systems Group* (Univ. of California Institute of Ecology, Davis, April 1969).

17 J. J. Spengler, in *Population: The Vital Revolution*, R. Freedman, ed. (Doubleday, New York, 1964), p. 67.

18 R. Chrisman, *Scanlan's* 1, 46 (August 1970).

19 A more extensive discussion of this point is given in an article by P. R. Ehrlich and A. H. Ehrlich, in *Global Ecology: Readings Toward a Rational Strategy for Man*, J. P. Holdren and P. R. Ehrlich, eds. (Harcourt, Brace, Jovanovich, New York, 1971).

20 J. L. Freedman, A. Levy, J. Price, R. Welte, M. Katz, P. R. Ehrlich, in preparation.

21 J. Lederberg, *Washington Post* (15 Mar. and 22 Mar. 1970).

22 C. Smith, D. Simpson, E. Bowen, I. Zlotnik, *Lancet* 1967-II, 1119, 1128 (1967).

23 Associated Press wire service, 2 Feb. 1970.

24 P. R. Ehrlich and J. P. Holdren, *BioScience* 19, 1065 (1969).

25 See L. Brown [*Seeds of Change* (Praeger, New York, 1970)] for a discussion of unemployment problems exacerbated by the Green Revolution.

26 G. Woodwell, *Science* 168, 429 (1970).

27 *New York Times*, 22 Oct. 1970, p. 18; *Newsweek* 76, 50 (2 Nov. 1970).

28 S. S. Epstein, *Environment* 12, No. 7, 2 (Sept. 1970); *New York Times* service, 17 Nov. 1970.

29 G. S. Krantz, *Amer. Sci.* 58, 164 (Mar.–Apr. 1970).

30 R. A. Bryson and W. M. Wendland, in *Global Effects of Environmental Pollution*, S. F. Singer, ed. (Springer-Verlag, New York, 1970).

31 J. Platt, *Science* 166, 1115 (1969).

57 The Ecological Necessity of Confronting the Problem of Human Overpopulation

Garrett Hardin

The Tragedy of the Commons

Population, as Malthus said, naturally tends to grow "geometrically," or, as we would now say, exponentially. In a finite world this means that the per capita share of the world's goods must steadily decrease. Is ours a finite world?

A fair defense can be put forward for the view that the world is infinite; or that we do not know that it is not. But, in terms of the practical problems that we must face in the next few generations with the foreseeable technology, it is clear that we will greatly increase human misery if we do not, during the immediate future, assume that the world available to the terrestrial human population is finite. "Space" is no escape.[1]

A finite world can support only a finite population; therefore, population growth must eventually equal zero. (The case of perpetual wide fluctuations above and below zero is a trivial variant that need not be discussed.) When this condition is met, what will be the situation of mankind? Specifically, can Bentham's goal of "the greatest good for the greatest number" be realized?

No – for two reasons, each sufficient by itself. The first is a theoretical one. It is not mathematically possible to maximize for two (or more) variables at the same time. This was clearly stated by von Neumann and Morgenstern,[2] but the principle is implicit in the theory of partial differential equations, dating back at least to D'Alembert (1717–83).

The second reason springs directly from biological facts. To live, any organism must have a source of energy (for example, food). This energy is utilized for two purposes: mere maintenance and work. For man, maintenance of life requires about 1600 kilocalories a day ("maintenance calories"). Anything that he does over and above merely staying alive will be defined as work, and is supported by "work calories" which he takes in. Work calories are used not only for what we call work in common speech; they are also required for all forms of enjoyment, from swimming and automobile racing to playing music and writing poetry. If our goal is to maximize population it is obvious what we must do: We must make the work calories per person approach as close to zero as possible. No gourmet meals, no vacations, no sports, no music, no literature, no art. . . . I think that everyone will grant, without argument or proof, that maximizing population does not maximize goods. Bentham's goal is impossible.

In reaching this conclusion I have made the usual assumption that it is the acquisition of energy that is the problem. The appearance of atomic energy has led some to question this assumption. However, given an infinite source of energy, population growth still produces an inescapable problem. The problem of the acquisition of energy is replaced by the problem of its dissipation, as J. H. Fremlin has so wittily shown.[3] The arithmetic signs in the analysis are, as it were, reversed; but Bentham's goal is still unobtainable.

The optimum population is, then, less than the maximum. The difficulty of defining the optimum is enormous; so far as I know, no one has seriously tackled this problem. Reaching an acceptable and stable solution will surely require more than one generation of hard analytical work – and much persuasion.

We want the maximum good per person; but what is good? To one person it is wilderness, to another it is ski lodges for thousands. To one it is estuaries to nourish ducks for hunters to shoot; to another it is factory land. Comparing one good with another is, we usually say, impossible because goods are incommensurable. Incommensurables cannot be compared.

Theoretically this may be true; but in real life incommensurables *are* commensurable. Only a criterion of judgment and a system of weighting are needed. In nature the criterion is survival. Is it better for a species to be small and hideable, or large and powerful? Natural selection commensurates the incommensurables. The compromise achieved depends on a natural weighting of the values of the variables.

Man must imitate this process. There is no doubt that in fact he already does, but unconsciously. It is when the hidden decisions are made explicit that the arguments begin. The problem for the years ahead is to work out an acceptable theory of weighting. Synergistic effects, nonlinear variation, and difficulties in discounting the future make the intellectual problem difficult, but not (in principle) insoluble.

Has any cultural group solved this practical problem at the present time, even on an intuitive level? One simple fact proves that none has: there is no prosperous population in the world today that has, and has had for some time, a growth rate of zero. Any people that has intuitively identified its optimum point will soon reach it, after which its growth rate becomes and remains zero.

Of course, a positive growth rate might be taken as evidence that a population is below its optimum. However, by any reasonable standards, the most rapidly growing populations on earth today are (in general) the most miserable. This association (which need not be invariable) casts doubt on the optimistic assumption that the positive growth rate of a population is evidence that it has yet to reach its optimum.

We can make little progress in working toward optimum population size until we explicitly exorcize the spirit of Adam Smith in the field of practical demography. In economic affairs, *The Wealth of Nations* (1776) popularized the "invisible hand," the idea that an individual who "intends only his own gain," is, as it were, "led by an invisible hand to promote . . . the public interest."[4] Adam Smith did not assert that this was invariably true, and perhaps neither did any of his followers. But he contributed to a dominant tendency of thought that has ever since interfered with positive action based on rational analysis, namely, the tendency to assume that decisions reached individually will, in fact, be the best decisions for an entire society. If this assumption is correct it justifies the continuance of our present policy of laissez-faire in reproduction. If it is correct we can assume that men will control their individual fecundity so as to produce the optimum population. If the assumption is not correct, we need to reexamine our individual freedoms to see which ones are defensible.

Tragedy of Freedom in a Commons

The rebuttal to the invisible hand in population control is to be found in a scenario first sketched in a little-known pamphlet[5] in 1833 by a mathematical amateur named William Forster Lloyd (1794–1852). We may well call it "the tragedy of the commons," using the word "tragedy" as the philosopher Whitehead used it: "The essence of dramatic tragedy is not unhappiness. It resides in the solemnity of the remorseless working of things."[6] He then goes on to say, "This inevitableness of destiny can only be illustrated in terms of human life by incidents which in fact involve unhappiness. For it is only by them that the futility of escape can be made evident in the drama."

The tragedy of the commons develops in this way. Picture a pasture open to all. It is to be expected that each herdsman will try to keep as many cattle as possible on the commons. Such an arrangement may work reasonably satisfactorily for centuries because tribal wars, poaching, and disease keep the numbers of both man and beast well below the carrying capacity of the land. Finally, however, comes the day of reckoning, that is, the day when the long-desired goal of social stability becomes a reality. At this point, the inherent logic of the commons remorselessly generates tragedy.

As a rational being, each herdsman seeks to maximize his gain. Explicitly or implicitly, more or less consciously, he asks, "What is the utility *to me* of adding one more animal to my herd?" This utility has one negative and one positive component.

1 The positive component is a function of the increment of one animal. Since the herdsman receives all the proceeds from the sale of the additional animal, the positive utility is nearly +1.
2 The negative component is a function of the additional overgrazing created by one more animal. Since, however, the effects of overgrazing are shared by all the herdsmen, the negative utility for any particular decision-making herdsman is only a fraction of −1.

Adding together the component partial utilities, the rational herdsman concludes that the only sensible course for him to pursue is to add another animal to his herd. And another; and another. . . . But this is the conclusion reached by each and every rational herdsman sharing a commons. Therein is the tragedy. Each man is locked into a system that compels him to increase his herd without limit – in a world that is limited. Ruin is the destination toward which all men rush, each pursuing his own best interest in a society that believes in the freedom of the commons. Freedom in a commons brings ruin to all.

Some would say that this is a platitude. Would that it were! In a sense, it was learned thousands of years ago, but natural selection favors the forces of psychological denial.[7] The individual benefits as an individual from his ability to deny the truth even though society as a whole, of which he is a part, suffers. Education can counteract the natural tendency to do the wrong thing, but the inexorable succession of generations requires that the basis for this knowledge be constantly refreshed.

[. . .]

In an approximate way, the logic of the commons has been understood for a long time, perhaps since the discovery of agriculture or the invention of private property in real estate. But it is understood mostly only in special cases which are not sufficiently generalized. Even at this late date, cattlemen leasing national land on the western ranges demonstrate no more than an ambivalent understanding, in constantly pressuring federal authorities to increase the head count to the point where overgrazing produces erosion and weed-dominance. Likewise, the oceans of the world continue to suffer from the survival of the philosophy of the commons. Maritime nations still respond automatically to the shibboleth of the "freedom of the seas." Professing to believe in the "inexhaustible resources of the oceans," they bring species after species of fish and whales closer to extinction.[8]

The National Parks present another instance of the working out of the tragedy of the commons. At present, they are open to all, without limit. The parks themselves are limited in extent – there is only one Yosemite Valley – whereas population seems to grow without limit. The values that visitors seek in the parks are steadily eroded. Plainly, we must soon cease to treat the parks as commons or they will be of no value to anyone.

What shall we do? We have several options. We might sell them off as private property. We might keep them as public property, but allocate the right to enter them. The allocation might be on the basis of wealth, by the use of an auction system. It might be on the basis of merit, as defined by some agreed-upon standards. It might be by lottery. Or it might

be on a first-come, first-served basis, administered to long queues. These, I think, are all the reasonable possibilities. They are all objectionable. But we must choose – or acquiesce in the destruction of the commons that we call our National Parks.

Pollution

In a reverse way, the tragedy of the commons reappears in problems of pollution. Here it is not a question of taking something out of the commons, but of putting something in – sewage, or chemical, radioactive, and heat wastes into water; noxious and dangerous fumes into the air; and distracting and unpleasant advertising signs into the line of sight. The calculations of utility are much the same as before. The rational man finds that his share of the cost of the wastes he discharges into the commons is less than the cost of purifying his wastes before releasing them. Since this is true for everyone, we are locked into a system of "fouling our own nest," so long as we behave only as independent, rational, free-enterprisers.

The tragedy of the commons as a food basket is averted by private property, or something formally like it. But the air and waters surrounding us cannot readily be fenced, and so the tragedy of the commons as a cesspool must be prevented by different means, by coercive laws or taxing devices that make it cheaper for the polluter to treat his pollutants than to discharge them untreated. We have not progressed as far with the solution of this problem as we have with the first. Indeed, our particular concept of private property, which deters us from exhausting the positive resources of the earth, favors pollution. The owner of a factory on the bank of a stream – whose property extends to the middle of the stream – often has difficulty seeing why it is not his natural right to muddy the waters flowing past his door. The law, always behind the times, requires elaborate stitching and fitting to adapt it to this newly perceived aspect of the commons.

The pollution problem is a consequence of population. It did not much matter how a lonely American frontiersman disposed of his waste. "Flowing water purifies itself every 10 miles," my grandfather used to say, and the myth was near enough to the truth when he was a boy, for there were not too many people. But as population became denser, the natural chemical and biological recycling processes became overloaded, calling for a redefinition of property rights.

[. . .]

Freedom to Breed is Intolerable

The tragedy of the commons is involved in population problems.

In a world governed solely by the principle of "dog eat dog" – if indeed there ever was such a world – how many children a family had would not be a matter of public concern. Parents who bred too exuberantly would leave fewer descendants, not more, because they would be unable to care adequately for their children. David Lack and others have found that such a negative feedback demonstrably controls the fecundity of birds.[9] But men are not birds, and have not acted like them for millenniums, at least.

If each human family were dependent only on its own resources; *if* the children of improvident parents starved to death; *if*, thus, overbreeding brought its own "punishment" to the germ line – *then* there would be no public interest in controlling the breeding of families. But our society is deeply committed to the welfare state,[10] and hence is confronted with another aspect of the tragedy of the commons.

In a welfare state, how shall we deal with the family, the religion, the race, or the class (or indeed any distinguishable and cohesive group) that adopts overbreeding as a policy to secure its own aggrandizement?[11] To couple the concept of freedom to breed with the belief that everyone born has an equal right to the commons is to lock the world into a tragic course of action.

Unfortunately this is just the course of action that is being pursued by the United Nations. In late 1967, some 30 nations agreed to the following:

> The Universal Declaration of Human Rights describes the family as the natural and fundamental unit of society. It follows that any choice and decision with regard to the size of the family must irrevocably rest with the family itself, and cannot be made by anyone else.[12]

It is painful to have to deny categorically the validity of this right; denying it, one feels as uncomfortable as a resident of Salem, Massachusetts, who denied the reality of witches in the 17th century. At the present time, in liberal quarters, something like a taboo acts to inhibit criticism of the United Nations. There is a feeling that the United Nations is "our last and best hope," that we shouldn't find fault with it; we shouldn't play into the hands of the archconservatives. However, let us not forget what

Robert Louis Stevenson said: "The truth that is suppressed by friends is the readiest weapon of the enemy." If we love the truth we must openly deny the validity of the Universal Declaration of Human Rights, even though it is promoted by the United Nations. We should also join with Kingsley Davis[13] in attempting to get Planned Parenthood-World Population to see the error of its ways in embracing the same tragic ideal.

[. . .]

Managing the Commons

Ethical implications of carrying capacity

It should be clear by now that the idea of the commons did not suddenly arise out of nothing in the year 1968. Passing references to the problem occur as far back as Aristotle, and Lloyd certainly saw it clearly in 1833. H. Scott Gordon's work in 1954 saw the beginning of a new concern with the problems presented by this politico-economic system. Yet the fact remains that a widespread recognition of these problems did not develop until after 1968. Why the delay? Two reasons are apparent.

First, a favorable climate of opinion was needed for remarks about the commons to be noticed. This was created in the 1960s by the rapid growth of the environmental movement, which alerted people to the consequences of distributional systems. Second, it was necessary that the properties of the commons be stated in no uncertain terms if people were to consider the matter seriously. It was necessary that the human tragedy of adhering to a commons-type distribution be emphasized. A good, solid fortissimo minor chord had to be sounded. Before 1968 most of the sounds were either mere grace notes or extended passages played pianissimo. The down-playing was for good reason, of course: the clear message of the commons threatened cherished beliefs and practices. Abandoning any traditional practice requires a political upset (though revolution may be too strong a word).

We have seen how the problem of the commons has been evaded in the exploitation of ocean fisheries. Understandably, it is evaded even more in the question of human populations. Both problems require for their rational resolution a clear understanding of the concept of carrying capacity and a willingness to fashion laws that take this concept into account.

Let us first look at the concept as it applies to other animals and plants, to the non-human populations we would like to exploit for our own benefit.

The carrying capacity of a particular area is defined as *the maximum number of a species that can be supported indefinitely by a particular habitat, allowing for seasonal and random changes, without degradation of the environment and without diminishing carrying capacity in the future.* There is some redundancy in this definition, but redundancy is better than inadequacy. Using deer as an example, the true carrying capacity of a region must allow for the fact that food is harder to get in winter than in summer and scarcer in drought years than in "normal years." If too many head of deer are allowed in the pasture they may overgraze it to such an extent that the ground is laid bare, producing soil erosion followed by less plant growth in subsequent years. Always, by eating the grasses that appeal to them, herbivores selectively favor the weed grasses that are not appealing, thus tending to diminish the carrying capacity for themselves and for their progeny in subsequent years.

The concept of carrying capacity is a time-bound, posterity-oriented concept. This is one of the reasons that it threatens the "conventional wisdom" (Galbraith's term) of the present time, which leans heavily on short term economic theory. The theory of discounting, using commercially realistic rates of interest, virtually writes off the future.[14] The consequences have been well described by Fife and Clark. Devotion to economic discounting in its present form is suicidal. How soon is it so? "In the long run," an economist would say, since disaster is more than five years off. "In the short run," according to biologists, since disaster occurs in much less than the million or so years that is the normal life expectancy of a species. Here we see a standing issue of dispute between economists and biologists, with their different professional biases in reckoning time.

Game management methods of maintaining the carrying capacity of a habitat impinge upon ethical theory. Officially, Judeo-Christian ethics is absolutist in form, rich in proscriptions such as "Thou shalt not kill." Can we base game management on such principles? Obviously we cannot. Time after time, in an area where men have eliminated such "varmints" as coyotes and wolves, prey species (e.g., deer) have multiplied far beyond the carrying capacity of their habitat, which they then severely damage thus reducing its carrying capacity in the future.[15] Taking for granted the legitimacy of human desire to maximize

gains from the deer-pasture, is "Thou shalt not kill" a good ethical rule? *It depends.* If the herd size is less than the carrying capacity we might insist on this rule; but if the herd has grown beyond carrying capacity we should deliberately kill animals, until the size of the herd is brought to a safe level.

For the maximum yield of venison we should keep the herd at that level at which the first derivative of the population function is a maximum; but for safety, allowing for unforeseen random fluctuations, the population level should be kept a bit above the point of fastest population growth.

This analysis was focussed wholly on the interests of man, the exploiter of nature. Much the same conclusion is reached if we focus entirely on the species being exploited. Whenever there are too many animals in a habitat the animals themselves show all the signs of misery, if our empathic projections are to be trusted at all. The animals become skinny and feeble; they succumb easily to diseases. The normal social instincts of the species become ineffectual as starving animals struggle with one another for individual survival.

In a state of nature the unsavory consequences of exceeding the carrying capacity are prevented by natural predation. Putting entirely to one side the exploitative goals of animal husbandry, whenever men maintain a population of animals free of predators they should, if they are humane, pursue a regular program of killing animals so as to keep the herd size below the carrying capacity of the habitat.

We see that the ethics of game management is not an absolutist ethics but a relativistic or situational ethics.[16] The foundation of situational ethics is this: *The morality of an act is determined by the state of the system at the time the act is performed.* Ecology, a system-based view of the world, demands situational ethics.

Unfortunately, situational (ecological) ethics creates difficult problems for the law. It is difficult to write statute law if we are deprived of the simplicity of flat, unqualified *dos* and *don'ts.* Qualifications can be written into law, but it is hard to foresee all the particularities of future situations. Our insufficiently informed efforts leave "loopholes" for rascals to crawl through. When found, loopholes can be plugged, of course; but that takes time. The legislative process is a slow one. Situational ethics seems almost to demand an administrative approach; by statute, administrators can be given the power to make instant, detailed decisions within a legally defined framework. Rules promulgated by an administrative agency are called administrative law.

On paper, the system may look fine, but the general public is understandably afraid of it. Administrative law gives power to administrators, who are human and hence fallible. Their decisions may be self serving. John Adams called for "a government of laws, and not of men." We rightly esteem this as a desirable ideal. The practical question we must face is how far can we safely depart from the ideal under the pressure of ecological necessity? This is the harrowing *Quis custodiet* problem;[17] it has no easy solutions.[18]

When a well-defined problem is virtually ignored as long as the commons problem was – more than a hundred years – we naturally suspect the interference of taboo. This plausible supposition is, by its very nature, nearly unprovable. Taboo is a composite thing:[19] there is "the primary taboo, surrounding the thing that must not be discussed; around this is the secondary taboo, a taboo against even acknowledging the existence of the primary taboo."

A taboo may be sustained in part for good tactical reasons: breaking it may open up a nest of problems not yet ripe for productive discussion. We may speculate – we can hardly know – that the long avoidance of the commons problem was due to a subconscious awareness of the intractable *Quis custodiet* problem, which would have been activated by any attempt to depart from the system of the commons.

Moreover, the theory on which the commons problem is based rests on the concept of carrying capacity, which so far we have assumed is static. This is a justifiable assumption when we are speaking of a deer pasture in the wild, a habitat we propose to leave wild for esthetic reasons. But when we talk about cattle pastures, fish culture in fresh water ponds, and oyster culture in estuaries, we are talking about areas in which it is possible to increase the carrying capacity by technological intervention. Much of what we have called progress in the last two centuries has resulted from increasing the carrying capacity of the earth by technological means. Agricultural productivity, for instance, has increased by more than an order of magnitude since the time of Malthus, whose theory clearly assumed a static carrying capacity. Malthus' historical failure has understandably made many intelligent people very skeptical of any theory founded on the idea of a static carrying capacity.

Thus has it come about that many of the decisions made at the present time (insofar as they are explicitly rational) are based on balancing today's demand against tomorrow's supply, a type of bookkeeping that is frowned upon by certified public accountants. For the past two centuries we've gotten away with this practice because Science and Technology have generated miracles. But can such progress continue without end? The chorus of those who say it must come to an end grows ever larger.[20] Whom shall we believe: the Technological Optimists, or the Limits Lobby? If we are wrong, which way of being wrong is more dangerous? What is the proper policy for the true conservative?[21]

The concept of carrying capacity calls for the conservative, balanced-equation type of thinking that has led to the triumphs of thermodynamics[22] and modern chemistry. But applied to human problems connected with exploiting the environment the concept of carrying capacity has been perceived as a threatening one. As regards populations of non-human animals and plants, we are just now beginning to grapple with the implications of carrying capacity. When it comes to humanity itself, it is doubtful if we yet have the courage to systematically examine all possibilities. [. . .]

For more than three centuries intellectual and emotional fashions have increasingly veered toward the global outlook. Our thoughts have been significantly molded by John Donne's "No man is an island . . ." and Karl Marx's ". . . to each according to his needs." The thoughts engendered by these banners are generous thoughts, whereas speaking of local responsibility for local environments seems to many to be a miserly and selfish way of looking at the world's problems. There are a thousand to praise generosity for every one who has a kind word to say for selfishness. Yet biology clearly tells us that survival requires a respect for carrying capacity, and points to the utility of territorial behavior in protecting the environment and insuring the survival of populations. Surely posterity matters. Surely there's something to be said for selfishness.

Altruism versus selfishness: It is all too easy to polarize the argument, to maintain the univalence of facts. But the facts are ambivalent, as wise men have recognized for millennia. A Talmudic saying puts the matter rather well:

> If I am not for myself, who will be for me?
> If I am for myself only, what am I?
> If not now – when?

The Immorality of Being Softhearted

I think it is time for some plain talking about foreign aid and population control, both domestic and foreign. What we call "foreign aid" is of two sorts: military aid, and peaceful gifts like food, agricultural machines, and dams. I am not competent to analyze the morality and wisdom of military aid. In this discussion "foreign aid" refers only to the peaceful gifts, about which a biologist has something to say.

As part of foreign aid our government now offers overcrowded countries both food and contraceptive devices. Most people think that family planning equals population control. This is not true. As Kingsley Davis has shown, a nation can be 100 percent converted to the philosophy of family planning, and still its population will grow out of control.

When I was in Kenya in 1968 I was appalled to learn the results of an attitude survey among families there. The average Kenyan family wants a bit more than six children – far more than enough for mere replacement. Such desires cause a population to grow "exponentially," that is, out of control. Davis has found such intolerable desires in every country of the world in which the necessary surveys have been made. When families want too many children family planning will not control population.

If we were birds it wouldn't matter. Natural selection would soon correct our blunders. Each species of bird tends to produce the best number of eggs. Suppose a species normally produces five eggs in a clutch. Those birds that produce fewer eggs per clutch will leave fewer descendants and so will gradually be eliminated from the germ line. That's easy to understand. More surprising is the fact that birds that produce more than five eggs per clutch will also be gradually eliminated from the line. Under the conditions in which the species lives, five is about all a mated pair can take care of. If they produce six or seven offspring at a time there is heavier mortality in the brood, and the parents leave not more, but fewer, offspring. There is no need for bird lovers to try to sell planned parenthood to the birds! Under natural conditions reproductive errors are automatically corrected.

But we aren't birds. We are deeply committed to the "welfare state." We will not allow the children of improvident parents to starve to death. Consequently the errors of parents in reproduction are not corrected by natural selection.

Unfortunately, the policy-makers of the United Nations do not seem to understand this. In late 1967 some thirty nations agreed to the following statement of principle: "The Universal Declaration of Human Rights describes the family as the natural and fundamental unit of society. It follows that any choice and decision with regard to the size of the family must irrevocably rest with the family itself, and cannot be made by anyone else."

Runaway feedback

From a biological standpoint it is crystal clear that this Declaration of Human Rights would be acceptable only if the survival of the children *also* depended irrevocably on the family itself. To make the family sovereign in determining the number of its children, but not responsible for their survival, is to produce a society at the mercy of the heavy breeders. The result is "runaway feedback." In a welfare state nothing succeeds like breeding. It is a pity that the United Nations has called for family sovereignty without coupling it to family responsibility.

It is a mistake to think that we can control the breeding of mankind in the long run by an appeal to conscience. The reason is very simple. People vary. Confronted by appeals to limit breeding some people will undoubtedly respond to the plea more than others. Those who have more children will produce a larger fraction of the next generation than those with more susceptible consciences. Overbreeding will become worse, generation by generation.

The argument assumes that conscience or the desire for children (no matter which) is hereditary – but hereditary only in the most general formal sense. The result will be the same whether the attitude is transmitted by gene or by social indoctrination. To appeal to conscience is to set up a selective system that works toward the elimination of conscience from the race.

How then shall we control population? This question must be divided into two parts. Controlling population within our own country is one problem. Controlling populations in all other countries is quite a different problem. The difference is created by sovereignty.

Within our own country we are sovereign. It is we who must control ourselves – no one else will do it for us. The thought of population control is repugnant to us, but we must eventually come to it. Without conscious, deliberate control our population will grow without limit until, as Harrison Brown said, our country will be "covered completely and to a considerable depth with a writhing mass of human beings, much as a dead cow is covered with a pulsating mass of maggots."

At that point nature would control population for us, through epidemic diseases and the insane behavior produced by overcrowding. We cannot choose between control and no control. We can only choose between nature's control and human control. Personally, I prefer human control. All control means some loss of freedom, but I think deliberate human control instituted at a level below that at which nature steps in will mean less loss of freedom.

By what means shall we control our population? There is no easy answer. We will need a great deal of ingenuity. The control does not have to be as crude as "a policeman in every bedroom." We can do better than that. Raymond B. Cowles has suggested that we create a "non-baby bonus." Beginning at the age of fifteen each girl would receive a generous sum on each Christmas Day if she has not had a child during the preceding twelve months. The sum would be $500, or $1,000, or whatever it took to motivate the girls adequately.

It would not be necessary to continue this bonus forever. It might be stopped at the twenty-fifth year. Older women are less fertile than younger women. The size of the bonus, and the years during which it is proffered, can be varied as experience shows that the system is producing either too many or too few children.

In resurrecting Cowles' scheme I do not offer it as either the complete or the final answer to controlling population. I offer it only as a prototype of a rational system for persuading people to control their breeding in their own interest, without an unworkable appeal to conscience. A breed of people that is clever enough to send rockets to the moon surely has the wit to avoid breeding itself into misery without invoking a police state.

International dilemma

So much for the domestic situation. What about the foreign problem – how can we help a foreign country to escape overpopulation?

Clearly, the worst thing we can do is send food. The child who is saved today becomes a breeder tomorrow. We send food out of compassion; but if we desired to increase the misery in an overpopulated nation, could we find a more effective way for doing so? Atomic bombs would be kinder. For a few

moments the misery would be acute, but it would soon come to an end for most of the people, leaving a very few survivors to suffer thereafter. Food-bombs increase the number of survivors to suffer from chronic malnutrition.

How can we help an overpopulated nation? I submit that only three kinds of aid are defensible: luxuries, contraceptives, and knowledge.

Luxuries may seem a perverse gift to send a starving country, but such a gift makes sense. Radios, television sets, sewing machines, bicycles, and perhaps automobiles (if we can afford to be so generous) can help a people to live better, without subsidizing further breeding. The phrase "the revolution of rising expectations" is used to describe what is taking place all over the world. It is in our interest to help bring about this revolution, to show poor people what life might be like so that they will be motivated to change their traditional ways. In effect, we should say to them: "Stop having so many children, and you can live a better life."

We can show them that they can stop having so many children if they will only use contraceptives. It is not enough, however, to send only the contraceptive chemicals and physical devices. We must send also the knowledge of how to use them. Getting this knowledge to them may be a bit ticklish. There is a danger that if we instruct them directly our well-meaning attempts may backfire. We may be accused of "genocide." Such an accusation is actually unjustified because refusal to use contraceptives can equally well be called genocide. The overbreeding of poor people is a genocidal threat to the contraceptors of the world. We must point this out to the soft-hearted alarmist who would put a stop to the export of contraceptives and contraceptive know-how.

To convey contraceptive information to poor people we should establish a short hierarchical system: our experts teach their experts, and then their experts teach their people. The face-to-face contact in the last link of the information chain must be native-to-native. In this way, a contraceptive program will become their program rather than ours.

Does this mean, then, that we should send absolutely no food at all to an overpopulated nation? Ideally, yes; but politically, such idealism is not practical. The billions of dollars worth of food that we are sending now cannot be cut off as with a knife. We will have to de-escalate gradually. But at every stage of the de-escalation we should insist on a *quid pro quo* in the form of evidence of increased contraceptive efforts, and in actual increased population control.

Some tenderhearted people will cry "Blackmail!" when they hear such a plan. But we should refuse to be moved by their outcry.

A banker makes many conditions before he will agree to lend money to a supplicant. Among these conditions is evidence of responsibility on the part of the supplicant. A country that gives food to other countries must also insist on evidence of responsible actions. Only by such insistence can the donor nation make sure that the next generation in the recipient nation has a chance at a decent life. Making these tough conditions is the kindest thing we can do for the needy peoples of the world.

And, ultimately, for the whole world.

Notes

1 G. Hardin, *J. Hered.* 50, 68 (1959); S. von Hoernor, *Science* 137, 18 (1962).

2 J. von Neumann and O. Morgenstern, *Theory of Games and Economic Behavior* (Princeton Univ. Press, Princeton, NJ, 1947), p. 11.

3 J. H. Fremlin, *New Sci.*, no. 415 (1964), p. 285.

4 A. Smith, *The Wealth of Nations* (Modern Library, New York, 1937), p. 423.

5 W. F. Lloyd, *Two Lectures on the Checks to Population* (Oxford Univ. Press, Oxford, England, 1833), reprinted (in part) in *Population, Evolution, and Birth Control*, G. Hardin, ed. (Freeman, San Francisco, 1964), p. 37.

6 A. N. Whitehead, *Science and the Modern World* (Mentor, New York, 1948), p. 17.

7 G. Hardin, ed. *Population, Evolution, and Birth Control* (Freeman, San Francisco, 1964), p. 56.

8 S. McVay, *Sci. Amer.* 216 (no. 8), 13 (1966).

9 D. Lack, *The Natural Regulation of Animal Numbers* (Clarendon Press, Oxford, 1954).

10 H. Girvetz, *From Wealth to Welfare* (Stanford Univ. Press, Stanford, Calif., 1950).

11 G. Hardin, *Perspec. Biol. Med.* 6, 366 (1963).

12 U. Thant, *Int. Planned Parenthood News*, no. 168 (February 1968), p. 3.

13 K. Davis, *Science* 158, 730 (1967).

14 Garrett Hardin, "The rational foundation of conservation." *North American Review*, 259(4) 1974: 14–17.

15 David R. Klein, "The introduction, increase, and crash of reindeer on St. Matthew Island." *Journal of Wildlife Management*, 32(1968): 350–67.

16 Joseph Fletcher, *Situation Ethics* (Philadelphia: Westminster Press, 1966).

17 Garrett Hardin, *Exploring New Ethics for Survival: The Voyage of the Spaceship Beagle* (New York: Viking, 1972) (Chap. 16).

18 P. MacAvoy, ed. *The Crisis of the Regulatory Commissions* (New York: Norton, 1970).

19 Garrett Hardin, *Stalking the Wild Taboo* (Los Altos, Calif.: Kaufmann, 1973) (p. xi).

20 Donella H. Meadows, Dennis L. Meadows, Jørgen Randers, and William W. Behrens III, *The Limits to Growth* (New York: Universe Books, 1972). Mihajlo Mesarovic and Eduard Pestel, *Mankind at the Turning Point* (New York: Dutton, 1974). Unlike the "first report to the Club of Rome," the "second report" does not aggregate the world's natural resources but seeks to deal with them on a regional basis. In going from facts to implications, however, this second report is not always consistent. See Garrett Hardin, "Will humanity learn from nature?" *Sierra Club Bulletin*, 60(8) 1975: 41–3.

21 It is one of the ironies of history that those who are generally labelled as economic "conservatives" at the present time are people who believe in limitless growth and hence see no need for what scientists regard as truly *conservative* thinking, that is, thinking in which the variables are conserved, and in which equations balance. For a particularly emotional defense of the conventional wisdom see Melvin J. Grayson and Thomas R. Shepard, Jr., *The Disaster Lobby: Prophets of Ecological Doom and Other Absurdities* (Chicago: Follett, 1973).

A book with a similar message, by the editor of the English journal *Nature*, is more sophisticated but scarcely better: John Maddox, *The Doomsday Syndrome* (New York: McGraw-Hill, 1972). For the most intellectual criticism of the limits to growth thesis see H. S. D. Cole, Christopher Freeman, Marie Jahoda and K. L. R. Pavitt, *Models of Doom: A Critique of The Limits to Growth* (New York: Universe Books, 1973). This, the American edition of the "Sussex Report", has the merit of including a postscript by the Meadows, et al. that throws much light on the nature of the controversy.

22 Nicholas Georgescu-Roegen, *The Entropy Law and the Economic Process* (Cambridge, Mass.: Harvard University Press, 1971). This is the only book published to date that sets economic theory on a firm foundation of thermodynamics, thus bringing together economics and ecology. (Etymologically, this is as it should be, since both words use the Greek root *oikos*, home. Both are concerned with the management of the "home," which classical economics sees almost entirely as made up of men only, with other organisms and the physical environment playing the role of "givens" – to which little attention is *given*. In the perspective of ecology, however, all organisms, as well as nonliving elements of the environment, are viewed as coexisting and interacting variables in this earthly home of ours.)

58   How Poverty Breeds Overpopulation

Barry Commoner

The world population problem is a bewildering mixture of the simple and the complex, the clear and the confused.

What is relatively simple and clear is that the population of the world is getting larger, and that this process cannot go on indefinitely because there are, after all, limits to the resources, such as food, that are needed to sustain human life. Like all living things, people have an inherent tendency to multiply geometrically – that is, the more people there are the more people they tend to produce. In contrast, the supply of food rises more slowly, for unlike people it does not increase in proportion to the existing rate of food production. This is, of course, the familiar Malthusian relationship and leads to the conclusion that the population is certain eventually to outgrow the food supply (and other needed resources), leading to famine and mass death unless some other countervailing force intervenes to limit population growth. One can argue about the details, but taken as a general summary of the population problem, the foregoing statement is one which no environmentalist can successfully dispute.

When we turn from merely stating the problem to analyzing and attempting to solve it, the issue becomes much more complex. The simple statement that there is a limit to the growth of the human population, imposed on it by the inherent limits of the earth's resources, is a useful but abstract idea. In order to reduce it to the level of reality in which the problem must be solved, what is required is that we find the *cause* of the discrepancy between population growth and the available resources. Current views on this question are neither simple nor unanimous.

One view is that the cause of the population problem is uncontrolled fertility, the countervailing force – the death rate – having been weakened by medical advances. According to this view, given the freedom to do so people will inevitably produce children faster than the goods needed to support them. It follows, then, that the birthrate must be deliberately reduced to the point of "zero population growth".

The methods that have been proposed to achieve this kind of direct reduction in birthrate vary considerably. Among the ones advanced in the past are: (a) providing people with effective contraception and access to abortion facilities and with education about the value of using them (i.e., family planning); (b) enforcing legal means to prevent couples from producing more than some standard number of children ("coercion"); (c) withholding of food from the people of starving developing countries which, having failed to limit their birthrate sufficiently, are deemed to be too far gone or too unworthy to be saved (the so-called "lifeboat ethic").

It is appropriate here to illustrate these diverse approaches with examples. The family planning approach is so well known as to need no further exemplification. As to the second of these approaches, one might cite the following description of it by Kingsley Davis, a prominent demographer, which is quoted approvingly in a recent statement by "The Environmental Fund" that is directed against the family planning position: "If people want to control population, it can be done with knowledge already available . . . For instance, a nation seeking to stabilize its population could shut off immigration and permit each couple a maximum of two children, with possible license for a third. Accidental pregnancies beyond the limit would be interrupted by abortion. If a third child were born without a license, or a fourth, the mother would be sterilized." (Quoted from the Environmental Fund's Statement "Declaration on Population and Food"; original in *Daedalus*, Fall, 1973.)

The author of the "lifeboat ethic" is Garrett Hardin, who stated in a recent paper (presented in San Francisco at the 1974 annual meeting of the American Association for the Advancement of

From *Ramparts*, vol. 13, no. 10 (1975): 21–4, 59. © 1975 by Barry Commoner. Reprinted with permission from the author.

Science) that: "So long as nations multiply at different rates, survival requires that we adopt the ethic of the lifeboat. A lifeboat can hold only so many people. There are more than two billion wretched people in the world – ten times as many as in the United States. It is literally beyond our ability to save them all . . . Both international granaries and lax immigration policies must be rejected if we are to save something for our grandchildren."

Actually, this recent statement only cloaks, in the rubric of an "ethic," a more frankly political position taken earlier by Hardin: "Every day we [i.e., Americans] are a smaller minority. We are increasing at only one percent a year; the rest of the world increases twice as fast. By the year 2000, one person in 24 will be an American; in one hundred years only one in 46 . . . If the world is one great commons, in which all food is shared equally, then we are lost. Those who breed faster will replace the rest . . . In the absence of breeding control a policy of 'one mouth one meal' ultimately produces one totally miserable world. In a less than perfect world, the allocation of rights based on territory must be defended if a ruinous breeding race is to be avoided. It is unlikely that civilization and dignity can survive everywhere; but better in a few places than in none. Fortunate minorities must act as the trustees of a civilization that is threatened by uninformed good intentions." (*Science*, vol. 172, p. 1297; 1971.)

The Quality of Life

But there is another view of population which is much more complex. It is based on the evidence, amassed by demographers, that the birthrate is not only affected by biological factors, such as fertility and contraception, but by equally powerful *social* factors.

Demographers have delineated a complex network of interactions among these social factors. This shows that population growth is not the consequence of a simple arithmetic relationship between birthrate and death rate. Instead, there are circular relationships in which, as in an ecological cycle, every step is connected to several others.

Thus, while a reduced death rate does, of course, increase the rate of population growth, it can also have the opposite effect – since families usually respond to a reduced rate of infant mortality by opting for fewer children. This negative feedback modulates the effect of a decreased death rate on population size. Similarly, although a rising population increases the demand on resources and thereby worsens the population problem, it also stimulates economic activity. This, in turn, improves educational levels. As a result the average age at marriage tends to increase, culminating in a reduced birthrate – which mitigates the pressure on resources.

In these processes, there is a powerful social force which, paradoxically, both reduces the death rate (and thereby stimulates population growth) and also leads people voluntarily to restrict the production of children (and thereby reduces population growth). That force, simply stated, is the quality of life – a high standard of living, a sense of well-being and of security in the future. When and how the two opposite effects of this force are felt differs with the stages in a country's economic development. In a pre-modern society, such as England before the industrial revolution or India before the advent of the English, both death rates and birthrates were high. But they were in balance and population size was stable. Then, as agricultural and industrial production began to increase and living conditions improved, the death rate began to fall. With the birthrate remaining high the population rapidly increased in size. However, later, as living standards continued to improve, the decline in death rate persisted but the birthrate began to decline as well, reducing the rate of population growth.

For example, at around 1800, Sweden had a high birthrate (about 33/1000), but since the death rate was equally high, the population was in balance. Then as agriculture and, later, industrial production advanced, the death rate dropped until, by the mid-nineteenth century, it stood at about 20/1000. Since the birthrate remained constant during that period of time, there was a large excess of births over deaths and the population increased rapidly. Then, however, the birthrate began to drop, gradually narrowing the gap until in the mid-twentieth century it reached about 14/1000, when the death rate was about 10/1000.[1] Thus, under the influence of a constantly rising standard of living the population moved, with time, from a position of balance *at a high death rate* to a new position of near-balance *at a low death rate*. But in between the population increased considerably.

This process, *the demographic transition*, is clearly characteristic of all western countries. In most of them, the birthrate does not begin to fall appreciably until the death rate is reduced below about 20/1000.

However, then the drop in birthrate is rapid. A similar transition also appears to be under way in countries like India. Thus in the mid-nineteenth century, India had equally high birth and death rates (about 50/1000) and the population was in approximate balance. Then, as living standards improved, the death rate dropped to its present level of about 15/1000 and the birthrate dropped, at first slowly and recently more rapidly, to its present level of 42/1000. India is at a critical point; now that death rate has reached the turning point of about 20/1000, we can expect the birthrate to fall rapidly – provided that the death rate is further reduced by improved living conditions.

One indicator of the quality of life – infant mortality – is especially decisive in this process. And again there is a critical point – a rate of infant mortality below which birthrate begins to drop sharply and, approaching the death rate, creates the conditions for a balanced population. The reason is that couples are interested in the number of *surviving* children and respond to a low rate of infant mortality by realizing that they no longer need to have more children to replace the ones that die. Birth control is, of course, a necessary adjunct to this process; but it can succeed – barring compulsion – only in the presence of a rising standard of living, which of itself generates the necessary motivation.

This process appears to be just as characteristic of developing countries as of developed ones. This can be seen by plotting the present birthrates against the present rates of infant mortality for all available national data. The highest rates of infant mortality are in African countries; they are in the range of 53.175/1000 live births and birthrates are about 27.52/1000. In those countries where infant mortality has improved somewhat (for example, in a number of Latin American and Asian countries) the drop in birthrate is slight (to about 45/1000) until the infant mortality reaches about 80/1000. Then, as infant mortality drops from 80/1000 to about 25/1000 (the figure characteristic of most developed countries), the birthrate drops sharply from 45 to about 15.18/1000. Thus a rate of infant mortality of 80/1000 is a critical turning point which can lead to a very rapid decline in birthrate in response to a further reduction in infant mortality. The latter, in turn, is always very responsive to improved living conditions, especially with respect to nutrition. Consequently, there is a kind of critical standard of living which, if achieved, can lead to a rapid reduction in birthrate and an approach to a balanced population.

Thus, in human societies, there is a built-in control on population size. If the standard of living, which initiates the rise in population, *continues* to increase, the population eventually begins to level off. This self-regulating process begins with a population in balance, but at a high death rate and low standard of living. It then progresses toward a population which is larger, but once more in balance, at a low death rate and a high standard of living.

Demographic Parasites

The chief reason for the rapid rise in population in developing countries is that this basic condition has not been met. The explanation is a fact about developing countries which is often forgotten – that they were recently, and in the economic sense often still remain, colonies of more developed countries. In the colonial period, western nations introduced improved living conditions (roads, communications, engineering, agricultural and medical services) as part of their campaign to increase the labor force needed to exploit the colony's natural resources. This increase in living standards initiated the first phase of the demographic transition.

But most of the resultant wealth did not remain in the colony. As a result, the second (or population-balancing) phase of the demographic transition could not take place. Instead the wealth produced in the colony was largely diverted to the advanced nation – where it helped *that* country achieve for itself the second phase of the demographic transition. Thus colonialism involves a kind of demographic parasitism. The second, population-balancing phase of the demographic transition in the advanced country is fed by the suppression of that same phase in the colony.

It has long been known that the accelerating curve of wealth and power of Western Europe, and later of the United States and Japan, has been heavily based on exploitation of resources taken from the less powerful nations: colonies, whether governed legally, or – as in the case of the US control of certain Latin American countries – by extra-legal and economic means. The result has been a grossly inequitable rate of development among the nations of the world. As the wealth of the exploited nations was diverted to the more powerful ones, their power, and with it their capacity to exploit, increased. The gap between the wealth of nations grew, as the rich were fed by the poor.

What is evident from the above considerations is that this process of international exploitation has had another very powerful but unanticipated effect: rapid growth of the population in the former colonies. An analysis by the demographer, Nathan Keyfitz, leads him to conclude that the growth of industrial capitalism in the western nations in the period 1800–1950 resulted in the development of a one-billion excess in the world population, largely in the tropics. Thus the present world population crisis – the rapid growth of population in developing countries (the former colonies) – is the result not so much of policies promulgated by these countries but of a policy, colonial exploitation, forced on them by developed countries.

[. . .]

There is a grave imbalance between the world's wealth and the world's people. But the imbalance is not the supposed disparity between the world's *total* wealth and *total* population. Rather, it is due to the gross *distributive* imbalance among the nations of the world. What the problem calls for, I believe, is a process that now figures strongly in the thinking of the peoples of the Third World: a return of some of the world's wealth to the countries whose resources and peoples have borne so much of the burden of producing it – the developing nations.

Wealth Among Nations

There is no denying that this proposal would involve exceedingly difficult economic, social and political problems, especially for the rich countries. But the alternative solutions thus far advanced are at least as difficult and socially stressful.

A major source of confusion is that these diverse proposed solutions to the population problem, which differ so sharply in their moral postulates and their political effects, appear to have a common base in scientific fact. It is, after all, equally true, scientifically, that the birthrate can be reduced by promulgating contraceptive practices (providing they are used), by elevating living standards, or by withholding food from starving nations.

But what I find particularly disturbing is that behind this screen of confusion between scientific fact and political intent there has developed an escalating series of what can be only regarded, in my opinion, as inhumane, abhorrent political schemes put forward in the guise of science. First we had Paddock's "triage" proposal, which would condemn whole nations to death through some species of global "benign neglect". Then we have schemes for coercing people to curtail their fertility, by physical and legal means which are ominously left unspecified. Now we are told (for example, in the statement of "The Environmental Fund") that we must curtail rather than extend our efforts to feed the hungry peoples of the world. Where will it end? Is it conceivable that the proponents of coercive population control will be guided by one of Garrett Hardin's earlier, astonishing proposals:

> How can we help a foreign country to escape over-population? Clearly the worst thing we can do is send food . . . Atomic bombs would be kinder. For a few moments the misery would be acute, but it would soon come to an end for most of the people, leaving a very few survivors to suffer thereafter. ("The Immorality of Being Softhearted", *Stanford Alumni Almanac*, Jan., 1969)

There has been a long-standing alliance between pseudo-science and political repression; the Nazis' genetic theories, it will be recalled, were to be tested in the ovens at Dachau. This evil alliance feeds on confusion.

The present confusion can be removed by recognizing *all* of the current population proposals for what they are – not scientific observations but value judgments that reflect sharply differing ethical views and political intentions. The family planning approach, if applied as the exclusive solution to the problem, would put the burden of remedying a fault created by a social and political evil – colonialism – voluntarily on the individual victims of the evil. The so-called "lifeboat ethic" would compound the original evil of colonialism by forcing its victims to forego the humane course toward a balanced population, improvement of living standards, or if they refuse, to abandon them to destruction, or even to thrust them toward it.

My own purely personal conclusion is, like all of these, not scientific but political: that the world population crisis, which is the ultimate outcome of the exploitation of poor nations by rich ones, ought to be remedied by returning to the poor countries enough of the wealth taken from them to give their peoples both the reason and the resources voluntarily to limit their own fertility.

In sum, I believe that if the root cause of the world population crisis is poverty, then to end it we must abolish poverty. And if the cause of poverty is the grossly unequal distribution of the world's wealth, then to end poverty, and with it the population crisis, we must redistribute that wealth among nations and within them.

Note

1   This and subsequent demographic information is from: Agency for International Development. *Population Program Assistance*, December, 1971.

---

59   More People, Greater Wealth, More Resources, Healthier Environment

Julian L. Simon

This is the economic history of humanity in a nutshell. From 2 million or 200,000 or 20,000 or 2,000 years ago until the 18th century there was slow growth in population, almost no increase in health or decrease in mortality, slow growth in the availability of natural resources (but not increased scarcity), increase in wealth for a few, and mixed effects on the environment. Since then there has been rapid growth in population due to spectacular decreases in the death rate, rapid growth in resources, widespread increases in wealth, and an unprecedently clean and beautiful living environment in many parts of the world along with a degraded environment in the poor and socialist parts of the world.

That is, more people and more wealth have correlated with more (rather than less) resources and a cleaner environment – just the opposite of what Malthusian theory leads one to believe. The task before us is to make sense of these mind-boggling happy trends.

The current gloom-and-doom about a 'crisis' of our environment is wrong on the scientific facts. Even the US Environmental Protection Agency acknowledges that US air and water have been getting cleaner rather than dirtier in the past few decades. Every agricultural economist knows that the world's population has been eating ever-better since the Second World War.

Every resource economist knows that all natural resources have been getting more available not more scarce, as shown by their falling prices over the decades and centuries. And every demographer knows that the

death rate has been falling all over the world – life expectancy almost tripling in the rich countries in the past two centuries, and almost doubling in the poor countries in only the past four decades.

Population Growth and Economic Development

The picture is now also clear that population growth does not hinder economic development. In the 1980s there was a complete reversal in the consensus of thinking of population economists about the effects of more people. In 1986, the National Research Council and the National Academy of Sciences completely overturned its 'official' view away from the earlier worried view expressed in 1971. It noted the absence of any statistical evidence of a negative connection between population increase and economic growth. And it said that 'The scarcity of exhaustible resources is at most a minor restraint on economic growth'.[1] This U-turn by the scientific consensus of experts on the subject has gone unacknowledged by the press, the anti-natalist environmental organisations, and the agencies that foster population control abroad.

Long-run Trends Positive

Here is my central assertion: Almost every economic and social change or trend points in a positive

From *Economic Affairs* (April 1994): 22–5, 26–9. © 1994 by *Economic Affairs*. Reprinted with permission from Blackwell Publishing Ltd.

direction, as long as we view the matter over a reasonably long period of time.

For a proper understanding of the important aspects of an economy we should look at the long-run trends. But the short-run comparisons – between the sexes, age groups, races, political groups, which are usually purely relative – make more news. To repeat, just about every important long-run measure of human welfare shows improvement over the decades and centuries, in the United States as well as in the rest of the world. And there is no persuasive reason to believe that these trends will not continue indefinitely.

Would I bet on it? For sure. I'll bet a week's or month's pay – anything I win goes to pay for more research – that just about any trend pertaining to material human welfare will improve rather than get worse. You pick the comparison and the year.

Let me quickly review a few data on how human life has been doing, beginning with the all-important issue, life itself.

The Conquest of Too-early Death

The most important and amazing demographic fact – the greatest human achievement in history, in my view – is the decrease in the world's death rate. Figure 59.1 portrays the history of human life expectancy at birth. It took thousands of years to increase life expectancy at birth from just over 20 years to the high twenties in about 1750. Then life expectancy in the richest countries suddenly took off and tripled in about two centuries. In just the past two centuries, the length of life you could expect for your baby or yourself in the advanced countries jumped from less than 30 years to perhaps 75 years. What greater event has humanity witnessed than this conquest of premature death in the rich countries? It is this decrease in the death rate that is the cause of there being a larger world population nowadays than in former times.

Then starting well after the Second World War, the length of life you could expect in the poor countries has leaped upwards by perhaps 15 or even 20 years since the 1950s, caused by advances in agriculture, sanitation, and medicine (figure 59.2).

Let me put it differently. In the 19th century the planet Earth could sustain only 1 billion people. Ten thousand years ago, only 4 million could keep themselves alive. Now 5 billion people are on average living longer and more healthily than ever before. The increase in the world's population represents our victory over death.

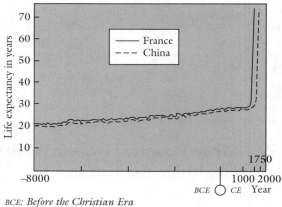

BCE: *Before the Christian Era*

Figure 59.1 History of human life expectancy at birth (3000 BCE–2000 CE).

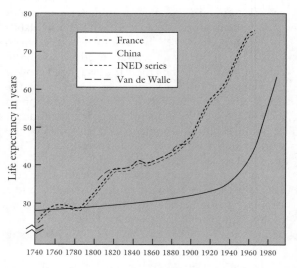

Figure 59.2 Female expectation of life at birth. *Source*: Official Statistics.

Here arises a crucial issue of interpretation: One would expect lovers of humanity to jump with joy at this triumph of human mind and organisation over the raw killing forces of nature. Instead, many lament that there are so many people alive to enjoy the gift of life. And it is this worry that leads them to approve the Indonesian, Chinese and other inhumane programmes of coercion and denial of personal liberty in one of the most precious choices a family can make – the number of children that it wishes to bear and raise.

The Decreasing Scarcity of Natural Resources

Throughout history, the supply of natural resources has worried people. Yet the data clearly show that natural resource scarcity – as measured by the economically-meaningful indicator of cost or price – has been decreasing rather than increasing in the long run for all raw materials, with only temporary exceptions from time to time: that is, availability has been increasing. Consider copper, which is representative of all the metals. In figure 59.3 we see the price relative to wages since 1801. The cost of a ton is only about a tenth now of what it was two hundred years ago.

This trend of falling prices of copper has been going on for a very long time. In the 18th century BCE in Babylonia under Hammurabi – almost 4,000 years ago – the price of copper was about a thousand times its price in the USA now relative to wages. At the time of the Roman Empire the price was about a hundred times the present price.

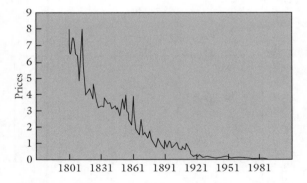

Figure 59.3   Copper prices indexed by wages.

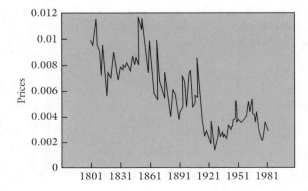

Figure 59.4   Copper prices divided by CPI.

In figure 59.4 we see the price of copper relative to the consumer price index. Everything we buy – pens, shirts, tyres – has been getting cheaper over the years because we have learned how to make them more cheaply, especially during the past 200 years. Even so, the extraordinary fact is that natural resources have been getting cheaper even faster than consumer goods.

So, by any measure, natural resources have been getting more available rather than more scarce.

In the case of oil, the shocking price rises during the 1970s and 1980s were not caused by growing scarcity in the world supply. And indeed, the price of petroleum in inflation-adjusted dollars has returned to levels about where they were before the politically-induced increases, and the price of gasoline is about at the historic low and still falling. Taking energy in general, there is no reason to believe that the supply of energy is finite, or that the price of energy will not continue its long-run decrease indefinitely. I realise that it sounds weird to say that the supply of energy is not finite or limited: for the full argument, please see my 1981 book.[2] (Science is only valuable when it arrives at knowledge different from common sense.)

Food – 'A Benign Trend'

Food is an especially important resource. The evidence is particularly strong for food that we are on a benign trend despite rising population. The long-run price of food relative to wages is now perhaps only a tenth as much as it was in 1800 in the USA. Even relative to consumer products, the price of grain is down because of increased productivity, as with all other primary products.

Famine deaths due to insufficient food supply have decreased even in absolute terms, let alone relative to population, in the past century, a matter which pertains particularly to the poor countries. Per-person food consumption is up over the last 30 years. And there are no data showing that the bottom of the income scale is faring worse, or even has failed to share in the general improvement, as the average has improved.

Africa's food production per person is down, but by 1994 almost no-one any longer claims that Africa's suffering results from a shortage of land or water or sun. The cause of hunger in Africa is a combination of civil wars and collectivisation of agriculture, which periodic droughts have made more murderous.

Consider agricultural land as an example of all natural resources. Although many people consider land to be a special kind of resource, it is subject to the same processes of human creation as other natural resources. The most important fact about agricultural land is that less and less of it is needed as the decades pass. This idea is utterly counter-intuitive. It seems entirely obvious that a growing world population would need larger amounts of farmland. But the title of a remarkably prescient article by Theodore Schultz in 1951 tells the story: 'The Declining Economic Importance of Land'.[3]

The increase in actual and potential productivity per unit of land has grown much faster than population, and there is sound reason to expect this trend to continue. Therefore, there is less and less reason to worry about the supply of land. Though the stock of usable land seems fixed at any moment, it is constantly being increased – at a rapid rate in many cases – by the clearing of new land or reclamation of wasteland. Land also is constantly being enhanced by increasing the number of crops grown per year on each unit of land and by increasing the yield per crop with better farming methods and with chemical fertiliser. Last but not least, land is created anew where there was no land.

The One Scarce Factor

There is only one important resource which has shown a trend of increasing scarcity rather than increasing abundance. That resource is the most important of all – human beings. Yes, there are more people on earth now than ever before. But if we measure the scarcity of people the same way that we measure the scarcity of other economic goods – by how much we must pay to obtain their services – we see that wages and salaries have been going up all over the world, in poor countries as well as rich. The amount that you must pay to obtain the services of a barber or cook – or economist – has risen in the United States over the decades. This increase in the price of people's services is a clear indication that people are becoming more scarce even though there are more of us.

Surveys show that the public believes that our air and water have been getting more polluted in recent years. The evidence with respect to air indicates that pollutants have been declining, especially

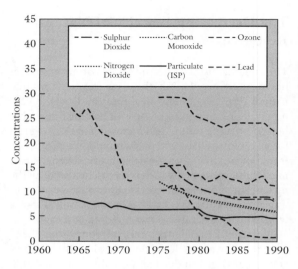

Figure 59.5 National ambient concentrations of pollutants: USA, 1960–90.

Source: Council on Environmental Quality, Environmental Quality, *22nd Annual Report*, 1992, p. 276. Council on Environmental Quality, Environmental Quality 1981, *12th Annual Report*, 1981, p. 243. Sulphur: 1964 thru 1972: EPA (1973): 32 stations.

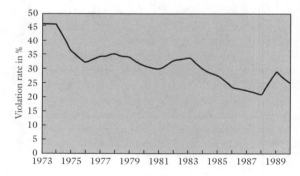

Figure 59.6 National ambient water quality in rivers and streams, USA, 1973–90: fecal coliform bacteria (200+ cells per 100 ml).

Source: *Statistical Abstracts of the United States*, various issues.

the main pollutant, particulates (see figure 59.5). With respect to water, the proportion of monitoring sites in the USA with water of good drinkability has increased since the data began in 1961 (figure 59.6).

Every forecast of the doomsayers has turned out flat wrong. Metals, foods, and other natural resources have become more available rather than more scarce throughout the centuries. The famous Famine 1975 forecast by the Paddock brothers – that we would see millions of famine deaths in the US on television in the 1970s – was followed instead by gluts in agricultural markets. Paul Ehrlich's primal scream about 'What will we do when the [gasoline] pumps run dry?' was followed by gasoline cheaper than since the 1930s. The Great Lakes are not dead; instead they offer better sport fishing than ever. The main pollutants, especially the particulates which have killed people for years, have lessened in our cities. Socialist countries are a different and tragic environmental story, however!

[. . .]

Population Density Favours Economic Growth

The research-wise person may wonder whether population density is a more meaningful variable than population growth. And, indeed, such studies have been done. And again, the statistical evidence directly contradicts the common-sense conventional wisdom. If you make a chart with population density on the horizontal axis and either the income level or the rate of change of income on the vertical axis, you will see that higher density is associated with better rather than poorer economic results.

You can check for yourself: if you fly over Hong Kong – just a few decades ago a place seemingly without prospects because of insoluble resource problems – you will marvel at the astounding collection of modern high-rise apartments and office buildings. Take a ride on its excellent smooth-flowing highways for an hour or two, and you will realise that a very dense concentration of human beings does not prevent comfortable existence and exciting economic expansion – as long as the economic system gives individuals the freedom to exercise their talents and to take advantage of opportunities. And the experience of Singapore demonstrates that Hong Kong is not unique. Two such examples do not prove the case, of course. But these dramatic illustrations are backed by the evidence from the aggregate sample of countries, and hence do not mislead us.

[. . .]

The most important benefit of population size and growth is the increase it brings to the stock of useful knowledge. Minds matter economically as much as, or more than, hands or mouths. Progress is limited largely by the availability of trained workers. The more people who enter our population by birth or immigration, the faster will be the rate of progress of our material and cultural civilisation.

Here we require a qualification that tends to be overlooked: I do not say that all is well everywhere, and I do not predict that all will be rosy in the future. Children are hungry and sick; people live out lives of physical or intellectual poverty, and lack of opportunity; war or some new pollution may finish us off. What I am saying is that for most relevant economic matters I have checked, the aggregate trends are improving rather than deteriorating.

Also, I do not say that a better future happens automatically or without effort. It will happen because women and men will struggle with problems with muscle and mind, and will probably overcome, as people have overcome in the past – *if the social and economic system gives them the opportunity to do so.*

The Explanation of These Amazing Trends

Now we need some theory to explain how it can be that economic welfare grows along with population, rather than humanity being reduced to misery and poverty as population grows.

The Mathusian theory of increasing scarcity, based on supposedly fixed resources (the theory that the doomsayers rely upon), runs exactly contrary to the data over the long sweep of history. It makes sense therefore to prefer another theory.

The theory that fits the facts very well is this: More people, and increased income, cause problems in the short run. Short-run scarcity raises prices. This presents opportunity, and prompts the search for solutions. In a free society, solutions are eventually found. And in the long run the new developments leave us better off than if the problems had not arisen.

To put it differently, in the short run more consumers mean less of the fixed available stock of goods to be divided among more people. And more workers labouring with the same fixed current stock of capital means that there will be less output per worker. The latter effect, known as 'the law of diminishing returns', is the essence of Malthus's theory as he first set it out.

But if the resources with which people work are not fixed over the period being analysed, the Malthusian logic of diminishing returns does not apply. And the plain fact is that, given some time to adjust to shortages, the resource base does not remain fixed. People create more resources of all kinds.

When we take a long-run view, the picture is different, and considerably more complex, than the simple short-run view of more people implying lower average income. In the very long run, more people almost surely imply more available resources and a higher income for everyone.

I suggest you test this idea against your own knowledge: Do you think that our standard of living would be as high as it is now if the population had never grown from about 4 million human beings perhaps 10,000 years ago? I do not think we would now have electric light or gas heat or cars or penicillin or travel to the moon or our present life expectancy of over 70 years at birth in rich countries, in comparison to the life expectancy of 20 to 25 years at birth in earlier eras, if population had not grown to its present numbers.

Scarcity and Discovery

Consider this example of the process by which people wind up with increasing rather than decreasing availability of resources. England was full of alarm in the 1600s at an impending shortage of energy due to the deforestation of the country for firewood. People feared a scarcity of fuel for both heating and for the iron industry. This impending scarcity led to the development of coal.

Then in the mid-1800s the English came to worry about an impending coal crisis. The great English economist, Jevons, calculated that a shortage of coal would bring England's industry to a standstill by 1990; he carefully assessed that oil could never make a decisive difference. Triggered by the impending scarcity of coal (and of whale oil, whose story comes next), ingenious profit-minded people developed oil into a more desirable fuel than coal ever was. And in 1990 we find England exporting both coal and oil.

Another element in the story: Because of increased demand due to population growth and increased income, the price of whale oil for lamps jumped in the 1840s, and the US Civil War pushed it even higher, leading to a whale oil 'crisis'. This provided incentive for enterprising people to discover and produce substitutes. First came oil from rapeseed, olives, linseed, and camphene oil from pine trees. Then inventors learned how to get coal oil from coal. Other ingenious persons produced kerosene from the rock oil that seeped to the surface, a product so desirable that its price then rose from $0·75 to $2·00 a gallon. This high price stimulated enterprisers to focus on the supply of oil, and finally Edwin L. Drake brought in his famous well in Titusville, Pennsylvania. Learning how to refine the oil took a while. But in a few years there were hundreds of small refiners in America, and soon the bottom fell out of the whale oil market, the price falling from $2·50 or more at its peak around 1866 to well below one dollar. And in 1994 we see Great Britain exporting both coal and oil.

Here we should note that it was not the British government that developed coal or oil, because governments are not effective developers of new technology. Rather, it was individual entrepreneurs who sensed the need, saw opportunity, used all kinds of available information and ideas, made lots of false starts which were very costly to many of those individuals but not to others, and eventually arrived at coal as a viable fuel – because there were enough independent individuals investigating the matter for at least some of them to arrive at sound ideas and methods. And this happened in the context of a competitive enterprise system that worked to produce what was wanted by the public. And the entire process of impending shortage and new solution left us better off than if the shortage problem had never arisen.

The Role of Economic Freedom

Here we must address another crucial element in the economics of resources and population – the extent to which the political-social-economic system provides personal freedom from government coercion. Skilled people require an appropriate social and economic framework that provides incentives for working hard and taking risks, enabling their talents to flower and come to fruition. The key elements of such a framework are economic liberty, respect for property, and fair and sensible rules of the market that are enforced equally for all.

The world's problem is not too many people, but lack of political and economic freedom. Powerful evidence comes from an extraordinary natural experiment that occurred starting in the 1940s with three pairs of countries that have the same culture and history, and had much the same standard of living when they split apart after the Second World War – East and West Germany, North and South Korea, Taiwan and China. In each case the centrally planned communist country began with less population 'pressure', as measured by density per square kilometre, than did the market-directed economy. And the communist and non-communist countries also started with much the same birth rates.

The market-directed economies have performed much better economically than the centrally-planned economies. The economic-political system clearly was the dominant force in the results of the three comparisons. This powerful explanation of economic development cuts the ground from under population growth as a likely explanation of the speed of nations' economic development.

The Astounding Shift in the Scholarly Consensus

So far I have been discussing the factual evidence. But in 1994 there is an important new element not present 20 years ago. The scientific community of scholars who study population economics now agrees with almost all of what is written above. The statements made above do not represent a single lone voice, but rather the current scientific consensus.

The conclusions offered earlier about agriculture and resources and demographic trends have always represented the consensus of economists in those fields. And the consensus of population economists also is now not far from what is written here.

In 1986, the US National Research Council and the US National Academy of Sciences published a book on population growth and economic development prepared by a prestigious scholarly group. This 'official' report reversed almost completely the frightening conclusions of the 1971 NAS report. 'Population growth at most a minor factor . . .' As cited earlier in this paper, it found benefits of additional people as well as costs.[4]

A host of review articles by distinguished economic demographers in the past decade has confirmed that this 'revisionist' view is indeed consistent with the scientific evidence, though not all the writers would go as far as I do in pointing out the positive long-run effects of population growth. The consensus is more towards a 'neutral' judgement. But this is a huge change from the earlier judgement that population growth is economically detrimental.

By 1994, anyone who confidently asserts that population growth damages the economy must turn a blind eye to the scientific evidence.

Summary and Conclusion

In the short run, all resources are limited. An example of such a finite resource is the amount of space allotted to me. The longer run, however, is a different story. The standard of living has risen along with the size of the world's population since the beginning of recorded time. There is no convincing economic reason why these trends towards a better life should not continue indefinitely.

The key theoretical idea is this: The growth of population and of income create actual and expected shortages, and hence lead to price rises. A price increase represents an opportunity that attracts profit-minded entrepreneurs to seek new ways to satisfy the shortages. Some fail, at cost to themselves. A few succeed, and the final result is that we end up better off than if the original shortage problems had never arisen. That is, we need our problems though this does not imply that we should purposely create additional problems for ourselves.

I hope that you will now agree that the long-run outlook is for a more abundant material life rather than for increased scarcity, in the United States and in the world as a whole. Of course, such progress does not come automatically. And my message certainly is not one of complacency. In this I agree with the doomsayers – that our world needs the best efforts of all humanity to improve our lot. I part company with them in that they expect us to come to a bad end despite the efforts we make, whereas I expect a continuation of humanity's history of successful efforts. And I believe that their message is self-fulfilling, because if you expect your efforts to fail because of inexorable natural limits, then you are likely to feel resigned; and therefore literally to resign. But if you recognise the possibility – in fact the probability – of success, you can tap large reservoirs of energy and enthusiasm.

Adding more people causes problems, but people are also the means to solve these problems. The main fuel to speed the world's progress is our stock of knowledge, and the brakes are (a) our lack of imagination, and (b) unsound social regulation of these activities.

The ultimate resource is people – especially skilled, spirited, and hopeful young people endowed with liberty – who will exert their wills and imaginations for their own benefit, and so inevitably benefit not only themselves but the rest of us as well.

Notes

1   National Research Council, Committee on Population, and Working Group on Population Growth and Economic Development, *Population Growth and Economic Development: Policy Questions*. Washington DC: National Academy Press. 1986.
2   J. L. Simon, *The Ultimate Resource*. Princeton, NJ: Princeton University Press, 1981.
3   T. W. Schultz, 'The Declining Economic Importance of Land', *Economic Journal*, vol. LXI. December 1951, pp. 725–40.
4   National Research Council, *op. cit.*

60   Population: Delusion and Reality

Amartya Sen

Few issues today are as divisive as what is called the "world population problem." With the approach this autumn of the International Conference on Population and Development in Cairo, organized by the United Nations, these divisions among experts are receiving enormous attention and generating considerable heat. There is a danger that in the confrontation between apocalyptic pessimism, on the one hand, and a dismissive smugness, on the other, a genuine understanding of the nature of the population problem may be lost.[1]

Visions of impending doom have been increasingly aired in recent years, often presenting the population problem as a "bomb" that has been planted and is about to "go off." These catastrophic images have encouraged a tendency to search for emergency solutions which treat the people involved not as reasonable beings, allies facing a common problem, but as impulsive and uncontrolled sources of great social harm, in need of strong discipline.

Such views have received serious attention in public discussions, not just in sensational headlines in the popular press, but also in seriously argued and widely read books. One of the most influential examples was Paul Ehrlich's *The Population Bomb*, the first three sections of which were headed "Too Many People," "Too Little Food," and "A Dying Planet."[2] A more recent example of a chilling diagnosis of imminent calamity is Garrett Hardin's *Living within Limits*.[3] The arguments on which these pessimistic visions are based deserve serious scrutiny.

If the propensity to foresee impending disaster from overpopulation is strong in some circles, so is the tendency, in others, to dismiss all worries about population size. Just as alarmism builds on the recognition of a real problem and then magnifies it, complacency may also start off from a reasonable belief about the history of population problems and fail to see how they may have changed by now. It is often pointed out, for example, that the world has coped well enough with fast increases in population in the past, even though alarmists had expected otherwise. Malthus anticipated terrible disasters resulting from population growth and consequent imbalance in "the proportion between the natural increase of population and food."[4] At a time when there were fewer than a billion people, he was quite convinced that "the period when the number of men surpass their means of subsistence has long since arrived." However, since Malthus first published his famous *Essay on*

From *The New York Review of Books*, vol. 41, no. 15 (September 22, 1994). © 1994, NYREV, Inc. Reprinted with permission from *The New York Review of Books* and Dr. Amartya Sen.

Population in 1798, the world population has grown nearly six times larger, while food output and consumption per person are considerably higher now, and there has been an unprecedented increase both in life expectancies and in general living standards.[5]

The fact that Malthus was mistaken in his diagnosis as well as his prognosis two hundred years ago does not, however, indicate that contemporary fears about population growth must be similarly erroneous. The increase in the world population has vastly accelerated over the last century. It took the world population millions of years to reach the first billion, then 123 years to get to the second, 33 years to the third, 14 years to the fourth, 13 years to the fifth billion, with a sixth billion to come, according to one UN projection, in another 11 years.[6] During the last decade, between 1980 and 1990, the number of people on earth grew by about 923 million, an increase nearly the size of the total world population in Malthus's time. Whatever may be the proper response to alarmism about the future, complacency based on past success is no response at all.

Immigration and Population

One current worry concerns the regional distribution of the increase in world population, about 90 percent of which is taking place in the developing countries. The percentage rate of population growth is fastest in Africa – 3.1 percent per year over the last decade. But most of the large increases in population occur in regions other than Africa. The largest absolute increases in numbers are taking place in Asia, which is where most of the world's poorer people live, even though the rate of increase in population has been slowing significantly there. Of the worldwide increase of 923 million people in the 1980s, well over half occurred in Asia – 517 million in fact (including 146 million in China and 166 million in India).

Beyond concerns about the well-being of these poor countries themselves, a more self-regarding worry causes panic in the richer countries of the world and has much to do with the current anxiety in the West about the "world population problem." This is founded on the belief that destitution caused by fast population growth in the third world is responsible for the severe pressure to emigrate to the developed countries of Europe and North America. In this view, people impoverished by overpopulation in the "South" flee to the "North." Some have claimed to find empirical support for this thesis in the fact that pressure to emigrate from the South has accelerated in recent decades, along with a rapid increase in the population there.

There are two distinct questions here: first, how great a threat of intolerable immigration pressure does the North face from the South, and second, is that pressure closely related to population growth in the South, rather than to other social and economic factors? There are reasons to doubt that population growth is the major force behind migratory pressures, and I shall concentrate here on that question. But I should note in passing that immigration is now severely controlled in Europe and North America, and insofar as Europe is concerned, most of the current immigrants from the third world are not "primary" immigrants but dependent relatives – mainly spouses and young children – of those who had come and settled earlier. The United States remains relatively more open to fresh immigration, but the requirements of "labor certification" as a necessary part of the immigration procedure tend to guarantee that the new entrants are relatively better educated and more skilled. There are, however, sizable flows of illegal immigrants, especially to the United States and to a lesser extent to southern Europe, though the numbers are hard to estimate.

What causes the current pressures to emigrate? The "job-worthy" people who get through the immigration process are hardly to be seen as impoverished and destitute migrants created by the sheer pressure of population. Even the illegal immigrants who manage to evade the rigors of border control are typically not starving wretches but those who can make use of work prospects in the North.

The explanation for the increased migratory pressure over the decades owes more to the dynamism of international capitalism than to just the growing size of the population of the third world countries. The immigrants have allies in potential employers, and this applies as much to illegal farm laborers in California as to the legally authorized "guest workers" in automobile factories in Germany. The economic incentive to emigrate to the North from the poorer Southern economies may well depend on differences in real income. But this gap is very large anyway, and even if it is presumed that population growth in the South is increasing the disparity with the North – a thesis I shall presently consider – it seems unlikely that this incentive would significantly change if the Northern income level were, say, twenty times that of the Southern as opposed to twenty-five times.

The growing demand for immigration to the North from the South is related to the "shrinking" of the world (through revolutions in communication and transport), reduction in economic obstacles to labor movements (despite the increase in political barriers), and the growing reach and absorptive power of international capitalism (even as domestic politics in the North has turned more inward-looking and nationalistic). To try to explain the increase in immigration pressure by the growth rate of total population in the third world is to close one's eyes to the deep changes that have occurred – and are occurring – in the world in which we live, and the rapid internationalization of its cultures and economies that accompanies these changes.

Fears of Being Engulfed

A closely related issue concerns what is perceived as a growing "imbalance" in the division of the world population, with a rapidly rising share belonging to the third world. That fear translates into worries of various kinds in the North, especially the sense of being overrun by the South. Many Northerners fear being engulfed by people from Asia and Africa, whose share of the world population increased from 63.7 percent in 1950 to 71.2 percent by 1990, and is expected, according to the estimates of the United Nations, to rise to 78.5 percent by 2050 AD.

It is easy to understand the fears of relatively well-off people at the thought of being surrounded by a fast growing and increasingly impoverished Southern population. As I shall argue, the thesis of growing impoverishment does not stand up to much scrutiny; but it is important to address first the psychologically tense issue of racial balance in the world (even though racial composition as a consideration has only as much importance as we choose to give it). Here it is worth recollecting that the third world is right now going through the same kind of demo-graphic shift – a rapid expansion of population for a temporary but long stretch – that Europe and North America experienced during their industrial revolution. In 1650 the share of Asia and Africa in the world population is estimated to have been 78.4 percent, and it stayed around there even in 1750.[7] With the industrial revolution,

the share of Asia and Africa diminished because of the rapid rise of population in Europe and North America; for example, during the nineteenth century while the inhabitants of Asia and Africa grew by about 4 percent per decade or less, the population of "the area of European settlement" grew by around 10 percent every decade.

Even now the combined share of Asia and Africa (71.2 percent) is considerably below what its share was in 1650 or 1750. If the United Nations' prediction that this share will rise to 78.5 percent by 2050 comes true, then the Asians and the Africans would return to being proportionately almost exactly as numerous as they were before the European industrial revolution. There is, of course, nothing sacrosanct about the distributions of population in the past; but the sense of a growing "imbalance" in the world, based only on recent trends, ignores history and implicitly presumes that the expansion of Europeans earlier on was natural, whereas the same process happening now to other populations unnaturally disturbs the "balance."

Collaboration versus Override

Other worries involving the relation of population growth to food supplies, income levels, and the environment reflect more serious matters.[8] Before I take up those questions, a brief comment on the distinction between two rival approaches to dealing with the population problem may be useful. One involves voluntary choice and a collaborative solution, and the other overrides voluntarism through legal or economic coercion.

Alarmist views of impending crises tend to produce a willingness to consider forceful measures for coercing people to have fewer children in the third world. Imposing birth control on unwilling people is no longer rejected as readily as it was until quite recently, and some activists have pointed to the ambiguities that exist in determining what is or is not "coercion."[9] Those who are willing to consider – or at least not fully reject – programs that would use some measure of force to reduce population growth often point to the success of China's "one child policy" in cutting down the national birth rate. Force can also take an indirect form, as when economic opportunities are changed so radically by government regulations that people are left with very little choice except to behave in ways the government would approve. In China's case, the government may refuse to offer housing to families with too many children – thus penalizing the children as well as the dissenting adults.

In India the policy of compulsory birth control that was initiated during the "emergency period" declared by Mrs. Gandhi in the 1970s was decisively rejected by the voters in the general election in which it – along with civil rights – was a major issue. Even so, some public health clinics in the northern states (such as Uttar Pradesh) insist, in practice, on sterilization before providing normal medical attention to women and men beyond a certain age. The pressures to move in that direction seem to be strong, and they are reinforced by the rhetoric of "the population bomb."

I shall call this general approach the "override" view, since the family's personal decisions are over-ridden by some agency outside the family – typically by the government of the country in question (whether or not it has been pressed to do so by "out-side" agencies, such as international organizations and pressure groups). In fact, overriding is not limited to an explicit use of legal coercion or economic compulsion, since people's own choices can also be effectively overridden by simply not offering them the opportunities for jobs or welfare that they can expect to get from a responsible government. Override can take many different forms and can be of varying intensity (with the Chinese "one child policy" being something of an extreme case of a more general approach).

A central issue here is the increasingly vocal demand by some activists concerned with population growth that the highest "priority" should be given in third world countries to family planning over other public commitments. This demand goes much beyond supporting family planning as a part of development. In fact, proposals for shifting international aid away from development in general to family planning in particular have lately been increasingly frequent. Such policies fit into the general approach of "override" as well, since they try to rely on manipulating people's choices through offering them only some opportunities (the means of family planning) while denying others, no matter what they would have themselves preferred. Insofar as they would have the effect of reducing health care and educational services, such shifts in public commitments will not only add to the misery of human lives, they may also have, I shall argue, exactly the opposite effect on family planning than the one intended,

since education and health care have a significant part in the voluntary reduction of the birth rate.

The "override" approach contrasts with another, the "collaborative" approach, that relies not on legal or economic restrictions but on rational decisions of women and men, based on expanded choices and enhanced security, and encouraged by open dialogue and extensive public discussions. The difference between the two approaches does not lie in government's activism in the first case as opposed to passivity in the second. Even if solutions are sought through the decisions and actions of people themselves, the chance to take reasoned decisions with more knowledge and a greater sense of personal security can be increased by public policies, for example, through expanding educational facilities, health care, and economic well-being, along with providing better access to family planning. The central political and ethical issue concerning the "override" approach does not lie in its insistence on the need for public policy but in the ways it significantly reduces the choices open to parents.

The Malthus-Condorcet Debate

Thomas Robert Malthus forcefully argued for a version of the "override" view. In fact, it was precisely this preference that distinguished Malthus from Condorcet, the eighteenth-century French mathematician and social scientist from whom Malthus had actually derived the analysis of how population could outgrow the means of living. The debate between Condorcet and Malthus in some ways marks the origin of the distinction between the "collaborative" and the "override" approaches, which still compete for attention.[10]

In his Essay on Population, published in 1798, Malthus quoted – extensively and with approval – Condorcet's discussion, in 1795, of the possibility of overpopulation. However, true to the Enlightenment tradition, Condorcet was confident that this problem would be solved by reasoned human action: through increases in productivity, through better conservation and prevention of waste, and through education (especially female education) which would contribute to reducing the birth rate.[11] Voluntary family planning would be encouraged, in Condorcet's analysis, by increased understanding that if people "have a duty toward those who are not yet born, that duty is not to give them existence but to give them happiness." They would see the value of limiting family size "rather than foolishly . . . encumber the world with useless and wretched beings."[12]

Even though Malthus borrowed from Condorcet his diagnosis of the possibility of overpopulation, he refused to accept Condorcet's solution. Indeed, Malthus's essay on population was partly a criticism of Condorcet's enlightenment reasoning, and even the full title of Malthus's famous essay specifically mentioned Condorcet. Malthus argued that

> there is no reason whatever to suppose that anything beside the difficulty of procuring in adequate plenty the necessaries of life should either *indispose* this greater number of persons to marry early, or *disable* them from rearing in health the largest families.[13]

Malthus thus opposed public relief of poverty: he saw the "poor laws" in particular as contributing greatly to population growth.[14]

Malthus was not sure that any public policy would work, and whether "overriding" would in fact be possible: "The perpetual tendency in the race of man to increase beyond the means of subsistence is one of the great general laws of animated nature which we can have no reason to expect will change."[15] But insofar as any solution would be possible, it could not come from voluntary decisions of the people involved, or acting from a position of strength and economic security. It must come from overriding their preferences through the compulsions of economic necessity, since their poverty was the only thing that could "indispose the greater number of persons to marry early, or disable them from rearing in health the largest families."

Development and Increased Choice

The distinction between the "collaborative" approach and the "override" approach thus tends to correspond closely to the contrast between, on the one hand, treating economic and social development as the way to solve the population problem and, on the other, expecting little from development and using, instead, legal and economic pressures to reduce birth rates. Among recent writers, those such as Gerard Piel[16] who have persuasively emphasized our ability to solve problems through reasoned decisions and actions have tended – like Condorcet – to find the solution of the population problem in economic and social development. They advocate a broadly collaborative

approach, in which governments and citizens would together produce economic and social conditions favoring slower population growth. In contrast, those who have been thoroughly skeptical of reasoned human action to limit population growth have tended to go in the direction of "override" in one form or another, rather than concentrate on development and voluntarism.

Has development, in fact, done much to reduce population growth? There can be little doubt that economic and social development, in general, has been associated with major reductions in birth rates and the emergence of smaller families as the norm. This is a pattern that was, of course, clearly observed in Europe and North America as they underwent industrialization, but that experience has been repeated in many other parts of the world.

In particular, conditions of economic security and affluence, wider availability of contraceptive methods, expansion of education (particularly female education), and lower mortality rates have had – and are currently having – quite substantial effects in reducing birth rates in different parts of the world.[17] The rate of world population growth is certainly declining, and even over the last two decades its percentage growth rate has fallen from 2.2 percent per year between 1970 and 1980 to 1.7 percent between 1980 and 1992. This rate is expected to go steadily down until the size of the world's population becomes nearly stationary.[18]

There are important regional differences in demographic behavior; for example, the population growth rate in India peaked at 2.2 percent a year (in the 1970s) and has since started to diminish, whereas most Latin American countries peaked at much higher rates before coming down sharply, while many countries in Africa currently have growth rates between 3 and 4 percent, with an average for sub-Saharan Africa of 3.1 percent. Similarly, the different factors have varied in their respective influence from region to region. But there can be little dispute that economic and social development tends to reduce fertility rates. The regions of the third world that lag most in achieving economic and social development, such as many countries in Africa, are, in general, also the ones that have failed to reduce birth rates significantly. Malthus's fear that economic and social development could only encourage people to have more children has certainly proved to be radically wrong, and so have all the painful policy implications drawn from it.

This raises the following question: in view of the clear connection between development and lower fertility, why isn't the dispute over how to deal with population growth fully resolved already? Why don't we reinterpret the population problem simply as a problem of underdevelopment and seek a solution by encouraging economic and social development (even if we reject the oversimple slogan "development is the most reliable contraceptive")?

In the long run, this may indeed be exactly the right approach. The problem is more complex, however, because a "contraceptive" that is "reliable" in the long run may not act fast enough to meet the present threat. Even though development may dependably work to stabilize population if it is given enough time, there may not be, it is argued, time enough to give. The death rate often falls very fast with more widely available health care, better sanitation, and improved nutrition, while the birth rate may fall rather slowly. Much growth of population may meanwhile occur.

This is exactly the point at which apocalyptic prophecies add force to the "override" view. One claim, then, that needs examination is that the world is facing an imminent crisis, one so urgent that development is just too slow a process to deal with it. We must try right now, the argument goes, to cut down population growth by drastic and forceful means if necessary. The second claim that also needs scrutiny is the actual feasibility of adequately reducing population growth through these drastic means, without fostering social and economic development.

Population and Income

It is sometimes argued that signs of an imminent crisis can be found in the growing impoverishment of the South, with falling income per capita accompanying high population growth. In general, there is little evidence for this. As a matter of fact, the average population of "low-income" countries (as defined by the World Bank) has been not only enjoying a rising gross national product (GNP) per head, but a growth rate of GNP per capita (3.9 percent per year for 1980–92) that is much faster than those for the "high-income" countries (2.4 percent) and for the "middle-income" ones (0 percent).[19]

The growth of per capita GNP of the population of low-income countries would have been even higher had it not been for the negative growth rates of many countries in sub-Saharan Africa, one region in which a number of countries have been experiencing economic decline. But the main culprit causing this state of affairs is the terrible failure of economic production in sub-Saharan Africa (connected particularly with political disruption, including wars and military rule), rather than population growth, which is only a subsidiary factor. Sub-Saharan Africa does have high population growth, but its economic stagnation has contributed much more to the fall in its per-capita income.

With its average population growth rate of 3.1 percent per year, had sub-Saharan Africa suddenly matched China's low population growth of 1.4 percent (the lowest among the low-income countries), it would have gained roughly 1.7 percent in per-capita GNP growth. The real income per person would still have fallen, even with that minimal population growth, for many countries in the region. The growth of GNP per capita is *minus* 1.9 percent for Ethiopia, *minus* 1.8 percent for Togo, *minus* 3.6 percent for Mozambique, *minus* 4.3 percent for Niger, *minus* 4.7 percent for Ivory Coast, not to mention Somalia, Sudan, and Angola, where the political disruption has been so serious that no reliable GNP estimates even exist. A lower population growth rate could have reduced the magnitude of the fall in per capita GNP, but the main roots of Africa's economic decline lie elsewhere. The complex political factors underlying the troubles of Africa include, among other things, the subversion of democracy and the rise of combative military rulers, often encouraged by the cold war (with Africa providing "client states" – from Somalia and Ethiopia to Angola and Zaire – for the superpowers, particularly from the 1960s onward). The explanation of sub-Saharan Africa's problems has to be sought in these political troubles, which affect economic stability, agricultural and industrial incentives, public health arrangements, and social services – even family planning and population policy.[20]

There is indeed a very powerful case for reducing the rate of growth of population in Africa, but this problem cannot be dissociated from the rest of the continent's woes. Sub-Saharan Africa lags behind other developing regions in economic security, in health care, in life expectancy, in basic education, and in political and economic stability. It should be no great surprise that it lags behind in family planning as well. To dissociate the task of population control from the politics and economics of Africa would be a great mistake and would seriously mislead public policy.

Population and Food

Malthus's exact thesis cannot, however, be disputed by quoting statistics of income per capita, for he was concerned specifically with food supply per capita, and he had concentrated on "the proportion between the natural increase of population and food." Many modern commentators, including Paul Ehrlich and Garrett Hardin, have said much about this, too. When Ehrlich says, in his *Population Bomb*, "too little food," he does not mean "too little income," but specifically a growing shortage of food.

Is population beginning to outrun food production? Even though such an impression is often given in public discussions, there is, in fact, no serious evidence that this is happening. While there are some year-to-year fluctuations in the growth of food output (typically inducing, whenever things slacken a bit, some excited remarks by those who anticipate an impending doom), the worldwide trend of food output per person has been firmly upward. Not only over the two centuries since Malthus's time, but also during recent decades, the rise in food output has been significantly and consistently outpacing the expansion of world population.[21]

But the total food supply in the world as a whole is not the only issue. What about the regional distribution of food? If it were to turn out that the rising ratio of food to population is mainly caused by increased production in richer countries (for example, if it appeared that US wheat output was feeding the third world, in which much of the population expansion is taking place), then the neo-Malthusian fears about "too many people" and "too little food" may have some plausibility. Is this what is happening?

In fact, with one substantial exception, exactly the opposite is true. The largest increases in the production of food – not just in the aggregate but also per person – are actually taking place in the third world, particularly in the region that is having the largest absolute increases in the world population, that is, in Asia. The many millions of people who are added to the populations of India and China may be constantly cited by the terrorized – and terrorizing – advocates of the apocalyptic view, but it is precisely in these countries that the most rapid rates of growth

Table 60.1 Indices of Food Production Per Capita

	1979–1981 Base Period	1991–1993
World	100	103
Europe	100	102
North America	100	95
Africa	100	94
Asia	100	122
including		
India	100	123
China	100	139

Source: FAO Quarterly Bulletin of Statistics.

in food output per capita are to be observed. For example, between the three-year averages of 1979–81 and 1991–3, food production per head in the world moved up by 3 percent, while it went up by only 2 percent in Europe and went down by nearly 5 percent in North America. In contrast, per capita food production jumped up by 22 percent in Asia generally, including 23 percent in India and 39 percent in China.[22] (See table 60.1.)

During the same period, however, food production per capita went down by 6 percent in Africa, and even the absolute size of food output fell in some countries (such as Malawi and Somalia). Of course, many countries in the world – from Syria, Italy, and Sweden to Botswana in Africa – have had declining food production per head without experiencing hunger or starvation since their economies have prospered and grown; when the means are available, food can be easily bought in the international market if it is necessary to do so. For many countries in sub-Saharan Africa the problem arises from the fact that the decline in food production is an integral part of the story of overall economic decline, which I have discussed earlier.

Difficulties of food production in sub-Saharan Africa, like other problems of the national economy, are not only linked to wars, dictatorships, and political chaos. In addition, there is some evidence that climatic shifts have had unfavorable effects on parts of that continent. While some of the climatic problems may be caused partly by increases in human settlement and environmental neglect, that neglect is not unrelated to the political and economic chaos that has characterized sub-Saharan Africa during the last few decades. The food problem of Africa must be seen as one part of a wider political and economic problem of the region.[23]

The Price of Food

To return to "the balance between food and population," the rising food production per capita in the world as a whole, and in the third world in general, contradicts some of the pessimism that characterized the gloomy predictions of the past. Prophecies of imminent disaster during the last few decades have not proved any more accurate than Malthus's prognostication nearly two hundred years ago. As for new prophecies of doom, they cannot, of course, be contradicted until the future arrives. There was no way of refuting the theses of W. Paddock and P. Paddock's popular book *Famine – 1975!*, published in 1968, which predicted a terrible cataclysm for the world as a whole by 1975 (writing off India, in particular, as a basket case), until 1975 actually arrived. The new prophets have learned not to attach specific dates to the crises they foresee, and past failures do not seem to have reduced the popular appetite for this creative genre.

However, after noting the rather dismal forecasting record of doom-sayers, we must also accept the general methodological point that present trends in output do not necessarily tell us much about the prospects of further expansion in the future. It could, for example, be argued that maintaining growth in food production may require proportionately increasing investments of capital, drawing them away from other kinds of production. This would tend to make food progressively more expensive if there are "diminishing returns" in shifting resources from other fields into food production. And, ultimately, further expansion of food production may become so expensive that it would be hard to maintain the trend of increasing food production without reducing other outputs drastically.

But is food production really getting more and more expensive? There is, in fact, no evidence for that conclusion either. In fact, quite the contrary. Not only is food generally much cheaper to buy today, in constant dollars, than it was in Malthus's time, but it also has become cheaper during recent decades. As a matter of fact, there have been increasing complaints among food exporters, especially in the third world, that food prices have fallen in rela-

tion to other commodities. For example, in 1992 a United Nations report recorded a 38 percent fall in the relative prices of "basic foods" over the last decade.[24] This is entirely in line with the trend, during the last three decades, toward declining relative prices of particular food items, in relation to the prices of manufactured goods. The World Bank's adjusted estimates of the prices of particular food crops, between 1953 and 1955 and 1983 and 1985, show similarly steep declines for such staples as rice (42 percent), wheat (57 percent), sorghum (39 percent), and maize (37 percent).[25]

Not only is food getting less expensive, but we also have to bear in mind that the current increase in food production (substantial and well ahead of population growth, as it is) is itself being kept in check by the difficulties in selling food profitably, as the relative prices of food have fallen. Those neo-Malthusians who concede that food production is now growing faster than population often point out that it is growing "only a little faster than population," and they are inclined to interpret this as evidence that we are reaching the limits of what we can produce to keep pace with population growth.

But that is surely the wrong conclusion to draw in view of the falling relative prices of food, and the current difficulties in selling food, since it ignores the effects of economic incentives that govern production. When we take into account the persistent cheapening of food prices, we have good grounds to suggest that food output is being held back by a lack of effective demand in the market. The imaginary crisis in food production, contradicted as it is by the upward trends of total and regional food output per head, is thus further debunked by an analysis of the economic incentives to produce more food.

Deprived Lives and Slums

I have examined the alleged "food problem" associated with population growth in some detail because it has received so much attention both in the traditional Malthusian literature and in the recent writings of neo-Malthusians. In concentrating on his claim that growing populations would not have enough food, Malthus differed from Condorcet's broader presentation of the population question. Condorcet's own emphasis was on the possibility of "a continual diminution of happiness" as a result of population growth, a diminution that could occur in many different ways – not just through the deprivation of food, but through a decline in living conditions generally. That more extensive worry can remain even when Malthus's analysis of the food supply is rejected.

Indeed, average income and food production per head can go on increasing even as the wretchedly deprived living conditions of particular sections of the population get worse, as they have in many parts of the third world. The living conditions of backward regions and deprived classes can decline even when a country's economic growth is very rapid on the average. Brazil during the 1960s and 1970s provided an extreme example of this. The sense that there are just "too many people" around often arises from seeing the desperate lives of people in the large and rapidly growing urban slums – *bidonvilles* – in poor countries, sobering reminders that we should not take too much comfort from aggregate statistics of economic progress.

But in an essay addressed mainly to the population problem, what we have to ask is not whether things are just fine in the third world (they obviously are not), but whether population growth is the root cause of the deprivations that people suffer. The question is whether the particular instances of deep poverty we observe derive mainly from population growth rather than from other factors that lead to unshared prosperity and persistent and possibly growing inequality. The tendency to see in population growth an explanation for every calamity that afflicts poor people is now fairly well established in some circles, and the message that gets transmitted constantly is the opposite of the old picture postcard: "Wish you weren't here."

To see in population growth the main reason for the growth of overcrowded and very poor slums in large cities, for example, is not empirically convincing. It does not help to explain why the slums of Calcutta and Bombay have grown worse at a faster rate than those of Karachi and Islamabad (India's population growth rate is 2.1 percent per year, Pakistan's 3.1), or why Jakarta has deteriorated faster than Ankara or Istanbul (Indonesian population growth is 1.8 percent, Turkey's 2.3), or why the slums of Mexico City have become worse more rapidly than those of San José (Mexico's population growth rate is 2.0, Costa Rica's 2.8), or why Harlem can seem more and more deprived when compared with the poorer districts of Singapore

(US population growth rate is 1.0, Singapore's is 1.8). Many causal factors affect the degree of deprivation in particular parts of a country – rural as well as urban – and to try to see them all as resulting from overpopulation is the negation of social analysis.

This is not to deny that population growth may well have an effect on deprivation, but only to insist that any investigation of the effects of population growth must be part of the analysis of economic and political processes, including the effects of other variables. It is the isolationist view of population growth that should be rejected.

Threats to the Environment

In his concern about "a continual diminution of happiness" from population growth, Condorcet was a pioneer in considering the possibility that natural raw materials might be used up, thereby making living conditions worse. In his characteristically rationalist solution, which relied partly on voluntary and reasoned measures to reduce the birth rate, Condorcet also envisaged the development of less improvident technology: "The manufacture of articles will be achieved with less wastage in raw materials and will make better use of them."[26]

The effects of a growing population on the environment could be a good deal more serious than the food problems that have received so much attention in the literature inspired by Malthus. If the environment is damaged by population pressures this obviously affects the kind of life we lead, and the possibilities of a "diminution in happiness" can be quite considerable. In dealing with this problem, we have to distinguish once again between the long and the short run. The short-run picture tends to be dominated by the fact that the per-capita consumption of food, fuel, and other goods by people in third world countries is often relatively low; consequently the impact of population growth in these countries is not, in relative terms, so damaging to the global environment. But the problems of the local environment can, of course, be serious in many developing economies. They vary from the "neighborhood pollution" created by unregulated industries to the pressure of denser populations on rural resources such as fields and woods.[27] (The Indian authorities had to close down several factories in and around Agra, since the façade of the Taj

Mahal was turning pale as a result of chemical pollution from local factories.) But it remains true that one additional American typically has a larger negative impact on the ozone layer, global warmth, and other elements of the earth's environment than dozens of Indians and Zimbabweans put together. Those who argue for the immediate need for forceful population control in the third world to preserve the global environment must first recognize this elementary fact.

This does not imply, as is sometimes suggested, that as far as the global environment is concerned, population growth in the third world is nothing to worry about. The long-run impact on the global environment of population growth in the developing countries can be expected to be large. As the Indians and the Zimbabweans develop economically, they too will consume a great deal more, and they will pose, in the future, a threat to the earth's environment similar to that of people in the rich countries today. The long-run threat of population to the environment is a real one.

Women's Deprivation and Power

Since reducing the birth rate can be slow, this and other long-run problems should be addressed right now. Solutions will no doubt have to be found in the two directions to which, as it happens, Condorcet pointed: (1) developing new technology and new behavior patterns that would waste little and pollute less, and (2) fostering social and economic changes that would gradually bring down the growth rate of population.

On reducing birth rates, Condorcet's own solution not only included enhancing economic opportunity and security, but also stressed the importance of education, particularly female education. A better-educated population could have a more informed discussion of the kind of life we have reason to value; in particular it would reject the drudgery of a life of continuous child bearing and rearing that is routinely forced on many third world women. That drudgery, in some ways, is the most immediately adverse consequence of high fertility rates.

Central to reducing birth rates, then, is a close connection between women's well-being and their power to make their own decisions and bring about changes in the fertility pattern. Women in many third world countries are deprived by high birth frequency of the freedom to do other things in life, not to mention the medical dangers of repeated pregnancy and high maternal mortality, which are both characteristic of many developing countries. It is thus not surprising that reductions in birth rates have been typically associated with improvement of women's status and their ability to make their voices heard – often the result of expanded opportunities for schooling and political activity.[28]

There is nothing particularly exotic about declines in the birth rate occurring through a process of voluntary rational assessment, of which Condorcet spoke. It is what people do when they have some basic education, know about family planning methods and have access to them, do not readily accept a life of persistent drudgery, and are not deeply anxious about their economic security. It is also what they do when they are not forced by high infant and child mortality rates to be so worried that no child will survive to support them in their old age that they try to have many children. In country after country the birth rate has come down with more female education, the reduction of mortality rates, the expansion of economic means and security, and greater public discussion of ways of living.

Development versus Coercion

There is little doubt that this process of social and economic change will over time cut down the birth rate. Indeed the growth rate of world population is already firmly declining – it came down from 2.2 percent in the 1970s to 1.7 percent between 1980 and 1992. Had imminent cataclysm been threatening, we might have had good reason to reject such gradual progress and consider more drastic means of population control, as some have advocated. But that apocalyptic view is empirically baseless. There is no imminent emergency that calls for a breathless response. What is called for is systematic support for people's own decisions to reduce family size through expanding education and health care, and through economic and social development.

It is often asked where the money needed for expanding education, health care, etc., would be found. Education, health services, and many other means of improving the quality of life are typically highly labor-intensive and are thus relatively inexpensive in poor countries (because of low wages).[29]

While poor countries have less money to spend, they also need less money to provide these services. For this reason many poor countries have indeed been able to expand educational and health services widely without waiting to become prosperous through the process of economic growth. Sri Lanka, Costa Rica, Indonesia, and Thailand are good examples, and there are many others. While the impact of these social services on the quality and length of life have been much studied, they are also major means of reducing the birth rate.

By contrast with such open and voluntary developments, coercive methods, such as the "one child policy" in some regions, have been tried in China, particularly since the reforms of 1979. Many commentators have pointed out that by 1992 the Chinese birth rate has fallen to 19 per 1,000, compared with 29 per 1,000 in India, and 37 per 1,000 for the average of poor countries other than China and India. China's total fertility rate (reflecting the number of children born per woman) is now at "the replacement level" of 2.0, compared with India's 3.6 and the weighted average of 4.9 for low-income countries other than China and India.[30] Hasn't China shown the way to "solve" the population problem in other developing countries as well?

China's Population Policies

The difficulties with this "solution" are of several kinds. First, if freedom is valued at all, the lack of freedom associated with this approach must be seen to be a social loss in itself. The importance of reproductive freedom has been persuasively emphasized by women's groups throughout the world.[31]

The loss of freedom is often dismissed on the grounds that because of cultural differences, authoritarian policies that would not be tolerated in the West are acceptable to Asians. While we often hear references to "despotic" Oriental traditions, such arguments are no more convincing than a claim that compulsion in the West is justified by the traditions of the Spanish Inquisition or of the Nazi concentration camps. Frequent references are also made to the emphasis on discipline in the "Confucian tradition"; but that is not the only tradition in the "East," nor is it easy to assess the implications of that tradition for modern Asia (even if we were able to show that discipline is more important for Confucius than it is for, say, Plato or Saint Augustine).

Only a democratic expression of opinion could reveal whether citizens would find a compulsory system acceptable. While such a test has not occurred in China, one did in fact take place in India during "the emergency period" in the 1970s, when Indira Gandhi's government imposed compulsory birth control and suspended various legal freedoms. In the general elections that followed, the politicians favoring the policy of coercion were overwhelmingly defeated. Furthermore, family planning experts in India have observed how the briefly applied programs of compulsory sterilization tended to discredit voluntary birth control programs generally, since people became deeply suspicious of the entire movement to control fertility.

Second, apart from the fundamental issue of whether people are willing to accept compulsory birth control, its specific consequences must also be considered. Insofar as coercion is effective, it works by making people do things they would not freely do. The social consequences of such compulsion, including the ways in which an unwilling population tends to react when it is coerced, can be appalling. For example, the demands of a "one-child family" can lead to the neglect – or worse – of a second child, thereby increasing the infant mortality rate. Moreover, in a country with a strong preference for male children – a preference shared by China and many other countries in Asia and North Africa – a policy of allowing only one child per family can easily lead to the fatal neglect of a female child. There is much evidence that this is fairly widespread in China, with very adverse effects on infant mortality rates. There are reports that female children have been severely neglected as well as suggestions that female infanticide occurs with considerable frequency. Such consequences are hard to tolerate morally, and perhaps politically also, in the long run.

Third, what is also not clear is exactly how much additional reduction in the birth rate has been achieved through these coercive methods. Many of China's longstanding social and economic programs have been valuable in reducing fertility, including those that have expanded education for women as well as men, made health care more generally available, provided more job opportunities for women, and stimulated rapid economic growth. These factors would themselves have reduced the birth rates, and it is not clear how much "extra lowering" of fertility rates has been achieved in China through compulsion.

For example, we can determine whether many of the countries that match (or outmatch) China in life expectancy, female literacy rates, and female participation in the labor force actually have a higher fertility rate than China. Of all the countries in the world for which data are given in the *World Development Report 1994*, there are only three such countries: Jamaica (2.7), Thailand (2.2), and Sweden (2.1) – and the fertility rates of two of these are close to China's (2.0). Thus the additional contribution of coercion to reducing fertility in China is by no means clear, since compulsion was superimposed on a society that was already reducing its birth rate and in which education and jobs outside the home were available to large numbers of women. In some regions of China the compulsory program needed little enforcement, whereas in other – more backward – regions, it had to be applied with much severity, with terrible consequences in infant mortality and discrimination against female children. While China may get too much credit for its authoritarian measures, it gets far too little credit for the other, more collaborative and participatory, policies it has followed, which have themselves helped to cut down the birth rate.

China and India

A useful contrast can be drawn between China and India, the two most populous countries in the world. If we look only at the national averages, it is easy to see that China with its low fertility rate of 2.0 has achieved much more than India has with its average fertility rate of 3.6. To what extent this contrast can be attributed to the effectiveness of the coercive policies used in China is not clear, since we would expect the fertility rate to be much lower in China in view of its higher percentage of female literacy (almost twice as high), higher life expectancy (almost ten years more), larger female involvement (by three quarters) in the labor force, and so on. But India is a country of great diversity, whose different states have very unequal achievements in literacy, health care, and economic and social development. Most states in India are far behind the Chinese provinces in educational achievement (with the exception of Tibet, which has the lowest literacy rate of any Chinese or Indian state), and the same applies to other factors that affect fertility. However, the state of Kerala in southern India provides an interesting comparison

with China, since it too has high levels of basic education, health care, and so on. Kerala is a state within a country, but with its 29 million people, it is larger than most countries in the world (including Canada). Kerala's birth rate of 18 per 1,000 is actually lower than China's 19 per 1,000, and its fertility rate is 1.8 for 1991, compared with China's 2.0 for 1992. These low rates have been achieved without any state coercion.[32]

The roots of Kerala's success are to be found in the kinds of social progress Condorcet hoped for, including among others, a high female literacy rate (86 percent, which is substantially higher than China's 68 percent). The rural literacy rate is in fact higher in Kerala – for women as well as men – than in every single province in China. Male and female life expectancies at birth in China are respectively 67 and 71 years; the provisional 1991 figures for men and women in Kerala are 71 and 74 years. Women have been active in Kerala's economic and political life for a long time. A high proportion do skilled and semi-skilled work and a large number have taken part in educational movements.[33] It is perhaps of symbolic importance that the first public pronouncement of the need for widespread elementary education in any part of India was made in 1817 by Rani Gouri Parvathi Bai, the young queen of the princely state of Travancore, which makes up a substantial part of modern Kerala. For a long time public discussions in Kerala have centered on women's rights and the undesirability of couples marrying when very young.

This political process has been voluntary and collaborative, rather than coercive, and the adverse reactions that have been observed in China, such as infant mortality, have not occurred in Kerala. Kerala's low fertility rate has been achieved along with an infant mortality rate of 16.5 per 1,000 live births (17 for boys and 16 for girls), compared with China's 31 (28 for boys and 33 for girls). And as a result of greater gender equality in Kerala, women have not suffered from higher mortality rates than men in Kerala, as they have in the rest of India and in China. Even the ratio of females to males in the total population in Kerala (above 1.03) is quite close to that of the current ratios in Europe and America (reflecting the usual pattern of lower female mortality whenever women and men receive similar care). By contrast, the average female to male ratio in China is 0.94 and in India as a whole 0.93.[34] Anyone drawn to the Chinese experience of compulsory birth control must take note of these facts.

Table 60.2   Fertility Rates in China, Kerala, and Tamil Nadu

	1979	1991
China	2.8	2.0
Kerala	3.0	1.8
Tamil Nadu	3.5	2.2

Sources. For China, Xiche Peng, *Demographic Transition in China* (Oxford University Press, 1991). Li Chengrui. *A Study of China's Population* (Beijing; Foreign Language Press, 1992), and *World Development Report 1993*. For India, *Sample Registration System 1979–80* (New Delhi: Ministry of Home Affairs, 1982) and *Sample Registration System: Fertility and Mortality Indicators 1991* (New Delhi: Ministry of Home Affairs, 1993).

The temptation to use the "override" approach arises at least partly from impatience with the allegedly slow process of fertility reduction through collaborative, rather than coercive, attempts. Yet Kerala's birth rate has fallen from 44 per 1,000 in the 1950s to 18 by 1991 – not a sluggish decline. Nor is Kerala unique in this respect. Other societies, such as those of Sri Lanka, South Korea, and Thailand, which have relied on expanding education and reducing mortality rates – instead of on coercion – have also achieved sharp declines in fertility and birth rates.

It is also interesting to compare the time required for reducing fertility in China with that in the two states in India, Kerala and Tamil Nadu, which have done most to encourage voluntary and collaborative reduction in birth rates (even though Tamil Nadu is well behind Kerala in each respect).[35] Table 60.2 shows the fertility rates both in 1979, when the one-child policy and related programs were introduced in China, and in 1991. Despite China's one-child policy and other coercive measures, its fertility rate seems to have fallen much less sharply than those of Kerala and Tamil Nadu. The "override" view is very hard to defend on the basis of the Chinese experience, the only systematic and sustained attempt to impose such a policy that has so far been made.

Family Planning

Even those who do not advocate legal or economic coercion sometimes suggest a variant of the "override" approach – the view, which has been getting increasing support, that the highest priority should be given simply to family planning, even if this means diverting resources from education and health care as well as other activities associated with development. We often hear claims that enormous declines in birth rates have been accomplished through making family planning services available, without waiting for improvements in education and health care.

The experience of Bangladesh is sometimes cited as an example of such success. Indeed, even though the female literacy rate in Bangladesh is only around 22 percent and life expectancy at birth no higher than 55 years, fertility rates have been substantially reduced there through the greater availability of family planning services, including counseling.[36] We have to examine carefully what lessons can, in fact, be drawn from this evidence.

First, it is certainly significant that Bangladesh has been able to cut its fertility rate from 7.0 to 4.5 during the short period between 1975 and 1990, an achievement that discredits the view that people will not voluntarily embrace family planning in the poorest countries. But we have to ask further whether family planning efforts may themselves be sufficient to make fertility come down to really low levels, without providing for female education and the other features of a fuller collaborative approach. The fertility rate of 4.5 in Bangladesh is still quite high – considerably higher than even India's average rate of 3.6. To begin stabilizing the population, the fertility rates would have to come down closer to the "replacement level" of 2.0, as has happened in Kerala and Tamil Nadu, and in many other places outside the Indian subcontinent. Female education and the other social developments connected with lowering the birth rate would still be much needed.

Contrasts between the records of Indian states offer some substantial lessons here. While Kerala, and to a smaller extent Tamil Nadu, have surged ahead in achieving radically reduced fertility rates, other states in India in the so-called "northern heartland" (such as Uttar Pradesh, Bihar, Madhya Pradesh, and Rajasthan), have very low levels of education, especially female education, and of general health care (often combined with pressure on the poor to accept birth control measures, including sterilization, as a qualifying condition for medical attention and other public services). These states all have high fertility rates – between 4.4 and 5.1. The regional contrasts within India strongly argue for the collaborative approach, including active and educated participation of women.

The threat of an impending population crisis tempts many international observers to suggest that priority be given to family planning arrangements in the third world countries over other commitments such as education and health care, a redirection of public efforts that is often recommended by policy-makers and at international conferences. Not only will this shift have negative effects on people's well-being and reduce their freedoms, it can also be self-defeating if the goal is to stabilize population.

The appeal of such slogans as "family planning first" rests partly on misconceptions about what is needed to reduce fertility rates, but also on mistaken beliefs about the excessive costs of social development, including education and health care. As has been discussed, both these activities are highly labor intensive, and thus relatively inexpensive even in very poor economies. In fact, Kerala, India's star performer in expanding education and reducing both death rates and birth rates, is among the poorer Indian states. Its domestically produced income is quite low – lower indeed in per capita terms than even the Indian average – even if this is somewhat deceptive, for the greatest expansion of Kerala's earnings derives from citizens who work outside the state. Kerala's ability to finance adequately both educational expansion and health coverage depends on both activities being labor-intensive; they can be made available even in a low-income economy when there is the political will to use them. Despite its economic backwardness, an issue which Kerala will undoubtedly have to address before long (perhaps by reducing bureaucratic controls over agriculture and industry, which have stagnated), its level of social development has been remarkable, and that has turned out to be crucial in reducing fertility rates. Kerala's fertility rate of 1.8 not only compares well with China's 2.0, but also with the US's and Sweden's 2.1, Canada's 1.9, and Britain's and France's 1.8.

The population problem is serious, certainly, but neither because of "the proportion between the natural increase of population and food" nor because of some impending apocalypse. There are reasons for worry about the long-term effects of population growth on the environment, and there are strong reasons for concern about the adverse effects of high birth rates on the quality of life, especially of women. With greater opportunities for education (especially female education), reduction of mortality rates (especially of children), improvement in economic security (especially in old age), and greater participation of women in employment and in political action, fast reductions in birth rates can be expected to result through the decisions and actions of those whose lives depend on them.

This is happening right now in many parts of the world, and the result has been a considerable slowing down of world population growth. The best way of dealing with the population problem is to help to spread these processes elsewhere. In contrast, the emergency mentality based on false beliefs in imminent cataclysms leads to breathless responses that are deeply counterproductive, preventing the development of rational and sustainable family planning. Coercive policies of forced birth control involve terrible social sacrifices, and there is little evidence that they are more effective in reducing birth rates than serious programs of collaborative action.

Notes

1   This paper draws on my lecture arranged by the "Eminent Citizens Committee for Cairo '94" at the United Nations in New York on April 18, 1994, and also on research supported by the National Science Foundation.

2   Paul Ehrlich, *The Population Bomb* (Ballantine, 1968). More recently Paul Ehrlich and Anne H. Ehrlich have written *The Population Explosion* (Simon and Schuster, 1990).

3   Garrett Hardin, *Living within Limits* (Oxford University Press, 1993).

4   Thomas Robert Malthus, *Essay on the Principle of Population As It Affects the Future Improvement of Society with Remarks on the Speculation of Mr. Godwin, M. Condorcet, and Other Writers* (London: J. Johnson, 1798), Chapter 8; in the Penguin classics edition, *An Essay on the Principle of Population* (1982), p. 123.

5   See Simon Kuznets, *Modern Economic Growth* (Yale University Press, 1966).

6   Note by the Secretary-General of the United Nations to the Preparatory Committee for the International Conference on Population and Development, Third Session, A/Conf.171/PC/5, February 18, 1994, p. 30.

7   Philip Morris Hauser's estimates are presented in the National Academy of Sciences publication *Rapid Population Growth: Consequences and Policy Implications*, Vol. 1 (Johns Hopkins University Press, 1971). See also Simon Kuznets, *Modern Economic Growth*, Chapter 2.

8   For an important collection of papers on these and related issues see Sir Francis Graham-Smith, FRS, editor, *Population – The Complex Reality: A Report of the Population Summit of the World's Scientific Academies,*

issued by the Royal Society and published in the US by North American Press, Golden, Colorado. See also D. Gale Johnson and Ronald D. Lee, editors, *Population Growth and Economic Development, Issues and Evidence* (University of Wisconsin Press, 1987).

9   Garrett Hardin, *Living within Limits*, p. 274.

10   Paul Kennedy, who has discussed important problems in the distinctly "social" aspects of population growth, has pointed out that this debate "has, in one form or another, been with us since then," and "it is even more pertinent today than when Malthus composed his *Essay*," in *Preparing for the Twenty-first Century* (Random House, 1993), pp. 5–6.

11   On the importance of "enlightenment" traditions in Condorcet's thinking, see Emma Rothschild, "Condorcet and the Conflict of Values," forthcoming in *The Historical Journal*.

12   Marie Jean Antoine Nicholas de Caritat Marquis de Condorcet's *Esquisse d'un Tableau Historique des Progrès de l'Esprit Humain*, Xe Epoque (1795). English translation by June Barraclough, *Sketch for a Historical Picture of the Progress of the Human Mind*, with an introduction by Stuart Hampshire (Weidenfeld and Nicolson, 1955), pp. 187–92.

13   T. R. Malthus, *A Summary View of the Principle of Population* (London: John Murray, 1830); in the Penguin classics edition (1982), p. 243; italics added.

14   On practical policies, including criticism of poverty relief and charitable hospitals, advocated for Britain by Malthus and his followers, see William St. Clair, *The Godwins and the Shelleys: A Biography of a Family* (Norton, 1989).

15   Malthus, *Essay on the Principle of Population*, Chapter 17; in the Penguin classics edition, *An Essay on the Principle of Population*, pp. 198–9. Malthus showed some signs of weakening in this belief as he grew older.

16   Gerard Piel, *Only One World: Our Own to Make and to Keep* (Freeman, 1992).

17   For discussions of these empirical connections, see R. A. Easterlin, editor, *Population and Economic Change in Developing Countries* (University of Chicago Press, 1980); T. P. Schultz, *Economics of Population* (Addison-Wesley, 1981); J. C. Caldwell, *Theory of Fertility Decline* (Academic Press, 1982); E. King and M. A. Hill, editors, *Women's Education in Developing Countries* (Johns Hopkins University Press, 1992); Nancy Birdsall, "Economic Approaches to Population Growth" in *The Handbook of Development Economics*, edited by H. B. Chenery and T. N. Srinivasan (Amsterdam: North Holland, 1988); Robert Cassen, et al., *Population and Development: Old Debates, New Conclusions* (New Brunswick: Overseas Development Council/Transaction Publishers, 1994).

18   World Bank, *World Development Report 1994* (Oxford University Press, 1994), Table 25, pp. 210–11.

19   World Bank, *World Development Report 1994*, Table 2.

20   These issues are discussed in my joint book with Jean Drèze, *Hunger and Public Action* (Oxford University Press, 1989), and the three volumes edited by us, *The Political Economy of Hunger* (Oxford University Press, 1990), and also in my paper "Economic Regress: Concepts and Features," *Proceedings of the World Bank Annual Conference on Development Economics 1993* (World Bank, 1994).

21   This is confirmed by, among other statistics, the food production figures regularly presented by the United Nations Food and Agricultural Organization (see the *FAO Quarterly Bulletin of Statistics*, and also the *FAO Monthly Bulletins*).

22   For a more detailed picture and references to data sources, see my "Population and Reasoned Agency: Food, Fertility and Economic Development," in *Population, Economic Development, and the Environment*, edited by Kerstin Lindahl-Kiessling and Hans Landberg (Oxford University Press, 1994); see also the other contributions in this volume. The data presented here have been slightly updated from later publications of the FAO.

23   On this see my *Poverty and Famines* (Oxford University Press, 1981).

24   See UNCTAD VIII, Analytical Report by the UNCTAD Secretariat to the Conference (United Nations, 1992), Table V-S, p. 235. The period covered is between 1979–81 to 1988–90. These figures and related ones are discussed in greater detail in my paper "Population and Reasoned Agency," cited earlier.

25   World Bank, *Price Prospects for Major Primary Commodities*, Vol. II (World Bank, March 1993), Annex Tables 6, 12, and 18.

26   Condorcet, *Esquisse d'un Tableau Historique des Progrès de l'Esprit Humain*; in the 1968 reprint, p. 187.

27   The importance of "local" environmental issues is stressed and particularly explored by Partha Dasgupta in *An Inquiry into Well-Being and Destitution* (Oxford University Press, 1993).

28   In a forthcoming monograph by Jean Drèze and myself tentatively called "India: Economic Development and Social Opportunities," we discuss the importance of women's political agency in rectifying some of the more serious lapses in Indian economic and social performance – not just pertaining to the deprivation of women themselves.

29   See Jean Drèze and Amartya Sen, *Hunger and Public Action* (Oxford University Press, 1989), which also investigates the remarkable success of some poor countries in providing widespread educational and health services.

30   World Bank, *World Development Report 1994*, p. 212; and *Sample Registration System: Fertility and Mortality*

Indicators 1991 (New Delhi: Ministry of Home Affairs, 1993).

31 See the discussions, and the literature cited, in Gita Sen, Adrienne German, and Lincoln Chen, editors, *Population Policies Reconsidered: Health, Empowerment, and Rights* (Harvard Center for Population and Development Studies/International Women's Health Coalition, 1994).

32 On the actual processes involved, see T. N. Krishnan, "Demographic Transition in Kerala: Facts and Factors," in *Economic and Political Weekly*, Vol. 11 (1976), and P. N. Mari Bhat and S. I. Rajan, "Demographic Transition in Kerala Revisited," in *Economic and Political Weekly*, Vol. 25(1990).

33 See, for example, Robin Jeffrey, "Culture and Governments: How Women Made Kerala Literate," in *Pacific Affairs*, Vol. 60 (1987).

34 On this see my "More Than 100 Million Women Are Missing," *New York Review of Books*, December 20, 1990; Ansley J. Coale, "Excess Female Mortality and the Balance of the Sexes: An Estimate of the Number of 'Missing Females'," *Population and Development Review*, No. 17 (1991); Amartya Sen, "Missing Women," *British Medical Journal*, No. 304 (March 1992); Stephan Klasen, "'Missing Women' Reconsidered," *World Development*, forthcoming.

35 Tamil Nadu has benefited from an active and efficient voluntary program of family planning, but these efforts have been helped by favorable social conditions as well, such as a high literacy rate (the second highest among the sixteen major states), a high rate of female participation in work outside the home (the third highest), a relatively low infant mortality rate (the third lowest), and a traditionally higher age of marriage. See also T.V. Antony, "The Family Planning Programme – Lessons from Tamil Nadu's Experience," *Indian Journal of Social Science*, Vol. 5 (1992).

36 World Bank and Population Reference Bureau, *Success in a Challenging Environment: Fertility Decline in Bangladesh* (World Bank, 1993).

61   A Special Moment in History

Bill McKibben

We may live in the strangest, most thoroughly different moment since human beings took up farming, 10,000 years ago, and time more or less commenced. Since then time has flowed in one direction – toward *more*, which we have taken to be progress. At first the momentum was gradual, almost imperceptible, checked by wars and the Dark Ages and plagues and taboos; but in recent centuries it has accelerated, the curve of every graph steepening like the Himalayas rising from the Asian steppe. We have climbed quite high. Of course, fifty years ago one could have said the same thing, and fifty years before that, and fifty years before *that*. But in each case it would have been premature. We've increased the population fourfold in that 150 years: the amount of food we grow has gone up faster still; the size of our economy has quite simply exploded.

But now – now may be the special time. So special that in the Western world we might each of us consider, among many other things, having only one child – that is, reproducing at a rate as low as that at which human beings have ever voluntarily reproduced. Is this really necessary? Are we finally running up against some limits?

To try to answer this question, we need to ask another: *How many of us will there be in the near future?* Here is a piece of news that may alter the way we see the planet – an indication that we live at a special moment. At least at first blush the news is hopeful. *New demographic evidence shows that it is at least possible that a child born today will live long enough to see the peak of human population.*

Around the world people are choosing to have fewer and fewer children – not just in China, where the government forces it on them, but in almost every nation outside the poorest parts of Africa. Population growth rates are lower than they have been at any time since the Second World War. In the past three decades the average woman in the developing world, excluding China, has gone from bearing six children to bearing four. Even in Bangladesh the average has fallen from six to fewer than four;

From *The Atlantic Monthly* (1998): 55–60, 72–3, 76–8. © 1998 by Bill McKibben.

even in the mullahs' Iran it has dropped by four children. If this keeps up, the population of the world will not quite double again; United Nations analysts offer as their mid-range projection that it will top out at 10 to 11 billion, up from just under six billion at the moment. The world is still growing, at nearly a record pace – we add a New York City every month, almost a Mexico every year, almost an India every decade. But the rate of growth is slowing; it is no longer "exponential," "unstoppable," "inexorable," "unchecked," "cancerous." If current trends hold, the world's population will all but stop growing before the twenty-first century is out.

And that will be none too soon. There is no way we could keep going as we have been. The *increase* in human population in the 1990s has exceeded the *total* population in 1600. The population has grown more since 1950 than it did during the previous four million years. The reasons for our recent rapid growth are pretty clear. Although the Industrial Revolution speeded historical growth rates considerably, it was really the public-health revolution, and its spread to the Third World at the end of the Second World War, that set us galloping. Vaccines and antibiotics came all at once, and right behind came population. In Sri Lanka in the late 1940s life expectancy was rising at least a year every twelve months. How much difference did this make? Consider the United States: if people died throughout this century at the same rate as they did at its beginning, America's population would be 140 million, not 270 million.

If it is relatively easy to explain why populations grew so fast after the Second World War, it is much harder to explain why the growth is now slowing. Experts confidently supply answers, some of them contradictory: "Development is the best contraceptive" – or education, or the empowerment of women, or hard times that force families to postpone having children. For each example there is a counterexample. Ninety-seven percent of women in the Arab sheikhdom of Oman know about contraception, and yet they average more than six children apiece. Turks have used contraception at about the same rate as the Japanese, but their birth rate is twice as high. And so on. It is not AIDS that will slow population growth, except in a few African countries. It is not horrors like the civil war in Rwanda, which claimed half a million lives – a loss the planet can make up for in two days. All that matters is how often individual men and women decide that they want to reproduce.

Will the drop continue? It had better. UN mid-range projections assume that women in the developing world will soon average two children apiece – the rate at which population growth stabilizes. If fertility remained at current levels, the population would reach the absurd figure of 296 billion in just 150 years. Even if it dropped to 2.5 children per woman and then stopped falling, the population would still reach 28 billion.

But let's trust that this time the demographers have got it right. Let's trust that we have rounded the turn and we're in the home stretch. Let's trust that the planet's population really will double only one more time. Even so, this is a case of good news, bad news. The good news is that we won't grow forever. The bad news is that there are six billion of us already, a number the world strains to support. One more near-doubling – four or five billion more people – will nearly double that strain. Will these be the five billion straws that break the camel's back?

Big Questions

We've answered the question *How many of us will there be?* But to figure out how near we are to any limits, we need to ask something else: *How big are we?* This is not so simple. Not only do we vary greatly in how much food and energy and water and minerals we consume, but each of us varies over time. William Catton, who was a sociologist at Washington State University before his retirement, once tried to calculate the amount of energy human beings use each day. In hunter-gatherer times it was about 2,500 calories, all of it food. That is the daily energy intake of a common dolphin. A modern human being uses 31,000 calories a day, most of it in the form of fossil fuel. That is the intake of a pilot whale. And the average American uses six times that – as much as a sperm whale. We have become, in other words, different from the people we used to be. Not kinder or unkinder, not deeper or stupider – our natures seem to have changed little since Homer. We've just gotten bigger. We appear to be the same species, with stomachs of the same size, but we aren't. It's as if each of us were trailing a big Macy's-parade balloon around, feeding it constantly.

So it doesn't do much good to stare idly out the window of your 737 as you fly from New York to Los Angeles and see that there's *plenty* of empty space down there. Sure enough, you could crowd lots more people into the nation or onto the planet. The entire world population could fit into Texas, and each person could have an area equal to the floor space of a typical US home. If people were willing to stand, everyone on earth could fit comfortably into half of Rhode Island. Holland is crowded and is doing just fine.

But this ignores the balloons above our heads, our hungry shadow selves, our sperm-whale appetites. As soon as we started farming, we started setting aside extra land to support ourselves. Now each of us needs not only a little plot of cropland and a little pasture for the meat we eat but also a little forest for timber and paper, a little mine, a little oil well. Giants have big feet. Some scientists in Vancouver tried to calculate one such "footprint" and found that although 1.7 million people lived on a million acres surrounding their city, those people required 21.5 million acres of land to support them – wheat fields in Alberta, oil fields in Saudi Arabia, tomato fields in California. People in Manhattan are as dependent on faraway resources as people on the Mir space station.

Those balloons above our heads can shrink or grow, depending on how we choose to live. All over the earth people who were once tiny are suddenly growing like Alice when she ate the cake. In China per capita income has doubled since the early 1980s. People there, though still Lilliputian in comparison with us, are twice their former size. They eat much higher on the food chain, understandably, than they used to: China slaughters more pigs than any other nation, and it takes four pounds of grain to produce one pound of pork. When, a decade ago, the United Nations examined sustainable development, it issued a report saying that the economies of the developing countries needed to be five to ten times as large to move poor people to an acceptable standard of living – with all that this would mean in terms of demands on oil wells and forests.

That sounds almost impossible. For the moment, though, let's not pass judgment. We're still just doing math. There are going to be lots of us. We're going to be big. But lots of us in relation to what? Big in relation to what? It could be that compared with the world we inhabit, we're still scarce and small. Or not. So now we need to consider a third question: *How big is the earth?*

Any state wildlife biologist can tell you how many deer a given area can support – how much browse there is for the deer to eat before they begin to suppress the reproduction of trees, before they begin to starve in the winter. He can calculate how many wolves a given area can support too, in part by counting the number of deer. And so on, up and down the food chain. It's not an exact science, but it comes pretty close – at least compared with figuring out the carrying capacity of the earth for human beings, which is an art so dark that anyone with any sense stays away from it.

Consider the difficulties. Human beings, unlike deer, can eat almost anything and live at almost any level they choose. Hunter-gatherers used 2,500 calories of energy a day, whereas modern Americans use seventy-five times that. Human beings, unlike deer, can import what they need from thousands of miles away. And human beings, unlike deer, can figure out new ways to do old things. If, like deer, we needed to browse on conifers to survive, we could cross-breed lush new strains, chop down competing trees, irrigate forests, spray a thousand chemicals, freeze or dry the tender buds at the peak of harvest, genetically engineer new strains – and advertise the merits of maple buds until everyone was ready to switch. The variables are so great that professional demographers rarely even bother trying to figure out carrying capacity. The demographer Joel Cohen, in his potent book *How Many People Can the Earth Support?* (1995), reports that at two recent meetings of the Population Association of America exactly none of the more than 200 symposia dealt with carrying capacity.

But the difficulty hasn't stopped other thinkers. This is, after all, as big a question as the world offers. Plato, Euripides, and Polybius all worried that we would run out of food if the population kept growing; for centuries a steady stream of economists, environmentalists, and zealots and cranks of all sorts have made it their business to issue estimates either dire or benign. The most famous, of course, came from the Reverend Thomas Malthus. Writing in 1798, he proposed that the growth of population, being "geometric," would soon outstrip the supply of food. Though he changed his mind and rewrote his famous essay, it's the original version that people have remembered – and lambasted – ever since. Few other writers have found critics in as many corners. Not only have conservatives made Malthus's name a byword for ludicrous alarmism, but Karl Marx called his essay "a libel on the human race," Friedrich Engels believed that "we are forever secure from the fear of overpopulation," and even Mao Zedong attacked Malthus by name, adding, "Of all things in the world people are the most precious."

Each new generation of Malthusians has made new predictions that the end was near, and has been proved wrong. The late 1960s saw an upsurge of Malthusian panic. In 1967 William and Paul Paddock published a book called *Famine – 1975!,* which contained a triage list: "Egypt: Can't-be-saved. . . . Tunisia: Should Receive Food. . . . India: Can't-be-saved." Almost simultaneously Paul Ehrlich wrote, in his best-selling *The Population Bomb* (1968), "The battle to feed all of humanity is over. In the 1970s, the world will undergo famines – hundreds of millions of people will starve to death." It all seemed so certain, so firmly in keeping with a world soon to be darkened by the first oil crisis.

But that's not how it worked out. India fed herself. The United States still ships surplus grain around the world. As the astute Harvard social scientist Amartya Sen points out, "Not only is food generally much cheaper to buy today, in constant dollars, than it was in Malthus's time, but it also has become cheaper during recent decades." So far, in other words, the world has more or less supported us. Too many people starve (60 percent of children in South Asia are stunted by malnutrition), but both the total number and the percentage have dropped in recent decades, thanks mainly to the successes of the Green Revolution. Food production has tripled since the Second World War, outpacing even population growth. We may be giants, but we are clever giants.

So Malthus was wrong. Over and over again he was wrong. No other prophet has ever been proved wrong so many times. At the moment, his stock is especially low. One group of technological optimists now believes that people will continue to improve their standard of living precisely *because* they increase their numbers. This group's intellectual fountainhead is a brilliant Danish economist named Ester Boserup – a sort of anti-Malthus, who in 1965 argued that the gloomy cleric had it backward. The more people, Boserup said, the more progress. Take agriculture as an example: the first farmers, she pointed out, were slash-and-burn cultivators, who might farm a plot for a year or two and then move on, not returning for maybe two decades. As the population grew, however, they had to return more frequently to the same plot. That meant problems: compacted, depleted, weedy soils. But those new problems meant new solutions: hoes, manure, compost, crop rotation, irrigation. Even in this century, Boserup said, necessity-induced invention has meant that "intensive systems of agriculture replaced extensive systems," accelerating the rate of food production.

Boserup's closely argued examples have inspired a less cautious group of popularizers, who point out that standards of living have risen all over the world even as population has grown. The most important benefit, in fact, that population growth bestows on an economy is to increase the stock of useful knowledge, insisted Julian Simon, the best known of the so-called cornucopians, who died earlier this year. We might run out of copper, but who cares? The mere fact of shortage will lead someone to invent a substitute. "The main fuel to speed our progress is our stock of knowledge, and the brake is our lack of imagination," Simon wrote. "The ultimate resource is people – skilled, spirited, and hopeful people who will exert their wills and imaginations for their own benefit, and so, inevitably, for the benefit of us all."

Simon and his ilk owe their success to this: they have been right so far. The world has behaved as they predicted. India hasn't starved. Food is cheap. But Malthus never goes away. The idea that we might grow too big can be disproved only for the moment – never for good. We might always be on the threshold of a special time, when the mechanisms described by Boserup and Simon stop working. It is true that Malthus was wrong when the population doubled from 750 million to 1.5 billion. It is true that Malthus was wrong when the population doubled from 1.5 billion to three billion. It is true that Malthus was wrong when the population doubled from three billion to six billion. Will Malthus still be wrong fifty years from now?

[. . .]

When we think about overpopulation, we usually think first of the developing world, because that's where 90 percent of new human beings will be added during this final doubling. In *The Population Bomb*, Paul Ehrlich wrote that he hadn't understood the issue emotionally until he traveled to New Delhi, where he climbed into an ancient taxi, which was hopping with fleas, for the trip to his hotel. "As we crawled through the city, we entered a crowded slum area. . . . the streets seemed alive with people. People eating, people washing, people sleeping. People visiting, arguing, and screaming. . . . People, people, people, people."

We fool ourselves when we think of Third World population growth as producing an imbalance, as Amartya Sen points out. The white world simply went through its population boom a century earlier (when Dickens was writing similar descriptions of London). If UN calculations are correct and Asians and Africans will make up just under 80 percent of humanity by 2050, they will simply have returned, in Sen's words, "to being proportionately almost exactly as numerous as they were before the European industrial revolution."

And of course Asians and Africans, and Latin Americans, are much "smaller" human beings: the balloons that float above their heads are tiny in comparison with ours. Everyone has heard the statistics time and again, usually as part of an attempt to induce guilt. But hear them one more time, with an open mind, and try to think strategically about how we will stave off the dangers to this planet. Pretend it's not a moral problem, just a mathematical one.

- An American uses seventy times as much energy as a Bangladeshi, fifty times as much as a Malagasi, twenty times as much as a Costa Rican.
- Since we live longer, the effect of each of us is further multiplied. In a year an American uses 300 times as much energy as a Malian; over a lifetime he will use 500 times as much.
- Even if all such effects as the clearing of forests and the burning of grasslands are factored in and attributed to poor people, those who live in the poor world are typically responsible for the annual release of a tenth of a ton of carbon each, whereas the average is 3.5 tons for residents of the "consumer" nations of Western Europe, North America, and Japan. The richest tenth of Americans – the people most likely to be reading this magazine – annually emit eleven tons of carbon apiece.
- During the next decade India and China will each add to the planet about ten times as many people as the United States will – but the stress on the natural world caused by new Americans may exceed that from new Indians and Chinese combined. The 57.5 million Northerners added to our population during this decade will add more greenhouse gases to the atmosphere than the roughly 900 million added Southerners.

[. . .]

So if it is we in the rich world, at least as much as they in the poor world, who need to bring this alteration of the earth under control, the question becomes how. Many people who are sure that con-trolling population is the answer overseas are equally sure that the answer is different here. If those people are politicians and engineers, they're probably in favor of our living more efficiently – of designing new cars that go much farther on a gallon of gas, or that don't use gas at all. If they're vegetarians, they probably support living more simply – riding bikes or buses instead of driving cars.

Both groups are utterly correct. I've spent much of my career writing about the need for cleverer technologies and humbler aspirations. Environmental damage can be expressed as the product of Population × Affluence × Technology. Surely the easiest solution would be to live more simply and more efficiently, and not worry too much about the number of people.

But I've come to believe that those changes in technology and in lifestyle are not going to occur easily and speedily. They'll be begun but not finished in the few decades that really matter. Remember that the pollution we're talking about is not precisely pollution but rather the inevitable result when things go the way we think they should: new filters on exhaust pipes won't do anything about that CO_2. We're stuck with making real changes in how we live. We're stuck with dramatically reducing the amount of fossil fuel we use. And since modern Westerners are practically machines for burning fossil fuel, since virtually everything we do involves burning coal and gas and oil, since we're wedded to petroleum, it's going to be a messy breakup.

[. . .]

Changing the ways in which we live has to be a fundamental part of dealing with the new environmental crises, if only because it is impossible to imagine a world of 10 billion people consuming at our level. But as we calculate what must happen over the next few decades to stanch the flow of CO_2, we shouldn't expect that a conversion to simpler ways of life will by itself do the trick. One would think offhand that compared with changing the number of children we bear, changing consumption patterns would be a breeze. Fertility, after all, seems biological – hard-wired into us in deep Darwinian ways. But I would guess that it is easier to change fertility than lifestyle.

Perhaps our salvation lies in the other part of the equation – in the new technologies and efficiencies that could make even our wasteful lives benign, and table the issue of our population. We are, for instance, converting our economy from its old industrial base to a new model based on service and information. Surely that should save some energy, should reduce the clouds of carbon dioxide. Writing software seems no more likely to damage the atmosphere than writing poetry.

Forget for a moment the hardware requirements of that new economy – for instance, the production of a six-inch silicon wafer may require nearly 3,000 gallons of water. But do keep in mind that a hospital or an insurance company or a basketball team requires a substantial physical base. Even the highest-tech office is built with steel and cement, pipes and wires. People working in services will buy all sorts of things – more software, sure, but also more sport utility vehicles. As the Department of Energy economist Arthur Rypinski says, "The information age has arrived, but even so people still get hot in the summer and cold in the winter. And even in the information age it tends to get dark at night."

[. . .]

It's not just that we use more energy. There are also more of us all the time, even in the United States. If the population is growing by about one percent a year, then we have to keep increasing our technological efficiency by that much each year – and hold steady our standard of living – just to run in place. The President's Council on Sustainable Development, in a little-read report issued in the winter of 1996, concluded that "efficiency in the use of all resources would have to increase by more than fifty percent over the next four or five decades just to keep pace with population growth." Three million new Americans annually means many more cars, houses, refrigerators. Even if everyone consumes only what he consumed the year before, each year's tally of births and immigrants will swell American consumption by one percent.

We demand that engineers and scientists swim against that tide. And the tide will turn into a wave if the rest of the world tries to live as we do. It's true that the average resident of Shanghai or Bombay will not consume as lavishly as the typical San Diegan or Bostonian anytime soon, but he will make big gains, pumping that much more carbon dioxide into the atmosphere and requiring that we cut our own production even more sharply if we are to stabilize the world's climate.

The United Nations issued its omnibus report on sustainable development in 1987. An international panel chaired by Gro Harlem Brundtland, the Prime Minister of Norway, concluded that the economies of the developing countries needed to grow five to ten times as large as they were, in order to meet the needs of the poor world. And that growth won't be mainly in software. As Arthur Rypinski points out, "Where the economy is growing really rapidly, energy use is too." In Thailand, in Tijuana, in Taiwan, every 10 percent increase in economic output requires 10 percent more fuel. "In the Far East," Rypinski says, "the transition is from walking and bullocks to cars. People start out with electric lights and move on to lots of other stuff. Refrigerators are one of those things that are really popular everywhere. Practically no one, with the possible exception of people in the high Arctic, doesn't want a refrigerator. As people get wealthier, they tend to like space heating and cooling, depending on the climate."

In other words, in doing the math about how we're going to get out of this fix, we'd better factor in some unstoppable momentum from people on the rest of the planet who want the very basics of what we call a decent life. Even if we airlift solar collectors into China and India, as we should, those nations will still burn more and more coal and oil. "What you can do with energy conservation in those situations is sort of at the margin," Rypinski says. "They're not interested in fifteen-thousand-dollar clean cars versus five-thousand-dollar dirty cars. It was hard enough to get Americans to invest in efficiency; there's no feasible amount of largesse we can provide to the rest of the world to bring it about."

The numbers are so daunting that they're almost unimaginable. Say, just for argument's sake, that we decided to cut world fossil-fuel use by 60 percent – the amount that the UN panel says would stabilize world climate. And then say that we shared the remaining fossil fuel equally. Each human being would get to produce 1.69 metric tons of carbon dioxide annually – which would allow you to drive an average American car nine miles a day. By the time the population increased to 8.5 billion, in about 2025, you'd be down to six miles a day. If you carpooled, you'd have about three pounds of CO_2 left in your daily ration – enough to run a highly efficient refrigerator. Forget your computer, your TV, your stereo, your stove, your dishwasher, your water heater, your microwave, your water pump, your clock. Forget your light bulbs, compact fluorescent or not.

I'm not trying to say that conservation, efficiency, and new technology won't help. They will – but the help will be slow and expensive. The tremendous momentum of growth will work against it. Say that someone invented a new furnace tomorrow that used half as much oil as old furnaces. How many years would it be before a substantial number of American homes had the new device? And what if it cost more? And if oil stays cheaper per gallon than bottled water? Changing basic fuels – to hydrogen, say – would be even more expensive. It's not like running out of white wine and switching to red. Yes, we'll get new technologies. [. . .]

[But there] are no silver bullets to take care of a problem like this. Electric cars won't by themselves save us, though they would help. We simply won't live efficiently enough soon enough to solve the problem. Vegetarianism won't cure our ills, though it would help. We simply won't live simply enough soon enough to solve the problem.

Reducing the birth rate won't end all our troubles either. That, too, is no silver bullet. But it would help. There's no more practical decision than how many children to have. (And no more mystical decision, either.)

The bottom-line argument goes like this: The next fifty years are a special time. They will decide how strong and healthy the planet will be for centuries to come. Between now and 2050 we'll see the zenith, or very nearly, of human population. With luck we'll never see any greater production of carbon dioxide or toxic chemicals. We'll never see more species extinction or soil erosion. Greenpeace recently announced a campaign to phase out fossil fuels entirely by mid-century, which sounds utterly quixotic but could – if everything went just right – happen.

So it's the task of those of us alive right now to deal with this special phase, to squeeze us through these next fifty years. That's not fair – any more than it was fair that earlier generations had to deal with the Second World War or the Civil War or the Revolution or the Depression or slavery. It's just reality. We need in these fifty years to be working simultaneously on all parts of the equation – on our ways of life, on our technologies, and on our population.

As Gregg Easterbrook pointed out in his book *A Moment on the Earth* (1995), if the planet does manage to reduce its fertility, "the period in which human numbers threaten the biosphere on a general scale will turn out to have been much, much more brief" than periods of natural threats like the Ice Ages. True enough. But the period in question happens to be our time. That's what makes this moment special, and what makes this moment hard.

B Industrial Agriculture

62 Nature as the Measure for a Sustainable Agriculture
Wes Jackson

63 Putting Food Production in Context: Toward a Postmechanistic Agricultural Ethic
David R. Keller and E. Charles Brummer

62 Nature as the Measure for a Sustainable Agriculture

Wes Jackson

At the Land Institute in Salina, Kansas, we use the prairie as our standard or measure in attempting to wed ecology and agriculture. When Wendell Berry dedicated our new greenhouse in March 1988, he traced the literary and scientific history of our work at the institute. To set the stage for understanding the institute's place in the grand scheme of things, I shall review the history he provided (Berry, *What Are People For?*, 1990).

Berry first cited Job:

> . . . ask now the beasts, and they shall teach thee;
> and the fowls of the air, and they shall tell thee:
> Or speak to the earth, and it shall teach thee; and
> the fishes of the sea shall declare unto thee.

Later Berry mentioned other writings. At the beginning of *The Georgics* (36–29 BC), Virgil advised that

> . . . before we plow an unfamiliar patch
> It is well to be informed about the winds,
> About the variations in the sky,
> The native traits and habits of the place,
> What each locale permits, and what denies.

Toward the end of the 1500s, Edmund Spenser called nature "the equall mother" of all creatures, who "knittest each to each, as brother unto brother." Spenser also saw nature as the instructor of creatures and the ultimate earthly judge of their behavior. Shakespeare, in *As You Like It*, put the forest in the role of teacher and judge; Touchstone remarks, "You have said; but whether wisely or no, let the forest judge."

Milton had the lady in *Comus* describe nature in this way:

> She, good cateress,
> Means her provision only to the good
> That live according to her sober laws
> And holy dictate of spare Temperance.

And Alexander Pope, in his *Epistle to Burlington*, counseled gardeners to "let Nature never be forgot" and to "consult the Genius of the Place in all."

"After Pope," Berry (1990) has stated, "so far as I know, this theme departs from English poetry. The later poets were inclined to see nature and

From F. Herbert Borkmann and Stephen R. Kellert, eds., *Ecology, Economics, Ethics: The Broken Circle* (New Haven and London: Yale University Press, 1991), pp. 43–5, 51–8. © 1991 by Wes Jackson. Reprinted with permission from the author.

humankind as radically divided, and were no longer much interested in the issues of a *practical* harmony between the land and its human inhabitants. The romantic poets, who subscribed to the modern doctrine of the preeminence of the human mind, tended to look upon nature, not as anything they might ever have practical dealings with, but as a reservoir of symbols."

In my own region of the prairies, I think of Virgil's admonition: "Before we plow an unfamiliar patch/ It is well to be informed about the winds." What if the settlers and children of settlers who gave us the dust bowl on the Great Plains in the 1930s had heeded that two-thousand-year-old advice? What if they had heeded Milton's insight that nature "means her provision only to the good / That live according to her sober laws / And holy dictate of spare Temperance"? Virgil was writing about agricultural practices, whereas Milton was writing of the spare use of nature's fruits. It is interesting that the poets have spoken of both practice in nature and harvest of nature.

Berry pointed out that this theme surfaced again among the agricultural writers, first in 1905 in a book by Liberty Hyde Bailey entitled *The Outlook to Nature*. The grand old dean at Cornell wrote, "If nature is the norm then the necessity for correcting and amending abuses of civilization becomes baldly apparent by very contrast. The return to nature affords the very means of acquiring the incentive and energy for ambitious and constructive work of a high order." In *The Holy Earth* (1915) Bailey advanced the notion that "most of our difficulty with the earth lies in the effort to do what perhaps ought not to be done." He continued, "A good part of agriculture is to learn how to adapt one's work to nature. . . . To live in right relation with his natural conditions is one of the first lessons that a wise farmer or any other wise man learns."

J. Russell Smith's *Tree Crops*, published in 1929, contributed to the tradition. Smith was disturbed with the destruction of the hills because "man has carried to the hills the agriculture of the flat plain." Smith too believed that "farming should fit the land."

In 1940 Sir Albert Howard's *An Agriculture Testament* was published. For Howard, nature was "the supreme farmer": "The main characteristic of Nature's farming can therefore be summed up in a few words. Mother earth never attempts to farm without live stock; she always raises mixed crops;

great pains are taken to preserve the soil and to prevent erosion; the mixed vegetable and animal wastes are converted into humus; there is no waste; the processes of growth and the processes of decay balance one another; ample provision is made to maintain large reserves of fertility; the greatest care is taken to store the rainfall; both plants and animals are left to protect themselves against disease."

It may appear that our work at the Land Institute is part of a succession in a literary and scientific tradition, for we operate with the assumption that the best agriculture for any region is one that best mimics the region's natural ecosystems. That is why we are trying to build domestic prairies that will produce grain. We were ignorant of this literary and scientific tradition, however, when we began our work. I did have a background in botany and genetics and could see the difference between a prairie and a wheat field out my windows at the Land Institute, but as Berry said about the poets and scientists he quoted, understanding probably comes out of the familial and communal handing down of agrarian common culture rather than from any succession of teachers and students in the literary culture or in the schools. As far as the literary and scientific tradition is concerned, Berry pointed out that it is a series, not a succession. The succession is only in the agrarian common culture. I came off the farm out of a family of farmers, and apparently my "memory" of nature as measure is embedded in that agrarian common culture. George Bernard Shaw said that, "perfect memory is perfectl forgetfulness." To know something well is not to know where it came from. That is probably the nature of succession in the nonformal culture.

[. . .]

Nature as Measure in Agricultural Research

Rather than deal with problems *in* agriculture here and now, we at the Land Institute address the problem *of* agriculture, which began when agriculture began some eight to ten thousand years ago. We have seen that nature is an elusive standard. Nevertheless, it seems to us at the Land Institute less elusive than any other standard when sustainability is our primary objective. The nature we look to at the Land Institute is the never-plowed native prairie.

We have around one hundred acres of such land at the institute, and when we compare prairie with the ordinary field of corn or wheat, important differences become apparent. From our typical agricultural fields, valuable nutrients run toward the sea, where for all practical purposes most of them are gone for good. The prairie, on the other hand, by drawing nutrients from parent rock material or subsoil, all the while returning chemicals produced by life, actually builds soil. The prairie, like nearly all of nature, runs mostly on contemporary sunlight, whereas our modern agricultural fields benefit from the stored sunlight of extinct ancient floras. Diversity does not necessarily yield stability overall; nevertheless, the chemical diversity inherent in the diverse plant species of the prairie confronts insects and pathogens, making epidemics, so common to agricultural monocultures, rare on the prairie. Because no creature has an all-consuming enzyme system, diversity yields some protection. The prairie therefore does not require the introduction of chemicals with which species have had no evolutionary experience.

So what are the basic differences between a prairie and an agricultural field? A casual examination of the ordinary differences will help us to see that the prairie features perennials in a polyculture, whereas modern agriculture features annuals in a monoculture. Our work at the Land Institute is devoted primarily to exploring the feasibility of an agriculture that features herbaceous perennials grown in a mixture for seed production – that is, domestic prairies – as substitutes for annual monocultures grown in rows on ground that can erode.

We address four basic questions in our experiments at the institute. First, can herbaceous perenniality and high seed yield go together? Because perennial plants must divert some photosynthate to belowground storage for overwintering, it may be difficult to breed perennials to produce as much seed as annual crops that die after reproducing. Perennial species differ greatly in both relative and absolute amounts of energy devoted to seed production, however, so theoretically there seems to be no reason why a fast-growing, well-adapted species could not yield adequate seed while retaining the ability to overwinter.

Before we begin to breed for stable high seed yields in an herbaceous perennial, we determine its genetic potential. Whether we start with a wild introduced species or a wild native, the development of perennial seed-producing polycultures will require that we select for varieties that perform well in polyculture. The potential improvement, therefore, depends on the range of existing genetic variability in the wild. To assess this variation requires an adequate sample drawn from the geographic range of the species and then an evaluation of the collection within a common garden.

Now our second question: Can a polyculture of perennial seed producers outyield the same species grown in monoculture? Overyielding occurs when interspecific competition in a plant community is less intense than intraspecific competition. Thus, we believe that through differences in resource use and timing of demand, multispecies fields typically yield more per unit area than do monospecific stands.

Our third question is, Can a perennial polyculture provide much of its own fertility? Specifically, can such internal factors as nitrogen fixation and weathering of primary minerals compensate for nutrients removed in harvested seed? To answer this question, we must document nutrient cycling in the soil, nutrient content of seed, and capacity of crop plants to enrich the soil.

As our fourth and final question we ask, Can a perennial mixture successfully contend with phytophagous insects, pathogens, and weeds? If we are to protect a crop, a combination of breeding for resistant lines and studies on the effects of species diversity must converge. Insect pests can be managed through a combination of attracting predators and preventing insects from locating host plants. A mixture of species, and of genotypes within species, may reduce the incidence and spread of disease. Weeds may be controlled either allelopathically or via continuous shading of the soil surface by the perennials.

Though we keep all four of these questions in mind, the most pressing biological question at the Land Institute is whether perennials and high seed yield can go together. To answer this question, we started a plant inventory that had the following steps: (1) we reviewed the literature of seed yield in winter-hardy herbaceous perennials; (2) we collected seed and plants in nature and developed an herbary of approximately three hundred species, each grown in five-meter-long rows; and (3) we planted more than forty-three hundred accessions of more than one hundred species representing seven grass genera. Our inventory continues even though we are currently focusing on five species plus a hybrid of our making.

The relationship between perennials and high yield also involves the issue of sustained production. Prairies, after all, feature perennials, but they do not feature high seed yield. Ultimately, we have to explore the optimum balance between sustainability and yield.

In addition to the inventory of potentially high-yielding species, other sorts of inventories, such as an inventory of the vegetative structure, are necessary for long-term considerations. Because perennial roots are a major feature of our work, an inventory of the soil relationships in the prairie and in our plots is also essential. The ecological inventory includes more than analysis of the phytomass ratios; it also includes an ongoing inventory of the insects and pathogens in our herbary and in our experimental plots. We always compare the results with those from our prairie, the system that represents the least departure from what was here before white settlement.

The inventory phase will probably never end. The ecological inventory is particularly long-lasting because of the countless number of interactions over time. Even research on the question of perennials and high yield will require several years, for it amounts to an investigation of long-term demographic patterns in perennial seed production, a field that is largely unexplored. Studies thus far at the Land Institute have shown increases, decreases, and oscillations in seed yield over time. But we always come back to these questions: What was here? What will nature permit us to do here? And what will nature help us to do here? Wendell Berry once wrote in a letter, "When we cut the forest and plowed our prairies we never knew what we were doing because we never knew what we were undoing." It is now a matter of practical necessity to learn what we were undoing.

In a 1986 preliminary investigation, Jon Piper, the institute's ecologist, asked, How much aboveground plant life is supported each year by the prairie, and what are the proportions of grasses, legumes, and composites? Those plant families comprise most of our temperate agricultural species. Net production of the plants at Piper's grassland sites (five hundred to seven hundred grams per square meter) was similar to that of many midwestern crops. At their peaks, grasses composed 67 to 94 percent of plant matter, and legumes and composites represented 16 and 11 percent of vegetation, respectively. Piper concluded from these encouraging results that "a sustainable agricultural system for central Kansas is feasible if perennial grasses were featured followed by nearly equal proportions of legumes and composites."

In 1985 we began to examine insects and plant pathogens qualitatively in nine experimental plots at the Land Institute. Every week from May through August, and every other week from September through October, insects were collected with a sweep net or from individual plants. All diseased plants were sent to the Disease Diagnosis Laboratory at Kansas State University for pathogen identification. All sampled plots showed a diversity of both beneficial and harmful insects. Several foliar diseases were present, but few were serious. We continued that inventory in 1986 but with important modifications. The prairie was sampled using sweep nets every third week. Over the years, we have sampled the prairie, the herbary, and the experimental plots for insects and pathogens and have made numerous comparisons.

A final example of this soft approach to sustainable-agriculture research is the design of the large polyculture experiment we intend to establish in 1991. For that experiment, we think about the species components we intend to introduce, the planting density of each species, the ratios of species to one another, and so forth.

Three Final Questions

We have three final questions to consider. First, is perennial polyculture or ecosystem agriculture inherently more complicated and therefore less likely to succeed than monoculture agriculture, be it of the annual or the perennial variety?

My answer is, not necessarily. The disciplines of science are divided to explore the various levels in the hierarchy of structure from atoms to molecules, cells, tissues, organs, organ systems, and organisms. At each level of aggregation, it is the emergent qualities more than the contents that define the discipline. A physicist may have learned about the structure and workings of an atom in great detail. Though some understanding of atoms is necessary for a chemist, the chemist does not need to know the atom with the same intricacy of detail as the physicist. A chemist mostly studies reactions. On up the hierarchy, we see that chemistry is important to a cell biologist but does not define cell biology, and a good cell biologist does not need to have a chemist's detailed knowledge. Cell biology as a field is not more complicated than chemistry or physics, though cells are more complex than molecules or atoms.

Likewise, ecosystem agriculture will be more complex than monoculture agriculture, but the management of agro-ecosystems may not be more complicated. Ecosystem agriculturalists will take advantage of the natural integrities of ecosystems worked out over the millennia.

When we deal with nature's designs, a great deal of ignorance on our part is tolerable. Much error is forgiven. Ignorance is tolerable until we begin to impose our own designs on nature's landscape. Even then certain kinds of ignorance and large amounts of forgetfulness will be tolerated. (Not knowing is a kind of ignorance preferred over knowing things that just are not so. At least one does not have to unlearn what is not known.) When we impose our own designs on nature's landscape, we do so with the presumption that we know what we are doing, and we have to assume responsibility for our mistakes. By imitating nature's patterns, we should be able to reduce error by taking advantage of nature's complexity, thus minimizing complications for ourselves. Farmers and scientists alike may not know why certain associations of plants and animals grant sustainability, just that they do. And though there is little wrong with finding out why certain associations work, from the point of view of a farmer interested in running a sustainable farm, knowing why is not always necessary.

Our second question is, How crucial is species diversity, and if it is necessary, how much and what kind are optimum? As mentioned earlier, diversity does not necessarily lead to stability. Numerous diverse ecosystems are less stable than simpler ones. We can raise a question about the inherent value of diversity by considering two extremes. At one extreme, we could assemble a diverse hodgepodge of species, plants that have never grown together in an ecosystem. At the other extreme, we could assemble plant species that have histories of growing together – on the prairie, let us say. In the latter case, natural integrities have evolved to the point that large numbers of genetic ensembles interact in a species mix. This area warrants much research.

Another important consideration is associated with the diversity question. As species are selected for future experimentation, we may need to determine to what extent the genetic profile is tuned to interspecific versus intraspecific complementarity. In all of our important domestic grains, the genetic assembly of an individual plant resonates against members of its own kind (intraspecific complementarity). On a prairie, that is not the case. Prairie plants are more tuned to interact with different species (interspecific complementarity).

The third question we ask is this: Is it true that, for any biotic system, internal control uses material and energy resources more efficiently than external control? In a hierarchy of structure – beginning with an individual plant, then the field (an ecosystem), then the farm (a larger ecosystem), and then the farm community (an even larger ecosystem) – it will be necessary to think about the efficient use of material and energy resources.

This philosophical consideration is of great practical importance. Consider a plant's resistance to an insect. If a plant uses its genetic code to make a chemical that is distasteful to an insect, thereby granting itself protection, we would call that internal control. If we, perhaps unknowingly, remove that ability through breeding, the plant is susceptible and we apply an insecticide on the plant's surface to grant it protection. That is external control. Yield increases, but the resource cost for protection is paid from the outside, and seemingly the total cost would be greater.

Another example is nitrogen fertility. If the feedstock for commercial nitrogen fertilizer is natural gas, the total energy cost would be higher than if the plant fixed its own nitrogen. In the first case, we are using what we might call vertical energy, or time-compressed energy; in the second case, we are using horizontal, or contemporary, energy from the sun. As our supplies of vertical energy run out and we are forced to use horizontal energy, then the answer to our major question becomes crucial, for at that point the energy source becomes a land-use problem.

A third example is weed control. If the roots of a plant produce an herbicide to keep back most weeds, then weed protection comes from within the plant (allelopathy). The plant's production of such an herbicide will come at a cost in yield. But let us say that a plant lacks the ability to produce the herbicide and that mechanical weeding is necessary. If we pay the cost on the farm the way we used to – that is, harvest biomass from a pasture or field to feed horses supplying the power for mechanical weed removal – then it seems obvious that the overall cost will be higher.

We are faced with extremely difficult choices and, I believe, extremely difficult times. Our goal must be a harmony between the human economy and nature's economy that will preserve both. In the greenhouse dedication speech mentioned earlier,

Wendell Berry pointed out that such a goal is traditional: "The world is now divided between those who adhere to this ancient purpose and those who by intention do not, and this division is of far more portent for the future of the world than any of the presently recognized national or political or economic divisions."

Recalling his outline of the literary and scientific traditions, Berry concluded, "The remarkable thing about this division is its relative newness. The idea that we should obey nature's laws and live harmoniously with her as good husbanders and stewards of her gifts is old. . . . And I believe that until fairly recently our destructions of nature were more or less unwitting – the by-products, so to speak, of our ignorance or weakness or depravity. It is our present principled and elaborately rationalized rape and plunder of the natural world that is a new thing under the sun."

---

63   Putting Food Production in Context: Toward a Postmechanistic Agricultural Ethic

David R. Keller and E. Charles Brummer

Agriculture is a defining characteristic of human civilization. Its development as a means of providing sustenance marked the transition from a nomadic existence to an urban lifestyle. And no other human activity has transformed so much of the earth's surface as farming (Vitousek et al. 1997). Oddly, the amount of attention given to the underlying values of agriculture is inversely proportionate to the environmental impact of agricultural activity. In academia, two disciplines obviously relevant to agriculture – agronomy and environmental philosophy – have addressed the effects of pesticides and soil erosion or the value of wilderness as compared with that of cultivated land but have not evaluated the fundamental assumptions implicit in the practice of agriculture. Even more surprising, dialogue between agronomists and philosophers is rare.

The Metaphysics of Industrial Agriculture

Any ethic presupposes a metaphysical foundation (Keller 1997). The code of ethics developed by contemporary industrial agriculture rests upon a conception of nature based on the mechanistic worldview that has increasingly defined modern Western science since the Renaissance. The hallmark of this perspective, as expounded by numerous scientists, philosophers, and theologians, is that nature is a grand and exquisite machine operating by the deterministic laws of physics. The astronomer Johannes Kepler first applied this thinking to the heavens. "My aim," he said, "is to show that the celestial machine is to be likened not to a divine organism but rather to a clockwork" (Oelschlaeger 1991) – a view shared by Galileo, Hobbes, Descartes, Newton, and others. Derivative of the mechanical view of nature is the belief that natural systems are understandable, predictable, and manipulatable. Indeed, the social responsibility of science is often couched in terms of prediction and manipulation, and adherents to the mechanical view tend to be optimistic about achieving these goals.

Connected with the metaphysics of mechanism is the idea that nature, as machine, has no intrinsic value. This axiology of nature is manifested in Western religion, philosophy, and science. Whereas paganism held the earth to be sacred, Christianity increasingly held it to be profane and subject to man's desires: "And the Lord God took the man, and put him into the garden of Eden to dress it and to keep it" (Genesis 2:15). For pre-Christian pagans, economic activities such as plowing or mining were barred on religious grounds, to prevent cutting or digging into Mother Earth (Jackson 1987, Merchant

From *BioScience*, vol. 52, no. 3 (2002): 264–71.

1990). The shift in religious worldview about the ontology of the natural order was synchronous with expanding economic exploitation of natural resources (White 1967), as lamented by the Roman poet Ovid (Figure 63.1; trans. Mandlebaum [1993]) in the *Metamorphoses*:

> And now the ground,
> which once – just like the sunlight and the air –
> had been a common good, one all could share,
> was marked and measured by the keen surveyor –
> he drew long confines, the boundaries.
> Not only did men ask of earth its wealth,
> its harvest crops and foods that nourish us,
> they also delved into the bowels of earth:
> there they began to dig for what was hid
> deep underground beside the shades of Styx.

A—STREAM.   B—DITCH.   C—MATTOCK.   D—PIECES OF TURF.   E—SEVEN-PRONGED FORK.
F—IRON SHOVEL.   G—TROUGH.   H—ANOTHER TROUGH BELOW IT.   I—SMALL WOODEN TROWEL.

Figure 63.1   From Agricola ([1556] 1912).

In science and philosophy, the mechanistic view maintains that only quantifiable (or primary) properties – namely, the parameters of classical physics such as size, shape, speed, mass, distance, and time – belong to the natural order. Qualitative (or secondary) properties – such as the taste, smell, sight, and touch of Descartes's piece of wax ([1641] 1989), Hobbes' "phantasms" ([1651] 1985), or the blue color and sweet scent of Locke's violet ([1690] 1985) – emanate from human consciousness. In and of itself, then, brute nature is absolutely devoid of qualitative value.

Consistent with – but not necessarily logically derivative of – mechanistic metaphysics is the epistemological doctrine of the fact–value (or is–ought) gap. Inspired by David Hume's ([1740] 1992) observation about the propensity of many thinkers to derive value-laden prescriptions from value-free descriptions, many scientists and philosophers have asserted the existence of an insurmountable gap between science and ethics. As the English philosopher Bertrand Russell (1961) remarked, "[Q]uestions as to 'values' lie wholly outside the domain of knowledge. That is to say, when we assert that this or that has 'value,' we are giving expression to our own emotions, not to a fact." Using this line of reasoning, one can garner facts independent of values. A clear example of this type of thinking occurred during the Manhattan Project, when scientists developing the atomic bomb adopted the view that they were to focus only on nuclear physics without making value judgments about the practice of detonating nuclear devices. (One of the scientists, J. Robert Oppenheimer, later renounced his dedication to the fact–value gap, telling President Truman he felt as though he had "blood on his hands" [Kunetka 1982].)

The implications of mechanistic metaphysics and the fact–value gap for the practicing farmer, the agribusinessman, and the agricultural scientist are profound. English philosopher John Locke ([1689] 1996) persuasively argued that nature itself has no inherent value, but that human beings, through labor, can transform the latent extrinsic (or resource value) of land into useful products. Thus, the mechanistic view of nature promulgates an economic model of human–nature interactions. The farmer is to produce as much food as possible, and neither the producer nor the consumer should make value judgments about the noneconomic worth of the land. After all, values are epiphenomena of human subjectivity and human activity; they are not embedded in the land.

Agriculture and the Production Paradigm

Modern agriculture has become highly industrialized in order to reliably produce the largest amount of plant and animal product possible while minimizing labor inputs. Through the incorporation of numerous components manufactured externally to the farm, including fertilizers, pesticides, and technology, the modern system manipulates the land to make it amenable to industrial processes. Typically, crops are produced as large-hectarage monocultures consisting of a single genotype planted across an entire field (figure 63.2). Most farms using modern agricultural methods cultivate only a few crops grown in simple rotations such as wheat–fallow or maize–soybean. Similarly, most animals are grown in feedlots or climate-controlled buildings in order to closely monitor feed efficiency and to guarantee uniform meat, egg, or milk products. Cycling of nutrients is not a major consideration of most industrial agricultural systems because the addition of externally derived fertilizers is cheaper and simpler than collecting, storing, and using manure.

Under the production paradigm, the prime directive is to improve the productivity of a select set of plants and animals. Solutions for problems arising in the system are discovered through scientific research leading to the development, production, and implementation of new technology. Finding these solutions can be expensive, but molecular biological advances, such as the sequencing of the genome of the model plant *Arabidopsis thaliana* (Arabidopsis Genome Initiative 2000) and the development of large-scale gene exploration methods (Somerville and Somerville 1999), promise to supply solutions to a host of genetically based problems more easily, more quickly, and more simply than currently available methods permit (Briggs 1998, Chory et al. 2000).

Therefore, at the heart of the production paradigm is the realization of the greatest possible quantity of agricultural product. Other factors, such as ecological

Figure 63.2   The increasing industrialization and decreasing diversity in farming in the latter half of the 20th century is shown in this comparison between an aerial photograph of a 9-square-mile section of Humboldt County, Iowa, taken in 1953 (left) showing substantial diversity of crops in small fields on many farms, and the cropping sequence in 1999 (right), which shows only maize (corn, C) and soybean (B) crops and many farms that are either no longer present or no longer involved with farming operations, as designated with an X. Aerial photograph from Lee Burras.

or aesthetic values of the agroecosystem, receive scant attention outside limited areas within academia, as can be easily visualized by driving through the corn or wheat belts of the United States.

Ecological Shortfalls of the Production Paradigm

Simplified systems of modern, industrial agriculture bear little resemblance to highly complex natural ecosystems. Within natural ecosystems, various biotic and abiotic components form an intricate network of interactions, allowing the systems to be both functional and adaptive under a wide range of conditions (Hulot et al. 2000, Williams and Martinez 2000). These ecosystems provide many services to the biosphere and hence to human survival and enjoyment (Balvanera et al. 2001). The value of these ecosystem services is considerable (Costanza et al. 1997), although as David Ehrenfeld remarked, "I am afraid that I do not see much hope for a civilization so stupid that it demands a quantitative estimate of the value of its own umbilical cord" (Stevens 1997). Agricultural systems based on the production paradigm do not recognize these hard-to-quantify, yet ecologically important, values. Although the structure, functioning, and values of natural systems could provide important clues about developing sustainable agricultural systems (Tilman 1999), little effort is devoted to investigating them.

Complex natural systems often exhibit emergent properties, characteristics that are not predictable from an analysis of the system's components (Odum 1986), such as stability in the face of perturbation. Because these properties are absent from simplified modern agricultural systems that lack important components present in natural systems, the rationale of developing such systems has been repeatedly questioned (Drinkwater et al. 1998, Matson et al. 1997, Tilman 1999). Critics outside the academic scientific community, such as Wendell Berry, Wes Jackson, and others, have made particularly pointed attacks on the insular, noncritical agricultural research community, which has focused most of its resources on the promulgation of the production paradigm. In rebuttals to these critiques, production-oriented proponents argue that the appropriate course of action is to modify existing systems toward increased sustainability (Sinclair and Cassman 1999). Consequently, a never-ending stream of new technologies, including pesticides and herbicides, chemical fertilizers, genetically engineered crops, and precision machinery, has been developed and applied (Lewis et al. 1997). Even though these modifications have not resulted in sustainable systems, it is hoped they eventually will.

Thus, the design of agricultural systems is based on commodity production and its attendant economics; the importance of modeling farming systems after natural systems, based on ecological principles, is widely overlooked. The American ecologist Aldo Leopold named the schism between the economic and ecological models of farming the "A–B cleavage" (Leopold [1949] 1987). The economic model (A) considers the value of the land to be its resource or productive potential, as espoused by Locke ([1689] 1996). Conversely, the ecological model (B) considers the land to be a living thing, including not only soil but also the plants and animals living in and on it and the water and energy flowing through it. In model (B), ecosystem components have types of value above and beyond direct economic value alone. The production paradigm of current agricultural systems clearly espouses model (A). Some adherents of the production paradigm reject outright the values suggested in model (B); others admit their existence but consider them only to the extent that they do not interfere with production of agricultural commodities.

From an ecological perspective, however, the productionist program fails doubly: It does not consider positive ecological benefits that could arise through different farming system architectures – increasing migratory bird habitat by restoring drained wetlands, for example – but it externalizes many costs associated with current production practices. An externality is a consequence – favorable or unfavorable – of an activity for which those affected by the activity are not compensated (Samuelson 1980). Because they are hard to track and tabulate, economists often lump together such consequences in cost-benefit analyses and label them externalities. Despite the dual character of externalities, the term has become a euphemism in economics and politics for masking the negative environmental consequences of public policy decisions regarding agricultural and other practices. As suggested above, many factors relating to the ontology of agroecological systems are not amenable to quantification. The severing of links in food webs by biocides, pollution related to soil erosion (figure 63.3) and the use of fertilizers, and the reduction of biodiversity are often

Figure 63.3   Erosion on industrially farmed landscapes can be extensive, as exemplified by these photographs taken in Boone County, Iowa, in the late 1990s. Wintertime wind erosion from row crop fields causes "black snow" in the ditches (top left); no soil is blown off a rare, neighboring pasture (top right). Water (lower left) and wind erosion (lower right) from newly seeded soybean fields does not occur in the oat–alfalfa intercrop in the foreground of the lower right photograph, which was seeded approximately 2 months before the soybeans.

written off as externalities and excluded in the decisionmaking process about prudent agricultural policy. In the estimation of American philosopher Paul Thompson (1995),

> Productionism is an absurd philosophical position on the face of it. It is contradicted by the oldest of old saws: man does not live by bread alone. There are no sophisticated philosophical defenses of productionism. Arguably, no individual has ever believed in it. Statements of the productionist norm must be found in slogans or aphorism, such as [Nixon administration secretary of agriculture] Earl Butz's injunctions to "plant fencerow to fencerow," and to "get big or get out."

Yet we continue to conduct agricultural research, business, and practice as if productivity were the

ultimate goal. Current high-yield agriculture and its attendant modern technologies are justified not on ecological grounds but by claiming to be the only means to feed the world's growing population (Thompson 1995, Briggs 1998). Since industrial agriculture significantly benefits the corporations selling the technologies deemed essential to "feeding the world," we may rightly question the validity and sincerity of such claims. Currently, Western countries produce so much of some commodities, such as maize and soybeans, that prices are at historically low levels, necessitating governmental intervention to avoid bankrupting farmers. In the United States, both land grant universities and the USDA Agricultural Research Service routinely hire scientists to find alternate uses for these crops. Therefore, the current need in the West is not increased production. That starving people live in a world with abundant food suggests that "what is missing is the 'purchasing power' of the poor" (Latham 2000). The imperative of "feeding the world" through industrial agriculture is a dogma with little foundation.

In 1962, Rachel Carson (1994) decried the "arrogance" of thinking pesticides (or more accurately, biocides) could control nature. Despite 40 years of trying, we are still incapable of controlling even (or perhaps especially) the simplest agroecosystems: Weeds, insects, pathogens, and nematodes continue to exact an immense toll in money and labor from our agricultural enterprise. If the system that we use to produce food does so in an environmentally unsound – that is, unsustainable – manner, then no matter how much it produces now, it will produce far less in the future, when the world's population very well might need it. Clearly, the development of stable and sustainable agricultural systems is needed first and foremost. The huge food surpluses that currently exist give us a remarkable chance to explore other avenues toward the dual goals of productivity and sustainability.

Fertile Ground for the 21st Century: Postmechanistic Agriculture Ethics

We have argued that (a) modern agricultural practice has evolved from the mechanistic worldview dominating modern science, (b) current technique involves the simplification, homogenization, and manipulation of agroecosystems, and (c) these systems are ecologically unsound and unsustainable. We would add that (d) rethinking agricultural practice within a postmechanistic – rather than a mechanistic – framework provides the basis for the development, maintenance, and improvement of sustainable agroecosystems.

The history of the hegemony of mechanism in the Western intellectual tradition suggests the need for a new metaphysics (Whitehead [1925] 1967). To this end, the word *postmechanistic* may be used to describe the rejection of the purely mechanical view of nature. In science, postmechanism involves the adoption of an indeterministic, stochastic view of nature, exemplified in physics by Heisenberg's uncertainty principle. In philosophy, postmechanism involves the elaboration of an "organismic" metaphysics and axiology (Whitehead [1929] 1978, Ferré 1996). The implica-

tions for ethics of rejecting the mechanistic view of nature, closing the fact–value gap, and recognizing that nature is imbued with value are that moral decisions ought to be taken in context: ecology entails ethics (Keller and Golley 2000).

A postmechanistic agricultural ethic does not suggest that mechanism is not important in improving agricultural systems. Just as Newtonian mechanics continues to be useful at explaining many physical phenomena despite the development of quantum mechanics, mechanistic investigations and explanations are still relevant to a postmechanistic agriculture. With respect to a postmechanistic ethic, we contend that the methods used to mechanistically dissect agriculture and its components need to be revised (as described below) and that nonmechanistic aspects of agricultural systems – ecological and qualitative values – need to be given consideration when constructing sustainable systems. Postmechanism is relevant to agriculture because it lays the groundwork for a more sustainable agricultural practice in at least five ways.

First, agricultural science and practice must become context-sensitive and holistic in methodology. Reductive techniques, exemplified by modern genetics and molecular biology, have resulted in substantial improvements in our understanding of the natural world. Yet, they need to be balanced with synthesis – namely, consideration of the unique ecological relationships of biota to each other and to the nonbiotic environment intrinsic to each agricultural system. It is unlikely that we will soon understand the mechanics of any plant or animal, given the complex interactions of the component parts of each one, let alone the myriad stochastic factors inherent in an agroecosystem.

Living systems are machinelike in many respects, but they cannot be understood solely in terms of deterministic and predictable cause-and-effect relationships (Rosen 1991). Biologist Richard Lewontin (2000) suggested that metaphors are useful and necessary, but that "there is a great risk of confusing the metaphor with the thing of real interest. We cease to see the world as if it were like a machine and take it to be a machine." Nevertheless, the nature-as-machine view is still popular with biologists:

In order to most efficiently and safely manipulate plants to meet growing societal needs, we must create a wiring diagram of a plant through its entire life cycle: from germinating seed to production of the next generation of seeds in mature flowers. . . . The ultimate expression of our goal is nothing short of a virtual plant which one could observe growing on a computer screen, stopping this process at any point in that development, and with the click of a computer mouse, accessing all the genetic information expressed in any organ or cell under a variety of environmental condition. (Chory et al. 2000)

The fact that a plant of a given genetic constitution develops differently across environmental conditions disabuses botanists of the very hope of completely understanding its developmental trajectory, simply because the environment is continuously changing in unpredictable ways.

The agroecosystem includes endemic micro- and macroflora and fauna, the micro- and macroclimate, and the soil, all of which affect the growth and development of crop plants. Although some aspects of agroecosystems are deterministic and predictable, significant, and perhaps insurmountable, gaps remain in our understanding of biology across hierarchical levels from the gene to the landscape. Therefore, agricultural research and the activity of farming must be gauged in terms of the unique ecological conditions of each locale. Folk wisdom, often unwelcome in academic journals, is revalidated when this approach is used. The consequence of context-dependent agriculture is that universal farming principles are not achievable. The same industrial equipment, the same chemicals, and the same seeds will not be equally effective in diverse locations.

Second, the role of diversity in agroecosystems must be considered (Brummer 1998). In some instances, increased diversity has been shown to have positive effects at various ecological scales. For example, complex landscapes improve biological control of pests (Thies and Tscharntke 1999), diverse mixtures of crops promote effective nutrient cycling (Drinkwater et al. 1998), species diversity improves biomass productivity and stability (Tilman et al. 2001), and genetic diversity within fields decreases disease pressure (Zhu et al. 2000). These examples suggest that biological diversity buffers the agroecosystem against perturbation. Thus many species that are not recognizably important on the economic model (A) function indirectly in the production of crops. Other research has indicated that the relationships among diversity, productivity, and stability are not clear, and examples contrary to those listed above may be found in the ecological literature. This conflicting literature suggests that the important

point is that the relationships are context dependent – what works in one situation may not work on another – and we must become more attuned to this reality. While the exact relationship between ecological diversity and stability remains controversial, diversity is a major indicator of the health and well-being of a biotic community (Golley 1998) and provides an important hedge for food stability against the vagaries of uncontrollable factors. This argues that a total systems approach to agricultural sustainability is needed (Lewis et al. 1997).

Third, technology may not offer the solution for all agricultural problems. Agricultural science currently exists in the modern, Panglossian world where no hurdle cannot be overcome with more money, more study, and increased technological implementation. Although technology itself is not necessarily a problem, we have been deploying ever more expensive "magic bullets" to solve emerging agricultural problems; that they inevitably become ineffectual strongly suggests that the structure of our current systems is not sufficiently robust to encompass both high productivity and environmental sustainability. Overlooked by the current mechanistic approach are simple alternatives, such as crop management methods based on genetic or species diversity, that produce a more complex agroecosystem, an emergent property of which could be elimination of some previously intractable problems. A recent report demonstrating that rice mixtures grown across thousands of hectares in China had a superior ability to withstand blast infection compared to monocultures supports this possibility (Zhu et al. 2000). By working in conjunction with crop management and ecosystem-scale research efforts rather than in isolation, plant improvement research can devote greater emphasis to the more important goals of increasing yield and nutritional quality of an entire cropping system (Serageldin 1999).

Ultimately, we can either attempt to impose order into agricultural systems through large-scale external inputs (and a creative accounting of costs), or we can bring order to the agroecosystem by mimicking natural ecosystems and taking advantage of the complexity inherent in them. Constructing plants, animals, and entire agroecosystems by reducing each to its components and then assembling agricultural systems "from first principles" (Somerville and Somerville 1999) does not allow for the expression of emergent solutions to the problems that will confront these systems when they are deployed in the real world.

Fourth, all externalities of agricultural activity ought to be included in cost-benefit analyses when comparing alternate methodologies. Unmitigated market forces invariably lead to undesirable consequences (prostitution, trafficking in addictive drugs, bribery, nepotism, monopolization, to name a few). Agriculture is no exception. The current system appears economically sensible because many costs – such as those associated with soil erosion, nitrogen and pesticide pollution, depletion of aesthetic value by monocultures and factory farms, and diminution of rural communities – are not included. The prescription for this axiological myopia involves legal changes that require the inclusion of externalities in public policy debates about agricultural practice. Once these externalities are considered, alternatives to industrial agriculture may appear significantly more cost-effective.

Fifth, and finally, the preceding points lead to the conclusion that a plurality of methods is desperately needed in agriculture. The techniques of industrial agriculture are treated as sacrosanct: Plant biology, and indeed agricultural science in general, do not stand for criticism, or even for ideas opposed to the dominant paradigm. Writer and farmer Wendell Berry summarized the situation clearly: "Why should our universities sponsor an active criticism of the fine arts . . . but no criticism of farming or forestry or mining or manufacturing? This question, of course, can be answered by a crude evolutionism – those who survive do not bite the corporations that feed them – but it ought to give some anxiety to a conservationist" (Berry 2000).

A sustainable agriculture cannot be attained by adopting a single farming system, industrial or otherwise, or by ignoring important values associated with the system we choose. Instead, a sustainable agriculture will arise through an aggregation of systems, each adapted to a particular region, to particular farmers, and to particular purposes. This panoply of farming options cannot be easily commodified or industrialized. Land grant and governmental research institutions primarily promulgate the industrial paradigm. Admittedly, some improvements have been made to industrialized systems. The incorporation of integrated pest management strategies and conservation tillage have lessened the environmental impact of farming to a degree. But numerous alternatives – including completely organic systems and perennialized landscapes – that could lead to sustainability of both farms and rural communities have received little attention relative to industrialized agriculture. The current industrialized system may be the one best suited to particular situations, but without more effort, little possibility exists that improvements outside the current paradigm can be developed. Land grant institutions can and should facilitate methodological pluralism.

The key to the successful development of a sustainable agriculture requires vigorous debate among all interested parties, with multiple points of view aired and evaluated. Discussion and dissension need to be interdisciplinary. To develop and apply a postmechanistic agricultural ethic, academics involved in agricultural issues – agronomists, animal scientists, ecologists, philosophers, anthropologists, economists, writers, and others – must become engaged in the dialogue about appropriate agricultural technique. The historical separation among the disciplines is an impediment to postmechanistic agricultural ethics.

Moreover, the discussion ought to take place free from corporate constraints. Land grant universities need to vigorously pursue research, teaching, and praxis that is based on ecology, not solely on economics. No longer can we expect to blithely conduct research or promote a new technology that does not clearly advance a context-sensitive postmechanistic agricultural ethic. Although many scientists involved in some aspect of agricultural research (and particularly those in very basic plant molecular genetics) feel their work will lead to improved environmental health (Briggs 1998), rigorous evaluation of their research and claims in terms of ecological integrity is lacking. Far more consideration should be given to the effect that particular genes, genotypes, crops, or cropping systems may have on altering the agroecosystem and agricultural landscape. A recent report suggests that widespread adoption of herbicide-resistant crops could have negative implications for seed-eating birds (Watkinson et al. 2000), a finding that clearly underscores why the relationship between reductive genetic manipulation and ecosystem functioning needs to be considered.

In short, land grant institutions, rather than being appendages of corporate interests, should be havens for discussion and dissension free from market forces. The German philosopher Friedrich Nietzsche's ([1885] 1995) admonition is strangely appropriate: "Far from the market place and from fame happens all that is great: far from the market place and from fame the inventors of new values have always dwelt." The agricultural industry is not excluded from this discussion,

Figure 63.4   This aesthetically pleasing mixture of row crops (maize and soybean) with hay and pasture and grazing cattle on an entirely organic farm in Harlan County, Iowa, represents one step toward affirming a postmechanistic agricultural ethic.

a variety of noneconomic values in the land: ecological, aesthetic, historical, political, social, even spiritual. Our concept of agriculture is that it is more than simply food production: It is the act of affirming as many of these values as possible (figure 63.4).

We call on land grant institutions, federal and state agricultural agencies, and the food-consuming public to recognize the plenitude of values involved in the activity of farming. A postmechanistic agricultural ethic encourages the farmer to facilitate the emergence of the special properties of his or her unique place, rather than to repress the intrinsic beauty and value of the land through simplification and homogenization. A reworking of Earl Butz's injunction is appropriate for the 21st century: Get sustainable or get out. Farming, after all, is a dynamic and complex enterprise; we should be loath to diminish, in any way, its wonder and surprise.

but in order to make a significant contribution to the sustainable agriculture of the future, it will need to place the good of the agroecosystem above the full economic exploitation it currently pursues.

A specter hangs over future improvements in agricultural sustainability. Current governmental farm policies often discourage the development of a context-sensitive agriculture by subsidizing a few commodity crops, such as maize and soybeans in the United States. Government policies need to be structured so that they advance, rather than subvert, ecological integrity. Instead of providing funds to maintain a commodity-based agricultural system, governmental investments should focus on the development of agricultural systems that will revitalize and stabilize agroecosystems (Stauber 1997) – in other words, farmers should be supported to farm small areas well, rather than to farm large areas poorly.

Conclusion

Notwithstanding the supersession of deterministic Newtonian mechanics by indeterministic quantum mechanics in physics, the mechanistic view of nature has maintained its hegemony on Western thinking in general and is clearly manifested in current industrial agricultural practice. Contrary to modern industrial technique, postmechanistic technique sees farming as a multifaceted activity that, in addition to mechanistic investigation and practice, involves the recognition of

References

Agricola G. [1556] 1912. *De re metallica*, Hoover H.C, Hoover L.H., trans. Mining Magazine (London), p. 337.

Arabidopsis Genome Initiative. 2000. Analysis of the genome sequence of the flowering plant *Arabidopsis thaliana*. Nature 408: 796–815.

Balvanera H. Daily G.C., Ehrlich P.R., Ricketts T.H., Bailey S.-A., Kark S., Kremen C., Pereira H. 2001. Conserving biodiversity and ecosystem services. *Science* 291: 2047.

Berry W. 2000. *Life Is a Miracle*. Washington (DC): Counterpoint Press.

Briggs S.P. 1998. Plant genomics: More than food for thought. *Proceedings of the National Academy of Sciences* 95: 1986–8.

Brummer E.C. 1998. Diversity, stability, and sustainable American agriculture. *Agronomy Journal* 90: 1–2.

Carson R. [1962] 1994. *Silent Spring*. Boston: Houghton Mifflin.

Chory J., et al. 2000. Functional genomics and the virtual plant: A blueprint for understanding how plants are built and how to improve them. *Plant Physiology* 123: 423–5.

Costanza R., et al. 1997. The value of the world's ecosystem services and natural capital. *Nature* 387: 253–60.

Descartes R. [1641] 1989. Meditations on first philosophy. Page 84 in Cottingham J., Stoothoff R., Murdoch D., trans. and eds. *Descartes: Selected Philosophical Writings*. New York: Cambridge University Press.

Drinkwater L.E., Wagoner P., Sarrantonio M. 1998. Legume-based cropping systems have reduced carbon and nitrogen losses. *Nature* 396: 262–5.

Ferré F. 1996. *Being and Value: Toward a Constructive Metaphysics*. Albany (NY): State University of New York Press.

Golley F.B. 1998. *A Primer for Environmental Literacy*. New Haven (CT): Yale University Press.

Hobbes T. [1651] 1985. *Leviathan*. MacPherson C.B., ed. New York: Penguin Books.

Hulot F.D., Lacroix G., Lescher-Moutoué F., Loreau M. 2000. Functional diversity governs ecosystem response to nutrient enrichment. *Nature* 405: 340–4.

Hume D. [1740] 1992. *A Treatise on Human Nature*. New York: Oxford University Press.

Jackson W. 1987. *Altars of Unhewn Stone: Science and the Earth*. San Francisco: North Point Press.

Keller D.R. 1997. Gleaning lessons from deep ecology. *Ethics and the Environment* 2: 139–48.

Keller D.R., Golley F.B. 2000. *The Philosophy of Ecology: From Science to Synthesis*. Athens: University of Georgia Press.

Kunetka J.W. 1982. *Oppenheimer: The Years of Risk*. Englewood Cliffs (NJ): Prentice-Hall.

Latham J.R. 2000. There's enough food for everyone, but the poor can't afford to buy it. *Nature* 404: 222.

Leopold A. [1949] 1987. *A Sand County Almanac and Sketches Here and There*. New York: Oxford University Press.

Lewis W.J., van Lenteren J.C., Phatak S.C., Tumilson J.H. III. 1997. A total system approach to sustainable pest management. *Proceedings of the National Academy of Sciences* 94: 12243–8.

Lewontin R. 2000. *The Triple Helix: Gene, Organism, and Environment*. Cambridge (MA): Harvard University Press.

Locke J. [1690] 1985. An essay concerning human understanding. Page 491 in Cahn S., ed. *Classics of Western Philosophy*, 2nd edn. Indianapolis (IN): Hackett Publishing.

Locke J. [1689] 1996. Second treatise of government. In Morgan M., ed. *Classics of Moral and Political Theory*. 2nd edn. Indianapolis (IN): Hackett Publishing.

Matson P.A., Parton W.J., Power A.G., Swift M.J. 1997. Agricultural intensification and ecosystem properties. *Science* 277: 504–9.

Merchant C. 1990. *The Death of Nature: Women, Ecology and the Scientific Revolution*. San Francisco: Harper Collins.

Nietzsche F. [1885] 1995. *Thus Spoke Zarathustra*. New York: Random House.

Odum E.P. 1986. Introductory review: Perspectives of ecosystem theory and application. Pages 1–11 in Polunin N. ed. *Ecosystem Theory and Application*. New York: John Wiley and Sons.

Oelschlaeger M. 1991. *The Idea of Wilderness: From Prehistory to the Age of Ecology*. New Haven (CT): Yale University Press.

Ovid. 1993. *Metamorphoses*. Mandlebaum A., trans. New York: Harcourt.

Rosen R. 1991. *Life Itself: A Comprehensive Inquiry into the Nature, Origin, and Fabrication of Life*. New York: Columbia University Press.

Russell B. 1961. *Religion and Science*. New York: Oxford University Press.

Samuelson P. 1980. *Economics*. 11th edn. New York: McGraw-Hill.

Serageldin I. 1999. Biotechnology and food security in the 21st century. *Science* 285: 387–9.

Sinclair T.R., Cassman K.G. 1999. Green revolution still too green. *Nature* 398: 556.

Somerville C., Somerville S. 1999. Plant functional genomics. *Science* 285: 380–3.

Stauber K. 1997. Envisioning a thriving rural America through agriculture. Pages 105–17 in Lockeretz W., ed. *Visions of American Agriculture*. Ames: Iowa State University.

Stevens W.K. 1997. How much is nature worth? For you, $33 trillion. *New York Times*, 20 May, sec. C.

Thies C., Tscharntke T. 1999. Landscape structure and biological control in agroecosystems. *Science* 285: 893–5.

Thompson P.B. 1995. *The Spirit of the Soil*. New York: Routledge and Kegan Paul.

Tilman D. 1999. Global environmental impacts of agricultural expansion: The need for sustainable and efficient practices. *Proceedings of the National Academy of Sciences* 96: 5995–6000.

Tilman D., Reich P.B., Knops J., Wedin D., Mielke T., Lehman C. 2001. Diversity and productivity in a long-term grassland experiment. *Science* 294: 843–5.

Vitousek P.M., Mooney H.A., Lubchenco J., Melillo J.M. 1997. Human domination of Earth's ecosystems. *Science* 277: 494–9.

Watkinson A.R., Freckleton R.P., Robinson R.A., Sutherland W.J. 2000. Predictions of biodiversity response to genetically modified herbicide-tolerant crops. *Science* 289: 1554–7.

White L. 1967. The historical roots of our ecologic crisis. *Science* 155: 1203–7.

Whitehead A.N. [1925] 1967. *Science and the Modern World*. New York: Free Press.

Whitehead A.N. [1929] 1978. *Process and Reality: An Essay in Cosmology*. New York: Free Press.

Williams R.J., Martinez N.D. 2000. Simple rules yield complex food webs. *Nature* 404: 180–3.

Zhu Y., et al. 2000. Genetic diversity and disease control in rice. *Nature* 406: 718–22.

C Socioeconomic Environmental Justice

64 Environmental Justice for All
    Robert D. Bullard

65 Just Garbage
    Peter S. Wenz

64 Environmental Justice for All

Robert D. Bullard

People of color have always resisted actions by government and private industry that threaten the quality of life in their communities. Until recently, this resistance was largely ignored by policymakers. This activism took place before the first Earth Day in 1970; however, many of these struggles went unnoticed or were defined as merely part of the "modern" environmental movement. This chapter outlines a framework that can be used to address disparate impact, unequal protection, and environmental discrimination.

Anatomy of Early Struggles

In 1967, students at predominantly African American Texas Southern University in Houston were involved in a campus riot triggered by the death of an eight-year-old African American girl, who had drowned at a garbage dump. Student protesters questioned why a garbage dump was located in the middle of the mostly African American Sunnyside neighborhood.[1] The protests got out of hand. Police were met with rocks and bottles. Gunshots were fired. A police officer, struck by a ricocheting bullet, was killed. Nearly 500 male students were cleared from the dormitories, and many of the leaders were arrested. The Kerner Commission classified the disturbance at Texas Southern University as a "serious disorder."[2]

In 1968, Reverend Martin Luther King, Jr., went to Memphis on an environmental justice mission – better working conditions and pay for striking African American garbage workers. King was killed in Memphis before he could complete this mission. Nevertheless, garbage and landfills did not disappear as an environmental justice issue.

In 1979, residents of Houston's Northwood Manor subdivision (a suburban neighborhood of African American home owners) filed the first lawsuit charging environmental discrimination. More than 83 percent of the Northwood Manor residents owned their homes. In *Bean v. Southwestern Waste Management,* Houston residents charged Browning-Ferris Industries with locating a municipal solid waste landfill in their community. An early attempt to place a similar facility in the same area in 1970 – when the area was mostly white – had been defeated by the Harris County Board of Supervisors.

Houston has a long history of locating its solid waste facilities in communities of color, especially in African American neighborhoods. From the early 1920s through the late 1970s, all five of the city-owned sanitary landfills and six of its eight municipal

From *Unequal Protection: Environmental Justice and Communities of Color* (San Francisco, CA: Sierra Club Books, 1994), pp. 3–22. © 1994 by Robert D. Bullard. Reprinted with permission from the author and Sierra Club Books.

solid waste incinerators were located in mostly African American neighborhoods. Similarly, three of the four privately owned solid waste landfills were located in mostly African American communities during this period. African Americans, however, made up only 28 percent of the city's population. Despite the overwhelming statistical evidence, the plaintiffs lost their lawsuit, and the Whispering Pines landfill was built in Northwood Manor.[3]

Some proponents of the Whispering Pines landfill suggested that the African American neighborhood would benefit from the waste facility by way of the jobs and taxes it would provide. However, Charles Streadit, president of Houston's Northeast Community Action Group, addressed the benefits and liabilities associated with the landfill in his neighborhood:

> Sure, Browning-Ferris Industries [owner of the Whispering Pines landfill] pays taxes, but so do we. We need all the money we can get to upgrade our school system. But we shouldn't have to be poisoned to get improvements for our children. When my property values go down, that means less for the schools and my children's education. . . . A silent war is being waged against black neighborhoods. Slowly, we are being picked off by the industries that don't give a damn about polluting our neighborhood, contaminating our water, fouling our air, clogging our streets with big garbage trucks, and lowering our property values. It's hard enough for blacks to scrape and save enough money to buy a home, then you see your dream shattered by a garbage dump. That's a dirty trick. No amount of money can buy self-respect.[4]

The aforementioned examples show a clear link between civil rights and environmental justice. However, it was not until the early 1980s that a national movement for environmental justice took root in several mainstream civil rights organizations. The environmental justice movement took shape out of the 1982 protests in Warren County, North Carolina. This mostly African American and rural county had been selected as the burial site for 30,000 cubic yards of soil contaminated with highly toxic PCBs (polychlorinated biphenyls). Oil laced with PCBs had been illegally dumped along roadways in fourteen North Carolina counties in 1978; the roadways were cleaned up in 1982.[5]

More than 500 protesters were jailed over the siting of the Warren County PCB landfill. Demonstrations were led by a number of national civil rights advocacy groups, including the United Church of Christ Commission for Racial Justice, the Southern Christian Leadership Conference, and the Congressional Black Caucus. African American civil rights activists, political officials, religious leaders, and local residents marched in protest against "Hunt's Dump" (named for Texas's governor at that time, James Hunt). Why had Warren County been selected for the PCB landfill? Opponents contend that the decision made more political sense than environmental sense.[6]

Although the demonstrations were unsuccessful in halting construction of the landfill, the protests marked the first time African Americans had mobilized a national, broad-based group to oppose what they defined as environmental racism. The demonstrations also prompted District of Columbia delegate Walter Fauntroy, who was chairman of the Congressional Black Caucus, to initiate the 1983 US General Accounting Office (GAO) study of hazardous waste landfill siting in the Environmental Protection Agency's Region IV.[7] Fauntroy had been active in the protests and was one of the many who went to jail over the landfill.

The 1983 GAO study found a strong relationship between the location of off-site hazardous waste landfills and the race and socioeconomic status of the surrounding communities. The study identified four off-site hazardous waste landfills in the eight states (Alabama, Florida, Georgia, Kentucky, Mississippi, North Carolina, South Carolina, and Tennessee) that constitute the EPA's Region IV. The four sites included Chemical Waste Management (Sumter County, Alabama); SCA Services (Sumter County, South Carolina); Industrial Chemical Company (Chester County, South Carolina); and the Warren County PCB landfill (Warren County, North Carolina).

African Americans made up the majority of the population in three of the four communities where off-site hazardous waste landfills were located. In 1983, African Americans were clearly overrepresented in communities with waste sites, since they made up only about one-fifth of the region's population, yet African American communities contained three-fourths of the off-site landfills. These ecological imbalances have not been reversed a decade later. In 1992, African Americans constituted about one-fifth of the population in Region IV. However, the two operating off-site hazardous waste landfills in the region were located in zip code regions where African Americans made up the majority of the population.

A new form of environmental activism has emerged in communities of color. Activists have not limited their attacks to well-publicized toxic contamination issues but have begun to seek remedial action on neighborhood disinvestment, housing discrimination and residential segregation, urban mass transportation, pollution, and other environmental problems that threaten public safety.

Activist groups of color have begun to build a national movement for justice. In October 1991, the First National People of Color Environmental Leadership Summit was held in Washington, DC. The Summit demonstrated that it is possible to build a multi-issue, multiracial environmental movement around *justice*. Environmental activism was shown to be alive and well in African American, Latino American, Asian American, and Native American communities.

The four-day Summit was attended by more than 650 grass-roots and national leaders representing more than 300 environmental groups of color. The Summit was planned *by* people of color. Delegates came from all fifty states, including Alaska and Hawaii, as well as from Puerto Rico, Chile, Mexico, and the Marshall Islands. Delegates attended the Summit to share their action strategies, redefine the environmental movement, and develop common plans for addressing environmental problems affecting people of color in the United States and around the world.

Grass-roots groups organized themselves around a number of environmental issues, ranging from the siting of landfills and incinerators to lead pollution. At the Summit, delegates adopted the "Principles of Environmental Justice," which they are using as a guide for organizing, networking, and relating to other groups. The common thread that runs throughout the grass-roots groups of color is their demand for a *just* environment.

The Environmental Justice Framework

There is general agreement that the nation's environmental problems need immediate attention. The head of the US Environmental Protection Agency, writing in the agency's *EPA Journal*, stressed that "environmental

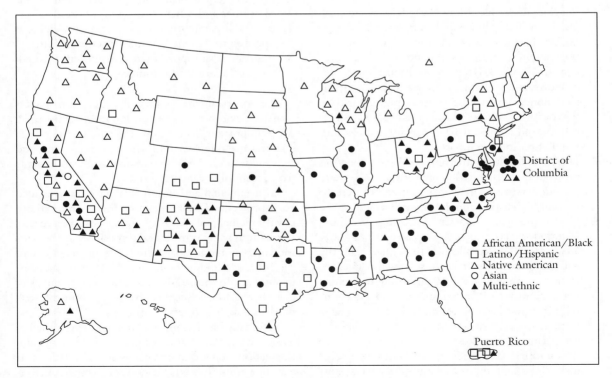

Figure 64.1   People of color grassroots environmental groups.

protection should be applied fairly."[8] However, the nation's environmental laws, regulations, and policies are not applied uniformly across the board, resulting in some individuals, neighborhoods, and communities being exposed to elevated health risks.

Environmental decision making operates at the juncture of science, technology, economics, politics, and ethics. A 1992 study by staff writers from the *National Law Journal* uncovered glaring inequities in the way the federal EPA enforces its laws. The authors write:

> There is a racial divide in the way the US government cleans up toxic waste sites and punishes polluters. White communities see faster action, better results and stiffer penalties than communities where blacks, Hispanics and other minorities live. This unequal protection often occurs whether the community is wealthy or poor.[9]

After examining census data, civil court dockets, and the EPA's own record of performance at 1,177 Superfund toxic waste sites, the *National Law Journal* report revealed the following:

1. Penalties under hazardous waste laws at sites having the greatest white population were 500 percent higher than penalties with the greatest minority population, averaging $335,566 for white areas, compared to $55,318 for minority areas.
2. The disparity under the toxic waste law occurs by race alone, not income. The average penalty in areas with the lowest income is $113,491, 3 percent more than the average penalty in areas with the highest median incomes.
3. For all the federal environmental laws aimed at protecting citizens from air, water, and waste pollution, penalties in white communities were 46 percent higher than in minority communities.
4. Under the giant Superfund cleanup program, abandoned hazardous waste sites in minority areas take 20 percent longer to be placed on the national priority list than those in white areas.
5. In more than half of the 10 autonomous regions that administer EPA programs around the country, action on cleanup at Superfund sites begins from 12 percent to 42 percent later at minority sites than at white sites.
6. At minority sites, the EPA chooses "containment," the capping or walling off of a hazardous waste dump site, 7 percent more frequently than

the cleanup method preferred under the law, permanent "treatment," to eliminate the waste or rid it of its toxins. At white sites, the EPA orders treatment 22 percent more often than containment.[10]

These findings suggest that unequal environmental protection places communities of color at special risk. The environmental justice framework attempts to uncover the underlying assumptions that may influence environmental decision making. It also rests on an analysis of strategies to eliminate unfair, unjust, and inequitable conditions and decisions. The basic elements of the framework consist of five basic characteristics:

1. Incorporates the principle of the right of all individuals to be protected from environmental degradation,
2. Adopts a public health model of prevention (elimination of the threat before harm occurs) as the preferred strategy,
3. Shifts the burden of proof to polluters and dischargers who do harm or discriminate or who do not give equal protection to racial and ethnic minorities and other "protected" classes,
4. Allows disparate impact and statistical weight, as opposed to "intent," to infer discrimination,
5. Redresses disproportionate risk burdens through targeted action and resources.

The goal of an environmental justice framework is to make environmental protection more democratic. More important, it brings to the surface the *ethical* and *political* questions of "who gets what, why, and in what amount."[11] Who pays for, and who benefits from, technological expansion?

Environmental and health laws have not provided equal protection for all Americans. Most of the nation's environmental policies distribute the costs in a regressive pattern while providing disproportionate benefits for whites and individuals who fall at the upper end of the education and income scale.[12] Numerous studies, dating back to the 1970s, reveal that communities of color have borne greater health and environmental risk burdens than has society at large.[13]

Nationally based conservation and environmental groups have played an instrumental role in shaping this nation's environmental laws and regulations. It was not until recently, however, that these nongovernmental organizations (NGOs) paid attention to environmental and health threats to poor, working-class persons and to communities of color.

The environmental justice movement attempts to address environmental enforcement, compliance, policy formulation, and decision making. It defines environment in very broad terms, as the places where people live, work, and play. The question of environmental justice is not anchored in a scientific debate but rests on an ethical analysis of environmental decision making.

Current decision-making models have proven to be inadequate in protecting at-risk communities. Emphasis on defining risk as the probability of fatality addresses only part of the health threats. Should endangered communities have to wait for a "body count" for government to act? Many communities would say no to this question.

Often, environmental stressors result in adverse health effects short of death. The health effects might be developmental, reproductive, respiratory, neurotoxic, or psychological in nature. As a consequence, the assignment of "acceptable" risk, use of averages, and siting of risky technologies (i.e., incinerators, landfills, chemical plants, smelters, etc.) often result from value judgments that serve to legitimate the imposition of inequitable social policies.

Endangered Communities

Millions of Americans live in housing and physical environments that are overburdened with environmental problems including older housing with lead-based paint, congested freeways that criss-cross their neighborhoods, industries that emit dangerous pollutants into the area, and abandoned toxic waste sites.

Virtually all of the studies of exposure to outdoor air pollution have found significant differences in exposure by income and race.[14] African Americans and Latino Americans are more likely than whites to live in areas with reduced air quality. For example, National Argonne Laboratory researchers D. R. Wernette and L. A. Nieves found the following:

> In 1990, 437 of the 3,109 counties and independent cities failed to meet at least one of the EPA ambient air quality standards. . . . 57 percent of whites, 65 percent of African Americans, and 80 percent of Hispanics live in 437 counties with substandard air quality. Out of the whole population, a total of 33 percent of whites, 50 percent of African Americans, and 60 percent of Hispanics live in the

136 counties in which two or more air pollutants exceed standards. The percentage living in the 29 counties designated as nonattainment areas for three or more pollutants are 12 percent of whites, 20 percent of African Americans, and 31 percent of Hispanics.[15]

The public health community has very little information to explain the magnitude of some of the health problems related to air pollution. However, we do know that persons suffering from asthma are particularly sensitive to the effects of carbon monoxide, sulfur dioxides, particulate matter, ozone, and nitrogen oxides.[16] African Americans, for example, have a significantly higher prevalence of asthma than does the general population.[17]

In the heavily populated Los Angeles air basin, more than 71 percent of African Americans and 50 percent of Latino Americans live in areas with the most polluted air, while only 34 percent of whites live in highly polluted areas.[18] For a few days in 1992, the attention of the entire world was affixed on the flames of Los Angeles. Even before the uprising, however, *San Francisco Examiner* reporter Jane Kay described the zip code region in which the now riot-torn South Central Los Angeles neighborhood is located as the "dirtiest" zip code (90058) in California.[19] This 1-square-mile area is saturated with abandoned toxic waste sites, freeways, smokestacks, and wastewater pipes from polluting industries.

Efforts to rebuild South Central Los Angeles and the other neighborhoods scarred by the uprising will need to incorporate environmental justice initiatives – rebuilding will need to encompass more than replacing the burned-out liquor stores, pawnshops, check-cashing centers, and fast food operations.

A "green" initiative will need to incorporate strategies employing incumbent residents in cleanup and rebuilding efforts that adopt environmentally sound technologies. Moreover, redlining practices must be vigorously attacked if any serious rebuilding of South Central Los Angeles is to take place. A partnership is needed between community institutions and businesses and the various government agencies (environmental protection, housing, public health, public works, human services, job training, education, business development, law enforcement, etc.) to create sustainable neighborhoods.

Threatened communities in southeastern Louisiana's petrochemical corridor (the 85-mile stretch along the Mississippi River from Baton

Rouge to New Orleans) typify the industrial madness that has gone unchecked for too long. The corridor has been dubbed "Cancer Alley" by some environmentalists.[20] Health concerns raised by residents and grass-roots activists who live in Alsen, Saint Gabriel, Geismer, Morrisonville, and Lions, all of which are located in close proximity to polluting industries, have not been adequately addressed by local, state, and federal agencies, including the federal EPA and the Agency for Toxic Substances and Disease Registry (ATSDR).

A few contaminated African American communities in Cancer Alley have been bought out or are in the process of being bought out by industries under their "good neighbor" programs. Dow Chemical, the state's largest chemical plant, is buying out residents of mostly African American Morrisonville.[21] The communities of Sunrise and Reveilletown (founded by former slaves) no longer exist. The buyout settlements are often sealed. Few of the recent settlement agreements allow for health monitoring or surveillance of affected residents once they are dispersed.[22]

Some settlements have even required the "victims" to sign waivers that preclude them from bringing any further lawsuits against the polluting industry. These practices have resulted in the scattering of residents, making it difficult to carry out follow-up or long-term health monitoring.

A few health assessments have been conducted by federal agencies, but few of these reports have found their way into the hands of residents of the affected communities. An environmental justice framework could assist communities in Cancer Alley as they negotiate buyout agreements or contemplate litigation or some other risk reduction strategy.

Industrial encroachment into Chicago's South Side neighborhoods is yet another example of endangered communities. Chicago is the nation's third largest city and one of the most racially segregated cities in the country. More than 92 percent of the city's 1.1 million African American residents live in racially segregated areas. The Altgeld Gardens housing project, located on the city's Southeast Side, is one of these segregated enclaves.

Altgeld Gardens is encircled by municipal and hazardous waste landfills, toxic waste incinerators, grain elevators, sewer treatment facilities, smelters, steel mills, and a host of other polluting industries. Because of the physical location, Hazel Johnson, a community organizer in the neighborhood, has dubbed the area a "toxic doughnut." Others see their community as a "toxic soup," where residents perform the role of human guinea pigs.

The Southeast Side neighborhood is home to 150,000 residents, of whom 70 percent are African American and 11 percent are Latino American. It also has 50 active or closed commercial hazardous waste landfills, 100 factories (including seven chemical plants and five steel mills), and 103 abandoned toxic waste dumps.[23] Currently, health and risk assessment data collected by the state of Illinois and the federal EPA for facility permitting have failed to take into account the cumulative and synergistic effects of having so many "layers" of poisons in one community.

Altgeld Gardens residents wonder at what point government will declare a moratorium on permitting any new noxious facilities in their neighborhood. Can a "saturation threshold" be determined without the necessary studies (one such study would be mandated under the proposed Environmental Justice Act of 1992) that delineate the cumulative health impacts of all of the polluting industries in the area? All of the polluting industries (lead smelters, landfills, incinerators, steel mills, foundries, metal-plating and metal-coating operations, grain elevators, etc.) imperil the health of nearby residents and should be factored into any future facility permitting decision.

Environmental justice advocates have sought to persuade the various levels of government (federal, state, and local) to adopt a framework that addresses distributive impacts, concentration, enforcement, and compliance concerns. They have taken their fight to city halls, state capitals, and the US Congress.

In 1990, New York City adopted a "fair share" legislative model designed to ensure that every borough and every community within each borough bear its fair share of noxious facilities. Public hearings have begun to address risk burdens in New York City's boroughs. Proceedings from a hearing on environmental disparities in the Bronx point to concerns raised by African Americans and Puerto Ricans who see their neighborhoods threatened by garbage transfer stations, salvage yards, and recycling centers. The report reveals the following:

> On the Hunts Point peninsula alone there are at least thirty private transfer stations, a large-scale Department of Environmental Protection (DEP) sewage treatment plant and a sludge dewatering facility, two Department of Sanitation (DOS) marine transfer stations, a citywide privately regulated medical waste incinerator, a proposed DOS resource

recovery facility and three proposed DEP sludge processing facilities.

That all of the facilities listed above are located immediately adjacent to the Hunts Point Food Center, the biggest wholesale food and meat distribution facility of its kind in the United States, and the largest source of employment in the South Bronx, is disconcerting. A policy whereby low-income and minority communities have become the "dumping grounds" for unwanted land uses works to create an environment of disincentives to community-based development initiatives. It also undermines existing businesses.[24]

In 1992, Chicago congresswoman Cardiss Collins offered an amendment to the bill reauthorizing the Resource Conservation and Recovery Act (RCRA), requiring "community information statements" that assess the demographic makeup of proposed waste site areas and the cumulative impact a new facility would have on the existing environmental burden.

In a similar vein, in 1992 Georgia congressman John Lewis, a longtime civil rights activist, and former senator Al Gore (now vice president) introduced their version of an Environmental Justice Act. (The 1993 version of the Environmental Justice Act was introduced in the House by John Lewis and in the Senate by Max Baucus, a Democrat from Montana.) The act (S. 2806 and H. R. 5326) was designed to "establish a program to ensure nondiscriminatory compliance with environmental, health, and safety laws and to ensure equal protection of the public health."

Some communities form a special case for environmental justice and risk reduction. Because of more stringent state and federal environmental regulations, Native American reservations, from New York to California, have become targets for risky technologies. Native American nations are quasi-sovereign and do not fall under state jurisdiction. Historically, reservations were "lands the feds forgot," and their inhabitants "must contend with some of America's worst pollution."[25]

Few reservations have infrastructures to handle the risky technologies that are being proposed for their communities, and more than 100 waste disposal facilities have been proposed for Native American lands.[26] Reservation inhabitants have among the worst poverty, unemployment, education, and health problems of all Americans. Targeting Native American land for disposal of wastes is a form of "garbage imperialism."

Toxic Waste Time Bombs

The hazardous waste problem continues to be one of the most "serious problems facing the industrial world."[27] Toxic time bombs are not randomly scattered across the urban landscape. In New Jersey (a state with one of the highest concentrations of uncontrolled toxic waste dumps), hazardous waste sites are often located in communities that have high percentages of poor, elderly, young, and minority residents.[28]

Few national studies have been conducted on the sociodemographic characteristics of populations living around toxic waste sites. Although the federal EPA has been in business for more than two decades, it has yet to conduct a national study of the problems of toxic wastes in communities of color. In fact, the United Church of Christ Commission for Racial Justice, a church-based civil rights organization, conducted the first national study on this topic.[29]

The Commission for Racial Justice's landmark study, *Toxic Wastes and Race in the United States*, found race to be the single most important factor (i.e., more important than income, home ownership rate, and property values) in the location of abandoned toxic waste sites.[30] The study also found that (1) three out of five African Americans live in communities with abandoned toxic waste sites; (2) 60 percent (15 million) African Americans live in communities with one or more abandoned toxic waste sites; (3) three of the five largest commercial hazardous waste landfills are located in predominantly African American or Latino American communities and account for 40 percent of the nation's total estimated landfill capacity; and (4) African Americans are heavily over-represented in the populations of cities with the largest number of abandoned toxic waste sites.[31]

In metropolitan Chicago, for example, more than 81.3 percent of Latino Americans and 76 percent of African Americans live in communities with abandoned toxic waste sites, compared with 59 percent of whites. Similarly, 81.3 percent of Latino Americans and 69.8 percent of African Americans in the Houston metropolitan area live in communities with abandoned toxic waste sites, compared with 57.1 percent of whites. Latino Americans in the Los Angeles metropolitan area are nearly twice as likely as their Anglo counterparts to live in a community with an abandoned toxic waste site.[32]

The mounting waste problem is adding to the potential health threat to environmental high-impact

Table 64.1   Estimated percentages of children (living in cities with population over 1 million) 0.5–5 years old with blood levels greater than 15 µg/dl, by race and income (1988)

Race	< $6,000	Income $6,000–$15,000	> $15,000
African American	68%	54%	38%
White	36%	23%	12%

Source: Agency for Toxic Substances and Disease Registry, *The Nature and Extent of Lead Poisoning in Children in the United States: A Report to Congress* (Atlanta: US Department of Health and Human Services, 1988)

areas. Incineration has become the leading technology for disposal of this waste. This technology is also becoming a major source of dioxin, as well as lead, mercury, and other heavy metals released into the environment. For example, millions of pounds of lead per year will be emitted from the nation's municipal solid waste incinerators in the next few years. All of this lead is being released despite what we know about its hazards to human health.

Hazardous waste incinerators are not randomly scattered across the landscape. A 1990 Greenpeace report, *Playing with Fire*, found that (1) the minority portion of the population in communities with existing incinerators is 89 percent higher than the national average; (2) communities where incinerators are proposed have minority populations 60 percent higher than the national average; (3) average income in communities with existing incinerators is 15 percent less than the national average; (4) property values in communities that are hosts to incinerators are 38 percent lower than the national average; and (5) average property values are 35 percent lower in communities where incinerators are proposed.[33]

Environmental scientists have not refined their research methodologies to assess the cumulative and synergistic effects of all of society's poisons on the human body. However, some health problems cannot wait for the tools to catch up with common sense. For example, the nation's lead contamination problem demands urgent attention. An environmental strategy is needed to address childhood lead poisoning. It is time for action.

The Politics of Lead Poisoning

Why has so little been done to prevent lead poisoning in the United States? Overwhelming scientific evidence exists on the ill effects of lead on the human body. However, very little has been done to rid the nation of lead poisoning – a preventable disease tagged the "number one environmental health threat to children" by the federal Agency for Toxic Substances and Disease Registry.[34]

Lead began to be phased out of gasoline in the 1970s. It is ironic that the "regulations were initially developed to protect the newly developed catalytic converter in automobiles, a pollution-control device that happens to be rendered inoperative by lead, rather than to safeguard human health."[35] In 1971, a child was not considered at risk for lead poisoning unless he or she had 400 micrograms of lead per liter of blood (or 40 micrograms per deciliter [µg/dl]). Since that time, the amount of lead that is considered safe has continually dropped. In 1991, the US Public Health Service changed the official definition of an unsafe level to 10 µg/dl. Even at that level, a child's IQ can be slightly diminished and physical growth stunted. Lead poisoning is correlated with both income and race (see table 64.1).[36]

A coalition of environmental, social justice, and civil libertarian groups are now joining forces to address the lead problem. The Natural Resources Defense Council, the NAACP Legal Defense and Education Fund, the American Civil Liberties Union, and the Legal Aid Society of Alameda County, California, won an out-of-court settlement worth $15 million to $20 million for a blood lead-testing program. The lawsuit, *Matthews v. Coye*, involved the failure of the state of California to conduct federally mandated testing for lead of some 557,000 poor children who receive Medicaid. This historic agreement will probably trigger similar actions in other states that have failed to live up to federally mandated screening requirements.[37]

Conclusion

Despite the recent attempts by federal environmental and health agencies to reduce risks to all Americans, environmental inequities still persist. Some children, workers, and communities are disproportionately affected by unhealthy air, unsafe drinking water, dangerous chemicals, lead, pesticides, and toxic wastes.

If this nation is to achieve environmental justice, the environment in urban ghettos, barrios, reservations, and rural poverty pockets must be given the same protection as that provided to the suburbs. All communities – African American or white, rich or poor – deserve to be protected from the ravages of pollution.

The current emphasis on waste management and pollution control regulations encourages dependence on disposal technologies, which are themselves sources of toxic pollution. Pushing incinerators and risk technologies off on people under the guise of economic development is not a solution to this nation's waste problem. It is imperative that waste reduction programs mandated by federal, state, and local government be funded that set goals for recycling, composting, and using recycled materials.

An environmental justice framework needs to be incorporated into a national policy on facility siting. In addition to the standard technical requirements, environmental justice proposals will need to require implementation of some type of "fair share" plan that takes into account sociodemographic, economic, and cultural factors of affected communities. It is clear that current environmental regulations and "protectionist" devices (zoning, deed restrictions, and other land use controls) have not had the same impact on all segments of society.

The federal EPA needs to take the lead in ensuring that all Americans are protected. It is time for this nation to clean up the health-threatening lead contamination problem and prevent future generations from being poisoned. No segment of society should be allowed to become a dumping ground or be sacrificed because of economic vulnerability or racial discrimination.

In order for risk reduction strategies to be effective in environmental high-impact areas and for vulnerable populations, there needs to be sweeping changes in key areas of the science model and environmental health research. At minimum, these changes must include a reevaluation of the attitudes, biases, and values of the scientists who conduct environmental health research and risk assessment and the officials who make policy decisions.

Acceptance of the public as an active and equal partner in research and environmental decision making is a first step toward building trust within affected communities. Government agencies and other responsible parties need to incorporate principles of environmental justice into their strategic planning of risk reduction.

We need a holistic methodology in documenting, remediating, and preventing environmental health problems. Prevention is the key. Environmental justice demands that lead poisoning – the number one environmental health problem affecting children – be given the attention and priority it deserves. It is the poorest among the nation's inhabitants who are being poisoned at an alarming rate. Many of these individuals and families have little or no access to regular health care.

The solution lies in leveling the playing field and protecting all Americans. Environmental decision makers have failed to address the "justice" questions of who gets help and who does not, who can afford help and who cannot, why some contaminated communities get studied while others are left off the research agenda, why some communities get cleaned up at a faster rate than others, why some cleanup methods are selected over others, and why industry poisons some communities and not others.

Finally, a national environmental justice action agenda is needed to begin addressing environmental inequities that result from procedural, geographic, and societal imbalances. Federal, state, and local legislation is needed to target resources for those areas where societal risk burdens are the greatest. States that are initiating fair share plans to address interstate waste conflicts need also to begin addressing intrastate environmental siting imbalances. It is time for environmental justice to become a national priority.

Notes

1   Robert D. Bullard, *Invisible Houston: The Black Experience in Boom and Bust* (College Station: Texas A & M University Press, 1987), pp. 110–11.

2   National Advisory Commission on Civil Disorders, *Report of the National Advisory Commission on Civil Disorders* (New York: Dutton, 1968), pp. 40–1.

3   See Robert D. Bullard, *Dumping in Dixie: Race, Class, and Environmental Quality* (Boulder, CO: Westview Press, 1990), chap. 3.

4   Interview with Charles Streadit, president of the Houston Northeast Community Action Group, May 30, 1988.

5   Ken Geiser and Gerry Waneck, "PCBs and Warren County," *Science for the People* 15 (July–August 1983): 13–17.

6   Ibid.

7   General Accounting Office, *Siting of Hazardous Waste Landfills and Their Correlation with Racial and Economic Status of Surrounding Communities* (Washington, DC: General Accounting Office, 1983), p. 1.

8   William K. Reilly, "Environmental Equity: EPA's Position," *EPA Journal* 18 (March–April 1992): 18.

9   Marianne Lavelle and Marcia Coyle, "Unequal Protection," *National Law Journal*, September 21, 1992, pp. S1–S2.

10   Ibid., p. S2.

11   See Robert D. Bullard and Beverly H. Wright, "The Politics of Pollution: Implications for the Black Community," *Phylon* 47 (March 1986): 71–8; Bullard, *Dumping in Dixie*, pp. 25–43.

12   See R. B. Stewart, "Paradoxes of Liberty, Integrity, and Fraternity: The Collective Nature of Environmental Quality and Judicial Review of Administrative Action," *Environmental Law* 7 (1977): 474–6; Leonard Gianessi, H. M. Peskin, and E. Wolff, "The Distributional Effects of Uniform Air Pollution Policy in the US," *Quarterly Journal of Economics* 56 (May 1977): 281–301.

13   See W. J. Kruvant, "People, Energy, and Pollution," pp. 125–67 in *The American Energy Consumer*, ed. D. K. Newman and Dawn Day (Cambridge, MA: Ballinger, 1975); Robert D. Bullard, "Solid Waste Sites and the Black Houston Community," *Sociological Inquiry* 53 (Spring 1983): 273–88; United Church of Christ Commission for Racial Justice, *Toxic Wastes and Race in the United States: A National Study of the Racial and Socioeconomic Characteristics of Communities with Hazardous Waste Sites* (New York: United Church of Christ Commission for Racial Justice, 1987); Michel Gelobter, "The Distribution of Air Pollution by Income and Race" (paper presented at the Second Symposium on Social Science in Resource Management, Urbana, Illinois, June 1988); Dick Russell, "Environmental Racism," *Amicus Journal* 11 (Spring 1989): 22–32; Bullard, *Dumping in Dixie*; Paul Ong and Evelyn Blumenberg, "Race and Environmentalism" (Los Angeles: University of California, Los Angeles, Graduate School of Architecture and Urban Planning, March 1990); Eric Mann, *LA's Lethal Air: New Strategies for Policy, Organizing, and Action* (Los Angeles: Labor/Community Strategy Center, 1991); Leslie A. Nieves,

"Not in Whose Backyard? Minority Population Concentrations and Noxious Facility Sites" (paper presented at the annual meeting of the American Association for the Advancement of Science, Chicago, February 1991); D. R. Wernette and L. A. Nieves, "Breathing Polluted Air: Minorities Are Disproportionately Exposed," *EPA Journal* 18 (March–April 1992): 16–17; Robert D. Bullard, "In Our Backyards: Minority Communities Get Most of the Dumps," *EPA Journal* 18 (March–April 1992): 11–12; Bunyan Bryant and Paul Mohai, eds., *Race and the Incidence of Environmental Hazards* (Boulder, CO: Westview Press, 1992).

14   See Gelobter, "The Distribution of Air Pollution."

15   Wernette and Nieves, "Breathing Polluted Air," pp. 16–17.

16   See Mann, *LA's Lethal Air*.

17   See H. P. Mak, H. Abbey, and R. C. Talamo, "Prevalence of Asthma and Health Service Utilization of Asthmatic Children in an Inner City," *Journal of Allergy and Clinical Immunology* 70 (1982): 367–72; I. F. Goldstein and A. L. Weinstein, "Air Pollution and Asthma: Effects of Exposure to Short-Term Sulfur Dioxide Peaks," *Environmental Research* 40 (1986): 332–45; J. Schwartz, D. Gold, D. W. Dockey, S. T. Weiss, and F. E. Speizer, "Predictors of Asthma and Persistent Wheeze in a National Sample of Children in the United States," *American Review of Respiratory Disease* 142 (1990): 555–62.

18   Ong and Blumenberg, "Race and Environmentalism"; Mann, *LA's Lethal Air*.

19   Jane Kay, "Fighting Toxic Racism: LA's Minority Neighborhood Is the 'Dirtiest' in the State," *San Francisco Examiner*, April 7, 1991.

20   Conger Beasley, "Of Pollution and Poverty: Keeping Watch in 'Cancer Alley,'" *Buzzworm* 2 (July–August 1990): 39–45.

21   James O'Byrne, "Death of a Town," *Times Picayune*, February 20, 1991.

22   Bullard, *Dumping in Dixie*, pp. 65–9; James O'Byrne and Mark Schleifstein, "Invisible Poisons," *Times Picayune*, February 18, 1991.

23   Greenpeace, "Home Street, USA," *Greenpeace* (October–November 1991): 8–13.

24   Fernando Ferrer, "Testimony by the Office of Bronx Borough President," *Proceedings of the Public Hearing on Minorities and the Environment: An Exploration into the Effects of Environmental Policies, Practices, and Conditions on Minority and Low-Income Communities* (Bronx, NY: Bronx Planning Office, September 20, 1991), p. 27.

25   Robert Tomsho, "Dumping Grounds: Indian Tribes Contend with Some of the Worst of America's Pollution," *Wall Street Journal*, November 29, 1990; Jane Kay, "Indian Lands Targeted for Waste Disposal

Sites," *San Francisco Examiner*, April 10, 1991; Bradley Angel, *The Toxic Threat to Indian Lands: A Greenpeace Report* (San Francisco: Greenpeace, 1992).

26 Angel, *Toxic Threat to Indian Lands.*

27 Samuel S. Epstein, Lester O. Brown, and Carl Pope, *Hazardous Waste in America* (San Francisco: Sierra Club Books, 1983), pp. 33–9.

28 Michael R. Greenberg and Richard F. Anderson, *Hazardous Waste Sites: The Credibility Gap* (New Brunswick, NJ: Rutgers University, Center for Urban Policy Research, 1984), pp. 158–9; Bullard, *Dumping in Dixie*, pp. 4–5.

29 United Church of Christ Commission for Racial Justice, *Toxic Wastes and Race.*

30 Ibid., pp. xiii–xiv.

31 Ibid., pp. 18–19.

32 United Church of Christ Commission for Racial Justice, *Toxic Wastes and Race.*

33 Pat Costner and Joe Thornton, *Playing with Fire* (Washington, DC: Greenpeace, 1990).

34 Agency for Toxic Substances and Disease Registry, *The Nature and Extent of Lead Poisoning in Children in the United States: A Report to Congress* (Atlanta: US Department of Health and Human Services, 1988).

35 Peter Reich, *The Hour of Lead* (Washington, DC: Environmental Defense Fund, 1992), p. 42.

36 Agency for Toxic Substances and Disease Registry, *Nature and Extent of Lead Poisoning.*

37 Bill Lann Lee, "Environmental Litigation on Behalf of Poor, Minority Children; *Matthews v. Coye:* A Case Study" (paper presented at the annual meeting of the American Association for the Advancement of Science, Chicago, April 1992).

65   Just Garbage

Peter S. Wenz

Environmental racism is evident in practices that expose racial minorities in the United States, and people of color around the world, to disproportionate shares of environmental hazards.[1] These include toxic chemicals in factories, toxic herbicides and pesticides in agriculture, radiation from uranium mining, lead from paint on older buildings, toxic wastes illegally dumped, and toxic wastes legally stored. In this chapter, which concentrates on issues of toxic waste, both illegally dumped and legally stored, I will examine the justness of current practices as well as the arguments commonly given in their defense. I will then propose an alternative practice that is consistent with prevailing principles of justice.

A Defense of Current Practices

Defenders often claim that because economic, not racial, considerations account for disproportionate impacts on nonwhites, current practices are neither racist nor morally objectionable. Their reasoning recalls the Doctrine of Double Effect. According to that doctrine, an effect whose production is usually blameworthy becomes blameless when it is incidental to, although predictably conjoined with, the production of another effect whose production is morally justified. The classic case concerns a pregnant woman with uterine cancer. A common, acceptable treatment for uterine cancer is hysterectomy. This will predictably end the pregnancy, as would an abortion. However, Roman Catholic scholars who usually consider abortion blameworthy consider it blameless in this context because it is merely incidental to hysterectomy, which is morally justified to treat uterine cancer. The hysterectomy would be performed in the absence of pregnancy, so the abortion effect is produced neither as an end-in-itself, nor as a means to reach the desired end, which is the cure of cancer.

Defenders of practices that disproportionately disadvantage nonwhites seem to claim, in keeping with the Doctrine of Double Effect, that racial

From Laura Westra and Peter S. Wenz, eds., *Faces of Environmental Racism: Confronting Issues of Global Justice* (Lanham, MD: Rowman & Littlefield Publishers Inc., 1995), pp. 57–71. © 1995 by Rowman & Littlefield Publishers, Inc.

effects are blameless because they are sought neither as ends-in-themselves nor as means to reach a desired goal. They are merely predictable side effects of economic and political practices that disproportionately expose poor people to toxic substances. The argument is that burial of toxic wastes, and other locally undesirable land uses (LULUs), lower property values. People who can afford to move elsewhere do so. They are replaced by buyers (or renters) who are predominantly poor and cannot afford housing in more desirable areas. Law professor Vicki Been puts it this way: "As long as the market allows the existing distribution of wealth to allocate goods and services, it would be surprising indeed if, over the long run, LULUs did not impose a disproportionate burden upon the poor." People of color are disproportionately burdened due primarily to poverty, not racism.[2] This defense against charges of racism is important in the American context because racial discrimination is illegal in the United States in circumstances where economic discrimination is permitted.[3] Thus, legal remedies to disproportionate exposure of nonwhites to toxic wastes are available if racism is the cause, but not if people of color are exposed merely because they are poor.

There is strong evidence against claims of racial neutrality. Professor Been acknowledges that even if there is no racism in the process of siting LULUs, racism plays at least some part in the disproportionate exposure of African Americans to them. She cites evidence that "racial discrimination in the sale and rental of housing relegates people of color (especially African Americans) to the least desirable neighborhoods, regardless of their income level."[4]

Without acknowledging for a moment, then, that racism plays no part in the disproportionate exposure of nonwhites to toxic waste, I will ignore this issue to display a weakness in the argument that justice is served when economic discrimination alone is influential. I claim that even if the only discrimination is economic, justice requires redress and significant alteration of current practices. Recourse to the Doctrine of Double Effect presupposes that the primary effect, with which a second effect is incidentally conjoined, is morally justifiable. In the classic case, abortion is justified only because hysterectomy is justified as treatment for uterine cancer. I argue that disproportionate impacts on poor people violate principles of distributive justice, and so are not morally justifiable in the first place. Thus, current practices disproportionately exposing nonwhites to toxic substances are not justifiable even if incidental to the exposure of poor people.

Alternate practices that comply with acceptable principles of distributive justice are suggested below. They would largely solve problems of environmental racism (disproportionate impacts on nonwhites) while ameliorating the injustice of disproportionately exposing poor people to toxic hazards. They would also discourage production of toxic substances, thereby reducing humanity's negative impact on the environment.

The Principle of Commensurate Burdens and Benefit

We usually assume that, other things being equal, those who derive benefits should sustain commensurate burdens. We typically associate the burden of work with the benefit of receiving money, and the burdens of monetary payment and tort liability with the benefits of ownership.

There are many exceptions. For example, people can inherit money without working, and be given ownership without purchase. Another exception, which dissociates the benefit of ownership from the burden of tort liability, is the use of tax money to protect the public from hazards associated with private property, as in Superfund legislation. Again, the benefit of money is dissociated from the burden of work when governments support people who are unemployed.

The fact that these exceptions require justification, however, indicates an abiding assumption that people who derive benefits should shoulder commensurate burdens. The ability to inherit without work is justified as a benefit owed to those who wish to bequeath their wealth (which someone in the line of inheritance is assumed to have shouldered burdens to acquire). The same reasoning applies to gifts.

Using tax money (public money) to protect the public from dangerous private property is justified as encouraging private industry and commerce, which are supposed to increase public wealth. The system also protects victims in case private owners become bankrupt as, for example, in Times Beach, Missouri, where the government bought homes made worthless due to dioxin pollution. The company responsible for the pollution was bankrupt.

Tax money is used to help people who are out of work to help them find a job, improve their credentials, or feed their children. This promotes economic growth and equal opportunity. These exceptions prove the rule by the fact that justification for any deviation from the commensuration of benefits and burdens is considered necessary.

Further indication of an abiding belief that benefits and burdens should be commensurate is grumbling that, for example, many professional athletes and corporate executives are overpaid. Although the athletes and executives shoulder the burden of work, the complaint is that their benefits are disproportionate to their burdens. People on welfare are sometimes criticized for receiving even modest amounts of taxpayer money without shouldering the burdens of work, hence recurrent calls for "welfare reform." Even though these calls are often justified as means to reducing government budget deficits, the moral issue is more basic than the economic. Welfare expenditures are minor compared to other programs, and alternatives that require poor people to work are often more expensive than welfare as we know it.

The principle of commensuration between benefits and burdens is not the only moral principle governing distributive justice, and may not be the most important, but it is basic. Practices can be justified by showing them to conform, all things considered, to this principle. Thus, there is no move to "reform" the receipt of moderate pay for ordinary work, because it exemplifies the principle. On the other hand, practices that do not conform are liable to attack and require alternate justification, as we have seen in the cases of inheritance, gifts, Superfund legislation, and welfare.

Applying the principle of commensuration between burdens and benefits to the issue at hand yields the following: In the absence of countervailing considerations, the burdens of ill health associated with toxic hazards should be related to benefits derived from processes and products that create these hazards.

Toxic Hazards and Consumerism

In order to assess, in light of the principle of commensuration between benefits and burdens, the justice of current distributions of toxic hazards, the benefits of their generation must be considered. Toxic wastes result from many manufacturing proc-

esses, including those for a host of common items and materials, such as paint, solvents, plastics, and most petrochemical-based materials. These materials surround us in the paint on our houses, in our refrigerator containers, in our clothing, in our plumbing, in our garbage pails, and elsewhere.

Toxins are released into the environment in greater quantities now than ever before because we now have a consumer-oriented society where the acquisition, use, and disposal of individually owned items is greatly desired. We associate the numerical dollar value of the items at our disposal with our "standard of living," and assume that a higher standard is conducive to, if not identical with, a better life. So toxic wastes needing disposal are produced as by-products of the general pursuit of what our society defines as valuable, that is, the consumption of material goods.

Our economy requires increasing consumer demand to keep people working (to produce what is demanded). This is why there is concern each Christmas season, for example, that shoppers may not buy enough. If demand is insufficient, people may be put out of work. Demand must increase, not merely hold steady, because commercial competition improves labor efficiency in manufacture (and now in the service sector as well), so fewer workers can produce desired items. More items must be desired to forestall labor efficiency-induced unemployment, which is grave in a society where people depend primarily on wages to secure life's necessities.

Demand is kept high largely by convincing people that their lives require improvement, which consumer purchases will effect. When improvements are seen as needed, not merely desired, people purchase more readily. So our culture encourages economic expansion by blurring the distinction between wants and needs.

One way the distinction is blurred is through promotion of worry. If one feels insecure without the desired item or service, and so worries about life without it, then its provision is easily seen as a need. Commercials, and other shapers of social expectations, keep people worried by adjusting downward toward the trivial what people are expected to worry about. People worry about the provision of food, clothing, and housing without much inducement. When these basic needs are satisfied, however, attention shifts to indoor plumbing, for example, then to stylish indoor plumbing. The process continues with needs for a second or third bathroom, a kitchen disposal, and a refrigerator attached to the plumbing so that ice is made automatically in the freezer, and cold water can be obtained without even opening the refrigerator door. The same kind of progression results in cars with CD players, cellular phones, and automatic readouts of average fuel consumption per mile.

Abraham Maslow was not accurately describing people in our society when he claimed that after physiological, safety, love, and (self-) esteem needs are met, people work toward self-actualization, becoming increasingly their own unique selves by fully developing their talents. Maslow's Hierarchy of Needs describes people in our society less than Wenz's Lowerarchy of Worry. When one source of worry is put to rest by an appropriate purchase, some matter less inherently or obviously worrisome takes its place as the focus of concern. Such worry-substitution must be amenable to indefinite repetition in order to motivate purchases needed to keep the economy growing without inherent limit. If commercial society is supported by consumer demand, it is worry all the way down. Toxic wastes are produced in this context.

People tend to worry about ill health and early death without much inducement. These concerns are heightened in a society dependent upon the production of worry, so expenditure on health care consumes an increasing percentage of the gross domestic product. As knowledge of health impairment due to toxic substances increases, people are decreasingly tolerant of risks associated with their proximity. Thus, the same mindset of worry that elicits production that generates toxic wastes, exacerbates reaction to their proximity. The result is a desire for their placement elsewhere, hence the NIMBY syndrome – Not In My Back Yard. On this account, NIMBYism is not aberrantly selfish behavior, but integral to the cultural value system required for great volumes of toxic waste to be generated in the first place.

Combined with the principle of Commensurate Burdens and Benefits, that value system indicates who should suffer the burden of proximity to toxic wastes. Other things being equal, those who benefit most from the production of waste should shoulder the greatest share of burdens associated with its disposal. In our society, consumption of goods is valued highly and constitutes the principal benefit associated with the generation of toxic wastes. Such consumption is generally correlated with income and wealth. So other things being equal, justice requires that people's proximity to toxic wastes be related positively to their income and wealth. This is exactly opposite to the predominant tendency in our society, where poor people are more proximate to toxic wastes dumped illegally and stored legally.

Rejected Theories of Justice

Proponents of some theories of distributive justice may claim that current practices are justified. In this section I will explore such claims.

A widely held view of justice is that all people deserve to have their interests given equal weight. John Rawls's popular thought experiment in which people choose principles of justice while ignorant of their personal identities dramatizes the importance of equal consideration of interests. Even selfish people behind the "veil of ignorance" in Rawls's "original position" would choose to accord equal consideration to everyone's interests because, they reason, they may themselves be the victims of any inequality. Equal consideration is a basic moral premise lacking serious challenge in our culture, so it is presupposed in what follows. Disagreement centers on application of the principle.

Libertarianism

Libertarians claim that each individual has an equal right to be free of interference from other people. All burdens imposed by other people are unjustified unless part of, or consequent upon, agreement by the party being burdened. So no individual who has not consented should be burdened by burial of toxic wastes (or the emission of air pollutants, or the use of agricultural pesticides, etc.) that may increase risks of disease, disablement, or death. Discussing the effects of air pollution, libertarian Murray Rothbard writes, "The remedy is simply to enjoin anyone from injecting pollutants into the air, and thereby invading the rights of persons and property. Period."[5] Libertarians John Hospers and Tibor R. Machan seem to endorse Rothbard's position.[6]

The problem is that implementation of this theory is impractical and unjust in the context of our civilization. Industrial life as we know it inevitably includes production of pollutants and toxic substances that threaten human life and health. It is impractical to secure the agreement of every individual to the placement, whether on land, in the air, or in water, of every chemical that may adversely affect the life or health of the individuals in question. After being duly informed of the hazard, someone potentially affected is bound to object, making the placement illegitimate by libertarian criteria.

In effect, libertarians give veto power to each individual over the continuation of industrial society. This seems a poor way to accord equal consideration to everyone's interests because the interest in physical safety of any one individual is allowed to override all other interests of all other individuals in the continuation of modern life. Whether or not such life is worth pursuing, it seems unjust to put the decision for everyone in the hands of any one person.

Utilitarianism

Utilitarians consider the interests of all individuals equally, and advocate pursuing courses of action that promise to produce results containing the greatest (net) sum of good. However, irrespective of how "good" is defined, problems with utilitarian accounts of justice are many and notorious.

Utilitarianism suffers in part because its direct interest is exclusively in the sum total of good, and in the future. Since the sum of good is all that counts in utilitarianism, there is no guarantee that the good of some will not be sacrificed for the greater good of others. Famous people could receive (justifiably according to utilitarians) particularly harsh sentences for criminal activity to effect general deterrence. Even when fame results from honest pursuits, a famous felon's sentence is likely to attract more attention than sentences in other cases of similar criminal activity. Because potential criminals are more likely to respond to sentences in such cases, harsh punishment is justified for utilitarian reasons on grounds that are unrelated to the crime.

Utilitarianism suffers in cases like this not only from its exclusive attention to the sum total of good, but also from its exclusive preoccupation with future consequences, which makes the relevance of past conduct indirect. This affects not only retribution, but also reciprocity and gratitude, which utilitarians endorse only to produce the greatest sum of future benefits. The direct relevance of past agreements and benefits, which common sense assumes, disappears in utilitarianism. So does direct application of the principle of Commensurate Burdens and Benefits.

The merits of the utilitarian rejection of common sense morality need not be assessed, however, because utilitarianism seems impossible to put into practice. Utilitarian support for any particular conclusion is undermined by the inability of anyone actually to perform the kinds of calculations that utilitarians profess to use. Whether the good is identified with happiness or preference-satisfaction, the two leading contenders at the moment, utilitarians announce the conclusions of their calculations without ever being able to show the calculation itself.

When I was in school, math teachers suspected that students who could never show their work were copying answers from other students. I suspect similarly that utilitarians, whose "calculations" often support conclusions that others reach by recourse to principles of gratitude, retributive justice, commensuration between burdens and benefits, and so forth, reach conclusions on grounds of intuitions influenced predominantly by these very principles.

Utilitarians may claim that, contrary to superficial appearances, these principles are themselves supported by utilitarian calculations. But, again, no one has produced a relevant calculation. Some principles seem *prima facie* opposed to utilitarianism, such as the one prescribing special solicitude of parents for their own children. It would seem that in cold climates more good would be produced if people bought winter coats for needy children, instead of special dress coats and ski attire for their own children. But utilitarians defend the principle of special parental concern. They declare this principle consistent with utilitarianism by appeal to entirely untested, unsubstantiated assumptions about counterfactuals. It is a kind of "Just So" story that explains how good is maximized by adherence to current standards. There is no calculation at all.

Another indication that utilitarians cannot perform the calculations they profess to rely upon concerns principles whose worth is in genuine dispute. Utilitarians offer no calculations that help to settle the matter. For example, many people wonder today whether or not patriotism is a worthy moral principle. Detailed utilitarian calculations play no part in the discussion.

These are some of the reasons why utilitarianism provides no help to those deciding whether or not disproportionate exposure of poor people to toxic wastes is just.

Free market approach

Toxic wastes, a burden, could be placed where residents accept them in return for monetary payment, a benefit. Since market transactions often satisfactorily commensurate burdens and benefits, this approach may seem to honor the principle of commensuration between burdens and benefits.

Unlike many market transactions, however, whole communities, acting as corporate bodies, would have to contract with those seeking to bury wastes. Otherwise, any single individual in the community could veto the transaction, resulting in the impasse attending libertarian approaches.[7] Communities could receive money to improve such public facilities as schools, parks, and hospitals, in addition to obtaining tax revenues and jobs that result ordinarily from business expansion.

The major problem with this free market approach is that it fails to accord equal consideration to everyone's interests. Where basic or vital goods and services are at issue, we usually think equal consideration of interests requires ameliorating inequalities of distribution that markets tend to produce. For example, one reason, although not the only reason, for public education is to provide every child with the basic intellectual tools necessary for success in our society. A purely free market approach, by contrast, would result in excellent education for children of wealthy parents and little or no education for children of the nation's poorest residents. Opportunities for children of poor parents would be so inferior that we would say the children's interests had not been given equal consideration.

The reasoning is similar where vital goods are concerned. The United States has the Medicaid program for poor people to supplement market transactions in health care precisely because equal consideration of interests requires that everyone be given access to health care. The 1994 health care debate in the United States was, ostensibly, about how to achieve universal coverage, not about whether or not justice required such coverage. With the exception of South Africa, every other industrialized country already has universal coverage for health care. Where vital needs are concerned, markets are supplemented or avoided in order to give equal consideration to everyone's interests.

Another example concerns military service in time of war. The United States employed conscription during the Civil War, both world wars, the Korean War, and the war in Vietnam. When the national interest requires placing many people in mortal danger, it is considered just that exposure be largely unrelated to income and market transactions.

The United States does not currently provide genuine equality in education or health care, nor did universal conscription (of males) put all men at equal risk in time of war. In all three areas, advantage accrues to those with greater income and wealth. (During the Civil War, paying for a substitute was legal in many cases.) Imperfection in practice, however, should not obscure general agreement in theory that justice requires equal consideration of interests, and that such equal consideration requires rejecting purely free market approaches where basic or vital needs are concerned.

Toxic substances affect basic and vital interests. Lead, arsenic, and cadmium in the vicinity of children's homes can result in mental retardation of the children.[8] Navaho teens exposed to radiation from uranium mine tailings have seventeen times the national average of reproductive organ cancer.[9] Environmental Protection Agency (EPA) officials estimate that toxic air pollution in areas of South Chicago increase cancer risks one hundred to one thousand times.[10] Pollution from Otis Air Force base in Massachusetts is associated with alarming increases in cancer rates.[11] Non-Hodgkin's Lymphoma is related to living near stone, clay, and glass industry facilities, and leukemia is related to living near chemical and petroleum plants.[12] In general, cancer rates are higher in the United States near industries that use toxic substances and discard them nearby.[13]

In sum, the placement of toxic wastes affects basic and vital interests just as do education, health care, and wartime military service. Exemption from market decisions is required to avoid unjust impositions on the poor, and to respect people's interests equally. A child dying of cancer receives little benefit from the community's new swimming pool.

Cost-benefit analysis (CBA)

CBA is an economist's version of utilitarianism, where the sum to be maximized is society's wealth, as measured in monetary units, instead of happiness or preference satisfaction. Society's wealth is computed by noting (and estimating where necessary) what people are willing to pay for goods and services. The more people are willing to pay for what exists in society, the better off society is, according to CBA.

CBA will characteristically require placement of toxic wastes near poor people. Such placement usually lowers land values (what people are willing to pay for property). Land that is already cheap, where poor people live, will not lose as much value as land that is currently expensive, where wealthier people live, so a smaller loss of social wealth attends placement of toxic wastes near poor people. This is just the opposite of what the Principle of Commensurate Burdens and Benefits requires.

The use of CBA also violates equal consideration of interests, operating much like free market approaches. Where a vital concern is at issue, equal consideration of interests requires that people be considered irrespective of income. The placement of toxic wastes affects vital interests. Yet CBA would have poor people exposed disproportionately to such wastes.[14]

In sum, libertarianism, utilitarianism, free market distribution, and cost-benefit analysis are inadequate principles and methodologies to guide the just distribution of toxic wastes.

LULU Points

An approach that avoids these difficulties assigns points to different types of locally undesirable land uses (LULUs) and requires that all communities earn LULU points.[15] In keeping with the Principle of Commensurate Benefits and Burdens, wealthy communities would be required to earn more LULU points than poorer ones. Communities would be identified by currently existing political divisions, such as villages, towns, city wards, cities, and counties.

Toxic waste dumps are only one kind of LULU. Others include prisons, half-way houses, municipal waste sites, low-income housing, and power plants, whether nuclear or coal fired. A large deposit of extremely toxic waste, for example, may be assigned twenty points when properly buried but fifty points when illegally dumped. A much smaller deposit of properly buried toxic waste may be assigned only ten points, as may a coal-fired power plant. A nuclear power plant may be assigned twenty-five points, while municipal waste sites are only five points, and one hundred units of low-income housing are eight points.

These numbers are only speculations. Points would be assigned by considering probable effects of different LULUs on basic needs, and responses to questionnaires investigating people's levels of discomfort with LULUs of various sorts. Once numbers are assigned, the total number of LULU points to be distributed in a given time period could be calculated by considering planned development and needs for prisons, power plants, low-income housing, and so on.

One could also calculate points for a community's already existing LULUs. Communities could then be required to host LULUs in proportion to their income or wealth, with new allocation of LULUs (and associated points) correcting for currently existing deviations from the rule of proportionality.

Wherever significant differences of wealth or income exist between two areas, these areas should be considered part of different communities if there is any political division between them. Thus, a county with rich and poor areas would not be considered a single community for purposes of locating LULUs. Instead, villages or towns may be so considered. A city with rich and poor areas may similarly be reduced to its wards. The purpose of segregating areas of different income or wealth from one another is to permit the imposition of greater LULU burdens on wealthier communities. When wealthy and poor areas are considered as one larger community, there is the danger that the community will earn its LULU points by placing hazardous waste near its poorer members. This possibility is reduced when only relatively wealthy people live in a smaller community that must earn LULU points.

Practical Implications

Political strategy is beyond the scope of this chapter, so I will refrain from commenting on problems and prospects for securing passage and implementation of the foregoing proposal. I maintain that the proposal is just. In a society where injustice is common, it is no surprise that proposals for rectification meet stiff resistance.

Were the LULU points proposal implemented, environmental racism would be reduced enormously. To the extent that poor people exposed to environmental hazards are members of racial minorities, relieving the poor of disproportionate exposure would also relieve people of color.

This is not to say that environmental racism would be ended completely. Implementation of the proposal requires judgment in particular cases. Until racism is itself ended, such judgment will predictably be exercised at times to the disadvantage of minority populations. However, because most people of color currently burdened by environmental racism are relatively poor, implementing the proposal would remove 80 to 90 percent of the effects of environmental racism. While efforts to end racism at all levels should continue, reducing the burdens of racism is generally advantageous to people of color. Such reductions are especially worthy when integral to policies that improve distributive justice generally.

Besides improving distributive justice and reducing the burdens of environmental racism, implementing the LULU points proposal would benefit life on earth generally by reducing the generation of toxic hazards. When people of wealth, who exercise control of manufacturing processes, marketing campaigns, and media coverage, are themselves threatened disproportionately by toxic hazards, the culture will evolve quickly to find their production largely unnecessary. It will be discovered, for example, that many plastic items can be made of wood, just as it was discovered in the late 1980s that the production of many ozone-destroying chemicals is unnecessary. Similarly, necessity being the mother of invention, it was discovered during World War II that many women could work in factories. When certain interests are threatened, the impossible does not even take longer.

The above approach to environmental injustice should, of course, be applied internationally and intranationally within all countries. The same considerations of justice condemn universally, all other things being equal, exposing poor people to vital dangers whose generation predominantly benefits the rich. This implies that rich countries should not ship their toxic wastes to poor countries. Since many poorer countries, such as those in Africa, are inhabited primarily by nonwhites, prohibiting shipments of toxic wastes to them would reduce significantly worldwide environmental racism. A prohibition on such shipments would also discourage production of dangerous wastes; as it would require people in rich countries to live with whatever dangers they create. If the principle of LULU points were applied in all countries, including poor ones, elites in those countries would lose interest in earning foreign currency credits through importation of waste, as they would be disproportionately exposed to imported toxins.

In sum, we could reduce environmental injustice considerably through a general program of distributive justice concerning environmental hazards. Pollution would not thereby be eliminated, since to live is to pollute. But such a program would motivate significant reduction in the generation of toxic wastes, and help the poor, especially people of color, as well as the environment.

Notes

1   See the introduction to L. Westra and P. S. Wenz, eds., *Faces of Environmental Racism* (Lanham, MD: Rowman & Littlefield) for studies indicating the disproportionate burden of toxic wastes on people of color.

2   Vicki Been, "Market Forces, Not Racist Practices, May Affect the Siting of Locally Undesirable Land Uses," in *At Issue: Environmental Justice*, ed. by Jonathan Petrikin (San Diego, Calif.: Greenhaven Press, 1995), 41.

3   See *San Antonio Independent School District v. Rodriguez*, 411 R.S. 1 (1973) and *Village of Arlington Heights v. Metropolitan Housing Development Corporation*, 429 U.S. 252 (1977).

4   Been, 41.

5   Murray Rothbard, "The Great Ecology Issue," *The Individualist* 21, no. 2 (February 1970): 5.

6   See Peter S. Wenz, *Environmental Justice* (Albany, NY: State University of New York Press, 1988), 65–7 and associated endnotes.

7   Christopher Boerner and Thomas Lambert, "Environmental Justice Can Be Achieved Through Negotiated Compensation," in *At Issue: Environmental Justice*.

8   F. Diaz-Barriga et al., "Arsenic and Cadmium Exposure in Children Living Near to Both Zinc and Copper Smelters," summarized in *Archives of Environmental Health* 46, no. 2 (March/April 1991): 119.

9   Dick Russell, "Environmental Racism," *Amicus Journal* (Spring 1989): 22–32, 24.

10 Marianne Lavelle, "The Minorities Equation," *National Law Journal* 21 (September 1992): 3.

11 Christopher Hallowell, "Water Crisis on the Cape," *Audubon* (July/August 1991): 65–74, especially 66 and 70.

12 Athena Linos et al., "Leukemia and Non-Hodgkin's Lymphoma and Residential Proximity to Industrial Plants," *Archives of Environmental Health* 46, no. 2 (March/April 1991): 70–4.

13 L. W. Pickle et al., *Atlas of Cancer Mortality among Whites: 1950–1980*, HHS publication # (NIH) 87-2900 (Washington, DC: U.S. Department of Health and Human Services, Government Printing Office: 1987).

14 Wenz, 216–18.

15 The idea of LULU points comes to me from Frank J. Popper, "LULUs and Their Blockage," in *Confronting Regional Challenges: Approaches to LULUs, Growth, and Other Vexing Governance Problems*, ed. by Joseph DiMento and Le Roy Graymer (Los Angeles, Calif.: Lincoln Institute of Land Policy, 1991), 13–27, especially 24.

D Environmental Ethics and Economic Policy

66 A Declaration of Sustainability
Paul Hawken

67 The Steady-State Economy
Herman E. Daly

68 Making Capitalism Sustainable
John Elkington

69 The Ignorance Argument: What Must We Know to be Fair to the Future?
Bryan Norton

70 Environmental Justice and Intergenerational Debt
Clark Wolf

66 A Declaration of Sustainability

Paul Hawken

I recently performed a social audit for Ben and Jerry's Homemade Inc., America's premier socially responsible company. After poking and prodding around, asking tough questions, trying to provoke debate, and generally making a nuisance of myself, I can attest that their status as the leading social pioneer in commerce is safe for at least another year. They are an outstanding company. Are there flaws? Of course. Welcome to planet Earth. But the people at Ben & Jerry's are relaxed and unflinching in their willingness to look at, discuss, and deal with problems.

In the meantime, the company continues to put ice cream shops in Harlem, pay outstanding benefits, keep a compensation ratio of seven to one from the top of the organization to the bottom, seek out vendors from disadvantaged groups, and donate generous scoops of their profits to others. And they are about to overtake their historic rival Häagen-Dazs, the ersatz Scandinavian originator of super-premium ice cream, as the market leader in their category. At present rates of growth, Ben & Jerry's will be a $1 billion company by the end of the century. They are publicly held, nationally recognized, and rapidly growing, in part because Ben wanted to show that a socially responsible company could make it in the normal world of business.

Ben and Jerry's is just one of a growing vanguard of companies attempting to redefine their social and ethical responsibilities. These companies no longer accept the maxim that the business of business is business. Their premise is simple: Corporations, because they are the dominant institution on the planet, must squarely face the social and environmental problems that afflict humankind. Organizations such as Business

From *The Utne Reader* (Sept./Oct. 1993): 54–61. © 1993 by Paul Hawken. Reprinted by kind permission of the author.

for Social Responsibility and the Social Venture Network, corporate "ethics" consultants, magazines such as *In Business* and *Business Ethics,* non-profits including the Council on Economic Priorities, investment funds such as Calvert and Covenant, newsletters like *Greenmoney,* and thousands of unaffiliated companies are drawing up new codes of conduct for corporate life that integrate social, ethical, and environmental principles.

Ben and Jerry's and the roughly 2,000 other committed companies in the social responsibility movement here and abroad have combined annual sales of approximately $2 billion, or one-hundredth of 1 percent of the $20 trillion sales garnered by the estimated 80 million to 100 million enterprises worldwide. The problems they are trying to address are vast and unremittingly complex: 5.5 billion people are breeding exponentially, and fulfilling their wants and needs is stripping the earth of its biotic capacity to produce life; a climactic burst of consumption by a single species is overwhelming the skies, earth, waters, and fauna.

As the Worldwatch Institute's Lester Brown patiently explains in his annual survey, *State of the World,* every living system on earth is in decline. Making matters worse, we are having a once-in-a-billion-year blowout sale of hydrocarbons, which are being combusted into the atmosphere, effectively double glazing the planet within the next 50 years with unknown climatic results. The cornucopia of resources that are being extracted, mined, and harvested is so poorly distributed that 20 percent of the earth's people are chronically hungry or starving, while the top 20 percent of the population, largely in the north, control and consume 80 percent of the world's wealth. Since business in its myriad forms is primarily responsible for this "taking," it is appropriate that a growing number of companies ask the question, How does one honorably conduct business in the latter days of industrialism and the beginning of an ecological age? The ethical dilemma that confronts business begins with the acknowledgment that a commercial system that functions well by its own definitions unavoidably defies the greater and more profound ethic of biology. Specifically, how does business face the prospect that creating a profitable, growing company requires an intolerable abuse of the natural world?

Despite their dedicated good work, if we examine all or any of the businesses that deservedly earn high marks for social and environmental responsibility, we are faced with a sobering irony: If every company on the planet were to adopt the environmental and social practices of the best companies – of, say, the Body Shop, Patagonia, and Ben and Jerry's – the world would still be moving toward environmental degradation and collapse. In other words, if we analyze environmental effects and create an input-output model of resources and energy, the results do not even approximate a tolerable or sustainable future. If a tiny fraction of the world's most intelligent companies cannot model a sustainable world, then that tells us that being socially responsible is only one part of an overall solution, and that what we have is not a management problem but a design problem.

At present, there is a contradiction inherent in the premise of a socially responsible corporation: to wit, that a company can make the world better, can grow, and can increase profits by meeting social and environmental needs. It is a have-your-cake-and-eat-it fantasy that cannot come true if the primary cause of environmental degradation is overconsumption. Although proponents of socially responsible business are making an outstanding effort at reforming the tired old ethics of commerce, they are unintentionally creating a new rationale for companies to produce, advertise, expand, grow, capitalize, and use up resources: the rationale that they are doing good. A jet flying across the country, a car rented at an airport, an air-conditioned hotel room, a truck full of goods, a worker commuting to his or her job – all cause the same amount of environmental degradation whether they're associated with the Body Shop, the Environmental Defense Fund, or R. J. Reynolds.

In order to approximate a sustainable society, we need to describe a system of commerce and production in which each and every act is inherently sustainable and restorative. Because of the way our system of commerce is designed, businesses will not be able to fulfill their social contract with the environment or society until the system in which they operate undergoes a fundamental change, a change that brings commerce and governance into alignment with the natural world from which we receive our life. There must be an integration of economic, biologic, and human systems in order to create a sustainable and interdependent method of commerce that supports and furthers our existence. As hard as we may strive to create sustainability on a company level, we cannot fully succeed until the institutions surrounding commerce are redesigned. Just as every act of production and consumption in an industrial society leads to further environmental degradation, regardless of intention or ethos, we need to imagine – and then design – a system of commerce where the opposite is true, where doing good is like falling off a log, where the natural, everyday acts of work and life accumulate into a better world as a matter of course, not a matter of altruism. A system of sustainable commerce would involve these objectives:

1 It would reduce absolute consumption of energy and natural resources among developed nations by 80 percent within 40 to 60 years.
2 It would provide secure, stable, and meaningful employment for people everywhere.
3 It would be self-actuating as opposed to regulated, controlled, mandated, or moralistic.
4 It would honor human nature and market principles.
5 It would be perceived as more desirable than our present way of life.
6 It would exceed sustainability by restoring degraded habitats and ecosystems to their fullest biological capacity.
7 It would rely on current solar income.
8 It should be fun and engaging, and strive for an aesthetic outcome.

Strategies for Sustainability

At present, the environmental and social responsibility movements consist of many different initiatives, connected primarily by values and beliefs rather than by design. What is needed is a conscious plan to create a sustainable future, including a set of design strategies for people to follow. For the record, I will suggest 12.

1. Take back the charter

Although corporate charters may seem to have little to do with sustainability, they are critical to any long-term movement toward restoration of the planet. Read *Taking Care of Business: Citizenship and the Charter of Incorporation,* a 1992 pamphlet by Richard Grossman and Frank T. Adams (Charter Ink, Box 806. Cambridge, MA 02140). In it you find a lost history of corporate power and citizen involvement

that addresses a basic and crucial point: corporations are chartered by, and exist at the behest of, citizens. Incorporation is not a right but a privilege granted by the state that includes certain considerations such as limited liability. Corporations are supposed to be under our ultimate authority, not the other way around. The charter of incorporation is a revocable dispensation that was supposed to ensure accountability of the corporation to society as a whole. When Rockwell criminally despoils a weapons facility at Rocky Flats, Colorado, with plutonium waste, or when any corporation continually harms, abuses, or violates the public trust, citizens should have the right to revoke its charter, causing the company to disband, sell off its enterprises to other companies, and effectively go out of business. The workers would have jobs with the new owners, but the executives, directors, and management would be out of jobs, with a permanent notice on their résumés that they mismanaged a corporation into a charter revocation. This is not merely a deterrent to corporate abuse but a critical element of an ecological society because it creates feedback loops that prompt accountability, citizen involvement, and learning. We should remember that the citizens of this country originally envisioned corporations to be part of a public-private partnership, which is why the relationship between the chartering authority of state legislatures and the corporation was kept alive and active. They had it right.

2. Adjust price to reflect cost

The economy is environmentally and commercially dysfunctional because the market does not provide consumers with proper information. The "free market" economies that we love so much are excellent at setting prices but lousy when it comes to recognizing costs. In order for a sustainable society to exist, every purchase must reflect or at least approximate its actual cost, not only the direct cost of production but also the costs to the air, water, and soil; the cost to future generations; the cost to worker health; the cost of waste, pollution, and toxicity. Simply stated, the marketplace gives us the wrong information. It tells us that flying across the country on a discount airline ticket is cheap when it is not. It tells us that our food is inexpensive when its method of production destroys aquifers and soil, the viability of ecosystems, and workers' lives. Whenever an organism gets wrong information, it is a form of toxicity. In fact, that is how pesticides work. A herbicide kills because it is a hormone that tells the plant to grow faster than its capacity to absorb nutrients allows. It literally grows itself to death. Sound familiar? Our daily doses of toxicity are the prices in the marketplace. They are telling us to do the wrong thing for our own survival. They are lulling us into cutting down old-growth forests on the Olympic Peninsula for apple crates, into patterns of production and consumption that are not just unsustainable but profoundly shortsighted and destructive. It is surprising that "conservative" economists do not support or understand this idea, because it is they who insist that we pay as we go, have no debts, and take care of business. Let's do it.

3. Throw out and replace the entire tax system

The present tax system sends the wrong messages to virtually everyone, encourages waste, discourages conservation, and rewards consumption. It taxes what we want to encourage – jobs, creativity, payrolls, and real income – and ignores the things we want to discourage – degradation, pollution, and depletion. The present US tax system costs citizens $500 billion a year in record-keeping, filing, administrative, legal, and governmental costs – more than the actual amount we pay in personal income taxes. The only incentive in the present system is to cheat or hire a lawyer to cheat for us. The entire tax system must be incrementally replaced over a 20-year period by "Green fees," taxes that are added onto existing products, energy, services, and materials so that prices in the marketplace more closely approximate true costs. These taxes are not a means to raise revenue or bring down deficits, but must be absolutely revenue neutral so that people in the lower and middle classes experience no real change of income, only a shift in expenditures. Eventually, the cost of non-renewable resources, extractive energy, and industrial modes of production will be more expensive than renewable resources, such as solar energy, sustainable forestry, and biological methods of agriculture. Why should the upper middle class be able to afford to conserve while the lower income classes cannot? So far the environmental movement has only made the world better for upper middle class white people. The only kind of environmental movement that can succeed has to start from the bottom up. Under a Green fee system the incentives to save on taxes will create positive, constructive acts that are affordable for everyone. As energy prices go up to

three to four times their existing levels (with commensurate tax reductions to offset the increase), the natural inclination to save money will result in carpooling, bicycling, telecommuting, public transport, and more efficient houses. As taxes on artificial fertilizers, pesticides, and fuel go up, again with offsetting reductions in income and payroll taxes, organic farmers will find that their produce and methods are the cheapest means of production (because they truly are), and customers will find that organically grown food is less expensive than its commercial cousin. Eventually, with the probable exception of taxes on the rich, we will find ourselves in a position where we pay no taxes, but spend our money with a practiced and constructive discernment. Under an enlightened and redesigned tax system, the cheapest product in the marketplace would be best for the customer, the worker, the environment, and the company. That is rarely the case today.

4. Allow resource companies to be utilities

An energy utility is an interesting hybrid of public-private interests. A utility gains a market monopoly in exchange for public control of rates, open books, and a guaranteed rate of return. Because of this relationship and the pioneering work of Amory Lovins, we now have markets for "negawatts." It is the first time in the history of industrialism that a corporation has figured out how to make money by selling the absence of something. Negawatts are the opposite of energy: They represent the collaborative ability of a utility to harness efficiency instead of hydrocarbons. This conservation-based alternative saves ratepayers, shareholders, and the company money – savings that are passed along to everyone. All resource systems, including oil, gas, forests, and water, should be run by some form of utility. There should be markets in negabarrels, negatrees, and negacoal. Oil companies, for example, have no alternative at present other than to lobby for the absurd, like drilling in the Arctic National Wildlife Refuge. That project, a $40 billion to $60 billion investment for a hoped-for supply of oil that would meet US consumption needs for only six months, is the only way an oil company can make money under our current system of commerce. But what if the oil companies formed an oil utility and cut a deal with citizens and taxpayers that allowed them to "invest" in insulation, super-glazed windows, conservation rebates on new automobiles, and the scrapping of old cars? Through Green fees, we would pay them back a return on their conservation investment equal to what utilities receive, a rate of return that would be in accord with how many barrels of oil they save, rather than how many barrels they produce. Why should they care? Why should we? A $60 billion investment in conservation will yield, conservatively, four to ten times as much energy as drilling for oil. Given Lovins' principle of efficiency extraction, try to imagine a forest utility, a salmon utility, a copper utility, a Mississippi River utility, a grasslands utility. Imagine a system where the resource utility benefits from conservation, makes money from efficiency, thrives through restoration, and profits from sustainability. It is possible today.

5. Change linear systems to cyclical ones

Our economy has many design flaws, but the most glaring one is that nature is cyclical and industrialism is linear. In nature, no linear systems exist, or they don't exist for long because they exhaust themselves into extinction. Linear industrial systems take resources, transform them into products or services, discard waste, and sell to consumers, who discard more waste when they have consumed the product. But of course we don't consume TVs, cars, or most of the other stuff we buy. Instead, Americans produce six times their body weight every week in hazardous and toxic waste water, incinerator fly ash, agricultural wastes, heavy metals, and waste chemicals, paper, wood, etc. This does not include CO_2, which if it were included would double the amount of waste. Cyclical means of production are designed to imitate natural systems in which waste equals food for other forms of life, nothing is thrown away, and symbiosis replaces competition. Bill McDonough, a New York architect who has pioneered environmental design principles, has designed a system to retrofit every window in a major American city. Although it still awaits final approval, the project is planned to like this: the city and a major window manufacturer from a joint venture to produce energy-saving super-glazed windows in the town. This partnership company will come to your house or business, measure all windows and glass doors, and then replace them with windows with an R-8 to R-12 energy-efficiency rating within 72 hours. The windows will have the same casements, molding, and general appearance as the old ones. You will receive a $500 check upon installation, and you will pay for the new windows over a 10- to 15-year period in your utility or tax bill. The total bill is less than the cost of the energy the windows will save. In other words, the windows will cost the home or business owner nothing. The city will pay for them initially with industrial development bonds. The factory will train and employ 300 disadvantaged people. The old windows will be completely recycled and reused, the glass melted into glass, the wooden frames ground up and mixed with recycled resins that are extruded to make the casements. When the city is reglazed, the residents and businesses will pocket an extra $20 million to $30 million every year in money saved on utility bills. After the windows are paid for, the figure will go even higher. The factory, designed to be transportable, will move to another city; the first city will retain an equity interest in the venture. McDonough has designed a win-win-win-win-win system that optimizes a number of agendas. The ratepayers, the homeowners, the renters, the city, the environment, and the employed all thrive because they are "making" money from efficiency rather than exploitation. It's a little like running the industrial economy backwards.

6. Transform the making of things

We have to institute the Intelligent Product System created by Michael Braungart of the EPEA (Environmental Protection Encouragement Agency) in Hamburg, Germany. The system recognizes three types of products. The first are *consumables*, products that are either eaten, or, when they're placed on the ground, turn into dirt without any bio-accumulative effects. In other words, they are products whose waste equals food for other living systems. At present, many of the products that should be "consumable," like clothing and shoes, are not. Cotton cloth contains hundreds of different chemicals, plasticizers, defoliants, pesticides, and dyes: shoes are tanned with chromium and their soles contain lead; neckties and silk blouses contain zinc, tin, and toxic dye. Much of what we recycle today turns into toxic by-products, consuming more energy in the recycling process than is saved by recycling. We should be designing more things so that they can be thrown away – into the compost heap. Toothpaste tubes and other non-degradable packaging can be made out of natural polymers so that they break down and become fertilizer for plants. A package that turns into dirt is infinitely more useful, biologically speaking, than a package that turns into a plastic park bench.

Heretical as it sounds, designing for decomposition, not recycling, is the way of the world around us.

The second category is *durables*, but in this case, they would not be sold, only licensed. Cars, TVs, VCRs, and refrigerators would always belong to the original manufacturer, so they would be made, used, and returned within a closed-loop system. This is already being instituted in Germany and to a lesser extent in Japan, where companies are beginning to design for disassembly. If a company knows that its products will come back someday, and that it cannot throw anything away when they do, it creates a very different approach to design and materials.

Last, there are *unsalables* – toxins, radiation, heavy metals, and chemicals. There is no living system for which these are food and thus they can never be thrown away. In Braungart's Intelligent Product System, unsalables must always belong to the original maker, safeguarded by public utilities called "parking lots" that store the toxins in glass-lined barrels indefinitely, charging the original manufacturers rent for the service. The rent ceases when an independent scientific panel can confirm that there is a safe method to detoxify the substances in question. All toxic chemicals would have molecular markers identifying them as belonging to their originator, so that if they are found in wells, rivers, soil, or fish, it is the responsibility of the company to retrieve them and clean up. This places the problem of toxicity with the makers, where it belongs, making them responsible for full-life-cycle effects.

7. Vote, don't buy

Democracy has been effectively eliminated in America by the influence of money, lawyers, and a political system that is the outgrowth of the first two. While we can dream of restoring our democratic system, the fact remains that we live in a plutocracy – government by the wealthy. One way out is to vote with your dollars, to withhold purchases from companies that act or respond inappropriately. Don't just avoid buying a Mitsubishi automobile because of the company's participation in the destruction of primary forests in Malaysia, Indonesia, Ecuador, Brazil, Bolivia, Canada, Chile, Siberia, and Papua New Guinea. Write and tell them why you won't. Engage in dialogue, send one postcard a week, talk, organize, meet, publish newsletters, boycott, patronize, and communicate with companies like General Electric. Educate non-profits, organizations, municipalities, and pension funds to act

affirmatively, to support the ecological CERES (formerly *Valdez*) Principles for business, to invest intelligently, and to *think* with their money, not merely spend it. Demand the best from the companies you work for and buy from. You deserve it and your actions will help them change.

8. Restore the "guardian"

There can be no healthy business sector unless there is a healthy governing sector. In her book *Systems of Survival*, author Jane Jacobs describes two overarching moral syndromes that permeate our society: the commercial syndrome, which arose from trading cultures, and the governing, or guardian, syndrome that arose from territorial cultures. The guardian system is hierarchical, adheres to tradition, values loyalty, and shuns trading and inventiveness. The commercial system, on the other hand, is based on trading, so it values trust of outsiders, innovation, and future thinking. Each has qualities the other lacks. Whenever the guardian tries to be in business, as in Eastern Europe, business doesn't work. What is also true, but not so obvious to us, is that when business plays government, governance fails as well. Our guardian system has almost completely broken down because of the money, power, influence, and control exercised by business and, to a lesser degree, other institutions. Business and unions have to get out of government. We need more than campaign reform: We need a vision that allows us all to see that when Speaker of the House Tom Foley exempts the aluminum industry in his district from the proposed Btu tax, or when Philip Morris donates $200,000 to the Jesse Helms Citizenship Center, citizenship is mocked and democracy is left gagging and twitching on the Capitol steps. The irony is that business thinks that its involvement in governance is good corporate citizenship or at least is advancing its own interests. The reality is that business is preventing the economy from evolving. Business loses, workers lose, the environment loses.

9. Shift from electronic literacy to biologic literacy

That an average adult can recognize one thousand brand names and logos but fewer than ten local plants is not a good sign. We are moving not to an information age but to a biologic age, and unfortunately our technological education is equipping us for corporate markets, not the future. Sitting at home with virtual reality gloves, 3D video games, and interactive cable TV shopping is a barren and impoverished vision of the future. The computer revolution is not the totem of our future, only a tool. Don't get me wrong. Computers are great. But they are not an uplifting or compelling vision for culture or society. They do not move us toward a sustainable future any more than our obsession with cars and televisions provided us with newer definitions or richer meaning. We are moving into the age of living machines, not, as Corbusier noted, "machines for living in." The Thomas Edison of the future is not Bill Gates of Microsoft, but John and Nancy Todd, founders of the New Alchemy Institute, a Massachusetts design lab and think tank for sustainability. If the Todds' work seems less commercial, less successful, and less glamorous, it is because they are working on the real problem – how to live – and it is infinitely more complex than a microprocessor. Understanding biological processes is how we are going to create a new symbiosis with living systems (or perish). What we can learn on-line is how to model complex systems. It is computers that have allowed us to realize how the synapses in the common sea slug are more powerful than all of our parallel processors put together.

10. Take inventory

We do not know how many species live on the planet within a factor of ten. We do not know how many are being extirpated. We do not know what is contained in the biological library inherited from the Cenozoic age. (Sociobiologist E. O. Wilson estimates that it would take 25,000 person-years to catalog most of the species, putting aside the fact that there are only 1,500 people with the taxonomic ability to undertake the task.) We do not know how complex systems interact – how the transpiration of the giant lily, *Victoria amazonica*, of Brazil's rainforests affects European rainfall and agriculture, for example. We do not know what happens to 20 percent of the CO_2 that is off-gassed every year (it disappears without a trace). We do not know how to calculate sustainable yields in fisheries and forest systems. We do not know why certain species, such as frogs, are dying out even in pristine habitats. We do not know the long-term effects of chlorinated hydrocarbons on human health, behavior, sexuality, and fertility. We do not know what a sustainable life is for existing inhabitants of the planet, and certainly not for future populations. (A Dutch study calculated that your fair share of air travel is one trip across the Atlantic in a lifetime.) We do not know how many people we can feed on a sustainable basis, or what our diet would look like. In short, we need to find out what's here, who has it, and what we can or can't do with it.

11. Take care of human health

The environmental and socially responsible movements would gain additional credibility if they recognized that the greatest amount of human suffering and mortality is caused by environmental problems that are not being addressed by environmental organizations or companies. Contaminated water is killing a hundred times more people than all other forms of pollution combined. Millions of children are dying from preventable diseases and malnutrition.

The movement toward sustainability must address the clear and present dangers that people face worldwide, dangers that ironically increase population levels because of their perceived threat. People produce more children when they're afraid they'll lose them. Not until the majority of the people in the world, all of whom suffer in myriad preventable yet intolerable ways, understand that environmentalism means improving their lives directly will the ecology movement walk its talk. Americans will spend more money in the next 12 months on the movie and tchotchkes of *Jurassic Park* than on foreign aid to prevent malnutrition or provide safe water.

12. Respect the human spirit

If hope is to pass the sobriety test, then it has to walk a pretty straight line to reality. Nothing written, suggested, or proposed here is possible unless business is willing to integrate itself into the natural world. It is time for business to take the initiative in a genuinely open process of dialogue, collaboration, reflection, and redesign. "It is not enough," writes Jeremy Seabrook of the British Green party, "to declare, as many do, that we are living in an unsustainable way, using up resources, squandering the substance of the next generation however true this may be. People must feel subjectively the injustice and unsustainability before they will make a more sober assessment as to whether it is worth maintaining what is, or whether there might not be more equitable and satisfying ways that will not be won at the expense either of the necessities of the poor or of the wasting fabric of the planet."

Poet and naturalist W. S. Merwin (citing Robert Graves) reminds us that we have one story, and one story only, to tell in our lives. We are made to believe by our parents and businesses, by our culture and televisions, by our politicians and movie stars that it is the story of money, of finance, of wealth, of the stock portfolio, the partnership, the country house. These are small, impoverished tales and whispers that have made us restless and craven; they are not stories at all. As author and garlic grower Stanley Crawford puts it, "The financial statement must finally give way to the narrative, with all its exceptions, special cases, imponderables. It must finally give way to the story, which is perhaps the way we arm ourselves against the next and always unpredictable turn of the cycle in the quixotic dare that is life; across the rock and cold of lifelines, it is our seed, our clove, our filament cast toward the future." It is something deeper than anything commercial culture can plumb, and it is waiting for each of us.

Business must yield to the longings of the human spirit. The most important contribution of the socially responsible business movement has little to do with recycling, nuts from the rainforest, or employing the homeless. Their gift to us is that they are leading by trying to do something, to risk, take a chance, make a change – any change. They are not waiting for "the solution," but are acting without guarantees of success or proof of purchase. This is what all of us must do. Being visionary has always been given a bad rap by commerce. But without a positive vision for humankind we can have no meaning, no work, and no purpose.

---

67   The Steady-State Economy

Herman E. Daly

The Concept of a Steady-State Economy

The steady-state economy (SSE) is defined by four characteristics:

1   A constant population of human bodies.
2   A constant population or stock of artifacts (exosomatic capital or extensions of human bodies).
3   The levels at which the two populations are held constant are sufficient for a good life and sustainable for a long future.
4   The rate of throughput of matter-energy by which the two stocks are maintained is reduced to the lowest feasible level. For the population this means that birth rates are equal to death rates at low levels so that life expectancy is high. For artifacts it means that production equals depreciation at low levels so that artifacts are long lasting, and depletion and pollution are kept low.

Only two things are held constant – the stock of human bodies and the total stock or inventory of artifacts. Technology, information, wisdom, goodness, genetic characteristics, distribution of wealth and income, product mix, and so on are *not* held constant. In the very long run, of course, nothing can remain constant, so our concept of a SSE must be a medium-run concept in which stocks are constant over decades or generations, not millennia or eons.

Three magnitudes are basic to the concept of a SSE:

1   *Stock* is the total inventory of producers' goods, consumers' goods, and human bodies. It corresponds to Irving Fisher's (1906) definition of

From Herman E. Daly and Kenneth N. Townsend, eds., *Valuing the Earth*, 2nd edn: *Economics, Ecology, Ethics* (Cambridge, MA: MIT Press, 1993), pp. 325–63. © 1992 Massachusetts Institute of Technology, by permission of The MIT Press.

capital and may be thought of as the set of all physical things capable of satisfying human wants and subject to ownership.

2 *Service* is the satisfaction experienced when wants are satisfied, or "psychic income" in Fisher's sense. Service is yielded by the stock. The quantity and quality of the stock determine the intensity of service. There is no unit for measuring service, so it may be stretching words a bit to call it a magnitude. Nevertheless, we all experience service or satisfaction and recognize differing intensities of the experience. Service is yielded over a period of time and thus appears to be a flow magnitude. But unlike flows, service cannot be accumulated. It is probably more accurate to think of service as a "psychic flux" (Georgescu-Roegen, 1966, 1971).

3 *Throughput* is the entropic physical flow of matter-energy from nature's sources, through the human economy and back to nature's sinks; it is necessary for maintenance and renewal of the constant stocks (Boulding, 1966; Daly, 1968; Georgescu-Roegen, 1971).

The relationship among these three magnitudes can best be understood in terms of the following simple identity (Daly, 1974):

$$\frac{service}{throughput} \equiv \frac{service}{stock} \times \frac{stock}{throughput}$$

[. . .]

In the SSE a different behavior mode is adopted with respect to each of the three basic magnitudes. (1) *Stock* is to be "*satisficed*" – maintained at a level that is sufficient for an abundant life for the present generation and ecologically sustainable for a long (but not infinite) future.[1] (2) *Service* is to be *maximized*, given the constant stock. (3) *Throughput* is to be *minimized*, given the constant stock. In terms of the two ratios on the right-hand side of the identity, this means that the ratio (service/stock) is to be maximized by maximizing the numerator with the denominator constant, while the ratio (stock/throughput) is maximized by minimizing the denominator with the numerator constant. These two ratios measure two kinds of efficiency: service efficiency and maintenance efficiency.

Service efficiency (service/stock) depends on allocative efficiency (does the stock consist of artifacts that people most want and are they allocated to the most important uses?), and on distributive efficiency (is the distribution of the stock among alternative people such that the trivial wants of some people do not take precedence over the basic needs of others?). Standard economics has much of value to say about allocative efficiency, but it treats distribution under the heading of social justice rather than efficiency, thus putting it on the sidelines of disciplinary concern. Although neoclassical economists carefully distinguish allocation from distribution in static analysis, they seem not to insist on any analogous distinction between intertemporal allocation (one person allocating over different stages of his lifetime) and intertemporal distribution (distribution between different people, that is, present people and future people). Intertemporal distribution is a question of ethics, not a function of the interest rate. The notion of optimal allocation over time must be confined to a single lifetime unless we are willing to let ethics and distributional issues into the definition of optimum. Neoclassical economics seems inconsistent, or at least ambiguous, on this point.

Maintenance efficiency (stock/throughput) depends on durability (how long an individual artifact lasts) and on replaceability (how easily the artifact can be replaced when it finally does wear out). Maintenance efficiency measures the number of units of time over which a population of artifacts yields its service, while service efficiency measures the intensity of that service per unit of time. Maintenance efficiency is limited by the entropy law (nothing lasts forever; everything wears out). Service efficiency may conceivably increase for a very long time, since the growing "magnitude," service, is nonphysical. There may, however, be physical limits to the capacity of human beings to experience service. But the definition of the SSE is in terms of physical stocks and throughput and is not affected by whether or not service could increase indefinitely.

[. . .]

The above concepts allow us to make an important distinction between growth and development. *Growth* refers to an increase in service that results from an increase in stock and throughput, with the two efficiency ratios constant. *Development* refers to an increase in the efficiency ratios, with stock constant (or alternatively, an increase in service with throughput constant). Using these definitions, we may say that a SSE develops but does not grow, just as the planet earth, of which it is a subsystem, develops without growing.

How do these concepts relate to GNP, the more conventional index of "growth"? GNP makes no distinction among the three basic magnitudes. It simply adds up value estimates of some services (the service of those assets that are rented rather than purchased, including human bodies, and omitting the services of all owned assets not rented during the current year, with the exception of owner-occupied houses), plus the value of the throughput flow (maintenance and replacement expenditures required to maintain the total stock intact), plus the value of current additions to stock (net investment). What sense does it make to add up benefits, costs, and change in inventory? Services of the natural ecosystem are not counted, and, more important, services sacrificed are not subtracted. In fact, defensive attempts to repair the loss of ecosystem services are added to GNP. The concept of a SSE is independent of GNP, and what happens to GNP in the SSE simply does not matter. The best thing to do with GNP is to forget it. The next best thing is to try to replace it with two separate social accounts, one measuring the value of service (benefit) and the other measuring the value of throughput (cost). In this way costs and benefits could be compared, although this aggregate macrolevel comparison is not at all essential, since regardless of how it turns out the behavior modes remain the same with respect to each of the three basic magnitudes. If we really could get operational cost and benefit accounts, then we might optimize the level of stocks by letting it grow to the point where the marginal cost of an addition to stock just equals the marginal benefit. But that is so far beyond our ability to measure that satisficing will for a long time remain a better strategy than optimizing. Aggregate economic indices should be treated with caution, since there are always some kinds of stupid behavior that would raise the index and thus become "justified."

Neither the concept nor the reality of a SSE is new. John Stuart Mill (1881) discussed the concept in his famous chapter on the stationary state. Historically, people have lived for 99 percent of their tenure on earth in conditions very closely approximating a steady state. Economic growth is essentially a phenomenon of the last 200 years, and only in the last 50 years has it become the dominant goal of nations. Growth is an aberration, not the norm. Development can continue without growth and is, in fact, more likely under a SSE than under a growth economy.

[. . .]

Social Institutions

The social institutions of control for a SSE are of three kinds: those for maintaining a constant population, those for maintaining a constant stock of physical wealth, and those governing distribution. In all cases the guiding design principle for social institutions is to provide the necessary control with a minimum sacrifice of personal freedom, to provide macrostability while allowing for microvariability, to combine the macrostatic with the microdynamic (Luten, n.d.).

The distribution institution

The critical institution is likely to be that of the minimum and maximum limits on income and the maximum limit on wealth. Without some such limits private property and the whole market economy lose their moral basis, and there would be no strong case for extending the market to cover birth quotas and depletion quotas as a means of institutionalizing environmental limits. Exchange relations are mutually beneficial among relative equals. Exchange between the powerful and the powerless is often only nominally voluntary and can easily be a mask for exploitation, especially in the labor market, as Marx has shown.

There is considerable political support for a minimum income, financed by a negative income tax, as an alternative to bureaucratic welfare programs. There is no such support for maximum income or maximum wealth limits. In the growth paradigm there need be no upper limit. But in the steady-state paradigm there must be an upper limit to the total, and consequently an upper limit to per capita income as well. A minimum wealth limit is not feasible, since we can always spend our wealth and could hardly expect to have it restored year after year. The minimum income would be sufficient. But maximum limits on both wealth and income are necessary, since wealth and income are largely interchangeable, and since, beyond some point, the concentration of wealth becomes inconsistent with both a market economy and political democracy. John Stuart Mill (1881) put the issue very well:

> Private property, in every defense made of it, is supposed to mean the guarantee to individuals of the fruits of their own labor and abstinence. The guarantee to them of the fruits of the labor and abstinence of others, transmitted to them without any merit or exertion of their own, is not of the essence

of the institution, but a mere incidental consequence, which, when it reaches a certain height, does not promote, but conflicts with, the ends which render private property legitimate.

According to Mill, private property is legitimated as a bastion against exploitation. But this is true only if everyone owns some minimum amount. Otherwise, private property, when some own a great deal of it and others have very little, becomes the very *instrument* of exploitation rather than a guarantee against it. It is implicit in this view that private property is legitimate only if there is some distributist institution (as, for example, the Jubilee year of the Old Testament) that keeps inequality of wealth within justifiable limits. Such an institution is now lacking. The proposed institution of maximum wealth and income plus minimum income limits would remedy this severe defect and make private property legitimate again. It would also go a long way toward legitimating the free market, since most of our blundering interference with the price system (e.g., farm programs, minimum wage, rent controls) has as its goal an equalizing alteration in the distribution of income and wealth. Thus such a distributist policy is based on impeccably respectable premises: private property, the free market, opposition to welfare bureaucracies and centralized control. It also heeds the radicals' call of "power to the people," since it puts the source of power, namely property, in the hands of the many people, rather than in the hands of the few capitalist plutocrats and socialist bureaucrats.

The concept of private property here adopted is the classical view of John Locke, Thomas Jefferson, and the Founding Fathers. It is emphatically not the apologetic doctrine of big business that the term *private property* evokes today. Limits are built into the very notion of property, according to Locke (quoted in McClaughry, 1974, p. 31):

> Whatsoever, then, a man removes out of the state that nature hath provided and left it in, he hath mixed his labor with it, and joined to it something that is his own, and thereby makes it his property. But how far has God given property to us to enjoy? As much as anyone can make use of to any advantage of life before it spoils, so much may he by his labor fix his property in. Whatever is beyond this is more than his share, and belongs to others.

Clearly, Locke had in mind some maximum limit on property, even in the absence of general scarcity.

Locke assumed, reasonably in his time, that resources were superabundant. But he insisted that the right to property was limited. Growing resource scarcity reinforces this necessity of limits. [. . .]

Maximum limits on income and wealth were an implicit part of the philosophy of all the prominent statesmen of early America except Alexander Hamilton.

Maximum income and wealth would remove many of the incentives to monopolistic practices. Why conspire to corner markets, fix prices, and so forth, if you cannot keep the loot?

[. . .]

Transferable birth licenses

This idea was first put forward in 1964 by Kenneth Boulding (1964, pp. 135–6). Hardly anyone has taken it seriously, as Boulding knew would be the case. Nevertheless, it remains the best plan yet offered, if the goal is to attain aggregate stability with a minimum sacrifice of individual freedom and variability. It combines macrostability with microvariability. Since 1964 we have experienced a great increase in public awareness of the population explosion and an energy crisis, and we are now experiencing the failures of the great "technological fixes" (green revolution, nuclear power, and space). This has led at least one respected demographer to take Boulding's plan seriously, and more will probably follow (Heer, 1975).

So many people react so negatively to the birth license plan that I should emphasize that the other two institutions (distributive limits and depletion quotas) do not depend on it. The other two proposals could be accepted and the reader can substitute his own favorite population control plan if he is allergic to this one.

The plan is simply to issue equally to every person (or perhaps only to every woman, since the female is the limitative factor in reproduction, and since maternity is more demonstrable than paternity) an amount of reproduction licenses that corresponds to replacement fertility. Thus each woman would receive 2.1 licenses. The licenses would be divisible in units of one-tenth, which Boulding playfully called the "deci-child." Possession of ten deci-child units confers the legal right to one birth. The licenses are freely transferable by sale or gift, so those who want more than two children and can afford to buy the extra licenses, or can acquire them by gift, are free to do so. The original distribution of the licenses is on the basis of strict equality, but exchange is permitted, leading to a reallocation in conformity with differing preferences and abilities to pay. Thus distributive equity is achieved in the original distribution, and allocative efficiency is achieved in the market redistribution.

[. . .]

There is an understandable reluctance to couple money and reproduction – somehow it seems to profane life. Yet life is physically coupled to increasingly scarce resources, and resources are coupled to money. If population growth and economic growth continue, then even free resources, such as breathable air, will become either coupled to money and subject to price or allocated by a harsher and less efficient means. Once we accept the fact that the price system is the most efficient mechanism for rationing the right to scarce life-sustaining and life-enhancing resources, then perhaps rather than "money profaning life" we will find that "life sanctifies money." We will then take the distribution of money and its wise use as serious matters. It is not the exchange relationship that debases life (indeed, the entire biosphere runs on a network of material and energy exchanges), it is the underlying inequity in wealth and income beyond any functional or ethical justification that loads the terms of free exchange against the poor. The same inequality also debases the "gift relationship," since it assigns the poor to the status of a perpetual dependent and the rich to the status of a weary and grumbling patron. Thus gift as well as exchange relationships require limits to the degree of inequality if they are not to subvert their legitimate ends. The sharing of resources in general is the job of the distributist institution. Allocation of particular resources and scarce rights is done by the market within the distribution limits imposed.

[. . .]

Depletion quotas

The strategic point at which to impose control on the throughput flow seems to me to be the rate of depletion of resources. If we limit aggregate depletion, then, by the law of conservation of matter and energy, we will also indirectly limit aggregate pollution. If we limit throughput flow, then we also indirectly limit the size of the stocks maintained by that flow. Entropy is at its minimum at the input (depletion) end of the throughput pipeline and at its maximum at the output (pollution) end. Therefore, it is physically easier to monitor and control depletion than pollution.

[. . .]

An example will illustrate the reason for putting the control (whether tax or quota) on resources rather than on commodities. Suppose the government taxes automobiles heavily and that people take to riding bicycles instead of cars. They will save money as well as resources (Hannon, 1975). But what will the money saved now be spent on? If it is spent on airline tickets, resource consumption would increase above what it was when the money was spent on cars. If the money is spent on theater tickets, then perhaps resource consumption would decline. However, this is not certain, because the theater performance may entail the air transport of actors, stage sets, and so on, and thus indirectly be as resource-consumptive as automobile expenditures. If people paid the high tax on cars and continued buying the same number of cars, then they would have to cut other items of consumption. The items cut may or may not be more resource-intensive than the items for which the government spends the revenue. If the revenue is spent on B-1 bombers, there would surely be a net increase in resource consumption. The conclusion is that the tax or quota should be levied on the resource itself rather than on the commodity.

[. . .]

How would a depletion quota system function? The market for each resource would become two-tiered. To begin with, the government, as a monopolist, would auction the limited quota rights to many buyers. Resource buyers, having purchased their quota rights, would then have to confront many resource sellers in a competitive resource market. The competitive price in the resource market would tend to equal marginal cost. More efficient producers would earn differential rents, but the pure scarcity rent resulting from the quotas would have been captured in the depletion quota auction market by the government monopoly. The total price of the resource (quota price plus price to owner) would be raised as a result of the quotas. All products using these resources would become more expensive. Higher resource prices would compel more efficient and frugal use of resources by both producers and consumers. But the windfall rent from higher resource prices would be captured by the government and become public income – a partial realization of Henry George's ideal of a single tax on rent (George, 1951).

The major advantage is that higher resource prices would bring increased efficiency, while the quotas would directly limit depletion, thereby increasing conservation and indirectly limiting pollution. Pollution would be limited in two ways. First, since pollution is simply the other end of the throughput from depletion, limiting the input to the pipeline would naturally limit the output. Second, higher prices would induce more recycling, thereby further limiting materials pollution and depletion up to the limit set by the increased energy throughput required by recycling. The revenue from the depletion quota auction could help finance the minimum-income component of the distributist institution, offsetting the regressive effect of the higher resource prices on income distribution. Attempts to help the poor by underpricing resources are totally misguided, because the greatest benefit of subsidized prices for energy, for example, goes to those who consume the most energy – the rich, not the poor. This is hardly progressive.

[. . .]

A coordinated program

Let us now consider all three institutions as a unified program.

The allocation among firms of the limited aggregate of resources extracted during a given time period would be accomplished entirely by the market. The distribution of income within the maximum and minimum boundaries imposed would also be left to the market. The initial distribution of reproductive licenses is done outside the market on the basis of strict equity – one person, one license – but reallocation via market exchange is permitted in the interest of efficiency. The combination of the three institutions presents a nice reconciliation of efficiency and equity and provides the ecologically necessary macrocontrol of growth with the least sacrifice in terms of microlevel freedom and variability. The market is relied upon to allocate resources and distribute incomes within imposed ecological and ethical boundaries. The market is not allowed to set its own boundaries, but it is free within those boundaries. Setting boundaries is necessary. No one has ever claimed that market equilibria would automatically coincide with ecological equilibria or with a reasonably just distribution of wealth and income. Nor has anyone ever claimed that market equilibria would attain demographic balance. The very

notions of "equilibrium" in economics and ecology are antithetical. In growth economics equilibrium refers not to physical magnitudes at all but to a balance of desires between savers and investors. As long as saving is greater than depreciation, then net investment must be positive. This implies a *growing* flow of physical inputs from and outputs to nature, that is, a biophysical disequilibrium. Physical conditions of environmental equilibrium must be imposed on the market in aggregate quantitative physical terms. Subject to these quantitative constraints, the market and price system can, with the institutional changes just discussed, achieve an optimal allocation of resources and an optimal adjustment to its imposed physical system boundaries. The point is important because the belief is widespread among economists that internalization of externalities, or the incorporation of all environmental costs into market prices, is a sufficient environmental policy and that once this is accomplished the market will be able to set its own proper boundaries automatically. This is not so. Nor, as we have already seen, is it possible to incorporate all ecological costs in rigged money prices.

The internalization of externalities is a good strategy for fine-tuning the allocation of resources by making relative prices better measures of relative marginal social costs. But it does not enable the market to set its own absolute physical boundaries with the larger ecosystem. To give an analogy: Proper allocation arranges the weight in a boat optimally, so as to maximize the load that can be carried. But there is still an absolute limit to how much weight a boat can carry, even optimally arranged. The price system can spread the weight evenly, but unless it is supplemented by an external absolute limit, it will just keep on spreading the increasing weight evenly until the evenly loaded boat sinks. No doubt the boat would sink evenly, *ceteris paribus*, but that is less comforting to the average citizen than to the neoclassical economist.

Two distinct questions must be asked about these proposed institutions for achieving a steady state. First, would they work if people accepted the goal of a steady state and perhaps voted the institutions into effect? Second, would people ever accept either the steady-state idea or these particular institutions? I have tried to show that the answer to the first question is probably "yes." Let the critic find any remaining flaws; better yet, let him suggest improvements. The answer to the second question is clearly "no" in the short run. But several considerations make acceptance more plausible in the not-too-long run.

The minimum-income side of the distributist institution already has some political support in the United States; the maximum limits will at first be thought un-American. Yet, surely, beyond some figure any additions to personal income would represent greed rather than need, or even merit. Most people would be willing to believe that in most cases an income in excess of, let us say, $100,000 per year has no real functional justification, especially when the highly paid jobs are usually already the most interesting and pleasant.

In spite of their somewhat radical implications, the proposals presented in this chapter are, as we have seen, based on impeccably respectable conservative institutions: private property and the free market.

[. . .]

All three of the institutions we have discussed are capable of gradual application during the transition to a steady state. The birth quota does not have to be immediately set at negative or zero growth, or even at replacement, but could begin at any currently prevailing level and gradually approach replacement or lower fertility. Initially the certificate price would be zero, and it would rise gradually as the number of certificates issued to each person was cut from, for instance, 1.1, to 1.0, to 0.9, or to whatever level is desired. The depletion quotas could likewise be set at present levels or even at levels corresponding to a slower rate of increase than in the recent past. They could be applied first to those materials in shortest supply and to those whose wastes are hardest to absorb. Initial prices on quota rights would be low but then would rise gradually as growth pressed against the fixed quotas or as quotas were reduced in the interest of conservation. In either case the increased scarcity rent would become revenue to the government. The distribution limits might begin near the present extremes and slowly close to a more desirable range. The three institutions are amenable to any degree of gradualism we may wish. However, the distribution limits must be tightened faster than the depletion limits if the burden on the poor is to be lightened. All three control points are price system parameters, and altering them does not interfere with the static allocative efficiency of the market.

But it is also the case that these institutions could be totally ineffective. Depletion quotas could be endlessly raised on the grounds of national defense,

balance of payments, and so forth. Real estate and construction interests, not to mention the baby food and toy lobbies and the military, might convince Congress to keep the supply of birth licenses well above replacement level. People at the maximum income and wealth limit may succeed in continually raising that limit by spending a great deal of their money on TV ads extolling the Unlimited Acquisition of Everything as the very foundation of the American Way of Life. Everything would be the same and all justified in the sacred name of growth. Nothing will work unless we break our idolatrous commitment to material growth.

A definite US policy of population control at home would give us a much stronger base for preaching to the underdeveloped countries about their population problem. So would the reduction in US resource consumption resulting from depletion quotas. Without such a base to preach from we will continue to waste our breath, as we did at the 1974 Population Conference in Bucharest.

Thus we are brought back to the all-important moral premises. A physical steady state, if it is to be worth living in, absolutely requires moral growth. Future progress simply must be made in terms of the things that really count rather than the things that are merely countable. Institutional changes are necessary but insufficient. Moral growth is also necessary but insufficient. Both together are necessary and sufficient, but the institutional changes are relatively minor compared to the required change in values.

On Moral Growth

Let us assume for a moment that the necessity of the steady state and the above outline of its appropriate technologies and social institutions are accepted. Logic and necessity are not sufficient to bring about social reform. The philosopher Leibnitz observed, "If geometry conflicted with our passions and interests as much as do ethics, we would contest it and violate it as much as we do ethics now, in spite of all the demonstrations of Euclid and Archimedes, which would be labeled paralogisms and dreams" (quoted in Sauvy, 1970, p. 270). Leibnitz is surely correct. However logical and necessary the above outline of the steady state, it is, on the assumption of static morality, nothing but a dream. The physically steady economy absolutely requires moral growth beyond the present level.

Economists and other social scientists of positivistic bias seem to consider appeals to morality as cheating, as an admission of intellectual defeat, like bending the pieces of a jigsaw puzzle. In economics there is a long and solid tradition of regarding moral resources as static and too scarce to be relied upon. In the words of the great British economist Alfred Marshall, "progress chiefly depends on the extent to which the *strongest* and not merely the *highest* forces of human nature can be utilized for the increase of social good" (quoted in Robertson, 1956, p. 148).

Presumably self-interest is stronger and more abundant than brotherhood. Presumably "progress" and "social good" can be defined independently of the driving motive of society.

Another British economist, D. H. Robertson, once asked the illuminating question: What is it that economists economize? His answer was "love, the scarcest and most precious of all resources" (Robertson, 1956, p. 154). Paul Samuelson quotes Robertson approvingly in the latest edition of *Economics*, his influential textbook. Nor are economists alone in ruling out reliance on moral resources. The reader will recall that in his "Tragedy of the Commons" biologist Garrett Hardin identifies a class of problems with no technical solution. He rules out moral solutions as self-eliminating on a somewhat far-fetched evolutionary analogy, and advocates a political solution: mutual coercion mutually agreed upon. This is fine, but where is the mutual agreement to come from if not from shared values, from a convincing morality? Political scientist Beryl Crowe (1969), in revisiting the tragedy of the commons, argues that the set of no-technical-solution problems coincides with the set of no-political-solution problems and that Hardin's "mutual coercion mutually agreed upon" is politically impossible. Between them they present a convincing case that "commons problems" will not be solved technically nor politically, assuming static morality. Mutual coercion does not substitute for, but presupposes, moral growth.

[. . .]

The morality of the steady state is that of the Sermon on the Mount. Growthmania requires the negation of that morality. If we give our first attention to the evils of the day, we will have moral growth though not so much economic growth. If we anxiously give our first attention to tomorrow's larger income, we will have economic growth but little or no moral growth. Since economic growth is reaching physical limits anyway, we may now find the Sermon on the Mount more appealing and easier to accept.

[. . .]

There are other sources of moral support for the steady state besides the Sermon on the Mount. From the Old Testament we have two creation myths, the Priestly and the Yahwistic, one that gives value to creation only with reference to man, and one that gives value to creation independently of man. In Western thought the first tradition has dominated, but the other is there waiting to receive its proper emphasis. Also, Aldo Leopold's "land ethic" is extremely appealing and would serve admirably as the moral foundation of the steady state. Finally Karl Marx's materialism and objection to the alienation of man from nature can be enlisted as a moral foundation of the steady state. Marx recognized that nature is the "inorganic body of man" and not just a pile of neutral stuff to be dominated (Marx, 1963, p. 127).

In writing this chapter, I've considered the steady state only at a national level. Clearly the world as a whole must eventually adjust to a steady state. Perhaps ultimately this recognition will promote unity among nations – or, conversely, the desire for unity may promote the recognition. However, when nations cannot even agree to limit the stock of "bads" through disarmament, it is hard to be optimistic about their limiting the stocks of "goods." There is no alternative except to try, but national efforts need not wait for international agreement.

Finally, one rather subtle yet very powerful moral force can be enlisted in support of the steady-state paradigm. That is wholeness. If the truth is the whole, as Hegel claimed, then our current splintered knowledge is so far from truth that it is hardly worth learning. I believe this is why many of our best university students do not work very hard at their studies. Why continue mining the deep, narrow, disciplinary shafts sunk into man's totality by the intellectual fragment makers? Why deepen the tombs in which we have buried the wholeness of knowledge? Why increase the separation of people by filling separate heads with separate fragments of knowledge? The malaise reflected in these questions is very grave, and is, in my view, a major reason for the new surge of interest in ecology. Ecology is whole. It brings together the broken, analyzed, alienated, fragmented pieces of man's image of the world. Ecology is also a fad, but when the fad passes, the movement toward wholeness must continue. Unless the physical, the social, and the moral dimensions of our knowledge are integrated in a unified paradigm offering a vision of wholeness, no solutions to our problems are likely. John Stuart Mill's idea of the stationary state seems to me to offer such a paradigm.

[. . .]

Probably the rule of right action most accepted in practice is Jeremy Bentham's greatest good for the greatest number. Economists have avoided the difficult problem of defining *good* by substituting the word *goods*, in the sense of commodities. The principle thus became the greatest per capita product for the greatest number. More products per capita and more people to enjoy those products lead, in this view, to the greater social good. Our commitment to growth is no doubt based in considerable degree on this principle, which implies that right action is that which leads to more goods for more people.

But there are two problems with the greatest per capita product for the greatest number. First, as others have pointed out, the dictum contains one too many "greatests." It is not possible to maximize more than one variable. It is clear that numbers of people could be increased by lowering per capita product, and per capita product could be increased by lowering numbers, since resources taken from one goal can be devoted to the other. Second, it makes a big difference whether "greatest number" refers to those simultaneously alive or to the greatest number ever to live *over time*.

To resolve the first of these difficulties, we must maximize one variable only and treat some chosen level of the other as a constraint on the maximization. For one of the "greatests" we must substitute *sufficient*. There are two possible substitutions: the greatest per capita product for a sufficient number, or a sufficient per capita product for the greatest number. Which is the better principle? I suggest that we adopt the latter, and that "greatest number" be understood as greatest number over time, which takes care of the second problem. The revised principle thus becomes *sufficient per capita product for the greatest number over time*.

It is hard to find any objection to maximizing the number of people who will ever live at a material level sufficient for a good life. However, this certainly does *not* mean maximizing the number alive at any one time. On the contrary, it means the avoidance of any destruction of the earth's capacity to support life, a destruction that results from over-loading the life support system by having too many people – especially high-consuming people – alive at once. The opportunity cost of those extra lives in the present is fewer people alive in all subsequent time periods, and consequently a reduction in total lives ever to be lived at the sufficient level. Increasing per capita product beyond the sufficient level (extravagant luxury) may also overburden life support systems and have the same long-run life-reducing effect as excess population.

Maximizing number while satisficing per capita product does not imply that quantity of life is a higher value than quality. It does assume that beyond some level of sufficiency further increase in per capita goods does not increase quality of life and, in fact, may well diminish it. But sufficiency is the first consideration. To put it more concretely, the basic needs of all present people take priority over future numbers, but the existence of more future people takes priority over the trivial wants of the present. The impact of this revised utilitarian rule is to maximize life, or, what is the same thing, to economize the long-run capacity of the earth to support life at a sufficient level of individual wealth. The sufficient level may be thought of as a range of limited inequality rather than a single specific per capita income applicable to everyone. Some inequality is necessary for fairness.

This modified utilitarian principle certainly offers no magic philosopher's stone for making difficult choices easy. But it does seem superior to the old Benthamite rule in that it draws our attention to the concept of sufficiency, and it extends our time horizon. It forces us to face the question of purpose: sufficient *for what?* needed for what? It will be very difficult to define sufficiency and build the concept into economic theory and practice. But I think it will prove far more difficult to continue to operate on the principle that there is no such thing as enough.

Note

1 To *satisfice*, as used here, means to seek enough rather than the most. The concept of "enough" is difficult to define but even more difficult to deny.

References

Boulding, Kenneth E. 1964. *The Meaning of the Twentieth Century*. New York: Harper & Row.

Boulding, Kenneth E. 1966. "The Economics of the Coming Spaceship Earth." In Henry Jarrett, ed., *Environmental Quality in a Growing Economy.* Baltimore: Johns Hopkins University Press.

Crowe, Beryl. 1969. "The Tragedy of the Commons Revisited." *Science*, 28 November.

Daly, Herman E. 1968. "On Economics as a Life Science." *Journal of Political Economy*, May/June.

Daly, Herman E. 1974. "The Economics of the Steady State." *American Economic Review*, May.

Fisher, Irving. 1906. *The Nature of Capital and Income.* London: Macmillan.

George, Henry. 1951. *Progress and Poverty.* New York: Robert Schalkenbach Foundation. (Originally published in 1879.)

Georgescu-Roegen, Nicholas. 1966. *Analytical Economics.* Cambridge: Harvard University Press.

Georgescu-Roegen, Nicholas. 1971. *The Entropy Law and the Economic Process.* Cambridge: Harvard University Press.

Hannon, Bruce. 1975. "Energy, Growth, and Altruism." Urbana: University of Illinois, Center for Advanced Computation (mimeographed).

Heer, David M. 1975. "Marketable Licenses for Babies: Boulding's Proposal Revisited." *Social Biology*, Spring.

Luten, Daniel S. "Teleoeconomics: The Microdynamic, Macrostatic Economy." Department of Geography, University of California, Berkeley (mimeographed).

McClaughry, John. 1974. "The Future of Private Property and Its Distribution." *Ripon Quarterly*, Fall.

Marx, Karl. 1963. *Karl Marx's Early Writings.* Trans. and ed. T. B. Bottomore. New York: McGraw-Hill.

Mill, John Stuart. 1881. "Of Property." In *Principles of Political Economy.* Book 2. New York: Appleton-Century-Crofts.

Robertson, D. H. 1956. *Economic Commentaries.* London: Staples Press.

Sauvy, A. 1970. *The General Theory of Population.* New York: Basic Books.

68   Making Capitalism Sustainable

John Elkington

Is Capitalism Sustainable?

Capitalism and sustainability, however much we may wish it otherwise, do not make easy bedfellows. As *Fortune* recently put it:

> Corporations were put on this earth, after all, to make money, and to some minds, profit maximization will never seem all that different from greed. But profits, of course, pay for the latest equipment and technology that produce economic growth and more jobs. If corporations weren't greedy like that, they'd go out of business and then we'd all be in trouble.[1]

Well maybe. But the sustainability lobby points out that we are in trouble already, often because of the self-interested way in which most corporations have interpreted their missions. So, it asks, can the capitalist system change not only its spots but also its very nature? Can these corporate cannibals, in short, not only learn to use more civilized tools but also begin to shift their diet towards inputs that are less ecologically, socially, and economically damaging?

Meanwhile, although it is far from clear that capitalism is significantly more environmentally damaging than the alternatives, it has been in the spotlight recently both because of its rising global power and because of what some would have us believe is the "end of history." In 1989, Francis Fukuyama wrote an influential article arguing that the world was seeing the development of a quite remarkable consensus on the legitimacy of liberal democracy as a system of government. This system, he suggested, had conquered rival ideologies such as hereditary monarchy, fascism, and communism. In this narrow sense, he believed that we were seeing the end of history, the "end point of mankind's ideological evolution" and the "final form of human government."

From John Elkington, *Cannibals with Forks: The Triple Bottom Line of 21st Century Business* (Capstone Publishing Ltd, 1999), pp. 24–5, 25–6, 35, 37, 38–9, 70–6, 79–81, 84–6, 87–8, 92–4, 94–6 (notes). © John Elkington, 1997, 1999. Reprinted with permission from Wiley-Blackwell.

The almost immediate crackdown by the Chinese communists after the Tiananmen Square protests in 1989, and the 1991 Iraqi invasion of Kuwait and ensuing Gulf War led many critics to argue that Fukuyama – who followed up with a controversial book, *The End of History and The Last Man*[2] in 1992 – was wrong. Whatever the facts, some analysts fear that the world may potentially be even more unstable after the end of the "Cold War" than it was when the West and the Soviet Union were poised in nuclear deadlock. Certainly, the potential for "rogue" states to develop their own nuclear, chemical, or biological arsenals appears much greater now that many of the defence industry skills of the old USSR are available on the open market. In this context, any transition to more sustainable forms of economic development will have to cope with – and may even trigger – major political dislocations. If we fail to wake up to and manage these challenges in time, they may well derail key elements of the sustainability transition.

[. . .]

Stripped to its essence, capitalism – of whatever brand – is an economic (and, necessarily, political) system in which individual owners of capital are (relatively) free to dispose of it as they please and, in particular, for their own profit. As we will see, there are many different ways of calculating, defining and valuing capital, but a key question for all capitalist societies in the 21st century will be whether their particular version can be sustained in the face of broader economic, political, social, and environmental challenges? This question is becoming more urgent as we see a shift in the balance of international power, with nations tending to lose power and transnational corporations tending to become increasingly powerful.

[. . .]

It is not yet remotely clear whether capitalism can ever become sustainable, as that term is currently understood. But there is enough evidence to suggest that the free enterprise model offers the best hope of moving in that direction – provided that it is suitably shaped by social and regulatory pressures. Its real strength is that, more than any other model subjected to large-scale testing, it promises to help harness human creativity and innovation to the sustainability cause.

[. . .]

Marx, it turns out, was right in much of his analysis but his prognosis was deeply flawed; Kruschev's,

too. Even so, the last thing 21st century corporations will be able to do is put their corporate feet up. On top of all the other changes under way, the sustainability transition will destroy some industries and force the radical restructuring of others. It will be the unmaking of tens of thousands of companies and businesses around the world. But it will also provide the seedbed conditions for hundreds of thousands, indeed millions, of new businesses.

[. . .]

[W]e are still a long way from sustainability. Systems thinking tells us that sustainability cannot be defined for a single corporation. Instead, it must be defined for a complete economic–social–ecological system, and not for its component parts.[3] Think of an industry directly based on a renewable natural resource, such as the fishing industry. A captain of a fishing vessel might fish for his entire life without depleting fish stocks in an area, but if he were joined by a sufficiently large fleet of identical vessels, the fishery could be destroyed. The behavior of the captain and his vessel would not have changed, but in the first case it would be sustainable and in the second not.

Worse, as Paul Hawken has pointed out in *The Ecology of Commerce*,[4] is that:

> we are faced with a sobering irony: If every company on the planet were to adopt the environmental and social practices of the best companies – of, say, the Body Shop, Patagonia, and Ben and Jerry's – the world would still be moving toward environmental degradation and collapse.

Ultimately, Paul Hawken argues, the problem we face is not so much a management problem as a *design* problem. "In order to approximate a sustainable society," he concludes, "we need to describe a system of commerce and production in which each and every act is inherently sustainable and restorative." This is the challenge implicit in the sustainability transition. Even the best companies [. . .] will only be sustainable when the institutions and markets surrounding them have been redesigned to support and promote sustainability.[5] This recognition, in turn, will require triple bottom line campaigners to invest much greater efforts in such fields as the recalibration of international trade agreements and the operations of global financial markets. In many respects, the challenge has only just begun.

The Triple Bottom Line

Driving companies towards sustainability will require dramatic changes in their performance against the triple bottom line. Some of the most interesting challenges, however, are found not within but *between* the areas covered by the economic, social, and environmental bottom lines. These "shear zones" are illustrated in figures 68.1–68.7 and typical agenda items are covered in the three "shear zone" panels.

Like the ancient Trojans dragging the vast wooden horse through a great gap torn in the walls of their long-besieged city, some of the world's best business brains spent the 1990s struggling to take on board the emerging sustainability agenda. Many of their colleagues warned that success would end in disaster, just as it had done for the Trojans. Sustainable development, they argued, was a treacherous concept; basically, communism in camouflage. By the middle of the last decade of the 20th century, however, their fevered brows were being soothed by the concept of "eco-efficiency," promoted by the World Business Council for Sustainable Development (WBCSD). And then, as some had feared, the trap was sprung.

Communism had nothing to do with it. But the sustainability agenda, long understood as an attempt to harmonize the traditional financial bottom line with emerging thinking about the environmental bottom line, turned out to be more complicated than some early business enthusiasts had imagined. Today we think in terms of a "triple bottom line," focusing on economic prosperity, environmental quality, and – the element which business had preferred to overlook – social justice.

None of this was new, of course. *Our Common Future*, the 1987 report of the World Commission on Environment and Development, had made it perfectly clear that equity issues, and particularly the concept of inter-generational equity, were at the very heart of the sustainability agenda.[6] But most of the hundreds of companies that limbered up for the 1992 Earth Summit by signing the Business Charter for Sustainable Development, devised by the International Chamber of Commerce (ICC), had little idea of the deeper logic of sustainable development. As far as they, and the thousands of companies which have signed up since, were concerned, the basic challenge was simply one of "greening," of making business more efficient and trimming costs.

When the *Harvard Business Review* turned its spotlight on to the sustainability agenda in 1997, ten years after the publication of *Our Common Future*, it noted that, "Beyond greening lies an enormous challenge – and an enormous opportunity. The challenge is to develop a sustainable global economy: an economy that the planet is capable of supporting indefinitely."[7] This represents a profound challenge. Although some parts of the developed world may be beginning to turn the corner in terms of ecological recovery, the planet as a whole is still seen to be on an unsustainable course.

"Those who think that sustainability is only a matter of pollution control are missing the bigger picture," explained Stuart Hart, director of the Corporate Environmental Management Program at the University of Michigan:

> Even if all the companies in the developed world were to achieve zero emissions by the year 2000, the earth would still be stressed beyond what biologists refer to as its carrying capacity. Increasingly, the scourges of the late twentieth century – depleted farmland, fisheries, and forests; choking urban pollution; poverty; infectious disease; and migration – are spilling over geopolitical borders. The simple fact is this: in meeting our needs, we are destroying the ability of future generations to meet theirs.

And these problems are not simply economic and environmental, either in their origins or nature. Instead, they raise social, ethical, and, above all, political issues. The roots of the crisis, Hart concluded, are "political and social issues that exceed the mandate and capabilities of any corporation." But here is the paradox: "At the same time, corporations are the only organizations with the resources, the technology, the global reach, and, ultimately, the motivation to achieve sustainability."

There is no question that some of these issues can have – indeed, already have had – a profound impact on the financial bottom line. Think of the companies and industries making or using such products as asbestos, mercury, PCBs, PVC, and CFCs and it is clear that the long-term sustainability of major slices of any modern economy is already being called into question.

Worryingly, at least on current trends, things can only get worse. "It is easy to state the case in the negative," as Hart pointed out. "Faced with impoverished customers, degraded environments, failing political systems, and unraveling societies, it will be increasingly difficult for corporations to do business. But," he stressed:

the positive case is even more powerful. The more we learn about the challenges of sustainability, the clearer it is that we are poised at the threshold of an historic moment in which many of the world's industries may be transformed.

The level of change implied by the sustainability transition is extraordinary. As the Worldwatch Institute put it in a recent *State of the World* report:

> We are only at the beginning of this restructuring. New industries are emerging to reestablish natural balances – based on technologies that can produce heat and light without putting carbon into the atmosphere; on metals made out of the scrap of past buildings and cars; on papers made out of what was once considered wastepaper. Some homes and offices are heated entirely by the sun or from electricity generated by the wind.[8]

But sustainable capitalism will need more than just environment-friendly technologies and, however important these may be, markets which actively promote dematerialization. We will also need to address radically new views of what is meant by social equity, environmental justice and business ethics. This will require a much better understanding not only of financial and physical forms of capital, but also of natural, human, and social capital.

Business leaders and executives wanting to grasp the full scale of the challenge confronting their corporations and markets will need to carry out a sustainability audit [. . .] against the emerging requirements and expectations driven by sustainability's triple bottom line. In the spirit of the management dictum that what you can't measure you are likely to find hard to manage, we should ask whether it is even possible to measure progress against the triple bottom line?

The answer is yes, but the metrics are still evolving in most areas – and need to evolve much further if they are to be considered in an integrated way. In the following pages, we briefly focus on the relevant trends in relation to the economic, environmental and social bottom lines. In each case, we headline some of the current thinking on accountability, accounting, performance indicators, auditing, reporting and benchmarking. But we also look at the new concepts and requirements emerging at the interfaces between each of these great agendas, in the "shear zones" (see figures 68.1–68.4).

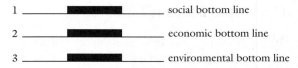

Figure 68.1   SustainAbility is developing the concept of the "triple bottom line" of sustainable development. Society depends on the economy – and the economy depends on the global ecosystem, whose health represents the ultimate bottom line.

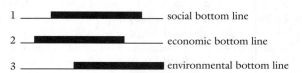

Figure 68.2   The three bottom lines are not stable; they are in constant flux, due to social, political, economic and environmental pressures, cycles and conflicts. So the sustainability challenge is tougher than any of the other challenges in isolation.

Figure 68.3   Think of each bottom line as a continental plate, often moving independently of the others. People often forget their dependence on wealth creation; and most of us are ignorant of our impacts on the ultimate bottom line.

Figure 68.4   As the plates move under, over, or against each other, "shear zones" emerge where the social, economic, and ecological equivalents of tremors and earthquakes occur. The main shear zones are illustrated in figures 68.5–68.7.

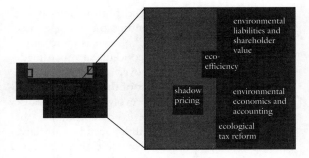

Figure 68.5 *In the economic/environmental shear zone*, some companies already promote eco-efficiency. But there are even greater challenges ahead, such as environmental economics and accounting, shadow pricing, and ecological tax reform.

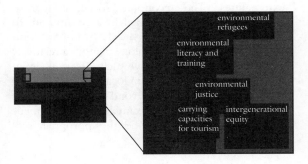

Figure 68.6 In the *social/environmental shear zone*, business is working on environmental literacy and training issues, but new challenges will be sparked by e.g. environmental justice, environmental refugees, and intergenerational equity.

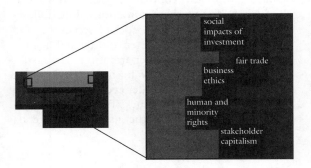

Figure 68.7 In the *economic/social shear zone*, some companies are looking at the social impacts of proposed investment, but bubbling under are issues like business ethics, fair trade, human and minority rights, and stakeholder capitalism.

The Economic Bottom Line

Let's begin in the area where business should feel most at home. Given that we are using the "bottom line" metaphor, however, we need to understand exactly what it means in its traditional usage. A company's bottom line is the profit figure used as the earnings figure in the earnings-per-share statement, part of standard accounting practice. In trying to assess a company's conventional bottom line performance, accountants pull together, record and analyze a wide range of numerical data. This approach is often seen as a model for environmental and social accounting, but the challenge can be even tougher in these emerging areas of corporate accountability.[9]

Economic capital

So how should a would-be sustainable corporation assess whether its business operations are economically sustainable? Obviously, a critical first step is to understand what is meant by economic capital. In the simplest terms, your capital is the total value of your assets minus your liabilities. In traditional economic theory, capital as a factor of production can come in two main forms: *physical capital* (including machinery and plant) and *financial capital*. But as we move into the knowledge economy, the concept is gradually being extended to include such concepts as *human capital* – a measure of the experience, skills, and other knowledge-based assets of the individuals who make up an organization. We will also consider the *intellectual capital* concepts adopted by companies like Skandia.

Among the questions business people need to ask in this area are the following. Are our costs competitive – and likely to remain so? Is the demand for our products and services sustainable? Is our rate of innovation likely to be competitive in the longer term? How can we ensure that human or intellectual capital does not migrate out of the organization? Are our profit margins sustainable?[10] Longer term, too, the concept of economic capital will need to absorb much wider concepts, such as *natural capital* and *social capital*, both of which are discussed below.

Accountability

In most countries, companies have an obligation to give an account of their financial performance. In the case of limited companies, directors are accountable to shareholders. This responsibility is partly discharged by the production and – in the case of public companies – publication of an annual report and accounts. An annual general meeting (AGM) theoretically provides shareholders with an opportunity to oversee the presentation of audited accounts, the appointment of directors and auditors, the fixing of their remuneration, and recommendations for the payment of dividends.

Typically, there has been little, if any, overlap between the areas covered by financial auditors in serving the interests of shareholders and the issues of interest to other stakeholders in terms of the environmental and social bottom lines. But one area where we see a growing degree of overlap between a company's economic and environmental performance is "eco-efficiency" [. . .]. At the same time, too, there are early signs that, as the sustainability agenda becomes a board-level issue, we will see growing overlaps with the whole corporate governance agenda [. . .].

Accounting

By the very nature of their work and training, most traditional accountants are short-sighted. Typically, the so-called accounting period is 12 months. Internal accounts are often prepared on a monthly or quarterly basis, with full results produced annually. Worldwide, however, the pressure to perform on a quarterly basis is intensifying as Anglo-Saxon approaches to stock management and investment banking spread.

In preparing their accounts, accountants are guided by a range of reasonably well-established concepts. These include the *ongoing concern concept* (with assets not stated at break-up value, unless there is evidence that the company is no longer viable), the *consistency concept* (which calls for accounts to be prepared on a consistent basis, allowing accurate comparisons between quarters or years), the *prudence concept* (accounts should be prepared on a conservative basis, recording income and profits only when they are achieved, and making provision for foreseeable losses) and *depreciation* (with the value of most assets progressively written off over time).

Despite 500 years – counting early clay tablets, some would say at least 5,000 years – of evolution in mainstream accounting, there remain huge controversies over how companies account for acquisitions and disposals, record extraordinary and exceptional items, value contingent liabilities, capitalize costs, and depreciate their assets. [. . .]

We have tended to see the bottom line as the hardest of realities, representing the unappealable verdict of impartial markets.[11] But it is increasingly clear that such accounting concepts are man-made conventions that change over space and time. Bottom lines are the product of the institutions and societies in which they have evolved. And, because accounting inevitably involves compromises, the bottom line turns out to be influenced by subjective interpretations, quite apart from "creative" accounting. So, for example, when Rover was taken over by BMW and subjected to Germany's stricter valuation criteria, a 1995 "profit" of £91 million became a £158 million "loss."

A key concept in relation to all three dimensions of sustainability – but particularly relevant in relation to environmental and societal costs – is that of "externalities." These economic, social, or environmental costs are not recorded in accounts. So, to take an economic example, the decision of a company to locate a high-technology plant in a relatively undeveloped region may have such effects as drawing technical talent away from local firms, or forcing up property prices locally beyond what local people can afford. We will look at examples of environmental and social externalities under the appropriate sections below.

[. . .]

Environmental Bottom Line

The social agenda for business probably has a longer history than the environmental agenda. Think of the early controversies around slavery, child labor, and working conditions. But, following a flurry of interest in social accounting and auditing in the 1970s, the environmental agenda has tended to attract greater attention. The result, paradoxically, is that many business people these days feel happier being challenged on environmental issues than on social issues. This fact has had a marked impact on the way the sustainability agenda is defined by business.

Natural capital

How can a would-be sustainable corporation work out whether it is environmentally sustainable? Again, a critical first step is to understand what is meant by natural capital. The concept of natural wealth is both complex and still evolving. If you try to account for the natural capital embodied in a forest, for example, it is not simply a question of counting the trees and trying to put a price-tag on the lumber they represent. You have to account for the underlying natural wealth which supports the forest ecosystem, producing – as just one stream of benefits – timber and other commercial products. Wider forest functions that need to be added into the equation include contributions to the regulation of water (in the atmosphere, water table, soils, and surface waters) and of greenhouse gases like carbon dioxide and methane.[12] And then there are all the flora and fauna, including commercial fisheries, whose health is linked to the health of the forest.

Natural capital can also be thought of as coming in two main forms: "critical natural capital" and renewable, replaceable, or substitutable natural capital. The first form embraces natural capital which is essential to the maintenance of life and ecosystem integrity; the second forms of natural capital which can be renewed (e.g. through breeding or relocation of sensitive ecosystems), repaired (e.g. environmental remediation or desert reclamation), or substituted or replaced (e.g. growing use of man-made substitutes, such as solar panels in place of limited fossil fuels).[13]

Among the questions business people will need to ask are the following. What forms of natural capital are affected by our current operations – and will they be affected by our planned activities? Are these forms of natural capital sustainable given these, and other, likely pressures? Is the overall level of stress properly understood and likely to be sustainable? Is the "balance of nature" or the "web of life" likely to be significantly affected?

The interesting thing about a company's ecological bottom line is that the carrying capacity of most ecosystems varies in relation to the number – and behavior – of the economic actors operating within them. As a result, these bottom lines will vary over time and space. The more efficient the actors, however, the more actors can be sustained. [. . .]

Accountability

In many countries, companies are held accountable by regulators for aspects of their environmental performance. In the USA, the Toxic Release Inventory (TRI) requires companies producing more than certain threshold limits of over 600 chemicals to report their emissions. Some countries, like the Netherlands, also back up their regulations with voluntary programs designed to push companies towards sectorally agreed targets.

Just as often, however, business is held to account by environmentalist and media campaigns, which may bear little relation to regulated or voluntarily agreed targets. And as companies begin to challenge their supply chains, a new dimension of pressure is being introduced. While planning this book, for example, I was invited by Volvo to help facilitate their first environmental conference for supplier companies. The company's top management told the 500-plus audience that Volvo had started off by focusing on safety, then added quality. Now, they said, environmental performance was increasingly in the spotlight – and suppliers would find environmental aspects being covered in Volvo's regular supplier audits.

Accounting

The field of environmental accounting is relatively embryonic, but is generating a growing literature.[14] Among other things, it aims to: re-balance the treatment of environmental costs and benefits in conventional accounting practice; separately identify environmental related costs and revenues within the conventional accounting systems; devise new forms of valuation which encourage better management decisions and increased investment in environmental protection and improvement; develop new performance indicators to track progress; and experiment with ways in which sustainability considerations can be assessed and incorporated into mainstream accounting.[15]

As far as environmental externalities go, many companies have been forced to take on to their books impacts and effects which were once externalized. Take the case of T&N, which as Turner & Newall was once one of the world's largest asbestos producers. For years, the company argued that the risks involved in the use of asbestos were acceptable. Eventually, however, the tide turned, not only against Turner & Newall but against the entire asbestos industry. At the time of writing, T&N had already paid out over £350 million over ten years to meet asbestos claims – and was busily selling off corporate assets to fund a further £323 million provision.[16] And, in an attempt to draw a line under its asbestos legacy, the company had announced a £515 million charge against annual profits to meet future personal injury claims and insurance costs. It was not alone in experiencing such problems.

[. . .]

Social Bottom Line

Some in the sustainable development community insist that sustainability has nothing to do with social, ethical or cultural issues. A sustainable world, they argue, could equally well be more equitable or less equitable than today's world. The real issues, they say, relate to resource efficiency. Like King Canute, they are trying to hold back the tide by sheer force of will, or prejudice. Their views may be a useful counterbalance to attempts to turn sustainability into a new form of communism, but in the end our progress against the social bottom line is going to be critically important in determining the success or failure of the sustainability transition. If we fail to address wider political, social and ethical issues, the backlash will inevitably undermine progress in the environmental area.

Social capital

So, how should a would-be sustainable corporation think about social capital? In part, it comprises human capital, in the form of public health, skills and education. But it also must embrace wider measures of a society's health and wealth-creation potential.

[. . .] Fukuyama says that social capital is "a capability that arises from the prevalence of trust in a society or in certain parts of it." It is a measure of "the ability of people to work together for common purposes in groups and organizations." This ability is likely to be critical to the sustainability transition. It can be developed (or eroded) at every level in a society, from the basic family unit to the major institutions of international government. It depends on the acquisition and maintenance of such virtues as loyalty, honesty and dependability.

The central benefits flow from a lowering of social friction. So, for example, Fukuyama notes that:

> if people who have to work together in an enterprise trust one another because they are all operating according to a common set of ethical norms, doing business costs less. Such a society will be better able to innovate organizationally, since the high degree of trust will permit a wide variety of social relationships to emerge.

In the same way, the degree of trust between a corporation or industry and their external stakeholders is likely to be a key factor determining their long-term sustainability. Conversely, "widespread distrust in a society imposes a kind of tax on all forms of economic activity, a tax that high-trust societies do not have to pay."

A key assumption in the work SustainAbility has done in recent years is that sustainable development is most likely – and will be achieved at the lowest overall cost to the economy – in those societies where there are the highest levels of trust and other forms of social capital. This, in turn, is likely to depend on the levels and equity of investment in human capital. According to Ismail Serageldin, the World Bank's vice president of environmentally sustainable development, human capital requires "investments in education, health and nutrition." Developing and spreading the necessary skills and training, particularly in the emerging economies and developing countries, will require new forms of public–private partnership.

Among the questions business people will need to ask are the following. What are the crucial forms of social capital in terms of our ability to become a sustainable corporation? What are the underlying trends in terms of the creation, maintenance, or erosion of these forms of capital? What is the role of business in sustaining human capital and social capital? To what extent are such concepts as environmental justice and intra- and inter-generational equity likely to change the ways in which we define and measure social capital?

Accountability

Whatever its critics may choose to believe, business is part of society. Governments try to regulate and otherwise control the social impacts associated with industry and commerce, but history is full of examples where the agenda was created outside the intertwined worlds of government and business. Whether it was the crusade to end slavery or the various campaigns to end child labor in European and North American factories, business people have long found their freedom of action being increasingly constrained by emerging social movements.

As globalization gathers steam, the interface between the economic and social bottom lines becomes increasingly problematic. Consider the abortive attempt by Germany's Krupp Hoesch to take over its rival Thyssen. This represented an attempt to make the German steel industry more competitive in the face of intensifying international competition. But, faced with massed rallies by tens of thousands of Ruhr steel-workers concerned about the implications for their jobs and protesting about "casino capitalism" and calling for "people before profit," Krupp – and its partner banks, Deutsche, Dresdner, and Goldman Sachs – backed down.[17] The decision was widely hailed by German politicians as evidence that the country's social consensus economy works; that "social responsibility" had prevailed. But there are short-term definitions of responsibility and longer-term definitions. The two companies may achieve the necessary efficiencies without redundancies, but if globalization continues Germany may simply have postponed the day of reckoning. In doing so, it may be ensuring that the inevitable economic and social quakes are worse than they need to have been.

[. . .]

Accounting

Social accounting aims to assess the impact of an organization or company on people both inside and outside. Issues often covered are community relations, product safety, training and education initiatives, sponsorship, charitable donations of money and time, and employment of disadvantaged groups. "Socio-economic sustainability," says Professor Tom Gladwin, "requires poverty alleviation, population stabilization, female empowerment, employment creation, human rights observance and opportunity on a massive scale."[18]

As far as social externalities are concerned, an example from Japan would be *karoshi*, the word for death caused by overwork. The case of Ichiro Oshima is not unusual. By the time he committed suicide, he had worked eighteen months with only half a day off. The advertising agency executive started work at 7am each day, often returning home at two in the morning. What was unusual was that his parents decided to sue his employer.[19] A flurry of litigation in the country has been forcing Japanese corporations to introduce "no overtime" days, in an attempt to give employees time off to spend with their families. How can such social costs be captured? Clearly, social accounting is another area where a great deal of further work is needed.

[. . .]

Accounting for the Triple Bottom Line

It is clear that progress – or the lack of it – can be measured against a wide range of indicators associated with each of the three bottom lines of sustainability. But the next step will be to tackle this agenda in an integrated way. Key tools will be sustainability accounting, auditing and reporting. In many respects these concepts are still "black boxes," more talked about in generalities than defined in precise terms, but there is now fascinating work under way in each of these areas.

Ultimately, as Professor Rob Gray and his colleagues put it, sustainability reporting "must consist of statements about the extent to which corporations are reducing (or increasing) the options available to future generations."[19] This is an extremely complex task, but one which will probably look much easier once we have worked our way through a decade or two of experimentation in sustainability accounting, auditing and reporting. A key area of activity in this respect will be "full cost pricing" – underpinned by new forms of full cost accounting. The idea of full cost pricing is that all the costs associated with a product or service should be internalized, and, as a result, reflected in its price. Even where no markets exist for the values being considered, the "shadow pricing" approach can provide at least some guidance on relative values.

Very often, we will be unable to say whether or not a particular company or industry is "sustainable," but we will become increasingly sophisticated in terms of our ability to assess whether or not it is moving in the right direction. The triple bottom line approach clearly complicates matters. It is one thing to suggest, as some do, that a sustainable corporation is one which "leaves the biosphere no worse off at the end of the accounting period than it was at the beginning," but when we include the social and ethical dimensions of sustainability the range of sustainability-related issues and impacts grows dramatically. This does not mean that we should not try to move in this direction, but simply that we should be very careful about over-hyping the likely early benefits or pace of progress.

Notes

1   *Fortune*, 15 April 1996, page 26.
2   Francis Fukuyama, *The End of History and the Last Man*, Hamish Hamilton, 1992.

3   Module 3, *From SMAS to SMAS: The EPE workbook for implementing sustainability in Europe*, Version 1.1, edited by Andrea Spencer-Cooke, SustainAbility for European Partners for the Environment, May 1996.

4   Paul Hawken, *The Ecology of Commerce: How business can save the planet*, Phoenix, 1993.

5   Paul Hawken, "A Declaration of Sustainability," *Utne Reader*, September/October 1993.

6   World Commission for Environment and Development, *Our Common Future*, Oxford University Press, 1987.

7   Stuart L. Hart, "Beyond Greening: Strategies for a sustainable world," *Harvard Business Review*, January–February 1997.

8   Hal Kane, "Shifting to sustainable industries," *State of the World 1996*, Worldwatch Institute.

9   Many of the definitions under the "Economic bottom line" section are based on the *Oxford Dictionary of Business*, Oxford University Press, 1996.

10 Daniel Blake Rubenstein, *Environment Accounting for the Sustainable Corporation: Strategies and techniques*, Quorum Books, 1994.

11 Simon Caulkin, "When black means red," *Observer*, 14 April 1996.

12 Daniel Blake Rubenstein, *ibid.*

13 Jan Bebbington and Rob Gray, "Sustainable development and accounting: incentives and disincentives for the adoption of sustainability by transnational corporations," in *Environmental Accounting and Sustainable Development: The final report*, Limperg Institute, The Netherlands, 1996.

14 See, for example, Rob Gray, Jan Bebbington and Diane Walters, *Accounting for the Environment*, Paul Chapman Publishing Ltd, 1993; Daniel Blake Rubenstein, *Environmental Accounting for the Sustainable Corporation: Strategies and techniques*, Quorum Books, 1994; and Wouter van Dieren (editor), *Taking Nature Into Account: Towards a sustainable national income*, a report to the Club of Rome, Copernicus, 1995.

15 Rob Gray, Jan Bebbington and Diane Walters, *Accounting for the Environment*, Paul Chapman Publishing Ltd, 1993.

16 Tim Burt, "T&N raises £42m for asbestos costs," *Financial Times*, 15 April 1997.

17 Michael Woodhead, "A Pyrrhic victory for Germany," *Sunday Times*, 30 March 1997.

18 Thomas N. Gladwin, Tara-Shelomith Krause and James J. Kennelly, "Beyond Eco-efficiency: Towards socially sustainable business," *Sustainable Development* 3, 35–43, April 1995.

19 Skandia, *Intellectual Capital Development*, 1996 (booklet and CD).

---

69   The Ignorance Argument: What Must We Know to be Fair to the Future?

Bryan Norton

It is often noted that "sustainability" has come to "mean all things to all people," and indeed the term is used in many confusing ways; but we should not go too far in emphasizing the ambiguity of the term. It does, after all, have a clear, core meaning: sustainability is about the future and our concern toward it.

It thus seems reasonable to say that sustainability has to do with our intertemporal moral relations and concerns our obligations to future generations. [. . .] Opinion polls show that overwhelming majorities of people in modern democratic societies believe we should protect resources and natural wonders for the future. [. . .] Surely this widespread impulse is at least partially responsible for the widespread interest in, and acceptance of, sustainability as a public policy goal.

Intertemporal Ethics as Economics

[. . .] I will refer to the "bequest package" that one generation leaves for the next – a bequest package is

From Daniel W. Bromley and Jouni Paavola, eds., *Economics, Ethics and Environmental Policy: Contested Choices* (Oxford: Blackwell Publishing, 2002), pp. 35, 36–9, 40–2, 43–52. © 2002 by Blackwell Publishing Ltd. Reprinted with permission from Blackwell Publishing Ltd. Edited by the author.

the sum total of accumulated capital, the technology, the institutions, and resources. The bequest package portends the sum total of *actual* impacts that one generation has on all subsequent generations. Given the prospective viewpoint of this essay, discussion of proposed bequests will of necessity refer to intended bequests, not actual bequests.

However great the difference between the two, we must assume they are related: the intentions of earlier generations must at least matter in the formation of the actual bequest. Otherwise, we would not take intergenerational obligations seriously. Accepting an obligation to protect the future from negative impacts of our own decisions requires at least some faith in our ability to foresee those impacts and at least some of their consequences for future people, as well as some means to avoid identified unacceptable consequences. As we shall see shortly, the problem of ignorance about the future lies at the heart of one of the most interesting and lively theoretical debates about the meaning of sustainability.

[. . .]

In this [essay] I explore intergenerational moral relationships in order to clarify the term "sustainability." I begin by addressing the economist's approach to the obligations to posterity, which will get us quickly to the issue of ignorance and the limits it may place on possible definitions and ideals of sustainability. Economists, much more than philosophers, have been seriously engaged in attempts to define sustainability and have succeeded in laying the foundations for the debate on intergenerational obligations. For example, many of those who explore obligations to the future take it for granted that discounting of future values will occur in evaluation processes; those who disagree usually propose alternative levels of discounting, different ways of computing the discount rates, or qualifications of the discounting practice. Economists have thus shaped the academic and policy discourse about intertemporal ethics. Their success in setting the agenda for the discussion of sustainability is due to an ingenious conceptual simplification – one that is based on an assumption regarding the role of knowledge in the process of choosing a fair bequest package. Accepting these assumptions, it is reasonable to consider our obligations to the future as a problem of finding a fair tradeoff between consumption today and foregone consumption today, in order to protect the consumption opportunities of future people.

I call this reduction of intergenerational equity to cross-temporal comparisons of welfare opportunities the "Grand Simplification" (GS). This simplification provides the theoretical foundation for the treatments of "sustainability" advocated by most mainstream economists and many philosophers. According to this view, sustainability is about affording each generation equal opportunity to enjoy undiminished welfare, by comparison to the welfare opportunities available to earlier generations. Philosophers who address the question of our obligations to the future have been supportive of such a simplification; they cede to the economists the intellectual territory where our actual obligations to future generations are to be determined. With the exception of the philosopher O'Neill (1993) and the economist Bromley (1998), there has been little resistance to the economizing of intergenerational morality. Here we will use the economists' version of this simplification to set the stage for a broader evaluation of the GS and its effects on both economics and philosophy.

Economists – especially growth theorists – have outlined a position that has come to be called *weak sustainability*. This view has been challenged by "ecological economists," who defend *strong sustainability*. Weak sustainability is based on the intuition that what we owe the future is to avoid actions that will make them *poorer* than we are in terms of opportunities to achieve welfare equal to ours. This is a weak requirement. Quite simply, each generation is required to maintain and pass on to their successors the economic capital they have inherited. No environmental goals should be given priority over other investments that have equal or greater expectation of return in terms of capital accumulation. Fairness is a matter of choosing the proper mix of investment and consumption.

Strong sustainability presents more stringent sustainability requirements. Strong sustainability theorists have defined a category of social value, called "natural" capital, which is not created by humans, and is deemed essential to the well-being of the people of the future. Strong sustainability requires the protection of natural capital (in addition to the more general requirement that each generation maintain the stocks of man-made capital) as a significant aspect of one generation's bequest to the next.[1] Strong sustainability requires an adequate and appropriate definition of natural capital, and I am not convinced such a definition can be provided (Holland, 1999; Norton, 1999). Strong sustainability theorists and others who wish to articulate more stringent sustainability requirements must provide good reasons to go beyond weak sustainability which, as we shall see, offers an initially attractive simplification of an otherwise perplexing moral problem.

In a series of lectures and papers, Robert Solow has forwarded a view according to which "sustainability" can be fully defined, characterized, and measured within neoclassical economic theory (Solow, 1974, 1986, 1992, 1993). He argues that all we could possibly owe the future is that they be as well off, economically, as we are (weak sustainability). Solow's basic idea is that the obligation to sustainability "is an obligation to conduct ourselves so that we leave to the future the option or the capacity to be as well off as we are." He doubts that "one can be more precise than that." A central implication of Solow's view is that, while to talk about sustainability is "not empty, . . . there is no specific object that the goal of sustainability, the obligation of sustainability, requires us to leave untouched" (1993: 181). Sustainability, he says, is "a problem about saving and investment. It becomes a choice between current consumption and providing for the future" (1993: 183). Within this set of definitions, the future cannot fault us as long as we leave the next generation as able to fulfill their needs and desires as we have been. This position challenges strong sustainability and calls into question most of the environmentalists' programs, which include many more specific items of obligation. Solow's argument is worth examining in detail.

First, Solow dismisses a "straw man" of "absurdly strong sustainability" – the theory that we should leave the world completely unchanged for the future. "But you can't be obligated to do something that is not feasible" (1993: 180), he argues. Solow concludes that, since we cannot leave nature exactly as it is, there are no limits at all to the substitution of human-made wealth for natural resources. We should simply try to maintain an expanding total stock of capital. From this viewpoint, sustainability is a matter of balancing consumption with adequate investment, so that in the future there will be enough wealth to invest and to support people's desires to consume. On this view, financial assets, technology, labor, and natural resources are interchangeable elements of capital. Having dismissed the straw man, Solow asserts our total ignorance regarding the preferences of future people: "we realize that the tastes, the preferences, of future generations are something that we don't know about" (1993: 181). So, he argues, the best that we can do is to maintain a non-

diminishing stock of capital. Solow says that "Resources are, to use a favorite word of economists, fungible in a certain sense. They can take the place of each other" (1993: 181). Because we do not know what people in the future will want, and because resources are intersubstitutable anyway, all we can be expected to do is to avoid impoverishing the future by overconsuming and under-saving. Provided that we maintain capital stocks across time, each generation will have an undiminished opportunity to achieve as high a standard of living as their predecessors. The ability of economies to find replacements for any scarce resource, if coupled with adequate economic capital for investment, will allow people of the future to fulfill whatever needs and wants they actually happen to have.

This argument reduces intergenerational obligations to fair tradeoffs across generations. The argument is appealing because it does seem wrong to expect earlier, poorer generations to sacrifice for the benefit of successors who turn out to be richer than they. According to this line of reasoning, provided that we manage tradeoffs between the present and the future such that people in the future have the opportunity to be as well off as we are, we will have achieved a fair tradeoff between obligations to the present and concerns for the future. Nothing more could be expected of us.

The GS is theoretically appealing because it cuts through a lot of confusing issues, and provides a clear and simple view of how to fulfill obligations to future generations. This weak sustainability approach is also practically attractive: it offers a criterion to judge whether or not a given society is "sustainable" – one can use economic growth and savings rates as a starting point for calculations – and therefore points the way for further research and experimentation. Even better, this sustainability requirement will no doubt be politically welcome – it suggests that changing over to sustainable development as a social goal involves little change from currently accepted goals of having an efficient, constantly growing economy, with a savings rate of greater than zero.

Environmentalists will – and should – be skeptical here; it seems as if Solow has swept away all concerns about environmental protection, submerging them under the more general calculations about savings and consumption. For him, the problem is to find good investments; investments that will grow rapidly enough to increase the wealth of the society even as they support increasing levels of consumption.

[. . .]

It is not surprising that Solow and other economists find the Grand Simplification attractive; it defines sustainability in a way that can be measured by the very techniques they can offer. It is more surprising that the few philosophers who have discussed obligations to the future have almost universally endorsed the GS. John Rawls (1971) argued that what we owe the future is to maintain a fair savings rate. Brian Barry has addressed obligations to the future several times, and in each case he advocates a position almost identical to Solow's (see, for example, Barry, 1989: 515–23). Other philosophical advocates of the GS include John Passmore (1974), the author of the first book-length treatment of environmental ethics, and the legal theorist Martin Golding (1981). So the GS has directly or indirectly shaped virtually the entire academic and public discourse about what sustainability is and what it means in normative and ethical terms.

Grandly Oversimplified?

I have raised several problems with the GS elsewhere (Norton, 1999), but here I want to concentrate on its foundational argument, ignorance, to show that the GS rests on shaky foundations. Solow's premise about the extent of our ignorance is stated so strongly as to defy plausibility. Solow seems to suggest that we have no idea what the future will be like, what challenges will be faced, and what people will want or need. Ignorance of what people will want wipes away any specific obligations beyond the next generation, because in a system of dynamic technological change we cannot identify any resources that will be crucial to tomorrow's production possibilities. It makes no sense to distinguish between unacceptable and acceptable use of resources – there are only "efficient" and "inefficient" ways to generate human welfare. As long as the future is wealthier, future people will have no right to complain that they were treated unfairly.

Solow's approach is about as simple as one can imagine, given that we address a problem as knotty as that of intergenerational equity. But simplicity, by itself, is not the goal of analysis. The theory should only be as simple as it can be, *given that it is adequate to the task at hand*. I have argued elsewhere that the problem of intergenerational equity is philosophically and morally complex (Norton, 1999). For example, there is a problem about the horizon of moral concern: How far into the future do our moral obligations extend? This can be called the *distance problem*. There is also what I call the *typology of effects problem*: How can we decide which of our actions (and associated impacts) are governed by moral principles? And which effects are simply matters to be decided by market forces? If I cut down a mature tree and plant a seedling of the same species, it seems unlikely that I have significantly harmed people of the future, although there will be a period of recovery. As long as there are many trees left for others, my seedling will eventually replace my consumption, and no harm is done. If, on the other hand, I clear-cut an entire watershed and set in motion severe and irreversible erosion and siltation of a stream, I may have significantly harmed the future. I have irreversibly limited resources available to future persons, and I have restricted their options for pursuing their own well-being. It may be difficult to provide a theoretically justifiable definition, or a practical criterion, for separating cases of these two types.[2] But the ignorance argument sweeps this distinction away altogether and calls into question the goal of separating culpable from nonculpable actions that affect the future. If one is at all gripped by these philosophical problems, one should be left with a nagging concern. How can a question of fairness to future generations be decided without any attention to important moral issues such as the *distance* problem and the *typology of effects* problem?

Let us now look in more detail at Solow's use of the ignorance argument to reach the Grand Simplification. The Grand Simplification: (1) foreshortens our obligations to only the next generation, cutting off our obligations to the future entirely arbitrarily;[3] (2) assumes the fungibility of resources across uses and across time, denying the possibility of shortages or unfulfilled demands for natural resources; and (3) rules out *ex cathedra* the possibility that some courses of action will be economically efficient, and remain that way, but still impose uncompensated and noncompensable harms on future people.

The Grand Simplification is so grand because it resolves the distance problem by erasing all specific concerns for distant generations and because it sidesteps the typology of effects problem by assuming the fungibility of resources. Thus, all we need do is to avoid impoverishing the future by overspending and under-saving, which can be achieved simply by maintaining a fair savings rate. This simplification is based on no better foundation than an implausibly strong statement of the ignorance problem,[4] coupled with the implicit fungibility assumption according to which resources "can take the place of each other." These assumptions should not be considered as an empirical theory but, rather, as a proposed conceptual model for judging the sustainability of proposed policies and activities (Daly and Cobb, 1989; Norton, 1995). Solow's approach must therefore be examined not just for the verifiability of its assertions, but also with respect to the appropriateness of its assumptions and conceptual commitments to the task of understanding what we owe the future. Operationally, these assumptions ensure the substitutability of resources, committing their advocate to the idea that, for any resource that may become scarce, there is a substitute that will stand in as an acceptable replacement for the loss.

This discussion has been mainly abstract and theoretical. It is appropriate to ask: What harm would result if we apply the GS, with discounting, to guide our resource use? This question cannot be answered conclusively unless we have some independent criterion for determining what we *should* do for the future. If we had such, the problem we are struggling with would already be solved. To avoid begging the question at issue, we must take a less direct approach to evaluating the consequences of the GS. For example, we can compare recommendations of the GS with intuitions of morally reflective individuals. Or, we can compare the bequest package that would be prepared by advocates of the GS with the package recommended by forward-looking environmentalists. In the remainder of this section, I will examine how well the GS does in comparison to our everyday intuitions and how much its recommendations diverge from the views of most environmentalists.

I have explored many examples of intuitions that conflict with the recommendations of the GS in Norton (1999). Here we will look at a few of them on our way toward a deeper examination of the role of ignorance in our choice of policies for long-term sustainability. If we take Solow's ignorance argument seriously, it seems as if we don't even know that people of the future will prefer clean water to water polluted with toxins. Perhaps future people will like to bathe in toxic wastes. This is not plausible; and one doubts that Solow meant his claim to be construed so generally. Surely there are some things we know about future preferences. What we

know about them, together with extrapolations of risks from present behaviors, implies that some of our actions – such as careless storage of toxic wastes – could gravely harm people in the future. But if Solow admits that interventions in the market are necessary to rule out some specific actions as too risky, he must offer a criterion to identify these actions. The following question is unavoidable: Given what we reasonably believe about future tastes, what effects of our activities can be predicted to be benign and which are likely to be harmful? But once we raise this question, the question about the typology of effects immediately returns to center stage. And then the Grand Simplification unravels. We are back to trying to figure out what we owe, to how many generations, with a knowledge base that contains some near certainties and a great deal of uncertainty.

The generic recommendations of advocates of the GS diverge in important ways, also, from the commitments of environmentalists, who believe we owe specific things to the future, such as clean water, biodiversity, and natural areas. Wilderness protection and protection of special places such as Chesapeake Bay highlight this disagreement between Solow's theory and the intuitions of environmentalists, a disagreement that extends far beyond the measures of consumption and welfare opportunities. [. . .] Solow claims that not only do we not know what the future will want but that "to be honest, it is none of our business" (Solow, 1993: 182). A comparison of this passage with attitudes of environmentalists tells us a lot about the difficult relations between mainstream economists and environmentalists.

When environmentalists assert an obligation of the present generation to protect special places from severe degradation, they may well make assumptions about what will be valued in the future. They might, for example, assume that people in the future will greatly value these special places. But environmentalists also believe that people in the future *should* value these special places. Imagine that our generation, through conscientious effort and some sacrifice, succeeds in protecting many special places. Further, suppose that our children's generation continues the protection, but that the next generation prefers development over preservation and systematically destroys the natural legacy we have left them. If we could somehow learn that our grandchildren or greatgrandchildren will desecrate the heritage we so carefully preserved for them, I submit that we would not, as passively as Solow says, accept this as none of our business. On the contrary, we might well increase efforts to educate today's population and to build lasting institutions that will perpetuate our deeply held values and ideals. Environmentalists accept responsibility to protect places – and in doing so they also accept responsibility to foster a *commitment to protection*. [. . .] Environmentalists hope to save the wonders of nature, but they also accept a responsibility to perpetuate a love and respect for the nature they have loved enough to protect (Sagoff, 1974; Sax, 1980).

I noted above that environmentalists would balk at Solow's ignorance argument. It is now clear that their disagreement with Solow is not based mainly on a belief that they are able to *predict* what people in the future will in fact prefer. It is, rather, that they *accept moral responsibility* for inculcating certain values, and for ensuring that those values are perpetuated in future generations. This analysis suggests that wilderness areas and other natural wonders are not valued by present and future preservationists simply as opportunities for preference-satisfaction and for welfare gain.

Two directions are open to us to explore the preservationist values. One possibility is to attribute intrinsic value directly to nature or its elements. This approach has led mostly to futile discussions of what has and what lacks intrinsic value, and will not be discussed here at any greater length. The other alternative is to understand the value placed on special places without either positing intrinsic value in nature or falling back upon the requirements of weak sustainability only. One can argue that there are ways in which we could harm future people *even if they are as well off as we are*. We can define a class of harms to future people that would leave them worse off than they would have been had these impacts been avoided. If such a class can then be defined independently of effects on productivity, on capital accumulation, and on social wealth, we would have identified a category of "noneconomic" obligations to the future. These are the values that people are referring to when they say that certain possessions or experiences are "priceless." Loss of such a value can represent a harm, despite any level of compensation represented by wealth or income.

While it would take more space than is available here to make a conclusive case that such obligations exist, the fact that such a class can be coherently defined shows that there is a possibility of developing a stronger notion of sustainability, and of doing so in at least partially noneconomic terms. Having already admitted that weak sustainability may state a necessary condition of sustainable living, I now explore whether there may be other obligations that would govern our behavior toward the future. It seems reasonable to seek such long-term obligations not in concerns to fulfill future consumer preferences, but in our debt to prior generations who have developed our society, created our culture, and established a community with reasonably democratic and noncoercive institutions, and formed a distinctive relationship to a geographical place.

Sustainability and Community-Based Obligations

Many environmentalists believe it is possible to harm the future in a way that could not be morally repaired, even if those in the future turn out to be wealthier than we are. I suggest we explore the idea of non-compensable harm by reference to violations of obligations to a multigenerational community. These include obligations not to destroy the natural and cultural history of a "place" in which humans and nature have interacted to create an organic process, a process that can be understood multigenerationally. The communitarian, unlike the welfare economist, sees goods beyond individual ones, rejecting the economist's model of decision making as based solely on aggregation of the individualistic values of *Homo economicus*. The communitarian recognizes also community-based values that connect a human community to its natural context.

Environmentalism can be understood within the broadly communitarian political ontology of the conservative philosopher Edmund Burke, who defined a society as "a partnership not only between those who are living, but between those who are living, those who are dead and those to be born" (1910: 93–4). What environmentalists need to add to Burke's political community is a stronger sense of human territoriality and a more explicit recognition that both our past and our future are entwined with the broader community of living things and ecophysical systems that form the habitat and the context of multigenerational human communities. Nature protectionists do not, as citizens in Burkean communities, evaluate special places as possibilities for present or future consumption, but rather as shrines, as occasions for present and future people to recollect, and stay in touch with, their authentic natural and cultural history. This is a history of humans as evolved animals, and also as cultural beings who have evolved culturally within a particular natural setting. These are cultural beings who cannot deny their wild origins (Leopold, 1949: 199–200; Thoreau, 1960: 144).

Here, I think, we have reached the nub of the matter. What holds the supporters of the GS together is methodological individualism, the view that *the* good must be an aggregation of *individual* goods. Countering this, I recommend that noneconomic obligations to the future be considered as community-based goods (O'Neill, 1993). We have these obligations because, as members of a community and a culture, we benefit from sacrifices and investments made by members of prior generations. While these benefits include economic goods, they are not reducible to such because they include the political and cultural practices that give meaning and continuity to the culture. Adam Smith (1776) talked of these practices and sensibilities as the "bonds of sympathy" and considered them an essential foundation of economic life. These bonds cannot be valued in economic terms. To do so is to commit an egregious category mistake (Sagoff, 1988: 92–4). These concerns are best understood by paying attention to the moral and cultural sentiments of persons and communities, and by emphasizing the ways in which these sentiments form an essential part of a person's personal and community identity.[5]

Some obligations to the future are obligations to build a community and culture that lasts. We would have failed the future if we fail to develop institutions, ideas, and practices that create lasting communities in real places, communities with the moral and institutional strength to protect special places as symbols of the natural history and emergent culture of the community. Failure to do so, I believe, could leave people of the future worse off than we are in an important respect, even if they are vastly wealthier than we are. To see how this might be true, suppose our generation systematically converts all old-growth forests and wilderness areas to farming and mining, producing one form of "wealth," but making it impossible for future persons to experience unspoiled wilderness or other natural places. If they are wealthy, they can perhaps provide themselves Disney-type facsimiles of wilderness. As long as they have adequate income to afford such substitutes, they will

have been adequately compensated – according to advocates of weak sustainability – for the loss of natural resources. Environmentalists, of course, would reject this reduction of all value to opportunities to produce and consume in the future. We can harm the future by failing to create and maintain a culture and a community respectful of its past, including both the human and natural history of the common heritage.

Successful protection of wilderness and special places such as the Chesapeake Bay requires a successful transmission of love, respect, and caring for these places to the persons who will live in subsequent generations – including a sense of moral obligation to continue to protect them. Solow, who is committed to the individualistic, utilitarian view of mainstream welfare economics, sees the value of an object as identical to its ability to fulfill preferences that people happen to have as individual consumers. Rejection of this individualistic value theory is at the very heart of the environmentalists' position. They not only work to protect natural resources and places in the present, but they also attempt to project their values into the future. The questions of how people come to have, and to change, their preferences, and of whether we can judge some preferences morally superior to others, are interesting and important questions for understanding intergenerational equity issues. But these questions have not been given attention by economists, because such questions are exogenous to the discourse of welfare economics.[6] Accordingly, the vocabulary of the economist models all values as fulfillments of individual preferences and cannot express a central aspect of environmentalists' concern for the future.

As noted above, not all economists agree with Solow's simplistic concern with capital and wealth accumulation, so there is a basis for developing an alternative understanding of sustainability from within economics. For example, Bromley (1998) has argued, congruent with the argument developed here, that identifying a rational bequest is more a matter of *what* is left as a legacy for the future than it is a question of *how much* is left. Bromley explicitly favors looking to the present – to commitments of present people – as the source of guidance in choosing sustainability goals and principles, and not to speculations about the opportunities of the future to consume. Bromley's approach, like the one adopted here, must rest the matter of intergenerational morality on political will and on institutional development, rather than on counting wealth and "fungible" capital. The development of a worthy bequest for subsequent generations will require us to address hard moral questions about ourselves and the nature of society we want to build and transmit.

From within Solow's perspective, making moral judgments about the preferences of future people is irrelevant to sustainability. The advocate of weak sustainability cares only about the economic means available to satisfy whatever preferences future people happen to have. But for the environmentalist, it makes sense to say that those people in the future, who have lost all interest in nature, are worse off in ways that have little to do with their ability to fulfill their actual preferences. This claim may be controversial. Solow would no doubt argue that it is meaningless and that it is an advantage of his value calculus that claims such as this fall by the wayside. But, environmentalists do exhibit commitment regarding the values that future people express and act upon, and this commitment cannot be expressed in the utilitarian calculus of economists. Can we help the environmentalists to make sense of their claim as a *moral* claim? If we can do so, we will have gone a long way toward clarifying the meaning of "noncompensable harm," and toward a stronger sense of sustainability.

What We Owe the Future

The formulation of intergenerational moral problems as utility tradeoffs, and as responding – in the manner of Solow and others – to the preferences of future persons, dooms any hopes of specifying stronger sustainability principles. If specifying our obligations to the future depends upon predicting in detail what individuals in the future will want or need, then assertions of obligations to the future will, at best, be plagued by unavoidable uncertainties. If we can be fair to the future only if we can predict their needs and preferences in detail, then there will always be an impossible task at the heart of all specific ("strong") sustainability requirements. From this perspective, the reduction of sustainability to weak sustainability – the reduction of future obligations to determining a fair savings rate – is simply a figment of the assumptions introduced in order to characterize the moral problem in utilitarian and economistic terms. Prior theoretical commitments to utilitarianism and economic operationalization of intertemporal welfare comparisons determine the

contours of the playing field on which intergenerational obligations are discussed and determined. By insisting that intergenerational moral obligations be measured in terms of comparisons of aggregated welfare, utilitarians define intergenerational fairness so as to require information that cannot be available at the time when crucial decisions about what to protect must be made. The collapse of sustainability into weak sustainability on the basis of ignorance is preordained by the chosen theoretical scaffolding.

This outcome can be traced to the utilitarian dogma that normative questions must be construed as empirical questions with empirical answers. This dogma brings the question of *prediction* of wants, needs, and demands center stage in discussions of our obligations to the future; and it is this dogma that undermines any attempt to specify stronger sustainability requirements within the broadly utilitarian framework of analysis. At its deepest level, the Grand Simplification rests not upon the *fact* of our ignorance about future values but, rather, on a deep and unquestioned commitment to reduce all moral questions to descriptive questions – to questions that can be fully resolved on an empirical basis. The commitment of economists to the empirical resolubility or dismissal of moral questions pushes them toward a commitment to measuring and comparing quantities of welfare across time. This tendency puts extraordinary weight on our ability to *predict* future values and preferences. Furthermore, this commitment renders the analytic framework of welfare economics unable to express the core ideas of environmentalists.

There is a name for the mistake committed by those who seek to construe sustainability as comparisons of measurable quantities of well-being over time: it has been called the "descriptivist fallacy" by J. L. Austin (1962: 5–7). Austin argues that many of our sentences that look like ordinary statements have purposes other than to describe. As examples, Austin mentions "I do" when uttered in the context of a marriage ceremony; "I name this ship the *Queen Elizabeth*," while striking the ship's bow with a bottle of champagne; and "I bequeath this watch to my brother," in the context of a will. He argues that to utter these sentences is not to *describe* the doing of what is being done but, rather, to *do* it. Austin proposes that we characterize such uses of language as "performatives," and that there can be many types of performatives, including "contractual" and "declaratory" ones. Later, Austin says: "A great many of the acts which fall within the province of

Ethics . . . have the general character, in whole or in part, of conventional or ritual acts."

Reflecting on the views of environmentalists, we found that they embrace a *commitment*, not only to save special places, but also to create and sustain institutions and traditions necessary to carry on the commitment indefinitely. These acts must include the creation of a place-based literature and narratives, as well as public and private "trusts" set up to secure, for example, habitat for indigenous species. All of these actions signal commitments to continuity between the past and the future; they are best understood in Austin's sense as "performatives." They are founded on the commitments that a community makes to continuity with its past, to its natural and cultural histories, and to a future in which its roots in nature are revered, protected, learned from, and cared for. These commitments are, one might say, "community performatives," and represent a community-based commitment to love and protect one's natural as well as one's social history.

One might ask whether my argument has not simply circled back to Solow's implication that sustainability of special places simply reflects aggregate preferences of the society. In what way is my final position on sustainability "stronger" than Solow's? In my approach to the problem, each generation has an obligation to contribute to the cultural fabric of the community of which it is a member. And, if those communities and their members feel that their natural as well as their cultural history embodies and expresses their deepest values – as passed down from earlier generations and augmented in the present – then they have an obligation to create institutions and cultural supports for those values. To do less would be to sever important cross-generational ties, to leave the future with a diminished connection with its past, and a poorer cultural legacy to pass on to their children. This, I have argued, could impose upon the future a noncompensable harm – they would be worse off for our carelessness, regardless of their opportunity to fulfill, in the absence of cultural and moral guidance from us, whatever preferences they happen to have. Unlike Solow's calculations, the search for a stronger sense of sustainability must take place in the present, and it must search the hearts and minds of humans who are committed to building a community that reflects both cultural and natural ideals. Ignorance of people's future preferences need not deter this search. Further, my approach demands a stronger sense of community; a sense of community that recognizes bonds to an ongoing project, as well as obligations in the distribution of opportunities to consume.

Applying Austin's idea, and based on the analysis of this [essay], a new way of thinking about intergenerational morality emerges. If we see the problem as one of a community making choices and articulating moral principles – a question of which moral values the community is willing to commit itself to – the problems of ignorance about the future become less obtrusive. On the more communitarian approach suggested here, lack of knowledge of the detailed tastes of future people provides no real threat to the intellectual and practical task of specifying a fair bequest package for the future, because deciding what is owed the future is not only about fulfilling the needs that people in the future will in fact have, but it also has to do with affecting what those preferences will be through the creation of communally validated social values. The question at issue is a question about the present; it is a question of whether the community will, or will not, take responsibility for the long-term impacts of its actions, and whether the community has the collective moral will to create or contribute to a community that represents its own distinct expression of the nature–culture dialectic as it emerges in a place. Will members of the community consciously and conscientiously choose and implement a bequest package – a trust or legacy – that they will pass on to future generations? We do not then ask what the future will want or need – we ask by what process a community might specify its legacy for the future.

If one wishes to study such questions empirically, there is information available. One might, for example, study how communities engaged in landscape or ecosystem management achieve, or fail to achieve, consensus on environmental goals and policies. While empirical studies such as these may contribute to community-based environmental management, I suggest that the foundation of a stronger sustainability commitment lies more in the community's articulated moral commitments to the past and to the future than in any *description* of consequences for individual welfare. That we owe something beyond mere riches to the future follows from the fact that we inherited far more than mere riches from the past. But whatever information we need to answer the question of what, in particular, we owe the future must be discoverable in the present. It will have to do with what is important to our culture today – not with what people in the future will prefer.

This basic point makes all the difference in the way information is used in defining sustainability, and it changes the way we should think about environmental values and valuation. If the argument of this [essay] is correct, then the problem of how to measure sustainability, while important, is logically subsequent to the prior question of commitment to preserving a natural and cultural legacy. So, we face the prior task – and I admit it is a difficult and complex one – of developing processes by which democratic communities can explore their common values, their differences, and choose which places and which ecosystems and which traditions will be saved, achieving as much consensus as possible, and continuing debate about differences. Commitments, made by earlier generations, represent the voluntary, morally motivated contribution of the earlier generation to the ongoing community. While choosing measurable indicators is logically subsequent to commitment to moral goals, the tasks of choosing measurable indicators can, and must, proceed simultaneously with the articulation of long-term environmental goals. It cannot be otherwise, because the choices that are made by real communities regarding which indicators are relevant to their moral commitments represent, in effect, an operationalization of moral commitments. The task of choosing community values similarly cannot be sharply separated from the specification of certain indicators that would track the extent to which actual choices and practices achieve those commitments. The specification of a legacy, or bequest, for the future must then ultimately be a political problem, to be determined in political arenas. The best way to achieve consensus in such arenas is to involve members of communities in an articulation of values, in a search for common management goals, and to include in that process a publicly accountable search for accurate indicators to correspond to proposed management goals.

The advantages of this shift in perspective are now evident: this approach suggests that the key terms, "sustainable" and "sustainable development," are not themselves abstract *descriptors* of states of societies or cultures, in general but, rather, refer to many sets of commitments of specific societies, communities, and cultures to perpetuate certain values, to project them into the future, and to build a strong sense of community and a respect for the "place" of that community, complete with institutions to support these values. The problem of how to measure success and failure in attempts at living sustainably is now the problem, for each community, of choosing a fair natural legacy for the future, democratically, and then operationalizing these commitments as concrete goals to be measured by democratically agreed-upon indicators. The problem of tradeoffs is still a key issue, but it is more manageable because it is no longer dominated by the constraints imposed by our ignorance about the future. The tradeoffs problem no longer appears as a problem of comparing aggregated welfare at different times, but as a problem of allocating resources to various, sometimes competing, social goals.

Here, it is undeniable – as the economists will be quick to point out – that, ultimately, people in the present must balance their concern and investments for the future against the needs of today. There are situations in which setting aside special places will compete with other values. But now the question is transformed. If we think less about intertemporal tradeoffs, and work toward creating fair and lasting institutions – institutions that sustain and provide fair access to resources now and in the future – these practices might be the most effective first steps that can be taken today. If we see the problem as one of commitment of today's people not to see certain of their values and commitments eroded, the fact of our (partial) ignorance of future desires and needs – while a limitation in some ways – is not really relevant to the environmentalists' case. They must make the case that, to the extent that the community has committed itself to certain values and associated management goals, these goals are deserving of social resources and "investments" in the future. The task for the environmentalists is a daunting one, given the competing demands upon society's limited resources. To the extent that a community and its members see the creation of a legacy for the future as a contribution to an ongoing dialectic between their culture and its natural context, and to the extent that they accept responsibility for their legacy to the future, they have embraced a commitment that gives meaning and continuity to their lives. To create the institutions necessary to accomplish this goal, one must start today, and one must work with the information that is available today. The recommendation that emerges from this essay is that the moral resources to begin, and carry forward, this task will be found in strong communities, not in attempts to guess and anticipate what people in the future will want.

Notes

1 See, for example, Daly and Cobb (1989).
2 See Page (1983) for an excellent discussion of this problem, and a demonstration that criteria of economic efficiency cannot solve it.
3 Presentism, so stated, might be thought to justify discounting. But many authors have argued that applying discounting across generations begs important moral questions. See Ramsey (1928), Pigou (1932), Parfit (1983), and Page (1988).
4 See Callahan (1981), Kavka (1981), Page (1983), and Barry (1989) for convincing reasons that this strong ignorance premise is implausible.
5 See Holland and O'Neill (1996) and Holland and Rawls (1993) for a useful discussion of the inseparability of cultural and ecological ideals. Also see Ariansen (1997). Ariansen suggests that some choices we make with respect to protecting our environment represent "constitutive" values. Loving and protecting special places and special features of a place, on this view, may be constitutive of a person's sense of self and of community membership. Careless destruction of these special features, correlatively, might be considered a kind of "cultural suicide." Ariansen's insight provides one interesting direction for the explication of what I call noncompensable harms.
6 I have argued elsewhere that the economists' theoretical/methodological commitment to "consumer sovereignty" is a key source of disagreement between environmentalists and economists. See Norton (1994) and Norton, Costanza, and Bishop (1998).

References

Ariansen, P. 1997: The non-utility value of nature: an investigation into biodiversity and the value of natural wholes (translation from Norwegian text). In *Communications of the Norwegian Forest Research Institute (Meddelelser fra Skogforsk)*. Aas: Agricultural University of Norway, 47.

Austin, J. L. 1962: *How to Do Things with Words*. Oxford: Oxford University Press.

Barry, B. 1989: *Democracy, Power, and Justice*. Oxford: Clarendon Press.

Bromley, D. W. 1998: Searching for sustainability: the poverty of spontaneous order. *Ecological Economics*, 24, 231–40.

Burke, E. 1910: *Reflections on the Revolution in France*. London: Dent.

Callahan, D. 1981: What obligations do we have to future generations? In E. Partridge (ed.), *Responsibilities to Future Generations*. Buffalo, NY: Prometheus Books, 73–85.

Daly, H. and Cobb, J. 1989: *For the Common Good*. Boston: Beacon Press.

Golding, M. 1981: Obligations to future generations. In Ernest Partridge (ed.), *Responsibilities to Future Generations*. Buffalo, NY: Prometheus Books, 61–72.

Holland, A. 1999: Sustainability: should we start from here? In A. Dobson (ed.), *Fairness and Futurity*. Oxford: Oxford University Press, 46–68.

Holland, A. and O'Neill, J. 1996: The integrity of nature over time. *Thingmount Working Paper 96-08*. Lancaster, UK: Department of Philosophy, Lancaster University.

Holland, A. and Rawls, K. 1993: Values in conservation. *Ecos*, 14, 14–19.

Kavka, G. 1981: The futurity problem. In E. Partridge (ed.), *Responsibilities to Future Generations*. Buffalo, NY: Prometheus Books, 113–15.

Leopold, A. 1949: *A Sand County Almanac*. Oxford: Oxford University Press.

Norton, B. G. 1994: Economists' preferences and the preferences of economists. *Environmental Values*, 3, 331–2.

Norton, B. G. 1995: Evaluating ecosystem states: two paradigms of environmental evaluation. *Ecological Economics*, 14, 113–27.

Norton, B. G. 1999: Ecology and opportunity: intergenerational equity and sustainable options. In A. Dobson (ed.), *Fairness and Futurity*. Oxford: Oxford University Press, 118–50.

Norton, B. G., Costanza, R., and Bishop, R. 1998: The evolution of preferences: why "sovereign" preferences may not lead to sustainable policies and what to do about it. *Ecological Economics*, 24, 193–212.

O'Neill, J. 1993: Future generations, present harms. *Philosophy*, 68, 35–51.

Page, T. 1983: Intergenerational justice as opportunity. In D. MacLean and P. Brown (eds.), *Energy and the Future*. Totowa, NJ: Rowman and Littlefield, 38–58.

Page, T. 1988: Intergenerational equity and the social rate of discount. In V. K. Smith and J. Krutilla (eds.), *Environmental Resources and Applied Welfare Economics*. Washington, DC: Resources for the Future.

Parfit, D. 1983: Energy policy and the further future: the social discount rate. In D. MacLean and P. Brown (eds.), *Energy and the Future*. Totowa, NJ: Rowman and Littlefield, 166–79.

Passmore, J. 1974: *Man's Responsibility for Nature*. New York: Charles Scribner's Sons.

Pigou, A. C. 1932: *The Economics of Welfare*. London: Macmillan.

Ramsey, F. 1928: A mathematical theory of saving. *Economic Journal*, 38, 543–59.

Rawls, J. A. 1971: *A Theory of Justice*. Cambridge, MA: Harvard University Press.

Sagoff, M. 1974: On preserving the natural environment. *Yale Law Journal*, 84, 205–67.

Sagoff, M. 1988: *The Economy of the Earth*. Cambridge: Cambridge University Press.

Sax, J. 1980: *Mountains Without Handrails*. Ann Arbor, MI: University of Michigan Press.

Smith, A. 1976 [1776]: *The Theory of Moral Sentiments.* New York: Garland.

Solow, R. M. 1974: The economics of resources or the resources of economics. *American Economic Review Papers and Proceedings*, 64, 1–14.

Solow, R. M. 1986: On the intergenerational allocation of natural resources. *Scandinavian Journal of Economics*, 88, 141–9.

Solow, R. M. 1992: *An Almost Practical Step Toward Sustainability.* Invited lecture on the occasion of the 40th anniversary of Resources for the Future, Washington, DC.

Solow, R. M. 1993: Sustainability: an economist's perspective. In R. and N. Dorfman (eds.), *Economics of the Environment: Selected Readings.* New York: W. W. Norton, 179–87.

Thoreau, H. D. 1960: *Walden.* New York: The New American Library.

70   Environmental Justice and Intergenerational Debt

Clark Wolf

Anyone familiar with the crippled appearance of any utopia fifty years after the death of its writer understands that no one can make a world for his grandchildren. (John B. Wolf, 1952)

No one, wrote my grandfather in the quotation above, can "make a world for his grandchildren." As he argued, our present ideas about what would be good for our distant descendants will be cramped by the limitations of our own time and our own understanding. Later generations will have different tastes and different ideas, and we may hope that they will possess knowledge of things we cannot imagine. So the attempt to "create the world" in which they will live, if we do it badly, is more likely to impose inappropriate constraints on their lives than to liberate them.

Still, our present choices can expand the range of opportunities that will be available to our descendants. By working to secure peace, by extending the scope of democracy and the protection of rights, we make it more likely that their lives will be secure. By expanding knowledge and promoting appropriate technologies, we may provide them with opportunities we cannot even imagine. Our present choices can constrain opportunities as well, and there are increasing grounds for concern that our way of life might create serious hardships in the future. I would like to suggest that we should understand important parts of this problem as a matter of intergenerational debt and saving, and that we can understand many of our most important obligations to the future using a simple economic model. While only some of the debts we incur are financial, the simple model of saving and expense provides an essential insight into the structure of our obligation to the future.

National Debt as a Problem of Intergenerational Justice

I will begin with the very practical problem of intergenerational financial debt. The National Debt of the United States of America rose to unprecedented levels during the first decade of the twenty-first century. By July 2008 the US national debt was US$9,508,168,461,845,50. This bewildering number needs to be put in perspective: This was about 67 percent of the 2007 Gross Domestic Product of the US. Given an estimated US population of 304,361,218, this amounts to an average individual debt of US$31,239,75. But the US debt was increasing at the rate of about 1.72 billion dollars every day, so the *per capita* debt burden changes regularly. President Bush proposed a budget for 2008 of about US$3 trillion, which would add about 240 billion dollars to the deficit in 2008 even if no additional spending were to take place. Of course, the US typically exceeds its planned budget by a significant amount, so this value is a

Originally published as "Justice and Intergenerational Debt," in *Intergenerational Justice Review*, Issue 1 (2008): 13–17. Reprinted with minor revisions by permission of Stiftung für die Rechte zukünftiger Generationen.

radical underestimate. (The current US debt burden can easily be found online: just look up "US National Debt Clock" on any search engine to find many sites devoted to this issue.)

What does the United States purchase with this massive pile of borrowed cash? In 2008, public frustration often focused on the portion spent on the wars in Iraq and Afghanistan and other costs associated with President Bush's "War on Terror." Effort was taken to hide the cost of these wars by making sure that the expenses associated with them never appeared in a single item on any official spreadsheet. The costs have been carefully sequestered under different headings in the budget, making it difficult to say exactly how much the US has spent on these military adventures.

But while we should be concerned to ask what is being purchased with this loan, it is at least as important to ask who will eventually pay it off. Debts come due, and an ever-increasing debt load cannot be maintained forever. Older Americans may take comfort in the thought that this debt probably won't be paid in our lifetimes. But just as individual debts eventually make it more difficult for people to pay for the things they want and need, national debts can constrain a nation's ability to accomplish important social goals.

Jefferson and Madison on Intergenerational Debts

Thomas Jefferson was deeply concerned about the possibility that the choices of one generation might come to bind or constrain later generations. In one context his concern was associated with his interest in the US Constitution: he argued that the document should be rewritten every 19 years so that it would represent the continuing and ongoing consent of each new generation as it arrives. Nineteen years was the appropriate interval, urged Jefferson, because, given the birth and death rates, it was the period after which a new majority would be in place. But Jefferson was also concerned about intergenerational *debt*: the possibility that a profligate generation might mortgage the future of the nation by borrowing vast sums of money, spending it irresponsibly, and passing on to later generations the burden of paying it off. He urged that public debts must be retired by the generation that incurred them, and that it would impose "solid and salutary" discipline on the government if this could be made a requirement of law. It is especially interesting to note that he thought that this

financial discipline would discourage ruinous conflicts and wars, since the cost of war would then be carried by those who would take the nation to war. It is much easier to urge war when the cost of conflict can be transferred to a later administration, and ultimately to the younger generation.

Jefferson's statement that "The earth belongs in usufruct to the generations of the living" is often quoted as implying that we are stewards who hold resources in trust for later generations. Surely this is part of Jefferson's meaning: usufructuary rights are stewardship rights or tenant rights. But Jefferson was also concerned that, as stewards, we must avoid passing the costs of our present activities on to later generations. If later generations inherit the cost of debts but none of the benefits these debts were incurred to purchase, then they have been treated unjustly by the previous generation. So, at any rate, was Jefferson's argument.

James Madison's response to Jefferson was thoughtful and measured. He urged that it would introduce too much instability to require that the Constitution be rewritten at regular intervals, and that the process would "engender pernicious fractions that might not otherwise come into existence, and agitate the public mind more frequently and more violently than might be expedient." While he acknowledged Jefferson's principle that "the earth belongs in usufruct to the generations of the living," he allowed that the present generation might be responsible for *improvements* that would render later generations better off than their predecessors. These improvements, he urged, constitute the basis of a debt that the living owe to the dead, which can best be paid off by "obedience to the will of the Authors of the improvements." With respect to the problem of monetary debt, Madison noted that some debts might be incurred "principally for the benefit of posterity." In such cases, he saw no reason why the debts might not be passed on with the benefits, even if they could not be retired before the new generation arrived. Madison praised the spirit of Jefferson's argument, and urged that it should always be "kept in view as a salutary restraint on living generations from *unjust and unnecessary* burdens on their successors." While he argued against legislative provision prohibiting the acquisition of intergenerational debt, Madison clearly shared Jefferson's concern that it is unjust for present generations to pass on a debt burden to their successors *except* where those burdens are fully compensated.

Intergenerational Debt, Sustainability, and "Hicksian Income"

Characteristically, debts accrue interest over time. But when we borrow and spend, we don't simply incur the burden of interest, we also forgo the benefits we might have gained from present investments. Just as borrowing shifts consumption from the future to the present, investments can shift it from the present to the future. Sir John Hicks described this dynamic long ago, and the resultant view of saving and consumption has come to be known as "Hicksian income":

> The Purpose of income calculations in practical affairs is to give people an indication of the amount they can consume without impoverishing themselves. Following out this idea, it would seem that we ought to define a man's income as the maximum value which he can consume during a week, and still be expected to be as well off at the end of the week as he was at the beginning. Thus when a person saves, he plans to be better off in the future, when he lives beyond his income, he plans to be worse off. Remembering that the practical purpose of income is to serve as a guide for prudent conduct, I think it is fairly clear that this is what the central meaning must be. (Hicks, *Value and Capital*. Oxford University Press, 1948)

A person's Hicksian income might be considered the amount she or he can *sustainably* consume, or, alternatively, the amount one can consume without accruing either debt or credit. When we consume at our Hicksian income rate, we maintain the same underlying stock of capital, so we are neither poorer nor richer over time. Of course, people have varied needs at different points in life, so even the most prudent people do not usually consume at the Hicksian income rate. For example, one might decide to consume less when younger, in anticipation of greater needs in old age. When young people decide to stay in school instead of entering the job market earlier in life, they are "saving," in a sense, since they are forgoing present income and consumption in order to build up their personal capital so that they will be able to earn more over the course of their lives.

One kind of careless imprudence is exemplified by the person who fails to save appropriately over time, burning through the stock of capital early on. Those who are blessed with a large stock of capital early in life may not be personally imprudent when they behave like this, as long as the capital stock they hold at the beginning is large enough that it won't be used up over the course of life. But those who burn through capital in this way are using up resources that will not be available later. Profligate heirs won't leave a fortune for their descendants because they consume at a rate faster than their Hicksian incomes would allow.

As individual persons, our saving and consumption rates are usually planned around the lifecycle changes we expect to live through. But as *nations*, or as a *global society*, we might plan for a longer time horizon. A nation that lives beyond the means provided by its Hicksian income consumes its capital resources, leaving later generations impoverished. And a global community that behaves in the same way will impoverish the human population of the earth. Just as individuals need to plan for different needs at varying stages in their lifecycle, nations and global communities also need to plan consumption and saving to accommodate for expected needs. In the case of nations and of the global community, however, changing needs are not created by a natural lifecycle but by changing the size and constituency of our population. Populations with different age constituencies have very different ability to address their own needs. To plan for a larger population with more people whose needs must be met, we may need to insure that available resources will expand to meet their needs. Where population is growing and needs are expanding, it will not be sufficient to pass on the same fundamental stock from one generation to the next. If we want the members of subsequent generations to have fully adequate life opportunities, we may need to *increase* the stock of resources that will be available to them.

Of course, people are not just consumers. We might expect each generation to provide for the circumstances of its own economic welfare. Instead of focusing on the availability of raw capital resources, it might be more appropriate for us to insure that future generations will enjoy circumstances that will enable them to maintain or increase the marginal rate of per capita productivity so that they will be able to support themselves. While the future productivity rate does not depend *only* on the availability of raw capital stocks, the focus on future productivity will not allow us to *ignore* these stocks either. Nor will it allow us to ignore the rate of intergenerational debt: intergenerational debt can be understood as a drag on future productive possibilities.

Still, it would be a mistake to think of our legacy to the future only in terms of the debts we accrue. We provide future generations with knowledge and capital improvements, not just with debts. These benefits constitute at least partial compensation for the disadvantages represented by the debts we pass on. But it is appropriate for us to ask whether our capital improvements constitute effective and appropriate compensation for the burdens we leave behind. Jefferson and Madison don't specifically speak of Hicksian income, of course. But they both express concern that a profligate administration might impose inappropriate debts on subsequent generations. And in both Madison and Jefferson, we find support for the underlying idea that such debts are unjust if they are not fully compensated. To avoid perpetrating injustice of this sort, we must pass on to later generations productive resources fully sufficient to provide them with adequate opportunities. And if our own opportunities were more replete than this, perhaps we owe the future more.

Non-Monetary Debts

The idea of Hicksian income is tightly tied to Jefferson and Madison's conception of unjust intergenerational debt: Where a nation consumes at a rate higher than its Hicksian income, it passes on uncompensated disadvantage to later generations. Of course the calculation is more complicated than the simple description above might seem to imply: we cannot simply look at growing national debt – to know whether a nation is consuming beyond its means, it is necessary to look at the entire package that is passed on to those who inherit the debt. If the economy has grown, is this compensation for the burden? If knowledge has been created, can we consider this to be adequate compensation?

Many of the costs we pass on to later generations are non-monetary, but they have precisely the same structure as a monetary debt. Where our present actions damage or degrade the natural environment, we pass on a burden that can be measured in terms of the rate at which the environment can recover from our assaults. The rate of recovery translates to a measure of the cost we pass on, since future generations will not only need to forgo the direct benefits they might have enjoyed if we had passed on

more intact environmental resources; the cost of present environmental damage also includes the investment they would need to make in order to recover the resource to its condition before our damage.

Consider, for example, the management of the ocean fisheries, which are currently being harvested at a rate much faster than they can regenerate. Our present consumption standard means that we will pass on to later generations a resource that is depleted, and stands in need of recovery. At some point, fisheries collapse. Recovery after collapse is a complicated matter, since a new environmental equilibrium may arise that simply does not include the depleted species. But in the interval before collapse, when recovery is still possible, we can model the cost of recovery as the payment of interest on an environmental debt. If later generations simply wish to maintain the resource in its depleted state, they might pay no more than the "interest" on the environmental debt we pass on to them. That is, they might continue to harvest fish but at a lower rate that will permit them to pass on to subsequent generations a fishery that is no more damaged (but no less damaged) than the one we will pass on to them. If later generations of US citizens were to decide to pay only the *interest* on the current debt instead of retiring the principle, they would be making a similar decision.

But in order to restore the fishery resource, future generations would need to consume at a rate much lower than the "sustainable" rate. The resources needed to pay down the environmental debt burden are much greater than those necessary to maintain a depleted system. But over time, a depleted system will produce at a lower rate. The fishery will produce less fish over time if it is a *depleted* system than it would if it were a healthy fishery managed at a sustainable rate of consumption. And unless later generations behave much better than we are currently behaving, it is quite possible that this resource will never recover.

Other intergenerational environmental burdens can be modeled in exactly the same way, but the recovery period can be much longer. By some estimates, a 40-acre farm's worth of Iowa topsoil flows down the Mississippi river every day. Topsoil regenerates itself when Iowa land is left as prairie, but the time period required is very long. Topsoil regenerates over *geological* time, so when it is gone it is as if it were gone forever. To be sure, it is possible to organize agricultural systems so that there is little topsoil loss, but the high-input productionist agriculture favored in the United States (and increasingly, elsewhere in the world) does not conserve the resource on which it depends. Iowa is blessed with a thick layer of the most fertile soil to be found anywhere in the world, and at present it seems to many people that it is an inexhaustible resource. But just like our fishery practices, our agricultural practices involve passing on an environmental debt. In this case, it is unlikely that the principle will ever be retired.

Our climate debt is one of the most disturbing debts we presently accrue. Some greenhouse gases (GHGs) have a very long "lifetime" in the atmosphere of the Earth. In this case, the "interest" rate on our present consumption is measured by the rate at which the earth's atmosphere can absorb and digest our emissions. So if we chose to pay only the *interest* on the climate debt incurred through the course of the Industrial Revolution, we would produce GHGs at the rate at which the Earth's atmosphere and its biological systems, can metabolize them. Call this rate M.

When we produce GHGs at a rate higher than M, we are consuming an exhaustible capital stock. We can think of M as the rate of interest on our climate debt, and if we were to live within our means, on our Hicksian climate income, we would at least need to pay the interest on the loan we inherited by dumping GHGs in the atmosphere at a rate no *faster* than M. For three important reasons, this is especially difficult in the case of climate. First, the earth's climate is a lagging indicator of its present GHG burden. This means that the climate implications of present and past emissions have not arrived yet. Even if we were to cease our production of GHGs immediately, global changes would continue on more or less the same course for a long time – perhaps for 50–100 years. Second, environmental changes caused by climate change are likely to affect the rate of global GHG production as well as the rate of global heat absorption from the sun. As permafrost melts, especially in the arctic north, it is releasing naturally present GHGs at an unprecedented rate. Much of the gas released is methane, which is many times more potent, as a GHG, than carbon dioxide. Finally, the rate of global GHG metabolism, M, is itself subject to change as a result of environmental degradation. As forests are turned into pasture in South America, as natural areas are transformed into housing subdivisions in California, the earth's environmental systems are able to fix carbon at a lower rate. The corresponding reduction in M constitutes an *increase* in the environmental rate of interest associated with our inherited GHG debt. The sustainable rate of GHG emission is thus increasing over time.

Fixed Stock Resources

Where the resources we consume, like Iowa topsoil, are regenerated at geological rates of time, we should consider them to be a non-renewing finite stock. Soil and oil are available to us in a fixed quantity, and if we consume them, we cannot expect to do so at a sustainable Hicksian rate. The best we can hope is that as we use these resources up, we may provide later generations with economic substitutes for them, so that our depletion will not leave the future worse off overall. But can we reasonably hope that our improvements in computer technology will compensate later generations for the loss of a stable climate, along with the other debts, financial and environmental, that we seem prepared to pass on to them?

Growing out of our Debts?

There are economists who urge that the US national debt is not a problem. It is an advantage that other nations are willing to continue to lend us money, and if the economy grows quickly enough the debt may come to seem smaller when we compare it to the size of the US economy itself. If we cripple the economy in an effort to pay our debts, it is urged, then we will pass on less, not more, to future generations. By diminishing the rate of economic growth, we diminish their economic prospects and the opportunities that will be available to them. In response to the present threat of economic recession, the US President and Congress are apparently prepared to take out an additional loan to provide an economic stimulus package.

But when we consider the financial debt in the context of all the non-monetary loans we continue to draw, can we reasonably hope that the process can continue over time? In the quotation at the head of this article, my grandfather, John B. Wolf, urged that we should avoid making decisions for our descendants, because we are likely to make the wrong ones. We can't know what they will want or need or value, so our efforts to promote their welfare may be a hopeless shot in the dark. But by mortgaging their welfare to purchase present advantages, we risk promoting their *illfare*. We need to begin to live within our means, within the economic and environmental budget that represents our Hicksean income. Failure to do this, as Jefferson and Madison would have urged, is a violation of our obligations of intergenerational justice.

I close with a quotation from Bertrand Russell, who saw more clearly than most that the rate of consumption in the modern world must create debts that will one day come due. Writing on this subject many decades ago, he wrote:

> I cannot be content with a brief moment of riotous living followed by destitution, and however clever the scientists may be, there are some things that they cannot be expected to achieve. When they have used up all the easily available sources of energy that nature has scattered carelessly over the surface of our planet, they will have to resort to more laborious processes, and these will involve a gradual lowering of the standard of living. Modern industrialists are like men who have come for the first time upon fertile virgin land, and can live for a little while in great comfort with only a modicum of labor. It would be irrational to hope that the present heyday of industrialism will not develop far beyond its present level, but sooner or later, owing to the exhaustion of raw material, its capacity to supply human needs will diminish, not suddenly but gradually. (*New Hopes for a Changing World*. Simon and Schuster, 1952, p. 37)

If we wish to avoid imposing our debts on our grandchildren, we need immediately to begin to live within our means.

E   Globalization

---

71   The Environmental Limits to Globalization

David Ehrenfeld

Introduction

The popular outcry against globalization is usually cast in social and economic terms: developed versus undeveloped, north versus south, exploiters versus exploited, rich versus poor. The wrongs evoked are socioeconomic and therefore political, bringing to mind visions of low-wage or semienslaved workers laboring in Third World factories and on Third World farms to produce the goods and the growing number of the services consumed in the United States and other industrial nations. But there is another, *nonpolitical*, side of globalization that demands attention – the impact of globalization on the environment. The environmental and social effects of globalization are intimately interconnected and equally important, yet it is the latter that receive nearly all of the attention.

The social changes wrought by the globalization process are still in flux, and the outcomes over the next few decades are unclear. For example, as production and wealth skyrocket in China and India, as cars replace bicycles and skyscrapers spring up everywhere, will these countries be able to maintain their own supply of cheap labor and the new moneyed class without bloody internal upheavals that threaten national stability? And what will happen as fewer people in the once-rich countries have incomes that allow them to buy the digital cameras, toys, building supplies, and tropical produce that are the lifeblood of global commerce? The complexity of the situation beggars simplistic answers.

The overall environmental changes brought about or accelerated by globalization are, however, much easier to describe for the near future, even if the long-term outcomes are still obscure. Climate will continue to change rapidly (Watson 2002); cheap energy and other resources (Youngquist 1997; Hall et al. 2003; Smil 2003), including fresh water (Aldhous 2003; Gleick 2004), will diminish and disappear at an accelerating rate; agricultural and farm communities will deteriorate further while we lose more genetic diversity among crops and farm animals (Fowler & Mooney 1990; Bailey & Lappé 2002; Wirzba 2003); biodiversity will decline faster as terrestrial and aquatic ecosystems are damaged (Heywood 1995); harmful exotic species will become ever more numerous (Mooney & Hobbs 2000); old and new diseases of plants, animals, and humans will continue to proliferate (Centers for Disease Control and Prevention 1995–present; Lashley & Durham 2002); and more of the great ocean fisheries will become economically – and occasionally biologically – extinct (Myers & Worm 2003). Although critics have

From *Conservation Biology*, vol. 19, no. 2 (April 2005): 318–20, 321, 322–3, 323–6. © 2002 by Conservation Biology. Reprinted with permission from Blackwell Publishing Ltd.

taken issue with many of these forecasts (Lomborg 2001; Hollander 2003), the critics' arguments seem more political than scientific; the data they muster in support of their claims are riddled with errors, significant omissions, and misunderstandings of environmental processes (Orr 2002). Indeed, these environmental changes are demonstrably and frighteningly real. And because of these and related changes, one social prediction can be made with assurance: globalization is creating an environment that will prove hostile to its own survival.

This is not a political statement or a moral judgment. It is not the same as saying that globalization ought to be stopped. The enlightened advocates of globalization claim that globalization could give the poorest residents of the poorest countries a chance to enjoy a decent income. And the enlightened opponents of globalization assert that the damage done by globalization to local communities everywhere, and the increasing gap it causes between the rich and the poor, far outweigh the small amount of good globalization may do. The debate is vitally important, but the fate of globalization is unlikely to be determined by who wins it. Al Gore remarked about the political impasse over global warming and the current rapid melting of the world's glaciers: "Glaciers don't give a damn about politics. They just reflect reality" (Herbert 2004). The same inexorable environmental reality is even now drawing the curtains on globalization.

Often minimized in the United States, this reality is already painfully obvious in China, which is experiencing the most rapid expansion related to globalization. Nearly every issue of *China Daily*, the national English-language newspaper, features articles on the environmental effects of globalization. Will efforts in China to rein in industrial expansion, energy consumption, and environmental pollution succeed (Fu 2004; Qin 2004; Xu 2004)? Will the desperate attempts of Chinese authorities to mitigate the impact of rapid industrialization on the disastrously scarce supplies of fresh water be effective (Li 2004; Liang 2004)? The environmental anxiety is palpable and pervasive.

The environmental effects of globalization cannot be measured by simple numbers like the gross domestic product or unemployment rate. But even without such summary statistics, there are so many examples of globalization's impact, some obvious, some less so, that a convincing argument about its effects and trends can be made.

The Disappearance of Cheap Energy

Among the environmental impacts of globalization, perhaps the most significant is its fostering of the excessive use of energy, with the attendant consequences. This surge in energy use was inevitable, once the undeveloped four-fifths of the world adopted the energy-wasting industrialization model of the developed fifth, and as goods that once were made locally began to be transported around the world at a tremendous cost of energy. China's booming production, largely the result of its surging global exports, has caused a huge increase in the mining and burning of coal and the building of giant dams for more electric power, an increase of power that in only the first 8 months of 2003 amounted to 16% (Bradsher 2003; Guo 2004).

The many environmental effects of the coal burning include, most importantly, global warming. Fossil-fuel-driven climate change seems likely to result in a rise in sea level, massive extinction of species, agricultural losses from regional shifts in temperature and rainfall, and, possibly, alteration of major ocean currents, with secondary climatic change. Other side effects of coal burning are forest decline, especially from increased nitrogen deposition; acidification of freshwater and terrestrial ecosystems from nitrogen and sulfur compounds; and a major impact on human health from polluted air.

Dams, China's alternative method of producing electricity without burning fossil fuels, themselves cause massive environmental changes. These changes include fragmentation of river channels; loss of floodplains, riparian zones, and adjacent wetlands; deterioration of irrigated terrestrial environments and their surface waters; deterioration and loss of river deltas and estuaries; aging and reduction of continental freshwater runoff to oceans; changes in nutrient cycling; impacts on biodiversity; methylmercury contamination of food webs; and greenhouse gas emissions from reservoirs. The impoundment of water in reservoirs at high latitudes in the northern hemisphere has even caused a small but measurable increase in the speed of the earth's rotation and a change in the planet's axis (Rosenberg et al. 2000; Vörösmarty & Sahagian 2000). Moreover, the millions of people displaced by reservoirs such as the one behind China's Three Gorges Dam have their own environmental impacts as they struggle to survive in unfamiliar and often unsuitable places.

Despite the importance of coal and hydropower in China's booming economy, the major factor that enables globalization to flourish around the world – even in China – is still cheap oil. Cheap oil runs the ships, planes, trucks, cars, tractors, harvesters, earthmoving equipment, and chain saws that globalization needs; cheap oil lifts the giant containers with their global cargos off the container ships onto the waiting flatbeds; cheap oil even mines and processes the coal, grows and distills the biofuels, drills the gas wells, and builds the nuclear power plants while digging and refining the uranium ore that keeps them operating.

Paradoxically, the global warming caused by this excessive burning of oil is exerting negative feedback on the search for more oil to replace dwindling supplies. The search for Arctic oil has been slowed by recent changes in the Arctic climate. Arctic tundra has to be frozen and snow-covered to allow the heavy seismic vehicles to prospect for underground oil reserves, or longlasting damage to the landscape results. The recent Arctic warming trend has reduced the number of days that vehicles can safely explore: from 187 in 1969 to 103 in 2002 (Revkin 2004). Globalization affects so many environmental systems in so many ways that negative interactions of this sort are frequent and usually unpredictable.

Looming over the global economy is the imminent disappearance of cheap oil. There is some debate about when global oil production will peak – many of the leading petroleum geologists predict the peak will occur in this decade, possibly in the next two or three years (Campbell 1997; Kerr 1998; Duncan & Youngquist 1999; Holmes & Jones 2003; Appenzeller 2004; ASPO 2004; Bakhtiari 2004; Gerth 2004) – but it is abundantly clear that the remaining untapped reserves and alternatives such as oil shale, tar sands, heavy oil, and biofuels are economically and energetically no substitute for the cheap oil that comes pouring out of the ground in the Arabian Peninsula and a comparatively few other places on Earth (Youngquist 1997). Moreover, the hydrogen economy and other high-tech solutions to the loss of cheap oil are clouded by serious, emerging technological doubts about feasibility and safety, and a realistic fear that, if they can work, they will not arrive in time to rescue our globalized industrial civilization (Grant 2003; Tromp et al. 2003; Romm 2004). Even energy conservation, which we already

know how to implement both technologically and as part of an abstemious lifestyle, is likely to be no friend to globalization, because it reduces consumption of all kinds, and consumption is what globalization is all about.

[. . .]

Loss of Agricultural Biodiversity

Among the many other environmental effects of globalization, one that is both obvious and critically important is reduced genetic and cultural diversity in agriculture. As the representatives of the petrochemical and pharmaceutical industries' many subsidiary seed corporations sell their patented seeds in more areas previously isolated from global trade, farmers are dropping their traditional crop varieties, the reservoir of our accumulated genetic agricultural wealth, in favor of a few, supposedly high-yielding, often chemical-dependent seeds. The Indian agricultural scientist H. Sudarshan (2002) has provided a typical example. He noted that

> Over the last half century, India has probably grown over 30,000 different, indigenous varieties or landraces of rice. This situation has, in the last 20 years, changed drastically and it is predicted that in another 20 years, rice diversity will be reduced to 50 varieties, with the top 10 accounting for over three-quarters of the sub-continent's rice acreage.

With so few varieties left, where will conventional plant breeders and genetic engineers find the genes for disease and pest resistance, environmental adaptations, and plant quality and vigor that we will surely need?

A similar loss has been seen in varieties of domestic animals. Of the 3831 breeds of ass, water buffalo, cattle, goat, horse, pig, and sheep recorded in the twentieth century, at least 618 had become extinct by the century's end, and 475 of the remainder were rare. Significantly, the countries with the highest ratios of surviving breeds per million people are those that are most peripheral and remote from global commerce (Hall & Ruane 1993).

Unfortunately, with globalization, remoteness is no longer tenable. Here is a poignant illustration. Rural Haitians have traditionally raised a morphotype of longsnouted, small black pig known as the

Creole pig. Adapted to the Haitian climate, Creole pigs had very low maintenance requirements, and were mainstays of soil fertility and the rural economy. In 1982 and 1983, most of these pigs were deliberately killed as part of swine disease control efforts required to integrate Haiti into the hemispheric economy. They were replaced by pigs from Iowa that needed clean drinking water, roofed pigpens, and expensive, imported feed. The substitution was a disaster. Haitian peasants, the hemisphere's poorest, lost an estimated $600 million. Haiti's ousted President Jean-Bertrand Aristide (2000), who, whatever his faults, understood the environmental and social effects of globalization, wrote

> There was a 30% drop in enrollment in rural schools . . . a dramatic decline in the protein consumption in rural Haiti, a devastating decapitalization of the peasant economy and an incalculable negative impact on Haiti's soil and agricultural productivity. The Haitian peasantry has not recovered to this day. . . . For many peasants the extermination of the Creole pigs was their first experience of globalization.

[. . .]

Loss of Wild Species

The reduction of diversity in agriculture is paralleled by a loss and reshuffling of wild species. The global die-off of species now occurring, unprecedented in its rapidity, is of course only partly the result of globalization, but globalization is a major factor in many extinctions. It accelerates species loss in several ways. First, it increases the numbers of exotic species carried by the soaring plane, ship, rail, and truck traffic of global trade. Second, it is responsible for the adverse effects of ecotourism on wild flora and fauna (Ananthaswamy 2004). And third, it promotes the development and exploitation of populations and natural areas to satisfy the demands of global trade, including, in addition to the agricultural and energy-related disruptions already mentioned, logging, over-fishing of marine fisheries, road building, and mining. To give just one example, from 1985 to 2001, 56% of Indonesian Borneo's (Kalimantan) "protected" lowland forest areas – many of them remote and sparsely populated – were intensively logged, primarily to supply international timber markets (Curran et al. 2004).

Surely one of the most significant impacts of globalization on wild species and the ecosystems in which they live has been the increase in introductions of invasive species (Vitousek et al. 1996; Mooney & Hobbs 2000). Two examples are zebra mussels (*Dreissena polymorpha*), which came to the Great Lakes in the mid-1980s in the ballast water of cargo ships from Europe, and Asian longhorn beetles (*Anoplophera glabripennis*), which arrived in the United States in the early 1990s in wood pallets and crates used to transfer cargo shipped from China and Korea. Zebra mussels, which are eliminating native mussels and altering lake ecosystems, clog the intake pipes of waterworks and power plants. The Asian longhorn beetle now seems poised to cause heavy tree loss (especially maples [*Acer* sp.]) in the hardwood forests of eastern North America. Along the US Pacific coast, oaks (*Quercus* sp.) and tanoaks (*Lithocarpus densiflorus*) are being killed by sudden oak death, caused by a new, highly invasive fungal disease organism (*Phytophthora ramorum*), which is probably also an introduced species that was spread by the international trade in horticultural plants (Rizzo & Garbelotto 2003). Estimates of the annual cost of the damage caused by invasive species in the United States range from $5.5 billion to $115 billion. The zebra mussel alone, just one of a great many terrestrial, freshwater, and marine exotic animals, plants, and pathogens, has been credited with more than $5 billion of damage since its introduction (Mooney & Drake 1986; Cox 1999). Invasive species surely rank among the principal economic and ecological limiting factors for globalization.

Some introduced species directly affect human health, either as vectors of disease or as the disease organisms themselves. For example, the Asian tiger mosquito (*Aedes albopictus*), a vector for dengue and yellow fevers, St Louis and LaCrosse encephalitis viruses, and West Nile virus, was most likely introduced in used truck tires imported from Asia to Texas in the 1980s and has spread widely since then. Discussion of this and other examples is beyond the scope of this article.

Even the partial control of accidental and deliberate species introductions requires stringent, well-funded governmental regulation in cooperation with the public and with business. Many introductions of alien species cannot be prevented, but some can, and successful interventions to prevent the spread of introduced species can have significant environmental and economic benefits. To give just one example, western Australia has shown that government and industry can cooperate to keep travelers and importers from bringing harmful invasive species across their borders. The western Australian HortGuard and GrainGuard programs integrate public education; rapid and effective access to information; targeted surveillance, which includes preborder, border, and postborder activities; and farm and regional biosecurity systems (Sharma 2004). Similar programs exist in New Zealand. But there is only so much that governments can do in the face of massive global trade.

Some of the significant effects of globalization on wildlife are quite subtle. Mazzoni et al. (2003) reported that the newly appearing fungal disease chytridiomycosis (caused by *Batrachochytrium dendrobatidis*), which appears to be the causative agent for a number of mass dieoffs and extinctions of amphibians on several continents, is probably being spread by the international restaurant trade in farmed North American bullfrogs (*Rana catesbeiana*). These authors state: "Our findings suggest that international trade may play a key role in the global dissemination of this and other emerging infectious diseases of wildlife."

Even more unexpected findings were described in 2002 by Alexander et al., who noted that expansion of ecotourism and other consequences of globalization are increasing contact between free-ranging wildlife and humans, resulting in the first recorded introduction of a primary human pathogen, *Mycobacterium tuberculosis*, into wild populations of banded mongooses (*Mungos mungo*) in Botswana and suricates (*Suricata suricatta*) in South Africa.

The Future of Globalization

The known effects of globalization on the environment are numerous and highly significant. Many others are undoubtedly unknown. Given these circumstances, the first question that suggests itself is: Will globalization, as we see it now, remain a permanent state of affairs (Rees 2002; Ehrenfeld 2003a)?

The principal environmental side effects of globalization – climate change, resource exhaustion (particularly cheap energy), damage to agroecosystems, and the spread of exotic species, including pathogens (plant, animal, and human) – are sufficient to make this economic system unstable and short-lived. The socioeconomic consequences of globalization are

likely to do the same. In my book *The Arrogance of Humanism* (1981), I claimed that our ability to manage global systems, which depends on our being able to predict the results of the things we do, or even to understand the systems we have created, has been greatly exaggerated. Much of our alleged control is science fiction; it doesn't work because of theoretical limits that we ignore at our peril. We live in a dream world in which reality testing is something we must never, never do, lest we awake.

In 1984 Charles Perrow explored the reasons why we have trouble predicting what so many of our own created systems will do, and why they surprise us so unpleasantly while we think we are managing them. In his book *Normal Accidents*, which does not concern globalization, he listed the critical characteristics of some of today's complex systems. They are highly interlinked, so a change in one part can affect many others, even those that seem quite distant. Results of some processes feed back on themselves in unexpected ways. The controls of the system often interact with each other unpredictably. We have only indirect ways of finding out what is happening inside the system. And we have an incomplete understanding of some of the system's processes. His example of such a system is a nuclear power plant, and this, he explained, is why system-wide accidents in nuclear plants cannot be predicted or eliminated by system design. I would argue that globalization is a similar system, also subject to catastrophic accidents, many of them environmental – events that we cannot define until after they have occurred, and perhaps not even then.

[. . .]

As globalization collapses, what will happen to people, biodiversity, and ecosystems? With respect to people, the gift of prophecy is not required to answer this question. What will happen depends on where you are and how you live. Many citizens of the Third World are still comparatively self-sufficient; an unknown number of these will survive the breakdown of globalization and its attendant chaos. In the developed world, there are also people with resources of self-sufficiency and a growing understanding of the nature of our social and environmental problems, which may help them bridge the years of crisis.

Some species are adaptable; some are not. For the nonhuman residents of Earth, not all news will be bad. Who would have predicted that wild turkeys (*Meleagris gallopavo*), one of the wiliest and most evasive of woodland birds, extinct in New Jersey 50 years ago, would now be found in every county of this the most densely populated state, and even, occasionally, in adjacent Manhattan? Who would have predicted that black bears (*Ursus americanus*), also virtually extinct in the state in the mid-twentieth century, would now number in the thousands (Ehrenfeld 2001)? Of course these recoveries are unusual – rare bright spots in a darker landscape.

Finally, a few ecological systems may survive in a comparatively undamaged state; most will be stressed to the breaking point, directly or indirectly, by many environmental and social factors interacting unpredictably. Lady Luck, as always, will have much to say. [. . .]

Awareness of the environmental limits that globalized industrial society denies or ignores should not, however, bring us to an extreme position of environmental determinism. Those whose preoccupations with modern civilization's very real social problems cause them to reject or minimize the environmental constraints discussed here (Hollander 2003) are guilty of seeing only half the picture. Environmental scientists sometimes fall into the same error. It is tempting to see the salvation of civilization and environment solely in terms of technological improvements in efficiency of energy extraction and use, control of pollution, conservation of water, and regulation of environmentally harmful activities. But such needed developments will not be sufficient – or may not even occur – without corresponding social change, including an end to human population growth and the glorification of consumption, along with the elimination of economic mechanisms that increase the gap between rich and poor. The environmental and social problems inherent in globalization are completely interrelated – any attempt to treat them as separate entities is unlikely to succeed in easing the transition to a postglobalized world. Integrated change that combines environmental awareness, technological innovation, and an altered world view is the only answer to the life-threatening problems exacerbated by globalization (Ehrenfeld 2003*b*).

If such integrated change occurs in time, it will likely happen partly by our own design and partly as an unplanned response to the constraints imposed by social unrest, disease, and the economics of scarcity. With respect to the planned component of change, we are facing, as eloquently described by Rees (2002), "the ultimate challenge to human intelligence and self-awareness, those vital qualities we humans claim as uniquely our own. *Homo sapiens* will either . . . become

fully human or wink out ignominiously, a guttering candle in a violent storm of our own making." If change does not come quickly, our global civilization will join Tainter's (1988) list as the latest and most dramatic example of collapsed complex societies.

Is there anything that *could* slow globalization quickly, before it collapses disastrously of its own environmental and social weight? It is still not too late to curtail the use of energy, reinvigorate local and regional communities while restoring a culture of concern for each other, reduce nonessential global trade and especially global finance (Daly & Cobb 1989), do more to control introductions of exotic species (including pathogens), and accelerate the growth of sustainable agriculture. Many of the needed technologies are already in place. It is true that some of the damage to our environment – species extinctions, loss of crop and domestic animal varieties, many exotic species introductions, and some climatic change – will be beyond repair. Nevertheless, the opportunity to help our society move past globalization in an orderly way, while there is time, is worth our most creative and passionate efforts.

The citizens of the United States and other nations have to understand that our global economic system has placed both our environment and our society in peril, a peril as great as that posed by any war of the twentieth century. This understanding, and the actions that follow, must come not only from enlightened leadership, but also from grassroots consciousness raising. It is still possible to reclaim the planet from a self-destructive economic system that is bringing us all down together, and this can be a task that bridges the divide between conservatives and liberals. The crisis is here, now. What we have to do has become obvious. Globalization can be scaled back to manageable proportions only in the context of an altered world view that rejects materialism even as it restores a sense of communal obligation. In this way, alone, can we achieve real homeland security, not just in the United States, but also in other nations, whose fates have become so thoroughly entwined with ours within the global environment we share.

References

Aldhous, P. 2003. How to slake a planet's thirst; the world's forgotten crisis. *Nature* 422: 243, 251–3.

Alexander, K. A., E. Pleydell, M. C. Williams, E. P. Lane, J. F. C. Nyange, and A. L. Michel. 2002. Mycobacterium tuberculosis: an emerging disease of free-ranging wild-life. *Emerging Infectious Diseases* 8: 598–601.

Ananthaswamy, A. 2004. Beware the ecotourist. *New Scientist* 181 (6 March): 6–7.

Appenzeller, T. 2004. The end of cheap oil. *National Geographic* 205(6): 80–109.

ASPO. 2004. The Association for the Study of Peak Oil and Gas, Newsletter No. 40, April. Association for the Study of Peak Oil and Gas, Uppsala, Sweden. Available from http://www.peakoil.net/ (accessed August 2004).

Bailey, B. and M. Lappé, editors. 2002. *Engineering the farm: ethical and social aspects of agricultural biotechnology.* Island Press, Washington, DC.

Bakhtiari, A. M. S. 2004. World oil production capacity model suggests output peak by 2006–07. *Oil and Gas Journal* 102(16): 18–20.

Bradsher, K. 2003. China's boom adds to global warming problem. *The New York Times,* 22 October: A1, A8.

Browne, J. 2004. Beyond Kyoto. *Foreign Affairs* 83: 20–32.

Campbell, C. J. 1997. *The coming oil crisis.* Multi-Science and Petroconsultants S.A., Brentwood, United Kingdom.

Centers for Disease Control and Prevention. 1995–present. *Emerging infectious diseases.* National Center for Infectious Diseases, Centers for Disease Control and Prevention, Atlanta.

Cox, G. W. 1999. *Alien species in North America and Hawaii: impacts on natural ecosystems.* Island Press, Washington, DC.

Curran, L. M., S. N. Trigg, A. K. McDonald, D. Astiani, Y. M. Hardiono, P. Siregar, I. Caniago, and E. Kasischke. 2004. Lowland forest loss in protected areas of Indonesian Borneo. *Science* 203: 1000–3.

Daly, H. E., and J. B. Cobb Jr. 1989. *For the common good.* Beacon Press, Boston.

Duncan, R. C., and W. Youngquist. 1999. Encircling the peak of world oil production. *Natural Resources Research* 8: 219–32.

Ehrenfeld, D. 1981. *The arrogance of humanism.* Oxford University Press, New York.

Ehrenfeld, D. 2001. Strangers in our own land. *Orion* 20: 8–11.

Ehrenfeld, D. 2003*a*. Globalisation: effects on biodiversity, environment and society. *Conservation and Society* 1: 99–111.

Ehrenfeld, D. 2003*b*. The Joseph strategy: transforming the cheap energy economy. *Orion* 22: 18–28.

Fowler, C., and P. Mooney. 1990. *Shattering: food, politics, and the loss of genetic diversity.* University of Arizona Press, Tucson.

Fu, J. 2004. Efforts to promote energy saving. *China Daily,* 4 June: 2.

Gerth, J. 2004. Forecast of rising oil demand challenges tired Saudi fields. *The New York Times,* 24 February: A1, C2.

Gleick, P. H. 2004. *The world's water 2004–2005: the biennial report on freshwater resources.* Island Press, Washington, DC.

Goldsmith, J. 1994. *The trap.* Carroll and Graf, New York.

Grant, P. M. 2003. Hydrogen lifts off – with a heavy load. *Nature* 424: 129–30.

Guo, N. 2004. Power use record set; peaks early. *China Daily,* 14 June: 1.

Hall, C., P. Tharakan, J. Hallock, C. Cleveland, and M. Jefferson. 2003. Hydrocarbons and the evolution of human culture. *Nature* 426: 318–22.

Hall, J. G., and J. Ruane. 1993. Livestock breeds and their conservation: a global overview. *Conservation Biology* 7: 815–26.

Heywood, V. H. 1995. *The global biodiversity assessment.* Cambridge University Press, United Nations Environment Programme, Cambridge.

Herbert, B. 2004. Masters of deception. *The New York Times,* 16 January: A21.

Hollander, J. M. 2003. *The real environmental crisis: why poverty, not affluence, is the environment's number one enemy.* University of California Press, Berkeley.

Holmes, B., and N. Jones. 2003. Brace yourself for the end of cheap oil. *New Scientist* 179 (2 August): 9–10.

Kerr, R. A. 1998. The next oil crisis looms large – and perhaps close. *Science* 281: 1128–31.

Lashley, F. R., and J. D. Durham, editors. 2002. *Emerging infectious diseases: trends and issues.* Springer-Verlag, New York.

Li, J. 2004. Water price hikes expected in Beijing. *China Daily,* 4 June: 3.

Liang, C. 2004. Effective measures urged to save water. *China Daily,* 9 June: 2.

Lomborg, B. 2001. *The skeptical environmentalist: measuring the real state of the world.* Cambridge University Press, Cambridge.

Mazzoni, R., A. A. Cunningham, P. Daszak, A. Apolo, E. Perdomo, and G. Speranza. 2003. Emerging pathogen of wild amphibians (*Rana catesbeiana*) farmed for international trade. *Emerging Infectious Diseases* 9: 995–8.

Mooney, H. A., and J. A. Drake, editors. 1986. *Ecology of biological invasions of North America and Hawaii.* Springer-Verlag, New York.

Mooney, H. A., and R. J. Hobbs, editors. 2000. *Invasive species in a changing world.* Island Press, Washington, DC.

Myers, R., and B. Worm. 2003. Rapid worldwide depletion of predatory fish communities. *Nature* 423: 280–3.

Orr, D. W. 2002. The labors of Sisyphus. *Conservation Biology* 16: 857–60.

Perrow, C. 1984. *Normal accidents: living with high-risk technologies.* Basic Books, New York.

Qin, C. 2004. Handling pollution vital to progress. *China Daily,* 4 June: 1.

Rees, W. E. 2002. Globalization and sustainability: conflict or convergence? Bulletin of Science, *Technology and Society* 22: 249–68.

Revkin, A. C. 2004. Alaska thaws, complicating the hunt for oil. *The New York Times*, 13 January: F1, F4.

Rizzo, D. M., and M. Garbelotto. 2003. Sudden oak death endangering California and Oregon forest ecosystems. *Frontiers in Ecology & the Environment* 1: 197–204.

Romm, J. J. 2004. *The hype about hydrogen: fact and fiction in the race to save the climate.* Island Press, Washington, DC.

Rosenberg, D. M., P. McCully, and C. M. Pringle. 2000. Global scale environmental effects of hydrological alterations: introduction. *BioScience* 50: 746–51.

Smil, V. 2003. *Energy at the crossroads: global perspectives and uncertainties.* MIT Press, Cambridge, Massachusetts.

Sudarshan, H. 2002. Foreword. In V. Ramprasad. *Hidden harvests: community based biodiversity conservation.* Green Foundation, Bangalore.

Tainter, J. A. 1988. *The collapse of complex societies.* Cambridge University Press, Cambridge.

Tromp, T. K., R.-L. Shia, M. Allen, J. M. Eiler, and Y. L. Yung. 2003. Potential environmental impact of a hydrogen economy on the stratosphere. *Science* 300: 1740–2.

Vitousek, P. M., C. M. D'Antonio, L. L. Loope, and R. Westbrooks. 1996. Biological invasions as global environmental change. *American Scientist* 84: 468–78.

Vörösmarty, C. J., and D. Sahagian. 2000. Anthropogenic disturbance of the terrestrial water cycle. *BioScience* 50: 753–65.

Watson, R. T., editor. 2002. *Climate change 2001: synthesis report: third assessment report of the intergovernmental panel on climate change.* Cambridge University Press, Cambridge.

Wirzba, N., editor. 2003. *The essential agrarian community: the future of culture, community, and the land.* University Press of Kentucky, Lexington.

Xu, D. 2004. Industrial output cools down. *China Daily*, 11 June: 1.

Youngquist, W. 1997. *GeoDestinies.* National Book Co., Portland, Oregon.

PART IX

WHAT IS THE FUTURE OF ENVIRONMENTAL ETHICS?

72   The Future of Environmental Ethics
     Holmes Rolston III

72   The Future of Environmental Ethics

Holmes Rolston III

Environmental ethics has a future as long as there are moral agents on Earth with values at stake in their environment. Somewhat ironically, just when humans, with their increasing industry and development, seemed further and further from nature, having more power to manage it, just when humans were more and more rebuilding their environments with their super technologies, the natural world emerged as a focus of ethical concern. Environmental alarms started with prophets such as Aldo Leopold, Rachel Carson, John Muir, and David Brower, and have, over recent decades, become daily news.

A massive *Millennium Ecosystem Assessment*, sponsored by the United Nations, involving over 1,300 experts from almost 100 nations, begins: "At the heart of this assessment is a stark warning. Human activity is putting such strain on the natural functions of Earth that the ability of the planet's ecosystems to sustain future generations can no longer be taken for granted" (Millennium Ecosystem Assessment, 2005a, p. 5).

The once almost-president Al Gore has turned to leading a campaign to wake us up to the threat of global warming, which he considers the biggest issue facing the world today, repeatedly calling it a moral challenge. John Kerry, the former Democratic presidential candidate, together with his wife, Teresa Heinz Kerry, urge our thinking of *This Moment on Earth: Today's New Environmentalists and Their Vision for the Future* (2007).

Paul Hawken calls environmentalism "the largest movement in the world," considering the number and force of environmental organizations around the globe (Hawken, 2007). If that seems exaggerated, remember that the United Nations Conference on Environment and Development (UNCED) at Rio de Janeiro in 1992 brought together the largest number of world leaders that have ever assembled to address any one issue. That conference drew 118 heads of state and government, delegations from 178 nations, virtually every nation in the world, 7,000 diplomatic bureaucrats, 30,000 advocates of environmental causes, and 7,000 journalists. The issues that coalesced there have been gathering over the last five hundred years, and they will be with us for another five hundred. *Agenda 21*, produced as UNCED faced the 21st century, is perhaps the most complex and comprehensive international document ever attempted (UNCED, 1992a).

All this certainly sounds like the environment is on the world agenda, and also on the ethical frontier, for the foreseeable future. Environmental ethics is, at times, about saving things past, still present, such as whooping cranes or sequoia trees. But environmentalism does not have much future if it is only museum work. Environmental ethics is about once and future nature. Diverse combinations of nature and culture have worked well enough over many millennia, but no more. We face a future without analogy in our past. Our modern cultures threaten the stability, beauty, and integrity of Earth, and thereby of the cultures superposed on Earth. An inter-human ethics must serve to find a satisfactory fit for humans in their communities; and, beyond that, an environmental ethics must find a satisfactory fit for humans in the larger communities of life on Earth.

We worried throughout much of the past century that humans would destroy themselves in inter-human conflict. That fear – at least of global nuclear disaster – has subsided somewhat only to be replaced by a new one. The worry for the next century is that, if our present heading is uncorrected, humans may ruin their planet and themselves with it. American Indians had been on the continent for 15,000 years, but with the coming of the Europeans in 1492 a disruption was imminent. We are living at another of the ruptures of history, worried whether European-Western civilization is self-destructing and, again, triggering disruptions around the globe.

Specially written for this volume.

1. Culture and Nature: Managed Planet? End of Nature?

Possibly with the ever-increasing transformation of nature, whatever residual nature remains may cease to be of significance for what it is in itself, with value attached more and more to the artifacted characteristics we superimpose on what was once wild nature. There will typically be degrees of modification: the relatively natural, the relatively cultured – or agri-cultured, the mostly manufactured. Nature is mixed with human labor or industry. Always in the past, continuing in the present, humans have had to rest their cultures upon a natural life support system. Their technosphere was constructed inside the biosphere.

In the future the technosphere could supercede the biosphere. Evolutionary history has been going on for billions of years, while cultural history is only about a hundred thousand years old. But certainly from here onward, culture increasingly determines what natural history shall continue. In that sense, it is true that Earth is now in a post-evolutionary phase. Culture is the principal determinant of Earth's future, more than nature; we are passing into a century when this will be increasingly obvious. The next millennium, some are even saying, is the epoch of the "end of nature." The new epoch is the Anthropocene.

That puts us indeed at a hinge point of history. Let's ask whether we ought to open this door. Henri Bergson, writing early in the last century, was prophetic. With the coming of the industrial age, when science joined with technology, we crossed the threshold of a new epoch.

> In thousands of years, when, seen from the distance, only the broad outlines of the present age will still be visible, our wars and our revolutions will count for little, even supposing they are remembered at all; but the steam-engine, and the procession of inventions of every kind that accompanied it, will perhaps be spoken of as we speak of the bronze or of the chipped stone of prehistoric time: it will serve to define an age. (Bergson, 1911, p. 146)

The transition from muscle and blood, whether of humans or of horses, to engines and gears shifts, by many orders of magnitude, the capacity of humans to transform their world, symbolized by the bulldozer. The pace change is from horse and buggy to jet plane. Even more recently, the capacity to produce has been augmented by the capacity for information transfer.

Consider the transition from handwriting to printing, from communication by written mail to radio and television, from information processing in books to information processing by computers. All this has occurred in a few hundred years, much of it in decades that your parents and grandparents can recall. In the course of human history, there have been epochal changes of state, such as the transition from hunter/gatherer cultures to agriculture, from oral to written cultures, the discovery of fire, the discovery of iron, the discovery of the New World, of Earth as a planet to circumnavigate, the discovery of motors, gears, electricity, electronics. This new century will indeed launch a new millennium: the super-industrial age. The high-technology age. The postnatural world? In the future we will have increasingly only "virtual nature." After Teflon, who wants clay?

"We live at the end of nature, the moment when the essential character of the world . . . is suddenly changing." Bill McKibben worries that already "we live in a postnatural world," in "a world that is of our own making." "There's no such thing as nature anymore" (McKibben, 1989, p. 175, p. 60, p. 85, p. 89).

Michael Soulé faces this prospect:

> In 2100, entire biotas will have been assembled from (1) remnant and reintroduced natives, (2) partly or completely engineered species, and (3) introduced (exotic) species. The term *natural* will disappear from our working vocabulary. The term is already meaningless in most parts of the world because anthropogenic [activities] have been changing the physical and biological environment for centuries, if not millennia. (Soulé, 1989, p. 301)

"Dominate" remains a disliked word, since it has echoes of the abuse of power. But "manage" is still quite a positive term. Humans, now and increasingly, want "ecosystem management," they will say, if ecologists. If religious, they want to be "good stewards." Humans want "sustainable development," they will say, if economists. With so much power and inclination to impose their will on nature, re-making it to their preferences, one does need to ask whether nature will (and ought) increasingly vanish.

Daniel Botkin predicts: "Nature in the twenty-first century will be a nature that we make. . . . We have the power to mold nature into what we want it to be." Of course he, like everybody else, urges us "to manage nature wisely and prudently," and, to that end, ecology can "instrument the cockpit of the biosphere." That sounds like high-tech engineering which brings wild nature under our control, remolding it into an airplane that we fly where we please. So it first seems, although Botkin − the ecologist in him returning − does go on to warn that it is important to recognize that "the guide to action is our knowledge of living systems and our willingness to observe them for what they are" and "to recognize the limits of our actions" (Botkin, 1990, pp. 192–3, pp. 200–1).

J. Baird Callicott puts it this way:

> Nature as Other is over. . . . We are witnessing the shift to a new idea, in which nature is seen as an organic system that includes human beings as one of its components. . . . A new dynamic and systemic postmodern concept of nature, which includes rather than excludes human beings, is presently taking shape. From the point of view of this new notion of nature, human technologies should be evaluated on their ecological merits. (Callicott, 1992, p. 16)

Spontaneous wild nature dies, and what lives on is not such nature *redivivus*, but a transformed, managed nature, a civilized nature, one also, hopefully, with ecological merits.

Before we ask what *ought* to be in the future, we should take a look at what *is* at present. Certainly, nature now bears the marks of human influence more widely than ever before. In one survey, using three categories, researchers find the proportions of Earth's terrestrial surface altered as follows: (1) Little disturbed by humans, 51.9%. (2) Partially disturbed, 24.2%. (3) Human dominated, 23.9%. Factoring out the ice, rock, and barren land, which supports little human or other life, the percentages become: (1) Little disturbed, 27.0%. (2) Partially disturbed, 36.7%. (3) Human dominated, 36.3%. Most terrestrial nature is dominated or partially disturbed (73.0%). Still, nature that is little or only partially disturbed remains 63.7% of the habitable Earth (Hannah, et al., 1994).

In another study, researchers found that humans now control 40% of the planet's land-based primary net productivity, that is, the basic plant growth which captures the energy on which everything else depends (Vitousek, et al., 1986). That is worrisome, but it does leave 60% still in the spontaneously wild. Also, of course, there is the sea, polluted and over-fished, but less affected than the land; and the oceans cover most of the Earth. Lately, scientists have been realizing there is great sub-surface biotic diversity.

The conclusion to draw is not that wild nature is impossible on Earth, but that it is threatened. Much remains, some can be restored. Is it the case, for instance, that, owing to human disturbances in the Yellowstone Park ecosystem, we have lost any possibility

of having a "natural" park in the 21st century? In an absolute sense this is true, since there is no square foot of the park in which humans have not disturbed the predation pressures. There is no square foot of the park on which rain falls without detectable pollutants.

But it does not follow that nature has absolutely ended, because it is not absolutely present. Answers come in degrees. Events in Yellowstone can remain 99.44% natural on many a square foot, indeed on hundreds of square miles, in the sense (recalling the language of the US *Wilderness Act*) that they are substantially "untrammeled by man." We can put the wolves back and clean up the air, and we have recently done both. Where the system was once disturbed by humans and subsequently restored or left to recover on its own, wildness can return. Perhaps the Colorado River is a "virtual" river, because it is so managed and controlled that it is no longer wild. But we do not yet have a "virtual Yellowstone." Or even a "virtual Adirondacks." Bill McKibben, who lives in the Adirondacks, in a subsequent book has *Hope, Human and Wild* (McKibben, 1995). Nature in part has ended, yet there is wild hope.

Environmental philosophy invites the inquiry whether we humans can launch a millennium of culture in harmony with nature. After all, the technosphere remains in the biosphere. We are perhaps in a post-evolutionary phase. Not many new species will evolve by natural selection, not at least by such selection unaltered by human changes. But we are not in a post-ecological phase. The management of the planet must conserve some environmental processes, if only for our survival, and it ought to conserve many more, if we are to be wise.

Environmental ethics ought to seek a complementarity. Think of an ellipse with its twin foci. Some events are generated under the control of one focus, *culture*; such events are in the *political* zone, where "polis" (town) marks those achievements in arts, industry, technology where the contributions of spontaneous nature are no longer evident in the criteria of evaluation. At the other end of the ellipse, a *wild* region of events is generated under the focus of spontaneous *nature*. These events take place in the absence of humans; they are what they are in themselves − wildflowers, loons calling, or a storm at sea. Although humans come to understand such events through the mediation of their cultures, they are evaluating events generated under the natural focus of the ellipse.

A domain of *hybrid* or *synthetic* events is generated under the simultaneous control of both foci, a resultant of integrated influences from nature and culture, under the sway variously of more or less nature and culture. "Symbiosis" is a parallel biological word. In the symbiosis zone, we have both and neither, but we do not forget there remain event-zones in which the principal determinant is culture, and other zones in which the principal determinant remains spontaneous nature. We do not want the ellipse to collapse into a circle, especially not one that is anthropocentric.

✓ Nature as it once was, nature as an end in itself, is no longer the whole story. Nature as contrasted with culture is not the whole story either. An environmental ethic is not just about wildlands, but about humans at home on their landscapes, humans in their culture residing also in nature. This will involve resource use, sustainable development, managed landscapes, the urban and rural environments. Further, environmental ethicists, now and in the future, can and ought to sometimes wish nature as an end in itself. That will prove an increasing challenge.

2. Global Warming: "Too Hot to Handle?"

But wait. There is one human activity that might make everything on Earth unnatural: global warming. Upsetting the climate upsets everything: air, water, soils, forests, fauna and flora, ocean currents, shorelines, agriculture, property values, international relations, because it is a systemic upset to the elemental givens on Earth. The Intergovernmental Panel on Climate Change, sponsored by the United Nations, meeting in Paris in 2007, released a bleak and powerful assessment of the future of the planet, with near certainty that unprecedented warming is human caused (Intergovernmental Panel on Climate Change, 2007).

John T. Houghton is one of the principal figures in the Intergovernmental Panel on Climate Change, also long a professor of atmospheric physics at Oxford. He was once Director General of the UK Meteorological Office (often called the MET). Houghton jarred political leaders with the claim that global warming already threatens British national security more than global terrorists, and that politicians were neglecting this "one duty above all others ... to protect the security of their people" (Houghton, 2003). The heat is first climatological, but secondly economic and political, and in the end moral.

✓ Global warming is a threat of first magnitude and is at the same time "a perfect moral storm," that is, utter or consummate (Gardiner, 2006). The storm is absolute, comprehensive, inclusive, ultimate; there is an unprecedented convergence of complexities, natural and technological uncertainties, global and local interactions, difficult choices scientifically, ethically, politically, socially. There are differing cross-cultural perspectives on a common heritage. There are intergenerational issues, distributional issues, concerns about merit, justice, benevolence, about voluntary and involuntary risk. There is a long lag time, from decades to hundreds of years. Surely but gradually, local *goods* cumulate into global *bads*. There are opportunities for denial, procrastination, self-deception, hypocrisy, free-riding, cheating, and corruption. Individual and national self-interest is at odds with collective global interests. This is Garrett Hardin's "tragedy of the commons," now taken at the pitch.[1]

Each person's lifestyle – at home, at work, at leisure, shopping, voting – has an ever-enlarging "ecological footprint," most of all with global warming where effects of our actions are globally dispersed – CO_2 in the air moving around the globe. There is fragmented agency; six billion persons differentially contribute to degrading a common resource (the atmosphere), all persons equally depending on climate, but with radically different powers to affect it. Even in the powerful nations, there is a sense of powerlessness. What can only one do? Any sacrifice I make (paying more for wind power) is more likely to benefit some over-user (heating his trophy home), than it is to better the commons. Institutional, corporate, and political structures force frameworks of environmentally disruptive behavior on individuals (such as high use of cars), and yet at the same time individuals support and demand these frameworks as sources of their good life (they love their SUVs).

The global character makes an effective response difficult, especially in a world without international government, where, for other reasons (such as cultural diversity, national heritages, freedom of self-determination), such government may be undesirable. Some global environmental problems can be solved by appeals to national self-interest, where international agreements serve such national interests. But the damage needs to be evident; the results in immediate prospect (such as with over-fishing agreements, whaling, the Law of the Sea, the Convention on Trade in Endangered Species, or the Montreal Protocol on ozone depleting hydrocarbons). Global warming is too diffuse to get into such focus. Cost-benefit analyses are unreliable in the face of such uncertainties. Who wins, who loses, who can do what, with what result?

Meanwhile we discount the future and shrug our shoulders: we have to look out for ourselves and the future will too. That's the way it has always been. Meanwhile too, the damage is done before we know it and is more or less irreversible.

Generally the developed nations are responsible for global warming, since they emit most of the carbon dioxide. Although global warming affects rich and poor, generally the poorer nations are likely to suffer the most. These nations may have semi-arid landscapes or low shorelines. Their citizen farmers may live more directly tied to their immediate landscapes. Being poor, they are the least able to protect themselves. They are in no position to force the developed nations to make effective response, particularly with effects on future generations or their or any other landscapes.

Tim Flannery, a scientist named "Australian of the Year" for his work, raises alarm about *The Weather Makers* (2005), fearing a runaway greenhouse effect, where earlier negative feedback processes, tending to keep equilibrium in atmospheric and ocean circulations, have been replaced by positive feedback processes spinning Earth into dis-equilibrium where humans will be powerless to halt the process. These may also be called non-linear or cascading shifts. We are smarter than ever, so smart that we are faced with overshoot. Our power to make changes exceeds our power to predict the results, exceeds our power to control even those adverse results we may foresee.

Where mitigating action is possible (such as limiting emissions), the present generation may bear costs, the benefits are gained by future generations. Postponing action will push much heavier costs onto those future generations; prevention is nearly always cheaper than cleanup. But the preventers live in a different generation from those who must cleanup. Classically, parents and grandparents do care about what they leave to children and grandchildren. But this intergenerational inheritance is not so local; it is rather diffuse. Americans gain today. Who pays what costs when, nobody knows. Notice, however, that by 2050, when many of these adverse effects will be taking place, 70% of all persons living on Earth today will still be alive.

Global warming simultaneously affects all life on Earth. Climates have changed in the past. In prehistoric times, with melting ice, species moved north variously from 200 to 1,500 meters per year, as revealed by fossil pollen analysis. Spruce invaded what previously was tundra, at a rate of about 100 meters per year. But plants cannot track climate changes of this order of magnitude. Some natural processes will remain (it still rains on whatever plants are there); but the system is more and more upset.

The plants that can survive tend to be ones that are weedy (kudzu and Japanese honeysuckle). The five hundred wilderness areas will be something like city weedlots, with tatterdemalion scraps of nature that have managed to survive catastrophic upsets. The situation is complex again. Global warming is compounded in effects if there are toxics or pollutants on the landscape, if there are extinctions that upset the ecology, or if there is deforestation and soil loss. These multiple factors combine to drive ecosystems across thresholds beyond which they crash.

Is there any hope, human or wild? Whether we have hope will depend considerably on what we think about human nature and our capacities to face an unprecedented crisis.

3. Human Nature: Human Uniqueness vs. "Pleistocene Appetites"

Can we be *Homo sapiens*, the wise species, as we have named ourselves? We may have engines and gears, but we still have muscle and blood appetites. The next decades will increasingly see tensions between nature and human nature. One might first think that, since humans presumably evolved as good adapted fits in their environments, human nature will complement wild nature. Biologists may call this "biophilia," an innate, genetically based disposition to love animals, plants, landscapes with trees, open spaces, running water (Wilson, 1984).

Critics find this a half truth because disconfirming evidence is everywhere. True, people like a house with a view, with a garden, but they do like a house, a big one. People are builders; their construction industry is what is destroying nature. People prefer culturally modified environments. "Man is the animal for whom it is natural to be artificial" (Garvin, 1953, p. 378). Neil Evernden says that *Homo sapiens* is "the natural alien" (Evernden, 1993). The really natural thing for humans to do (our genetic disposition) is to build a culture differentiating (alienating) ourselves from nature. Human agriculture, business, industry, development consumes most of our lives, and the search for nature is only avocational recreation.

Biophilia might be a positive Pleistocene relic. But other genetic legacies are problematic. Any residual biophilia is weak before our much more powerful desires for the goods of culture. Our evolutionary past did not give us many biological controls on our desires for goods that were in short supply. We love sweets and fats, of which in Pleistocene times humans could seldom get enough. But now we overeat and grow fat. Generally, that is a model for the whole overconsumption problem.

There are few biological controls on our desires to amass goods, to consume; for most people it has always been a struggle to get enough (indeed, for most it still is). When we can consume, we love it, and overconsume. Consumer capitalism transmutes a once-healthy pattern of desires into avarice. With escalating opportunities for consumption, driven by markets in search of profits, we need more self-discipline than comes naturally. Our self-interested tendencies overshoot; we love ourselves (egoism) and find it difficult to know when and how to say enough.

√⌈For all of human history, we have been pushing back limits.⌋Humans have more genius at this than any other species. Especially in the West, we have lived with a deep-seated belief that life will get better, that one should hope for abundance, and work toward obtaining it. Economists call such behavior "rational"; humans will maximize their capacity to exploit their resources. Moral persons will also maximize human satisfactions, at least those that support the good life, which must not just include food, clothing, and shelter, but an abundance, more and more goods and services that people want. Such growth is always desirable.

In the West we have built that into our concept of human rights: a right to self-development, to self-realization. Such an egalitarian ethic scales everybody up and drives an unsustainable world. When everybody seeks their own good, there is escalating consumption. When everybody seeks everybody else's good, there is, again, escalating consumption.

⌈Humans are not well equipped to deal with the sorts of global level problems we now face. The classical institutions – family, village, tribe, nation, agriculture, industry, law, medicine, even school and church – have shorter horizons. Far-off descendants and distant races do not have much "biological hold" on us. Across the era of human evolution, little in our behavior affected those remote from us in time or in space, and natural selection shaped only our conduct toward those closer. Global threats require us to act in massive concert of which we are incapable. If so, humans may bear within themselves the seeds of their own destruction. More bluntly, more scientifically put: our genes, once enabling our adaptive fit, will in the next millennium prove maladaptive and destroy us.⌋

Both policy and ethics will be required to enlarge the scope of concern. Humans are attracted to appeals to a better life, to quality of life, and if environmental ethics can persuade large numbers of persons that an environment with biodiversity, with wildness, is a better world in which to live than one without these, then some progress is possible – using an appeal to still more enlightened self-interest, or perhaps better: to a more inclusive and comprehensive concept of human welfare. That will get us clear air, water, soil conservation, national parks, some wildlife reserves and bird sanctuaries. Environmental ethics cannot succeed without this, nor is this simply pragmatic; it is quite true. This may be the most we can do at global scales, even national scales, with collective human interests.

We may prove able to work out some incentive structures. The European Union has transcended national interests with surprising consensus about environmental issues. Kofi Annan, Secretary General of the United Nations, praised the Montreal Protocol, with its five revisions, widely adopted (191 nations) and implemented, as the most successful international agreement yet. All the developed nations, except the United States and Australia, have signed the Kyoto Protocol. The Convention on International Trade in Endangered Species of Wild Fauna and Flora (CITES) has been signed by 112 nations. There are over 150 international agreements (conventions, treaties, protocols, etc.) registered with the United Nations, that deal directly with environmental problems (United Nations Environment Programme, 1997; Rummel-Bulska and Osafo, 1991).

⌈Humans have proved capable of advanced skills never dreamed of in our ancient past – flying jet planes, building the Internet, decoding their own genome, and designating world biosphere reserves. It would be tragic in the future if we let our left-over Pleistocene appetites become a useful alibi for continuing our excesses. *Homo sapiens* can and ought to be wiser than that.⌋

4. Sustainable Development vs. Sustainable Biosphere

The United Nations Conference on Environment and Development entwined its twin concerns into "sustainable development." No one wants unsustainable development, so sustainable development is likely to remain the favored model. The duty seems unanimous, plain, and urgent. Only so can this good life continue. Over 150 nations have endorsed sustainable development. The World Business Council on Sustainable Development includes 130 of the world's largest corporations.

Proponents argue that sustainable development is useful just because it is a wide angle lens. The specifics of development are unspecified, giving peoples and nations the freedom and responsibility of self-development. This is an orienting concept that is at once directed and encompassing, a coalition-level policy that sets aspirations, thresholds, and allows pluralist strategies for their accomplishment.

Critics reply that sustainable development is just as likely to prove an umbrella concept that requires little but superficial agreement, bringing a constant illusion of consensus, glossing over deeper problems with a rhetorically engaging word. There are two poles, complements yet opposites. Economy can be prioritized, the usual case, and anything can be done to the environment, so long as the continuing development of the economy is not jeopardized thereby. The environment is kept in orbit with economics at the center. One ought to develop (since that increases social welfare and the abundant life), and the environment will constrain that development if and only if a degrading environment might undermine ongoing development. The underlying conviction is that the trajectory of the industrial, technological, commercial world is generally right – only the developers, in their enthusiasm, have hitherto failed to recognize environmental constraints.

At the other pole, the environment is prioritized. A "sustainable biosphere" model demands a baseline quality of environment. The economy must be worked out "within" such quality of life in a quality environment (clean air, water, stable agricultural soils, attractive residential landscapes, forests, mountains, rivers, rural lands, parks, wildlands, wildlife, renewable resources). Winds blow, rains fall, rivers flow, the sun shines, photosynthesis takes place, carbon recycles all over the landscape. These processes have to be sustained. The economy must be kept within an environmental orbit. One ought to conserve nature, the ground-matrix of life. Development is desired, but even more, society must learn to live within the carrying capacity of its landscapes.

"Sustainable" is an economic but also an environmental term. The Ecological Society of America advocates research and policy that will result in a "sustainable biosphere." "Achieving a sustainable biosphere is the single most important task facing humankind today" (Risser, Lubchenco, Levin, 1991). The fundamental flaw in "sustainable development" is that it sees the Earth as resource only. The underlying conviction in the sustainable biosphere model is that the current trajectory of the industrial, technological, commercial world is generally wrong, because it will inevitably overshoot. The environment is not some undesirable, unavoidable set of constraints. Rather, nature is the matrix of multiple values; many, even most of them, are not counted in economic transactions. In a more inclusive accounting of what we wish to sustain, nature provides numerous other values (aesthetic experiences, biodiversity, sense of place and perspective), and these are getting left out. The *Millennium Ecosystem Assessment* explores this in great detail.

A central problem with contemporary global development is that the rich grow richer and the poor poorer. Many fear that this is neither ethical nor sustainable.

> Global inequalities in income increased in the 20th century by orders of magnitude out of proportion to anything experienced before. The distance between the incomes of the richest and poorest country was about 3 to 1 in 1820, 35 to 1 in 1950, 44 to 1 in 1973, and 72 to 1 in 1992. (United Nations Development Programme (UNDP), 2000, p. 6)

> For most of the world's poorest countries the past decade has continued a disheartening trend: not only have they failed to reduce poverty, but they are falling further behind rich countries. (United Nations Development Programme (UNDP), 2005, p. 36)

The assets of the world's top three billionaires exceed the combined gross national product (GNP) of all of the least developed countries. The richest two percent own more than half of global household wealth (United Nations University, World Institute for Development Economics Research, 2006). The distribution of wealth raises complex issues of merit, luck, justice, charity, natural resources, national boundaries, global commons. But by any standards this seems unjustly disproportionate. The inevitable result stresses people on their landscapes, forcing environmental degradation, more tragedy of the commons, with instability and collapse. The rich and powerful are equally ready to exploit nature and people.

Such issues come under another inclusive term, "environmental justice." Now the claim is that social justice is so linked with environmental conservation that a more fair distribution of the world's wealth is required for any sustainable conservation even of rural landscapes, much less of wildlife and wildlands. Environmental ethicists may be faulted for overlooking the poor (often of a different race, class, or sex) in their concern to save the elephants. The livelihood of such poor may be adversely affected by the elephants, who trash their crops. Or it may be adversely affected because the pollution dump is located on their already degraded landscapes – and not in the backyard (or even on the national landscapes) of the rich. They may be poor because they are living on degraded landscapes. They are likely to remain poor, even if developers arrive, because they will be too poorly paid to break out of their poverty.

Ethicists ought to speak the truth to power. They may suffer for it. Joseph E. Stiglitz, Nobel laureate, Chief Economist for the World Bank, became increasingly ethically concerned.

> While I was at the World Bank, I saw firsthand the devastating effect that globalization can have on developing countries, and especially the poor within those countries. . . . Especially at the International Monetary Fund . . . decisions were made on the basis of what seemed a curious blend of ideology and bad economics, dogmas that sometimes seemed to be thinly veiling special interests . . . The IMF's policies, in part based on the outworn presumption that markets, by themselves, lead to efficient outcomes, failed to allow for desirable government interventions in the market, measures which can guide economic growth and make *everyone* better off. (Stiglitz, 2002, p. ix, p. xiii, p. xii)

Nor are governments, pushed by such financial interests, always willing so to guide economic growth. Stiglitz wrote in April 2000:

> I was chief economist at the World Bank from 1996 until last November, during the gravest global economic crisis in a half-century. I saw how the IMF, in tandem with the US Treasury Department, responded. And I was appalled. (Stiglitz, 2000, p. 56)

For such concern he was pressured into resigning and his contract with the World Bank was terminated. Ethicists need now and forever in the future to remember Lord Acton: "Power tends to corrupt and absolute power corrupts absolutely" (Acton, 1887, 1949, p. 364). This reconnects us with the worries we had earlier about those Pleistocene appetites driving humans, rich and poor, ever to want more, more, more.

Sustainable development is impossible without a sustainable biosphere. Thirty percent of the *Millennium Ecosystem Assessment* Development Goals depend on access to clean water. A third of the people on the planet lack readily available safe drinking water. Consider the conclusion of some of its principal authors:

> We lack a robust theoretical basis for linking ecological diversity to ecosystem dynamics and, in turn, to ecosystem services underlying human well-being. . . . The most catastrophic changes in ecosystem services identified in the MA (*Millennium Assessment*) involved nonlinear or abrupt shifts. We lack the ability to predict thresholds for such changes, whether or not such a change may be reversible, and how individuals and societies will respond. . . . Relations between ecosystem services and human well-being are poorly understood. One gap relates to the consequences of changes in ecosystem services for poverty reduction. The poor are most dependent on ecosystem services and vulnerable to their degradation. (Carpenter et al., 2006)

People and their Earth have entwined destinies; that past truth continues in the present, and will remain a pivotal concern in the new millennium.

5. Biodiversity: "Good for me" vs. "Good of its kind"

"The biospheric membrane that covers the Earth, and you and me, . . . is the miracle we have been given" (Wilson, 2002, p. 21). Earth's biodiversity is in more jeopardy today than previously in the history of life. If we do not shift our present development course, "at least a fifth of the species of plants would be gone or committed to early extinction by 2030, and half by the end of the century" (Wilson, 2002, p. 102). The *Millennium Ecosystem Assessment*, reporting a multi-national consensus of hundreds of experts, concluded: "Over the past few hundred years, humans have increased species extinction rates by as much as 1,000 times background rates that were typical over Earth's history" (Millennium Ecosystem Assessment, 2005b, p. 3).

The causes are complex: over-hunting, over-fishing, destruction of habitat, pollution, invasive species, global warming. Measures of loss are multiple: numbers of species, percentages, genetic populations, ecosystems degraded, hotspots lost. Biodiversity (including but more inclusive than "endangered species") is in subspecies, genetically distinct populations, in diverse habitats and ecosystems. Most species on Earth are yet undescribed – so far only about 10% of fungi, and less for most invertebrates and microorganisms. We hardly know what we are losing. Predictions are difficult. Nevertheless, all the measures find biocide quickening in speed and intensity.

Paleontologists trace an evolutionary natural history with ongoing turnover extinctions and replacements. Anthropogenic extinction (caused by human encroachments) is radically different. One opens doors; the other closes them. In natural extinctions, nature takes away life when it has become unfit in habitat, or when the habitat alters, and supplies other life in its place. Through evolutionary time, nature has provided new species at a higher rate than the extinction rate; hence, the accumulated diversity. Life rebounds even after the six catastrophic extinctions, which often open up novel opportunities for dramatic respeciation. Artificial extinction shuts down tomorrow because it shuts down speciation. There is no respeciation on Walmart parking lots. Humans dead-end these lines.

But that evolutionary epic is over, critics will say. Most of the species that ever existed in the past are extinct by natural causes, and in the next century more will go extinct by human causes. That may be a pity, but it is inevitable. Nor is it immoral, since humans are worth more than beetles and fungi. We do need to sustain the biosphere, our life support system, as the ecologists were just claiming. So save what is "good for us," but, beyond that, we have no duties to the living things as "goods of their kind." Biodiversity for medical, agricultural, industrial, recreational, scientific uses? Yes, these are instrumental values. But intrinsic value in animals and plants, a "good of their own" that claims our care? That goes too far.

"Human beings are at the centre of concerns . . ." So the *Rio Declaration* begins, formulated at the United Nations Conference on Environment and Development (UNCED), and signed by almost every nation on Earth. This document was once to be called the *Earth Charter*, but the developing nations were more interested in asserting their rights to develop, more ecojustice, more aid from the North to the South, and only secondarily in saving the Earth. The Rio claim is, in many respects, quite true. The human species is causing all the concern. Environmental problems are people problems, not gorilla or sequoia problems. The problem is to get people into "a healthy and productive life in harmony with nature" (UNCED, 1992b).

Wilfred Beckerman and Joanna Pasek put it this way:

> The most important bequest we can make to posterity is to bequeath a decent society characterized by greater respect for human rights than is the case today. Furthermore, while this by no means excludes a concern for environmental developments – particularly those that many people believe might seriously threaten future living standards – policies to deal with these developments must never be at the expense of the poorest people alive today. One could not be proud of policies that may preserve the environment for future generations if the costs of doing so are borne mainly by the poorest members of the present generation. (Beckerman and Pasek, 2001, p. vi)

That is certainly humane, and no one wishes to argue that the poorest should bear the highest of these costs, while the rich gain the benefits. We are not proud of a conservation ethic that says: the rich should win, the poor lose. That was what appalled Joseph Stiglitz about the World Bank, the IMF, and the US Treasury.

But look at how this plays out with World Health Organization policy:

> Priority given to human health raises an ethical dilemma if "health for all" conflicts with protecting the environment. . . . Priority to ensuring human survival is taken as a first-order principle. Respect for nature and control of environmental degradation is a second-order principle, which must be observed unless it conflicts with the first-order principle of meeting survival needs. (World Health Organization, Commission on Health and Environment, 1992, p. 4)

Again, that seems quite humane. But in India this policy certainly means no tigers. In Africa it means no rhinos. Both will only remain in Western zoos. To *preserve*, even to *conserve*, is going to mean to *reserve*. If there are biodiversity reserves, with humans on site or nearby, humans must limit their activities. Else there will always be some hungry persons, who would diminish the reserve. The continued existence in the wild of most of Earth's charismatic endangered species depends on some 600 major reserves for wildlife in some 80 countries (Riley and Riley, 2005). If these are not policed, the animals will not be there.

Michael L. Rosenzweig wants a "win-win ecology" so that "the Earth's species can survive in the midst of human enterprise" (Rosenzweig, 2003). All these you-can-have-your-cake-and-eat-it-too solutions are welcome, so far as they go. A bumper sticker reads: Re-cycling: Everyone wins. That, some say, is an aphoristic model for the whole human/nature relationship. If we are in harmony with nature, everyone wins, equally people, rhinos, and tigers.

The conservatives (the skeptics?) will say that win-win is all that is politically, economically, sociologically, biologically, feasible, even imaginable. The best you can do is enlighten self-interest. Remember those Pleistocene urges for more and more. This will be especially true in a free-market democracy, which is what most of the world seems to want today. So the best strategy is to argue that persons living abundant lives need to experience the wonderland natural world (those biophilia instincts). Biodiversity was formerly too much devalued, as if it were nothing but consumable resources. Biodiversity in place benefits people. Ecotourists who come to see tigers and rhinos will bring in more money than will cutting the timber and grazing cattle there.

Nevertheless, there is something suspicious about these claims. They seem humane; they also hide an arrogance about human superiority. Let's make a comparison. What if Americans were to say: Always prefer Americans, first order. All other nations are second order. "We will not do anything that harms our economy," said George W. Bush rather bluntly, "because first things first are the people who live in America" (Bush, quoted in Seelye, 2001). Didn't John Houghton earlier, in his warning about global warming, say that the first duty of political leaders is to protect the security of the people within their nations?

But Houghton did not say that the security of the British is first order, that of the Americans second order. Bush did say that the economic health of the American companies takes bedrock priority. And we are suspicious when one group says to another: We will deal with you only in ways that are first beneficial to us. Maybe we begin to see why Joseph Stiglitz, concerned about the world's poor, was "appalled" by the IMF and US Treasury. None of this bodes well for inter-human justice, much less for interspecific ethics.

Analogously, what if humans say (as did the World Health Organization): First things first are people. Wildlife, plants, non-humans, second. "You non-humans can live, only if you are worth more to us

alive than dead." That is the cash value of the policy: Always prefer humans, first order. The other ten million species on the planet come second to us.

Ought not really superior humans be willing to sacrifice something for these ten (or more) million other species on Earth? There is something morally naive about living in a reference frame where one species takes itself as absolute and values everything else relative to its utility, even if we phrase it that we are taking ourselves as primary and everything else as secondary. If true to their specific epithet, ought not *Homo sapiens* value this host of life as something with a claim to care in its own right? If we humans continue as we are headed and cause extinctions surpassing anything previously found on Earth, then future generations, rich or poor, are not likely to be proud of our destroying "the miracle we have been given" either.

Nobody wants to be a loser, so maybe we can put it this way: Humans will win when, and only when, they change their goals. Humans will come to be corrected from a misperception: "good for us," "instrumental value" is all that counts. We will win because we get our values right. The loser will be worse off by his lights, but his lights are wrong (nature all and only a resource). If he or she gets things in the right light ("good kinds," "goods of their own," "intrinsic values," "respect for life," "the wonderland Earth"), there is no loss, only gain.

Consider abolishing slavery. Slave-owners lost their slaves as resources. But when the right thing was done, the result was win-win in the long term. Within the next century blacks increasingly prospered and so did the whites. Similarly with the liberation of women or minorities. White males lost some jobs, but the talents and skills of women and blacks, formerly often wasted, now are fully utilized in the work force; family incomes are higher, marriages are richer, and so on. In environmental ethics, there is a parallel. The person re-forms his or her values and becomes a winner because now living in a richer and more harmonious relationship with nature.

At this point, critics will protest that we insist that humans can win but then redefine winning. We win by moving the goal posts. And that's cheating, like showing a net positive balance in your checkbook by revising the multiplication tables. You will win, by losing at the old game and playing a new game. Some persons did lose, in the sense that losing had when our argument started. They lost timber, or jobs, or opportunities for development, or grazing their cattle.

Yes, you do have to move the goal posts to win. That might be cheating if the game is football. But in environmental ethics, there is a disanalogy. You move the goal posts because you discover that they are in the wrong place. And that is really to win, because getting to the wrong goal is not winning. Moving the goal posts, these "losers" at the exploitation game will come to live in a community with a new worldview, that of a sustainable relationship with the biodiverse Earth, and that is a new idea of winning. All they really lose is what it is a good thing to lose: an exclusively exploitative attitude toward nature – similar to that once held about slaves. What they gain is a good thing to gain: a land ethic.

"Every form of life is unique, warranting respect regardless of its worth to man." That is how the UN *World Charter for Nature* begins (United Nations General Assembly, 1982). This charter is as nonanthropocentric as the *Rio Declaration* is anthropocentric. One hundred and twelve nations endorsed this charter, though the United States vigorously opposed it. This statement was largely aspirational; few took it to require any serious changes in policy. But in a vision for the future, we need aspirations. It is possible, we should notice, for humans to be at the center of concerns and also for every form of life to have its worth regardless of humans. Both can be true.

6. Earth Ethics

We have been traveling into progressively less familiar ethical terrain. We need a logic and an ethic for Earth with its family of life. Ecosystems are ultimately our home, from which the word *ecology* is derived (Greek: *oikos*, house). In the twentieth century, the commons problem became transnational; at the turn of the millennium it has become global. Our citizenship in nations is not well synchronized with our residence in geographic places, nor with our sense of global dwelling on our home planet.

People are fighting for what is of value in nature but as citizens of nations that have economic policies and political agendas, demanding loyalties in support. Their access to natural resources comes filtered through political and industrial units that are not formed, or continued, with these ecologies in mind. They want resources, but political alignments can often mean suboptimal and unjust solutions to the problems of resource distribution. "Nationalizing" natural resources can be as much part of the problem as part of the answer, especially when the sovereign independence of nations is asserted without regard for the interdependencies of these nations – both those with each other and those of the global ecosystems. When biological resources are taken to be national possessions in dispute, rather than an Earth commons to be shared, it can become difficult to find a way to share them.

In previous environmental ethics, one might have spoken loosely, perhaps poetically, or romantically of valuing Earth. But that would not have been taken as a serious cognitive claim, no more than was the *World Charter for Nature*. Earth is a mere thing, a big thing, a special thing for those who happen to live on it, but still a thing, and not appropriate as an object of intrinsic or systemic valuation. Thinking this way, we can, if we insist on being anthropocentrists, say that it is all valueless except as our human resource.

But we will not be valuing Earth objectively until we appreciate this marvelous (miraculous?) natural history. This really is a superb planet, the most valuable entity of all, because it is the entity able to produce and sustain all the Earthbound values. At this scale of vision, if we ask what is principally to be valued, the value of life arising as a creative process on Earth seems a better description and a more comprehensive category than to speak of a careful management of planetary natural resources that we humans own. Such a fertile Earth, interestingly, is the original meaning of the word "nature," that which "springs forth," "gives birth," or is "generated." This was once explained in the mythology of a "Mother Earth"; now we have it on scientific authority.

Dealing with an acre or two of real estate, perhaps even with hundreds or thousands of acres, we usually think – and perhaps will continue to do so – that the Earth belongs to us, as private property holders. Dealing with a landscape, we think that the earth belongs to us, as citizens of the country geographically located there. So we have our nation states with their territories. But on the global scale, Earth is not something we own. Earth does not belong to us; rather we belong to it. We belong on it. The challenging philosophical question for the new millennium is how we humans belong in this world, not how much of it belongs to us. The question is not of property, but of community. Biospheric Earth is really the relevant survival unit. And with that global vision, we may want to return to our regional landscapes, and think of ourselves as belonging there too, with a deeper sense of place.

In the next millennium, it will not be enough to be a good "citizen," or a "humanist," because neither of those terms have enough "nature," enough "earthiness" in them. "Citizen" is only half the truth; the other half is that we are "residents" on landscapes. Humans are Earthlings. Earth is our dwelling place. From here onward, there is no such thing as civic competence without ecological competence. Many a citizen who is celebrated for his or her humanity is quite insensitive to the boding ecological crisis, or, even were there no crisis, in enjoying the values the natural world carries all around them. Until that happens, no one is well educated for the next century, the century in which many of these problems will have to be solved – if ever they are solved. Somewhat paradoxically, the two new areas in an undergraduate education, differing from the classical education of the past century is that graduates need to be (1) computer literate and (2) environmentally literate.

Our responsibility to Earth might be thought the most remote of our responsibilities; it seems so grandiose and vague beside our concrete responsibilities to our children or next-door neighbors. But not so: the other way round, it is the most fundamental of our responsibilities, and connected with these local ones. Responsibilities increase proportionately to the level and value of the reality in jeopardy. The highest level that we humans have power to affect, Earth, is the most vital phenomenon of all.

Boutros Boutros-Ghali, speaking as the UN Secretary-General, closed the Earth Summit: "The Spirit of Rio must create a new mode of civic conduct. It is not enough for man to love his neighbour; he must also learn to love his world" (Boutros-Ghali, 1992a, p. 1). "We must now conclude an ethical and political contract with nature, with this Earth to which we owe our very existence and which gives us life" (Boutros-Ghali, 1992b, vol. IV, pp. 66–9). This does not deny that we must continue to love our neighbors, but it enlarges the vision from a social contract to a natural contract. The challenge is to think of Earth as a precious thing in itself because it is home for us all; Earth is to be loved, as we do a neighbor, for an intrinsic integrity.

Views of Earth from space are the most impressive photographs ever taken, if one judges by their worldwide impact. They are the most widely distributed photographs ever, having been seen by well over half the persons on Earth. Few are not moved to a moment of truth, at least in their pensive moods. The whole Earth is aesthetically stimulating, philosophically challenging, and ethically disturbing. "Once a photograph of the Earth, taken from *the outside* is available . . . a new idea as powerful as any in history will be let loose" (Fred Hoyle, quoted in Kelley, 1988, inside front cover). We had to get off the planet to see it whole.

A virtually unanimous experience of the nearly two hundred astronauts, from many countries and cultures, is the awe experienced at the first sight of the whole Earth – its beauty, fertility, smallness in the abyss of space, light and warmth under the sun in surrounding darkness and, above all, its vulnerability. In the words of Edgar Mitchell, Earth is "a sparkling blue-and-white jewel . . . laced with slowly swirling veils of white . . . like a small pearl in a thick sea of black mystery" (quoted in Kelley, 1988, at photographs 42–5).

"I remember so vividly," said Michael Collins, "what I saw when I looked back at my fragile home – a glistening, inviting beacon, delicate blue and white, a tiny outpost suspended in the black infinity. Earth is to be treasured and nurtured, something precious that *must* endure" (Collins, 1980, p. 6). Earth is a fragile planet, a jewel set in mystery. We humans too belong on the planet; it is our home, as much as for all the others. Humans are certainly a dominant species – what other species takes pictures of Earth from space? But the glistening pearl in space may not be something we want to possess, as much as a biosphere we ought to inhabit with love. Environmental ethics is the elevation to ultimacy of an urgent world vision. We are searching for an ethics adequate to respect life on this Earth, an Earth Ethics. That is the future of environmental ethics.

Note

1 A "tragedy of the commons" occurs when individuals, sharing a resource held in common, each act in self-interest and the collective result progressively degrades the collective resource, illustrated by shepherds placing more and more sheep on land held in common (Hardin, 1968).

References

Acton, Lord (John Emerich Edward Dalberg-Acton), 1949. *Essays on Freedom and Power*, Gertrude Himmelfarb (ed.). (Glencoe, IL: Free Press).

Beckerman, Wilfred, and Joanna Pasek, 2001. *Justice, Posterity, and the Environment*. (New York: Oxford University Press).

Bergson, Henri, 1911. *Creative Evolution*, Arthur Mitchell (trans.). (London: Macmillan and Co.).

Botkin, Daniel B., 1990. *Discordant Harmonies: A New Ecology for the Twenty-first Century*. (New York: Oxford University Press).

Boutros-Ghali, Boutros, 1992a. Extracts from closing UNCED statement, in an UNCED summary, *Final Meeting and Round-up of Conference*, June 14. UN Document ENV/DEV/RIO/29, 14 June.

Boutros-Ghali, Boutros, 1992b. Text of closing UNCED statements, in *Report of the United Nations Conference on Environment and Development*, 1992, vol. IV, pp. 66–9. UN Document A/CONF.151.26 (Vol. IV).

Callicott, J. Baird, 1992. "La Nature est morte, vive la nature!" *Hastings Center Report* 22 (no. 5, September/October): 16–23.

Carpenter, Stephen R., et al, 2006. "Millennium Ecosystem Assessment: Research Needs," *Science* 314 (13 October): 257–8.

Collins, Michael, 1980. "Foreword," in Roy A. Gallant, *Our Universe*. (Washington, DC: National Geographic Society).

Evernden, Neil, 1993. *The Natural Alien: Humankind and Environment*. (Toronto: University of Toronto Press).

Flannery, Tim, 2005. *The Weather Makers: The History and Future Impact of Climate Change*. (New York: Atlantic Monthly Press).

Gardiner, Stephen M., 2006. "A Perfect Moral Storm: Climate Change, Intergenerational Ethics and the Problem of Moral Corruption," *Environmental Values* 15: 397–413.

Garvin, Lucius, 1953. *A Modern Introduction to Ethics*. (Cambridge, MA: Houghton Mifflin).

Hannah, Lee, David Lohse, Charles Hutchinson, John L. Carr, and Ali Lankerani, 1994. "A Preliminary Inventory of Human Disturbance of World Ecosystems," *Ambio* 23: 246–50.

Hardin, Garrett, 1968. "The Tragedy of the Commons," *Science* 162 (December 13): 1243–8.

Hawken, Paul, 2007. *Blessed Unrest: How the Largest Movement in the World Came into Being and Why No One Saw It Coming*. (New York: Viking).

Houghton, John, 2003. "Global Warming is Now a Weapon of Mass Destruction," *The Guardian*, 28 July, p. 14.

Intergovernmental Panel on Climate Change, 2007. *Climate Change 2007: The Physical Science Basis*. Online at www.ipcc.ch.

Kelley, Kevin W, (ed.), 1988. *The Home Planet*. (Reading, MA: Addison-Wesley).

Kerry, John, and Teresa Heinz Kerry, 2007. *This Moment on Earth: Today's New Environmentalists and Their Vision for the Future*. (New York: Perseus Group, Public Affairs Books).

McKibben, Bill, 1989. *The End of Nature*. (New York, NY: Random House).

McKibben, Bill, 1995. *Hope, Human and Wild*. (Little, Brown and Company).

Millennium Ecosystem Assessment, 2005a. *Living Beyond our Means: Natural Assets and Human Well-Being: Statement from the Board*. (Washington, DC: World Resources Institute).

Millennium Ecosystem Assessment, 2005b. *Ecosystems and Human Well-being: Biodiversity Synthesis*. (Washington, DC: World Resources Institute).

Riley, Laura, and William Riley, 2005. *Nature's Strongholds: The World's Great Wildlife Reserves*. (Princeton, NJ: Princeton University Press).

Risser, Paul G., Jane Lubchenco, and Samuel A. Levin, 1991. "Biological Research Priorities – A Sustainable Biosphere," *BioScience* 47: 625–7.

Rosenzweig, Michael L., 2003. *Win-Win Ecology: How the Earth's Species Can Survive in the Midst of Human Enterprise*. (New York, NY: Oxford University Press).

Rummel-Bulska, Iwona, and Seth Osafo, (eds.), 1991. *Selected Multilateral Treaties in the Field of the Environment, II*. (Cambridge, MA: Grotius Publications).

Seelye, Katharine Q., 2001. "Facing Obstacles on Plan for Drilling for Arctic Oil, Bush Says He'll Look Elsewhere," *The New York Times*, March 30, 2001, p. A13.

Soulé, Michael E., 1989. "Conservation Biology in the Twenty-first Century: Summary and Outlook," in David Western and Mary Pearl, (eds.), *Conservation for the Twenty-first Century*. (Oxford: Oxford University Press).

Stiglitz, Joseph E., 2002. "The Insider: What I Learned at the World Economic Crisis," *The New Republic* 222 (no. 16/17, April 17 and 24): 56–60.

Stiglitz, Joseph E., 2002. *Globalization and Its Discontents*. (New York, NY: Norton).

United Nations Conference on Environment and Development (UNCED) 1992a. *Agenda 21*. Document No. A/CONF.151/26. http://www.un.org/esa/sustdev/documents/agenda21/index.htm.

United Nations Conference on Environment and Development (UNCED), 1992b. *The Rio Declaration*. UNCED Document A/ CONF.151/5/Rev. 1, 13 June.

United Nations Development Programme (UNDP), 2000. *Human Development Report 2000*. (Oxford, UK: Oxford University Press).

United Nations Development Programme (UNDP), 2005. *Human Development Report 2005*. (New York, NY: United Nations Development Programme).

United Nations Environment Programme, 1997. *Register of International Treaties and Other Agreements in the Field of the Environment*. (Nairobi: United Nations Environment Programme).

United Nations General Assembly, 1982. *World Charter for Nature*, UN General Assembly Resolution No. 37/7 of 28 October.

United Nations University, World Institute for Development Economics Research, 2006. "The World Distribution of Household Wealth," online at www.wider.unu.edu.

Vitousek, Peter M., Paul R. Ehrlich, Anne H. Ehrlich, and Pamela A. Matson, 1986. "Human Appropriation of the Products of Biosynthesis," *BioScience* 36: 368–73.

Wilson, Edward O., 1984. *Biophilia*. (Cambridge, MA: Harvard University Press).

Wilson, Edward O., 2002. *The Future of Life*. (New York, NY: Alfred A. Knopf).

Wolff, Edward N., 2002. *Top Heavy: The Increasing Inequality of Wealth in America and What Can Be Done About It*. (New York, NY: The New Press).

World Health Organization, Commission on Health and Environment, 1992. *Our Planet, Our Health: Report of the WHO Commission on Health and Environment*. (Geneva: World Health Organization).

BIBLIOGRAPHY

Abbey, Edward. "Earth First! and *The Monkey Wrench Gang.*" *Environmental Ethics* 5, no. 1 (Spring 1983): 94–5.

Anker, Peder. "Deep Ecology in Bucharest." The *Trumpeter: Journal of Ecosophy* 24, no. 1 (2008): 56–67.

Aquinas, Thomas. *Summa Contra Gentiles.* Trans. Joseph Rickaby. Westminster, MD: The Carroll Press, 1950.

Attfield, Robin. *The Ethics of Environmental Concern.* 2nd edn. Athens: University of Georgia Press, 1991.

Attfield, Robin. *Environmental Ethics: An Overview for the Twenty-First Century.* Malden, MA: Polity, 2003.

Attfield, Robin, and Andrew Belsey, eds. *Philosophy and the Natural Environment*, Royal Institute of Philosophy Supplement 36. New York: Cambridge University Press, 1994.

Bacon, Francis. *The Great Instauration.* In James Spedding, Robert Leslie Ellis, and Douglas Denon Heath, eds., *The Works*, vol. VIII. Boston, MA: Taggard and Thompson, 1863.

Baum, Dan. "Wise Guise." *Sierra* (May/June 1991): 71–93.

Beckerman, Wilfred, and Joanna Pasek. *Justice, Posterity, and the Environment.* New York: Oxford University Press, 2001.

Bentham, Jeremy. *The Principles of Morals and Legislation.* Amherst, NY: Prometheus Books, 1988.

The *Bible. New Oxford Annotated Bible.* New Revised Standard Version. 3rd edn. New York: Oxford University Press, 2001.

Blackstone, William T., ed. *Philosophy and Environmental Crisis.* Athens: University of Georgia Press, 1974.

Bookchin, Murray. "Social Ecology Versus Deep Ecology." *Socialist Review* 88, no. 3 (1988): 11–29.

Bookchin, Murray. *The Ecology of Freedom: The Emergence and Dissolution of Hierarchy.* Oakland, CA: AK Press, 2005.

Brennan, Andrew. *Thinking About Nature: An Investigation of Nature, Value, and Ecology.* Athens: University of Georgia Press, 1988.

Breton, Ana. "Dog Found Badly Beaten After Apparent Burglary." *Salt Lake Tribune* (August 19, 2008): B6.

Brower, David, ed. *Wilderness: America's Living Heritage.* San Francisco, CA: Sierra Club Books, 1961.

Buchanan, Robert A. *Technology and Social Progress.* Oxford: Pergamon Press, 1965.

Bullard, Robert D. "Environmental Justice for All." In Robert D. Bullard, ed., *Unequal Protection: Environmental Justice and Communities of Color.* San Francisco, CA: Sierra Club Books, 1994, pp. 3–22.

Bullard, Robert D. "Overcoming Racism in Environmental Decision-Making." *Environment* 36, no. 4 (May 1994): 10–44.

Burdick, Alan. "It's Not the Only Alien Invader." *New York Times Magazine* (November 13, 1994): 48–55, 78, 80–1, 86–7.

Cafaro, Philip. "Thoreau, Leopold, and Carson: Toward an Environmental Virtue Ethics." *Environmental Ethics* 23, no. 1 (Spring 2001): 3–17.

Callicott, J. Baird. "Non-anthropocentric Value Theory and Environmental Ethics." *American Philosophical Quarterly* 21, no. 4 (October 1984): 299–309.

Callicott, J. Baird. "On the Intrinsic Value of Nonhuman Species." In Bryan Norton, ed., *The Preservation of Species: The Value of Biological Diversity.* Princeton, NJ: Princeton University Press, 1986, pp. 138–72.

Callicott, J. Baird. "The Metaphysical Implications of Ecology." *Environmental Ethics* 8, no. 4 (Winter 1986): 301–16.

Callicott, J. Baird. *In Defense of the Land Ethic: Essays in Environmental Philosophy.* Albany: State University of New York Press, 1989.

Callicott, J. Baird. "The Case against Moral Pluralism." *Environmental Ethics* 12, no. 2 (Summer 1990): 99–124.

Callicott, J. Baird. "The Role of Technology in the Evolving Concept of Nature." In Frederick Ferré and Peter Hartel, eds., *Ethics and Environmental Policy: Theory Meets Practice*. Athens: University of Georgia Press, 1994, pp. 58–83.

Callicott, J. Baird. *Beyond the Land Ethic: More Essays in Environmental Philosophy*. Albany: State University of New York Press, 1999.

Callicott, J. Baird, and Robert Frodeman, eds. *Encyclopedia of Environmental Ethics and Philosophy*, vols. 1 and 2. Farmington Hills, MI: Macmillan Reference USA.

Carson, Rachel. *Silent Spring*. Boston, MA: Houghton Mifflin, 1994.

Cavanagh, Rebecca. "Boy, 7, Feeds Live Zoo Animals to Croc." *Northern Territory News* (October 3, 2008).

Cerrell Associates. "Political Difficulties Facing Waste-to-Energy Conversion Plant Siting." Prepared for the California Waste Management Board. Cerrell Associates, Los Angeles, 1984.

Clements, Frederic E. *Plant Succession: An Analysis of the Development of Vegetation*. Carnegie Institution of Washington Publication no. 242. Washington, DC: Carnegie Institution, 1916.

Cobb, John B. Jr. "The Population Explosion and the Rights of the Subhuman World." *IDEC International* 9, North American edn. (September 12, 1970): 40–62.

Cohen, Michael P. *The Pathless Way: John Muir and American Wilderness*. Madison: University of Wisconsin Press, 1984.

Collingwood, Robin G. *The Idea of Nature*. New York: Oxford University Press, 1960.

Commoner, Barry. *The Closing Circle: Nature, Man, and Technology*. New York: Alfred A. Knopf, 1971.

Commoner, Barry. "Response to 'One Dimensional Ecology.'" *Bulletin of the Atomic Scientists*, vol. 28 (May 1972), p. 56.

Commoner, Barry. "How Poverty Breeds Overpopulation (and not the other way around)." *Ramparts* 13, no. 10 (August/September 1975): 21–5, 58–9.

Cronon, William. "The Trouble with Wilderness." *New York Times Magazine* (August 13, 1995): 42–3.

Cronon, William. "The Trouble with Wilderness: A Response." *Environmental History* 1, no. 1 (1996): 47–55.

Cronon, William, ed. *Uncommon Ground: Rethinking the Human Place in Nature*. New York: W. W. Norton & Company, 1996.

Curry, Patrick. *Ecological Ethics: An Introduction*. Malden, MA: Polity, 2007.

Daly, Herman E. *Steady-State Economics*. 2nd edn. Washington, DC: Island Press, 1991.

Daly, Herman E., and Kenneth N. Townsend, eds. *Valuing the Earth: Economics, Ecology, Ethics*. Cambridge, MA: The MIT Press, 1993.

Darwin, Charles. *The Descent of Man, and Selection in Relation to Sex*. Princeton, NJ: Princeton University Press, 1981.

Descartes, René. *Discourse on the Method*. Trans. Elizabeth Anscombe. London: Thomas Nelson and Sons, 1966.

Descartes, René. *The Philosophical Writings of Descartes*, vol. 3: *The Correspondence*. Trans. John Cottingham, Robert Stoothoff, Dugald Murdoch, and Anthony Kenny. New York: Cambridge University Press, 1991.

Devall, Bill, and George Sessions. *Deep Ecology: Living as if Nature Mattered*. Salt Lake City, UT: Peregrine Smith Books, 1985.

Diamond, Jared M. *Collapse: How Societies Choose to Fail or Succeed*. New York: Viking, 2005.

Diamond, Jared M. "The Ends of the World as We Know Them." *New York Times* (January 1, 2005): A13.

Domsky, Darren. "Evaluating Callicott's Attack on Stone's Moral Pluralism." *Environmental Values* 10, no. 3 (August 2001): 395–415.

Donahue, Debra L. *The Western Range Revisited: Removing Livestock from Public Lands to Conserve Native Biodiversity*. Norman: University of Oklahoma Press, 1999.

Ehrenfeld, David. "The Environmental Limits to Globalization." *Conservation Biology* 19, no. 2 (April 2005): 318–26.

Ehrlich, Paul R. *The Population Bomb*. New York: Galantine Books, 1968.

Ehrlich, Paul R., and John P. Holden. "Impact of Population Growth." *Science* 171 (March 26, 1971): 1212–17.

Elkington, John. *Cannibals with Forks: The Triple Bottom Line of the 21st Century Business*. Stony Creek, CT: New Society Publishers, 1998.

Elliot, Robert. "Meta-Ethics and Environmental Ethics." *Metaphilosophy* 16, nos. 2 & 3 (April/July 1985): 103–17.

Elliot, Robert, ed. *Environmental Ethics*. New York: Oxford University Press, 2004.

Evernden, Neil. *The Social Creation of Nature*. Baltimore, MD: The Johns Hopkins University Press, 1992.

Ferré, Frederick. *Philosophy of Technology*. Englewood Cliffs, NJ: Prentice-Hall, 1988.

Ferré, Frederick. "Personalistic Organicism: Paradox or Paradigm?" In Robin Attfield and Andrew Belsey, eds., *Philosophy and the Natural Environment*, Royal Institute of Philosophy Supplement 36. New York: Cambridge University Press, 1994, pp. 59–73.

Ferré, Frederick. "Persons in Nature: Toward an Applicable and Unified Environmental Ethics." *Ethics and the Environment* 1, no. 1 (1996): 15–25.

Foreman, Dave. "Earth First!" *The Progressive* 45, no. 10 (October 1981): 39–42.

Foreman, Dave. "More on Earth First! and *The Monkey Wrench Gang*." *Environmental Ethics* 5, no. 1 (Spring 1983): 95–6.

Fox, Warwick. "Deep Ecology: A New Philosophy of Our Time?" *The Ecologist* 14, nos. 5–6 (1984): 194–200.

Fox, Warwick. *Toward a Transpersonal Ecology: Developing New Foundations for Environmentalism*. Albany: State University of New York Press, 1995.

Fox, Warwick, ed. *Ethics and the Built Environment*. New York: Routledge, 2000.

Fox, Warwick. *A Theory of General Ethics: Human Relationships, Nature, and the Built Environment*. Cambridge, MA: The MIT Press, 2006.

Gallup, Gordon C. Jr. "Chimpanzees: Self-Recognition." *Science* 167, no. 3914 (January 2, 1970): 86–7.

Gilligan, Carol. *In a Different Voice: Psychological Theory and Women's Development*. Cambridge, MA: Harvard University Press, 1982.

Glacken, Clarence J. *Traces on the Rhodian Shore: Nature and Culture in Western Thought from Ancient Times to the End of the Eighteenth Century*. Berkeley: University of California Press, 1967.

Goodpaster, Kenneth E. "On Being Morally Considerable." *Journal of Philosophy* 75, no. 6 (June 1978): 308–25.

Goodpaster, Kenneth E., and Kenneth M. Sayre, eds. *Ethics and Problems of the 21st Century*. Notre Dame, IN: University of Notre Dame Press, 1979.

Grossman, Karl. "Environmental Racism." *Crisis* 98 (April 1991): 14–17, 31–2.

Hamilton, Edith, and Huntington Cairns, eds. *Plato: The Collected Dialogues*. Princeton, NJ: Princeton University Press, 2005.

Hardin, Garrett. "The Tragedy of the Commons." *Science* 162 (December 1968): 1243–8.

Hardin, Garrett. "The Immorality of Being Softhearted." *The Relevant Scientist* 1, issue 1 (November 1971): 17–18.

Hardin, Garrett. "Ethical Implications of Carrying Capacity." In Garrett Hardin and John Baden, eds., *Managing the Commons*. New York: W. H. Freeman and Company, 1977, pp. 112–25.

Hargrove, Eugene C. "Weak Anthropocentric Intrinsic Value." *The Monist* 75, no. 2 (April 1992): 183–207.

Hargrove, Eugene. "Ecological Sabotage: Pranks or Terrorism?" *Environmental Ethics* 4, no. 4 (Winter 1982): 291–2.

Hargrove, Eugene. Response to Abbey and Foreman. *Environmental Ethics* 5, no. 1 (Spring 1983): 96.

Hargrove, Eugene C. *Foundations of Environmental Ethics*. Englewood Cliffs, NJ: Prentice-Hall, 1989.

Hawken, Paul. "A Declaration of Sustainability." *Utne Reader* 59 (September/October 1993): 54–61.

Hawken, Paul. *The Ecology of Commerce: A Declaration of Sustainability*. New York: HarperBusiness, 1993.

Hobbes, Thomas. *Leviathan*. Ed. C. B. MacPherson. New York: Penguin Books, 1985.

Horkheimer, Max. *Eclipse of Reason*. New York: Oxford University Press, 1947.

Hudson, William, ed. *The Is–Ought Question*. New York: Macmillan, 1969.

Hume, David. *A Treatise of Human Nature*. Ed. P. H. Nidditch. 2nd edn. New York: Oxford University Press, 1978.

Jackson, Wes. "Nature as the Measure for a Sustainable Agriculture." In F. Herbert Bormann and Stephen R. Kellert, eds., *Ecology, Economics, Ethics: The Broken Circle*. New Haven, CT: Yale University Press, 1991, pp. 43–58.

Jamieson, Dale. *Ethics and the Environment: An Introduction*. Cambridge, UK: Cambridge University Press, 2008.

Johnson, Lawrence E. *A Morally Deep World: An Essay on Moral Significance and Environmental Ethics*. New York: Cambridge University Press, 1993.

Jonas, Hans. *The Phenomenon of Life: Toward a Philosophical Biology*. New York: Harper & Row, 1966.

Kant, Immanuel. *Grounding for the Metaphysics of Morals*. 2nd edn. Trans. James W. Ellington. Indianapolis, IN: Hackett Publishing Company, 1985.

Kant, Immanuel. *Observations on the Feeling of the Beautiful and Sublime*. Trans. John T. Goldthwait. Berkeley: University of California Press, 1991.

Kant, Immanuel. *Lectures on Ethics*. Trans. Peter Heath. New York: Cambridge University Press, 1997.

Kant, Immanuel. *The Metaphysics of Morals*. Trans. Mary Gregory. New York: Cambridge University Press, 1996.

Katz, Eric, Andrew Light, and David Rothenberg, eds. *Beneath the Surface: Critical Essays in the Philosophy of Deep Ecology*. Cambridge, MA: The MIT Press, 2000.

Keller, David R. "Gleaning Lessons from Deep Ecology." *Ethics and the Environment* 2, no. 2 (1997): 139–48.

Keller, David R., and Frank B. Golley, eds. *The Philosophy of Ecology: From Science to Synthesis*. Athens: University of Georgia Press, 2000.

Keller, David R., and E. Charles Brummer. "Putting Food Production in Context: Toward a Postmechanistic Agricultural Ethic." *BioScience* 52 (March 2002): 264–71.

Keller, David R. "The Fallacy of Safe Space." In David Rothenberg and Wandee Pryor, eds., *Writing on Air*. Cambridge, MA: The MIT Press, 2003, pp. 287–93.

Kerr, Richard A., and Richard Stone. "A Human Trigger for the Great Quake of Sichuan?" *Science* 323 (January 16, 2009): 322.

King, Roger J. H. "How to Construe Nature: Environmental Ethics and the Interpretation of Nature." *Between the Species* 6 (Summer 1990): 101–8.

King, Roger J. H. "Environmental Ethics and the Built Environment." *Environmental Ethics* 22, no. 2 (Summer 2000): 115–31.

Kormondy, Edward J. "Natural and Human Ecosystems." In Frederick Sargent, ed., *Human Ecology*. 2nd edn. Amsterdam: North Holland, 1974, pp. 27–43.

Leopold, Aldo. "The Ecological Conscience." *Journal of Soil and Water Conservation* 3 (July 1948): 109–12.

Leopold, Aldo. *A Sand County Almanac and Sketches Here and There*. New York: Oxford University Press, 1949.

Light, Andrew, ed. *Social Ecology After Bookchin*. New York: The Guilford Press, 1998.

Light, Andrew. "The Urban Blindspot in Environmental Ethics." *Environmental Politics* 10, no. 1 (2001): 7–35.

Light, Andrew, and Eric Katz, eds. *Environmental Pragmatism*. New York: Routledge, 1996.

Light, Andrew, and Holmes Rolston III, eds. *Environmental Ethics: An Anthology*. Malden, MA: Blackwell, 2003.

Litonjua, Augusto A., Vincent J. Carey, Scotte T. Weiss, and Diane R. Gold. "Race, Socioeconomic Factors, and Area of Residence are Associated with Asthma Prevalence." *Pediatric Pulmonology* 28, no. 6 (1999): 394–401.

Locke, John. *Two Treatises of Government*. Ed. Peter Laslett. New York: Cambridge University Press, 2005.

Loope, Lloyd L., Ole Hamman, and Charles P. Stone. "Comparative Conservation Biology of Oceanic Archipelagoes: Hawaii and the Galápagos." *BioScience* 38, no. 4 (April 1988): 272–82.

Lovejoy, Arthur O. *The Great Chain of Being*. Cambridge, MA: Harvard University Press, 2001.

Lovelock, James E. "Gaia As Seen Through the Atmosphere." Letter to the Editor. *Atmospheric Environment* 6, no. 8 (1972): 579–80.

Lovelock, James E. *Gaia: A New Look at Life on Earth*. New York: Oxford University Press, 1979.

Malthus, Thomas. *An Essay on the Principle of Population*. 1st edn. London: Oxford University Press, 1798.

Malthus, Thomas. *An Essay on the Principle of Population*. Ed. Patricia James. New York: Cambridge University Press, 1989.

Manes, Christopher [Miss Ann Thropy]. "Population and AIDS." *Earth First!* 7, no. 5 (May 1987).

Marsh, George Perkins. *Man and Nature*. Ed. David Lowenthal. Cambridge, MA: Belknap Press of Harvard University Press, 1967.

Marx, Karl. *Capital: A Critical Analysis of Capitalist Production*, vol. I. Trans. Samuel Moore and Edward Gaveling. New York: International Publishers, 1947.

Marx, Karl, and Frederick Engels. *Collected Works*, vols. 4, 20. Trans. Richard Dixon et al. New York: International Publishers, 1975, 1976.

Mayr, Ernst. *The Growth of Biological Thought: Diversity, Evolution, and Inheritance*. Cambridge, MA: The Belknap Press of Harvard University Press, 1982.

McKeon, Richard, ed. *The Basic Works of Aristotle*. New York: Random House, 1941.

McKibben, Bill. "A Special Moment in History." *Atlantic Monthly* (May 1998): 55–78.

McKibben, Bill. *Maybe One: A Case for Smaller Families*. New York: Plume Books, 1999.

McLaughlin, Andrew. "The Heart of Deep Ecology." In George Sessions, ed., *Deep Ecology for the Twenty-First Century*. Boston: Shambhala Publications, 1995, pp. 85–93.

Merchant, Carolyn. *The Death of Nature: Women, Ecology, and the Scientific Revolution*. San Francisco: Harper Collins, 1990.

Merchant, Carolyn. "Ecofeminism and Feminist Theory." In Irene Diamond and Gloria Orenstein, eds., *Reweaving the World: The Emergence of Ecofeminism*. San Francisco: Sierra Club Books, 1990, pp. 100–5.

Meyer, William B. *Human Impact on the Earth*. New York: Cambridge University Press, 1996.

Midgley, Mary. *Animals and Why They Matter*. Athens: University of Georgia Press, 1983.

Mill, John Stuart. *Nature, the Utility of Religion, and Theism*. London: Longmans, Green, Reader, and Dyer, 1874.

Mill, John Stuart. *Principles of Political Economy with Some of Their Applications to Social Philosophy*. Books III–V. Toronto: University of Toronto Press, 1965.

Millgram, Elijah, ed. *Varieties of Practical Reasoning*. Cambridge, MA: MIT Press, 2001.

Muir, John. *Our National Parks*. Boston: Houghton Mifflin, 1901.

Muir, John. *The Yosemite*. New York: Century, 1912.

Muir, John. *A Thousand Mile Walk to the Gulf*. Boston: Houghton Mifflin, 1916.

Murphy, Jamie. "Could It Happen in West Virginia?" *Time* (December 17, 1984).

Naess, Arne. "The Shallow and the Deep, Long-Range Ecology Movement: A Summary." *Inquiry: An Interdisciplinary Journal of Philosophy and the Social Sciences* 16 (1973): 95–100.

Naess, Arne. "The Deep Ecology Movement: Some Philosophical Aspects." *Philosophical Inquiry* 8 (1986): 10–31.

Naess, Arne. "Self-Realization: An Ecological Approach to Being in the World." The *Trumpeter: Journal of Ecosophy* 4, no. 3 (1987): 35–42.

Naess, Arne. *Ecology, Community, and Lifestyle: Outline of an Ecosophy*. Trans. and rev. David Rothenberg. New York: Cambridge University Press, 1989.

Naess, Arne. "The Shallow and the Deep Ecology Movement." Trans. Erling Schøller. In Peder Anker, "Deep Ecology in Bucharest." The *Trumpeter: Journal of Philosophy* 24, no. 1 (2008): 59–66.

Nash, Roderick Frazier. *The Rights of Nature: A History of Environmental Ethics*. Madison: University of Wisconsin Press, 1989.

Newton, Isaac. *Opticks.* London: G. Bell & Sons, 1931.

Newton, Isaac. The *Principia: Mathematical Principles of Natural Philosophy.* Trans. Bernard Cohen and Anne Whitman. Berkeley: University of California Press, 1999.

Newton, Lisa H. *Ethics and Sustainability: Sustainable Development and the Moral Life.* Upper Saddle River, NJ: Pearson Education, 2003.

Nielsen, Kai. "Problems of Ethics." In Paul Edwards, ed., *The Encyclopedia of Philosophy,* vol. 3. New York: Macmillan and Free Press, 1967, pp. 117–34.

Norton, Bryan G. "Conservation and Preservation: A Conceptual Rehabilitation." *Environmental Ethics* 8, no. 3 (Fall 1986): 195–220.

Norton, Bryan G. *Toward Unity Among Environmentalists.* New York: Oxford University Press, 1991.

Norton, Bryan G. "The Ignorance Argument: What Must We Know to be Fair to the Future?" In Daniel W. Bromley and Jouni Paavola, eds., *Economics, Ethics, and Environmental Policy: Contested Choices.* Malden, MA: Blackwell Publishers, 2002, pp. 35–52.

Norton, Bryan G. *Sustainability: A Philosophy of Adaptive Ecosystem Management.* Chicago: University of Chicago Press, 2005.

O'Connor, James. "Socialism and Ecology." *Capitalism, Nature, Socialism* 2, no. 3 (1991): 1–12.

Odum, Eugene P. *Fundamentals of Ecology.* 1st edn. Philadelphia: Saunders, 1953.

Oelschlaeger, Max. *The Idea of Wilderness: From Prehistory to the Age of Ecology.* New Haven: Yale University Press, 1991.

O'Neill, John. "The Varieties of Intrinsic Value." *The Monist* 75, no. 2 (1992): 119–38.

Palmer, Clare. "A Bibliographic Essay on Environmental Ethics." *Studies in Christian Ethics* 7, no. 1 (1994): 68–93.

Parikh, Jyoti K., ed. *Sustainable Development in Agriculture.* Boston: Dordrecht, 1988.

Passmore, John. *Man's Responsibility for Nature: Ecological Problems and Western Traditions.* New York: Charles Scribner's Sons, 1974.

Passmore, John. "Attitudes to Nature." In R. S. Peters, ed., *Nature and Conduct.* New York: St Martin's Press, 1975, pp. 251–64.

Pastor, Manuel Jr., Jim Sadd, and John Hipp. "Which Came First? Toxic Facilities, Minority Move-In, and Environmental Justice." *Journal of Urban Affairs* 23, no. 1 (2001): 1–21.

Pellow, David N. "The Politics of Illegal Dumping: An Environmental Justice Framework." *Qualitative Sociology* 27, no. 4 (Winter 2004): 511–25.

Pinchot, Gifford. *Breaking New Ground.* New York: Harcourt, Brace and Company, 1947.

Pinchot, Gifford. *The Fight for Conservation.* Seattle: University of Washington Press, 1967.

Plumwood, Val. "Nature, Self, and Gender: A Critique of Rationalism." *Hypatia* 6, no. 1 (Spring 1991): 3–22.

Plumwood, Val. *Feminism and the Mastery of Nature.* New York: Routledge, 1993.

Regan, Tom. "An Examination and Defense of One Argument Concerning Animal Rights." *Inquiry: An Interdisciplinary Journal of Philosophy and the Social Sciences* 22, nos 1–4 (1979): 189–219.

Regan, Tom. "Animal Rights, Human Wrongs." *Environmental Ethics* 2, no. 2 (Summer 1980): 99–120.

Regan, Tom. "The Case for Animal Rights." In Peter Singer, ed., *In Defense of Animals.* New York: Basil Blackwell, 1985, pp. 13–26.

Regan, Tom. *The Case for Animal Rights.* 2nd edn. Berkeley: University of California Press, 2004.

Richards, Bradley W. *The Savage View: Charles Savage, Pioneer Mormon Photographer.* Nevada City, CA: Carl Mautz Publishing, 1995.

Richardson, Susan A. "It Takes a Movement to Secure Environmental Justice." *Austin American Statesman* (July 24, 1997): A15.

Rodman, John R. "The Liberation of Nature?" *Inquiry: An Interdisciplinary Journal of Philosophy and the Social Sciences* 20 (1977): 83–145.

Rolston, Holmes III. "Is There an Ecological Ethic?" *Ethics: An International Journal of Social and Political Philosophy* 85 (1975): 93–109.

Rolston, Holmes III. *Science and Religion: A Critical Survey.* Philadelphia: Temple University Press, 1987.

Rolston, Holmes III. *Environmental Ethics: Duties to and Values in the Natural World.* Philadelphia: Temple University Press, 1988.

Rolston, Holmes III. *Genes, Genesis, and God: Values and Their Origins in Natural and Human History.* New York: Cambridge University Press, 1999.

Rothenberg, David. *Hand's End: Technology and the Limits of Nature.* Berkeley: University of California Press, 1993.

Rothenberg, David, ed. *Wild Ideas.* Minneapolis: University of Minnesota Press, 1995.

Rothenberg, David, and Wandee Pryor, eds. *Writing on Air.* Cambridge, MA: The MIT Press, 2003.

Russell, Bertrand. *Religion and Science.* New York: Oxford University Press, 1961.

Sagoff, Mark. "Animal Liberation and Environmental Ethics: Bad Marriage, Quick Divorce." *Osgoode Hall Law Journal* 22, no. 2 (1984): 297–307.

Sagoff, Mark. "Environmental Science and Environmental Ethics." In Henk A. M. J. ten Have, ed., *Environmental Ethics and International Policy.* Paris: UNESCO Publishing, 1985, pp. 145–63.

Sandler, Ronald, and Philip Cafaro, eds. *Environmental Virtue Ethics.* New York: Rowman & Littlefield Publishers, 2005.

Schweitzer, Albert. *Civilization and Ethics*. Trans. C. T. Campion. London: A. & C. Black, 1923.

Sears, Paul B. "Ecology – A Subversive Subject." *BioScience* 14, no. 7 (July 1964): 11–13.

Sen, Amartya. "Population: Delusion and Reality." *New York Review of Books* 41, no. 15 (September 22, 1994).

Sessions, George. "Spinoza and Jeffers on Man in Nature." *Inquiry: An Interdisciplinary Journal of Philosophy and the Social Sciences* 20 (1977): 481–528.

Sessions, George. "Spinoza, Perennial Philosophy and Deep Ecology." Paper presented at Dominican College, San Raphael, CA, June 29–July 4, 1979. Unpublished manuscript, dated September, 34 pages.

Shelley, Mary. *The Last Man*. New York: Oxford University Press, 1994.

Shepard, Paul. "Virtually Hunting Reality in the Forests of Simulacra." In Michael E. Soulé and Gary Lease, eds., *Reinventing Nature? Responses to Postmodern Deconstruction*. Washington, DC: Island Press, 1995, pp. 17–29.

Shrader–Frechette, Kristin S. *Environmental Ethics*. 2nd edn. Lanham, MD: Rowman & Littlefield, 1998.

Simon, Julian L. "More People, Greater Wealth, More Resources, Healthier Environment." *Economic Affairs* 14, no. 3 (April 1994): 22–9.

Simon, Julian L. *The Ultimate Resource*. 2nd edn. Princeton, NJ: Princeton University Press, 1996.

Singer, Peter. "Animal Liberation." Review of Stanley Godlovitch, Roslind Godlovitch, and John Harris, eds., *Animals, Men and Morals. The New York Review of Books* 20, no. 5 (April 5, 1973): 17–21.

Singer, Peter. "All Animals Are Equal." *Philosophical Exchange* 1, no. 5 (Summer 1974): 103–16.

Singer, Peter, ed. *In Defense of Animals*. New York: Basil Blackwell, 1985.

Singer, Peter. *Animal Liberation*. New York: HarperCollins, 2002.

Soulé, Michael E. "What is Conservation Biology?" *BioScience* 35, no. 11 (December 1985): 727–34.

Sterba, James P. "A Biocentrist Strikes Back." *Environmental Ethics* 20, no. 4 (Winter 1998): 361–76.

Sterba, James P. *The Triumph of Practice Over Theory in Ethics*. New York: Oxford University Press, 2005.

Stone, Charles P., and J. O. Keith. "Control of Feral Ungulates and Small Mammals in Hawaii National Parks: Research and Management Strategies." In C. G. J. Richards and T. Y. Ku, eds., *Control of Mammal Pests*. New York: Taylor & Francis, 1987, pp. 277–9.

Stone, Christopher D. "Should Trees Have Standing? Toward Legal Rights for Natural Objects." *Southern California Law Review* 45, no. 2 (1972): 450–501.

Stone, Christopher D. *Should Trees Have Standing? Toward Legal Rights for Natural Objects*. Los Altos, CA: W. Kaufmann, 1974.

Summerhays, John, and Harriet Croke. *Air Toxics Emissions Inventory for the Southeast Chicago Area*. Washington, DC: U.S. Environmental Protection Agency, 1987.

Sylvan [Routley], Richard. "Is There a Need for a New, an Environmental, Ethic?" *Proceedings of the XV World Congress of Philosophy*, no. 1 (paper presented at the session on "Philosophy and Science, Morality and Culture, Technology and Man," Varna, Bulgaria, 1973), Sofia, Bulgaria, 1973, no. 1, pp. 205–10.

Sylvan, Richard. "A Critique of Deep Ecology," part II. *Radical Philosophy* 41 (1985): 1–22.

Sylvan [Routley], Richard, and Val Plumwood [Routley]. "Against the Inevitability of Human Chauvinism." In Kenneth E. Goodpaster and Kenneth M. Sayre, eds., *Ethics and Problems of the 21st Century*. Notre Dame, IN: University of Notre Dame Press, 1979, pp. 36–59.

Sylvan, Richard, and David Bennett. *The Greening of Ethics: From Anthropocentrism to Deep-Green Theory*. Tucson: University of Arizona Press, 1994.

Taylor, Paul W. "The Ethics of Respect for Nature." *Environmental Ethics* 3, no. 3 (Fall 1981): 197–218.

Taylor, Paul W. *Respect for Nature: A Theory of Environmental Ethics*. Princeton, NJ: Princeton University Press, 1986.

Tennyson, Alfred. "In Memoriam A. H. H." In Christopher Ricks, ed., *The Poems of Tennyson*, vol. 2. Berkeley: University of California Press, 1987, pp. 304–459.

Thompson, Paul B. *The Spirit of the Soil: Agriculture and Environmental Ethics*. London: Routledge, 1995.

Thoreau, Henry David. *Excursions*. Boston, MA: Houghton Mifflin Company, 1893.

Thoreau, Henry David. *The Works of Thoreau*. Ed. Henry S. Canby. Boston: Houghton Mifflin Company, 1937.

Tribe, Laurence H. "Ways Not to Think about Plastic Trees: New Foundations for Environmental Law." *Yale Law Journal* 83, no. 7 (June 1974): 1315–48.

VanDeVeer, Donald. "Interspecific Justice." *Inquiry: An Interdisciplinary Journal of Philosophy and the Social Sciences* 22, nos 1–2 (Summer 1979): 55–79.

Varner, Gary. "No Holism without Pluralism." *Environmental Ethics* 13, no. 2 (Summer 1991): 175–9.

Varner, Gary. *In Nature's Interests? Interests, Animal Rights, and Environmental Ethics*. New York: Oxford University Press, 1998.

Vogel, Steven. "Nature as Origin and Difference: On Environmental Philosophy and Continental Thought." *Philosophy Today* 42 (SPEP Supplement 1998): 169–81.

Ward, Chip. "Stupid Is As Stupid Does: What if the Crown of Creation is a Dunce Cap?" *Catalyst* (January 2008): 12–15.

Warren, Karen J. "The Power and Promise of Ecological Feminism." *Environmental Ethics* 12, no. 3 (Summer 1990): 125–46.

Watson, Richard A. "A Critique of Anti-anthropocentric Biocentrism." *Environmental Ethics* 5, no. 3 (Fall 1983): 245–56.

Wenz, Peter S. "Just Garbage." In Laura Westra and Peter S. Wenz, eds., *Faces of Environmental Racism: Confronting Issues of Global Justice.* Lanham, MD: Rowman & Littlefield, 1995, pp. 57–71.

Weston, Anthony. "Beyond Intrinsic Value: Pragmatism in Environmental Ethics." *Environmental Ethics* 7, no. 4 (Winter 1985): 321–39.

Weston, Anthony, ed. *An Invitation to Environmental Philosophy.* New York: Oxford University Press, 1999.

White, Lynn. "The Historical Roots of Our Ecologic Crisis." *Science* 155 (March 10, 1967): 1203–7.

Wilson, Edward O. "The Little Things that Run the World." *Conservation Biology* 1 (December 1987): 344–6.

Wolf, Clark. "Justice and Intergenerational Debt." *Intergenerational Justice Review* 1 (2008): 13–17.

Zimmerman, Michael E., J. Baird Callicott, George Sessions, Karen J. Warren, and John Clark, eds. *Environmental Philosophy: From Animal Rights to Radical Ecology.* 2nd edn. Upper Saddle River, NJ: Prentice-Hall, 1998.

Zimmerman, Michael E., J. Baird Callicott, Karen J. Warren, Irene J. Klaver, and John Clark, eds. *Environmental Philosophy: From Animal Rights to Radical Ecology.* 4th edn. Upper Saddle River, NJ: Prentice-Hall, 2005.